THE COLLECTED WORKS OF
SAMUEL TAYLOR COLERIDGE . 12

MARGINALIA

General Editor: KATHLEEN COBURN
Associate Editor: BART WINER

THE COLLECTED WORKS

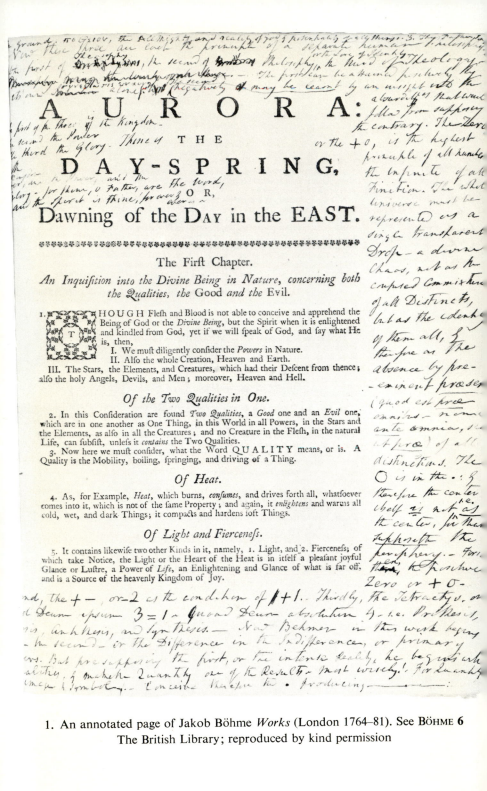

AURORA:

THE
DAY-SPRING,
OR,
Dawning of the Day in the EAST.

❀❀❀❀❀❀❀❀❀❀❀❀❀❀❀❀❀❀❀❀❀❀❀❀❀❀❀❀❀❀❀❀❀❀

The First Chapter.

An Inquisition into the Divine Being in Nature, concerning both the Qualities, the Good *and the* Evil.

1. THOUGH Flesh and Blood is not able to conceive and apprehend the Being of God or the *Divine Being*, but the Spirit when it is enlightened and kindled from God, yet if we will speak of God, and say what He is, then,

    I. We must diligently consider the *Powers* in Nature.

    II. Also the whole Creation, Heaven and Earth.

    III. The Stars, the Elements, and Creatures, which had their Descent from thence; also the holy Angels, Devils, and Men; moreover, Heaven and Hell.

Of the Two Qualities in One.

2. In this Consideration are found *Two Qualities*, a *Good* one and an *Evil* one; which are in one another as One Thing, in this World in all Powers, in the Stars and the Elements, as also in all the Creatures; and no Creature in the Flesh, in the natural Life, can subsist, unless it *contains* the Two Qualities.

3. Now here we must consider, what the Word Q U A L I T Y means, or is. A Quality is the Mobility, boiling, springing, and driving of a Thing.

Of Heat.

4. As, for Example, *Heat*, which burns, *consumes*, and drives forth all, whatsoever comes into it, which is not of the same Property; and again, it *enlightens* and warms all cold, wet, and dark Things; it compacts and hardens soft Things.

Of Light and Fierceness.

5. It contains likewise two other Kinds in it, namely, 1. Light, and 2. Fierceness; of which take Notice, the Light or the Heart of the Heat is in itself a pleasant joyful Glance or Lustre, a Power of *Life*, an Enlightening and Glance of what is far off, and is a Source of the heavenly Kingdom of Joy.

1. An annotated page of Jakob Böhme *Works* (London 1764–81). See BÖHME **6**
The British Library; reproduced by kind permission

THE COLLECTED WORKS OF

Samuel Taylor Coleridge

Marginalia

I

Abbt to Byfield

EDITED BY

George Whalley

ROUTLEDGE & KEGAN PAUL

BOLLINGEN SERIES LXXV
PRINCETON UNIVERSITY PRESS

This edition of the text by Samuel Taylor Coleridge is
copyright © 1980 by Princeton University Press

The Collected Works, sponsored by Bollingen Foundation,
is published in Great Britain
by Routledge & Kegan Paul Ltd
39 Store St, London WC1E 7DD
ISBN 0 7100 0249
and in the United States of America
by Princeton University Press, Princeton, New Jersey
ISBN 0-691-09879-4
LCC 68-10201
The Collected Works constitutes
the seventy-fifth publication in Bollingen Series

The present work, number 12 of the Collected Works,
is in 5 volumes, this being 12: I

Designed by Richard Garnett

Printed in Great Britain
at the University Press, Cambridge

THIS EDITION
OF THE WORKS OF
SAMUEL TAYLOR COLERIDGE
IS DEDICATED
IN GRATITUDE TO
THE FAMILY EDITORS
IN EACH GENERATION

IN THE PREPARATION OF
THIS FIRST VOLUME OF MARGINALIA
THE EDITOR IS INDEBTED FOR SPECIAL KNOWLEDGE
AND CO-OPERATION

TO

James D. Boulger
Merton A. Christensen
Hans Eichner
Richard Haven
Lore Metzger

CONTENTS

———■ I ■———

Marginalia

[† designates a "Lost Book"—a book reported to contain marginal notes in C's hand but which the editor has not been able to find and for which no transcript of marginalia is known to exist.]

Contents

LIST OF ILLUSTRATIONS

FOREWORD

THE first generation of editors of Coleridge's work, Henry Nelson Coleridge and Sara Coleridge—encouraged evidently by Coleridge himself—published a quantity of the notes he wrote in the margins and on the flyleaves of his own and other people's books. The impression left by this part of their work was that marginalia, though sometimes sustained enough to be considered as a running commentary on the books they were written in, were important primarily as extensions of his published work and as an immethodical component in the fragmentary record of his work-in-progress. None of the early editors had all the marginalia under his hands at any one time, and so could hardly appreciate that they represented a huge stream of discourse even more remarkable for its copious singleness than for the number and variety of topics embraced. In 1892, after the books had begun to drift away from the family and the first major public collection of Coleridgiana had been formed in the British Museum Library, a large group of annotated books—including most of those that the early editors had not seen fit to publish—became inaccessible to scholars; for sixty years there was no way that all the marginalia could be assembled. Yet during that interval Coleridge's reputation had become such that there were many reasons for wishing to see them brought together: perhaps they could be seen as the embodiment of "unity in multeity"; perhaps they represented a kind of writing as distinct as his published writings are from his notebooks, or his notebooks from his letters; perhaps they could be read as the sustained record of the responses of a brilliant, patient, and versatile mind to the events and issues of his own time and to the intellectual and imaginative heritage of Europe.

This edition, therefore, not out of archaeological zeal or literary-historical piety, ventures to attempt completeness. The record, of course, is not complete. But some 8000 notes have been recovered from about 450 titles (nearly 700 volumes) written by some 325 authors. We know of another seventy books that Coleridge annotated but of which there is now no textual record. Of other books

xiii

that we know Coleridge owned or used, 650 have been identified with some precision; by advancing only a little way into the penumbra of conjecture one could identify another couple of hundred books that at some time passed through his hands or sat on his shelves.

In preparing this edition, the work of the early editors, both published and in manuscript, has been indispensable. The work of later editors, which has usually been selective or piecemeal, has also been of great value, particularly in identifying and tracing annotated books that lay outside the two large collections in the British Museum and Victoria College. I intended that any previous publication of marginalia would be recorded in the headnotes to individual books, where prominent recognition could be given to the many scholars who have in the past been concerned to preserve Coleridge's marginal notes. In the final stage of revising the manuscript of this book—a collectaneum that nothing could prevent from being both long and detailed—it was deemed necessary to reduce the length of the main text in whatever way was possible. To my regret, notices of previous publication have therefore been transferred to an Appendix in the final volume; there, where the information is given in concentrated form, the acknowledgment may be more pointed (though less honorific) than it would have been if it had been distributed at large through the headnotes. The only direct use that has been made of previously published text, however, has been for the notes in books now lost or mislaid. The policy in this edition has been to turn back afresh to the original manuscripts wherever they could be found, and in the case of books that have disappeared to rely upon the earliest and most reliable transcripts in preference to printed versions.

In an undertaking of this scope, and with little precedent as guide, my debts are extensive and of many kinds, and many of them are of long standing. It is a very great pleasure to recall the names of those who have helped me since I first began this work (or something like it) in 1946. If scholarship were anything like money-lending, this would be a grim rehearsal of debts hopelessly past due, bearing an accumulation of compound interest that would force me to remove ⸜ to Antarctica, leaving no forwarding address. Fortunately, in the field of learning nothing is one's own until it has been given away, and the ledger entries read to me more like a canticle composed on the names of eminent predecessors, benefactors, colleagues, friends. Which makes it sorrowful, so glacial the slowness with which the work has advanced, to recall—among those who I hoped would share some sense of accomplishment in the book—how many death has undone. At first I marked their names with an obelisk, but found the repetition of that mark too grievous; and am bold in this place to deny death his insignia, being certain that he has little reason to be proud and less cause to be celebrated.

My first debt is to members of the Coleridge family, for the inherited treasure of the early family editors, for the use of books and manuscripts that were for a long time kept safe within the family, and for permission to copy and print from them. Permission to prepare and publish Coleridge's marginalia was graciously given by Mr Alwyne Coleridge, the poet's great-great-grandson, who also not only allowed me to study books and manuscripts in his keeping, but honoured me with his collaboration as a fellow-editor. I remember with special gratitude and affection Mr Walter Coleridge, the Reverend Antony Coleridge, and the Reverend Nicholas Coleridge, for the use of their books and manuscripts and for many hospitable kindnesses. A few others through the Wordsworth connexion played a similarly important role: Miss Joanna Hutchinson, Mrs Eleanor Rawnsley, and Mrs Dorothy Dickson.

I am grateful to others who had some of Coleridge's books and manuscripts in their possession and allowed me to copy out what was written in them: Cecil Bald, Kathleen Coburn, Gerard P. D. Coleridge, Professor S. G. Dunne, Lord Elwyn, John Louis Haney (who also made generous contributions from his life-long study of the provenance of Coleridge's books), Mrs Koblenzer-Hill and Dr Peter J. Koblenzer, George Lyward, Professor E. L. McAdam, Sir John Murray, John Grey Murray, Carl H. Pforzheimer, Gordon N. Ray, Miss G. H. Savery (who gave me Coleridge's copy of Pomponius Mela—Basle [1595]—now in the Victoria College Library), Mrs Wallace Southam, Robert H. Taylor, the Honourable Josiah Wedgwood, and Richard Wordsworth.

I wish to thank the staff of the two principal Coleridge collections for their courteous and intelligent assistance over the years: the British Museum Library (now the British Library, Reference Division), and especially David Foxon, Mr H. Sellars, Miss Anne O'Donovan, Ian Willison, Dennis E. Rhodes, and D. L. Paisey; and the Coleridge Collection in the Victoria College Library, University of Toronto, and especially Miss Lorna D. Fraser. For similar privileges and courtesies I am grateful to: The Athenaeum, Philadelphia; Birmingham University Library; the Bodleian Library, and Desmond Neill; the Boston Public Library, and John

Alden; the Bristol Central Library, and James Ross and W. S. Haugh; the University of California Library; Cambridge University Library; the William Andrews Clark Memorial Library, Los Angeles, and William E. Conway; Columbia University Library; the Wordsworth Collection in the Cornell University Library, and George Healey; the Dove Cottage Library and Trustees, and Miss Nesta Clutterbuck, Stephen Gill, and Robert Woof; the William R. Perkins Library in Duke University, and John L. Sharpe III; the Folger Shakespeare Library, and Louis B. Wright; the Houghton Library of Harvard University, and (in the early years) William H. Bond; the Henry H. Huntington Library and Art Gallery; the University of Illinois Library; the Lilly Library of Indiana University, and Geneva Warner; Johns Hopkins University Library; Keats House, Hampstead; Keele University Library, and Dr Ian Fraser; the Library of Congress; Manchester College Library, Oxford; the Mitchell Library, Sydney, New South Wales; Nagoya University Library, Tokyo; the Berg Collection in the New York Public Library, and Dr Lola L. Szladits; the University of Pennsylvania Library; the J. Pierpont Morgan Library; the Carl H. Pforzheimer Library, and Mihai H. Handra; Princeton University Library, and Howard C. Rice Jr; the Rothschild Library; the John Rylands Library of the University of Manchester; St John's College Library, Cambridge; the School of Oriental and African Studies in the University of London; Stanford University Library; the Swedenborg Society, London; the Humanities Research Center in the University of Texas, and David Farmer; University College Library in the University of London; the University of Vermont Library; the Victoria and Albert Museum; the State Library of Victoria, Australia; Washington University Libraries, and William Matheson; Dr Williams's Library; the Wisbech Museum and Literary Institute; the Beinecke Rare Book and Manuscript Library in Yale University, and Marjorie G. Wynne. For the examination of associated books and manuscripts I acknowledge the help of Christ's Hospital, the Highgate Literary and Scientific Institution, the Library Company of Philadelphia, the Coleridge Cottage at Nether Stowey, the Redpath Library in McGill University, and Messrs Josiah Wedgwood & Sons Ltd, Stoke-on-Trent. I owe a special debt of gratitude to the staff of the Douglas Library in Queen's University, and especially to H. Pearson Gundy.

If certain individuals and institutions had not collected and cherished Coleridge's books and manuscripts, this edition could not with any confidence have been attempted; but once the work had been conceived, it could not have been sustained without the advice, encouragement, and learned generosity of many persons. Beginning as a study of Coleridge's reading and an attempt to identify all the books he owned and annotated, this edition assumed its present shape and purpose in 1961, when Kathleen Coburn and Rupert Hart-Davis invited me to prepare for the *Collected Works of Samuel Taylor Coleridge* an edition of all the marginalia, grafting into it whatever was appropriate from the earlier study—"the old *Cormorant*". My first and most important debt is to Kathleen Coburn, who, at the beginning, advised me upon the study of Coleridge's reading and where best to carry it out, provided me with essential materials that nobody else at that time had access to, and generously allowed me to take some part in her own work-in-progress. To say that this edition is in the nature of a collaboration would be—in the obsolete and Coleridgian sense—preposterous (that is, upside-down or overthwart), but there is no calculus for measuring or defining the depth, extent, and vitality of the part she has played in it.

The scope of Coleridge's knowledge and interests make heavier editorial demands than any one person is likely to be able to meet single-handed. I have therefore drawn upon the special knowledge and expert judgement of a group of coeditors whose names are given on the fly-title to each of the volumes. Each coeditor undertook to prepare the primary copy for particular groups of marginalia by checking and completing my transcript of the text of those marginalia from the manuscript originals (when these existed), selecting textus and providing translation for it when necessary, and adding their commentary in the form of footnotes. In order to secure uniformity in conventions of transcription I have made myself responsible for a final reading of all the transcripts against the originals; and in order to bring the contributed entries into harmony with the editorial style that was progressively evolved, I have added to and revised the coeditors' notes in consultation with them. The name of the co-editor is placed at the end of the headnote to each entry prepared in this way. For some of the German entries more than one coeditor is shown; in most of these cases it is not possible to specify the contribution of each because the work has been co-operative, carried out over a considerable period of time and often at a distance.

The alphabetical arrangement of the entries distributes the work of coeditors in an accidental manner: only five of the coeditors are represented in Volume I: James Boulger in the entries for Adam,

Birch, and Blanco White; Merton Christensen in the single entry for Heinrichs's edition of Revelation; Hans Eichner for Abbt and the *Athenaeum*; Richard Haven in the single large entry for Jakob Böhme; Lore Metzger in relatively brief entries for Argens and Blumenbach. Subsequent volumes will show more clearly the contribution of these and other individual coeditors. James Boulger undertook a number of miscellaneous theological entries, mostly of eighteenth- and nineteenth-century authors; Merton Christensen has dealt with the technical biblical commentaries of Eichhorn, Paulus, and Schleiermacher, and with the works of Emanuel Swedenborg; Alwyne Coleridge prepared the entries for Hartley Coleridge's *Northern Worthies* and Henry Nelson Coleridge's *Six Months in the West Indies*; Lore Metzger prepared a considerable group of German philosophers and scientists—Heinroth, Herder, Jacobi, Kluge, Lessing, Mendelssohn, Mesmer, Oken, Rehberg, and Schubert; Hans Eichner drafted materials related to his studies in German Romantics—Flögel, Goldfuss, Hoffbauer, Novalis, Rehberg, Hans Sachs, A. W. Schlegel, and Wieland; Willem Schrickx prepared the entries for Fichte, Hegel, Heinroth, and Schubert; and John Beer prepared the Leighton marginalia, which are almost inseparably part of his edition of *Aids to Reflection*. Mrs Irene Wells made a first transcript of the textus and marginalia for all the Kant and Schelling entries; and James Mays reworked the text of the marginalia on Tennemann's *Geschichte der Philosophie* from a version originally prepared by Kathleen Coburn. Professor Hermann Boeschenstein gave valuable detailed advice upon the text of the German entries. I very much regret that the work of coeditors, in many cases begun more than ten years ago, should have taken as long as it has to reach the eye of the public. The other entries, representing nearly three-quarters of the titles, I have prepared myself.

From the very beginning, the need for clear visual presentation of this material was paramount. I am especially grateful to Richard Garnett, not only for finding a hitherto unrecognised book with Coleridge's annotations in it, but particularly for discovering, out of prolonged reflection upon the intransigencies of a uniquely awkward manuscript, an elegant typographical design that conceals from the reader the difficulties encompassed and makes the text a model of clarity and a pleasure to look at. Some time before two-colour printing had become common in contemporary books, this design received enthusiastic encouragement from John D. Barrett and Bollingen Foundation. Lorna Arnold has brought all the Latin and

Greek under her expert scrutiny, and from her untiring zeal in abstruse research has added many exact connexions and many touches of detail that I should have been proud to claim for my own. In the final preparation of the manuscript, I have enjoyed the cheerful, generous, and thoroughly professional co-operation of the Associate Editor of the *Collected Coleridge*, Bart Winer; his knowledge of Coleridge is hard for even seasoned Coleridgians to keep pace with; his uncanny memory and wide reading have rescued me from many *bêtises* and have spared my readers many a *lacrymabilis lacuna*; his detailed contributions and his sense of style pervade the whole edition.

I wish to record my thanks to Earl Leslie Griggs for his edition of the *Letters*, without which all studies of Coleridge would be impoverished, and to express my gratitude for the hospitality he extended to me early in my career by inviting me to California to read through the transcripts of all the letters he was preparing for publication.

There is no "Coleridge Centre"; all the individual titles of the *Collected Works* have been prepared independently of each other. Yet there has been from the beginning the freest interchange of specialised information among the editors as far as it was possible for anybody to guess who might already have an answer to what questions. If the demands of academic life and the vagaries of defective postal systems have prevented an ideal and continuous interaction, the Associate Editor has always stood as transmitter at the centre of the spider's web. I cannot easily identify the debts I owe to editors in this series who have finished their work before me; in most cases I have had access to the manuscript and proofs of their work long before publication. I therefore name my fellow-editors in order of publication: Barbara Rooke (*The Friend*), Lewis Patton (*Lectures 1795* and *The Watchman*), Peter Mann (*Lectures 1795*), R. J. White (*Lay Sermons*), John Colmer (*Church and State*), David Erdman (*Essays on His Times*), and Robin Jackson (*Logic*). In various ways I am grateful to other editors whose work has not yet appeared: John Beer (editor of *Aids to Reflection* and coeditor of the Leighton marginalia), Edward Bostetter, Reginald Foakes (whose work on the Shakespeare lectures is intimately related to the marginalia on four copies of Shakespeare's works), Robin and Heather Jackson (whose work on the *Shorter Works and Fragments* is in places interwoven with the marginalia), Trevor Levere (but for whose knowledge of early-nineteenth-century science and the history of the *Naturphilosophie* many of Coleridge's speculative flights might seem to lie only a little this side of alchemy), Thomas McFarland (for the zest and scope of his book *Coleridge and the Pantheist Tradition*), and Carl Woodring (whose unravelling of the *Table Talk* has come upon certain threads of marginalia). Particularly I wish to thank Robin Jackson, who, over a period of years, has at my request made a number of detailed contributions to this edition, not least by securing transcripts of annotations in fugitive books.

I am grateful to a number of persons for answering my questions and for sharing with me the fruits of their thought and learning: W. P. Albrecht, John Baird, Owen Barfield, Paul Betz, Roberta Florence Brinkley, Jane Campbell, John Carter, Beatrice Corrigan, Basil Cottle, Mrs Warren E. Cox, Joyce Crick, Brooke Crutchley, Bertram R. Davis, H. O. Dendurent, Madeleine Doran, John W. Elliott, Dorothy Emmett, James Evans, Barker Fairley, Dame Helen Gardner, Mary Lynn Johnson Grant, Lawrence Hanson, George Healey, David Hoeniger, Humphry House, H. W. Howe, Bishop Hunt, the Honourable Angela James, Paul Kaufman, the Honourable Rachel Kay-Shuttleworth, Paul Magnuson, James Mays, Mary Moorman, Burton Pollin, Robert Presson, Mark Reed, Anne and Ferdinand Renier, Sir Francis Rennel of Rodd, Basil Savage, Elisabeth Schneider, Chester Shaver, Sir Samuel Scott, J. Gordon Spaulding, Reynolds Stone, Sir Ralph Vaughan Williams, William Walsh, Oliver Warner, George Watson, Reginald Watters, Alvin Whitley, Elizabeth Mary Wilkinson, Basil Willey, Jon Wittreich, D. H. Woodward, Robert Woof, Jonathan Wordsworth.

I wish to thank the editors of *The Times Literary Supplement*, the *University of Toronto Quarterly*, and *The Book-Collector* for their earlier publishing of certain materials that are now incorporated, with substantial revision, into the Introduction and the second Annex to it.

Among my colleagues of many years in Queen's University I wish to thank—in the English Department, Antony Alpers, William Barnes, John Baxter, Frederick Colwell, A. C. Hamilton, Norman MacKenzie, John Matthews, Isaac Newell, Colin Norman, Grant Sampson, and John Stedmond; in the Philosophy Department, Sandy Duncan, Martyn Estall, and Joseph Russell; in the Classics Department, Eric Smethurst and Ross Kirkpatrick; in the German Department, Hans Eichner and Tony Riley; in the Department of Spanish and Italian, James McDonald. Successive Heads of the English Department have advanced my work in many ways, not least by recommending leave at statutory and other intervals: Henry Alexander, Malcolm Ross, John Stedmond and Douglas Spettigue. I am grateful to successive Principals of Queen's University for taking an interest in what I was doing and for endorsing the recommendations of my colleagues: Dr William A. Mackintosh, Dr Alex J. Corry, Dr John J. Deutsch, and Dr Ronald L. Watts.

I owe a considerable debt to research assistants for the initiative and accuracy that has marked their work: Ann Bonnycastle, Heather Bremer, Colin Clair, Susan Moore, Jonathan Slattery, and Oliver Stonor. For preparing complex copy without reduplicative error I am grateful to Mary Ellen Barrett, Mrs Begg, Mrs Boesch, Shirley Carter, Freda Gough, Pat Hanman, Betty Hakkak, Lynda Hendrickson, Miss A. C. Jones, Mrs Legaré, Eva Palfalvy, Marion Lent, and Chris Somerville.

Long before the *Collected Works* was more than a pipe-dream, and even before Coleridge was more to me than the author of the *Ancient Mariner,* certain mentors set my feet along paths that I am now glad to have followed: at Bishop's University, Anthony Preston and William Raymond; at Oriel College, Oxford, William Maclagan; and at King's College, London, Geoffrey Bullough. For endorsing the conviction that scholarship is an imaginative activity, and for showing that it is best conducted with a light heart, I recall with admiration and affection the names of Sir Rupert Hart-Davis, Sir Herbert Read, Professor Ivor A. Richards, and Professor Douglas Bush. For fruitful influences of which they may not have been aware, I thank Cecil Bald, Edmund Blunden, Helen Darbishire, and James R. MacGillivray. I am particularly grateful to those who invited me to the University of Wisconsin as visiting professor and treated me as a guest at an important turning-point in this work. I acknowledge in silence those who, over the years, have shown in their affection, generosity, and hospitable tact that they regarded this work as of deeper personal import and wider human implication than works of scholarship are commonly thought to be. My greatest debt is to Elizabeth, my wife, and to Katharine, Christopher, and Emily, my children, who have outlived the burden of an albatross more menacing at times than we could ever have foreseen it would be.

The preparation of this edition has been generously supported by the Humanities Research Committee of Queen's University, the Nuffield Foundation, the British Council, the Humanities Research Council of Canada, by several grants from the Canada Council, by fellowships from the Nuffield Foundation, the John Simon Guggenheim Memorial Foundation, and the Killam Programme, and by sustaining grants from Bollingen Foundation and Princeton University Press. I wish to acknowledge particularly the generous and perceptive encouragement given me by John D. Barrett and Vaun Gillmor of Bollingen Foundation.

At the end I can only say, as Michael Drayton said in the foreword to his *Poly-olbion*, and as David Jones said again at the end of his preface to *In Parenthesis*: "if I have not done her right, the want is in my ability, not in my love".

Hartington, Ontario, December 1976   GEORGE WHALLEY

EDITORIAL PRACTICE,
CONVENTIONS,
AND ABBREVIATIONS

MARGINALIA

T HE term "marginalia" (singular, *marginale*) refers to anything written by Coleridge in the margins and other blank spaces in the text of a printed book, on flyleaves, end-papers, or the inside or outside of a paper wrapper. Notes written by Coleridge on separate slips of paper and inserted between the leaves of a book (sometimes later tipped in) are also treated as marginalia when they clearly refer to the text of the book in which they are found. Coleridge's notes of acquisition and presentation inscriptions are not treated as marginalia unless (as in Bowles's *Sonnets*) they bear a direct critical relation to the text of the book; when such a note occurs in an annotated book, it is recorded in the headnote. (See also "Marked Books", below.) Coleridge's marginalia were written almost entirely in printed books and pamphlets; but his annotations on two manuscripts (Wordsworth's *Prelude*, and John Leslie's unpublished *Life of Josiah Wedgwood*) and one note scribbled in the margin of a cutting from a copy of the *Morning Post* have been identified. Marginal notes written on proofs or copies of his own published works, being mostly revisions or extensions of what he had given to the public, are not included in this edition, but are distributed through the volumes of the *Collected Works*—except for the *Annual Anthology* and *Omniana*, which, as special cases, are included in this edition.

The text of each marginal note is printed literatim from the original manuscript whenever the original has survived and has been available to the editor. For annotated books that have disappeared, or have been inaccessible during the period of study (1948–76), the text is printed from a manuscript transcript or from a published text, whichever in the editor's judgement lies textually closest to Coleridge's original. When the text of a marginal note is defective or incomplete—from cropping, deterioration of the writing, or other physical damage—manuscript and printed versions have been consulted in the attempt to restore the missing or defective parts of the text. Variants between the text of this edition and the text of earlier transcripts and published versions, which often diverge widely from the original, have not been recorded, but in problematical cases they are noted selectively.

Coleridge's eighteenth-century and idiosyncratic spellings are reproduced, as are his slips of the pen and accidental repetitions. Words and phrases cancelled *currente calamo* or in revision are also reproduced. His directions for assembling the parts of a discontinuous note are transferred from the text to the textual notes. His use of capitals and punctuation has been followed. Because Coleridge sometimes, but inconsistently, used enlarged minuscules for capitals, and because he does not always form his punctuation marks precisely, the editor has sought to record—as far as consistency is possible over a considerable period of time in a large number of subtly ambiguous situations—what he took to be Coleridge's intention in punctuation and capitals rather than to attempt a facsimile rendering of the marks on the page. Two or more dashes at the end of a sentence are printed as a single dash, and his use of " it's " as the genitive of " it " is printed as " its ". His ampersand (which has a distinctive form) has not been expanded to "and". His paragraph mark " ʃʃ ", which follows the practice of some printers of his day, is transcribed as a single paragraph mark. His Greek is printed as he wrote it, with or without accents, and with the not infrequent inversion of breathings that may give a clue to his pronunciation; but breathings placed on the first vowel of an initial diphthong have been transferred to the second vowel. Two common Greek ligatures that he often used have been silently expanded to ου and στ. Otherwise, any editorial intrusion into the manuscript is recorded in a textual note.

Where pencil notes are so badly rubbed, cropped, or offset as to be virtually illegible, the transcript is occasionally lineated to correspond with the lines of the manuscript in order to provide a framework for possible later conjectural reconstructions. In the very few cases in which a note has proved wholly illegible, a serial number has been assigned to record the presence of the unread note. The geometrical diagrams that appear from time to time in the marginalia are printed fair on a scale proportionate to the handwriting of the original but with no attempt to reproduce the accidental effects of his uncertain draftsmanship; his special symbols of relation (x, ⅹ, ⅹ, etc) and other special characters that exist in the printer's fount are printed in typographical form; only unique sketches or devices are reproduced exactly as Coleridge drew them.

TEXTUS

This term (plural *textūs*) is here—in defiance of its traditional denotation (a manuscript or book of the Gospels or of the whole Bible)—used to refer to that part of the book which prompted Coleridge to write a marginal note and to which a marginal note refers.

Coleridge usually begins his annotation at or near the place in the text that has seized his attention. Sometimes he marks the textus with a line in a margin, sometimes with a marginal "X" or " + " or with one of his distinctive sigla (which are not here reproduced), the note being written in a convenient place on the page, on the facing page, or on a flyleaf. Except when he has marked the textus with a line in the margin, the extent of the textus is matter for the editor's judgement. Textus has been chosen in such a way as to provide any key words or phrases that are needed to understand Coleridge's note, to give an adequate context for the discourse, and to convey something of the style and tone of the printed original.

Textus is printed literatim from the copy of the book originally annotated, or in the absence of the original from a copy of the same edition. The typographical peculiarities of the printed original (to which Coleridge is usually sensitive) are followed in order to preserve something of the visual savour of the original; but ligatures and suspensions have been silently expanded, in Latin textus " & " is printed "et" (treating it as the ligature that it is), and in a few cases an obvious typographical error in the original has been silently corrected, provided Coleridge himself has not drawn attention to it. When the textus is in a language other than English, a translation is given below the textus; but titles of German works are not translated, nor are the German subtitles in the generic references translated. Because of Coleridge's strong sense of the integrity of words, a reader usually needs the *ipsissima verba* of the textus under his eye; summary of textus has therefore been introduced sparingly.

SUBMARGINALIA

Coleridge's marginalia vary in kind and extent from (at one extreme) impromptu essays of considerable length to (at the other extreme) the marking of notable or questionable passages with " ! " or " ? " or "Qu?", or with no more than a line in the margin. It is desirable to present the marginalia in the character of substantive critical comment and reflective discourse; it is also desirable to have record of everything he wrote in the books. Yet it would be undesirable to confuse the effect of the marginalia, or to inflate the number of them, by treating minute or trivial details at the same level as sustained discourse. In order to avoid the submerged judgement of silent omission, the editor has recognised a class of "submarginalia"—corrections, alterations, and marks made by Coleridge that do not imply a substantive critical comment and that are not included in the textus to a marginal note. (His simple corrections of typographical errors are normally recorded in the headnote.) Because it is often difficult to identify two or three characters hastily scribbled as Coleridge's or to be sure that underlining and lines in the margins are his, these have been assigned to Coleridge with much caution, especially when it is clear that a book passed through other hands before and after he annotated it. (The annotated copy of Hartley Coleridge's *Worthies of Yorkshire and Lancashire* raises special difficulties of this kind.)

Submarginalia are normally printed within the sequence of the marginalia and are given the serial number of the preceding marginal note with A, B, C, etc added. (In the few instances in which a submarginal note occurs before the first marginal note, it is numbered A.) When marked passages are numerous enough to interfere with the flow of the marginalia (as in AURELIUS), they are assembled in an Annex. Passages marked according to an announced system of qualitative sigla (as in ADAM and AURELIUS) are treated as submarginalia, even though they represent an implicit critical judgement. These are usually assembled in an Annex; but when, together with marginalia, they give a clear account of Coleridge's progressive response to the whole text as he was reading it, these are printed within the sequence of marginalia (as in ATHENAEUM and BROWNE *Religio*).

USE OF COLOUR

Coleridge's marginal notes are printed in the second colour, as are his marks in the margins, his underlinings, cancellations, corrections, and insertions in textus. His marginal lines are not reproduced, but are noted either in the headline to the entry or in a textual note.

Words written by Coleridge in a margin by way of correction to the printed text, or marked for insertion in the textus, are carried into the body of the textus (in the second colour) if he has cancelled the printed word or phrase; otherwise such additions, and any brief comments of his that best make their point by direct association with a certain place in the textus, are printed (in the second colour) within the type-area and marked off from the textus by].

All editorial matter is printed in black; except that the editor's footnote indicators, and the few editorial interpolations in the text of the marginalia themselves, are printed in the second colour. All editorial interpolations are indicated by textual notes, except that the editorial restoration of cropped or defaced words is placed in [ ] without comment.

CONVENTIONS USED IN TRANSCRIPTION

[wild]	A reading supplied by the editor when the word has been lost from the ms by cropping or physical damage
[not][a]	A word inserted by the editor to supply an unintentional omission on Coleridge's part, or to clarify the sense of an elliptical or ambiguous phrase. The accompanying textual note [a] accounts for the insertion
[? wild]	An uncertain reading
[? wild/world]	Possible alternative readings
⌐wild¬	A reading restored from erasure or obliteration, or from damage to the ms other than cropping—normally accompanied by a textual note
[...]	An illegible word or phrase
[.....]	A passage of undetermined extent illegible through rubbing or offsetting, or lost by cropping or other physical damage
⟨ ⟩	A word or passage inserted between the lines, or marked for insertion from another part of the page (in which case a textual note is provided). An inserted word or passage is not so marked when it follows immediately upon a cancellation in the ms

ARRANGEMENT OF ENTRIES

Each marginal note is identified by a "headline" and is preceded by its textus whenever a textus is identifiable or appropriate. The headline gives in bold type the serial number of the marginal note (in a series that applies only to that book); the page(s) on which the note is written in the original ms; and an indication whether the note is in ink or pencil (no comment means ink). When a note is physically separated from its textus—for example, on a flyleaf—the formula "referring to p ..." follows the page-reference, and Coleridge's own reference is printed as part of his marginal note. After a vertical rule |, a "generic reference" is given according to the author's subdivision of the book (into e.g. Book, Part, Chapter, Section, etc) so that the textus can be readily traced in an edition other than that actually annotated. In order to provide the reader with a broad context for the marginal note, the generic reference includes the author's title (if any) to the section in which the textus is found. The exact location of the textus is not recorded since the beginning of a marginal note is usually in close physical relation to the textus, or else the exact textus is identified by one of Coleridge's marks or indicators, or by a specific reference to page, part, paragraph, etc.

The annotations are printed in a single sequence in the order in which they appear in the book; with two exceptions. (*a*) Any note written on a flyleaf or elsewhere that clearly refers—usually by page reference—to an identifiable place in the printed text is placed in the series of marginalia as though it had been written on the page(s) it refers to. When a detached note refers to a textus on which a marginal note is also written, the marginal note is printed before the detached note, on the assumption that Coleridge preferred to write first on the printed page, using flyleaves and other accidental blank spaces for (among other purposes) longer extensions of notes begun in the text, for postscripts to marginal notes, and for general critical and reflective summaries. (In a few books Coleridge has written on a flyleaf a series of references to pages on some or all of which marginal notes also appear; then the detached reference is treated as the first paragraph of the marginal note.) (*b*) In a few places, because of the order in which Coleridge happened to write three or more notes on the same page, the physical order of the notes does not consort with the order of the textus to which they refer. In such a case, the annotations are printed in the order of their textus. If the chronological order of writing such notes can be discerned, the details are placed in a textual note.

BOOK-ENTRIES

An annotated book is described in three elements that are printed before the beginning of the sequence of marginalia in that book: the author's full name, with year of birth and death; the title of the book; and a "headnote". A work of two or more volumes is treated as a single book.

The title-page of the book is normally cited in full, but omitting mottoes and the author's name (unless the name is a grammatically integral part of the catch-word title). Imprints are given descriptively, with Latin place-names anglicised and dates in arabic figures. Publisher and printer are omitted, except when there is some significant connexion with Coleridge, or when the book is of intrinsic bibliographical interest beyond its association with Coleridge—in either of which cases the information is given in a bibliographical note added to the title-description. The format is given as an approximate indication of the shape and size of the volume(s). If the date or circumstances of publication provide a terminus for dating the marginalia, or if the annotated copy is in some way exceptional, this information is given in the bibliographical note.

The headnote opens with a statement of the present location of the book. The entry "Not located" means that the location of the book was not known to the editor at the time of going to press; but some of the un-located books passed through the editor's hands before they disappeared, and the entry "Not located" does not necessarily mean that the text of the marginalia is drawn from a secondary source. (Details of provenance, and especially the transmission through the early auction sales at which many of Coleridge's books were dispersed, are given in an Appendix in the final volume.)

A description of the unique annotated copy is then given, with an account of any inscription, signature, bookplate, marks, or notes that show who owned or used the book before, during, or after the time of Coleridge's annotation. This is followed by an account of any marks or inscriptions (other than marginalia) by Coleridge himself, together with any known details of Coleridge's acquiring, borrowing, or using the book, his acquaintance (if any) with the author, and—as far as this is not included in the editor's footnotes—his critical response to the book. The headnote ends with a summary account of CONTENTS (for collective works), MS TRANSCRIPTS (if any), DATE of the marginalia (with evidence for dating), and—when applicable—the COEDITOR(S). (An account of the previous publication of marginalia is given in an Appendix in the final volume.)

FOOTNOTES

Coleridge sometimes footnoted details in his annotations: these are indi-cated by the traditional symbols *, †, ‡, etc (the distinctive form of his own indicators not being reproduced), and are printed full measure below the marginal note they refer to. The editor's footnotes are indicated by superior arabic numerals in a series that begins with each marginal note; the footnotes themselves (printed in two columns at the foot of the page) are indicated by a corresponding number in bold type with the serial number of the marginal note as prefix (e.g. 27[2]). The order of the editor's footnotes follows the order that can be expected in reading: when Coleridge's marginal note includes an asterisk or dagger the reader turns from the body of the note to Coleridge's footnote and then returns to the body of the note. Textual notes, indicated by superior italic letters, are printed above the editor's footnotes in a smaller type.

AUTHOR-ENTRIES

The annotated books are arranged in alphabetical order of authors. When Coleridge has annotated more than one work by the same author, the books are entered in alphabetical order of title; when he has annotated more than one edition of the same work, the books are normally entered in chronological order of publication.

Some of the larger author-entries are provided with a "general note" preceding the first book-entry, in order to correlate and summarise information about the relation of the various works and copies as far as this cannot be adequately managed in the headnotes to the separate books, and to discuss Coleridge's reaction to the work of the author as a whole.

When Coleridge has annotated more than one copy of a work, or more than one edition of the same work, each is designated COPY A, COPY B, etc for convenience in identifying and referring to each unique book: for example, ANDERSON COPY A, B, and C are three sets of the same, though bibliographically variant, multi-volume compendium of British poetry. But (contrary to normal library practice) the designation has been broadened to include different versions of substantially the same work: for example, SHAKESPEARE COPY A, B, C, and D are four different editions of Shakespeare's works, only one of which includes the non-dramatic writings; and BARCLAY COPY A and COPY B are two editions of Barclay's *Argenis*, one in English translation (1629), the other in Latin (1649).

For works more than one copy or edition of which was annotated an index to annotations is provided, when appropriate (as e.g. BAXTER *Reliquiae* and BROWNE *Religio*), to show the relative distribution of marginalia through the copies. An index is also provided to show which parts of a collective work or edition were annotated and as a finding list (e.g. DONNE *Poems*); and such an index is provided to display the distribution of annotations through the individual copies of a collective edition (e.g. ANDERSON and BEAUMONT & FLETCHER).

Anonymous works are entered alphabetically by title; but when the author of an anonymous work has been reliably identified, the book is entered under the author's name. Pseudonymous works are entered under the author's true name (when known). Renaissance authors are entered under their Latin names, according to the custom of their time and Coleridge's usage. Compilations and periodicals are entered alphabetically by title, except for "Anderson's Poets" and "Chalmers's Poets", which are entered under their editors' names. A few annotations have been discovered that are now separated from the books in which they were originally written, the books not identifiable; these are entered under the heading "UNIDENTIFIED" and arranged according to topic.

FORM OF REFERENCE TO MARGINALIA

In the editorial matter, reference to a particular marginal note is made by adding the serial number of the note (in bold type) to an abbreviated identification of the unique annotated book in the form AUTHOR *Title* COPY, using only the elements essential to identification. For example, "BARTRAM" refers to the only annotated book in this edition written by an author named Bartram; the form of entry also implies that only one Bartram (William, as it happens) is represented by an annotated book. "ANDERSON COPY C" refers to COPY C of the only title entered under "Anderson". "DONNE *Sermons* COPY A" refers to a copy of John Donne's *Sermons* and indicates that there is at least one other annotated "copy"; the form of entry also implies that only one author of the name of "Donne" is represented in the edition, and that Coleridge annotated at least one other work of Donne's besides the *Sermons*. The presence of an initial before the author's surname in an abbreviated title implies that two or more authors of the same surname are represented by annotated books; and the reference "Jeremy TAYLOR" implies that there are annotated books written by two or more Taylors whose initial was "J.". References to marginalia that had not been finally prepared for the press at the time of writing are given in the same form, but with a page-reference in place of the serial number. Reference to a particular textus is made in the form "ADAM 27 textus". Reference to a particular footnote is made by referring to the marginal note to which the footnote applies, in the form "BAXTER *Reliquiae* COPY B 100 n 4." A precise location in a long annotation can be given in the form "BÖHME 45 at n 6".

SOME SPECIAL TERMS

FLY-PAGES—all blank pages at the front and back of a volume, outside the first and last page on which anything is printed. The term refers, not to the bibliographical definitions of "flyleaves" (blank leaves inserted by the binder between the end-paper and the first or last gathering of printed matter), but to all blank pages available to receive annotation at the front and back of a volume, including end-papers, flyleaves, original paper wrappers, and even (on occasion) the blank recto of an engraved portrait that faces a title-page; it includes also any blank pages that are part of the first or last gathering (signature) of the volume and yet are *outside* the first and last printed page. (The verso of a half-title, for example, is not a fly-page because it lies "inside" the printed half-title.) In order to provide an economical and unambiguous reference to those parts of a book which are most subject to revision in rebinding, fly-pages are identified by page-numbers counted *outward* from the first and last page that carries any print, the series ending (except in the case of the outside of a wrapper) with the paste-down (abbreviated "p–d"). Front fly-pages have the prefix $^-$; back fly-pages have the prefix $^+$. For example, "p $^-$1" is the blank page immediately preceding the first page on which printing appears, and is usually a verso but may be a recto; "p $^-$4 (p–d)" is a front paste-down and is followed by three blank fly-pages—and since the front paste-down must be a verso, p $^-$1 in this book would have to be a recto; "p $^+$2" is the second blank page after the last printed page (which is often the page bearing only the printer's imprint), and could be either recto or verso.

ANNEX—matter printed at the end of a book-entry and typographically distinct from the marginalia. Annexes are used mostly for gathering together passages that are marked but not annotated (as in ADAM and AURELIUS); but an Annex can be used to present documentary material that is intimately related to the marginalia but that cannot conveniently be introduced in the editor's footnotes (as in BÖHME and BROWNE *Works*).

MS TRANSCRIPT—a manuscript copy of marginalia (occasionally by Coleridge himself), usually not now accompanying the book in which the notes were written. Many of these transcripts were made by the early editors and their amanuenses in preparing *Literary Remains* and other edited collections of Coleridge's manuscripts. A special type of transcript—here referred to as a "MS Facsimile"—was made by transcribing all or some of Coleridge's marginalia from the original annotated copy into another copy of the same book, usually a copy of the same edition as the original, with some attempt to reproduce the placing and visual quality of the original notes. Most of the known ms facsimiles were made by or for the Gillmans before they transferred the originals to Joseph Henry Green; but James Dykes Campbell made a few, and a few others—particularly of Donne's *Poems*—were made by persons unknown. For a few books such a copy is the only authority for Coleridge's annotations. None of the known ms facsimiles is to be regarded as a forgery, even though Thomas J. Wise owned some of them and described some of those in his possession as though they were originals.

QUASI-MARGINALIA—notes written by Coleridge in a notebook or on separate sheets of paper, of a kind that might well have been written in the book they refer to if it had been convenient or appropriate for him to do so. These typically include the title of the book referred to and page-references. The clearest examples are the early notes on Godwin's *St Leon* in *CN* I 254 (written perhaps from Godwin's proof-sheets or a prepublication copy of the book), some detailed notes written in Malta referring to Henry Peter Brougham's *Inquiry into the Colonial Policy of the European Powers* (the copy apparently belonged to the Governor of Malta), and the notes on Blake's *Songs of Innocence and Songs of Experience* in *CL* IV 836–8 (written from C. A. Tulk's copy—in any case a book that one cannot imagine anybody writing notes in). But Coleridge so often wrote in his notebooks with a book open in front of him, especially in the later years, that the category explodes into a kind of writing common enough in the notebooks and elsewhere, and a serious question arises whether writing done free of the constraints of margins and fly-pages can properly be regarded as a kind of marginalia. No quasi-marginalia have been included in a series of true marginalia in this edition, but some are noticed in the editor's footnotes, and are printed there, or in an Annex, when they are obvious extensions of the annotations actually written in the book.

APPENDIX—a separate list, table, or summary ancillary to the main text of the marginalia. All appendixes are assembled in the final volume of this edition.

LOST BOOK—a book described as annotated by Coleridge but now lost without any transcript of the marginalia having been made. All Lost Books are entered in the alphabetical series of annotated titles and are provided with a headnote in the usual form. In an Appendix the "*Lost List*" brings together in one series the details of Lost Books and of the unlocated annotated books for which some version of the marginalia is preserved.

MARKED BOOK—a book known by its markings (other than marginalia) to have belonged to Coleridge or to have been used by him. The most obvious members of this category are those books which bear his name in full or in initials, in his own or another hand; but the term also applies to any book with a presentation inscription to or from Coleridge. A book shown as Coleridge's in an authoritative handlist—especially Wordsworth LC and the Green List—is treated as a marked book, even though the book itself may have disappeared, for many of the books shown as his in those lists have been certainly identified as his and a certain number of them are annotated. (If all the missing Marked Books were to be recovered, some would probably be found to contain marginalia.) The small distinctive label inscribed "S. T. C." (usually attached to a title-page), EHC's marking "Green Bequest" (often on a slip of paper inserted in the book, but sometimes written in), and John Duke Coleridge's monogram "C" found in many books from the Ottery Collection are also taken as presumptive evidence that the book was Coleridge's—an assumption often corroborated by other evidence. Coleridge's own statement that he owned or annotated a certain book is taken at face value, even though the book may have disappeared. Descriptions in auction sale catalogues have been judged according to context. In an Appendix in the last volume a list is given of books (some of them annotated) that have been ascribed to Coleridge but that are now known not to have been his.

ABBREVIATIONS

Place of publication is London, unless otherwise noted. Special abbreviations that apply only to certain author-entries or book-entries are given in the appropriate general note or headnote.

Allsop	[Thomas Allsop] *Letters, Conversations and Recollections of S. T. Coleridge* (2 vols 1836)
AM	S. T. Coleridge *The Rime of the Ancient Mariner*
AP	*Anima Poetae: from the Unpublished Notebooks of S. T. Coleridge* ed E. H. Coleridge (1895)
A Reg	*The Annual Register* (1758–)
AR (1825)	S. T. Coleridge *Aids to Reflection* (1825)
Ashley LC	Thomas J. Wise *The Ashley Library: A Catalogue of Printed Books, Manuscripts and Autograph Letters Collected by Thomas James Wise* (11 vols 1922–36). Coleridge items are principally in Vols I, VIII, X. Items from Wise's collection now in the BM bear the prefix "Ashley" in the press-mark
AV	The "Authorised Version"—or "King James Version"—of the Bible, in modern orthography
BCP	*The Book of Common Prayer and Administration of the Sacraments and other rites and ceremonies of the Church according to the use of the Church of England*

BL (1817)	S. T. Coleridge *Biographia Literaria; or Biographical Sketches of My Literary Life and Opinions* (2 vols 1817)
BL (1847)	S. T. Coleridge *Biographia Literaria* ed. H. N. and Sara Coleridge (2 vols 1847)
BL (1907)	S. T. Coleridge *Biographia Literaria...with His Aesthetical Essays* ed. J. Shawcross (2 vols Oxford 1907)
BM	British Library, Reference Division, formerly "British Museum Library"
BMC	*The British Museum Catalogue of Printed Books*
BNPL	*New York Public Library Bulletin* (New York 1897–)
B Poets	*The Works of the British Poets* ed Robert Anderson (13 vols Edinburgh & London 1792–5; vol 14 1807). The annotated copies are referred to as "ANDERSON"
Bristol LB	George Whalley "The Bristol Library Borrowings of Southey and Coleridge" *Library* IV (Sept 1949) 114–31
C	Samuel Taylor Coleridge
C&S	S. T. Coleridge *On the Constitution of the Church and State, According to the Idea of Each* (2nd ed 1830)
C&S (*CC*)	S. T. Coleridge *On the Constitution of the Church and State* ed John Colmer (London & Princeton 1976)= *CC* x
C & SH	George Whalley *Coleridge and Sara Hutchinson and the Asra Poems* (1955)
Carlisle LB	Carlisle Cathedral Library Borrowings 1801–2
Carlyon	Clement Carlyon *Early Years and Late Reflections* (4 vols 1836–58)
C at H	L. E. Watson *Coleridge at Highgate* (London & New York 1925)
CC	*The Collected Works of Samuel Taylor Coleridge* general ed Kathleen Coburn (London & Princeton 1969–)
CH	*Coleridge: The Critical Heritage* ed J. R. de J. Jackson (1970)
CIS	S. T. Coleridge *Confessions of an Inquiring Spirit and Some Miscellaneous Pieces* ed H. N. Coleridge (1849)
CL	*Collected Letters of Samuel Taylor Coleridge* ed Earl Leslie Griggs (6 vols Oxford & New York 1956–71)
C Life (C)	E. K. Chambers *Samuel Taylor Coleridge* (Oxford 1938)

C Life (G)	James Gillman *The Life of Samuel Taylor Coleridge* (1838)
C Life (H)	Lawrence Hanson *The Life of Samuel Taylor Coleridge: the Early Years* (1938)
C Life (JDC)	James Dykes Campbell *Samuel Taylor Coleridge* (1894)
CM (*CC*)	S. T. Coleridge *Marginalia* ed George Whalley (London & Princeton 1979–) = *CC* XII
CN	*The Notebooks of Samuel Taylor Coleridge* ed Kathleen Coburn (New York, Princeton & London 1957–)
C Pantheist	Thomas McFarland *Coleridge and the Pantheist Tradition* (Oxford 1969)
CRB	*Henry Crabb Robinson on Books and Their Writers* ed Edith J. Morley (3 vols 1938)
CR (*BCW*)	*Blake, Coleridge, Wordsworth, Lamb, etc. being Selections from the Remains of Henry Crabb Robinson* ed Edith J. Morley (Manchester 1922)
CRC	*The Correspondence of Henry Crabb Robinson with the Wordsworth Circle* ed Edith J. Morley (2 vols Oxford 1927)
CRD	*Diary, Reminiscences, and Correspondence of Henry Crabb Robinson* ed Thomas Sadler (2 vols 1872)
CR Life	Edith J. Morley *The Life and Times of Henry Crabb Robinson* (1935)
C Talker	R. W. Armour and R. F. Howes *Coleridge the Talker* (1949)
C 17th C	*Coleridge on the Seventeenth Century* ed R. F. Brinkley (Durham NC 1955)
CW	*The Complete Works of S. T. Coleridge* ed W. G. T. Shedd (7 vols New York 1853)
DC	Derwent Coleridge
De Q	Thomas De Quincey
De Q to W	John E. Jordan *De Quincey to Wordsworth. A Biography of a Relationship* (Berkeley & Los Angeles 1962)
De Q Works	*The Collected Writings of Thomas De Quincey* ed David Masson (14 vols Edinburgh 1889–90)
Diels	Hermann Diels *Die Fragmente der Vorsokratiker* ed Walther Kranz (3 vols Zürich 1971)
DNB	*Dictionary of National Biography* (1885–)
Durham LB	Durham Cathedral Library Borrowings 1801

DW	Dorothy Wordsworth
DW (S)	Ernest de Selincourt *Dorothy Wordsworth* (Oxford 1933)
DWJ	*Journals of Dorothy Wordsworth* ed Ernest de Selincourt (2 vols Oxford 1939)
DWJ (M)	*Journals of Dorothy Wordsworth. The Alfoxden Journal 1798* [and] *The Grasmere Journals 1800–1803* ed Mary Moorman (Oxford 1971)
EC	*The English Catalogue of Books (including the original "London" Catalogue* [of 1786 for 1700–86]) *...issued in the United Kingdom...1801–1836* ed R. A. Peddie and Q. Waddington (London 1914)
EHC	Ernest Hartley Coleridge
EOT (*CC*)	S. T. Coleridge *Essays on His Times in "The Morning Post" and "The Courier"* ed David V. Erdman (3 vols London & Princeton 1977) = *CC* III
Farington Diary	Joseph Farington *The Farington Diary* ed James Greig (8 vols 1922–8)
Friend (*CC*)	S. T. Coleridge *The Friend* ed Barbara E. Rooke (2 vols London & Princeton 1969) = *CC* IV
Gillman SC (1843)	*Catalogue of a valuable collection of books, including the Library of James Gillman, Esq* (Henry Southgate 1843). Marked copies: BM S–C Sg 64(2) and a53
G Mag	*The Gentleman's Magazine* (1731–1907)
Göttingen LB	A. D. Snyder "Books Borrowed by Coleridge from the Library of the University of Göttingen, 1799" *Modern Philology* xxv (1928) 377–80.
Green List	VCL MS 8. A handlist of Coleridge's books prepared by Mrs J. H. Green c 1863
Green SC (1880)	*Catalogue of the Library of Joseph Henry Green... sold by auction* (Sotheby Jul 1880). Marked copy: BM S–C S 805(1)
Green SC (1884)	*Catalogue of scarce and valuable books, including a remarkable collection of Coleridgeiana* (Scribner & Welford, New York 1884)
HC	Hartley Coleridge
HCL	*Letters of Hartley Coleridge* ed Grace Evelyn and Earl Leslie Griggs (Oxford 1936)
HC Poems	*Poems by Hartley Coleridge, with a memoir of his life by his brother* ed Derwent Coleridge (2 vols 1851)
HCR	Henry Crabb Robinson
HEHL	The Henry E. Huntington Library and Art Gallery, San Marino, California

Highgate List	Wordsworth LC entries 1186–1299: a handlist in WW's hand of books "Sent to Coleridge" in c 1829
HNC	Henry Nelson Coleridge
H Works	*The Complete Works of William Hazlitt* ed P. P. Howe (12 vols 1930–4)
IS	*Inquiring Spirit: a New Presentation of Coleridge from His Published and Unpublished Prose Writings* ed Kathleen Coburn (London & New York 1951)
JDC	James Dykes Campbell
JW	John Wordsworth
JWL	*Letters of John Wordsworth* ed C. H. Ketcham (Ithaca NY 1969)
L	*Letters of Samuel Taylor Coleridge* ed E. H. Coleridge (2 vols 1895)
L & L	*Coleridge on Logic and Learning* ed Alice D. Snyder (1929)
LB	William Wordsworth [and S. T. Coleridge] *Lyrical Ballads with Other Poems* (Bristol 1798 &c); the edition referred to indicated by a bracketed date. "*LB*" following a place-name (e.g. *Durham LB*) means "Library Borrowing"
LCL	Loeb Classical Library
Lects 1795 (CC)	S. T. Coleridge *Lectures 1795: On Politics and Religion* ed Lewis Patton and Peter Mann (London & Princeton 1971) = *CC* I
LL	*The Letters of Charles Lamb to Which Are Added Those of His Sister Mary Lamb* ed E. V. Lucas (3 vols 1935)
LL (M)	*The Letters of Charles and Mary Anne Lamb* ed Edwin W. Marrs, Jr (Ithaca NY 1975–)
L Life	E. V. Lucas *The Life of Charles Lamb* (1921)
LLP	*Letters from the Lake Poets to Daniel Stuart* [ed Mary Stuart and E. H. Coleridge] (1889)
L Works	*The Works of Charles and Mary Lamb* ed E. V. Lucas (6 vols 1912)
Logic (CC)	S. T. Coleridge *Logic* ed J. R. de J. Jackson (London & Princeton 1979) = *CC* XIII
Lost List	A handlist prepared by George Whalley of books known to have been annotated by Coleridge but not located at the time this edition went to press. An incomplete version was published in *Book Collector* XVII (1968) 428–42 and XVIII (1969) 223. A complete list is given in an Appendix

LR	*The Literary Remains of Samuel Taylor Coleridge* ed H. N. Coleridge (4 vols 1836–9)
LS	S. T. Coleridge *A Lay Sermon, Addressed to the Higher and Middle Classes, on the Existing Distresses and Discontents* (1817)
LS (1852)	S. T. Coleridge *Lay Sermons. I. The Statesman's Manual. II. Blessed are ye that sow beside all Waters* [i.e. *A Lay Sermon*] ed Derwent Coleridge (1852)
LS (*CC*)	S. T. Coleridge *Lay Sermons* [being *The Statesman's Manual* and *A Lay Sermon*] ed R. J. White (London & Princeton 1972) = *CC* v
M Chron	*The Morning Chronicle* (1769–1862)
Method	*S. T. Coleridge's Treatise on Method as Published in the Encyclopaedia Metropolitana* ed Alice D. Snyder (1934)
Migne *PG*	*Patriologiae cursus completus…series Graeca* ed J. P. Migne (162 vols Paris 1857–1912)
Migne *PL*	*Patriologiae cursus completus…series Latina* ed J. P. Migne (221 vols Paris 1844–64)
Minnow	*Minnow among Tritons: Mrs S. T. Coleridge's Letters to Thomas Poole, 1799–1834* ed Stephen Potter (1934)
Misc C	*Coleridge's Miscellaneous Criticism* ed T. M. Raysor (1936)
M Post	*The Morning Post* (1772–1937)
Mrs C	Sara Coleridge née Fricker (wife of C)
MS Leatherhead	A manuscript formerly in the collection of the Rev Gerard H. B. Coleridge when Vicar of Leatherhead
MW	Mary Wordsworth née Hutchinson (wife of WW)
N	Notebook of Samuel Taylor Coleridge (numbered or lettered) in ms. References are given by folio
NEB	*The New English Bible* (Oxford & Cambridge 1964)
NEB Gk	*The Greek New Testament being the text translated in the New English Bible 1961* ed R. V. G. Tasker (Oxford & Cambridge 1964)
NED	S. T. Coleridge *Notes on English Divines* ed Derwent Coleridge (2 vols 1853)
NLS	S. T. Coleridge *Notes and Lectures upon Shakespeare and Some Other Old Poets and Dramatists with Other Literary Remains* ed Sara Coleridge (2 vols 1849)
NT Gk Lex	W. Bauer *A Greek-English Lexicon of the New Testament and Other Early Christian Literature* ed & tr W. F. Arndt and F. W. Gingrich (Chicago & Cambridge 1968)

NTP	S. T. Coleridge *Notes, Theological. Political and Miscellaneous* ed Derwent Coleridge (1853)
NYPL	New York Public Library
ODCC	*The Oxford Dictionary of the Christian Church* ed F. L. Cross (London 1971)
OED	*The Oxford English Dictionary being a corrected re-issue...of "A New English Dictionary on Historical Principles"* (12 vols Oxford 1970)
OLD	*Oxford Latin Dictionary* (Oxford 1968–)
Omniana	*Omniana, or Horae otiosiores* ed Robert Southey [with articles by C] (2 vols 1812)
p–d	paste-down. See "Editorial Practice" p xxx, above
P Lects (1949)	*The Philosophical Lectures of Samuel Taylor Coleridge* ed Kathleen Coburn (London & New York 1949)
Poole	M. E. Sandford *Thomas Poole and His Friends* (2 vols 1888)
Prelude	William Wordsworth *The Prelude or Growth of a Poet's Mind* ed Ernest de Selincourt, rev Helen Darbishire (Oxford 1959)
"*Prometheus*"	S. T. Coleridge "On the *Prometheus* of Aeschylus: An Essay...read at the Royal Society of Literature, May 18, 1825" as printed in *LR* ii 323–59.
Proto-*Prometheus*	The ms draft of "*Prometheus*" written c 1821: Duke University
PW (EHC)	*The Complete Poetical Works of Samuel Taylor Coleridge* ed E. H. Coleridge (2 vols Oxford 1912)
PW (JDC)	*The Poetical Works of Samuel Taylor Coleridge* ed J. D. Campbell (1893)
RES	*Review of English Studies* (1925–)
RS	Robert Southey
RSV	The [American] Revised Standard Version of the Bible: NT 1946, OT 1952
RV	The Revised Version of the Bible: NT 1881, OT 1885, Apocr 1895
RX	John Livingston Lowes *The Road to Xanadu* (rev ed Boston 1930)
SC	Sara Coleridge (daughter of C, and wife of HNC)
SC Life	Earl Leslie Griggs *Coleridge Fille. A Biography of Sara Coleridge* (Oxford 1940)
SC Memoir	*Memoir and Letters of Sara Coleridge* [ed Edith Coleridge] (2 vols 1873)
SH	Sara Hutchinson

Sh C	*Coleridge's Shakespearean Criticism* ed T. M. Raysor (2nd ed 2 vols 1960)
SHL	*The Letters of Sara Hutchinson* ed Kathleen Coburn (London & Toronto 1954)
SL	S. T. Coleridge *Sibylline Leaves* (1817)
S Letters (Curry)	*New Letters of Robert Southey* ed Kenneth Curry (2 vols New York & London 1965)
S Letters (Warter)	*A Selection from the Letters of Robert Southey* ed J. W. Warter (4 vols 1856)
S Life (CS)	*Life and Correspondence of Robert Southey* ed C. C. Southey (6 vols 1849–50)
S Life (Simmons)	Jack Simmons *Southey* (1945)
SM	S. T. Coleridge *The Statesman's Manual: or, The Bible, the Best Guide to Political Skill and Foresight. A Lay-Sermon Addressed to the Higher Classes of Society* (1816)
SM (1852)	S. T. Coleridge *The Statesman's Manual* in *Lay Sermons* ed Derwent Coleridge (1852)
SM (*CC*)	S. T. Coleridge *The Statesman's Manual* in *Lay Sermons* ed R. J. White (London & Princeton 1972)
Southey SC (1844)	*Catalogue of the Valuable Library of the Late Robert Southey* (Sotheby, May 1844). Marked copy: BM S–C S 252(1)
Studies	*Coleridge: Studies by Several Hands on the Hundredth Anniversary of his Death* ed E. Blunden and E. L. Griggs (1934)
TL	S. T. Coleridge *Hints Towards the Formation of a More Comprehensive Theory of Life* ed Seth B. Watson (1848)
TT	*Table Talk of Samuel Taylor Coleridge* ed H. N. Coleridge (rev ed 1836). Cited by date
UL	*Unpublished Letters of Samuel Taylor Coleridge* ed Earl Leslie Griggs (2 vols 1932)
V & A	Victoria and Albert Museum
VCL	Victoria College Library, University of Toronto
Watchman (*CC*)	S. T. Coleridge *The Watchman* ed Lewis Patton (London & Princeton 1970) = *CC* II
WL (*E2*)	*Letters of William and Dorothy Wordsworth; the Early Years* ed Ernest de Selincourt, rev Chester L. Shaver (Oxford 1967)
WL (*L*)	*Letters of William and Dorothy Wordsworth; the Later Years* ed Ernest de Selincourt (3 vols Oxford 1939)

WL (M2)	*Letters of William and Dorothy Wordsworth; the Middle Years* ed Ernest de Selincourt, rev Mary Moorman (2 vols Oxford 1969–70)
W Life	Mary Moorman *William Wordsworth, A Biography* (2 vols Oxford 1957–65)
Wordsworth LC	Wordsworth Library Catalogue. Harvard MS Eng 880. A handlist of books in WW's library at Rydal Mount from c 1823. Serial numbers supplied by George Whalley. Edition of the ms by Chester Shaver in preparation
Wordsworth SC (1859)	*Catalogue of the...Library of...William Wordsworth* (Preston 1859)
W Mem	Christopher Wordsworth *Memoirs of William Wordsworth* (2 vols 1851)
W Prose	*The Prose Works of William Wordsworth* ed W. J. B. Owen and J. W. Smyser (3 vols Oxford 1974)
WPW	*The Poetical Works of William Wordsworth* ed Ernest de Selincourt and Helen Darbishire (5 vols Oxford 1940–9)
WW	William Wordsworth

CHRONOLOGICAL TABLES

S. T. COLERIDGE
1772–1834

1772	(21 Oct) C b at Ottery St Mary, Devonshire, to the Rev John and Ann (Bowdon) Coleridge, youngest of their 10 children	George III king (1760–1820) Wordsworth 2 years old Scott 1 year old *M Post* began
1774		Southey b
1775		American War of Independence Charles Lamb b
1776		Adam Smith *Wealth of Nations* Gibbon *Decline and Fall*
1778	C at Ottery Grammar School	Hazlitt b Rousseau and Voltaire d
1780		(Jun) Gordon Riots
1781	(4 Oct) C's father died	Kant *Kritik der reinen Vernunft* Schiller *Die Räuber*
1782	(Jul) Enrolled at Christ's Hospital preparatory school for girls and boys, Hertford (Sept) Christ's Hospital, London, with C. Lamb, G. Dyer, T. F. Middleton, Robert Allen, J. M. Gutch, Le Grice brothers	Priestley *Corruptions of Christianity* Rousseau *Confessions*
1783		Pitt's first ministry (–1801)
1784		Samuel Johnson d
1785	Walked the wards of London Hospital with his brother Luke	De Quincey b Paley *Principles of Moral and Political Philosophy*
1787	First contribution to Boyer's *Liber Aureus*	
1788	(early summer) Elected Grecian; met Evans family	
1789		(14 Jul) French Revolution Blake *Songs of Innocence* Bowles *Sonnets*
1790		Burke *Reflections on the Revolution in France*

1791 (Sept) Jesus College, Cambridge, Exhibitioner, Sizar, Rustat Scholar; met S. Butler, Frend, Porson, C. Wordsworth, Wrangham

(Mar) John Wesley d
Paine *Rights of Man* pt I (pt II 1792)
Boswell *Life of Johnson*
Anti-Jacobin riots at Birmingham

1792 (3 Jul) C's prize-winning Greek *Ode on the Slave-Trade* read at Encaenia

Pitt's attack on the slave-trade
Fox's Libel Bill

1793 (Jan) Failed by a technicality to win Craven Scholarship
(May) Attended Cambridge trial of Frend
(15 Jul) First poem in *Morning Chronicle*
(2 Dec) Enlisted in 15th Light Dragoons as Silas Tomkyn Comberbache

(21 Jan) Louis XVI executed
(1 Feb) France declared war on England and Holland
(Mar-Dec) Revolt of La Vendée
(16 Oct) Marie Antoinette executed
(16 Oct) John Hunter d
Godwin *Political Justice*
Wordsworth *An Evening Walk* and *Descriptive Sketches*

1794 (7–10 Apr) Returned to Cambridge
(Jun) Poems in *Cambridge Intelligencer*; set out with Joseph Hucks to Oxford; met Southey, planned pantisocracy; Welsh tour
(Aug) Joined Southey and Burnett in Bristol; met Thomas Poole; engaged to Sara Fricker
(Sept) Returned to Cambridge; with RS published *The Fall of Robespierre* (Cambridge); *Monody on Chatterton* published with *Rowley Poems* (Cambridge)
(Dec) Left Cambridge; sonnets in *M Chron*; "Noctes Atticae" with Lamb at Salutation and Cat
(24 Dec) Began *Religious Musings*

(23 May) Suspension of Habeas Corpus
(28 Jul) Robespierre executed; end of the Terror
(Oct–Dec) State Trials: Hardy, Tooke, and Thelwall acquitted of charge of treason
(–1795) Paine *Age of Reason*
Paley *Evidences of Christianity*

1795 (end Jan) RS brought C back from London to Bristol; lodgings with RS and Burnett; met Joseph Cottle
(Feb) Political lectures
(Feb/May) *Moral and Political Lecture* published
(May–Jun) Lectures on Revealed Religion
(16 Jun) Lecture on the Slave-Trade Portrait by Peter Vandyke
(Aug–Sept) Quarrel with RS; pantisocracy abandoned; met WW in Bristol
(4 Oct) Married Sara Fricker
(26 Nov) Lecture on the Two Bills
(3 Dec) *Conciones ad populum* published

(Jun–Jul) Quiberon expedition
(26 Sept) WW and DW to Racedown
(Nov) Directory began
(3 Nov) Treason and Convention Bills introduced
(18 Dec) Two Acts put into effect
Lewis *Ambrosio, or the Monk*

(Dec) *An Answer to "A Letter to Edward Long Fox"* and *Plot Discovered* published; *Watchman* planned

1796 (9 Jan–13 Feb) Tour of Midlands to sell *The Watchman*; met Erasmus Darwin and Joseph Wright (painter)
(1 Mar–13 May) *The Watchman* in ten numbers
(16 Apr) *Poems on Various Subjects*
(19 Sept) Hartley C b; reconciliation with RS
(31 Dec) *Ode on Departing Year* in *Cambridge Intelligencer*; move to Nether Stowey

(Jul) Robert Burns d
(Sept) Mary Lamb's violent illness
(Nov) Catherine of Russia d
England treating for peace with France
Threats of invasion of England
Jenner performs first smallpox vaccination

1797 (Mar) WW at Stowey
(5 Jun) C at Racedown
(Jul) DW, WW, and Lamb at Stowey; DW and WW in Alfoxden House
(16 Oct) *Osorio* finished; *Poems, to which are now added, Poems by Charles Lamb and Charles Lloyd*
(13–16 Nov) Walk with Wordsworths to Lynton and *Ancient Mariner* begun

(Feb) Bank of England suspended cash payments
(Apr–Jun) Mutinies in the British fleet
(9 Jul) Burke d
(17 Oct) France and Austria sign peace treaty
(Nov) Frederick William II of Prussia d
(Nov) *Anti-Jacobin* began

1798 (Jan) C's Unitarian sermons at Shrewsbury; Hazlitt heard C preach; Wedgwood annuity £150 accepted
(Mar) *Ancient Mariner* completed
(Apr) *Fears in Solitude*
(14 May) Berkeley C b
(18 Sept) *Lyrical Ballads* published; WW, DW, Chester, and C to Hamburg; met Klopstock
(Oct) C to Ratzeburg

(Feb–Oct) Irish rebellion
(Apr) Helvetic Republic
(12 Jun) Malta taken by French
(Jul) Bonaparte invaded Egypt
(9 Jul) *Anti-Jacobin* last number
(1–2 Aug) Nelson's victory in Battle of the Nile
Lloyd *Edmund Oliver*
Bell introduced Madras system of education in England

1799 (10 Feb) Berkeley C died
(11 Feb) C at University of Göttingen
(c 6 Apr) C had news of Berkeley's death
(May) Ascent of the Brocken
(29 Jul) In Stowey again
(Sept–Oct) Devon walking tour with RS; met Humphry Davy in Bristol; experiments with nitrous oxide
(Oct–Nov) First Lakes tour, with WW
(26 Oct) Met Sara Hutchinson

(Nov) Directory overthrown
(Dec) Constitution of Year VIII; Bonaparte First Consul
Schiller *Die Piccolomini* and *Wallensteins Tod* published
Royal Institution founded

(27 Nov) Arrived in London to accept *M Post* offer
(Dec) DW and WW at Town End (later Dove Cottage)

1800 (Jan–16 Apr) *M Post* reporter and leader-writer; translating *Wallenstein* at Lamb's
(Apr) To Grasmere and WW
(May–Jun) In Stowey and Bristol
(24 Jul) Moved to Greta Hall, Keswick
(Sept–Oct) Superintended printing of *Lyrical Ballads* (2nd ed)

(25 Apr) Cowper d
(14 Jun) Battle of Marengo
Burns *Works* ed Currie
(Aug) Union of Great Britain and Ireland
(5 Sept) Malta after long siege fell to English

1801 (Jan) *Lyrical Ballads* (1800) published; prolonged illnesses
(Jul–Aug) With SH at Stockton
(15 Nov) In London writing for *M Post*
Christmas at Stowey

(Mar) Pitt resigned over Emancipation
Addington ministry (–1804)
(Jul) Bonaparte signed Concordat with Pope
Davy lecturer at Royal Institution
RS *Thalaba*

1802 (Jan) In London; attended Davy's lectures at Royal Institution; writing for *M Post*
(Mar–Nov) In the Lakes, severe domestic discord
(4 Apr) *Dejection*
(Aug) Scafell climb; visit of the Lambs
(Sept–Nov) Writing for *M Post*
(Nov) Tour of S Wales with Tom and Sally Wedgwood
(23 Dec) Sara C b

(25 Mar) Peace of Amiens
(18 Apr) Erasmus Darwin d
(8 May) Bonaparte Consul for life
(2 Oct) WW married Mary Hutchinson
(Oct) French army entered Switzerland
Edinburgh Review founded
Cobbett's *Weekly Political Register* founded
Paley *Natural Theology*
Spinoza *Opera* ed Paulus (1802–3)

1803 (Jan–Feb) In Somerset with Wedgwoods and Poole; with Lamb in London; made his will
(Jun) *Poems* (1803) published
(summer) Hazlitt, Beaumonts, and S. Rogers in Lakes visited C; Hazlitt's portrait of C
(15–29 Aug) Tour of Scotland with WW and DW
(30 Aug–15 Sept) Continued tour alone
(20 Dec) To Grasmere on way to London

(Feb) Act of Mediation in Switzerland
(30 Apr) Louisiana bought by U.S. from France
(18 May) England declared war on France
(25 May) Emerson b
(Sept) Emmet's execution in Ireland
Cobbett *Parliamentary Debates* (later Hansard)
Hayley *Life and Posthumous Writings of Cowper*
Chatterton *Works* ed RS and Cottle
Malthus *Principles of Population* (2nd ed)

1804 (Jan) Ill at Grasmere, then to London; portrait by Northcote

(12 Feb) Kant d
(Mar) Code Napoléon

(27 Mar) To Portsmouth
(9 Apr–18 May) In convoy to Malta
(by Jul) Private secretary to Alexander Ball, High Commissioner at
Malta
(Aug–Nov) Sicily, two ascents of
Etna; stayed with G. F. Leckie

(Apr) 2nd Pitt ministry (–1806)
(18 May) Napoleon made Emperor
(12 Dec) Spain declared war on
Britain
Blake *Jerusalem*

1805 (Jan) Appointed Acting Public Sec-
retary in Malta; news of loss of
John Wordsworth in *Abergavenny*
(Sept–Dec) In Sicily
(Dec) To Naples and Rome

(Apr) Third Coalition against
France
(9 May) Schiller d
(26 May) Napoleon King of Italy
(17 Oct) Napoleon's victory at Ulm
(21 Oct) Nelson's victory at
Trafalgar
(2 Dec) Austerlitz
Hazlitt *Principles of Human Action*
Knight *Principles of Taste*
Scott *Lay of the Last Minstrel*
RS *Madoc*

1806 (Jan) In Rome, met Washington Allston, the Humboldts, Tieck, and
Schlegel; to Florence and Pisa
(23 Jun) Sailed from Leghorn
(17 Aug) Landed in England; London, job-hunting and recovering
his books and papers; at Parn-
don with the Clarksons and to
Cambridge
(26 Oct) In Kendal with Wordsworths and SH
(Nov) Keswick, determined to separate from Mrs C
(21 Dec) Joined Wordsworths and
SH at Coleorton; crisis of jealous
disillusionment with them

(Jan) Pitt d; "Ministry of all the
Talents" under Grenville, who
resigned (Mar 1807) after rejection of Bill to open all comis-
sions to RCs
(6 Aug) Holy Roman Empire
ended
(26 Aug) Palm executed
(13 Sept) Fox d
British blockade
(Oct) Jena
(Nov) Berlin Decree and Continental System
Arndt *Geist der Zeit* (–1818)

1807 Coleorton; heard WW read *Prelude*
and wrote *Lines to William
Wordsworth*
(4 Apr) Left for London with Words-
worths
(Jun) With his family at Stowey
(Aug) Met De Quincey; alone in
Bristol and at Stowey with Poole
(Nov) In London

(Mar) Portland ministry (–1809)
(25 Mar) Abolition of slave-trade
(Jul) Peace of Tilsit
(2 Sept) Bombardment of Copen-
hagen by British fleet
(Dec) Peninsular War began
Davy and oxymuriatic acid
WW *Poems in Two Volumes*
RS *Letters from England by Don
Espriella*; *Specimens of the
Later English Poets*
C. and M. Lamb *Tales from
Shakespeare*

1808 (15 Jan–Jun) In rooms at *Courier*
office, Strand; lectures at Royal

Bell-Lancaster controversy
Sir Arthur Wellesley to Portugal

Institution on poetry and principles of taste; illnesses, Bury St Edmunds
(Feb–Mar) WW in London
(1 May) Wordsworths moved to Allan Bank
(Jun–Aug) Bristol, Leeds, Keswick
(Jul) Review of Clarkson's *History of the Abolition of the Slave-Trade*
(1 Sept) Arrived Allan Bank, Grasmere; instructed Mrs C to send all his books there
(Nov) First prospectus of *The Friend*; Kendal
(Dec) Took up residence at Allan Bank

Crabb Robinson *Times* correspondent in Peninsula
(1 May) Hazlitt married Sarah Stoddart
(30 Aug) Convention of Cintra signed
(Dec) Napoleon invaded Spain; Dr T. Beddoes d
Dalton *New System of Chemical Philosophy* and publication of atomic theory
Lamb *Specimens of English Dramatic Poets*
Scott *Marmion*
John and Leigh Hunt's *Examiner* began
Goethe *Faust* pt i

1809 (1 Jun–15 Mar 1810) *The Friend*, 27 numbers plus supernumerary
(7 Dec–Jan 1810) "Letters on the Spaniards" in *Courier*

(Feb) *Quarterly Review* founded
(9 Mar) Byron *English Bards and Scotch Reviewers*
(May) Napoleon captured Vienna
WW *Convention of Cintra* pamphlet
(21 Sept) Canning–Castlereagh duel
Perceval ministry (–1812)
Schlegel *Über dramatische Kunst und Litteratur*

1810 (Mar) SH left Grasmere for Wales; last number of *Friend*
(Oct) To London; Montagu precipitated quarrel with WW; with Morgans in Hammersmith
(Nov) Personal association with HCR began

(Mar) Battle over admission of press to House of Commons
(May) First Reform Bill since 1797 introduced
(Jul) Napoleon annexed Holland
George iii recognised as insane
WW *Guide to the Lakes*
Mme de Staël *De l'Allemagne*
Scott *Lady of the Lake*
RS *Curse of Kehama*

1811 (Mar–Apr) Miniature painted by Matilda Betham; met Grattan
(20 Apr) First table-talk recorded by John Taylor Coleridge
(Apr–Sept) Contributions to *Courier*; J. Payne Collier met C
(18 Nov–27 Jan 1811) Lectures on Shakespeare and Milton at Scot's Corporation Hall, Collier, Byron, Rogers, HCR attending; George Dawe bust of C

(5 Feb) Prince of Wales made Regent
RC claims in Ireland; scheme to set up representative assembly in Dublin
(Nov to 1815) Luddite uprisings
Shelley *Necessity of Atheism*

1812 (Feb–Mar) Last journey to the Lakes to collect copies of *Friend*
(Apr) With the Morgans, Berners Street, Soho

(11 May) Perceval shot; Liverpool PM, resigned but resumed after Canning (pro-Catholic) declined to serve with Wellesley

(May–Aug) Lectures on drama in Willis's Rooms; portrait by Dawe

(May) Lamb and HCR patch up WW quarrel

(Jun) Catherine Wordsworth d

(Jun) *The Friend* reissued

(3 Nov–26 Jan 1813) Shakespeare lectures in Surrey Institution

(Nov) Half Wedgwood annuity withdrawn; RS and C *Omniana*

(Dec) Thomas Wordsworth d

(18 Jun) U.S. declared war on Great Britain

(22 Jun) Napoleon opened war on Russia

(Oct–Dec) Retreat from Moscow

Combe *Tour of Dr Syntax in Search of the Picturesque*

Byron *Childe Harold* bk I

1813　(23 Jan) *Remorse* opened at Drury Lane

Morgan's financial affairs deteriorating, he escaped to Ireland in Sept

(2 Sept) Met Mme de Staël

(Oct–Nov) Moved to Bristol; lectures on Shakespeare and education

(Dec) Established the Morgans at Ashley Cottage near Bath, returned ill to Bristol

(1 May) Wordsworths moved to Rydal Mount

(May) Grattan's Bill for Relief of Roman Catholics abandoned

(Jul–Aug) Peace Congress at Prague failed

(10 Aug) Austria declared war on Napoleon

(Sept) RS Poet Laureate

(autumn) Wellington successful in Peninsula; Switzerland, Holland, Italy, Rhineland, Spain, Trieste, Dalmatia freed of French rule

RS *Life of Nelson*

Northcote *Memoirs of Reynolds*

Leigh Hunt imprisoned for libel (1813–15)

1814　(Apr) Lectures at Bristol on Milton, Cervantes, Taste; lecture on French Revolution and Napoleon; under medical care of Dr Daniel for addiction and suicidal depression

(3 May) Charles Danvers d

(1 Aug) *Remorse* performed in Bristol

(Aug–Sept) Allston portrait of C; Allston's exhibition of paintings; essays "On the Principles of Genial Criticism" in *Felix Farley's Bristol Journal*

(10 Sept) Joined the Morgans at Ashley Cottage

(20 Sept–10 Dec) "To Mr. Justice Fletcher" in *Courier*

(c 5 Dec) Moved with the Morgans to Calne, Wilts, to be treated by Dr Page

(1 Jan) Invasion of France by Allies

(1 Mar) Castlereagh's treaty with Austria, Prussia, and Russia against Napoleon

(6 Apr) Napoleon abdicated

(May) First Treaty of Paris; Napoleon exiled to Elba; Restoration of the Bourbons

(8–9 Jun) Cochrane perjury trial

(Sept–Jun 1815) Congress of Vienna

(24 Dec) Peace of Ghent signed by Britain and U.S.

Inquisition re-established in Spain

WW *Excursion*

Scott *Waverley*

Cary's *Dante* completed

1815　(Jun) *Remorse* performed at Calne

(Jul–Sept) Dictating *Biographia Literaria*

(Mar–Jun) The Hundred Days: Napoleon escaped from Elba to France

(Aug–Sept) *Sibylline Leaves* and *Biographia Literia* sent for publication in Bristol

(6 Apr) Allies mobilise vs Napoleon
(18 Jun) Waterloo
Restoration of Louis XVIII
Napoleon from Plymouth to St Helena
(20 Nov) Second Treaty of Paris
WW *Poems* of 1815; *The White Doe of Rylstone*
Scott *Guy Mannering*

1816 (Feb) Grant from Literary Fund, and gift from Byron
(Mar) London: illness
(10 Apr) Sent *Zapolya* to Byron
(15 Apr) Accepted as patient and house-mate by Dr Gillman, Moreton House, Highgate
(May–Jun) *Christabel* published (three editions); renewed acquaintance with Hookham Frere; offered Stuart tract or essays on Catholic Question
(Dec) *Statesman's Manual* published; Hazlitt's antagonistic reviews in *Examiner* (Jun, Sept, Dec) and *Edinburgh Review* (Dec)

(24 Apr) Byron left England
(21 Jun) Motion for relief of Roman Catholics rejected in the Lords
(7 Jul) Sheridan d
Parliamentary Committee on Education of the Poor
(Nov) *Cobbett's Political Register* reduced price to 2d
(2 Dec) Spa Fields Riot
Shelley *Alastor and Other Poems*
Peacock *Headlong Hall*
Maturin *Bertram*
J. H. Frere ms tr of Aristophanes

1817 (Apr) Second *Lay Sermon* published
(14 Apr) *Remorse* revived
(Jul) *Biographia Literaria*, *Sibylline Leaves* published
(summer) Met Joseph Henry Green
(Sept) Met Henry Cary
(Nov) *Zapolya* published; C's tr of Hurwitz's *Hebrew Dirge* for Princess Charlotte; Tieck visited C

(13 Feb) RS *Wat Tyler*
(4 Mar) Habeas Corpus suspended
(27 Mar) Sidmouth Circular on libels
(Apr) *Blackwood's Magazine* founded as *Edinburgh Monthly Magazine*
(May) Motion for Relief of Roman Catholics rejected in the Lords
(6 Nov) Princess Charlotte d
Elgin Marbles purchased by government and placed in BM
Keats *Poems*
Hazlitt *The Characters of Shakespeare's Plays*
Moore *Lalla Rookh*
Ricardo *Principles of Political Economy*
Cuvier *Le règne animal*

1818 (Jan) "Treatise on Method" in *Encyclopaedia Metropolitana* published
(Jan–Mar) Lectures on poetry and drama
(Jan) Met Thomas Allsop
Annotated 1817 Catholic Emancipation debate in copy of Hansard

(28 Jan) Habeas Corpus restored and never again suspended
(1 Jun) Parliamentary motion for universal suffrage and annual parliaments defeated
(Jun) Westmorland election
Keats *Endymion*

(Apr) Two pamphlets supporting Peel's Bill against exploitation of child-labour

(summer) Portrait by Thomas Phillips

(Nov) *The Friend* (3-vol edition)

Portrait by C. R. Leslie

(Dec) Lectures on the History of Philosophy (–Mar 1819); literary lectures (–Mar 1819)

(Aug) *Blackwood's* and *Quarterly* attacks on Keats

Hallam *Middle Ages*

Hazlitt *Lectures on the English Poets*

Lamb *Collected Works* (Vol II dedicated to C)

Peacock *Nightmare Abbey*

1819 (Mar) Financial losses in bankruptcy of publisher Rest Fenner

(29 Mar) Lectures ended

(11 Apr) Met Keats in Millfield Lane; HC elected Fellow of Oriel; revived interest in chemistry; occasional contributions to *Blackwood's* (to 1822)

(May) Grattan's Motion for Relief of Roman Catholics defeated

(Jun) Grey's Bill to abolish Declaration against Transubstantiation defeated

1820 (May) HC deprived of Oriel Fellowship

(Aug) Green began to act as weekly amanuensis to record C's work on Old and New Testament

(Oct) DC to St John's Cambridge

(Dec) High opinion of new friend, Hyman Hurwitz

(29 Jan) George III d; accession of George IV

Cato Street Conspiracy

(Feb) Parliament dissolved

(Jun) Grattan d; Plunkett became main Irish spokesman

Revolution in Spain and Portugal

(Aug–Nov) Trial of Queen Caroline

Crawfurd *History of the Indian Archipelago*

Godwin *Of Population*

Keats *Lamia and Other Poems*

Lamb *Essays of Elia*

Shelley *Prometheus Unbound*

RS *Life of Wesley*

WW *The River Duddon*

1821 (Apr–May) Projected 3 Letters to C. A. Tulk MP on Catholic Question

(Jul) Reunion with brother George

(autumn) Invitation to lecture in Dublin declined

HNC essay on C in *Etonian*

(Feb) Plunkett's Motion for Relief of Roman Catholics with two securities (ban on foreign correspondence and veto on appointments) passed by Commons, rejected in Lords after intervention of Grenville (Apr)

(Feb) Keats d

Napoleon d

Greek War of Liberation

De Quincey *Confessions of an English Opium Eater*

Hazlitt *Lectures on Elizabethan Drama*

Mill *Elements of Political Economy*

RS *Vision of Judgment*

1822 (spring) C's "Thursday-evening class" began; SC's tr of Martin Dobrizhoffer *An Account of the Abipones, an Equestrian People of Paraguay*
(Nov) Meeting with Liverpool and Canning at Ramsgate
(Nov–Feb 1823) Mrs C and SC visit C at Highgate
(29 Dec) HNC began recording *Table Talk*
Edward Irving's first visit

(30 Apr) Canning's Catholic Peers Bill carried in Commons, rejected in the Lords
(Jul) Shelley d
(Aug) Castlereagh d; Canning became Foreign Secretary
(Nov–Dec) Faction-fights between Orangemen and Catholics in Ireland
Byron *Vision of Judgment*
Grattan *Speeches*
Shelley *Hellas*
Blanco White *Letters from Spain*
WW *Ecclesiastical Sketches*

1823 (21 Mar) HNC and SC secretly engaged
(Jul) Met Edward Irving
(Sept) Sought admission to BM through Sir Humphry Davy
(Oct) Rydal Mount library catalogue perhaps begun, possibly under supervision of SC
(Nov, before 10th) Gillmans moved to 3 The Grove; C's attic study

(Apr) Plunkett's Motion for Relief of Roman Catholics abandoned for lack of support
(May) First meeting of Catholic Association in Dublin; in London (Jun)
War between France and Spain
Hazlitt *Liber Amoris*
RS *History of the Peninsular War*

1824 (Mar) Elected Royal Associate, RSL, with annuity of £100
DC took BA Cambridge
(Jun) Carlyle and Gabriel Rossetti called at Highgate
(Jun–Jul) DC seriously ill at Highgate
John Taylor Coleridge became editor of *Quarterly Review*

(Apr) Byron d
Foundation of London Mechanics' Institution
Cary tr *The Birds* of Aristophanes
Godwin *History of the Commonwealth of England*
RS *The Book of the Church*

1825 (Apr) Prati called on C and introduced him to Vico's work
(May) *Aids to Reflection* published
(18 May) "On the *Prometheus* of Aeschylus" delivered to RSL
(May) 6 essays promised to publisher, J. A. Hessey
(Jun) Partnership of C's publishers, Hessey & Taylor, dissolved
(Jul) Blanco White visited C at Highgate
(Nov) Corrected proofs of Hurwitz's *Hebrew Tales*; proposed three lectures on projected London University
(Dec) Received Blanco White's *Letters from Spain* and *Poor Man's Preservative*

(Feb–May) Burdett's Motion for the Relief of Roman Catholics passed in Commons, defeated in the Lords
(May) Liverpool's speech on Coronation Oath; quoted with approval by Canning
(Aug) Frere arrived in England
Brougham *Practical Observations upon the Education of the People*
Butler *The Book of the Roman-Catholic Church*
Hazlitt *Spirit of the Age*
Mill *Essays on Government*
Blanco White *Poor Man's Preservative Against Popery* and *Practical and Internal Evidences Against Catholicism*

1826	(spring) Intensive work on Daniel and the Apocalypse	General Election with Corn Laws and Catholic Emancipation as main issues
	(summer) Frere spent long periods with C	England sent troops to Portugal
	(Sept) Frere obtained promise of sinecure of £200 from Liverpool for C	HNC *Six Months in the West Indies*
		Turner *History of Henry VIII*
	(Dec) C occupied his renovated book-room	RS *Vindiciae Ecclesiae Anglicanae*
		Blanco White *A Letter to Charles Butler*
1827	(Feb) Lord Dudley Ward intended to speak to Liverpool on C's behalf	(Feb) Liverpool seized with paralysis
	(10 May) Thomas Chalmers called at Highgate; C's serious illness; visit from Poole	(Mar) Burdett's Bill rejected in Commons; Canning PM
	(15 Jul) DC ordained	(8 Aug) Canning d
	(6 Dec) DC married Mary Pridham	(Aug) Goderich ministry
	Sir George Beaumont d, leaving £100 to Mrs C	University of London founded
		Blake d
		Hallam *Constitutional History*
		Hare *Guesses at Truth*
		Irving tr of *The Coming of Messiah*
		Keble *Christian Year*
		Tennyson *Poems by Two Brothers*
1828	(22 Apr) Fenimore Cooper met C	(Jan) Wellington ministry
	(21 Jun–7 Aug) Netherlands and Rhine Tour with Dora and WW	(Apr) Repeal of Test and Corporation Acts
	(Aug) *Poetical Works* (3 vols); John Sterling called at Highgate	(May) Burdett's Bill for Relief of Roman Catholics passed in Commons, rejected in Lords (Jun)
	Hyman Hurwitz appointed Professor of Hebrew, London University	(Aug) Peel and Wellington in correspondence over the Catholic Question
	(Aug) Onset of prolonged intermittent illness, with strong presentiment of death	(Dec) Lord Liverpool d
		Russia goes to war with Turkey
		Brougham *A Speech on the Present State of the Law of the Country*
		Hazlitt *Life of Napoleon* vols I, II
1829	(Jan–Feb) Refused to sign Petition against Catholic Emancipation	Meetings held throughout the country to petition against Catholic Emancipation
	(spring) Illness delayed writing of *Church and State*	(Jan) King agrees to discussion of Catholic Emancipation in Cabinet
	(c May) *Poetical Works* (2nd ed)	
	Poetical Works of Coleridge, Shelley, and Keats (Galignani Paris)	(Feb–Mar) Bill passed to suppress the Catholic Association
	(3 Sept) SC married her cousin HNC; Lady Beaumont left C £50; Poole visited Highgate	(10 Mar) 1st reading in the Commons of Catholic Relief Bill
	(17 Sept) C wrote his will	(10 Apr) 3rd reading in Lords passed
	(Sept) Mrs C left Greta Hall for good	

(Oct) Rydal Mount library catalogue checked and signed by WW's clerk, John Carter; also perhaps checked by SC and HNC
HNC and SC living in Gower Street
(Dec) *On the Constitution of the Church and State* published

(31 Apr) George iv gave reluctant assent
(May) Sir Humphry Davy d
Arnold *Sermons*
Hurwitz *The Elements of the Hebrew Language*
RS *Sir Thomas More*
[Isaac Taylor] *Natural History of Enthusiasm* (May)

1830 (c Apr) *On the Constitution of the Church and State* (2nd ed)
(Jun) HNC and SC settled in Hampstead; Herbert Coleridge b
(2–17 Sept) C remade his will
(18 Sept) Hazlitt d
Republication of *The Devil's Walk* "by Professor Porson"

Reform agitation
(Jun) Death of George iv; accession of William iv
(Nov) Grey ministry
Greece independent
Comte *Cours de philosophie positive*
Lyell *Principles of Geology*
Tennyson *Poems Chiefly Lyrical*

1831 Last meetings with WW; *Aids to Reflection* (2nd ed)
(May) Royal Society of Literature annuity withdrawn; refused personal grant from Grey; Frere made up the loss
Active interest in Parliamentary Reform

(Mar) Lord John Russell introduced Reform Bill in Commons
Dissolution of Parliament
Second Reform Bill rejected by Lords
Final Reform Bill introduced
Hegel d
J. S. Mill *The Spirit of the Age*
(Jul) Review of *C&S* in *Eclectic Review*
Walsh *Popular Opinions on Parliamentary Reform*

1832 Legacy of £300 from Steinmetz
(Sept) Portrait by Moses Haughton

Grey resigned; Wellington failed to form ministry; Grey recalled
(May) Reform Bill passed
Scott d
Green *Address Delivered in King's College*
Martineau *Illustrations of Political Economy*
Park *The Dogmas of the Constitution*

1833 HC's *Poems* dedicated to C
(24–9 Jun) To Cambridge for meetings of British Association
(Jul) Harriet Martineau visited C
(5 Aug) Emerson called at Highgate
HC's *Northern Worthies* published

Arnold *Principles of Church Reform*
Carlyle *Sartor Resartus*
Keble's sermon on "National Apostacy" began Oxford Movement
Lamb *Last Essays of Elia*
Mill "Corporation and Church Property"
Smith *Seven Letters on National Religion*
Tracts for the Times (Newman et al)

1834 (Mar–Jul) *Poetical Works* (3rd ed)   New Poor Law
3 vols published separately   (Feb) Augustus Hare d
(Apr) Instructed Hurst to dispose of (Dec) Malthus d
his share in the editions of *AR* and (27 Dec) Lamb d
C&S   Bentham *Deontology*
(25 Jul) C died at Highgate 6.20 A.M.
Autopsy performed shortly thereafter
(2 Aug) C immured in vault in Highgate Churchyard

CHRONOLOGY OF THE LOCATION AND DISPERSAL OF COLERIDGE'S BOOKS AND MANUSCRIPTS

1834 (25 Jul) C died at 3 The Grove, Highgate; J. H. Green named literary exectuor by C's will, the working library and mss being in the physical possession of the Gillmans
(3 Sept) HNC formulated his plans for editing the literary materials under the general direction of Green; tacit arrangements made for the disposal of books and mss while editorial work in progress
(by Oct) The last of the books that C had left at Allan Bank in 1810 sent by the Wordsworths to Green
(27 Dec) Lamb died, bequeathing his library to his sister Mary

1835 (10 Jan) SH sent Green copies of marginalia from WW's books
(4 Jun) Poole sent letters and mss to Green

1836 (7 Jun) HC sent Green transcripts of marginalia and mss, with list of C's books "in Wordsworth's library acknowledged as mine"
(23 Jun) SH died
Green purchased C's library and mss (according to the terms of C's will)
(c Sept) *Literary Remains* I and II published, marking the end of the first phase of editing C's miscellaneous literary mss

1837 (Feb) Carl Aders's fortune lost; Eliza Aders gave HCR books annotated by C
(early summer) HNC and SC moved from Hampstead to Chester Place, Regent's Park
Green gave up his medical practice in London and retired to Hadley near Barnet
(8 Sept) Thomas Poole died; his library dispersed without record

1839 (May) Aders's pictures sold and his library (possibly including books annotated by C) dispersed
(1 Jun) James Gillman died, bequeathing his library to his widow Anne

1841 DC moved from Helston to Chelsea, bringing his association books and mss into relation with the materials held by HNC and SC

1843 (26 Jan) HNC died
(21 Mar) RS died; BM declined to acquire his library but purchased a selection not including C association books

(31 Mar) Gillman's library, including books annotated by C, sold at auction by Southgate; Mrs Gillman left The Grove

1844 First BM acquisition of a book annotated by C, originally from Gillman sale

1845 (24 Sept) Mrs C died

1846 Ernest Hartley Coleridge, son of DC, b

1847 (May) Mary Lamb died; by Apr 1848 most of Lamb's library had been destroyed by executor Edward Moxon, except for a few books, including some annotated by C, which were sold to Scribner, New York

1848 (Feb) Small part of Lamb's library sold at private sale by Scribner, New York

1849 (6 Jan) HC died; his books and papers passed to DC

1850 (23 Apr) WW died, his books and mss bequeathed to his widow Mary

1852 (3 May) SC died; DC took over the materials for completing her editorial work

1859 (17 Jan) Mary Wordsworth died
(Jul) WW's library sold at auction at Rydal
(8 Dec) Thomas De Quincey died

1862 (Apr) Library of Herbert C (1830–61), including a few books annotated by C, sold at auction by Sotheby

1863 (13 Dec) Green died, bequeathing his library to his widow and entailing the C books and mss to DC

1865 Joseph Cottle died; his C memorabilia remained in his family and were gradually dispersed

1867 HCR died, appointing Edwin Wilkins Field his literary executor; his mss and a few books annotated by C given to Dr Williams's Library

1879 (17 Sept) Mrs Ann Green died, bequeathing the C materials to DC; some confusion in identifying and transferring the bequest

1880 (Jul) Green's library, inadvertently including a quantity of C's annotated books and a few mss, sold at auction by Sotheby
(4 Aug) BM acquired a large group of C's annotated books from purchases made by Wilson at the Green Sale, thus laying the foundation of the greatest Coleridge collection; description of these by Helen Zimmern in *Blackwood's* 1882

1883 DC died, bequeathing his library and the C books and mss to EHC

1884 Annotated books purchased by Stibbs at the Green Sale in 1880 sold at auction by Scribner, New York, providing a major source for C association books in U.S. (though many of these were lost)

1888 (Jul) Philological part of DC's library, including a few books annotated by C, sold at auction by Sotheby

1892 (c Aug) EHC transferred to his cousin John Duke Coleridge, 1st Baron Coleridge, C's notebooks and an important part of the mss and annotated books (here referred to as the "Ottery Collection"). At this time, and in 1894, he disposed of a group of C mss to the BM, reserving to himself the balance of the inherited collection (here called the "Leatherhead Collection")

1894 John Duke Coleridge died; the "Ottery Collection" passed to his son Bernard, 2nd Baron Coleridge

1920 EHC died, bequeathing his library to his eldest son, Gerard Coleridge

1943 Gerard Coleridge retired from Leatherhead to Cornwood in Devon; some C association books acquired by Blackwell at this time were offered in catalogues 1945–8

1945 Gerard Coleridge died, bequeathing the "Leatherhead Collection" to his three sons, the main part of the collection being held by Alwyne H. B. Coleridge

1951 The "Ottery Collection" acquired by the Pilgrim Trust and presented to the BM

1954 The S. T. Coleridge part of the "Leatherhead Collection", with a few omissions, acquired by Victoria College, Toronto

1963–4 The balance of the "Leatherhead Collection", mostly letters and papers of HC, DC, HNC, SC, and EHC, acquired by the University of Texas

1968 Walter H. P. Coleridge (son of EHC) died; his collection of C association books acquired by the BM

EDITOR'S INTRODUCTION

THE POINTER, NOT THE GREYHOUND

THERE is no body of marginalia—in English, or perhaps in any other language—comparable with Coleridge's in range and variety and in the sensitiveness, scope, and depth of his reaction to what he was reading. It is difficult in small compass to convey the swift brilliance, the warmth of personal feeling or the sharp relentlessness, the acute play of intelligence, the felicities of phrasing, the outbursts of humour, with words and phrases rescued from oblivion or coined for the occasion, and preposterous philological speculation driven to self-mocking extremes of grotesquerie in the impulse to initiate or sustain a line of reflection. Agile and—like a musician— capable of swift unprepared changes of mood, tonality, and texture, he moves effortlessly across the range of his multifarious concerns, at times tender, at times learned to the point of pedantry; and always, at or just below the surface, the deft sense of verbal possibilities that is the poet's gift.

He finds his beloved Baxter writing of some children at confirmation that, far from having "the spirit of Christ", they "do live a carnal and careless life", and exclaims in the margin, "Poor little sinful darlings!" Of Laud he can say, "What an appetite for persecution the Fellow had!" and attack a philosopher with colloquial and affectionate informality—"Master Cudworth! this is not quite fair!" Colquhoun's definition of poverty in *A Treatise on Indigence* as "a most necessary and indispensable ingredient in society" is to Coleridge "invidious" and he rephrases it with indignant irony: a poor man is "he whose bare wants can not be supplied without such unceasing Labour from the hour of waking to that of sleeping, as precludes all improvement of mind—& makes the intellectual Faculties to the majority of mankind as useless a boon as pictures to the Blind. Such a man is poor indeed: for he has been robbed by his unnatural Guardians of the very house-loom of his *human nature*, stripped of the furniture of his Soul." In his persistent assault on the superficial and narrow-minded, and in his warm appreciation of

lvii

what deserves enduring praise, his landmarks stand firm in his judgement of their excellence. Of Andrew Fuller's examination of the Calvinistic and Socinian systems he says: "10 Fullers + 10 × 10 Dr. Priestleys, piled on each other, would not reach the calf of Spinoza's Leg"; Mrs Lucy Hutchinson "As a portrait-painter [in words]... unites the grace and finish of Vandyke with the life and substantive Reality of Rembrandt"; and "Montaigne's Essays are made delightful by their frank autobiographical Vein, ⟨by⟩ his amiable Whimsies, his love and admiration of Plutarch, and by a hundred Finenesses, that *quiver* one and a hundred Genialities, that make one warm and *comfortable*".

Often the context does not prepare us for the flash of insight. On a flyleaf of one of the twelve dull volumes of Tennemann's history of philosophy he writes: "Let the attempt of Plotinus have ended in a failure—yet who could see the courage and skill with which he seizes the reins, and vaults into the Chariot of the Sun, with what elegance he curbs and turns the ethereal steeds, without sharing in his enthusiasm—and taking honour to the human mind even to have fallen from such magnificent Daring!... " In another philosophical work, Hutton's *Principles of Knowledge*, he remarks: "'I can not walk *with* them, because I could walk *in* them,' said a Wag of a very much too large Pair of Shoes. Something of the sort might be applied to this Work.... In short, there is Sense, and Strong Sense: but it loses itself in its own enormous House, in the Wilderness of the multitudinous Chambers & Passages.—As poor Sarah Stoddart (afterwards, poor Lass! Mrs Hazlitt) complained to me of her Brother's Lectures & Remonstrances—'He drives it *in, in, in,* (to my head) till he drives it out, out, out, again. I feel as if there was a Hole thro' my head and nothing remaining but a Buz.'" Yet for all the sure-footedness of his judgements of others he can pause in modest self-scrutiny, saying: "I have fallen into a mistake in the above. The contemptuous tone in which he [Cowley] spoke is not the one to apply to the whole *Miscellany*, but only to the juvenile part of it. It gives me pleasure to have observed this & to correct the mistake in this manner rather than erase the note."

Sara Coleridge, not long before her death and after nearly eighteen years of editorial devotion to her father's writing, said: "Indeed, he seems ever at my ear, in his books, more especially his marginalia—speaking not personally to me, and yet in a way so natural to my feelings, that *finds* me so fully, and awakens such a strong echo in my mind and heart, that I seem more intimate with him now than I ever was in my life."[1] In May 1808 Coleridge had said of his way of writing in his notebooks: "I write more unconscious that I am writing, than in my most earnest modes I *talk*—I am not then so unconscious of talking, as when I write in these dear, and only once profaned, Books, I am of the act of writing—So much so, that even in the last minute or two that I have been writing on my writing, I detected that...I was only *thinking*."[2] His marginalia come into being with this same lyrical immediacy. Whether he is borne aloft on the wings of an exhilarating affirmation or moving about cautiously from puzzlement or affection, whether he is making heavy weather in the Hessian boots of a dogged intransigence, insisting, reiterating, nailing down a true position in the face of some common sophism or pretentious fantasy, it is always the same intelligence, the same hospitable receptivity that combines respect with a deep sense of human propriety. His over-arching imagination secures at a stroke both the integrity of what he is reading and the armed vision of his response. And the marginalia show Coleridge reading, thinking, speaking; they trace out his way of thinking and knowing and getting to know—even the process of what he ingeniously called his "intellecturition".[3] In a marginal note of 1 September 1825 on *Reliquiae Baxterianae* he wrote:

Mr Kenyon yesterday...observed, that R[obert] S[outhey] could not *mediate* and that I could not *militate*—that even when it was Southey's own purpose to sit as an Arbiter, he was sure, before he was aware, to stand up as a Partizan, and drop the Scales in order to wield the Sword—while I was so engaged in tracing the diverging Branches to a common Trunk both for Right and Wrong that both Parties took to the Sword against me. S. saw all Difference as Diversity; while I was striving to reduce supposed Contraries into compatible Opposites, whose worst error consisted in their reciprocal Exclusion of each other. S. found positive falsehoods where I saw half-truths, and found the falsehood in the partial Eclipse. S. = a Grey-hound: S. T. C. a Pointer.—I have amplified our common Friend's Observation in my own metaphorical way; but I give the conclusion in his own words—In short, Southey should write Books and you write notes on them.[4]

---

[1] *SC Life* 430. See also the closing phrases of the prefatory note to Thomas Browne in *Blackwood's*, p cxv, below.

[2] *CN* iii 3325; cf i 921. At a crucial point in his argument C was capable of omitting the word "not"—an idiosyncrasy that he thought was of some psychological interest: cf *CN* i Introduction xxx–xxxi and ii 3217.

[3] C used the word "intellecturition" in BÖHME 122.

[4] BAXTER *Reliquiae* COPY B 80, dated 1 Sept 1825. HNC presumably had this note in mind—unless the epigram was a commonplace of C's later conversation—when he wrote to RS about the notes in *The Life of Wesley*: "Some of the remarks are

Elsewhere, Coleridge—taking up Southey's charge that he was always "nosing every nettle along the Hedge"—said: "I do not care two pence for the *Hare*; but I value most highly the excellencies of scent, patience, discrimination, free Activity; and find a Hare in every Nettle I make myself acquainted with."[1]

No doubt there were times of illness or languor or confused purpose when Coleridge read a book to pass the time, as an anodyne, to avert crisis, to defer decision. In Malta he noted that "Books are conversation at present. Evil as well as Good in this, I well know/ but Good too as well as Evil."[2] Usually, however, and even at times of distress and inanition, books were literally food for thought. The notebooks and marginalia show very clearly that reading was for Coleridge a strenuous activity, and that almost anything he took up to read could instantly arouse his mind to intense reflective and organising energy, seeking as it were to engage "the whole soul" of the man. In the *Biographia Literaria* he said that "Intelligence is a self-development", that we may conceive of it under "a metaphor borrowed from astronomy" as "an indestructible power with two opposite and counteracting forces, which ... we may call the centrifugal and centripetal forces. The intelligence in the one tends to *objectize* itself, and in the other to *know* itself in the object."[3] "What are my motives but my impelling thoughts—", he asked in a note on Tetens's *Philosophische Versuche*; "and what is a Thought but another word for 'I thinking'?"

The marginal notes seldom have the confessional intimacy that many passages in the notebooks have—margins of books are too public for that sort of writing. Yet at times they find a freedom seldom found even in the notebooks, where more often the dominant is intellectual struggle and the search for self-articulation. The limits of the margins of a page—a physical confinement only—could shift the emphasis from the self, could persuade him to listen as well as speak, and so encourage dialogue out of his energetic reaction to the author of the book, or even the owner of it. To read a book could be to enter the immediate presence of the writer transfigured in the embodiment of what he meant to say. So the marginalia are often ringed about with silence in the way poems are: we often overhear

---

beautiful—& make me think of what your friend Mr Kenyon once said, I believe—that *you* were born to write delightful books, & S. T. C. to write

notes on them." Ms Leatherhead. Cf also *CN* ii 2347.
[1] *IS* 143–4.
[2] *CN* ii 2526.
[3] *BL* ch 12 (1907) i 188.

his voice, table-talking (as it were) to one companion; and then the dialogue becomes (in the words of one of his favourite poets) "a dialogue of one". What Coleridge wrote in the margins of books, then, were not simply expressions of opinion or statements of conclusive thoughts or sustained reflective dialogue; they can be seen also as an essential physical deposit or secretion in a process of self-knowing, self-realisation, "self-production".[1] The very act of writing assumed for him peculiar importance: for "Form is factitious *Being*, and Thinking is the Process. Imagination the Laboratory, in which Thought elaborates Essence into Existence."[2] As he was to say years later, "I lived with my Thoughts, as my fellow-creatures."[3]

A particular blend of active imagination and "wise passiveness" in Coleridge's reading was guided by one of his favourite maxims: "Until I understand a writer's ignorance, I presume myself ignorant of his understanding."[4] This principle he extended in an unpublished note of 1825 on the anonymous *Eternal Punishment Proved to Be Not Suffering* (1817): "Every book worthy of being read at all must be read in and by the same Spirit, as that by which it was written. Who does not do this, reads a [Sun-]Dial by Moonshine." Of Sir Thomas Browne he said in a note on *Religio Medici*: "A library was a living world to him, and every book a man, absolute flesh and blood! and the gravity with which he records contradictory opinions is exquisite." And of himself, in the same note: "I have never read a book in which I felt greater similarity to my own *make* of mind—active in enquiry, & yet with an appetite to believe,—in short, an affectionate & elevated Visionary!"[5] In December 1804, writing about the intellectual effect of St Paul's writing, he noted: "No Book of itself teaches a language in the first instance, but having by symp[athy] of Soul learnt it we then understand the Book—i.e. the Deus minor in his Work."[6]

In a notebook entry of May 1808, he said that "All minds must think by some *symbols*—the strongest minds possess the most vivid Symbols in the Imagination"; and the need for symbols "ingenerates a *want*, ποθον, *desiderium*, for vividness of Symbol: which something that is *without*, that has the property of *Outness* ... can alone fully gratify".[7] In a mind as active and fertile as Coleridge's,

---

[1] *CN* iii 3670.
[2] *CN* ii 3158.
[3] N F° f 5.
[4] E.g. *BL* ch 12 (1907) i 160.
[5] Browne *Religio* 33.

[6] *CN* ii 2326.
[7] *CN* iii 3325. For other uses of the term "outness" see e.g. *CN* ii 2540, iii 3592, 3605.

and with a "memory capacious & systematizing", "If one thought leads to another, so often does it blot out another. ... My Thoughts crowd each other to death."[1] The advantage of reflecting while reading, and reading while reflecting—given the right kind of book —was that the book itself provided not only a commanding stimulus but also a shaping matrix: it provided the outness of "Symbols" and could—in the intellectual field—serve much the same directing and crystallising function that occurs in the symbolic activity of poetry. To lose touch with the symbolic structure could encourage free fantasy—a disadvantage if sustained reflection was the endeavour. As reader, as critic, Coleridge often thought that the only way to be faithful to a book or poem was to place at the disposal of what he was reading all possible resources—of understanding, imagination, learning, feeling—and to allow a relevant selection and concentration of these to occur under the shaping control of the thing-to-be-known. The test in the end was what could be digested into a coherent order. When, for example, he was pondering Kant's argument for the existence of God, he came to the reluctant conclusion (after repeated readings) that an infinite regress was involved, and remarked that "The Stomach of my Understanding does not reject it; but neither does it assimilate it"—a different use of the digestive tract than *la jeunesse dorée* refers to as "gut reaction". So the marginal notes are sometimes characteristically

Hints & first Thoughts, often too cogitabilia rather than actual cogitata a *me*, [and] may not be understood as my fixed opinions—but merely as the suggestions of the disquisition; & acts of obedience to the apostolic command of Try all things: hold fast that which is good.[2]

Coleridge wrote marginal notes for a variety of discernible purposes—in preparing lectures, to provide critical advice for an author (or reviewer), as instruction to a person younger than himself and less deeply informed, as memoranda to himself of his own concentrated reflection upon difficult or obscure texts. Yet, even when a purpose for the writing can be clearly identified, he can begin writing "unconscious that I am writing", and we are in the presence of the powerful heuristic *nisus* of his mind: he is "only *thinking*".

---

[1] *CN* III 3342. The phrase about his memory is from *CL* I 71 (4 Mar 1791).
[2] *CN* III 3881. "Try all things"—a variant of 1 Thess 5.21—evidently in the sense of "test by inquiry or experiment" with the implied sense of "separate the good from the bad". For the first quotation see KANT *Vermischte Schriften* COPY C II +4.

If we assume that the more important the book the more copious the notes, we often find the emphasis inverted. The only note on his copy of the 1737 edition of Dante is the single word "Pacchiaretti" —a corrupt version of the name of a Spanish wine he enjoyed; the word appears in various places, always without a hint of what he meant by writing it.[1] On his copy of Ariosto there is nothing but the sketch for an original Italian stanza form. There is only a single note on Bartram's *Travels*, for Plato only a handful on Thomas Taylor's translation of four of the dialogues; none on Aristotle or Bacon or Cudworth, on Bruno, Fracastorius, or Vico; none on Augustine, Origen, Aquinas, or Davy; none on Wordsworth beyond six stylistic notes written in ink on a blank page at the end of the manuscript of the 1805–6 *Prelude*. Yet there are bulkier notes on Bishop Blomfield's 38-page *Charge* than on Hegel's *Wissenschaft der Logik*; many more notes on Southey's *Life of Wesley* than on Milton's prose works; more on Böhme than on John Donne's *Sermons*; only a few on Hartley's *Observations*; few on August Wilhelm Schlegel but many on Emanuel Swedenborg; fewer on Kant than perhaps was to be expected. No doubt accidents of occasion played their part; his marginalia were usually initiated by some peculiar interest, and he did not always return pen-in-hand to books that had seized his attention before he was in the habit of annotating while he read. Least of all is the process predictable; and not least interesting are some of the notes that bear no relation to the books they are written in.

The notes on Böhme, written over a period of several years, are the most difficult and abstruse notes Coleridge ever wrote, and in their nature and function are central and prototypal. Böhme's *Works*, in the translation Coleridge used, present the reader with formidable problems of interpretation; all is cast in the quaint and private symbolism of a visionary as gravely unconscious of the traditions of philosophical discourse as of orthodox biblical scholarship. Coleridge wrestled resolutely with Böhme's figurative vocabulary, and with some success, especially in the *Aurora*, the most heavily and frequently annotated part of the four thick quarto volumes. But a reader must not expect to find in these

---

[1] He also wrote the word in RS's copy of Pascal's *Provinciales* in the autumn of 1803; and see e.g. *CN* I 371 and n, II 1959 (Mar 1804), 3040 (May 1807). In a letter of Nov 1798 (*CL* I 439) he mentioned "A Spanish Wine—I have forgot the name"; but when he reworked the German letters into "Satyrane's Letters" for *The Friend* he supplied "Pacchiaretti". *Friend* (*CC*) II 216.

marginalia a running commentary that will make Böhme intelligible. From time to time the notes do come to terms with the obscurities of the original, and they never seem to lose sight of the coherence of Böhme's imagined scheme; but mostly Coleridge's response to the text is refracted towards certain philosophical and theological issues that were of crucial importance to himself. We can see him evolving, adjusting, refining his own scheme of creation, his understanding of the relation of God to the natural world, and the relation of those positions to the emergent chemical theories that were eventually to join hands with physics in modern molecular and subatomic theory. There is perhaps no more dramatic record of his patient inquiry into the subtle and pervasive problem that taxed his attention for many years—the discerning of unrecognised pantheisms. That Böhme's eccentric and long-winded work could have evoked such a sustained process of radical philosophical enquiry, self-scrutiny, and original speculation is some indication of the fertility of Coleridge's response.

A similar engagement over a long period of time is to be seen—though with differing emphasis and line of vision—in the notes on Richard Baxter, on Kant, on Thomas Browne, on the Bible; it is, in private, the very process that was to bring into public print *Aids to Reflection*, a book of Coleridge's that is most like a continuous, stabilised, and coherent example of his activity as an annotator. That work, the evolution of which can be traced through three distinct sets of marginalia, was the one prose work that in his lifetime was successful.[1]

Another similar project Coleridge conceived in 1832, when in convalescence he hoped to be "capable of resuming my literary labours" and thought—"by way of a light *prelude*, a sort of unstiffening of my long dormant joints & muscles"—to reprint "as nearly as possible except in quality of the *paper* a fac Simile of John Asgill's Tracts, with a Life & Copious Notes—to which I would affix Postilla et Marginalia i.e. my MSS. Notes, blank leaf & marginal, on Southey's Life of Wesley, and sundry other Works".[2] He

[1] A similar process can be seen projected into the earlier (1808) abortive project for "a complete '*Rifacciamento*', or '*Umarbeitung*', of the *Geist der Zeit*" by Ernst Arndt; he intended to "add a long Preface, but throughout by notes or marked Interpolations, joined to softenings, omissions, and the lowering of the dyther-ambic style prevalent in the original, make almost a new work". *CL* III 109. C certainly did some work on this, but another translation pre-empted the market. We have no trace of an annotated copy of *Geist der Zeit*.

[2] *CL* VI 901: to H. F. Cary 22 Apr 1832.

sought help from H. F. Cary, then second in command to the Keeper of Printed Books in the British Museum, and wrote a detailed account of the project to Henry Nelson Coleridge, asking him to interest Lockhart or Croker so that he might get John Murray as publisher.

Coleridge had been given a copy of Asgill's *Tracts* (1715) by William Kirkpatrick on 28 January 1827. He was delighted with Asgill's intelligence, courage, and wit, and by his style, "idiomatic, simple, perspicuous, at once significant & lively—i.e. expressive of *the* thought and of a manly proportion of *feeling* appropriate to it". He wrote twelve notes in the book, some of them long; but he explained to Henry Nelson Coleridge that the tracts themselves could scarcely convey his intention, nor could "the few MSS Notes, which the paucity & scant dimension of the Blank Leaves, & the lankness of the Margins allowed me to incorporate or rather inatramentate with the papyr[i] cacatiss[imi] of the Volume itself—".[1] He had found a neglected writer whose work he admired. The marginal notes were not merely a record of what he had thought and felt when he read the book; they aroused thoughts that he needed to unravel elsewhere and at greater length.

The proposal that went to Murray included, beyond three sections devoted to the text of Asgill, a life of Asgill, three essays (on Whiggism, the history of the Church of England clergy from Cranmer to the present, and proofs of Asgill's orthodoxy taken from post-Reformation Divines), and—as two separate sections—"My Marginalia & Post-illa on Baxter, [and] Southey's Life of Wesley—".[2] The volume of Asgill's tracts runs to some 375 octavo pages; Coleridge's preface, additions, notes, and appended marginalia would presumably have carried the volume well over 500 pages. What lends impetuosity to the scheme is not simply his admiration for Asgill but his feeling that here—given suitable elucidation— Asgill could speak to the present. To Coleridge, with his sense of the life and immediacy of the original, the connexions have the clarity almost of axioms; Murray, who had a good eye for a controversial pamphlet, thought otherwise.

The Asgill episode points to one characteristic way in which Coleridge's mind worked. In his public writing, in conversation, in letters, and in his notebooks he loved to propose a large question

---

[1] *CL* vi 905. The complaint against restriction of space for marginal notes is unusual; but there are e.g. two such complaints in the notes on the folio Jeremy TAYLOR *Polemicall Discourses*.
[2] *CL* vi 906.

and to follow it wherever it might lead. At times, perhaps when initiative was weaker or from love of subtle reflection, he liked to choose a text as starting-point—either a condensed gnomic phrase like "Extremes meet" or the extended and evolving argument of a book he was reading. The habit made him as a young man "a *mottophilist*, and almost a motto-*manist*".[1] He would allow his mind to work from his direct meditative response to the text in a pattern of indirection, obliquity, digression. Then, since the digressions grew not from a hidden desire to evade issues but rather from an awareness that truth is manifold, single, and continuously evolving, the digressions themselves could become fertile:

[This] will *seem*, perhaps it may *be*, somewhat fanciful, not to say whimsical, that is, maggotty—but there are worse things run in people's heads than maggots. . . . A Maggot may catch a Fish, and a Fish may have a Diamond Ring in it's Guts (such cases are read of) or the Seal of Solomon. Or it may become a Bee and make honey, or a Silkworm & help adorn Buckingham-house and give bread to Spital-fields. At the worst, it will turn to a Fly, and make a Buz in one of my Flycatchers. So let it wriggle into Light— into ink, at least, and end this maggotty digression.[2]

This digressive habit of mind, which both amused and irritated Keats,[3] and provided an easy target for unsympathetic reviewers of the prose works, is nevertheless a key to Coleridge's method and a mark of his distinctive genius. In the marginalia, taken together and read in their own right rather than as a running commentary on a text, there is a unique opportunity to study the energy that can flow from attention to a text and a vigorous personal and imaginative response to it. Henry Nelson Coleridge, in his Preface to *Literary Remains* III (1838), put the matter accurately and succinctly:

Although the Author in his will contemplated the publication of some at least of the numerous notes left by him on the margins and blank spaces of books and pamphlets, he most certainly wrote the notes themselves

[1] *CL* I 293.

[2] BM MS Egerton 2801 f 57: after 1827. C called some of the later note-books "Flycatchers", describing them variously as day-books "for bird-liming Small Thoughts", "for holding for Trial doubtful thoughts", and "for impounding Stray Thoughts". In a marginal note on JOANNES Scotus Erigena (5) he refers to himself as a "Philo-Parenthesist".

[3] Keats's brilliant account of his one meeting with C is in his letter of 16 Apr 1819. Writing on "Negative Capability" in Dec 1817, he had said: "Coleridge, for instance, would let go by a fine isolated verisimilitude caught from the Penetralium of mystery, from being incapable of remaining content with half knowledge. This pursued through Volumes would per-haps take us no further than this. . . ". *Letters of John Keats* ed H. E. Rollins (Cambridge, Mass. 1958) II 88–9, I 193–4.

without any purpose beyond that of delivering his mind of the thoughts and aspirations suggested by the text under perusal. His books, that is, any person's books—even those from a circulation library—were to him, whilst reading them, as dear friends; he conversed with them as with their authors, praising, or censuring, or qualifying, as the open page seemed to give him cause; little solicitous in so doing to draw summaries or to strike balances of literary merit, but seeking rather to detect and appreciate the moving principle or moral life, every one and single, of the work in reference to absolute truth.[1]

These qualities, however, are less clearly to be seen when marginalia have been published in isolated groups, or according to some undeclared principle of selection. When Cuthbert Southey republished his father's *Life of Wesley* in 1846, he printed many of Coleridge's marginalia as footnotes by way of running commentary; but the notes had been strictly selected after a tense correspondence with Sara Coleridge, who objected to his omitting any of the notes for reasons of alleged theological impropriety; Coleridge's reason for bequeathing his annotated copy to Southey could only with great difficulty be inferred from Cuthbert's published version. Similarly, Derwent Coleridge added to his edition of his brother Hartley's *Lives of the Northern Worthies* (1852) some of the notes his father had written in Henry Nelson Coleridge's copy of the first edition, entitled *The Worthies of Yorkshire and Lancashire*, and drew attention to them on his title-page; but he omitted all the most pungent notes, presumably for personal reasons, although those are the notes most typical of Coleridge's critical candour. For example, where, in the life of Lady Anne Clifford, Hartley had made some offhand remarks about the alleged priestly practice of remitting sins "for a *consideration*", his father has written in the margin: "These petulant crudities of indigested thoughts from the primæ viæ of Reflection, these temerities of interpocular Talk, vex my Spirit in dear Hartley's Writings. . . . I would put H. on a year's *Fast* from all Review and Magazine Reading—as one means of getting rid of the constant itch to be witty—which always implies a want of faith in the interest of the Matter itself, of which he is treating".[2] The notes on Shakespeare, Daniel, and Donne—again selected—became part of the glossarial underpinning of scholarly editions during the later nineteenth century, and the notes on Beaumont and Fletcher and on Jonson would also no doubt have found a permanent home in scholarly editions of those playwrights if their work had been more frequently edited. T. K. Abbott added Coleridge's marginal notes on

[1] *LR* III ix–x. [2] See H. COLERIDGE 24.

Kant's *Logik* to his edition of *Kant's Introduction to Logic* (1885), and Agnes Arber intended to include the notes written on Spinoza's *Opera* in a book she did not live to finish; both were apparently matters of respectful curiosity. Many marginalia, which have been printed in isolation largely for their epigrammatic or critical interest, have tended to seem occasional or more judicial than they were in their original form and intent.[1]

Many books that Coleridge annotated became his "dear friends". But not all. Charactistically he paid close attention to the front-matter of a book—dedication, addresses to the reader, introduction—but needless to say he did not always annotate the whole of a book, nor did he invariably finish reading a book he had started. His eleventh and last note on Hegel's *Wissenschaft der Logik* appears on p 91 of the first part, leaving more than 900 pages un-marked—which, however, is not to say that he did not read any further. In some cases a considerable part of a book still remains unopened after a century and a half; yet there is at least one book in which he has written a marginal note between the unopened gatherings. Like any other reader, he made his judgements as he went along, sometimes mustering his conclusions into a summary state-ment. On the inside cover of Weishaupt's *Ueber Wahrheit und sitt-liche Volkommenheit*, the three volumes of which make up almost 1100 pages he has written:

I have no recollection of any work so verbose as this—Such a forest of *Leaves*—An apple brought d[own] a whole basket of leaves—taken away, & again brought, the very same apple, another huge basket of other leaves [&] so forth. It is most wearisome.

His judgement was not always patient or charitable or even polite, as witness a note on the wrapper of Herder's *Kalligone*:

Dec. 19. 1804. Malta.—And thus the Book impressed me, to wit, as being, Rant, abuse, drunken Self-conceit that kicking and sprawling in the 6 inch-deep Gutter of muddy Philosophism from the drainings [of] a hundred Sculleries dreams that he is swimming in an ocean of the Translucent & the Profound—I never read a more disgusting Work, scarcely so disgusting a one except the Meta-critik of the same Author. I always, even in the perusal of his better works ... thought him a painted Mist with no sharp outline—but this is a mere Steam from a Heap of Mans dung.

---

[1] HNC and SC included in their editions of C's published works many of C's marginal afterthoughts, either incorporating them silently into the text or appending them in footnotes. C's annotations on his own works are not included in *CM* but are printed in the relevant volumes of *CC*.

On Herder *On the Resurrection* he wrote—"All this Trash might be silenced by one Question ..."; on Thomas Abbt—"Of all the contemptible Ass-flings of infidel Wantonness this is surely the most asinine and contemptible! And in German too! And not a Translation from the French!"; on Paullini's *Disquisitio curiosa an mors naturalis plerumque sit substantia verminosa*—"I cut open this book Oct. 1, 1803, the leaves having remained uncut an exact Century, 8 years of the time in my possession. It is verily and indeed a Book of Maggots"; on Schelling's *Denkmal der Schrift von den göttlichen Dingen*—"In addition to the harsh quarrelsome and vindictive Spirit that displays itself in this Denkmal, there is a Jesuitical dishonesty in various parts that makes me dread almost to think of Schelling. I remember no man of any thing like his Genius & intellectual Vigor so serpentine & unamiable." Yet Coleridge regarded Schelling's *System des transcendentalen Idealismus* as "A book, I value, I reason and quarrel wit[h] as with myself when I am reasoni[ng]." This is an important clue. For Coleridge, to read a book was to venture a personal encounter.

It is often said, that Books are companions—they are so, dear, very dear, Companions! But I often when I read a book that delights me on the whole, feel a pang that the Author is not present—that I cannot *object* to him this & that—express my sympathy & gratitude for this part, & mention some fact that self-evidently oversets a second. Start a doubt about a third—or confirm & carry a fourth thought. At times, I become restless: for my nature is very social.[1]

Coleridge did not share Southey's Dibdinish bibliomania. His choice of old books and neglected authors turned upon his judgement of their vitality, their timelessness, which is also their timeliness, their place in the community of civilised thinking and perception. The history of philosophy given in the lectures of 1818–19 was to be conceived as "a tendency of the Human Mind to exhibit the powers of the Human Reason—to discover by it's own strength the origin & laws of Man and the world".[2] In this perspective he could consider Heraclitus, Plato, the Church Fathers, Bacon, the Caroline divines,

[1] *CN* II 2322: Dec 1804. But cf Allsop II 47: "In one respect, and in one only, are books better than conversation...". See also his advice in c 1826–7 on keeping a notebook record of successive readings of the same books in order to determine whether one's mind continues growing: there would be (he said) peculiar value in "the liveliness...in which the words unsought-for and untrimmed ...were the first-born of your first impressions, when you were either enkindled by admiration of your writer, or excited by a humble disputing with *him*, re-impersonated in his Book...". N 23 ff 24ᵛ–26.

[2] *CL* v 26.

and Wordsworth as simultaneously active in the workings of the human reason and the human spirit. The heterodox geniuses whom he wished to vindicate in the eyes of the thinking world were canonised for him by their power, the clarity of their vision, the integrity of their intellectual purpose—no matter how quaint, cumbersome, crabbed, or perverse their terminology. Giordano Bruno, Swedenborg, George Fox, Jakob Böhme, Spinoza, John Wycliffe, Martin Luther, Giambattista Vico: these were sacred names to him. In Jeremy Taylor and the Cambridge Platonists, and in one or two of the pre-Socratics and Neoplatonists, he was delighted and reassured to find his own theory of imagination and fancy anticipated and some of his psychological perceptions supported. Coleridge's ear could catch far off the hound-call of a fine intelligence.

In general, once Coleridge had developed his "propensity to marginal annotation" he usually wrote his notes in ink and seems to have been stimulated rather than inhibited by the chance limitations of the margins. The spaces presented by a printed page were, for him, as much as paper, type, or binding, an essential physical feature of a book; as for a typographer, space assumed constructive value, was a positive element of design. In books that he annotated heavily he made good use of what space was at hand, seldom grumbling about lack of it, his annotations overflowing as occasion suggested (sometimes taxing the ingenuity of an editor to unravel where one annotation left off and another began) into the spaces at chapter openings and endings, the backs of fly-titles, title-pages, and frontispiece engravings. Flyleaves and paste-downs were a special luxury, when needed, and he had little hesitation about writing a note on a title-page.

On the few occasions when he had several extra sheets of writing paper bound at the beginning and end of a German book, he did not always fill them up. When the Gillmans gave him an interleaved Shakespeare he wrote 200 notes in it, but they are terse and a little constricted, the pages far from filled, as though he found so much space a little menacing. Yet on occasion a commodious space could be too small for what engaged his mind, as when he found Bishop Blomfield's view of the proper relation between clerisy and the Church "not a question to be discussed *marginally*—large and tempting as the Margins of this Charge happen to be!—" It may be that he never quite outgrew the "Mahometan Superstition-dread as to the destruction of Paper" induced in the early years by the scarcity and high price of paper.[1] Although sometimes, usually in the earlier annotated books, he would draw up on a flyleaf a list of memorable pages or passages, he preferred not to have to take his eye off the printed text. It is uncanny how deftly, time and time again, he has fitted a note to the space that happened to be available, the last word of the cadence dropping into the last scrap of space with the precision of a lecturer ending an elaborate discourse on the dot of the hour.

On 14 May 1826 Coleridge noted that he had "tried to make a Crow-quill [into] a Pen/ a chance Rook-feather, and from the shorter wing-feathers. Could I procure the largest and longest, I think I should succeed/ and the pens would be very useful for marginal notes."[2] Why?—perhaps because they would give finer writing? We don't know. In his few public remarks about his marginal notes he suggested that he "pencilled" them, perhaps to convey the immediacy and informality of the notes or to show that he was aware that a book can be disfigured by indelible writing. But the pencils of his day were unreliable, and left "too perishable a record"; the reason he gave for copying out in ink on a flyleaf some notes he had written in the body of Kant's *Vermischte Schriften* was that "pencil marks are treacherous memorials or rather Confidants that soon lose the power of being treacherous".[3] In his use of pencil —except in the German books—there is no sign of a uniform policy; apparently it was not, for example, a mark of respect when he wrote in other people's books. It is true that most of the marginalia he wrote in Wordsworth's copy of Anderson's *British Poets* are in pencil, but more than half the notes on Wordsworth's copy of Donne's *LXXX Sermons* are in ink, and so are all the notes in Wordsworth's two volumes of Ritson. Most of the notes he wrote in Poole's books are in ink, and the notes he wrote in Lamb's books are typically in ink—which is not surprising from what we know of Lamb's way of handling books. But one wonders by what feat of half-fraternal indulgence Southey allowed Coleridge to write a number of notes in ink in his prized copy of Mather's *Magnalia Christi Americana* or in his rare copy of Pereira's *Antoniana Margarita*.[4]

---

[1] *CN* III 2446: 11 Feb 1805. Surely it was shortage of paper that induced WW to dismember a copy of C's *Poems* (1797) (now at Dove Cottage) and write drafts of his own poems in the blank spaces. For RS on the high cost of paper see e.g. *S Letters* (Curry) I 471.

[2] N 26 f 2.

[3] See e.g. BÖHME **93**.

[4] In spring 1824 RS commended Cotton Mather's *Magnalia Christi*

On the evidence of the books that have survived it is clear that Coleridge sometimes used pencil because he had nothing else handy to write with; and sometimes no doubt he used a pen for the same reason. But a strong impression is left—even allowing that pencil notes are more likely to have been overlooked, rubbed out, or effaced, and the books lost over the years—that he preferred to use pen and ink for his marginal notes, partly from prudence, that the record be permanent, but also, it may be, because he preferred the irrevocable commitment of ink.

The German books introduce the one systematic principle in the use of pencil for marginalia. Printed on a soft absorbent paper, the German books forced him to choose between writing on the text in pencil or turning to the flyleaves and paper wrappers to use ink, and the choice seems to have been an agitating one. For the German paper he had no good word, turning Catullus' indelicate phrase "cacata charta" through a number of variations.[1] His most expansive comment on this recurrent vexation came in a note written on 19 February 1826 on the front flyleaves of his second copy of Eichhorn's *Commentarius in Apocalypsin Joannis*, which he had just bought at Priestley's in High Holborn:

With *such* paper (plusquam Germanico-cacistη (κακιστη) and no greater number of pages, five Shillings should have ⟨been⟩ supererogatory—But Booksellers are themselves absolute Papishes in this article of Miscreance, and Master Priestley ⟨κατ᾽ εξοχὴν⟩ a *super-rogue*!... But I *wanted* the Book: and so $\genfrac{}{}{0pt}{}{\text{Good-by,}}{?\text{Good } \textit{Buy}?}$ Half Guinea!...

Mem. I have had, for years, the first Volume, among my Odd Books—& should have so filled the Margins before this time, that it would have been fairly worth the 10½ Blood-drops ⟨wrung⟩ from the pinched Hippocratic Nose of my Poverty, (£0,,10,,6) to any Friend of mine of an Apocalyptic Turn—But the villainous paper, the spongy Goodwin Sands, that would suck in a Galleon of Ink-wit, baffles every attempt/ tho' you still see sundry black Wrecks hulling shapeless in the Margins.

N.B. The Reward of my Thanks offered to Sir Humphrey Davy, Guy de Lussac, Dʳ Woolaston, or any other of the Chemical Magnates of this All-chemical Generation, for the discovery of a new Pounce or other Additament, fluid or solid, that shall render the papyrus cactoria of German Books as retentive of the *forms*, as it is absorbent of the *Stuff*, of Marginal Msspta—. It will be an act of true Christian Charity to prevent such a waste of our poor Scholar's Ink-hum

---

Americana to his friend C. W. Williams Wynn as "one of the most extraordinary books in the world". *S Letters* (Curry) II 265. For RS overtracing C's pencil notes in his own books, see p xciii, below.

[1] *CL* III 365.

Two other salvoes of late date are of record. In October 1833 Coleridge opened a new notebook bound in full red morocco (now called Notebook R), and wrote a title in it:

Marginalia intentionalia or a Substitute for Margins, when the Book, I am reading happens to have next to none (ex. gr. MY BIBLE) or when, as in German Books, the paper retains the Ink but the Ink will not retain the Leettrs.—The Ink simply *runs*: but the words run *away*. Likewise as a compromise between my cacoethes annotandi and my Virtue when it is a *gay* Book and not my own. S. T. Coleridge Octr 1833.

Shortly before his death he was prepared—on one occasion, at least— "in awe of the precisians of the Book Society" to "put down my reflections on separate paper", but those notes have been lost;[1] we know there were other occasions when he was less fastidious. To a note of October 1827 he added in pencil: "See the Marginal Notes in Cocceius, Vol 5—Mem.—To transcribe them into this Book—". A little later he overtraced the pencil note in ink and added:

but which, tho' they were long & numerous, I neglected to do till the ten Folios were reclaimed by the Owner, ⟨Mr Tudor, whom the notes scared & scandalized—⟩. So has it been with Volumes of my Marginalia, written indiscriminately in other men's Books.[2]

Notebook R did not fill up with "Marginalia intentionalia", nor yet with notes transcribed from vulnerable locations; indeed there is not much in it but the "Essay on Faith" transcribed in Watson's hand. But on 19 November 1833 he transcribed into Notebook 54 "in remembrance of *German* Printing, Anglicè, *blotting*: Paper" a note on Heinrichs's *Apocalypsis Graece* that would otherwise have eluded us (for Henry Nelson Coleridge left it out of his transcript):

This vile, this ⟨"vel⟩ Cacata indigna Papyrus," which will not receive Plumbago (i.e. black lead pencil) and makes Ink go mad, yea, run out of its *Senses*—this alone has saved Master Heinrichs, page after page, from a sound *, †, and †† flagellation for his inveterate Prosaism.—Verily, it provokes me to see such a Dodo attempting to *tread* an Eagle.

The notes written in pencil on the text of the German books are now dismally rubbed and confusingly offset upon each other. At times Coleridge could not reconstruct them himself; now they are much fainter from the leaves having been pressed together for a century and a half or more. To make matters worse, some of the books have been clumsily guillotined in rebinding, and the German

---

[1] *CL* VI 988. Cf Cary's discovery of some marginal notes by C in a library book in 1814, noticed below, p lxxxv n 2.

[2] N 35 f 6^v. He took up the lament again in N 44 f 33^v (16 Jul 1830).

books have suffered heavily. Losses to the beginnings and ends of words in the side margins can usually be reconstructed, but when the note has been cropped at the head or foot of a page the loss is irreparable. In some cases, the owner of a book has folded in the edges of the annotated leaves to save them from the guillotine, but not often enough, and the early editors—to judge from their transcripts—seldom saw the notes before they were cropped. Many of the German books were rebound by J. H. Green, their original paper wrappers having fallen into serious disrepair, but it does not appear that transcripts of the notes in those books were made before the guillotine fell. In at least one case—Schelling's *Philosophische Schriften*—a binder cropped notes before Coleridge himself had written all he wanted to write: "The Book-binder has docked my former notes", he wrote in the book; "but I understand enough to find that my first impressions were the same as my present ones." In February 1846 Sara Coleridge told Henry Taylor that "He did sometimes forget to finish a note, in some instances most tantalizingly. Perhaps he broke off to think, and then either did not satisfy himself, or forgot to record his conclusions. Some of his *marginalia* have been cruelly docked by binders, some rubbed out."[1]

As for the handwriting, Lamb was correct enough in saying that Coleridge wrote "no very clerkly hand".[2] Yet his writing, though variable, is usually quite legible to anybody familiar with the handwriting of the period; and his preference for writing his marginal notes in ink has relieved his editors of some dismay. Many of the pencil notes—particularly in the volumes of Kant and Schelling—are extremely difficult to read, in places indecipherable. There are some very difficult passages in ink too, but the difficulties are usually local rather than endemic, confined to a group of entries or to single words or phrases when there has been some notable conflict between pen and paper, or when the writing is crowded into that last

---

[1] *SC Mem* II 26–7.

[2] "The Two Races of Men" *L Works* II 30. In Lamb's phrase there is probably some Blue-coat byplay and perhaps also a touch of self-mockery. In the Writing School at Christ's Hospital boys were trained to write the florid hand used for engrossing documents and for keeping fair copies of correspondence, accounts, invoices, ship's logs, and the like: this represented a level in the schoolboy hierarchy to which C as Grecian and Lamb as Deputy Grecian were greatly superior. Nevertheless, Lamb—who wrote a hand no more ceremonious than C, and is not known to have mastered the craft of engrossing—made his livelihood as a clerk in the East India House. "A bold free hand, and a fearless flourish" is what Lamb liked, and may have been claiming—though jocularly—for himself (*LL* II 381).

fraction of space at the foot of a page where the pen-hand is always at some disadvantage, or—having nowhere else to go—has slid into the gutter. When parts of a note are capriciously disposed about the page or entangled in notes previously written, or when a note has been (as in the Brerewood and Byfield volume) very heavily revised, the problem is not so much one of legibility as of keeping a cool head. The local difficulties of legibility are resolved more often by a swift unprejudiced glance (that is, by luck) than by systematic analysis. Familiarity with Coleridge's syntax and the peculiarities of his exceptional vocabulary help a little, no doubt, in dealing with passages that might defy an acute but uninformed palaeographical eye; but Coleridge, working often well beyond the boundaries of any dictionary, very quickly teaches a transcriber to be wary about jumping to plausible conclusions on slender visual evidence.

At least, to read Coleridge's hand—unlike Wordsworth's or Yeats's—an editor does not have to be clairvoyant. Coleridge's nature was too impulsive and generous to allow him to write consistently in a neat fair hand—or indeed to write consistently the same hand at any period of his life. In the careless exuberant hand of the early years some of the letter-forms can be ambiguous, but the writing is large; in contrast, some of the writing of the late years is small and rapid, with fewer ambiguous letter-forms perhaps, occasionally very fine, in a few places almost microscopically small. But there is small neat writing that is unquestionably of early date, and large sprawling writing that is undoubtedly of late date; the transcriber's eye has to be ready for variety as well as plenty. There are idiosyncrasies of spelling (e.g. "knowlege", "compleat", "shew") and of punctuation (especially the oblique stroke, from which a parenthesis is sometimes indistinguishable in form). In trying to make an exact literal transcript, it is often difficult to decide whether an initial letter is meant to be a capital or miniscule (his capitals sometimes being enlarged miniscules); whether a medial mark is a comma or an oblique stroke; whether a terminal mark is a full point or a dash; and sometimes a terminal -n has a descending curl that looks like an inattentively formed -s but is seldom, if ever, so intended.

With notable exceptions, the marginalia are generally legible. There are various reasons for this. Some of the marginal notes were deliberately legible, being written for somebody else to read. Most of the marginal notes seem to have been written in more favourable physical conditions than the notebooks often were and usually in a fairly equable state of mind. Also the printed books have suffered little from exposure or hard use, and—except for the pencil notes and the intrusions of the binder's guillotine—are in much the same condition now as they were when they were written. Some pencilled notes were overtraced in ink (a few by Coleridge himself) not always with complete accuracy; but at least there are no deletions or obliterations by a later hand as there are in some of the notebooks. Altogether, when account is taken of all the difficulties of Coleridge's handwriting—and they are not inconsiderable—and as long as the writing has not been seriously amputated or defaced, there is usually less difficulty in establishing a fairly reliable text than in unravelling and dating the layers of notes in the books that he annotated over and over again through a span of years.

A HABIT INDULGED

I am in the habit of making marginal observations on the books I read—a habit indulged by the partiality of my friends. For the last 20 years there is scarce a book so bepenned or bepenciled, but some one or more instances will be found noticed by me of the power of the visual and its substitution for the conceptual. . . .

Coleridge wrote this on the half-title of Kluge's *Magnetismus*. Some of the notes on Kluge seem to have been written in 1817, some in 1827; unfortunately this particular note cannot be confidently dated, but it may suggest 1797 as roughly the earliest date for marginalia. Coleridge's two other references to early marginal notes were also made years later. In a letter of 8 April 1825 he said that all the elements of his philosophical opinions existed for him before he had "even seen a book of German Metaphysics, later than Wolff and Leibnitz, or could have read it, if I had", and that he could prove this from "Writings (Letters, Marginal Notes and those in books that have never been in my possession since I first left England for Hamburgh, &c.)"—that is, since September 1798.[1] As far as marginalia are concerned, this could involve a lapse of memory; and so could his statement in *Church and State* (published December 1829) that the annotations on Isaac Taylor would "remind some of my old school-fellows of the habit for which I was even then noted".[2]

An entry in a Sotheby sale catalogue for 17 December 1908, lot 284, seems at first sight to support the statement made in the note

[1] *CL* VI 421–2.
[2] *C&S* (*CC*) 166. Part of the same paragraph is quoted below, pp cxvi–cxvii.

on Kluge. The lot was bought by Dobell for £1 and has now disappeared; it is known only from the catalogue description:

Philosophical Transactions of the Royal Society. 18 vol. 1792–1809. This interesting copy was formerly in the library of Thos. Poole of Nether Stowey. ... Several of the volumes contain profuse pencil notes, in the margins, in the handwriting of Coleridge dating from 1796 onwards until his leaving the village.

Some of Poole's books with Coleridge's notes have survived, but Poole's library as a whole has vanished almost without trace.[1] Poole may have made a note in the volumes identifying the hand as Coleridge's; there is no *prima facie* reason to doubt that the cataloguer identified the notes correctly. We know from Lowes's *Road to Xanadu* the links between these volumes and the *Ancient Mariner*. Whether the notes were actually written between 1796 and, say, 1799 is another question; the cataloguer may have been guessing. If these volumes of the *Philosophical Transactions* should turn up again, what I think they will show is that there are notes in them in Coleridge's hand, that at least some of them are in pencil, that Poole may have attested the hand somewhere in the set, that Coleridge has not dated the notes himself, and that internal evidence would show that although a few notes may have been written as early as 1796, most, if not all, were written in 1807. If these notes were in fact written from 1796 to 1798, they precede by about five years all other evidence of copious annotation.

Coleridge's known writings in printed books before 1800 are few and slight; scarcely recognisable as marginalia at all, they give little indication of what was eventually to follow. In 1793 he wrote out a 12-line Bowles-like poem in a prayer-book (now lost) in the chapel of Jesus College, Cambridge; and in July of the same year he wrote on the front and back flyleaves of a copy of William Collins's *Poetical Works* what appears to be the earliest form of his two poems *Cupid Turn'd Chymist* and *On Presenting a Moss Rose to Miss F. Nesbitt*. On a front flyleaf of the Bible that Joseph Cottle gave him as a wedding present (second-hand) Coleridge made family entries

---

[1] Thomas Poole's collection of letters to and from C and Mrs C is, however, preserved in BM Add MS 35345. By the time C visited Poole in Nether Stowey in Feb 1803, Poole had given Thomas Ward his house in Castle Street, with the original book-room, and had moved to "The Old House" in St Mary Street, where among many alterations and improvements he had a large book-room made in the attic with new dormer windows. See Berta Lawrence *Coleridge and Wordsworth in Somerset* (Newton Abbot 1970) 48–51 and illustration facing p 52.

in 1795, 1796, and 1800; a passage from Romans 9 and three stanzas from a poem of Davenant's, written on a back flyleaf, may also have been made in the Stowey days. He may have made the few manuscript corrections that we now have in the text of Thomas Burnet's *De statu mortuorum* late in 1795, but his copy of Burnet's *Telluris theoria sacra*, acquired at the same time and important in the conception of the *Ancient Mariner*, has no notes in it. On 18 December 1796 he wrote an extended presentation inscription to Mrs Thelwall on the front flyleaf of a copy of Bowles's *Sonnets*; bound with it— as was his original intention—is a copy of the "Sheet of Sonnets" with three marginal notes and a few textual corrections. An inscription with Latin epigram in *Catulli Tibulli Propertii Opera* records that the book was a gift from his brother George on 29 August 1799. If we ignore corrections and comments written on proofs of his own poems, the earliest surviving notes that may properly be called marginalia seem to be three brief pencilled notes in the copy of Bürger's *Gedichte* that he bought in Hamburg on 22 September 1798, and a little cluster of notes written on a back flyleaf of Vol I of Hartley's *Observations on Man* (1791), which seem to belong to late 1799 but may be a little earlier.

Considering the amount of reading and writing Coleridge had done in preparing his Bristol lectures, the poems of the *annus mirabilis*, and *The Watchman*, it is indeed surprising that no marginalia survive from those years. To mark books for reference is so obvious and convenient a thing to do that he must surely have done it, at least in his own books. But he had very few books of his own, and to write marginal notes is only one way of recording immediate impressions; another way was to write them in his notebooks (which he had been doing since 1794 with increasing frequency), and yet another was to write on separate sheets of paper. A quantity of Coleridge's detached papers have been preserved, among them a set of "Notes on Atheism" based upon his Bristol Library reading apparently at the turn of the year 1796–7.[1] In the Gutch Memorandum Book there is a set of notes written between late December 1799 and

---

[1] BM MS Egerton 2801 ff 212ᵛ–215, unwatermarked. The practice of making abstracts from books and more or less accurate extracts—with or without running commentary—did not stop as his writing of marginalia increased. See e.g. "Prognostics of the Weather", a long abstract from Theophrastus by way of *Nicholson's Journal* made in Sept 1807 (*CN* II App F); extracts from William Dampier's *Voyages and Adventures* and from Franklin's *Narrative of a Journey to the Shores of the Polar Sea*, both apparently of late date, are preserved in BM MS Egerton 2800.

January 1800 while he was reading Godwin's *St Leon* at Godwin's request and for Godwin's benefit; these notes might as well have been written on a flyleaf or end-paper of the book itself if it had been appropriate to do so—a list of page references with terse comments beside some of them, elliptical memoranda to write from or speak from.[1] But in notebooks before 1800 there seems to be only one other entry that might conceivably be regarded as quasi-marginalia.[2]

In July 1800 Coleridge took up residence in Greta Hall, Keswick. His reasons for moving there were his desire for the company of the Wordsworths and the propinquity of Sara Hutchinson, whom he had first met at Sockburn in November 1799. The interior of the house was still not all finished, but it was a big house with far more usable space than the Coleridges had ever dreamed of before. To whatever books he had accumulated in Nether Stowey and London he now added the box of German books that he had finally recovered from the hazards of its journey from Hamburg. Within a few days of settling in he told his friend James Tobin that

In the way of books, we are extraordinarily well off for a country place. My landlord has a respectable library, full of dictionaries and useful modern things; *ex gr.*, the Scotch Encyclopaedia....But there is at some distance Sir Wilfred Lawson's magnificent library, and Sir Wilfred talks of calling upon me, and of course I keep the man in good humor with me, and gain the use of his books.[3]

When he was about to leave for Dove Cottage on his way to the Mediterranean, Coleridge entered in a notebook a glimpse of his study in Greta Hall:

When in a state of pleasurable & balmy Quietness I feel my Cheek and Temple on the nicely made up Pillow in Caelibe Toro meo, the fire-gleam on my dear Books, that fill up the whole side from ceiling to floor of my

---

[1] See *CN* I 254 for C's quasi-marginalia on *St Leon*. For a group of extracts with commentary, not unlike marginalia, see the notes on Kant's *Grundlegung zur Metaphysik der Sitten* in *CN* I 1704, 1705, 1710, 1711, 1723 (Dec 1803; one annotation in KANT *Grundlegung* is dated 6 Dec 1803).

[2] *CN* I 388 on Dr John Brown in the *Jena Recensent*.

[3] *CL* I 614: 25 Jul 1800. C told Poole that Jackson's library was "as large as yours". *CL* I 618. Jackson's books, being in C's part of the house, were available for regular use by C and later by RS. Jackson died in Sept 1809; it does not appear what happened to his books, but RS was indignant that Jackson did not bequeath them to HC. C did not in fact use Lawson's library much, if at all, but it was injudicious dispersal of part of the Lawson library that may have enabled him to gather in a number of rare Caroline political tracts: see *Friend* (*CC*) I 411 and n, but see also "CROM-WELLIAN TRACTS" headnote.

Tall Study—& winds, perhaps are driving the rain, or whistling in frost, at my blessed Window, whence I see Borrodale, the Lake, Newlands—wood, water, mountains, omniform Beauty...then what visions have I had, what dreams.[1]

Soon after arriving at Greta Hall he revised some of his own poems in the recently published *Annual Anthology* II, but his notes and comments on his copy seem to have been written later; he wrote one note on Wordsworth's copy of Percy's *Reliques* on 5 September 1800 (his own copy having been left behind in London), and at some time in that year two notes on Mendelssohn's *Jerusalem* and perhaps the one note on Vincent's *The Greek Verb Analysed* (1795)—the book itself possibly the relic of an earlier reviewing chore. Early in 1801 he wrote a note in Fichte *Ueber den Begriff der Wissenschaftslehre*, and late in the year two notes in Wordsworth's copy of Cowley's *Works*, a note in Cave's *Scriptorum ecclesiasticorum historia* (in which he found the memorable epithet μυριόνους in December),[2] and a passage from Pico della Mirandola in Horne Tooke's Ἔπεα πτερόεντα (which has not survived). Two other books annotated in that year are connected with Sara Hutchinson: on the back flyleaves of Matthisson's *Gedichte* he jotted down a record of the building of "Sara's Seat" on 26 March and 10 October, and in a copy of Bartram's *Travels* that had originally belonged to James Tobin he addressed a single note to her on 19 December.

But Coleridge was not all the time at Greta Hall. Often he was at Dove Cottage, or walking the fells; sometimes he was in London, and in August 1803 there was the Scotch Tour with the Wordsworths. In two books of Lamb's he wrote notes rather more sustained than he had written in Greta Hall (this was in November 1801–February 1802, when he saw much of Lamb in London, or in March 1803, when he stayed with Lamb to console him on the recurrence of Mary's insanity)—Dyer's *Poems*, Godwin's *Thoughts Occasioned by Dr. Parr's Spital Sermon* (1801). But the one marginal note on John Fitzgibbon's speech on the bill for the relief of His Majesty's Roman Catholic Subjects (Dublin 1798), which Lamb bound into the same volume with the other two, seems to be of much later date. In March 1803 he wrote two notes in a copy of Jeremy Taylor's Ἐνιαυτος that Lamb had owned since 1798. And it seems to have been in London, not Greta Hall, that he wrote the first notes (eventually there were to be more than thirty) in a copy of Sir Thomas

---

[1] *CN* I 1718; cf I 1577, III 3727.   [2] *CN* I 1070.

Browne's *Religio Medici* presented—or intended to be presented—to Sara Hutchinson.

In October 1803 Coleridge told his brother George that for the last three years he had been reading on an average not less than eight hours a day. In that context the paucity of surviving marginalia is perhaps striking: in Klopstock's *Messias* a saucy epigram, in Voss's *Poeticarum institutionum libri tres* one note (April 1803), in Christopher Wordsworth's *Letters ... on the Uses of the Definitive Article* (1802) six notes and a series of page references, one note (in October) in Paullini's *Disquisitio curiosa an mors naturalis plerumque sit substantia verminosa*, and on 6 December two notes in Kant's *Grundlegung zur Metaphysik der Sitten* (the earliest dated marginalia on Kant). On 22 September, while Southey was unpacking his books at Greta Hall, Coleridge picked up with delight the tetraglot edition of Pascal's *Les Provinciales*—apparently his first venture into Italian—and wrote in it three marginal notes in ink, and in pencil the word "Pachiaretti" and George Fricker's address in London. Something less casual occurred on the night of 1/2 November. Immediately after writing one of the most moving of the Greta Hall notebook entries—the one in which he listens to "The Voice of the Greta, and the Cock-crowing" and hears "the low voice of quiet change, of Destruction doing its work by little & little"[1]—he took up Volume II of his set of Anderson's *British Poets*, read a pencil note that Wordsworth had written on Shakespeare's sonnets, and at half-past three in the morning wrote through four pages of the text a note addressed to "My sweet Hartley" (who was then seven years old), the subject paederasty.

When illness detained him on his journey to London and the Mediterranean at the turn of the year, he may have written the few notes in Wordsworth's copy of Anderson; certainly it was at that time that he wrote the five long notes for Southey in his copy of the new edition of Malthus's *Essay on the Principles of Population*, advising him how to review it, and sent it off—with the customary apologies for delay—on 11 January 1804. Out of this strange patchwork of marginalia written in the three and a half years that Coleridge lived in Greta Hall one fact at least emerges: of the surviving annotated books for those years as many belonged to other people as to Coleridge himself.

The habit of annotating books, like most benign habits, took hold slowly and tentatively. The practice was initiated, no doubt, by his

[1] *CN* I 1635.

way of working, but it was established as a habit by instincts of affection and love. In London on his way to Malta Coleridge began to annotate two particular books. In Jeremy Collier's translation of *The Emperor Marcus Antoninus His Conversation with Himself* (otherwise known as Marcus Aurelius' *Meditations*) he wrote little beyond comments on Collier's deplorable prose style, although he was later to add matter more personal and more weighty. The other book was the 1658–9 folio of Sir Thomas Browne's "*Works*"— a volume containing *Pseudodoxia Epidemica, Religio Medici, Hydriotaphia*, and *The Garden of Cyrus*—and the marginalia he began writing in it then are informed by his affection for Charles Lamb and his love for Sara Hutchinson. These notes are energetic, personal, wide-ranging.

The inscriptions by Lamb and Coleridge in the volume of Browne leave no doubt about the date and occasion of acquisition. Lamb wrote: "C Lamb 9th March 180[4] bought for S T Coleridge"; and Coleridge added:

N.B. It was on the 10th; on which day I dined & punched at Lamb's—& exulted in the having procured the Hydriotaphia, & all the rest lucro posito.

Between the two inscriptions Sara Hutchinson has written "Given by S. T. C. to S. Hutchinson March 1804", but this was probably written many years later. At midnight of 10 March 1804 Coleridge wrote on three front flyleaves a long letter to "My dear Sara"— which in 1819 (after some modification) was to be the first of Coleridge's annotations to be published.[1] Whether or not he did in fact send the book to Sara before he sailed on 7 April is not certain: this may have been the copy of "Sir T. Brown's works, sent down to me to P[ortsmouth] by mistake ... packed up with Greenough's neatness".[2] If he did send the book to Sara before he left London on 27 March, it is difficult to imagine when he worked through the text of the *Pseudodoxia* deleting and revising what he seems to have thought would offend Sara's sense of delicacy.[3] Eventually the book was to accumulate more than fifty notes: whatever was written in it before he went to Malta, he annotated it again in 1808 and probably in 1811; the book was in Coleridge's possession in 1818, and

[1] See below, p cxv.
[2] *CN* ii 2014. *CN* ii does not provide evidence that C was using an edition of Thomas Browne in Malta.

[3] For similar heavy deletion see AURELIUS **12A, 56A**.

further notes were added in 1824; it may have been in his possession when he died.

When Coleridge sailed for Malta in April 1804 he took a mixed collection of books with him, some of them (including some volumes of Anderson's *British Poets*) in a box that for a time he thought he had lost. In the Mediterranean he added to his collection certain Italian and other books that were to remain in his library until his death. On the return voyage some of his books and papers were thrown overboard; after he reached London it took several agitating weeks to recover the surviving boxes of books and papers delayed in the distractions of war; it is not certain that in the end he recovered everything. A number of the books that we know he acquired in the Mediterranean have now been lost. Most of the "Malta books" that have survived are very lightly annotated. The exceptions are a little surprising—a few notes in Nicolson and Burn's *History and Antiquities of Westmoreland and Cumberland* (perhaps another hope for completing *Christabel*) and a few written in Syracuse in August 1804 in Rehberg's *Ueber der Verhältniss der Metaphysik zu der Religion* written in Syracuse in August 1804. The inside of the grey paper wrapper of Rehberg is inscribed in an unusually large hand: "Sara Hutchinson | S. T. Coleridge"; the annotated copy of the beautifully printed Plotinus, also acquired in Syracuse, bears Sara's name as well as his own; his copy of Tetens has the names of Sara, William, Dorothy, and Mary in it, written apparently soon after he had had word in Malta that John Wordsworth had been drowned. In trying to renounce Sara he had numbed the agonies of intolerable decision to the level of a haunting regret; the death of John, who might have married Sara, denied him the prospect of a natural resolution. The unreliable wartime communications with England had broken the contact with Lamb. He could speak to himself in his notebooks then, but seems to have had little taste for speaking to himself in the margins of his books. In Pisa in June 1806 he wrote:

> Come, come, thou bleak December Wind,
> And blow the dry Leaves from the Tree!
> Flash, like a Love-thought, thro' me, Death
> And take a Life, that wearies me.[1]

Within two days of stepping ashore at Stangate Creek on 17 August 1806, feeling "as light as a blessed ghost", he said, "I am now going to Lamb's".[2]

For the weeks between his coming ashore in August and his arrival

---

[1] *CN* II 2866.   [2] *CL* II 1177.

in Keswick at the end of October there are no marginalia unless the two notes in Colquhoun's *Treatise on Indigence* are a relic of some work for Daniel Stuart, the proprietor of the *Courier*. But the notebooks show him reading Guarini on his way north, and doing some careful study of Pindar's prosody in Schmied's edition, possibly with *Christabel* in mind. At Greta Hall he wrote references in his notebooks that suggest that he had brought with him Lamb's copy of Fulke Greville and perhaps wrote his notes in it at that time; and he may have been reading Hutton's *Principles of Knowledge* (at least he left a letter of Wordsworth's between the leaves as a bookmark). It must have been at Coleorton that he wrote the few notes on a blank page at the end of the manuscript of *Prelude* VI, a part of the poem that Wordsworth had written while Coleridge was in the Mediterranean; but these were proposals for revisions. At Coleorton there was—as far as we know—no flowering of marginalia. On 4 April 1807, restless and in dismay, Coleridge left for London; he was expected to return but did not do so.

From early June 1807 until the second week in September Coleridge was with Thomas Poole in Nether Stowey. It was a period of recuperation: at the beginning he was (as he told Cottle) "the wretched wreck of what you knew me, rolling, rudderless", but he could report to Davy three months later that he had "received such manifest benefit from horse exercise, a gradual abandonment of fermented & total abstinence from spirituous liquors, & by being alone with Poole & the renewal of old times by wandering about among my dear old walks, of Quantock & Alfoxden, that I have now seriously set about composition, with a view to ascertain whether I can conscientiously undertake...a series of Lectures at the Royal Institution".[1] The occasion is marked by an impressive cluster of sustained marginal notes. Poole, distressed at Coleridge's lack of initiative, urged him to begin preparing the lectures he had contracted to give at the Royal Institution in December, and entreated him to write in his books. So Coleridge annotated Stillingfleet's *Origines Sacrae*, Hayley's *Life of Milton*, Parnell's *Historical Apology*, and Andrew Fuller's *Calvinistic and Socinian Systems*, and wrote a searching series of personal notes in Adam's *Private Thoughts on Religion*.[2] This may have been the occasion of his annotating Poole's

---

[1] *CL* III 22, 29.

[2] Poole must have given this copy of ADAM to C: it was among the books C left behind at Allan Bank in 1810 and was one of the consignment of books sent to Highgate in c late 1829.

copy of the *Philosophical Transactions*;[1] perhaps he wrote also the few notes in his own copy of Ralegh's *History of the World* and rather more in Robert Robinson's *Miscellaneous Works*, and possibly some of the notes in his own copy of Junius. His annotating zeal even overflowed into a Stowey Book Society work on miracles (unidentified), for which "accident" he duly apologised.[2]

Coleridge, addressing himself to the books that Poole set before him, apparently felt the soothing relief that comes from concentration. The books were more markedly theological than in the earlier years, for it was in the Mediterranean that he had first seriously tried to come to terms with the central doctrines of Christianity.[3] Although the notes are not copious, they are swift-moving, unguarded, firm and supple in style, persuasive in tone, written as freely and confidently as he could speak to the sympathetic listener Tom Poole. The annotations on Adam and the systematic marking of that text show to what focus of self-awareness his reading tended; on the other hand, the marginalia on Stillingfleet show with what self-possession he could pass from an analysis of miracles to calculate the displacement of Noah's Ark and the depth of the Noachic floodwaters. Poole's great pleasure during this visit was Coleridge's conversation, and it was at this time that Lord Egmont noticed that Coleridge "talked very much like an angel". At Nether Stowey the marginalia began to find the quality that he himself was later to attribute to them—that they gave "much more nearly than any of his printed works, the style of Coleridge's conversation".[4]

From Nether Stowey Coleridge moved to Bristol. The date for the Royal Institution lectures was approaching. He fell ill, and only after several trips back and forth to Bristol finally settled in the *Courier* office in London in time for the first literary lectures to begin on 15 January 1808. Dorothy Wordsworth could still say:

---

[1] See above, p lxxvii.

[2] *CL* III 32. Cf *Poole* II 200. The "Definition of Miracle" printed immediately after the marginalia on ROBINSON in *CIS* 159–61 may be a relic of this "desecration". On 24 Feb 1814 H. F. Cary found in a copy of SELDEN *Table Talk* in the Westminster Library, Jermyn Street, marginalia written by C; he copied some of the notes into his diary, but the book itself has not been preserved. That story, or something like it, may have had some currency in London—see *QR* Jul 1837 p 16: "It is grievous to think how many volumes covered with Coleridge's notes are now wearing out in circulating libraries, or lying buried in private collections." For HC's plea that C should *not* write notes in pamphlets he was sending him see *HCL* 131.

[3] See e.g. the letter to Clarkson of 13 Oct 1806: *CL* II 1193–9.

[4] See below, p cxv.

"how Coleridge does rise up, as it were, almost from the dead!"[1] Yet the lectures began disastrously, were interrupted by cancellations for illness, and in the end stopped *sine die* on 13 June. Wordsworth, alarmed by the possibility that Coleridge was dying—a fear Coleridge himself felt at this time—came to London in late February and stayed for seven weeks, irritated by Coleridge's inaccessibility and incensed that the cause of his illness was all too clear. Yet one curious—almost incredible—relic of that visit is the copy of Richard Payne Knight's *Analytical Inquiry into the Principles of Taste*, in which Coleridge wrote a few notes and Wordsworth many—the largest series of Wordsworth marginalia so far identified. During the early months of 1808 in London, when he was giving his first literary lectures, Coleridge extended the annotations on Marcus Aurelius and Thomas Browne, engaging in them the personal and literary concerns that began at that time to find a distinctive voice in the notes he was writing in some of Lamb's books: the annotations on Samuel Daniel's *Poetical Works* were written in Lamb's copy, and the copy of Chapman's *Homer* that he annotated for Sara Hutchinson was also associated with Lamb. At this time Coleridge probably began to annotate Shakespeare and may have added to his comments on Anderson. He wrote only a few notes in Milton's prose works, in Scapula's lexicon, perhaps in Berkeley's *Siris*, and in two books secured for him by De Quincey—Hermann's *De emendenda ratione graecae grammaticae* and the *Homeric Hymns*. The river of annotation began to flow through the four volumes of the "Law Edition" of Jakob Böhme's *Works* (also provided by De Quincey).

It might have been expected that once Coleridge had left Greta Hall to Southey, and his own study there deserted, the practice of annotating books would dwindle to almost nothing until he had been able to establish stable living conditions. The reverse, as we have seen, was the case. From the time he left Coleorton in 1807 until he joined the Wordsworths at Allan Bank at the end of 1808, the momentum steadily increased, in spite of the preparation for his lectures, the sudden paralysing illnesses, the waverings after the lectures ended, the travels and crises that finally brought *The Friend* into being. It is difficult to avoid the conclusion that in 1808, as had been the case in early 1804 on the point of sailing for Malta, two persons stand at the evocative centre of many of his most vivacious and penetrating marginalia—Lamb and Sara Hutchinson.

Although Coleridge wrote Sara Hutchinson's name in several of

[1] *WL* (*M* 2) I 188.

his books, in the same way that in his notebooks he joined her name to the names of the Wordsworths as a loving memento, the number of annotated books that he actually inscribed to her is small. (The intimacy between them continued with interruptions only from November 1799 to October 1810.) Yet the marginalia written for her are extensive and of peculiar interest.

The first book we know Coleridge gave Asra was a copy of the "Sheet of Sonnets", inscribed on her first brief visit to Greta Hall: "The Editor to Asahara, the Moorish Maid, Dec. 1800, Greta Hall, Keswick." On 10 December 1801 he gave James Tobin's copy of Bartram's *Travels* to her; and the one note chimes with a distinctive word-usage in the notes on Thomas Browne's *Religio Medici*. That work he annotated apparently in 1802, and he may have given it to her at that time; if he did, he took it back again. When Lamb found and bought for Coleridge a copy of Browne's "*Works*" in folio on 9 March 1804, Coleridge wrote a long critical letter to Sara Hutchinson in it and intended to send the book to her at that time; he wrote other notes in it in 1808 and again in 1818 and 1824. Among the notes on the *Pseudodoxia Epidemica* there is a reference to Withering's *British Plants* (from which Asra had entered in Notebook 21 a long series of vernacular names of flowers). In September 1801 Coleridge had noted how

Endeavoring to make the infinitely beloved Darling understand all my knowledge I learn the art of making the abstrusest Truths intelligible; & interesting even to the unlearned.[1]

Indeed an affectionate and unimportunate didacticism does inform many of the notes written for Asra—as at the end of Book I of the *Pseudodoxia Epidemica*.[2]

The only other annotated book Coleridge is known to have given to Sara Hutchinson is a copy of Chapman's *Homer*. The letter of about 12 February 1808 sent with the book includes a glowing appreciation of Chapman's translation; it also shows the same critical eagerness as the long inscription in the form of a letter addressed to her in Thomas Browne's "*Works*" four years earlier, but is less extended, less lyrical, and less personal. He sent the book in a box containing "The Piranesi Folios for William" and, for Sara, "a little but very neat N. Testament, Chapman's Homer/ which is be-

---

[1] *CN* I 984. Cf a fragmentary note of Apr 1805: "...explaining it—& by all sweet images conveying to *her* understanding, truth, and to *my* own, simplicity & the power of uttering abstrusest Truths as from the mouth of Childhood...". *CN* II 2536.

[2] Below, p cxv.

come very scarce & valuable, & a new work—Huber's History of Bees". The notes on the text of Chapman are not overtly didactic, nor do they condescend; if the letter of presentation were not in the book, we should simply hear Coleridge talking critically to himself in an alert and buoyant mood.

Perhaps Coleridge gave or sent other books to Sara, with or without inscription. When they were together, as they were to be again in Allan Bank, there was no need for marginalia to share enjoyment; for them a brief inscription in the shorthand of vivid memory would be eloquent enough. Only at a distance did Coleridge reach out towards her by writing in the margins of a book.

The notes in Chapman's *Homer* represent a new vein of sustained critical comment; but the notes written in the same year in Samuel Daniel's *Poetical Works* have an even deeper implication—the book belonged to Charles Lamb. At that time, and earlier, Lamb had been picking up books for Coleridge as gifts or on request; but the earliest letters to Coleridge that have survived show him drawing attention, with his uncanny critical insight, to unusual books. Lamb communicated his enthusiasm for old and neglected books so strongly, and so unstintingly shared his delight in new discoveries and old loves, that Coleridge—through their close identification with each other since boyhood—sometimes thought the discoveries were his own even when they were not.

We find Lamb recommending Walton's *Compleat Angler* to Coleridge in June 1796 (as to Robert Lloyd in 1801), Amory's *Life of John Buncle* in June 1797, Chapman's *Homer* in 1802. By 1806 Lamb was already at work on his *Specimens of English Dramatic Poetry*, and the aura of that fascination reached Coleridge long before the book was published in 1808.[1] These are only a few identifiable moments in a rich and continuing reciprocal process. Lamb blessed Coleridge for first bringing him in 1796 to Jeremy Taylor for consolation, and came to be even more extravagantly eloquent than Coleridge on the subject of Taylor's genius. It was Lamb's copy of the *Polemicall Discourses* that Coleridge "marginated" more densely than any other book, and once he had embarked on that policy of "spoiling" he seems never to have returned the book to its owner.

Lamb's pleasure at the notes written in his Daniel and in Sidney's

[1] Lamb lent C the ms of the *Specimens*, perhaps for use in a lecture, in Feb 1808: see *CL* iii 51.

Arcadia encouraged Coleridge in 1811 (if he needed any encouragement) to write extensive notes in Lamb's copy of Donne's *Poems* (1669) and in his Beaumont and Fletcher; in that year he wrote his first notes in Lamb's copy of Taylor's *Polemicall Discourses*.[1] Beyond these there are only three others that have survived the destruction of Lamb's library: *The History of Philip de Commines* (annotated about 1811–12), Petvin's *Letters Concerning Mind* (annotated in 1820), and Reynolds's *Triumphe of Gods Revenge Agaynst the Cryinge, and Execrable Sinne of Murther* (annotated perhaps early in Highgate). One other annotated book did not come back to Lamb; it is the subject of a letter of August–September 1819 that became the first draft for Elia's essay "The Two Races of Men":

Dear C.,
   Why will you make your visits, which should give pleasure, matter of regret to your friends? You never come but you take away some folio that is part of my existence. With a great deal of difficulty I was made to comprehend the extent of my loss. My maid Becky brought me a dirty bit of paper, which contained her description of some book which Mr. Coleridge had taken away. It was "Luster's Tables," which, for some time, I could not make out. "What! has he carried away any of the *tables*, Becky?" "No, it wasn't any tables, but it was a book that he called Luster's Tables." I was obliged to search personally among my shelves, and a huge fissure suddenly disclosed to me the true nature of the damage I had sustained. That book, C., you should not have taken away, for it is not mine; it is the property of a friend, who does not know its value, nor indeed have I been very sedulous in explaining to him the estimate of it; but was rather contented in giving a sort of corroboration to a hint that he let fall, as to its being suspected to be not genuine, so that in all probability it would have fallen to me as a deodand; not but I am sure it is Luther's as I am sure that Jack Bunyan wrote the "Pilgrim's Progress;" but it was not for me to pronounce upon the validity of testimony that had been disputed by learneder clerks than I. So I quietly let it occupy the place it had usurped upon my shelves, and should never have thought of issuing an ejectment against it.... I have several such strangers that I treat with more than Arabian courtesy; there's a copy of More's fine poem, which is none of mine; but I cherish it as my own.... So you see I had no right to lend you that book; I may lend you my own books, because it is at my own hazard, but it is not honest to hazard a friend's property; I always make that distinction. I hope you will bring it with you, or send it by Hartley; or he can bring that, and you the "Polemical Discourses," and come and eat some atoning mutton with us one of these days shortly.... So come all four—men and books I mean—my third shelf (northern compartment)

---

[1] Lamb's work on the *Specimens* was already under way in 1806. The first edition (1808) included, in a long note on the extract from Jonson's *Philaster*, an enthusiastic appreciation of Donne's *Elegie* XVI and the full text of the poem.

from the top has two devilish gaps, where you have knocked out its two eye-teeth.

Your wronged friend, C. Lamb.[1]

Whether or not Coleridge went to eat atoning mutton, he began writing marginal notes in "Lusters' Tables"—that is, *Colloquia Mensalia; or, Dr Martin Luther's Divine Discourses at His Table* (1652)—from about 25 September 1819.

Lamb's friend, the original owner of the book, was Edward White—an old acquaintance in the East India House. Assisted no doubt by Lamb's acknowledged deviousness, White had already forgotten the book or later gave it to Lamb, and Lamb may in the end have given up hope of retrieving his beloved folio, for Coleridge had it with him in Highgate when he died, and had written more than a hundred notes in it. Whether it passed back and forth between Lamb and Coleridge during those fifteen years we do not know. With the Luther, as with Taylor's *Polemicall Discourses*, the first principle of book-ownership as ascribed to Coleridge by Lamb seems handsomely to have applied: "the title to property in a book ... is in exact ratio to the claimant's powers of understanding and appreciating the same".[2]

Lamb elaborated the theme in "The Two Races of Men". The Elia essays, he admitted, were "a tissue of truth and fiction impossible to be extricated, the interlacings shall be so delicate, the partitions perfectly invisible";[3] but the books he mentions in the essay are worth noticing: *Opera Bonaventurae*, "Brown on Urn Burial"—"C. will hardly allege that he knows more about that treatise than I do, who introduced it to him, and was indeed the first (of the moderns) to discover its beauties"—a volume of Dodsley's *Old Plays*, Burton's *Anatomy of Melancholy*, Walton's *Compleat Angler*, Amory's *Life of John Buncle*.[4] In some of these there is certainly an element of playful fiction. But not all the details are circumstantial moonshine.

The missing volume of Dodsley had indeed a sombre history, and only a year or eighteen months earlier Lamb would have been rubbing salt in an open wound by mentioning it in public.[5] If Coleridge did indeed have Amory's *Buncle* then—and he certainly had

---

[1] *LL* II 284–5. The "copy of More's fine poem" was probably C's—hence Lamb's sly reference to it. If so, it would be the *Philosophical Poems*, Lamb thinking of the whole volume as the *Song of the Soul*.

[2] "The Two Races of Men" *L Works* II 29.

[3] *LL* II 282.

[4] *L Works* II 29.

[5] For the details of this unpleasant incident see DONNE *Poems* 3 n 1.

it at some time because he wrote at least one note in it—it came back to Lamb eventually and was one of the few of his surviving books to be sold in New York in 1848 (but now adrift). The thread of Burton's *Anatomy of Melancholy* is more labyrinthine. As in the case of Amory's *Buncle*, Lamb did not say that Coleridge wrote notes in Burton; but Coleridge did so. In "The Two Races of Men" Lamb accused James Kenney of taking away to France for the edification of his bride Lamb's copy of Fulke Greville's *Certaine Learned and Elegant Workes*, annotated by Coleridge. With Elian mercuriality Lamb said nothing in public about his Beaumont and Fletcher, or the *Polemicall Discourses*, or the copy of Donne's *Poems* that bears most moving tribute to Coleridge's and Lamb's long critical acquaintance. The main theme of "The Two Races" is book-borrowing, and Lamb closed it with his panegyric on Coleridge as an enricher of books.[1]

One further transaction needs to be noted as a clue to the special quality in their exchange of books. On a March day in 1829 Lamb found in a stall in the Barbican "one of whom I have oft heard and had dreams, but never saw in the flesh—that is, in sheepskin—The whole theologic works of THOMAS AQUINAS!" His "arms aked with lugging it a mile to the stage, but the burden was a pleasure, such as old Anchises was to the shoulders of Aeneas—or the Lady to the Lover in old romance, who having to carry her to the top of a high mountain—the price of obtaining her—clamber'd with her to the top, and fell dead with fatigue".[2] In October he wrote to Gillman to apologise for not knowing, because of his infrequent visits to Highgate, that Coleridge had been in "indifferent health":

A little school divinity, well applied, may be healing. I send him honest Tom of Aquin; that was always an obscure great idea to me: I never thought or dreamed to see him in the flesh, but t'other day I rescued him from a stall in the Barbican, and brought him off in triumph. He comes to greet Coleridge's acceptance, for his shoe-latchets I am unworthy to unloose. Yet there are pretty pro's and con's, and such unsatisfactory learning in him. ... Well, do not break your lay brains, nor I neither, with these curious nothings. They are nuts to our dear friend, whom hoping to see at your first friendly hint that it will be convenient, I end with begging our very kindest loves to Mrs. Gillman.[3]

This sounds like a gift, but Lamb evidently intended otherwise, for he wrote a little later asking for the loan of two of Coleridge's volumes of Thomas Fuller and added: "Also give me back Him of

---

[1] See below, p cxvi.
[2] *LL* iii 213.
[3] *LL* iii 230.

Aquinum."[1] I should like to be persuaded that Coleridge ignored this plea and that these are the five great folios from a broken set of twenty that Derwent Coleridge inherited and that are now in the Victoria College Library, where they still make the arms ache to lift them down from the shelves. But it is not so. Coleridge had in fact left behind at Allan Bank in 1810 his own five volumes of Aquinas; they were kept at Rydal Mount until his death; these are the ones that eventually went to Derwent. Lamb did get back his Aquinas.

Before the outstanding marginalia of 1808 had developed in 1811 into a blaze of literary brilliance in the notes on Donne, Beaumont and Fletcher, and Shakespeare, Coleridge had spent much of 1809–10 with the Wordsworths in Grasmere writing and publishing *The Friend.* They had been in their new house Allan Bank since late May 1808. Although Coleridge did not establish there until December, he wrote to his wife on 9 September (while he was still travelling about to make final arrangements for publication) asking her to "send me a good lot of books by each Carrier—no odds, with what you begin—as many each time as you conveniently can—& lastly the Shelves".[2] Most of his library was then set up in the room the Wordsworths had given him for a study—the room where, of all the rooms in that smoke-ridden house, the chimney smoked least.

At Allan Bank Coleridge annotated a few of Wordsworth's books —a copy of Donne's *LXXX Sermons* (eight notes only; the heavy annotation of another copy of Donne's *Sermons* came later), a volume of Ritson's *Ancient Songs* and a volume of his *Select Collection of English Songs,* Thomas Taylor's translation of four Plato dialogues, and the spurious *Memoirs of the Count de Bonneval.* But most of the books he annotated were his own: some German books, a copy of *Reliquiae Baxterianae,* a copy of Chillingworth, Herbert's *Temple,* Henry More's *Philosophical Poems.* None of these is profusely annotated. He wrote a few notes in De Quincey's copy of Leibniz's *Theodicee,* which raises a question about the reliability of De Quincey's statement that he lent Coleridge so many books in Grasmere that there were at one time five hundred of his German books in Allan Bank. On 15 March 1810 the last number of *The Friend* was published; on the 23rd Sara Hutchinson went to Wales; early in May Coleridge went back to Keswick—for ten days, he said, but he stayed for five months and was never to live with the Wordsworths again.

[1] *LL* iii 234.   [2] *CL* iii 121.

In the summer of 1810 Coleridge stayed on at Greta Hall, bemused and undecided after the demise of *The Friend*; "as at Grasmere, he has done nothing but read".[1] If writing marginalia at Poole's in 1807 helped him to recover self-respect and concentration, the marginal notes he wrote at Greta Hall that summer show that to write in the books he was reading could also be a consolatory occupation. Most of the annotations were, for lack of most of his own books, in Southey's books. The notes in Gilbert White's *Natural History of Selborne*, Burnet's *Life of William Bedell*, and *The Works of the Holy Mother St. Teresa of Jesus* are neither long nor numerous, but at this time he also wrote a large number of notes in James Sedgwick's anonymous *Hints...on the Nature and Effect of Evangelical Preaching*.

On 18 October he accepted Basil Montagu's offer to travel to London in his coach. They stopped at Grasmere on their way, and Wordsworth (in Dorothy's absence) privately warned Montagu that there were certain domestic disadvantages in having Coleridge as a house-guest for an indefinite period. In London Montagu clumsily repeated to Coleridge part of what he understood Wordsworth to have told him. Coleridge suddenly felt as though the whole world of affection that had supported him for twelve years or more had collapsed; at one stroke, as it turned out, he had lost the Wordsworths and Sara Hutchinson. He was to return only once more to the North, in February 1812, to collect the sheets of *The Friend*; he drove through Grasmere without stopping to speak to the Wordsworths. During that short stay at Greta Hall he was to write notes in at least two of Southey's books: Pereira's *Antoniana Margarita* and Mather's *Magnalia Christi Americana*, both books precious to Southey. For all his fastidious taste for books, Southey by this time, and later, cherished the notes Coleridge wrote in his books, even though some of the observations were uncomplimentary to him. In Volume I of Sedgwick's *Evangelical Preaching* Southey wrote: "The marginal notes in this book are S. T. Coleridge's, written in pencil by him, & traced in ink by me 'that nothing be lost.' R. Southey. June 13. 1819." He was to do the same with other pencil notes of Coleridge's, not least in the copy of his own *Life of Wesley* (1820). In 1813, however, he started to rifle Coleridge's books at Greta Hall, paying for what he took; among them, the heavily annotated copy of Flögel's *Geschichte der komischen Litteratur*.[2]

[1] *WL* (*M* 2) I 412.
[2] RS had just returned from London, indignant at C's inability to pull himself together. He wrote to Charles

During the years 1810–16, between the estrangement from the Wordsworths and the domestication with the Gillmans in Highgate, Coleridge had no settled place to live. He was sometimes in lodgings, sometimes with the Morgans in Hammersmith or Soho, with the Beaumonts or Lambs, in Bristol with Josiah Wade or in lodgings in Bristol when he was undergoing once more the terrible ordeal of attempting to withdraw from opium; then with the Morgans in Ashley Cottage near Bath, and finally in Calne, Wiltshire. During this six-year period, although he was often dangerously ill, the old mountaineer's spirit was not defeated: he did a good deal of work and, as far as the hazards of sudden illnesses allowed, lived a crowded social life. For several months in 1811 he was the leader-writer for the *Courier*; in 1812 he rewrote *Osorio* into *Remorse* and saw the play through its successful presentation in London at Drury Lane early in 1813. He gave several series of lectures: in London, on Shakespeare and Milton, November 1811 to January 1812; on the drama, May to August 1812; on Shakespeare, November 1812 to January 1813; then two series in Bristol, one on Shakespeare and education, October and November 1813, and a miscellaneous set in April 1814. The preparation for these lectures, mostly literary in subject, left a rich deposit of marginal notes, especially in Shakespeare, Jonson, and Beaumont and Fletcher, but also in a variety of other books.

It is difficult to identify what books Coleridge had with him from time to time in 1810–16, and difficult to identify all the marginalia that belong to that period, or to be sure that a good number have not disappeared. As far as books were concerned, he seems to have travelled like a tortoise with his house on his back. From the letters that survive from this ill-documented period, it is clear that as he moved about he left behind him a trail of his own books and books

---

Danvers in Bristol on 9 Dec 1813 "for the purpose of speaking thro you to Coleridge" about family matters, and added: "One thing more respecting Coleridge. I took from his German books the two volumes of Romances £2–2, the volume of Minnesingen £1–1, the Hist. of Comic Literature 4 vol. £1–8, The Book about Fools 7/, Eschenburg 7/, PlattDeutsches Worter Buch 16/, and Bliomberis [?] 5, sum total £6–6. I suppose they are priced at as much as they cost. Had he been here I would willingly have taken many more, and shall now be glad of Lessing, of all the historical works, and of any others which he would recommend, at their original cost." *S Letters* (Curry) II 89. Most of these German books seem to have been at Greta Hall; the Wordsworths had sent the German books from Allan Bank in May 1812, most of them to C in London and a few (a "parcel") to RS in Greta Hall.

borrowed from other people; books borrowed from Lamb, from Henry Crabb Robinson (whom he had first met in November 1810), from his old friends in Bristol, and from other acquaintance more recent and casual.

There are disappointingly few reliable means of dating the notes that accumulated in the German books before the middle of 1812; certainly he began writing notes in Kant's *Metaphysische Anfangs-gründe* in July 1811. As he planned to reissue *The Friend* in early 1812, and was preparing his lectures on the drama, he felt a pressing need to have his German books at hand. This was awkward because he had left them with many other books with the Wordsworths in October 1810 and had had no communication with them since; but he needed the books badly enough to ask his wife to persuade the Wordsworths to let him have them. On 3 May 1812 Dorothy wrote to William, who had come to London in an intransigent frame of mind to try to resolve Coleridge's sense of outrage:

We have packed up three Boxes of Coleridge's German Books, and sent him a parcel by coach—You may judge we had a busy day last Sunday but one in looking over all the German books, to find out those that were to be sent by coach—and another parcel to be sent to Keswick for Southey. All this we did on the Sunday and packed two chests, and on Friday we packed the third Chest, and Tom Wilson, who was here to put down the carpet, nailed and corded them, and yesterday a Cart which had brought us coals, carried them off.... Coleridge wrote to Mrs C specifying the Books to be sent immediately by the Coach, which he wanted for his present labours—[1]

So "the 'Hessians', as we used to call Coleridge's German books" made their way south,[2] with consequences for the marginalia and for the 1812 lectures on the drama. In January he asked his wife to send his quarto manuscript book and the two volumes of *Poetae graeci veteres* ("For I want them hourly") and asked her to send him William Sotheby's "Folio Edition of all Petrarch's Works, which I left at Grasmere"—he found it embarrassing to have kept the volumes by mischance since some time before he sailed to Malta.[3]

---

[1] *WL* (*M* 2) II 18.

[2] *SHL* 165, Nov–Dec 1819. Since "Hessians" are sometimes German boots, the family name for C's German books may commemorate the corrupt text of some sibylline communication between Keswick and Grasmere. The cryptographic solution of this nice point is encouraged by J. C. T. Oates's article "An Old Boot at Cambridge" in the *Book Collector* x (1961) 291–300, which concludes with the advice: "*ne sutor ultra crepidam*—which means, roughly, bibliographers should be-ware of boots".

[3] *CL* III 431. The Petrarch did not reach its owner until early 1816: see *CL* IV 635, 655.

A request to Mrs Morgan in London to send him two notebooks and the two volumes of Schlegel's *Vorlesungen* in Bristol in October 1813 shows under what difficulties he sometimes worked from scattered books (the annotated *Vorlesungen* has been lost without trace of the notes). Through the early months of 1813 the Morgans' financial affairs had been deteriorating steadily. In September—by which time Morgan had run away to Ireland to escape his creditors—Coleridge needed some ready money on their account or his own, and asked Daniel Stuart to send the Morgans the few books he had left in the *Courier* office because "I am compelled to sell my Library". He did not sell his library, but a letter to Charlotte Brent in mid-November shows that he had pawned forty of his books, a watch, and a snuff-box for £6.[1] In that same month he wrote to the Reverend Mr J. Eden in Bristol asking him for the loan of his copy of Southey's pamphlet on Bell's system of education, adding wistfully—"And as I am in a most unnatural Dearth of Books here, should you have any two or three Volumes that you have found interest in, critical, controversial, or historical, of recent date, you would by entrusting them to me for a day or two oblige Your respectful & obliged S. T. Coleridge."[2]

When Coleridge and the Morgans finally settled at Calne early in 1815, he had come to rest with some of his books for the first time in five years, and was to stay there for a year. Though he was in fragile health, he could have repeated George Herbert's thanksgiving—

> And now in age I bud again,
> After so many deaths I live and write.

He gathered together his poems for *Sibylline Leaves* and, thinking to write an introduction to that volume, dictated the *Biographia Literaria*, a book that looked back towards a prophetic notebook entry of

---

[1] *CL* III 446, 442, 455.

[2] *CL* III 455. It was Eden who gave C a message in May 1814 that a Mr Russel was leaving for the East Indies and wanted his 3-vol Milton back. For the account of how C searched for Vol III through "two chaos chest[s] of Books", how he ran the book down at Hood's and made himself ill in recovering it, see *CL* III 496. In the series of confused moves of the Morgan household some of C's books may have inadvertently been withheld from his use—as was the case with Sotheby's Petrarch after Mrs C had sent it to London. See *CL* IV 655. The Morgans moved from Hammersmith in Mar 1812 to Berners St and then in Oct 1813 to poor lodgings off Fitzroy Square. Morgan's books were deposited at Bishopsgate St presumably when they left Berners St.

September–October 1803[1] and perhaps even farther back to the projected "life of Lessing".

In spite of the medical advice and strenuous treatment Coleridge had received in Bristol in 1814, his addiction to opium had not been broken and his general state of health in 1815 was still alarming. In his search for medical counsel he was introduced in April 1816 to James Gillman, a physician in his early thirties practising in Highgate. Both Gillman and his wife were captivated at the first meeting; Coleridge was immediately received into the family as patient, housemate, and friend. Leaving the Morgans, who had sheltered him affectionately since 1808 and had shared their shifting household with him ever since the breach with the Wordsworths, he now began a new life at Moreton House at the top of Highgate Hill.

To write notes in books was now part of his habit of mind and work. An increasing number of friends lent him books with the express invitation to annotate them; and on his own account, and for his own purposes, he wrote notes in his own books with astonishing certainty of touch and in remarkable profusion. When he took up residence with the Gillmans, at the age of forty-four, he entered upon the three years of his greatest productivity, and the marginalia—stimulated rather than inhibited by the books he was writing and the lectures he was giving—increased steadily both in volume and in the number of books annotated. His friends now knew where they would find him; old friends, and many new ones, came to see him, to listen to him. He went into London to dine with the Beaumonts, with Basil Montagu, Daniel Stuart, John Hookham Frere, and the Aderses (German, collectors of paintings, lovers of music and books, friends of Crabb Robinson and Lamb);[2] and sometimes he was a little lionised and was often the brilliant focus of these dinners.

In the early and middle years the friends who had provided books that he could annotate were relatively few: in Bristol Joseph Cottle, Josiah Wade, James Tobin, and Thomas Poole, and later Henry Daniels and W. B. Elwyn; in addition to the immediate Keswick–Grasmere circle there had been Thomas Clarkson, William Jackson

---

[1] "Seem to have made up my mind to write my metaphysical works, as *my Life*, & *in* my Life—intermixed with all the other events/ or history of the mind & fortunes of S. T. Coleridge." *CN* I 1515.

[2] Some account of Carl and Eliza Aders is given in DE WETTE *Theodor* headnote.

(the landlord of Greta Hall), Sir George Beaumont, James Losh. Since the end of 1810 Henry Crabb Robinson had provided German books unstintingly, often making his own suggestions. Lamb could only occasionally visit Highgate, but his books were still accessible; and in 1818 Lamb's *Works* appeared, the second volume bearing a splendid dedication to Coleridge. At Highgate the bookish acquaintance quickly multiplied. Almost as soon as he arrived there he met the Hebrew scholar Hyman Hurwitz. In 1817 he first met Henry Francis Cary, Charles Augustus Tulk, and the man who was to be named in Coleridge's will as the "dear friend, the companion, partner, and helpmate of my worthiest studies", Joseph Henry Green. In that year Ludwig Tieck came to Highgate to renew their Mediterranean meeting, and they talked happily about Shakespeare. George Frere lent him a copy of Baxter's *Reliquiae*, and when John Hookham Frere came home from public service in Malta there was good talk about Aristophanes and prosody. Carl Aders lent him German books and arranged for others to be bought for him in Germany. A neighbour, Mrs Milne, lent him an edition of Shakespeare in which he may well have written more than the note on *Romeo and Juliet* that we know about (though the book itself is now lost). Mr Bage, the bookseller and stationer from whom he bought notebooks, lent him a copy of Fielding's *Joseph Andrews*, and he wrote notes in that. William Kirkpatrick gave him a volume of Asgill's tracts and the *Spes Israelis*. In 1825 the strange young revolutionary Gioacchino de' Prati lent him Vico's *Scienza nuova*; Coleridge certainly read it, but there is no record that he annotated it. Young men brought their books—his two nephews, Henry and Edward, J. H. B. Williams, Julius Hare, F. D. Maurice, John Sterling.[1] Joseph Blanco White and Edward Irving were drawn into the magnetic field, and—even though they appeared mothlike across the line of vision and presently disappeared from view—he wrote extensive notes in books that they had written and presented to him. The most open-handed providers were Crabb Robinson, Green, and the Gillmans. It was for James and Anne Gillman that he wrote the greatest number of marginalia on request; and it was the Gillmans who, when they had to part with cherished annotated books, wrote out the notes as best they could into the margins of other copies in order to have facsimiles of the originals.

---

[1] Thomas Allsop gave a list of about thirty of Lamb's friends and associates during the later years of his life. Many of these were also in various degree friends or acquaintances of C's. Allsop I 203.

Early in 1823 Coleridge was well enough known as a literary figure about London to be placed on charge in a facetious police report in the *London Magazine* for "idling about the suburbs of town".[1] In October or November of that year, Moreton House now proving uncomfortably small for the Gillmans' growing family, they moved across Pond Square to No 3 The Grove, one of a fine row of houses built in the late seventeenth century by one William Blake in order to finance the charity school for girls that he had founded in Highgate. The Gillmans had a copy of a curious undated pamphlet that Blake had written in about 1670 to solicit subscriptions for the school; Coleridge wrote one note in it, but it is not certain that he knew that there was any connexion between William Blake and The Grove.

One of the reasons for the move to The Grove "from small and warm to comfortably large but *not* draftless rooms",[2] was to provide Coleridge with a more suitable work-place. The move was made discreetly while he was on holiday at Ramsgate and was completed by the time he returned to Highgate on 10 November 1823.[3] According to Lucy Watson, grand-daughter of the Gillmans, he at first had a room on the second floor next to the room occupied by James and Anne Gillman, but "going up to reconnoitre one day the floor above, he was so delighted with the well-known view of Caen Wood and the adjacent valley that he requested his hosts to let his books and belongings be moved to this quaint upper chamber".[4] He was installed in his "Bed and Book-room" by the beginning of December; on the 10th he told Allsop, "You will be delighted with my new Room", and to William Worship expatiated upon the view "from the attic in which I and my books are now installed".[5] But the move was ill-omened. He had scarcely set himself up in the attic when Mrs Gillman, going down the steep uncarpeted stairs without a light, tripped at the top and took a serious fall, breaking her arm.[6] What

[1] *London Magazine* VII (Mar 1823) 158: "The Literary Police Office, Bow-street. Edward Herbert's letters to the Family of the Powells. No VIII. Literary police, Bow-street." "Samuel Taylor Coleridge was brought up for idling about the suburbs of town, without being able to give a satisfactory account of himself. He was taken up for sleeping at Highgate in the day-time. The magistrates committed him to the Muses' Treadmill for two months, hard labour. It is supposed his *feet* will be all the better for this exercise. This is the same person, though much altered, who passed himself off as the Ancient Mariner, at a marriage in the metropolis some time back."

[2] *CL* v 311.

[3] *CL* v 308.

[4] *C at H* 51.

[5] *CL* v 335, 313.

[6] *CL* v 317, 335; see also 314.

with the upset of the move and Mrs Gillman's accident, and the distress of an illness that afflicted him until well into February 1824, his books were still in great confusion as late as mid-February.[1] Even if he had been in good health and not harassed by difficulties with the proofs of *Aids to Reflection*, it might well have taken him some time to get his library in order, for the room was very much an attic room providing little convenient space for shelving many books. The one window faced north; the room certainly had a splendid view, but it must always have been rather dark. Here the greater part of his reading and writing was done in the last ten years of his life.

The number of friends, disciples, and donors increased, and Coleridge began to write marginalia on request more than ever before. But nobody induced in his notes the tone that had been—and still continued to be—associated with Lamb, though some of the notes specially written for Anne Gillman have something of the same courtly-affectionate, slightly bantering, pedagogic tone that some of the notes for Sara Hutchinson had had. Notes written for the young—for Henry and Edward Coleridge, and sometimes for Derwent—seem to have been written from a consciousness of wisdom, yet on the whole they are seldom sententious and are sometimes exuberantly playful. Over Southey's books, and Blanco White's and Edward Irving's, he could become disputative and sharp in a way that he seldom had been in his earlier hard-hitting notes; and this tone, brought to epigrammatic trenchancy by his sense of Southey's baleful influence on Hartley's prose style, dominates the notes he wrote in *The Worthies of Yorkshire and Lancashire* in 1832–3. Otherwise the marginalia written at Highgate seem to have crystallised from a mind enclosed in its own reflection, yet flowing out of the same unself-conscious spontaneity, the same fidelity to their source, that had originally secured the habit of writing in books as he read them.

In Highgate, where he was able to work more consistently than for a long time, Coleridge annotated old books that he had never annotated before and new books as they came out, and also returned to books that already had his marginal notes in them. He did not systematically complete or revise as though for publication any series of notes previously written. He would sometimes reread favourite books, and in looking through his earlier notes write new notes farther on in a book than he had annotated before, or be content with corrections and afterthoughts in the form of comments

[1] *CL* v 328.

on his own notes; sometimes he would intersperse a new series of notes through the earlier ones, or occasionally—for reasons not always discernible—begin afresh in a separate copy. His energy and concentration were prodigious.

A few examples suggest the variations in pattern of the marginal notes. Of more than a hundred notes in seventeen volumes (eleven titles) of Kant—written "at so many different and distant times" that they are impossible to disentangle chronologically—Coleridge wrote the first in 1800 and some as late as 1824. The notes in seven volumes of Schelling, however, though rather more numerous than the notes on Kant, seem all to have been written within a short period, perhaps about 1815–17; yet the marginalia in ten volumes of Steffens— slightly more numerous than those on Schelling and more technical —seem to fall into two groups, perhaps 1815–18 and 1823–6. The biblical commentaries of Eichhorn, which he used rather like work-books, accumulated almost 200 notes written mostly between 1812 and 1827; Tennemann's *Geschichte der Philosophie*, originally a work-book for the Philosophical Lectures of 1818–19, includes some very long notes dated 1822, 1824, and 1827. He began to annotate his volumes of Böhme in 1808–9 and the folio of Jeremy Taylor's *Polemicall Discourses* in 1811; the one has almost 200 notes in it, strongly concentrated in the one work *Aurora*, the other has more than 250 notes, more evenly distributed and some of them of exceptional length; the latest dated notes in both are for 1826 but Coleridge probably went on annotating both of them later than that. He said that Luther's *Colloquia Mensalia* was "next to the Scriptures my main book of meditation, deep, seminative, pauline, beyond all other works in my possession, it *potenziates* both my Thoughts and my Will";[1] he wrote more than a hundred notes in it from 1819 to 1829 and probably later. By contrast the total of almost a hundred notes in three editions of Leighton's *Works* were written in three distinct and separate series, in 1814, 1817, and 1822–3, and had run their seminal course when *Aids to Reflection* went to press in 1824. The notes in one copy of *Reliquiae Baxterianae* were written from 1811, the notes in the other from 1817; but it looks as though both copies may sometimes have been in use together, with indiscriminate alternation.

One heavily annotated book of special personal import belongs to Highgate—Southey's *Life of Wesley*. Coleridge wrote more than a

---

[1] *CL* vi 561: to Edward Coleridge 8 Feb 1826.

hundred notes in his copy between 1820 and 1832, called it "my darling Book and favourite of my Library", and insisted that it be given to Southey after his death. The last book Coleridge read through, in June and July 1834, was *The Remains of Bishop Daniel Sandford* (2 vols Edinburgh 1830). Henry Nelson Coleridge said that Coleridge "wrote several notes [in it], one exquisite" on the Bishop's "courteous demeanour to his daughters". The book has not been preserved, but that one note exists in transcript.

Coleridge died on 25 July 1834 at half-past six in the morning. In the middle of the previous day "his mind [was] in perfect vigour & clearness—he remarked that his intellect was quite unclouded & he said 'I could even be witty' ".[1] Almost four years earlier he had set down, in the final version of his will, his wishes for the disposition of his books and papers after his death. In his epitaph Coleridge had prayed for forgiveness rather than fame. Whether as he died he had any hope of fame, he must have been confident that what he had written and had never managed to "sheave and cart and house" was now in safe hands.

LIBRARY CORMORANT

From his early childhood Coleridge was guilty of what André Gide called "this unpunished vice of reading" and suffered also from that "worst voluptuousness" that Donne speaks of—"an Hydroptique immoderate desire of humane learning and languages". From the age of eight to fourteen, he said in a late autobiographical fragment, he was "a playless Helluo Librorum"—a glutton for books. When he was a Bluecoat schoolboy, a chance encounter with a clergyman in London made him free of "a great Circulating Library in King's Street, Cheapside", and he "*read thro'* the whole Catalogue, folios and all—whether I understood them or did not understand them". This "preposterous pursuit" left him isolated from his schoolfellows in "the wide, wild wilderness of useless, unarranged Book-knowlege, and book-thoughts".[2] What with his conversations with his father (who died when Coleridge was nine—a real Parson Adams, yet a grammarian, an amateur astrologer, and a knowledgeable

[1] *CL* vi 992.

[2] N F⁰ ff 90ᵛ–92ᵛ; parts of the autobiographical note were printed seriatim in *C Life* (G). Lamb's portrait of C as a Bluecoat, in "Christ's Hospital Five and Thirty Years Ago", does not provide independent evidence of C's learning at that period: as Lamb acknowledged, most of the detail came from C himself.

Hebraist), and from the indiscriminate reading in his boyhood and his not-much-more systematic reading as an undergraduate, he had come to the conviction by his early twenties—if not earlier—that "all the knowlege, that can be acquired, [is] child's play—the universe itself—what an immense heap of *little* things"; and his mind felt "as if it ached to behold & know something *great*—something *one* & *indivisible*".[1] In November 1796 he told the harried revolutionary John Thelwall that

I am, & ever have been, a great reader—& have read almost every thing—a library-cormorant—I am *deep* in all out of the way books, whether of the monkish times, or of the puritanical aera—I have read & digested most of the Historical Writers—; but I do not *like* History. Metaphysics, & Poetry, & "Facts of mind"— (i.e. Accounts of all the strange phantasms that ever possessed your philosophy-dreamers from Tauth, the Egyptian to Taylor, the English Pagan,) are my darling Studies.—In short, I seldom read except to amuse myself—& I am almost always reading.—Of useful knowlege, I am a so-so chemist, & I love chemistry—all else is *blank*,—but I *will* be (please God) an Horticulturist & a Farmer.[2]

Some leniency must be allowed the guileless vanity of young genius. For the Bristol years 1795–8 there is record of his borrowings, and the borrowings of his friends and associates, from the Bristol Library Society; there is record also of his borrowings from the Göttingen University Library in 1799, from the Carlisle and Durham Cathedral libraries in 1801–2, and fragmentary but incomplete record of the use of other libraries—an ancient library in Kendal, the Red Cross Street (or Dissenters) Library, the Westminster Library, Sion College Library, the British Museum; and he was always drawing levies upon the libraries of his friends, even (he hoped) of such distant acquaintances as Sir Wilfred Lawson and possibly Sir Joseph Banks. His own library altogether grew more rapidly than it dwindled by dispersal, as in his restless movements he left behind sometimes large deposits, sometimes casual strays in ones and twos. So vivid was his continuous commerce with books that certain bookish incidents were to remain indelibly in his mind with the tantalising importunity of a poetic image. In March 1810, in a constellation of remembered images associated with Sara Hutchinson—images "which never fail instantly to awake into vivider flame the for ever and ever Feeling of you"—he found embedded in memory, at a distance of eight years, "All Books—my Study at Keswick ... Books of abstruse Knowlege—the Thomas

[1] *CL* I 349.   [2] *CL* I 260.

Aquinas & Suarez from the Durham Library".[1] And in November 1827, more than thirty years after the event, another book-recollection came back to him with the clarity of a dream:

—by the bye, I must get the Book—which I have never seen since in my 24th year [1795] I walked with Southey on a desperate hot summerday from Bath to Bristol with a Goose, 2 Vol. of [Andrew] Baxter on the Immortality of the Soul, + the Giblets, in my hand—I should not wonder if I found that Andrew had thought more on the subject of Dreams than any other of our Psychologists, Scotch or English—[2]

As a lover of White's *Natural History of Selborne* and a watchful observer of birds, he probably meant what he said when he described himself to Thelwall in November 1796 as a "library-cormorant". Even in the first thirty years of his life he read a great many books, some of them curious, some strange, some massive and dull, some commonplace enough, some commanding his attention for the rest of his life. But the seductive enthusiasm of John Livingston Lowes should not persuade us—nor was this Lowes's intention—that Coleridge had in fact read *everything*. The cormorant is indeed a voracious bird; but he is not nit-witted like the booby or—as sailors say of his half-brother the gannet—an indiscriminate glutton. For books, Coleridge had a keen appetite, some discrimination, and an almost flawless digestion.

But what books did he own then, in the *annus mirabilis*? Probably a small and miscellaneous collection, a function of his omnivorous interests and small income—some treasures, like the Casimir and Bentley's Horace that he had rescued from a bookseller after his withdrawal from the Dragoons, a number of his university books and standard texts, classical and other (of which we can see clear traces in the Rydal Mount catalogue), probably some school-books like Tooke's *Pantheon* and the rare North American Bible (now lost) that Lamb had helped him dog-ear at Christ's Hospital,[3] and an increasing number of books of questionable virtue that he had received for review or had picked up at a venture. He had his own copy of Anderson's *British Poets* (12 volumes, price £8); a few oddities too, no doubt, like Paullini's discourse on the worminess of death, which he bought in 1795 but did not open until eight years later, and the little volume of Neoplatonic works that he commissioned Thelwall to buy for him.[4] In Bristol he had access to

---

[1] *CN* III 3708.
[2] N 35 f 36.
[3] *CL* I 262.
[4] See *CL* I 262. The book was

Iamblichus *De mysteriis Aegyptorum etc* [Selections, tr M. Ficino] (1607). DC's copy, perhaps given him by C, is in VCL.

Joseph Cottle's bookshop and became a member of the Bristol Library Society—a well-stocked library with an intelligent policy of acquisition; in Nether Stowey he used Tom Poole's library and the Stowey Book Society. His first major acquisition was £25 worth of German books bought in Hamburg with a publisher's advance— perhaps a hundred volumes.[1] It is doubtful whether he was ever again able to make a single purchase of books on that scale, though in the middle and later years he must have run up some considerable accounts with booksellers, to judge from some of the lists of desiderata in the notebooks and surviving correspondence especially with Boosey and Bothe.

Coleridge never had much money to spend on books. A few details have survived. After returning from Germany he bought some theological folios "for their weight" in the "Book-Golgotha" of a druggist in Exeter.[2] When he got to Keswick he rescued a group of Caroline and Civil War tracts from shops where (he said) they were being used as "winding-sheets for pilchards" after the dissolution of a gentleman's library nearby.[3] In July 1802 his friend Thomas Wilkinson gave him "a parcel of old Books" including an unidentified "old System of Philosophy by some FANTASTIC or other", which he conned through with the child Hartley and described delightedly to Sara Hutchinson.[4] From time to time Lamb bought him books from barrows in the Barbican, for a few shillings or even a few pence, a pastime that seems to have had no attractions for Coleridge himself. We know that by March 1801 Coleridge, like Wordsworth, was indebted to Longman for a copy of the 4-volume Withering *British Plants* and a botanical microscope that went with it as a bargain offer. (The microscope is recorded in Wordsworth's *Stanzas Written in Thomson's "Castle of Indolence"*.) At Syracuse in October 1804 G. F. Leckie gave him a splendid Greek edition of Arrian and Epictetus (Amsterdam 1683), but afterwards "retracted the Gift";[5] and perhaps Leckie had something to do with the beautiful Basle 1580 edition of Plotinus that Coleridge acquired in Syracuse at this time. When, in February 1826, he had to pay 10s 6d

[1] C told the Wedgwoods that he had spent £30 on German books. *CL* I 519. When he left for Germany he had indeed a credit for £30, but records of his German accounts at Cornell show that he had only £25 to spend with his Hamburg bookseller, William Remnant.

[2] *CL* I 531: 29 Sept 1799.
[3] See e.g. *CN* I 781, *Friend* (*CC*) I 428. The phrase is from Catullus by way of Milton.
[4] *CL* II 827.
[5] *CN* II 2236. A full description of this copy of Arrian is given in *CN* II 2236n.

to replace a missing volume of Eichhorn on the Apocalypse he grumbled wittily at the deplorable paper it was printed on. At Calne 29 March 1815 he bought for £4 10*s* the 4-volume Stockdale edition (1811) of Ben Jonson and Beaumont and Fletcher. Poole gave him at least one of the books he had annotated at Stowey in 1807. Mr West, a surgeon of Calne, gave him a copy of the Brerewood and Byfield sabbatarian controversy, and Coleridge—though he eventually annotated it—cherished it for its parchment wrapper, "which I conjecture to be part of a Record, that had belonged to Canterbury Cathedral, of the Pilgrims, offerings, miraculous Cures &c at the Shrine of Thomas of Becket", and thought to transcribe the manuscript from the wrapper if he could and send it to the *Gentleman's Magazine*.[1] In 1818 somebody gave him a bundle of Cromwellian tracts, some of which he annotated. In November 1820 Green gave him a copy of Proclus' commentary on the Platonic theology.[2] William Sotheby, who had drawn from Coleridge in 1802 some of his most perceptive utterances on poetry, gave him in 1827 the huge hexaglot *Georgics* that Coleridge intended to present to his daughter Sara on her wedding day.[3] Edward Irving gave him his one incunable—Hugh of St Victor *De sacramentis Christianae fidei* (Strassburg 1485) with initial capitals in red and blue neatly executed throughout. William Kirkpatrick, who gave him a copy of Asgill in 1827, also gave him the *Spes Israelis* of Menasseh ben Israel, but that has disappeared. We do not know how he came by his treasured *Reinecke Foss* (Rostock 1592) or his "obscure old Edition of the New Testament" (1622).

   The growth of Coleridge's library was not merely haphazard. He studied catalogues and drew up lists of desiderata; he commissioned Southey, Lamb, De Quincey, Morgan, Crabb Robinson, Green, Carl Aders, and others to buy books for him; from time to time he had regular arrangements with booksellers other than those who

---

[1] *CL* IV 594.

[2] *N* 29 f 38.

[3] In thanking Sotheby for the book, he promised to "deliver [it] to my Daughter on her Wedding Day—as the most splendid way, that I can command, of marking my sense of the Talent and Industry, that have made her Mistress of the Six Languages comprized in the Volumes". *CL* VI 691. He also said that "I will avail myself of some one of those focal states of my Being, in which Head and Heart converge, and record on the blank leaves all, I know, think, and feel, of the work, and it's author"; but he wrote in it only a long inscription, by coincidence on Sara's wedding-day, expressing the hope that "she will never willingly part with this Volume or alienate the same", and endorsed this hope by making specific bequest of it to SC in his will. *CL* VI 1000.

published his works. But he never forgave a Mr Hare for not lending him the rare Brunos from the Roxburghe Sale, and it is difficult to refrain from guessing that one motive for his tentative agreement to make a verse translation of *Faust* for John Murray was the hope of getting for nothing a set of the latest edition of Goethe's works. He used what public libraries were available to him, but in his day there were few public collections of books of the sort he needed, and when he came to Highgate he was too far away from the rapidly growing British Museum Library to use it regularly (though Coleridge is reported to have visited H. F. Cary there after he took up residence in the Museum in 1826). Quite early on he had acquired some cheap plain edition of the classics, and in about 1807 gave thanks for such bounty in a note written in Casaubon's edition of Persius:

When I recollect, that I have the whole works of Cicero, of Livy, and Quintilian, with many others, the whole works of each in a single Volume, either thick Quarto with thin paper & small yet distinct print, or thick Octavo or duodecimo of the same character & that they cost me in the proportion of a Shilling to a Guinea for the same quantity of worse matter in modern Books, or Editions, I am a poor man yet one whom "βιβλίων κτήσεως ἐκ παιδαρίου δεινὸς ἐντέτηκε πόθος [a terrible longing to acquire books has filled ever since childhood]" feel the liveliest Gratitude for the Age which produced such Editions...

Like many a reader, he preferred not to be hurried. As time went on he needed to have his own books to work from, and as he came to rely increasingly upon his own marginal notes, many of his own books—and some books that did not belong to him—became indispensable.

In November 1802 Coleridge told his wife: "I love warm Rooms, comfortable fires, & food, books, natural scenery, music &c; but I do not care what *binding* the Books have, whether they are dusty or clean".[1] Some of his Mediterranean books were stained with sea-water; and he had no objection to dust, crumbling calf, spiders' webs, traces of bookworms. But he had too great respect for any book to open its leaves with a buttery knife, as Wordsworth is scandalously (and probably unjustly) alleged to have done;[2] and none of his books shows that he approved of the technique of accelerated ageing

---

[1] *CL* II 881.

[2] "William Wordsworth and Robert Southey" *Tait's Magazine* Jul 1839: *De Q Works* II 313. According to De Q's laborious account, the book was not WW's but De Q's, and the assault was provoked by the unlovely title on the spine: "Burke's Works". Books that have survived from WW's library suggest that he may have handled some of them roughly, but not barbarously.

that Lamb practised (as witness his folio edition of Beaumont and Fletcher in the British Museum) by introducing cheese-crumbs, port, and tobacco-ash into the gutters of his books.[1] When he came upon an offensive passage in Lamb's copy of Fulke Greville he refrained from tearing out the leaf on the unassailable ground that "I make it part of conscience never to mutilate a book". But annotation was not mutilation, nor can restraint from annotation be taken as a mark of respect for a rare or valuable book. He rightly withheld his pen from Tulk's copy of Blake's *Songs of Innocence and Songs of Experience*; but in his one incunable he wrote a note that has nothing to do with Hugh of St Victor, and wrote several notes in his Asgill and the volume of Brerewood and Byfield, curious books though not intrinsically valuable. Only once did he waver towards finery, in a note on his German version of Sidney's *Arcadia*: "Would I were rich enough to procure a handsome *authentic* Russia-leather Binding for this, the Renard the Fox, & a few other Jewels." He had a reasonable eye for typography and layout, learned (one imagines) from Joseph Cottle, whose early Bristol books have never received the admiration they deserve. But Coleridge's primary devotion was to the text of a book. If it was readable, well; and as time went on, if the paper would take ink, better; if the book was also his own, best of all.

As Coleridge's books slowly accumulated from the Nether Stowey days onward, the physical location of his books became of increasing importance to him. When he set up house in Greta Hall, Keswick, in July 1800, he had a "library" for the first time, and as soon as he was settled he wrote in the character of "Gentleman-poet and Philosopher in a mist" to William Godwin to say that

I have, or have the use of, no inconsiderable collection of Books—in *my* Library you will find all the Poets & Philosophers, & many of our best old Writers—below in our Parlor, belonging to my Landlord, but in my possession, are almost all the usual Trash of the Johnsons, Gibbons, Robertsons, &c with the Encyclopaedia Britannica, &c &c. Sir Wilfrid

---

[1] See *LL* I 322–3: Lamb to C 11 Oct 1802. "...a book reads the better, which is our own, and has been long known to us, that we know the topography of its blots and dog's-ears, and can trace the dirt in it to having read it at tea with buttered muffins, or over a pipe, which I think is the maximum". In Nov 1831 C made the following apology to a Highgate neighbour: "I plead guilty to the stains and spots on the cover of this book [unidentified], and penitently take them on my own covering, hoping, they will be considered by you as only *skin-deep*, relatively to the character of your obliged friend and servant." *CL* VI 873

Lawson's magnificent Library is at some 8 or 9 miles distant—and he is liberal in the highest degree in the management of it.[1]

Lamb visited Greta Hall in September 1802 and has left one of the few glimpses of Coleridge's study there:

Coleridge had got a blazing fire in his study; which is a large antique, ill-shaped room, with an old-fashioned organ, never played upon, big enough for a church, shelves of scattered folios, an Aeolian harp, and an old sofa, half-bed, &c. And all looking out upon the last fading view of Skiddaw and his broad-breasted brethren . . .[2]

When Coleridge was about to leave for Dove Cottage on his way to the Mediterranean, he inadvertently preserved another glimpse of the room that had provided the vivid setting of many memorable notebook entries in 1802 and 1803, recording his pleasure in "the fire-gleam on my dear Books, that fill up the whole side from ceiling to floor of my Tall Study".[3]

During the first three and a half years at Greta Hall, in spite of what he had told James Tobin, Poole, and Godwin, Coleridge was neither a recluse scholar nor a virtuoso—not a Thomas Gray or a Horace Walpole. He went up to London at least twice and stayed for some weeks. He went back and forth to the Wordsworths, and, although Dove Cottage was already overcrowded, they kept a place for him there so that he could come at any time, leave books and papers, work if he wished, whether there was anybody else in the house or not. This explains perhaps the marginalia in some of Wordsworth's books written at this time, the joint inscription

[1] *CL* I 619.

[2] *LL* I 315. For a detailed description of the rooms see H. W. Howe *Greta Hall* (priv ptd 1977). When HC was paying a visit to Greta Hall shortly before C's death he wrote to SC of his anguish at finding many changes in the house where his childhood had been spent, and particularly in C's study. "The organ room is out of tune, not at all comparable to what it was with its bare wall, whereon the Damp had played the Geographer —mapping out Ejuxrias and Eutopias, with shores embayed, and winding rivers long and wide, and forests vast of mouldy greenery, sharp jutting capes to cleave the long-back waves . . .". *HCL* 159.

In late Jul 1800 Lamb had written:

"*Your Books* are all safe.—Only I have not thought it necessary to fetch away your last batch, which I understand are at Johnson's the Bookseller; who has got quite as much room, & will take as much care of them as myself—and you can send for them immediately from him—". *LL* (M) I 216. Some of the books are identified in his next letter to C, 6 Aug 1800: " . . . three ponderous German dictionaries, one volume (I can find no more) of German and French ditto, sundry other German books unbound, as you left them, Percy's Ancient Poetry, and one volume of Anderson's Poets." Ibid I 216–17. These books left for Kendal by wagon early in Nov 1802. *CL* II 880.

[3] See above, pp lxxix–lxxx.

"W. W. + S. T. C." in some of Wordsworth's books, and the mixing of sets of books, as may have happened at some time with two copies of Anderson's *British Poets*. Dorothy Wordsworth, in a letter of 14 June 1802 to Mary and Sara Hutchinson, recorded the transfer of a major cache of books from Greta Hall to Dove Cottage; on which occasion, as on others, he came to Grasmere over Helvellyn rather than by the easier familiar road over Dunmail Raise:

> ... in the evening Coleridge came over Grisdale Hawes with a wallet of books—he had had a furious wind to struggle with, and had been attacked by a vicious cow, luckily without horns, so he was no worse—he had been ill the day before—but he looked and *was* well—strong he must have been for he brought a load over those Fells that I would not have carried to Ambleside for five shillings.[1]

When Southey came to Greta Hall with his family in September 1803, grieving for the death of his daughter Margaret in Bristol, he had regarded his stay as temporary, and had left most of his books in Bristol, London, and Burton. Only a few weeks after Coleridge had sailed for Malta it seemed that the Coleridge and Southey families would be obliged to leave the house, and Dorothy knew that Coleridge would be "Heart-struck at the thought of no more returning to his old Books in their old Book-case looking to Skiddaw—his study, his study fire-side, Newlands and Borrowdale all taken from him".[2] That crisis passed and, although the house was still partly unfinished and in some respects inconvenient and uncomfortable, Southey stayed on, but restless, hoping to move back to the West Country. In February 1807 Coleridge wrote from Coleorton to inquire about Southey's plans, hoping that if Southey were to leave (taking Mrs Coleridge with him) he himself would be able to secure Greta Hall and share it with the Wordsworths. (The Wordsworths had agreed "*very very* reluctantly", one of their reasons being "the convenience of [Coleridge] having his books already there".[3]) Southey's response to the inquiry was instant: he decided to remain in Greta Hall, began at once to improve the house and grounds, sent to Bristol and elsewhere for all his books, and—hearing that Coleridge was on his way to Bristol—sent stern instructions to Charles Danvers to say that Coleridge was on no account to be allowed to "get at my books, and carry any of them off with him"—"in the first place he spoils every decent book on which he

---

[1] *WL* (*E* 2) 362. Ambleside is less than four miles from Grasmere, Keswick about fourteen by the main road. Perhaps on this occasion C walked across White Moss Common; or even, as on other occasions, over Helvellyn.

[2] *WL* (*E* 2) 510.

[3] *WL* (*M* 2) i 137.

lays his hands, and in the next place the moment it is in his hands he considers it to all intents and purposes as his own, and makes no scruple of bescrawling it, of giving it away".[1] Southey need not have worried. By the time Coleridge reached Bristol he was too distracted with other more personal concerns to be casting greedy eyes on Southey's books.

By the spring of 1807, when Coleridge went to Nether Stowey to meet his wife and announce their separation to the family in Ottery St Mary, he knew that Greta Hall was no longer his own home, even though his books remained there in the Organ Room and even though he would be able to visit from time to time. Eighteen months later, when he was about to take up residence with the Wordsworths at Allan Bank, he instructed his wife to send all his books from Keswick, and finally the bookcases. This transfer of his library, essential to his writing of *The Friend*, was to have serious consequences. When he set off for London with Basil Montagu on 18 October 1810 he had no premonition that, within a matter of days, he would be involved in a desolating estrangement from the Wordsworths, that it would lose him the companionship of Sara Hutchinson, that it would separate him from a large part of his library. He took south with him only one box, containing his clothes and whatever books he expected to need at once—"a rope and a couple of nails will suffice to secure it".[2]

When the Wordsworths moved first to Grasmere Vicarage in June 1811, and then to Rydal Mount in May 1813, they took Coleridge's books with them. Dorothy had sent him a number of his German books in the spring of 1812; at least 400 volumes remained. Whether, after he had joined the Gillman household in Moreton House, Highgate, Coleridge could have housed there the books he had left with the Wordsworths we do not know; possibly not, because the reason for leaving Moreton House was that it was too small for the family, let alone a library. Once the Gillmans had moved to The Grove in November 1823 there was certainly room for the books in that "large & handsome Mansion", particularly after Coleridge's attic room had been reconstructed late in 1826; but not until late 1829 or early 1830 were any more of the books at Rydal Mount sent to him, and then only about a third of them.

---

[1] *S Letters* (Curry) I 446–7.
[2] As he later told the Morgans: *CL* III 301. In mid-Aug 1814 he was worried how to get "a Box of Books & Cloathes" transported to Ashley Cottage (*CL* VI 1031)—presumably this same box.

We should know nothing in detail about those books if it were not for a handlist of the books in the Rydal Mount library drawn up evidently in 1823 and revised and checked in about 1829. Coleridge's books were then intermixed with Wordsworth's but were given a distinctive mark in the list. The whole catalogue runs to 1181 titles; 315 of these are shown as Coleridge's.[1] The titles are so sketchily entered that if we did not have other information about Coleridge's books—and Wordsworth's—many would be impossible to identify with any certainty. The list is of peculiar interest as being the only handlist we have of any major group of Coleridge's books drawn up during his lifetime. From various markings in the list, and from a four-page list of 114 titles in Wordsworth's hand marked "The above sent to Coleridge", we can identify some thirty books that Coleridge had annotated before he left them behind at Allan Bank in October 1810, and certain other books that he received in Highgate in late 1829 or early 1830 and did not annotate. Notations in the list show that certain of Coleridge's books were lent or given to Hartley and Derwent, three to Edward Irving, and two to Southey. The list may have been drawn up in the first place by Sara Coleridge and Edith Southey in 1823; the Coleridge books were apparently checked —probably in connexion with Wordsworth's "Highgate" list—in about October 1829 by Wordsworth's clerk, John Carter, and apparently also by Sara Coleridge and Henry Nelson on their honeymoon. This was also the time when Mrs Coleridge was leaving Greta Hall for the last time, a time (one would suppose) for clearing up any of Coleridge's effects that remained in Keswick and Grasmere. But about two hundred of Coleridge's books may have remained at Rydal Mount until after his death.[2]

---

[1] The handlist of the Rydal Mount library (called Wordsworth LC in this edition) is in the Houghton Library, Harvard, catalogued as MS Eng 880. It is being edited by Professor Chester Shaver. The list is divided into twelve divisions: Classics, Theology, Philosophy, Law & Politics, Poetry, History, "Voyages Travels, Geog: &c", Natural History, Books of Amusement, Novels & Romances, Translations, and Modern Languages (43 of the 113 titles in the last section being C's). C's books were marked in the list with a "C" when the list was first formed, and were checked off—with a few corrections and additions—on later occasions.

[2] The full details of these transactions, and the inferences from which they have been reconstructed, will be discussed in an Appendix in the final volume; but see also ANNEX B p clviii n 1, below.

Southey died on 21 March 1843. That there should have been in his library so few books annotated by Coleridge is a sombre comment upon their relationship. Their friendship had developed swiftly in 1795, when they shared lodgings, borrowed books together from the Bristol Library Society and Joseph Cottle's bookshop, jointly prepared lectures that they hoped would provide passage-money to America. It was broken with the dissolution of pantisocracy late in 1795, to be renewed in 1799. Coleridge's compassion in receiving the stricken Southey and his family into Greta Hall in September 1803, and Southey's generosity in harbouring the Coleridge family from 1804 until Coleridge's return from the Mediterranean, arose as much from their feeling for each other as friends as from their relation as brothers-in-law—on both parties the necessity involved some sort of virtue. But Southey's mounting indignation at Coleridge's erratic and (as he thought) irresponsible behaviour after deciding to separate from his wife gave at times an unattractive and censorious edge to his remarks about his brother-in-law. By 1813 Southey's failure to appreciate Coleridge's state of mind in his darkest years drove a gulf between them for the rest of their lives that was deeper even than the rift with the Wordsworths. It is true that from time to time congenial letters passed between them and when they were both in London at the same time they were quizzically civil to each other. But the relationship was always haunted by the fact of Southey's meddling contribution to Coleridge's disastrous marriage, and Southey's unflagging industry and generosity tacitly accused the man of higher genius of improvidence, lack of method, and weakness of will. Against these accusations Coleridge had no permanent defence. There were also profound differences of opinion about politics and the social order. Yet after Coleridge's last visit to Greta Hall in 1812, Southey—at least in the Highgate years—sent him specimens of his prolific literary output, and Coleridge responded by sending a copy of anything he published. With the exception of *Joan of Arc* (1798), the *Annual Anthology* II (1800), and *Omniana* (1812), all of which were in effect joint productions, Coleridge annotated nothing of Southey's (as far as we know) earlier than *The Life of Wesley* (1820); it is unfortunate that *The Life of Nelson* (1813) was published at an inopportune time in their relationship—marginal notes on that most durable of Southey's writings would be well worth having. In the 1830 edition of *Pilgrim's Progress* Coleridge wrote more than half of his notes on Southey's 104-page "Life of Bunyan". The last two of

Southey's books to reach him have only a few notes written in them: *Lives of the British Admirals* I (1833) and *The Doctor* I and II (1834)—the second of these being one of the very last books Coleridge was to annotate.

On 14 August 1834, less than a month after Coleridge's death, Southey wrote:

Those whom I knew in early life, are now falling fast around me. I commenced old man myself on Tuesday last, that day being the completion of my sixtieth year. It is just forty years since I became acquainted with Coleridge; he had long been dead to me, but his decease naturally wakened up old recollections. The papers are left to a Mr. Green, one of his metaphysical disciples. If everything worth preserving be collected his remains will be found not inconsiderable in quantity. There are seven volumes in process, besides scattered pieces. I know not what manuscripts he may have left, and do not suppose there will be anything complete, or approaching to completion; but *perhaps* many fragments, *probably* much that has been taken down from his Conversation, and *certainly* a great number of letters. Whoever edits these will have a difficult and delicate task. All who are of his blood were in the highest degree proud of his reputation but this was their only feeling concerning him.[1]

William Wordsworth died on 23 April 1850 at the age of eighty, his wife surviving him until January 1859. If there is little trace of Coleridge in Southey's library, his presence is discreetly pervasive in Wordsworth's. Of the fifteen books associated with Coleridge, seven bear either the signatures of both Wordsworth and Coleridge or the curious double-autograph inscription:

W. W.
+
S. T. C.[2]

The inscription "S. T. Coleridge + W. Wordsworth" is also found in a tattered and incomplete copy of Pomponius Mela *De situ orbis* [Basle 1522] in the library of St John's College, Cambridge—a little sixteenth-century book with folded maps that show rivers in the shape of trees, and the oceans with ships under sail and a few sea monsters; here *terra incognita* is confidently outlined and the Fortunate Islands are plotted; but there is no record of the Fields of Sleep.

Finally a word needs to be said about Coleridge's "Bed and Book-room" in the attic of No 3 The Grove, Highgate. When he first occupied it in November 1823 it was a real attic room, with half the

---

[1] *S Letters* (Warter) IV 381–2.
[2] A similar inscription—"W. W. +   S. T. C."—appears without comment in *CN* III 4146 of c Apr 1812.

2. Coleridge's "Bed and Book-room" at No 3 The Grove, Highgate, from
the watercolour by George Scharf (1788–1860) painted shortly after
Coleridge's death
Coleridge Cottage, Nether Stowey, The National Trust; reproduced by
kind permission

ceiling sloping down to the eaves at the north-facing back of the house. Late in 1826 Gillman had the roof lifted to give the room "rectangular dignity" and the room assumed the shape that we see in the watercolour drawing made by George Scharf shortly after Coleridge's death.[1] The large book-case that fills the easterly wall was at that time installed, or modified from what was already there, greatly increasing its capacity for the rational disposition of books. It is still in the room, filled (when last seen) with books on sailing and rock-climbing. Here for the last seven and a half years of his life the treasures that his mind fed upon were marshalled as he could wish, ready to hand, and in this room he died.

THE HARVEST ON THE GROUND

In *Blackwood's Edinburgh Magazine* for November 1819 an item of less than two pages was printed under the title "Character of Sir Thomas Brown as a Writer". It opened with a few words addressed to the Editor:

It is well known to those who are in habits of intercourse with Mr Coleridge, that not the smallest, and, in the opinion of many, not the least valuable part of his manuscripts exists in the blank leaves and margins of books; whether his own, or those of his friends, or even in those that have come in his way casually, seems to have been a matter altogether indifferent. The following is transcribed from the blank leaf of a copy of Sir T. Brown's Works in folio, and is a fair specimen of these *Marginalia*; and much more nearly than any of his printed works, gives the style of Coleridge's conversation. G. J.[2]

The piece of marginalia that was then printed is a letter Coleridge had originally addressed to Sara Hutchinson in March 1804 in a copy of Sir Thomas Browne's "*Works*" (1658-9)—*Pseudodoxia Epidemica, Religio Medici, Hydriotaphia,* and *The Garden of Cyrus*—

---

[1] The change was made while C was in Ramsgate 11 Oct–14 Dec 1826. He reported on 29 Dec that "Our house [has been] repaired from top to bottom and so altered for the better. G[illman] has done wonders...I am specially delighted with my room." *CL* vi 658–9. For a drawing of the north elevation of the house showing the modified attic room see *C at H* facing 52; this corresponds well with Scharf's watercolour drawing of the in-terior (which was reproduced in *L* facing ii 616, and is also reproduced in *CL* facing vi 659). "Rectangular dignity" is Lucy Watson's phrase. The original line of the sloping roof can be seen on the west wall in Scharf's drawing.

[2] *Bl Mag* Nov 1819 p 197. The full text of the *Bl Mag* version, collated with the manuscript, is given in BROWNE *Works* ANNEX [*a*].

the letter in which "The Huntsmen are up in Arabia" (and sometimes in America). Since "G. J." is the reversed initials of James
Gillman, Coleridge's host in Highgate, it is reasonable to assume
that Coleridge had edited the annotation on Browne and may have
written the prefatory note. This was the first of Coleridge's marginal
notes to appear in public with acknowledgement and the first public
notice of his practice of writing them. A year later (December 1820)
Charles Lamb, writing under the pseudonym of "Elia", gave similar
witness in the *London Magazine* in the essay entitled "The Two
Races of Men"—the men who lend books and the men who borrow
them. If a man were "blessed with a moderate collection" of books,
and his heart overflowed to lend them:

> let it be to such a one as S. T. C.—he will return them (generally antici-
> pating the time appointed) with usury; enriched with annotations, tripling
> their value. I have had experience. Many are these precious MSS. of his—
> (in *matter* oftentimes, and almost in *quantity* not unfrequently, vying with
> the originals)—in no very clerkly hand—legible in my Daniel; in old
> Burton; in Sir Thomas Browne; and those abstruser cogitations of the
> Greville, now, alas! wandering in Pagan lands.[1]

These two notices, with their air of privileged disclosure, are the
only allegedly independent accounts of Coleridge's practice of
writing notes in the margins of his own and other people's books. In
Aids to Reflection (1825) he identified a passage in the text as "the
first marginal Note I had pencilled on Leighton's Pages, and thus
(remotely, at least), the occasion of the present Work". And just
before the section entitled "Conclusion", he printed, without
comment, a "*Marginal Note written (in 1816) by the Editor in his
own Copy of Wall's work*".[2] Then in *Church and State* (1830) he
printed a set of three long notes that he had written in Isaac Taylor's
anonymous *Natural History of Enthusiasm* (1829), saying that this
was an example of the "Marginalia, which, if brought together from
the various books, my own and those of a score others, would go
near to form as bulky a volume as most of those old folios, through

---

[1] *L Works* II 31. Cf De Q's statement: "Coleridge often spoiled a book
but in the course of doing this, he enriched that book with so many and
so valuable notes, tossing about him,
with such lavish profusion, from such
a cornucopia of discursive reading,
and such a fusing intellect, commentaries so many-angled and so many-
coloured that I have envied many a

man whose luck has placed him in the
way of such injuries." *De Q Works* II
314.

[2] *AR* (1825) 158; the other is at pp
375–6. "Wall's work" is William Wall
*Conference Between Two Men That
Had Doubts About Infant Baptism* (1st
ed 1720); C's copy is lost and the
edition not identified.

which the larger portion of them are dispersed".[1] In 1830 Coleridge might have been suspected of a little exaggeration, but we now know there were no grounds for suspicion. During his lifetime nobody outside a small and scattered group of intimates—probably not even Lamb—could have guessed at the quantity and variety of the marginalia that Coleridge wrote over a period of more than thirty years.

Coleridge made his own assessment of this body of material as early as March 1820, in a letter to Thomas Allsop. A London business-man twenty years younger than Coleridge, Allsop had attended Coleridge's literary lectures from January to March 1818, fell under his spell, and was now his close friend. Even in 1820, almost four years after he had come to safe harbour with the Gillmans, his pathetically small financial needs could not be met even from the burst of publications produced with remarkable energy since he had come to Highgate.[2] Coleridge now unfolded in some detail the work he had in progress; discussed the prospects of completing what he hoped to do, in the face of ill health and public neglect and the need to meet his obligations to his hosts in Highgate and to his scattered family. He said that he had five works in hand, four of which

I have literally nothing more to do, than *to transcribe*; but ... from so many scraps & *sibylline* leaves, including Margins of Books & blank Pages, that unfortunately I must be my own Scribe—& not done by myself, they will be all but lost—or perhaps (as has been too often the case already) furnish feathers for the Caps of others—some for this purpose, and some to plume the arrows of detraction to be let fly against the luckless Bird, from whom they had been plucked or moulted![3]

The four works were "Characteristics of Shakespear's Dramatic Works" (possibly a recension of the notes and marginalia used in his lectures since 1808); a philosophical analysis of the genius and works of Dante, Spenser, Milton, Cervantes, and Calderón, with shorter studies of Chaucer, Ariosto, Donne, and Rabelais (again probably a recension of materials—including marginal notes—associated with his literary lectures); the history of philosophy (probably to be based on the "Philosophical Lectures" delivered between December 1818 and March 1819, but amplified with

[1] *C&S (CC)* 166–72. See above, p lxxvi and n 2.
[2] *SM, Christabel, LS, BL, SL,*   *Zapolya, The Friend,* and the Introduction to *EM.*
[3] *CL* v 27. The ostrich image first appeared in Oct 1802: *CN* i 1248.

material in the notebooks and the notes written in the volumes of
Tennemann, Stanley, and others); letters on the Old and New Testa-
ments (to be drawn together from his biblical observations preserved in his notebooks, and not least from the heavily annotated
Eichhorn volumes). The fifth work was the *Opus Maximum*. These,
he reckoned, would make about ten large volumes, not counting the
Opus Maximum. "Gifted with powers confessedly above mediocrity",
he had had an education "of which ... I have never yet found a
Parallel"; he had devoted himself "to a Life of unintermitted
Reading, Thinking, Meditating and Observing"; his published
work gave evidence that "I have not been useless in my generation".
And yet—and did he in this mean to echo not only the sombre 44th
chapter of Ecclesiasticus but also one of the saucy couplets Touch-
stone improvised to tease Rosalind?—

from circumstances the *main* portion of my Harvest is still on the ground,
ripe indeed and only waiting, a few for the sickle, but a large part only
for the *sheaving*, and carting and housing—but from all this I must turn
away, must let them rot as they lie, & be as tho' they had never been: for I
must go to gather Blackberries, and Earth Nuts, or pick mushrooms &
gild Oak-Apples for the Palates & Fancies of chance Customers.[1]

Coleridge lived for fourteen years after that, and published another
two books as well as three editions of his *Poetical Works*; but he
did not succeed in completing or publishing any of the five works he
had outlined to Thomas Allsop. To judge from what we now know
of the "scraps & *sibylline* leaves, including Margins of Books &
blank Pages"—and from what Coleridge's literary executor, Joseph
Henry Green, was to find in several years of rueful labour—the task
of "*sheaving*, and carting and housing" was much more formidable
to others than in a sanguine moment Coleridge supposed it would
have been for him.

Perhaps the thought of gathering in a harvest from the marginalia
had something to do with the agreement he had reached with
Blackwood's Edinburgh Magazine at about this time. In the first
issue of *Blackwood's*, October 1817 (after its reconstitution from the
Edinburgh Monthly Magazine), Coleridge had been so seriously
abused by Hazlitt that he considered taking action for libel. Yet
early in 1819 he found himself being courted by William Blackwood
to become a regular contributor. Blackwood needed a distinguished
and experienced writer, Coleridge needed the money; and an agreement was finally reached—far more limited than Coleridge had been

[1] *CL* v 30.

trying to insist on—that Coleridge should provide two sheets of copy for each issue for a fee of £20 a sheet. After reluctantly sending "two sheets *probationary*" in June 1819, he was hard-pressed for copy: his heart was not in the undertaking. The first identifiable contributions were in the November 1819 issue: the poem *Fancy in Nubibus* and the "Character of Sir Thomas Brown as a Writer"— the prefatory note to which has already been noticed, above. If Coleridge had thought that he would use an arrangement with *Blackwood's* to publish a sequence of his selected marginal notes, it was not to be. By January 1822 the agreement had lapsed.

On 21 June 1823 he committed to a notebook a project for a selection from the notebooks and marginalia:

When shall I find time & *ease* to reduce my Pocket-books and Memorandums to an Index—or *Memoriæ Memorandum*? If—aye! and alas! If—if I could see the last sheet of my Assertio Fidei Christianæ, et Eterni temporizantis; having previously beheld my Elements of Discourse, Logic, Dialectic, & Noetic, or Canon, Criterion, & Organon, with the philosophic Glossary—in one printed volume, & the Exercises in Reasoning as another—*if*—what then? Why, then I would publish all that remained unused, Travels & all; under the Title—of Excursions abroad & at Home, what I have seen & what I have thought and with a little of what I have felt, in the words in which I told and talked them to my Pocketbooks, the Confidantes who have *not* betrayed me, the Friends whose Silence was *not* Detraction, and the Inmates before whom I was not ashamed to complain, to yearn, to weep—or even to pray!—

To which are added Marginal notes from many books old Books and one or two new ones—

Sifted through the Mogul Sieve of Duty towards my Neighbor—
by Εστησε.[1]

He seems to have recognised that the marginal notes—like the notebooks, though less intimately and perhaps with less of "what I have felt"—bore the vital imprint of his mind in his commerce with other lives and other minds often at a great remove in time and space—minds with which he discovered fellowship through their tact of judgement and candour of perception.

Coleridge never gave up the hope of collecting and publishing a considerable group of his marginal notes. In August of the year before his death he noted: "Should the Aids of Reflection be again reprinted, and I should add another Volume—Mem.—I should like the size to be a large Octavo (unless the 2 were divided into 3. Volumes) . . ." and then sketched out a title or advertisement:

[1] Quoted in *CN* I Introduction pp xviii–xix; cf *CN* III 3881.

Aids to Reflection, including Meditations, Discourses, and Marginal Comments on various Writers, by S. T. C./ The second Volume may be had separately under the title of Marginalia, &c.[1]

The connexion with *Aids to Reflection* is significant. That book, first conceived as a selection of "Beauties" drawn from the works of Archbishop Leighton, had grown and changed with the annotation of three different copies of Leighton's *Works* until it became virtually a sequence of marginal reflections on aphorisms picked out of Leighton.[2]

It took ten years for *Aids to Reflection* to achieve its final form out of the first personal and tentative notes written in 1814; but by 1819, if not earlier, there already existed groups of marginalia that he regarded as substantial enough to deserve studying by other people. On 28 March 1819, on the verso of the title-page of his copy of Richard Field *Of the Church* (1635), he addressed his younger son Derwent, then nineteen and due to begin reading for holy orders at Cambridge the next year:

This one Volume thoroughly understood and appropriated will place you in the highest rank of *doctrinal* Church of England Divines (of such as now are) and in no mean rank as a true doctrinal Church Historian.

Next to this I recommend Baxter's own Life edited by Sylvester, with my Marginal MSS notes. Here . . . you will see the strength, and beauty of the Church of England—i.e. its Liturgy, Homilies, and Articles. . . .

Thirdly, Eichhorn's introductions to the O. & N. Testament, and to the Apocrypha, and his Comment on the Apoc[al]ypse (to all which my Notes and your own previous studies will supply whatever antidote is wanting)—these will suffice for your *Biblical* Learning, and teach you to attach no more than the supportable weight to these and such like outward evidences of our holy and spiritual Religion.—

So having done, you will be in point of professional knowlege such a Clergyman as will make glad the heart of your loving Father S. T. Coleridge[3]

Derwent evidently did not take the copy of Field away with him— it is not clear in any case that his father meant him to keep it—and Coleridge went on writing notes in it, and as the notes on Baxter accumulated they continued to seem to him important enough to warrant publication.

In the account given in *Blackwood's* and in *Church and State* Coleridge had drawn attention to the fact that the notes were written

---

1 N Q f 77.
2 See above, p cxvi.
3 FIELD *Of the Church*, note on title-page and front flyleaves; also in *CL* IV 929. For sixty more notes on this volume see *CM* II under FIELD.

not only in his own books, but also in his friends' books, and in books that came his way by chance. The notes written in his friends' books include several deprecatory or mock-deprecatory comments on the practice. In Lamb's copy of Samuel Daniel's *Poetical Works* Coleridge addressed a letter to Lamb on a front flyleaf, dated 10 February 1808; it ends—"Have I injured thy Book—? Or wilt thou 'like it the better there*fore?*' But I have done as I would gladly be done by—thee, at least.—"[1] On 7 June 1809 Lamb wrote to congratulate Coleridge on "the appearance of 'The Friend'" and to say that he had fetched away from the *Courier* office what books of his he could find—Dodsley's *Old Plays* (one volume missing, which was to cause trouble later), Sidney's *Arcadia*, and "'Daniel,' enriched with manuscript notes":

I wish every book I have were so noted. They have thoroughly converted me to relish Daniel, or to say I relish him, for, after all, I believe I did relish him. You well call him sober-minded. Your notes are excellent. Perhaps you've forgot them.[2]

"Ostrich oblivion" was one of the idiosyncrasies that Lamb liked affectionately to ascribe to Coleridge; and the grave byplay continued in the spring of 1811 in Lamb's copy of Donne's *Poems* (1669):

[on a front flyleaf]
N.B. Tho' I have scribbled in it, this is & was Mr Charles Lamb's Book, who is likewise the Possessor & (I believe) lawful Proprietor of all Volumes of the "old Plays" excepting one.

[between two notes on "This beautiful & perfect Poem" *Sweetest Love, I doe not goe*]
N.B. Spite of Appearances, this Copy is the better for the Mss. Notes. The Annotator himself says so. S. T. C.

[on a back flyleaf]
I shall die soon, my dear Charles Lamb! and then you—will not be vexed that I had bescribbled your Books. 2 May, 1811.

The last note on Lamb's copy of Beaumont and Fletcher is similar:

N.B. I will not be long here, Charles!—& gone, you will not mind my having spoiled a book in order to leave a Relic.[3]
                   S. T. C. —   Octr 1811.—

[1] DANIEL *Poetical Works*, note on a front flyleaf of Vol II; also in *CL* III 54. The "letter" evidently flowed out of a conversation they had had the night before. There are also notes by Lamb in the volume.
[2] *LL* II 75.

[3] If this last word is a direct reference to Donne's *The Relique*, the second and third stanzas of that poem may be taken *mutatis mutandis* as a brilliant image of the relationship that informed the marginalia written by C in Lamb's books.

A few other apologies of various date differ in tone from the apologies to Lamb. Halfway through the nearly 150 notes written in John James Morgan's copy of Shakespeare, he remarked (in 1808?): "As Morgan allows me thus to spoil his Book, I will remark here the fineness of Shakespear's sense of musical period . . .". Other such notes arise from a sense of the integrity of the book or the sensibility of the owner of the book. He wrote, in July 1810, in Southey's copy of White's *Natural History of Selborne* (now, and perhaps then, in a Cottonian binding): "I trust, that this Note will not be considered as lessening the value of this sweet delightful Book"; in George Frere's copy of Duncan Forbes's *Works*, in August 1817: "The desire to record this regret of mine has tempted me to the liberty of disfiguring this Leaf in a Book of yours". In Allan Cunningham's copy of Howie's *Biographia Scoticana*, writing in ink, he closed the third of nine notes with a flourish:

> . . . S. T. Coleridge, who intreats & trusts in, Allan Cunningham's pardon for thus bescrawling a leaf of his Book. A. C. may be assured that S. T. C. is not so devoid either of genial Taste, or of gratitude for pleasures enjoyed, as to have treated a Book of A. Cunningham's own creation so irreverentially

An introductory note written on 11 September 1830 in a copy of the Bishop of London's 38-page *Charge Delivered to the Clergy of the Diocese* that the author[1] had presented to Henry Nelson Coleridge is at once deferential and self-justifying—Henry being Coleridge's nephew and twenty-six years his junior:

> I am almost afraid, my dear Henry! that this being an Author's = presentation Copy, and this Author a Bishop, and this Bishop a Bishop of LONDON, I may be thought, at least *felt*, by you to have indulged my propensity to marginal Annotations somewhat out of place. But . . .

He continued to cover two large blank flyleaves with objections to the Bishop's reasoning.

There is no sign that Coleridge in any way undervalued the quality of his marginal notes, whether in his own or in other men's books; and when he thought—as he sometimes did—of the difficulty of recovering notes from books that did not belong to him (as, for instance, those he had written in Mr Tudor's copy of Cocceius' commentaries on the Bible) he was dismayed. But by the time he wrote his will in September 1829 he had clearly appreciated that, whether or not he would be able to publish his marginalia himself, his annotated books and the notes written elsewhere would be of

[1] Charles James Blomfield.

importance to his literary executor, his editors, and the beneficiary relicts of his estate.

Twenty-one years earlier, in February 1808, Coleridge had made a memorandum regarding his library:

In case of my speedy Death it would answer to buy an 100£ worth of carefully chosen Books, in order to attract attention to my Library, & to give accession to the value of Books, by their co-existing with co-appurtenants; as for instance Plato, Aristotle, Plotinus, Porphyry, Proclus— Schoolmen. Interscholastic. Bacon. Hobbes. Lock—Berkley, Leibnitz. Spinoza. Kant & the critical Fichte & Wissenschaftslehre. Schelling— Boem. &c.[1]

In late 1813, the pawning of forty of his books—with a watch and a prized snuffbox—for only £6 must have made him realise the huge chasm that lay between the market value of his books and the value that his own need and use placed on them.[2] When he wrote his will he knew that the value of his library now turned on the fact that it was *his* library, that it would be of value to those who knew how to use it rather than to collectors of rarities or curiosities, that his books and papers must be held together if possible until the editing could be finished, and that manuscripts lying outside his own possession must also be gathered in, if only in transcript:

I hereby give and bequeath to Joseph Henry Green . . . all my Books, manuscripts, and personal Estates and Effects whatsoever . . . upon Trust, to sell & dispose of such part thereof, as shall not consist of money, according to his discretion, and to invest the Produce thereof. . . . And my Will is, that notwithstanding any thing herein and before contained, & it is my desire, that my Friend, Mr Joseph Henry Green, shall in lieu of selling my Books have the option of purchasing the same at such price as he shall himself determine, in as much as their chief value will be dependent on his possession of them.

The proceeds from the publication of "any of the Notes or Writings made by me in the same Books, or any of them; or . . . any other manuscripts or writings of mine, or any letters of mine, which should any be hereafter collected from, or supplied by, my Friends & Correspondents" were to be paid into the estate for the benefit of his family. To "preclude any delicacy that might result from the

---

[1] See *CN* III 3276 and n.

[2] Compared with the prices fetched by association books at auction since 1945, the prices paid for C's books 1840– 80 seem pathetically low: see below, ANNEX B, "The Dispersal of Coleridge's Books". In 1859 WW's library realised only £380.11.9, yet one observer at the sale thought that the books "went at high prices". See below, p clxviii n 3.

said disposition", he explained in a separate paragraph that his motives arose "from the peculiar character of the Books".[1]

Henry Nelson Coleridge worked closely with his uncle on the second editions of *Aids to Reflection* and *Church and State* and on the 3-volume 1834 edition of the *Poetical Works* published shortly before Coleridge's death.[2] There is no record of discussions with Green and Henry about the posthumous editing and publishing of the manuscript remains. That no such discussions occurred is inconceivable. Little more than a month after Coleridge's death, Henry wrote to Thomas Poole on 3 September 1834, asking—on Green's behalf, by authority of the will—for "notes or letters", and outlined the editorial plan:

I have not had very much detailed conversation with him [J. H. Green] upon the subject, but in a general way he seemed to propose that I should undertake the collection & arrangement of what may be called the Literary & Critical part of what is left; that Messrs Julius Hare & Stirling should do as much for the critical & didactic Divinity; that Mr. Gillman should collect the Letters, & that he, Mr Green, should reserve the Philosophy to himself.[3]

He was already "drawing out selections from my memoranda of Coleridge's Table Talk" and thought this "would fill a small volume". A year later, after the *Table Talk* had been published, he told Poole that he was "making progress with a publication of at least two volumes of literary remains, containing what is most popular". But, he continued, "the task of selection & arrangement is, I assure you, a very anxious & laborious one—so fragmentary are the materials in my possession. Yet they are more continuous than I expected". By April 1836 the first volume was printed, but he was still writing to Josiah Wade through Poole for copies of "MS. or marginal notes"; "It has been a task of considerable difficulty, in consequence of the exceedingly scattered state of my materials, &

---

[1] BM Add Ch 66314. The text of the will was printed in *Poetical and Dramatic Works* (1836) liii–lx. For the full text of the will in Somerset House (probated 15 Aug 1834) see *CL* VI 998–1002.

[2] SC stated that *PW* (1834) "was arranged mainly, if not entirely, at the discretion of his earliest Editor, H. N. Coleridge": *PW* (EHC) II 1170.

[3] BM Add MS 35344 f 110. Green's letter to Poole of 11 Jun 1835 (ff 202–

3ᵛ) gave much the same plan for publication. In his letter of 3 Sept 1834 (f 111) HNC told Poole that "Before his death—a short time—he [C] talked of a new arrangement of the B. Literaria", and was himself considering a biographical memoir of the sort that he later began but was not able to complete for *BL* (1847). For Green's discussion of the responsibilities that he was to assume after C's death see *CL* VI 861 (May 1831), 977 (Mar 1834).

especially of my not having them all before me at once".[1] The first two volumes of *Literary Remains* were published together by William Pickering in 1836. The dedication to Joseph Henry Green is followed by a Preface dated 11 August 1836 and, after the Preface, with the title "L'Envoy" there is printed a notebook entry of Coleridge's made on about 10 March 1818 while his next-to-last course of literary lectures was still under way:

⟨S. T. C.=⟩ who with long and large arm still collected precious Armfuls in whatever direction he pressed forward, yet still took up so much more than he could keep together that those who followed him gleaned more from his continual droppings than he himself brought home—Nay, made stately Corn-ricks therewith, while the Reaper himself was still seen only with a strutting Armful of newly cut Sheaves.—But I should misinform you grossly, if I left you to infer that his Collections were a heap of incoherent Miscellanea—No!—the very Contrary—Their variety conjoined with the too great Coherency, the too great both desire & power of referring them in systematic, nay, genetic subordination was that which rendered his schemes gigantic & impracticable, as an Author—& his Conversation less instructive, as a man/—*Inopem sua Copia* fecit, too much was given, all so weighty & brilliant as to preclude choice, & too many to be all received—so that it passed over the Hearers mind like a roar of waters—[2]

A substantial part of the cumulus of manuscripts, if the letters and notebooks be ignored as too personal at that time for more than a careful and veiled selection, were the marginalia—as copious almost as his conversation, as dense at times as the most unyielding of his published prose, as eloquently self-revealing sometimes as the cadences of the moon-gloss to the *Ancient Mariner*, and now in the end—though the main portion of his library was on Highgate Hill—scattered as though a sand-devil had got amongst them more than once. For the five years after Coleridge's death marginal notes commanded a great part of Henry Nelson Coleridge's attention, with his wife and many of Coleridge's friends patiently transcribing annotations and textus. Annotated books were seldom far from the minds and needs of the first generation of editors as they worked in succession to prepare editions of all Coleridge's published writings, until in 1853, after the death of both Sara and Henry, Coleridge's younger son Derwent published the last of their series of marginalia as *Notes Theological, Political, and Miscellaneous*.

Whether Coleridge had any clear scheme for preparing his marginal notes for publication, we do not know. If it is assumed, as

---

[1] BM Add MS 35344 ff 120, 127.

[2] From *CN* III 4400 rather than from HNC's smoother revision in *LR*

I xiii–xiv; but reading *inopem* instead of C's *inopes* to mean "His *wealth* made him penniless".

seems reasonable, that he discussed with Henry Nelson Coleridge at some time the future use of these notes, then presumably the presentation of them in *Literary Remains* represents something of Coleridge's own view of the way it might be done. The three specimens that he himself supervised for publication show that he did not consider bibliographical detail of much importance, not even to the extent of recording the exact title and edition of the book annotated; and that he felt free both to alter in some details the text he was annotating and—as any author would be tempted to do—to revise his own notes. The same holds true of the few marginal notes transcribed into the notebooks; and in some books he can be seen revising his own notes, sometimes, as in Richard Byfield's *Doctrine of the Sabbath Vindicated* (1631), so extensively that he had to write out a second draft, still revising as he copied.

Coleridge's was a unifying, organising, transforming mind, "systematizing" as well as "copious". If he had attempted an edition of his marginalia, surely he would not have been able to refrain from tinkering with them, rewriting, refining, fruitfully digressing, freshly inventing. Fascinated though he was with his own "inner goings-on" and with all the multifarious ways of mind that he could discern in other people and in the authors behind the books he read, it is doubtful whether he would have tried to put together—by minute transcription and an attempt at accurate dating —a case history of his own mind, using the marginal notes as the demonstrative materials for it. It is doubtful, for example, whether in any version he may have had in mind he would have presented two distinct sets of notes on Baxter's *Reliquiae*, or two on Donne's *LXXX Sermons*, or three on Leighton, or four on Shakespeare (not counting the annotated editions now lost), or three on Anderson's *British Poets*. Surely he would have selected and merged, as Henry Nelson and Sara Coleridge in their own way felt they should. Possibly he would somehow have preserved—as they tended not to do— interesting comparisons of his "early" and "later" views of the same work. As Chapter 22 of *Biographia Literaria* shows, Coleridge had a strong dramatic sense of the ways of mind and of the possible ways of presenting them. In September 1825, when he allowed Edward Coleridge to read "some of the Memorandum Books of old date", he charged him to "read them *dramatically*—i.e. as the portrait and impress of the mood and the moment—birds of passages—or Bubbles—But I would have them sacred to your eyes".[1]

[1] *CL* v 492–3.

But the early editors had in mind a purpose different from any Coleridge might have had; and our purpose is of necessity different from either. Not being Coleridge, we cannot with confidence venture any selecting or merging. Our concern is no longer—as it was with the first editors—simply to regard as paramount the substance of what he wrote in the margins of books and to put the best possible public face upon those private writings.

Hartley Coleridge spoke of "the infinite care, industry, and skilfulness" shown by Sara and Henry Nelson Coleridge.[1] Coleridgians of this generation have inherited from them a concern that nothing be lost. In 1893, when there was a squabble in *Notes and Queries* over the alleged failure of the ·literary executors to honour the possibilities held by Coleridge's manuscripts and the books from Green's library, C. A. Ward wrote:

... a man like Coleridge cannot write on a subtle and abstruse theme [like Logic], however devoid of good fruit and useless the theme may be in itself, without dropping pearls and diamonds of light crystallized by the way; he is the diamond-clad Esterhazy, and where he steps diamonds drop; so that whatever he may have left us will repay our looking after it before it is too late. Oblivion is always a gaping chasm, and night is on our track.[2]

From what we now know is involved in refashioning Coleridge's life and work and the life of his mind, it is even less pardonable than it was eighty years ago to assume with any confidence that there is some threshold of alleged triviality below which we need not pay attention.

SOME EDITORIAL CONSIDERATIONS

Energy, dynamics, integration, polarity, process, growth—these are the keys to Coleridge's method. Close attention therefore has to be paid to the chronology of his writings, particularly the informal writings that he did not prepare for publication. The need for accurate dating arises not simply from a desire for historical or biographical precision but as a way both of delineating the abiding elements in his thinking and of perceiving the variables evolving

---

[1] ANNEX A, below, assesses the editorial purposes and ideals that have guided the work of those who preserved and published notes that Coleridge wrote in the margins of books. ANNEX B provides hints for constructing search diagrams for the considerable number of annotated books that are still missing, and may also provide clues to the identity of annotated books of which we have as yet no record.

[2] *N&Q* 28 Jan 1893 pp 64–5.

into clarity. The aim is to provide aids towards apprehending the unity and the multeity of his mind.

Coleridge did not regularly date his marginal notes; nor did he regularly write his name in his books, and when he did he only rarely gave the date of acquisition.[1] Single notes and small series of notes are therefore often difficult to date. In general he was more likely to date notes in the Highgate years than earlier, and a marginal note is more often dated in the manuscript if he had already written some notes in the same book, and that is truer of the later years than of the earlier. (There is, for example, no date written anywhere in the notes on Marcus Aurelius.) Even when he did put a date to some notes, he never provided any systematic marking that would help to separate the successive layers or sequences of notes (in Böhme, Jeremy Taylor, Luther, Tennemann), and the manuscript gives least help with the perplexing pencil notes that accumulated in the several readings of Kant and Schelling. It is therefore extremely difficult to separate out notes of different date in any single book.

The evidence of the handwriting itself is of limited value for dating, except perhaps sometimes in the broadest terms of "early" (that is, up to about 1808) and "late" (that is, from about 1823 onwards); it sometimes helps to associate annotations on a given work. Variations in paper and circumstance—to say nothing of Coleridge's state of health or frame of mind—the instability of the hand as it reached the foot of the page in a thick volume, the hazards of reed pens and quills that had to be cut, unreliable pencils, and

---

[1] C was not systematic about writing his name in his books. When he did, it was usually in the form "S. T. Coleridge" and was not usually accompanied by a date. He was fond of using his initials "S. T. C." as his name (see ANNUAL ANTHOLOGY 10 n 3), but he seldom, if ever, signed his initials on a flyleaf or title-page as mark of ownership. When these initials appear in the front of a book, they are usually marks of identification made by the various people who held some of C's books during his lifetime, or through whose hands books passed during the process of dispersal. Again, C did not regularly initial his marginalia, and when he did it is difficult to see why he did, since (for example) it is not necessarily when he was writing in somebody else's book. Placed at the end of a marginal note, these initials need to be watched warily: they have often been added afterwards by somebody who wished to identify and/or authenticate the note as C's; and in transcripts by HNC, SC, and EHC the initials "S. T. C." have often been added in order to make a clear distinction between textus and marginal note. The statement in a sale catalogue that a book contains C's autograph signature or initials can be confirmed only by examining the original; the statement is often incorrect.

(in the last years only) recalcitrant steel pens—all these compound to reduce detection to the level of guesswork or haruspication when it comes to dating. Although alternation between pen and pencil will sometimes identify the notes deposited in two different readings, in most cases no such distinction holds. Coleridge preferred to write his marginal notes in ink if the paper would let him, but it is pretty clear that an occasional note or group of notes was written in pencil simply because there was no serviceable pen at hand or perhaps no charged ink-pot.

In some cases it can be seen that a set of notes was written at a single "reading", depending on the extent of the notes, the length of the book, and the physical circumstances; we need to take into account the prodigious energy and concentration that Coleridge at times commanded. Even if there are only (say) ten notes in a book, one of them dated 1816 and another dated 1825, it can be very difficult to tell which of the notes were written in 1816, which in 1825, and even more difficult to tell whether any of them were written between those dates, or before 1816, or after 1825, and these discriminations can scarcely be attempted if the original manuscript has not survived.

Known details in the history of Coleridge's reading, especially from his letters and notebooks, can help to date marginalia; but sometimes suggestive parallels can be misleading. In the late High-gate years marginalia are found that are (as it were) interwoven with notebook entries dated while the marginal notes were being written. Internal evidence sometimes provides links with historical and biographical events and with the text of letters, notebooks, other marginalia, miscellaneous manuscripts, and published works. But because of the scope and accuracy of Coleridge's memory, the persistence of many of his central thoughts and concerns, and his ability to recall precisely, at a great distance, his first wording of anything, topical parallels and verbal coincidences have to be used warily, and in combination with as many different kinds of evidence as can be brought to bear. Occasionally a piece of evidence will turn up in other people's letters, in diaries, in records of conversation; but the value of that evidence depends upon the trustworthiness of the witness and his ability to observe accurately—not always the same thing.

Altogether the problems of dating some of the marginalia are intricate and many-faceted. Some questions of conjectural dating have been resolved, though not always to the same level of reliability. Much remains to be done. Probably some of the sets of notes, and a number of single notes, cannot be dated more closely than within limiting dates, the limits varying from instance to instance. But a good number of the marginalia date themselves beyond question, and others can be dated fairly reliably. These together provide a structure of reference from which, in the end, it should be possible to bring most of the "precious armfuls" into a finely co-ordinated sequential image of the mind that sowed the seeds in the first place.

Something needs to be said about the editor's "pestilent glosses" (the phrase is Henry VIII's), the notes on Coleridge's notes that with gratuitous efflorescence form dense nebulae at the foot of almost every page of this text. In a postscript to a long footnote in *Aids to Reflection*, Coleridge himself has provided what seems a suitable defence:

P.S. In a continuous work, the frequent insertion and length of Notes would need an Apology: in a book of Aphorisms and detached Comments none is necessary, it being understood beforehand, that the Sauce and Garnish are to occupy the greater part of the dish. S. T. C.[1]

Some of the footnotes provide references to books that Coleridge often had in mind; some—probably not many—are offered by way of unravelling what Coleridge has written: he can at times be allusive and even oracular when writing to himself, and—as Donne recognised—"darke texts need notes". Many of the footnotes make connexions with other things Coleridge wrote. A good many of them try to show along what routes certain words, phrases, images, came into his mind and were at his disposal in shaping and articulating his thinking; these are complementary to the dating as a means of tracing out the configuration and dynamics of his inner life.

The "sources" found in books that Coleridge is known to have read or probably read are not necessarily links in a known causal chain; they are the resources of an active imagination. To note them is to record the tactual and affectionate workings of the mind, things

---

[1] *AR* (1825) 222–3n. Cf *CL* v 98–9: "A blessing, I say, on the inventors of Notes! You have only to imagine the lines between the ( ) [in this case, 32 lines of type] to be printed in smaller type at the bottom of the page—& the Writer may digress, like Harris, the Historian, from Dan to Barsheba & from Barsheba in hunt after the last Comet, without any breach of continuity." When C spoke disparagingly of "your ponderous Note-makers" (in POETAE MINORES GRAECI) his objection was not to notes but to ponderosity.

assimilated and forgotten as well as things remembered; to delineate the marvellous continuity sensed when we touch the threads of a living tissue of figures, thoughts, tales, words, tunes, rhythms. In the landscape of Coleridge's reading there loom some obvious and commanding presences—Plato, Shakespeare, Milton, the Bible and the Book of Common Prayer, Kant, Hooker and Baxter, Spinoza and Lessing, Heraclitus, Pindar, Homer, Aristotle. But other figures too, of smaller stature, though sometimes no less momentous. Coleridge's memory was nourished by vivid events of heightened perception: by chance illuminations and imperious dreams; by contemporary persons and events, even by the serious reviewing of his day; by personal discoveries luminous for the fact or occasion of discovering them and treasuring them for their ancestry whether common or personal or recondite. To touch upon these is to tell over names in a continuous ceremony of landfalls and departures.

All his life Coleridge was astonishingly alert to contemporary events and issues; yet he was also all the time preoccupied with old and abiding things. To live within the web of antiquity, as he did, is one thing; now that we live outside it and try to persuade ourselves that it is well that we do, there is strangeness in the "sting of *pleasure*" a man may have felt in recognising what he had somehow always known and had forgotten. It is the grace of scholarship to recover and so to reinitiate these ritual acts of recognition; for it is not only the "Commentator and Interpreter" of the Bible who needs to unite "sound Learning, sober Judgement, and that rare Gift of Imagination which enables the possessor to think, feel, and reason in the form and character of a distant age".[1]

Whatever an editor may attempt in tracing sources, however, is bound to be incomplete and at best ancillary. What Coleridge has written is of first concern. A connexion, a reference, a distant recollection was clear to him when he wrote it, if not always afterwards. An editor may well pray for "the hounding scent of Sympathy and . . . the Key of previous and superior Insight".[2] But an editor can hint merely; he cannot enjoin.

"Sensibility indeed, both quick and deep", Coleridge said in the *Biographia*, "is not only a characteristic feature, but may be deemed a component part, of genius. But it is not less an essential mark of true genius, that its sensibility is excited by any other cause more powerfully than by its own personal interests; for this plain reason, that the man of genius lives most in the ideal world, in which the

---

[1] See IRVING *Sermons* I ⁺1.   [2] See RHENFERD p 208.

present is still constituted by the future or the past; and because his feelings have been habitually associated with thoughts and images, to the number, clearness, and vivacity of which the sensation of *self* is always in an inverse proportion."[1] Possibly by noting threads and echoes, and being alert to "the *Optics* and *Acoustics* of the inner sense", we can revive what he called "the history of my own mind for my own improvement",[2] and share in the committal of his selfless self-identification and the continuity of his mind in his discourse with himself, with other persons, with the world. The articulated patterns of coming-into-being, of finding and losing and remembering, and somehow at times in a flash recognising what otherwise could not have been known—these patterns declare both the searching impulse and the living tissue of his mind.

---

[1] *BL* ch 2 (1907) I 30.

[2] *Friend (CC)* I 145. *CN* II 2368 (cf III 3325 f 14).

Annex A

HARVESTING THE MARGINALIA
1834–1955

THE FIRST GENERATION

THE first editors of Coleridge's marginalia were all members of his family: his nephew Henry Nelson Coleridge (1798–1843), his daughter Sara (1802–52), and his younger son Derwent (1800–83). Responsibility for the literary part of Coleridge's writing, both published and unpublished, was delegated by Coleridge's literary executor Joseph Henry Green to Henry Coleridge.[1] After Henry's death, his wife Sara, who had gradually become indispensable to him in his editing, continued his work as they had planned it. When Sara realised that she would not live to complete all her plans she introduced her brother Derwent to the minutiae of the materials and their editorial methods, and persuaded him to see into print the editions she had virtually completed and to undertake the editions with with which she had intended to round out the whole editorial programme. When that editorial impulse came to an end in 1853, the first generation of editors had brought into circulation carefully considered editions of all Coleridge's published works and a quantity of hitherto unpublished manuscript. In that same year, as a distant gesture of tribute to Coleridge and his editors, there appeared in New York *The Complete Works of Samuel Taylor Coleridge* in seven volumes, edited by W. G. T. Shedd of the University of Vermont—a complete reprint of all the editions Henry and Sara Coleridge had made down to and including 1849.[2] No other such attempt was made for more than a hundred years.

In his Preface to *Literary Remains* I and II (1836) Henry Nelson Coleridge stated what he took his editorial responsibilities to be:

Mr. Coleridge by his will, dated in September, 1829, authorized his executor [Joseph Henry Green], if he should think it expedient, to publish any of the notes

---

[1] See Introduction, above, p cxxiv, at n 3.

[2] *CW* included *TT* and *LR*, and *TL* (which was not edited by HNC) was added as an appendix to *AR*. But *EOT* and the new marginalia in *NTP*, both of which were published after 1849, were necessarily excluded. All prefatory and supplementary essays were omitted "because of their prevailing reference to topics and controversies of local and temporary interest". The order of presentation in *CW* implies an unexpected estimate of the relative importance of the works for American readers: I. *AR* and *SM*; II. *The Friend*; III. *BL*; IV. *NLS*; V. *LR* III and IV and *CIS*; VI. *C&S, LS*, and *TT*; VII *Poetical Works*. For some account of C's reputation in America see A. D. Snyder "American Comments on Coleridge a Century Ago" in *Studies* and "On Reading Coleridge" in *S. T. Coleridge* ed R. L. Brett (1971) 20–1.

or writing made by him (Mr. C) in his books, or any other of his manuscripts or writings, or any letters which should hereafter be collected from, or supplied by, his friends or correspondents. Agreeably to this authority, an arrangement was made, under the superintendance of Mr. Green, for the collection of Coleridge's literary remains; and at the same time the preparation for the press of such part of the materials as should consist of criticism and general literature, was entrusted to the care of the present Editor. The volumes now offered to the public are the first results of that arrangement.[1]

Although he did not say so in his Preface, we know that the two largest groups of manuscripts at his disposal were the large series of notebooks and the marginal notes written in books. The notebooks, because of their intimate nature and highly allusive character, could not be published as they stood. Henry's nervousness about any biographical reconstruction of Coleridge's life prevented him from making any use of the notebooks beyond the unidentified inclusion of some extracts in the *Table Talk*, in his reconstruction of literary lectures in *Literary Remains*, and in his extension of the *Omniana*. With marginal notes he was more confident, not least because of the authority given by Coleridge's will: these contained little personal material that might prove embarrassing in print, and if there were danger of public outrage over minute points of political or theological orthodoxy, these could be softened by deft revising and by omission. He quickly discovered that marginalia could supply point and substance in reconstructing lectures, for instance; he also recognised that marginalia of sufficient intrinsic interest offered an almost inexhaustible source of copy that could be published with (it seemed) very little editorial intervention—once suitable transcriptions had been made. From the beginning of his work, even in the first book he completed, *Table Talk*, marginalia provided a great deal of solid flesh to clothe a variety of skeletons.

Henry Nelson Coleridge, born in the year of publication of *Lyrical Ballads*, educated at Eton and King's College, Cambridge (of which he became a Fellow), was a classical scholar of sufficient standing to be invited in his early thirties to stand for the chair of humanities at Glasgow University. In 1825, for reasons of health, he visited the West Indies with his cousin William Hart Coleridge, who had been appointed first bishop of Barbados. His account of the trip—*Six Months in the West Indies*, published anonymously in 1826—aroused some indignation in the Coleridge family because in it he made fun of his aunt Edith, because of its "gay, laughing Epicureanism", and perhaps also because of certain not-very-carefully-concealed indications of his love for "Eugenia", i.e. his cousin Sara, the daughter of the black sheep of the Coleridge family.[2] He had first met Sara in December 1822 and became secretly engaged to her a few weeks later. In 1826 he became barrister-at-law, and by July 1829, when he went to Keswick to marry Sara, his practice was established, though not remunerative. Sara, at the age of twenty-seven, was mistress of six languages (as Coleridge noticed) and an author in her own right,

[1] *LR* I viii.
[2] The book was withdrawn immediately after publication at the insistence of HNC's father and was reissued in the same year in revised form. A copy of the first edition annotated by C has been preserved.

having published two considerable translations: Dobrizhoffer's *An Account of the Abipones, an Equestrian People of Paraguay* (3 vols 1822)[1] and *The History of the Chevalier Bayard* (1825), from sixteenth-century French.

After their honeymoon in Cumberland, Henry and Sara took a house in Gower Street, not far from Lincoln's Inn, so that Sara should not be lonely after her busy life in Greta Hall. But with the Gillmans' help they soon found a house in Hampstead and moved there in June 1830. Only a little more than a mile's walk across Hampstead Heath from The Grove, Sara was able to spend a good deal of time with her father, whom she had seen very little of as a child, and as an adult only on her one visit to London in 1822–3. During the first year in Hampstead her first child, Herbert, was born, and early in the autumn of 1832 her daughter Edith. Later in that autumn she suffered a breakdown, and was no sooner recovering in 1833 than she bore twins who died at birth. The delicate state of her health made it difficult for her to sustain the shock of her father's death in July 1834.

Immediately after Coleridge's death, Henry Nelson Coleridge proceeded at once with the *Table Talk* (2 vols 1835), for which he had been collecting materials since 1822, and then with *Literary Remains* I and II (1836). Sara had been persuaded in 1834 to publish a group of poems composed for her children—*Pretty Verses for Children*. The little book was so enthusiastically received that she published, shortly after they left Hampstead for Chester Place in Regent's Park, her very Coleridgian book *Phantasmion*. Without wishing to do so, she had become something of a minor literary celebrity. The house in Chester Place was larger than the house in Hampstead and closer to Lincoln's Inn so that Henry could be with her more continuously than had been possible in Hampstead; but her ill-health persisted. After moving to Chester Place she suffered three miscarriages and in 1840 lost a second daughter at birth. Somehow Henry, himself in poor health, managed to look after her with great solicitude while he pursued his double career as barrister and as editor of Coleridge's works, supplementing his income with occasional reviewing. It was against this personal background that their editing was achieved.

A list of the publications of the first generation of editors gives some impression not only of their remarkable industry but also of the importance of marginalia in the construction of their work (the extent of marginalia is roughly indicated by three sigla: † some marginalia, not essential to the body of the work, or not noticed as marginal notes; * subsets of marginalia presented as such; ** marginalia formally presented and comprising virtually the whole text):

1835 † *Table Talk* (ed Henry Nelson Coleridge) 2 vols: revised in 1 vol 1836

1836 *† *Literary Remains* I, II (ed Henry Nelson Coleridge)

1837 *The Friend* (ed Henry Nelson Coleridge) 3 vols: reissued 1844,

---

[1] C considered the translation "unsurpassed for pure mother English by any thing I have read for a long time". *TT* 4 Aug 1832.

1850, 1863, 1865, and thereafter in the Bohn and Bell editions

1838 ** *Literary Remains* III (ed Henry Nelson Coleridge)

1839 ** *Literary Remains* IV (ed Henry Nelson Coleridge)
Church and State + *Statesman's Manual* + *Lay Sermon* (ed Henry Nelson Coleridge) in 1 vol

1840 † *Confessions of an Inquiring Spirit* (ed Henry Nelson Coleridge)

1843 [Henry Nelson Coleridge died 26 Jan]
Aids to Reflection (ed Henry Nelson Coleridge) 2 vols

1844 *Poems* (ed Sara Coleridge): reissued with small revisions 1848

1847 † *Biographia Literaria* (ed Henry Nelson Coleridge and Sara Coleridge) 2 vols

1849 *† *Notes and Lectures on Shakespeare* (ed Sara Coleridge) 2 vols: 1st part of the topical redistribution of *Literary Remains*

1850 *Essays on His Own Times* (ed Sara Coleridge) 3 vols

1852 [Sara Coleridge died 3 May]
Poems (ed Sara Coleridge and Derwent Coleridge)
Dramatic Works (ed Derwent Coleridge)
Statesman's Manual + *Lay Sermon* (1839 ed, revised Derwent Coleridge)
Church and State (1839 ed, revised Derwent Coleridge)

1853 ** *Notes on English Divines* (ed Sara Coleridge, published Derwent Coleridge): 2nd part of the topical redistribution of *Literary Remains*

** *Notes Theological, Political, and Miscellaneous* (ed Derwent Coleridge): 3rd part of redistribution of *Literary Remains* + about one third new material[1]

From the beginning Henry directed the editorial work and took all the editorial decisions. Sara, as far as her health and domestic responsibilities allowed, helped him by transcribing, collating, proof-reading. With characteristic modesty, though well schooled and widely read, she undertook a rigorous programme of reading in order to extend her editorial capacity, and although Henry was at first a little in awe of her learning and intelligence, she soon provided the perfect complement to him in his literary work: to his own scholarly flair and lawyer-like thoroughness her brilliance and imaginative power provided a fruitful counterpoise, and Henry came to rely more and more upon her breadth of learning and the acuity of her critical judgement.

In the Preface to *Literary Remains* I Henry said that he was "painfully sensible that he could bring few qualifications for the undertaking, but such as were involved in a many years' intercourse with the author himself, a patient study of his writings, a reverential admiration for his genius, and an affectionate desire to help in extending its beneficial

---

[1] In 1863 DC reissued, with additions, the *Poems* and *Dramatic Works* of 1852 as *Poetical Works* in 3 vols. See also p cl and n 1, below.

influence".[1] Since December 1822 he had been in close and continuous relation with Coleridge and had been recording his conversation for what became the *Table Talk*; he had assisted Coleridge in preparing the second edition of *Church and State* (1830) and the second edition of *Aids to Reflection* (1831); in preparing the three-volume *Poetical Works* of 1834 he had played a major, if not a commanding, rôle; he had studied all Coleridge's published writing and was familiar with a considerable part of his unpublished manuscripts. The two essays he had written on Coleridge, in 1821 and 1834,[2] showed that he was not insensitive to poetry, that he had a well-developed intelligence and something of the scholar's sense of the deft disposition of related materials.

Both Henry and Sara were informed to some extent by filial piety, but they were not blinded by it. As their confidence in each other grew, they entered into their editorial work with great intellectual zest, reinforced by their respect for each other, savouring the delight of their growing technical accomplishment in the "delicate and perplexing task" of presenting Coleridge's work and thought to the world as faithfully as they could. That Sara's contribution soon began to add intellectual force and scholarly depth to Henry's editing there can be little doubt. The ebullient and slightly naïve quality of Henry's first editing arose from his confident expectation of a sympathetic audience that did not have to be persuaded of the quality of Coleridge's genius. That confidence was soon to be shaken. They were shocked and wounded by public attacks on Coleridge that appeared in the reviews as soon as he had died—particularly by the patronising unfairness of De Quincey's self-aggrandising breaches of confidence. They were distressed by the conceited tactlessness (as they saw it) of Thomas Allsop in publishing (1836) self-revealing letters that Coleridge had written to him, and by the sentimentality and patent inaccuracies of Joseph Cottle's *Early Recollections* (1837–9). They became wary and a little defensive. Their editorial purpose toughened and darkened as they became aware of hostility and of damaging misconceptions that they had to face and that they would have to outface as soon as they could muster the scholarly confidence to deal with them.

As far as the day-to-day conduct of their editorial work was concerned, there must have been considerable difficulty in the physical disposition of the primary materials, even though Green may have transferred to Henry Coleridge—as far as he could discreetly separate them from the Gillmans

---

[1] *LR* I viii.

[2] The first essay was published pseudonymously in the *Etonian*: see *CH* 461–70. Except that HNC seems to have attended C's literary lectures in Jan–Mar 1818, it was to be more than two years before he had any close personal acquaintance with his "Uncle Sam"; yet the essay gives a vivid account of C as a person and of his conversation. *CH* 169–70. The *QR* essay of 1834 is reprinted in *CH* 620–

51. On 17 Sept 1834 HNC wrote to Poole: "If the last August Quarterly Review falls in your way—you may read ⟨in⟩ it a paper by me on S. T. C.'s poetry written while he was alive, but not published in time for him to read. It is adequate—but right, I believe, as far as it goes—& at all events will, I hope, do him some little justice." BM Add MS 35344 f 113. In the text of the essay HNC had said "the author still lives".

—the materials needed for their work. In Hampstead they had been only a mile away from the Gillmans' house; in Regent's Park they were four miles from Highgate, an hour's journey; but in 1836 Green gave up his practice in Lincoln's Inn Fields and retired to Hadley near Barnet, more than nine miles from Regent's Park—a serious inconvenience if they had to consult materials in Green's possession.[1] It appears that by 1837 Henry and Sara had solved any logistic difficulties by concentrating in Chester Place all they needed for their immediate work, either in original or in transcript, and that from that time onward only an occasional visit to Highgate or Hadley was needed.[2]

Henry Coleridge's first conception of *Literary Remains* was probably set by a current and well-established tradition—the tradition recognised, for example, by Mathias's *The Works of Thomas Gray, to Which Are Subjoined Extracts Philological, Poetical, and Critical from the Author's Original Manuscripts* (2 vols 1814)—of which Coleridge himself had annotated a copy. Whatever of the author's manuscripts could, with a little judicious tinkering and smoothing, be made to look enough like finished work from the author's pen could be expected to arouse interest, and the more diverse the manuscripts, the better; for a poet, poems if possible, but in order to show the author's many-sidedness, other things as well. In April 1836, when *Literary Remains* I had finished printing, Henry told Poole that he wanted to "*add* to the fame & also to the useful-

[1] For some details of the journey from Highgate to the West End from C's point of view see *CL* vi 925. J. H. Green set up practice in Lincoln's Inn Fields in 1815 and in 1828 was appointed to the chair of surgery at King's College; for his agonies of decision at that time, and C's advice to him, see *CL* vi 471ff. In 1836 he gave up his practice and moved to The Mount, Hadley, where he lived for the rest of his life. A memoir of him is prefixed to his posthumous *Spiritual Philosophy* (1865).

[2] A letter from HNC to Gillman dated "Thursday 10 [? Sept 1835]" gives some impression of the early editorial difficulties: "The last papers delivered to me by Mrs Gillman are valuable indeed, & I think with them & Mr Green's notes, I shall be able to arrange a splendid morsel at least of the various lectures. One difficulty I have had—as to the references. I have fortunately hit them all out except as to Spenser. Do you think he used the vol. of your collection of poets [CHALMERS]? I must collate, when I come back. No edition of mine

leads me to his paging. If you will be so good as to send the Shakespeare by the bearer, Sara will transcribe in my absence, & will send them back with McDiarmid. Baxter & Donne must still wait. I wish you could tell the Highgate carrier to call at my chambers for Hooker & some other book, I forget what—wch are done; He should call before three. You spoke of some notes on Luther's T. Talk;—they would be interesting, I should think. I shall be away six weeks, I fear, & leave Sara in a bad state.... We can discover no traces of Fenelon." Sara has added a PS: "I will write to dear Mrs Gillman as soon as I have *myself* made a thorough search for Fenelon which I have hitherto been too weak to do. But I have no hopes of finding it, Mama having sought in vain, & none of us having any remembrance of its coming hither." Original in possession of B. H. Blackwell & Co, Oxford, in 1949. R. F. Brinkley "Coleridge Transcribed" *RES* xxv (1948) 220–1 summarised this letter, dating it "[Jan 1836]".

ness & influence of the author" and had "good hopes that the volumes will be popular".[1] In the Preface he said that

The materials were fragmentary in the extreme—Sibylline leaves;—notes of the lecturer, memoranda of the investigator, out-pourings of the solitary and self-communing student. The fear of the press was not in them. Numerous as they were, too, they came to light, or were communicated, at different times, before and after the printing was commenced; and the dates, the occasions, and the references, in most instances remained to be discovered or conjectured. To give to such materials method and continuity, as far as might be,—to set them forth in the least disadvantageous manner which the circumstances would permit,—was a delicate and perplexing task...[2]

The construction of those first two volumes is indeed ingenious, and marginal notes provided a major component in the jigsaw. If we removed from them all marginal notes—which for the most part were unobtrusively blended into the whole construction—they would lack much of their substance and richness and much of their air of coherence.

The two volumes were conceived as a single collection arranged under six divisions: uncollected poems, a course of literary lectures, Coleridge's contribution to Southey's *Omniana* (with additions, mostly undesignated, from notebooks), "Shakespeare, with Introductory Matter on Poetry, the Drama, and the Stage", the Royal Society of Literature essay "On the *Prometheus* of Aeschylus", and a sampling of marginal notes.

Henry Coleridge's reconstruction of the literary lectures is a good example both of his ingenuity in handling fragmentary materials and of his use of marginalia as primary materials. The fullest set of lecture notes he had been able to find in the notebooks was for the course of literary lectures of January–March 1818, a series he had attended. These notes, incomplete though they were, provided a matrix to be filled out to something like consistent length for each lecture, the notebook materials being used as the primary text.

For the first two of the fourteen lectures he had no primary material at all; for the first he used a note taken at the lecture by Gillman, and for the second a note taken by William Hammond. For Lecture 3 he found brief notes in a notebook and amplified these by inserting marginalia on writers included in the published prospectus of the lecture—Petrarch and Spenser.[3] He could find no record of Lectures 4–6 and left those blank. Lecture 7, on Jonson, Beaumont and Fletcher, and Massinger, was covered by a notebook, and the extensive marginalia on the first three were withheld for Volume II. To seven pages of notes for Lecture 8 on Cervantes and *Don Quixote*, the longest up to this point, he added ten pages of marginalia. Lecture 11 interposes eight pages of marginalia on *Robinson*

---

[1] BM Add MS 34344 f 127.

[2] *LR* I viii. One gathering, preserved at VCL, shows that HNC was still considering the internal proportions of the text while the volumes were printing.

[3] *CN* III 4389. The only surviving marginalia on Spenser are the few in ANDERSON COPY B and COPY C. What HNC printed looks less like marginalia than lecture notes with page-references to C's unidentified working edition.

Crusoe between five pages of lecture notes and a three-page note on the education of children. Lecture 12—on dreams, apparitions, and alchemists —adds to nine pages of lecture notes six pages of topically related marginalia from Hillhouse's *Hadad*, John Smith's *Select Discourses*, and the "Life of Henry Earl of Morland" (that is, Henry Brooke *Fool of Quality*), those marginal notes, however, having been written in 1824 and 1827. Lecture 13 is entirely from a notebook; and Lecture 14 "On Style" overflows without typographical transition into more than thirty pages of marginalia covering the period 1802–20, all on the general subject of prose style, followed by two fragmentary essays (of 1810 and 1818). Henry put a date to all these groups of marginal notes; and as these dates are seldom within five years of the date of the lectures it seems that, unable to find material of date coinciding with the lectures, and aware of the degree of assimilation of most of this material in Coleridge's mind and the continuity of his thought on much of it, he did not consider the chronological disparities to be significant.[1]

In Volume II of *Literary Remains* marginalia play a major part but are visually and editorially more unobtrusive than they had been in Volume I. The first 167 pages are devoted to "Shakespeare, with Introductory Matter on Poetry, the Drama, and the Stage". The given structure for the literary lectures had been fragile enough, but it was a framework; here there is none, because of the number of different times Coleridge had addressed himself in public to the criticism of Shakespeare and Elizabethan drama, and because the notebook records were fragmentary and chronologically indistinct. In the attempt to give some coherence to Coleridge's Shakespeare criticism Henry's arrangement proceeded from general considerations of Shakespeare and his art, the history of the theatre and the order of the plays, to detailed notes on single plays arranged play by play. Much of the general material came from notebooks and miscellaneous manuscripts, but some of it is from the annotated copies in which some lecture notes are written and in which Coleridge himself had sometimes marked the transitions to and from a notebook or other manuscript.

The notes on individual plays, submitting to the need for order, convenience, and authority, were redisposed from two annotated copies of Shakespeare; the notes are not identified as marginalia, the annotated editions are not cited, and the separate notes are not assigned to their source to allow a consideration of the identity of each set of marginalia.[2] After the

---

[1] In a footnote to Lecture 10 HNC said: "Nothing remains of what was said on Donne in this Lecture. Here, therefore, as in previous like instances, the gap is filled up with some notes written by Mr. Coleridge in a volume of Chalmers's Poets, belonging to Mr. Gillman.... Numerous and elaborate notes by Mr. Coleridge on Donne's Sermons are in existence, and will be published hereafter." *LR* I 148–9n. He probably did not know of the

important set of marginalia in Lamb's copy of Donne's *Poems*. After C's death Lamb was too distracted and ill to collaborate with Green and HNC; his own death on 27 Dec 1834 may have interrupted transcription of C's notes or suddenly rendered Lamb's books inaccessible to the editors.

[2] But in a footnote to II 96, in an extended note on *The Tempest*, he added what C "writes in the margin". Although the notes on Shakespeare

Shakespeare section, there are fifty-five pages of notes on Ben Jonson and on Beaumont and Fletcher; although these are not announced as marginal notes, they look like marginalia and are in fact marginalia.

The material on Elizabethan drama is followed by a reprint of the Royal Society of Literature essay "On the *Prometheus* of Aeschylus" (which had been delivered as a lecture in 1825 but, as it happened, was almost hot off the press when Henry republished it),[1] accompanied by two brief technical notes on the text of Aeschylus; then a group of miscellaneous marginalia entitled "Notes"—the word Henry normally used in his text to refer to marginalia (though also using the term "notes" indiscriminately to refer to notebook entries and miscellaneous manuscripts).[2] Although "style" seems to provide one topical thread for this group of notes, the selection may have been intended to offer a glimpse of the range and variety of the marginalia, for this is the one place in the first two volumes in which marginal notes stand by themselves.

It does not appear that when he planned *Literary Remains* I and II Henry had any intention of attempting a formal presentation of marginal notes on a large scale. The sampling of notes on thirteen titles at the end of Volume II happened to consort well with the traditional view of what a collection of literary reliques would include; the selection may have been whatever at that time he had conveniently at hand, or to please Coleridge's friends who had "communicated" most of them.[3] The executor's request for manuscripts had gone out as soon as Coleridge's will was probated, and some people who owned annotated books evidently responded promptly. The impression given by the Coleridge family papers at Victoria College and the University of Texas is that Henry and Sara made a considerable effort to trace, gather, and transcribe marginal notes. To transcribe marginalia, even when the annotated books have been assembled, is a laborious task because of the attention that has to be given to the textus

show fewer marked changes in critical judgement than (say) the marginalia on Böhme, the two sets of notes cover a period of at least ten years, and each set of notes implies that C had a distinct purpose in writing them.

[1] "On the *Prometheus* of Aeschylus" was first published in the *Transactions of the Royal Society of Literature* Vol II Pt ii (1834), issued to members on 4 Jul 1834. It is possible that C did not live to see either a copy of Vol II Pt ii or the twenty offprints of his essay to which he was entitled. See *N&Q* Feb 1969 pp 52–5.

[2] The notes were taken from Chalmers's *English Poets*, Selden's *Table Talk* (the Westminster Library copy), Benjamin Wheeler's *Theological Lectures*, a sermon of Walter Birch (a

friend of H. F. Cary), Fénelon (HNC never managed to identify the actual book, nor have I), Fielding's *Tom Jones* and *Jonathan Wild*, Barry Cornwall's *Dramatic Scenes*, C's copies of Fuller's *Holy State and Profane State*, *Appeal of Injured Innocence*, and *Church History*, Asgill's *Collection of Tracts*, and the copy of Thomas Browne's "*Works*" addressed to SH.

[3] HNC acknowledged communication of marginalia in *LR* II from H. F. Cary (three titles), James Gillman (three titles), and WW. Other notes were acknowledged in Vol III to Gillman ("for the greatest part"), WW, DC, and Edward Coleridge; and in Vol IV to RS, Green, Gillman, Alfred Elwyn (of Philadelphia), Mr Money, HC, and Edward Coleridge.

that belongs to each marginal note. It is fortunate that they and their friends were prepared to go to that trouble: beyond the quantity of marginal notes that Henry and Sara eventually published or used in their editions, a number of their transcripts preserve notes in books of which we have no other record, and in other cases take us a step closer to the lost original manuscript than the printed text of them does.

In the Preface to *Literary Remains* I Henry Nelson Coleridge had promised to present more than those two volumes contained:

The contents of these volumes are drawn from a portion only of the manuscripts entrusted to the Editor: the remainder of the collection, which, under favourable circumstances, he hopes may hereafter see the light, is at least of equal value with what is now presented to the reader as a sample.

Yet we find nowhere any statement of his policy regarding marginalia, and it is not even clear whether he had originally planned *Literary Remains* as a two-volume set or as the four volumes that it finally became.[1] The emphasis in Volumes I and II is strongly "literary"; the general impression they leave is that the marginal notes are fragmentary curiosities or notable flashes of critical insight. There is no hint that the marginalia represented a huge mass of records of sustained reflection over a period of many years, the spontaneous deposit of Coleridge's commerce with many of the books that were to him of greatest importance. Although the *Table Talk* was to become one of the most widely read of books associated with Coleridge's name, it seemed fragmentary and occasional to people who knew him and his conversation well, and Henry's desire to make *Literary Remains* "popular" had produced two volumes that were more brilliant than consistent, less clearly indicative of the scope and penetration of Coleridge's mind than Green, Gillman, Poole, and others had hoped.[2]

---

[1] *LR* I ix. The "seven volumes in process" that RS mentioned in 1834 (quoted above, p cxiv) would be 2 vols of *TT*, 3 vols of *The Friend*, and *LR* I and II. See also the letter quoted in p cxxiv, above.

[2] In 1836 Gillman told Green that "I have thought much since yesterday of the order and arrangement of Coleridge's Works for Publication—H.N.C.'s plan is very summary—his present arrangement of the two Volumes I do not like—they remind me of a fishing Smack, going to Market with Herrings and such like Fish, all thrown into the Hold together, Heads & Tails, to take the chance of the Market, and there's an end of them." Sotheby Sale 20 Jul 1971, lot 490. HC was more favourably impressed: "I am, on the whole, greatly pleased with them. There is

little in the book that is new to me. Some of the marginal notes can hardly be intelligible to any but those who are familiar with the books in which they were written, and a few contain opinions not strictly consonant with my father's later judgment. But Henry has performed a laborious task, with infinite care, industry and skilfulness." *HCL* 205–6. Before reading *TT*, however, HC had been nervous. "I hope Henry has been very, very careful as to what he has recorded. Dear papa often said things which he would not himself have published: and I have heard him utter opinions both in Religion and in Politics not very easy to reconcile with what he has published. And things of this sort would be welcomed with a savage exultation by such miscreants as begrudge Southey the just reward of his mani-

Yet Henry had always been impressed by Coleridge's many-sidedness. In his 1821 essay he had recognised Coleridge and Wordsworth as determinate influences in setting "the peculiar character, and its distinguishing excellence" of "the poetry, the philosophy, and the criticism of the present day".[1] And at the end of his *Quarterly* essay of 1834 he had said:

> Can we lay down the pen without remembering that Coleridge as poet is but half the name of Coleridge? This, however, is not the place, nor the time, to discuss in detail his qualities or his exertions as a psychologist, moralist, and general philosopher. That time may come, when his system, as a whole, shall be fairly placed before the world, as we have reason to hope it will soon be...[2]

He was no doubt somewhat constricted by the limitations of the assignment Green had given, but he evidently intended not to limit his work very strictly to the fields of literature and criticism. The marginal notes were bound to draw him into deeper waters, not only because of the gravity of many of them but because no matter what the subject of a book Coleridge was annotating it could easily touch and set vibrating the complex web of his manifold concerns—and often did. He probably did not feel competent to present Coleridge's mind "as a whole", but he could escape from getting drawn in that direction only by ignoring marginalia altogether or by using them in a topical and illustrative manner. Perhaps partly in response to the wishes of family and editorial friends, he decided that he could not ignore the marginalia and that he must somehow make a more daring presentation of some of them.

Volumes III and IV of *Literary Remains*, planned together but issued separately in 1838 and 1839, are entirely different from Volumes I and II. Except for the "Formula Fidei", the "Nightly Prayer" (1831), and the "Letter to a Godchild" (1834) in Volume III, and the "Essay on Faith" in Volume IV, they consist entirely of marginalia—nearly a quarter of a million words (of notes and textus); many of the sets of notes are much more extensive and continuous than anything in Volumes I and II, Volume

---

fold labours for the benefit of his species and the honour of his Maker." *HCL* 174. But when he had read the book he wrote to HNC: "What makes you think that I dislike your 'Table Talk'? I might have fears lest it should be Mali exempli—fears which Allsop has shewn not to be wholly groundless. I might tell Derwent, that the book gave me no feeling of my father's manner, which it does not pretend to do, but the execution of the work I greatly admire, and Derwent well observes that it were sad indeed if so much excellent criticism, so much moral, religious, and political wisdom were to perish with the lips that uttered." *HCL* 181.

[1] *CH* 469.

[2] *CH* 650. In the essay HNC glossed the phrase "his system" with a statement of C's, also printed in *TT* 12 Sept 1831. "My system, if I may venture to give it so fine a name, is the only attempt that I know, ever made, to reduce all knowledge into harmony. It opposes no other system, but shows what was true in each; and how that which was true in the particular in each of them, became error, *because* it was only half the truth.... I wish, in short, to connect by a moral copula, natural history with political history; or, in other words, to make history scientific, and science historical;—to take from history its accidentality, and from science its fatalism." *CH* 651.

III consisting of annotations on eleven books and Volume IV of those on fifteen.[1] As far as Coleridge's marginal notes ever belong strictly to the same category as the books they are written in, all these notes are on theology, biblical criticism, and ecclesiastical history. The material is arranged chronologically according to the order in which the books themselves were published; only the intrusion of Heinrichs's edition of Revelation (1821) in the middle of Volume III (so placed because of the close relation of these notes to the notes on Henry More immediately preceding), and the placing of Luther and St Teresa at the beginning of Volume IV, break that scheme. Volume III deals with the sixteenth century and the first half of the seventeenth century; Volume IV picks up the seventeenth century, continues through the eighteenth century, and closes with half a dozen nineteenth-century books, four of them published in 1825 or later.

The Preface to these volumes, much longer than the Preface to Volumes I and II, is—like the other Preface—ingratiating in tone, yet a bit defensive and a little defiant. The "graver character of the general contents" required some explanation beyond what Henry had said two years earlier.[2] On the one hand, he wished to affirm Coleridge's innocence of intention in writing the notes; on the other hand, he seems to have wanted to establish the theological propriety of Coleridge's notes or at least to offer an account that would place them in a privileged position, secure against improperly literal interpretation and hostile objection:

Although the Author in his will contemplated the publication of some at least of the numerous notes left by him on the margins and blank spaces of books and pamphlets, he most certainly wrote the notes themselves without any purpose beyond that of delivering his mind of the thoughts and aspirations suggested by the text under perusal. His books, that is, any person's books—even those from a circulating library—were to him, whilst reading them, as dear friends; he conversed with them as with their authors, praising, or censuring, or qualifying, as the open page seemed to give him cause; little solicitous in so doing to draw summaries or to strike balances of literary merit, but seeking rather to detect and appreciate the moving principle of moral life, ever one and single, of the work in reference to absolute truth. Thus employed he had few reserves, but in general poured forth, as in a confessional, all his mind upon every subject,—not keeping back any doubt or conjecture which at the time and for the purpose seemed worthy of consideration. In probing another's heart he laid his hand upon his own. He thought pious frauds the worst of all frauds.... Further he distinguished so strongly between that internal faith which lies at the base of, and supports, the whole moral and religious being of man, and the belief, as historically true, of several incidents and relations found or supposed to be found

---

[1] Strictly thirteen in *LR* III and seventeen in *LR* IV: in *LR* III the notes from two copies of Donne's *Sermons*, and from two copies of Bunyan's *Pilgrim's Progress*, are combined; and in *LR* IV the notes from three copies of Leighton's *Works* are combined. In each case the merged notes are treated as a single series and there is no indication that more than one copy was annotated.

[2] It is difficult not to feel that SC had a hand in this Preface, or may even have written it; and there can be little doubt that she shared in editing the volumes. But HNC's name appears alone on the title-pages, and it is convenient to refer to him as author of the Preface and editor of the text.

in the text of the Scriptures, that he habitually exercised a liberty of criticism with respect to the latter, which will probably seem objectionable to many of his readers in this country.

His friends have always known this to be the fact; and he vindicated this so openly that it would be folly to attempt to conceal it... to suppress this important part of his solemn convictions would be to misrepresent and betray him.[1]

If we are "to find firm footing in Biblical criticism", he continued, "if the indisputable facts of physical science are not for ever to be left in a sort of admitted antagonism to the supposed assertions of Scripture", our thought must be carried through "by the aid, and in the light, of those truths of deepest philosophy which in all Mr. Coleridge's works, published or unpublished, present themselves to the reader with an almost affecting reiteration".

But to do justice to those works and adequately to appreciate the Author's total mind upon any given point, a cursory perusal is insufficient; study and comprehension are requisite to an accurate estimate of the relative value of any particular denial or assertion; and the apparently desultory and discontinuous form of the observations now presented to the Reader more especially, calls for the exercise of his patience and thoughtful circumspection.

He ended by saying that he had "not permitted any thing to appear before the public which Mr. Coleridge saw reason to retract" and expressed confidence that "nothing contained in the following pages can fairly be a ground of offence to any one".

As long as marginalia could be used as ancillary and amplifying materials in a literary context, Henry was at ease; but once marginalia became the centre of attention in matters of philosophy, politics, morals, and religion he felt that he was on dangerous ground. He urged careful study of the marginalia in *Literary Remains* III and IV but gave the reader little or no help in doing so. He had published a splendid block of marginal notes, but his way of presenting them seems to us now to have deflected or masked the full impact of the radical and searching mind that had produced them. Aware of the "strange seas of thought" that Coleridge's mind had traversed, he knew that the trade-winds of Coleridge's mind were for seasoned mariners, and may have supposed that apprentice readers would have to learn their seafaring by taking trial outings in lighter airs; they might be persuaded that notes written in private, without reserve, and with a candour and incisiveness that some might find scandalous, were in fact orthodox, conservative, and thoroughly respectable.

The history of the publication of Coleridge's marginalia is more a

---

[1] *LR* III ix–xi. In support of HNC's general position H. St J. Hart's introductory note to his issue of *CIS* (1956) may be quoted: "The influence of Coleridge in keeping within the Church of England scholars who were disturbed by the controversies of the early and middle nineteenth century was acknowledged at the time, and has since been studied. Coleridge, the anticipator, seemed to have seen all the problems in advance, and in advance he seemed to many to have provided his church with a satisfying apologetic, reconciling Christianity with modern thought."

history of editorial intention than a story of increasingly refined scholarly purpose and accomplishment. Except that Henry and Sara preserved some marginal notes that would now be otherwise lost to us, their work is not very useful to a modern editor. In his edition of *The Friend*, published the year before *Literary Remains* iii, Henry had been concerned primarily to refine the text to Coleridge's best and latest known intention, drawing upon annotated copies; he had not yet attempted the level of minute annotation that he and Sara were to reach in their edition of the *Biographia* (1847). But there is a marked difference between his editing of *The Friend* and his editing of the marginalia in *Literary Remains* both in respect of textual integrity and of editorial assistance for the reader. In *Literary Remains* there are practically no notes explanatory or discursive apart from an occasional identification of a classical reference, and no cross-references to Coleridge's published writings except to identify specific references that Coleridge himself made in the manuscript. Because the style of presentation of marginal notes established in *Literary Remains* iii and iv is the style that has been followed with few exceptions ever since, it is important to understand both the editorial intention and its technical limitations.

What matters most in an edition of manuscript materials is the accuracy and integrity of the text. In this, Henry Nelson Coleridge is not above reproach. In general, in order to make his copy "readable" he smoothed out what he took to be stylistic roughness and normalised spelling, capitals, and punctuation. He omitted in silence notes that were difficult to read or seemed to him trivial—which is understandable; but he also omitted notes he may have found hard to stomach and modified others to provide what he thought would be, to the public, a more acceptable statement.[1] Passages that were cropped or illegible he silently restored to some semblance of plausible intelligibility. In matters of technical scholarship his sketchiness has deprived us of a good deal of detailed information and internal evidence for which we should now be grateful. He paid so little attention to bibliographical detail that he sometimes failed to record the actual edition that Coleridge annotated; in some cases he referred the marginal notes systematically to the most recent authoritative edition of the work (rather than to the edition actually annotated), and in a few cases of books now lost he altered Coleridge's page-references to the paging of his chosen edition, thus destroying the chance of identifying the edition

---

[1] Cf *C 17th C* viii: "Henry Nelson Coleridge in *Literary Remains* sometimes suppressed passages, occasionally even changed the meaning of the original, and frequently revised the wording of a comment in such a way that the flavor of Coleridge's personality is lost. Thomas Poole noticed these things at the time of publication and wrote to Henry Nelson reproving him for misrepresenting Coleridge. The editor admitted toning down certain comments but denied making his uncle 'speak of any supposed politics of my own.' The changes are so numerous that to collate the text of the original source with the passage in the *Literary Remains* would increase this volume to an intolerable size...." For a sample of such collation see 206–22 (on Hacket's *Scrinia Reserata*). R. F. Brinckley had previously dealt with this matter in "Coleridge Transcribed" *RES* xxiv (1948) 219–26. For a discussion of *C 17th C* see below, pp cliv–clv.

that Coleridge annotated. In dealing with "textus" he normalised the spelling and punctuation of the old editions (when he was not working from a modern edition) and often (through understandable fatigue) provided a passage so brief or truncated as to give no intelligible context for the marginal note that it had initiated. He combined into one series the marginal notes from two or three different sets, even though they may have been written ten, fifteen, or twenty years apart. In the Preface to *Literary Remains* III he said that because "Coleridge's mind was a growing and accumulating mind to the last, his whole life one of inquiry and progressive insight...the dates of his opinions are therefore in some cases important, and in all interesting";[1] but his dating is intermittent and his evidence for it is never recorded or discussed. He always printed a date when it appeared in the body of the manuscript and may also have preserved from manuscript some dates now lost to us. But he was not always right, and one cannot have uncritical confidence in his dating when he could say of the 190 pages of marginal notes he printed from Jeremy Taylor's *Polemicall Discourses* that "Most of those...belong to the year 1810, and were especially designed for the perusal of Charles Lamb", when the manuscript itself includes notes dated 1811, 1812, 1819, 1824, and 1826.

Except for his occasional interference with the integrity of the manuscript text, little of this represents a serious complaint. The editorial ideals and practices of the early nineteenth century were not the same as ours; and Henry Coleridge was undoubtedly deflected from a faithful reproduction of his text by his desire to "help in extending [the] beneficial influence" of Coleridge's writing—a motive that sometimes tempted him to rewrite so that Coleridge's words would be in tune with opinions current in the late 1830's. He saw his task as primarily to prepare substantial readable copy that "the general informed reader" could read in an armchair without a library at his elbow. Whether or not he was technically (and temperamentally) capable of a more rigorous presentation, he had no intention of being more exact than he was. If the pages of *Literary Remains* have a greater air of stylistic coherence and physical homogeneity than the original manuscripts had, that—within certain intuited limits of fidelity—was precisely what he had in mind. The revisions away from Coleridge's intended sense are not numerous, and many of the revisions are innocent of substantial distortion.[2] Both Henry and Sara were concerned to have Coleridge read, and to have him read intelligibly, and to remove adverse expectations that might interfere with sympathetic and "beneficial" reading.

Literary Remains III and IV represent a high-water mark in the publication of Coleridge's marginalia beyond which neither Henry nor Sara ever advanced. Henry added a few miscellaneous marginal notes to *Confessions of an Inquiring Spirit* (1840); in *Biographia Literaria* (1847) Sara printed

---

[1] *LR* III xv.

[2] R. A. Foakes's restoration of John Payne Collier's shorthand notes of C's lectures in 1811 also shows the recovery of C's voice from Collier's heavily reworked version of *Seven Lectures* (1856). See *Coleridge on Shakespeare* (1971).

the first marginalia on German philosophers, as a necessary armament in her defence of her father against the charge of plagiarism. *Literary Remains* was never reprinted in its original form; and the marginalia from the four volumes were later reorganised into a different arrangement with little or no revision.

After *Literary Remains* IV in 1839, Henry Coleridge published in a single volume *Church and State, The Statesman's Manual*, and *A Lay Sermon*, and in 1840 *Confessions of an Inquiring Spirit*. He continued to work on his two-volume edition of *Aids to Reflection* and on a new edition of the *Biographia*, but the remarkable spate of publication was checked in 1840. In the spring of 1842 he was suddenly stricken by a progressive paralysis and was forced to give up his practice of law.[1] He died less than a year later, on 26 January 1843; Sara wrote in her diary: "So ends the great charm of this world to me. He has made all things bright to me for 20 years—". She continued with the editing, desolate at first, determined to dispose her intellectual powers to scholarly exposition and defence of her father's work. She became more earnest and stern than she had been when Henry was alive, more blue-stockingish than when she had charmed London literary circles before her marriage. A growing morbidity inundated her youthful mercuriality but failed to undermine her literary judgement or her deep respect for the work she was editing.

Sara's contribution to the canon of marginalia was slight, and she made no attempt to correct the editorial shortcomings of the principles that had guided Henry in the four volumes of *Literary Remains*. Her main concern for the marginalia was to reissue the published notes in three topical divisions: literary, theological, and miscellaneous. As soon as she had completed for publication the two works that Henry had had in hand when he died—*Aids to Reflection* (2 vols 1843) and *Biographia Literaria* (2 vols 1847)—and had finished her own new edition of the *Poems* (1844), she rearranged the critical material in *Literary Remains* I and II into *Notes and Lectures on Shakespeare and Some Other Old Poets and Dramatists* (2 vols 1849) as the first part of that scheme. She gave pride of place to the materials on Shakespeare by placing these in her Volume I and moving the "Course of Lectures" (with its interpolated marginal notes) and the marginalia on Jonson and Beaumont and Fletcher from their prominent place in *Literary Remains* I to her Volume II. She preserved the group of marginalia on prose style, but dropped the miscellaneous section of annotated books that came at the end of *Literary Remains* II. *Notes and Lectures*, like its source, contained a large number of marginal notes, but it was intended mainly to provide a reasonably coherent and representative cross-section of Coleridge's critical practice. The book, kept in print until superseded in 1930, was generally thought to provide the basis for Coleridge's critical reputation at least until the critique of Wordsworth in the *Biographia* received due recognition in this century. Sara was not able to complete her threefold scheme, but she did make the selection and arrange-

---

[1] Although HNC made light of his own chronic "rheumatism" and was always most solicitous for SC, records in the HCR collection in Dr Williams's Library show that he had been suffering from a cancer of the spine.

ment of materials from *Literary Remains* III and IV that was to form the second division under the title *Notes on English Divines*.

In 1849 Sara's brilliant, lovable, and pathetic elder brother Hartley died.[1] Her other brother Derwent, a successful clergyman-schoolmaster, had moved from his headmastership of Helston Grammar School in 1841 to become the first Principal of St Mark's College, Chelsea. Since Sara's marriage he had not been particularly sympathetic to her, had raised objections to Henry's editing, and had quarrelled with her over points of theology. They were drawn together by Hartley's death and decided to collect and edit his poems, essays, and other writings. Sara was already too deeply committed to her work on *Essays on His Own Times* and the *Poems* to do anything practical about editing Hartley's work, but she gave Derwent advice from her own experience and helped him to make critical decisions. Within two years Derwent had completed an edition of Hartley's *Poems* (2 vols 1851), with a perceptive memoir that remains the best tribute to Hartley, and a collection of Hartley's *Essays and Marginalia* (1851).

After seeing *Essays on His Own Times* through the press in 1850, Sara began a new edition of her father's poems, the first to present them in chronological order.[2] But by September 1850 she knew she was dying of cancer, and as her strength began to fail she had to rely more and more upon Derwent's collaboration. She persuaded him to accept responsibility for completing her work and hurried to teach him what, from years of familiarity, she knew about her father's books and papers. Derwent took up these responsibilities with characteristic thoroughness, "pressing [her] for assistance" while she lived.[3] In the last weeks of her life she read proofs of the *Poems*, dictating notes and corrections after she was no longer able to write. She died on 3 May 1852, and the edition was published a few weeks after her death. Within about eighteen months Derwent completed Sara's editorial design, not only by reissuing *Church and State*

---

[1] The codicil of 2 Jul 1830 to C's will provided for an annuity held in trust for HC's support. The Deed of Release and Arrangement, dated 2 Dec 1846 (BM Add Ch 66314), noted that "the said Henry Nelson Coleridge and Joseph Henry Green mentioned in the said recital Codicil have both dep[d] this life without ever having acted in the trusts reposed in them by the said Codicil". HNC and Green may have been guilty of technical dereliction of responsibility, but they knew that the intention of the codicil was being fulfilled. Mrs C, who had looked after HC's haphazard finances ever since he went north in 1823, continued to administer them until her death in Sept 1845. Thereafter SC took over the responsibility until HC died.

[2] See *TT* 1 Jan 1834: "After all you can say, I still think the chronological order the best for arranging a poet's works. All your divisions are in particular instances inadequate and they destroy the interest which arises from watching the progress, maturity, and even the decay of genius." For SC's difficulties with the chronological arrangement, see her Preface reprinted in *PW* (EHC) II 1169.

[3] SC wrote in 1851: "My brother wishes to have some of the Esteesian remains prepared for new editions, and this cannot be done without work on my part, as I have been so long the housekeeper of the S. T. C. literary house." *SC Life* 248.

and the two *Lay Sermons* in separate volumes, and by preparing his own edition of the *Dramatic Works* as a companion to the *Poems*, but by preparing and publishing the two remaining sections of marginalia: *Notes on English Divines* (2 vols) and *Notes Theological, Political, and Miscellaneous*, both in 1853. About one third of the second of these consisted of hitherto unpublished material; according to the opening sentence of the Preface this "completed the publication of Coleridge's Marginalia". In the previous year he had published Hartley's *Lives of the Northern Worthies*, adding as footnotes to the text many of the marginal notes that Coleridge had written in a copy that had originally belonged to Henry; apart from these, and the new annotations in *Notes Theological*, Derwent had added nothing to the canon of marginalia. With the publication of *Notes Theological* in 1853 the editorial work on marginalia by the first generation came to an end.[1] In the course of almost twenty years of effort they had succeeded in publishing new editions of virtually all Coleridge's published work and had acquainted readers with a large body of marginal notes—by then comprising more than a third of the corpus of Coleridge's prose. But the text of the marginalia they had published was defective, the editorial underpinning scanty.

For many reasons, any later editor of Coleridge's work is grateful for what the first generation did. Yet they had inadvertently left the impression after 1853 that, except for a few curious odds and ends that might turn up, the marginalia were a closed book; they had failed to convey how many more marginalia remained uncollected and unpublished, and of what kinds. The new marginalia in *Notes Theological* looked like makeweight material used to plump out a thin volume. The German marginalia that Sara added to the *Biographia* (1847) were of first importance but incomplete in that she gave no indication of the mass of material they represented. Two important components remained virtually untouched: annotations on philosophical and scientific books and annotations on the Bible and biblical commentaries. By ill-fortune J. H. Green's work on the philosophical manuscripts, though long drawn out, left little trace in Coleridge studies. Julius Hare and John Sterling never seriously addressed themselves to their biblical assignment. The decline of interest in theological matters in this century led to the neglect of the whole large group of notes in *Literary Remains* III and IV (and in *Notes on English Divines*), and ironically confirmed the earlier impression that Coleridge's marginalia are fragmentary, that they become diffuse when they take a theological turn, that they are of some interest as part of the received corpus of English literary criticism but not worthy of special or separate attention, being (after all) only commentaries (no matter how various and brilliant) on what other people had written. For this reason, and no doubt for

---

[1] In 1854 DC published a new edition (the seventh) of *AR* and in 1863 combined the *Poems* and *Dramatic Works* of 1852, with some additions, into *Poetical Works* in 3 vols. He continued to supervise the reissue of the earlier editions of HNC and SC but did no more original editing of his father's work. In 1864 he published an edition of the poems of M. W. Praed, and in 1876 an edition of the poems of John Moultrie.

others, there have been since 1853 a few large collections of marginalia and several small ones, but no attempt at a detailed edition.[1]

LATER EDITORS OF MARGINALIA

In 1867, four years after J. H. Green's death, the Shakespearean scholar C. M. Ingleby delivered to the Royal Society of Literature an attack on Coleridge's literary executors for their alleged failure to collect and publish his manuscripts and the annotations from his books. Ingleby's contribution was not impressive: a brief account of ten annotated books he knew of, with a transcript of notes from two of them, three of the books known to him only from published descriptions, one in his own possession, the others in the hands of various booksellers.[2] Up to that time only the sale of Gillman's library in 1843 had released any number of Coleridge's annotated books. Herbert Coleridge's library had been sold in 1862, but Derwent had bought up the most interesting items in it. Crabb Robinson's death in 1867 released nothing because his library was not sold at auction and his Coleridge-annotated books went obscurely to Dr Williams's Library. The British Museum library had by then only six of Coleridge's annotated books.

The important turning-point was the sale of Green's library in 1880—not so much the sale itself, but the large number of Coleridge's annotated books that came to the British Museum immediately after the sale.[3] The acquisition was reported anonymously by Helen Zimmern, with substantial quotations from marginal notes, in *Blackwood's* in 1882, and J. P. Anderson appended to Hall Caine's *Life of Coleridge* (1887) a handlist of the British Museum holdings of Coleridge associated items. In harmony with this list, W. F. Taylor issued a privately printed tract in 1889 entitled *Critical Annotations of Samuel Taylor Coleridge*, a typographically elaborate (but textually inaccurate) presentation of the marginal notes in twelve titles in the British Museum.[4] In 1888 James Dykes Campbell, who was then working on his edition of the *Poetical Works* and the splendid "Narrative of the Life" that was to accompany it, had begun a series of detailed notes of "Coleridgeana" in the *Athenaeum*, which continued until

---

[1] In the *New CBEL* III (as in *CBEL* V) a separate section of the entry is devoted to editions, collections, and versions of C's marginalia, and with reports of scholarly attempts to identify and collect annotated books.

[2] "On the Unpublished Manuscripts of Samuel Taylor Coleridge" *Trans RSL* 2nd ser IX (1870) 132–3, 428–9. The books noticed were BÖHME (from De Q's description), RALEGH *History of the World* (in Ingleby's possession), FLEURY, the Rann edition of SHAKESPEARE (COPY C), BOERHAAVE, MORE *Philosophical Poems*, LAW *Serious Call*, BURNET *Life of Bedell*, Algernon SIDNEY *Works*, SOUTHEY *Joan of Arc* (from a published version).

[3] See Annex B p clxv, n 2, below.

[4] Taylor presented the notes book by book in alphabetical order of authors, stopping at FICHTE *Die Anweisung zum seeligen Leben*. He intended to prepare a complete series of all the BM holdings of marginalia, but did not go beyond *CA*. Both Aynard and Nidecker were aware of Taylor's work; Nidecker disapproved of the alphabetical arrangement.

1893. John Louis Haney's list entitled "Marginalia" in his *Bibliography of S. T. C.* (Philadelphia 1903), though much more wide-ranging than Anderson's list, was probably less influential than it deserved to be, partly because it was privately printed, and partly because on publication it was savagely reviewed by Thomas J. Wise, whose reputation as a bibliographer was as yet unchallenged and untarnished. Wise himself contributed little because his *Bibliography of Coleridge* (1913, supplement 1919) described only those annotated books which happened to be in his own possession.

The interest aroused by Campbell's edition of the poems, and by Ernest Hartley Coleridge's two-volume selection of letters in 1895 and in the same year his brilliantly selected and beautifully printed group of notebook entries entitled *Anima Poetae*, laid seeds that—as far as marginalia were concerned—were not to be fertilised until the publication of John Livingston Lowes's momentous *Road to Xanadu* (Boston 1927). In the interval one systematic attempt had been made to present in scholarly form (but within a restricted range of Coleridgian reference) one of the elements missing from the canon of published marginalia—annotations on German philosophers. Henri Nidecker published in the *Revue de littérature comparée* 1927–33 a series of annotated transcripts of marginalia in the British Museum on Kant, Schelling, Schubert, Hegel, Steffens (with parallels to the *Theory of Life*), and Oersted, as documents illustrating Coleridge's attitude to the *Naturphilosophie* and the introduction of the Kantian philosophy to England. Nidecker seems to have fulfilled his intention when the series stopped with the Coleridgian inscription "(À suivre)".[1]

The publication of T. M. Raysor's *Coleridge's Shakespearean Criticism* (2 vols 1930) and *Coleridge's Miscellaneous Criticism* (1936) did little to advance the systematic process of collecting and publishing Coleridge's marginalia. Indeed, both books tended to confirm the impression inadvertently left by the first generation of editors: that most of the important marginalia had already been published and that the most interesting were those which consorted with the early-twentieth-century vogue of "literary criticism". *Shakespearean Criticism* was an extended and reorganised version of *Notes and Lectures*; *Miscellaneous Criticism* was a selection of annotations, many of which had been previously published, with an emphasis on "criticism" that prevented it from being a modern reworking of *Notes Theological*.

In *Shakesperean Criticism* Raysor revised and extended the marginal notes on Shakespeare by collating them with the manuscript of the three annotated editions of Shakespeare that Henry and Sara Coleridge had used (COPY A, B, and D). He reserved the notes on Jonson and Beaumont and Fletcher for *Miscellaneous Criticism*, and in an appendix to that volume printed the marginalia from a fourth edition of Shakespeare that had come to light since 1930 (COPY C).[2] From the point of view of

---

[1] J. S. Aynard had printed in the *Revue germanique* in 1911 a selection of twelve notes from ten miscellaneous titles in the BM. In a later note to the *Revue de littérature comparée* (1922) he described the annotated SCHUBERT *Allgemeine Naturgeschichte* and printed six notes from it; the book had come from the Green sale and was then in his possession.

[2] When *Sh C* was reissued with some revision in the Everyman edition

establishing an accurate and complete text of marginalia—which was not Raysor's primary intention—both books are disappointing, even though whenever possible his texts were based on the original manuscripts. The considerable benefits of both books are somewhat vitiated by normalised spelling and punctuation, by the edging away from marginalia difficult to read or interpret, and generally by a willingness to smooth out the stylistic abruptness of some of the originals. What explanatory notes Raysor provided for the marginal notes were concerned largely with the textus and the correctness (or otherwise) of Coleridge's critical observations in the light of modern critical scholarship; he made little attempt to relate the marginal notes to the corpus of Coleridge's writing or to explicate serious difficulties and obliquities in them. It is startling to find in the preface to *Miscellaneous Criticism* a return to the "popular" expectations that Henry Nelson Coleridge had hoped to arouse in *Literary Remains* I and II, reinforced with the conviction that the "literary" marginalia were the only ones likely to interest a modern reader and that neither curiosity nor piety could redeem the rest.

This collection of Coleridge's criticism is considerably more extensive than those previously published.... I should not wish, however, to collect and publish all of Coleridge's innumerable marginalia, even if it were possible. I have, in some cases, printed critical notes in this book with much reluctance, merely because they had more or less established themselves in the canon of Coleridge's published work. In other cases, I have deliberately passed by Coleridge marginalia posthumously published in various periodicals, either because this book is limited to criticism of literature, or because it would be unfair to the writer to print trivialities never intended for the press. But I have exercised my veto cautiously, probably too cautiously, because of the consideration that others might value what I might wish to reject.[1]

The claim to have offered a "collection...considerably more extensive than those previously published" was excessive. The book consisted of all the "critical" material from *Literary Remains* II that in *Notes and Lectures* Sara had relegated to Volume II, the text of the marginalia somewhat improved by reference to the original manuscripts where they were accessible. To this Raysor added a selection of marginal notes on literary texts, most of which had been published before, "correcting" to manuscript wherever possible (but with the same leniency in points of detail as in *Shakespearean Criticism*). The principal additions consist of the notes in a second copy of Anderson's *British Poets* and the appended notes from a third copy of Shakespeare. The selection is perhaps more *variegated* than before, but hardly more *extensive*; of twenty-three authors represented by marginalia in this book, ten offered a better text and only four had not been previously published in *Literary Remains*, *Notes and Lectures*, or *Notes Theological*. Raysor's two editions, valuable though they have been especially in the field of Shakespeare studies, restricted rather than extended interest in the marginalia and—since it was not his intention to do

---

(2 vols 1960) Raysor unfortunately was not able to include the marginalia from COPY C that he had printed in an appendix to *Misc C*.

[1] *Misc C* ix.

so (in spite of close attention, in *Shakespearean Criticism*, to Coleridge's debts to the Germans)—evinced no interest in the unexplored areas of philosophical and biblical marginalia. But it may be remembered that the first book had been assembled and had received its final form—and probably the second too—before Lowes published *The Road to Xanadu*.

The Road to Xanadu drew attention to the earliest of the notebooks (the "Gutch Memorandum Book"), to the range and variety of Coleridge's reading, and to a number of marginalia on Coleridge's own poems. It remained for three successive publications by Kathleen Coburn to throw the marginalia into a context broader than that staked out by the first generation of editors and to hint at the need for a more complete and scrupulously edited collection of marginalia than had so far been attempted. The *Philosophical Lectures* (1949), in the use of marginal notes on Tennemann's *Geschichte der Philosophie* and on certain German philosophers (especially Kant and Schelling), gave a first savour of a large category of notes hitherto virtually unknown and by implication indicated how important marginalia would be in editing Coleridge's published works. *Inquiring Spirit* (1951) included a sampling of previously unpublished marginalia taken from all kinds of books that Coleridge annotated. The first volume of the *Notebooks* (1957), although it presented only one formal set of marginal notes (Volume I stops in January 1804), fulfilled the implications of *Philosophical Lectures* by making use in the editorial notes of a wide range of marginalia—as a glance at the index will show.

Florence R. Brinkley's *Coleridge on the Seventeenth Century* (1955), published shortly before the first volume of *Notebooks*, is not primarily an edition of marginalia, but a comprehensive collection of certain parts of Coleridge's observations, including marginalia, on a single broad topic. The book was designed to present, in the form of primary materials drawn from both published and unpublished sources (with strong emphasis on manuscripts), something like a complete account of Coleridge's views on every phase of seventeenth-century writing. The editor claimed for it only a "reasonable completeness". By focusing the book on the theme of Coleridge's critical response to seventeenth-century writing, the emphasis was removed from the marginalia themselves, even though they were to constitute a large proportion of the text. The formidable task of making a careful edition of even that body of marginalia was further lightened by omitting the marginal notes on Shakespeare. As in Raysor's two editions, marginalia were printed from manuscript wherever possible; but also there were virtually no editorial notes to help the reader with difficulties in Coleridge's text or to provide parallels among the marginalia themselves or between marginalia and other writings. There was, however, much less silent manipulation of the minutiae of the text of manuscripts than Raysor had allowed himself, and Brinkley's discussion of the marginalia was more sympathetic than Raysor's.

Coleridge on the Seventeenth Century runs to almost 700 pages of text, some two-thirds of which are marginalia. The topical arrangement—partly by theme, partly by author—placed the emphasis on subject-matter rather than on the Coleridge texts themselves. The claim for "reasonable completeness" applies well to the collections of published and manuscript material, but is more apparent than real as far as marginalia are concerned; the balance and proportions of the book have been controlled to tip the scales towards "literary" matters.[1] It is not fair to complain that Brinkley did not make the sort of book she never intended to make; but from the point of view of the history of editions of Coleridge's marginalia, the inclusion of some new marginalia and the rereading of previously published notes using the manuscripts are offset by an inconsistent method of transcription that leads to unevenness in the authority of the text, by the exclusion of the Shakespeare marginalia, and by including only about one-third of the notes in Jeremy Taylor's *Polemicall Discourses*. If all the marginalia in the seventeenth-century books represented in the volume had in fact been printed, the balance would have swung heavily towards the ecclesiastical.

After publication of *Notebooks* I in 1957 and II in 1961, there was no longer a possibility that Coleridge's marginalia could be edited selectively, according to principles of personal taste or an editor's expectations about the general "usefulness" of the materials. The marginalia evidently had a wider ambience, a greater importance in the corpus of Coleridge's unpublished writing, and a greater significance as an unparalleled phenomenon in the field of creative activity. They had to be collected as completely as possible, set down as accurately as possible, provided with as much of the ancillary evidence as would be likely to lead to the correct identification, dating, and understanding of them. Now that it is possible to publish such an edition, in spite of all the work done by Henry, Sara, and Derwent Coleridge, and later by Raysor, Brinkley, and others, an editor of the marginalia needs a stout heart as he gazes out upon the flurry of faded, stained, and tattered pages and gathers about his heels—as earlier editors on the whole had not—the blizzard of footnotes that, with the passage of time, the changes in taste, and the decay of so much of the learning that Coleridge loved, is one of the reasons for doing the work.

---

[1] After two quite short sections on "The Seventeenth Century" (34 pp) and "Philosophy" (80 pp), the first main section "The Old Divines" devotes 240 pp to sixteen authors, and is followed by "Science" (16 pp). The book closes with three "Literary" sections, "Literary Prose", "Poetry", and "Drama" (other than Shakespeare)—270 pp dealing with thirty-one authors.

THE DISPERSAL OF COLERIDGE'S
BOOKS

T HE attempt to identify and, if possible, to recover all the books in which
Coleridge wrote notes involves two kinds of searches: looking for the
whereabouts of books already known and looking for those not yet
identified as Coleridge's. During his lifetime no catalogue was made of
Coleridge's library, except for the Wordsworth Library Catalogue, which
shows what books of his were still in the Wordsworths' possession at
Rydal Mount from about 1823. From collation of other evidence it is
possible to identify thirty books in the list as having been annotated by
Coleridge.[1] The only other list of any substance is the Green Library
Catalogue, drawn up by Mrs Ann Green evidently near the end of her life
(when her eyesight was failing) in an attempt to record for the benefit of
her executors what books in her possession were Coleridge's and should
therefore be transferred to Derwent.[2] The list, made on two different
occasions, consists of 237 entries; but, as there are eight double entries in
it, it represents 229 titles.[3] Many of the entries are sketchy, the author's
name is omitted or the title garbled; but with the help of other information
most of them can be identified without question: some are annotated
books, some "marked" books. Altogether these represent only a fraction
of the Coleridge books that Joseph Henry Green had gathered in as
executor. A third smaller list of annotated books is the "Watson List"—
twenty-one titles of books (some of them "manuscript facsimiles") that
had been preserved in the Gillman family and had passed down to the
granddaughter, Mrs Lucy Watson, author of *Coleridge at Highgate*.
These three lists together would be almost meaningless if they could not
be compared with the actual books that have survived in collections both
public and private and with the published versions of marginalia particularly by the first generation of editors. With the duplications that occur

1 See p cxii, above, and p clxix,
below.
2 The documents associated with the
probating of C's will show that Green
undertook to supply to the Court of
Canterbury by the end of Feb 1835
an inventory of the estate, but no such
document has been traced—if indeed
Green ever submitted it; even if he
did, it is unlikely that it would include
a detailed catalogue of C's books.
3 VCL MS 8: a vellum-bound ms
book, here referred to as Green LC.

The book also contains a numerical
list of the notebooks and a "Catalogue
of *Copies* of Letters written by S. T.
Coleridge, now in the possession of
Bernard Lord Coleridge". Most of
the association books in this list did
in fact go to DC or eventually ended
up in the possession of the family; but
at least ten appeared in the Green sale;
of these seven are in libraries other
than the BM (mostly in the U.S.A.)
and twenty-four have disappeared.

in them the total list is only a small part of the more than 1100 titles of annotated and marked books that have been identified. Nevertheless, those three lists have peculiar authority both for their closeness to the source and because of the special knowledge of those who drew them up.

The search for the books that Coleridge annotated is complicated by the fact that he wrote notes in many books that did not belong to him. In establishing a list of books that can be deliberately looked for, a quantity of circumstantial evidence can be assembled from Coleridge's letters, notebooks, and miscellaneous manuscripts and from the letters, diaries, books, and biographies of persons who came within the circle of Coleridge's personal acquaintance.

The first principles of any search-procedure is to begin as soon as possible, especially as the area in which Coleridge's books may be found is, after the lapse of a century and a half, rather large. Whenever a library changes hands, random dispersal occurs, often on a ruinous scale. Books vanish through carelessness, generosity, loss, theft, and destruction, and the sorts of people who allow such erosions seldom keep records. (It is only fair to notice, however, that to make an accurate catalogue of even a modest collection of books is an arduous task that few, even out of greed or affection, are prepared to undertake.) But in the case of a private library intrinsically valuable or of important association, the act of dispersal may produce a moment of documentary stability; if the books are presented to a permanent library and catalogued, or if they are sold at auction and a catalogue is printed, the books will be described and we may be able eventually to find them. Auction catalogues, until about the middle of this century, were not always up to the standard that a professional bibliographer or librarian would applaud, and they vary greatly in the amount of detail recorded. But they are usually compiled by knowledgeable people and, although mistakes, oversights, and pardonable inaccuracies are not uncommon, they are—from the nature of the book-trade—seldom guilty of flagrant misrepresentation. In compiling a list of Coleridge's annotated books, auction catalogues have been of peculiar value.

Catalogues marked by buyers at sales are—after the books themselves—among the most treasured possessions of bibliophiles and collectors. For purposes of reconstructing Coleridge's library and the list of books associated with him, the most informative version of a sale catalogue is the copy used by the auctioneer, in which he will have noted the names of the buyers and the prices paid and will occasionally have corrected errors in description. The extensive collection of auctioneers' marked catalogues in the British Library has been specially useful in compiling a descriptive list of Coleridge's annotated and association books, in tracing their provenance, in judging where missing books are likely to turn up, in tracking down "ghosts", in piecing together information about annotated books of which no transcript exists, in finding whether an annotated book has been described by oversight as a marked book, and—since few published transcripts of marginalia are both complete and textually accurate—in recovering the originals from which notes have already been printed. Information drawn from sale catalogues is therefore recorded in an Appendix in the final volume of this edition.

In the case of Coleridge's books, and other people's books with his notes in them, the process of dispersal had been going on during his lifetime. At the time of his death, in July 1834, his literary executor, Joseph Henry Green, was confronted with a complex and delicate task (as Coleridge noted in his will) in assembling—if only for preliminary and methodical examination—all the books and manuscripts that he was entitled by the will to consider for publication. Most of Coleridge's working library, and some books that did not belong to him, were in his study in the Gillmans' house. A number of the Gillmans' own books had been annotated by him at their request and were their own property. They also made careful transcriptions in copies of the same edition as the originals ("manuscript facsimiles") of annotated books of which they were especially fond but which had to be turned over to Green. Green had books of his own that Coleridge had annotated, and as collaborator in Coleridge's philosophical studies he probably also had a number of Coleridge's own books and manuscripts in his possession. Henry and Sara Coleridge had some annotated books; Derwent had all Hartley's books, some of which had been his father's and were annotated, and probably also had whatever books Mrs Coleridge had finally brought from Greta Hall in 1829. All these fell within the ambit of Sara's work as soon as Derwent and she had settled their differences. If there were still any books at Greta Hall they can only have been a few strays and books that Southey considered his own property. At Rydal Mount there may still have been a substantial part of the collection left at Allan Bank in 1810—perhaps as many as 200 titles.

Somehow, without giving offence to anybody, Green resolved all the questions of ownership. We do not know by what means, by what date, or in what place Green assembled and sorted these materials and redistributed them according to the agreed editorial responsibilities—or even if he did anything as methodical as that. If the single instance of George Frere's copy of *Reliquiae Baxterianae* is typical, he identified and returned to their rightful owners the erratics that Coleridge had taken to his heart. The redistribution of the working materials must have been effective, for although among Henry Coleridge's transcripts and letters there are signs that (as was to be expected) a particular book might be hard to trace or be needed in one place when it was in another, it does not appear that the editors, once they had begun their work, were much troubled by the location or distribution of the materials. One reason, perhaps, was that each had decided to work from what he had on hand.

The last books from Rydal Mount seem to have arrived in London late in 1834. Sara Hutchinson wrote to Green on 10 January 1835 forwarding "the Copies of all the notes written by Mr Coleridge in the Books at Rydal Mount" and asking him to look out for, and return, the copy of Chapman's *Homer* that Coleridge had given her and that had been sent south by mistake—"I do not know whether it was sent to Highgate or to Helston"[1]—

---

[1] *SHL* 439. There were two copies of Chapman's *Homer* in the Rydal Mount library, one of them—presumably SH's—marked as C's because his marginalia were written in it without a presentation inscription. SH

"His books were sent from Rydal when I was absent—".[1] Immediately after Coleridge's death, Green and Henry Nelson Coleridge had written to Coleridge's friends, asking for letters, reminiscences, and transcripts of marginalia, but the list cannot have been long. Some of the friends— Lamb and Southey particularly—were not able to respond.[2] The search for marginalia in other people's books seems to have stopped after that first impulse. Henry Crabb Robinson, who had some annotated books, liked hunting down others, and was willing to make transcripts, received little encouragement from Green when he offered his services.[3]

seems not to have realised that the Rydal Mount books would legally be going to Green (in Lincoln's Inn), not to Gillman (in Highgate) or to Mrs C (who was then staying with DC in Helston). It is a reasonable guess, however, that Green used The Grove as the first collecting place.

[1] An unpublished letter of 7 Feb 1831 from RS to HNC raises a question whether in fact many of C's books remained with the Wordsworths after late 1830 or early 1831. RS wrote: "If you cannot tell how pleased I have been in opening the package that arrived after me, & disposing of the books, Sara can. There were about 350 volumes." (MS in possession of Nicholas Coleridge.) It is not certain that these were C's books, or that they came from Rydal Mount; but it is quite possible that C had instructed HNC to dispose of the remaining books at Rydal Mount that he no longer wanted after receiving the consignment of 1829—and who more likely to welcome them than pack-rat Southey? The transfer of 350 volumes to RS would have left behind at Rydal only the books that HC, SH, and WW had kept for themselves, and no doubt a few strays. The only reference to C's books being sent from Rydal after C's death (*SHL* 439) gives no hint of how many there were to send.

On 7 Jun 1836 HC wrote to Green from Grasmere, sending him an unpublished essay on faith and a detailed list of some of his father's books, including several "in Mr Wordsworth's Library, where however they are acknowledged as mine". Sotheby sale 20 Jul 1971, lot 488; I do not know whether the list of books is still with the letter. It appears that after the Wordsworths had returned the last of C's books late in 1834, Green made further inquiry whether there were still any other annotated books in the Wordsworths' possession.

[2] For the list of contributors to *LR* acknowledged by HNC see Annex A, p cxli n 3, above; for Lamb's failure to contribute see above, p cxl n 1. There is acknowledgment to RS for one book in *LR* IV, but he had not transcribed it himself, being at that time preoccupied with domestic distress. When SH wrote to Green in Jan 1835 she had just returned from looking after the Southey family ever since the previous Sept, when Edith Southey suffered a sudden mental collapse from which she never fully recovered before dying on 16 Nov 1837. After a secret engagement, RS married Caroline Bowles in Jan 1839. Only a few weeks later his mind began to fail; he was unable to do any more effective work, and died on 21 Mar 1843.

[3] In Dec 1835 HCR offered to lend Green his Spinoza "for the purpose of his extracting the marginalia of Coleridge"; in Jun 1836 he "rose early and copied some curious marginal notes in Lightfoot's works, by Coleridge, which I shall probably offer to Green and Nelson Coleridge for the intended publication"; in Mar 1837 he saw Green at St Thomas's Hospital and "lent him five books (German philosophy) with notes by Coleridge". *CRB* II 469, 496, 514. HNC and SC did not publish any of these.

In 1835 Green inherited a considerable fortune from his father. He gave up his practice in Lincoln's Inn Fields in 1836 and retired to Hadley.[1] In 1837 he exercised his option of buying Coleridge's books, and it was perhaps by this time that the Gillmans had finished making their manuscript facsimiles.[2] Also in 1837 Green resigned the chair of surgery at King's College, London, but his retirement to Hadley did not prevent him from retaining the surgeoncy at St Thomas's Hospital until 1852 or from maintaining an active rôle in the College of Surgeons and the Medical Council. Not the whole of the remaining twenty-eight years of his life was devoted to the dispiriting and abortive task of trying to complete Coleridge's philosophical system.[3] In effect he had isolated his own task and had delegated the remainder of the editorial work to Henry Coleridge almost from the beginning. But Henry correctly acknowledged in his Preface to *Literary Remains* I that "above and independently of all others, it is to Mr. and Mrs. Gillman, and to Mr. Green himself, that the public are indebted for the preservation and use of the principal part of the contents of these volumes".

Within twenty years of Coleridge's death virtually all his friends, and all the people who possessed or can be supposed to have possessed books annotated by him, had died. Hazlitt had died in 1830, four years before Coleridge, abandoned by everybody except Lamb.[4] Josiah Wade died in 1830, and the "considerable number of Letters, Books and Marginal Notes, and other papers written by Mr Coleridge" that he had were destroyed by fire in the Bristol riots in 1831.[5] As for Lamb—when Coleridge died, Lamb said: "Never saw I his likeness, nor probably the world can see again", and went about (his friends said) haunted by the fact that "Coleridge is dead". Too stricken to attend the funeral or to respond to Henry Coleridge's request for documents, he died five months later, on 27 December 1834.[6] Sara Hutchinson died on 23 June 1835; Coleridge had bequeathed her a mourning ring, and she had recovered her copy of Chapman's *Homer*. William Godwin, whose library Coleridge may have used from time to time, died in April 1837, and Thomas Poole on 8 September of the same year. George Dyer died in 1841, Francis Wrangham

---

[1] See Annex A, p cxxxviii n 1, above.

[2] Lucy Watson wrote in *C at H* 2: "From the manuscripts that came into his [J. H. Green's] possession he allowed my grandmother [Mrs Gillman] to copy anything that she might wish to preserve for herself. These copies she bequeathed to me."

[3] Green's *Spiritual Philosophy, Founded on the Teaching of the Late S. T. Coleridge*, ed John Simon, was published in two volumes in 1865. In view of the failure of Green's book, it is agreeable to notice HCR's appreciation of Green's Hunterian Oration of 1847, *Mental Dynamics; or, Ground-*

work of a Professional Education— "a more luminous exposure of some of Coleridge's principles than has been yet given to the world". *CRB* II 664. In 1839 Green had given the Hunterian Oration entitled *Vital Dynamics* (published 1840).

[4] Hazlitt seems not to have had any books annotated by C.

[5] See CAPPER headnote.

[6] HC wrote to DC in Sept 1835: "Hal [i.e. HNC] has taken Lamb to himself. He had a right to do so— but *that* would have suited me." *HCL* 178.

in 1842, Henry Nelson Coleridge and Southey in 1843, Henry Francis Cary in 1844, Josiah Wedgwood in 1846, Mary Lamb in 1847, Wordsworth in 1850, Sara Coleridge in May 1852, De Quincey in 1859. The last to go were Joseph Henry Green in 1863, Joseph Cottle in 1865, and Henry Crabb Robinson in 1867. A record of the libraries of some of these persons is preserved, but of some—particularly Thomas Poole's—there is no trace, and there is also no record of the libraries of others who probably had annotated books—the Beaumonts, Wade, Danvers, Prati, the Aderses, Charles Augustus Tulk, and the Mr Tudor who lent Coleridge his ten folio volumes of Cocceius' commentaries. Only the Gillman and Green libraries contained a large number of Coleridge's books, and it is from these two that the main lines of dispersal, and the history of the two great permanent collections, are to be traced.

James Gillman died in 1839; when Anne Gillman left The Grove in the spring of 1843, she offered her husband's library for sale at auction. With the sale of that library the posthumous dispersal of Coleridge's library begins. Thirteen of Gillman's most prized Coleridge books (some of them manuscript facsimiles of annotations in books that had been transferred to Green) were not offered for sale; these remained in the family until some of them passed into Thomas J. Wise's possession in 1952 or 1956 and are now in the Ashley collection of the British Museum. The rest of Gillman's books were sold at auction by Henry Southgate on 31 March 1843, the 229 lots realising £101.6.0. In the catalogue thirty items are shown as Coleridge's; the auctioneer added two annotated items belonging to "Strong"—Robert Robinson's *Miscellaneous Works* (4 vols Harlow 1807), now in the Huntington Library, and William Tindal's *Antiquities of...Evesham* (Evesham 1794), now lost. At the sale William Pickering bought seventeen lots of Coleridge books, Bohn seven, and the rest went to four other buyers. Only six of the books described as annotated by Coleridge are permanently preserved: Southey's *Omniana* and the anonymous *Odes and Addresses to Great People* (by Thomas Hood and John Hamilton Reynolds), both now in the British Library; Stanley's *History of Philosophy*, now in the Berg Collection of the New York Public Library; Blanco White's *Letters from Spain*, now at Keble College, Oxford; the curious little book by William Blake of Highgate called "Silver Drops", now in the University of Indiana; and Robinson's *Works*.[1] But a few other annotated books from this sale, not so described in the catalogue, have been identified since—e.g. Thomas Fuller's *Pisgah-Sight of Palestine*—and certain other books not noted as Coleridge's must have been his—e.g. the large-paper copy of Southey's *Poems* (1797).

Marginalia from ten, possibly eleven, of Pickering's purchases were first published by Derwent Coleridge in *Notes Theological*; the connexion may have been accidental. Pickering had published Coleridge's work since

[1] A second auctioneer's copy of the sale catalogue (BM S–C Sg a 53), recognised by Lorna Arnold in 1976, identifies the Gillman lots as 303–466, 468–501, 504–34; the two Strong items were entered as 467* and 471*. Many of the lots included several titles only one or two of which were specified. The copy of *Odes and Addresses* from this sale was the first BM acquisition (1844) of one of C's books; the BM acquired the copy of *Omniana* in 1864.

1828, but his dealings with Henry and Sara Coleridge were so uncongenial that the marginalia in these books may have been transcribed before Gillman's death.[1] Green may have agreed to the sale of these books because the notes had been transcribed, but it is more likely that they were in the sale from oversight or through the assiduity of the bookseller. To judge from the sale catalogue, only two important works have disappeared from this sale without record of their marginalia: Burnet's *History of His Own Times* (2 vols 1734) and Milton's *Paradise Lost* (1777). None of the books from this sale passed into Green's library.

The fate of Charles Lamb's "ragged regiment" is more melancholy. He bequeathed his library to his sister Mary, who lived until 1847, in her last years only intermittently lucid. The publisher Edward Moxon, who had married the Lambs' adopted daughter Emma Isola, had been appointed Lamb's executor but did not take possession of the books until after Mary's death, by which time some had drifted away. Crabb Robinson on 27 April 1848 gave an elliptical but indignant account of what then happened to the books:

I had a chat with...Talfourd about Moxon, who has really sold Lamb's books to some American. Talfourd is displeased with this, and reasonably. [Moxon] tells him that these were worth nothing, and that he got only £10 by them. This cannot be true, and if true so much the worse. Moxon told me at first that he would give the books to the University College; but afterwards said they were not worth their accepting.[2]

Moxon gave some books away indiscriminately to friends and, beyond the few sold for £10 to his friend Charles Welford, burned the rest. In February 1848 Bartlett & Welford of New York printed a catalogue of sixty titles, stating in a prefatory note that

[1] Though Pickering published the Coleridge editions for HNC, he accepted responsibility neither for the printing nor for the initial capital outlay. This burdensome arrangement, accentuated by the irregularity of Pickering's payments, troubled HNC when he was dying; but no solution was to be found, and SC continued with Pickering until relations, which had steadily deteriorated, broke down completely in 1851. Moxon then bought up from Pickering all the stocks of C's books and continued to issue the HNC and SC editions. Pickering died in 1854; the Gillman items were not included in his stock auctioned between Aug 1854 and Jan 1855. In the 1854 sale 696 unsold copies of Gillman's *Life of Coleridge* were sold in lots of a hundred at about 4*d* a copy: A. N. L. Munby "The Sales of William Pickering's Publications" *Book Collector* XXI (1972) 39. See also Geoffrey Keynes *William Pickering* (privately printed 1924).

[2] *CRB* II 675. Thomas Westwood, who had known the library during Lamb's life, was also indignant: "I have been told that his books were sold to the Yankees. Oh, pity! Oh, shame! They should have been held in honour and charge by some Londoner who was a London-lover—a haunter of the old streets and of the old book-stalls. There are some libraries the dispersion of which we feel as a positive pain, almost a disgrace—and Lamb's was of them. His books were his household gods, and he has himself told us that his household gods kept 'a terrible fixed foot.'" Quoted by E. V. Lucas *The Life of Charles Lamb* (New York 1905) II 426.

The notes, remarks, &c, referred to and quoted...in the following list, are warranted to be *all* in the autograph of Lamb (except when otherwise mentioned) ...no attempt has been made to re-clothe his "shivering folios;" they are precisely in the state in which he possessed and left them.

At a private sale in February 1848 these were sold for $479.75.[1] George T. Strong, a perceptive collector of early printed books and association items, bought (for $108.50) the last five titles in the catalogue, shown as "Books with notes by S. T. Coleridge": Amory's *Life of John Buncle*, Donne's *Poems* (1669), Reynolds's *Triumphe of Gods Revenge Agaynst the Cryinge, and Execrable Sinne of Murther*, *The History of Philip de Commines*, and Petvin's *Letters Concerning Mind*. An account of the five Coleridge books appeared in the *Literary World* in 1853 with transcripts of some of the notes; Strong himself sent transcripts to Derwent Coleridge, which were used in *Notes Theological*.[2] Strong's library was sold in 1878, and four of the five Coleridge books are now in permanent collections—in Yale, Harvard, Princeton, and the Huntington Library. Only the most modest item—Amory's *Life of John Buncle*—is missing from this group, but it must be lurking shyly somewhere because it was in the possession of the Rosenbach Company in 1947. A few other of Lamb's books with Coleridge's marginalia in them have been preserved, but his copy of Fulke Greville *Certaine Learned and Elegant Workes* (1633) from this sale has not appeared since it was sold at Sotheby's in 1903.

The first library belonging to an immediate member of the Coleridge family was auctioned at Sotheby's on 10 and 11 April 1862—the library of Herbert Coleridge, the brilliant son of Henry and Sara, who had died at the age of thirty-one, one of the founders of the *Oxford English Dictionary*. The catalogue described the collection as "including a series of the writings of S. T. & H. Coleridge ... some [13] having the autograph & notes of S. T. Coleridge". The 627 lots realised £241.14.6. Derwent attended the second day of the sale and bought twenty-seven lots, including four Coleridge association books. One of these was the presentation copy of Sotheby's limited edition of the hexaglot *Georgics*, which Coleridge had given to Sara as a wedding present, the volume he had wished she "should never part with". (The book has Edith Coleridge's signature in it, dated 1852—the year of her mother's death.)

---

[1] See R. L. Hine *Charles Lamb and His Hertfordshire* (1949) 122 and J. S. Finch *Princeton University Library Chronicle* IX (1947) 30–2. The books were sold at a private sale in Feb 1848. Buyers came from as far away as California and Oregon; the sale caused such excitement that it was described in the *Literary World* and the Dibdin Club immediately reprinted the catalogue with a description of the sale. John Keese, of the New York auctioneering firm of Cooley, Keese, and Hill, capitalising on the interest aroused by the Scribner sale, persuaded a number of buyers to offer their books again at sale by auction. The sale took place on the evening of 21 Oct 1848 in a scene of riotous enthusiasm (see *Literary World* 4 Nov 1848); but the volumes with C's notes were already in George Strong's possession.

[2] Strong's transcripts are now in the VCL collection. An account of the Lamb–C books was published in *Literary World* 30 Apr, 2 and 28 May 1853.

On 13 December of the following year, 1863, Joseph Henry Green died, leaving an estate of some £45,000 to his widow, Ann Eliza, "the Relict the sole Executrix". When in 1837 Green had exercised his option to buy Coleridge's books, the intention was to place funds in the trust held for Coleridge's widow and children. Although the books then became technically Green's property, there seems to have been some tacit agreement that if Green bought the books they would eventually devolve to Coleridge's heirs. Ann Green died on 17 September 1879. At the beginning of a long and detailed will appointing William Henry Freeman and Charles Norris Wild as executors of a "Personal Estate under £25,000", she bequeathed "to the Reverend Derwent Coleridge all the portraits books and writings which were bequeathed to my late dear husband by the late Samuel Taylor Coleridge"—Derwent being the sole survivor of Coleridge's family. He was then seventy-nine years old and had been vicar of Hanwell (near Ealing) since 1864; he may be forgiven if he did not exert a young man's energy in detaching all his father's books from Mrs Green's estate.[1] Presumably the Green Library Catalogue was not available to the executors, for eight titles in it were included in the sale. When, by provision of the will, Green's library was sold at auction by Sotheby, Wilkinson, and Hodge, it included 140 lots of Coleridge's books, the catalogue announcing that this "valuable collection of metaphysical, theological, and miscellaneous writings" included "Many Volumes enriched with the Autograph Notes of S. T. Coleridge the poet, and J. H. Green, including Coleridge's Manuscript Note Book and Shakespeare, 8 vols. *with important MS. Notes*". This is the largest single collection of Coleridge association books ever offered for public sale. Most of the books in the sale were Green's own books, but a good number seem originally to have been Coleridge's. Although it is impossible to tell from the sale catalogue which of the unmarked books in the Gillman and Green sales were Coleridge's, the two catalogues have proved to be a valuable indication of some of the (otherwise unidentifiable) editions that Coleridge had in Highgate and used there. The Green sale ran from 27 to 29 July 1880, the 956 lots realising £607.10.6. The 140 lots of association books—as shown in the catalogue, but not including 14 lots of marked or annotated copies of Coleridge's own works —fell fairly equally to John Wilson and Edward Stibbs, Wilson buying forty-eight, Stibbs fifty-five. The rest went to fifteen other buyers, only three of whom bought more than five lots and none more than seven.

Immediately after the sale, Wilson offered thirty-nine lots to the Trustees of the British Museum for £88.13.2; the Museum accepted all these, comprising fifty-three titles, and dated the acquisition 4 August 1880. Wilson submitted a supplementary list of five more titles on 20 August, of which the Museum accepted three (for £8.7.0, acquisition date 9 November 1880), rejecting the copy of John Anster's *Poems* (now in the Huntington

---

[1] A further provision of Mrs Green's will may have caused confusion: "and as to my books I desire that my executors will select such part thereof not exceeding fifty volumes in the whole as they may like to retain for themselves and that the residue thereof shall be sold".

Library) and Hölty's *Gedichte*, described as "With MS. notes by S. T. Coleridge", which has disappeared.[1] At that time there was no public collection of Coleridge's books to compare in range and interest with this single Green–Wilson–British Museum transaction; it was to form the nucleus of the present collection, which is now of unparalleled scope and richness. Up to 1880 the British Museum held only six of Coleridge's annotated books; in one transaction more than fifty titles were added.[2]

Of Wilson's other eight association purchases, four are of slight interest, being presentation copies inscribed to Coleridge: Heraud's *Legend of St Loy* (1825), Hetherington's *Twelve Dramatic Sketches* (1829), Moxon's *Sonnets* (1830), and Landor's *Gebir* (1831), now at Yale. Two others appear in a Wilson catalogue of 1880: Hölty's *Gedichte* (which the British Museum had declined) and Mandeville's *Fable of the Bees* (1724), now in the library of the University of Tokyo. Two other Wilson purchases, which have now disappeared, are described as bearing Coleridge's autograph signature: Scaliger's *De subtilitate* (Frankfurt 1607) and Henry More's *Enchiridion ethicum* (Amsterdam 1679).

The fate of the fifty-five lots of Coleridge association books bought by Stibbs is more complicated and more disastrous. In 1884 thirty-nine titles from Stibbs's purchases were offered for sale in New York by Scribner and Welford; Haney's 1903 list of marginalia includes thirty-five of these. Of the twenty-seven items bought by Stibbs and not sold by Scribner, only two have turned up, both in the United States—which suggests that all the Stibbs books may have gone there. Why they did not all go to Scribner or, if they did, why they were not catalogued does not appear; seven of the uncatalogued titles, described in the Green catalogue as annotated, were probably sold privately. Three of the Scribner items—Descartes's *Opera philosophica* (Amsterdam 1685), Opitz's *Teutsche Gedichte* (4 vols Frankfurt 1740), and Quarles's *Emblems* (1676)—which had not been shown as

---

[1] Information from BM library invoices.

[2] The BM acquisitions from the Green sale were noticed in *Athenaeum* II (1880) 273–4 with a brief description of the books and an expression of the BM's "good fortune to secure all the most important lots" from the Green sale. Helen Zimmern wrote anonymously at greater length in *Bl Mag* cxxxi (Jan 1882) 107–25; even at that time "Many pencillings...have been so rubbed as to have become wholly or partially illegible." She gave samples of the marginalia but closed her article with a common disclaimer: "We have omitted as not suited to these pages, a large number of theological notes, that very specially illustrate the instability of opinion in

Coleridge, to which we referred in the Commencement."

Readers of the annotated books now in the BM may find it convenient to identify the approximate sources of the books by the case-numbers.

C.28: the earliest acquisition (1844) —one book

C.43, C.44, C.45: books from the Green sale (4 Aug 1880), and a few acquisitions 1864–87 and 1912

C.126: books from the "Ottery Collection" (14 Jul 1951), and a few books identified 1948–56 as Coleridge's

C.132: books from the collection of W. H. P. Coleridge (acquired Jul 1968), and a few acquisitions since 1970

Ashley: books from T. J. Wise's Ashley Collection (acquired c 1938)

annotated in the Sotheby catalogue, were noticed in the Scribner catalogue as containing Coleridge marginalia. (The Descartes went to the
University of Vermont; the notes in it were published in 1934.) Of the
other thirty-six titles, five are now in the Harvard Library, two each in the
Berg Collection, Princeton, and Victoria College, and one each in Columbia, the Huntington, University of Pennsylvania, Queen's University, and
a private American collection. In 1903 Haney said that a "widely published appeal" had failed to bring to light any of the twenty-one titles
then missing from the Scribner sale; but eight have turned up since 1950,
and others may still be discovered. That some are lost beyond recall is
scarcely to be doubted, for the history of the one Stibbs item in the
British Museum—Rehberg's *Metaphysik zu der Religion* (Berlin 1789)—
suggests how slender was their chance of survival. The book was presented
to the Museum in 1934 by Bernard Flexner with a covering letter saying
that some years before he had "picked [it] out of a box of books on sale"
in New York. Yet the volume bears on the flyleaf the names of Sara
Hutchinson and S. T. Coleridge written by Coleridge in a large sprawling
hand, and on the back cover there is a note in his hand, signed and dated
"August 29th, Syracuse, 1804".

Of the untraced Stibbs items offered for sale in New York, many are
described as bearing only Coleridge's signature or initials. Three, however, would be worth recovering: Chiabrera's *Opere* (3 vols in 2, Venice
1782), Lacépède's *Les Ages de la nature* (2 vols in 1, Paris 1830), and
Mendelssohn's *Philosophische Schriften* (2 vols Carlsruhe 1780)—all of
which are catalogued as containing several manuscript notes.

The Stibbs purchases that were not included in the Scribner catalogue
have left even less trace. Many of them were presentation copies or had
only Coleridge's initials in them. Franciosini's *Grammatica spagnuola ed
italiana* (Venice 1734) survived to be offered in a Blackwell catalogue in
1945; Timpler's *Metaphysicae systema* (Frankfurt 1607) is in the Library
of Congress. The most serious losses seem to be: ten volumes of Garve's
works (Breslau 1792 etc), Lactantius' *Opera* (Basle 1521), and nine volumes
of Weishaupt, including *Anschauung und Erscheinungen* (Nuremberg 1788)
and *Regierungskunst* (Frankfurt 1795). Seven volumes of A. W. Schlegel
are said to have "a loose sheet of notes inserted"; and the *Vorlesungen
über dramatische Kunst und Literatur* (3 vols in 2, Heidelberg 1809–12),
described as bearing a note on "the Eichhornian hypothesis", which is
probably not the copy from DC's library that later belonged to Edward
Dowden and is now lost. Solger's *Erwin* and Mariana Starke's *Travels on
the Continent* are listed with a single note in Coleridge's hand in each. In
the same way that the Wilson purchases at the Green sale provided the
foundation for the British Museum collection of Coleridgiana, the Stibbs
purchases dispersed by Scribner and Welford in New York in 1884 provide
a focus to which a large proportion of the Coleridgiana held in the United
States can be traced. But the largest single nucleus formed from the Stibbs
dispersal consists of five titles at Harvard.

Few of the books taken by the other fifteen buyers have been preserved
in permanent collections. One of Bridges's four purchases—Cary's
translation of Aristophanes *The Birds* (1824)—is in the Harvard Library;

another—Schubert's *Allgemeine Naturgeschichte* (Erlangen 1826)—was once in the possession of J. S. Aynard in Paris and is now in the British Museum. Southey's *History of Brazil*, bought at the Green sale by Dr Riggall, is also now in the British Museum. The six lots bought by James Speirs formed the most interesting of the small groups. Only one of these was recorded by Haney in 1903—Swedenborg's *Wisdom of Angels*—and it has now disappeared. The other five came into the possession of the Coleridge family either by gift or purchase, evidently while Gerard H. B. Coleridge was still alive. One of these—Sotheby's *Poems*—went to the Victoria College Library with the "Leatherhead Collection"; another—*Sendschreiben an...Herrn...Teller* (Berlin 1799)—appeared in 1945 in a Blackwell catalogue of the overflow from G. H. B. Coleridge's library; the other three were all in the collection of the late Walter H. P. Coleridge and are now in the British Museum.

It seems proper to consider separately the books associated with Coleridge that appeared in the sales of the Southey and Wordsworth libraries. Fortunately both were sold at auction and were therefore catalogued with descriptive notes more or less accurate.

Southey's son Cuthbert tried to interest the British Museum Library in acquiring the 14,000-volume collection of Southey's books intact because of its association interest (Southey had been Poet Laureate since 1813) and because his collection of about 700 Spanish and Portuguese books and manuscripts was of some rarity. Because the British Museum already held copies of many of the books in Southey's library, the Trustees declined the offer. The library was auctioned at Sotheby's in 3861 lots; the sale, beginning on 8 May 1844, lasted for sixteen days and realised £2933.8.6. After the sale the British Museum bought from Rodd some 250 lots, including about eighty lots from the Spanish and Portuguese section.

Since most of Coleridge's books had been transferred to Allan Bank in 1808 and what little was left at Greta Hall had been taken by Mrs Coleridge to Helston when she left Keswick in the autumn of 1829, few if any of Coleridge's books could be expected to be in the Southey sale. Apart from a few copies of Coleridge's own works, only five titles are recognised in the catalogue as associated with Coleridge, all five being books that belonged to Southey and had been annotated by Coleridge. Only two of these are now in permanent collections: Burnet's *Life of Bedell* at Stanford University and James Sedgwick's anonymous *Hints on Evangelical Preaching* at Duke University. Of the other three, the annotated copy of Waterland's *Vindication* (1720) would be worth recovering because the notes would be earlier than those written in the copy given to Coleridge by Methuen in 1814. A transcript of the note in Pereira's *Antoniana Margarita* has survived, but the original is lost. There is no record of the notes in Rimius's *Narrative of the Rise and Progress of the Moravians* (2 vols in 1 1753–4).

There were two other annotated books in the sale that are not so described in the catalogue: Cotton Mather's *Magnalia Christi Americana* (now in the Huntington Library) and the copy of Flögel's *Geschichte der komischen Litteratur* (now at Harvard) that Southey had bought from

Coleridge in December 1813.[1] It is not certain that the annotated copy of Gilbert White's *Natural History of Selborne* (acquired by the British Museum in 1891) was included in the sale. The heavily annotated copy of Southey's *Life of Wesley* was not included in the sale; it was in Coleridge's possession when he died and was sent to Southey—as Coleridge had directed—by Henry Coleridge in about February 1835.[2] It remained in Cuthbert Southey's possession long after he had extracted some of the notes for his 1846 edition of the *Life* and is now in the Berg Collection in the New York Public Library.

In July 1859 Wordsworth's library was sold at auction "by Mr. John Burton. (Of Preston;) at that haunt of hallowed memories Rydal Mount, near Ambleside, Windermere". Wordsworth was not, like Coleridge, a bookish man, nor like Southey a collector; the library was of sentimental rather than intrinsic interest, not worth shipping to London for auction. John Brown, who organised the sale, was the keeper of the Queen's Hotel, Ambleside. The catalogue is a wretched jumble. The sale lasted three days and the 700 lots realised £380.11.9. An annotated copy of the catalogue shows that at this provincial sale West End manners were not expected, and few buyers attended:

In consequence, it was understood, of the disgraceful manner in which visitors to "Rydal Mount" gratified their abominable propensity of carrying away Souvenirs of the place in the shape of plants, pieces of wood and stone etc— etc, whereby the house and grounds were much disfigured, the Poet Laureate's Library was sold in a Coach House adjoining—

The number of people present at the Sale did not average more than about 50 each day—The principal purchasers were Kerslake, bookseller, Derby; The Rev[d] —— Graves, Ambleside; the Rev[d] Tatham, Rydale—[3]

---

[1] Two other books that RS bought from C in 1813 can also be recognised in the *Southey SC*: *Sammlung Deutscher Gedichte aus dem XII, XIII, und XIV Jahrhundert* (2 vols Berlin 1784) and *Sammlung von Minnesingern aus dem Schwaebischen Zeitpuncts XCL Dichter enthaltend* (2 vols in 1 Zurich 1758), neither annotated. These did not go to the BM.

[2] Letter from HNC to RS 1 Feb 1835: University of Texas (Coleridge Collection). SC told Henry Taylor on 26 Feb 1846: "I do not know how any of the Notes came to be effaced, never having seen the copy of 'The Life of Wesley', in which they were written by my father himself." *SC Mem* II 26–7.

[3] Dove Cottage MS. By 1 Jul HCR had received a copy of the sale catalogue but said: "The best have been already taken away." *CRB* II 785. The

only book he wanted was Mrs Barbauld's *Works* and hoped that his friend J. J. Tayler would get it for him. Tayler wrote to HCR about the sale on 25 Jul: "The books went at high prices, evidently for the associations attached to them, & for the autographs they contained, for they were not generally speaking of much value for their rarity, their editions or their condition. Kerslake of Bristol, the well known bookseller, seemed to me the chief purchaser.—" He bid for the Barbauld but it sold "for nearly double the sum you had mentioned"; and a first edition of *The Friend* went for £1.12.0—rather more than he was confident HCR wanted to pay. Tayler himself "got in one lot" two items that would be worth recovering: "a copy of Coleridge's Table Talk, with Wordsworth's autograph & some lead pencil notes, which have interest as

Only two books appeared in the sale that had been shown in the Words-worth Library Catalogue as associated with Coleridge: Thomas Shad-well's *Dramatick Works* (4 vols 1720) with Coleridge's signature in it and the copy of Chapman's *Homer* that Coleridge had given to Sara Hutchin-son fifty years earlier. Unnoticed as associated with Coleridge were the lightly annotated copy of Donne's *LXXX Sermons* (now at Harvard), the annotated Hillhouse's *Hadad* (now at Yale), a copy of William Frend's *Evening Amusements* that Coleridge had inscribed to his son Hartley in 1809, and the unmarked copy of Shelvocke's *Voyage* that had provided the albatross for the *Ancient Mariner*.[1]

Derwent Coleridge died in 1883, bequeathing his library to his son. Ernest Hartley Coleridge (b 1846) now had in his possession the large collection of manuscripts, notebooks, letters, miscellaneous papers, and books that had passed directly from Coleridge to Derwent—a collection preserved reasonably intact for almost fifty years by Coleridge's literary executor, Joseph Henry Green, and his widow. He also had—in addition to Derwent's considerable personal library—the residue of the Greta Hall library (brought to Helston by Mrs Coleridge in 1829), as well as Hartley's books and manuscripts (which included some of Coleridge's manuscripts and annotated books). Derwent had had the whole of this huge cumulus in his possession for only three years after Mrs Green's death. There had been some losses by direct gift to Henry and Sara Coleridge, and not all these had come home; there was some loss through the Gillmans, but not very much. The most serious loss had been in the transfer of the collection from the Greens to Derwent, but an important part of that loss had been rescued by the British Museum.

Although Ernest Hartley Coleridge was already by 1883 committed to a life of editing and miscellaneous writing, he must have decided at an early date—possibly before his father's death—that he would devote a good part of his energy to honouring the editorial responsibility that possession of Coleridge's papers and books implied. The time for candour was approaching; many letters previously, out of discretion, had been withheld and could now be published, possibly some parts of the notebooks. A life needed to be written to offset the bias, inaccuracy, and flaccidity of the attempts at biography made by Joseph Cottle, Thomas Allsop, and James Gillman. He began to clear the decks for his editorial work by offering for sale at Sotheby's in July 1888 "The Philological Library of the late

throwing light on the history of Coleridge's reputed plagiarisms & especially on the genesis of the Ancient Mariner, &...a small copy of Emer-son's Essays, also with Wordsworth's autograph. The Table Talk is a pre-sentation copy from the Editor, with H. N. Coleridge's inscription." *CR Life* II 834. The copy of *TT* with WW's notes has not, as far as I know, survived.

[1] The copy of Frend later belonged

to Joanna Hutchinson, and is now in the possession of Jonathan Words-worth. WW's copy of *Purchas His Pilgrimage*, now in the library of Worcester College, Oxford, bears a note by C. H. Wilkinson stating that it is "Probably the copy over which Coleridge fell asleep when reading the passage on p. 472, and then com-posed 'Kubla Khan' in his sleep". There is no evidence that it was.

Rev. Derwent Coleridge"; 90 lots were sold for £45.3.0. This sale is re-markable for the evidence it gives of Derwent's linguistic accomplishment,[1] but it included—presumably by mistake—one of Coleridge's annotated books, Hermann's *De emendenda ratione Graecae grammaticae*, with three marginal notes in Latin. Acquired by the British Museum on 15 August 1888, the book was not catalogued as Coleridge's until 1949.

In July 1891 Ernest Hartley Coleridge offered most of the rest of his father's library for sale, announced as "A Portion of the Library of the late Rev. Derwent Coleridge"; it comprised 294 lots and realised £185.3.6. This sale included sixteen of Coleridge's books, five of them with mar-ginalia: *Acta Seminarii Regii et Societatis Philologicae Lipsiensis*, John Payne Collier's *History of English Dramatic Poetry*, *The Poems of William Dunbar* (Vol i, Edinburgh 1834), Grotius' *De jure belli et pacis* (Amster-dam 1763), and Schleiermacher's *Critical Essay on the Gospel of St Luke* (1825). Only two of these have survived—the *Acta Seminarii* in the Hunting-ton Library, the Schleiermacher in the British Museum. These books may have been in the sale by mistake, because Ernest Hartley bought back from Iredale, who had bought nine of the sixteen association items in the sale, Coleridge's copy of Hayley's *Life of William Cowper*. There has been no trace of any of the other association books since then. But in 1890 Ernest Hartley Coleridge managed to buy from Iredale three volumes of Cole-ridge's four-volume set of Boccaccio's *Opere* (1723), which Iredale had acquired in 1887 from an unknown source. It is not clear how many strays Ernest Hartley Coleridge was able to recover. He had a strong sense of the continuity of the collection he had inherited, noting where appropriate—either by direct inscription or on an inserted card—"Green bequest". In Bede's *Ecclesiastical History* he noted:

This with other folios marked "S. T. C." were in my father's [Derwent's] library as long as I can remember—whether the volumes came to him on the death of Hartley Coleridge, 1849, or when his father died in 1834, I do not know.

He might well wonder. The book was not in the Wordsworth Library Catalogue. Hartley's name is not written in it, but there may have been a family tradition that it had once been his. Ernest Hartley had himself bought it from Iredale. It later appeared in a Blackwell's catalogue in 1945 after Gerard Coleridge's death and has now disappeared. Ernest Hartley's inscription in Fludd's *Philosophia Moysaica* suggests that he was not clear how the books had been transmitted from Coleridge's executor to Derwent: "This was among the books of S. T. Coleridge's bequeathed to Derwent Coleridge by Joseph Henry Green."

[1] The first sale catalogue of DC's library shows that he owned books printed in the following languages: German (including early forms), Dutch, Flemish, Anglo-Saxon, Old Norse, Icelandic, Norwegian, Swedish, Danish; Celtic, Welsh (including Bar-dic), Cornish, Breton, Irish, Gaelic, Manx; Latin, French, Italian, Rhaeto-Romanic, Spanish, Portuguese; Greek; Bohemian (Czech); Sanskrit, Bengali; Armenian; Finnish, Lappish, Hun-garian; Hebrew, Syriac, Chaldaic, Arabic, Ethiopian, Egyptian, Coptic; Maori, Hawaiian; Nepalese; Eskimo. He also had books on the dialects of Cumberland and Westmorland, North-ampton, and Dorset.

In the Victoria College Library there are many evidences of the care Ernest Hartley Coleridge devoted to the books and with what industry over how many years—at times with dismay and a sinking heart—he worked to organise and clarify what was in the collection. We must treat with respect all marginalia quoted or referred to by him and all editions cited in the *Letters, Poetical Works*, and *Anima Poetae*, even though he was not minutely accurate in transcribing and was capable on occasion of slips in citing titles and editions. A similar respect must be extended also to such material cited in the work of his close friend, James Dykes Campbell. Both of them, for a period of nine years after Derwent's death, carried out their Coleridge work with a larger group of the original materials under their hands than had ever before been gathered in one place; no such collection can ever again be assembled.

Ernest Hartley's primary intention was to write a life of Coleridge. For this purpose he spent some years studying and arranging the materials in his possession, tracking down and transcribing letters, miscellaneous manuscripts, and marginalia that were in the possession of other people, transcribing and digesting the notebooks. Now that a full biography was to be attempted, all the materials had suddenly assumed manifold, even paralysing, implications. A much greater subtlety and depth of purpose had to command the editorial work: he could no longer simplify the man and his work as Henry and Sara had. Determined to be both faithful and comprehensive, he fell victim to the sheer magnitude and complexity of the responsibility he had inherited. Then in about 1896 his work suffered a reverse from which it never fully recovered: a trunkful of manuscripts and working papers disappeared in transit between London and Torquay and was never found. The shock, interruption, and discouragement caused by the loss prevented him from completing the "Life of Coleridge".[1] The "Narrative" that his friend James Dykes Campbell wrote for his own edition of the *Poetical Works* (1893) remains the best and most perceptive biography we have.

In 1895 Ernest Hartley published a two-volume selection of the *Letters* and a beautiful little volume of selections from the notebooks—*Anima Poetae*—which provide a glimpse of dimensions in Coleridge's life and thought that had scarcely broken through the surface of the earlier and graver editions. Perhaps more than any other single work, *Anima Poetae* indicated that nothing less than everything that had come from Coleridge's pen would have to be published. In 1912 Ernest Hartley's two-volume edition of *The Complete Poetical Works* appeared, and in the same year the Royal Society of Literature published his pioneering study of *Christabel*. In 1918 he published an essay on the origins of the *Ancient Mariner*, the seed that—obscurely fertilised by Alois Brandl—grew into J. L. Lowes's *The Road to Xanadu*. Although he collected and transcribed some marginalia, he published none beyond those included incidentally in the *Poetical Works*.

---

[1] The fragmentary draft of EHC's life of C was published by Gerard Coleridge in *Studies* (1934).

It is very Coleridgian that what Ernest Hartley Coleridge achieved seems to be less than he might have achieved. Yet what he did achieve, both in his own name and through his friendship with James Dykes Campbell, is the foundation for modern Coleridge scholarship. There is a Coleridgian irony in the circumstance that Hartley, Derwent, Sara, Henry Nelson, and Herbert Coleridge all found a place in the *Dictionary of National Biography*, but not Ernest Hartley. The long-sustained effort, the pressure of other responsibilities, the shock of the irreparable loss of his working papers took their toll on him.[1] But it was financial considerations rather than despair over his work that induced him in 1892 to dispose of a major part of the collected Coleridge materials to his kinsman John Duke Coleridge, first Baron Coleridge and Lord Chief Justice, grandson of Coleridge's elder brother James. A large group of Coleridge's manuscripts, marked and annotated books, and the main series of the notebooks were transferred to Ottery St Mary, to comprise what was known to Coleridge scholars as the "Ottery Collection", though they had little or no access to it. The transfer of this part of the collection is recorded in many of the Ottery annotated books with John Duke Coleridge's distinctive monogram "C" and the date 1892, in some cases with a brief additional note. The collection was rich and immensely important, not only for containing most of the notebooks, but also because it included most of the philosophical and theological marginalia that the early editors had not been able to use or develop. The fact that the major notebooks were included implies that Ernest Hartley was determined to secure the integrity and safekeeping of the collection he had inherited.

In 1892 and again in 1895, Ernest Hartley disposed of substantial groups of manuscripts to the British Museum.[2] He kept in his own possession the literary and miscellaneous manuscripts and those books which were the background for his own work-in-progress as well as the transcripts and digests he had prepared from notebooks, letters, marginalia, and miscellaneous manuscripts, together with similar material inherited from Henry and Sara. When he died in 1920 he bequeathed his collection to his elder son, Gerard H. B. Coleridge, vicar of Leatherhead. This part of his original inheritance came to be known to Coleridgians as the "Leatherhead Collection". When Gerard Coleridge retired in 1945 he decided to reduce the size of his library while still holding the Coleridge collection intact. In the transfer a certain number of Coleridge items—none of them of first importance—came on the market, and with them the copy of Words-

---

[1] EHC's Coleridge publications began in 1889 with *Letters from the Lake Poets to Daniel Stuart*, then fell into two phases, with *Letters* and *AP* in 1895 and *PW* in 1912. Between these he worked on the new and enlarged edition of Byron, publishing the 7 vols of Byron's *Poetical Works* in 1898 (reissued 1905), with a separate edition of *Don Juan* in 1906. In 1904 he published his 2-vol *Life and Correspondence*

of John Duke, *Lord Coleridge*, in 1905 and in 1907 a selected edition of C's *Poems*, in 1907 the RSL study of *Christabel*. After *PW* (1912) he published only *The Life of Thomas Coutts, Banker* (2 vols 1920).

[2] E.g. BM Add MS 34225 is marked "Purchased of EHC 1 Aug 1892" and BM MS Egerton 2801—also from EHC—is marked 15 May 1895.

worth's *Poetical Works* (1837), now in the Royal Library, Windsor, annotated with Wordsworth's last thoughts and corrections.[1] Substantially intact, the "Leatherhead Collection" passed at Gerard Coleridge's death jointly to his three sons, who decided that, apart from a few family mementoes to be kept by each of the younger brothers Anthony and Nicholas, the collection should be held by the eldest brother Alwyne. For forty years that family duty and privilege was honoured also for the "Ottery Collection" by John Duke until his death in 1894, then by his son Bernard, and by his grandson Geoffrey Duke, until the time was ripe for people outside the family to attempt to do what the members of Coleridge's family had not yet succeeded in doing.

In 1951 the "Ottery Collection" was purchased by the Pilgrim Trust and presented to the British Museum, and in 1954 the "Leatherhead Collection" was acquired by Victoria College, Toronto. In this way the large family collection consolidated for less than ten years under Ernest Hartley's hands has been permanently preserved in two major collections, suffering only the inevitable attrition that occurs with time or when any collection is transferred from one person to another. The two collections are rather different in character. The British Museum, with more than eighty titles, already had the largest public collection of annotated and marked books (not counting Coleridge's own works) before the twelve titles in the Ashley Library were added. The "Ottery Collection" brought another 123 titles, making a total of 216. The Victoria College collection comprises 120 annotated and marked books. The two collections together contain almost exactly three times the number of annotated and marked books known to be held in all other collections combined. In 1968 a small group of choice annotated books came to the British Museum from the collection of Ernest Hartley's son Walter H. P. Coleridge. Some 150 books that are known to have Coleridge marginalia in them have still to turn up (but some sort of transcript of about eighty of these exists); no doubt some hitherto unrecognised annotated books exist and will sooner or later come to light.

Since 1945 the tendency for marked and annotated books to be lost and misplaced by oversight or through ignorance of their value has been reversed. Mounting prices in the saleroom wonderfully sharpen the perception; and in the postwar years—until recently—universities became aggressive, omnivorous, and well-funded collectors. The libraries of H. B. Smith (auctioned in 1914), Mark P. Robinson (1918), James B. Clemens (1945), and Walter P. Chrysler (1952) contained a number of valuable Coleridgiana, several of which have already found their way into permanent collections. It is inconceivable that many of the now-missing items will not have been cherished and eventually come into permanent collections, even though some may have been destroyed. Some of the choice groups of books affectionately preserved by members of the Coleridge,

---

[1] This annotated copy was edited by Helen Darbishire for Sir Owen Morshead for presentation to the members of the Roxburghe Club as *Some Variants in Wordsworth's Text in the Volumes of 1836–7 in the King's Library* (privately printed 1948).

Wordsworth, and Hutchinson families have tended to find a home in the end either in the British Museum or in the Dove Cottage Museum. Victoria College, Toronto, is still adding to its holdings. It is to be expected that there will be steady additions to the major American collections of Coleridgiana: Harvard, the Berg Collection in the New York Public Library, the Huntington Library, Yale, Cornell, the University of Texas, and no doubt other permanent collections that so far hold only one or two of Coleridge's books.

Although we shall never again be able to assemble in one place all the books that Green inherited, or Derwent, or Ernest Hartley Coleridge, it is to be hoped that many more will come to light to give testimony of the poet who, in cherishing them, "spoiled" them.

MARGINALIA

THOMAS ABBT
1738–1766

Thomas Abbts ... vermischte Werke. Erster Theil welcher die Abhandlung vom Verdienste enthält; Zweyter Theil welcher 1) vom Tode fürs Vaterland 2) Fragment der Portugiesischen Geschichte enthält ... Sechster Theil welcher Briefe und Fragmente enthält. Dritten Auflage, &c. Vols I, II, VI (of 6) in 2 vols. Berlin & Stettin 1772, 1770, 1781. 8°.

The first bound volume comprises Vols I, II; the second is Vol VI. C. F. Nicolai edited Vols I–III, Johann Erich Biester Vols IV–VI.

Princeton University Library

The signature "Fischer" is written on I ⁻3, with C's annotation 1 written around it. Bookplate of C. Sanders.

Autograph signature "S. T. Coleridge" in what appears to be an early hand on the title-pages of Vols I and VI, which suggests that the three volumes were already bound in this form when C owned them.

DATE. Uncertain. Perhaps 1810–12, after C met HCR, or later. In N 29 f 112 C remembered seeing in "Abbt's Essays" a contrast between Tom Jones and Sir Charles Grandison and noted: "Mem. to look for it". HNC's inclusion of this entry in his "Omniana 1809–16" in *LR* I 380–6 is an unreliable clue to the date of the Abbt marginalia.

COEDITOR. Hans Eichner.

---

1 I ⁻3–⁻1, referring to I 10–11 | Der Begriff vom Verdienste

Lasset uns di[e]se zerstreueten Stralen des Verdienstes sammeln, und in ein deutliches Bild ordnen.

   1) *Handlungen*, oder überhaupt *Thätigkeit*,

   2) den *andern* zum *Nutzen*,

   3) aus *freyer Entschliessung* und *reinen Absichten*, oder, welches einerley ist, aus *Wohlwollen*,

   4) zu einem *erheblichen Zwecke*

   5) durch *Seelenkräfte*, ausgeübt worden, diese können wir *Verdienst* nennen.

[Let us gather the scattered rays of merit and arrange them in a clear picture.

   1) *Actions*, or generally *activity*, carried out

3

2) for the *benefit* of *others*,
3) as a result of a *free choice* and with *pure intentions*, or, which comes to the same thing, as a result of *benevolence*,
4) to an *important end*,
5) through *moral powers*—these can be called *merit*.]

Page. 10–11.—In this inventory of the Ingredients of true Desert the 2nd and the 5th are superfluous. Handlung = an Action, does of itself imply Seelen-kräfte = moral & intellectual powers impulsive and co-operant: how much more then 1 An Action 2 for the benefit of others 3 by & with a determination of *free Choice*, & from pure Motives 4 to a useful and important *End*? In like manner, the 3rd & 4th involve the second: or the definition is false. Say, that I exert all the best powers of the good Principle within me in a long & at length successful Agony of Self-conquest in order to master a Habit of taking Stimulants & Narcotics injurious to my Health? If this be done with pure motives, it must be *as a Duty* & not merely selfishly —or rather Self becoming an object of Duty ipso facto becomes an object of Benevolence, & includes my social claims—the effects of my Conduct, ~~of~~ & its Consequences on the Happiness or Well-being of others.—

I doubt indeed, whether even the 5th be not either false or super-fluous (~~for~~ or indeed false at once): for by the precedent Instance of Fossombrone it is clear, that the Author intended by "erheblichem Zwecke" an end really important, and not one sincerely believed to be so by the Agent himself.)[1] Now this sophisticates the moral Idea of Worth & true Merit by the commixture of *Accidents*. The degree of natural Talent is always an accident quoad hominem.[2] i.e, it does not depend on the will of the Individual himself—the degree of acquired knowlege & ~~im~~ *cultivation* of natural Talent is very often so in great measure. The Judgments of men respecting the comparative Importance of Ends proposed are not only fallible, but influenced likewise by Events not connected with the meritorious Agent—& they too therefore partake of the accidental: ex. gr. a valuable Dis-covery made a month or years after the same had been already ~~published~~ made./ but without the knowlege of the second Person, as possibly was the case of Leibnitz: Sir I. Newton in the discovery of Infinitesimal Arithmetic—[3]

[1] Abbt suggests on I 9ff that some of the feats reported of the Capuchin Ludovico di Fossombrone would have been worthy of a Hannibal if they had not been performed simply in defence of a peaked cowl.

[2] "As far as he is a man".

[3] C is more charitable than those

2 I $^+$2, referring to I 14 | Von der Grösse des Geistes

Den *grossen Geist* sollen wir also hier vorfordern, um ruhig seine Eigenschaftern . . . zu beschauen. Wer kann aber . . . versprechen, nicht dabey in Feuer zu gerathen? Nur dem schwarzen und abgelebten Verschnittenen muthet es sein Herr an, die Reizungen einer jungen nackten Sklavinn, die zum Verkaufe angeboten wird, genau zu besichtigen, und hernach den Ausspruch zu thun, ob sie seines Herrn werth sey? Findet der scheussliche Unmann jede wollüstige Reizung wie eine aufbrechende Knospe . . . so wirft er den Schleyer über die *Schöne*; fällt auf sein Antlitz; und betet im Froste an. So verwahrloset sollen wir uns auch zeigen bey Betrachtung der vortreflichsten Sache in der Schöpfung? eines Geistes, der in seinem umkreise selbst ein Schöpfer ist?

[We are here to summon the *great mind*, in order calmly to observe . . . its properties. But who can . . . promise to do so without falling into a passion? Only the black and decrepit castrate is expected by his master accurately to examine the charms of a young, naked slave-girl who is offered for sale, and then to pronounce judgement whether she is worthy of her master. If the disgusting eunuch finds every lascivious charm like an opening bud . . . he will cast a veil over the *beautiful girl* and fall upon his face in frosty adoration. Are we to show ourselves equally depraved when we look upon the most excellent thing in creation—a mind that is itself a creator in its own sphere?]

p. 14. Almost without exception the unluckiest & most ill-chosen Illustration, I ever met with!—

3 I $^+$2, referring to I 149 | Von der Güte des Herzens und dem Wohlwollen

Das *gute Herz* ist allemal *weich*; aber *nicht* jedes *weiche* Herz ist <u>gut in allen Graden</u>.

[The *good heart* is always *tender*; but *not* every *tender* heart is *good in all degrees*.]

149. Das Gute Herz ist allemal weich—in any tolerable interpretation of weich = tender, this is false.[1]

4 VI $^+$1, referring to VI 16–23 | Briefe und Fragmente. Letter to Möser 3 Oct 1764

[Abbt expresses his disbelief in positive religions; he suggests, for example, that if God had revealed a specific religion to man, he

commentators who, without denying Leibniz's original contribution to the development of the infinitesimal calculus, claim that he knew about Newton's early method of calculation and probably formed his calculus upon Newton's fluxions with some change in notation and procedure. For Newton and Leibniz see also BAHRDT 1 nn. For other examples of "simultaneous discovery" see *C Pantheist* 47n.

3[1] Although Abbt's essay runs to 79 pages (I 110–88), C has written only this one brief objection on the text.

would have revealed it to all mankind at once, thus bringing about a fundamental and immediate elevation (*Erhöhung*) of man.]

p. 16–23. Of all the contemptible Ass-flings of infidel Wantonness this is surely the most asinine and contemptible! And in German too! And not a Translation from the French? Nay! for it is even *infragallican*: and what German could translate it? Possibly as a specimen of *per hyperbolen* of the French Lust of Blasphemy, and the Blasphemies of French Lust![1] For it is twofold Blasphemy, Blasphemy against Religion, & Blasphemy against common Sense!—O Tommy Abbot! this too well explains thy "Life & Character of Baumgarten",[2] & thy abuse of Möser![3]—S. T. C.

5   vi +2, pencil

capio a e meo ipsius commodo labores meos et eos in commune commodum transfero—
hos in meum ipsius commodum labores *sus*cipiendos existimo/[1]

[4][1] For C's strong and persistent bias against the French see e.g. ATHENAEUM 21.

[4][2] The sixth item in Vol IV (which was still part of the set when Green's library was sold) is "Leben und Charakter Gottlieb Alexander Baumgartens". Alexander Gottlieb Baumgarten (1714–62), professor of philosophy at Frankfurt-on-Oder from 1740, attempted to found a science or philosophy of the Beautiful, which he named "Aesthetics".

[4][3] Vol VI 3–37 comprises a group of letters from Abbt to Justus Möser (1720–94); in the second of these Abbt raises objections to Möser's *Brief an den Vikar in Savoyen*, which maintained against Rousseau that natural religion would not be universally acceptable.

[5][1] "I take my efforts from my own interest and transfer them to the common interest—I consider that these efforts are to be *under*taken for my own interest".

ACTA SEMINARII

Acta Seminarii Regii et Societatis Philologicae Lipsiensis. Adiecta bibliotheca critica. Curavit Christianus Daniel Beckius. Vol I (of 2). Leipzig 1811. 8º.

Henry E. Huntington Library

Inscribed by C on p ⁻2: "Given to Hartley Coleridge by his Father: with a promise on the part of the said H. C., that he will bonâ fide read thro' them. Highgate, Jan. 1. 1818.—" HC, twenty-two years old when C wrote this note, had been up at Oriel College since 1815, and was to receive a probationary fellowship in 1819. HC spent the Christmas vacation in Highgate from 13 Dec 1817 to 17 Jan 1818. *CL* IV 793, 803.

CONTENTS. This volume contains *inter alia* articles by Ludwig Baumgarten-Crusius, Gottfried Hermann (*De pronomine* αὐτός), Franz Passow (on Schneider's Greek lexicon and other recently published Greek and Latin dictionaries), C. A. Böttiger (on archaeology), and a group of *Iudicia de scriptis antiquis* by various authors.

DATE. Possibly 1811–17. The book may have come to C from HCR, who from Nov 1810 onward lent his German books to C and shared with him his enthusiasm for German literature and criticism. For C's interest in a "Greek & English Grammar on a perfectly new plan, & . . . a small but sufficiently compleat Greek & English Lexicon" in Jun 1807, see *CL* III 22. Though never formally completed, the grammar was used in draft form to teach Greek to HC and DC.

---

1 p 209 | Romanus de Timkowsky "Commentatio de dithyrambis"

[Footnote 7, quoting Catullus *Carmina* 63.19–26:]
    Simul ite, sequimini
 Phrygiam ad domum Cybelles, Phrygia ad nemora Deae,
 Ubi cymbalûm sonat vox, ubi tympana reboant,
 Tibicen ubi canit Phryx curvo grave calamo.

[Tr F. W. Cornish (LCL 1912): ". . . go together, follow to the Phrygian house of Cybele, to the Phrygian forests of the goddess, where the noise of cymbals sounds, where timbrels re-echo, where the Phrygian flute-player blows a deep note on his curved reed."]

Qʸ? Cymbalum casu objectivo, pro *"cymbalo"* assonat?[1]

1[1] "Is 'cymbalum' in the accusative case, instead of *'cymbalo'* assonat [the   voice sounds to the accompaniment of the cymbal]?" All commentators

7

2 p 344, pencil | Iudicia de scriptis antiquis

[A discussion of the authorship of Περὶ ὕψους (*De sublimitate, On the Sublime*), with copious quotations from the edition by B. Weiske (Leipzig 1809), including on p 343:] Tum illa τῆς οἰκουμένης εἰρήνη, et quod non oratores sed *adulatores tantum magnifici* fiebant, qui eloquentiam in exquisita principis laude ostentarent, temporibus Augusti egregie convenit, sed vix cadit in Aureliani saeculum.

["Then that phrase 'the universal peace', and the fact that they became not orators but 'merely extravagant flatterers' who showed off their eloquence in elaborate praise of the emperor, fits well with the times of Augustus but scarcely belongs to the age of Aurelian."]

To me, I confess, this Περι υψους seems a shewy shallow declamation worthy of a Sophist of Aurelian's Age: & scarcely worth disputing about.[1] s. t. c.

---

apparently take *cymbalum* as genitive plural, except those who, following Scaliger, read *nox* (night) for *vox* (voice or sound). C's suggestion perhaps does not too much strain the meaning of the accusative, but to take *cymbalum* as genitive plural is more natural. Footnote 7 describes the rites of Bacchus and Cybele, ending: "tympana pulsando et verba incondita iactando"—"to the beating of drums and the shouting of incoherent words".

2¹ C's generally low opinion of Περὶ ὕψους is surprising; this note is the most

impatient of his few recorded comments; see e.g. DYER *Poems* 3. Critical tradition has valued *On the Sublime* highly as a liberating inquiry into exaltation of style and for its penetrating insight into the emotional effects of great literature.

Controversy, not yet settled, about the authorship of Περὶ ὕψους began with Weiske's edition. Modern scholars on the whole place it late in the first or early in the second century B.C., whereas the supposititious author, Cassius Longinus, was contemporary with the Emperor Aurelian (215–75).

THOMAS ADAM
1701–1784

Private Thoughts on Religion, and other subjects connected with it, extracted from the diary of the Rev. Thomas Adam, late Rector of Wintringham. To which is prefixed a short sketch of his life and character. Second edition. York 1795. 12⁰.

British Museum C 43 a 8

Inscribed by Poole on p ⁻5: "*Thoˢ Poole* Given to me by the Earl of Egmont *15ᵗʰ June 1804*." The initials "S. T. C." are written on the title-page (possibly in C's hand).

John James Perceval, 3rd Earl of Egmont (c 1737–1822), was the brother of Spencer Perceval, assassinated in 1812. Enmore, the Egmont estate, is mentioned in C's *The Nightingale* (lines 50–1) as "a castle huge | Which the great lord inhabits not". Egmont's agent was William Cruikshank (d 1802), a friend of Thomas Poole; his daughter Ellen is the "most gentle maid" associated with the birds in *The Nightingale*, and his son John was the one whose dream provided C with the skeleton ship for *AM*. C and his wife visited Lord Egmont at Enmore in early summer 1807; Egmont told De Q afterwards that C "talks very much like an angel, and does nothing at all". *De Q Works* II 148. See also *Poole* I 174; II 182, 199, 200.

DATE. Jun–Sept 1807. Not in C's possession 1810–30: Wordsworth LC 350, 1186.

COEDITOR. James D. Boulger.

1   p ⁻4, pencil

= means assent to, sympathy
|| difference, either in opinion, or in consciousness of my own individual character, according to the §, against which the mark is pl[a]ced
? doubt.[1]

2   p 31, pencil | Ch 1 "Confessions"

=] I had a full conviction that I stand more in awe of P. L. than God.[1]
S. H.—[2]

[1][1] The marked passages, of interest because of the early date of the marking, are assembled in the ANNEX to this entry.

[2][1] In the previous paragraph Adam wrote: "I do not know the person whose good opinion I do not naturally love more than their soul."

[2][2] I.e. Sara Hutchinson.

9

3   p 51, pencil | Ch 3 "God"

=] Nothing but love can unite with and enjoy love.

As Light alone mixes with Light.[1]

4   p 83, pencil | Ch 4 "Human Depravity"

I should not have had the stone in my bladder or kidneys, or both, if I had not first had a stone in my heart.

? Is not anti-evangelical?[1]

5   p 92, pencil

The scripture affirms that the imagination of man's heart is evil continually; and it is a great point gained, and directs to a necessary subject of prayer, to know that the will is bound, and that none but God can set it free.

True or false, as it is taken: food or poison.

6   p 127, pencil | Ch 7 "Faith"

Christ came to teach a pure morality, and assert the necessity of a perfect law-keeping, but does not expect to find it in us; he therefore wrought it for us.

What poison may not a weak mind suck from this?

7   pp 160–5 | Ch 8 "Good Works"

Why then are works to be the great subject of inquiry at the day of
*] judgment? Because they are the visible effects of faith, and only good as springing from a root of faith, so that the want of them proves of course the want of faith.

* Explain it thus: God will judge each man before all men; consequently, he must judge relatively to man. But man knoweth not the heart of man,[1] scarcely each knoweth his own; there must therefore be outward & visible signs by which man may be enabled to judge of the inward state, & thereby justify the ways of God to man.[2] Now good works are these; and as such & only as such become

---

3[1] Cf *BL* ch 8 (1907) ı 89: "the law of causality holds only between homogeneous things...".

4[1] In N 30 f 13 e.g. C was to ask: "Illness Wickedness? or Wickedness Illness?"

7[1] Cf 1 Cor 2.11, Jer 17.9.

7[2] "Outward and visible sign" is part of the definition of a sacrament in the Church of England Catechism. The phrase "justify the ways of God to man" from *Paradise Lost* ı 26 has no direct verbal source in the Bible (see, however, Ps 145.17, Rev 15.3).

necessary. In short, there are two parties, God & the human Race— and both are to be satisfied: God, who seeth the root & knoweth the heart—therefore there must be Faith/ Man, who can judge only by the Fruits—therefore that Faith must bear fruits of Righteousness. But that, which God seeth, that alone justifieth/ what man seeth doth, in this LIFE, shew that justifying Faith *may* be the root of the things seen—in the life to come, will shew that it actually *is* & *was* the root. *Here* a good life presumes justification, as its only possible tho' still ambiguous Revelation; the absence of a good life not only presumes, but proves, the contrary. Good works may exist without saving principles, therefore cannot contain in themselves the principle of Salvation; but saving principles never did, never can, exist without good works. On a subject of such infinite importance I fear prolixity less than obscurity. Men often talk against Faith, yet themselves judge by the same principle: for what is Love without kind offices? and yet what noble mind values the offices except as *signs* of Love?[3]

8   p 166, pencil | Ch 9 "Christian Life"

Nothing is well done in our spiritual building but what is done =] with prayer and God's help. Fight and pray. Fly and pray.

Pray always?[1]

9   p 171

The world slides into our hearts by the avenues of sense, in cases we little think of. There may be danger in giving ourselves up fully to =] a warm sunshine, or the pleasures of a beautiful landscape. This may be thought morose indeed! But let the militant soul be upon its guard.

To certain characters this is true; but unfortunately those are most likely to act upon it, to whom it is not true—those, to whom a quiet Subjacence to sunshine & natural beauty would be often medicinal. S. T. C.

9A   p 172, pencil

=] Meekness of wisdom compels where Strength of reason cannot persuade.

[7³] This note on justification represents a central position in C's religious thought: see *AR* (1825) 305–9 (Aph XVIII). See LUTHER *Colloquia* *Mensalia* (1652) p 208. See also ANNEX Ch 8 pp 160–1.

[8¹] See BOOK OF COMMON PRAYER COPY B 1 n 1.

9B   p 189, pencil

=] The more I increase in notions only, the more guilt of knowledge and pride Sloth of heart.

10   p 197, pencil

Every spiritual person, at times, is lively, and feels a glow at his heart, in the exercise of faith, prayer, meditation, and reading the scripture; but though he has the same will and desire, yet, in spite of ?] all his efforts, is oftener dull, cold, and unaffected. I can account for this no way, but by the Spirit's agency and presence at one time more than another; because in other intellectual acts and appearances ?] it is not so. Whatever science a man is in pursuit of, the mind is ready at his call, though not always with the same vigour, yet with very little variation or interruption.

See p. 199[1]

11   p 200, pencil

=] "As yet hardenest thou thyself against me, that thou wilt not let sin go?" See the history of Pharaoh.

Oh!—

12   pp 218–19 | Ch 10 "Charity"

The difference between carnal and spiritual love is, that one is *] convergent, the other divergent; one is drawn to a point, like the rays in a burning glass, the other is diffusive, like the rays of the sun . . .

* But may not, must not, different persons be placed in different parts of the divergence? Tho' God be in the Sun, may there not be Mercury & Venus without injury to Saturn & Uranus? Or is this a Temp[t]ation? Sophistry tampering with carnal affections?

13   p 251 | Ch 16 "Miscellaneous"

Let us talk no more of the constitution of this or that country, and the excellence of one above another; it is in every man's power, through grace, to live under the best government in the world.

10[1] On p 199 C has marked a passage for "assent": "Conquest of temptation, deliverance from the power of evil habits, and a ready compliance with the will of God, in answer to prayer, is a much better proof of his favourable presence than joyous feelings. The latter may be mistaken; but the former are as sure a mark of the divine operation and blessing, as that a plentiful crop of corn has had the benefit of rain and sunshine."

Yes! having the Light. But does not Christian Charity command us to be zealous against manifest causes of spiritual Darkness? Does God forbid us to have our eyes open to, our hearts regardful of, clear & uniform Experience? And have we not c. & u. Exp: of the affects of Oppression & Ignorance[1]

14   pp 252–3

What is it to me whether the Americans are in a state of rebellion or not? Why do I not advert more to the rebellion of my own heart and will against God?

Have we then no duties to mankind? Or is it the Monk or Hermit only that performs them? Did not Christ weep over Jerusalem, even as over Lazarus?[1] He wept twice, once in justification of public, & once of private affections. I can easily conceive that such a reflection may arise virtuously from the sense of unchristian excess & of worldly Bustle in the Heart—& may act medicinally on the reflector —but there is danger in propounding such reflections as general Truths, in prescribing *my* medicine for every man's food. S. T. C.

Annex

On the first thirteen pages a number of passages have been marked in the margin with a vertical line in pencil. Although only one passage within these pages (p 10, to show a difference of opinion) is marked with one of the sigla established in **1**, these marks appear to be C's.

Ch 1 "Confessions"

p 1. "I know, with infallible certainty, that I have sinned ever since I could discern between good and evil . . .".

p 2. "I have not made a conscience of improving the talents thou gavest me for the benefit of others and the good of my own soul . . .".

"What pleases God does not please me; but often vexes, frets, hurts me, harrows up my soul."

"Sin is still here, deep in the centre of my heart, and twisted about every fibre of it."

p 3. "Is sin such a plague and burden to me, that I should think myself undone if there was no God to hear and answer my prayers for deliverance from it?"

"Who was it that said, 'I will not sin against my God?' Who says less? Why do not I say it?"

"My great controversy is with myself, and I am resolved to have none with others till I have put things upon a better footing at home."

13[1] The reading "affect", though unexpected, is correct.

14[1] Luke 19.41 and John 11.35.

"Past sin I see and lament; but not present sin, though struggling against it...".

p 4. "Devoted to ease and sloth, never easy but in doing nothing, and always contriving to have nothing to do."

"If I love God, I must love him for his holiness, and how then can I love sin? Nevertheless I have full conviction in myself that I do not hate it as I ought."

"I pray faintly, and with reserve, merely to quiet conscience, for present ease, and almost wishing not to be heard. In a full prayer for full deliverance there is hope."

pp 5–6. "Two things I know with infallible certainty, that I cannot help myself, and that I am unhelped. I have wishes, form resolutions, make efforts, say prayers, mention particular sins; but do not find that I am a jot better. The only hopeful thing in my case is, that I do not despair."

p 6. "I want one point of selfishness, which is to convert the word of God to my own use. All the reflections I make upon the pride, corruption, blindness, and deadly fall of man; upon the necessity of the daily cross, and death to the world, I bestow freely upon others; and am hindered by the deceitfulness of my own heart, and the artifice of the devil, from turning the edge of them upon myself."

p 8. "When I see others astonishingly blind to their failings, I suppose it to be my own case, and should think that man my friend who helps to open my eyes."

p 9. "St. Paul knew human nature but too well, when he said, 'their feet are swift to shed blood.' Romans iii. 15. I protest I am often catching myself at it; and do verily believe that, if we were sincere, we should find within ourselves abundant proof of the assertion."

pp 10–11 (after the first passage marked with a siglum). "When I return to a better temper, after having been under the impressions of black melancholy; that is, from being morose, sullen, discontented, impatient, quarrelsome; I cannot help saying, what a beast and a devil I was; meaning that I am so no longer. An open confession of this kind is looked upon as a mark of great ingenuousness, when, in truth, it is nothing but self-deception, counterfeit humility, and a stratagem to reinstate myself in my own good opinion, or the esteem of others. The stile of the confession should run in the present tense *I am, I am, I am*; for the nature is the same, though at present it may be smoothed over with a handsome appearance, as a filthy puddle is always the same, though it does not always smell alike."

p 11. " '...I will therefore still present myself before the throne of grace, notwithstanding the want of sensible consolations. Fear not, my soul, the operations of the Spirit are in secret, and the daily growth of the spiritual man as imperceptible as that of corn.' Mark iv. 27. John iii. 8."

"I have all my life long been considering what I would do in such and such circumstances, and putting off the season of working to some imaginary period, without ever duly considering what I can do at present, or using the opportunities and abilities I have."

p 12. "I know that I am hateful and contemptible, and yet I cannot help idolizing that painted thing which I myself am...".

p 13. "I would not give myself one hour's trouble for what the world calls immortal glory; and yet I am sure that a sense of reputation, or rather dread of shame, mixes itself with all I do."

Certain paragraphs—in addition to textus **8, 9B, 10, 11**—have been marked by C according to the sigla established in **1**, above.

= means assent to, sympathy

Ch 1 "Confessions"

p 16. "I am perpetually looking out for some fitness in myself, some procuring meritorious cause of God's acceptance of me, as if I could never be safe till I could challenge reward at his hands as a debt...".

p 17. "Till we have a full belief and apprehension of the scripture doctrine of the remission of sins, we are under a kind of necessity of denying, extenuating, and explaining away the guilt of them; and this seals us up in blindness, impenitence, and hardness of heart."

"We are apt to acquiesce in the bare act of prayer, and can be well enough content all our lives to go without the spiritual good things we pray for. The case is plain, we do not desire them."

"For a great part of my life I did not know that I was poor, and naked, and blind, and miserable. I have known it for some time, without feeling it. Thank God, I now begin to be pinched with it. Stand aside Pride, for a moment, and let me see that ugly thing myself."

p 18. "O, my God! grant me not the turbulent feverish transports of a sickly fancy, not the swellings of enthusiastic pride; but freedom from the detested rule of passion, and perpetual serenity from an humble, resigned, obedient, frame of spirit!"

p 24. "I have just enough to keep a sickly hope alive, but not the sense and enjoyment of spiritual health."

p 29. "So long as there is one speck of sin remaining, perfect happiness is impossible."

p 32. "I can see nothing without the Spirit's eyes, but as it were in a mist. I am fully persuaded of the truth of scripture, and what it tells me of sin, myself, God, Christ, and eternity; but with little more effect and true feeling than what I know and believe of some remote country in which I have no manner of concern."

p 39. "It was suggested to my heart and conscience, as by a heavenly voice, that God's command is for an absolute, immediate renunciation of sin, and a perpetual, full obedience, and that every thing short of such a purpose is prevarication, rebellion, misery, death."

Ch 2 "The Scriptures"

p 43. "The design of the Christian religion is to change men's views, lives, and tempers. But how? By the superior excellence of its precepts? By the weight of its exhortations, or the promise of its rewards?—No; but by convincing men of their wretched guilt, blindness, and impotence; by inculcating the necessity of remission, supernatural light and assistance, and actually promising and conveying these blessings."

p 44. "The religion of most men is fixed from nature; that is, worldly ease and convenience, before they come to the reading of the scripture.

The consequence is plain. In all points where it exceeds their standard, it will be pared away."

p 46. "'Son of man, can these dry bones live? Lord God, thou knowest.' Shew me a thought so interesting, so profound, so impressive, and so well expressed in a Pagan author."

"It is an awful, dreadful thing to come full into the light of scripture, and be upon a foot of sincerity with God."

p 48. "It is said of Socrates, that when he believed he was divinely admonished to do any thing, it was impossible to make him take a contrary resolution. How does his example shame those who pretend to receive and believe the scripture as a divine direction, and yet for the most part trample it under their feet?"

p 49. "There is but one kind of happiness in nature for intelligent creatures, viz. that by which God is happy: God is happy in his own will; therefore intelligent creatures can only be happy by their knowledge of, and conformity to, that will."

Ch 3 "God"

p 50. "All spiritual happiness is in God, and inseparable from him, and there is no possibility of the creature's receiving any but by being in him. The gospel only teaches the necessity of this union, and the precious means and mystery of it by Christ."

Ch 4 "Human Depravity"

p 63. "What is the reason of the frequent uneasiness betwixt man and wife; and of their sometimes giving full scope to their passions upon very trifling occasions; even amongst persons who behave with decency, calmness, and general good temper to all others? It is because they think their reputation safe in each other's hands, and therefore are not afraid to discover their natural sourness and malignity."

p 71. "Flying with horror from the thought that we are unfit to die, if God should take us this day and hour out of the world, keeps off the discovery of our true state more than any thing else, and fatally hinders our preparation for it."

p 81. "The more I attempt to murder time, the more life it has to murder me, soul and body: If I put my time in my pocket, it is no excuse to say that I do not carry it to the play-house."

"Time waits upon the soul early every morning, and says, What wilt thou have me to do to-day? It is a shame to say what the answer is, but will one day be known."

p 82. "A full sight of the corruption of human nature, if we exempt ourselves from it in whole or in part, will certainly be followed with a splenetic contempt of others, approaching to misanthropy."

p 83. "I see my sin in every person I meet."

"People never tell more lies than in their prayers."

"Sinning is putting poison into the sting of death."

"It is the hardest thing in the world to call out in earnest for help against one's self, and yet all depends upon it."

p 91. "Sin is against my retirements, against my prayers, against the sacrament, against the bowels and wounds of Christ, against my possession and enjoyment of him, against peace in life and comfort in death, against time, against eternity, against all my hopes."

p 92 (immediately following 5). "If God should do any thing but what he does, in any the minutest instance; send one drop of rain more or less; diminish one pain; heighten one enjoyment; add or take away one moment of life, the consequence might be very bad; and yet, what is almost all the praying in the world for, but to tell him that we are displeased with his will, and desire him to change it."

p 93. "Whenever I spy a fault in another, I am determined to look for two in myself, and they will not be far to seek."

p 97. "... But then, He [God] himself is ever and anon troubling the order of the world and the repose of individuals, by terrible inflictions. The consequence is plain, we are ignorant of our state, and live in a perpetual mistake. God does not make so great reckoning of this life as we do. He aims at the reformation of the heart...".

p 98. "Reading is for the most part only a refined species of sensuality, and answers man's purpose of shuffling off his great work with God and himself, as well as a ball or a masquerade."

Ch 5 "Repentance"

p 113. "... It is by a miracle that any man repents."

Ch 6 "Jesus Christ"

p 118. "Christ is God, stooping to the senses, and speaking to the heart of man."

Ch 8 "Good Works"

p 150. "Human perfection is reality of desire, and sincerity of endeavour, and that in Christ is accepted; perfect righteousness was attained only by Christ, and that is imputed...".

p 156. "Justification by sanctification is man's way to heaven, and it is odds but he will make a little serve the turn. Sanctification by justification is God's, and he fills the soul with his own fulness."

pp 156–7. "The maintainers of imputed righteousness must be content to undergo the mortification of being thought opposers or discouragers of good works: Though they constantly plead for them, and for their own doctrine as the best, if not the only sure way of attaining to them; do not come a whit behind their adversaries in the performance of them, and perform them more freely and sincerely, and upon more generous principles of love, gratitude, and obedience, than those who venture all upon their own actions, and make them the ground of their acceptance."

p 157. " 'Without holiness no man shall see the Lord.' But then holiness is not the foundation of our reward."

"It is impossible for God to forgive an unrepenting sinner; and he does not repent who does not purpose and wish to be changed."

"I know and believe that all I am, have, or can be, without charity is nothing: But I do not believe in charity for my acceptance with God."

p 158. "It is next to impossible to do good actions, merely because they are good, till we are in possession of that principle so strenuously asserted by Martin Luther, viz. That our Salvation is wholly of faith; and that good works are only a ground of comfort, as proofs of our faith, but signify nothing to our acceptance with God."

"It is impossible for a proud man to have so much as one virtue; he wants the very essence of all virtue, viz. disinterestedness and a pure love of rectitude."

p 159. "What, for instance, is the greatest affability and condescension, without a root of true humility; forbearance of the outward act, without inward purity; patience without thankfulness; beneficence without love...".

"Christ's cross truly believed will have two seemingly different effects; it will put me upon being as good as ever I can, and make me sensible that I am altogether vile."

p 160. "...and whenever obedience puts itself in the place of faith, St. Paul's words may fitly be applied to it, 'know that thou bearest not the root, but the root thee'". (7 follows.)

pp 160–1. "If I have faith in Christ, I shall love him; if I love him, I shall keep his commandments; if I do not keep his commandments, I do not love him; if I do not love him, I do not believe in him."

Ch 9 "Christian Life"

pp 162–3. "In heaven we shall have a perfect knowledge of sin, far beyond any thing we now conceive of it, in conjunction with the greatness of our deliverance; and the glory of redeeming mercy will be the eternal ground of our love and admiration. On earth it is the great exercise of faith, and one of the hardest things in the world, to see sin and Christ at the same time, or to be penetrated with a lively sense of our desert, and absolute freedom from condemnation: But the more we know of both, the nearer approach we shall make to the state of heaven; and are our own greatest enemies, if...we do not look unto Jesus."

p 163. "Repent, and believe; believe, and love; love, and obey; obey in love; and be as happy as you can be in this world."

p 166. (Before **8**.) "The spirit in the children of God is like an organ; one man is one stop; another, another; the sound is different, the instrument the same, but music in all."

p 168. "In case of sin allowed, or weakly resisted, the conscience will not be quieted with hopes and promises; no, nor with the blood of Christ."

p 171. (In **9** textus, but marked separately by C.) "The World slides into our hearts by the avenues of sense, in cases we little think of. There may be danger in giving ourselves up fully to warm sunshine, or the pleasures of a beautiful landscape."

p 174. "Peace with God, and peace with all the world, and with all nature.—See *Hosea* ii. 18. and the parallel places."

p 185. "Have a work to do daily, with a will to it, and a prayer upon it, and let that work be God's."

p 199. "Sensible communications may be, and are, often withheld from the best of men; the better they are, the more they desire perfect conformity to the will of God as their portion and happiness." (See also **10** n 1.)

"Happy man! when that hallelujah is the experience of my soul, 'The Lord God omnipotent reigneth!'"

Ch 10 "Charity"

p 208. "If I hate any one, I love none truly."

p 212. "Self neither can, nor perhaps ought to be totally excluded from religion: But where it is the great motive, can there be any religion?"

p 217. "Memorandum. To have no controversy (if possible) with any one but myself."

Ch 12 "Prayer"

p 234. "Nothing is more easy than to say the words of a prayer; but to pray hungering and thirsting is the hardest of all works."

"Praying with the heart, for the heart, is praying by the Spirit, whether with or without a form."

"Blessed be God, I do not only begin to pray when I kneel down, but leave not off praying when I rise up."

Ch 15 "Heaven"

pp 248–9. "Delight in the will of God is the perfection of all intelligent beings, the essence of happiness, the joy of angels, heaven upon earth, and the heaven of heaven."

Ch 16 "Miscellaneous"

p 252. "Hell is truth seen too late."

||difference, either in opinion, or in consciousness of my own individual character

Ch 1 "Confessions"

p 10. "Strange, that I should be conscious of such a nature, and yet unhumbled! but then at the worst, and in the worst of men, there is still a capability of goodness...".

p 16. "I see enough in others for a ground in all to be humble; and yet this very thing prevents me from being so."

p 19. "Little children have but one appetite, know what they want, and can be quieted with nothing else. Would to God I was so."

p 33. "I could tear my heart out for not being God's. I have been deceived all my life by sayings of philosophers, scraps of verses, and most of all by the pride of my own heart, into an opinion of self-power, which the scripture plainly tells me, and I find by repeated fruitless efforts, that I have not."

? doubt

Ch 2 "The Scriptures"

p 48. "It is impossible, in the nature of things, that so burdensome and expensive an institution, as that of Moses, should ever have been received by the Jews, but upon sufficient evidence of its being divine. *See Stillingfleet's Orig. Sac.* Vol. II. c. I. p 116."[1]

---

[1] Did Adam send C to Poole's copy   (1675) at this time?
of STILLINGFLEET *Origines Sacrae*

JOHANN CHRISTOPH ADELUNG
1732–1806

Deutsche Sprachlehre für Schulen. Dritte vermehrte und verbesserte Auflage. Mit alle gnädigen Privilegien. Berlin 1795. 8°.

Victoria College Library (Coleridge Collection)

Autograph signature "S. T. Coleridge" in an early hand at the head of the title-page.
In c 1817 C made up a small German grammar for HC based on this book. See *CN* III 4336.

DATE. Unknown; possibly 1798–9 in Germany.

COEDITOR. Lore Metzger.

1 p 306, pencil, cropped | Theil I *Von der Fertigkeit richtig zu reden*. Abschnitt ii "Von den Arten der Wörter oder den Redetheilen überhaupt". Kapitel 12 "Von den Präpositionen". §§540–1

§. 540. Anstatt, oder kürzer statt, bezeichnet das Verhältniss, da [in]stead of etwas an der Statt oder Stelle eines andern geschiehet: anstatt oder statt des Fürsten war ein Minister da. . . .

§. 541. Halb, halben und halber, von dem alten Hauptworte die Halbe, die Seite. Halb bezeichnet das Verhältniss des Ortes, die Gegend, Richtung oder Seite, lebt aber nur noch in ausserhalb,[1] innerhalb,[2] oberhalb [3] und unterhalb,[4] welche alle den Genitiv erfordern; also nicht innerhalb drey Tagen, sondern dreyer Tage. Halben und halber[5] bezeichnen einen Bewegungsgrund; beyde werden dem Substantive nachgesetzt, halber aber stehet am liebsten, wenn dasselbe keinen Artikel hat: ich thue es der Freundschaft halben, deiner Laster halben, Alters halber, Scheins halber; welche ohne Noth und Grund zusammen gezogen werden, scheinshalber.

[§ 540. *Anstatt* (instead of), or the abbreviated form *statt*, designates the relation of something happening instead of or in place of something else: *anstatt* or *statt* (instead of) the sovereign, the minister was there. . . .

§ 541. *Halb, halben* and *halber* (for the sake of, on account of), from the obsolete noun *die Halbe* (half), *die Seite* (side). *Halb* designates the relation of place, vicinity, direction or position but survives only in *ausserhalb* (without, outside of),[1] *innerhalb* (within, inside of),[2] *oberhalb* (above, on the upper side of)[3] and *unterhalb* (below, on the lower side

20

of),[4] all of which govern the genitive; hence not *innerhalb drey Tagen* (inside three days) but *dreyer Tagen* (inside of three days). *Halben* and *halber* (for the sake of)[5] denote a motive; both follow the noun, but *halber* is preferred when the noun is used without an article: I do it *der Freundschaft halben* (for friendship's sake), *deiner Laster halben* (on account of your vices), *Alters halber* (in consideration of age), *Scheins halber* (for appearance's sake), which without rhyme or reason is contracted as *scheinshalber*.]

[1]
   [wi]thout
2
   [wit]hin
[3]
   [on th]e higher side
4
   [on the l]ower side
5
   [on] account of

2   p 307, pencil, cropped | ɪ ii 12 §§542–4

§. 542. Kraft[1] und laut[2] sind eigentlich Substantiva, wovon das erste als Präposition das Verhältniss der wirkenden Ursache, und letzteres des Erkenntniss-grundes bezeichnet: kraft der Gesetze, kraft des mir aufgetragenen Amts; laut des königlichen Befehls, wofür im Curialstyle auch besage und inhalts gebraucht werden. Mittelst, edler vermittelst, von Mittel,[3] kündiget das Verhältniss eines Mittels, einer Beyhülfe an: mittelst göttlicher Hülfe, vermittelst deines Beystandes.

§. 543. Ungeachtet,[4] nicht so richtig unerachtet, und noch weniger ohnerachtet, druckt das Verhältniss der unterlassenen Rücksicht aus: Ungeachtet seiner Geschicklichkeit überging man ihn doch; am liebsten aber hinter dem Substantive, seiner Geschicklichkeit ungeachtet; alles dessen ungeachtet. Der Dativ, dem ungeachtet, oder wohl gar dem ohnerachtet, lässt sich mit nichts entschuldigen. Unweit[5] und das grossen Theils veraltete unfern bezeichnen das Verhältniss der Nähe: unweit der Stadt, des Hauses. Nicht so richtig ist hier der Dativ, unweit dem Hause, welche Form durch von ergänzet werden muss, unweit von dem Hause, in welchem Falle unweit als ein blosses Adverbium stehet. Vermöge[6] ersetzt das Verhältniss der wirkenden Ursache, des Mittels, des Grundes: das kann ich vermöge meines Rechtes nicht zugeben; vermöge des Testamentes ist Cajus Erbe.

§. 544. Während,[7] eigentlich das Participium des Verbi wären, ist für das Verhältniss der Dauer einer andern Handlung: während der Zeit, da dieses geschahe, nicht während Zeit; während unsers Gespräches geschahe es; während des Krieges; während dessen.

[§ 542. *Kraft* (by virtue of, by power of)[1] and *laut* (according to)[2] are actually nouns used as prepositions, the former pertaining to agent, the latter to motive: by power of the law, in pursuance of the duties of my office, according to royal command, for which legal style also uses *besage* (in conformity with) and *inhalts* (concerning). *Mittelst* (through), more formally *vermittelst*, and *von Mittel* (by means of)[3] indicate the relation of means or of assistance: through divine aid, by means of your support.

§ 543. *Ungeachtet* (notwithstanding),[4] or less correctly *unerachtet* (heedless of), or even less correctly *ohnerachtet* (regardless of), expresses the relation of disregard or heedlessness: he was passed over in spite of his ability. It is best placed after the noun: his ability notwithstanding; all that notwithstanding. The dative, *dem ungeachtet* (for all that), or even *dem ohnerachtet*, is utterly inexcusable. *Unweit* (not far from)[5] and the largely obsolete *unfern* designate the relation of proximity: not far from the city or from the house. The dative, *unweit dem Hause* (near the house), is less correct here and must be completed by *von* (from), *unweit von dem Hause* (not far from the house), in which case *unweit* becomes merely an adverb. *Vermöge* (by means of, by virtue of)[6] is substituted for the relation of agent, means or cause: I cannot concede this by reason of my rights, Cajus is heir by power of the testament.

§ 544. *Während* (during),[7] actually a participle of the verb *währen* (to continue, to endure), expresses the relation to the duration of another action: during the time that this happened and not *währender Zeit* (continually); it happened during our conversation, during the war, during the same.]

1

   by power [of]

2

   according [to]

3

   by mean[s of]

4

   notwiths[tanding]

5

   not far from—

6

   by means [of] &c &c.

7

   during

3 p 308, pencil, cropped | ɪ ii 12 §§544–5

Wegen[1] von dem Wurzellaute weg mit der adverbischen Ableitungs-
sylbe en, bezeichnet das Verhältniss der bewegenden Ursache; und
stehet sowohl vor als nach dem Substantive: wegen seines Fleisses,
seines Fleisses wegen. Es mit dem Dative zu verbinden, wegen seinem
Fleisse, ist im Hochdeutschen fehlerhaft. . . .

§. 545. 2. Den Dativ allein erfordern: aus, ausser, bey, entgegen,
mit, nach, nächst, zunächst, nebst, sammt, seit, von, zu, zuwider,
und die veralteten ab, binnen, und ob; wovon die vornehmsten in
folgenden Versen enthalten sind:

Daphnis an die Quelle.

2

Nach dich schmacht ich, zu dir eil ich, du gelibte Quelle du!

4

Ans dir schöpf ich, bey dir ruh ich, seh dem Spiel der Wellen zu;

6

Mit dir scherz ich, von dir lern ich heiter durch das Leben wallen,
Angelacht von Frühlingblumen, und begrüsst von Nachtigallen,

Ramler.

[*Wegen* (because of, on account of),[1] from the root syllable *weg* (way)
and the adverbial suffix *en*, designates the relation of causal agent and is
placed before as well as after a noun: because of his diligence, for his
diligence's sake. To use it with the dative, *wegen seinem Fleisse* (owing to
his diligence), is incorrect in High German. . . .

§. 545. 2. [Prepositions] governing only the dative: *aus* (out of), *ausser*
(beyond), *bey* (near, beside), *entgegen* (against, opposite), *mit* (with),
nach (after), *nächst* (next), *zunächst* (close to), *nebst* (beside), *sammt*
(together), *seit* (since), *von* (from), *zu* (to), *zuwider* (contrary to), and the
obsolete *ab*, *binnen*, and *ob* (during). The most important of these occur in
the following lines:

Daphne to the Spring

For you I yearn, to you I fly, my beloved spring!
From you I drink, near you I rest and watch the waves play;
With you I jest, from you I learn to journey serenely through life,
Smiled upon by spring flowers and greeted by nightingales.

Ramler.]

1
  [on] account of
2
  /to
4
  of/ by
6
  out/ from

AESCHYLUS
525–456 B.C.

Αἰσχυλου, Ἀγαμεμνων τριγλωττος. Graece. Textum ad fidem editionum, praesertim Blomfieldianae, recognovit, notasque anglice conscriptas et indices adjecit, Jacobus Kennedy...Teutsch. Übersetzt von Heinrich Voss. English. Translated by James Kennedy. Dublin 1829. 8º.

British Museum C 126 h 16

Inscribed by C on the title-page: "Given me by dear Mʳ Anster, on his visit to us fro[m] Ireland, July 1829. S. T. Coleridge. Grove, Highgate." Monogram "C" of John Duke Coleridge, 1st Baron Coleridge, on p ⁻4; "S. T. C." label on title-page.

Anster's visit, marked by intimate conversation, gave C unusual pleasure: *CL* vi 792–5. See also A NSTER, below.

DATE. Jul 1829.

1 pp 38–9, pencil, cropped | *Agamemnon* lines 140–3

> τόσον περ εὔφρων ἁ καλὰ
> * δρόσοις ἀέπτοις μαλερῶν [λεόντων]
> πάντων τ᾽ ἀγρονόμων φιλομάστοις
> θηρῶν ὀβρικάλοισιν.

[...so she, the beautiful, benevolent to the young—still unable to follow their mothers—of fierce lions and to the breast-loving offspring of all country-haunting wild beasts.]

* Qʸ. δρομοις αεπτοις? the syntax being, η καλη δρομοις αεπτοις ευφρων (ουσα) λεοντων παντων τε αγρονομων φιλομαστοις &c—/ She the beautiful in unfollowed races—benevolent to the young of all the wild beasts—.¹ There is a similar passage in the Psalms.²—I am

1¹ Of these lines the edition by J. D. Denniston and D. Page (Oxford 1957) says: "Text and interpretation are extremely doubtful", but no editor has found it necessary to alter δρόσοις (dewdrops). C's dictionaries would have told him that "dewdrops" was a familiar Greek figure for young creatures, and previous editions of the *Agamemnon*, including Blomfield's (1st ed Cambridge 1818), quoted examples of other words for "dew" as used to describe young animals. Kennedy in this ed makes no comment at this point. C's translation, if his emendation is accepted, gives an accurate account of the syntax and is more direct and economical than Kennedy's. Textus tr is the editor's, following the Greek as closely as possible.

1² Ps 84.3?

24

strongly disposed to [think the text of this] Pl[ay] unusually corrupt[3]
—The too [. . . . .]
Prometheus by an inferior mind./ The ill effect of the ponderou[s]
Epithets & similar tricks for inducing the reader to look at fleas [&]
flies thro' a magnifying Glass MILTON seems to have felt—see hi[s]
Paradise Regained./[4]

1[3] Wilomowitz gave a long list of corrupt readings for all Aeschylus' plays, most of which could never have been restored but for quotations in ancient sources outside the primary mss. E. Fraenkel (Oxford 1950) says that "Fate has not been too kind to the text of the *Agamemnon*", but the passage C is discussing happens to fall within the parts of the play (lines 1–310, 1067–1159) preserved in the Medicean MS, the least problematical of the mss of *Agamemnon*.

1[4] In *Paradise Regained* IV lines 343–7 the Son of God says of the poetry of the Greeks: "Remove their swelling epithets, thick laid | As varnish on a harlot's cheek; the rest | Thin sown with aught of profit or delight, | Will far be found unworthy to compare | With Sion's songs...". When C discussed the charge that his early poems were guilty of "a general turgidness of diction and a profusion of new-coined epithets", he cited Milton and Shakespeare as writers who, by authority of practice, enjoined purity of diction. *BL* ch 1 (1907) I 2n. The effect of C's proposed translation is to redistribute the accumulation of epithets, but his version, made to elucidate the syntax, does not attempt to include all the epithets that occur in the Greek original.

Αἰσχύλου Προμηθεύς Δεσμώτης. Aeschyli Prometheus vinctus. Ad fidem manuscriptorum emendavit notas et glossarium adjecit Carolus Jacobus Blomfield, &c. [Edition not identified] Cambridge 1810 or 1812. 8º

First use of the Porson Greek types. See BEAUMONT & FLETCHER COPY B **10** n 1.

Not located. Annotations printed from MS TRANSCRIPT.

Henry Francis Cary's copy, which C returned to him, together with his edition of the *Persae* (1814), on 6 Nov 1817 with the comment: "I hope, the Cambridge Professor will go thro' the remaining plays of Eschylus— They are delightful Editions." *CL* IV 781. Blomfield also edited *Septem contra Thebas* (1810), *Agamemnon* (1818), and *Choephoroe* (1824), as well as three of the lyric poets for *Poetae minores graeci* (1823), of which C owned a copy (not annotated). See also BLOMFIELD *A Charge* (1830).

MS TRANSCRIPT. VCL LT 50a: EHC.

DATE. c Oct 1817.

1   ? p 2 | *Prometheus vinctus* lines 14–15

> ἐγὼ δ' ἄτολμός εἰμι συγγενῆ θεὸν
> δῆσαι βίᾳ φάραγγι * πρὸς δυσχειμέρῳ.

[Tr H. W. Smith (LCL 1922): "But for me—I cannot nerve myself to bind amain a kindred god upon this rocky cleft assailed by cruel winter."]

* Anglicé *A Coomb*.[1]

2   ? p 2 | line 17

> εὐωριάζειν γὰρ πατρὸς λόγους βαρύ.

[Tr Smith: "For 'tis perilous to disregard the commandments of the Father."]

[1] In his "Glossarium" (p 90) Blomfield notes (in Latin): "Φάραγξ. A valley between steep mountain slopes. Stephanus, in the *Appendix* to his *Thesaurus*, and others translate it *precipice*, not accurately enough. The MS Lexicon of Cyrillus has φάραγξι— hollow places between mountains the *Etymologicum Magnum* p. 787, 41, φάραγξ—a cleft in the earth." C's word "combe" is not only supported by Blomfield's definition, but also shows his characteristic taste for a local term familiar to him in West Country usage. He used the word "coomb" only once in a poem—in line 2 of *Brockley Coomb. PW* (EHC) I 94.

Still I should prefer ἐξωριάζειν,[1] notwithstanding its being an ἅπαξ λεγομενον.[2] The ευ seems to my *tact* too free and easy a word: and yet "our" "*to trifle with*" seems the exact meaning.[3]

2[1] Ms TRANSCRIPT begins this note with the words "εὐωριάζεινα word introduced into the text against the authority of all editions and manuscripts." *LR* prints the sentence as though it were part of C's note, but it is evidently the transcriber's summary of Blomfield's note to line 17, which reads (in Latin): "Ἐξωριάζειν is the reading of all editions and MSS. Porson obelizes the word. Hesychius moreover has: 'εὐωριάζειν, to despise, take no thought, disregard. Sophocles uses the word in *The Syrian Women*.' Photius's *Lexicon* (in MS) has: 'εὐωριάζειν, to be heedless' and Porson

considered this to be the correct reading in this passage. Schutz silently writes ἐξωριάζειν in the Hesychius entry, whereas the word exists only in this place [i.e. in *Prometheus*]."

2[2] Most more recent editors agree with Blomfield in preferring εὐωριάζειν. C knew from Blomfield's note that ἐξωριάζειν was a word that "occurs only once".

2[3] The prefix εὐ means "well". As in his choice of the word "combe", C again shows a sensitive approach to possible subtle shades of meaning in the Greek. On "tact" see DANTE COPY B 4 n 1.

THE AGE

The Age. A poem. In eight books. London 1829. 8º.

British Museum C 43 c 10

Inscribed in pencil on p ‾3 (p-d) in an unidentified hand: "S. T. Coleridge MS Notes".

The author is not identified. *The Age* was published by Hurst, Chance & Co, the publisher of *C&S*; C's copy could have come to him either from the author or from the publisher on publication. The book was unfavourably reviewed in *Athenaeum* 29 Apr 1829 (p 259).

DATE. Probably 1829.

1   pp 184–5, 187–8, pencil | Bk v, near the end

> But faith like this, is seldom found; and youth
> Especially are weak ...
>   —They cannot bear
> The taunting laugh, the foul-mouthed stigma cast
> Upon them in their course, by men whose sense
> And rationality in all beside
> They estimate not lightly.—Or perchance
> X The rougher usage is withheld; the laugh
> Becomes the smile of pity, and the taunt
> Is softened to the milder charge of fond
> Enthusiasm and over righteous zeal ...
> What! shall the ardour of sincerity
> Inspiring the vain, frivolous pursuits
> Of honours, wealth, and unsubstantial fame
> Be justified by mortals,—when they treat
> X Sincerity and ardour in the cause
> Most fitting for the soul of man ...

I too will suppose myself speaking to a Theresa, but a Theresa in this World[1]—and I would say to her—Have you found any one among

1[1] Theresa is the central figure in the poem. Carried off at an early age by "Consumption, ghastly spectre" and now established as "pure and perfect" spirit in a grove of contemplation in heaven, she is joined by her brother Lucius, who obliges her by singing "a song of the world" (pp 5–6). The anonymous author's intention is clearly stated:

28

those whom you calledl dear friends, who has tried to taunt, smile, or coax you out of "sincerity and ardour in the cause Most fitting for a human Soul"—that is, the renewal of the divine image within you by the watchful and zealous cultivation of whatever is truly and essentially your *Humanity*, that by which as you had the title, Man or woman, in contra-distinction from the Animal, given you by your Creator—when God said, But MAN we will create in our own image. —Man and Woman created he him.[2]—If you have found any such false Friend, turn from him as from a Poisoner. But if your friend should only seek to guard you against the snares of & "prejudices[a] of certain shrivelled, proselyting, censorious Religionists,"[3] who would have you regard Religion and the Christian Faith, as a particular *trade*, that is to engross all your thoughts in the ostensible technical forms and instruments of this trade—instead of being as it indeed is, the Spirit of Truth, of Love, and Light, and Purity, that should diffuse itself thro' your whole *humanity*, the friend, the helper and the perfecter of whatever can make you happy, and the occasion of innocent happiness to to those around you, of all honorable, all useful, all seemly things[4]—devotional habits and the Love of your blessed Saviour, the *man*, Jesus, and the faith in him, being the Key-stone of all—from such a friend neither be coaxed away, nor frightened away. S. T. Coleridge—

2   pp 231–2 | Bk VII §5

> Young, beautiful was she; her parents' joy,
> And the sole prop of their declining age.
> And happy was she,—and perhaps had been
> For ever happy,—but in evil hour,
> Her lover took her to the theatre;—
> Thence date her sorrow and her misery.

Not in the fictions of poetry but in the records of our criminal Courts may we find similar results and consequences not less tragic, from

---

[a] At the turn of the page C has written: "(turn over to p. 187—"

The Age
To sing I purpose; with its characters,
Its virtues, vices, signs, realities,
And vain pretensions—chiefly as relate
To thee, O Britain, isle beloved, my home,
My country...

and he proposes to "sound an awful warning, and to bear | Witness against an age of fools and crime".

[1][2] Cf Gen 1.26–7.

[1][3] This phrase does not appear in *The Age* and seems to be C's improvisation in the manner of the poem.

[1][4] Cf Phil 4.8.

evening attendance on the Conventicle. Many a poor wretch has dated her fall, from the evil hour, Her Lover took her to the Methodist Barn, or half-lit Chapel.—But neither Theatre nor Conventicle can be wisely considered as the *cause* of the depravity, tho' both may be accessories; and the latter more influentially, perhaps, than the former. For religious (more accurately, irreligious) Fanaticism is a species of Concupiscence—alike in its source, in its manifestations and in its products sensual.[1] S. T. Coleridge.

THOMAS AMORY

c 1691–1788

LOST BOOK

The Life of John Buncle, Esq. [Edition not identified.] (1st ed: 2 vols London 1756.)

Not located; marginalia not recorded. *Lamb SC* (1848) 56. *Lost List*.

Charles Lamb's copy with C's marginalia. Lamb first introduced the book to C in Jun 1797: *LL* I 110.

---

[2][1] See also DE WETTE 13.

ANALYSIS

Analysis of the Report of a Committee of the House of Commons on the Extinction of Slavery. With notes by the editor [? Thomas Pringle]. London 1833. 8⁰.

"Printed for the Society for the Abolition of Slavery Throughout the British Dominions". Dated "January 1833". The *Analysis* is an abstract of the "655 closely printed folio pages" of evidence heard by the Parliamentary Committee sitting from 6 Jun to 11 Aug 1832.

Bound as second in "Pamphlets on the Slave Trade", a volume comprising three tracts on the slave-trade 1821–33 (two of them annotated by C) made up after C's death.

British Museum C 126 h 14(2)

Inscribed in ink on the title-page: "S. T. Coleridge Esq with Mʳ Pringles best regards".

Thomas Pringle (1789–1834), after emigrating with his family to South Africa in 1820, returned to England in 1826 and became secretary to the Anti-Slavery Society, of which Clarkson and Wilberforce were vice-presidents. Clarkson recommended that Pringle write the history of the abolition of the slave-trade, adding: "You have all the documents before you in the minutes of the Committee". *Poetical Works of Thomas Pringle* ed L. Ritchie (1838) xcvi. There is a strong inference that Pringle, already an experienced editor, edited this *Analysis*.

In Mar 1828 C wrote to Pringle, admiring his poem *Afar in the Desert*, which he had read in George Thompson's *Travels and Adventures in Southern Africa* (2 vols 1827), saying that he had ordered a copy of Thompson's book and inviting Pringle to visit him in Highgate. *CL* vi 732. Pringle responded by presenting C with a copy of his *Ephemerides* (1828), the first volume of South African poetry to be published. In 1831, as C knew, Pringle had taken a hand in trying to have C's RSL annuity restored. *CL* vi 867–8.

In c Jun 1833 C wrote to Pringle—possibly in response to receiving the copy of the *Analysis*—declaring himself "an ardent & almost life-long Denouncer of Slavery". *CL* vi 939–41. The correspondence from Aug 1833 onwards—by which time Pringle was living in Highgate and editing *Friendship's Offering*—is concerned with the poems that were to be published in the 1834 issue (*CL* vi 949–53, 954–5, 957, 962), but on at least one occasion C returned to the subject of slavery (*CL* vi 952–3).

DATE. 1833, before Aug.

1 title-page verso, pencil

We, the undersigned Members of the Legislatures of Jamaica, Antigua &c &c having thought proper, on sundry and grievous provocations to disinheritimpropriate the King of Great Britain of that large & valuable Mass of devoted Loyalty, known commonly under the name of "prepared to sacrifice the last shilling in our purse & the last drop of blood in our veins"/ do hereby set up the same, as forfeited goods, to foreign Auction:—

General Andrew Jackson!—say, what shall it be put up at?—Favor us with the first Bid!—[1]

Make haste!—we espied Louis Philippe, Emperor Nicholas, with Nicholas Senior from below stairs, & Ibrahim Pacha and the Ex-dey of Algiers./[2]

2 pp 1, 4, pencil

[Constitution and terms of reference of the committee]

Mem.—Would it not be well for the Government to enquire, of each estate, in Jamaica for instance, & then in the other Islands,—Who *are* the *real* Possessors, in distinction from the nominal? What & how many of them, are mortgaged or otherwise made liable for their products, equal to or beyond the now marketable Value of the Estates? *Then* we should know, how far the temulent Members of the Colonial Legislatures are or are not the bonâ fide Proprietors.—It surprizes me, that the *Mortgagees* in London, Bristol & Liverpool, in so many cases the true Owners, are not more on the Alert! That they do not see how clearly *their* interest connects them with the Government, and with its efforts & objects.

3 pp 2–3, pencil

[The two Propositions which the Committee was charged to investigate:] 1st. That the Slaves, if emancipated, would maintain them-

---

1[1] Andrew Jackson (1767–1845), who had won the Battle of New Orleans at the end of the War of 1812, had been elected President of the U.S. for a second term in 1832. The doctrine of "manifest destiny" may have suggested to C that American expansion might soon absorb the British colonies.

1[2] A collection of unsavoury rogues: Louis Philippe (1773–1850), proclaimed King of the French at the July Revolution in 1830; Nicholas of Russia (1796–1855), Emperor since 1825, notorious for his stern suppression of the Polish uprising in 1830–1; "Old Nick" from down below; Ibrahim Pasha (1789–1848), Egyptian general, governor of Syria in 1833 after a series of spectacular victories in Syria and against the Turks; Hussein Pasha, the last Dey of Algiers, expelled by the French in 1830.

selves, would be industrious, and disposed to acquire property by labour.

*] 2nd. That the dangers of convulsion are greater from freedom withheld, than from freedom granted to the slaves.

* Assuredly, *this* should have been the *first* position. Then, supposing it to have been proved, the other would have been corroborative —in other words, 1. That the danger of speedy Emancipation is less & less imminent than that of rejection or indefinite Delay—2. That the ~~danger~~ Evil of the former is exaggerated, ~~and~~ as far as it rests on the assumption that no motive can be substituted for that of the Lash & immediate physical Compulsion—[1]

4   p 6, pencil

[Among the witnesses before the Committee, seeking to demonstrate the inexpediency of early emancipation, was] WILLIAM ALERS HANKEY, Esq., a banker of London . . . late treasurer of the London Missionary Society, who is a proprietor of 300 slaves in the island of Jamaica, but who has never visited the West Indies.

Is it quite fair or consistent with the facts thus to place M[r] Hankey in the same list with Capt[n] Williams, the Scotts, Shands &c?—[1]

5   p 7, pencil

During that time he [William Shand] had under his charge 18 or 20,000 slaves, residing occasionally in almost every parish in the island.

I cannot but find a too great disposition to widen the difference between the Friends of immediate and the Advocates of Gradual Emancipation/ To me they appear to differ much more in the *word* than in the measure itself.

3[1] See also 5 and 9, which continue this line of argument. Cf also Henry GREY, Viscount Howick *Corrected Report of the Speech of Viscount Howick...on Colonial Slavery* (1833), bound in this same volume of tracts. Grey was a member of the parliamentary committee.

4[1] Three of the twenty-one slave-owners who gave evidence against early or immediate emancipation: the names are listed on pp 5–7 with biographical summary. Capt Charles Hampden Williams RN gave evidence on the strength of five days ashore in West Indian slave estates; Robert Scott had owned 400 slaves during his seven years in the West Indies; William Shand, resident in the West Indies for thirty-four years, a magistrate and member of Assembly, had handled between 18,000 and 20,000 slaves.

6   p 22, pencil | Evidence of W. Taylor, Esq (*pro*)

[Taylor gives an account of the estate of Mr Wildman, a humane man who forbad corporal punishment; yet his overseers inflicted it.]

How unhappy a state of mind must that of a humane and religious Planter's be.[1]

7   pp 59–61, pencil | Evidence of the Rev P. Duncan (*pro*)

Inconveniences might possibly arise, both to master and slave, from any great and sudden change, like that of emancipation, as they arise more or less from all great changes. But it is Mr. Duncan's firm opinion, that, even if the Negroes were emancipated at a stroke, there would not be that loss or disturbance which must ensue if emancipation is long delayed. Emancipation might take place with perfect tranquillity, if a proper police were established. [Duncan then spoke of the possible transfer of land to freed Negroes in return for labour, of the superior character of the "religiously-instructed slaves", and of the violent opposition of most planters to religious instruction because it encouraged the slaves' desire for freedom.]

As to plans of emancipation, Mr. Duncan thought that all partial plans would fail of their effect. The best was that of emancipating all children born after a certain day, but even that was attended with great and perhaps insuperable difficulties. Still that would be better than nothing. The only plan not attended with very great, perhaps insuperable difficulties, is a general emancipation. Not that there are not great difficulties in the way of that measure, but they were more easily overcome.

Preparatives. 1. Stipendiary Magistracy. 2. Organized Police/ 3. Means of Instruction, Schools, Chapels/. *Then*, from Jan[y] 1835,

---

6[1] In N Q a leaf has been tipped in between f 25[v] and f 26 with a note by C referring to p 28 of this *Analysis*. Possibly it was once loose in this pamphlet. "...Decrease in the Negro Population accounted for in part by the frequent miscarriages of the Females caused by *whipping* in the earlier periods of Pregnancy. Merciful Heaven! and this, ~~with~~ and all the other atrocities of which this is but a specimen, to obtain Sugar from the W. Indian Islands at 10[d] a pound which we might get elsewhere for 6[d]!— That is, for the sake of making two or three hundred superfluous Rich Men in a Nation already pauperized by having too many! And lastly, utterly failing in this insane purpose, and producing instead a squad of bankrupt, over-mortgaged Proprietors with a retinue of rapacious, needy, dishonest, and cruel Attorneys, Managers, and Overseers, the ever-rising Scum, to the periodical depuration of which by the [...] of Emigration Scotland mainly owes her character of Probity and Religion. S. T. C."

all Children, born in marriage, free by birth.[1] 2. The Slave Population to be emancipated, each year, one tenth, for three days/ At the close of the year following, wholly emancipated—their places being then filled by the 10th of the following class, now half-emancipated—& so on, the priority being the premium of 1. moral good conduct & industry. 2. Progress in religious instruction. 3. Ability to read the Gospel—

At the end of the tenth year all would be free—or from incurable depravity under the control of Law. And from the very beginning all would be so far emancipated, that they would cease to be Mancipia = things, & become Persons,[2] tho' not at first jure suo, but sub tutelâ, as Wards & Clients of the Law./[3]

7[1] C inserted a hypothetical date. Grey left the date open in his *Speech* (p 61). After the Whigs came into power, the Emancipation Bill was passed in Aug 1833, releasing 800,000 slaves and providing a fund of £20 million to compensate slave-owners; see also *CL* VI 939n for a summary of proceedings. The outcome of the debate was in doubt when C wrote his notes.

7[2] *Mancipia*—pieces of property legally acquired; the word was used especially of slaves considered as chattels. The "sacred distinction between Person and Thing, which is the Light and the Life of all Law, human and divine" (TAYLOR *Polemicall Discourses*—1674—i 898) had been a central insistence of C's for many years, and is a key to his views on marriage and social organisation as well as slavery. He had formulated his position clearly by Oct 1809. See *Friend* (*CC*) II 125=I 189–90; cf *TT* 18 Dec 1831 and *LS* (*CC*) 219–20 and n. See also *CN* III 3317, *CL* VI 929. When C wrote: "Men, I still think, ought to be weighed not counted. Their *worth* ought to be the final estimate of their value" (*LS—CC—*211), he can hardly have foreseen, after the slave-trade had been finally abolished, the incredulous shock of horror that Primo Levi was to feel in 1944 when, at the mustering of Italian Jews for transport to Auschwitz, a

corporal in reply to his officer's question "Wieviel Stück?" reported that "there were six hundred and fifty 'pieces' and that all was in order". Primo Levi *Se questa e un huomo* (Turin 1958) tr Stuart Woolf (1959) 7.

In a footnote (pp 178–81) to the evidence given by Wildman, the editor corrected him on "the law as to slave evidence" by quoting two sections of the statute of 1831. The two following sections on p 180 are marked in the margin in pencil. "CXXX... And provided also, that no free person shall be convicted on the testimony of any slave or slaves of any crime or offence, as aforesaid, unless the complaint shall have been made within twelve months after the commission thereof, and unless the crime or offence shall have been committed subsequent to the commencement of this act. And provided also, that no free person, accused *of any crimes herein before mentioned,* shall be committed for trial, or required to enter into any recognizance to appear and take his or her trial upon the evidence of any slave, *unless* such evidence shall be corroborated by some other slave or free person clearly and consistently deposing to the same fact, being examined apart as aforesaid." "CXXXII. And, in order to remove as much as possible any temptation to commit perjury by those slaves who shall be required to give evidence, be it enacted, that the court

8   pp 196–7, pencil | Committee's objection to evidence of J. B. Wildman, Esq
(*contra*)

But to affirm, as he [Wildman] does, that the influence of real
Christianity must precede a man's restoration to the enjoyment of
his natural, and civil, and even political rights, is a proposition
which we find it very difficult to understand. . . . Would he then
propose that men's natural and civil rights should be restrained in
proportion to their want of Christian knowledge and Christian
practice?

It is scarcely fair to suppose that Mr W. meant this—or ~~morale~~ than
~~that distingu~~ a competent acquaintance with the duties and obligations, under which the Slave would pass when emancipated—ex. gr.
with the necessity of working for his maintenance, and ⟨with⟩ the
Rights of *Property* on the part of others, as well ⟨as with⟩ the personal
Immunities belonging to himself as a freed-man.

9   p 213, pencil | at the end

1. The danger of emancipation less and less imminent than that of
rejection or indefinite Delay.

   2. The Evil of emancipation ~~not~~ is asserted on the assumption that
the Negroes emancipated can by no motive be induced to work—&
this unproved, and met with many facts & probable presumptions
to the contrary.

   N.B.—The first position, if proved, suffices to decide the question
practically—tho' the second were erroneous or doubtful. But the
proof of the second will add wonderfully to the force of the first.

---

shall not be at liberty to exercise the
power given by this act for declaring
any slave free and discharged from all
manner of servitude, where the owner
of such slave has been convicted of
particular offences, if *any slave* shall
have been sworn upon the trial as a
witness on the part of the prosecution."

   7³ At first the slaves would not be
"their own masters" but would be
"under guardianship" or tutelage.

"ANDERSON'S BRITISH POETS"

The Works of the British Poets. With prefaces, biographical and critical, by Robert Anderson, M.D. [1750–1830], &c. 13 vols. Edinburgh & London 1792–5. 8⁰.

Vol XIV was issued separately in 1807. Each volume regularly has two title-pages, one engraved (imprinted London), the other in type (imprinted Edinburgh). Individual sets vary as to consistency of title-pages and fly-titles, and in the date of single volumes.

B Poets, issued at £8 in boards, was the earliest compendious edition of English poetry published at a moderate price; it became the source at which C, WW, and RS developed their comprehensive grasp of the canon of English poetry. WW acknowledged his obligation to Anderson in a note to *Yarrow Visited*: "Through these Volumes I became first familiar with Chaucer, and so little money had I then to spare for books, that, in all probability, but for this same work, I should have known little of Drayton, Daniel, and other distinguished poets of the Elizabethan age, and their immediate successors, till a much later period of my life. I am glad to record this, not from any importance of its own, but as a tribute of gratitude to this simple-hearted old man". *WPW* III 450–1. In Sept 1814, after meeting Anderson, WW wrote to him urging him to add further volumes to the collection, and provided him—with RS's help—with a list of suggested authors. *W Life* (Moorman) II 259 and n 3. With their small print and two-column layout, these books would be difficult to read through, and one could hardly browse in them with much pleasure (especially by candlelight). That the edition was "full of blunders" and typographical errors C noted in SANNAZARO *Opera omnia* (Frankfurt 1709), in "The Historie and Gestes of Maxilian" (*CW* IV 440n), and elsewhere. Yet the importance of these volumes to both C and WW, especially in the early years, can scarcely be exaggerated.

C annotated three copies of *B Poets*, but only one of them—COPY A—certainly belonged to him; COPY B was connected with John Morgan; COPY C was originally JW's, then WW's.

CONTENTS

I. Chaucer, Sackville, Surrey, Wyatt

II. Davies, Hall, Shakespeare, Spenser

III. Carew, Drayton, Suckling

IV. William Browne, Crashaw, Daniel, Davenant, Donne, Drummond, G. Fletcher, P. Fletcher, Jonson

V. Butler, Cowley, Denham, Milton, Waller

VI. Dorset, Dryden, Duke, Halifax, W. King, Montague, Otway, J. Philips, Pomfret, Rochester, Roscommon, E. Smith, Sprat, Walsh

VII. Addison, Congreve, Fenton, Garth, Granville, Hughes, Parnell, Prior, Rowe, Sheffield, Tomkins, Yalden

VIII. Blackmore, Blair, Broome, Gay, Hammond, Hill, Pattison, Pitt, Pope, Savage, Somerville, Tickell

IX. Akenside, Collins, J. Dyer, Hamilton, Harte, Mallet, A. Philips, Shenstone, Swift, Thomson, Watts

X. J. Armstrong, Boyce, T. Brown, Cawthorne, Churchill, Cooper, Cunningham, Goldsmith, Grainger, Gray, Green, R. Lloyd, Lyttleton, Moore, Smollett, W. Thompson, West, P. Whitehead, Young

XI. Blacklock, Bruce, Chatterton, Cotton, Dodsley, Glover, Graeme, Jago, Jenyns, Johnson, Langhorne, Logan, Lovibond, Mickle, Penrose, J. Scott, C. Shaw, Smart, the Wartons, W. Whitehead, Wilkie

XII. Dryden tr Virgil, Persius, Juvenal; Pitt tr Virgil *Aeneid*; Pope tr Homer; Rowe tr Lucan; West tr Pindar

XIII. "C" tr *The Rape of Helen*; Cooke tr Hesiod; Creech tr Lucretius; Fawkes tr Theocritus, Bion, Moschus, Sappho, Museus, Apollonius Rhodius; Grainger tr Tibullus

AUTHOR INDEX TO THE MARGINALIA

	Volume	COPY A (C's copy)	COPY B (Morgan copy)	COPY C (JW's copy)
Browne, William	IV	7	12	
Butler, Samuel	V	10		
Cowley	V		31	
Crashaw	IV	8, 9	17–25	
Creech	XIII	14		13
Daniel	IV	3–6	10–11	
Davenant	IV	9C		
Denham	V		32, 33	
Donne	IV	2		
Drayton	III		3–9	10B
Dyer	IX		34A	
Fletcher, Phineas	IV		13–15	
Jonson	IV		16	
Mallet	IX		35, 36	
Milton	V		26–30	
Shakespeare	II	1		10
Spenser	II		1, 2	1–9
Thomson	IX		34	
Waller	V			11, 12
Young, Edward	X	11–13		

Copy A

The Works of the British Poets, &c. 12 vols (lacking VIII) of 13. Edinburgh & London 1792–5. 8º.

Folger Shakespeare Library

C's copy, and the first annotated of the three, acquired by Apr 1796: see *PW* (EHC) II 1136, and *CN* I 84, 171, and index. The early history of COPY A is so uncertain that this set has sometimes been thought to have been WW's because of the large number of notes and markings in his hand and because the only dated note written in it by C is a comment on a ms note of WW's. But there can no longer be serious doubt that this was C's copy. WW's earliest references to *B Poets* are late enough for him to have been using COPY A after C had moved to Greta Hall in Jul 1800; by the time C had withdrawn somewhat from Dove Cottage in the early summer of 1803, COPY C had arrived from London and WW no longer needed to rely upon C's. In 1800 C left a volume of this set behind in his London lodgings, but we do not know which one; Lamb recovered it for him (*LL* I 197), but it seems not to have reached Greta Hall until about Nov 1802 (*CL* II 880). C intended to take some of the volumes to the Mediterranean, and wrote to his wife from Malta in Jun 1804: "I have been haunted by the Thought that I have lost a box of Books, containing Shakespere (Stockdale's), the 4 or 5 first Volumes of the British Poets, Young's Syllabus (a red-paper Book), Condilliac's Logic, Thornton on Public Credit &c—" *CL* II 1139. Wherever and however the box was mislaid, the contents were evidently recovered by some time after his return.

This set has been heavily annotated by HC, to whom C had addressed **1** in Nov 1803, and into whose possession the volumes eventually passed. HC stamped "H Coleridge" on the title-pages of Vols V, IX, and XI, and signed his name on the fly-title of Donne in Vol IV. DC, in his edition of HC's *Poems* (2nd ed 1851) I cxxxiii, described HC's sitting-room in Nab Cottage, where he lived from 1840 until his death in 1849: "Within arm's length of an old cushioned chair, with claws and grotesque arms, the book he [HC] most used, Anderson's British Poets." His notes in Vols I and II are mostly in pencil, but elsewhere mostly in ink: these were published in the posthumous edition of HC's *Essays and Marginalia* ed DC (1851) II 1–128, some of C's notes being included. That Vol VIII, with Pope as principal author, had been lost by the time of HC's death is attested by DC in *HC Poems* (1st ed 1851) ccxiii and HC *Essays and Marginalia* II 79.

On the title-page verso of Vol IV HC has written:

> Whereas this third Volume of Anderson's Poets doth contain certain notes & observations written by the late Samuel Taylor Coleridge of blessed Memory with his own hand—as I Hartley Coleridge am ready to make affirmation

This is to give Notice

That any Person or Persons presuming to exscind—cut out—purloin—or
abstract the said notes & observations—or any thereoff—or any line,
word, syllable or letter thereof—shall be prosecuted with the utmost
severity of the Law.

As witness my Hand

December 21.ˢᵗ 1843   Hartley Coleridge

Ye Autographs-secreting thieves—
Keep scissors from these precious leaves,
And likewise thumbs, profane and greasy
From pages hallowed by S.T.C.—

Pencilled below this in another hand: "This refers to Vol 2 also
see pages 665, 666, 667, 668 and most of the other Vols"; and on a front
flyleaf of Vol II: "see pages 665, 666, 667, 668 signed by S. T. Coleridge
W.W.—p 352." The initials "EW" are written in ink on the engraved title-page of Vol IV.

Sheets of HC's notes are tipped into the front and back of several
volumes, and a leaf of his writing is pasted into Vol XIII. A printed sheet
with running headline "Notes on British Poets" pp 47–8—on Dryden from
HC's *Essays and Marginalia* II—with literal corrections in ink, is tipped
into Vol XII.

In addition to HC's notes and a small number by C, there are some
notes by WW, mostly in pencil, and a few by RS (e.g. II 27, IV 259). The
RS notes seem to have been written shortly after he took up residence in
Greta Hall in Sept 1803: C refers to them in **1**, dated 2 Nov 1803. Throughout this set many passages have been marked in various ways, not always
in association with marginal notes; ascription of these markings to any
of the four known annotators is conjectural and hazardous. Some of the
notes on Chaucer in Vol I are certainly WW's, and probably many of the
markings. C admitted to a "reverential Love of Chaucer" (see e.g. *IS*
152, *CL* II 951, III 56) but the markings of Chaucer in COPY A are probably
to be associated with WW's "translations" of Chaucer, all of which were
made in Dec 1801: see *WPW* IV 209–33, 358–65. WW's notes are as widely
dispersed as C's and more numerous, appearing in Vols I, II, III, IX at least,
and concentrated mostly on Spenser in Vol II. His notes vary in tone from
"very fine", written at the end of *Faerie Queene* III x (II 212), and "This
Legend of Courtesy [Sir Calidore] taking it all together is to me exceedingly delightful" (II 352), to a stern note on Drayton *Ideas* (III 550)—
"These sonnets seem to me not worth reading—flat, far-fetch'd conceits,
with scarcely a single natural thought throughout the whole—" and some
unexpectedly insensitive remarks on the *Faerie Queene*: I v is "heavy with
allegory & mythology" (II 38); II ix is marked "allegory again" (II 126);
of II vi, "first part very pleasant, conclusion intolerable" (II 108), and II iv
he finds is "poisoned with Allegory" (II 99). Several of the Shakespeare
Sonnets in Vol II have been marked with an X; the divergence from C's
choice in COPY C **10** is wide enough to suggest that these marks are WW's,

as the remark written above Sonnet 116 certainly is—"The best sonnet, I think". See also COPY C **10** n 1.

It would be agreeable to think that C gave COPY A to his son in 1820 when, after the Oriel disaster, C was encouraging him to establish himself in London as a writer, or in 1822 when HC went North, never to see his father again. But the history is probably more like this: the broken set remained in Greta Hall—otherwise why should C have had to use COPY B? —and it could have been transferred to Allan Bank in 1808 and left there when C went south in 1810. If COPY A had been left at Allan Bank, WW could have turned it over to HC before Wordsworth LC was drawn up in 1823. If—as seems more likely—the volumes were at Greta Hall, Mrs C could have given them to HC, either when he came to the Lakes in 1822 or when she finally left Greta Hall in 1829.

DATE. Uncertain. **1** is dated 2 Nov 1803; **3** is repeated almost verbatim in *CN* II 2224 (49) of c 1807.

SHAKESPEARE

1   II 665–8 | *The Sonnets*. WW's ms note in pencil at the end

These sonnets ⟨beginning at 127,⟩ to his Mistress, are worse than a game at a puzzle-peg. They ⟨are⟩ abominably harsh obscure & worthless. The others are for the most part much better, have many fine lines very fine lines & passages. They are also in many places warm with passion. Their chief faults, and heavy ones they are, are sameness, tediousness, laboriousness, quaintness, & elaborate obscurity.—

⟨With exception of the Sonnets to his Mistress (& even of these the expressions are unjustly harsh)⟩ I can by no means subscribe to the above pencil mark of W. Wordsworth;[1] which however, it is my wish, should never be erased. It is *his*: & grievously am I mistaken, & deplorably will Englishmen have degenerated, if the being *his* will not, ⟨in times to come,⟩ give it a Value, as of a little reverential Relict —the rude mark of his Hand left by the Sweat of Haste in a St Veronica Handkerchief![2] And Robert Southey! My sweet Hartley! if thou livest, thou wilt not part with this Book without sad necessity & a pang at Heart. O be never weary of reperusing the four first Volumes of this Collection, my eldest born![3]—To day thou art to be

1[1] For WW's choice among the Shakespeare sonnets, and for C's appraisal of these sonnets, see COPY C **10** and n 1 and ANNEX.

1[2] According to complex and variable legend, St Veronica's napkin was the linen cloth offered by Veronica to Jesus on the way to Golgotha and which (in Gibbon's plangent but inexact version) "Christ in his agony and bloody sweat applied to his face", the napkin miraculously receiving the indelible imprint of Jesus's features. Cf HC's note, above, forbidding erasure of C's notes.

1[3] See BIBLE COPY A **2**.

christened, being more than 7 years of age, o with what reluctance & *distaste* have I permitted this ~~silly~~ unchristian, & in its spirit & consequences anti-christian, Foolery to be performed upon *thee*, Child of free Nature.[4] On thy Brother Derwent, & thy Sister Sara, somewhat; but chiefly on thee.[5] These Sonnets then, I trust, if God preserve thy Life, Hartley! thou wilt read with a deep Interest, having learnt to love the Plays of Shakespere, co-ordinate with Milton, and subordinate only to thy Bible. To thee, I trust, they will help to explain the mind of Shakespere, & if thou wouldst understand these Sonnets, thou must read the Chapter in Potter's Antiquities on the Greek Lovers—of whom were that Theban Band of Brothers, over whom Philip, their victor, stood weeping; & surveying their dead bodies, each with his Shield over the Body of his Friend, all dead in the place where they fought, solemnly cursed those, whose base, fleshly, & most calumnious Fancies had suspected their Love of Desires against Nature.[6] This pure Love Shakespere

1⁴ C's dread of HC's baptism invaded a dream six days earlier (*CN* I 1620), but he is otherwise silent about the matter in both letters and notebooks. The christening was postponed to 8 Nov 1803. *DWJ*. C discusses "the strongest argument of all against Infant Baptism, & that which alone weighed at one time with me", in a note on TAYLOR *Polemicall Discourses* i 180; cf *CN* I 1516, BAXTER *Reliquiae* COPY A **8, 11, 12**, CHILLINGWORTH COPY B **11**, *CL* IV 581. An essay on baptism is to be found in *AR* (1825) 356–76. On the "Child of free Nature" see *Frost at Midnight* lines 54–64: *PW* (EHC) I 242.

1⁵ DC, born 14 Sept 1800, was christened shortly after birth in expectation of his death; see BIBLE COPY A **4**. His sister Sara, born 23 Dec 1802, was baptised shortly before 1 Feb 1803 (*CL* II 919; see also BIBLE COPY A ANNEX [*b*]).

1⁶ John Potter (c 1674–1747), abp of Canterbury, in his *Archaeologia Graeca: or the Antiquities of Greece* (2 vols Oxford 1697–9) II 262–6, Ch 9 "Of their Love of Boys", states that the Greek love of boys was wholly virtuous, and that the boys who were beloved wore special marks and en-joyed special status. The "Theban Band of Brothers" in this story was the ἱερὰ φάλαγξ of lovers, distinguished for being the first to defeat the Spartans in combat. Philip's words, according to Potter, were "Let them perish, who suspect that these Men either did, or suffer'd any Thing base." For use of Potter's *Archaeologia* in perhaps 1808 see *CN* III 3297. Writing in 1830 in praise of the training that he had received at Christ's Hospital, C said that "we had Potter (both his Historical volumes & his Antiquities) ... at our fingers' ends". *CL* VI 843. C's copy, now lost, was included in Wordsworth LC.

The possibility of love between males returned to C's mind on several occasions, sometimes—as in BLANCO WHITE *Practical Evidence* **13**—in the image of "two Boy friends—like two butterflies that climb the air". Cf *CN* III 3247, 4115 f 27, 4198. When C deals directly with the subject, Shakespeare comes to mind, as in the unpublished Greek Vocabulary (N 25 f 135): ἀΐτης—"The Beloved, between man and man: Of the nature of this connection and the probability of its innocence Shakespeare's Sonnets afford a curious proof—". In *TT* 14 May 1833

For I have sworn thee fair: more perjur'd I,
To swear, against the truth, so foul a lie!

CLIII.

Cupid lay'd by his brand, and fell asleep:
A maid of Dian's this advantage found,
And his love-kindling fire did quickly steep
In a cold valley-fountain of that ground;
Which borrow'd from this holy fire of love
A dateless lively heat, still to endure,
And grew a seething bath which yet men prove,
Against strange maladies a sovereign cure.
But at my mistress' eye love's brand new-fired,
The boy for trial needs would touch my breast;
I sick withal, the help of bath desired,
And thither hied, a sad distemper'd guest,
  But found no cure; the bath for my help lies
  Where Cupid got new fire; my mistress' eyes.

CLIV.

The little love-god lying once asleep,
Laid by his side his heart-inflaming brand,
Whilst many nymphs that vow'd chaste life to
  keep,
Came tripping by; but in her maiden hand
The fairest votary took up that fire
Which many legions of true hearts had warm'd;
And so the general of hot desire
Was sleeping by a virgin hand disarm'd.
This brand she quenched in a cool well by,
Which from love's fire took heat perpetual,
Growing a bath and healthful remedy
For men diseas'd; but I, my mistress' thrall,
  Came there for cure, and this by that I prove,
  Love's fire heats water, water cools not love.

beginning at 127.

*These sonnets to his Mistress, are worse than ⟨⟩
a puzzle-peg. They are abominably harsh obscure & worthless.
The others are for the most part much better, have
many fine lines very fine lines & passages. They
are also in many places warm with passion: Their
chief faults and heavy ones they are, are sameness,
tediousness, ⟨⟩ quaintness, &
elaborate obscurity. — with exception of the
sonnets to his Mistress && even of these the exceptions are unp[...] hard⟩
I can by no means subscribe to the above pencil mark
of W. Wordsworth; which however, it is my wish,
should never be erased. It is his: & grievously am
I mistaken, & deplorably will Englishmen have
degenerated, if the being his will not ⟨in times to come⟩ give it a
value, as of a little reverential Relict — the very
mark of his Hand left by the sweat of haste in a
St Veronica Handkerchief! — And Robert Southey!
& sweet Hartley! if thou livest, thou wilt not part with
my book without that sad necessity & a pang at Heart.
Be never weary of reperusing the four first volumes of
this Collection, my eldest born! To-day thou art [...]
e christened, being more than 7 years of age, O with
what reluctance & distaste have I permitted [...]*

A page of *The Works of the British Poets* ed Robert Anderson (12 vols Edinburgh & London 1792–5). See ANDERSON COPY A 1

he Folger Shakespeare Library, Washington, D.C.; reproduced by kind permission

appears to have felt—to have been no way ashamed of it—or even to have suspected that others could have suspected it/ yet at the same time he knew that so strong a Love would have been made more compleatly a Thing of Permanence & Reality, & have been blessed more by Nature & taken under her more especial protection, if this Object of his Love had been at the same Time a possible Object of Desire/ for Nature is not bad only—in this Feeling, he must have written the 20th Sonnet, but its possibility seems never to have entered even his Imagination.[7] It is noticeable, that not even an Allusion to that very worst of all possible *Vices* (for it is wise to think of the Disposition, as a *Vice*, not of the absurd & despicable Act, as a *crime*) not even any allusion to it in all his numerous Plays —whereas Johnson, Beaumont & Fletcher, & Massinger are full of them.[8] O my Son! I pray fervently that thou may'st know inwardly how impossible it was for a Shakespere not to have been in his heart's heart chaste. I see no ⟨elaborate⟩ obscurity ~~nothing of his puzzle peg~~ & very little quaintness—nor do I know any Sonnets that will bear such frequent reperusal: so rich in metre, so full of Thought & *exquisitest* Diction.

S. T. Coleridge, Greta Hall, Keswick, Wed. morning, ½ past 3, Nov. 2. 1803.[9]

DONNE

2 IV 42 | *On the Blessed Virgin Mary*

In that, O Queen of queens! thy birth was free
From that which others doth of grace bereave,

his view was more circumspect; but on that occasion he expressed the clear view that "the sonnets could only have come from a man deeply in love, and in love with a woman". Cf ATHENAEUM **19** textus.

1[7] Sonnet xx—"A woman's face, with nature's own hand painted"—is a love poem addressed to a young man. It is not one of the sonnets appraised by C in ANDERSON COPY C, but it is probably the sonnet C referred to in *TT* 14 May 1833 as the "one sonnet which, from its incongruity, I take to be a purposed blind".

1[8] Though there seems to be no specific reference to paederasty in C's notes on the Elizabethan and Jacobean dramatists, he frequently insists upon the moral (and sexual) purity of Shakespeare's writing compared with Jonson, Beaumont and Fletcher, and Massinger: see e.g. *BL* ch 15 (1907) II 16, examples grouped in *C 17th C* 646, 657, 668–9, 678, and *Sh C* II 93.

1[9] This note was written immediately after C had written *CN* I 1635—one of the most moving and eloquent of all the Greta Hall entries, in which he listens to "The Voice of the Greta, and the Cock-crowing" and hears "the low voice of quiet change, of Destruction doing its work by little & little". The notebook entry was written between "20 minutes past 2 °clock" and about 3 o'clock on the same night.

When in their mother's womb they life receive,
God, as his sole-born daughter, loved thee.

Singular to meet in so serious a poem so full an assertion of the Virgin's *Immaculate Conception*.[1]

DANIEL

3 IV 204 | Epistles. *To the Lord Henry Howard* lines 1–22

Praise, if it be not choice, and laid aright,
Can yield no lustre where it is bestow'd;
Nor any way can grace the giver's art,
(Though 't be a pleasing colour to delight)
For that no ground whereon it can be shew'd,
Will bear it well, but virtue and desert.

And though I might commend your learning, wit,
And happy utt'rance; and commend them right,
As that which decks you much, and gives you grace,
Yet your clear judgment best deserveth it,
Which in your course hath carried you upright,
And made you to discern the truest face,

And best complexion of the things that breed
The reputation and the love of men;
And held you in the tract of honesty,
Which ever in the end we see succeed;
Though oft it may have interrupted been,
Both by the times, and men's iniquity.

A curious instance how rhymes may be *wasted*, and the Poet have all the restraint & trouble, while the Reader has none of the effect—except indeed now & then a perplexed suspicion of a *jingle* in the monotonous blank verse.[1]

2[1] H. J. C. Grierson, in his edition of the *Poems of John Donne* (2 vols Oxford 1912), ascribed this poem to Henry Constable (1562–1613). For further annotations on Donne's poems see CHALMERS 3–7, DONNE *Poems*.

3[1] C later annotated DANIEL *Poetical Works* (1718). *To the Lord Henry Howard* is the second in a group of eight *Epistles* in which Daniel was apparently looking for an informal yet shapely tune proper to the verse-letter; all are in iambic pentameter and all use rhyme to provide a discreet armature.

Whatever pattern the ear constructs from the *abcabc* scheme, the effect is not so much of colloquial ease but of accidents of rhyme, for the distance of hence C's feeling that he was reading blank verse marred by occasional accidents of rhyme, for the distance of three lines between rhyme-sounds seems too great for assured recognition by ear. C also described the scheme in *CN* II 2224 [49], repeating this note almost verbatim; see also 3210 and n. But Daniel, evidently preoccupied with a threefold rhyme-pattern in the

4　ɪᴠ 204 | *To the Lady Margaret, Countess of Cumberland* lines 1–16, 33–40

He that of such a height hath built his mind,
And rear'd the dwelling of his thoughts so strong,
As neither fear nor hope can shake the frame
Of his resolved pow'rs; nor all the wind
Of vanity or malice pierce to wrong
His settled peace, or to disturb the same:
What a fair seat hath he, from whence he may
The boundless wastes and weilds of man survey?
　　And with how free an eye doth he look down
Upon these lower regions of turmoil?
Where all the storms of passions mainly beat
On flesh and blood: where honour, pow'r, renown,
Are only gay afflictions, golden toil;
Where greatness stands upon as feeble feet,
As frailty doth; and only great doth seem
To little minds, who do it so esteem. . . .
　　Nor is he mov'd with all the thunder-cracks
Of tyrants threats, or with the surly brow
Of pow'r, that proudly sits on others crimes;
Charg'd with more crying sins than those he checks.
The storms of sad confusion, that may grow
Up in the present for the coming times,
Appal not him; that hath no side at all,
But of himself, and knows the worst can fall.

A noble Poem in all respects.

4A　ɪᴠ 205 | lines 78–81, 116–19

Where no vain breath of th' impudent molests,
That hath secur'd within the brazen walls　　*heart?*
Of a clear conscience, that (without all stain)
Rises in peace, in innocency rests;

　．　　．　　．　　．　　．　　．　　．

This concord, madam, of a well-tun'd mind
Hath been so set by that *i*all-working hand
Of heav'n, that though the world hath done his worst
To put it out by discords most unkind;[1]

Epistles, is not always unsuccessful; in *To the Lady Margaret*—which C admired (see **4**)—the *abcabc* scheme is clinched with a couplet to form a satisfactory and variable 8-line stanzaic paragraph. See also Dᴀɴɪᴇʟ **3**.

4A[1] *Poems of Daniel and Defence of Rhyme* ed A. C. Sprague (Chicago 1965) reads "hath" and "all-working" in main text without comment.

5   IV 206 | *To the Lady Lucy, Countess of Bedford*

> And though books, madam, cannot make this mind,
>   Which we must bring apt to be set aright;
>   Yet do they rectify it in that kind,
> And touch it so, as that it turns that way
>   Where judgment lies. And though we cannot find
>   The certain place of truth; yet do they stay,
> And entertain us near about the same;
>   And give the soul the best delight, that may
>   Enchear it most, and most our spir'ts enflame
> To thoughts of glory, and to worthy ends.

Annex these Lines as a Note and modest answer to the lines in Milton's Paradise Regained in Christ's Reply—Par. Regained, B. IV.

> "However, many Books
> Wise men have said, are wearisome,["] &c.[1]

6   IV 209–10 | *The Passion of a Distressed Man*

> *Pars Altera.*
> Will not her safety being thus attain'd,
> Raise her proud heart t' a higher set of scorn,
> When she shall see my passions are distain'd
> With blood; although it were to serve her turn?
> Since th' act of ill, though it fall good to us,
> Makes us yet hate the doer of the same.

> .   .   .   .

> *Resumptio*
> But that were to be cruel to all three;
> Rebel to nature, and the gods arrest,
> Whose ordinances must observed be:
> Nor may our frailty with the heav'ns contest.

.   .   .   .

5[1] *Paradise Regained* IV 321–30:

> However, many books,
> Wise men have said, are wearisome;
>   who reads
> Incessantly, and to his reading brings
>   not
> A spirit and judgment equal or
>   superior
> (And what he brings, what needs he
>   elsewhere seek?)
> Uncertain and unsettled remains,
> Deep vers'd in books, and shallow in
>   himself,
> Crude or intoxicate, collecting toys,
> And trifles for choice matters, worth
>   a spunge;
> As children gathering pebbles on the
>   shore.

C cited this passage again in ANDERSON COPY B **29**. DC included this note as HC's in *Essays and Marginalia* (1851). Cf *BL* ch 9 (1907) I 98.

This Resumption has done away the chief possible merit of this moot case, by destroying its only possible moral—viz. that for our *Lives* we are not answerable, but for our actions—If therefore Life be offered me at the price of aฅ bad action, let it be one or 20, the Murder is with the Offerer—I die not only innocent, but virtuous. Better a thousand die, than one commit a crime; for ⟨of⟩ what a *crime* is, it were impiety to pretend to be ignorant, what *Death* is, it were presumptuous to pretend to know.—

WILLIAM BROWNE

7   IV 320 | *Britannia's Pastorals* Song III (near the end)

<blockquote>

A little thence, a fourth with little pain

conn'd (?)   Cou'd all their lessons and them sung again;

So numberless the songsters are that sing

too   In the sweet groves of the <u>two</u> careless spring,

That I no sooner could the hearing lose

Of one of them, but straight another rose,

And perching deftly on a quaking spray

Nigh tir'd herself to make her hearer stay,

*   Whilst in a bush two <u>nightingales</u> together

Shew'd the best skill they had to draw me thither:

</blockquote>

* Licentia poetica. Nightingales never visit Devon or Cornwall.[1]

CRASHAW

8   IV 702 | Anderson's Life of Crashaw

On his arrival at Rome, he became Secretary to a Cardinal there; and obtained the office of a Canon in the Church of Loretto; where he died of a fever soon after his election, in 1650.

No wonder! not improbably, the wretches sent him to Loretto on purpose to get rid of him & all future applications for him from the

---

[1] On the basis of his own direct observation of nightingales in the Quantocks (see *The Nightingale* of Apr 1798, esp lines 43–86: *PW*—EHC —I 264–7), C might well accuse Browne of poetic licence. A recent note on the distribution of nightingales tends to confirm C's statement. See H. F. Witherby, F. C. R. Jourdain, N. F. Ticehurst, and B. W. Tucker *Handbook of British Birds* (5 vols 1949) II 189. There are numerous evidences of C's alert attention to birds throughout his life: see e.g. *CN* II App F. For C on William Browne see COPY B **12** n 1.

Queen: for Loretto is notorious for its deadly Air—aria cattivissima[1] —which has baffled all the miracles of the Virgin & all the treasures of the Popes.[2]

9 iv 703

Tenderness and piety seem to have been the peculiar characteristics of this amiable poet, at every period of his life. The reader of sensibility, who peruses his *Verses to St. Teresa*, whatever he may think of his tender bigotry, will hardly suspect that his piety was not perfectly sincere.

> O! thou undaunted daughter of desires,
> By all thy dower of lights and fires;
> By all the eagle in thee, all the dove;
> By all thy lives and deaths of love;
> By thy large draughts of intellectual day;
> And by thy thirsts of love, more large than they;
> By all thy brim-fill'd bowls of fierce desire;
> By thy last morning's draught of liquid fire;
> By the full kingdom of that final kiss,
> That seal'd thy parting soul, and made thee his;
> By all the heavens thou hast in him,
> Fair sister of the seraphim;
> By all of him we have in thee,
> Leave nothing of myself in me;
> Let me so read thy life, that I
> Unto all life of mine may die.

very strange, that these "Verses to S[t] Teresa" are not to be found in this Collection. There are 3 poems on S[t] Teresa, but in neither of the three are these Lines to be found.[1]

8[1] Loretto, a place of pilgrimage, was celebrated for its Santa Casa, said to have been the house where Jesus, Mary, and Joseph lived in Nazareth, miraculously removed to Italy by angels. Pilgrims will have brought back information that in many parts of Italy epidemic outbreaks of malaria were not unusual.

8[2] For C on Crashaw see COPY B 19 n 1.

9[1] At iv 746 Anderson prints *The Flaming Heart* in the short version of 1648, omitting the last 24 lines. In the Life of Crashaw—where C found them —Anderson quotes the last 16 lines of the short version and apparently did not reprint them in his text because he had already printed them in the Life. This was a favourite poem of C's; in May 1821 he said that the "lines on St. Theresa" were "present to my mind whilst writing the second part of Christabel; if, indeed, by some subtle process of the mind they did not suggest the first thought of the whole poem". Allsop i 194, 195–6. The "3 poems on S[t] Teresa" are *Hymn to the*

9A IV 724 | *On Hope*

have

> The fates ~~of~~ not a possibility
> Of blessing thee;
> If things then from their ends we happy call,
> 'Tis Hope is the most hopeless thing ~~at~~ all.

of

9B IV 729 | *To the Queen, upon Her Numerous Progeny*

> For, lo! the gods, the gods
> Come fast upon thee; and those glorious <u>odes</u>!
> Swell thy full honours to a pitch so high
> As fits above thy best capacity.
> Are they not <u>odes</u>? and glorious?[1]

odds

odds

DAVENANT

9C IV 766, marked with ink line in margin | Preface [to *Gondibert*] "To His Much Honoured Friend, Mr. Hobbes"

For wise poets think it more worthy to seek out truth in the passions, than to record the truth of actions; and practise to describe mankind just as we are persuaded or guided by instinct; not particular persons, as they are lifted, or levelled by the force of fate; it being nobler to contemplate the general history of nature, than a selected diary of fortune.[1]

BUTLER

10 V 663 | *Miscellaneous Thoughts*

> The world has long endeavour'd to reduce
> Those things to practice that are of no use,
> And strives to practise things of speculation,
> And bring the practical to contemplation,
> And by that error renders both in vain,
> By forcing Nature's course against the grain.

a very profound remark: the sum and substance of all true philosophy.[1]

Name and Honour of the Admirable Saint Teresa (IV 720–2), *An Apology for the Precedent Hymn* (IV 722), and *The Flaming Heart, upon the Book and Picture of the Seraphical Saint Teresa* (IV 746–7). In 1807 C noted three couplets from Crashaw, two of them from the first two of these poems. *CN* II 3102–4. For more extensive notes on Crashaw see COPY B **17–25**.

9B[1] C made the same correction in COPY B **23**.

9C[1] C copied this same passage into a notebook in Apr–Jun 1810: *CN* III 3769.

A note on Milton in pencil on V 168, ascribed to C in *Misc C*, is HC's.

10[1] C quoted five couplets from *Miscellaneous Thoughts* in *BL* ch 7 (1907) I 82.

YOUNG

11   x v | Anderson's Life of Young

In 1721, *The Revenge*, a tragedy, was acted at the theatre in Drury-Lane, and met with very great success. This is his best dramatic performance. . . . The first design seems suggested by "Othello" and "Abdelazar"; but he has, in some respects, greatly improved on both. The reflections, the incidents, and the diction, are original. The moral observations are so introduced and so expressed, as to have all the novelty that can be required.

othello!! and Abdelazar!—Alexander the Great, and Corporal Drillman of Cap^tn Noke's Company &c!¹ and the Revenge *improves on* othello! Candid Critic*s*! Most tasteful, tho' not learned, Dr Anderson!²

12   x vii

It is related by Ruffhead, that, when he determined on the church, he addressed himself to Pope, for instructions in theology; who, in a frolic, advised the diligent perusal of ┌Thomas Aquinas. With this treasure, he retired from interruption, to an obscure place in the suburbs. Pope hearing nothing of him during half a year, and apprehending he might have carried the jest too far, sought after him, and found him just in time to prevent what Ruffhead calls "an irretrievable derangement."

it F This vulgar joke–anecdote against Thomas Aquinas reminds me of Fielding's observation of Aristotle, that he was not ⟨quite⟩ so great a Blockhead, as he was deemed by young Gentlemen who had never read his works.¹ It is plain, however, from Young's writings that he really had formed his mind on the scholastic writers—an

11¹ That Young in *The Revenge* drew upon *Othello* and Aphra Behn's *Abdelazer, or the Moor's Revenge* (1676), as Anderson suggests, may be conceded; but, C observes elliptically, to utter *Othello* and *Abdelazer* in the same breath is like comparing Alexander with the sergeant of the soft-shoe company commanded by Capt Noke.

11² C borrowed a volume of Young's *Works* (1774–8) in Mar–Apr 1795 (*Bristol LB* 41) and was affected by what he read there: *CN* I 33–4, 36, 566n. For a possible reading of Young in *B Poets* in Nov 1799 see *CN* I 587.

12¹ The initial letter of *anecdote* is clearly a Greek α, to recall the meaning of the Greek word: see DAVISON 10 n 4. Fielding's observation is in *Amelia* bk III ch 10. C echoed it again, with elaboration, in *SM* (*CC*) 103. C borrowed Aquinas from the Durham Cathedral library 25 Jul to 24 Aug 1801. *Durham LB* 2. See also *CN* I 973 A and n. C later owned a 5-vol set of Aquinas.

Edition of the Night Thoughts with a running Commentary from Aquinas & his followers would perhaps surprize such of our modern Critics, as can construe Latin.   S. T. Coleridge—

13 x ix

In them [i.e. pieces that Young refused to reprint] he would only appear, perhaps, in a less respectable light as a poet; and though despicable as a dedicator, he would not pass for a worse Christian, or for a worse man. This enviable praise, which cannot be claimed by every writer, is due to the author of the *Night Thoughts*.

No?—what [!] are the vile Lies of a Preferment-hunter's ~~fancy~~ Flattery no detraction from Honor, Honesty, & Christianity!

CREECH

14 xiii 404 | Tr of Lucretius: Notes on Bk ii

First, then, that weight is not a property of atoms is evidently proved from the difference in weight of bodies: for take a cube of gold, and hollow it half through, and weigh it against a solid cube of wood of the same dimension; that gold, though it has lost half its matter, and consequently half its weight by the hollow, is twenty times heavier than the wood; from whence the consequence is natural and easy.* For if weight were a property of matter, it would be impossible that a hollow piece of gold should outweigh the wood, because the wood cannot contain a ten times greater vacuity than that hollow.

* A very shallow argument. and easily eluded unless it be ill expressed—[1]

14[1] For authorship of the Notes on Creech's Lucretius see COPY C **13** n 1.

Copy B

The Works of the British Poets, &c. 12 vols (lacking xi) of 13. Edinburgh & London 1793–5. 8⁰.

Victoria and Albert Museum (Forster Collection)

A set, probably not his own, which C used and annotated for a time from c 1807.

All the volumes have the bookplate of John Forster; his autograph signature is written on the engraved title-pages of Vols i–v. The present uniform binding belongs to the late nineteenth century, as is confirmed by the cropping of e.g. **22** on iv 742 and of some notes and markings made after the volumes had left C's hands.

COPY B, having more than twice as many C marginalia as either of the other two sets, has a quite separate history, being connected not with the Grasmere–Keswick setting, but with the middle years in London and the West Country. The temporary loss of the first four or five vols of COPY A on the way to Malta may account for C's using COPY B when he was giving his first series of literary lectures in London in 1808. This set is closely related to John James Morgan, but it is not clear whether the set belonged to Morgan before C joined his household, whether Morgan bought it for C to use, or even whether C could have bought it for Morgan; it seems never to have belonged to C. (The heavy marking and glossing of Chaucer in Vol i, once thought to be WW's, is now seen to be the work of S. C. Hall.)

These volumes are so heavily marked that it is best to begin the description with evidence of the owner next before Forster. Notes signed "S. C. H." are written on i 592, 593, ii 701, v 561, ix 175, 674 (the last two being comments on C's notes); the words "extract 18 stanzas", on ii 1682, against Sir John Davies *On the Immortality of the Soul*, are in the same hand. Samuel Carter Hall (1800–89) made the acquaintance of C and the Gillmans when he founded the *Amulet* in 1826. Although C badly needed the fees that Hall offered for his unpublished poems, and looked forward to receiving them, the relationship soon broke down through Hall's unscrupulousness in handling C's mss and his unreliability in meeting promises of payment. See *CL* vi 698 and n, 775–6. Hall used this set of *B Poets*—possibly before C's death—in preparing *The Book of Gems* (3 vols 1836–8). It does not appear how Hall acquired the volumes, whether by loan, gift, or purchase, or from whom; the fact that HNC and SC did not include the marginalia in *LR* or their later collections suggests strongly that the volumes were not at The Grove at the time of C's death or for some time before. Hall's object in *The Book of Gems* was "to collect and arrange, in a popular and attractive form, the most perfect specimens of the Poets, illustrated by the pencils of the Artists, of Great Britain". The tables of contents to Hall's volumes, and the nature of his one-page biographical notes, suggest emphatically that *B Poets* provided the framework for his selections; finding Anderson's text inaccurate, he made astute anthologist's use of passages that had already been marked in the volumes before he had them. In his notes on Drayton, Phineas Fletcher, and Crashaw he included five of C's marginalia, acknowledging C's authorship but not the source, and used other Coleridge notes without acknowledgment.

The text of Chaucer in Vol I is heavily marked in pencil. On I 595 a note in ink at the beginning of Surrey's *Songes and Sonnettes*—"These copies of Anderson are full of errors—they must not be transcribed in any other edit."—and a note in ink on Drayton on I +2 look a little like WW's hand but are probably Hall's. Directions such as "begin here" and "Doubtful", written in pencil on I 34, 151, 153, 218, 230, 239, 531, and numerous pencil glosses interpreting or modernising middle-English words are probably Hall's. In Vols II, III, and IV many passages are marked in the margin with pencil lines, chiefly in the works of Drayton, Suckling, Donne, Daniel, and Jonson; fewer passages are marked in Vols V, VI, IX, XII.

In Vols I, IV, V, VI, X, XII words beginning with the letter *A* have been picked out in the text in pencil and rewritten in the margins as though for reference. Three hands seem to be involved: an unidentified mature hand, which accounts for most of them; an immature hand in Vol IX, possibly a child's; in Vols IX and X a number are initialled "JJM" in a distinctive monogram that is identified as John James Morgan's by SHAKESPEARE *Works* (8 vols 1773) [COPY A], which C annotated in preparing his early lectures. The presence of Morgan's initials strengthens the impression that C used this set in preparing his literary lectures of 1808 and 1811–12. It also raises the question whether the volumes could have been given by Morgan to C, or by C to Morgan. Morgan died in 1820, six years before Hall first met C; it is possible that, if the set belonged to Morgan (as seems likely), Mrs Morgan may have sold it to Hall when she was in need.

John James Morgan (d 1820) had been an acquaintance of C's since the early Bristol days, and from 1807 until 1816 he and his wife Mary and her sister Charlotte Brent were important in C's life—and he in theirs. The Morgans nursed C through a three-weeks' illness in Bristol in Nov 1807; he lived with them in Hammersmith off and on from Nov 1810 until late Mar 1812, giving an increasing amount of his time, energy, and small resources to try to disengage Morgan from deepening financial trouble: see e.g. *CL* VI 162, 436–7. After the collapse of Morgan's fortune he escaped to Ireland, but returned in May 1814 and by Dec had established his family and C at Calne, Wiltshire. Here Morgan was responsible for getting *BL* into writing (see *CN* II 3186n). When C left Calne for London and took up residence with the Gillmans in Highgate on 15 Apr 1816, his long intimacy with the Morgans was interrupted, never to be restored. They remained in touch, but after Morgan's death Mary and Charlotte lived in conditions of penurious distress from which C and his friends could do little to relieve them. See e.g. *LL* II 263 and n, and *S Letters* (Curry) II 443.

DATE. c 1807, and later. See **23** n 1 and **29** n 3, below.

SPENSER

1 II 38 | *Faerie Queene* I v 6

> Their shining shieldes about their wrestes they tye,
> And burning blades about their heads doe blesse,*
> The instruments of wrath and heavinesse:

* Licentiously careless as Spenser is in the orthography of words varying the final vowels as the Rhyme requires, I scarcely can reconcile myself to the belief, that he would misuse a word in so arbitrary a manner, as to employ bless for "brandish". May it not have been class for clash?[1]

2 II 220-1 | *Faerie Queene* III xii 14

> And after them Dissemblaunce and Suspect
> Marcht in one rancke, yet an unequal paire;
> For she was gentle and of milde aspect,
> Courteous to all, and seeming debonaire,
> Goodly adorned, and exceeding faire;
> Yet was that all but paynted and pourloynd,
> And her bright browes were deckt with borrowed haire;*
> Her deeds were forged, and her words false coynd,
> And alwaies in her hand two clewes of silke she twynd:

* Here, as too often in this great Poem, that which is and may be known, but cannot *appear* from the given point of view, is confounded with the visible. It is no longer a mask-figure, but the character of a Dissembler. Another common fault in St. xvi. Grief represents two incompatibles, the Grieved and the Aggriever.[1] Indeed this Confusion of agent and patient occurs so frequently in his allegorical Personages, that Sp. seems to have deemed it within the Laws & among the legitimate privileges of Allegory.

[1] Beside C's note Hall has written: "May not blesse mean to wound= French blesser? To 'wound the air': so Macbeth: not unusual". The use of "bless" as "wave about, brandish"— unconnected with either the normal English meaning (originally "to mark with blood") or the meaning derived from *blesser*, "to wound"—is peculiar to Spenser and was much used by him: see also e.g. *Faerie Queene* I viii 22, VI viii 13.

[1] *Faerie Queene* III xii 16:

Grief all in sable sorrowfully clad,
Downe hanging his dull head with
  heavy chere,
Yet inly more than seeming sad;
A paire of pincers in his hand he had,
With which he pinched many people
  to the hart.

The word "many" in the last line above is in Anderson's text but not in most editions of Spenser.

DRAYTON

3 III iii–[ii] | Anderson's Life of Drayton

Aubrey's MSS. call him the son of a butcher; but his biographers, whether from ignorance, or disbelief of the fact, or from a ridiculous delicacy, take no notice of this circumstance.

Aubrey's authority, unsupported by circumstances or internal probability is $1-1=0$: and in this instance is of no weight against the fact in the very next §, that at 10 years old he was a Proficient in Latin, and a Page to a Person of Quality.

I do not say, that it is impossible; but only that it is improbable, in an age when the Pages of Noblemen were almost always the Children of Gentlemen/ and there is more than enough to weigh down the gossiping Testimony of such a credulous omnium gatherum Dreamer, as old Aubrey;[1] or *Anderson*—[a]

4 III iv

It is probable, however, that he had indulged himself in forming expectations on James's coming to the throne, but was disappointed; for, in the preface to his *Poly-Olbion*, and his Epistles to Browne and Sandys, he moralizes on the times, with the peevish dissatisfaction of one who thinks himself neglected or ill-treated.

This miserable Imitation of the slanderous aphorising Detraction of D[r] Johnson.—[1]

5 III iv

In 1626, the addition of Poet Laureat is affixed to his name, in a copy of recommendatory verses prefixed to "Holland's poems": probably as a mark of his excellency in the art of poetry; for that appellation was not formerly restricted, as it is now, to his majesty's

---

[a] *Misc C* 240 reverses the order of the two paragraphs

3[1] John Aubrey (1626–97), whose unpublished antiquarian notes C could not have read, was known to him in Aubrey's *Miscellanies* (1721), a copy of which was in Green's library. For notes on witch-trials and other matters drawn from this edition see *CN* III 4390–3 (Mar 1818).

4[1] For S. C. Hall's recognition of Anderson's debt to Dr Johnson in this edition see **34** n 1 and **35** n 1, below. For C's distaste for Johnson's style and mentality see e.g. *TT* 1 Nov 1833, *IS* 185, and AURELIUS **1** n 3. For "aphorising" see ATHENAEUM **13** n 1.

servant, known by that title, who, at that time, is presumed to have been Jonson.

J. *succeeded* Mr D.[1]

6 III iv

The MSS. abovementioned [Aubrey's] say . . . that his [Drayton's] epitaph was written by Quarles, and not by Jonson, to whom it is commonly attributed.

The epitaph, which was written in letters of gold, runs as follows.

MICHAEL DRAYTON, Esquire.

1631.

A memorable poet of his age,
Exchang'd his laurel for a crown of glory,
Do, pious marble, let thy readers know
What they, and what their children owe
To DRAYTON's name, whose sacred dust
We recommend unto thy trust.
Protect his memory, and preserve his story:
Remain a lasting monument of his glory;
And when thy ruins shall disclaim
To be the treasurer of his name,
His name that cannot fade shall be
An everlasting monument to thee.

A noble Epitaph; more sweet and rhythmical than Johnson commonly is, and more robust and dignified, than Quarles.[1]

7 III v

. . . his verse of twelve syllables, though generally harmonious, is antiquated and unsuitable to the dignity and importance of his

---

5[1] Unconfirmed tradition holds that Samuel Daniel (1562–1619) succeeded as poet laureate on Spenser's death in 1599. From 1603 until his death in 1637 Ben Jonson carried out the functions of laureate without officially holding the title. Drayton, who had been rebuffed in 1603 for his too-zealous courting of King James's favour, did not in fact assume the title of poet laureate.

6[1] The epitaph in Westminster Abbey has been variously ascribed to Jonson, Quarles, and Thomas Randolph.

Nothing of Quarles's is reprinted in *B Poets*. C evidently had some familiarity with the *Emblems* of both Quarles and Withers by 1 Jul 1796, when he commended them to Lamb: *LL* I 32. In N 25 ff 85–6 C made an assessment of the first three books of the *Emblems* (1736) and copied out the poem *Peace, peace, my dear!*

subject, and his continual personification of woods, mountains, and rivers, are tedious, and must be read for information than pleasure.

why, antiquated?—[1]

8 III v

His *Nymphidia: the Court of Fayrie* ... is a most pleasing effort of a sportive fancy.... It is a fine prelude to the witches Cauldron in Macbeth, and only exceeded by the stronger genius of Shakspeare.

a *Prelude*? Did not the Scotchman know the meaning of the word? The Nymphidia was first *published* in 1627: and Shakespear *died* in 1616. It is a manifestation Imitation (a lovely & spirited one) of Shakespear's Tempest, Midsummer Night's Dream, & Macbeth.—[1]

9 III vi

His *Sonnets* possess, in a high degree, those distinctions which have been esteemed the most delicate improvements in English versification, and are scarce inferior to the best compositions of that kind in our language.

What could Dr A. have meant? The Sonnets are not *metrically* Sonnets; but poems in 14 lines—and it would be difficult to point out one good one. Drayton knew better than to call them *Sonnets*. The best, I think, of these "*Ideas*" is the 59th—which is original in conception, and humorously executed.—[1]

7[1] The Alexandrine had been carried into English from French through renderings of the *chansons de geste* and is to be found in some early English romances, sometimes in Chaucer, experimentally in Ralegh, and occasionally in Shakespeare. But it was Drayton who first ventured to defy the tacit principle that English verse cannot accumulate lines longer than decasyllables without serious danger of monotony, by casting his long poem *Polyolbion* in that measure. Indeed Drayton, far from cultivating "antiquated" forms, was "an untiring experimenter" and had "a singular faculty of catching, and even anticipating, the *aura* of the time, so that he is by turns representative of strictly Elizabethan, of Jacobean, and even of Caroline poetry". G. Saintsbury *The History of English Prosody* (3 vols 1923) II 98.

8[1] *Nimphidia* was indeed first published in 1627. Approximate dates for completion of the three plays are: *Midsummer Night's Dream* 1595, *Macbeth* 1606, *Tempest* 1611. Drayton was in any case a friend of Shakespeare's. C's contempt for Anderson as a Scotsman recurs in **13, 34, 35, 36**, and in **35** Thomson narrowly escapes the same condemnation. See also **35** n 1, below. *CN* III 4134 offers a long jocular excursus, written in 1811–12, on the shortcomings of the Scots.

9[1] In Anderson's edition all Drayton's 14-line poems come under the single title of *Ideas*. No LIX *To Proverbs* —"As love and I late harbour'd in one inn"—is marked with a pencil line. C quoted four lines of IX in *BL* ch 19 (1907) II 73.

DANIEL

10   IV 165 | *Civil Wars* VI xxviii

[Daniel claims in xxvi–xxvii that the use of artillery in war brought ruin to a happy Europe.]

> It was the time when fair Europa sat
> With many goodly diadems address'd,
> And all her parts (in flourishing estate)
> Lay beautiful, in order, at their rest.
> No swelling member, unproportionate,
> Grown out of form, sought to disturb the rest:
> The less subsisting by the greater's might;
> The greater by the lesser kept upright. *

* A Theory framed in Fancy (in strictness, not Θεωρια, but αθεωρια, *or* at best ημιθεωρια)[1] never fails to produce a distortion of Faith.*a* Consult the contemporary Historians of the 12, & 13 Centuries & compare them with Daniel's flattering statement. S T C.

11   IV 166–7, pencil | *Civil Wars* VI xxxff

[Nemesis calls upon Pandora to spread evils abroad, using elaborate mythological machinery to give an account of the invention of artillery.]

Nothing can be more *out of keeping*, as the Painters say,[1] than the introduction of these fictions in so grave & prosaic, tho' rhymed, History. They read like a stupid Lie, told in cold blood, for Lying's sake.—[2]

a "Fact" intended?

10[1] C's word "Theory" at the outset suggests some such version as "not theory, but non-theory, *or* at best half-theory". But a pun lurks in θεωρία—contemplation, beholding—and this is needed too: "not attention, but inattention, *or* at best half-attention". Cf *TT* 29 Jun 1833.

11[1] "Keeping", originally a painter's term—that may have come to C from Beaumont, Northcote, Allston, or Hazlitt—for the maintenance of proper relation between nearer and more distant objects in a picture, or more generally the maintenance of harmony in composition (*OED* 9a, 1715); "in or out of keeping" (*OED* 9c) is dated c 1790. C's most striking use of the word is in c 1809: "... poetry demands a *severer keeping*—it admits nothing that Prose may not often admit; but it *oftener* rejects. In other words, it presupposes a more continuous state of Passion". *CN* III 3611; see also 3240 and 4250. Cf also *Sh C* II 231, *CN* III 3524, *CL* V 34.

11[2] For a more extensive note on this passage, written Feb 1808, see DANIEL **12**.

11A IV 227 | *A Description of Beauty* st 7

> Old trembling age will come,
>> With wrinkl'd cheeks and stains,
>> With motion troublesome;
>> With skin and bloodless <u>weaves</u>, *veins*
>> That lively visage <u>reaven</u>,[a] *wanes*
>> And made deform'd and old,
>> Hates sight of glass it lov'd so to behold.

11B IV 227 | st 11

> Pluck, pluck betime thy flow'r,
> That springs, and parcheth both in one short hour.

WILLIAM BROWNE

12 IV 255 | Anderson's Life of Browne

He was born at ~~Tavistock~~, in Devonshire, in the year 1590.
Ottery St Mary, the Birth-place of S. T. Coleridge.—[1]

PHINEAS FLETCHER

13 IV 379 | Anderson's Life of Phineas Fletcher

No one of Fletcher's figures is more consistently habited than his
Death:

> A dead man's skull supplied his helmet's place,*
> A bone his club, his armour <u>sheets</u> of lead;
> Some more, some less fear his *all-frighting* face;
> But most, who sleep in <u>downie</u> pleasure's bed.

> [*The Purple Island*] Canto XII. Stanza 38.

!! Yet the first of these † terrific attributes is suggested by Spenser,
who has given it to Meleager . . .

* How natural it is for a common-place ⟨mind⟩ to be delighted with
common-place Images, if tricked out in language! and yet not less,

  † say rather, Surgeon's apprentice's Tricks!—

a So misprinted; "reaves" is required by the rhyme-scheme

12[1] Browne's birthplace is regularly given as Tavistock. C may have confused birth and death here, for he wrote in Nov–Dec 1809: ". . . he is a dear fellow, & I love him, that W. Browne who died at Ottery, & with whose family my own is united in Marriage—or rather connected & acquainted". *CN* III 3652; see 3652n. A William Browne was buried in Tavistock on 27 Mar 1643; another William Browne died at Ottery St Mary in Dec 1645. Browne's history after 1640 is not recorded.

tho' differently, struck by the most *outrèe*.—Sympathy with the ~~common-place~~ Trivial; Wonderment at the Monstrous; are the ground springs of a Scotch Critic's Judgement.[1] S. T. C.

14   IV 380

The *Piscatory Eclogues*, his next great work, do equal credit to his abilities, and equally deserve being brought forward to notice. However unfavourably the name of Piscatory Eclogue may be regarded, after the censure of Addison, it cannot be denied that he has imitated the Eclogues of Sannazarius,[1] who first attempted this species of composition, with admirable success.

as a congener of the Pastoral, Piscatory Eclogues were rightly condemned by Addison:[2] for from elementary causes, i.e. independently of accidental Associations, our feelings have nothing *fishy* in them. The coldness, the slime, the *imparticipability* (what a word!) of their Habits,[3] their voicelessness—the tools of Death & Deceit—

13[1] C quoted four lines from *The Purple Island* in a *M Post* article of 10 Jan 1800. *EOT* (*CC*) I 96n. In a note of Aug–Sept 1815 he applied a new phrase to his definition of symbol, and chose three lines from *The Purple Island* as descriptive of Napoleon: *CN* III 4253. For a "Scotch Critic's Judgement" see **35** n 1, below, and DONNE *Poems* 1.

14[1] C owned and annotated a copy of SANNAZARO *Opera omnia* (Frankfurt 1709). The notes seem to be of early date—perhaps the Malta period. Sannazaro's *Arcadia*, the prototype for Sidney's *Arcadia*, had a considerable vogue, passing through many editions up to about 1888.

14[2] See *Guardian* No 28. "*Sannazarius*...hath changed the Scene in this kind of Poetry [pastoral] from the Woods and Lawns, to the barren Beach and boundless Ocean: Introduces Sea-calves in the room of Kids and Lambs, Sea-mews for the Lark and the Linnet, and presents his Mistress with Oisters instead of Fruits and Flowers. How good soever his Stile and Thoughts may be; yet who can pardon him for his arbitrary Change of the sweet Manners and pleasing Objects of the Country, for what in their own Nature are uncomfortable and dreadful? I think he hath few or no Followers, or if any, such as knew little of his Beauties, and only copied his Faults, and so are lost and forgotten." See also No 32. The *Guardian* ran a series of essays—Nos 22, 23, 28, 30, 32—to enhance Ambrose Philips's pastorals above Pope's. In *Rambler* No 36 Johnson echoed the *Guardian* essays with customary gravity, declaring that he was "afraid it will not be found easy to improve the pastorals of antiquity, by any great additions or diversifications". He objected to Sannazaro's substituting fishermen for shepherds on two grounds: that the sea has "much less variety than the land", and because of "the ignorance of maritime pleasures, in which the greater part of mankind must always live".

14[3] *OED* records the use of "imparticiple"—incapable of being participated or shared—by Thomas Taylor in his translation of Proclus in 1789 (which C annotated), but not C's use of "imparticipability".

the immediate Loss of Life, so that they are always [considered]*a* as Food &c &c—

15 IV 408–9 | *The Purple Island* VI xx

> But sing that civil strife and home dissension
> 'Twixt two strong factions with like fierce contention,
> * Where never peace is heard nor ever peace is <u>mention.</u>

* Is not this a use (to me unmet with elsewhere) of mention quasi mentio—i.e. in mente.—Pax neque in voce, neque vel in mente versata est./ *Quere.* mentire—nonne vult, a mente ire? Our "Lie" & the German "Lügen", strongly mark a primitive Language—a Græcomanist, ⟨indeed⟩ might derive it from λυειν, i.e. to dissolve the compact between man & man[1]—That the Consonants were originally appropriate to classes of Thoughts, I cannot doubt—spite of the at first sight laugh-compelling Facts to the contrary. Thus Low, and Lofty. But may not Lofty be a compound—off the low?[2]

JONSON

16 IV 522: verso of fly-title facing the Life

It was not possible, that so bold and robust an Intellect as that of Ben Jonson could be devoted to any form of intellectual Power vainly or even with mediocrity of Ef Product.[1] He could not but be a Species of himself: tho' like the Mammoth and Megatherion fitted & destined to live only during a given Period, and then to exist a Skeleton, hard, dry, uncouth perhaps, yet massive and not to be contemplated without that mixture of Wonder and Admiration,[2] or more accurately, that middle somewhat between both for which we want a term—not quite even with the latter, but far above the mere former. In this Light, a Heretic as to the ordinary Notion

a Word supplied by the editor

15[1] "Mention as though it were *mentio*—i.e. in the mind. Peace dwelt neither in the voice nor in the mind. *Query.* mentire [to lie]—doesn't it mean a mente ire [to go from the mind]?" A characteristic piece of C's heuristic etymology. The root of *mentiri* is indeed *men-* (cf Sanscrit *man*, "think"), from which *mens* (mind), *memini* (remember). Originally *mentiri* meant "to invent" rather than 'to lie". The word λύειν means "to loose", *lügen* "to lie"; modern ety-mologists find no connexion between λύειν and *lügen*.

15[2] Cf BÖHME **57** and n 3.

16[1] C wrote more than fifty notes on *The Dramatic Works of Ben Jonson* in the 4-vol "Stockdale Edition" of Beaumont & Fletcher and Jonson, of which BEAUMONT & FLETCHER COPY B is part.

16[2] The mammoth (originally a Russian word), an extinct elephant that ranged both hemispheres in the Pleistocene age. The skeleton of a

(if words echoed sine noscendo can be called Notion)[3] but in compleat sympathy with the practical Feeling of my contemporary, I regard B. Jonson the ~~Dramatist~~ Play-wright—& hold his ~~Plays~~ Dramas of worth far inferior to his Poems, and the Plays themselves chiefly valuable for the many & various passages which are not dramatic.—In Harmony of metre, in rhythm, in sweetness of words, he is indeed greatly inferior to Juvenal; but in all other excellencies superior—and in none more so, than those which (in *kind*) they both possessed in common.—Jonson's philosophy more profound, his morality more pure, his Observation more acute & active, and his Figures more alive and individual. *S. T. C.*

16A   IV 551 | *Epigrams*: Epitaph to Shakespeare

> And tell how farther didst our Lily outshine,
> Or Sporting ~~kid~~ Kyd, or Marlow's mighty line.

CRASHAW

17   IV 703, pencil | Anderson's Life of Crashaw, quoting *The Flaming Heart*

[See COPY A **9** textus.]

It is strange, that this very poem is omitted in this Collection.[1]

18   IV 707, pencil, overtraced | *Steps to the Temple: The Weeper* vi

> Not in the evening's eyes, .
> When they red with weeping are   *
> For the sun that dies,
> Sits sorrow with a face so fair:

* Better—Tho' they red with weeping were

mammoth found in a cave in Virginia was reported in *G Mag* LXXII (1802) i 493, and a plaster cast of the bones was exhibited in Pall Mall in 1803. *G Mag* LXXIII (1803) i 322. Rembrandt Peale issued for the occasion *An Historical Disquisition on the Mammoth*, drawing heavily upon Cuvier; it was extracted in *G Mag* LXXIV (1804) i 237–9.

The megatherium, an extinct ground sloth—"a SLOTH of...stupendous magnitude", according to Peale—was widely distributed through N and S America in the Pleistocene age; attaining a length of 18 feet and impressive weight, it is known to us in fossils. The name *megatherium* (lit. a large beast) was coined by Cuvier—"the *Handel* of French Physiology" (*CN* III 4357)—in 1797. For another example of C's interest in such matters, see *CN* III 3958 (Jul 1810), 4436.

16[3] Echoed "without knowing"—"notion" from the past participle of *noscere*, "to know". For C's definition of "notion" see *SM (CC)* 113.

17[1] For the connexion between *The Flaming Heart* and *Christabel* see COPY A **9** n 1. See also *CN* II 3102–7 and nn.

Two notes in ink on IV 701, 702 (on Anderson's Life of Crashaw), included in *Misc C*, are not C's.

19 IV 707, pencil, overtraced

Who but must regret, that the Gift of Selection, and, of course, of Rejection, had ⟨not⟩ been bestowed on this sweet poet in some proportion to his Power and Opulence of Invention! I have ventured throughout to mark the Stanzas, by the mere omission of which the ⟨finer⟩ Poems would have increased in weight, no less than Polish.[1] However ⟨justly⟩ the modern Chemists may triumph over the doctrine of Phlogiston or positive Levity, there exists undeniably a poetic Phlogiston which adds by being abstracted and diminishes by its presence.[2] *S. T. Coleridge*

20 IV 706, referring to IV 719, pencil, overtraced | *On a Prayer-Book Sent to Mrs. M. R.*

. . . .

Amorous languishments, luminous trances,
Sights which are not seen with eyes,
Spiritual, and soul piercing glances,
Whose pure and subtle lightning flies
Home to the heart, and sets the house on fire,

19[1] Stanzas III, IV, V, X, XI (last couplet), XVII, XXI are marked for deletion. Other passages marked for deletion: (*a*) IV 719, *On a Prayer-Book*, the two lines cited in **20** are deleted, then restored by someone else; (*b*) IV 726, *Music's Duel* lines 73–82: "In that sweet...blushing day", and lines 113–18: "The sweet-lipp'd sisters... look higher"; (*c*) IV 728, *Upon the Death of the desired Mr. Herrys. Another*, last 40 lines from "Now all their steely...". C made the same point about Crashaw to Allsop in c 1821: "Crashaw seems in his poems to have given the first ebullience of his imagination, unshapen into form, or much of, what we now term, sweetness. In the poem, Hope, by way of question and answer, his superiority to Cowley is self-evident. In that on the name of Jesus equally so; but his lines on St. Theresa are the finest. Where he does combine richness of thought and diction nothing can excel [him], as in the lines [in *The Flaming Heart*] you so much admire". Allsop I 194–5. See also **17** n 1, above.

19[2] Phlogiston was a hypothetical substance or "principle" given off during combustion. But when experiments showed that matter gained in mass after combustion the theory could only be maintained if phlogiston had negative mass or "levity". Originated by J. J. Becher and popularised by G. E. Stahl in 1731, the phlogiston theory was defended by Priestley all his life, even after 1774, when he had himself isolated "dephlogisticated air", named "oxygen" by Lavoisier. Through his interest in Priestley's work, and through his early acquaintance with Thomas Beddoes and Humphry Davy, C was familiar with the theory of phlogiston and with the controversy (see e.g. *CN* I 1098 of Jan–Feb 1802). This note is an interesting instance of C using an outmoded chemical analogy for an imaginative process. See also BÖHME **101** n 2.

And melts it down in sweet desire;
~~Yet doth not stay~~
~~To ask the windows leave to pass that way.~~

Delicious deaths, soft exhalations
Of soul, dear and divine annihilations;
    A thousand unknown rites;
    O joys and rarify'd delights!

A hundred thousand goods, glories, and graces,
    And many a mystic thing,
    Which the divine embraces
Of the dear Spouse of Spirits, with them will bring,
    For which it is no shame,
That dull mortality must not know a name.

    Of all this store
Of blessings, and ten thousand more;
    (If, when he come,
    He find the heart from home),
    Doubtless he will unload
Himself some other where,
    And pour abroad
    His precious sweets,
On the fair soul whom first he meets.

O fair! O fortunate! O rich! O dear!
    O happy! and thrice happy she,
    Selected dove,
    Who'er she be,
    Whose early love
    With winged vows,
Makes haste to meet her morning Spouse
And close with his immortal kisses.
    Happy indeed who never misses,
    To improve that precious hour,
    And every day
    Seize her sweet prey;
All fresh and fragrant as he rises,
Dropping with a balmy show'r
A delicious dew of spices.

O let the blissful heart hold fast
Her heav'nly armful, she shall taste,
At once ten thousand paradises
    She shall have power
    To rifle and deflower
The rich and roseal spring of those rare sweets,
Which with a swelling bosom there she meets.
Boundless and infinite————
————bottomless treasures,
    Of pure inebriating pleasures.
Happy proof! she shall discover
    What joy, what bliss,
How many heav'ns at once it is,
To have her God become her lover.

With the exception of only two lines ("Yet doth not stay To ask the windows leave to pass that way") I recollect few Poems of equal Length so perfect in suo genere, so passionately supported, & closing with so grand a Swell, as that (719) *On a Prayer-book, sent to Mʳˢ M. R.*[1] *S. T. C.*

21 IV 721 | *A Hymn to the Name and Honour of the Admirable Saint Teresa*

Love, thou art absolute sole lord
Of life and death.————To prove the word,
We'll now appeal to none of all
Those thy old soldiers, great and tall
Ripe men of martyrdom, that could reach down,
With strong arms their triumphant crown:
Such as could with lusty breath,
Speak loud into the face of death,
Their great Lord's glorious name; to none
Of those whose spacious bosoms spread a throne
For love at large to fill: spare blood and sweat,
And see him take a private seat,
Making his mansion in the mild
And milky soul of a soft child.
Scarce hath she learn'd to lisp the name,

20[1] The offending passage (lines 75–6) has been cancelled in pencil in the text; the whole poem is 124 lines long. In COPY A IV 719 HC has written beside *On a Prayer-book*: "This poem was a special favourite with S. T. Coleridge." The Latin phrase means "in their own kind".

Of martyr; yet she thinks it shame
Life should so long play with that breath,
Which spent can buy so brave a death.
She never undertook to know,
What death with love should have to do;
Nor hath she e'er yet understood,
Why to show love, she should shed blood,
Yet though she cannot tell you why,
She can love, and she can die.
Scarce hath she blood enough, to make
A guilty sword blush for her sake;
Yet hath she a heart dare hope to prove,
How much less strong is death than love.
Be love but there, let poor six years
Be pos'd with the maturest fears
Man trembles at, you straight shall find
Love knows no nonage, nor the mind.
'Tis love, not years, nor limbs, that can
Make the martyr or the man.
Love touch'd her heart, and lo it beats
High, and burns with such brave heats!
Such thirsts to die, as dares drink up
A thousand cold deaths in one cup.
Good reason; for she breathes all fire,
Her weak breast heaves with strong desire,
Of what she may with fruitless wishes
Seek for amongst her mother's kisses.
    Since 'tis not to be had home,
She'll travel for a martyrdom.
No home for her's confesses she,
But where she may a martyr be.
She'll to the Moors and try with them,
For this unvalued diadem,
She'll offer them her dearest breath,
With Christ's name in't, in change for death.
She'll bargain with them, and will give
Them God, and teach them how to live
In him; or if they this deny,
For him, she'll teach them how to die.
So shall she leave amongst them sown,
Her Lord's blood, or at least her own.

Farewell, then, all the world! adieu,
Teresa is no more for you:
Farewell all pleasures, sports, and joys,
(Never till now esteemed toys):
Farewell whatever dear may be,
Mother's arms or father's knee:
Farewell house, and farewell home,
She's for the Moors and martyrdom.

. . . .

an admirable Poem; but the two first §s *most* admirable. Here indeed præcipitatur liber Spiritus.[1]

21A iv 721

Mistress attended by such bright
Souls as thy shining-fels shall come,   self
And in her first ranks make thee room.

22 iv 724, heavily cropped | *On Hope, By Way of Question and Answer, Between A. Cowley and R. Crashaw*

[It is in]teresting [to] observe [...] Cowley's [...] the Wit [...] Thoughts or [em]otions; [Cr]ashaw's [wi]t indeed [...], but the [wi]t of [im]ages—[is more pro]perly, [wi]tty *Fancy*.[1]

21[1] "Here indeed the free spirit is precipitated (hurried along with abandon)". C had used "precipitates" of the nightingale's song in *The Nightingale* line 44. *PW* (EHC) i 265. C later described the ease of an accomplished poet in the phrase from Petronius *Satyricon* 118 which he probably had in mind here (even though in Petronius "the free spirit must plunge headlong"): "praecipitandum liberum spiritum". *TT* 14 May 1833.

22[1] No more can be deciphered in the ms. Collier's report of the sixth of the 1811–12 lectures, delivered before C had clearly articulated the relation between imagination and fancy, provides an exact gloss to this marginal note; indeed the marginal note, if not written at much the same time as the lecture, may even represent a draft for the position declared in the lecture. In discussing the outstanding quality of Shakespeare's wit, C said that "in at least nine times out of ten in Shakespeare, the wit is produced not by a combination of words, but by a combination of images"; and "when the pleasure is produced not only by surprise, but also by an image which remains with us and gratifies for its own sake, then I call it fancy. I know of no mode so satisfactory of distinguishing between wit and fancy." *Sh C* ii 90–1. Cf *CN* iii 4503 ff 135ᵛ–135. In that context the contrast between Crashaw and Cowley could be reconstructed as follows: "It is interesting to observe how Cowley's [wit of words differs from] the Wit [of images in Crashaw, whether aroused by] Thoughts or emotions; Crashaw's wit indeed is [not only the wit of words], but the wit of images—is more properly, witty Fancy."

22A   IV 727

> The timorous maiden-blossoms on each bough,
> Peep'd forth in their first blushes: so that now
> A thousand ruddy hopes smil'd in each bud,

22B   IV 728

> While he sweetly 'gan to show
> His swelling glories, Auster spied him,

23   IV 729 | *To the Queen, upon Her Numerous Progeny*

> For, lo! the gods, the gods
> Come fast upon thee; and those glorious odes   odds*
> Swell thy full honours to pitch so high
> As fits above thy best capacity.
> Are they not odes? and glorious? . . .   odds*

* i.e. supernumerary glories.[1]

23A   IV 735, pencil | *Out of the Italian*

> Chronology's the book of history, and bears
> The just account of days, & months, and years.

23B   IV 739 | *To the Name Above Every Name*

> Nor yield the noblest nest
> Of warbling seraphims, to the cares of love,   ears

24   IV 741 | *In the Glorious Epiphany of Our Lord God*

Crashaw is too too apt to weary out a Thought.

25   IV 753 | *On the Birth of a Princess*

Anderson could not read Latin. This same Poem stands in the very page preceding, 752[1]

23[1] *CN* II 3105 (1807) following immediately on the transcript of three couplets from Crashaw, reads: "a supernumerary excellence—". See *CN* II 3105n.

25[1] The text of the poem "Cresce, O dulcibus imputanda Divis", against which C has drawn a line in ink, is printed in Latin in both cases. The title *Natalis Principis Mariae* is on IV 752; but on IV 753 the title reads *On the birth of a Princess, the fifth child of Charles I* "(Not printed in any former edition)", and a footnote gives the source as *Concentus et gratulatio musarum Cantabrigiensium ad serenissimum Britanniarum Regem Carolum*, &c (Cambridge 1637).

MILTON

26 v iv–[vi], pencil, overtraced | Anderson's Life of Milton

He was now in his 52d year, blind, infirm, and poor; for he lost his paternal property by the civil wars, and his acquired by the Restoration. But neither his infirmities, nor the vicissitudes of Fortune, could depress the vigour of his mind, or prevent him from executing a design he had long conceived, of writing an Heroic Poem.

The great work of Paradise Lost was finished in 1665. . . . He sold the copy to Samuel Simmons for Five Pounds in hand, Five Pounds more when 1300 should be sold, and the same sum on the publication of the second and third Editions, for each edition. Of this agreement Milton received in all Fifteen Pounds; and his widow afterwards sold her claims for Eight.

In the nature of things this is impossible. Say rather it is self contradictory, as illustrating what it is meant to illustrate, the paultry payment for the P. L. I do not doubt the Fact, that is too well established! but I as little doubt that these 5 pounds were means to transfer the Property legally, & I could venture to determine that they were devoted by Milton to charitable purposes A man might incautiously sell any Copy-right for 5£; but would any man in his senses who wished to sell it, have bargain'd that after 1300 Copies, he should have 5£ more. If the sum was greater than now, was not likewise Paper Printing &c cheaper in the same proportion? I do not know the price at which the first Edition of Paradise Lost was sold —say only five Shillings—yet $1300 \times 5 = 6500^s = 325£$. Say that the expences of Publication, Paper, Printing, &c cost an 100£ (in all probability not above 50£) still the net profit would be 225£; & this a man with his eyes open (for he states the number of the Edition, 1300) *sells* for 10£.[1] Nay, and nothing more was demanded, even tho' by the Sale of the first Edition the Success of the Poem must have been then proved!—and this too by Milton, who remain'd *the admired* of all parties, & the revered of a very numerous one, and with whose name "all Europe rung from side to side"/[2]—

[1] The original price for a copy of *Paradise Lost* was 3*s*. C's calculation would then produce a net profit of £95 at the higher cost of production, £145 at the lower.

[2] This phrase may be a conflation of two of Milton's sonnets—xv *To the Lord General Fairfax* line 1: "Fairfax, whose name in arms through Europe rings . . ." and xxii *To Cyriack Skinner* line 12: "Of which all Europe talks from side to side". These sonnets are printed in *B Poets* v 171, 172.

Even so, I doubt not that it was Milton's injunction to his Widow to pursue the same course, & not degrade the divine Muse by Merchandize. STC

26A   v 41–2 | *Paradise Lost* v 1–120

[C has numbered the lines of *Paradise Lost* v 1–120, writing the numerals in the margin in ink, in fives.]

27   v 45–7 | *Paradise Lost* v 469–74

> O Adam, one Almighty is, from whom
> All things proceed, and up to him return, |
> If not deprav'd from good, created all   *
> Such to perfection, one first matter all, |
> Indued with various forms, various degrees
> Of substance, and in things that live, of life;

* There is nothing wanting to render this a perfect enunciation of the only true System of Physics, but to declare the "*one first matter all*" to be a one Act or Power consisting in two Forces or opposite Tendencies, φυσις διπλοειδης potentialiter sensitiva;[1] and all that follows, the same in different Potencies.[2] For matter can neither be *ground* or distilled into spirit. The Spirit is an Island harbourless, and every way inaccessible All its contents are its products: all its denizens indigenous. Ergo, as matter could exist only for the Spirit, and as for the Spirit it cannot exist, Matter as a *principle* does not exist at all—; but as a mode of Spirit, and derivatively, it may and does exist: it being indeed the intelligential act in its first Potency.[3]

The most doubtful position in Milton's ascending Series is the Derivation of Reason from the Understanding—without a medium.[4]

S. T. C.

27[1] "A two-formed [? bipolar] nature potentially sensitive".

27[2] For C's scheme of bipolarity, see BöHME, esp **6**, **35–38**, **54**, **95**, **101**, **137**, **139–142**; it was much elaborated in the notebooks after c 1817.

27[3] Cf Copy G of *SM*: "A safer definition of Matter is that which opposes it to Spirit or Power—thus
Spirit = id quod *est* et non videtur [that which *is* and does not appear]
Matter = id quod merè videtur [that which merely appears]

Body = id quod est et videtur [that which is and appears]...".
SM (*CC*) 81n (but rendering *videtur* "appears", following C's own wording in the note). See also ARGENS **18**.

27[4] The "medium" between reason and understanding is presumably imagination: see e.g. a note in the ms "On the Divine Ideas" printed in *C 17th C* 694. The passage in Milton occurs in *Paradise Lost* v 482–90, where the angel Raphael is instructing

28   v 123, each line marked with an ink dot | *Paradise Regained* IV 564–81

> As when Earth's son Antaeus (to compare
> Small things with greatest) in Irassa strove
> With Jove's Alcides, and oft foil'd, still rose,
> Receiving from his mother Earth new strength,
> Fresh from his fall, and fiercer grapple join'd,
> Throttled at length in th' air, expir'd and fell;
> So, after many a foil, the Tempter proud,
> Renewing fresh assaults, amidst his pride
> Fell whence he stood to see his Victor fall.
> And as that Theban monster that propos'd
> Her riddle, and him who solv'd it not devour'd,
> That once found out and solv'd, for grief and spite
> Cast herself headlong from th' Ismenian steep;
> So struck with dread and anguish fell the Fiend,
> And to his crew, that sat consulting, brought
> Joyless triumphals of his hop'd success,
> Ruin and desperation, and dismay,
> Who durst so proudly tempt the Son of God

O that these 18 Lines had been omitted! Here as in one other Instance in the Par. Lost, Power & Fertility injure Strength & Majesty.[1]

29   v [125–6] | "Of That Sort of Dramatic Poem Which Is Called Tragedy"

Division into act and scene, referring chiefly to the stage (to which this Work never was intended) is here omitted.

It suffices if the whole drama be found not produced beyond the fifth act.

The Submission of Milton's Mind to the Ancients indiscriminately/ spite of the Declaration, in Par. Reg. B. IV. (in this Vol. p. 121)[1] is

Adam upon the order of the universe and its relation to God.

...flours and thir fruit
Mans nourishment, by gradual scale sublim'd
To vital Spirits aspire, to animal,
To intellectual, give both life and sense,
Fansie and understanding, whence the soule
Reason receives, and reason is her being,

Discursive, or Intuitive; discourse
If oftest yours, the latter most is ours,
Differing but in degree, of kind the same.

28[1] C does not identify the offending passage—perhaps the pun on the fallen angels in Bk VI, mentioned in DANIEL 11 and DONNE *Poems* 51.

29[1] *Paradise Regained* IV 321–30, noticed in COPY A **5** and quoted in **5** n 1.

here curiously exemplified—The Play has *no* acts: for Aristotle prescribes none, & the Greek Tragedies knew of no such division— But yet it is not extended beyond the 5th Act—for a line of Horace (a mere ipse dixit without one reason assigned, & therefore probably founded on some accident of the Roman Stage) enjoins the non quinto productior actu.2—Into such contradictions could over- weening Reverence of Greek & Latin Authorities seduce the greatest & most judicious of men!—And from the same Cause must we ex- plain the stern censure on the Heterogeneous (Comic Stuff with Tragic Gravity) as applied to Shakespear.—Milton had not reflected, that Poetry is capable of subsisting under two different modes, the Statuesque—as Sophocles—& the Picturesque, as Shakespear—the former producing a Whole by the separation of Differents, the latter by the balance, counteraction, inter-modification, & final Harmony of Differents.—Of this latter Shakespear is is the only Instance.3 In all other Writers Tragi-Comedy merits all, that Milton has here affirmed concerning it. S. T. C.

29A   v 148 | *Comus* lines 624–5

> Which when I did, he on the tender grass
> Would'st sit, and hearken even to extasy,

29B   v 170 | Sonnet xi

> Hated not learning worse than toad or asp,
> When thou taught'st ~~in~~ Cambridge, and King Edward Greek.

29² Horace *Ars poetica* 189–90: "neve minor neu sit quinto productior actu | fabula quae posci vult et spec- tanda reponi". Tr E. H. Blakeney (LCL 1928): "A play which is to be in demand and, after production, to be revived, should consist of five acts— no more, no less."

29³ For C's defence of Shakespeare's mixing of "Comic Stuff with Tragic Gravity" in disregard of Aristotle, see *CN* III 3288 (lecture note of 1808); *BL* ch 23 (1907) II 182–3; *Sh C* II 122 (lecture report 1818). "Statuesque" in its first English use (in contrast to "picturesque" in his Shakespeare lectures of 1811) is attributed by *OED* to C. In *Sh C* I 196, in which ms lecture notes—not reports— are quoted, T. M. Raysor says (n 5), of C's statement "Ancients, statuesque, moderns pic- turesque...": "C is merely con- densing Schlegel's first lecture". But the contrast here between Sophocles and Shakespeare was made also by Lessing; and Schiller as well as Schlegel, in comparing poetry to the other arts of painting and sculpture, applied the word "plastisch" to the ancients—not quite C's "statuesque" and rather different in connotation, especially in the context of drama. See also De Q's tr of *Laocoon: De Q Works* XI 194–6, n on 195.

30 v 193 | *De Idea Platonica quemadmodum Aristoteles intellexit*

This is not, as has been supposed, a Ridicule of Plato; but of the gross Aristotelean Misinterpretation of the Platonic Idea, or Homo Archetypus.[1]

COWLEY

31 v 290 | *Ode Upon His Majesty's Restoration and Return* IX

> The martyrs' blood was said, of old, to be
> The seed from whence the Church did grow:
> The royal blood which dying Charles did sow,
> Becomes no less the seed of royalty:
> 'Twas in dishonour sown,
> We find it now in glory grown:

Cromwell's Exploits, the intimate connection of his name with vast Events, might easily have blended in the mind of a Genius, his name & the idea of magnanimous Liberty conquered and enforced. And in such a Spirit is Milton's panegyric of Cromwell conceived.[1] But how is it possible not to feel the degradation of a man of mind who could submit thus to flatter the wretched progeny of the Stuarts.[2]

DENHAM

32 v 679 | *On Mr. Abr Cowley's Death, and Burial Amongst the Ancient Poets*

> He not from Rome alone, but Greece,
> Like Jason, brought the Golden Fleece:
> * To him that language (though to none
> Of th' others) as his own was known.[1]

* It seems improbable, that Spenser who stood for a Fellowship against Bishop Andrews, should have been ignorant of Greek—/[2]

30[1] This poem of Milton's, a burlesque of Aristotle's criticism of Plato's doctrine of ideal forms, speaks from the point of view of a literal-minded Aristotelian to ask where the ideal form of man is to be found. Line 22 has the phrase *ingens hominis archetypus gigas*—"the huge archetype of man, a giant".

31[1] Sonnet *To the Lord General Cromwell, May 1652.*

31[2] On "the heartless Brotheller, Charles II" see HOOKER *Works* (1682)

1; also BUNYAN COPY A 11 and n 1.

32[1] Greek was "that language" known to Cowley; "th' others", named in succession earlier in Denham's poem, are Chaucer, Spenser, Shakespeare, Jonson, and John Fletcher.

32[2] Lancelot Andrewes (1555–1626), bp of Winchester, was the first divine to be appointed to prepare the "King James" version of the Bible. See also DONNE *Sermons* COPY B 1 n 3. Andrewes, a brilliant contemporary of

33   v 686 | *The Progress of Learning* Preface

> My early mistress, now my ancient Muse,
> That strong Circean liquor cease t' infuse,
> Wherewith thou didst intoxicate my youth;
> Now stoop, with disinchanted wings, to truth.

Much as I despise pretended Plagiarisms, as if no two men could have originated the same Thought,[1] yet considering Pope's admiration of Denham I think it probable that from this couplet he took his

> Yet not in Fancy's Maze I wander'd long
> But stoop'd to Truth, and moraliz'd my song.[2]

THOMSON

34   ix 174–5 | Anderson's Life of Thomson

He had recommendations to several persons of distinction, particularly to Mr. Forbes ... who ... received him kindly. ... He obtained likewise the notice of Hill, whom, being friendless and indigent, and glad of kindness, he courted with every expression of servile adulation.

Damn this Scotch Scoundrel of a Biographer—he cannot avoid stabbing & mangling his own Countryman, the Honor, yea, the Redeemer of Scotland. What? was it difficult to account for a young Poet's over-warm expressions from over-warm feelings of gratitude & ignorance of the World?—[1]

Spenser's at both the Merchant Taylors' school and at Pembroke Hall, Cambridge, was elected Fellow of Pembroke in 1576, the year in which Spenser proceeded MA and left Cambridge; he was an avid and omnivorous scholar, master of Latin, French, and Italian, and—as his Irish friend Lodowick Bryskett declared in 1583—"perfect in the Greek tongue".

33[1] Cf *CN* ii 2546 of 14 Apr 1805: "What is the right, the virtuous Feeling, and consequent action, when a man having long meditated & perceived a certain Truth finds another, a foreign Writer, who has handled the same with an approximation to the Truth, as he ⟨had previously⟩ conceived it?—Joy!—Let Truth make her Voice *audible*!" C knew of the case of Newton and Leibniz (see ABBT **1**,

BAHRDT **1**, AURELIUS **66**). On Laplace and Kant see BÖHME **106** n. 1.

33[2] *Epistle to Dr Arbuthnot* lines 340–1. But Pope wrote: "That not in Fancy's Maze he wander'd long | But stoop'd to Truth and moraliz'd his song".

34[1] Hall has added: "Anderson was not the guilty party—Mr Coleridge ought, one might suppose, to have known it—the language is Johnson's. But Anderson borrows wholesale—the very words—without acknowledg^t. SCH." For C on Thomson as inferior to Cowper but a "*born poet*" see *BL* ch 1 (1907) i 16n. For C on Thomson's blank verse see *CL* iv 782 and cf *TT* 20 Mar 1834; and for the difference between his own "mood and Habit of mind" and Thomson's see *CL* iv 974.

JOHN DYER

34A   ix 551 | *Grongar Hill*

Come, with all thy various dues,   hues[1]
Come, and aid thy sister muse;

MALLET

35   ix 673–4 | Anderson's Life of Mallet

[The poem] was published in 1728, under the title of the *Excursion*, a desultory and capricious view of such scenes of nature as his fancy led him, or his knowledge enabled him to describe. It has the beauties and faults of the "Seasons" of his friend Thomson, which were then in their full blossom of reputation.

Is it possible that a man should have written this?—O Lord! Yes! any thing is possible from a Scotchman! & N. B. Thomson was born only ten miles from the Borders, so that the Air from Cumberland might easily have anglicized him—& I should only find what I had expected, if it came out that his *real* Father was an Englishman.[1]

36   ix 675

In 1740, he was employed ... to prefix a *Life of Bacon* to a new edition of his works, in 4 vols. folio; which was written with great elegance and judgment. ... It ranks with the best pieces of biography in our language.

The Devil, it does!—Poor Language!—But Anderson, perhaps, meant the Scotch Language.[1]

34A[1] The reading of the 1761 ed is "hues".

35[1] Hall has added: "Notwithstanding this severe remark of Coleridge upon Anderson—Dr Johnson is as guilty. He makes precisely the same remark: 'He has Thomson's beauties and his faults.' S. C. H."

Thomson is one of a group of Scotsmen whom C exempted from the charge of being "a dull Frenchman and a superficial German"—the others being Hume, Robertson, Smollett, Reid, Dugald Stewart, Burns, Walter Scott, Hogg, and Campbell—and added to Thomson's name: "if this last instance be not objected to as savouring of geographical pedantry ...". *Friend* (*CC*) I 423. See also **8 n 1**, above. David Mallet (c 1705–65), a Scotsman by birth, was a friend of Thomson's.

36[1] C owned a copy of *The Works of Francis Bacon* (4 vols 1740) with Mallet's "New Life". He cited this edition and copied a long extract from it in May 1808 (*CN* III 3331), but he had been using it as early as c Jan–Feb 1801 (*CN* I 913).

Copy C

The Works of the British Poets, &c. 13 vols. Edinburgh & London 1794–5. 8°.

Dove Cottage Library

Inscribed on the engraved title-page of Vol I: "Wm Wordsworth from his dear Brother John". Late in life WW referred to this set as having been "my brother's companion in more than one voyage to India, and which he gave me before his departure from Grasmere, never to return" (*WPW* II 450–1), but his recollection was faulty in detail. JW bought his copy of *B Poets* in May 1801 or shortly before, after he had left Grasmere in Sept 1800 for what turned out to be the last time. During his long stay at Dove Cottage Jan–Sept 1800 JW had developed a desire to read widely in English poetry; he reported his purchase of *B Poets* to DW in May 1801. *JWL* 123. He was then on the point of making his first voyage in command of the *Earl of Abergavenny* and did not return from India and China until 10 Sept 1802. By then he had read enough to tell DW in Nov that "I shall send Wm Anderson's Poets I only whish for Spenser out of the whole collection but that I shall buy in London". *JWL* 128–9. On 17 Dec he promised to send a box containing the volumes of *B Poets* when he had fulfilled some commissions for SH to accompany them. *JWL* 134. Neither the Wordsworth letters nor DW's journal records the arrival of the books at Dove Cottage. JW made another voyage to China May 1803–Aug 1804 (on which C hoped, for a time, to accompany him) but did not visit Grasmere on his return. On setting out on another voyage to the East, the *Abergavenny* struck the Shambles off Portsmouth on 4 Feb 1805 and JW was drowned.

In addition to C's notes, there are a few other notes and marks, some by WW and others in an unidentified hand. The text of Chaucer in Vol I is virtually unmarked (cf COPY A), but line numbers are written in the Prologue to the *Canterbury Tales* and in *The Knight's Tale*, and there are short notes in I 101, 401, 520, +1. On V 479 two lines are revised in pencil; VI 240, two notes in pencil by WW; XI 462, corrections in the headline; XI 365, two lines marked in pencil; XII ⁻4, draft of a pun in French on *âne/âme*. Vertical lines against the text of Spenser's *Faerie Queene* (II 39, 52, 59, 61, 70, 72, 73) could be JW's, or C's.

DATE. c 1806–10.

SPENSER

1 II 81, pencil | at the end of *Faerie Queene* I xii

617 Stanzas in Book I
9
――――――――
5048 Lines

5553

2 ɪɪ 172, pencil | *Faerie Queene* ɪɪɪ iv

A lovely, thrice lovely Canto/

3 ɪɪ 400, pencil | *Faerie Queene* vɪ x 2, 4

>   Another quest, another game, in vew
>   He hath, the guerdon of his love to gaine,
>   With whom he myndes for ever to remaine,
>   And set his rest amongst the rusticke sort,
>   Rather than hunt still after shadowes vaine
>   Of courtly favour, fed with light report
>   Of every blaste, and sayling alwaies in the port.
>
> .   .   .   .
>
>   The glaunce whereof their dimmed eies would daze,
>   That never more they should endure the shew
>   Of that sunne-shine that makes them looke askew;
>   Ne ought in all that world of beauties rare
>   (Save onely Glorianaes heavenly hew,
>   To which what can compare?) can it compare,
>   The which, as commeth now by course, I will declare.

A striking, & *rare*, instance of *inconsistency* in the Poet.[1] His Court
& Faery Queene become here a vulgar Court & an ordinary Sovereign
& the parenthetic words in Stanza IV are but an insufficient redemption.

3A ɪɪ 517 | *Epithalamion* lines 67–8

>   And eke, ye lightfoot Maids! which keep the door,   *deer*[1]
>   That on the hoary mountain use to towre,

4 ɪɪ 519, pencil | *Epithalamion* lines 250–3

>   Pour out the wine without restraint or stay,
>   Pour not by cups, but by the belly-full: + +
>   Pour out to all that wull,
>   And sprinkle all the posts and walls with wine,

>   + + Brim the deep Bowls, the ample Goblets fill!
>   Fill out to all, that will:—[1]

3[1] In a literary-critical project as early as 1796 C gave prominence to Spenser (*IS* 152–3): this project became more substantial in 1803–4 (*CL* ɪɪ 955, 960, 1054), and by 1807 had become the nucleus for his literary lectures (see *CL* ɪɪɪ 30, and cf Dᴀɴɪᴇʟ 4). See also *CN* ɪɪ 3197.

  3A[1] The correct reading is "deer".

  4[1] Cf *TT* 24 Jun 1827.

5   II 519, pencil | lines 261–77

> Ring ye the bells, ye young men of the town,
> And leave your wonted labours for this day;
> This day is holy; do you write it down,
> That ye for ever it remember may:
> This day the sun is in its chiefest hight,
> With Barnaby the bright . . .
> But for this time it ill ordained was,
> To chuse the longest day in all the year,
> And shortest night, when longest fitter were;

Better su⟨i⟩ted for a night of assignation, than of marriage

6   II 520, pencil | lines 328–35, 349–52

> Like as when Jove with fair Alcmena lay,
> When he begot the great Tirynthian groom;
> Or like as when he with thy self did lie,
> And begot Majesty;
> And let the maids and young men cease to sing;
> Ne let the woods them answer, nor their eccho ring.
>
> Let no lamenting cries nor doleful tears
> Be heard all night within, nor yet without;
> .   .   .   .
> Ne let th' unpleasant quire of frogs still croking
> Make us to wish their choking;
> Let none of these their drery accents sing,
> Ne let the woods them answer, nor their eccho ring.

X But only let my Voice mid our caressings
   Sometimes sound ~~out~~ forth the Blessings,
The thanks, which I from year to year shall sing,
While them my Heart shall answer & their echo ring.

7   II 521, pencil | lines 353–404

> But let still Silence true night-watches keep,
> That sacred Peace may in assurance reign,
> And timely Sleep, when it is time to sleep,
> May pour his limbs forth on your pleasant plain;
> The whiles an hundred little winged Loves,
> Like divers-fethered doves,
> Shall fly and flutter round about your bed,

And in the secret dark, that none reproves,
Their pretty stealths shall work, and snares shall spread,
To filch away sweet snatches of delight,
Conceal'd through covert night.
Ye Sons of Venus! play your sports at will,
For greedy Pleasures, careless of your toyes,
Think more upon her Paridise of joyes
Then what you so, all be it good or ill.
All night, therefore, attend your merry play
For it will soon be day:
Now none doth hinder you that say or sing,
Ne will the woods now answer, nor your eccho ring.

Who is the same which at my window peeps?
Or whose is that fair face which shines so bright?
Is it not Cynthia, she that never sleeps,
But walks about high heaven all the night?
O! fairest Goddess! do thou not envy   **X**
My love with me to spy;
For thou likewise didst love, though now unthought,
And for a fleece of wool, which privily
The Latmian shepherd once unto thee brought,
His pleasures with thee wrought:
Therefore to us be favourable now,
And sith of womens labours thou hast charge,
And generation goodly doost enlarge,
Encline thy will t' effect our wishful vow,
And the chaste womb inform with timely seed,
That may our comfort breed;
Till which we cease our hopful hap to sing,
Ne let the woods us answer, nor our eccho ring.

And thou, great Juno! which with awful might
The laws of wedlock still doost patronize,
And the religion of the faith first plight,
With sacred rites hast taught to solemnize,
And eke for comfort often called art
Of women in their smart,
Eternally bind thou this lovely band,
And all thy blessing unto us impart.   **X**
And thou, glad Genius! in whose gentle hand

The bridale bowre and genial bed remain,
Without blemish or stain,   *
And the sweet pleasures of their love's delight
With secret aid doost succour and supply
Till they bring forth the fruitful progeny,
Send us the timely fruit of this same night,

X These two Stanzas may be made into one, thus/

all the night/
Thee oft the fruitful Wife invok'd of yore
To aid ~~their~~ her Travail sore
If ~~not~~ bless thou can'st, o bless this lovely Band,
And ~~from my~~ all thy aid for *my* Beloved store!
And thou, Glad Genius! &c[1]

8 II 521, referring to II 520, pencil | line 400 (in **7** textus)

Without blemish or stain,   *

* With Bleshmish none or Stain/

9 II 521, pencil | at the end of *Epithalamion*

All that could be wished to raise this admirable Composition from its present rank, i.e. among the very best 3 or 4 Odes in our Language, to an undoubted Supremacy, ~~would~~ is that Spenser had substituted two or three Stanzas of moral Tenderness from moral anticipations relative to marriage Life for two or three of the least beautiful of those relating to things & feelings purely bodily.—[1]

SHAKESPEARE

10 II 645, fly-title to the Sonnets

T first class of goodness.
I 2nd or next higher.
Ɨ 3rd or higher still
ᵀᵀ*a* 4th or highest.

The figures mark how many lines the praise is meant to extend to.
N.B. If the marks be placed on the left, or before the Number of the

a In writing the sigla against the individual sonnets C has consistently written this in the form Ⅱ. In the ANNEX, however, this siglum has been printed in the form II given in **10**, so that it does not seem to imply a class lower than "4th or highest"

7[1] C's detailed intention is not perfectly clear from the marked copy; his general intention was to dissolve the carnality of the original: see **9** and n 1, below.

9[1] See also **5**, above, and cf *CN* III 4388 f 146ᵛ.

Sonnet, the manner or style is praised, if on the right or behind it, the thoughts or matter: if over the number, both style and thought:—all according to the feelings & taste of S. T. C.[1]

DRAYTON

10A   III 622 | *The Muses Elysium* Nymphal VI line 7

  To make one leaf the next ~~to~~ kiss,   leaf[1]

WALLER

11 V 478 | Epistles VIII. *To Van Dyck*

 { No; for this theft thou hast climb'd higher
 { Than did Prometheus for his fire.

See p. 482—repeated—[1]

12 V 482, pencil | Epistles XXI. *To Mr. George Sandys*

 { To light this torch thou hast climb'd higher
 { Than he who stole celestial fire.

see p. 478.

10[1] C quoted from the well-known Sonnets 107 and 110 in the Gutch Notebook at an early date (*CN* I 215) and in 1803, writing about WW, echoed Sonnet 86, which he was to quote in *BL* ch 2 (1907) I 23. *CN* I 1546 and n. Comprehensive interest in the Sonnets appeared in Mar 1808 in his lectures to the Royal Institution when he first publicly declared his admiration for the poetry of the early Shakespeare.

The selection in ANDERSON COPY C—see ANNEX, below—seems to be the best record we have of C's assessment of the Sonnets. At the time of the 1808 lectures C had drawn up a short list of Sonnets: "for deep feeling"—Nos 64, 97, 98, 109; "for his own belief of his own greatness"—107; "Concerning his time of Life"—73. *CN* III 3289. When this list is compared with the selection in COPY C (see prefatory summary in ANNEX, below), it is seen that of these six three (98, 107, 109) appear in the "4th" or highest" class, two in the 3rd class (73, 97), and one in the 2nd class (64).

Another selective list of Sonnets is given in *CN* II 2428—a series of transcriptions or quotations from memory with personal variations, representing Sonnets 76, 91, 92, 97, 98, 105, 109, 113: three of these are in the 4th or highest class of the COPY C selection, four in the 3rd class, and one in the second.

An interesting comparison can be made between the COPY C appraisal and WW's (earlier) marking of twenty-four of Shakespeare's Sonnets in COPY A Vol II: Sonnets 30, 31, 33, 48, 54 (line 14), 78, 79, 80, 81 (line 12), 94, 95, 98, 102, 105–10, 112, 113, 116 ("The best sonnet, I think"), 134 (line 14 redrafted), 136 ("a very droll sonnet!"). WW's list includes four of the eight Sonnets C placed unreservedly in the 4th or highest class, two of C's eight in the 3rd class, and two of C's eight in the 2nd class. Thirteen of WWs choice are not in C's selection, but of these Sonnet 110 was quoted by C in *CN* I 215 and 105 was in C's "Asra" selection (*CN* II 2428).

10A[1] The tercentenary ed (Oxford 1932) prints the line as Anderson has it.

11[1] For C on Waller's technical accomplishment in *Go, Lovely Rose*, see *BL* ch 19 (1907) II 71.

CREECH

13 XIII 370 | Notes on Creech's Lucretius Bk I[1]

But indeed Cartes proposes his ambient attending circle, as the only way to solve the phenomenon of motion in a fall, which he thought he had sufficiently before evinced: but his arguments are weak and sophistical. For, in the first of his Meditations, he never takes notice of impenetrability, in which the very essence of matter consists; and in the second part of his Principles, he mistakes the notion of a void, and confounds substance and body.

Poor Des Cartes! never was a great man more calumniated. He does notice inpenetrability; because he denies it to be a property of matter, and refers it very philosophically to repulsion, which he proves a spiritual power.[2]

Annex

C has marked Shakespeare's Sonnets selectively in this copy according to the scheme set forth in **10**, above. Four sigla indicate four classes of "goodness"; the placing of the siglum, to the left or right of the number of the sonnet, or above it, shows whether the "goodness" is in respect of style or thought or both. The following table summarises the classification; the first line only of each of the selected Sonnets, with C's markings, is then given from Anderson's text, except when marking requires more extended text.

13[1] *CL* II 674—"Creech's account of Space in his notes to Lucretius"— shows that C did not appreciate that the notes were not by Creech but by an unknown writer annotating Creech often with qualification and disagreement. The notes were first published in the 1714 ed.

13[2] Descartes asserts impenetrability in the *Meditations*: see Reply to Objections VI §10 "...for true bodily extension is such as to prevent any interpenetration of parts". Throughout the *Principia* he assumes impenetrability, for he derives motion from the fact that two pieces of matter cannot occupy the same space in the plenum. As he derives all physical phenomena from extension and motion (see *BL* ch 13—1907—I 195-6),

Descartes has no need for attraction and repulsion or for any *forces*.

In his eagerness to defend Descartes, however, C is attributing to him his own views as expressed in *BL* ch 7 (1907) I 88. In the *Meditations* Descartes was concerned with the *existence* of material things, in the *Principia* with their nature and properties. As SC and Shawcross both point out, C's views were held explicitly by Leibniz: see esp *Nouveaux essais sur l'entendement humain* II xxi § 2, cited by SC in *BL* (1847) I 131; but as neither SC nor Shawcross points out, Leibniz in that place also makes a connexion between impenetrability, power, and soul.

For C on attraction and repulsion generally see AURELIUS **51** and n 2.

	T first class of goodness	**I** 2nd or next higher	**I** 3rd or higher still	**TT** 4th or highest
left manner or style	XVII (pt), XXIII	CXIV	XXXIII (pt), XLI, LXXIII, CVI	LXXXVI
right thoughts or matter	VII (pt)	XVI, XLIX, LIV (pt), LXX	~~XXXIII~~ (pt)	
over style and thought	XV, XVIII, XXXII, L	XXVII, XXX, XLI, LXIV, LXXXVI, XCIII (pt), CV, CXLIII	XXIX, XXXI, LXVI, LXXVI, XCII, XCVII, CXI, CXIII	XXXVI, LXVIII, XCI, XCVIII, CVII, CIX, CXVI, CXXIX

VII T.8

Lo in the orient when the gracious light
Lifts up his burning head, each under eye
Doth homage to his new-appearing sight,
Serving with looks his sacred majesty;
And having climb'd the steep-up heavenly hill,
Resembling strong youth in his middle age,
Yet mortal looks adore his beauty still,
Attending on his golden pilgrimage;

T

XV

When I consider every thing that grows...

XVI I

But wherefore do not you a mightier way...

XVII

Who will believe my verse in time to come,
If it were fill'd with your most high deserts?
Though yet heaven knows, it is but as a tomb
Which hides your life, and shews not half your parts.
If I could write the beauty of your eyes,
And in fresh numbers number all your graces,
The age to come would say, this poet lies,
Such heavenly touches ne'er touch'd earthly faces.
So should my papers, yellow'd with their age,
Be scorn'd, like old men of less truth than tongue;
And your true rights be term'd a poet's rage,
And stretched metre of an antique song:
    But were some child of yours alive that time,
    You should live twice;—in it, and in my rhime.

T

XVIII

Shall I compare thee to a summer's day?...

T XXIII

As an unperfect actor on the stage...

I

XXVII

Weary with toil, I haste me to my bed...

I

XXIX

When in disgrace with fortune and mens eyes,..

I

XXX

When to the sessions of sweet silent thought...

I

XXXI

Thy bosom is endeared with all hearts...,

T

XXXII

If thou survive my well-contented day...

I.3. XXXIII I.3

Full many a glorious morning have I seen
Flatter the mountain tops with sovereign eye,
Kissing with golden face the meadows green,
Gilding pale streams with heavenly alchymy;

TT

XXXVI

Let me confess that we two must be twain...

I

I XLI

Those pretty wrongs that liberty commits...

XLIX I

Against that time, if ever that time come...

T

L

How heavy do I journey on the way,
When what I seek,—my weary travel's end,—
Doth teach that ease and that repose to say,

"Thus far the miles are measur'd from thy friend!"
The beast that bears me, tired with my woe,
Plods dully on, to bear that weight in me,
As if by some instinct the wretch did know
His rider lov'd not speed, being made from thee:
The bloody spur cannot provoke him on
That sometimes anger thrusts into his hide,
Which heavily he answers with a groan,
More sharp to me than spurring to his side;
    For that same groan doth put this in my mind,
    My grief lies onward, and my joy behind.

LIV I 12.

O how much more doth beauty beauteous seem,
By that sweet ornament which truth doth give!
The rose looks fair, but fairer we it deem
For that sweet odour which doth in it live.
The canker-blooms have full as deep a dye,
As the perfumed tincture of the roses,
Hang on such thorns, and play as wantonly
When summer's breath their masked buds discloses:
But, for their virtue only is their shew,
They live unwoo'd and unrespected fade;
Die to themselves. Sweet roses do not so;
Of their sweet deaths are sweetest odours made:
    And so of you, beauteous and lovely youth,
    When that shall fade, my verse distills your truth.

I

LXIV

When I have seen by Time's fell hand defac'd
The rich-proud cost of out-worn bury'd age;
When sometime lofty towers I see down-raz'd,
And brass eternal slave to mortal rage;
When I have seen the hungry ocean gain
Advantage on the kingdom of the shore,
And the firm soil win of the watry main,
Increasing store with loss, and loss with store;
When I have seen such interchange of state,
Or state itself confounded to decay;
Ruin hath taught me thus to ruminate—
That Time will come and take my love away.
    This thought is as a death, which cannot choose
    But weep to have ~~that which it~~ what it so fears to love.

I

LXVI

Tir'd with all these, for restful death I cry...

⊓

LXVIII

Thus is his cheek the map of days outworn...

LXX I

That thou art blam'd shall not be thy defect...

Ɨ LXXIII

That time of year you may'st in me behold...

Ɨ

LXXVI

Why is my verse so barren of new pride?...

I

⊓ LXXXVI

Was it the proud full sail of his great verse...

⊓

XCI

Some glory in their birth, some in their skill...

Ɨ

XCII

But do thy worst to steal thyself away...

Ɨ 12.

XCIII

So shall I live, supposing thou art true,
Like a deceived husband; so love's face
May still seem love to me, though alter'd new;
Thy looks with me, thy heart in other place:
For there can live no hatred in thine eye,
Therefore in that I cannot know thy change.
In many's looks the false heart's history
Is writ, in moods and frowns and wrinkles strange,
But heaven in thy creation did decree,
That in thy face sweet love should ever dwell;
Whate'er thy thoughts or thy heart's workings be,
Thy looks should nothing thence but sweetness tell.
　How like Eve's apple doth thy beauty grow,
　If thy sweet virtue answer not thy show!

Ɨ

XCVII

How like a winter hath my absence been...

⊓

XCVIII

From you have I been absent in the spring...

I

CV

Let not my love be call'd idolatry...

ICVI

When in the chronicle of wasted time...

⊓

CVII

Not mine own fears, nor the prophetic soul...

⊓

CIX

O never say that I was false of heart...

I

CXI

O for my sake do thou with fortune chide...

I

CXIII

Since I left you, mine eye is in my mind...

ICXIV

Or whether doth my mind, being crown'd with you...

⊓

CXVI

Let me not to the marriage of true minds...

⊓

CXXIX

The expence of spirit in a waste of shame...

I

CXLIII

Lo as a careful house-wife runs to catch...

ANNUAL ANTHOLOGY

The Annual Anthology. [Edited by Robert Southey.] Vol II (of two). Bristol 1800. 8⁰.

Yale University (Beinecke Library)

Inscribed by RS on the title-page (of Vol II): "S. T. Coleridge from Robert Southey." On II ⁻6 EHC noted: "The omission of pages 118–123 is common to all copies of the work—but one. EHC—The work is often improperly described as imperfect." The bibliographical details of other copies of *Annual Anthology* II do not support EHC's statement. The BM copy, however, has a bookseller's note on Vol I: "as usual no leaf B8 in Vol I". The cancellation of the leaf has removed pp 31/2.

This volume is accompanied by a copy of Vol I (1799) that C did not annotate and that may not have been his. He wrote to his brother George on 29 Sept 1799: "Oh—I left the Annual Anthology [Vol I] behind!— Save, O save it from Edward's papyrologiophagous *Caco*daemony!—It can come with the rest.—" *CL* I 532. It is not known whether C recovered his copy of Vol I, or—if he did—whether he marked or annotated it. In this copy of Vol I two corrections in ink, one on a poem of William Taylor's (I 1), the other on a poem of RS's (I 25), may be in RS's hand.

The two volumes were edited and partly written by RS. A number of poems are unsigned or signed with initials or pseudonyms. There was nothing of C's in Vol I. On 10 Nov 1799, however, C wrote to RS that *Christabel*—"were it finished & finished as spiritedly as it commences"— would not make a good poem to open Vol II. *CL* I 545.

In Sept 1799 C had noted that in Vol I "Southey [is] a Salmon dressed with Shrimp Sauce." *CN* I 456, recalled in I 1582. In Nov he objected that "The great & master fault of the last anthology [i.e. Vol I] was the want of arrangement/ it is called a Collection, & meant to be continued annually; yet was distinguished in nothing from any other single volume of poems, equally good.—Your's ought to have been a cabinet with proper compartments, & papers in them. Whereas it was only the Papers.—Some such arrangement as this should have been adopted/ First, Satirical & Didactic. 2. Lyrical. 3. Narrative. 4. Levities...But still, my dear Southey! it goes grievously against the Grain with me, that *you* should be editing anthologies." *CL* I 545–6. Although Vol II shows no such subdivisions, some poems are grouped together: 20 sonnets by various authors are numbered in sequence (as in Vol I), and 17 epigrams. To Vol II C contributed 15 poems (including *Lewti*, *A Christmas Carol*, and *This Lime-Tree Bower*) and 12 epigrams.

When RS left Bristol on 14 Apr 1800 on his way to Portugal he had already begun to work on Vol III. In some expectation of death he appointed C his

88

literary executor and turned over to Charles Danvers and Humphry Davy the editing of Vol III; it was never realised.

DATE. Between 1800 and 1810. Vol II was published shortly after 2 Feb 1800; C brought a copy to the Wordsworths on 31 Jul 1800. *S Letters* (Curry) I 223; *DWJ*. C may have made the alterations to his own poems shortly after publication, possibly in connexion with *LB* (1800). The identification of authors seems to have come at a later date: the fact that C failed to recognise Amos Cottle's poem in Vol II (see **13**C n 1) suggests that he was not writing the identifications close to the date of publication; yet he did remember Sherive (see **1** n 4), who seems not to be mentioned anywhere else by C. It was in mid-Aug that Lamb fulminated at the phrase "gentle-hearted Charles" in *This Lime-Tree Bower* (*LL* I 203), and C's alterations to that poem in this copy ingeniously eliminate one occurrence of the offending phrase. In Oct 1803 C recalled his earlier epigram about RS's handling of Vol I (*CN* I 1582). In Feb 1804 C parodied in hexameter a line of William Taylor's found in Vol II; but he was then staying with James Tobin, who, as a contributor, must surely have had a copy. *CL* II 561. These few details are inconclusive. C's identifications of the authors were evidently made without consulting RS. This copy seems to have been left in C's library at Greta Hall, where RS's notes were made later, probably on more than one occasion.

1 II ⁻2, lightly cropped

Explanation of the Signatures

R. S. Y.	Robert Southey
S.	Ditto
Theoderit	Ditto
*	
Erthusyo	Ditto
R.	Ditto
Esteesi (id est, S. T. C.)[1]	S. T. Coleridge
J. W. T.	Mr James Tobin[2]

* Anagrams of—The Editor, & R. Southey.—

1[1] For the import and use of the name grecized from C's initials, see **10** and n 3, below. A complete transcript of the notes and markings in this copy of *AA* is included in Kenneth Curry "The Contributors to *The Annual Anthology*" *Papers of the Bibliographical Society of America* XLII (1948) 50–65, where the identification of contributors is based on this copy of Vol II, RS's marked copy of both volumes (Harvard), Alexander Dyce's copy (V & A), and other evidence.

1[2] James Webbe Tobin (1767–1814), son of Azariah Pinney's Bristol partner, lived in London with his brother John (1770–1804), attorney, and dramatist of posthumous reputation, from 1795 until John's death. He was a member of the Bristol Library Society and met C in Bristol in c 1797 (if not earlier) and visited the Wordsworths at Alfoxden with Tom Wedgwood in the same year. He is the "dear Brother Jem" of the rejected line in the prefatory stanza C contributed to

F. R. S.	Rev[d] Francis Wrangham[3]
C. H. S.	Rev[d] M[r] Sherive[4]
Byondo	Robert Southey
O. A.	M[rs] Opie[5]
Cordomi (i.e. Heart at home)—[6]	S. T. Colerid[ge]
Ryalto,	M[r] William Taylor of Norwi[ch][7]
Aepio	M[rs] Opie

WW's *We Are Seven. WPW* I 361–2. James was for a time assistant to Humphry Davy at the Pneumatic Institute, Davy having first come to Bristol in 1799: see **16A** n 1, below. While C was in London early in 1804, waiting to sail for Malta, he stayed with the Tobin brothers at 7 Barnard's Inn from mid-March. *CL* II 1085. James was one of the small group who finally saw C off from London, "*advising* and *advising* to the last moment". *CL* II 1129; and see *CN* II 2032. After seeing to the posthumous publication of his brother's plays, James Tobin left England in 1809, then totally blind, and spent the rest of his life managing his father's plantation in Nevis and working for the abolition of slavery. The copy of BARTRAM that C presented to SH was originally his.

1[3] Francis Wrangham (1769–1842), classical scholar, minor poet, epigrammatist, translator, and bibliophile, after being disappointed in his hope of a Cambridge fellowship was curate at Cobham, Surrey, when C's first surviving letter to him was written on 26 Sept 1794 (*CL* I 107). The correspondence concerned C's "translation —or rather Imitation—of your excellent Bru[n]toniad"—*Hendecasyllabi ad Bruntonam e Granta exituram*. Wrangham's privately printed *Poems* of 1795 is of historical interest in as much as it includes C's "imitation" and a verse translation of the "anonymous" French poem *La Naissance de l'amour* (actually Vicomte de Ségur *L'Education de l'amour*) signed "Wordsworth". *PW* (EHC) I 66; *WPW* I 298–9 and nn. In 1795 Wrangham became rector of

Hunmanby near Scarborough, Yorkshire, within easy visiting distance of Grasmere and Keswick. *CL* I 657, II 750. Wrangham's bibliophily, learning, wit, and scholarship were dear to C's heart. A warm friendship continued through C's lifetime, each sending the other copies of their books on publication. For Wrangham's monograph on Richard Bentley ([1816]), and a copy of the private and limited edition of his *Scraps* (1816) with C's marginal notes, see WRANGHAM. A presentation copy of Wrangham's *Thirteen Practical Sermons* (1800) is in VCL. Wrangham contributed two sonnets to *AA* I and six poems to Vol II.

1[4] Identified by Kenneth Curry as the Rev Christopher Hardy Sherive of Wadham College, Oxford (BA 1787, MA 1791), who died in 1800. He contributed six poems to Vol II, none to Vol I.

1[5] Amelia Opie née Alderson (1769–1853), who married the painter John Opie in 1795 after rejecting the suit of Thomas Holcroft. RS's friend, she contributed five poems to Vol I, two to Vol II. Her work as novelist and poet did not attract notice until the publication of *Father and Daughter* (1801) and *Poems* (1802).

1[6] C used this signature to only two poems (pp 192, 193): *Something Childish, but very Natural. Written in Germany* and *Home-Sick. Written in Germany. PW* (EHC) I 313–14.

1[7] William Taylor of Norwich (1765–1836) suggested the plan of *AA* to RS (*Memoir of the Life and Writings of William Taylor* I 228, 239)— a fact that RS may have acknowledged by placing one of Taylor's six

2 II 10 | RS *St Juan Gualberto* st 27

> In after years, what he, good <u>man! had wrote,</u>*
>
> [*] good Christian! wrote—
> So exquisite a poem should not be deformed by false grammar.

3 II 19, written at the end of the poem[1]

An inimitable poem, original both in conception & execution. It is a poet's natural *conversation*; but the conversation of a *Poet* by nature. *S. T. C.*

4 II 23 | C *Lewti* lines 8–9[1]

> But the rock shone brighter far,*
> The rock half shelter'd from my view,
>
> * Two lines expressing the wetness of the Rock—[2]

5 II 26 | lines 68–9[1]

> The nightingale sings o'er her head;
> ~~Had I the enviable power~~
> (O beating Heart!) had I the power[2]

[signed at the end:] Esteesi[3]

---

contributions at the beginning of Vol I; Taylor contributed nothing to Vol II. Although he was particularly RS's friend, he was intermittently important to C as one of the few enthusiasts for German literature in England in the early years of the century. His translation of Bürger's ballad *Lenore* published in the *M Mag* in Mar 1796 transported Lamb (*LL* I 37) and was an early landmark in C's discovery of German poetry: see e.g. *CN* I 340 and n, *CL* I 438. Taylor's German scholarship, however, was seriously discredited by the publication of his *Historic Survey of German Poetry* (3 vols 1828–30), largely pieced together from many of the 1754 articles he contributed to the *M Rev*.

3[1] The poem consists of 47 stanzas.

4[1] *PW* (EHC) I 253. *Lewti* had been printed as part of *LB* (1798) but was cancelled in type and *The Nightingale* substituted. D. F. Foxon "The Printing of *Lyrical Ballads*" *Library* 5 ser IX (1954).

4[2] EHC does not include C's note.

5[1] *PW* (EHC) I 256.

5[2] EHC notes this revision. The final form of the line was "Voice of the Night! had I the power".

5[3] In the Harvard copy RS has noted beside this poem: "W. Wordsworth when a boy, corrected by S. T. C."; and opposite the title in the contents: "A school-poem of W. W. Corrected by S. T. C." WW's original —*Beauty and Moonlight*—is given in *WPW* I 263–4 (cf II 531). Far from simply "correcting" WW's poem, C has transformed it into a poem as peculiarly Esteesean as his later (1806) translation of a poem of Ludwig Tieck's as "Glycine's Song" in *Zapolya* (*CN* II 2791). See also *CN* I 315n, 316n.

5A　II 33 | C *To a Young Lady*[1]

[signed:] *LABERIUS.* S. T. C.

6　II 34 | RS *The Battle of Blenheim*

a lovely poem!

6A　II 45 | RS *Ode to Silence, alias Unanimity*

[signed:] Southey

7　II 59, cropped | C *Recantation*[1]

Written when fears were entertained of an Invasion—& Mr Sheridan & Mr Tierney were absurdly represented as having *recanted*, because tho' [? opposed] to the war in its origin, they [. . . . .][2]

8　II 69 | J. G. *Lines to Sarah*

[signed:] J. G.oodwin[1]

A very vile Poem, Mister J. Goodwin! take a Brother Bard's Word for it![2]

5A[1] *PW* (EHC) I 252. The poem had been signed "LABERIUS" also in its published version in *M Post*.

7[1] *PW* (EHC) I 299–303; the note is given at I 299n.

7[2] Perhaps the sense of the cropped sentence—unlike the version proposed by EHC—is: "they changed their position when the revolutionaries betrayed their original principles". George Tierney (1761–1830), bitter opponent of Pitt to the point of a (bloodless) duel, and Richard Brinsley Sheridan (1751–1816), who made a famous speech in support of the French Revolution in 1794, both supported the principles that informed the French Revolution "in its origin", and opposed the Revolutionary War. Disgusted by the excesses of the Terror, they deplored the corruption of those principles of liberty, fraternity, and equality which they wished to continue to espouse. Emotionally, this was also the history of C's reaction to the French Revolution, and WW's. The title of C's poem is ironic: only in party-political terms—a position that C always refused to adopt—was this change of attitude a "recantation". See also Carl Woodring *Politics in the Poetry of Coleridge* (Madison 1961) 139–43.

8[1] George Goodwin contributed *Omar at the Tomb of Azza* (II 219–22) and *Fragments* (II 281–3); but possibly "J. Goodwin" is James Bones (d 1809), who became a scholar of Christ's College, Cambridge, in 1788, and who in Nov 1793 after taking his BA and before entering holy orders changed his name to Goodwin. In the Harvard copy RS has noted: "God knows who." But in this copy C's note has been extended in pencil in an unidentified hand—possibly (in view of the use of the initial lower-case letters) RS's: "Possibly Goodwin, but as probably any name beginning in G. about its very vileness Doctors differ. some par[ts] are *more than decent*."

8[2] On II 70–3 RS's *The Mad Woman*, signed "R.", is stroked through in ink, presumably by RS, the poem being a crude and derivative attempt at a "lyrical ballad".

9 II 74–5 | C *Lines Written in the Album at Elbingerode* lines 5, 28[1]

~~Homeward~~ Downward I dragg'd thro' fir-groves evermore,

. . . .

Thy sands and high white cliffs! Ø̶ My native Land,[2]
[signed:] C.oleridge

10 II 82, 81 | C *A Christmas Carol*[1]

IX

Strange prophecy! could half the screams
Of half the men, that since have died
To realize War's kingly dreams,
Have risen at once in one vast tide,
The choral music of Heavens multitude
Had been o'erpower'd and lost amid the uproar rude![2]

[signed on p 81:] ESTEESI[3]

10A II 89 | RS *History*

[signed:] Southey

9[1] *PW* (EHC) I 315–16.
9[2] These revisions are not noted by EHC. Both represent the final form of the text.
10[1] *PW* (EHC) I 338–40.
10[2] The cancelled stanza did not appear in any later published version of the poem. EHC does not notice that this stanza existed or that it was deleted in *AA*.
10[3] The poem ends on p 82 with st 9 and the printed signature "*ESTEESI*"; after cancelling the last stanza, C wrote his signature at the end of st 8, on p 81, in the same form. When first published in *M Post*, 25 Dec 1799, the poem had been signed "ΕΣΤΗΣΕ", which proved to be the definitive (though not invariable) form of the name C took for himself by vocalising his initials. As a child, and by the Ottery members of the family throughout his life, C was called "Sam", a name that he himself used in the Bristol period 1795–8 (see *Bristol LB*); to HNC and his generation he was "Uncle Sam". But he disliked the name his parents had given him as much as he disliked his facial features: see *CL* II 1126 (16 Apr 1804), and cf

Rev Samuel JOHNSON *Works* (1710) 315—"Nothing can *reconcile* me to my *wobbling* name, Samuel". 'Εστησε was, he said, "Punic Greek", signifying "*He hath stood*" (*CL* II 867)—a personal affirmation not much less strong than Luther's celebrated declaration *Hier steh Ich*. Cf *CL* IV 902. In 1805 C had a seal cut which he used on his letters from Malta, consisting of a triangle with "ΕΣΤΗΣΕ" above and "S.T.C." below: it is reproduced on the title-pages of *PW* (EHC) and *CC*, and on the half-titles of *CN*. (See also *CL* II 1160.) When he was drafting his own epitaph in 1833 he could say that he had become "better known by the initials of his Name than by the Name itself", and the initials assume a key place in all drafts of the epitaph and in the final version; in the introductory comment to one draft he placed them in an epigrammatic sequence:"ἔστησε: κεῖται · ἀναστήσει–. [he hath stood; he lies at rest; he will rise again] Hic Jacet, qui stetit, restat, resurget [Here lies one who hath stood, awaits, will rise again]." See TODTENTANZ and *CL* VI 963.

10B II 105 | C *To a Friend* line 35[1]

   These with stopp'd nostrils and glove-guarded hand[2]

10C II 111, 114, 126, 135, 136 | RS *On a Dull Fellow, Vezins & Regnier, Eclogue: The Wedding, To a Bee, To a Friend Expressing a Wish to Travel*

[each signed:] Southey

11 II 140–3 | C *This Lime-Tree Bower My Prison* lines 1–27, 41–4, 64–70[1]

   Well, they are gone, and here must I remain,
   This lime-tree bower my prison! ~~I have lost~~
   ~~Such beauties and such feelings, as had been~~
   ~~Most sweet to have remember'd, even when age~~
   ~~Had dimm'd my eyes to blindness!~~ They, meanwhile,
   My friends, whom I may never meet again,
   On springy heath along the hill-top edge
   Wander in gladness,* ~~and wind down, perchance~~
   To that still roaring dell, of which I told;
   The roaring dell, o'erwooded, narrow, deep,
   And only speckled by the mid-day sun;
   Where its slim trunk the Ash from rock to rock
   Flings arching like a bridge; that branchless Ash
   Unsunn'd and damp, whose few poor yellow leaves
   Ne'er tremble in the gale, yet tremble still
   Fann'd by the water-fall! And there my friends,
   Behold the dark-green file of long lank weeds,
   That all at once (a most fantastic sight!)
   Still nod and drip beneath the dripping edge
   Of the dim clay-stone.
            Now my friends emerge
   Beneath the wide wide Heaven, and view again
   The many-steepled track magnificent
   Of hilly fields and meadows, and the sea
   With some fair bark perhaps which lightly touches
   The slip of smooth clear blue betwixt two isles
   ~~Of purple shadow!~~ Yes! they wander on
   In gladness all . . .

10B[1] *PW* (EHC) I 159.

10B[2] The reading "nostrils" was also made by C in his copy of the earlier Bristol newspaper appearance of the poem. After *AA* the reading was always "nostril".

11[1] *PW* (EHC) I 178–81. For the earliest version, sent to RS in a letter of 17 Jul 1797, see *CL* I 334–6. Between the letter and the *AA* version C had carried out careful revision (sharpening specific detail and dissolving generalities) and had also expanded the opening section of the poem.

  *   Wander in gladness, pausing oft to view
      The many-steepled Track[2] magnificent
      Of hilly Lawn and Pasture, and the Sea
      With all its shadows. Yes! they wander
      In gladness all; &c[3]

.   .   .   .

      Less gross than bodily,* ~~a living thing~~
      ~~Which *acts* upon the mind—and with such hues~~
      ~~As cloath the Almighty Spirit, when he makes~~
      ~~Spirits perceive his presence.~~ . . .

  *   Less gross than bodily, within ~~the~~ his soul
      Kindling unutterable Thanksgivings
      And Adorations, such perchance as rise
      Before the Almighty Spirit, when he makes
      Spirits perceive his presence.[4]

.   .   .   .

      Awake to love and beauty! ~~And sometimes~~
       1   2   5   4   3
      ~~'Tis well to be bereft of promis'd good,~~
      ~~That we may lift the soul, and contemplate~~
      ~~With lively joy the joys we cannot share.~~
      ~~My gentle-hearted Charles!~~[5] ~~W~~When the last Rook
      Beat its straight path along the dusky air
      Homewards, I blest it! deeming ~~its black~~ that its wing[6]

11A   II 149, 150 | RS Sonnet V "I marvel not, O Sun!", Sonnet VI "Fair be thy fortunes"

[each signed:] Southey

11B   II 156 | C Sonnet XII

[in the title:] *To W. Linley Esq.*[1]
[signed:] Coleridge

11[2] This word was retained in *SL* and *PW* (1828), and thereafter became "tract".

11[3] This revision is not noted by EHC.

11[4] The printed *AA* version of these four lines is substantially the same as in the letter. The biblical personifications of this ms revision were not retained in *SL*, and one line was omitted.

11[5] This ms deletion gets rid of the phrase Lamb objected to without leaving a scar in the text, but the cancelled passage remained in all later printings—another indication that C probably did not have this copy by him when he was preparing *SL*.

11[6] The final version reads "deeming its black wing". EHC does not notice the *AA* variant.

11B[1] *PW* (EHC) I 236.

11C II 157, 164 | RS Sonnet XIII "Porlock, thy verdant vale", Sonnet XX "She comes majestic"

[each signed:] Southey

12 II 174 | C *The British Stripling's War-Song* line 13[1]

My own shout of onset, ~~when the Armies advance,~~
in the heart[a] of my Trance,

12A II 191 | RS *The Death of Wallace*
[signed:] Southey

13 II 213–15 | C *Ode to Georgiana* lines 12–16, 56–7, 68–77[1]

Emblazonments and old ancestral crests,
With many a bright obtrusive form of Art,
Detain'd your eye from Nature: stately vests,
Rich viands and the pleasurable wine, X[b]
Were your's unearn'd by toil . . .

X That veiling strove to deck your charms &c[2]

. . . .
 *   Than the poor ~~Reptile~~ Catterpillar owes
             ~~Its~~ The gaudy Parent ButterFly![3]

* originally written—

             Than Catterpillars are to Butterflies.—

. . . .
           The ANGEL of the Earth, who while he guides
              His chariot planet round the goal of Day,
           All trembling gazes on the eye of God,
              A moment turn'd his awful Face away;
δ to be   And as he view'd you, from his aspect sweet
Omitted   New influences in your being rose,
           Blest intuitions and communions fleet,

---

a Both EHC and Curry read "heat"
b C's "X" is written between the lines to indicate that the line written in the margin was omitted in error

12[1] *PW* (EHC) I 317. This revision was not printed in any later version.
13[1] *PW* (EHC) I 335–8.
13[2] Although EHC noted the insertion of this line, he seems not to have appreciated that it had been omitted by error of transcription or printing. The final word of the line is "divine,".
13[3] This deletion is not noted by EHC. The final version was "the poor caterpillar owes | Its gaudy parent fly."

With living Nature in her joys and woes!
Thenceforth your soul rejoiced to see
The shrine of social Liberty!

13A II 235 | C *Fire, Famine and Slaughter*[1]

[signed:] ESTEESI

13B II 242 | C *The Raven*[1]

[signed:] ESTEESI

13C II 253 | *An Elegy Written in a London Church-Yard. A Parody*

[signed:] C. Bedford[1]

14 II 267 | C Epigrams I and II[1]

I

O would the Baptist come again
And preach aloud with might and main
Repentance to our viperous Race!
But should this miracle take place,
I hope, ere Irish ground he treads,
He'll lay in a good Stock of Heads!

II

Occasioned by the Former

I hold of all our viperous Race
The greedy creeping Things in Place
Most vile, most venomous; and then
The United Irishmen!
To come on earth should John determine,

13A[1] *PW* (EHC) I 237–40.
13B[1] *PW* (EHC) I 169–71.
13C[1] Grosvenor Charles Bedford (1773–1839), schoolfellow of RS at Westminster and his lifelong friend. For a biographical sketch of Bedford see *S Letters* (Curry) II 481–2. He contributed one poem to Vol I and—if C is correct—only this one parody to Vol II. But C's ascription has been crossed out in pencil and "Amos Cottle" added by RS. (Curry did not notice this ms ascription of C's in his table of contents.) In the Harvard copy also RS ascribed this poem to Amos Cottle. Amos, younger brother of Joseph Cottle, died on 28 Sept 1800 at the age of thirty-two; Lamb at the time, in one of the funniest letters he ever wrote to C, made cruel capital of Joseph's grief. *LL* I 216–17. His *Icelandic Poetry, or the Edda of Saemund* (1797) was the earliest attempt at an English verse rendering of part of the poetic *Edda*; he worked it out from the parallel Latin version in the standard Copenhagen ed (1787, 3 vols to 1818). He contributed one poem to each volume of *AA*.
14[1] *PW* (EHC) II 959: Nos 25, 26.

Imprimis, we'll excuse his Sermon.
Without a word the good old Dervis
Might work incalculable service,
At once from Tyranny and Riot
Save Laws, Lives, Liberties, and Moneys,
If sticking to his ancient *Diet*
He'd but cup our *Locusts* and *wild Honeys*!

Dull & profane

14A   II 269 | C Epigram III "Hoarse Maevius" line 5[1]

~~But~~ yet folks say, Maevius is no Ass!

[signed at the end:] Esteesi

14B   II 269–70 | C Epigrams IV–X[1]

[each signed:] Esteesi

15   II 270 | RS Epigram XI

Doris can find no taste in tea,
Green to her drinks like Bohea;
Because she makes the tea so small
She never tastes the tea at all.

Flat! flat! flat! Flat as a Flounder![1]

15A   II 271 | C Epigrams XIII, XIV[1]

[each signed:] Esteesi

15B   II 271–2 | Epigrams XV–XVII

[each signed:] Tobin[1]

15C   II 276 | RS *Dramatic Fragment*

[signed:] Southey

15D   II 288 | *Lines on the Portrait of a Lady*

[signed:] Satterthwaite[1]

14A[1] *PW* (EHC) II 955: No 16.
14B[1] *PW* (EHC) II 954–6, 958: Nos 10, 22, 27, 28, 15, 29, 18.
15[1] For a similar comment see BEAUMONT & FLETCHER COPY A 11.
15A[1] *PW* (EHC) II 961: Nos 30, 31.

15B[1] For James Tobin see **1** n 2, above. As Curry points out, EHC printed Epigram XVI (which is signed simply "1798") as C's on the authority of *PW* (1877) II 166. *PW* (EHC) II 953: No 6.
15D[1] James Satterthwaite (c 1772–1827), successively of St John's,

16 II 292 | C *To an Unfortunate Woman ... at the Theatre* lines 13, 19[1]

Mute the ~~Lavrac~~ Sky-lark and forlorn,

. . . .

Upwards to the Day-star sp[r]ing,

[signed at the end:] Coleridge

16A II 296 | *Lines Descriptive of Feelings Produced by a Visit*

[signed:] K. Humphry Davy[1]

16B II 299 | RS *Song of the Araucans*

[signed:] Southey[1]

Trinity, and Jesus, and fellow of Jesus 1795–1806, was one of C's confederates in the undergraduate "defence" of William Frend at Cambridge in 1793. The hand at first sight looks like RS's, but that is unlikely considering that he ascribed this poem mistakenly to C in the Harvard copy.

16[1] *PW* (EHC) I 171–2. "Skylark" and "spring" are both in the final version.

16A[1] Humphry Davy (1778–1829), chemist. This is the only poem identified in Vol II as Davy's; it is not noticed in the *Fragmentary Remains* ed John Davy (1858), but the style and subject make the identification certain. Davy contributed five poems to Vol I, one dated 1795, the others 1796; one has his name in the title (I 281), the others are signed "D." (I 93, 120, 172, 179). These poems show that while Davy was still in Cornwall, and before meeting RS or C, he showed a precocious talent for verse composition informed by strong feeling for the maritime county of his birth. His five poems in *AA* mark the friendship he formed immediately with RS in response to the earlier passion for verse, which he was never wholly to renounce. By the time Vol II was being put together, Davy—though he found time to see *LB* (1800) through the press in London for WW—had turned his attention almost exclusively to chemistry and the Royal Institution.

C first met Davy in Oct 1799, after returning from Germany, and was immediately impressed and charmed by a man six years his junior who showed comparable versatility and genius. *CL* I 559. In Oct 1800 C wrote a letter of enthusiastic comment and technical advice on a poem of Davy's (*CL* I 630); and in the "Apologetic Preface" to *Fire, Famine, and Slaughter* (c 1815) he was to refer to Davy (not by name) as "a man who would have established himself in the first rank of England's living poets, if the Genius of our country had not decreed that he should rather be in the first rank of its philosophical and scientific benefactors". *PW* (EHC) II 1097–8.

See also AURELIUS **17** n 2 and **51** n 1, BARCLAY COPY A **3** n 3. For C's later disillusionment, esp at the time of Davy's knighthood (1812), see BÖHME **17** n 3.

16B[1] Other names have been written in pencil, the hand not identified: on II 145, 146, 162, 163 "Wrangham—". On II 192 RS has written "Coleridge —" below the printed "Cordomi", and "ditto" twice on 193. On II 197 RS has written "Hucks—", i.e. Joseph Hucks (c 1772–1800), C's companion on the walk through Wales in the summer of 1793.

JOHN ANSTER
1793–1867

Poems. With some translations from the German. Edinburgh 1819. 12⁰.

Henry E. Huntington Library

C's copy, probably presented to him by the author.

JDC, who once owned this copy, recorded that "the first few leaves ... were cut open and annotated by Coleridge". *PW* (JDC) cx n. In 1975 a number of gatherings were still unopened.

Whether or not C first met John Anster in Apr–May 1821 (cf *CN* III 4465), an important relationship was formed in Jul 1821: the presentation inscriptions in corrected copies of *LS* (Jul 1821) and of *SM* (Aug 1821) seem to point to the occasion. *LS* (*CC*) 235, 238; see also M. J. Ryan "Coleridge and Anster" *Dublin Magazine* II (1927). To C's inscription to Anster in *LS*, Anster added a variant of the opening lines of *To Two Sisters*—"To meet, to know, to love—and then to part | Formed the sad tale of many a worthy heart". *LS* (*CC*) 238; cf *CL* v 334.

If, as seems likely, this copy of Anster's *Poems* marks the first meetings between C and Anster Apr–Jul 1821, that may also have been the time when C received from him his copy of Charles Phillips's anonymous *Calumny Confuted* (1817), not annotated.

Anster, a Dubliner and one-time scholar of Trinity College, Dublin, invited C in Nov 1821 to deliver a course of lectures there and nearly prevailed. *CL* v 187; *C Life* (JDC) 249. On a visit to C in Jul 1829 Anster presented him with the triglot AESCHYLUS *Agamemnon*.

An epigraph from WW is printed on the title-page of the *Poems*; a note to p 242 quotes from *Joan of Arc* I.

CONTENTS. *The Times: a reverie. 1815*; *Lines on the Death of ... Princess Charlotte*; *Zamri, a fragment*; "Miscellaneous Poems"; "Translations" of poems by S. E. W. von Sassen, Klopstock, Haller, Schiller, Körner, Goethe.

DATE. 1821 or early 1822.

1   pp 4–8, pencil | *The Times* pt i

> Hast thou beheld the obedient march of waves,
> The appointed flow, the regulated fall,
> The rise, and lapse alternate? even as soon
> Shall they rebel against th~~r~~at silent ~~maid~~ Queen,

Who walks in joy among ~~the~~ her company
Of stars, and casts her chain upon the deep,
As poet struggle with the awful Power,
That wakes the slumbering spirit into song;
As Man forbid the soul to undulate
Through all its depths, what time the breath of heaven
Moves o'er the darkness:—
                          Speake there not a voice,
Voice of The present ~~voice of~~ God?—"Let there be light,"
It said, and light was over air and earth,
And with its glory garmented the deep:—

It said: and there was Light. O'er Air and Earth
Was and with glory &c

~~Even~~ And such a voice was heard on Chebar's banks,
Loud as the rushing of a thousand streams,
When in the shadow of the Deity
The Prophet sate, or hung 'mid earth and heaven,
                    +
And, in the fearful vision, saw display'd
The burning glory of the living God!
And, 'tis my faith, a portion of that power,
A ray of that divinest light, a breath
Of that eternal spirit, hath been given,
In later days to strengthen and to cheer,
To govern and to guide those favour'd men,
Whose lips are destin'd hallow'd[a] to proclaim to Earth   on/
The ways of God, his providence, his power.

    For me, and such as I am, humbler lay
Is more appropriate beseeming.[a] Not to me was given
Ethereal impulse; yet the ardent mind   Empyreal
Brooks not inglorious silence! yet my cares
Are often solac'd by some lighter muse!
When sorrow prest me, when the heavy hand
Of sickness weigh'd on the dejected mind,
And cursed me in the merry time of youth
With the dim eye, and feeble foot of age;
?   When Hope's reviving glow with health return'd,

?   Yet oft as Hope with tremulous Health return'd,

[a] C has written his revision above the word underlined

Some spirit still was near to whisper song,
A form that, angel-like, hung o'er my bed
Of pain, to reconcile the soul to death,
And, angel-like, illumes my brighter hours.

A form angelic, oer my bed of pain
It hung &c
And angel-like still*ᵃ*   my

    What hour more fitting for her visitations,

And for such visitings what hour more fit,

    Than when the silence of the night hath lull'd
The spirit?—when the stir of intercourse,
The fretting bustle, all that jarring clash'd
To drown the music of the mind, hath ceas'd?   *quell*/
What scene more suited to her agency
Canst thou conceive?—Round my broad window's arch
The ivy's wreaths are wound, and through the frame
A few short shoots have found unbidden way;
The woodbine's pillar'd blossom in the breeze
Moves slowly, and upon the moonlight ground
The shadow casts an ever-varying stain;—
The sound of waters, too, is here,—that stream,
Whose banks I love to call the poet's haunt,
Soothes with its ceaseless murmur,—opposite
My window is a poplar, all whose leaves
Flutter most musical;—the moonshine there
Plays strange vagaries,—now a flood of light
Spreads like a sheet of snow along the plain,—
        +
Now all is darkness, save that through the boughs
On the green circle, like a summer shower
Slow falling from unagitated leaves,
Some glancing drops of light are chequering still;—
Now is the ivy colour'd with the beams,—
Now on my floor they lie in quietness,—
Now float with mazy flow most restlessly,
(At rest, or quivering, still how beautiful!)
Like Fancy sporting with the poet's soul!

    They come—in midnight visitings they come—
But not such forms as in the calm of night

ᵃ After "still" C has left a space for a word not yet chosen; and at the end of the line another space, for which "hours" was probably assumed

Seek the soft twilight of the gentle moon!—
What form is yonder?—never hath the dream
Of night been bodied in a wilder shape!
Stern is his brow, and gloomy, and his height
Is as the shadow on the burial ground,
When the moon's light upon some sculptur'd form

Moónlight
the dead Moonshine[1]
still

In cold reflection lies! ...

1A   p 149 | *Solitude* lines 5–10

—Was there when fearless Sidney fell,
No angel form to guard his cell?
And when around the tyrant's throne,
    The courtly sons of flattery stood,
Oh, saw ~~ye~~ he then this pomp alone?—
Dwelt not his ear on Sidney's groan?

1[1] Anster had used the word "moonshine" 20 lines earlier. The word does not often occur in C's poems but has peculiar force when it does: see *AM* line 78 and *Christabel* line 146.

JEAN BAPTISTE DE BOYER,
MARQUIS D'ARGENS
1704–1771

Des Herrn Marquis d'Argens ... Kabbalistische Briefe, oder philosophischer, historischer und kritischer Briefwechsel zwischen zween Kabbalisten, verschiedenen Elementargeistern und dem höllischen Astaroth. Aus dem Französischen nach der neuesten Haager Ausgabe übersetzt. 8 pts in 2 vols. Danzig 1773–7. 8º.

British Museum C 43 a 2

DATE. Perhaps Mar 1810: on the basis of parallels in *CN* III 3750–3.

COEDITOR. Lore Metzger.

1   I i 55 | Letter 5

Mariana [addressing Spinoza:] Die Begierde, deinen Namen auf die Nachwelt zu bringen, beherrschete dich in so grossem Maasse, dass du von dem Pöbel zerfleischet und in Stücken zerrissen zu werden wünschetest, um nur dein Andenken durch eine so grausame Todesart verewiget zu wissen.

[The desire to hand down your name to posterity dominated you to such a high degree that you wished to be slaughtered and torn to pieces by the mob merely to see your memory immortalised through such a gruesome form of death.]

Detestable Calumny! If ever man of Genius was free from the lust of a wide reputation, Spinoza was he. To the very last he was unsatisfied, whether the good produced thro' his Ethics by the propagation of Truth would not be over balanced by the evil of being so generally misunderstood—he could not endure, that his name should be attached to his opinions—& dreaded as a curse the giving name to a *Sect*. He queried, whether those who thought enough to understand his work would not—without the work arrive of themselves at the same truths—& wished it to be suppressed.[1]

[1] 1 Only two of Spinoza's works were published in his lifetime: the *Principia philosophiae* (1663) and *Tractus theologico-politicus* (1670), the second anonymously. In the edition that C annotated—HCR's copy of *Opera quae supersunt omnia* (2 vols Jena 1802–3)—Vol II is entitled *Opera posthuma*

2 I i 64–5

[Mariana:] Du [Spinoza] nimmst nach deinen verkehrten Begriffen an, die Materie bestehe von Ewigkeit her, ja diese Materie sey Gott selbst; sie könne denken und sey beseelet, und daraus ziehest du die Folge, gleichwie unser Körper einen Theil der Materie des ganzen Weltgebäudes ausmachet, so sey unsre Seele gleichfalls ein kleiner Theil jenes allgemeinen Weltgeistes, den du an die Stelle des höchsten Wesens setzen wolltest.

[You assume according to your mistaken conceptions that matter has existed from eternity, indeed that this matter is God Himself; [that] it can think and has a soul; and from this you deduce that just as our body constitutes a part of the matter of the whole universe, so similarly our soul [constitutes] a small part of that spirit of the universe which you wished to put in place of the supreme being.]

This Coxcomb Frenchman probably never looked into the Ethic of Sp..; but certainly did not, could not, understand a Sentence of it.[1] What is matter in Sp:?—One of the two modes of contemplating the divine Being, into which all other modes are reducible—viz. Thought and Extension. The system is false indeed: for Sp. had no right to include Power, Life, & Will under Thought—but so far from being Materialism it is evidently a dogmatic Idealism—& its radical error consists in its dogmatism, in its identifying—Hoc *videtur*, et hoc *est*.—[2]

3 I ii 50 | Letter 27

[Paraphrasing Athenagoras:] "... [Die Poeten und die Philosophen] empfanden aus einem natürlichen Eindrucke, dass es ihre Pflicht wäre, sich um die Erkenntniss der Gottheit zu bemühen. Da sie sich aber mit gar zu grosser Zuversicht ihrer Einbildungskraft überliessen, so haben sie sich in ihren Untersuchungen geirrt, weil sie nicht das Wesen der Gottheit an ihr selbst untersuchten. Sie

and comprises *Ethica, Tractatus politicus, De intellectus emendatione*, letters, and the Hebrew grammar; these works were first published together in Amsterdam in 1677. The anonymous preface to *Opera posthuma* mentions that Spinoza was commissioning the printing of the *Ethics* at the time of his death and he wished the title-page to bear only his initials, apparently because (quoting *Ethics* pt 4 Appendix cap xxv) he did not wish "that his system should be known by his name". In a notebook entry of Jun 1810 C similarly vindicated Spinoza: *CN* III 3869.

2[1] For Spinoza's concept of matter see *Ethics* I Prop xiv–xv—a passage that C did not annotate. *CN* III 3751 (Mar 1810) draws on the text of Argens I i 66—a passage that appears after **2** textus.

2[2] Identifying "This *appears* (*is seen*) and this *is*".

haben sie in sich selber gesucht, wo sie doch ihren Wohnsitz nicht hat. Daher sind alle die verschiedentlichen Meynungen, und jene Streitigkeiten über das göttliche Wesen, über die Materie, über die Form, über die Welt gekommen. Die Christen sind freylich nicht in diese Irrthümer gerathen, weil sie an den Propheten, und an den Büchern der Schrift sichrere Führer hatten."

[The philosophers and poets felt, by a natural impulse, that it was their duty to occupy themselves about the knowledge of God. Since, however, they abandoned themselves with much too much confidence to their imaginations their inquiries went astray, because they did not investigate the essence of God in God himself. They looked for it in themselves, where it has not its dwelling. It is for this reason that they are all of different opinions and that the notorious disputes have arisen over the divine essence, over matter, form, and the world. The Christians, of course, had not fallen into this error, because they had surer guides, in the Prophets and Holy Writ.]

In other words, the christians avoided these errors, as long as they neither thought or wrote concerning the same subjects.

4 I iv 112 | Letter 89

Eine ausgemachte Sache ist es, dass unter den berühmtesten Mathematikern sehr viele Streitigkeiten herrschen: sie widersprechen einander beständig; die Antworten und Gegenantworten häufen sich unter ihnen eben so sehr, als unter den andern Gelehrten. Wir erfahren dieses von den Neuern, und es ist ausgemacht, dass die Alten eben so wenig einig waren; ein Beweis, dass es auf diesem Wege viele verborgene Schleifwege giebt, dass man sich leicht verirren und die Spur der Wahrheit verlieren kann.

[It is an acknowledged fact that there are very many disputes amongst the most distinguished mathematicians; they contradict one another incessantly, and replies and counter-replies accumulate amongst them as much as among other scholars. We find that this is true of the moderns and it is certain that the ancients were just as little in agreement; a proof that on this road there are many obscure side-paths, so that one can easily go astray and lose the track of the truth.]

Just such a proof, as this: In a long and intricate calculation A. made a mistake, which B. detected—ergo, there is no Certainty in ~~maa~~arithmetic!!!

5 I iv 113

Sie [die Mathematiker] glauben zum Exempel beweisen zu können, dass es *unendliche und doch auf allen Seiten umgränzte Grössen gäbe*; wie getrauen sie sich wohl eine Deutlichkeit in einem solchem

Satze zu finden? Sind wohl alle ihre gelehrten Reden im Stande das
Licht der Natur ganz auszulöschen, und die Vernunft umzukehren,
die uns zeiget, dass das *Endliche* mit dem *Unendlichen* nie einerley
sey, und dass das *Unendliche* aufhört unendlich zu seyn, sobald man
es umgränzen kann?

[The mathematicians believe that they can demonstrate for example that
infinite, yet on all sides limited, magnitudes exist; how do they dare to find
significance in such a statement? Are not, perhaps, all their learned discourses such as totally to extinguish the light of nature and to overthrow
reason, which shows us that the *finite* is never identical with the *infinite*
and that *infinity* ceases to be infinite as soon as it can be limited?]

This instance of Infinites is a mere sophism, founded in a transfer of
definitions—Define infinity so as to exclude *all* limits, of extension
not less than number, & doubtless I limited Infinity is nonsense,
but take the definition of the Geomete[r]ᵃ and attach it to some other
Sound, and the contradiction disappears—it being purely verbal, or
etymonic—[1]

6 I iv 114–15

Der berümte *Gassendi* hat sehr wohl angemerkt, *dass die Mathe-
matiker, besonders die Messkünstler ihre Herrschaft in dem Reiche
der Abstractionen und Ideen errichtet hätten.* ... Wir finden im
Newton ein Beyspiel davon: ohngeachtet ihm die Geometrie zu
erkennen gab, dass die Materie ins unendliche theilbar sey, so
getraute er sich doch nicht diesen Satz in der Naturlehre anzuwenden.
... Er nahm hierauf die Atomen des *Epicurs* an und behauptete, es
*sey unmöglich, dasjenige in verschiedene Theile zu zertheilen, was doch
durch die Anstalt Gottes selbst als ein ursprüngliches Eins wäre
erschaffen worden.*

[The famous *Gassendi* has very well remarked *that the mathematicians,
especially the surveyors, have established their dominion in the realm of
abstractions and ideas.* ... This we find exemplifed in *Newton*: although
geometry taught him that matter is infinitely divisible, he did not dare
apply this axiom to natural science. ... He thereupon adopted the
atomism of *Epicurus* and asserted that *it was impossible to divide into
separate parts that which through divine providence itself was created as a
primal unity.*]

What philosophic Mathematician ever supposed Geometry to be any

ᵃ Letter supplied by the editor

5[1] This observation on notions of   ἄπειρον: see Böhme **31** n 7.
"infinity" clarifies C's use of τὸ

thing else, than a system of the conceivable and inconceivable in the mind's constructive Intuitions? It is wholly *ideal*.[1]

Newton's solid atoms are utter aliens from Geometry, in which the mind exclusively contemplates its own energies: and *applies* them not otherwise, than hypothetically. Newton erred by introducing *Dogmatismc Realism* into the *Ideal world*—Solid atoms are not an *hypothesis*, as Gravity is; but a mere *Hypopoesis*.[2]

7 I iv 124 | Letter 90

Wenn hierauf *Montagne* sagt, *dass ein vortrefliches Gedächtniss mit einer schwachen Urtheilskraft verbunden wäre*, so könnte man ihm leicht das Gegentheil aus den angeführten Stellen beweisen . . .

[When *Montaigne* replies *that an excellent memory is related to a weak power of judgement*, one could easily prove to him the opposite from the cited passages. . .]

Strange! He has just quoted the passage himself, & M. says, that it *sometimes* is the case, & therefore the two qualities must be different/ & surely he says the truth.[1]

6[1] A frequent assertion of C's. Cf "Philosophy has *hitherto* been DIS-CURSIVE; while Geometry is *always* and *essentially* INTUITIVE." *BL* ch 12 (1907) I 171. See also e.g. *CN* III 3455, *BL* ch 10 (1907) I 109n.

6[2] The distinction between hypothesis (supposition) and hypopœēsis (suffiction) is clarified in *CN* III 3587 (Jul–Sept 1809). See also *BL* ch 5 (1907) I 72. C's argument is that if Newton's concept of "solid atoms" were a concept of "philosophic mathematics", it would be a hypothesis (supposition), an act of "the mind's constructive Intuition" in "the *Ideal world*"; but since it is an assertion based on the allegedly deductive assumption that the substratum of the physical world must itself have physical properties—"solidity"—the concept is a hypopœesis (suffiction). For a similar criticism of Newton's concept of an "Ether, or *most* subtle Fluid, as the ground and immediate Agent in the phaenomena of universal Gravitation" see *AR* (1825) 394n.

7[1] "Even Montaigne, whose writings are full of occurrences and quota-tions that necessarily presuppose a great capacity and exceptional ease of memory, believed that he himself had a very poor memory." The passage from Montaigne then appears in German on I i 121–2, citing *Essays* Vol I ch 9 ["Of Liars"]. "There is not a man whom it would so ill become to boast of memory as myself; for I own I have scarce any, and do not think that, in the world there is another so defective as mine. My other faculties are all mean and common; but in this respect, I think myself so singular and rare, as to deserve a more than ordinary character. Besides the inconvenience I naturally suffer from this defect of memory, (for in truth, the necessary use of it considered, Plato might well call it a great and powerful goddess,) in my country when they would signify that a man is void of sense, they say that he has no memory; and when I complain of the defect of mine, they reprove me, and do not think I am in earnest by accusing myself for a fool; for they do not discern the difference betwixt memory and understanding, in which they make me worse than I

8 I iv 126

Was die Ursachen anbelangt, denen man die Schwächung des Gedächtnisses beymessen kann, so sind deren sehr viele; Krankheiten, Wunden am Haupte, Erschütterungen des Gehirns, grosser Schrecken, schwere Fälle . . .

[There are a great many causes to which the weakening of the memory can be attributed: diseases, head injuries, brain concussions, great shock, serious falls. . .]

Despondence, or hopeless Passion is another Cause—the state of the Stomach yet another.[1]

9 I iv 132 | Letter 91

Der Kayser *Gracian* verliehe dem Dichter *Ausonius* das Consulat für seine Schriften . . .

[The emperor *Gratian* awarded the consulship to the poet *Ausonius* for his writings. . .]

He was Gratian's Tutor.[1]

10 I iv 134

[Footnote d:] Hier sind die Verse des Virgils, ich habe sie wohl mehr als hundert mal durchgelesen, und sie sind mir allemal schöner vorgekommen. Eines der grössten Genies auf der Welt sagte, er könnte sich nicht satt daran lesen.

> *Quis pater, ille virum qui sic comitatur euntem?*
> *Filius, anne aliquis magna de stirpe nepotum? . . .*[1]

really am; for, on the contrary, we rather find, by experience, that a strong memory is liable to be accompanied with a weak judgment; and, as I acquit myself in nothing so well as the friend, they do me another wrong in this respect that, by the same words with which they accuse my infirmity, they represent me as ungrateful." *The Essays of Michael Seigneur de Montaigne, Translated into English* (3 vols 1776) I 34.

8[1] C spoke from his own experience: see e.g. BAXTER *Reliquiae* COPY B 5. He offered an antidote: "a condition free from anxieties; sound health, and above all...a healthy digestion"—echoing the old Salernitan tag that recurred in his letters from Aug 1801. *BL* ch 7 (1907) I 88; see e.g. *CL* II 751.

CN III 3750 is based on another passage on the same page of Argens's text.

9[1] Decimus Magnus Ausonius (c 310–95), Roman poet and rhetorician, wrote his best poem, *Mosella*, while he was tutor at the court of Valentinian to the heir-apparent Gratian. He was made consul by Gratian four years after his accession, in 379. In his speech of gratitude to Gratian for his consulship he refers to his tutorship but not to his poems.

10[1] Virgil *Aeneid* 6.863–86—the much praised and pathetic passage in which the ghost of Anchises tells Aeneas of the early death and unfulfilled promise of the young Marcellus, their descendant to be, the adopted son of Augustus.

[Here are Virgil's lines; I have already perused them over a hundred times, and each time they have seemed to me more beautiful. One of the greatest geniuses on earth has said that he could not read them often enough.

Who, father, is he who attends the hero?
A son, or one of the illustrious line of his descendants?...]

That the lines are beautiful, especially in the metre and composition, *singultus* quasi numerorum, *sobs* of Harmony,[2]—this I see and feel— But that they are wonderful, super-excellent, &c &c, I deny—for what is there that might not have been said of any other hopeful young Roman who had died in his youth—what one distinct Image? what one deep feeling that goes to the human heart? I see not one.—[3]

11 I iv 256 | Letter 104

Wenn es wahr wäre, emsiger *Ben-Kiber*, dass Samuel nicht wirklich erschienen wäre, sondern die Zauberinn dem Saul nur ein Blendwerk vorgemacht hätte, wie hätte sie denn diesem Prinzen eben die Gesichtszüge, eben die Gestalt und Kleidung des Propheten vorstellen können?

[If it were true, diligent *Ben-Kiber*, that Samuel did not really appear but that the witch deluded Saul with a false semblance, how could she have presented to the prince the exact features, form, and dress of the prophet?]

It does not appear from the Text, that Samuel did appear to Saul— The Witch sees and describes him: and Saul hears a Voice.[1] What if the Witch had been previously lessoned by some friend of David's who had discovered Saul's Intention/ OR rather who had advised it.— The Witch knows Samuel & then Saul—& yet Saul does not know him except by his Witch's Description—

12 II v 288–9 | Letter 134

Mit den Empfindungs-Werkzeugen geht es eben so, wie mit den Sinnen. Der Mensch hat das Vermögen zu sprechen; seine Zunge, sein Schlund lernen ohne Schwierigkeit Worte bilden, und ver-

---

10[2] Lit. "*Sobs* as of numbers". C's version seems to imply that the sobs are intrinsic to the versification. The source of the Latin phrase is not known.

10[3] Cf "If you take from Virgil his diction and metre, what do you leave him?" *TT* 8 May 1824. See also *CL*

II 743 and H. N. COLERIDGE "Life of Hesiod" (*QR* 1832) **5** and n 3.
11[1] 1 Kings 28; cf *TT* 1 May 1823. In *CN* III 3753 (Mar 1810) C wrestled with these same questions about the Witch of Endor. See also BIBLE COPY B **10** n 1.

schiedene Töne articuliren. Dieses Vorzuges sind die Thiere beraubet; ihre Zunge kömmt ihrem Verstande nicht zu Statten.

[The tools of perception work just as the senses do. Man has the capacity to speak; his tongue, his throat learn to form words without difficulty and to articulate different tones. Animals are deprived of this advantage; their tongue does not serve their intelligence.]

Answer: the Parrot and the whole Genus of Pies.[1]—Dogs have been taught to speak—and I doubt not, that were the human Body possessed for ten generations by a mere animal Soul, and if a human & rational Soul were given to the 11th generation, there would be nearly as great difficulties to overcome in those men's organs of Speech, as in the Dogs—. So if Dogs had Reason for ten generations, consecutively, I doubt not, that in the eleventh they would have acquired a facility in articulating Sounds—.[2] We forget, how long the Infant is in bringing his organs to that power—& this by a willing effort continuously pursued for 8 or even 12 months—whereas a Dog is exercised only every now & then, & by *pain* & terror.—

13　ii v 297

Man findet auch unter den Elephanten treffliche Tanzmeister. Die Römer gaben bey ihren Schauspielen oftmals sehr schöne Ballets, die überaus schwer auszuführen waren, und von Elephanten getanzt wurden.

[Elephants can also be found to excel at dancing. The Romans often presented with their plays very beautiful ballets that were extremely difficult to execute and were danced by elephants.]

This story of the Elephant suggests a startling question/ How comes it, that in all these pretended proofs of the Reason of Animals only single extraordinary Incidents are mentioned?—There have been prophets—is that a proof that *mankind* possess the faculty of prophecy? Our proofs of human Reason are drawn from every voluntary act of every human Being—not from wonders? How comes it, that these strange stories excite so much wonder—were they not at war with our constant & regular experience?[1]

14　ii v 299

Ich habe zu Aix im Tollhausen ein junges siebzehnjähriges Mädchen gesehen, welches blind, taub und stumm gebohren war. . . .

12[1] The traditional association is with the magpie.
12[2] See **13** and n 1, below.

13[1] The question of animals possessing reason is discussed in *Friend* (*CC*) i 154–6, 160–1, *LR* ii 334, and *AR* 1825) 212–14, 234–42. Cf *CN* i 1831.

[In the madhouse in Aix I saw a young seventeen-year-old girl who was born blind, deaf, and dumb. ...]

[Argens says that she was so well-known that everybody who came to Aix would go to see her out of curiosity. Having seen her more than thirty times—most recently in c 1770, but he did not know whether she was still alive two years later—he was able to give a detailed account of her. She was cared for by an old woman who regularly brought her food, which she tore into pieces with her teeth, and gave her water to drink by holding a big earthenware crock to her mouth. She lay all the time on a pile of straw, crawling under the straw in cold weather. She could not bear to have any clothes on, and if clothes were put on her she would rip them off. She would often claw at her belly with her fingernails, and if anybody struck her or pricked her with a needle she would let out a loud cry like a goat. Yet she had an air of astonishing fineness, her body very clean and her skin healthy.]

This Girl was evidently not merely blind, deaf, & dumb, but had some disease of the Brain or nervous system which made the Body no fit instrument of the developement of the Understanding—this disease was the *Cause* of the Blindness, &c &c/ for others have been known, whose loss being confined to the Senses, have been instructed & humanized—Let a being born blind, deaf & dumb; yet otherwise healthy, be transported to a race of intelligent men who had formed a language of Smell & Touch, & be educated among them/—[1]

15   II v 306 | Letter 135

Wir sehen aus dieser Stelle, mein fleissiger *Ben-Kiber*, dass der Wein, sobald der Gebrauch desselben bekannt geworden war, dem dritten Theile des menschlichen Geschlechtes zur Ursache des Unglücks gereichen musste.

[We learn from this passage, my diligent *Ben-Kiber*, that wine, as soon as its use became known, was to become the source of misfortune for a third part of the human race.]

Filial Impiety was the *Cause*; the Wine only the accidental *occasion*.[1]

14[1] Cf *CN* I 987. On the sense of touch see BÖHME **24** n 9

15[1] The story is of Noah's drunkenness in Gen 9.20–5. But the offence that brought down Noah's curse of servitude on Canaan—"a third part of the human race"—was that Ham had seen "the nakedness of his father" when he lay drunk and "uncovered in his tent".

16 II v 317 | Letter 136

Num sollte aber die vornehmste Sorge eines Mannes, der lehren und unterrichten will, keine andre seyn, als sich nach jedermanns Fassungskraft dergestalt zu richten, dass er den Beyfall der Gelehrten habe, Leuten von Einsicht gefalle, und auch vom gemeinsten Volke völlig verstanden werde. Mir ist ausser dem Apostel *Paulus* kein Prediger bekannt, der jemals Schriften herausgegeben hätte, die in diesem Geschmack abgefasst wären.

[Now, the chief care of a man who wishes to teach and instruct should be no other than so to adapt himself to everyone's powers of comprehension that he has the approval of scholars, pleases men of discernment, and is perfectly understood by the most ordinary people. Except the Apostle *Paul,* I know of no preacher who ever published writings that were composed in this style.]

!! St Paul fully intelligible by the most ordinary *Vulgar!!*[1]

17 II vii 230–1 | Letter 169

Die *Engländer* fiengen an, Theil an dem Streite zu nehmen; es gab unter ihnen Leute, welche behaupteten, die Lehre des *David Nieto* wäre nichts anders, als was ihre Philosophen den *Spinozismus* nennten . . .

[The *English* began to take part in the dispute; there were among them those who maintained that the teachings of *David Nieto* were nothing but what their philosophers called *Spinozism...*]

Spinozism does not consist in making Nature to be God; but in making God to be Nature.[1] David Nieto denied any intermediate plastic power, Spirit without intelligence/ and held Nature to be a mere general Term, such as Art, Agency, &c[2]—this conclusion is wise & scriptural/ and the opinion of almost all Christian Divines— Boyle has shewn the dangerous consequences of this Nature, con-

16[1] C often adverted to the difficulty of Paul's style and thought. See e.g. *CN* III 3903, 3976, and *SM* (*CC*) 54–5.

17[1] C frequently discussed the specific definition of Spinoza's pantheism as a refined distinction that many of Spinoza's critics failed to grasp. See e.g. *BL* ch 14 (1907) II 12–13, BAXTER *Reliquiae* COPY A 2 n 2, *TT* 10 Mar 1827.

17[2] David Nieto (1654–1728), Jewish theologian born in Venice, came to London in 1701 as rabbi to Spanish and Portuguese Jews. He published theological works in Spanish and Latin. "Plastic" (from πλάσσειν, to shape), a favourite word of Cudworth's, found its way into *The Eolian Harp* and into C's coined phrase for the imagination, the "esemplastic" or "esenoplastic" power. Cf *Dejection* line 86: "My shaping spirit of Imagination".

sidered as an ens reale[3]—Grew's plastic spirit &c[4]—A Spirit cannot be organized—therefore no justification from the analogy of a machine or automaton/ and θif all the works of the universe, animate & inanimate, now are & for millions of years have been, the products of an unintelligent power, why not ab eterno? Quicquid *est*, possibile est.[5]—Spinozism consists in the exclusion of intelligence and consciousness from Deity—therefore it is Atheism. Pantheism is an erroneous, but not *of necessity* an irreligious opinion: for it leaves all the relations of Man to God the same/ and excludes no attribute from Deity—[6]

18 ii viii 81 | Letter 80, to Eberhard Weismann

Ihnen gesunde Vernunft beybringen wollen, heisst etwas Unmögliches versuchen. Auf den, der so was unternehmen wollte, würde ich anwenden, was ein deutscher Gelehrter von denen sagte, die immer beweisen wollten, dass *Plato* an die Erschaffung der Materie geglaubt hätte: *dergleichen Leute wollen einen Mohren bleichen.*

[To make you listen to reason means to attempt the impossible. To anyone who would undertake something like that I would apply what a German scholar said of those who always wish to prove that *Plato* believed in the creation of matter: *such people want to turn black into white.*]

There is a preliminary Question to be asked. Did Plato hold the existence of *Matter* in the modern or atomic Sense?—If he made its essence negation το μη ov, how *could* he believe the creatio[n][a] i.e. the actualiz[ing] of *nothin*[g]?[1]—Did Matter mean aught but limit &

---

[a] The writing has overrun the edge of the page here and in two words following; the *g* of "nothing" can be seen on p 83

17[3] See Robert Boyle (1627–91) *A Free Inquiry into the Vulgarly Receiv'd Notion of Nature* (1685–6), esp sec iv. For the scholastic term *ens reale*—a real being or entity—see Böhme 7 n 3.

17[4] C annotated a copy of Nehemiah Grew *Cosmologia sacra* (1701) in 1832–3. "Plastic spirit" is not a phrase used by Grew; but a note on a front flyleaf of Grew points to the implied difficulty here: "Matter may be *imagined* without Spirit: Spirit may be *conceived* without Matter; but Matter cannot be *conceived* without Spirit, nor Spirit be *imagined* without Matter.

—Again, Matter *implies* Spirit, for Spirit is *the* Substance; but Spirit does not *necessarily* imply (or rather *supersume*) Matter: for Matter is only *an* Accident of Spirit."

17[5] Why not "from everlasting? Whatever *is* is possible".

17[6] Repeated in *BL* ch 12 (1907) i 170n. See also Aristophanes tr Cary **1** n 4.

18[1] The Greek phrase means "the not-being". In the marginalia on Böhme C was preoccupied with the transition from undifferentiation (τὸ ἄπειρον) to real being: see e.g. Böhme **31** n 7.

multitude with Plato? Plato taught the το εν = το αγαθον² to be the Ground of all positive Being—all Beings were material as far as they were defined by negations of the το εν—³

18² "The one = the good".

18³ This is not a quotation from Plato but a summary in a Neoplatonic mode. At one extreme of Neoplatonic teaching about the world, "the one and good", the supreme reality, is above all being, the chain of being descending by a series of emanations to formless matter, pure negation, evil, not-being:

see e.g. Plotinus 1.87, 2.3.17. At the other extreme of doctrine, deriving primarily from the *Timaeus*, is the view that from the good only good could come and that therefore the physical world is good and beautiful: see e.g. Plotinus 4.8.6 and the note on the triangle as "unity in multeity" in BÖHME 116 n 3.

LUDOVICO ARIOSTO
1474–1533

Orlando Furioso di M. Lodovico Ariosto. Con gli argomenti in ottava rima di M. Lodovico Dolce, et con le allegorie à ciascun canto, di Tomaso Porcacchi da Castiglione Aretino. Diligentemente corretto, & di nuove figure adornato. Con la tavola di tutte le cose, che nell' opera si contengono. Venice 1713. 8°.

New York Public Library (Berg Collection)

Inscribed in ink by SC on the title-page: "S. T. Coleridge Gretahall Keswick"; and on p ‾2: "Given to me by Ernest Hartley Coleridge, Oct. 1901 S. T. Coleridge's writing at end of book. Writing on title-page either his wife's or his daughter's. R. Garnett." A note by EHC is pasted to p ‾3 (p–d): "To Richard Garnett C.B. LLD from Ernest Hartley Coleridge October 2 1901. The inscription *S. T. Coleridge, Greta Hall, Keswick*, is, probably in the youthful handwriting of Sara Coleridge. The blank leaf at the end, 'Il Metro Spenseriano' etc is, certainly, in S. T. C.'s own handwriting. Ernest Hartley Coleridge Oct. 2. 1901. N.B. It is only a guess of mine with regard to the handwriting of the inscription. It might have been Mrs Coleridge who wrote her husbands name in his books to keep them distinct from Southeys—but I *think* it might have been the daughter and not the mother."

A plus (+) in ink marks passages on pp 31 and 43; there is no indication that they are C's.

DATE. c Sept–Oct 1804: on the evidence of *CN* II 2224.

1 p ⁺3*ᵃ*

Il Metro Spenseriano Inglesi parmi migliore d' ottava rima/[1]

fastose	11 syl.
figlio	dᵒ
rose	dᵒ
giglio	dᵒ

> *ᵃ* The last leaf of the text pasted to the free end-paper so that only p ⁺2 is exposed

1[1] Tr: "The English Spenserian Stanza seems to me better than *ottava rima*." In about 1820 C spoke of the Spenserian stanza as "that wonder-work of metrical Skill and Genius! that nearest approach to a perfect Whole, as bringing the greatest possible variety into compleat Unity by the never interrupted interdependence of the parts!—that 'immortal Verse', that

> winding bout
> Of linked sweetness long drawn out
> Untwisting all the chains that tie
> The hidden soul of Harmony."

He was then comparing Spenser's difficult and subtle stanza with "the

116

piglio	dº
~~dispettose~~	
ingrata	dº
meraviglio	dº
~~vergognose~~	
nata	dº
fata	13.²

fastose	
figlio	
rose	
giglio	undeci Syllablee
piglio	con pause
grata	~~usale~~ solite³
meraviglio	
nata	

fata	13 Syll: la pausa essendo sempre dopo la sesta Syllable.⁴

stanza of Prior in which two elegiac Quatrains are put atop a couplet ending with an Alexandrine...these ten-line Paragraphs...which have about the same claims to be stanzas, as the King and three Fidlers to enter *solus*". BM MS Egerton 2800 (in *IS* 158); see also *CN* III 3318, 4357. *Ottava rima*, the staple stanza for Ariosto and Tasso, consists of eight hendecasyllabic lines rhymed *ababacc*. In Spenser's nine-line stanza the final Alexandrine imparts terminal weight and its final rhyme links it to the last line of the second quatrain. Both in the statement on Ariosto and in the later praise of the Spenserian stanza, C is sensitive to the unifying effect of the interlocked rhyming, as well as the cadential effect of the Alexandrine.

1² C provides Italian rhyme-words for an Italian Spenserian stanza, amplifying the English ten- and twelve-syllable lines to eleven- and thirteen-syllable lines to take care of the Italian feminine ending. C seems to have contrived the words himself: there is no corresponding group in the edition of *Opere* that he was using. The scheme is written out a second time more clearly,

after cancelling the variants for lines 5 and 7, which would produce an alternative rhyme-scheme (*ababacacc*) in which the emphasis is shifted from the second rhyme-word (as in Spenser's practice) to the first rhyme-word. In *CN* II 2224 C considers a variety of metrical movements and stanza forms; the experiments most closely related to Italian procedure and with the Italianate Spenserian here sketched out are Nos 19–49.

1³ Tr: "hendecasyllables with the usual pauses".

1⁴ "The pause being always after the sixth Syllable." This one elliptical note gives little hint of the scope of C's interest in Ariosto. In early summer 1805 he declared: "Dante, Ariosto, Giordano Bruno [shall] be my Italy", and in Sept referred to "the *first Canzone* of the darling Ariosto". *CN* II 2598, 2670. Later comments are much less laudatory—see e.g. *CN* III 4115 f 27ᵛ, 4388 ff 147–6ᵛ—but C could say that he preferred Ariosto to Tasso (*TT* 12 Jul 1827), and that he considered him the greatest of the major Italian poets of the Renaissance (*CN* II App A).

ARISTAENETUS

fl mid-fifth century A.D.

LOST BOOK

Ἀρισταινετου Ἐπιστολαι. Aristaeneti Epistolae graecae. . . . Cum Latina interpretatione et notis [by Josias Mercerus]. Tertia editio, &c. Paris 1610. 12°.

Not located; marginalia not recorded. Parke-Bernet Cat. 18 Feb 1941, lot 140: "With autograph of Coleridge on the title-page. The signature of Coleridge and the name of the place where he purchased the book appear on the inside of the front cover. A few notes in the volume are believed to be in Coleridge's hand." Appeared again in Parke-Bernet Cat. 29 Jan 1951, lot 125, and again in Parke-Bernet Cat. 18 Oct 1955, lot 270, this last time without mention of any notes. *Lost List.*

ARISTOPHANES

c 445–c 385 B.C.

The Birds of Aristophanes. Translated by the Rev. Henry Francis Cary, A.M. With notes. London 1824. 8⁰.

Harvard University (Houghton Library)

Inscribed on p ⁻2: "S. T. Coleridge Esq: with the translator's affectionate remembrances." An ink mark against an early part of the long footnote that C annotated (p 62n) may be C's. Bookplate of J. A. and C. W. Loeb on p ⁻5 (p–d).

In the Preface (p x) Cary mentions the unpublished translation of *The Frogs* by John Hookham Frere, lines of which C had printed in *The Friend* (*CC*) I 18; and in a footnote to p 61 he refers the reader to "an excellent description of the Sophists" in *The Friend* (*CC*) I 436–44. In Lecture 5 of the Philosophical Lectures (18 Jan 1819) C had outlined *The Birds* at some length, apparently as a compliment to Frere. *P Lects* (1949) 181–2.

For C's acquaintance with Cary see DANTE COPY B; and for C on Aristophanes see FLÖGEL 32.

DATE. 12 Feb 1827.

1   pp 64–5, cropped | I vi

[The Chorus tells how Chaos, Night, and Hell existed before all other things, then how Night laid an egg from which Eros emerged. In a long footnote Cary reports through Cudworth Salmasius' reconstruction of Aristophanes' scheme based on the assumption that what Aristophanes had got hold of was "really a piece of the old atheistic cabala".] "... As if not only the substance of matter, and those inanimate bodies of the elements, fire, water, air, and earth, were, as Aristotle somewhere speaks, according to the sense of those atheistic theologers, φύσει πρότερα τοῦ θεοῦ, θεοὶ δὲ καὶ ταῦτα, *first in order of Nature before God, as being themselves also Gods,* but also brute animals at least, if not men too. And this is the atheistic creation of the world, Gods, and all out of *senseless and stupid matter, or dark Chaos, as the only Original Numen; the perfectly inverted order of the universe."

[*] Master Cudworth![1] This is not quite fair! Theis "Atheistic"

[1] Ralph Cudworth (1617–88), one of the Latitudinarian Cambridge Pla-   tonists, whose *True Intellectual System of the Universe* (2 vols 1743) C had

119

Scheme of Creation may be "senseless & stupid", if you please;[2] but the Elements, φυσει προτερα του Θεου, θεοι δε και ταυτα, are for that reason the first & *therefore* lowest (prima et infima) Evolutions ~~εκ~~ of Chaos—i.e. εκ του Θειου.[3] [. . . . .] the Absolute [. . . . .] intellectual Pantheism is moral Atheism, I both admit, & have strenuously contended—but it is not Epicurean Atheism, or the godless lifeless Phantasm of crass Materialism.[4] S. T. Coleridge 12 Feby 1827. Grove, H[ighga]t[e]

---

borrowed from the Bristol Library 15 May to 1 Jun 1795 and 9 Nov to 13 Dec 1796 (*Bristol LB* 55, 90), using it in preparing his Lectures on Revealed Religion, esp I and V; see *Lects 1795* (*CC*) 96–9n, 101n, 105n. Cudworth has important bearings upon the Conversation Poems and was to have provided material for the projected "Hymns on the Elements". *CN* I 174 (16), 200, 201; cf *CL* V 28. *CN* I 203, 246, 247 show that in 1795–6 C had paid particular attention to the passage cited by Cary.

1[2] C seems to have lost the thread of Cary's long and high-spirited note (pp 62–4). What Cary has actually done is to quote the commonly held view "that Aristophanes here mixes up the opinions of poets and philosophers...in order to make one and the other appear more ridiculous". He then quotes extensively from Erasmus Darwin to show how vulnerable Darwin would be to Aristophanes' satirical attack. He then quotes Cudworth as saying that Salmasius' view is "not without some reason". The phrase "senseless and stupid" is applied by Cudworth to "matter" (in his reconstruction of Salmasius), not

to the theory (which he is sympathetically advancing).

1[3] The Greek phrase means "from/ out of the divine"; the longer phrase is translated by Cary. For the distinction between ὁ θέος and τὸ θεῖον see BÖHME 6. From C's point of view, though the Greeks made the error of omitting God from their cosmogony, yet by deriving their elements from the divine ground, or chaos, they were in the error of intellectual pantheism or moral atheism rather than in the more serious error of Epicurean atheism or crass materialism. For the Coleridgian cosmogony see BÖHME **68, 94, 110, 136** n 2, and **139**.

1[4] See also BÖHME **110, 159**. Cf a note on JOANNES Scotus Erigena *De divisione naturae* (Oxford 1681) pp [iv], 1. In c 1820 C told Allsop: "Not one man in ten thousand has either goodness of heart or strength of mind to be an atheist. And, were I not a Christian, *and that only in the sense in which I am a Christian*, I should be an atheist with Spinosa". Allsop I 89. Cf *TT* 4 Apr 1832. "Crass Materialism" is the position represented by "the sensual and the proud" in *Dejection* V.

JOHN ASGILL
1659–1730

A Collection of Tracts written by John Asgill, Esq; from the year 1700. to the year 1715. Some relating to divinity: and others to the history of the monarchy, the succession of the crown, and constitution of the government of Great Britain. 8 pts in 1 vol. London 1715. 8º.

British Museum C 126 d 2

Inscribed on p ⁻3 (p–d): "8/0 Rivington WGK 11 Octr 1822"; and in another hand: "Valuable Wm G. K." The first inscription is repeated in pencil on p ⁻2, and below it "24 Melchidezek", C's note 1 being written over. Inscribed on the title-page: "Matt: Lawrance". A note by EHC, referring to *CW* v 545 and *TT* 10 Jun 1832, tipped in at i 32/33.

Inscribed by C on p ⁻3 (p–d): "28 Jany 1827. This Book given me by Mr Kirkpatrick—together with the Spes Israel by R. Menasseh Ben Israel. S. T. Coleridge." The signature "S. T. Coleridge" is also written at the top of p ⁺3 (p–d). "S. T. C." label on the title-page, and monogram of John Duke Coleridge on p ⁻2.

"Wm G. K."—i.e. William George Kirkpatrick (c 1801–28), the only son of James Achilles Kirkpatrick of Hyderabad and nephew of the orientalist William Kirkpatrick (1754–1812), matriculated at Merton College, Oxford, in Jun 1820.

There were several editions of Manasseh ben Israel (1604–57) *Spes Israelis*, first published in Amsterdam in 1650 and in London with an English translation in the same year. C's copy has disappeared.

On p ⁻1, in pencil, a tabular construction of letters as for a cipher, the consonants arranged in order vertically in groups of four. Below this, also in pencil, a series of five interrelated sigla has been evolved from the equilateral triangle; there is further tabular presentation of the alphabet and the un-Greek word αρεδφογυ [? Dear Gough]. On pp ⁺1, ⁺2, ⁺3, also in pencil, there are sketches for the spine of this volume with short titles of the Asgill tracts. The writing in all these is not unlike C's in form, but smaller, more precise, and more ceremonious than appears elsewhere in the volume. All these pencillings—like the reference to Archimedes on i 84— were evidently in the book before C received it: they arrested his attention so little that he wrote his notes 1–3 in the front of the book, and 12 and 13 in the back, without respect for them.

On 22 Apr 1832 C told H. F. Cary (Assistant Keeper of Printed Books in the BM since 1826) that he had planned "a reprint, as nearly as possible except in quality of the *paper* a fac Simile of John Asgill's Tracts, with a

121

Life & Copious Notes—to which I would affix Postilla et Marginalia—. Now can you direct me to any sources of Information respecting John Asgill, a prime Darling of mine—the most honest of all Whigs, whom at the close of Queen Anne's Reign the scoundrelly Jacobite Tories twice expelled from Parliament...". *CL* VI 901–2. A few days later he wrote to HNC with definite proposals for publication by John Murray—an elaborate affair, to include marginalia on Baxter and on RS's *Life of Wesley*: see *CL* VI 904–6. Murray did not respond, and the work went no further.

CONTENTS. (i) An Argument proving, that according to the covenant of eternal life reveal'd in the Scriptures, man may be translated from hence into that eternal life, without passing through death (1715). (ii) [Mr. Asgill de Jure Divino.] The Assertion is, that the title of the House of Hannover to the succession of the British monarchy ... is a title hereditary, and of divine institution (1715). (iii) An Essay for the Press (1712). (iv) Mr. Asgill's Defence upon his expulsion from the House of Commons ... in 1707 (1712). (v) Mr. Asgill's Extract of the several Acts of Parliament for settling the succession of the crown in the House of Hannover (1714). (vi) The Pretender's Declaration abstracted from two anonymous pamphlets (1715). (vii) The Succession of the House of Hannover vindicated, against the Pretender's second declaration in folio (1714). (viii) The Pretender's Declaration [from Plombiers] English'd (1715).

DATE. Feb 1827 to 1828, with a personal note added in 1832: 2 Feb 1827 (**10**), 1828 (**13**), 1832 (PS to **13**).

1   p ‾2 | *An Argument Proving That ... Man May Be Translated*

If I needed an illustrative example of the distinction between Reason and the Understanding, ~~or~~ between spiritual *Sense*, and *Logic*, this first treatise of Asgill would supply it.[1]—Excuse the defect of all *Idea* or spiritual Intuition[a] of God—and allow yourself to bring him as Plaintiff or Defendant into a common Law-court—and *then* I cannot conceive a more clear & clever piece of Special pleading than Asgill has here given.[2]—The language E X C E L L E N T—idiomatic, simple, perspicuous, at once significant & lively—i.e. expressive of *the* thought and of a manly proportion of *feeling*.[b] appropriate to it.

In short, it is the ablest attempt to exhibit a Scheme of Religion without Ideas, that the inherent contradiction in the thought renders possible.[3]

[a] C has written "Intitution", for which "Intuition" makes better sense in the context than "Institution", as read by *C 17th C* 496
[b] C has put a full point after "feeling". The last three words of the sentence and the sentence that follows are written in a slightly different hand, either as a considered afterthought or on another occasion

[1] For C's distinction between reason and understanding see BAXTER *Catholick Theologie* **14** n 3.
[2] Asgill was a man of law: see headnote and cf **3** below.
[3] See a full statement in a letter to HNC 7 May 1832, printed inaccurately in *C 17th C*, now in *CL* VI 901–3.

2 p ‾1, concluded on title-page verso

In him is Life: and that Life is the *Light* of Men.[1] And as long as the Light abides within its own sphere—i.e. appears as Reason; so long it is commensurate with the Life and its adequate Representative. But not so when this Light shines downward into the Understanding[a] of the Individual Here it is always more or less refracted, and differently in every different Individual, and ⟨it⟩ must be re-converted into *Life* to rectify itself and regain its universality—(*all-common-*⟨*ness,*⟩ as the German more expressively says,)[2]—Hence in Faith and Charity the Church is Catholic. So likewise in the fundamental Articles of Belief, which constitute the Right REASON of Faith. But in the minor doctrines dogmata & in modes of exposition & the vehicles of Faith and Reason to the Understandings, Imaginations and Affections of Men, the Churches may differ, and in this difference supply one Object for Charity to exercise itself on, by mutual forbearance.—

O! there is a deep philosophy in the proverbial phrase, "His Heart sets his Head right." In our commerce with Heaven, when the Balance of Trade is vastly in our favour we we must cast our local Coins and Tokens into the Melting-pot of Love, to pass by weight of Bullion. And where the Balance of Trade is so immensely in our favor, we have little right to complain, tho' they should not pass for half the nominal value, they go for in our own Market.[3] S. T. C.

3 p ‾1, concluded on title-page[b]

It is of minor importance, *how* a Man represents to himself his Redemption by the Word Incarnate, according to within what scheme of his Understanding he concludes it or by what ⟨*supposed*⟩ analogies (tho' actually no better than metaphors) he tries to conceive it, provided he has a lively *Faith* in Christ, a the Son of the Living God, as his Redeemer. The *Faith* may be and must be the same in all who

---

[a] The beginning of this note, written in the space above **3**, breaks where the previously written **2** prevented C from writing any more on p ‾1. Above the first line of **2** he has squeezed in the direction "(*turn over the title-page*)"; the note is resumed on title-page verso with "*Continued from Line 6th of P. 2, blank leaf*"

[b] The last of **2** and the first six lines of **3** are written over the pencil draft for a cipher and the triangular sigla discussed in headnote, above

2[1] John 1.4 (var).

2[2] I.e. *Allgemeinheit*.

2[3] Cf N Q ff 7–8: "The Church doctrines are the bank notes the scriptures the bullion which the notes represent and which the bank i.e. the church must be ready to bring forward when fairly demanded." On "*bullion-money*" see John TAYLOR *Essay on Money* (1830), and for the phrase "Balance of Trade" see e.g. *CN* III 3455. The *Edinburgh Encyclopaedia* (1830) IV 370 refers to "The exploded doctrine of a balance of trade".

are thereby saved; but every man, more or less, construes it into an intelligible *Belief* thro' the ~~co~~ shaping and colouring Optical Glass of his individual Understanding.

Mr Asgill has given a very ingenious Common-Law Scheme. Valeat quantum valebit![1] It would make a figure among the Benchers of the Temple.[2] I prefer the belief, that Man was made to know that a finite free Agent could not stand by the coincidence & independent harmony of a separate Will ~~from~~ with the Will of God. Only by the Will of God can he obey God's Will. Man fell as a *Soul* to rise a *Spirit*. The first Adam was a living *Soul*; the last a life-making Spirit.[3] S. T. C.

4 i [2] | Preface

To them that knew not the reason, it look'd like a Whym *for the Man in the Gospel to walk about the Streets with his Bed upon his Back on the Sabbath-day* ...

? Whym! Whim. Unde *der*?—Is it the same with the German *Wahn*?[1]

4A i 43 | *Argument*

2dly. *A Deed-~~R~~Poll*, in which the Parties need not be named, but are described by the first Prescription of the Deed ...

5 i 46-7

And I am so far from thinking this Covenant of Eternal Life to be an Allusion to the forms of Title amongst Men, that I rather adore it as the Precedent for them all, from which our imperfect Forms are taken: Believing with that great Apostle, That *the things on Earth are but the Patterns of things in the Heavens, where the Originals are kept.*

Aye! This, *this* is the Pinch of the Argument, which Asgill should have *proved*, not merely asserted. Are these Human Laws and these

---

3[1] "Let it prosper as far as it proves valid!"

3[2] Cf *TT* 30 Jul 1831. "Benchers"— senior members of the two Inns of Court, the Inner Temple and Middle Temple.

3[3] 1 Cor 15.45: "The first man Adam was made a living soul: the last Adam was made a quickening spirit."

4[1] "Whence *der*[ived]?" *Wahn* originally meant "expectation, hope, opinion" but by C's time had acquired the meaning of "error, illusion". For the uncertain derivation of "whim" see *OED* under "whim-wham", which gives a possible origin in Old Norse and Scandinavian: e.g. *hvima* (to wander with the eyes), with related notions of dizziness, unsteadiness (which Webster prefers).

Forms of Law *absolutely* good and wise, or only *conditionally*/ i.e. the limited powers & intellect, and the corrupt Will of Men being considered.—S. T. C.

6 i 64–7

And hence, tho the Dead shall not arise with the same Identity of Matter with which they died, yet being in the same Form, they will not know themselves from themselves, being the same to all Uses, Intents, and Purposes. . . .

But then as God (in the Resurrection) is not bound up to use the same Matter, neither is he obliged to use a different Matter.

Whenever the Body to be raised, doth remain so intire from Corruption that the Form of it is not spoiled, God uses that Form again (as it is) without composing any other Matter.

The great objection to this part of Asgill's Scheme, which has had & still, I am told, has many Advocates among the chief Dignitaries of our Church, is—that it either takes Death, as the utter extinction of Being—or it supposes a continuous or at least a renewal of Consciousness after Death. The former involves all the irrational, and all the immoral, consequences of Materialism. But if the ~~granted~~ latter be granted, the ~~whole~~ proportionality, adhesion and symmetry of the whole Scheme are gone—& the infinite Quantity (i.e. immortality under the curse of estrangement from God) is rendered a mere supplement tacked on to the finite and comparatively insignificant, if not doubtful, evil—namely, the dissolution of the organic Body. See what a poor hand Asgill makes of it, *p. 26.*[1]

7 i 66

So from the words of *David, Thou wilt not leave my Soul in the Grave*; there was a Conception rais'd of the separate Existence of the Soul . . . And that it is translated *Soul*, is an *Anglicism*, not understood in other Languages, which have no other word for *Soul* but the same which is for Life.

? Seele, ✕ Leben—German:[a] Ψυχή ✕ Ζωή—Greek.[1]

a C first wrote " ? Seele—German, ✕ Leben", then put a mark of transposition to produce the reading given in the text

6[1] C has not marked the passage, which reads: "By which God shew'd, that if Man had had more than his Life to give, God would have had it of him. And therefore to signify the height of this Resentment, God raises man from the Dead to demand further

Satisfaction of him." C continues his argument in **7** and **8**. This passage is also referred to in a note on a back flyleaf of LUTHER *Colloquia Mensalia* (1652).

7[1] Expanded, this note would read: "Query? Is not *Seele* (soul) distinct

8 i 67

Then to this Figure God added Life, by breathing it into him from himself, whereby this inanimate Body became a living one.

And what was *Life*? Something? or Nothing?—And had not, first, the Spirit, and next the Word, of God, infused Life into the *Earth* of which Man as an animal & all other animals were made/ & then *in addition* to this breathed into *Man* a living *Soul*—which he did *not* breathe into the other Animals?[1]

8A i 68, marked with a pencil line in the margin

... every Body shall have its own Spirit, and every Spirit its own Body.

9 p ⁻3 (p–d), referring to i 75

... (in the day of Restitution of all things) every Body shall have its own Spirit, and every Spirit its own Body.

A man so $\underline{\kappa\alpha\tau'\ \dot{\epsilon}\xi o\chi\acute{\eta}\nu}$[1] clear-headed, so remarkable for the perspicuity of his Sentences, and the luminous Orderliness of his Arrangement—in short, so consummate an Artist in the statement of his Case, and in the inferences from his Data, as John Asgill must be allowed by all competent Judges to have been—WAS HE *in earnest or in jest* from p. 75 to the end of the first Treatise?[2]—*My* belief is, that He himself did not know.

Asgill was a thorough HUMORIST: and so much of WILL, with a spice of THE WILFUL, goes to the making up of a Humorist's Creed, that it is no easy matter to determine, how far such a man might not have a pleasure in humming ~~himself~~ his own mind, and believing in order to ~~make~~ enjoy a dry laugh at himself for the Belief.[3]—S. T. C.—

9A i 78, marked with a pencil line in the margin

But when that is done [i.e. when "I have done all my Heart's desire"], I know no Business I have with the Dead, and therefore do as much

---

from *Leben* (life) in German in the same way that ψυχή (soul) is distinct from ζωή (life) in Greek?" Cf AURELIUS **27, 37, 45.**

8[1] Cf *AR* (1825) 4–5.

9[1] A phrase often used by C: "especially", "outstandingly", "eminently".

9[2] The closing pages of the *Argu-*

ment defy summary; **9A** offers a fair sample. Asgill admits (p 77) that while he was writing he "felt two Powers within" himself: "one *bids me write*, and the other bobs my Elbow".

9[3] C found in Asgill "the very soul of Swift", and considered his irony—like Defoe's—"often finer than Swift's". *TT* 30 Jul 1831, 30 Apr 1832.

28 Jany 1827.

8/ Riverston

Novr 1829.

This Book given me
by Mr Kirkpatrick
together with the Spes
Israel by R. Menasseh
Ben Israel.
S. T. Coleridge

Valuable

Wm G. K.

"A man so κατ' ἐξοχὴν clear-headed, so
remarkable for the perspicuity of his Sentences
and the luminous Orderliness of his Arrangement,
in short, so consummate an Artist in the
statement of his Case, and in the inferences
from his Data, as John Asgill must be allowed
by all competent Judges to have been — was he
in earnest or in jest from p. 75 to the End of
the first Treatise? — My belief is, that
He himself did not know.... Asgill was
a thorough Humorist: and so much of Will,
with a spice of the Wilful, goes to the making
up of a Humorist's Creed, that it is no easy
matter to determine, how far such a man might
not have a pleasure in humming his own mind,
and believing in order to — — — a dry laugh
at himself for the Belief." S. T. C. —

4. A flyleaf of John Asgill *A Collection of Tracts* (London 1715) annotated
by Coleridge. See ASGILL headnote and **9**
The British Library; reproduced by kind permission

depend that I shall not go hence by *returning to the Dust*, which is the Sentence of that Law from which I claim a Discharge: But that I shall *make my Exit by way of Translation*, which I claim as a Dignity belonging to that Degree in the Science of Eternal Life, of which I profess my self a Graduate, according to the true intent and meaning of the Covenant of the Eternal Life reveal'd in the Scriptures.

9B   i 84, marked with a pencil line in the margin

And according to this Art, it cannot be denied, That the whole weight of this Terrestrial Globe is moveable by the strength of a Hair, and the force of a Man's Breath, only by getting far enough off from the Center before he gives the Puff.[1]

10   recto of advertisement leaf, completed on iv [88] advertisement

That Asgill's Belief, professed and maintained in the first of these Tracts, is unwise and odd, I can more readily grant than that [it][a] is altogether *irrational* and absurd. I am even strongly inclined to conjecture, that so early as St Paul's Apostolate there were persons (whether sufficiently numerous to form a Sect or party, I cannot say) who held the same tenet as Asgill's, and in a more intolerant and exclusive a Sense: and that it is to such Persons that St Paul refers in the justly admired 15th C. of the Coirrinthians:[1] and that the inadvertence to this has led a numerous class of Divines to a misconception of the Apostle's Reasoning and a misinterpretation of his words, in behoof of the Socinian notion, that the Resurrection of Christ is the only Argument of Proof for the Belief of a Future State—and that this was the great end and purpose of this Event.[2] Now this assumption is so destitute of support from the other Writers of the N. T. and so discordant with the whole spirit and gist of St Paul's Views and Reasoning in every where else, that it is a priori probable, that the apparent exception in Corinth. XVth is only apparent. And this the hypothesis, I have here advanced, would enable one to shew, and[b] to exhibit the true bearing of the Texts.— Asgill contents himself with maintaining that Translation without

---

a Word supplied by the editor
b Here C has written ʌ at the foot of p [89] and repeated it at the foot of p [88] to mark the continuation of the note

9B[1] Somebody—not C and probably not the writer of the sketch of the binding on the back flyleaves—has made the sensible suggestion in pencil: "vide Archimedes Paraboles".

10[1] In the Church of England service at the burial of the dead the lesson is 1 Cor 15.20–58.
10[2] On the Socinians see BAHRDT 1 n 1.

Death is *one* & the best, mode of passing to the Heavenly State. *Hinc* itur ad astra.[3] But his earliest Predecessors contended that it was the *only* mode—& to these*ᵃ* Sᵗ Paul justly replies: If in this Life only we have Hope, we are of all men most wretched.[4] *S. T. Coleridge.* Febʸ 2. 1827.

11 iv 28–9 | *Mr Asgill's Defence upon His Expulsion*: Introduction

For as every Faith (or Credit) that a Man hath attain'd to, is the Result of some Knowledg or other; so that whoever hath attain'd that Knowledg, hath that Faith (for whatever a Man knows, he cannot but believe:)

So this *All* Faith being the Result of all Knowledg, 'tis easy to conceive that whoever had once attain'd to all that Knowledg, nothing could be difficult to him.

And thus, tho this extreme Notion in the Science of Faith be intelligible only and not imitable;

Yet the lesser degrees of Knowledg in that Science are both intelligible and imitable.

This discussion on Faith is one of the very few instances in which Asgill has got out of his Depth. According to all usage of words Science & Faith are incompatible in relation to the same object— while according to Asgill Faith is merely the power, which Science confers on the Will. A. says—what we know, we must believe. I retort—what we only *believe*, we do not know. The minor here is excluded by, and not included in, the major.—[1]

12 p +2, referring to iv 28

Tract IV. P. 28.—Mem.—Minors by difference of Quantity are included in their Majors; but Minors by difference of quality are excluded by them or superseded. Apply this to Belief and Science or certain Knowlege—On the confusion of the ~~first~~ second, (mⁿⁱˢ by diff. of Qᴜᴀʟɪᴛʏ) with the first, rests Asgill's erroneous exposition of Faith.

ᵃ Here, at the foot of the page, C has written ∧∧∧, and at the head of the same page: "∧∧∧ from the bottom of *this* page"

10[3] A variant of Virgil *Aeneid* 9.641: "sic itur ad astra". C's version translates: "*Hence* we get to the stars/heaven".

10[4] 1 Cor 15.19 (var).

11[1] Cf e.g. Dᴏɴɴᴇ *Sermons* ᴄᴏᴘʏ ʙ 30. See also the "Essay on Faith": *LR* ɪᴠ 425–38.

13   pp +2–+3 (p–d)

Charm when one's foot is asleep—which I have tried 50 times when a little Boy at the Blue-coat School, and always found efficacious— It had been in the School time out of mind, possibly from the first foundation under Edward VI. ⟨Tho' now from "the march of intellect" perhaps exploded and non-extant. S. T. C. 1832/⟩[a]

> Foot! Foot! Foot! is fast asleep.
> Thumb, thumb, thumb, in Spittle we steep.
> Crosses three we'll make to ease us,
> Two for the Thieves and one for Christ Jesus.

And the same for a cramp in the Leg, only substituting for the first couplet the following—

> The Devil is tying a knot in my Leg—
> Mark, Luke, and John, unloose it, I beg!
> Crosses three &c/
>
> *S. T. C.*

And getting out of bed, in which the Cramp most frequently occurred, and pressing the sole of the foot on the cold floor, and then repeating this charm with the acts configurative therein prescribed, I can safely affirm, that I do not remember an instance, in which the Cramp did not go away after a few Seconds.[1]

⟨P.S.⟩[b] I should not wonder, if it were equally good for a Stitch in the Side; but I cannot say, that I ever tried it for *that*.

S. T. Coleridge.
1828

Grove, Highgate

---

[a] This last sentence, judging from the colour of ink and form of writing, is an afterthought crowded into the space between "Edward VI" and the beginning of the rhyme. C clearly wrote the date "1832" at the end of it; somebody later wrote "28" in ink over the original "32" to consort with the date 1828 at the end of the note on p +3

[b] The "P.S." is written full left between the last line "after a few Seconds" and the first line of the next paragraph, a little crowded. Unlike the insertion noted in *a* above, there is no change in ink or hand from the note to the postscript

13[1] Cf a recollection of childhood in Oct 1797: "I suppose, you know the old prayer—

> Matthew! Mark! Luke! & John!
> God bless the bed which I lie on.
> Four angels round me spread,
> Two at my foot & two at my bed
> [*for* head]—

This prayer I said nightly—& most firmly believed the truth of it.— Frequently have I, half-awake & half-asleep, my body diseased & fevered by my imagination, seen armies of ugly Things bursting in upon me, & these four angels keeping them off.—". *CL* I 348.

CHARLES BOWKER ASH
b 1781

Adbaston; or Days of Youth. A descriptive poem. Bath 1814.

Not located: marginalia not recorded. *Lost List.*

In the Advertisement to the 2nd ed of *Adbaston* in *The Poetical Works of C. B. Ash, of Adbaston* (2 vols 1831) Ash wrote (I xiii): "Since this Poem was first printed at Bath in 1814, it has been revised, and several alterations have been made in it, for which I am chiefly indebted to the friendly suggestions of MR. COLERIDGE, Author of 'The Remorse' and other works, who, in the kindest manner, not only gave me considerable encouragement, but, entirely without my knowledge or solicitation, took much trouble in making many marginal notes in a copy, that, afterwards, fell into my hands by accident, from which, it is hoped, advantage has been gained." I find no reference to Ash by C. "Mᵣ Sam Ash—Kings Square—Bristol", a linen merchant, appears in the list of subscribers to the 1809–10 *Friend*. *Friend (CC)* II 411. The poem may have come to C's attention through some mutual friend while C was in Bristol and Calne 1814–15.

ATHENAEUM

Athenaeum. Eine Zeitschrift von August Wilhelm Schlegel und Friedrich Schlegel. 3 vols (4 pts) in 1 vol. Berlin 1798, 1799, 1800. 8°. Vols I, II ed A. W. and Friedrich Schlegel; Vol III ed F. Schleiermacher.

British Museum C 132 c 2

Autograph signature "Joseph Henry Green" on p ⁻1. Before rebinding in the BM, the volume had a label pasted to p ⁻3 (p–d): "Buchhandlung von Ferd. Dümmler in Berlin under den Linden No. 19." A partial transcript of the marginalia, made by EHC on a loose sheet, is tipped in at the end of the volume.

These marginalia belong to the earliest phase of C's friendship with Joseph Henry Green (1791–1863), whom he first met on 13 Jun 1817, when he was invited to dine at Green's to meet Ludwig Tieck and two other visitors from Germany. (C had met Tieck in Rome early in 1806.) HCR, who had not met Green before, was also invited, found it "an afternoon and evening of very high pleasure indeed", and wrote a long account in his diary. *CRB* I 207. But C, even though in Sept 1814 he had proposed to John Murray a "comprest critical account of the 4 Stages of German Poetry from Hans Sachs to Tiek and Schlegel" (*CL* III 528), was "not in his element", HCR thought. Yet his response to the meeting was prompt and enthusiastic: next day he told Thomas Boosey the bookseller about the meeting, ordered "all the works, you may have, of LUDWIG TIECK" as well as a book of Schelling, another by Steffens, and Solger's *Erwin*. *CL* IV 737–9, 744–6; cf 666–7, 794. It turned out that Green, who had "studied the German Philosophies both in Books, and at the feet of the Gamaliels" (*CL* IV 848), also had literary and critical interests: he owned books by Schlegel and by Tieck; in Dec 1817 he tried to engage C in literary-critical discussion (*CL* IV 793); in Jul 1818 he persuaded C to read Novalis's *Heinrich von Ofterdingen* (*CL* IV 870), and had already lent him the Tieck–Wackenroder *Phantasien* in Jun 1817 (*CL* IV 743, 911). By 16 Jan 1819 Green must have lent C a number of German books; for on that day C, asking for a short loan of Goethe's *Farbenlehre*, "piously resolve[d] on Tuesday to put my Books in some order, but at all events to select your's and send all of them that I do not want". *CL* IV 911. In all this there is no mention of the *Athenaeum*, but Mme de Staël's visit to England in 1813 could have drawn C's attention to this manifestolike periodical, and the early months of C's acquaintance with Green would be a time for Green to lend it to him. That C, when he wrote these marginalia, was not much concerned about the history of "romanticism" is shown by his neglect of the now-celebrated Fragment 116 (in modern notation) on I 28–30, which lies between **21** and **22**.

131

For a reference to *Athenaeum* I i (*Die Sprachen*) see *TT* 4 Sept 1833. This section is unmarked in Green's copy, but C may have had the book with him on the occasion when the *TT* remark was recorded, for he also spoke at some length on "elegy" and A. W. Schlegel—the subject of **17–18**: see *TT* 23 Oct 1833.

CONTENTS. I i: I A. W. Schlegel *Die Sprachen*; II Novalis *Blüthenstaub* (**1–16**); III A. W. and F. Schlegel *Elegien aus dem Griechischen* (**17–19**); IV A. W. Schlegel *Beyträge zur Kritik der neuesten Litteratur* (**20**).

I ii: I *Fragmente* (**21–29**); II *Über Goethe's Meister.*

II i: I F. Schlegel *Ueber die Philosophie*; II A. W. Schlegel *Die Gemählde*; III A. L. Hülsen *Ueber die natürliche Gleichheit der Menschen.*

II ii: I A. W. Schlegel *Die Kunst der Griechen*; II A. W. Schlegel *Ueber Zeichnungen zu Gedichten und John Flaxman's Umrisse*; III A. W. Schlegel *Der rasende Roland*; IV *Notizen* (**30**).

III i: I F. Schlegel *An Heliodora*; II F. Schlegel *Ideen*; III A. L. Hülsen *Natur-Betrachtungen auf einer Reise durch die Schweiz*; IV F. Schlegel *Gespräch über die Poesie*; V *Notizen.*

III ii: I F. Schlegel *An die Deutschen*; II F. Schlegel *Gespräch über die Poesie*; III Novalis *Hymnen an die Nacht*; IV Sophie Brun *Lebensansicht*; V A. W. and F. Schlegel *Idyllen aus dem Griechischen*; VI A W. and F. Schlegel *Sonnette*; VII *Notizen*; VIII F. Schlegel *Ueber die Unverständlichkeit.*

DATE. c summer/autumn 1817 to 1818: see above. The consideration of genius, talent, and wit in **5**, **14**, **23**, **31** recalls *CL* IV 666–7 (4 Sept 1816) and *Friend* (*CC*) I 419–23. See also the long letter to Tulk, Sept–Nov 1817: *CL* IV 767–76 and cf 873–6.

COEDITOR. Hans Eichner.

1   I i 70–1, pencil | *Blüthenstaub* [No 3: by Novalis[1]]

Der Weltstaat ist der Körper, den die schöne Welt, die gesellige Welt, beseelt. Er ist ihr nothwendiges Organ.

[The world-state is the body, the cultivated world, the social world, is the soul, to which it is the necessary organ.]

I should say, the *Materia* objecta et circumstans[2]—that, which the Soil and the Elements are to the living Plant, whose *Organ*s is its own Body. The World is to the sublimated *civilized* World, and this again to the *cultivated* World (= die schöne Welt) at once an Object, and medium, and a partially assimilable Stuff.[3]

1[1] Only four of the aphorisms published under the title *Blüthenstaub* are by Friedrich Schlegel: 15, 20, 26, 31. Of these C noticed only Nos 20 and 26: see **4C** and **8**, below.

1[2] "*Matter* presented to it [as an object] and surrounding it".

1[3] For the general distinction between civilisation and cultivation see e.g. *Friend* (*CC*) I 493 and n, 500–2. On organisation and mechanism see e.g. *CN* III 4319.

2   1 i 71, pencil

G. = bene. N. = nebulous, misty. D. = doubtful, or of an unlucky likeness to nonsense. ? = I don't understand it.[1]

2A   1 i 71 | [No 4]

G.] Lehrjahre sind für den poetischen, akademische Jahre für den philosophischen Jünger. Akademie sollte ein durchaus philosophisches Institut seyn; nur Eine Facultät; die ganze Einrichtung zur Erregung und zweckmässigen Übung der Denkkraft organisirt.

[Years of apprenticeship are for the poetic, academic years for the philosophic disciple. An academy ought to be a completely philosophical institute: only one faculty; the whole institution organised for the purpose of the stimulation and suitable training of intellectual power.]

2B   1 i 71 | [No 6]

G.] Ganz begreifen werden wir uns nie, aber wir werden und können uns weit mehr, als begreifen.

[We shall never understand ourselves completely, but we shall do and can do very much more than understand ourselves.]

3   1 i 71, pencil | [No 7]

Gewisse Hemmungen gleichen den Griffen eines Flötenspielers, der um verschiedene Töne hervorzubringen, bald diese bald jene Öffnung zuhält, und willkührliche Verkettungen stummer und tönender Öffnungen zu machen scheint.

[Certain inhibitions are like the finger movements of a flute-player, who, in order to produce different notes, closes now this, now that finger-hole and seems with arbitrary concatenations of the stops to link silences with tones.]

I called the Insects Commas, Fish ; ; Birds Colons. Man the Full Stop.

3A   1 i 71 | [No 8]

N.] Der Unterschied zwischen Wahn und Wahrheit liegt in der Differenz ihrer Lebensfunkzionen. Der Wahn lebt von der Wahrheit; die Wahrheit lebt ihr Leben in sich. Man vernichtet den Wahn, wie man Krankheiten vernichtet, und der Wahn ist also nichts, als logische Entzündung oder Verlöschung, Schwärmerey oder Philisterey. Jene hinterlässt gewöhnlich einen scheinbaren Mangel an Denkkraft, der durch nichts zu heben ist, als eine abnehmende

---

2[1] In order to secure the continuity of C's reaction to the text, the marked passages have been placed in sequence with the marginalia.

Reihe von Inzitamenten, Zwangsmitteln. Diese geht oft in eine trügliche Lebhaftigkeit über, deren gefährliche Revoluzionssymptome nur durch eine zunehmende Reihe gewaltsamer Mittel vertrieben werden können. Beyde Disposizionen können nur durch chronische, streng befolgte Kuren verändert werden.

[The distinction between delusion and truth lies in the difference between their functions in life. Delusion lives on truth; the truth lives its life in itself. One destroys delusion as one destroys illnesses, and delusion is therefore nothing but logical inflammation or extinction, gushing enthusiasm or philistinism. The former usually leads to an apparent inability to think that can be remedied only by a decreasing series of inciting, forcing agents. The latter often changes into a deceptive vivacity, whose dangerous revolutionary symptoms can only be cured by an increasing series of powerful agents. Both dispositions can only be changed by chronic, strictly observed treatment.]

3B   ɪ i 72 | [No 11]

G.] Das Höchste ist das Verständlichste, das Nächste, das Unentbehrlichste.

[The highest is the most comprehensible, the nearest, the most indispensable.]

3C   ɪ i 72 | [No 12]

?] Wunder stehn mit naturgesetzlichen Wirkungen in Wechsel: sie beschränken einander gegenseitig, und machen zusammen ein Ganzes aus. Sie sind vereinigt, indem sie sich gegenseitig aufheben. Kein Wunder ohne Naturbegebenheit und umgekehrt.

[Miracles interact with effects of the laws of nature: they mutually limit one another and add up to a whole. They combine by annulling one another. No miracle without natural event and vice versa.]

3D   ɪ i 74 | [No 16]

N. D.] Die Fantasie setzt die künftige Welt entweder in die Höhe, oder in die Tiefe, oder in der Metempsychose zu uns. Wir träumen von Reisen durch das Weltall: ist denn das Weltall nicht in uns? Die Tiefen unsers Geistes kennen wir nicht.—Nach Innen geht der geheimnissvolle Weg. In uns, oder nirgends ist die Ewigkeit mit ihren Welten, die Vergangenheit und Zukunft. Die Aussenwelt ist die Schattenwelt, sie wirft ihren Schatten in das Lichtreich.[1] Jetzt scheint es uns freylich innerlich so dunkel, einsam, gestaltlos, aber wie ganz anders wird es uns dünken, wenn diese Verfinsterung

---

3D[1] This sentence is **4** textus.

vorbey, und der Schattenkörper hinweggerückt ist. Wir werden mehr geniessen als je, denn unser Geist hat entbehrt.

[The imagination places the future world either above us, or below us, or in metempsychosis. We dream of journeys through the universe—as if the universe were not in us! We do not know the depths of our mind.—The mysterious way leads within. Eternity with its world, the past and future, is within us or nowhere. The external world is the world of shadows, it casts its shadow into the realm of light. Admittedly, now it seems to be so dark within us, so lonely and shapeless; but how utterly different will it appear to us when the eclipse has passed and the body casting the shadow has moved away. We shall have more joy than ever before, for our mind will have known deprivation.]

4   1 i 74, pencil | textus included in 3D

Die Aussenwelt ist die Schattenwelt, sie wirft ihren Schatten in das Lichtreich.

[The external world is the world of shadows, it casts its shadow into the realm of light.]

Do Shadows cast Shadows? If not, the World without must be a Substance-world. An opake body interposing between me and a Lichtreich will bedarken *me*; but how ⟨can⟩ the Shadow affect the Lichtreich?

4A   1 i 74 | [No 18]

G.] Wie kann ein Mensch Sinn für etwas haben, wenn er nicht den Keim davon in sich hat? Was ich verstehn soll, muss sich in mir organisch entwickeln; und was ich zu lernen scheine, ist nur Nahrung, Inzitament des Organismus.

[How can a man have the organ of apprehension for something unless he has the seed of it in himself? That which I am to understand must develop organically in myself; and that which I seem to learn is only nutriment, incitement of the organism.]

4B   1 i 74 | [No 19]

D. N.] Der Sitz der Seele ist da, wo sich Innenwelt und Aussenwelt berühren. Wo sie sich durchdringen, ist er in jedem Punkte der Durchdringung.

[The seat of the soul is where the internal and the external worlds touch. Where they penetrate each other, it is in every point of penetration.]

4C   1 i 75 | [No 20: by Friedrich Schlegel]

N.] Wenn man in der Mittheilung der Gedanken zwischen absolutem Verstehen und absolutem Nichtverstehen abwechselt, so darf das schon eine philosophische Freundschaft genannt werden. Geht es uns doch mit uns selbst nicht besser. Und ist das Leben eines denkenden Menschen wohl etwas andres als eine stete innere Symphilosophie?

[If one alternates in the communication of thoughts between absolute comprehension and absolute incomprehension, this can already be called a philosophic friendship. After all, we do not do any better with ourselves. And is the life of a person who thinks anything but a constant inner symphilosophy?]

5 ɪ i 75, pencil | [No 21]

Genie ist das Vermögen von eingebildeten Gegenständen, wie von wirklichen zu handeln, und sie wie diese zu behandeln.

[Genius is the faculty of dealing with imagined objects as if they were real, and also of treating them like real objects.]

This may be one of the characters of Genius, but assuredly not the definition. Rather, it describes Talent united with a vivid Fancy.[1]

6 ɪ i 75–6, pencil | [No 22]

N.] Das willkührlichste Vorurtheil ist, dass dem Menschen das Vermögen ausser sich zu seyn, mit Bewusstseyn jenseits der Sinne zu seyn, versagt sey. Der Mensch vermag in jedem Augenblicke ein übersinnliches Wesen zu seyn. . . . Je mehr wir uns aber dieses Zustandes bewusst zu seyn vermögen, desto lebendiger, mächtiger, genügender ist die Überzeugung, die daraus entsteht. . . . Es ist kein Schauen, Hören, Fühlen; es ist aus allen dreyen zusammen-*] gesetzt, mehr als alles Dreyes: eine Empfindung unmittelbarer Gewissheit, eine Ansicht meines wahrhaftesten, eigensten Lebens. . . . Für den Schwachen ist das Faktum dieses Moments ein Glaubens-artikel. . . . Hier ist viel Unterschied zwischen den Menschen. Einer hat mehr Øffenbarungsfähigkeit, als der andere. Einer hat mehr Sinn, der andere mehr Verstand für dieselbe. Der letzte wird immer N.] in ihrem sanften Lichte bleiben, wenn der erste nur abwech-selnde Erleuchtungen, aber hellere und mannichfaltigere hat. . . .

[It is the most arbitrary prejudice that man is denied the ability to be beside himself, to be consciously beyond his senses. At every moment, man can be a supersensual being. . . . The more we can be conscious of

---

this state of mind, the more vivid, more powerful, more satisfying is the conviction arising from it. . . . It is not seeing, hearing, feeling; it is composed of all three, is more than all three: a feeling of immediate certainty, a view of my truest, most personal life. . . . For the weak, the fact of this moment is an article of faith. . . . In this respect, there is great variation between people. One has more capacity for revelation than another. One has more feeling [*Sinn*] for it, another understands it better. The latter will always remain in its gentle light, while the former will only experience a series of illuminations, which will, however, be brighter and more varied. . . .]

* In other words (a materialist might retort) it is a *confusion*. And how a Zusammengesetztes of 3 Senses can be etwas übersinnliches, is a puzzle.

There is, I at least believe, something at the bottom of this; but the Aphorist has not succeeded in bringing it up.

6A I i 77 | [No 23]

G.] Scham ist wohl ein Gefühl der Profanazion. Freundschaft, Liebe und Pietät sollten geheimnissvoll behandelt werden. Man sollte nur in seltnen, vertrauten Momenten davon reden, sich stillschweigend darüber einverstehen. Vieles ist zu zart um gedacht, noch mehres um besprochen zu werden.

[Shame is probably a feeling of profanation. Friendship, love and reverence should be treated with reserve. One should speak of them only in rare moments of intimacy, agree on them tacitly. Many things are too delicate to be thought, still more too delicate to be discussed.]

7 I i 77, pencil | [No 24]

Selbstentäusserung ist die Quelle aller Erniedrigung, so wie im Gegentheil der Grund aller ächten Erhebung. Der erste Schritt wird Blick nach Innen, absondernde Beschauung unsers Selbst.

[Self-alienation is the source of all humiliation, just as, on the other hand, it is the source of all genuine elation. The first step is introspection, an isolating viewing of our self.]

For Selbst I would put *Geist*—of our *Spirit*, principium individualitatis—*a* 1

Reverence thy Soul in meekness, O my Son: knowing how weak and how mighty a thing it is. APOCRYPHA.[2] We can scarcely

a The first sentence is written at the end of the epigram, the second paragraph at the foot of the page

7[1] "Principle of individuality". Cf *CL* IV 690 (10 Nov 1816) and **31** (last sentence).

7[2] Ecclus 10.28 (var); also quoted in *Friend (CC)* I 95 (var). C might have taken a slightly different view of it if he had looked at the original: "My son, in all modesty, keep your self-respect and value yourself at your true worth". *NEB*.

think too highly of the *potential* in us, or too humbly of the Actual.[3]

7A　ɪ i 77 | [No 25]

G. G.] Derjenige wird nie als Darsteller etwas vorzügliches leisten, der nichts weiter darstellen mag, als seine Erfahrungen, seine Lieblingsgegenstände, der es nicht über sich gewinnen kann, auch einen ganz fremden, ihm ganz uninteressanten Gegenstand, mit Fleiss zu studiren und mit Musse darzustellen. Der Darsteller muss alles darstellen können und wollen. Dadurch entsteht der grosse Styl der Darstellung, den man mit Recht an Goethe so sehr bewundert.

[No one will ever produce an excellent description who is unwilling to describe anything but his own experiences, his favourite objects; who cannot persuade himself to study industriously and to describe at leisure even an object that is quite foreign and quite uninteresting to him. He who describes must be able and willing to describe everything. It is thus that the great descriptive style develops that is rightly so much admired in Goethe.]

8　ɪ i 78, pencil | [No 26: by Friedrich Schlegel]

Hat man nun einmal die Liebhaberey fürs Absolute und kann nicht davon lassen: so bleibt einem kein Ausweg, als sich selbst immer zu widersprechen, und entgegengesetzte Extreme zu verbinden. Um den Satz des Widerspruchs ist es doch unvermeidlich geschehen, und man hat nur die Wahl, ob man sich dabey leidend verhalten will, oder ob man die Nothwendigkeit durch Anerkennung zur freyen Handlung adeln will.

[If one has the predilection for the absolute and cannot do without it, one is left no alternative but to contradict oneself continually, and to combine opposite extremes. In that case, the law of contradiction is inevitably done for and one is only left the alternative of remaining passive or of elevating necessity to a free act by recognising it.]

And why? because Schelling overlooked the I AM in the Absolute[a] —and then confounded the *Absolute* with *Nature*—identified Earth, yea Hell, with Heaven. He terrestrialized the celestial by the abortive attempt to celestialize the Terrestrial.[1]

---

[a] The first phrase to "Absolute" is written at the end of the epigram, the rest at the foot of the page

7[3] Cf *BL* ch 12 (1907) ɪ 167: "They and they only can acquire the philosophic imagination, the sacred power of self-intuition, who within themselves can interpret and understand the symbol.... They know and feel, that the *potential* works *in* them, even as the *actual* works on them!"

8[1] This terse dispatch of Schelling's "mere Pantheism ... Plotinised Spino-

9 I i 78, pencil | [No 27]

Eine merkwürdige Eigenheit Goethe's bemerkt man in seinen Verknüpfungen kleiner, unbedeutender Vorfälle mit wichtigern Begebenheiten. Er scheint keine andre Absicht dabey zu hegen, als die Einbildungskraft auf eine poetische Weise mit einem mysteriösen Spiel zu beschäftigen.

[A strange peculiarity of Goethe's can be seen in his connecting small, insignificant events with more important happenings. In doing so, he seems to have no other intention than to occupy the imagination mysteriously and playfully in a poetic manner.]

Cum grano Salis ~~non~~ plusquam uno./[1]

9A I i 79 | [No 29]

N.] Humor ist eine willkührlich angenommene Manier. Das Willkührliche ist das Pikante daran: Humor ist Resultat einer freyen Vermischung des Bedingten und Unbedingten. Durch Humor wird das eigenthümlich Bedingte allgemein interessant, und erhält objektiven Werth. Wo Fantasie und Urtheilskraft sich berühren, entsteht Witz; wo sich Vernunft und Willkühr paaren, Humor. Persifflage gehört zum Humor, ist aber um einen Grad geringer: es ist nicht mehr rein artistisch, und viel beschränkter. Was Fr. Schlegel als Ironie karakterisirt, ist meinem Bedünken nach nichts anders als die Folge, der Karakter der Besonnenheit, der wahrhaften Gegenwart des Geistes. Schlegels Ironie scheint mir ächter Humor zu seyn. Mehre Nahmen sind einer Idee vortheilhaft.

[Humour is a capriciously adopted manner. Its capriciousness makes it poignant: humour is the result of a free mingling of the conditioned and the unconditioned. Through humour, that which is particularly conditioned becomes generally interesting and objectively valuable. Where imagination and judgement come into touch, wit arises; where reason and caprice come together, there arises humour. Persiflage belongs with humour, but ranks one degree lower: it is no longer purely artistic, and much more limited. What Friedrich Schlegel characterises as irony is to my mind nothing but the consequence, the character of circumspection, of true presence of mind. Schlegel's irony seems to me to be genuine humour. More than one name is of advantage to an idea.]

zism" (*CL* IV 885) was central to C's position. Nowhere else did he express it more neatly. Cf also *P Lects* Lect 13 (1949) 390–1. See *C Pantheist* esp ch 3 and Excursus Notes VI, XII. The question of pantheism and Spinoza is prominent in C's marginalia on Schelling. See also BAXTER *Reliquiae* COPY A 2 n 2.

9[1] "With a grain of Salt, ~~not~~ more than one."

9B I i 79 | [No 30]

G.] Das Unbedeutende, Gemeine, Rohe, Hässliche, Ungesittete, wird durch Witz allein Gesellschaftfähig. Es ist gleichsam nur um des Witzes willen: seine Zweckbestimmung ist der Witz.

[The insignificant, common, crude, ugly, unmannerly becomes permissible in good society only through wit. It exists, as it were, only for the sake of wit: its purpose is wit.]

10 I i 80, pencil | [No 33]

Wenn uns ein Geist erschiene, so würden wir uns sogleich unsrer eignen Geistigkeit bemächtigen: wir würden inspirirt seyn durch uns und den Geist zugleich. Ohne Inspirazion keine Geistererscheinung. Inspirazion ist Erscheinung und Gegenerscheinung, Zueignung und Mittheilung zugleich.

[If a spirit were to appear to us, we would at once come into possession of our own spirituality: we would be inspired simultaneously by ourselves and the spirit. Without inspiration no apparition. Inspiration is simultaneous apparition and counter-apparition, appropriation and communication.]

G. but wants unfolding[1]

11 I i 80, pencil | [No 35]

Interesse ist Theilnahme an dem Leiden und der Thätigkeit eines Wesens. . . .

[Interest is participation in the suffering and the activity of a being. . . .]

Superficial—if not false. Interesse = esse *inter*. Between A and B. there is a *draw-bridge* of communication. I pass over into him—he takes a place in me: i.e. I feel an interest in him—my feeling est inter me et alium.[1]

12 I i 81, pencil | [No 40]

In heitern Seelen giebts keinen Witz.

[In serene souls there is no wit.]

Negatur[1]

13 I i 82, pencil | [Nos 42–4]

Wir halten einen leblosen Stoff wegen seiner Beziehungen, seiner Formen fest. Wir lieben den Stoff, in so fern er zu einem geliebten Wesen gehört, seine Spur trägt, oder Ähnlichkeit mit ihm hat.

10[1] Cf the use of "unfold" in Böhme **5** and **109**.

11[1] "Interest is the same as to be *between* . . . is between me and another [person]." For the distinction between interest and concern see *AR* (1825) 175.

12[1] "*It is denied*". On wit see **14**, below.

Ein ächter Klub ist eine Mischung von Institut und Gesellschaft. Er hat einen Zweck, wie das Institut; aber keinen bestimmten, sondern einen unbestimmten, freyen: Humanität überhaupt. Aller Zweck ist ernsthaft; die Gesellschaft ist durchaus fröhlich.

Die Gegenstände der gesellschaftlichen Unterhaltung sind nichts, als Mittel der Belebung. Diess bestimmt ihre Wahl, ihren Wechsel, ihre Behandlung. Die Gesellschaft ist nichts, als gemeinschaftliches Leben: eine untheilbare denkende und fühlende Person. Jeder Mensch ist eine kleine Gesellschaft.

[We hold on to a lifeless substance because of its relations, its forms. We love the substance in so far as it belongs to a beloved being, bears its mark, or resembles it.

A genuine club is a mixture of institute and social gathering. It has a purpose, like the institute; but not a definite, but an indefinite, free purpose: humanity in general. All purpose is serious; the social gathering is completely lighthearted.

The topics of conversation at a social gathering are nothing but means of animation. This determines how they are chosen, changed, and treated. Society is nothing but social life: one indivisible thinking and feeling person. Every person is a small social gathering.]

These and too many others are really aphorising for aphorising sake.[1]

13A ɪ i 82–3 | [No 45]

N.] In sich zurückgehn, bedeutet bey uns, von der Aussenwelt abstrahiren. Bey den Geistern heisst analogisch, das irdische Leben eine innere Betrachtung, ein in sich Hineingehn, ein immanentes Wirken. So entspringt das irdische Leben aus einer ursprünglichen Reflexion, einem primitiven Hineingehn, Sammeln in sich selbst, das so frey ist, als unsre Reflexion. Umgekehrt entspringt das geistige Leben in dieser Welt aus einem Durchbrechen jener primitiven Reflexion. Der Geist entfaltet sich wiederum, geht aus sich selbst wieder heraus, hebt zum Theil jene Reflexion wieder auf, und D.] in diesem Moment sagt er zum erstenmal Ich. Man sieht hier, wie relativ das Herausgehn und Hineingehn ist. Was wir Hineingehn nennen, ist eigentlich Herausgehn, eine Wiederannahme der anfänglich Gestalt.

13[1] The contemptuously toned present participle of the noun-verb "aphorism" marks one limit in the semantic extension of the word—to make clever but superficial gnomic epigrams: *OED* cites Milton *On Reformation*—"Soyl'd and slubber'd with aphorising pedantry"—and C in *BL* ch 12 (1907) ɪ 192 — "certain immethodical aphorising Eclectics". Cf *CN* ɪ 108. See also *AR* (1825) 18–19n and 20.

[To withdraw into one's self means with us to abstract from the external world. Among spirits, analogically, life on earth signifies an inner contemplation, an entering into one's self, an immanent effect. Thus life on earth originates in an original reflexion, a primitive entering into, a collecting oneself in one's self, which is as free as our reflexion. Inversely, the spiritual life in this world originates in a piercing of that primitive reflexion. The spirit unfolds again, and at this moment, it says "I" for the first time. One sees here how relative this emerging and entering is. What we call entering is actually emerging, a resumption of the original shape.]

13B   I i 83 | [No 47]

G.] Wo ächter Hang zum Nachdenken, nicht bloss zum Denken dieses oder jenes Gedankens, herrschend ist, da ist auch Progressivität. Sehr viele Gelehrte besitzen diesen Hang nicht. Sie haben schliessen und folgern gelernt, wie ein Schuster das Schuhmachen, ohne je auf den Einfall zu gerathen, oder sich zu bemühen, den Grund der Gedanken zu finden. Dennoch liegt das Heil auf keinem andern Wege. Bey vielen währt dieser Hang nur eine Zeitlang. Er wächst und nimmt ab, sehr oft mit den Jahren, oft mit dem Fund eines Systems, das sie nur suchten, um der Mühe des Nachdenkens ferner überhoben zu seyn.

[Where a genuine inclination to think things out is dominant, not merely to think this or that thought, there is also progressiveness. Very many scholars do not have this inclination. They have learnt to infer and to conclude as a shoemaker learns to make shoes, without its ever occurring to them or their ever troubling themselves to discover the basis for their thoughts. Yet there is no other method. With many, this inclination lasts only for a while. It grows and decreases, [the latter] very frequently as they get older, often when they have found a system, which they only looked for so as to be rid of the effort of thinking things out.]

13C   I i 83 | [No 48]

G.] Irrthum und Vorurtheil sind Lasten, indirekt reizende Mittel für den Selbstthätigen, jeder Last gewachsenen. Für den Schwachen sind sie positiv schwächende Mittel.

[Error and prejudice are burdens, indirectly stimulating agents for independent minds that can cope with any burden. For the weak, they are positively debilitating agents.]

13D   I i 84–5 | [No 53]

G.] Formeln für Kunstindividuen finden, durch die sie im eigentlichsten Sinn erst verstanden werden, macht das Geschäft des artistischen Kritikers aus, dessen Arbeiten die Geschichte der Kunst vorbereiten.

[To find formulas for individual artists through which they are *understood* for the first time in the most proper sense of this word is the business of the artistic critic, whose labours prepare the way for the history of art.]

13E   i i 85 | [No 54]

G.] Je verworrener ein Mensch ist, man nennt die Verworrenen oft Dummköpfe, desto mehr kann durch fleissiges Selbststudium aus ihm werden; dahingegen die geordneten Köpfe trachten müssen, wahre Gelehrte, gründliche Encyklopädisten zu werden. Die Verworrnen haben im Anfang mit mächtigen Hindernissen zu kämpfen, sie dringen nur langsam ein, sie lernen mit Mühe arbeiten: dann aber sind sie auch Herrn und Meister auf immer. Der Geordnete kommt geschwind hinein, aber auch geschwind heraus. Er erreicht bald die zweyte Stufe: aber da bleibt er auch gewöhnlich stehn. Ihm werden die letzten Schritte beschwerlich, und selten kann er es über sich gewinnen, schon bey einem gewissen Grade von Meisterschaft sich wieder in den Zustand eines Anfängers zu versetzen. Verworrenheit deutet auf Überfluss an Kraft und Vermögen, aber mangelhafte Verhältnisse; Bestimmtheit, auf richtige Verhältnisse, aber sparsames Vermögen und Kraft. Daher ist der Verworrne so progressiv, so perfektibel, dahingegen der Ordentliche so früh als Philister aufhört. Ordnung und Bestimmtheit allein ist nicht Deutlichkeit. Durch Selbstbearbeitung kommt der Verworrene zu jener himmlischen Durchsichtigkeit, zu jener Selbsterleuchtung, die der Geordnete so selten erreicht. Das wahre Genie verbindet diese Extreme. Es theilt die Geschwindigkeit mit dem letzten und die Fülle mit dem ersten.

[The more confused a man is—one frequently calls confused people stupid—the further he can develop through industrious study of himself; orderly minds, on the other hand, must try to become genuine scholars, thorough encyclopaedists. The confused persons at first have to struggle with powerful obstacles, they find their bearings slowly, it costs them an effort to learn to work: but then they are lords and masters forever. The orderly mind finds his bearings quickly, but quickly loses them again. He soon reaches the second stage, but usually stops there. He finds the last steps difficult, and once he has acheived a certain degree of expertness, he can but rarely bring himself to return to the state of a beginner. Confusion indicates an excess of strength and ability, but faulty proportions; precision indicates correct proportions, but scanty ability and strength. This is why the confused person is so progressive, so perfectible, while the orderly mind so soon comes to a standstill as a philistine. Order and precision alone are not clarity. By working on himself the confused person reaches that heavenly transparency, that self-illumination, which the orderly mind achieves so rarely. The true genius combines these extremes. He shares the speed with the latter and the abundance with the former.]

14 I i 86–7, pencil | [No 57]

Witz, als Prinzip der Verwandtschaften ist zugleich das *menstruum universale*. Witzige Vermischungen sind z. B. Jude und Kosmopolit, Kindheit und Weisheit, Räuberey und Edelmuth, Tugend und Hetärie, Ueberfluss und Mangel an Urtheilskraft in der Naivetät und so fort ins Unendliche.

[Wit as a principle of affinities is at the same time the *universal stand-by*. Witty mixtures are for instance Jew and cosmopolitan, childhood and wisdom, brigandage and noble-mindedness, virtue and harlotry, superabundance and lack of judgement in naïvety, and so on ad infinitum.]

This is confounding instead of distinguishing—

It does not become Wit because it may happen to have some one property which Wit likewise has. Or else a circleular Orbit formed by two antagonist forces would be a piece of Wit—a capital Joke. The adlibitive is no less essential an ingredient of Witt—/[1]

14A I i 87 | [No 62]

G.] Das beste an den Wissenschaften ist ihr philosophisches Ingrediens, wie das Leben am organischen Körper. Man dephilosophire die Wissenschaften: was bleibt übrig? Erde, Luft und Wasser.

[What is best in the sciences is their philosophic ingredient, like life in the organic body. Dephilosophise the sciences, and what remains? Earth, air and water.]

15 I i 90–1, pencil | [No 74: by Novalis]

Nichts ist zur wahren Religiosität unentbehrlicher als ein Mittelglied, das uns mit der Gottheit verbindet. . . . In der Wahl dieses Mittelglieds muss der Mensch durchaus frey seyn.

[Nothing is more indispensable to true religiousness than an intermediary linking us with the deity. . . . In the choice of this intermediary, man must be absolutely free.]

Probably, by Friedrich Schlegel, and a covert excuse of his conver-

14[1] In *Friend* (*CC*) I 131–2 (=II 112) C distinguished between the wit of Voltaire and the witty humour of Erasmus, and later engaged the distinc- tion between wit and humour with his discussion of genius and talent: *Friend* (*CC*) I 420.

sion to (*the profession of*) the Roman Catholic Church.[1] But in fact
it is an attempt to establish Arianism *a priori* on a subjective ground:
for which the Romish Church will not thank him.[2]

15A   1 i 97 | [No 83]

G.] In den meisten Religionssystemen werden wir als Glieder der
Gottheit betrachtet, die, wenn sie nicht den Impulsionen des Ganzen
gehorchen[,] wenn sie auch nicht absichtlich gegen die Gesetze des
Ganzen agiren, sondern nur ihren eignen Gang gehn und nicht
Glieder seyn wollen, von der Gottheit ärztlich behandelt, und ent-
weder schmerzhaft geheilt, oder gar abgeschnitten werden.

[In most religious systems we are treated as members of the divinity: if
they do not obey the impulsions of the whole, if they act against the laws
of the whole even unintentionally, merely following their own course and
not wanting to be members, these are medically treated by the divinity and
are either painfully healed or even cut off.]

16   1 i 98, pencil | [No 84]

In jeder Berührung entsteht eine Substanz, deren Wirkung so lange,
als die Berührung dauert.

[At every contact a substance originates, the effect of which lasts as long
as the contact itself.]

In what sense does the writer take "Substance"? Dass eine Wirkung
entsteht,[1] I grant, *but* a Substance?—[2]

17   1 i 110, pencil | A. W. and F. Schlegel *Elegien aus dem Griechischen*

[This article consists of verse translations, by A. W. Schlegel, of
fragments of elegies by Phanocles and Hermesianax and of Callimachus' *Bath of Pallas,* and of introductions and comments by
F. Schlegel. The latter explains on p 110 that the modern view,

15[1] Friedrich Schlegel's conversion
to Roman Catholicism took place in
1808, ten years after the publication of
Blüthenstaub; the aphorism is by
Novalis. HCR noted on 21 Dec 1816
that C "praises Steffens, and complains of the Catholicism of Schlegel
and Tieck". *CRB* 1 200.

15[2] Arians denied the divinity of
Christ. For C on Arianism see e.g.
CHILLINGWORTH COPY B 1 and
DONNE *Sermons* COPY B 8.

16[1] "That an effect originates".

16[2] C was well aware that "What is
[a] Substance?" was a momentous
question both in philosophy and in
theology. Convinced that "Idealism"
is "the truest and most binding
realism" (*BL* ch 12—1907—1 178), he
was not prepared to accept the dualistic implications of the "*soul-and-
bodyists*" (*BL* ch 8—1907—1 91). See
also his note of c Aug–Sept 1809 "On
Certainty": *CN* III 3593. For C's use
of "substance" as *substans* see BIBLE
COPY B **136** n 2.

according to which the elegy is a song of lamentation, is erroneous; for, even though the word was often used in this sense in the sixth and fifth centuries B.C., there are elegies that are not mournful. Schlegel does not, however, provide a definition of his own.]

? Elegia, quasi ενλεγια—inward Discourse—a train of *Thoughts*, or Reflections on *any* subject/—but as these are most often occasioned by some *Desiderium*, Elegy came to be chiefly tho' not necessarily amorous or mournful.[1]

18   i i 110–11, pencil

[On p 111, Schlegel suggests that "if erotic gracefulness and culti-vation [*Bildung*] are the soul of the later Greek elegy, nothing more elegiac can be found than Hermesianax' precious fragment".]

This is the plague of the Germans. Why not say at once what the word Elegy means, then what it was made to mean, i.e./ what it comprehended/—then, to what it became more especially appropria-ted; and lastly, find out, if you can, some one character distinctive of the Elegy in all its various kinds—or if not, say so—and *propose* to confine the word to a determinate Genus.[1]

19   i i 112, pencil

Die Richtung dieser Liebe aufs männliche Geschlecht kann derjenige, welcher es nicht anerkennt, dass Schönheit das einzige Gesetz und die wahre Sittlichkeit der Empfindungen ist, dass der freye Mensch unnatürlich seyn darf, und dass manches, was an sich Verirrung ist, für eine bestimmte Zeit und Stufe der Entwicklung nothwendig und also auch gut seyn kann, am besten für blosse Poesie halten, ohne dabey länger zu verweilen, als um sich zu erinnern, dass Apollo und Hyakinthos Trotz jenes Fehlers doch wohl natürlicher und gesitteter seyn könnten, als alle, die dagegen reden.
[He who does not accept the fact that beauty is the only law and the true morality of the emotions, that the free man may be unnatural, and that

17[1] An attractive notion but ety-mologically ungrounded. The Greek ελεγεία is associated with ἔλεγος (flute-song) from some foreign word for a flute. The Schlegels and C are both correct in wishing to broaden the term *elegy*: most early types of elegiac have no relation to laments. C provided his own definition of elegy in *TT* 23 Oct 1833: "Elegy is the form of poetry natural to the reflective mind...." For his distinction between "the Elegiac Πόθος" and "the Lyrical Ὄρεξις", see *CL* vi 729.

18[1] Although C declared that one of the characteristics of the Germans was "distinctness" (*Friend—CC—*i 421), he often accused German philo-sophers of making imprecise distinc-tions. See e.g. *IS* 99.

some things that in themselves are aberrations are necessary and therefore can be good at a certain time and stage of development, will do best to consider this love's being directed towards the male sex as mere poetry and to dwell on it no longer than is required to recall that Apollo and Hyacinth in spite of this fault may very well be more natural and more civilised than all those who protest against such love.]

What *can* this mean?—The most charitable answer would be, that the Writer himself did not know.—[1]

20 I i 145, pencil | A. W. Schlegel *Beyträge zur Kritik der neuesten Litteratur*

Ein Hauptnachtheil der allgemeinen kritischen Institut ist es, dass sie die verschiedenartigsten Dinge auf einerley Fuss behandeln müssen. Zuerst die guten Bücher und die schlechten. Von jenen muss dargethan werden, dass sie gut, und von diesen, dass sie schlecht sind. Wie sehr diess auch dem heiligen Grundsatze der Gleichheit gemäss scheint, so kann die Gerechtigkeit doch niemals verpflichten, etwas überflüssiges zu thun. Entweder man nimmt an, dass alle Bücher schlecht sind, bis das Gegentheil erwiesen ist; so wird man sich bloss mit dem Vortrefflichen beschäftigen, und das Übrige *] mit Stillschweigen übergehn. Ein solches Journal haben wir nicht, und es würde sich aus mancherley Ursachen nicht lange halten können. Oder man nimmt an, dass alle Bücher gut sind, bis das Gegentheil erwiesen ist, und daraus wird das umgekehrte Verfahren entstehn.

[A major disadvantage of a general critical institute is that it must treat the most heterogeneous things on the same basis. First of all, the good books and the bad. It must be shown of the former that they are good and of the latter that they are bad. However much this may seem to be in accordance with the sacred principle of impartiality, fairness can never oblige one to do anything unnecessary. Either one assumes that all books are bad until the opposite is proven, in which case one will merely concern oneself with the excellent and pass over the rest in silence—we do not have such journal, and for a variety of reasons one would be unable to last for long—or one assumes that all books are good until the contrary is proven, and then the reverse process will take place.]

* The justness of this remark is proved by the Edinborough & Quarterly, which commenced on this plan & with this promise, but soon passed into collections of original Essays intermixed with the most palpable Favoritism or Hostility. What appertained to a Review was ⟨generally⟩ one or the other.[1]

19[1] For an earlier note on homo-sexuality see ANDERSON COPY A **1**.
  20[1] C in *BL* ch 22 discussed "the present mode of conducting critical journals"; as a professional journalist he deplored "personalities" and in-

21 I ii 5, pencil | "Fragmente"[1] [No 82: by Friedrich Schlegel]

Man hat von manchem Monarchen gesagt: er würde ein sehr liebens-
würdiger Privatmann gewesen seyn, nur zum Könige habe er nicht
getaugt. Verhält es sich etwa mit der Bibel eben so? Ist sie auch bloss
ein liebenswürdiges Privatbuch, das nur nicht Bibel seyn sollte?

[It has been said of many a monarch that he would have been a very
amiable private citizen, and that he was merely unfit to be a king. Is it not
like this with the Bible? Is the Bible also just an amiable private book that
merely should not have been the Bible?]

A. W. S. = a frog-man. Sub *writer*[2]

The whole history of civilization for the last 2000 years gives the
indignant Lie to this French-German most worthless Sneer.[3] The
more hybrid, the more hateful—thus a swimming Frog excites the
fancy of ⟨a⟩ Frog-man. Even so A. W. Schegel of a French Fop & a
German Scholar.[4]

22 I ii 25, pencil | [No 99: by Friedrich Schlegel]

Bey den Ausdrücken, Seine Philosophie, Meine Philosophie, erinnert
man sich immer an die Worte im Nathan: "Wem eignet Gott?
*] Was ist das für ein Gott, der einem Menschen eignet?"

[By the expressions "his philosophy", "my philosophy", one is always
reminded of the words in [Lessing's] *Nathan the Wise*: "To whom does
God belong? What sort of God would it be who belongs to one human
being?"]

* an equivoque. Was ist das für ein Gott, der *nur* einem eignet? No
God at all. But if had I said, "So fern ich ihn wille und liebe, auch
mir eignet Gott,["]1 and the same question were repeated, I might

---

sisted that reviewing should be conducted according to considered critical
principles. For his alarm and "pain"
when John Taylor Coleridge accepted
the editorship of the *QR* in 1825, see
e.g. *CL* v 422–3, 525–6.

21[1] Variously by Friedrich Schlegel,
A. W. Schlegel, Schleiermacher, and
Novalis. In the headline the number
assigned in modern editions to each
aphorism is given together with the
identity of the author—information
not reliably available to C.

21[2] Cf C's reference to Samuel
Johnson as "the Frog-critic. How
nimbly it leaps, how excellently it
swims..." *Sh C* I 73n.

21[3] This foolish suggestion offends
C's view of the Bible, not merely as a
book, but as the living Word. See *SM*
(*CC*) 31.

21[4] C sees in A. W. Schlegel signs
of French superficiality and a German
proneness to generalisation. See *Friend*
(*CC*) I 421–2 and e.g. *P Lects* (1949)
416 n 25. Schlegel had joined the
household of Mme de Staël in 1803
and remained with her until her death
in Jul 1817; during this time he published several works in French.

22[1] "What sort of God would it be
that belonged *only* to one human
being?... In so far as I desire him
and love him, God belongs to me too."

answer—God omnipresent, All every where, One for All, All in each.[2]

23 i ii 31, pencil | [No 119: by Friedrich Schlegel]

[The aphorism that contrasts talent and genius ends:] . . . Genie kann man eigentlich nie haben, nur seyn. Auch giebt es keinen Pluralis von Genie, der hier schon im Singularis steckt. Genie ist ne[h]mlich ein System von Talenten.

[. . . Actually one can never have genius, one can only be one. Also, the word "genius" has no plural, which in this case is already contained in the singular; for genius is a system of talents.]

I assert the contrary viz. that the Man of Genius *has*, not is, a Genius. Schlegel and I differ as Pelagianism and Free Grace. We *are* it only while we have it, as our pitying Angel, whom yet we may alienate.[1] S. T. C.

24 i ii 31, pencil

[Last sentence of **23** textus: "for genius is a system of talents".]

Negatur—[1]

25 i ii 35, pencil | [No 132: by A. W. Schlegel]

Dichter sind doch immer Narzisse.

[Poets are always Narcissuses.]

Too often; but not *always*, I hope.

A man may see his face in the Glass with pleasure (after restoration to full health, from sickness, for instance) and yet be no Narcissus.[1]

22[2] Cf BAXTER *Reliquiae* COPY A 2 and n 2.

23[1] Cf JACOBI *Ueber die Lehre des Spinoza* (Breslau 1789) 353: "Man *has*, God *is* Wisdom." Cf *TT* 21 May 1830, and *AR* (1825) 5, where the soul is said to be man's "proper *being*, his truest *self*, *the* man *in* the man". The marginal note has strong personal overtones for C. See e.g. his letter to RS 16 Feb 1807: "I felt as a man revisited by a familiar Spirit the first morning, that I felt that sort of stirring warmth about the Heart, which is with me the robe of incarnation of my genius, such as it is." *CL* III 5. For his sense of the loss of genius see e.g. *CN* II 3136, III 3324.

According to the Pelagian heresy man is saved by his own efforts—a form of subjectivism repugnant to C. He contrasts Schlegel's subjective self-assertion (for he evidently thought this Fragment was written by A. W. Schlegel) with his own acknowledged need of divine grace.

24[1] "It is denied", as in **12**.

25[1] Several letters record C's pleasure in greeting his reflection in the mirror after recovering from illness—as though in an act at once affirmative and incredulous he celebrated his return from the brink of the grave. But Clement Carlyon noticed, perhaps as early as the Göttingen days, how when

26 I ii 36, pencil | [No 138: by Friedrich Schlegel]

Die Tragiker setzen die Szene ihrer Dichtungen fast immer in die Vergangenheit. Warum sollte diess schlechtin nothwendig, warum sollte es nicht auch möglich seyn, die Szene in die Zukunft zu setzen, wodurch die Fantasie mit einem Streich von allen historischen Rücksichten und Einschränkungen befreyt würde?

[The tragic poets almost always set the scene of their plays in the past. Why should this be absolutely necessary? Why should it not also be possible to set the scene in the future, in which case the imagination would at once be freed from all historical considerations and limitations?]

No bad Hint for a Christmas Pantomime.[1]

27 I ii 37–8, pencil | [No 144: by Friedrich Schlegel]

Das goldne Zeitalter der römischen Litteratur war genialischer und der Poesie günstiger; das sogenannte silberne in der Prosa ungleich korrekter.

[The Golden Age of Roman literature was endowed with more genius and was more favourable to poetry; in prose, the so-called Silver Age was incomparably more correct.]

—more *compressed*, I would say, and marks an age, in which *Books* as the positive Pole worked formatively on the Conversation of the Higher Classes, as in the Age of Cicero the eloquence of the Senate & the Forum & the Conversation of the Higher Classes worked formatively on the Bookish./ In the one age the Man wrote as he talked—in the other, talked as they had read.[1]

28 I ii 75, pencil | [No 272: by Friedrich Schlegel]

Warum sollte es nicht auch unmoralische Menschen geben dürfen, so gut wie unphilosophische und unpoetische? Nur antipolitische oder unrechtliche Menschen können nicht geduldet werden.

[Why should not immoral persons be tolerated just as unphilosophical and unpoetical persons are? Only antipolitical or unjust people cannot be tolerated.]

The answer is: they *are*, Nay, not only tolerated but promoted.[1]

---

there was a mirror in a room C had a tendency to converse "between himself and the man I have so often seen him look at with admiration, when standing opposite to a mirror". Carlyon I 161.

26[1] This hint of a "Christmas Pantomime" may betray the hope that both C and Lamb had of writing for the theatre something light-hearted, popular, and lucrative.

27[1] Cf the "Wonderfulness of Prose" fragment in *LR* II 372–3.

28[1] A political observation that, without invoking the grand old Duke of York, was as valid in C's day as in ours.

29 I ii 143, pencil | [No 441: almost certainly by Friedrich Schlegel]

Liberal ist wer von allen Seiten und nach allen Richtungen wie von selbst frey ist und in seiner ganzen Menschheit wirkt; wer alles, was handelt, ist und wird, nach dem Mass seiner Kraft heilig hält, und an allem Leben Antheil nimmt, ohne sich durch beschränkte Ansichten zum Hass oder zur Geringschätzung desselben verführen zu lassen.

[That man is tolerant [*liberal*] who is free on all sides and in all directions as if on his own accord and who acts as a complete person; he who, as far as his strength permits, considers sacred everything that acts, is, and becomes, and who participates in the whole of life, without allowing himself to be tempted by narrow-minded views to hate or disdain it.]

Nonsense. The Liberal is he, who observes correctly, infers legitimately, and judges charitably.[1]

30 II 308, pencil | "Notizen." Review by F. E. D. Schleiermacher of *Anthropologie v. Immanuel Kant. Königsb. 98*

Die Germanischen Sprachen aus dem ersten Jahrhundert nach Christi Geburt waren schwerlich im achten noch verständlich; und hätten sie sich mit dem Fortgange der Zeit umgewandelt, und wären etwa in der Sprache des Kero und Otfried abgefasst gewesen: wie könnten wir ihrer Aechtheit und ihres Alterthums gewiss seyn? . . .

[The Germanic languages of the first century A.D. could hardly have still been comprehensible in the eighth; and if they [the "Bardic songs" alleged to have been collected by Charlemagne] had changed in the course of time and had been written, e.g. in the language of Kero and Otfried, how could we be sure of their genuineness and their age?[1]]

This presumption stands or falls with the proof of a Progression, and consequently a change in the state of manners.

31 pp +2–+3, pencil; perhaps an extension of **7** or **23**

All is, must be, *evolution* in Man/ the Moulds, and the matter that receives form from the Moulds.[1] But in some the Moulds seem to be

29[1] "Liberal" had at this time different connotations in English and German. Schlegel used the word almost invariably in the sense of "open-minded" or "tolerant".

On II 119 a sentence is marked in the margin in pencil with a heavy geometrical mark unlike C's practice; it is probably Green's. The passage reads in translation: "But if for once a foreign element is allowed to intrude, then it is probably just as legitimate to tell a biblical story in the Venetian dialect as to see the whole world through Greek spectacles."

30[1] Kero, the supposed author of the "Keronic Glossary", now better known as the *Abrogans* (c 765); Otfried, the author of a rhymed Gospel harmony (c 863–71). C had read Otfried's Gospel at Göttingen. *BL* ch 10 (1907) I 139.

31[1] The difference between "form as body, i.e. as shape" and form as

so easily formed as to appear almost preformed—while the fixed Matter that should fill them & filling supersede them, is deficient. In others there is the reverse—want, or posteriority, of the Moulds— *Genius*—where the Products finally perfecting into form give the [?motion/motive/motus] to a Mould, as a perpetuating *Shape* of the forma per se formata./[2]

Or shall we better understand the difference, as the Thing, and the *Relations*? the *hiccæity*,[3] and the diagnostics of *its* particularity? I.e. as the All, in its first self-sensation; but in order to its consequent self-affirmation, it must find itself a *part*—And as such is self-annihilated, reduced to the indistinction in the Multëity, till it can constitute itself[a] *that* part, & in admitting its dependence claim the privilege of an interdependence—A is being *that* particular it is from the Whole; but as A to B, so B to A—&c &c—till the Whole is

---

[a] What looks like a cancellation of two letters is a flaw in the paper

---

"forma efformans" (as outlined in *CN* III 4066 c Apr 1811) is fundamental to C's theory of imagination, growth, and evolution. The word "Moulds" is not usual in such a context, but it does occur again e.g. in BÖHME **162**, in which the "forms of Understanding" are referred to as "formæ formificæ, or potential moulds". The distinction is clearly given in *CN* III 4397 f 53[v] (c 10 Mar 1818) without using the word "Moulds": "Difference of Form as proceeding and Shape as superinduced".

31[2] See **31** n 1, above. The Latin phrase means "the form formed by/ through itself". See also *CN* II 2444 on "Form...is ab intra *evolved*".

31[3] "Hiccæity", and (later in this marginal note) "multëity" and "Sëity", are words of scholastic origin or derivation. Duns Scotus coined *haeccitas* and *seitas* for his own special uses; it is safe to assume that C came upon them in "their own natural home". A family of words in -*ëitas* (-*ëity*), fashioned to clarify aspects of "essence", commended themselves to C for an almost-Greek directness that Latin abstract nouns usually lack; the nature and function of these words are best preserved in

English if they are rendered plainly— "this-ness", "many-ness", "self-ness".

After Duns Scotus, neither *haeccitas* nor *seitas* had much serious currency. C, however, took up "hiccëity" (a legitimate form, not in *OED*) as a term of peculiar specificity; and, using "sëity" seldom, preferred the stronger variant "ipsëity", which Henry More had used in his *Immortality of the Soul*, a poem known to C. See also *CN* I 374.

"Multëity" — "many-ness" — is, however, a Coleridgian word formed on the analogy of the other two. For the earliest use of it *OED* quotes C's account of it in "On the Principles of Genial Criticism" (1814): *BL* (1907) II 230. In a similar note on "this scholastic term, *multeity*" C said that he was using the term because he needed "an unequivocal word...that would convey the notion in a positive and not comparative sense in kind, as opposed to the *unum et simplex*, not in degree, as contrasted with the *few*". *TL* (1848) 45n. In that case, the coining of the word can be seen as an extension of the principle of desynonymisation: the need to secure and clarify a distinction could lead him,

dependent on A—which by admission of a Whole *integrates* itself, as a representative Fluxion of the Whole.[4]

To live in the *relations* without sensation of the Sëity, or only as a per se indifferenced stuff (a tree sawed into equal planks, one of which I call *I*) is Talent, i.e. self-*application*, the prospective Self reflected from the application./ In Genius, the application manifests, but does not *constitute*, the distinct Self.—Genius is Individuality, Talent Individuation.

---

in the absence of suitable approximate synonyms, to invent the necessary missing term.

For "personëity" see BAXTER *Reliquiae* COPY B **42** n 1; for "omnëity" see BÖHME **118** n 1; and for a general comment on "the *ivitates* and *ëitates* of the Schoolmen" see *CN* III 4352.

31[4] It is not clear to what part of the *Athenaeum*—if any—the note refers; or what theme gave rise to it. C owned a copy of Thomas Simpson *A New Treatise on Fluxions* (1737); and on 17 Apr 1819 he wrote to a "Miss B" asking for "the Loan of the Volume of your Encyclopaedia, containing the article, Fluxions". *CL* IV 936. Originally a "fluxion" was a rate of change in a variable quantity; but as the Leibnizian notation and terminology superseded Newton's the word "fluxion" seems to have been used loosely as a synonym of "differential"—"the infinitesimal difference between consecutive values of a continuously variable quantity" (*OED*)—and so De Q is noted by *OED* as using the word. C seems to use "fluxion" here in that sense to accentuate his argument—meaning an infinitely small part, perhaps an instance of the "infinite minima" mentioned in *CN* III 4266 (Sept 1815).

EDWIN ATHERSTONE
1788–1872

LOST BOOK

The Last Days of Herculaneum; and Abradates and Panthea. Poems.
London 1821.

Not located; marginalia not recorded. *Green SC* (1880) 13: "With
autograph note by S. T. Coleridge". *Lost List*.

Gillman's library contained a copy, not shown as C's, of Atherstone's
Fall of Nineveh Bks I–VI (1828), possibly a presentation copy to C. *Gillman
SC* (1843) 405. In c Aug 1827, after negotiations between S. C. Hall and C
over contributions to Hall's *Amulet* (founded 1826) had broken down,
Atherstone—who had first introduced Hall to C—acted as Hall's agent,
regarding himself as a friend of C's. *CL* VI 698, 801, and nn. But in Jan
1827 C disapproved of Atherstone's approaches to his daughter, declined
to give him Tom Poole's address, and told Poole that "Nature wove him
well but with coarse threads. His Epic Poem in 24 Books on the Siege of
Nineveh, the whole of which with exception of one or two Proper Names
is to be of his own invention, is the most ridiculous thing, I ever heard of
—and I wasted some wisdom upon him to no purpose." *CL* VI 662.

MARCUS AURELIUS ANTONINUS
121–180

The Emperor Marcus Antoninus His Conversation with Himself. Together with the preliminary discourse of the learned Gataker. As also, the Emperor's Life, written by Monsieur D'acier, and supported by the authorities collected by Dr. Stanhope. To which is added The Mythological Picture of Cebes the Theban, &c. Translated into English from the respective originals, by Jeremy Collier, M.A. 2 pts in 1 vol. London 1701. 8°.

The 36 pages interpolated at 240/241 comprise Gataker's "Preliminary Discourse". The continuity of catchwords shows that this section was considered integral to the volume. *The Picture of Cebes* begins on i 241 immediately following Gataker's "Discourse".

Pierpont Morgan Library

Above the displayed lettering of the title, the initials "C∗ A S∗" are stamped in red; and lower on the title-page is the signature "C A Sturgeon", which is also written at the head of p 59. On the title-page, around the stamp and signature, is inscribed in two early hands: "Richard Brathwait Ex Libris Johannis Pughe Armigeri. Reddātur Haeredi.—Thomas Fryssbe Gogarthan Mathafarn Necnon De Rūg", and three or four illegible words in the upper right margin outside the enclosing rule.

This translation of Marcus Aurelius and Cebes was among the books C took to sea with him in the *Speedwell* for the voyage to Malta in spring 1804 (*CN* II 2014 and n). For C on the "Imperial Stoic" see *Friend* (*CC*) II 9 and *CL* III 158. On the *Picture of Cebes*, see *Misc C* 30. For the style of Jeremy Collier (1650–1726), as "carried out to the utmost extreme of slang and ribaldry", see *Misc C* 219; cf 224.

In view of the special interest that C was taking in prose style in 1802–3 (see **1** n 3, **16** n 1, below), it might seem that the earliest marginalia on AURELIUS could belong to the middle or end of 1803. But there is no definite evidence that C actually owned this copy before he arrived in London on 23 Jan 1804; and Collier's name does not appear in the note of Nov 1803 (cited in **62** n 2, below) that is the prototype for his reiterated comment on slangy prose. It appears that C acquired the book in London some time after 23 Jan 1804 and before leaving Portsmouth on 27 Mar on his way to Malta.

DATE. Mainly c 1804–1811; a few notes may have been added up to 1818–19; one note (**35**), associated with a letter of 1826 and *C&S*, is probably

later than any of the other notes. None of the notes is dated in ms. *CN*
II 2077 (see **59A** n 1, below)—an entry made in the *Speedwell* on 5 May
1804, when the ship was becalmed, heavy rain was falling, and C was sea-
sick—makes a comment on style that accords with some twenty marginalia
and with the heavy marking of the text. See ANNEX.

The notes—on the basis of handwriting and subject—seem to fall into
two chronological groups: (*a*) c late Jan to May 1804: the stylistic notes
(**1–17, 33, 50, 60, 64**) and the marking of nearly 200 words, phrases, and
passages in all books of the *Meditations* except VI and VIII, and with special
concentration in *The Picture*—that "absolute Dictionary of '*Slang*'";
(*b*) of the rest of the notes, many seem to have been written in Jan–Jun
1808 in London and .perhaps at Bury St Edmunds; but some seem to
belong to early 1811 in London, a few (e.g. **48**) may be as late as 1818–19,
and one is probably as late as 1826 or later (see **35** n 1, below).

1   pp i–iii | "The Life of the Emperour Marcus Antoninus"

This Translation is ridiculed by Pope in his Martinus Scriblerus.[1]—
It must be confessed, that the Style is often even ludicrous, from its
"colloquial barbarisms", as Johnson phrases it.[2] Yet there is a Life,
a Spirit, a Zest, which makes it more pleasing, say rather, less disgusting to me, than is the pompous enigmatic Jargon of modern
Prose since the publication of the Rambler.[3] I speak however only
of the Translation of M. Antonine: for that of of "the Picture of
Cebes" is an absolute Dictionary of "*Slang*". An amusing & instructive Essay might be written on idiomatic Language, in which
the reasons should be given, & exemplified, why certain Idioms ~~can~~

1[1] The Scriblerus Club, originally
Pope, Arbuthnot, Swift, Gay, Parnell,
and Robert Harley, the Earl of
Oxford, met from 1714 until about
1730. Authorship of individual Scrib-
lerus papers is difficult to establish. The
Memoirs—the work of Pope and
Arbuthnot—was first published in Vol
II of Pope's *Works* in 1735 after
Arbuthnot's death, and in later editions
of that volume the previously published Scriblerus papers were collected:
hence presumably C's ascription of
Scriblerus to Pope. Charles Kerby-
Miller, in his edition of *Memoirs of
...Martinus Scriblerus* (New Haven
1950) 184–5, says of C's note that it
can refer only to Ch 1 of the *Memoirs*:
"Despite the resemblance [to Collier]
it seems doubtful that a direct parody
was intended....It seems safe to
conclude that this part of the *Memoirs*

ridicules a type of style of which
Jeremy Collier is an outstanding
example." It is known, however, that
Pope used Collier's tr of Aurelius when
he was writing the *Essay on Man*.

1[2] *Rambler* No 208 (17 Mar 1752),
Johnson's farewell paper. C had already
considered "colloquial barbarisms" in
CN I 666. See also **7** and ANNEX [*d*].

1[3] For C on Johnson's *Rambler*
style see *TT* 1 Nov 1833; and for a comparison of the styles of Johnson, Junius,
and Gibbon, see *LR* I 239–40 (cf also
61). In Jul 1803 C had included in his
scheme for the "Bibliotheca Britannica" an extensive historical-critical
study of English prose style (*CL* II
955–6), and in Sept 1802 advised Basil
Montagu on an edition of prose
selections from Taylor, Hooker, Hall,
and Bacon (*CL* II 870; cf 877). See also
BURNET *Life* **5**.

give Passion and Color to Style, which wholly stripped of them become a sort of *Alien*: as ex. gr. Gibbon & the Scotch Quarto-Writers contrasted with the prose of Dryden, Cowley, and Addison/[4] and why others degrade the Diction, and render it mean & ludicrous. One cause of the latter I hold to be the indefiniteness* of the phrase, which marks a vulgar mind—as "to have a *mind* to a thing."[5] Now "Mind" being either the whole spiritual Being, or else the whole intellectual part of our Being, it marks an ignorance of the appropriate & definite words, "desire[']", "inclination", &c—A man talks as if Language were yet in its Infancy.—Of the *good* Idioms the greater part will be found to express, & to have originated in, Passion, or Imagination, or both: as to fall short of a thing—

   * or vice versâ false definiteness, as—"the Soldiers seemed to find refreshment in *cutting the throats* of their enemies—" instead of "slaughtering" &c[6]—The Image is disgusting, & it is false.

2 p lxxiv

And here the *Romans* made a horrible Slaughter of them, the Field was all strew'd with Carcasses, and the greatest trouble the Emperour had was to check the Heat and Fury of his Soldiers, who as weary as they were, seem'd to Refresh themselves by <u>cutting of the Throats of</u> the Enemy.

Now we know that Soldiers do very rarely *cut the throat* at all. They stab the body, or cleave the Head, &c. This is false Definiteness combined with a disgusting Image.

1[4] An example of C's sense of idiom is given in *CN* I 350: "Sterben—to die, decease, depart, depart this life, starve, breathe your last, expire, give up the ghost, kick up your heels, tip off, top over the Perch."

Edward Gibbon (1737–94) published his *History of the Decline and Fall of the Roman Empire* in 6 vols 1776–88; one detached marginal note on it by C has survived. In 1810 C complained of "the monotonous and effeminate structure of his Periods". *CN* III 3823. When he refers to "Addison" C is usually thinking of the *Spectator* papers, which he evidently read with care and a good deal of admiration (though not for the first time) when he was preparing to write *The Friend* 1809–10; see *LR* I 238. When he said in Jul 1801 that "Of Dryden I

am & always have been a passionate admirer. I have placed him among our greatest men" (*CL* II 743), it is not clear whether he was thinking of Dryden's prose or poetry; but when (in **61**, below) he compared Dryden and Cowley and found Dryden superior he was certainly thinking of Dryden as a prose-writer. In C's view it was Dryden who began the second great period of the English language. *TT* 5 Jul 1834.

The quarto format, being splendid in appearance, encouraged pretentious magnificence; and C enjoyed girding at the Scots. For the "Agricultural Quarto-mongers" see *CL* III 539.

1[5] The phrase "had a mind to" occurs e.g. immediately after **17** textus.

1[6] See **2**, below.

3 p lxxv

The *Thunder Legion* . . . attack'd the *Jazygian* Cavalry with so much Bravery, that they forced them to wheel off, and Ride for't.

Now here is the vulgar Indefiniteness—*for't*, or omitting the caco-phony, "*for it*" may mean 20 things/ "in order to escape". Such phrases imply a want of *sobriety* in the mind—or to borrow from the Style, I am condemning, it marks a sort of *Huddle* in the Ideas: and for this cause similar Idioms have a good effect in dramatic or im-passioned writing, as in Burns, &c—[1]

4 p [cxxviii] (blank page facing the opening of the *Meditations*)

I would advise, in general, that only one Paragraph should be read a time. First, because each is a Meditation, & well worthy of exciting it in the reader—secondly, because the Habit of passing from one thought to another not connected with it, both weakens the Memory, & injures the Understanding. This is one of the Causes why Re-views & Magazines leave no good or deep impression/—So, I would never suffer a ~~Child~~ Boy to read more than one paper at a time in the Spectator, &c—[1]

5 p [cxxviii]

O means a ~~vu~~ phrase vulgar from its indefiniteness—see page 1 & 2.—[1]

⊙ means a phrase vulgar by false definiteness.

3[1] From the Bristol days onwards C was enthusiastic about Burns's poems and in Dec 1796 wrote a poem for cir-culation "in aid of a subscription for the family of Robert Burns". *PW* (EHC) I 158. Burns was one of the poets C intended to consider in a book of critical studies in Jun 1802. *CL* II 829. A couplet from *Tam o'Shanter* stuck in C's memory as an example of "the capacity of the poet to give novelty and freshness, profundity and wisdom, entertainment and instruction, to the most familiar objects". *Sh C* II 159; cf 68 and *Friend* (*CC*) II 74. See also *CN* II 2431 f 5.

4[1] On 3 May 1808 C gave a lecture "of two hours and a quarter on Education"; see HCR's account of the lecture in *Sh C* II 9–12.

In May 1804 C had playfully con-sidered that he, WW, Lamb, and RS "should publish *a Spectator*" to gather amusing absurdities of the kind he had just noted in an Italian "Method of Learning"—perhaps a foretaste of RS's *Omniana. CN* II 2074; cf I 1633 and n and *Friend* (*CC*) II 186. But when he was considering what ideally *The Friend* should be he expressed alarm that the *Spectator* was firmly estab-lished as a guide to morals for the young. See *Friend* (*CC*) II 28–9. He thought it had "produced a passion for the unconnected in the minds of Englishmen". *CL* III 279, 281; and cf 254. See also **12, 21,** below.

5[1] See ANNEX [*a*], [*b*], below. For different sets of qualitative sigla see ANDERSON COPY C **10** n 1.

Φ means a phrase vulgar or ludicrous from its transiency, or dependence on an accidental Fashion—such as, *quizzing*, the *Ton*, &c
&c.

N.B. means that the passage seemed to me worthy of *particular*
attention.

MEDITATIONS

6   p 2 | ɪ vi

... This *Diognetus* help'd me to the Faculty of bearing Freedom and
Plain-dealing in others; brought me to Relish Philosophy, and apply
my self to't; and procured me the Instruction of those celebrated
Men, *Bacchius*, *Tandacides*, and *Marcianus*. He likewise put me
upon improving my self by writing Dialogues when I was a Boy,
prevail'd with me to prefer a Couch cover'd with Hides, to a Bed of
State; and reconcil'd me to other resembling Rigors of the Stoick
Discipline.

This Mr Collier seems to have had an antipathy to the vowel, "i"—
he literally *blinds* ~~them~~ all his poor innocent pronouns "/ɪt".

7   p 3 | ɪ vii

And to conclude with him, he procur'd me a Copy of *Epictetus*'s
Works.

Most of these barbarisms are capable of a double meaning, or perhaps treble. The sense enables you to decypher the phrase, instead
of the phrase leading to the Sense.

8   pp 4–5 | ɪ viii

To give him his due, his practice was a handsome Instance, that a
Man may be Master of his own Behaviour.

By X I mean to point out low misapplication of physical or bodily
words to the mind:[1] this no doubt depends on ⟨arbitrary⟩ custom,
in *great* measure—⟨but not entirely:⟩ ~~and~~ ex. gr. beautiful ~~by~~ in all
languages is applied ~~merely to~~ both morally & *materially*—but
handsome being a definite species of ~~the~~ personal Beauty is not so
used, except vulgarly. It is illogical, because that by which its
Meaning is particularized has no relation to the following Substantive: as if, for instance, instead of "a deformed Soul" I should
say "*a humpbacked Soul.*"

8[1] See ANNEX [*d*], below. The omission of X here was an oversight.

9　p 5 | i ix

By his Precedent I was instructed ... To bear with the ignorant and unthinking; to be Complaisant and Obliging to all People, even up to the Smoothness of Flattery; and yet at the same time not to suffer in <u>ones</u> Quality, or <u>grow a jot</u> the Cheaper for't.

I am sorry, that I have not the original with me: for I more than suspect, that many passages are rendered falsely—it should be, I believe, "with the innocent Flattery of a kind and soft Manner"/[1]

10　p 6 | i xi

Fronto, <u>my</u> Rhetorick Master, obliged me with the knowledge of Men: For the purpose, that Envy, Tricking, and Dissimulation, are the Character and Consequences of Tyranny; And that those we call Top Quality, have commonly not much of *Nature* in them.

ludicrous by association/ ["]My dancing-master" &c[1]

11　p 8 | i xv

And which is very remarkable, No Body ever fancied they were slighted by him; or had the Courage to think themselves his *Betters* ...

⌜This reminds me of Sir G. B.⌝[1]

9[1] See also **30** and **44**, below. For C's copy of the Greek original see *CN* III 4314n. Not only C, but also Matthew Arnold—one of the few defenders of Collier's translation—complained of Collier's imperfect acquaintance with Greek; but in this case C—lacking the Greek—is no more accurate than Collier. This particular passage seems to have stuck in C's memory: in May 1817 he sent the printer a Greek motto for *Friend* III (*CL* IV 729) ingeniously put together from I ix by elision, by transferring part of a sentence from I viii, and then doctoring the syntax of the last three words. His own translation reads: "From Sextus, and from the contemplation of his character, I learnt what it was to live a life in harmony with nature; and that seemliness and dignity of deportment, which ensured the profoundest reverence at the very same time that his company was more win-

ning than all the flattery in the world. ..." *Friend* (*CC*) I 377.

10[1] The absurdity may be heightened in C's mind by Hogarth's caricature of a dancing-master, which JW certainly knew and enjoyed (*JWL* 100); he is also a prominent figure in *The Rake's Progress*.

11[1] The whole note has been crossed out in ink, perhaps not by C, presumably to conceal the identity of "Sir G. B.". Sir George Beaumont (1753–1827), painter and patron of the arts, first met C in Jul 1803 and "disliked me at first" (*CL* II 1114), but friendship quickly developed and through C Beaumont soon became friend and benefactor to WW. C paid a visit to the Beaumonts at Dunmow in Essex in Feb 1804, exchanged letters with them after his return to London, and called on them in late March at their house in South Audley Street, where they seem to have come to see

12 p 8 | I xvi

From him a Prince might learn to love Business and Action, and be constantly <u>at it</u>.

O that Princes were made to learn this Book by Heart; & so educated as to *love* what they learnt. It is surprizing that neither M. Antoninus or Epictetus are in the Lists of School Books at any of the Public Schools.[1]

12A p 9

To understand the Critical Seasons, and Circumstances for Rigour, or Remissness; when 'twas proper to make up, and when to slacken the Reins of Government: ~~To have no *He-Sweet-Hearts*, and Boy-Favourites:~~[a] Not to stand upon Points of State and Prerogative.

13 p 10

He was Condescensive* and Familiar in Conversation.

* This is a good word, & we want it.[1] "Ive" always means habit or general power—Lambs are sport*ive*—Yonder Lamb is sport*ing*.[2]

14 p 11

'Twas none of <u>his</u> custom to Bath at unusual Hours ...

The vileness of this phrase, and similar ones, arises 1. from offending against Logic & Grammar—it ought to be "Customs"—2. because it deviates from a simpler, plainer phrase, without any assignable reason—It was not his Custom—3. It confuses the mind by a capricious Blending of the Negative with the Positive. N.B. This last I deem the great defect of the French Language.[1]

---

[a] C has obliterated these words so heavily that they cannot be read in this copy

---

C off. They made him an affectionate farewell with presents of books and other comforts to relieve the voyage. *CN* II 1998. For C's view of Beaumont in the spring of 1804 see *CL* II 1102–3; cf 1106–7, *CN* II 1983, 2193.

12[1] C would naturally join the names of Marcus Aurelius, the "Imperial Stoic", and Epictetus, the freed Roman slave banished from Rome—two of the three outstanding figures in the late Stoic period—for the posthumous philosophic writing of Epictetus (c 55–c 135) had a profound effect on Aurelius. The splendid edition of Arrian, which Leckie gave to C in Sicily in Oct 1804 as what turned out to be an Indian gift, includes Epictetus' *Enchiridion* and *Apophthegmata*: see *CN* II 2236 and n, III 3276. On reading for children see *CN* III 3390. *Friend* (*CC*) II 29–30, *Sh C* II 11.

13[1] The earliest use recorded in *OED* is 1652.

13[2] The choice of the key word may be a sportive gibe at Lamb.

14[1] In May 1802 C told Poole that "I have, you well know, read nothing

15   p 14 | I xvii

I had the Happiness of being acquainted with those celebrated Philosophers, *Apollonius, Rusticus*, and *Maximus*: For having a clear Idea of the Rules of Practice, and the true way of Living... 'tis impossible for me to miss the Road of Nature and right Reason, unless by refusing to be guided by the Dictates, and almost sensible Inspirations from Heaven.

The Contrary was one of the worst Faults in the characters of Sir R. Walpole & Mr Pitt—they shunned or undervalued all men eminent in Literature.[1]

15A   p 14

'Tis the Favour of these superior Beings [i.e. Apollonius et al]... That I never had any infamous Correspondence with *Benedicta* or *Theodotus*...
[Shoulder-note:] ~~The one most probably a famous *Wench*, and the other a Court *Catamite*.~~

16   p 15

... when I was willing to Relieve the Necessities of Others, I was never told that the *Exchequer*, or *Privy Purse*, were out of Cash. And farther, 'tis from them that my Wife is so very obsequious, and affectionate, and so remote from the Fancy of Figure and Expence...

Happy Ignorance!

---

in French but metaphysical French/ of French Books I know nothing—of French manners nothing—", and had declined an offer from a bookseller to travel in France and Switzerland "chiefly...from my ignorance of the French Language". *CL* II 799–800. C was usually rather violent about anything French, and in his 1808 lectures thanked God that he was totally ignorant of "that frightful jargon, the French language". *N&Q* 16 Oct 1875, cited by William Black from "a biography of Coleridge, written during his lifetime and prefixed to an edition of his poems issued at Philadelphia".

15[1] Sir Robert Walpole (1676–1745), 1st Earl of Orford, father of Horace Walpole and prime minister (1715–17

and 1721–42), had a reputation for coarse-mindedness that, though deserved, consorts ill with the fine collection of paintings he brought together at Houghton from 1720 onwards and that were to become one of the glories of the Hermitage in Leningrad. William Pitt the younger (1759–1806) was prime minister 1783–1801 and 1804–5. One a Whig, the other a Tory, neither was a patron of letters. C published a "Character of Pitt" in the *M Post* 19 Mar 1800, saying—among other uncomplimentary things—that "He has patronised no science, he has raised no man of genius from obscurity; he counts no one prime work of God among his friends." *EOT* (*CC*) I 225. See also *CN* III 4079.

17 pp 15–16

That Remedies were prescrib'd me in a Dream, against Giddiness, and Spitting of Blood; As I remember, it happen'd both at *Cajeta*, and *Chrysa* . . .

I am not convinced that this is mere Supersition. Providence is at once general & particular/ there is doubtless a sort of *divining* power in man/ Sensations awaken Thoughts congruous to them. I could say much on this Subject.[1] A Gentleman told Dr Beddoes a remarkable Dream: the Dr immediately examined his pulse, &c &c, bled him &c—and it was evident that in a day or two he would otherwise have had an apoplectic Fit.[2] My Father had a similar Dream 3 nights together before ~~my~~ his his Death, while he appeared to himself in full & perfect Health—He was blest by God with sudden Death. That was the only part of our Liturgy, which he objected to/ the prayer against sudden Death.[3]

18 p 16 | II ii

!!] II. This Being of mine, all that's on't, consists of Body, Breath, and that *Part which governs* . . .

Σωμα, Ψυχη, Νους.[1]

17[1] For C's "supposition of a diving power in the human mind", see *SM* (*CC*) 80–1, 83, 86–7, and cf *Friend* (*CC*) I 428–30. For an erroneous cause of superstition see *CN* III 3372; and on a prophetic dream see *CN* II 2418. The relation between sensation and thought was continually explored by C and is important in his theory of dreaming: see e.g. *CN* I 921, *Sh C* I 185, *Friend* (*CC*) I 106n, *SM* (*CC*) 80–1. For the dream that foretold death to his father see **17** n 3, below.

17[2] Dr Thomas Beddoes (1760–1808), physician, founded the Pneumatic Institute at Clifton in 1798 for the treatment of disease by the inhalation of gases, and appointed Humphry Davy as first superintendent of the Institute. See ANNUAL ANTHOLOGY 16A n 1. In Feb–Mar 1808 C resolved again to "place myself under the immediate Care of Dr Beddoes", when Beddoes died in Dec 1808 C said that "Dr Beddoes's Death has taken more Hope out of my Life, than any

event I can remember". *CL* III 73, 79, 162.

17[3] C had given an account of his father's death, and of the dream that foretold it, in one of his autobiographical letters to Poole in 1797. *CL* I 355; cf *CN* III 4396. C, who said that "I strongly resemble him in person & mind" (*CL* III 104; cf VI 754, 837), had a strong presentiment of sudden death in late 1807, in the spring of 1808 (see *CL* III 38, 90, 104; *CN* III 3273, 3276; DANIEL 3 n 9), and again in the spring of 1811 (BEAUMONT & FLETCHER COPY A 13, DONNE *Poems* 61). Cf *CN* III 3352, 3362, 3412, 3656, 3881, 4071. The reference to "the prayer" is to the ninth sentence of the Litany: "From lightning and tempest; from plague, pestilence, and famine; from battle and murder, and from sudden death, *Good Lord deliver us.*"

18[1] C, not having the Greek text in front of him, is guessing at the three terms into which Aurelius divides the self. The terms here are actually σαρκία

18A   p 17

Let it not quarrel with Fate ...

19   p 17 | II iii

III. *Providence* shines clearly through the Administration of the World: Even Chance it self is not without Steadiness and *Nature* at the bottom; being only an Effect of that Chain of Causes which are under a providential Regulation ...

a most profound Remark, and fruitful in consequences especially to men in governing situations.

19A   p 18

For *Generation*, and *Corruption*, are no more than Terms of Reference. ~~and Respect~~.

20   p 18 | II iv

IV. Remember how often you have postpon'd the minding your Interest, and slip'd those Opportunities the Gods have given you.

O me![1]

21   p 19 | II vii

... don't ramble from one Thing to another.

Most important maxim/ & of especial use in the present Age. The minds of men from great Cities, from Newspapers, Reviews, Magazines, "*Beauties*" or Selections, from Routs (2 or 3 perhaps in the same night) have become more & more discontinuous.[1]

καὶ πνευμάτιον καὶ τὸ ἡγεμονικόν, which Collier translates with reasonable accuracy (cf A. S. L. Farquharson, 1944: "flesh and vital spirit and the governing self"). In XII iii the three terms are σωμάτιον, πνευμάτιον, νοῦς ("body, vital spirit, mind"), and in III xvi—on which C wrote **37**—the terms are those noted here by C: Σῶμα, ψυχή, νοῦς. It is clear—as C understood, but not Collier—that to Aurelius ψυχή (and correspondingly πνευμάτιον) meant, in the threefold scheme, "animal spirit" or "life"— that which distinguishes man and animals from vegetable creation and inorganic bodies. The primary meaning of ψυχή is "life", but Collier is prob-

ably deflected by the later meaning of "soul". In IV xxi—on which C wrote **45**—Farquharson and C. R. Haines (LCL 1916), like Collier, translate ψυχαί "souls", but C is probably correct in saying that Aurelius is referring again to the "animal life" and not the personal identity. For C's further discussion of the tripartite division see **27, 37, 45, 54**.

20[1] For C's expressions of regret at misuse of his genius see e.g. *CN* II 2914, 2990, 3136; III 3324, 3420, 4070; *CL* III 22, 131.

21[1] On newspapers, reviews, and magazines see *Friend* (*CC*) II 28, 150; and on routs *CN* III 3325 and n.

22 p 20 | II viii

VIII. A Man can rarely miscarry by being ignorant of anothers Thoughts, but he that does not attend to his own, is certainly Unhappy.

N.B. Let me reflect on this this whole day.

23 p 20 | II x

For a Man that is Angry seems to quit his Hold unwillingly, to be teaz'd out of his Reason, and start out of Rule before he is aware.

This is a very ingenious Remark—and I believe, a true one. Many good men are subject to fits of Anger; but Libertinism never fails to harden the Heart.[1]

24 p 21 | II xi

XI. Manage all your Actions and Thoughts in such a Manner as if you were just going to step into the Grave; And what great matter is the Business of Dying; if the Gods are in being you can suffer nothing, for they'll do you no Harm: And if they are not, or take no Care of us Mortals; why then must I tell you, that a World without either Gods, or *Providence*, is not worth a Mans while to live in.

Most excellent!

25 p 22 | II xii

'Twill show one what sort of Bulk those People are off, upon whose Fancy and Good Word, the Being of ~~Fame~~ Reputation depends.[1]

26 p 24 | II xiv

XIV. Suppose you were to Live Three Thousand, or if you please, three Millions of Years, yet you are to remember that no Man can lose any other Life than that which he lives by, neither is he possess'd of any other than that which he Loses. From whence it follows, that the longest Life, as we commonly speak, and the shortest, come all to the same Reckoning.

The fallacy of this § consists in its proving too much: for it would prove that Life itself was no blessing—if it be loss to die at 20, then none at 19, 18, 17—& so on even to the womb.—[1]

23[1] On anger and sensuality see *CN* I 979 and n; and cf *Religious Musings* lines 135–41 (1796 var)—"petrify th' imbrothell'd Atheist's heart". *PW* (EHC) I 114n.

25[1] For the distinction between fame and reputation see esp *CN* III 3291 (Mar 1808) and 3671 (Jan 1810). Cf *CL* III 87 (14 Apr 1808).

26[1] Cf *CN* III 3362 (Sept 1808).

27　p 26 | II xvii

XVII. The Extent of Human Life is but a Point; *Matter* is in a perpetual Flux: The Faculties of Sence, and Perception, are Weak, and Unpenetrating: The Body slenderly put together, and but a Remove from Putrefaction: The Soul a rambling sort of a Thing.

This should have been translated *Life* not *Soul*/ the ancients always considered man as animal triplex, of body, *life*, and Reason/ now it is *Life*, not Reason, which Antonine describes as migratory—in the quaint *slang* of this most vulgar Translation "a rambling sort of thing[."] S[t] Paul adopts the same distinction—the Body, the Flesh or Life, & the Spirit.[1]

28　p 28 | III i, shoulder-note

The Stoicks allow'd Self-Murder.[1]

They did not allow any act of *Murder* but they considered a man's own Life & his Neighbours as subjected to the same Law of Morals.

27[1] Here the Heraclitan source of early Stoic physics and cosmology comes to the surface in Aurelius. C later placed great emphasis on the difference between soul and life: see e.g. ASGILL **7** and **8**. For Aurelius' tripartite analysis of the self see **18** n 1, above. C's own analysis is rather different: see e.g. *CL* III 152–3 (Dec 1808): "Are we not a union of Reason, Understanding, and Sense (i.e. the Senses)?..." The triad "spirit and soul and body" appears in 1 Thess 5.23 and is implicit in 1 Cor 15.

28[1] "Self-murder" is the English form of *Selbstmörder*, the normal German word for suicide; but because of the English legal doctrine that suicide is *felo de se*, a self-inflicted felony, "self-murder" is not a neutral term and provided a convenient ambiguity in the bitter debate about suicide and martyrdom in which John Donne played some part. The oath of allegiance to the English sovereign, rigorously imposed by James I from 1605 onwards, forced Roman Catholics to renounce allegiance to the Pope in all matters spiritual and civil; the penalty for refusal to subscribe was death on a charge of treason; a nice question (apart from the propriety of these pro-

ceedings) was whether those who were executed in these circumstances had suffered martyrdom or had committed "self-murder", for there was no difference between placing oneself in a situation from which death was almost certain to result and taking one's life by a deliberate act. The term "self-murder" was normally used by those who insisted that all acts of suicide were felonies and mortal sins (see e.g. Donne *The Flea* lines 17–18). Donne, in the title of *Biathanatos* (see **28** n 2, below), referred more discreetly, and with greater legal accuracy, to *self-homicide*, but also argued in *Pseudo-martyr* (1610) that executions "for the faith" under civil law were instances of "self-murder" rather than martyrdom, unless it could be shown that the person had acted according to a law superior to "the Law of Nature". In English law until 1870 suicide committed while of sound mind incurred forfeiture of estate to the crown and degrading disposal of the corpse.

C became interested in the romantic cult of suicide when he encountered it in Germany in 1798–9: see *CN* I 398 and n, 874n. In **57**, below, he notices again the distinction between "suicide" and "self-murder".

See Dr Donne's admirable "Biothanatos"^*a*—which was indeed written before he became a Clergyman; but yet at his Death he ordered it to be published.[2] It is a masterly Defence of the Stoic Doctrine upon Xtian Principles.[3]

29 p 29 | III ii

One thus prepared will perceive the Beauty of Life, as well as tha of Imitation; and be no less pleased to see a Tyger Grin in the *Tower* than in a *Painter's* Shop.

one might fancy, that Collier had intended this as a *Travesty* rather than a *Translation*.

a The first *o* in "Biothanatos" is unmistakable in the ms

28[2] C was using a copy of *Biathanatos* in Jan 1808 and early in 1811; see *CN* III 3243, 4050. For C's consistent spelling "Biathanatos", and for the full title of *Biathanatos*, see DONNE *Poems* **46** n 1. Donne wrote the book in 1607 or 1608, seven or eight years before he was ordained, appointed Chaplain to the King, and awarded the honorary D.D. at Cambridge (1615). The book was indeed first published posthumously but not until 1646, fifteen years after his death. C's version of the story is incorrect. In the spring of 1619, when Donne was preparing to go to Germany with Lord James Hay's embassy, he sent the ms with some poems to Sir Robert Ker, saying of *Biathanatos*: "It was written by me many years since...I have always gone so near suppressing it, as that it is onely not burnt...it is a Book written by *Jack Donne*, and not by D. *Donne*: Reserve it for me if I live, and if I die, I only forbid it the Presse, and the Fire: publish it not, but yet burn it not; and between those, do what you will with it." *Letters to Severall Persons of Honour* (1651) 21–2. When Donne's son John finally gained possession of the ms in c 1646 the author's express instructions not to publish may no longer have accompanied the ms. C early in 1811 had the account straight; see DONNE *Poems* **46**.

28[3] The early Stoics considered that to take one's life (or allow it to be taken) was in certain circumstances an affirmation of the dignity of man—if it were for the sake of one's country or friends, or in order to preclude disgrace or excessive humiliation whether in military defeat, incurable disease, severe mutilation, or even in the extremes of poverty. But they held that suicide was matter for personal judgment, the mind guided by an austere and courageous view of the possible nobility of man. (Hence the distinction between "suicide" and "self-murder" that C ascribes to the Stoics in **57**.) The Christian colour of later Stoicism refined the attitude to suicide but did not radically alter it.

Donne in *Biathanatos* does indeed argue for a position not unlike that of the Stoics, informed by his own impulse towards suicide and by his sense of the extreme delicacy of moral judgment in matters of conscience. In C, who in 1808 was in a similar state of mind and almost exactly the same age as the Donne of *Biathanatos*, the book evidently struck a much more responsive chord than it has in most other readers. For C's thoughts of suicide towards the end of his sojourn in the Mediterranean and in the months after his return see DONNE *Poems* **46** n 1.

30   p 30 | III iii

...*Heraclitus* who argued so much about the Worlds being set on Fire, perish'd himself by a Counter-Element, and was Drown'd in a Dropsy. *Democritus* was eaten up with Lice, and *Socrates* was dispatched by another sort of Vermin. And what are these Instances for? Why, to shew what we must all come to.

I wish I had the original by me. It would be curious to see the words, out of which Mr Collier has squeezed these *maggots* of Wit.[1]

30A   p 30 | III iv

N.B.] IV. For the Future, don't spend your Thoughts upon other People, unless you are put upon it by Common Interest. For the prying into foreign Business, that is musing upon the Talk, Fancies, and Contrivances of another, and guessing at the *what*, and *why*, of !] his Actions; All this does but make a Man forget himself, and Ramble from his own Reason. He ought therefore not to work his Mind to no purpose, nor throw a superfluous Link into the Chain of Thought; And more especially, to stand clear of Curiosity, and Malice, in his Enquiry.

31   p 31

...Let it be your way to think upon nothing, but what you could freely Discover, if the Question was put to you: So that if your Soul was thus laid open, there would nothing appear, but what was Sincere, Good-natur'd, and publick Spirited; not so much as one Libertine, or Luxurious Fancy, nothing of Litigiousness, Envy, or unreasonable Suspicion, or any thing else, which would not bear the Light, without Blushing. A Man thus qualified, may be allowed the first Rank among Mortals; he is a sort of Priest, and Minister of the Gods, and makes a right use of the Deity within him...[1]

most sublime.

30[1] For a bravura passage on wit and lice see *CL* III 369 (11 Feb 1812) and *CN* III 4073 (c Apr–May 1811). Later C was to take a more hospitable view of mental maggots: see *IS* 202–3 (from BM MS Egerton 2801 f 57). Collier's translation is not far from the original, except for two omissions. Farquharson reads: "Heraclitus, after many speculations about the fire which should consume the Universe, was waterlogged by dropsy, poulticed himself with cow-dung and died. Vermin killed Democritus; another kind of vermin Socrates. What is the moral? You went on board, you set sail, you have made the port."

31[1] See **54** n 1, below.

32 p 32

... General Kindness and Concern for the whole World, *is no more than a piece of Humanity.

* i.e. is the property, by which man is distinguished from the Brutes— that by which Human nature *is specified*.[1]

33 p 32 | III v

V. Be not Haled, Selfish, Unadvised, or Passionate in any Thing you do; Don't affect Quaintness, and Points of wit: neither Talk, nor Meddle more than is necessary.

hawl'd?—driven or dragged along by the passions or Affections.[1]

33A p 33

!!] And in a word, never throw away your Legs, to stand upon Crutches.[1]

34 p 35 | III ix

IX. The Happiness of your Life depends upon the Quality of your Thoughts, therefore guard accordingly: And take care that you entertain no Notions unsuitable to Virtue and reasonable Nature; Now in order to this, you must be wary in your Assent, Obedient to the Gods, and Benevolent to Mankind.

most important.

35 pp 36–7 | III x

Well then! Life moves in a very narrow Compass; yes, and Men live in a poor Corner of the World too: And the most lasting Fame will stretch but to a sorry Extent. The passage on't is uneven and craggy, and therefore it can't run far. The frequent Breaks of *Succession* drop it in the Conveyance: For alas! poor transitory Mortals, know little either of themselves, or of those who were long before them.

I have compared a human Soul to a Glow-worm creeping on in the night: a little, pleasing inch of Light before and behind and on either

---

32[1] For the distinction between man and brutes see e.g. *Friend* (*CC*) I 154–5.

33[1] See *OED* "hale/haul", 2: "... draw forcibly to, into, or out of a course of action, feeling, condition, etc.; to bring in violently, drag in".

33A[1] C was startled, even without looking at the Greek, which reads in Farquharson's version: "You should stand upright, not be held upright."

side,[a] and a World of Darkness all around.[1] Yea, even the vast Soununs[2] & Systems of Heavenly Truth partake, to us, of our own littleness, & are but Glow-worms, & Sparkles, in the black Ether—Reason enlarges them indeed somewhat by her Telescope; but their true dimensions are deduced by Faith availing herself of the Instruments of Reason. S. T. Coleridge[3]

36   p 37, referring to III xi

XI. To the foregoing Hints you may add this which follows. And that is, to survey and define every Object and Thought extraordinary; and that with such Penetration, as to dissect it throughout, pull off its Mask and Fucus, and view it in its naked Essence: To call the Whole, and the Parts by their true Names; and be truly informed of their Force and Nature, both Single, and in Composition. For nothing is so likely to raise the Mind to a pitch of Greatness, as to bring Accidents, Persons, and Pretensions to a true Test. For instance, To be ready to tell ones self, to what sort of purpose this

---

[a] After "side" a watery ink-blot developed at the margin while C was writing and has invaded "World of" and "around"

35[1] Cf "...the Light of the Glow-worm ... lighting inch by inch it's mazy path through weeds and grass, leaves all else before, behind, and around it in darkness". *CL* VI 595–6. C printed the whole letter with slight variation as an appendix to *C&S*: see *CC* 173–83.

C said that he had transcribed the substance of this letter from one of his papers written so long before that it was "a sere and ragged half-sheet... far too decrepit to travel per se". The setting of the transcript disarms any positivist judgement about the antiquity—or even the existence—of the putative original ms. There is no reason why the marginal note could not have been written in 1826 or when he was preparing *C&S* for publication shortly before Dec 1829—the verbal similarity between the letter and marginal note is close. Yet there are grounds for wondering whether both may be based on an earlier ms now lost.

35[2] C's correcting "Son" to "Sun" is an instance of a ms change so fre-quent as to seem habitual. See e.g. BAHRDT 2, BUNYAN COPY A 20, CHILLINGWORTH COPY B 2, DE WETTE 39. In DONNE *Sermons* COPY B 17 C commented on Donne's play on the two homonyms; see also *SM* (*CC*) 56n.

For C's early use of the "Sun/Son" identity see *CN* I 327, 349; cf *CL* II 927. For possible sources or indorsements see e.g. a passage in South's *Sermons* in *CN* I 327, also BÖHME 7, **116**.

35[3] In Jan 1804 C had thought of "a great metaphysician" who "looked at his own Soul with a Telescope" and so "added to the Consciousness hidden worlds within worlds". *CN* I 1798. He observed correctly that "the most powerful Telescope will not make a fixed Star appear larger than it does to an ordinary & unaided Sight". *CN* III 4065; cf *SM* (*CC*) 24. In *AR* (1825) 335 he also wrote: "By the eye of Reason through the telescope of faith, i.e. Revelation, we may see what without this telescope we could never have known to exist."

thing serves, and what sort of World 'tis which makes use on't?
what proportion of value it bears to the *Universe*, and what to Men
in particular; to Men I say, who are Citizens of that Great Capital,
in respect of which all other Towns, are no more than single Families.
To return: My Business is to examine nicely into the present Object;
to know what 'tis made on, and how long 'twill last; what Virtue it
requires of me, and gives occasion to, whether Fortitude, or Truth,
Good Nature, or Good Faith, Simplicity, Frugality, and so forth;
upon every Impression and Accident, a Man should be ready to pronounce, This was sent me by Heaven, This is a Consequence of
Destiny; This comes from Chance, over-ruled by Providence.

a § almost worthy of an Evangelist.[1]

36A   p 37, pencil

[Shoulder-note:] See Book 2. Sect. 1.

15 p

37   p 39 | III xvi

XVI. There are three things which belong to a Man, the Body, the
~~Soul~~ *Life*, and the Mind: And as to the Properties of the Division,
Sensation belongs to the body, Appetite to the ~~Soul~~ Life,[1] and
Reason to the Mind.

38   p 40

... lets find out the Mark of a Man of Probity: His distinction then
lies,* in keeping Reason at the Head of Practice, and being Easy in
his Condition.

* In the *unconditional* obedience of his Will to pure Reason. Most
of our modern Divines make Virtue to be the regulation of the Will
by *Prudence*—which is, of necessity, individual & empirical—Instead
of loving our Neighbour, as ourselves, & God above all, their
doctrine implies—"Act & feel so & so towards God & your neigh-

36[1] The various concerns that meet
in this passage of Aurelius present a
group of themes of continuous importance in C's notebooks and marginalia: the interest in naked essence, in
the relation between whole and parts
and between the cosmos and man as
microcosm; the insistence upon judgement according to accidents and ends,
chance and providence; the need "to

tell oneself" the purpose and consequence of "every Impression and
Accident". The presence of such a
piece of "pure Coleridge" in Aurelius'
Conversations explains why C should
return repeatedly to this little book for
purposes more urgent than the study
of prose style.
37[1] See **18** n 1, above.

bour, because you love yourself above all." See Paley's Chapter on Moral Obligation—in which, Virtue is boldly stated as a mere modification of selfish Prudence/[1]

39 p 41 | IV i

And if any thing comes cross, shee [Nature] falls to Work upon't, and like Fire converts it into Fuel.

a very noble Thought.[1]

40 p 42 | IV iii

. . . Consider, That Mankind were made for mutual Advantage; that Forbearance is one part of Justice, and that People misbehave themselves against their Will.

It would require more than a marginal note, to explain the compatibility of this Sentiment with the Faith in Free-Will. He means, that in the act of i.e. in the inward & primary act of Vice, Man *abdicates* his free-will—in the outward material *deed* he is a slave of necessity—even as we feel no indignation at any thing said in delirium, tho' that delirium has been induced by Drunkenness.—[1]

41 p 43

Pray Reflect, your Soul does not lie in your Lungs, nor your Reason in your Breath, so that if you are somewhat Asthmatick, or out of Order, 'tis no such great Matter. No, Not if your Mind will * retire, and take a view of her own Priviledge and Power. And when she has done this, Recollect her Philosophy about Pleasure and Pain; And to which she has formerly assented.

* This is the peccant part of Stoicism/ it seems always to suppose, that the mind can act ⟨with⟩ consciousness independent of its bodily organs.—*Recollect*! But what if the Disease has destroyed all power of recollection/[1] Here it is, that Xtianity is so immeasurably superior

---

38[1] In a letter to Beaumont in Dec 1808 C virtually repeated the wording of this note: *CL* III 153; cf 216. "Paley's Chapter on Moral Obligation", in *Principles of Moral and Political Philosophy* Bk II ch 2, is examined in *LS* (*CC*) 186–7n. For attacks on Paley's doctrine of prudence see e.g. *CN* III 3293 f 18 (Apr–Jun 1808 or 1818), *Friend* (*CC*) II 313; see also BLANCO WHITE *Practical Evidence* 1 n 1.

39[1] For C's use of the image of the fuel and the fire see *CN* II 3136. Cf *LS* (*CC*) 180.

40[1] See also DE WETTE 27 and cf *Friend* (*CC*) II 280–1. For the moral slavery of opium see e.g. *CL* VI 892 (23 Nov 1832): ". . . the curse of my existence, my shame and my *negro-slave* inward humiliation and debasement".

41[1] Cf *TT* 28 Sept 1830. See also *CN* III 3431 and *TT* 1 May 1830.

in Truth & practical Wisdom. The difference between it & Stoicism[2] is that between the roses of a healthy country maidens cheek, & the puffed flushed Countenance of incipient Dropsy.

42 p 45 | IV iv

... *Nothing* can no more produce *Something*, than Something can sink into Nothing: And thus in Proportion to the Reasoning upon my Constitution, our *Understanding* must have a Cause, and proceed from some Quarter or other.

It is strange, that Atheists should deny a hereafter/ they will not believe a Creator, because they cannot comprehend a transition from Nothing to Something, & yet find no difficulty in the Transition from Something to Nothing—which yet is just as difficult, & no reason for submitting to the Difficulty.[1]

42A p 46 | IV x

?] Take notice that all events turn upon Merit, and Congruity.[1]

43 p 46 | IV xi

XI. If a Man Affronts you, don't go into his Opinion, or Think just as He would have you: No, look upon Things as Reality presents them, and form your Judgment accordingly.

O that I had acted concerning — — under the Influence of this invaluable maxim!!![1]

41[2] The title of Aphorism xv of Moral and Religious Aphorisms in *AR* (1825) 91 is "The Christian no Stoic".

42[1] In *SM* App E, C discusses carefully what is implied in insisting with "rationalists" generally against "a Platonist" and the mainstream of Christian theology that "nothing is made out of nothing". *SM* (*CC*) 103–6.

42A[1] On reward and merit see *CN* I 1403.

43[1] On the assumption, presented by C's later cryptographic practice, that a sign twice repeated represents a letter twice repeated, "— —" presumably stands for "WW". (C's earliest recorded use of a systematic cipher is in *CN* II 2387 of 27 Dec 1804; a hyphen or dash is not an element in any version of his cipher.) "Concerning — —" may not refer to any single episode or person, but if to anyone, to the alienation from the Wordsworths, precipitated by Basil Montagu's disclosure of WW's confidences in Oct 1810 and formally (but never satisfactorily) resolved in 1812. See *CN* I 1471, III 4162, 4165. RS and C had quarrelled in 1795 over the principles of pantisocracy (which quarrel C analysed carefully in Oct 1803: *CN* I 1605); again, there was a "dreadful Rumpus" with William Godwin on 2 Feb 1804 and this left C frightened, remorseful, and humiliated (*CN* II 1890, *CL* II 1056–73). But neither of these incidents seems to warrant the rueful force of this reticent note.

44 pp 47–9 | IV xiv

XIV. At present your Nature is Distinguish'd, and stands apart; But e'er long <u>you'l vanish</u> into the *Whole*: Or if you please you'l be return'd into that Active and Prolifick *Reason* which gave you your Being.

? I regret, that I have not the original by me.[1]—I have not seen Tiedemann's Hist. of Stoicism,[2] but it is impossible that the account given in common of their Principles can be accurate—I believe, that they limited the name of their Sect to contain moral opinions—& left open theological ones—so that A. might express himself in contradiction to B. yet both be genuine Stoics. I conjecture, that in Theology some of the head Stoics were epicureans, others, as Brutus, Platonists, others Sceptics: and yet all considered as Stoics. But we have not one single *philosophical* Tract extant of their countless writings. What a Treasure the works of Chrysippus![3]—As to Seneca, nothing can be gathered from his Witticisms, any more than a *System* from Pope's Essay of Man, which implies 13 very different Systems. Seneca's Head was not capable of a System—his mind was discontinuous—a moral *wit*[4]

45 p 49 | IV xxi

XXI. If Humane Souls have a Being after Death, which way has the Air made Room for them from all Eternity? Pray now has the

44[1] Farquharson reads: "You came into the world as a part. You will vanish in that which gave you birth, or rather you will be taken up into the generative reason by the process of change." If what made C want "the original" was Collier's phrase "Prolifick Reason", he would have been rewarded by finding that it was λόγος σπερματικός—seminal reason. In *CN* III 4136 (c 1811–12) C used side by side the two phrases "rationes spermaticae" and "λογοι ποιητικοι"; the possible sources are considered in *CN* III 4136n.

44[2] Dietrich Tiedemann (1748–1803) *System der stoischen Philosophie* (3 vols Leipzig 1776). There is no definite evidence that C read the book.

44[3] Chrysippus of Soli (280–207 B.C.), head of the Stoa 232–207 B.C. in succession to Cleanthes, who had inherited the headship from the founder Zeno, was the last of the early Stoics. In his vigorous defence of Stoic doctrine against the attacks of the Academy, his work (fragments of which C seems to have met with in Cicero) established itself as orthodox Stoic doctrine, thereby preventing a reconstruction of Zeno's original doctrines. C could have found much in his familiar copy of Thomas S T A N L E Y *History of Philosophy* (1701) from Diogenes Laertius and Stobaeus about Chrysippus, especially in the section on Zeno.

44[4] Lucius Annaeus Seneca (c 4 B.C.– A.D. 65) was Epictetus' predecessor as a leading late Stoic. A copy of his works, with the works of Marcus Annaeus Seneca (Leyden 1609), bearing the autograph signatures of both C and WW, is at Cornell University. On "men of continuous and discontinuous minds" and the "conjunction disjunctive of Wit" see *CN* II 2112.

Earth been Capacious enough to receive all the Bodies buried in't?
"Souls" here means the *animal Life*; by no means, the immortal
Spirit—ψυχη, not πνευμα.[1]

46 pp 50–1 | shoulder-note at end of iv xxi

By *Form* the Stoicks meant God, or the Efficient Cause of all Things.

Not accurate. As far as animal Life is a compound, so far it is
mortal; but the Power & Principle of its composition (the *Form*)
is immortal—& tho' forming ~~an~~ a mysterious one with all, yet
must thro' all eternity remain distinct:[1] for how ⟨can⟩ that, which
God conceived as distinct, ever cease to be so? Is there aught perishable or mutable in Deity! The understanding the difference between Division & Distinction is the first step in the Solution of the
seeming Contradictions concerning Individuality & final Co-aduna-
tion,[2] both in the N. Test: & the writings of Epict: & Antonine/ if it
be not wrong to mention them together.—[3]

45[1] C probably has in mind St
Paul's distinction in 1 Cor 15.44—
between σῶμα ψυχικόν and σῶμα πνευ-
ματικόν (*NEB* "animal body" and
"spiritual body"), and between the
first Adam, who became a ψυχὴ ζῶσα,
and the last Adam, who became
πνεῦμα ζωοποιοῦν (*NEB* "an animate
being" and "a life-giving spirit"). AV
consistently translates ψυχή as "soul"
and πνεῦμα as "spirit". If C had had
the Greek original in front of him he
would have seen (as shown in **18** n 1)
that Aurelius merges ψυχή and πνευμάτιον.

46[1] In the phrase "forming a
mysterious one with all"—i.e. entering
into some sort of unity with all
creatures—C is skirting around the
pantheistic lure of Ἕν καὶ πᾶν by offering an inexplicit instance of "unity in
multeity". See also ATHENAEUM **22**.

46[2] On distinction and division see
BAXTER *Reliquiae* COPY B **82** n 1.
C had defined imagination in Sept 1802
as "the *modifying*, and *co-adunating*
Faculty". *CL* II 866. In the 1808
lectures he addressed himself again to

the definition, although the word
"coadunation" is not preserved in the
fragmentary record: "Imagination/
power of modifying one image or
feeling by the precedent or following
ones...combining many circumstances into one moment of thought to
produce that ultimate end of human
Thought, and human Feeling, Unity".
CN III 3247; cf *Friend* (*CC*) I 456. Cf
the account of the bond of life in *TL*
(tr): "the force from within, whose
function is to coadunate many things
into a single thing". *TL* (1848) 44. For
other uses of coadunation see *Friend*
(*CC*) I 90 (association of provinces),
CN III 3542 (relation between words
and things), *CN* II 2057 (poetic values
in *The Recluse*), KANT *Metaphysik der
Sitten* (2 vols Königsberg 1797) back
flyleaf ("Coadunation or spiritual Marriage"), *CN* III 4158 (unity of lovers),
DONNE *Sermons* COPY B **121** (faith
as coadunation of will with reason). See
also *CN* II 2994, 3154, III 3605.

46[3] For Epictetus and Aurelíus see
12 and n 1, above.

47 p 51 | IV xxiv

XXIV. If *you would* Live *at* your *Ease*, says *Democritus, Manage but a few Things*. I think it had been better, if He had said, Do nothing but what is necessary; and what becomes one made for *Society*; Nothing but what Reason prescribes, and in the Order too she prescribes it. For by this Rule a Man may both secure the Quality, and draw in the Bulk of his Business; And have the double Pleasure of making his Actions Good, and Few, into the Bargain. For the greatest part of what we say and do, being unnecessary; If this were but once retrench'd, we should have both more Leisure, and less Disturbance. And therefore before a Man sets forward He should ask himself this Question; Am I not upon the Verge of something unnecessary and impertinent? Farther; We should apply this Hint to what we *Think*, as well as to what we *Do*; For Impertinence of Thought; draws Unnecessary Action after it.

This § is what the Quakers act upon—the principle, on which their *character* is formed.[1]

48 p 53 | IV xxx

One Learned Man has nothing for his *Stomach*, nor Another for his *Lectures*; However they are resolved to starve on, and be *Wise* in Despight of Misfortune.

Ex. gr. S. T. C.[1]

49 p 55 | IV xxxiii

Those celebrated *Names* of *Camillus, Caeso*, and *Volesus* are Antiquated; Those of *Scipio, Cato*, and *Augustus* will have the same Fortune; and those of *Adrian*, and *Antoninus*, must follow.

This is not just. The name of Adam is as fresh as that of Scipio: & Scipio's as Lord Nelson's.[1]

47[1] In a notebook entry of 5 May 1804 (*CN* II 2077) C said that he had found in Aurelius' *Meditations* VII liv "the Sum & Essence of Quakerism": see **59** n 1, below. C devoted a considerable section of *LS* (*CC* 185–191) to an analysis of "the sensible, orderly and beneficent Society of the FRIENDS, more commonly called Quakers". In wealthy Quakers he noticed an unresolved coincidence of strict demeanour and active commercial instinct that put them for him among "the distinguished and world-honoured company of Christian Mammonists". Quietness, simple nobility, concentration, detachment, and a certain secular duplicity—these are the characteristics that Aurelius commends here; and these are all facets of the Quaker "character" as C saw it.

For a contrast between "original" and "modern" Quakers see *TT* 12 Jan 1834. See also *Friend* (*CC*) II 102 (I 69).

48[1] This could apply to any of the courses of lectures from 1811 onwards.

49[1] Publius Cornelius Scipio (236–

50   p 57 | IV xxxix

Nay farther, the Declension of your Health, or the Accidents in your Carcass need not affect you.

One would think that this great Master of the *Free & Easy* Style, had been a Carcass-butcher: he is so fond of the word.[1]

51   pp 58–60 | IV xlvi

Therefore don't forget the Saying of *Heraclitus*;* *That the Earth dies into Water, Water into Air, Air into Fire, and so Backward.*

* Expressed in the present chemical nomenclature/ Solids by increased repulsion of their parts become fluids, by a still greater repulsion aeriform Gasses, and it is possible that these may all be resolvible into imponderable & igniform natures, Light, Electricity, Magnetism, Heat—& that all these four may be but ~~the~~ detachments of one & same substance—the plastic Fire of the ancients—in different proportions of repulsion & attraction in se, acting on other proportions[1]—Then to comprehend attraction & Repulsion as one power is perhaps the point of the Pyramid of physical Science.[2]

184/3 B.C.), surnamed Africanus, won renown for his defeat of Hannibal, which brought the second Punic War to an end. Horatio Nelson (1758–1805) became a national hero at the battle of the Nile in Aug 1798 (which C celebrated in Germany: see DANTE COPY A **1** n 1), and his fame became even greater after his victory at Copenhagen in 1801. (Henry Nelson Coleridge, born 25 Oct 1798, received his second name in honour of Admiral Nelson.) For C on Nelson's death as reported in Naples see *Friend* (*CC*) II 365–6.

50[1] On the same page, in IV xli, the text reads: "Epictetus will tell you that you are a *Living Soul*, that drags a *Carcass* about with her." C has underlined the word "Carcass". For fuller development of this theme, see **62**, below.

51[1] On 24 Nov 1807 C said that Davy "has proved...that by a practicable increase of electric energy all *ponderable* compounds (in opposition to *Light & Heat*, magnetic fluid, &c) may be decomposed, & presented simple—& recomposed thro' an in-

finity of new combinations...." *CL* III 38; cf *CN* II 3192. C considered Davy's fundamental discoveries "more intellectual, more ennobling and impowering human Nature than Newton's". *CL* III 38, 41; cf *Friend* (*CC*) II 251–2 and BÖHME **9**. His mind turned at once to the possibility of applying the newly discovered chemical analogy and vocabulary to ethics and psychology: see **52**, below, and e.g. *CN* II 3192, III 3312, 3448, 3569. See also BÖHME **15**, and on impenetrability reduced to repulsion see ANDERSON COPY C **13** and n 2.

51[2] Beginning from hints gathered from Heraclitus, Giordano Bruno, and then from Davy's work, C's dynamic scheme resting upon the unity of "attraction" and "repulsion" seems finally to have crystallised around the work of Ruggiero Boscovich. *CN* III 3962. He achieved growing certainty about this principle and flexibility in applying it in annotating BÖHME 1809–10: see esp BÖHME **14** n 1, and cf **6** and **15**. An unexpected use of this principle occurs in Nov 1809, in a

52   pp 62–3 | IV li

LI. Always go the shortest way to work; Now the nearest Road to your Business lies through Honesty. Let it be your constant method then to deal clearly and above Board. And by this means you need not Fatigue it, you need not Quarrel, Flourish, and Dissemble like other People.

The straightest road is self-evidently the nearest: and strictly speakne-ing straightness implies ~~sub~~ smoothness. Now to prove that Honesty is the ~~nearest~~ strait road, & consequently both the shortest and the smoothest would be highly useful, but requires more than a geometrical metaphor/ tho' doubtless it is both wonderful and attended with awe to perceive t what an admirable *language* the mathematical properties of Quantity ~~furnish~~ are of moral & intellectual operations, as the chemical properties of material agency are of Life, Fancy, & Passion[1]

53   p 67 | V vii

VII. The *Athenians* us'd to be mighty Clamorous to *Jupiter* for Rain upon their own Lands, but not a word for other People.

Would that our episcalopal Clamourers would attend to this Hint in their Forms of Prayers for Fast-days—[1]

54   p 73 | V xiii

XIII. My Being consists of *Matter* and *Form*, that is, of Soul and Body; *Annihilation* will reach neither of them; For as they were never produced out of *Nothing*, so they will always remain *Something*: The consequence is, that every part of me will serve to make something in the *World*; and thus I shall be toss'd from one Figure to another, through an infinite succession of Change.

Understand this of the Body, & the fleshly vital Principle; these Antonine in this places calls "me", "my Being", "I", &c/ because the Spirit, (or principle of the Will, the Conscience, and the Reason) he is fond of considering ⟨as God⟩ & callings it ⟨the⟩ *God* within us—/ Something very like this is noticeable in many Texts of S[t] John's Gospel.[1]

---

discussion of taxation: see *Friend* (*CC*) II 161. *SM* (*CC*) 81 is late enough (1816) to be much more specific.

52[1] See *CN* II 3023 (Feb–May 1807): "In all processes of the Understanding the shortest way will be discovered the last.... The shortest *way* gives me the *knowlege* best; the longest way makes me more *knowing*."

53[1] See *Conciones*: *Lects 1795* (*CC*) 65–6 and n 4.

54[1] In Collier's version "the *God* within us" is not easy to discern, but it is clearly present in the Greek

55   p 75 | v xix

XIX. *'Tis Thoughts*, not *Things* which take hold of the Soul. Outward Objects can't force their Passage into the Mind, nor set any of its Wheels a going. No, The Impression comes from her self, and 'tis her *Notions* which affect Her. As for the contingencies of Fortune, they are either Great or Little, according to the Opinion she has of her own Strength.

very just.

56   pp 76–7, passage marked with an inked line in the margin | v xxi

XXI. Among all Things in the *Universe*, direct your Worship to the Greatest: And which is that? 'Tis that Being which Manages, and Governs all the Rest. And as you worship the best Thing in Nature, so you are to pay a proportionable Regard to the best Thing in your *Self*: You'l know it by its Relation to the Deity. The Quality of its Functions will discover it. 'Tis the Reigning Power *within you*, which disposes of your Actions, and your Fortune.

This Paragraph and the many others of the same kind ought to be remembered as fair interpreters of other Paragraphs in which the Emperor, tho' meaning the same christian Truths, expresses himself in a less christian-like phrases. Thus in those passages in which he seems to confound God with the universe, making all Things to be God, it is to be remembered that as a Platonic Stoic he considered matter & the visible world as something below entity or reality/ God is the supreme Reality[1]

56A   p 79 | v xxviii

XXVIII. Are you angry at a Rank Smell, or an ill scented Breath? Why if a Man's Lungs, or Stomach, are ulcerated, or ~~his Arm-pits~~[a] out of Order, how can he help it.

[a] C has obliterated these three words so heavily that they cannot be read

original. The sentence immediately following **33** textus reads (in Collier): "Take care that your Tutelar Genius* has a creditable Charge to preside over" and the shoulder-note reads: "*The Mind, or Powers of Reason." The Greek for Collier's "your Tutelar Genius" is ὁ ἐν σοὶ θεός, "the God within you"; and a similar phrase ὁ ἔνδον δαίμων, "the spirit within", occurs in *Meditations* II xiii, xvii. In any case the notion of "the *God* within us" had peculiar personal import for C. See e.g. *CN* III 3996, *PW* (EHC) I 360, and *CN* III 3911 ff 59ᵛ–60.

For "Texts of Sᵗ John's Gospel" see e.g. John 4.24, 6.63, 14.17, 15.2, 15.26, 16.13; and see also Rom 8.9–11, 1 Cor 3.16, 1 John 4.12, 15.

56[1] In *P Lects* Lect 6 C took a less generous view of Aurelius' position. *P Lects* (1949) 219–21.

57 p 79 | v xxix

XXIX. You may live *now* if you please, as you would chuse to do if you were near dying: But suppose People won't let you; why then give Life the Slip, but by no means make a Misfortune on't.

The Stoics justified Suicide indeed, but not Self-murder/[1] and on this principle,[a]

58 pp 93–5 | vi xxv

XXV. What abundance of Motions there are in the Body, what abundance of Thoughts and *Sensations* in the Mind at the same time? What a vast number of Operations are performed, and how much Business is Dispatch'd within us in a single Moment? He that considers this, won't wonder so much that infinitely more productions should start out together in the Universe: Or that the *Soul of the World* should by once exerting Himself look over, Actuate, and govern the whole *Mass* of *Matter*.

admirable. As every single idea has a unity ~~of~~ and consciousness, yet there are millions of ideas into which our mind is modified, so the ancients conceived that the aggregate of minds in any given Planet might form one self-conscious mind, even as the aggregates of countless conscious ideas form a mind in each Individual.[1] This "Soul of the World" is therefore considered equally distinct from God as a man is—tho' as being an incomparably more extensive and powerful agent, the ~~attributes~~ powers necessarily attributed to it are of necessity often the same with those attributed to Deity—Even as among us in the use of the vague word, Nature/ the most pious men talk of a lusus naturæ, a sport of Nature, an abortive effort of Nature, consequently mean something different from God—& yet of necessity often in other contemplations speak of the wisdom, exquisite contrivances, &c [of] Nature.[2]

59 p 121 | vii xlviii

Consider the Course of the Stars as if you were driving through the Sky, and kept them Company.

Sublime. A Thought for a Milton.[1]

[a] The note breaks off

57[1] See **28** nn 2, 3, above.

58[1] For C on the *anima mundi* see BAXTER *Reliquiae* COPY A 2, *P Lects* (1949) 92, *Friend (CC)* I 505, *AR* (1825) 395.

58[2] In his Royal Institution lectures in Mar 1808 C deplored the "happy medium & refuge, to talk of Shakspere as a sort of beautiful Lusus Naturae." *CN* III 3288, reworked into *BL* ch 15.

59[1] Or for the composition of the "Moon" gloss to *AM* (lines 263ff)? In *CN* II 2077 C noted, referring to

59A   pp 127–8, passage marked with an inked line in the margin | vii lxvii

LXVII. Which way are we to conclude that *Socrates* was a better Man in Virtue and Temper, than *Telauges*. To make out this, 'tis not enough to say, that he disputed better, and died Bolder. The Austerity and Discipline of his Life; his Bravery in slighting the Orders of the *Thirty Tyrants*, and refusing to apprehend an Innocent Person; The Gravity and Greatness in his Mien and Motion: (Tho the truth of this last particular may be question'd:) All this Glitter won't make the Character shine out. To prove the point, we must examine what sort of Soul *Socrates* carried about him: Could he be contented with the Conscience of an Honest and a Pious Man? Did he not Fret and Fume to no purpose at the Knavery, and Wickedness of the Age? Was he govern'd by no Bodies Ignorance? Did he never question the Equity of Providence, grow surpriz'd at his hard Fortune, and sink under the Weight of it? To conclude, Did he keep Pain and Pleasure at a due distance, and not dip his Soul too deep in his Senses? These Marks are the only Test of a Great Man; and 'tis to no purpose to pretend to that Character without them.[1]

60   p 153, pencil | viii liv

LIV. Let your Soul receive the Deity as your Blood does the Air, for the Influences of the one, are no less Vital than the other. This Correspondence is very Practicable: For there's an Ambient Omnipresent Spirit, which lies as open, and pervious to your Mind, as the Air you breath does to your Lungs: But then you must remember to be dispos'd to draw it.

a sublime though mysterious idea[1]

p 123: "Marcus Antoninus Book 7—§ 54 the Sum & Essence of Quakerism/." Aurelius § liv reads: "As long as a Man can make use of his Reason, and Act in concert with God's, he needs not question the Event. There can be no grounds to suspect Misfortune, provided you stick close to Nature, and manage within the Character of your condition." C underlined "stick close" and continued his note: "*N.B.* Jeremy Collier's Translation!—L'Estrange outheroded"—a clear link with these marginalia. L'Estrange's vice was "to be pert, frisky, & vulgar". *CN* i 1660.

59A[1] In *CN* ii 2077, referring to this passage, C noted: "§ 67 of B. 6

[actually vii] contains the sum of my Remark on the—not what he has done, but what is he?" See also FIELDING *Tom Jones* 4 at n 5: "If I want a servant or mechanic, I wish to know what *he does*—but of a Friend, I must know what he is...." There is another close parallel to **59A** in *CL* iii 216 (22 Jun 1808).

60[1] This is the last marginal note on the *Meditations*, almost at the end of Bk viii; but passages are marked in Bks ix–xii; see ANNEX [*g*]. In 1816 C transcribed in Greek variatim a passage from xii xxix (*CN* iii 4314); the passage is marked in this copy of Collier's translation with a pencil brace: see ANNEX [*g*] p 236.

THE PICTURE OF CEBES

61 p 241

This is worth reading as a Masterpiece of the *Black-guard Slang*, which passed for *easy* writing from the Restoration of Charles to the accession of Queen Anne—of the Royalist Party   I cannot remember any one, but Cowley, that was not more or less infected with it— Even Dryden, masterly as his Prose-style is, is not quite free from it.—[1]

62 pp 244–6

[After C had marked many phrases:] If a Man can't look through her [i.e. *Folly*], and untie her Riddle, tho' she does not chop him up at a Mouthful like the *Sphinx*, yet she will be sure to dispatch him by Degrees, sit as close to him as a Consumption . . .

and yet, this Translation of perhaps the finest specimen of simple, delicate & dignified Style in the whole Greek Literature, was not INTENDED as burlesque. I believe, Sir Roger L'Estrange was the Introducer of this Thames-Waterman's Language—was ably discipled by the facetious Tom Brown, & his Grub-street imitator, Edward Ward—& marvellous to say!—was honored ~~by~~ in the frequent adoption of it by Barrow/ indeed as frequent as the nature & precision of his Thoughts rendered it possible[1]—It lasted in full fragrance till the conclusion of the Reign of William the Third. One most remarkable is Burnet's own Translation of his own *Theoria Sacra*/—Such a Contrast, I suppose, scarcely exists elsewhere. His Latin Style marches to the Sound of silver Trumpets;

61[1] See **1** n 4, above. C had grouped Dryden, Cowley, and Addison as superior to Gibbon in Lect 14 of the 1818 Literary Lectures. *LR* I 238.

62[1] C has arranged his list in descending order of talent and respectability. Sir Roger L'Estrange (1616–1704), royalist pamphleteer, journalist, and translator, is best remembered for his extensive collection of *Fables of Aesop and Other Eminent Mythologists*. C owned a copy of L'Estrange's *Fables* (2 vols 1724–30). Thomas Brown (1663–1704), satirist and hack translator, is perhaps best remembered for the quatrain (after Martial) on Dr Fell. Edward Ward (1667–1731), coarse humorist, wrote an imitation of *Hudibras*.

Isaac Barrow (1630–77), a fine classical scholar, resigned the chair of mathematics at Cambridge in favour of his pupil Newton, to whom among British mathematicians he was considered second only. On 16 Oct 1803 C received from the Beaumonts a 2-vol ed of Barrow's *Sermons* in which Lady Beaumont had marked "the admirable Passage on Wit" that C acknowledged as "an old friend & favorite of mine". *CL* II 1017. C considered Barrow a landmark in the history of English prose style: *TT* 5 Jul 1834. He owned a copy of Barrow's *Works* (4 vols 1683–7).

his English *jigs* on to the Clare-Market Music of a [. . .]*ᵃ* Marrow-bones and Cleavers.²

63 p 245

She opens a Vein, and gives them a Glass of her Constitution: What sort of Drink is that? 'Tis Ignorance and Mistake.

unintelligible as well as vulgar/

63A p 247

?] Those, *says he*, who seem so merry and well pleas'd, have <u>receiv'd</u> a <u>Spill</u>, and sped in their Addresses to this Lady . . .

64 p 249

But I am tired of underscoring—Satis et plusquam satis.—¹

65 pp 263–4

Resumptions are very common with this Lady [Fortune], and there's no depending upon her Favour; And therefore the *Genius* advises People to be loose and indifferent with her, and neither be transported when she gives, nor dejected when she takes away. For she

---

ᵃ Three illegible words cancelled; one of them may be "chopper"

62² Thomas Burnet (c 1635–1715), master of the Charter house, was dismissed as chaplain to William III for interpreting the Mosaic account of the Fall as an allegory in his *Archaeologiae philosophiae* (1692); the epigraph to *AM* (1817) is from p 68 of this work. See Thomas BURNET.

A longer version of **62**, not including—perhaps significantly—mention of Collier, was set down in Nov 1803: *CN* I 1655. The note recurs, e.g. in the 1818 literary lectures: *LR* I 236–7 and *Friend* (*CC*) I 359. See also *TT* 3 Jul 1833, 5 Jul 1834. For a convenient group of C's observations on prose style see *C 17th C* 411–25 (but on p 415 Jeremy Collier is incorrectly identified as Joseph Collyer).

C is paraphrasing Colman on Dr Johnson's style—"marched to kettle-drums and trumpets". "Marrow-bones and Cleavers" produced (on occasion) rough percussive music for impromptu dancing in the streets. Since Clare Market, in Lincoln's Inn Fields, was noted for the slaughtering of sheep and oxen, C may well have heard this music. To catch a glimpse of Charles Lamb in the background may be illusory but is tempting. In a note addressed to Lamb in Jeremy TAYLOR *Polemicall Discourses* (1674) i 38 C celebrated the "noctes Atticæ at the Cat and Salutation, Blood Alley, Newgate Market, when Butchers grasped their Steels, and listened to our knock-down arguments".

64¹ After marking many words and phrases on pp 242–9 C wrote this note on p 249, but he continued to mark words up to p 264. C's Latin phrase—"Enough and more than enough"—seems to echo the closing words of Giordano Bruno's Ode "Id vere plusquam satis est", a poem that had so impressed him that in Apr 1801 he copied it into a notebook. *CN* I 929; cf *Friend* (*CC*) II 282. For another echo of these words, in the note bidding farewell to lecturing in 1819, see *CN* III 4504 and n.

never acts upon Reason, but throws out every thing at Peradventure. Therefore the Rule is never to be surpriz'd at any of her Proceedings . . .

This is the most defective Passage of the whole Treatise. It is not true, and it is of pernicious consequence, to represent Fortune as *wholly* mad, blind, deaf, and drunk. On the *average* each man receives what he pays for—the miser gives care & self-torment, and receives increase of Gold—the vain give clamour, & bustle, pretensions & flattery, & receive a *Buz*—the Wise man Self-conquest & neighbourly Love, and receives sense of Dignity, of Harmony, and Content. Each is paid in sort—Virtue is not rewarded by Wealth, nor is the Eye affected by Sound.[1] S. T. C.

66 p 265

For, to speak freely, a Man may have abundance of fine Notions in his Head, and run through all the *Sciences* as they call them, and yet love* Wine and Women, and Mony,† a great deal too much.

* Bolingbroke[1]

†Ex. gr. Leibnitz & Sir. I. Newton.[2]

67 p 269

To put an other Question to you, had you rather live scandalously, or Die bravely? I had rather Die upon those terms. You answer like a Man; From hence it follows that Death is no Evil, because 'tis sometimes more Eligible than Living. You are right.

Is the Tooth-ache no pain, because it is more eligible than a Fit of the Stone?—The Truth is here injured by being ill supported. There is an Equivoque/ Death is either the loss of Life, or it is the Pain and Terror which accompany it, whether considered as annihilation, or as an unknown Change of Being: in the latter Sense it is a part of *Life*;[1]

65[1] See the essay on fortune and luck in *The Friend* of 28 Dec 1809, esp *Friend* (*CC*) II 250.

66[1] Henry St John, 1st Viscount Bolingbroke (1678–1751), statesman, great orator, and notable profligate. His philosophical fragments were partly versified by Pope in the *Essay on Man* (see **44**, above); his collected *Works* were edited by Mallet in 5 vols in 1754. His "Deistic Atheism" (as C called it in N 29) was influential in C's day, but C considered that "Bolingbroke removed Love, Justice, and Choice, from power and intelligence, and yet pretended to have left unimpaired the conviction of a Deity". *Friend* (*CC*) II 44. For an adverse comparison of Bolingbroke's style with Cowley's see *TT* 12 Jul 1827.

66[2] For another joining of the names of Leibniz and Newton see A B B T **1** and B A H R D T **1**.

67[1] On 2 Feb 1808 C suspected that he was suffering from "the Stone". *CL* III 52. For his strong presentiment of death in 1807–8 see **17** n 3, above.

in the former sense it is indeed undeniable, that where Life is no Blessing, the *Loss* of it can be no Evil—but this is nugatory, barren of all consequence, not to say, comfort.[2]—S. T. C.—

68   i 270, at the end

... 'tis Precept, and Principles, not an Estate, which makes a Man good for something. Indeed, I think so. Which way then ... can *Wealth* be a real Advantage, if it can't improve the Owners, nor contribute to the making them better. How then can that be absolutely a good Thing, when a Man is sometimes the better for being without it.

This is the point, in which, I think, the Ancients did not explain themselves happily: with exception of Aristotle[1]—The Eyes & Ears, ⟨&c &c⟩ are not an ultimate, not an independent Good; yet they are a most important Adjunct, nay, necessary Component of the ultimate Good—as they are worse than worthless unless subordinated to the ultimate Good, so is this latter a non-existent without *them*. This is the Evil of disjoining what God has joined[2]—Yet I deny not that it is of use to point out the distinction between good, as *means*, & good, as the *end*; but then their mutual re-actions ought to be shewn at the same time—[3]

Annex

C has marked words, phrases, and passages according to the three sigla given in **5** and a fourth introduced in **8**. He has also underlined single words and phrases, without any siglum, by way of comment. Further, beyond passages here printed as textus, he has marked certain passages with a vertical line or a brace in the margin. In the following transcript the use of italics in the printed text has been ignored: all italics and small capitals represent C's underscoring.

[*a*] ○ a phrase vulgar from its definiteness

p 2 "meddle with other Peoples *Matters*"
p 3 "And to *conclude with* him"
p 5 "to suffer in *ones* Quality, or *grow a jot the Cheaper for't*"
p 9 "without *minding* being Lampoon'd"
p 24 "signifies *not a Farthing*" (also marked X as in [*d*], below)

67[2] The phrase "where Life is no Blessing" seems to anticipate *Youth and Age. PW* (EHC) I 440: c 1823.

68[1] In view of his long acquaintance with Thomas Stanley *The History of Philosophy* (1701) C may be thinking of the passage (pp 260–3) in which, under the heading of "Aristotle", Stanley summarises Stobaeus on the ethics of the Peripatetics.

68[2] Cf Matt 19.6, incorporated into the marriage service.

68[3] On the distinction between "good, as *means*" and "good, as the *end*" see *P Lects* Lect 6 (1949) 216.

[*b*] ☉ a phrase vulgar by false definiteness

p 1 "doing any Body *an ill Turn*" "endure the thought *on't* "

p 2 "TO THROW the Necessities of Nature into a little Compass" "He likewise *put* me upon improving my self"

p 3 "first *set* me *upon* correcting my Humour"

p 4 "To *give him his due*" "To *go on* with him" (X) "Scholars could seldom *throw him off the Hooks*" (X)

p 5 "nor *fall foul* upon People for improprieties of Phrase"

p 8 "Never . . . *lye Grinning* at a Disgust" (X)

p 24 "it signifies not a *Farthing*" (X)

p 121 "*up to the Ears* in Trading and Merchandize"

[*c*] ⚹ a phrase vulgar or ludicrous from its transiency or dependence on an accidental fashion

p 3 "Dress and Mien of a *Beau*"

p 6 "those we call *Top Quality*"

p 10 "His Dress was neither *Beauish*, nor Negligent"

p 60 "had *knocked so many Mens Brains out*"

p 123 "*stick close* to Nature"

[*d*] X low misapplications of physical or bodily words to the mind
(See also phrases marked in [*a*] and [*b*], above.)

p 6 "being supplanted, or *overtopp'd* by them"

p 10 "without *chopping* and changing of Measures"

p 14 "I *took up*, and recover'd: That when I *fell out* with Rusticus . . . I was not transported"

p 15 "Voluminous Reading, *Chopping Logicke*, or Natural Philosophy"

p 26 "What . . . will *stick by* a Man"

pp 35–6 "As for other speculations, *throw them all out of your Head*"

[*e*] *Phrases and words underlined, but not categorised by siglum*
(See also some passages in [*f*] and [*g*], below.)

p xxiv "his Inclinations were *eager*"

p xxxix "St. *Polycarp* was the first that was sacrificed"

p lxxiii "this Honour he accepted *this bout*"

MEDITATIONS

p 2 "apply my self *to't*" (see **6**)

p 4 "And as for his Learning . . . he was so far from being *smitten with himself*"

p 10 "if a . . . Country happen to *prove cross*"

p 15 "That I did not spend too much time in Voluminous Reading, *Chopping Logicke*, or Natural Philosophy" (follows on **17**)

p 16 "all *that's on't*" "As for your *Carcass*, value it no more" (see **50**) "nothing but a little *paltry* Blood and Bones"

p 17 "is concern'd *in't*"

p 25 "he does not know what *he would be at* in a Business"

p 30 "*March off* themselves" "you'll have done *drudging* for your *Carcass*" (see **50**) p 47 "make use *on't* "

p 56 "*Han't* you done with"

p 65 "*I'le jog on* in that Path which Nature *has Chalk'd out*, till my *Legs sink* under me"

p 120 "his business is to *stand Buff* against Danger and Death"

p 121 "the Transmutation and *shuffling* of the Elements"

p 123 "no grounds to suspect Misfortune, provided you *stick close to Nature*" (see **59**n)

p 125 "the right *Knack* of Living, resembles Wrastling more than Dancing"

p 129 "a brace of Lions should quarter upon your *Carcass*" (see **50**)

THE PICTURE OF CEBES

p 242 "*at a stand* about the Design" "a grave Man somewhat in Years, *making up*, begins to *discourse us* in this Manner" "this Picture should *puzzle* you" "none of our *Town Manufacture*" "a certain *out-landish Man*" "a Disciple of Pythagoras, and Parmenides; This *Genteleman*"

p 243 "he *talk'd at a strange significant rate*" "I have heard him . . . *read upon* the Argument" "Danger! *As how*? Why, says he, *if you mind what you are about*" "This Mythology is *as touchy a Business* to the Audience" "he *found his Account* in the Undertaking"

p 244 "she does *not chop him up at* a Mouthful like the Sphinx" "*ride him* as the Spleen does" "*then she goes to Pot* her self" "you *make us almost Wild* to hear you"

p 245 "Imposture . . . that *bubbles* the whole World" "when they have taken this *Stirrup Cup*" "*Does every body* take *their Mornings Draught* of this Liquor? Every body, but not all *Brimmers*" "don't you see a *parcel of Wenches* within the Gate" "these *Lasses frisk about them* . . . and then *lug them off* "

p 246 "Some to good Fortune, and some . . . to Ruin, *and the Gallows*" "having taken a Glass . . . are so *muddy-headed*" "ramble about . . . *as* you see" "how *those Gypsies* manage the People" "but Mad, and Deaf *into the bargain*"

p 247 "*mightily* shock'd" "others as *much out of sorts*" "Those . . . have *receiv'd a Spill*"

p 248 "dress'd like *Wenches*" "their Quality is very *Coarse*" "what do they stand staring *here for*? *To Spy out* those" "appear *mightily* transported"

p 249 "when Men *come to this pass*" (see **64**)

p 251 "Here *I put in again*"

p 253 "what makes them *sprawl* their Hands *out* with so much Fancy?"

p 254 "This must *needs be a delicate Place then*" "that People may know *where to have her*"

p 255 "this Lady *has an excellent Hand* at making Presents" "a Patient dangerously ill, is *undertaken by a Physician*" "In the place first *the Doctor* endeavours to remove the Cause . . . the Man is *set up*. But if he *won't take his Physick . . . she falls to Doctring of him presently*"

p 256 "*In earnest*, said I, *fine Ladies all!*"

p 257 "not to any *degree of Magot*, or Curiosity" "*snaped a Collop sometimes out of his Carkass*, and used him at a *miserable rate*" "tho' they *don't go it* may be *upon all four*"

p 258 "it has a *mighty satisfying Quality*" "conquering *at this rate*" "they shew him at *what a rate* of Scandal and Misery People live" "How often *they run their Heads against a Post*"

p 259 "Visit of an able *Doctor. What won't he be afraid of those scurvy Women any more*, which you said were *like Bears in a Bear-garden*"

p 261 "they return to *fetch* more"

p 262 "I shall *let you* into the whole *Business*"

p 264 "a Favour that will *stick by* them"

[*f*] *N.B.* the passage seemed to be worthy of particular attention

p 3 "By his Instructions I was perswaded to be easily reconcil'd to those who had misbehav'd themselves, and disoblig'd me. And of the same Master I learn't to Read an Author carefully. Not to take up with a superficial View, or resign to every Noisy Impertinent; but to look thro' the Argument, and go to the Bottom of the Matter."

p 4 "Apollonius taught me to give my Mind its due Freedom, and disengage it from dependance upon Change: And furnish'd me with such Precepts for Steadiness and Ballast, as not to Flote in Uncertainties, or be at a Loss about Design or Event; nor so much as to look towards any thing uncountenanc'd by Reason and Truth . . ."

"This great Man *let me* into the true secret of managing an Obligation, without either lessening my self, or being ungrateful to my Friend."

pp 5–6 "But to *set* them right, by speaking the Thing properly my self, and that either by way of Answer, Assent, or Enquiry; or by some such other remote, and Gentlemanly Correction."

p 6 "XII. Alexander the Platonist advised me, that without Necessity I should never pretend not to be at Leisure to assist a Friend. Nor make Business an Excuse to decline the Offices of Humanity."

"XIII. I learn'd of Catullus not to slight a Friend for making a Remonstrance, tho it should happen to be unreasonable, but rather to retrieve his Temper, and make him Easy." (marked N.B. N.B.; cf **43**)

p 7 "XIV. I am indebted to Severus for the due regard I have for my Family and Relations, and for keeping this Inclination from growing too strong for Justice and Truth."

"'Twas of him I learn'd not to grow Wise by Starts, and broken Fancies, but to be a constant Admirer of Philosophy and Improvement"

"Hope the best of Matters, and never question the Affection of his Friends"

"To be free in shewing a reasonable dislike of another"

"not to put his Friends to the Trouble of Divining what he would be at"

p 9 "To be constant to a Friend, without Tiring, or Fondness."

p 12 "notwithstanding if my Humour had been awaken'd, and push'd forward, I had been likely enough to have miscarried this way: But by the goodness of the Gods, I met with no Provocations to discover my Infirmities"

pp 15–16 "Remember to put your self in mind every Morning, That before Night 'twill be your Luck to meet with some Inquisitive Impertinence, with some ungrateful, and abusive Fellow; with some Knavish, Envious, or unsociable Churl or other. Now all this perverseness in them proceeds from their Ignorance of Good and Evil: And since its fallen to my share to understand the Natural Beauty of a good Action, and the Deformity of an ill One; since I am satisfied the Person disobliging is of Kin to me, and tho we are not just of the same Flesh and Blood, yet our Minds are nearly related, being both extracted from the Deity; since I am likewise convinc'd that no Man can do me a real injury, because no Man can force me to misbehave my self; For these Reasons, I can't find in my Heart to Hate, or to be Angry with one of my own Nature and Family. For we are all made for mutual Assistance, no less than the Parts of the Body are for the Service of the whole; From whence it follows that Clashing and Opposition is perfectly Unnatural: Now such an unfriendly Disposition is imply'd in Resentment and Aversion." (See also [*g*], below, i 37.)

p 18 "And let the Action be done with all the Dignity and Advantage of Circumstance"

p 19 "don't complain of your Destiny, and *have nothing of Insincerity, and Self-Love to infect you*"

p 23 "That is wonderfully busy to force a Passage into other Peoples Thoughts, and dive into their Bosom"

"And as for Men, their Actions should be well taken for the sake of Common Kindred."

"Which Incapacity of Discerning between Moral Qualities, is a greater Misfortune than that of a Blind Man, who can't distinguish between White and Black."

p 25 "A Man Lessens and Affronts himself when he is overcome by Pleasure, or Pain"

p 29–30 "The bending of an Ear of Corn, the Brow of a Lion, the Foam of a Boar, and many other Things, if you take them singly, are far enough from being handsome, but when they are look'd on as parts of somewhat else, and consider'd with Reference, and Connexion; are both Ornamental, and Affecting."[1] (See also **30A**.)

p 32 "That every ones Good Opinion is not worth the gaining; but only of those who live up to the Dignity of their Nature." (See also [*g*], below, i 31–2.)

p 33 "VI. If in the whole compass of Humane Life, you find any thing preferable to Justice and Truth, to Temperance, and Fortitude; To a Mind Self-satisfied with its own Rational Conduct ... never balk your Fancy, count it your Supream Happiness, and make the most *on't* you can. ... Now Use and Significancy, is the proper Test of this Quality: So that the Question will be whether a Thing is serviceable to your Rational Capacity; If so, close with the Offer; But if 'tis no more than a sensual Advantage, hold your Hand; And that you may Distinguish rightly, keep your Judgment Unbyass'd, and don't let it *stick* in the outside of Matters."

---

[1] Cf BROWNE *Religio* 13, on ugliness.

p 39 "To say no more on't, He that would view this Matter rightly, must Think a little, and look inward."

p 41 "III. 'Tis the Custom of People to go to unfrequented Places and Country Seats for Retirement; And this has been your Method formerly. But after all, this is but a Vulgar Fancy. For 'tis in your Power to withdraw into your self whenever you have a Mind to't. Now ones own Breast is a place the most free from Crowd and Noise in the World, if a Mans Retrospections are easy, his Thoughts entertaining, and his Mind well in Order. Your way is therefore to make frequent use of this Retirement, and Refresh your Virtue in't. And to this End, be always provided with a few short uncontested Notions, to keep your Understanding True, and make you easy in your Business."

p 53 "He that frets himself Sore because Things don't happen just as he would have them, is but a sort of an Ulcer of the World; By murmuring at the Course of Nature, he quits the Universal Body, and gains only the Distinction of a Disease. Never considering that the same Cause which produced the displeasing Accident, made him too. And lastly, He that is Selfish, narrow-Soul'd, and *sets up* for a Separate Interest, is a kind of Voluntary Out-Law, and Disincorporates himself from Mankind."

p 58 "XLIV. Whatever happens Here, is as Common, and well known as a Rose in the Spring, or an Apple in Autumn: Of this kind are Diseases, and Death, Calumny and Undermining; And several other Things, which Raise, and Depress the Spirits of unthinking People."

p 59 "And seem perfectly unacquainted with those things which occur daily. Farther, we must not Nod over Business, nor dream away Life, like People who fancy they are mightily employ'd, when they are fast in their Beds."

[g] *Passages* (other than those printed as textus) *marked in the margin with a line or brace but without a siglum*

pp xxiii–xxiv "He [Marcus Antoninus] was both Merciful and Just, and no less Indulgent to others than Rigorous to Himself; Deaf to the Charms of Vanity, immovable in his Enterprizes, and Resolutions, which were never fix'd and taken up without Mature Deliberation; being never swayed by Passion and Freak: He hated busy Informers, was Religious without Affectation, *untransported and free from Eagerness upon* all occasion; always under an Equality of Temper, always Master of himself, and resigned to the Reason of the Case; a perfect stranger to Disguise and Dissimulation, and always upon his Guard against the Excesses of Selflove; never uneasy nor impatient, very inclinable to pardon the greatest Crimes against himself; but not to be prevail'd on where Reasons of State and Publick Interest required Severity. His Laws had a Regard to the common Advantage of all Ranks and Nations under his Government; neither could any Prince be more tender of the Property and Privileges of the Subject. The Good of the Commonwealth was always his Rule to act by, from which he was never diverted by any Private Fancy, Interest, or Ambition of his own. To conclude, since his Designs were only to oblige Mankind, and Resign to Providence, he never strain'd his Politicks to the Prejudice of his Morals, but always kept within the compass of Justice and Truth."

p xxxii "Indeed, let the Difficulty of the Juncture be what it would, he was always Master of so much Fortitude, and Prudence, as never to be over-ruled beyond Justice, either out of Fear, or easyness of Temper."

p xxxiv "The Emperour was the only person not in Despair, his Confidence lay in the Protection of Heaven, for which he endeavour'd to qualify himself in the first Place, by the offering of Sacrifices"

p lx "That a Man that goes in to the Sentiment of another, is no less at his Liberty than if he had stuck close to his first Thought; For 'tis purely his own sense and Judgment that prevails with him to alter his Mind."

pp lxi–lxii "He loved to be throughly inform'd of what People said of him, not to punish those who took too much Liberty, but to learn what was liked, or dislik'd in his Management; The use that he made of Publick Censure, or Commendation, being only to recover a false step, or go on in a Defencible Method, with better Assurance. And when his Administration, or private Conduct were blam'd without Reason, his Custom was to reply to the Charger either by Letter or Word of Mouth, not so much to justify himself, as to undeceive those that spread the Report, and acquaint them with Matter of Fact."

p lxii "... 'tis the peculiar Privilege of Virtue, to raise up a Monarch to the Gods; and that a Prince remarkable for Justice; has the whole Worldfor his Temple, and all honest Men will be his Priests to worship him"

p lxiii "... provided he maintain'd his Ground, and stood firm to a reasonable Resolution"

p lxxxv "When he had the Command of the Army in Germany, some of his Auxiliaries happen'd to surprize a Detatchment of three thousand Sarmatians, by the Danube, very much in Disorder. Upon this Advantage they fell on, and cut them in Pieces: But Cassius instead of Rewarding the Captains of these Companies, had every Man of them Crucified; letting them know that they had no Liberty to fight without Orders. For how could they tell but that they might have fallen into an Ambush, and expos'd the Arms of the Empire to an Affront: Besides the Authority and Force of Discipline must be lost this way."

p xci "... for no body will believe there's any Truth in a Conspiracy till they see it Executed. 'Tis true, this fine Sentence belongs to Domitian, but I rather chuse to cite Adrian; because the Sententious Sayings of Tyrants have not the same Weight and Authority, as those which are deliver'd by a Good Prince. Let Cassius then take his Humour, for to give him his due, he is a great General, brave in his Person, and one that we can by no means spare as Affairs stand. As to what you insinuate, that his Death is the only Security for my Children; I say, if Cassius's Merits outshine theirs, let them smart for't..."

p cxv "The Bounties of Princes which have least Discretion are commonly most taking with the People; whereas Prudence and Reason goes for Covetousness with them: For they never distinguish between giving and squandring, and make their own craving Temper the Standard of Liberality: But after all, 'tis certain Rome never had a Prince more beneficent than Antoninus..."

MEDITATIONS

p 7 "XV. The Proficiency I made under Maximus was to Command my self, and not to be overborn with any Impotency of Passion or Surprize. To be full of Spirits under Sickness and Misfortune. To appear with Modesty, Obligingness, and Dignity of Behaviour."

p 12 ". . . he could either Take or Leave those Conveniences of Life with respect to which, most People are either uneasie without them, or intemperate with them. Now to hold on with Fortitude in one Condition, and Sobriety in the other, is an argument of a great Soul, and an impregnable Virtue. And lastly, when his Friend Maximus was Sick, he gave me an instance how I ought to behave my self upon the like occasion."

p 18 "IV. Remember how often you have postpon'd the minding your Interest, and slip'd those Opportunities the Gods have given you. 'Tis now high time to consider what sort of World you are part of, and from what kind of Government of it you are Descended: That you have a set Period assign'd to Act in. And unless you improve it to Brighten and Compose your Thoughts, 'twill quickly run off with you, and be lost beyond Recovery."

pp 31–2 ". . . he always resigns to Providence, and meets his Fate with Pleasure: He never minds other Peoples Thoughts or Actions, unless Publick Reason and General Good require it. No; He confines himself to his own Business, and contemplates upon his Post, and Station; And endeavours to do the First as it should be, and believe well of the Latter: I say of the Latter; for Fate is both inevitable, and convenient. He considers that all Rational Beings are of Kin; and that General Kindness and Concern for the whole World, is no more than a piece of Humanity. That every ones Good Opinion is not worth the gaining; but only of those who live up to the Dignity of their Nature. [The last sentence also marked *N.B.*] As for others, he knows their way of Living, and their Company; their Publick, and their Private Disorders; And, why indeed should he value the Commendation of such People, who are so Vitious and Fantastical, as not to be able to please themselves?"

pp 34–5 "VII. Don't be fond of any Thing, or think that for your Interest, which makes you break your Word, quit your Modesty, be of a Dissembling, Suspicious, or Outragious Humour; which puts you upon Hating any Person, and enclines you to any Practice, which wont bear the Light, and look the World in the Face. For he that values the Virtue of his Mind, and the Dignity of his Reason, before all other Things, is easy, and well fortified, and has nothing for a Tragedy to work on; He laments under no Misfortune, and wants neither Solitude nor Company; And which is still more, he neither flies Death, nor pursues it; but is perfectly indifferent about the Length, and Shortness of his Life. And if he was to expire this Moment, the want of Warning would not surprize him; He'd ne'er struggle for more time, but go off with Decency and Honour. Indeed, he is solicitous about Nothing but his own Conduct, and for fear he should fail in the Functions of Reason, Prudence, and Generosity."

p 38 "And then, if you will but stick to your Measures, and be True to the Best of your Self" "be always furnish'd with Rules and Principles" p 40 "To live in a Crowd of Objects, without suffering either in his Sense, his Virtue, or his Quiet."

p 50 "XXII. Don't run Riot; Keep your Understanding True, and your Intentions Honest."

pp 66–7 "These are much like a Vine, which is satisfied by being fruitful in its Kind, and bears a Bunch of Grapes without expecting any Thanks for it. A Fleet Horse or Greyhound, don't use to make a Noise when they have perform'd handsomly, nor a Bee neither when she has made a little Hony: And thus a Man that's rightly Kind, never proclaims a Good Turn, but does another as soon as he can; just like a Vine that bears again the next Season. Now we should imitate Those who are so obliging, as hardly to remember their Beneficence: But you'l say, a Man ought to understand the Quality of his own Actions."

p 67 "the privacy of doing a good-turn will never discourage you"

p 70 "Now think a little, and tell me what is there more delightful than downright Honesty and Religion, than Generosity and Greatness of Mind?"

p 72 "XI. What use do I put my Soul to, or what Hand do I make of my Reason? 'Tis a serviceable question this, and should frequently be put to ones self? I say, how does my sovraign Part stand affected? And what's the Furniture and Complexion of my Mind? Is there nothing of the Boy or the Beast in't? Nothing that's either Tyrannical, or Effeminate?"

p 78 "XXV. A Man misbehaves himself towards Me: what's that to me? The Action is his, and the Will that set him upon't is His, and therefore let him look to't. As for me, I am in the Condition Providence would have me, and am doing what becomes me."

p 109 "VI. How many Famous Men are dropt out of History, and forgotten? And how many Poets and Panegyrists, that promised to keep up other People's Names, have lost their own?"

pp 115–16 "XXVII. When any one misbehaves himself towards you, immediately bethink your self what Notions he has concerning Advantage and Disadvantage: When you have found out this, you'l pity him, and neither be angry, nor surprized at the Matter. It may be upon enquiry, you may find your Opinions upon these points much the same, and then you ought to pardon him; for you would have done the same thing your self upon the same Occasion. But if your Notions of Good and Evil, are different, and more just than his, then your Passion will yield to your Good Nature, and you'l easily bear with his Ignorance.

"XXVIII. Don't let your Head run upon that which is none of your own. But pick out some of the best of your Circumstances, and consider, how eagerly you would wish for them, were they not in your possession; but then you must take care to keep your satisfaction within compass..."

"XXIX. Fortifie at home, and rely upon your self. For a Rational Mind is born to the priviledge of Independance. Honesty, and the Inward Quiet consequent to it, is enough in all Conscience, to make you Happy."

p 117 "XXXII. Would you set off your Person, and recommend your self? Let it be done by Simplicity and Candour, by Modesty of Behaviour, and by Indifference to External Advantages..."

p 122 "L. By looking back into History, and considering the Fate and Revolutions of Government, you will be able to draw a Guess, and almost Prophecy upon the Future. For things Past, Present, and to Come, are strangely Uniform, and of a Colour; and are Commonly cast in the same Mould. So that upon the Matter, Forty years of Humane Life, may serve for a Sample of Ten Thousand."

pp 124–5 "LIX. When any Accident happens, call to mind Those who have formerly been under the same Circumstances, how full of Surprize, Complaint, and Trouble they were about the matter: And where are They now? They are gone, their Murmuring could not make them Immortal. To what purpose should you imitate their Behaviour: Can't you leave foreign Humours and Things, to their own Mismanagement and Bias? Your business is only to mind your Conduct, and give a Turn of Advantage to the Emergency. Now you may be the better for the Misfortune, if you will but take care, and do nothing but what is warrantable. Always remember, that Accidents are indifferent in themselves, and only good, or bad for us, accordingly as we use them.

"LX. Look Inwards, and turn over your self; For you have a lasting Mine of Happiness at home, if you will but Dig for't."

p 126 "LXIV. 'Tis a saying of Plato's, that no Body misses Truth by their Good-will."

p 127 "LXVI. Don't return the Temper of Ill-natur'd People upon themselves, nor treat them as they do the rest of Mankind."

p 159 "I suppose you understand the Plague too well not to run away from it? And what's the Plague? Why if you are a Knave, or a Libertine, you have the Tokens upon you. The Infection of the Mind is ten times worse then that of the Air: The Malignity is not near so fatal in the Blood, as in the Will; For the Brute only suffers in the first Case, but the Man in the other."

p 160 "IV. He that commits a Fault Abroad, is a Trespasser at Home; And he that injures his Neighbour, hurts himself, for to make himself an ill Man is a shrew'd Mischief."

"V. Omissions no less than Commissions, are oftentimes Branches of Injustice."

p 165 "XVIII. Examine the size of Peoples Sense and the Condition of their Understanding, and you'l never be fond of Popularity, or afraid of Censure."

"XX. Don't disturb your self about the Irregularities of other People, but let every bodies Fault lye at their own Doors."

p 170–1 "XXXI. Be always Easie, and Upright; Let Fortitude Guard without, and Honesty within; Keep your Mind, and your Motions true to the Interest of Mankind, for then you know your Faculties are in the right Posture, that Nature has set them."

p 177 "This is a sign that you had a mercenary View, and that you were but a Huckster in the Mask of a Friend"

p 178 "[You have humour'd your own] Nature, and acted upon your Constitution; and must you still have something over and above? This is just as if an Eye, or a Foot should demand a Sallery for their Service, and not see a Pin, or move a Step, without something for their Pains. For as these

Organs are contriv'd for particular Functions, which when they perform, they pursue their Nature, and attain their perfection; So Man is made to be Kind, and Oblige, and his Faculties are ordered accordingly. And therefore when he does a good Office, and proves serviceable to the World, he follows the Bent, and answers the End of his Being; and when he does so, he moves smoothly, and is always in the best Condition."

pp 178–9 "O My Soul are you ever to be rightly Good, Uncompounded, and Uniform, Unmask'd, and made more Visible to your self than the Body that hangs about you? Are you ever likely to Relish Good Nature, and General Kindness, as you ought? Will you ever be fully satisfied, get above Want, and Wishing, and never desire to fetch your pleasure out of any Thing Foreign, either Living, or Inanimate? Not desiring I say, either Time for longer Enjoyment, nor Place for Elbow-room, nor Climate for good Air, nor the Musick of good Company? Can you abstract your self thus from the World, and take your leave of all Mortals, and be contented with your present Condition, let it be what it will? And be persuaded that you are fully furnish'd, that all things will do well with you..."

p 191 "XX. That's best for every Man which God sends him; and the time of his sending too, is always a Circumstance of Advantage."

p 194 "XXIX. Consider the satisfactions of Life singly, and examine them as they come up; And then ask your self, if Death is such a terrible Bugbear in taking them from you?"

pp 196–7 "XXXII. Put it out of the Power of Truth to give you an ill Character; And if any Body reports you not to be an Honest, or a Good Man, let your Practice give him the Lye: This is all very feasible: For pray who can hinder you from being Just, Sincere, and Good Natur'd if you have a mind to it? To make all sure, you should resolve to live no longer then you can live Honestly; For, in earnest, you had much better be Nothing, than a Knave."

p 205 "IV. Have I oblig'd any Body, or done the World any Service? If so, the Action has rewarded me; This Answer will encourage Good Nature, therefore let it always be at Hand."

p 208 "IX. Never grow sour upon Peoples Malice, or Impertinence: Can they beat you off your Reason, or stop your Progress in Virtue; Not at all. Be not then Disconcerted, nor check your Good-nature towards them. If you meet with Opposition and Ill-will, you must neither be Diverted, nor Disturb'd, but keep your Point, and your Temper too. For as 'tis a Weakness to loose your Spirits, and be thrown off your Conduct, so 'tis likewise to be angry with Impertinent People: Upon the whole; They are both a sort of Deserters from Providence, who are either frighten'd from their Duty, or fall out with those of their own Nature, and Family."

p 217. "That to wish all People may do ill Things is to wish an impossibility, and no better then a piece of Distraction. But then to give them leave to plague other Folks, and desire to be priviledged your self, is a Foolish and a Haughty expectation."

p 218 "Now this is a very bad Character. There's Three of them: And whatever you are conscious degrades the Diviner part of you, makes your Mind Truckle to your Body, and your Reason to your Pleasure, look upon that as the Fourth."

pp 220–1 "XXVII. The Pythagoreans would have us look up into the Sky every Morning: To put us in mind of the Order, and Constancy of the Heavenly Bodies, of the Equality and Perpetuity of their Motion, of the Fineness and Purity of their Matter, and how frankly they lye open to Observation; for a Star never wears a Mask, nor puts any Cloaths on."

p 227 "VI. Accustom your self to Master things of the greatest difficulty, and which you seem to despair of; For if you observe, the Left-hand, tho' for want of Practice, 'tis insignificant to other Business, yet it holds the Bridle better than the Right, because it has been used to it."

p 229 "XI. What a mighty privilege is a Man born to, since 'tis in his power not to do any thing but what God Almighty approves, and to be satisfied with all the Distributions of Providence."

p 236 "XXIX. The best Provision for a happy Life, is to dissect every Thing, view it on all Sides, and Divide it into Matter and Form. To practise Honesty in good earnest, and speak Truth from the very Soul of you: And when you have done this, live easy and chearful; And crowd one Good Action so close to another, that there may not be the least Empty, or Insignificant space between them."

p 238 "XXXIII. The great Business of a Man, is to improve his Mind, and govern his Manners; this is minding the main Chance. As for all other Projects, and Pursuits, whether in our Power to compass or not, they are no better than Trifling, and Amusement."

p 239 "XXXV. He that likes no Time so well as that fixt by Providence, he that's indifferent whether he has room for a long Progress in Reason, and Regularity or not, or whether he has a few or a great many Years to view the World in; a Person thus qualified will never be afraid of dying."

"XXXVI. . . . No, you quit the Stage as fairly as a Player does that has his Discharge from the Master of the Revels: But I have only gone through three Acts, and not held out to the end of the Fifth. You say well; but in Life three Acts make the Play entire. He that appoints the Entertainment is the best Judge of the length on't . . ."

Gataker's "Discourse" p 16 ". . . the Glutton lays all upon the tip of his Tongue, and swallows his Estate like a poached Egg. And which is more, these Excesses make the Carkass smart as well as the Pocket."

KARL FRIEDRICH BAHRDT

1741–1792

Des Herrn D. Bahrdts Glaubens-Bekänntniss mit Anmerkungen von Joh. Friedrich Jacobi. Zelle 1780. 8º.

Victoria College Library (Coleridge Collection)

Monogram at the foot of the title-page in an unidentified hand reading perhaps "A W 34".

MS TRANSCRIPT. VCL BT 52: EHC transcript inserted in the volume. There is no clear sign that EHC made his transcript before C's long note was cropped.

DATE. c 1807–12, or later.

The long note **2**, which C evidently consulted when he was writing *AR* (1825) 313, was perhaps in the first place associated with the projected "Mysteries of Christianity" that was to be a supplement to the 1809–10 *Friend*: see *CL* III 279 (21 Jan 1810), *CN* III 3678 (c Jan–Feb 1810), 3847, 3892–3 (c Jun 1810). It appears that the suspension of *The Friend* in Mar 1810, the onset of ill-health and personal distress in London from late Oct 1810, and the demands of his work for the *Courier*, deflected him from a project that had to wait to be absorbed into *AR* some years later.

1 p 11

[Jacobi's footnote to Bahrdt's pronouncement that many Christian doctrines (including that of the divinity of Christ) are contrary both to scriptures and to reason. Many great men, Jacobi says, have found these doctrines consistent with their reason:] Sind denn *Neuton**, *Boyle*, *Leibnitz*,† *Boerhave*, *Werlhof*, *Haller*, *Pütter*, *Michaelis*, *Kaestner*, keine Geister von einem vorzüglichen Range? Haben sie keine Vernunft von einigem Wehrte?

[Are *Newton, Boyle, Leibniz, Boerhaave, Werlhof, Haller, Pütter, Michaelis, Kaestner* not outstanding minds? Does their power of reason not possess some merit?]

* a Socinian[1]   † credat qui credere vult!![2]

1[1] Sir Isaac Newton (1642–1727) was accused of Socinianism in his own lifetime, and certainly shows little enthusiasm for the trinitarian doctrine even in his published works. C had read some of Newton's theological writing as early as 1796 (*CN* I 82–3), and later came to regard him as one

197

2 pp 89–97, cropped

[Jacobi's footnote:][1] ...Zu dem Ende sandte er seinem eingebohrnen Sohn in die Welt, Joh. 3 Cap. 16 V. Begnadigungen, welche schlecht weg geschehen und deren man viele Tausende, ja Millionen theilhaftig machet, wenn solches gleich unter der Bedingung wahrer Besserung geschiehet, haben die allernachtheiligsten Folgen. ... Künftige Tugenden können die grösten Laster zudecken. Die Gesetze verlieren hierbey ihre Kraft und der Gesetzgeber erhält das

of "the Theists of the mechanic school". *BL* ch 12 (1907) I 184n.

"Socinian" originally meant a follower of the doctrine of Faustus Socinus (1539–1604), one of the earliest leaders (in Poland) of the anti-trinitarians. He argued that Luther and Calvin had not gone far enough in establishing that the human reason was the only sound basis for Protestantism. Eventually he attacked many of the chief Christian dogmas: the divinity of Christ, propitiatory sacrifice, original sin, human depravity, the doctrine of necessity, and justification by faith. C included him in his list of "Revolutionary Minds" in Nov 1803 (*CN* I 1646). Nevertheless, C considered the Socinian position dangerous and after renouncing Unitarianism—his early attraction to which was probably more political and intellectual than theological—was at pains to assail it. In a letter of 4 Oct 1806 he gives an account of the history of his attitude to Socinianism, for "I was for many years a Socinian". *CL* II 1189–90; see also the central trinitarian letter of 13 Oct 1806, *CL* II 1193–9. By the end of the eighteenth century Socinianism had taken on a "modern" colour, for Priestley had worked out from the mechanistic theories of Hartley the philosophical basis for the later Socinianism. In BÖHME **108** C referred to Socinianism as "the general term for all Heresies that deny or metaphorize the mystery of Redemption and Incarnation"; cf *CN* III 3581 § 7, 3675. In about May 1810 C planned "a full and free Examination of the Credibility of Socinian Christianity, or rather *Jesuism*" (*CN* III

3817; cf 3867, 3870); and in Apr 1814 declared that "it is not even *Religion*" (*CL* III 479)—a thought that carries directly into *AR*. This attack led to a serious misunderstanding with John Prior Estlin, his Unitarian Bristol friend of almost twenty years: see *CL* III 471, 477–8, 492. On Socinianism as pantheism (written at much the same time, 1814–15) see a note on WATERLAND *Vindication of Christ's Divinity* (Cambridge 1719) sig A3. For C's detailed account of Socinianism see *LS* (*CC*) 182–3n. See also *TT* 23 Jun 1834.

1[2] "Let him believe who will!" Leibniz often presents belief as a matter of will, e.g. *Nouveaux Essais* IV 20 § 12. He sought to reconcile Lutherans and Catholics by trying to persuade Catholics to be tolerant. Although C acknowledged in his early Unitarian days that Leibniz had helped him clarify his own views of the nature of God, he could not find in Leibniz, any more than in Locke, Berkeley, or Hartley, "an abiding place for my reason". *BL* chs 9, 10 (1907) I 93, 136. See also *CL* II 676, 702–3 (1801); *CN* II 2443, 2584, 2596, 2598 (c Feb–Jun 1805). C wrote several notes on LEIBNIZ *Theodicee* (Hanover & Leipzig 1763). For other linkings of the names of Newton and Leibniz see ABBT **1** and AURELIUS **66**.

2[1] This footnoted edition of Bahrdt's rationalistic "confession of faith"—by Johann Friedrich Jacobi (1712–91), an evangelical theologian and the uncle of Friedrich Heinrich Jacobi the philosopher—was one of fifteen attacks on and refutations of Bahrdt to be published soon after his work first appeared (1779).

Ansehen, als sey er sehr gleichgültig bey seinen Gesetzen und seine Drohungen seyn kein Ernst.... Weltliche Monarchen pflegen daher bey Gesetzen, auf deren Beobachtung das Wol ihrer Staaten beruhet und ihnen daher viel ankommt, nicht schlecht weg zu begnadigen.... So hat auch Gott ... neben der Gnade seinen Ernst, das Unendliche seiner Heiligkeit und Gerechtigkeit offenbahren wollen, damit er eine solche Güte erzeigte, welche den Sünder nicht zur Sicherheit, sondern zur Busse leitete, eine heilsame Gnade kund machte, die uns kräftig antriebe, alles ungöttliche Wesen zu verleugnen.... In dieser Absicht ist das Wort, der eingebohrne Sohn Gottes Mensch worden, hat diese Gnade den Menschen verkündiget ...die von ihnen verwirkte Strafen auf sich legen lassen, ist ein Fluch worden, damit er uns erlösete von dem Fluche des Gesetzes. Er versöhnete die Sünder Gotte, da sie noch seine Feinde waren, er ist daher ein Versöhn-Opfer, dessen Blut uns von der Sünde rein machet und er ist die Versöhnung für der ganzen Welt Sünde.

[... To this end he sent his only-begotten son into the world (John 3.16). Absolute pardons, which thousands—even millions—share, have the most detrimental consequences even when they are contingent on true reformation.... Future virtuous acts can cover up the greatest sins. Laws thereby lose their efficacy and the lawgiver appears indifferent toward his own laws and not serious about his threats.... Earthly monarchs therefore tend not to grant absolute pardons in relation to those laws that matter much to them because on their observance rests the well-being of their state.... Thus God also has ... made manifest, besides his mercy, his severity, the limitlessness of his holiness and justice in order to show that goodness which would lead the sinner not to certainty but to repentance; he proclaimed his salutary mercy to impel us strongly to renounce all ungodly conduct.... For this purpose the Word, the only-begotten Son of God, become man, proclaimed this mercy to men ... he has taken upon himself the punishment incurred by them, has become a curse in order to redeem us from the curse of the law. He atoned for those who sinned against God even while they were still his enemies; he is thus an atonement-sacrifice whose blood cleanses us of sin and he atones for the sin of the whole world.]

This Grotian Theory of Redemption nev[er] can satisfy a thinking mind, much less, a feeling Heart.[2] It is a *mystery*; but if this Theo[ry]

2[2] Hugo Grotius (or de Groot) (1583–1645), Dutch jurist, is best known for his work on international law *De jure belli et pacis* (1625): see also BAXTER *Reliquiae* COPY B **18** n 1. In the theological conflict in Rotterdam between Calvinists and Arminians Grotius sided with the Arminians or Remonstrants and suffered severely for his attempts at reconciliation. His theological work consists of annotations on the Old Testament (1644) and New Testament (1641–6) and the famous *De veritate religionis Christianae* (1627). Notebook entries for the 1820's show that C had by then, if not

were accurate, Redemption would be no myster[y]. What then? [What if a Planter would][a] not forgive a sincerely penitent Slave on the mere condition that his after-conduct should prove the sincerity of his repentance; but demanded, that his eldest Son should suffer the whole of the Punishment? Should we not smile, if we were [.....][b] [not horrified! Could] any thing be imagined more unjust? S[t] Pau[l's] *metaphors* must be explained by S[t] John's Letter: for the *Letter* is here the ~~Meta~~ Spirit.[3] But a Metaphor does not express the Thing: (for how then is it a Metaphor[?)] but the *effect* of the Thing. When I call the ~~Son~~un[4] the Lam[p] of Heav[en] I mea[n] that [the] effec[t] on us is th[e] same as tha[t] of a Lamp [,] not t[hat] the Su[n] is itse[lf] a Lam[p.] So when Pau[l] call[s] the my[st]erio[us] Working of the Incarnate Logos, Redemption, Satisfaction, Atonement, Sacrifice, we are to understand that it produces the same effects that a Redemption from Slavery, the Liquidation of a Debt[,] a re[conci]liati[on] t[o] [.....][c] a Sin-offering, would do: not that it *was* [th]ese things.[5] What then is it?—The privilege [of] being born anew in Christ by taking up his [C]ross, [i]n order to the possibility of which [t]he Logos must have become Man, [a]nd ~~have~~ suffer

---

[a] The first two words are cut in half, and for the last two-thirds of the line of ms only traces of ascenders survive. EHC suggests "[should we think of a Planter who would]" but that is too many words for the gap
[b] A whole line of ms is cut off, leaving traces of about four ascenders at the end of the line. EHC suggests "[not tempted to exclaim, can]"
[c] Again, guessing from ascenders but too wordily, EHC suggests "t[o an offended Deity by way of]"

---

earlier, some acquaintance with Grotius' biblical commentaries—possibly at second hand. An early reference to Grotius, in a letter to RS 2 Sept 1802, contains the kernel of his distaste for what he came to call the "Grotio-Paleyan scheme"—"the judicial, law-cant kind of evidence for Christianity which has been since so much in Fashion". *CL* II 861; see also 1189.

2[3] The primary reference is to 2 Cor 3.5–6: "Not that we are sufficient of ourselves to think any thing as of ourselves; but our sufficiency is of God; Who also hath made us able ministers of the new testament; not of the letter, but of the spirit: for the letter killeth, but the spirit giveth life." In this note C introduces a paradox that he was to explore more fully in *AR*.

See *AR* (1825) 198–200, 307–9n, 311ff. In this note the "*Letter*", or the text given, is John 3.16 (cited by Bahrdt), the announcement by John of a "most important doctrinal Truth": "For God so loved the world, that he gave his only begotten Son..."—the fact to which a "literal" interpretation of Redemption must be referred.

2[4] For this merging of "Son" and "Sun" see AURELIUS 35 n 2. Here, however, it seems a slip of the pen, understandable in the context, but significant nonetheless.

2[5] In *AR* (1825) 313–14 C considers in almost identical terms the points "from which the learned Apostle [Paul] has drawn the four principal Metaphors, by which he illustrates the blessed *Consequences* of Christ's Redemption of Mankind".

Anguish and Death/—[T]he [re]lation [of] the [o]ne to [t]he [o]ther [a]s [c]ause [to] [ef]fect, we [ca]nnot [un]der[s]tand: [fo]r they [be]long [to tr]ue Laws of Spirit, or the World of Noumena (κόσμος νοερος)[6] and all our forms of comprehension are confined to *Phænomena*, or objects of Sense. But for this reason there [can] be no reason a priori against the reality of such a relation—And this is the Sphere, in which Faith must exist, if i[t] exists at all. Thus, I cannot comprehend Freedo[m;] and if it were included in the world of Phænomena, it would involve a contradiction in Terms, an effect without a cause, a Dependence without a previous Link. But it is revealed to me by the Law of Conscience—and I believe the οτι εστι,[7] tho' (it being a Noumenon) it is impossible for me to explain the *How*, or to have any insight into its *possibility*. Sin is is a disease in the Will. The Will is a mystery[:] the Disease is a mystery: must we not therefore [e]xpect, that the Remedy should be a mystery? [I]t is thus, that the Mysteries of Christianity [i]ncrease each the other's credibility not [by] explanation, but by Harmony & [C]onsequentiality. Each has a ground of Faith peculiar to itself, and yet each implies [t]he [ot]her: [wh]ereas [in l]egendary [M]iracles, [ex]plained [b]y [M]iracles, the [i]mprobability [i]s increased [by] the [s]olution. [I]f a [m]an [t]ells me, [t]hat at Rome there are Cabbages as big as the Pantheon, he does not facilitate my *belief* of it by adding, that there was a Pot there to boil it in as large as S[t] Peter's.—For the C[a]bb[age] has no connection with the Pot & neither Pot or Cabbage have a word to say for themse[lves] why they should not have sentence passed on them, as Lies.—S. T. Coleridge.[*a*]

Altogether, I have never met with so repulsive an exposition (say rather, so disgraceful an *exposure*) of the System, which might not inaptly be named, the Pseudo-Pauline[,] & yet it is now in vogue— [I]t were hard to determine, whether the [g]rossness of the Anthropomorphism, or the disparateness of the attempted analogies, are more striking.

Every instance adduced is justifiable [e]ven in earthly governors only by their [w]eakness, [a]nd [t]he [im]per[f]ection of their knowledge. Apply the [su]pposed [c]ase to the Father of a Family— & the hollowness of the conclusions become evident. And how opposite to Christ's own declarations ~~ef~~ in the Parable of the Laborer who came in at the [e]l[even]th Hour? Or of the Prodigal

---

[*a*] Here p 95 ends; the note makes a fresh start on p 96. What follows continues the line of thought; there is no change in the ink or hand to suggest that the continuation was written at a different time

2[6] "Intellectual universe".   2[7] "[The fact] that it *is*".

Son?[8] O never, never could you destroy a Soul that loved him however imperfectly/—The[se] writers always suppose repentance; wherea[s] the gif[t] of Christian Repentance is itself a part of the Redemption. I almost wish, that the Church had confined itself to the expressi[on] of S[t] John: & Regeneration, and the grow[th] in to Christ by participation of his spiritual Humanity, had been the only literal Terms[9]

2[8] Matt 20.1–16; Luke 15.11–22.

2[9] For the "expression of John" (John 3.16) see 2 n 3, above. See also an earlier part of Jesus's reply to Nicodemus: "Except a man be born again, he cannot see the kingdom of God." John 3.3; cf 5.7. See also BAXTER *Catholick Theologie* 2.

PETER AUGUSTINE BAINES

1786–1843

Faith, Hope, and Charity. The substance of a sermon preached at the dedication of the Catholic chapel at Bradford, in the County of York, on Wednesday, July 27, 1825. [Second edition.] London 1827. 8⁰.

"Printed for the Defence Committee of the British Catholic Association".

Bound as No 1 in "PAMPHLETS—DIVINITY", a volume comprising eight tracts 1824–33 (three of them annotated by C) made up after C's death.

British Museum C 126 h 2(1)

DATE. 1827 or later.

COEDITOR. James D. Boulger.

1 p 2, pencil

Faith ... teaches us to believe, without doubting, doctrines which we cannot comprehend, on the testimony of God, who has taught them.

This is, me saltem judice,[1] the Queen Bee in the Hive of Romish— would that I dared say only of Romish—Error.[2] Yet the Sophism is palpable: inasmuch as the congruity of an asserted Revelation with Reason & Conscience is an indispensable part, or condition of its evidence. *S. T. C.*

2 pp 2–3, pencil

Charity, then, is something more than benevolence. What is it? It is a virtue which regards God as well as man. It would be a partial and imperfect virtue, indeed, if it excluded God; the most perfect,

1[1] "In my judgement at least".

1[2] C's first use of the queen bee as the image of a radical sophism that proliferates error seems to have been on 7 Feb 1805 (*CN* II 2434); the term is not distinct from his recurrent phrase πρῶτον ψεῦδος but is more potent and ominous inasmuch as he habitually refers it to the grounds of religion and morality. This particular error involves an unexamined identi-fication of moral terms in such a way as to induce a circular argument and so to inhibit or preclude the exercise of reason: e.g. identification of faith and opinion (CHILLINGWORTH COPY A 5, c Apr 1809), assumption of the literal truth of the Gospels (DONNE *Sermons* COPY A 6, 1809–10), faith as suspension of reason (as here), identi-fication of reason with understanding (*C&S*—*CC*—171).

the most amiable, the only adorable being, the first of benefactors, the best of friends, the most tender and loving of parents. ... It teaches us to worship him in the manner he requires, and consequently to follow the religion which we sincerely believe to have been established by Him. For should any man say to God, "I love thee, O God, but I will not worship thee in the manner which thou hast commanded, but in a manner which I consider as good or better;" would he not offer an affront to God?

If a man *sincerely* believes a particular form of Worship to be God's express will and ordinance, he must be *man* before he could "say to God, I will not so worship thee!" And what a precious Virtue this popish *Charity* must be, which according to this Baynes, Bishop of Siga (well for him had he complied with the advice, σιγα!)[1] consists in abstaining from an impossible crime!—But Baynes means by sincerely believing a doctrine an unquestioning Reliance on the words of a Priest, without knowing or caring either about the doctrine or the evidence of its divine origin. In ⟨short,⟩ Charity is Bigotry—which is Paddyism & the Inquisition.

3   p 5

... Catholics, as well as you, know the folly, and detest, as much as you, the impiety of giving divine honours to a lifeless piece of wood or ivory, however skilfully the sculptor may have fashioned it. ...

"*But do we not worship and pray to the saints?*" We worship *no creature whatever*, and therefore not the saints. "*But at least we pray to them?*" Yes, my Christian brethren, just as St Paul prayed to his own converts, or I pray to you.

Impudent Sophism! Do we pray to Capt[n] Parry & his Crew—O brave Heroes! hear us in your great mercy from your Car-boat in the frozen Ocean?[1]—Do we practically attribute omnipresence to our fellow-men?—

2[1] Baines entered the Benedictine order in 1804, became priest in 1810, bp of Siga in 1823, vicar-apostolic of the Eastern district in 1829. The Greek word σίγα means "Be silent!".

3[1] William Edward Parry (1790–1855; knighted 1829, rear-admiral 1852) was a commander under Ross in the Arctic in 1818 and led three expeditions in search of the Northwest Passage in 1819–20, 1821–3, 1824–5. In 1827 he tried to reach the North Pole from Spitzbergen over the ice by sledge-boat (car-boat), was stopped by adverse currents, but established a Farthest North that was to stand for fifty years. His *Narrative of the Attempt to Reach the North Pole* was published in 1827. Captain Parry's two elder brothers, Charles and Frederick, were C's companions—with Charles Greenough, Clement Carlyon, John Chester, and the younger Blumenbach —on the Harzreise, or "Carlyon-Parry-Green-ation", that C made in the spring of 1799.

RACHEL BAKER

b 1794

Remarkable Sermons of Rachel Baker and pious ejaculations, delivered during sleep, taken in shorthand, with remarks of Drs. Mitchell, Priestley, and Douglass. London 1815.

Not located; marginalia not recorded. *Green SC* (1880) 19: "With an interesting MS. note by S. T. Coleridge, of 44 lines." *Lost List.*

Rachel Baker was born in Pelham, Massachusetts, to a Presbyterian family. On 28 Nov 1811 she first talked in her sleep. Medical interest was aroused and records began to be made of her "pious ejaculations" in sleep. There is an "Account of Her Life" in the American book from which the London ed was apparently taken: *Devotional Somnium; or, a Collection of Prayers and Exhortations, uttered by Miss Rachel Baker, in the city of New York, in the winter of 1815, during her abstracted and unconscious states; to which pious and unprecedented exercises is prefixed, An Account of Her Life*, &c (New York 1815).

FRANCESCO BALDOVINI
1634–1716

Lamento di Cecco da Varlungo di Francesco Baldovini con la versione latina ed annotazioni. Si aggiungono la risposta della Sandra e la disdetta di Cecco nuovi idilli rusticali[.] Seconda edizione corretta ed accresciuta dell' idillio in Morte della Sandra, &c. Florence 1806. 8º (half-sheet).

Collection of Kathleen Coburn

Autograph inscription in ink on p ⁻2: "S. T. Coleridge Jan. 4. 1806." Bookplate of Phillips Brooks on p ⁻7 (p–d).

CN II App A (p 399) suggests that C bought this book "during his brief and penniless visit to Florence", because of his interest in Italian dialects.

CONTENTS. Pp 1–29, *Lamento di Cecco* (Italian text on verso pages, Latin version on recto); pp 31–46, Luigi Clasio *La Sandra da Varlungo idillio rusticale che risponde per le desinenze all' idillio del Baldovini*; pp 47–62, Cammillio Alisio *La Disdetta di Cecco da Varlungo idillio rusticale*; pp 63–74, Luigi Clasio *Lamento di Cecco da Varlungo in morte della Sandra idillio rusticale*; pp 75–132, Notes. The first edition of the *Lamento* was published in 1694.

DATE. Early 1806, after 4 Jan.

1 p 2, cropped | *Lamento di Cecco* st II lines 3–4

> Che, Diascol! t' ho fatt' io, Bocchin di mele,
> Che tu siei sì caparbia, e arrapinata?

[What the devil have *I* done to you, my darling, that you are so wilful and ill-tempered?]

[wha]t, the deuce!

2 p 2 | II 7–8

> Anzi mentre il me' cor <u>trassini</u> e struggi,
> I' ti vengo dirieto, e tu mi fuggi.

[... Rather, while you are tormenting and destroying me, I come after you and you flee from me.]

trattare, maltrattare[1]

2[1] Provided by the editorial note (p 77).

3 p 4, cropped | III 1–4

> Ma fuggi pure, e fuggi quanto il vento,
>   Ch' i' vo' seguirti infin drento all' Onferno;
> Che di star liviritta i' so contento,
> Purch' i' stia teco in mezzo al fuoco aterno.

[But flee, then, flee like the wind, for I shall follow you right into hell; for being in that very place I am content if I may be with you in the midst of the eternal fire.]

[ib]i rectà, i.e. in [q]uel luogo lì.[1]

4 p 4, cropped | IV 5–8

> Come i' ti veggo i' sono alto e biato,
> Comunche i' non ti veggo, i' vo 'n fracasso,
> E ch' e' si trovi al Mondo un, che del bene
> Ti voglia piùe, non è mai ver, non ene.

[When I see you I am exalted and happy; whenever I do not see you, I am broken, and it is not true that any man in the world loves you more than I do—not true.]

beato[1]
seu cado [in] ruinam [tur]bulentam.[2]
[non] ene, i.e. non è nessuno.[3]

5 p 4, cropped | v 1–2

> E pur tu mi dileggi, e non mi guati,
>   Se non con gli occhi biechi, e 'l viso arcigno.

[And yet you deride me, and you only look at me askance and with a surly expression.]

[d]eridi[1]

3[1] Both the Latin and Italian phrases are given in the editorial note (p 77): "in that very place". The Latin version on p 5 reads *illic*.

4[1] Provided by the note (p 78).

4[2] The note (p 78) gives the gloss *andare in rovina*—"to fall (go) in ruins". C's Latin gloss seems to seek the force of *fracasso*—"or 'I fall into confused ruins' ".

4[3] If C had read the note (p 78) carefully he would have seen that *non è mai ver, non ene* is an intensive repetition common with rustic people— "it is not true, not true". His own (inaccurate) version is "there is not any one [at all]".

5[1] From the note (p 78).

6 p 6, cropped | vɪɪ 1

> Donche al me' tribolío presto soccorri,

[So, quickly relieve my tribulation before I am in my grave...]

[al]la mia [tri]bolazione[1]

7 p 6 | vɪɪ 5–8

> Altro, Sandra, ci vuol, che far lo gnorri,
> Tu fai viste ch' i' canti, e i' me la batto.
> Guata il mie viso sì malconcio e grullo,
> E vedrai ch' i' mi muoio, e non mi brullo.

[It is more than a matter, Sandra, of playing the fool: you pretend that I am only singing when I am actually dying. See how drawn and stupefied my face is, and you will see that I am dying, not joking.]

me ne vo i.e. nell' altro mon[do][a][1]
burlo[2]

8 p 6 | vɪɪɪ 3–4

> Stia sempre in su' miei campi il tempo nero,
> E le pecore mie manichi il lupo.

[Let the dark weather remain over my fields, and let the wolf devour my sheep.]

mangi[1]

9 p 8, cropped | ɪx 5–6

> E sì da un ago il cor mi sentii punto,
> Che 'n vederti restai mogio e balordo;

[And as though my heart had been pierced by a needle, seeing you I was left stunned and dull ...]

mogio forte vult [dic]ere idem, [q]uod apud [An]glos *mopy/* [a] perfect *mope.*[1]

[a] Letters lost in the gutter in rebinding

6[1] The note (p 80) provides *tribolazione* for *tribolío*; C has expanded the phrase.

7[1] The whole phrase *me ne vo nell' altro Mondo* is given in the note (p 81).

7[2] From the note (p 81), which says that *brullare* is a metathesis for *burlare*.

8[1] From the note (p 82), which glosses *manichi* as *mangi, divori.*

9[1] "*Mogio* means perhaps the same as *mopy* in English usage"—an acute suggestion. The Latin version has *enervis* (weak, nerveless); the note (p 81) gives *sbalordito* (stunned, stupefied).

10 p 8, cropped | x 1–4

> I' non fo cosa piùe, che vadia a verso,
> Comincio un' opra, e non la so fornire;
> S' i' aro, i' do col bombere a traverso,
> S' i' fo una fossa, i' non ne so nescire.

[Nothing I do goes with the grain. I begin a piece of work and don't know how to make it go; if I plough, the ploughshare goes crooked; if I dig a ditch, I don't know how to get out of it.]

Anglicè, that goes *in tune*[1]
vomere, plough-[s]hare.[2]

11 p 8, cropped | xi 3

> Più no sciolvo, o merendo . . .

[I no longer breakfast or dine . . .]

[bre]akfast or [d]ine.[1]

12 p 8 | xi 5–6

> Solo ho disío di gaveggiar coresto
> Bel viso tuo sì gaio, e sì pulito;

[I desire only to devour that beautiful face of yours, so pleasant and so smooth...]

cotesto—to gaze on *"that there"* fair face of thine so gladsome & neat.[1]

13 p 10, cropped | xii 1–2

> Mal fu per me quel die, quand' unguannaccio
> Tu vienisti a' miei campi . . .

[Bad for me was that day, and evil the year, when you came to my fields...]

[ques]to malo [an]no—[1]

10[1] A happy suggestion.
10[2] From the note (p 83).
11[1] The note (p 84) is interesting, but C could have worked this out for himself from the common *merenda*, now "lunch" but earlier "late afternoon dinner".
12[1] C has turned *sì gaio, e sì pulito* neatly. The crux, however, is *coresto* (modern *cotesto*), derived from Latin *iste*—demonstrative adjective associated with the second person and a middle distance—"that fair face of yours". There is a note on *coresto* on p 85.
13[1] "This bad year". The phrase *in quest' anno* appears in the note (p 85); C has inserted the word *malo* to correspond to the (weaker) pejorative implication of the suffix *-accio*.

14   p 10 | xii 3–4

   E' mi salse intru l' ossa un fuoco, e un diaccio,
   Ch' i' veddi mille lucciole golare;

[And there came into my bones fire and ice, for I saw a thousand fireflies
fly[1] ...]

giaccio[2]
volare.[3]

14A   pp 14, 15 | [x]ix 2 (Italian and Latin)

   Ch' i' vo' vedere un po', come la vane,
   Nam spectare iuvat quo res tandem exeat,

[For I wish to see a little how things may go.[1] (Latin: For it is good to
see how things may turn out in the end.)]

14[1] The note (p 86) explains at
length that "to see a thousand fireflies (or glow-worms) fly" means "to
feel a great grief". In view of C's use
of the images of firefly and glow-worm
in crucial notes on love it is curious
that he did not comment on this
striking idiomatic figure or use it
elsewhere. Perhaps after all he did not
read the note and so took the phrase
at face-value.

14[2] *Giaccio* (tiller) in error for
ghiaccio (ice)—possibly a word familiar
to C's ear in Malta. *Diaccio*, the more
usual form, is not glossed in the note.
   14[3] *Volar* is suggested in the note
(p 86).
   14A[1] The reason for underlining is
not clear, unless perhaps the Latin
version helped resolve the Italian
phrase.

JOHN BANIM
1798–1842

MICHAEL BANIM
1796–1874

Tales by the O'Hara Family. Second Series. Comprising "The Nowlans", and "Peter of the Castle". [Anonymous.] 3 vols. London 1826. 12º.

Victoria College Library (Coleridge Collection)

Inscribed on the title-page of Vol I: "From the Author". Autograph signature of Edward Sterling on I ⁻1, II ⁻1. Marked "Green Bequest".

   Edward Sterling (1773–1847), journalist and member of *The Times* staff 1815–40, was the father of John Sterling (1806–44), who, having first met C in 1828 through Julius Charles Hare (1795–1850), became an admirer of C and for a time a vigorous exponent of his work. *L* II 771n, *CL* VI 932–3n. When John Banim was ill and suffering under savage reviews of *The Boyne Water* (1826), Edward Sterling befriended him. Because of hostile criticism *The Boyne Water* was not included in the series of *Tales by the O'Hara Family*, even though *The Nowlans* had been written "in furtherance of our Boyne Water". The second series of *Tales* probably came to C through John Sterling in the early months of their acquaintance and seems to have been in C's possession at the time of his death. It was John Banim's ambition to be recognised as the Walter Scott of Ireland. See *CRB* I 348–9, II 705.

DATE. 1828 or later.

1   I ⁻1, referring to I 228, pencil, below the signature of Edward Sterling | *The Nowlans* ch 10

[John Nowlan meets Frank Adams and accuses him of going to meet his sister Maggy Nowlan. Adams admits that this is so and says that he intends marriage and has made a proposal. Adams in turn charges John Nowlan with going to meet *his* sister, Letty Adams, and says that he knows she loves Nowlan. Nowlan, in extreme distress (being a priest), pleads his vow of celibacy; but Adams dismisses that objection with levity.]

P. 228. Let Mr Cooper in his envy of or Antipathy to England and

Englishmen invent or rather manufacture English Fools, English Scoundrels, English Cowards, ~~and~~ make Heroes and Bayards of Yankee Majors, and let ⟨a[n]⟩ American *Pirate* fight and take ⟨a⟩ British Man of War, of twice ~~their~~ his weight of Metal,[1] But to introduce a moral *Monster*, an olla podrida of Vices and Villainie[s,] a cold scheming black-hearted Miscre~~a~~tent—and (o marvellous!) in the person of a highly-gifted, highly educated Scholar and Gentleman, young and handsome—& finally, to make him an *Oxonian* and a *Protestant* in contrast with an erring but amiable *Catholic* Priest of ⟨pure⟩ *Irish* Breeding—o this was beneath a Writer of Banim's Genius. Tis such a cheap, hackneyed trick of Faction/ S. T. C.—

2   I 248, pencil

[Frank Adams, questioned by his uncle, denies that he has "paid any particular attentions to Miss Nowlan" and questioned about a "change in Letty's manner of late" dismisses his uncle's suggestion that she may be in love with John Nowlan.]

There is a *clumsiness* in this excess of Baseness, that disgusts one's Common Sense/—In short, the whole character is a woeful Failure. To render a *Villain* interesting in a Tale or Drama, the intellectual ~~must~~ superiority must be ever prominent—as in Iago, Edmund, Rich. III—./[1]

3   I 284, pencil | Ch 12

[At a dinner of welcome John Nowlan meets his former school-fellow Mike Horrogan; John regards "this specimen of a conversion from his own faith with mixed alarm and interest".]

1[1] James Fenimore Cooper (1789–1851) first met C at William Sotheby's on 22 Apr 1828 and later in the same month paid C a visit at Highgate. J. F. Cooper *Gleanings in Europe* ed R. E. Spiller (1930) II 332. The sea-battle C refers to is in *The Red Rover* (1827) vol III ch 10; the first English ed of that book in 1828 was published at Sotheby's instigation.

2[1] On 23 Dec 1810 C had told HCR that Shakespeare "delighted in portraying characters in which the intellectual powers were found in a preëminent degree, while the moral faculties were wanting", and cited Iago, Richard III, and Falstaff. *Sh C* II 165. C regularly developed this theme in his Shakespeare lectures from 1811 to 1818–19; on the first occasion HCR found C's "disquisitions" on these characters "full of paradox, but very ingenious and in the main fine", and Lamb, who had also heard the lecture, took up the theme with enthusiasm. *Sh C* II 181, cf 26, 141, 237; II 165. In the 1818–19 lectures (or perhaps earlier) C had dropped Falstaff from the group and substituted Edmund. *Sh C* II 259. He considered Iago to be Shakespeare's greatest triumph in portraying a character who was both highly intellectual and deeply wicked. *Sh C* I 52. See also *BL* ch 23 (1907) II 189.

"Have you imparted much to the crowd of poor famishing souls we left you with in the village, Mr. Horrogan?" asked Mr. Stokes....

"Nations to me, no, Sir, no," answered Mr. Horrogan, with a hoarse laugh that, when very much excited, was the climax of his sputtering titter—"poor creatures! they only shillooed at me, as usual, poor creatures, *you* see," (placing the genuine southern emphasis on the *you*) "when I was just beginning to lay down my syllogism, by which I intended to show, to a Q. E. D. that, sowls and bodies, they were all in darkness and error and peril; and then, it's my head they wanted to break;" (another ho[a]rse laugh)—"and I was forced to be off, in a ratio, I'm quite of opinion, with the velocity of a man riding far the bare life, *you* see."

To what gross improbabilities will not party spirit reconcile a man's imagination!—as, that such a Creature, as Mr Horrogan, could have been trusted by a Mr Stokes!—

4   I 288, pencil

[Mr Long:] "And yet I believe the people of Ireland understand their own religion ... none of us deny that; and if so, containing as it does, and as all Christian sects do, many of the great dogmas in which we believe, I scarce see how the darkness of Ireland can be called a religious darkness; unless, we call the creed of an Alfred, *] a Bede, a Fenelon, a More, a Ganganelli, or a Montesquieu, by such a name ...".

*An assumption that Alfred, Bede &c rested their faith on the doctrines, which Protestants rejected.

5   I 295, pencil

[Mr Long:] "... Although Camden authorizes us to assume for Ireland, in the sixth century, a great literary reputation; and although such assumption would not leave her unlearned, nor unenlightened at the visit of Henry II., in 1172, (her priests, alone, appearing as her tutors,) yet let us avoid that point altogether."

Much, I conceive, as Petersburg might be justly celebrated for its Astronomers & Mathematicians, i.e. its Learned *Societies*[1]—But

5[1] Catherine I founded the Academy of Science in St Petersburg in 1725, and by the time the University was founded in 1819 St Petersburg was renowned as a centre of scientific achievement. In Ireland the tradition of learning was much older than in St Petersburg, more widespread, and much more deep-rooted. E.g. the abbey of Clonard in the sixth century under the rule of Finnian accepted 3000 students at a time.

did the Irish People partake of this knowlege existing in her Monasteries?

6 i 298, pencil

"But why have not the priests done their duty since the wisdom of the legislature mercifully repealed the law [forbidding *Roman Catholics to teach in a school publicly, or in a private house, or as ushers to protestants*]?" asked Mr. Stokes ...

But Mr Banim can not but know, that for generations the unrepealed Law had not been acted on, in that no opposition was made to Catholic Schoolmasters.[1]

7 i 299, pencil

[Mr Long:] "... I recollect nearly forty years back; and, from my own observations, in different parts of Ireland, I can say that the Catholic priests have, during that period, been zealous and very successful too, in educating the poor of their flock."

Precious the effects!

6[1] For C's insistence on the obligations of the learned to "national civilization" see *C&S* (*CC*) e.g. 53–4. The act that provided the penalty of life-imprisonment for keeping a Catholic school in Ireland, not rigorously enforced for many years, was not abolished until 1778. By 1791 Catholic worship and the formation of Catholic schools were tolerated, and in 1793 Catholics in Ireland were admitted to the franchise, the universities, and the professions.

JOHANN CONRAD BARCHUSEN

1666–1723

Johannis Conradi Barchusen Elementa chemiae, quibus subjuncta est confectura lapidis philosophici imaginibus repraesentata. Leyden 1718. 4º.

University of Pennsylvania Library (E. F. Smith Collection)

Impression of a rubber stamp on the title-page: "J. H. B. Williams. 1817." This is crossed out in ink and the name "S. T. Coleridge Esqre" written beside it in ink. Inscribed on p $^{-}2$ in Williams's hand: " S. T. Coleridge E Dono J. H. B. Williams 7th Octr 1819." Inscribed by C on p $^{-}2$: "John Hartwell Bonnell Williams—Lord bless you, Sir! We have not room for half of you!" Bookplate of Charles F. Cox, New York, on front pastedown.

John Williams was for a time medical assistant to James Gillman; letters from C to him are preserved for Sept 1816 onwards. A notebook entry of 20 Oct 1819 shows C making efforts to prevent Williams from "acting as an ungrateful serpent to Mr Gillman": this is a draft for the detailed memorandum sent by C to Williams on the same day. N 21½ f 44^v; *CL* IV 957–62. The issue arose over Williams's desire to become Gillman's professional partner, a position for which Gillman did not consider him competent. The copy of FIELDING *Tom Jones* (4 vols 1773) that C annotated belonged first to Williams's father and has the bookplate of the Rev James Gillman.

DATE. c Oct 1819.

1 p $^{+}$1, referring to p 505 | Pt iii. Liber singularis de Alchimia vel Chrysopoeia §21 "Confectio lapidis philosophorum per imagines expressa"

Decima quarta docet aurum, leonem, per stibium, Chemicorum lupum, purgandum esse. Nam aurum cum antimonio fusum in regulum convertitur, qui ob gravitatem ad ima vasis subsidet, metallis interea vilioribus, quae auro antea erant immixta, scoriis inhaerentibus, ut autem Leo denuo in libertatem vindicetur, i.e. ad ipsi admixto stibio separetur, necesse est regulum igni intenso imponi, sic destructo antimonio aurum rursus sui juris fit.

[Fig 14 teaches that gold, the Lion, is to be purged by antimony, the wolf of the Chemists.[1] For gold fused with antimony is converted into a

1[1] In Fig 14 the creature looks more like a toad (as C's note attests). A toad also represented *stibium*, or antimony sulphide. The alchemists

215

regulus,[2] which from its weight sinks to the bottom of the vessel, while the baser metals, which had formerly been mixed with the gold, inhere in the dross; but for the Lion to be set free again, that is, for it to be separated from the antimony that has been mixed with it, the regulus must be placed on an intense heat, and so the antimony is broken down and the gold comes into its own again.]

p. 505—tabula precedent. Fig. 14.—Leo designat vires igneas ingenii poetici.—Cens. Anon. Edin.—vid.—Arcana recensendi—. N.b.—Hinc liquet, buffooned a *Bufone*—Poeta bufonatus, *toaded*, sive toad-eaten—Q?—teutonicè getödtet?[3]

probably did purify antimony, but their terminology cannot be accurately translated.

[12] According to p 126, when a metal or mineral is fused with antimony and poured into a conical or pyramidical vessel, the purer parts sink and make the form of a *regulus*. See also *OED* "regulus".

[13] Fig 14 (see Plate 5) consists of a twofold alchemical device: in a circle, a lion breathing a luxuriant stream of fire, which also burns beneath his feet; below, flanked by two small symbols (which, according to Barchusen's "Signorum apud Chemicos usitatorum explicatio", stand for *on the left* oil/fire, *on the right* mercury/distillation/water), a toad—i.e. wolf: see n 1, above—with the hind quarters and tail of the lion protruding from the toad's mouth. C's comment is a linked pun: "In Fig 14—the illustration preceding p 505—the Lion represents the fiery strength of poetic genius.—[Being devoured by] an Anonymous Edinburgh Critic—see Secret Files of a Reviewee—.N.b. Hence, it is clear, buffooned from *Bufo* [toad]—the Poet *bufonatus*—*toaded*, or toad-eaten—Query—in German '*getödtet*' killed [toaded/deaded]?"

5. Figure 14 from J. C. Barchusen *Elementa chemiae* (Leyden 1718).
See BARCHUSEN **1** and n 3
University of Pennsylvania Libraries; reproduced by kind permission

JOHN BARCLAY
1582–1621

Copy A

Io. Barclaii Argenis. Editio novissima. Cum clave. Hoc est, nominum propriorum elucidatione hactenus nondum edita. Amsterdam (Ex Officina Elzeviriana) 1659. 12°.

Harvard University (Houghton Library)

Inscribed at the head of p ⁻3: "wᵗ the Clavis"; and, perhaps in the same hand, at the head of pp ⁺4, ⁺5, written before C wrote 3, a few letters that look like algebraic expressions. A number of passages have been marked and words underlined throughout the volume, but the marks are not identifiable as C's.

When C was reading *Argenis* COPY A he was not fully informed about the translations of it: see COPY A 3; COPY B was RS's copy of the Le Grys–May translation. He evidently left his own copies of *Argenis* and *Satyricon* behind at Allan Bank in 1810: both are recorded in Wordsworth LC (90, 93) together with WW's copies (91, 92).

DATE. c Jul–Dec 1809. HNC in *LR* dated the notes 1803 without citing evidence, but the reference to Roscoe's *Leo the Tenth* in 3 cannot be earlier than 1805. C acquired his copy of *Argenis* and *Satyricon* apparently at the same time, some time after Feb 1808.

---

1 pp ⁻3–⁻2

Heaven forbid! this Work should not exist in its present form and Language! Yet I cannot avoid the Wish, that it had been, during the reign of James the first, moulded into an heroic poem in English Octava Rima;¹ or *epic* blank Verse/ which however at that time had not been invented, & which, alas! still remains the sole property of the Inventor—as if the Muses had given him an unevadible Patent for it! Of dramatic Blank Verse we have many & various Specimens —ex. gr. Shakspere's as compared with Massinger's—both excellent

---

1¹ C was by this time familiar with *ottava rima*, especially from his reading of Ariosto's *Orlando furioso*: see ARIOSTO **1** n 1. Not until 1817 did Byron pick up from J. H. Frere's *Whistlecraft* prospectus the facetious *ottava rima* for *Don Juan*.

217

in their kind/[2] of lyric, and of what may be called Orphic, or philosophic Blank Verse, perfect Models in Wordsworth[3]—of colloquial
Blank Verse excellent if tho' not perfect, examples in Cowper, &c[4]—
but of epic since Milton not one.—S. T. C.

2 pp ‾1, [2]

In what year did the last [of][a] the *great* Elzevirs die? ⟨*John & Dan:*⟩
The Euphormio is certainly a genuine Elzevir, 1655—"apud Elze-
virios"—but I fear both from type & accuracy that this is indeed no
more than Ex Officinâ Elzevirianâ.[1] S. T. C.—

a Leaf damaged

1[2] For C on dramatic blank verse
generally, see e.g. BEAUMONT &
FLETCHER COPY B 10 and cf 28, 41.

1[3] In Jan 1804 C had praised WW
as "the first & greatest philosophical
Poet". *CL* II 1034. Early in Jan 1807,
at Coleorton, C had listened to WW
reading aloud for the first time the
"1805" *Prelude*; and on 7 Jan had
written his own poem *To William
Wordsworth*, speaking of *The Prelude*
as "—an Orphic Tale indeed, | A Tale
divine of high and passionate thoughts|
To their own music chaunted!" *PW*
(EHC) I 406, MS W version.

1[4] The flexible blank verse used by
Cowper, especially in *The Task*, was
important in shaping the manner of
C's Conversation Poems, and important to WW—whether directly
from Cowper or by way of C's
practice—in discovering his distinctive voice in *Tintern Abbey*. C's early
enthusiasm is celebrated in the phrase
"the divine Chit-Chat of Cowper",
which he and Lamb gallantly ascribed
to each other in 1796 (e.g. *CL* I 279,
LL I 66). Cowper was to have been discussed in a series of critical essays in
Jul 1802. *CL* II 829, and see *CN* I
Index. For C's view in 1798 of Cowper
as "the best modern poet" see
H Works XVII 120, and cf XX 216.

2[1] An unidentified annotator has
tried to answer C's question by writing
on p ‾1 and title-page verso a note
saying *inter alia* that "The genuine
Elzevir Editions in 12mo." of Barclay
were the *Satyricon* (Leyden 1637) and

Argenis (Leyden 1630); the names,
dates, and associations of the "seven
great Elzevirs. (12 altogether)." are
then given.

The history of the Elzevirs, and of
the 1618 titles they produced in 129
years of family printing, is not without
its intricacies. The "last of the *great*
Elzevirs ... ⟨*John & Dan*⟩" were
working together at Leyden 1652–5;
Jean died in 1671, Daniel in 1680. The
golden age of Elzevirian printing was
in the time of Bonaventura and Abraham (1622–52), culminating in the
editions of Caesar, Terence, and Pliny
in 1635, and of Virgil in 1636. In Oct
1810 C noted a few details about the
Elzevirs from the *Encyclopaedia Londi-
nensis*, but they are too slight to settle
the questions he raises in this note.
CN III 3978.

The imprint of C's "Euphormio"
(from the actual wording of the title
*Euphormionis Lusinini sive Ioannis
Barclaii Satyricon*), i.e. *Satyricon*
(Leyden 1655), is "Apud Elzeviria-
nos" ("At the house of the Elzevirs"),
i.e. at the Leyden press of Jean and
Daniel. His *Argenis* (Amsterdam 1659)
is imprinted "Ex Officina Elzeviriana"
("From the Elzevir Press"), that is, at
the Amsterdam press of Daniel and
Louis. C seems to have wondered
whether the Elzevirian imprints were
systematic enough to give some indication of date or quality of production;
he may even have known that "ex
officina" was much used at Leyden in
the period of decline after 1681. But in

2A p 26, pencil | Bk I

> " Nec tu Lemniacis <u>Mauros</u> formosior armis   Mavors
> Fraena quatis, <u>Paviisve</u> soles mitescere blandus   Paphiis
> Cultibus...."[1]

[Tr Le Grys:
> " Not fairer's *Mars*, when clad in *Lemnian* armes,
> Hee rides, or smiles, pleas'd with faire *Venus* charmes...."]

2B p 67, lines 14–15, underlined in pencil

> Si qua fides, illic mortalia corpora primum
> Aspexere diem, <u>retinens cum terra supremi</u>
> ? <u>Aetheris informes animavit Apolline glebas.</u>

[Tr Le Grys:
> ... where first of all mortality
> (If we beleeve't) saw day; when from the skie,
> *Apollo* quickened the then formless clay.]

2C p 71, pencil

Sedulum esse, nihil temere loqui, assuescere labori, et imagine
patere?] sapientiae <u>parere,</u> tegere angustiores partes ingenii ...

[Tr Le Grys (adapted): " To bee diligent, to speake nothing rashly, to
accustome ones selfe to labour, and to obey (C's emendation: be con-
spicuous) with a shew of wisdome; and hide the weaker parts of the
wits..."][1]

---

fact both imprints were used often by both branches of the family, "ex officina" as early as 1601 by Louis senior at Leyden and "apud" as late as 1659 by Louis and Daniel at Amsterdam; and Daniel was associated with both imprints. It appears that C, basing his judgement on the superiority of his copy of *Satyricon*, may have thought that the imprint "apud" was the mark of "a genuine Elzevir" and that "Ex officina Elzeviriana" was the mark of a book not supervised by the masters themselves.

2A[1] C has provided the correct version for these two corruptions of the text.

C contrasted the "unpleasant" intermixture of verse and prose in Cowley's *A Vision, Concerning...Cromwell the Wicked* with the accep-

table "insertion of poems supposed to have been spoken or composed on occasions previously related in prose" in Boethius' *Consolations* and Barclay's *Argenis. BL* ch 22 (1907) II 97.

2C[1] Since Le Grys was using an earlier and more correct edition, his translation is here adapted to fit the textus. Le Grys reads: "to accustome onself to labour, and to the shew of wisdome; to obey and hide ...". The 1630 ed misplaced the comma after *labori* from its correct position before *sapientiae*, a mistake that led to the further corruption of (correct) *imagini* to *imagine*. This passage is part of one of the two quotations written in *CN* III 3536 (c Jul–Sept 1809), used variatim—and with omission of the word here altered—in *BL* ch 9 (1907) I 106.

3 pp +1–+5

It absolutely *distresses* me when I reflect that this Work, admired as
it has ⟨been⟩ by great men of all ages, and lately, I hear, by the
Poet Cowper,[1] should be only not *unknown* to general Readers. It
has been translated into English two or three times—how, I know not
—wretchedly, I doubt not. It affords matter for Thought, that the
last Translation—(or rather in all probability, miserable & faithless
Abridgement, of some former) was given under another name.[2]
What a mournful proof of the Incelebrity of this great, and amazing
Work, among both the *Public* and the *People*!/ for as Wordsworth,
the greatestr of the two *great* men of this Age—(at least, except
Davy & him I have *known, read of, heard of*, no others)[3] for as W.
~~most justly ob~~ did me the honor of once observing to me, the *People*
and the *Public* are two distinct Classes, and (as things go) the former
is likely to retain a better Taste, the less it is acted on by the Latter.
Yet *Telemachus* is in every mouth, in every school-boys & school-
girl's Hand.—[4]

It is aweful to say of a work, like the Argenis, the style and
latinity of which judged not according to classical pedantry, which
pronounces every ~~phrase~~ sentence right which can be found in any
book prior to Boetius, ~~and every one~~ however vicious the Age or

3[1] See William Hayley *Life and
Posthumous Works of William Cowper*
(3 vols Chichester 1803–4) I 243, letter
of Cowper to Samuel Rose 27 Aug
1787. In Apr 1805 the Wordsworths
had been reading a copy of Hayley's
Cowper. WL (*E2*) 577.

3[2] The *Argenis* was translated by
Kingsmill Long in 1625 and—as C
was to find not long after writing these
notes—by Sir Robert Le Grys and
Thomas May in 1629 (see COPY B).
The "last Translation...given under
another name" was perhaps *The
Phoenix; or, the History of Polyarchus
and Argenis* "translated from the
Latin by a Lady" (Clara Reeve) (4
vols 1772). Long had used "The
Loves of Poliarchus and Argenis" as
subtitle, and a similar title was used
for some English, Spanish, and French
translations.

3[3] C's admiration for Davy's genius
was perhaps at its highest in late 1807
and early 1808: see AURELIUS **51** n 1;

cf *Friend* (*CC*) II 251–2 (28 Dec 1809).
For C's changing view of Davy as "our
Prince of Chemists", on C's association with him, and on Davy's career
generally see BÖHME **117** n 1.

3[4] *Aventures de Télémaque*, the
most famous work of François de
Salignac de La Mothe Fénelon (1651–
1715), published in 1699, was frequently translated and widely circulated. By tracing the adventures of
Telemachus in search of his father
Ulysses, Fénelon made a political
romance intending "to change the
tastes and habits of the whole people,
and build up again from the very
foundations". C admired the "mystical writings of Fenelon" (*CN* III
3922) but the paternal-rationalist
utopianism of *Télémaque* was not to
his taste. A single marginal note by
C on Fénelon is preserved, but the
book it was written in has not been
identified.

affected the Author; and every ~~phrase~~ sentence, wrong, however natural & beautiful, which has been of the Author's own combination/[5] but according to the universal Logic of Thought as modified by feeling, is equal to Tacitus in energy and genuine conciseness, is perspicuous as Livy, and is free from the affectations, obscurities, and lust to *surprize*, of the former, and forms a sort of antithesis to the slowness and prolixity of the Latter. This remark does not however impeach even the *classicality* of the Language, which, considering the freedom & originality, ~~of~~ the easy motion and perfect Command of the Thoughts, is truly wonderful—of such a work it is aweful to say, that it would have been well if it had been written in English or Italian Verse/ Yet the Event seems to justify the Notion.— Alas! it is now too late. What ⟨modern⟩ work even of the size of Paradise Lost, much less of the Faery Queen—~~is read in~~ (N.B. are even *these* read?) would be *read* in the present Day; ~~unless~~ or even *bought* or likely to be *bought*, unless it be an INSTRUCTIVE Work, like Roscoe's 5 quartos of Leo X—or Boswell's 3 of D[r] Johnson's pilfered brutalities of Wit?[6]—It may be fairly objected, what work of surpassing merit has given the proof?—Certainly, none. Yet still there are ominous facts sufficient, I fear, to afford a certain prophecy of its reception, if ~~it~~ such were produced. S. T. C.

3[5] *The Consolations of Philosophy* by Anicius Manlius Severinus Boethius (c 480–c 524—C's copy of the Preston tr (1695) is in the BM unannotated—is one of the outposts of impressive Latinity that C, with his insistence upon judging by tact rather than by rule, was prepared to praise in the face of classical purists; the *Argenis* and Petrarch's Latin writings and some of Scaliger's verses were of the same company. But it was the poems, not the prose, of Boethius that C admired; see *BL* ch 22 (1907) II 116. See also 2A n 1, above.

3[6] William Roscoe (1753–1831) published *The Life and Pontificate of Leo the Tenth* in 4 (not 5) quarto vols

(Liverpool 1805); the 8° ed of 1806 was in 6 vols. C had made the acquaintance of Roscoe and his intellectual circle in Liverpool in Jul 1800 and knew of the Athenaeum Library there, though there is no record of his borrowing from it. See *CL* I 607–8, 615. Boswell's *Life of Johnson*, first published in 1791 in 2 vols, appeared in Malone's "revised and augmented" ed of 1793 in 3 vols; successive editions, until the early twentieth century, were in 4 vols.

The last phrase of this note is perhaps the most savage of all C's many gibes at Dr Johnson (but cf *CN* III 3321, 4104, 4188); for C shared Gibbon's distaste for Johnson's "bigoted though vigorous mind".

Copy B

Iohn Barclay His Argenis, translated out of Latine into English: the prose upon his Maiesties command: by Sir Robert Le Grys, Knight: and the verses by Thomas May, Esquire. With a clavis annexed to it for the satisfaction of the reader, and helping him to understand, what persons were by the author intended, under the fained names imposed by him upon them: and published by his Maiesties command. London 1629. 4º.

British Museum C 44 d 34

Inscribed on p ⁻1 (recto of frontispiece portrait): "Lib: Robᵗⁱ Gay Chyrurg. Lond. 1695." Autograph inscription on the title-page: "Southey". Inscribed in pencil on p ⁻4 (p–d): "p. 131 the design. 148–159"; and across the top left corner, also in pencil, "Coleridge Notes".

MS TRANSCRIPT. VCL BT 33 (omitting **2**).

DATE. c late 1809: see **2** n 1, below.

1 pp ⁻4–⁻3

That Charles the first commanded the Translation of this excellent work, & was so *impatient* for its early appearance (vide Sir Rob. Le Grice's Preface) is itself no mean proof of his Leaning towards Catholicism[1]—at least, that he abhorred the tenets of the Reformed Churches & was most charitable to the whole corrupt Mass of Popery—making certain Tenets of the Puritans, i.e. Predestination, Election, Reprobation, Final Perseverance, &c, the *pretexts*—while the Love of Liberty & the superior knowlege of the Puritans were his true Motives.—These purely *theological* Tenets had & still have their Advocates among the Romanists—& I question, whether a single Instance could be found in which their Belief & Disbelief had any practical consequences—except as far as that any serious exercise of the reasoning Faculties accompanied with moral Zeal tends to wean & unsensualize the human mind.[2] But thus it is!—Men dispute about Cricket, & *Fives*[3]—& forget, that both are valuable

[1] Le Grys simply says in his dedication: "... your Maiestie commanded, and it was my duty to obey". C has modernised the translator's name into the form of his Christ's Hospital friend Charles Valentine Le Grice.

[2] C had used this phrase in *Religious Musings* line 210 and *Destiny of Nations* line 81. *PW* (EHC) I 117, 134.

[3] Cricket seems to have been played in mediaeval England, but the first authoritative rules were not drawn up until 1774. Fives was a less ancient

only for that which is common to both—i.e. employment, exercise, health & agility & strength. *S. T. C.*

Judge too from this of the sincerity of Charles in his Relief of *Rochelle*—I verily am inclined to believe, that their Destruction was *designed, planned,* & rejoiced in, by Charles—such a Bigot was he to Arbitrary Rule/[4]— S. T. Coleridge

2 pp ⁻3–⁻2, outer edge slightly damaged near the foot

The most important Deduction from this great work (for a great work it is!) we may fairly deem to be the degeneracy of Genius, when it unnaturally weds itself with Cunning, Despair of Human Kind, & (that worst Pest of civilized Man!) the base Calculation of consequences as the grain of morality.[1] Cowards & Traitors! listening with half an ear to the plain, positive Injunction of Conscience, while their eyes are fixed on a Dæmon in the Distance, now flattering, now threatening them with obscure gestures, the interpretation of which forms their daily & hourly Superstition[.] Is it right?—He who says, I cannot tell, till I calculate the consequences, is already an *Atheis*[t] in its worst, nay, in its only sense.—To kno[w] the effects of this state of mind, compare the moral Breathings of even the mistaken Patriots of Charles the first & the Republic with the Loyalists (many of them men of superior Talents & amiable characters, as *Cowley*)—Think of Milton, Ludlow, Colonel Hutchinson, Harrington[2]—in short, compare only, in one feeling, the suspicion &

---

game of handball, of obscure origin; the earliest use of the word recorded in *OED* is 1636. C referred to cricket in *P Lects* Lect 9 (1949) 281 and to fives in *CN* III 4331 f 115. Keats is on record as suffering a black eye from a cricket ball; and see *H Works* xv 154, IX 86–9; in the second of these the poetic style of WW and of C is criticised as less dexterous than Cavanagh's style as a fives-player.

1[4] Charles I, after failing to raise the funds to wage war on the German Catholics, made two humiliating attempts to storm Cadiz in 1626. In 1627 he mounted an expedition to relieve the Protestants of La Rochelle, but that also failed shamefully.

2[1] The substance of this note was expanded in "Letters on the Spaniards" VII, *Courier* 22 Dec 1809:

EOT (*CC*) II 79–82. Paley's doctrine of the calculation of consequences as a basis for moral action struck C with peculiar revulsion: see e.g. AURELIUS **38** n 1.

2[2] Cowley, having been driven from his Cambridge fellowship in 1644, followed Queen Henrietta Maria to France, returned to England as a royalist spy in 1656, but after the Restoration was denied the mastership of the Savoy. The others comprise a list of men loyal to the Coleridgian idea of the state. Milton lost his eyesight as learned defender of the Protectorate but was not prosecuted after the Restoration. Edmund Ludlow (c 1616–92), regicide yet a resolute opponent of Cromwell, suffered exile at the Restoration. John Hutchinson (1615–64), regicide, withdrew from

hatred of God's Creatures with the Love & Hope of them—For this is the true Difference between the Philo-despotist, & the Republican—the latter of whom may, & under certain circumstances such as that of G. Britain at present, *will*, of necessity, be the most zealous & faithful Partizan of his King & the Constitution of his Country. A Republican is he, who under any constitution hopes highly of his fellow-citizens, attributes their vices to their circumstances, & takes the proper means (such as are in his power) to ameliorate them—gradually indeed, & not by placing Children in the *first Form*, or gifting Russian Slaves with the British Constitution/—but still looking on & hoping. The Despotist always assumes every vice of any of the People as common to all—& the present vices as essential & irremoveable.—

3   pp ⁻4, 93 | II v

He [*Vsimulca*, i.e. Calvin] denied that any man commits a sinne, but he whom the Gods compell to do it, and have predestined him to the same: that howsoever thou strive against sinne, be innocent in thy life among men, and liberall in the service of the Gods, he yet affirmes, that by this pietie thou art made nothing the dearer to the Gods. . . . Further, that there is no difference in sinnes, but in them that commit them: for those with whom the Gods were displeased, should they but steale a few Pot-herbs, did deserve whatsoever the Furies . . . could inflict: but the others, not with Parricide, not with Incest, could slake the friendship which the Gods had contracted with them.

Vide p. 93.*ᵃ*

A fine instance this of *saying* Truth and *conveying* Falsehood.[1] It is true, that these Tenets are *Calvinistic*, but most false, that to these the Spread of Calvinism was owing, or tho' characteristic of their Theology (i.e. the point in which they are unique) are or were

ᵃ On p ⁻4, above **1** but in a slightly different ink from the note. C *17th* C 434 mistakenly prefixes the direction to **1**

politics in alarm at Cromwell's ambitions but was imprisoned at the Restoration. (See Lucy HUTCHINSON *Life of Colonel Hutchinson*.) James Harrington (1611–77), political theorist, had attended Charles to the scaffold, but was imprisoned after the Restoration for attempting to change the constitution. C owned a copy of Harrington's *Oceana* (1700), which he

was reading—perhaps at Thomas Poole's instigation (*Poole* II 4)—as early as Jan 1800. *CN*I 638–41; cf 934. He regarded Harrington as one of the representative figures in the history of English liberty (*CN* II 2598) and in the later years referred to him many times.

3[1] See *Friend* (*CC*) I 43, 48–9, *CN* II 2397, and BAXTER *Reliquiae* COPY B **115** at n 7.

characteristic of the *Sect* in France.[2] No! the severity of their morals, & in their opinions not what they held, but what they did *not* hold, what they were emancipated from—Idolatry, Ignorance of the Scriptures, &c &c—these were the character of the Huguenots. It is always suspicious when the opinions of a numerous sect are attacked, omitting their moral conduct—if the latter be bad, the former cannot be good—if good, it proves that the opinions are not as bad as they sound.

[3]2 After Calvin was forced to leave France in 1535, because of the persecution aroused by his preaching of reformed doctrines, the French Calvinists developed their doctrines and actions along lines over which Calvin had no personal influence.

WILLIAM BARTRAM
1739-1823

Travels Through North & South Carolina, Georgia, East & West Florida, the Cherokee country, the extensive territories of the Muscogulges, or Creek Confederacy, and the country of the Chactaws; containing an account of the soil and natural productions of those regions, together with observations on the manners of the Indians. Embellished with copper-plates. Philadelphia 1791. 8⁰.

Dove Cottage Library

Autograph signature of J. W. Tobin (see ANNUAL ANTHOLOGY 1 n 2) on the title-page and back paste-down (p +1, a flyleaf having been torn out). Inscribed by C: "Sara Hutchinson from S. T. C. Dec. 9. 1801 "; the inscription, perhaps originally on a loose sheet or on a flyleaf that later came loose from the binding, has been cut out and pasted to p ⁻3 (p–d). Below this, in pencil in an unidentified hand, "S. T. Coleridge". On the dedication page the signature "S. Hutchinson" in ink.

The relation of Bartram's *Travels* to the *AM* and other poems of C's, first noticed by EHC, was explored in detail by Lowes: *RX* 8–10, 452–3 n 22; and see index. The detail has been refined and clarified in the light of notebooks of later date than the Gutch Notebook (see e.g. *CN* I 218–22, 228, and nn), but the copy of Bartram that C used in 1797 has not been identified. It is possible that he was using Tobin's copy in 1797 but there is no evidence one way or the other. In any case WW evidently had a copy of Bartram with him in Germany (see *RX* 453 n 22, 455 n 28); it is very likely that this was Tobin's copy. See *WL* (*E2*) 212.

Shortly after he had taken up residence in Greta Hall, Keswick, C wrote to ask Tobin to bring his copy of Bartram when he came to Keswick (*CL* II 727; 25 Jul 1800), but Tobin's visit, because of his failing eyesight, was postponed indefinitely and in Jan 1801 the book was sent, not to C, but to WW at Dove Cottage. *JWL* 83, 87, 107. The book may have arrived while C was staying at Dove Cottage 20 Dec–3 Jan, for it was evidently on that occasion that C read parts of the book to SH. On 26 Mar C copied into N 21 a passage from Bartram as "a fantastic analogue & similitude to Wordsworth's Mind"—a passage he was later to use in *BL* for the same purpose. *CN* I 926; *BL* ch 22 (1907) II 128–9.

After SH's death this copy of Bartram stayed in the Wordsworth family. It was not included in the sale of WW's library in 1859, and came to rest with other Wordsworth books at The Stepping Stones, Rydal, harboured among brilliantly coloured birds, insects, and butterflies that had been brought there from the Amazon a generation after C's death.

In Apr 1818 C provided himself with a copy of the London 1794 ed of Bartram. In it Mrs Gillman copied out C's desolate poem *O! Christmas Day*, and G. Gordon Wordsworth later transcribed into it the inscription that C had addressed to SH in 1801.

MS TRANSCRIPT. VCL 114: G. Gordon Wordsworth copy of the note, written in C's copy of the London 1794 ed.

DATE. 19 Dec 1801.

1 p ⁻3, written below the presentation inscription

This is not a Book of Travels, properly speaking; but a series of poems, chiefly descriptive, *occasioned* by the Objects, which the Traveller observed.—It is a *delicious* Book; & like all *delicious* Things, you must take but a *little* of it at a time.¹—Was it not about this time of the year, that I read to you parts of the "Introduction" of this Book, when William & Dorothy had gone out to walk?— I remember the evening well, but not what time of the year it was.—²

1¹ C used the word "delicious" in the same way in BROWNE *Religio* 2 and 33—notes written in 1802 in a book that he gave, or intended to give, to SH.

1² That C could not remember exactly "what time of the year it was" is understandable in view of the many visits to and fro between Keswick and Grasmere between Nov 1800 and Apr 1801. C was at Dove Cottage in Dec 1800 at the same time as SH on three occasions: 28 Nov–2 Dec, 4–6 Dec, and 20 Dec–3 Jan. On all three occasions he was ill and less likely than usual to want to join the Wordsworths and SH on their frequent walks. If Tobin's copy arrived at the beginning of Jan only the third of these is possible, but the incomplete record of *DWJ* makes 4 Dec 1800 a suggestive date. C had arrived in the morning but would eat nothing; DW and SH "walked round the 2 Lakes" on "a very fine morning". After tea "we" (which could well be only WW and DW) walked by moonlight to look at Langdale covered with snow, and after their return they all "Sat up till half-past one". The suggestion in Mark Reed *Chronology of Wordsworth* (Cambridge, Mass., 1967) 274 item 56, that the occasion was 25 or 26 Oct at Sockburn, seems less likely.

THOMAS BATEMAN

1778–1821

A Practical Synopsis of Cutaneous Diseases according to the arrangement of Dr. Willan, exhibiting a concise view of the diagnostic symptoms and the method of treatment. . . . Third edition. London 1814. 8⁰.

C's edition is not identified. 1st ed 1813; earliest ed in BM is the 3rd, with Advertisement dated 31 Oct 1814.

Not located. *Lost List.*

Dr Daniel's copy, lent to C c Jun 1814: *CL* III 509. Henry Daniel, surgeon, is entered in the 1812 list of members of the Royal College of Surgeons as not living within seven miles of London; he appears in the Bristol Directory of 1817 as living at 45 Queen Square, Bristol. The date of his death is not recorded.

In Jan 1804 C had made two emphatic observations on the skin as "a Terra Incognita in Medicine". *CN* I 1826, *CL* II 1027. In May 1814 C's Bristol friend William Hood, alarmed at C's state of mind and at a massive skin affection induced by large and frequent doses of laudanum, called the Bristol physician Henry Daniel to treat him. Daniel firmly and sensibly engaged C in a regimen of gradual withdrawal, spending "two or three hours a day with me", regularly reducing the amount of opium, and arranging for continuous supervision to preclude the strong possibility of suicide. See *CL* III 489–526. On 19 May C sent Daniel part of *The Pains of Sleep*: ". . . the lines may not be without interest to you . . . as one about to be entitled to my life-long, affectionate gratitude for my emancipation from a Slavery more dreadful, than any man, who has not felt it's iron fetters eating into his very soul, can possibly imagine". *CL* III 495–6. Daniel's reason for lending C the Bateman *Synopsis* is obvious. Cf J AHR-BÜCHER **20** for Bateman on musk.

DATE. 1814, c early Jun.

1   p 327 | Order VIII. Maculae: ii Naevus, etc.

. . . it would be insulting the understanding of the reader, to waste one word in refutation of the vulgar hypothesis, which ascribes them to the mental emotions of the mother,—an hypothesis totally irreconcilable with the established principles of physiology...[1]

Ἐπέχω, me nimiâ experientiâ invitum cogente.[2]

---

[1] In a footnote to p 323 Bateman wrote: "In consequence of the old notion, that those spots were impressed upon the foetus by the emotions of the mother, the term Naevus is commonly associated with the epithet *maternus*, and the appellations of *mutter-mahl*, *mother-spots*, *fancy-marks*, &c., have been given to them in different languages." Daniel, however, was "delighted" with C's comment and in agreement. *CL* III 509.

[2] "*I hesitate* unwillingly, from knowledge based on too much experience." "I hesitate" is C's rendering of ἐπέχω—see e.g. G. BURNET *History* 8 and H. COLERIDGE 18.

RICHARD BAXTER
1615–1691

Richard Baxter, originally a strict conformist, adopted Presbyterian views c 1600, and in 1642 on the outbreak of the Civil War—his sympathies being with the Puritans—removed to Coventry and acted as chaplain to the garrison there. As the Civil War approached its crisis, he withdrew to minister and write in retirement, composing in 1650 *The Saint's Everlasting Rest*, which is considered his best book. (See *Reliquiae* COPY B **10** and *CN* I 1041.) The Act of Uniformity (1662) drove him—a Presbyterian within the Church of England—from the English church; he lived in retirement until the Act of Indulgence (1672) allowed him to return to London. Charged with libelling the Church in his *Paraphrase of the New Testament* (1685), he was tried by Judge Jeffreys in the Bloody Assizes, abused, fined, and imprisoned for eighteen months. He spent the last four years of his life at Rutland House as assistant to Matthew Sylvester (c 1636–1708), who issued Baxter's autobiography in 1696, badly edited, under the title *Reliquiae Baxterianae*.

The earliest definite sign of C's interest in Baxter is a memorandum of Apr–May 1802 to write on "Presbyterians & Baxterians in the time of Charles 1 & 2nd". *CN* I 1181. Late in that same year Lamb bought him a copy of the *Holy Commonwealth* for 3s 6d (*LL* I 325, 346, 348–9); in *Friend* No 15 of 30 Nov 1809 C used a long quotation from that book as epigraph: *Friend* (*CC*) II 197.

Although the early marginalia in *Reliquiae* COPY A were written in c 1811, the rest of the notes on COPY A and all those on COPY B and the *Catholick Theologie* belong to Highgate. The grounds for C's admiration for Baxter appear in a record of Allsop's for Oct 1820: C affirmed that Baxter was "a century before his time, that he was a logician, and first applied the tri-fold or tri-une demonstration. . . . He also first introduced the method of argument, that the thing or reason given contains a positive and its opposite . . . Baxter tried to reconcile the almost irreconcilable tenets of Calvinism and Arminianism. He more than any other man was the cause of the restoration, and more than any other sectarian was he persecuted by Charles II." Allsop I 133–4. Notes in N 29 and the Logic MS both refer to the fact that Baxter had anticipated Kant's trichotomous theory: see *Reliquiae* COPY B **103** n 1 and *L&L* 128–9; for a cluster of C's notes on "Baxter and Trichotomy" see *C 17th C* 118–21.

C placed special value on his marginalia on Baxter's *Reliquiae* and intended to include them in his projected edition of Asgill in 1832: *CL* VI 906. He recognised between himself and Baxter some community of fate: see *Reliquiae* COPY B **34**.

230

Richard Baxter's Catholick Theologie: plain, pure, peaceable: for pacification of the dogmatical word-warriours ... In three books ... Written chiefly for posterity, when sad experience hath taught men to hate theological logical wars, and to love, and seek, and call for peace, &c. 4 pts in 1 vol. London 1675. F⁰.

British Museum Ashley 4777

Inscribed below the frontispiece portrait facing the title-page: "Roger Stephens his Lott", and on the title-page "E Hs". Autograph signature "Anne Gillman" on p ⁻3; heraldic bookplate of A. Steinmetz on p ⁻4 (p–d). The fact that this title appears in *Watson List* shows that the book belonged to the Gillmans, not to C's executors, and that it was later presented to Adam Steinmetz.

Passages are marked and underlined in ink on sigg a3ᵛ, a4ʳ, bʳ, bᵛ, b2ʳ, b2ᵛ, b4ʳ, c2ʳ, p 13, and in certain later sections of the volume; a few words are also added. The fact that this style of marking can be clearly distinguished from C's note **8** shows that the marks were not C's; further, the cropping of a marginal word before C annotated the same page shows that the marks were made by an earlier owner of the book.

DATE. c 1824–30. *AR* is referred to in **10**, and for discussions between C and H. F. Cary that may be connected with these marginalia see **10** n 3, below.

1   p ⁻3

How large a proportion of this Volume would have been superseded by a previous reduction of a few words, ex. gr. Thing, Cause, ~~Mind~~ Power &c—to a fixed Sense.—in the Writer's thoughts! Year after year, yea, day after day, I see more clearly or feel more livelily the importance of the Noetic Tetrad and the Logical Pentad, as the fundamental Form of all Thinking—and of Trichotomy in all *real* definition—1

Instead of the dichotomy Real ÷ Unreal—or Thing: which are mere *words*—for What *is* not cannot be Nothing ⊙ opposed—and Reality can have no opposite, we should say—:

Reality in finite existence has two forms actual & potential—/ the latter as truly *real* as the former—

⊙ irrelative + relative in correspondent antithesis to −. − relative in correspondent antithesis to +.

1¹ For the principle of trichotomy   COPY B **103** and n 1.
and the tetrad see BAXTER *Reliquiae*

⊙ Real

\+ Actual   − Potential

In God alone the Actual and the Real are one and the same or the divine Reality excludes all potentiality—Actus purissimus sine ullâ potentialitate.[2]

2 sig A2^{r-v} | Invocation

Rom. 10.9, 10. *If thou confess with thy mouth the Lord Jesus, and believe in thy Heart that God hath raised him from the dead, thou shalt be saved: For with the Heart man believeth unto Righteousness, and with the Mouth confession is made to salvation.*

Few points in the Christian Theology of more interest, and scarcely any that have attracted less attention, than the Evangelic & Pauline Sense of the term, *Saved*. Perhaps, I should have said, *Senses*: for either the total Work of Redemption, a *regenerated* Spirit born spiritually into Christ, may be intended by Salvation, tho' I do not at present recollect any special instance in the New Testament.[1] But generally "Saved" is taken in a narrower sense—viz. as the first admission within the pale of the alone saving Church, as the condition & inceptive of Redemption—not superseding the expediency, & where Means are afforded the necessity of a growth in the Faith, of an expansion of the Belief.

3 sig a2^r, a^v | The Preface

But in 1640, the *Oath* called "*Et Caetera*" being offered the Ministry, forced me to a yet more *searching Study* of the case of our *Diocesane Prelacie* (which else I had never been like to have gainsaid.) At a meeting of Ministers to debate the case, it fell to Mr. *Christopher Cartwrights* lot and mine to be the Disputers; and the issue of all (that and my studies) was, that I setled in the approbation of the

---

1[2] "Purest Actuality devoid of any potentiality". C used the phrase many times: see e.g. *CL* II 1195 (13 Oct 1806). In a note addressed to the Rev James Gillman in a copy of *C&S* (2nd ed 1830), he ascribed the phrase to Boethius (*C&S—CC*—234), but in *BL* ch 9 (1907) I 94 he mentioned "the length of time during which the scholastic definition of the *Supreme Being*, as 'actus purissimus sine ulla potentialitate,' was received in the schools of

Theology, both by the Pontifician and the Reformed divines". Cf Thomas Aquinas *Summa theologia* Pt I Quaestio 3 Art 2c: "Ostensum est autem, quaest. 2 art. 3, quod Deus est purus actus, non habens aliquid de potentialitate"; similar passages occur in Aquinas and the schoolmen passim.

2[1] In support of C's position, however, see Titus 3.5–7, Eph 2.2–10; and cf Matt 19.28–9, 1 Cor 15.1–2.

Episcopacy asserted by *Ignatius*, yea, and *Cyprian*, but such a dissent from the *English* frame, as I have given account of in my *Disputations* of *Church Government*.

In an honest and intelligent Mind this is the first & inevitable Consequent of the Ignorance respecting the true nature & purpose of a National Church and its Prelacy: and of its essential distinction from the Christian Church and its Episcopacy.[1] But what are distinct, yea, different, need not *therefore* be separated. Two distinct trusts and functions may be vested in and exercised by the same Person: nay, the perfection of the lower of the two Trusts may depend on this Union.—But bear in mind, that the Error in this case was common to both Parties—to the persecutingors, ~~Prelates~~ who demanded as Bishops, ⟨what they ought to have asked only as Prelates,⟩ no less than to the resisting Puritans—while the blame lies heavier* on the former.   S. T. Coleridge

* This may be easily shewn. For the *aggression* was on their part who required in the name of Christ what they were entitled to demand only in the name of *Cæsar*, & consequently respecting the *temporalities* of the National Church exclusively: and not on those who resisted or remonstrated against a Power assumed in the name of Christ, which, they clearly saw, Christ so far from having delegated to others had never assumed for himself

4 sigg a2ᵛ–a3ʳ

And though *Camero*'s moderation and great clearness took much with me, I soon perceived that his Resolving the cause of sin into necessitating objects and temptations, laid it as much on God (in another way) as the Predeterminants do.ᵃ And I found all godly mens Prayers and Sermons run quite in another strain, when they chose not the Controversie as pre-engaged.

For *me* this would be as weighty an argument as it was for Baxter— possibly, even a more convincing one, thro' my conviction that in prayer and earnest practical enforcement of the truths of Godliness the Spirit acts more *collectively*, is more total and entire, than it can be in any simply *intellectual* Effort—the *intellection* being indeed a noble *part* of our Humanity but yet only a *part*, & therefore with the

ᵃ From here to the end marked with an inked line in the margin

3[1] See *C&S* (*CC*) 113–28, in which in the section "The Idea of the Christian Church" the difference between a National Church and a Christian Church is examined under "four distinctions, or peculiar and essential marks".

deficiency of a fragment—which the mistaking the part for a whole converts into *defect* & positive error.[1]

5 sig a3ᵛ

I came by many years longer study to perceive, that most of the *Doctrinal* Controversies among Protestants ... are far more about *equivocal words*, than *matter*; and it wounded my soul to perceive what work both *Tyrannical*, and *unskilful Disputing* Clergie-men had made these thirteen hundred years in the world! And experience ... hath loudly called to me to Repent of my own *prejudices*, *sidings* and *censurings* of *causes* and *persons* not understood, and of all the mis-carriages of my Ministry and life, which have been thereby caused; and to make it my chief work to call men that are within my hearing to more peaceable *thoughts*, *affections* and *practices*: And my en-deavours have not been in vain ... But the Sons of the Coal were exasperated the more against me, and accounted him to be against *every man*, that called all men to Love and Peace, and was for no man as in a contrary way.

Who having the heart of a Christian can in the present day read the writings of Baxter, and not feel the deaf'ning & hard'ning effects of party-passion, which did make, & which alone could make, so many minds insensible or hostile!—

6 sig cʳ

14. And it greatly promoteth Schisms that good people are *un-acquainted with Church-history*, and know not how just *such Opinions and Schisms* as *their own* have in former ages *risen*, and how they have *miscarryed* and *dyed*, and what have been their *fruits*.

A most just Remark! O if instead of the chopped straw of their prudential discourses on given Texts, like School-boys' *Themes*, our Clergy would labor to *instruct* their Congregations—teach them what they are—and what their Fore-fathers were—and how both the one & the other came to be that which they were or are!—From the neglect of this, how languid is Protestantism!

4[1] The superiority of spirit to intellect, and the relation of the whole and parts, were abiding principles in C's view of imagination, reason, and life. In a note of Aug 1808 he noticed how "The *habit* of psychological Analysis makes additionally difficult the act of true Prayer". *CN* III 3555. Cf letter to Cottle Apr 1814, *CL* III 478–9.

7 sig c[v]

1. Christ first laid down the *Description* and *Measure* of *Christianity*, in the *Baptismal Covenant*; and ordained that all should be accounted *Christians in foro Ecclesiae* who by Baptism were solemnly devoted to him, in a professed Belief and Covenant, Dedication and Vow to God the *Father, Son and Holy Ghost*: These he would have called *Christians* or his *Disciples*, and this is their *Christening*, and so ever called in the Church. 2. And next he made it his new (that is *Last*) and *Great Command*, that *All his Disciples should Love each other*, and live in eminent *Unity and Peace*: which he accordingly wrought them to by the first pouring out of his Spirit, *Act.* 2. & 3. & 4.

Alas! this very text is regarded by sundry learned men as a proof of the post-apostolic Date of the Gospel, in which it occurs: and as a departure from the more simple form given in the Acts of the Apostles—[1]

8 sig c2[r]

... *Paul* often warneth them to *hold fast* the *form* of *sound words*, and summeth up (as 1 *Cor.* 15.1, 2, 3, 4.) the *Articles of their faith*, and chargeth them that so far as *they had attained, they should walk by the same rule, and mind the same things*, and *if in any thing they were otherwise minded*, stay till God revealed the matter to them, *Phil.* 3. ... And what cannot be *done* by *Light* and *Love*, is not to be done by them [i.e. ministers] at all: The Magistrate and not they, must use the Sword; but not to make men *believers* (for he cannot.)[a]

This again is most true—that the truth in Christ should be *propounded, declared, offered*—To as many as receive it, offer lovingly every aid & furtherance—but do not attempt to DISPUTE men into it

[a] Words and phrases in the last sentence are underlined, not by C, and an X placed in the margin. The marking here is typical of the non-Coleridgian marking throughout the volume

7[1] The two texts in question are Matt 28.19—"Go ye therefore, and teach all nations, baptizing them in the name of the Father, and of the Son, and of the Holy Ghost"—and Acts 2.38—"Then Peter said unto them, Repent, and be baptized every one of you in the name of Jesus Christ, for the remission of sins, and ye shall receive the gift of the Holy Ghost." The "Gospel according to St Matthew", which by tradition opens the NT, was for a long time assumed to be the earliest of the gospels. The Unitarians argued for the primitive simplicity of the version in Acts.

Biblical scholarship, working from beginnings made by C's contemporaries, has now concluded that Mark is the earliest, and that the order of composition was Mark, Luke, Matthew, John, Acts being written by "Luke" as a continuation of his gospel.

9 sig c2ᵛ

... it is to me a certainty, that the Apostles made and used the Creed for sense and substance as the very summary and test of Christianity, long before any Book of the New Testament was written (about twelve years, and almost sixty six before the whole.) [Baxter gives eight reasons for his certainty.]

All this may be substantially true; but for *Certainty*, I cannot receive it. Nay, I am persuaded that the so called Apostles' Creed was consequent on the Conversion of the Gentiles, and intended as a form of ᴘꜰ instruction for pagan Catechumens preparatory to Baptism.[1] How could John or Paul have sanctioned the *first* clause of the Creed, who both expressly attribute the making of the Heaven & Earth to the Son?—[2]

10 i 2–4 | ı i §§ 3, 7

3. We neither have, nor can have here in flesh any one proper *formal Conception* of the *Divine Nature*, that is formally suited to the truth in the object: But only Metaphorical or Analogical Conceptions; borrowed from things better known. ...

7. God is here seen in the *Glass* of his *Works*, with the *Revelation of his Word* and *Spirit*. And from these *works* we must borrow our conceptions.

How many perplexities and even contradictions would this good and great Man have escaped, had he rightly distinguished an Idea from

9[1] C refers to "the so called Apostles' Creed", recognising that the title had attached itself etiologically to a fanciful legend about its composition on the day of Pentecost (see Acts 2.1–4), constructed in support of the belief that the Apostles had composed and used that formula. Within the same tradition Baxter assumes that it was composed "Long before any Book of the New Testament". C, however, in a view that remained consistent with him except in points of detail, held that the Apostles' Creed was composed *after* the Gospels (being "*gathered out* of the Scriptures"), that it was not to be identified with the "Symbolon Fidei" (the doctrinal declaration "always repeated at Baptism" but never written

down), that its purpose was as elementary instruction for catechumens, and that it had been composed—or at least brought into prominence—to meet the requirements of the Church in its increasingly successful proselytising "consequent on the Conversion of the Gentiles". See *CN* ɪɪɪ 3880 (from which the quoted phrases are taken) of Jun 1810, and Bᴀxᴛᴇʀ *Reliquiae* ᴄᴏᴘʏ ʙ **58** n 2, **100** n 4.

9[2] "I believe in God the Father Almighty, Maker of Heaven and earth"—the first clause in both the Apostles' Creed and the Nicene Creed. Cf John 1.1–3 and Col 1.16. "Maker of Heaven and earth" does not appear in Rufinus; it is one of the later additions mentioned in *Reliquiae* ᴄᴏᴘʏ ʙ **58** and n 1.

a Conception, and rigorously observed the distinction! A *Conception* of God, whether in or out of the flesh, is an Absurdity; but the *Idea*, God (for a temptation to error lurks in the phrase, Idea *of* God) is for Man, yea, as the form, norm, ground and condition of all other Ideas may be affirmed to constitute his Reason. See AIDS TO REFLECTION.[1]—N.b.—R. B. has, with many others, been misled by translating the pauline εσοπτρον "glass", instead of "mirror"[2] —The Apostle alludes to the mirrors used in the Mysteries, & which are still frequently discovered in the tombs of the Ancients, & indicate that the Deceased had been an initiated person.[3]

11 i 8–10 | iv §§ 64, 65

64. The *Possibility* and *Futurity* of things, are not accidental notions, or relations of the things themselves; but are *termini diminuentes*, as

10[1] *AR* (1825) 158–60, 225–8.

10[2] 1 Cor 13.12: "For now we see through a glass [δι' ἐσόπτρου] darkly; but then face to face". The use of ἐν ἐσόπτρῳ in James 1.23 raises no difficulty—"a man beholding his natural face in a glass"; and the use of an associated verb in 2 Cor 3.18—"But we all, with open face beholding as in a glass [κατοπτιζόμενοι] the glory of the Lord, are changed into the same image"—is universally recognised as referring to a mirror. But on 1 Cor 13.12 commentators have been almost equally divided. Elsewhere (see n 3, below) C argued that "the true sense" was εἰς ἔσοπτρον—a phrase not found in NT Greek or Septuagint—"in a mirror". It seems odd of C to attack Baxter for accepting the AV version "through a glass" when he must have known that δι' ἐσόπτρου could mean "by means of a mirror" or "*through* a mirror" (the image appearing to be behind the surface), and when "glass" had for a long time been a word for a mirror even if the mirror was not made of glass. Perhaps C was anxious to introduce the possible connexion with the mirrors found in tombs: see n 3, below.

10[3] This statement is illuminated by a notebook entry of 1 Oct 1830 in which C speaks of "the *Names* of God" as "Symbols & Indices of God's indwelling Wisdom and omnific Love, vouchsafed to us who see dimly as in a mirror—i.e. by reflection & symbolicaly—/ for such (as my friend Mr Cary pointed out), is the true sense of St Paul's words—not *thro'* a Glass but εἰς ἐσόπτρον, but in a mirror—alluding to the Mirror in the Mysteries. So often found in the Tombs of the Ancients & marking that the Defunct had been an Initiate of the Mysteries. ..." N 47 ff 4–4^v. See also BROOKE **14** and n 3. H. F. Cary, informed in classical antiquities, was apparently the first to see a connexion between the mirrors in 1 Cor 13.12 and 2 Cor 3.18. The current interpretation of certain objects found in Etruscan tombs was that they were associated with the Bacchic, Eleusinian, or Cabiric rites of the dead. Francesco Inghirami, in *Monumenti Etruschi o di Etrusco nome disegnati* (6 vols Fiesole 1822–6), was the first to publish convincing arguments to show that the metal *paterae* ("dischi manubriati") found in Etruscan tombs were really household mirrors rather than sacred dishes. Cary met Inghirami in 1833 and discussed *patere* and *specchi* with him: *Memoir of Cary* (1847) II 205.

to the *Things*, and are spoken of *Nothing*. To say that a *Thing May be* or *Will be*, which now is not, is to say that *now* it *is nothing*.

65. *Nothing* is no *Effect*; and therefore hath *no Cause*: Therefore things *Possible* and *Future* as such, have no Cause.

§ 64. 65.—Surely, this is a mere misuse of the Equivoque in the word "*Thing*"—and the delusion would at once clear off on a just definition of "Being", or "Reality"—under which "Thing" would be subsumed as a *Mode*.—Again—Cause is a vague term. Substitute "*ground*"—and the fallacy of the assertion in §. 65. becomes evident. The Child beginning to walk *will* every now and then stumble. Who would venture to assert, that there was *no ground* of this? For in reason tho' not in the sensuous Fancy Negations are as true Causes as positives—/ The Frost burns, as truly as the Fire, tho' in both Cases the Heat is the Efficient.—But the merely *logical* character of the Category, "Cause" had not been disclosed to Baxter

12 i 9 | §§ 67–8

67. Therefore also God is no Cause of any Eternal Possibility or futurity.

68. Therefore the *Possibility* and *futurity* of things (conceived as an effect) hath no *Eternal Cause*: For there is nothing Eternal but God.

68. a direct contradiction of § 67. The production of finite, i.e. of non-absolute, Spirits was an eternal possibility.—

Evil or the Self-will was a consequent *eternal possibility*—/ Baxter merely plays on the word "*thing*".

13 i 11 | § 87

It's strange how some Learned men confound *Things and Nothings*, and the *Notions* and *Names* of *Nothings* with the *Nothings* named.

But excellent Baxter falls into the opposite error—and reduces into *Nothings* all that tho' they *are*, yet are not *things*—i.e. units that fill a space *exclusively*—or which he can imagine as so doing. The ground of his Error is the attribution of degree-lessness to Reality.[1]

13[1] In a ms addendum to *The Friend*, written variatim in four copies of the 1818 edition, he attacked the denial of "the reality of all finite existence...": "Are *we* then indeed NOTHING?...How and whence did this sterile and pertinacious Nothing acquire its *plural* Number? [Copies A, H, L read: "Whence this portentous transnihilation of Nothing into Nothings?"] And ... what is that inward Mirror, in and for which these Nothings have at least a relative existence?—" The note then goes on to discuss the implications of this for pantheism. *Friend* (*CC*) I 522–3n.

14 i 12

For Gods essence is the *prime Incomplexe Being*, and not a *Complexe proposition*, " *Deus est*": His *Properties, primary*, are *Omnipotent-vital-power, Intellect and Will*; But these also are the same *Incomplexe essence*, and not *propositions*: And his Intellect as an object of it self is not before his Intellect as an Actual Knowledge of himself, nor the cause of it: All the sense he can make of it is, that this proposition " *Deus est, et est Aeternus*, &c." if it *had had an eternal being*, would in order of nature have been conceivable *to us* before this " *Deus scit se esse*" or before *his knowledge* it self. ... But *God knoweth not* himself by propositions. Words (in mente vel in ore) are but *artificial organs* for blind creatures to know by.

But then, whispers the Spinosist, what do you *mean* by God? The incomprehensible?—This is what *we* contend, & you call us Atheists for. We contend that as God is the Ground of all Motion yet not moving, so he is the Ground of all intelligence but not intelligent—i.e.—God is the term by which we express the relation of cause to effect universally.[1]—But surely this is not the God, whom Christians adore!—not the Eternal I AM! not the *Father* of Spirits! not the Holy, the Merciful God![2]—But all these perplexities would have cleared away before a right view of the diversity of the *Reason* & the Understanding.[3]

14[1] On Spinoza's alleged atheism see e.g. *CN* I 1379 (Mar–Jul 1803), *CL* III 483 (1814), and *BL* ch 9 (1907) I 98–9. See also *Friend* (*CC*) I 516.

14[2] On the "Names" of God see **10** n 3, above. God is "I AM" in Exod 3.14, "the Father of spirits" in Heb 12.9, "eternal" in Deut 33.27, and is called "Merciful" and "Holy" passim.

14[3] For a central discussion of reason and understanding, see *SM* (*CC*) 60 n 2 and *AR* (1825) 208–28, esp 215–

18. For a formulation of the distinction in Oct 1806, see *CL* II 1198.

On i 13 a passage is marked in brown ink, probably not by C; but if marked before C used the book it will have attracted his attention: "And all this which men talk in the dark about God is non-sense, to trouble themselves and the world with, in false suppositions that God's Knowledge is such as ours, or that we can have sound conceptions and descriptions of it...".

Copy A

Reliquiae Baxterianae: or, Mr. Richard Baxter's narrative of the most memorable passages of his life and times. Faithfully publish'd from his own original manuscript, by Matthew Sylvester, &c. 3 pts (in 1 vol). London 1696. F°.

3 pts in two series of pagination, the second series beginning at Pt iii of the text; the Appendix forms a third series, to which is added the 18-page *Elisha's Cry After Elijah's God* by Matthew Sylvester.

Not located. Annotations reprinted from *NED. Lost List.*

The notes in this copy are identified in *NED* as "First Series". This may be the set of notes C referred to in his inscription in FIELD *Of the Church* (Oxford 1635) addressed to DC on 28 Mar 1819.

MS TRANSCRIPT. BM Add MS 32566 ff 9–12: brief summaries of about 25 of these marginalia made by the Rev John Mitford (1781–1859) in 1844, when the original was in the possession of William Pickering. Two of Mitford's notes represent one—or perhaps two—of C's notes not printed in *NED* and of which there is at present no other record: these are given in the ANNEX to this entry.

John Mitford, a contemporary of Richard Heber at Oxford and a friend of Lamb and of Bernard Barton, made important editions of Gray's poems and letters, prepared a dozen collective editions of English poets for Pickering's Aldine edition, and was editor of *G Mag* (then owned by Pickering) 1834–50. It does not appear by what process this agreeable, prosperous, and talented clergyman ("a pleasant layman spoiled", according to Lamb), an urbane but unpretentious conversationalist as well as a keen cricketer and a planter of exotic trees, came to be translated in *C 17th C* 321n into "Miss J. Mitford".

DATE. c 1811 and later. On 23 May 1814 C commended the book enthusiastically to J. J. Morgan. *CL* III 497–8. There is an insubstantial (and incorrect) reference to Baxter in Jul–Sept 1809 in *CN* III 3516, and a short quotation from the *Reliquiae* in late 1818 in *CN* III 4459; but there is no sign of the *Reliquiae* in the 1809–10 *Friend*, nor any positive indication when these notes were written. Some of the notes—especially **8** and **44[i]**—seem to look towards *AR*.

DISTRIBUTION OF MARGINALIA IN THE TWO COPIES

COPY A	textus page	COPY B
	i 2–14	3–6
2	22	7–8
	23–40	9–18
3	41	19

COPY A	textus page	COPY B
4	46	
	47	20
	59–114	21–38
5–7	116–25	
	127–38	39–47
8	141	48
9	142	49
	143	50
10	147	
	177–9	51, 52
11, 12	183–4	
13	185	53
	188–9	54, 55
14	193	
	194	56
15–17	197	
	198–226	57–64
18–25	242–5	
26–29	246	65
30, 31	247	
	248–70	66–75
32	271	
33	272	76
	273	77
34–43	274–307	
44[a]–[u]	308–32	78[a]–[j]
	337–43	79, 81
45–47	347–54	
	[365–7]	[82]
	368–9	83
48	369	84–86
49	370	87
	373–5	88–90 (116)
50, 51	384–7	
	398–405	91–93
52	411	
53	412	94
54	413	95, 96
55, 56	414–33	
	435	97
57–60	438–47	
61–64	ii 6–46	
	59–69	98–103
	144–91	104–110
	iii 36–45	111–113
65	55	114
66	57	

1 on a front flyleaf

In the notes, I have been bold enough marginally to write in this book, it will, I trust, be seen, that I am a bigot to no party. Highly do I approve of Baxter's conduct, affectionately admire and bless his peace-seeking spirit, and coincide with him as to the necessity of Church discipline in a Christian Church; but, on the other hand, I think his objections to the Liturgy, &c. &c., mistaken altogether, and even captious. His own system would have introduced an Hierocracy unexampled and insufferable, which yet he was the last man on earth to have meant or wished.

2 i 22 | 1 i § 34

1. That the Being and Attributes of God were so clear to me, that he was to my Intellect what the Sun is to my Eye, by which I see it self and all Things: And he seemed mad to me that questioned whether there were a God: that any Man should dream that the World was made of a Conflux of irrational Atoms, and Reason came from that which had no Reason, or that Man, or any Inferiour Being was independent; or that all the Being, Power, Wisdom and Goodness which we conversed with, had not a Cause which in Being, Power, Wisdom and Goodness, did excel all that which it had caused in the World, and had not all that *formaliter vel eminenter* in it self which it communicated to all the Creatures.

Ay! but this, alas, is not the true difficulty. No man in his senses can deny *God* in some sense or other, as *anima mundi, causa causarum*,[1] &c., but it is the *personal, living, self-conscious* God, which it is so difficult, except by faith of the Trinity, to combine with an infinite being infinitely and irresistibly causative. Τὸ ἓν καὶ πᾶν is the first dictate of mere human philosophy. Hence almost all the Greek philosophers were inconsistent Spinozists.[2]

2[1] "The soul of the world, the cause of causes". Cf AURELIUS **58**.

2[2] "The One and All" or "The One, that is, All"—the phrase that for C lies at the root of pre-Socratic, Neoplatonic, Spinozist, and Schellingian pantheism: see ATHENAEUM **22**. A central version of his oft-repeated formula for Spinoza's pantheism is part of a long note on HILLHOUSE *Hadad* (New York & London 1825) vi–xi (reprinted variatim in *TT* 10 Mar 1827): "...G = God. W = World.

W − G = 0. i.e. the World without God is an impossible Idea

G − W = 0 i.e. God without the World is do. Christian Theism

W − G = 0—i.e. as in the Spinosistic Scheme

G − W = G. i.e. But God without the World is God, the self-sufficing."

In a statement to HCR in Nov 1812 C said: "Did philosophy commence in an IT IS instead of an I AM, Spinoza would be altogether true." *CRB* I 112; and see ATHENAEUM **8** n 1, SPINOZA *Opera* (2 vols Jena 1802–3).

3 i 41 | § 57

But I remember some Principles which I think he misapplieth, as also doth Mr. *Thomas[a] Hooker* . . . That *the King* is *singulis major*, but *universis minor*; that he receiveth *his Power from the People*, &c. For I doubt not to prove that his Power is so immediately from God, as that there is no Recipient between God and him to convey it to him: Only . . . God by his Law, as an Instrument, conveyeth Power to that Person or Family whom the People consent to; and their Content is but a Conditio *sine quâ non*; and not any Proof that they are the Fountain of Power, or that ever the governing Power was in them; and therefore for my part I am satisfied that all *Politicks* err, which tell us of a *Majestas Realis* in the People, as distinct from the *Majestas Personalis* in the Governors . . . yet as to *governing Power* (which is the thing in question) the King is (as to the People) *Universis Major*, as well as *Singulis*: For if the Parliament have any Legislative Power, it cannot be as they are the Body or People . . . For if once Legislation (the chief Act of Government) be denied to be any part of Government at all, and affirmed to belong to the People as such, who are no Governors, all Government will hereby be overthrown.

Baxter here suffers himself to be deceived by the word *King*, which, in its Scriptural sense, does not mean a person, but the supreme power wherever rightfully vested.[1] In this sense, King, Lords, and Commons are our *King*, and in the execution of the laws, the King *represents* the whole, not *is*.

4 i 46 | § 68

[An account of an old woman who, after the massacre at Bolton, found an infant lying in the street by its dead mother and father, and] put it to her Breast for warmth, (having not had a Child her self of about 30 Years) the Child drew Milk, and so much, that the Woman nursed it up with her Breast Milk a good while . . .

The great naturalist, Ray, adduces, in treating of the male teat (vide his "Wisdom of God"), a yet stronger instance, that of a father whose breast furnished milk sufficient to preserve the life of the babe, whose

---

a Actually *Richard*: see COPY B 18A for C's correction

3[1] In his address on election as a Royal Associate of the Royal Society of Literature C spoke of "the lawful Representative of THE NATION, contra-distinguished from the People, as the Unity of the Generations of a people organized into a State—that is . . . the King, or the Sovereign". *CL* VI 864n. Cf *C&S (CC)* 41.

mother had perished as they were travelling through the waste plains (then so at least), in the North of Italy, and on seeming good authority.[1] I think that I have myself known a man who could have done it, under a conceived intense stimulus of pity and parental fondness.

5   i 116 | § 182

26. About the same time I fell into troublesom Acquaintance with one *Clement Writer* of *Worcester*. . . . His Assertion to me was, that no Man is bound to believe in Christ that doth not see confirming Miracles himself with his own Eyes.

By the Provocations of this Apostate, I wrote a Book [*The Unreasonableness of Infidelity*] . . . consisting of four Parts: The first, of the extrinsick Witness of the Spirit by Miracles, &c. to which I annexed a Disputation against *Clement Writer*, to prove that the Miracles wrought by Christ and his Apostles, oblige us to believe that did not see them. The Second part was of the intrinsick Witness of the Spirit, to Christ and Scripture. The Third was of the Sin or Blasphemy against the Holy Ghost. And the Fourth was to repress the Arrogancy of reasoning against Divine Revelations. All this was intended but as a supplement to the Second Part of *The Saints Rest*, where I had pleaded for the Truth of Scripture: But this Subject I have handled more fully in my *Reasons of the Christian Religion*.

Ay! but this was a natural consequence, honoured Baxter! of thy own step, who didst first introduce into England the Grotian *ab extra* mode of defending Christianity, which either leads to this conclusion or to Socinianism.[1]

4[1] John Ray (1627–1705) noticed this in *The Wisdom of God Manifested in the World of Creation* (pp 190–1 in the 1798 ed identified by *CN* III 4029 of 1810), one of Ray's most popular and least profound works. C noticed at least two other reports of males suckling: by Franklin in N 3½ f 134ᵛ, and by Humboldt in N 37 f 62.

5[1] Baxter had actually recommended "Grotius of the *Truth of Christian Religion*, which I lately saw is translated into English" in *The Saints Everlasting Rest* (1688) pt ii ch 7 p 245. In fairness to Baxter it may be suggested that in dealing with "Unbelievers and Anti-Scripturists" *ab extra* arguments are to some extent inevitable; and C evidently saw this as a natural outcome of Baxter's entering into controversy with an "Apostate". C affirms the defence *ab intra* in *CN* III 3911 (25 Jun 1810) as resting upon "the total State of the Spirit . . .". For Socinianism see e.g. BAHRDT **1** n 1, *CL* II 861, *CN* II 2640 and n. In *CN* I 1187 C spoke of the "pseudo-rationalism" of Paley—a description that C embraced in his often-used dismissive compound "Grotio-Paleyan".

6 i 123 | § 211

2. ... But fain they would have had my Controversal Writings, (about Universal Redemption, Predetermination, &c. in which my Judgment is more pleasing to them); but I was unwilling to publish them alone, while the Practical Writings are refused. And I give God thanks that I once saw Times of greater Liberty (though under an Usurper); or else as far as I can discern, scarce any of my Books had ever seen the Light.

A just though severe sarcasm: for observe Baxter and his writings were at least as inimical to Cromwell as to the Diocesans; nay, far, far more so. But the reign of Charles II. is the one great foul blotch of the Church of England.

7 i 125 | § 213

2. ... And those things which I was Orthodox in, I had either in-sufficient Reasons for, or a mixture of some sound and some in-sufficient ones, or else an insufficient Apprehension of those Reasons: so that I scarcely knew what I seemed to know*a* ...

Excellent.

8 i 141 | I ii § 6

And I found in all Antiquity, that though Infant Baptism was held lawful by the Church, yet some with *Tertullian* and *Nazienzen*, thought it most convenient to make no haste, and the rest left the time of Baptism to every ones liberty.... So that in the Primitive Church some were Baptized in Infancy, and some at ripe Age, and some a little before their Death; and none were forced, but all left free ...

But it is plain that Baxter and the other Pædo-Baptists have mis-understood the word "Infants" in the Greek and Latin Fathers, which should be translated *Minors*—all, in short, who had not the right of speaking for themselves, in courts of law. Thus wards, slaves, &c. were Νηπιοι, *Infantes*.[1] Absolute *Babe*-baptism began on the most charitable motives in Africa in the time of Cyprian.[2]

a Wherever—as here—*NED* italicises a passage not italicised in Baxter's printed text, it is assumed that the words were underlined by C in the annotated copy

8[1] Νήπιος, "foolish, infant"; and in the legal sense "not competent to speak for oneself" see Gal 4.1; *infans*, "not speaking, infant, of legal in-capacity".

8[2] This note seems to be based on Robert Robinson's *History of Baptism* (1790), which is not included in ROBINSON *Miscellaneous Works* (4 vols Harlow 1807). In *AR* (1825) 361n

9 i 142 | § 13

In the Presbyterian way I disliked 1. Their Order of *Lay-Elders* who had *no Ordination*, nor *Power to Preach*, nor to *administer Sacraments*: For though I grant that Lay-Elders, or the Chief of the People, were oft imployed to express the Peoples Consent, and preserve their Liberties, yet these were no *Church-Officers* at all, nor had any Charge of private Oversight of the Flocks ...

Now this is almost the only thing which I approve of and admire in the Presbyterian form, as constituting a medium and conducting link between the priest and the congregation, so that all may be one well-organised body spiritual without discontinuity; whereas our churches resemble insects, in which the head is connected with the body only by a *thread*, a conjunction disjunctive.

10 i 147 | § 26

[A letter of Mr Richard Vines to Baxter in reply to Baxter's "attempt for Concord with all, but especially the Episcopal Party".]

As finely perplexed, notably intertexed,[1] and luminously obscure an epistle as I ever remember to have read. The bursting plenitude of its nihility absolutely *overwhelms* and *crushes* a simple understanding. *Vines*, indeed! Ay, and brambles too! but without either grapes or blackberries![2]

11 i 183 | § 45

[How to find "Principles that we are all agreed in" with the Anabaptists.] 4. Those that do not take them [i.e. infants] for [Church] Members, if yet they have any more hope of them than of Heathen Children, or think it a Duty in any sort to dedicate them to God, let them bring them to the Congregation, and there ... either dedicate them to God, or profess their willingness to do it to the utmost of their Interest and Capacity, and desire God to accept them and bless them.

And what, in mercy's name, have the poor little heathen babies done, to be thus despondingly spoken of? Certainly no controversy can more senselessly produce anger and separation than that of baptism.

C asserted that "there exist no sufficient proofs that it *was*, the practice of the Apostolic Age", citing Baxter's authority in support of his view.

10[1] "Intertexed" — interwoven — a word also used in Jonson's *Underwoods* (*OED*).

10[2] Cf *EOT* (*CC*) ɪɪ 475 for a similar passage on vines—brambles—blackberries (in Latin).

For the Anti-pædo-Baptists lay no saving stress on the ceremony, and therefore their baptism amounts to no more than our Confirmation.

12   i 184

2. Let us declare that though one part be confident that Infant Baptism is a Duty, and the other that it is a Sin, yet we judge that they that Err here, while they sincerely desire to know the Truth, may be saved, notwithstanding that Errour.

A *hard* dispute! O mercy, mercy, dear Lord, on the intolerance of thy erring creatures! Did not the Lord himself say of *unbaptised* children "of such are the kingdom of heaven?"

13   i 185

[Replies to the objections of the Anabaptists.] 3. It must be no easie matter with us to believe, that the Head and Shepherd of the Church hath *de facto* had a Church of a false Constitution, as to the very Materials, and Enterance, from the beginning to this day, except a few within this twenty years that troubled it in a corner of the World; and that now in the end of the World, we must expect a right Constitution, as if Christ had slept, or regarded not his Church, or been the Head of a Body which he disowned: We cannot hastily believe such things. I say again, No Church, no Christ; for No Body, no Head: And if no Christ then, there is no Christ now. Take heed therefore how you un-Church, or disown the whole Church of Christ in the very frame, for so many Ages.

Might not the Baptist answer, "When Christ cometh, shall he find faith in the world? I say unto you, nay."[1] Besides, this reasoning compels a favourable judgment of the Romish European Church during ages by no means consonant with facts.

14   i 193 | § 49

And on the other Extream, *Cromwell* himself, and such others, commonly gave out that they could not understand what the Magistrate had to do in Matters of Religion; and they thought that all Men should be left to their own Consciences, and that the Magistrate could not interpose but he should be ensnared in the Guilt of Persecution . . .

13[1] Cf Luke 18.8, where the question is not answered.

One among a thousand proofs of Cromwell's attachment to the best interests of human nature!

15   i 197

10. Though it be not of necessity, yet would it be of great conveniency and use, if the Magistrate would be with us, or appoint some Substitute to represent him in all our Assemblies, that he may be a Witness of our Proceedings, and see that we do no wrong to the Commonwealth, and avoid all Suspicions that may be occasioned by Rumors: But principally that he may see how far it is meet for him in any case to second us by his Power.

The Magistrate's duty is not to punish or attempt to prevent *all* acts that may indirectly and in their remote consequences *injure* society: for if this were admitted, the statute *de Hereticis comburendis* might be justified:[1] but such acts as are directly incompatible with the *peace* and *security* of society, leaving all else to the influences of religion, education, sympathy, necessity of maintaining a character, &c. But Baxter's error was the error of his age, with the exception of a handful of Quakers, Independents, and philosophic Deists.[2]

16   i 197 | § 50

When *Cromwell's* Faction were making him Protector, they drew up a Thing which they called *"The Government of* England, *&c."* Therein they determined that all should have Liberty or free Exercise of their Religion, *who professed Faith in God by Jesus Christ.* After this he called a Parliament, which Examined this Instrument of Government; and when they came to those words, the Orthodox Party affirmed, *That if they spake* de re, *and not* de nomine *"Faith in God by Jesus Christ" could contain no less than the Fundamentals of*

15[1] The writ *De haeretico comburendo*—"On the need to burn a heretic"—first enacted in 1401 and suspended in 1533, was revived in 1554 (cf **35** n 1, below), and was finally abolished in 1677. See also COPY B **1** n 6.

15[2] C insists that the magistrate should not intrude upon the moral guidance of the church or upon the dictates of conscience—in short, that there can be no moral argument for government through state police. See also *C&S* (*CC*) xxxix; cf *SM* (*CC*) 92n.

For C on the Quakers generally see AURELIUS **47** n 1.

For the "Independents" see COPY B **2** n 5. Among the "philosophic Deists" C would number John Toland (1670–1722), Thomas Woolston (1670–1747), Anthony Collins (1676–1729), and Henry St John, 1st Viscount Bolingbroke (1678–1751): see e.g. *SM* (*CC*) 86 n 2, *Friend* (*CC*) I 426 and n 3. For a discussion of "philosophical Theists & Atheists" see *CN* III 4030.

Religion: whereupon it was purposed that all should have a due measure of Liberty who professed the *Fundamentals*.

The § 50 proves the danger of any, even the most moderate, test of religious faith.

17   i 197–8 | § 51

My own Judgment was this, that we must distinguish between the *Sense* (or *matter*) and the *Words*; and that it's only the *Sense* that is primarily and properly our *Fundamentals*: and the *Words* no further than as they are needful to express that *Sence* to others, or represent it to our own Conception: that the Word "Fundamentals" being Metaphorical and Ambiguous, the Word "Essentials" is much fitter ... that *quoad rem* there is no more *Essential* or *Fundamental* in Religion, but what is contained in our Baptismal Covenant, "*I believe in God the Father, Son and Holy Ghost, and give up my self in Covenant to him, renouncing the Flesh, the World and the Devil.*"

Baxter often expresses himself so as to excite a suspicion that he was inclined to Sabellianism.[1]

18   i 242–3 | "The Bishop's Answer to the first Proposals of the London Ministers"

§ 8. ... And we verily believe what Experience and the Constitutions of Kingdoms, Armies and even private Families sufficiently confirmeth ... that the Government of many is not only most subject to all the aforesaid Evils and Inconveniencies, but more likely also to breed and foment perpetual Factions both in Church and State, than the Government by one is or can be. And since no Government can certainly prevent all Evils that which is liable to the least and fewest is certainly to be preferred.

What a base appeal to the plan and passion of Charles II. for arbitrary power and despotic monarchy! what a wicked soothing and fomenting of it! From the furious insolent spirit of this answer, I suppose it to have been drawn up by or under Sheldon.[1]

[17][1] Against the orthodox doctrine of the "essential Trinity", Sabellius (fl A.D. 215) held a doctrine of "economic Trinity": that God was one indivisible substance with three fundamental modes or activities—as creator and lawgiver (Father), as redeemer (Son), and as the divine presence among men (Holy Ghost). The term "Sabellian" was later expanded, however, to include other forms of Monarchianism. For Sabellianism as the only one of "all the *Heresies* respecting the Person of Christ" that can be seen as "certainly clear from Polytheism" see *CN* III 3968. For Socinianism, see BAHRDT **1** and n 1.

[18][1] Gilbert Sheldon (1598–1677), successively Warden of All Souls, chaplain to Charles I, and (after im-

19 i 243 | § 9

... It being a great mistake, that the Personal Inspection of the Bishop is in all places of his Diocess at all times necessary. For by the same reason, neither Princes, nor Governours of Provinces, nor Generals of Armies, nor Mayors of great Cities, nor Ministers of great Parishes could ever be able to discharge their Duties in their several Places and Charges.

Answered by Christ's *"But it shall not be so among you."*[1]

20 i 243 | § 10

We confess the Bishops did (as by the Law they were enabled) depute part of the Administration of their Ecclesiastical Jurisdictions to Chancellors, Commissaries and Officials as Men better skill'd in the Civil and Canon Laws.

Still "The Law;"—as if the whole question had not been whether "the Law" ought not to be altered.

21 i 243

The reign of Charles I. was at once the glory and the shame of the English Diocesan Church; glory for the vast and various learning and stupendous talents of its Prelates and dignified Clergy; shame, for their atrocious cruelties, and rapid approximations to the superstitions, though not to the doctrinal errors of Popery. But the reign of Charles II., subtracting that which had attained its full growth in his father's life, was the mere infamy of the Church—a leprosy, some white discolorations from which are still eating, like a dry rot, into the walls of the Temple.

22 i 244 | § 16

We do not take the Oaths, Promises and Subscriptions by Law required of Ministers at their Ordination, Institution, &c. to be unnecessary. ... Upon all which consideration it is, that Officers in the

---

prisonment) bp of London, and abp of Canterbury. The Savoy Conference on the revision of the Book of Common Prayer was held in 1661 in his lodgings, he being then Master of the Savoy as well as bp of London. As adviser to Charles ii, he showed great severity to dissenters, yet is said to have sometimes protected them. See also below, **35**, **50**, and **62**.

19[1] See Matt 20.25–7: "Ye know that the princes of the Gentiles exercise dominion over them, and they that are great exercise authority upon them. But it shall not be so among you: but whosoever will be great among you, let him be your minister; and whosoever will be chief among you, let him be your servant." See also Mark 10.41–4.

Court, Freemen in Cities, and Corporate Towns, Masters and Fellows of Colledges in the Universities, &c. are required at their Admission into their several respective places to give Oaths for well and truly performing their several respective Duties, their liableness to punishment in case of Non-performance accordingly notwithstanding. Neither doth it seem reasonable that such Persons as have themselves with great severity prescribed and exacted antecedent Conditions of their Communion not warranted by Law, should be exempted from the tye of such Oaths and Subscriptions as the Laws require.

What a vindictive unchristian spirit of recrimination breathes here! Those who had the chief hand in drawing up the proposals, had opposed the former tyranny as firmly as that now impending.

23 i 245 | § 18

3. Nor [prayers] too tedious in the whole. It's well known that some Mens Prayers before and after Sermon, have been usually not much shorter, and sometimes much longer than the whole Church Service.

Petty womanish recrimination again! Does 15 prevent 10 from being 10? or A's being quite black justify B from being blacker than it ought to be?

24 i 245

4. Nor the Prayers too short. The Wisdom of the Church . . . hath thought it a fitter means for relieving the Infirmities of the meaner sort of People (which are the major part of most Congregations) to contrive several Petitions into sundry shorter Collects or Prayers, than to comprehend them altogether in a continued stile, or without interruption.

To this I fully agree.

25 i 245

5. Nor the Repetitions unmeet. . . . Not to mention the unhandsome Tautologies that oftentimes happen, and can scarce be avoided in the Extemporary and undigested Prayers that are made; especially by Persons of meaner Gifts.

But no one was then pleading for an extemporary service. This, too, is mere recrimination.

26 i 246 | § 21

As the Lord declared himself Jealous in Matters concerning the Substance of his Worship, so hath he left the Church at liberty for

Circumstantials to determine concerning Particulars according to Prudence as occasion shall require, so as the foresaid General Rules be still observed. And therefore the imposing and using indifferent Ceremonies, is not varying from the Will of God, nor is there made thereby any addition to, or detraction from the holy Duties of God's Worship.

Curious logic! The "using" may not be "varying", but the "imposing"—that is the contraband ware! There limps the "*Ergo*!"

27   i 246 | § 24

That the Ceremonies have been Matter of Contention in this or any other Church was not either from the Nature of the Thing enjoyned, or the enjoyning of the same by Lawful Authority: but partly from the weakness of some Men's Judgments unable to search into the Reason of Things: and partly from the unsubduedness of some Mens Spirits more apt to contend, than willing to submit their private Opinions to the Publick Judgment of the Church.

True Inquisitor's logic! But ought not the foreseen certainty of these evils to have modified and aided in forming the public judgment of the Church? Would not St. Paul have advised this, who even in things not essential bids the stronger give way to their weaker brethren?[1]

28   i 246 | § 27

The Separation that hath been made from the Church, was from the taking a Scandal where none was given ... chiefly occasioned by the Practice, and defended from the Principles of those that refused Conformity to the <u>Law</u>, the <u>just Rule</u> and <u>Measure</u> of the <u>Churches</u> Unity.

Christ's kingdom then *is* of this world! *The Law*![1]

29   i 246–7 | § 28

The Nature of Things being declared to be mutable, sheweth that they may therefore be changed, as they that are in Authority shall see it expedient; but it is no proof at all that it is therefore expedient that it should be actually changed.... The Change of Laws, although liable to some Inconveniencies, without great and evident

27[1] No single text supports this statement, but see e.g. Acts 20.35, Rom 15.1, 1 Cor 1.27, 6.4, 2 Cor 12.9–10, Col 3.12–25.

28[1] Cf John 18.36: "Jesus answered, My kingdom is not of this world...".

necessity, hath been by Wise men ever accounted a thing not only Imprudent, but of evil, and sometimes pernicious Consequence.

An evident sophism, εἰς ἄλλο γενός.[1] Baxter confines the remark to *religious* indifferent ceremonies; and adds a very wise reason, which is here passed over.

30   i 247 | § 29

... The Lord hath entrusted Governours to provide, not only that Things necessary in God's Worship be duly performed, but also that things advisedly enjoyned, though not otherways necessary, should be orderly and duly observed. The too great neglect whereof would so cut the Sinews of Authority, that it would become first infirm, and then contemptible.

In what part of the New Testament has the Lord troubled these Gentlemen with any concern in any part of the business? St. Paul cries Shame! on those Christians who appealed to Courts of *Law*, even in their matters of temporal interest.[1] This, indeed, is now a precept not practicable, but the *spirit* of it is still valid.

31   i 247 | § 32

But why they that confess that in the Judgment of all the things here mentioned [the Surplice, Cross after Baptism, and bowing at the Name of Jesus] are not to be valued with the Peace of the Church, should yet after they are established by Law, disturb the Peace of the Church, about them, we understand not.

This is the most plausible, and therefore *decantatissimum sophisma*[1] of the Herodian Diocesans. And yet a mere sophism it is. For whoever thought these things *of saving importance*, would err even to a most perilous heresy. *Ergo*, all true members of the Church of England must regard these holidays and ceremonies *at best*, as among the ἀδιάφορα, things of mutable expedience:[2] while the objectors considered them

29[1] A "transition to another kind", or as C explained in *AR* (1825) 215: "...the numerous Sophisms comprised by Aristotle under the head of Μετα-βασις εις αλλο γενος, *i.e.* Transition into a new kind, or the falsely applying to X what had been truly asserted of A, and might have been true of X, had it differed from A in its degree only. The sophistry consists in the omission to notice what not being noticed will be

supposed not to exist...". See also *AR* (1825) 312: a "clandestine passing over into a diverse kind". See Aristotle *Posterior Analytics* 75ᵃ38ff.

30[1] The gist of 1 Cor 6.1–7.

31[1] "The most-often-mouthed fallacy". *Decantatus*=repeated as in singing, sing-song, in an empty-headed manner.

31[2] "Indifferent"—which C glosses as "things of mutable expedience".

as *dangerous* follies, though not *condemnative*; inasmuch as they had a tendency to lead back men's minds to Popish superstitions, and had occasioned, yea, and still do occasion, the vulgar to elevate circumstantials into essentials.

32 i 271 | § 106 "The Reasons why we insist on the second Proposal"

2. If all Presentments and Appeals be made to the *Bishop* and his *Consistory alone*, it will *take from us* the *Parish Discipline* which granted us, and cast almost all Discipline out of the Church.

The incompossibility[1] of Christian discipline with a Church established by Law, and all the permitted acts of which have the force of penal or compulsory Laws, has always appeared to me the objection that bears hardest on Church Establishment. Where Law begins, Discipline ends. This Baxter did not at all times see clearly. But the Diocesan form of an Established Church, as it exists in England, adds to this inherent incongruity all possible external impediments. And yet

> Old Church! with all thy faults I *love* thee still.—[2]

Yea, with a filial, though not with a blind, adherence.

33 i 272

2. We beseech your Majesty to understand, that it is not our meaning by the Word "*abolishing*" to crave a Prohibition against *your own* or other Mens Liberty in the things in question; but it is a *full Liberty* that we *desire*; such as should be in *unnecessary things*; and such as will tend to the Concord of your People, *viz. that there be no Law or Canon for or against them, commanding, recommending or prohibiting them*: As now there is none for any particular Gesture in *singing of Psalms*, where *Liberty* preserveth an *uninterrupted Unity*.

Admirable!

34 i 274

A little before this, the Bishops Party had appointed . . . a meeting with some of us. . . . Accordingly Dr. *Morley*, Dr. *Hinchman*, and Dr. *Cosins* met Dr. *Reignolds*, Mr. *Calamy*, and my self; and after a

---

32[1] "Incompossibility"—total incapability of existing together (or of being valid together)—is recorded in *OED* as early as 1629. Randolph (1630)

ascribed the word to Duns Scotus.

32[2] Variant of Cowper *The Task* II 206: "England, with all thy faults, I love thee still".

few roving Discourses we parted without bringing them to any particular Concessions for Abatement . . .

This was the Dr. Cosins who formed and left the present Durham Library. He was deeply versed in the Schoolmen, *ipse plusquam satis scholasticus*. Yet I could find but one work of Duns Scotus's—that *De Sententiis*.[1]

35   i 276 | § 108

After all this a Day was appointed for his Majesty to peruse the Declaration as it was drawn up by the Lord Chancellor, and to allow what he liked and alter the rest, upon the hearing of what both sides should say. Accordingly he came to the Lord Chancellor's House, and with him the Duke of *Albermarle*, and Duke of *Ormond* (as I remember), the Earl of *Manchester*, the Earl of *Anglesey*, the Lord *Hollis*, &c. and Dr. *Sheldon* (then) Bishop of *London*, Dr. *Morley* (then) Bishop of *Worcester* . . .

This was the incendiary! this Sheldon the most virulent enemy and poisoner of the English Church. Alas! she still feels the *taint* in her very bones. I look on Gardner as canonisable compared with Sheldon.[1]

36   i 277 | § 110

. . . Thereupon he read, as an Addition to the Declaration, that "*others also be permitted to meet for Religious Worship, so be it, they do it not to the disturbance of the Peace: and that no Justice of Peace or Officer disturb them.*" When he had read it, he again desired them all to think on it, and give their Advice: But all were silent. The Presbyterians all perceived, as soon as they heard it, that it would secure the Liberty of the Papists . . .

34[1] John Cosin (1594–1672)—"no mean scholastic himself"—when prebendary and later bp of Durham, and as Master of Peterhouse, Cambridge, introduced elaborate services and church ornaments, for which he was accused of Romanism.

C used the Durham Cathedral library Jul–Aug 1801; see *CN* I 973n. He said that he was "burning Locke, Hume, & Hobbes" under the nose of Duns Scotus; see *CL* II 746. In Nov 1803 he asked Thelwall to bring a copy of Duns Scotus *De sententiis* from the Sandes Library in Kendal (*CL* II 1020); in the same month "Scotus" was one of the names in C's list of "Revolutionary Minds" (*CN* I 1646).

35[1] For Sheldon, see **18** n 1, above, and **62**, below. "Gardner" is Stephen Gardiner (c 1483–1555), bp of Winchester. In 1554 he secured re-enactment of the writ *De haeretico comburendo* (see **15** n 1, above) and displayed the grossest cruelty in his persecution of Protestants. It is clear from **62** why C regarded Sheldon as more despicable than Gardiner.

Another sad proof of the bad effects of imperfect theory respecting religious toleration. How easy would it otherwise have been to have excepted and excluded the Papists, not as religionists, but as having an actual temporal magistracy, under the false name of spiritual, obstinately independent of the supreme power, and owning a foreign Sovereign.

37   i 278 | § 112

And here you may note, by the way, the fashion of these Times, and the state of the Presbyterians: Any Man that was for a Spiritual serious way of Worship (though he were for moderate Episcopacy and Liturgy), and that lived according to his Profession, was called commonly a *Presbyterian*, as formerly he was called a *Puritan*, unless he joyned himself to *Independents*, *Anabaptists*, or some other Sect which might afford him a more odious Name.

I suspect that it would have puzzled the mild and kind-hearted old man sorely, if he (Baxter, I mean), had been asked: Well! and what would you have done with these sectaries, Independents, Socinians, &c. Hang them? Banish them? Dungeon them? The admission that even an avowed *Atheist* may, *for that cause only*, be rightfully punished by the civil magistrate, doth, by incontestable consequence justify and legitimate the whole fire and faggot system, *de Hereticis cujuslibet generis et omnium specierum*.[1] Even now unlimited toleration is only a thing, half *fashion*, half religious indifference. The *common* arguments in favour of it, such as those adduced by Locke,[2] had been fairly and fully and repeatedly confuted by both Romish and Protestant Divines; and the *true* grounds it would not perhaps *even now* be quite safe for a writer to bring forwards. We owe the blessing wholly to God, with no intervention or instrumentality of Human Wisdom.

37[1] The Latin phrase continues the sentence, "with regard to heretics of every class and all species"—an allusion to the title *De haeretico comburendo* in **15**, above.

37[2] John Locke (1632–1704) published his *Letter Concerning Toleration* in Latin in 1667; appearing in English tr in the same year, it attracted controversy in which Jonas Proast of Queen's College, Oxford, was principal opponent. Locke replied with three *Letters for Toleration* in 1689, 1690, and 1692; a fourth was incomplete when Locke died. He argued that there should be an established church exercising a toleration that legislated only against atheism and Catholicism as being inimical to religion and the state.

38   i 279 | § 116

... Before this, I was called to preach at Court before the King (by the Lord Chamberlain who had sworn me his Chaplain, and invited me under that Name): And after Sermon it pleased his Majesty to send the Lord Chamberlain to require me to print it. ... Yet when this Sermon came abroad, Dr. *Thomas Pierce* went up and down raging against me, for calling my self on the Title page "His Majesty's Chaplain" (which if I had not, it would have been taken as a Contempt) and for saying it was printed by his Majesty's Special Command: and he renewed all the Railings which in print he had lately vented against me.

Who dare presume himself secure from the sin of calumnious bigotry, (except by the opposite extreme of irreligious indifference,) when such men could be capable of such wicked outrages? But an infatuated ἀνακτοδουλεῖα, an absolute Carololatreia,[1] strongly marked in his fine Latin epitaph on Charles the First, combined with a raging zeal for Diocesan Episcopacy to overset him.[2]

39   i 280 | § 117

§ 117. ... I did thereupon write a little Collection out of the late Writings of *Grotius* (especially his *Discussio Apologetici Rivetiani*) to prove him to have turned Papist; and that Popery was indeed his Religion (though he communicated with no Church) (for he expressly pleadeth for our consenting to the Council of *Trent*, and all other general Councils as the Churches Law, and to the Pope's

---

[1] ᾿Ανακτοδουλεῖα—King-veneration; "Carololatria"—Charles-worship. In theological usage, as here, "-dulia" ("-douly", δουλεῖα) is the veneration paid to saints and angels, "latria" ("-latry", λατρεῖα) the worship due to God alone. In classical Greek δουλεῖα means "slavery", λατρεῖα "service, worship". C, in using several compounds of "-duly" and "-latry", sometimes makes play of the difference between the classical and theological meanings. See "bibliolatry" in CHILLINGWORTH COPY B 2; "hagiolatry" and "papoduly" in CHILLINGWORTH COPY B 4; "hierolatry" in BAXTER *Reliquiae* COPY B 30; "Mammonolatry" in BAXTER *Reliquiae* COPY B 47; "par-

thenolatries" and "hyperdulies" in BLANCO WHITE *Practical Evidence* 10. The coinage αξιολατροι—Wordsworth-worshippers—appears in a contemptuous sense in *CN* III 4243.

[2] Thomas Pierce (1622–91), controversialist and bitter enemy of the Calvinists, became chaplain in ordinary to Charles II. His "fine Latin epitaph" on Charles I is *Caroli* τοῦ μακαρίτου παλινγενεσία—*The Restoration of the Blessed Charles*—(1649 anon, later acknowledged), appended with other epitaphs of his to the *Rationes...Caroli* [? 1690], his Latin translation of *His Majesties Reasons Against the Pretended Jurisdiction of the High Court of Justice.*

Sovereign Government; so it be according to those Laws, and to the Mistressship of the Church of *Rome* over all other Churches . . .)

This surely must have been some mistake of Baxter's. That Grotius sighed for a reconciliation of the Roman and Protestant Churches is well known; but that he should go beyond the French Catholics, and even the Spanish, is to me incredible. Baxter seems not to have read the works themselves, but to have relied on the authority of the French author of *Grotius Papizans*.[1]

40 i 280

But Mr. *Pierce* was vehemently furious at my Book, and wrote a Volume against me full of <u>ingenuous</u> Lies and Railings; for he had no better way to defend *Grotius* or himself.

One of the very few improvements in our language since the time of the Restoration is the separation of "ingenious" and "ingenuous". The prior writers confound them.[1]

41 i 282 | § 123 Baxter's Letter to the Lord Chancellor upon the office of a Bishopric

My Lord . . . *I was, till I saw the Declaration, much dejected, and resolved against a Bishoprick as unlawful. But finding there more than on* Octob. 22. *his Majesty granted us* (*in the Pastor's* Consent, &c. *the Rural Dean with the whole Ministry enabled to exercise as much persuasive Pastoral Power as I could desire* (*who believe the Church hath no other kind of Power, unless communicated from the Magistrate*) *Subscription abated in the Universities, &c.*)

Even this says the Inquisition![1] But what right has a Christian pastor to admit, much less to invite, the *Wolf* of temporal power, even

---

39[1] Baxter cites the work at i 280: "a Book written (I think by *Vincentius*) a French Minister, called *Grotius Papizans*". The book is Jacobus Laurentius (1585–1644) *Hugo Grotius Papizans* (Amsterdam 1642). The book was reprinted at The Hague in 1830. Laurentius' claim to fame comes from this attribution of Roman Catholic sympathies to Grotius.

40[1] C made the same point in Thomas FULLER *Holy State* 1. OED cites examples of the confusion of "ingenuous" and "ingenious" from Shakespeare (1588) to Adam Smith (1776). Both words are derived from *in+gen*, in-born; but "ingenious" is from *ingenium* (inborn character, intelligence) and "ingenuous" from *ingenuus* (native, free-born, honourable).

C held that "all Languages perfect themselves by a gradual process of desynonimizing words originally equivalent" (*CN* III 4397 f 49ᵛ); see also *BL* ch 4 (1907) I 61, and cf *P Lects* Lect 5 (1949) 173–4. For some other examples of "The importance of desynonymizing" see *CN* III 4422.

41[1] See COPY B 1 n 6.

against the scabbiest sheep of his flock?[2] Oh! this, this was the dire error that ruined the otherwise good cause of these good men!

42   i 291 | § 149 Letter of thanks to Baxter from the Court and Governor in New England

All that we desire is Liberty to serve God according to the Scriptures...

That is, alas! alas! according to *our* interpretation of the Scriptures. So say not a few even of the Romanists.

43   i 307 | § 174

[At the Savoy Conference, instituted by Charles II to review and reform the liturgy, two of the assistants to the Commissioners were Baxter himself and Dr Lightfoot.] § 174. When I brought my Draught [for a revised prayer-book] to the Brethren, I found them but entering on their Work of Exceptions against the Common-Prayer... The chief Actors in that part were, Dr. Reignolds, Dr. Wallis, Mr. Calamy, Mr. Newcomen, Dr. Bates, Mr. Clarke, Dr. Jacomb &c. Dr. *Horton* never came among us at all, nor Dr. *Tuckney*, (alledging his backwardness to speak, though he had been the Doctor of the Chair in *Cambridge*) nor Dr. *Lightfoot* but once or twice...

A learned man, but a *shy cock*. His trimming, however, the effect perhaps of timidity, died with him; his works still remain a treasure to Christ's Church.[1]

44   i 308–32 | "The Exceptions against the Common-Prayer which I offered the Brethren when they were drawing up theirs"[1]

The Common-Prayer-Book is guilty of great Defectiveness, Disorder, and vain Repetitions; and therefore unfit to be the common imposed Frame of Worship to the God of Order, without Amendment, when we may do it.

I really grieve that such an eminent saint of God as Baxter should,

---

41[2] Cf BÖHME **16**, in which C speaks of his own life as "sickly and like a Sheep with the *Rot*". In 1805, when he wrote his name in a list with the names of WW, DW, MW, and SH, he added: "O blessed Flock! I the sole scabbed Sheep!" *CN* II 2623; cf 2005.

43[1] C's reference is to John Lightfoot (1602–75), a biblical scholar of substance and one of the greatest Hebraists England has ever produced. See also LIGHTFOOT *Works* (2 vols 1684).

44[1] The "Exceptions" run through i 308–33. C's sequential comments in COPY A, as in COPY B **78**, are here treated as a single annotation divided into lettered sections.

against the advice of his own friends, have preserved such weak and *pettish* criticisms.

44[a]　i 308

3. The Confession omitteth not only Original Sin, but all actual Sin.... Whereas *Confession* being the *Expression of Repentance*, should be more *particular*, as *Repentance* it self should be.

But this is public, common, prayer.

44[b]　i 308

4. When we have craved help for *God's Prayers*, before we come to them, we abruptly put in the Petition for speedy Deliverance "*O God make speed to save us: O Lord make haste to help us.*" without any Intimation of the Danger that we desire deliverance from, and without any other Petition conjoined.

　5. It is disorderly in the *Manner*, to sing the Scripture in a plain Tune after the manner of reading.

　6. "*The Lord be with you. And with thy Spirit*" being Petitions for Divine Assistance, come in abruptly, in the midst or near the end of Morning Prayer: And "*Let us Pray*" is adjoined when we were before in Prayer.

Oh! these seem to me very captious and unthinking objections. Had good Baxter considered the Liturgy *psychologically*, or as a grand composition of devotional *music*, gradually attuning, preparing, animating, and *working up*, the feelings of men to *public* and *common* prayer, and thanks, and glory-giving, he would have seen the excellence of much which he here condemns. Above all, he should have borne in mind that public prayer and private prayer, nay, I may add an intermediate, viz., domestic prayer, are quite distinct—much in each incongruous with the others—and that *common* prayer neither can, nor was ever intended to, supersede individual prayer. The direful lethargy of the *mumpsimus*[1] Church hirelings then distorted, and alas *still* too often distorts, the judgments of warm and earnest Gospel preachers.

　44[b][1] The word, often used to mean an old fogey, originally meant a person who obstinately adheres to old ways in spite of clear evidence that he is wrong, alluding to the story told by Richard Pace (c 1482–1536) in his *De fructu* (1517) of an illiterate English priest who, when corrected for mispronouncing the liturgical phrase *quod in ore sumpsimus*, replied: "I will not change my old mumpsimus for your new sumpsimus."

44[c] i 308

12. The *Litany*, which should contain all the ordinary Petitions of the Church, omitteth very many particulars, as may appear in our offered Forms compared with it: It were tedious to number the half of its omissions. And it is exceeding disorderly, following no just Rules of method...

Who might not suppose that Baxter required the soul to be *syllogising* all the while it was praying?

44[d] i 309

... Next is a Prayer against *Adversity* and *Persecutions*, which was done before: and both here and through the rest of the Prayers, the deprecation of *bodily suffering* hath very much too large a proportion, while *spirituals* are too *generally* and *briefly* touched; which is unbeseeming the Church of Christ, which mindeth not the things of the *flesh*, but of the *spirit*...

This is an especial trait of wisdom in the compilers of our Liturgy; it was to be *common* prayer. Now the spirit prayeth to the Spirit *ineffably*; but outward evils, taken as God's trials or chastisements, are to all men intelligible, and the combining them with devotional faith and feelings of the best practical influence.

44[e] i 310

Baxter seems constantly to overlook, that our Liturgy is a form of *common* prayer, for a promiscuous audience, and charitably framed to rouse the inattentive as often as possible; and to provide something that will suit each; *some* particularly, and which yet *all*, in a spiritual sense at least, may use pertinently.

44[f] i 310

The first Collect on *Good-fryday* hath no Petition, but that God will "*graciously behold this his Family*" (inconveniently also expressed: the Pronoun "*this*" seeming plainly to mean, that particular Congregation; which is not to be called *God's Family*, but part of it).

Why not? Should I not say "this family," though many of my sons and daughters were elsewhere?

44[g] i 311

That [Collect] on *Trinity* Sunday asketh nothing at all, but "*through the stedfastness of our Faith to be defended evermore from all ad-*

versity". A Petition so frequently repeated, even alone, as if we would perswade the Enemies of the Church, that we are a worldly carnal People; and principally seek the things that perish: when indeed it is a sin to pray to be "*evermore defended from all adversity*"; when God hath told us, *that through many tribulations we must enter into his kingdom*...

But surely the compilers did not mean "adversity" in this carnal sense; but for whatever opposes our permanent well-being.

44[h] i 311

No more reason is there for the order of the Requests [on specified Sundays after Trinity]...(which only prays God, whose Providence is never deceived, to put *away from us all hurtful things, and give us those things that be profitable*: all meer Generals; in which no *particular repentance* or *desires* are expressed).

But all this, and nine-tenths of the foregoing, asks impossible or inconvenient things. The different prayers were not of necessity to be strikingly appropriate to each day; but to bring in all at *some* time or other, which *could* not be presented to the mind at *each* time. They were *opportunities* for wise prayers, rather than the *occasions* of them.

44[i] i 313

The Conclusion that "*the Child is Regenerate*" and the Thanksgiving for "*Regenerating it by the Spirit*" are doubly faulty: First, in concluding that *all Children baptized are Regenerate*....Secondly in concluding all Infants regenerate by the Holy Ghost, when so many Learned Divines think that it is but a Relative Regeneration, that is ascertained them; and the Controversie is yet undecided.

It is now the fashion (see Prettyman and Magee)[1] to assert that

44[i][1] George Pretyman, later Tomline (1750–1827), tutor to the younger Pitt and bp of Winchester. C refers to Tomline's *A Refutation of Calvinism* (1811, 8th ed 1823). In ch 2 "Of Regeneration" Tomline limits the term "regeneration" to the sense of Tit 3.5—"Not by works of righteousness which we have done, but according to his mercy he saved us, by the washing of regeneration, and renewing of the Holy Ghost"—and argues that the term is properly applicable to baptism only.

William Magee (1766–1831), abp of Dublin, whose "statement or exposition (*ad normam Grotianam*)", in *Discourses on the Scriptural Doctrines of Atonement and Sacrifice* (1801), "of the doctrine of Redemption" disappointed C's "high expectations" and sadly chilled "the fervid sympathy" that Magee's introductory chapter had aroused. *AR* (1825) 400–1n. C referred to Magee as an "Arminian Church of England Divine" in N 35 f 30[v].

"regeneration" is used by all the best Fathers, as a mere synonym equipollent to Baptism; and so they try to evade the consequences drawn by the Anti-pædo-baptists against the baptism of infants, as insusceptible of those spiritual concomitances of the will, without which Regeneration (in a spiritual sense) seems either magical or a mere *word*. But how easily is the argument turned against them! If, in the opinion of the Primitive Doctors, Regeneration means Baptism, then Baptism must have meant Regeneration; but Regeneration implies a concomitance of the will: *Ergo*, &c.[2]

44[j]   i 314

In the Rubrick for Confirmation, the Order that Children shall be Confirmed when they can say the Creed, Lord's Prayer, and Ten Commandments, and answer the Questions of the Catechism, seems contrary to the first and third Reasons, which require that *Solemn Renewal* or *owning of their Covenant*, which ordinarily they are not ripe for, of many years after they can say the Catechism.

This does appear to *me* unanswerable except by an admission, which truth might dictate, yet Christian prudence hardly permit; viz., that an Established National Church is not only a most useful, but even a necessary thing; and yet that it *is* not and that it *ought* not to be, judged of by the rules of an *elect* Christian congregation. "Cast thy bread on the waters," &c., seems the proper motto of the Established Church of England.[1]

44[k]   i 314

The Prayers and Administration of Confirmation suppose all the Children brought to be Confirmed, to have the Spirit of Christ and the forgiveness of all their Sins; whereas a great number of Children at that Age...do live a carnal, careless Life, and shew no Love to God above all, no prevalent self-denial, Mortification, nor Faith in Christ, and Heavenly-mindedness, nor serious Repentance for the Life of Sin which they continue in after Baptism: Therefore to these Children Confirmation is not to be Administered, till besides the saying of the Catechism, they make a credible Profession of Faith,

44[i][2] The "*Ergo* &c" is "therefore infants *are* susceptible of those spiritual concomitances of the will...". C later developed this in *AR* (1825) 330–2. See also *CN* III 4401.

44[j][1] Eccles 11.1: "Cast thy bread upon the waters: for thou shalt find it after many days."

Repentance, and Obedience: And to them that do not thus, Confirmation is a gross and perilous Abuse.

Poor little sinful darlings! This was the cant of the age.

44[l] i 315

In the Communion of the Sick, the ancient Custom of the Church was, where time and place allowed it, to send the Deacon to the Sick, at the time of the Celebration, with a Portion of the Consecrated Bread and Wine, which is here omitted.

Me Judice,[1] a very wise omission; for the practice almost inevitably leads to superstition, and to the notion of some *magical* charm infused into the elements.

44[m] i 315

1. It is a great Disorder that we have so *many Prayers*, instead of *many Petitions in one Prayer*...whereas the Common-Prayer-Book, in its numerous Collects, doth make oft times as *many Prayers* as *Petitions*; and we undecently begin with a solemn Preface, and as Solemnly conclude, and then Begin again...

Baxter for ever forgets that at Kidderminster he had a *select* congregation, one perhaps of a thousand; but that the national Church has to provide for *promiscuous congregations*.

44[n] i 315

2. Hence it comes to pass that the holy and reverend Name of God is made the matter of unnecessary Tautologies, while half the Prayer is made up of his Attributes and Addresses to him, and with Conclusions containing the Mention of his Name and Kingdom, and the Merits of his Son; even in holy Worship we should fear using God's Name unreverently and in vain.

This is most true; but with what tenfold force does it apply to common *extemporary* prayer among Dissenters!

44[o] i 317 | "The Exceptions against the Book of Common-Prayer"

4. That in regard the Litany ... is so framed, that the Petitions for a great part are uttered only by the People, which we think not to be so

44[l][1] "In my Judgement".

consonant to Scripture, which makes the Minister the Mouth of the People to God in Prayer, the Particulars thereof may be composed into one solemn Prayer to be offered by the Minister unto God for the People.

No wonder that the bishops and their party conquered, when the excepters gave them such advantages. Many a proselyte has *the Church* gained from *the Meeting-house* through the disgust occasioned by the long-winded, preaching prayers of the dissenting ministers, and the utter exclusion of the congregation from all *active* share in the public devotion.

44[p]   i 321–4 | "Particulars to be taken into tender and serious Consideration"

N.] [i] By this Rubrick, and other places in the Common Prayer Books, the *Gloria Patri*, is appointed to be said *six times ordinarily* in every Morning and Evening Service, *frequently eight times* in a Morning; *sometimes ten...* for the avoiding of which appearance of evil, we desire it may be used but once in the Morning, and once in the Evening....

N.] [ii] In regard that the wages of sin is death; we desire that this Clause [in the Litany] may be thus altered, *From Fornication, and all other heinous, or grievous sins.*

N.] [iii] We desire the term *"All"* may be advised upon, as seeming liable to just Exceptions, and that it may be considered, whether it may not better be put indefinitely, *those that travel,* &c. rather than *universally.*

NN.] [iv] That instead of those short Prayers of the People [in the Communion Service], intermixed with the several Commandments, the Minister after the reading of all may conclude with a suitable Prayer.

Paragraphs marked thus—N., appear to me weak; those with NN. not only weak, but of ill consequence.

44[q]   i 326 | Of Publick Baptism

NN.] There being divers Learned, Pious, and Peaceable Ministers, who not only judge it unlawful to Baptize Children, whose Parents both of them are Atheists, Infidels, Hereticks, or Unbaptised, but also such whose Parents are Excommunicate Persons, Fornicators, or otherwise notorious and scandalous Sinners; We desire they may not be enforced to Baptize the Children of such, until they have made due Profession of their Repentance.

If it be right and efficacious to baptise children at all,[1] why should these poor darlings be excepted, for no other reason but that they are so unfortunate as to have wicked parents? If baptism be a good, the denial of it is a misfortune; and is it Christian charity to add misfortune to misfortune, and that to poor worse than orphan children?

44[r]   i 327 | Of Private Baptism

NN.] We desire that Baptism may not be administered in a private place at any time, unless by a lawful Minister, and in the presence of a competent Number...

Beyond all doubt every sincere Christian is so far a priest of the Gospel, as that, in case of necessity, he may and ought to baptise.

44[s]   i 329 | Of Confirmation

We conceive that it is not a sufficient qualification for Confirmation, that Children be able *memoriter* to repeat the Articles of the Faith ...and to answer to some Questions of this short Catechism; for it is often found that Children are able to do all this at four or five years old....

This is a sound and weighty objection, confirmed by constant experience.

44[t]   i 331 | Of the Form of Solemnization of Matrimony

N.] Seeing the Institution of Marriage was before the Fall, and so before the Promise of Christ, as also for that the said Passage in this Collect seems to countenance the Opinion of making Matrimony a *Sacrament*, we desire that Clause ["Consecrated the state of Matrimony to such an excellent Mystery"] may be altered or omitted.

44[u]   i 332 | Of the Order for the Burial of the Dead

"Forasmuch as it hath pleased Almighty God, of his great mercy to take unto himself the soul of our dear Brother here departed: We therefore commit his Body to the Ground in sure and certain hope of Resurrection to Eternal Life." These words cannot in Truth be said of Persons living and dying in open and notorious sins.

44[q][1] See **8** n 2, above, and BIBLE COPY B **138** n 1. For C's attitude towards the christening of his own children see ANDERSON COPY A **1** and nn 4, 5.

"We give thee hearty thanks for that it hath pleased thee to deliver this our Brother out of the miseries of this sinful world, &c." These words may harden the wicked, and are inconsistent with the largest rational Charity.

"That when we depart this Life, we may rest in him, as our hope is this our Brother doth." These words cannot be used with respect to those Persons who have not by their actual Repentance given any ground for the hope of their Blessed Estate.

Sound objections. Indeed, no month passes in which the common people do not make the same observation, when any one of notoriously bad character is burying.

45   i 347 | § 217

...I alledged the 20th *Canon Concil. Nicaen. &c. Concil. Trull.* and *Tertullian* oft, and with the common Consent of ancient Writers, who tell us, it was the Tradition and Custom of the universal Church, not to adore by Genuflexion on any Lord's Day, or on any Day between *Easter* and *Whitsuntide. Ergo,* not so to adore in taking the Sacrament.

I think that *this* one argument might have been fairly turned against Baxter; for by the implied allowance of genuflexion on *week* days, with the exception of the interval between Easter and Whitsuntide, it seems evident that the standing up was intended as a symbolical remembrancing of our Lord's resurrection and of our own: *ergo*—one of those mere arbitrary ceremonies which led to the final corruption and apostasy both of the Roman (or Western), and of the Greek or Oriental churches. It is, however, undeniable, that Baxter truly asserted the primitive custom to be that of receiving the sacrament sitting.

46   i 354 | § 224 "The Reply to the Bishops Disputants"

I. So to receive one another as Christ received us to the Glory of God the Father, and this not to doubtful Disputation, (or not to judge their doubtful Thoughts) and not to despise or judge one another, but to take each other for such as do what we do to the Lord, and let every Man be fully perswaded in his own Mind; and so as to distinguish the Points that we differ about from those in which God's Kingdom doth consist, in which whosoever serveth Christ is acceptable to God, and should be approved of Men; and so as to follow the things that edifie and make for Peace, and not lay a stumbling block or occasion of falling in our Brother's way, or destroy him by the uncharitable use of our Liberty, knowing it is Sin to him that esteemeth it Sin; but to forbear our selves to use those things in Controversie whereby our Brother stumbleth or is offended, because he is damned if he use them doubtingly; and therefore to have the belief of their lawfulness to our selves before God, and to bear with the Infirmities of the Weak, and please them to their E[d]ification, and not to please our selves, that so being like-minded one towards another, that with one mind and one mouth we may glorifie God: We say, Thus to receive is not consistent with the denial of Communion in the Sacrament for those Faults. But such was the Receiving required by the Apostle, *Rom.* 14. & 15.

This is a most beautiful paragraph, and the more so to a *true* taste for the seeming carelessness of its construction, like the *happily* dishevelled hair of a lovely woman.

47   i 354

He that can seriously ponder all these Expressions, and the Scope of the Holy Ghost, and yet can believe that all this Receiving is but such as consisteth with forbidding them Communion in the Lord's Supper, which then was so great a part of the daily Communion of the Church, and also may consist with the further Process against People and Ministers to Excommunication, and Prohibition to preach the Gospel, which is now pleaded for in our Case, is of so strange a temperature of Understanding, as that we can have little hope by any Scripture-Evidence to convince him.

Most true! Alas, that the *best* of all national churches should have had an era so disgraceful as that of the Restoration!

48   i 369 | § 241 "A Copy of the Proceedings of some Worthy and Learned Divines touching Innovations in the Doctrine and Discipline of the Church of England"

10. Some have maintained that the Lord's Day is kept meerly by Ecclesiastical Constitution, and that the Day is changeable.

So did the learned and saintly martyrs full of faith; yea, Luther himself.[1] Selden too condemns the sabbatical transferred to the dominical day, as the basest of Judaic superstitions.[2] The best argument for the

48[1] See Luther *The Greater Catechism* (*Der grosser Katechismus*), The Third Commandment.

48[2] The transcription may be in-

accurate here. C presumably means that Selden condemns the transfer of the Jewish superstitious observance of the Sabbath (Saturday), with all its

cheerfully serious observation of Sunday in rest, meditation, sober recreation, &c. is, that there *can* be no sound argument against it, or for the change of the day or interval. I consider it, in our present state, as a *command* of natural religion, favoured, though not compelled, by the Gospel revelation.[3] Were an angel to trumpet it from the clouds, the duty of observing it could not be more manifest to my reason than it already is.

49 i 370

15. Some have absolutely denied Original Sin, and so *evacuated the Cross of Christ*, as in a Disputation at *Oxon*.

Bishop Jeremy Taylor doth. If ever book was calculated to drive men to despair, it is Bishop Jeremy Taylor's on Repentance.[1] It first opened my eyes to Arminianism,[2] and that Calvinism is *practically* a far, far more soothing and consoling system.

50 i 384 | § 277

By this means there was a great Unanimity in the Ministers, and the greater Number were cast out: And as far as I could perceive, it was by some designed that it might be so. . . . It seemed to be accounted the one thing necessary, which no Reason must be heard against, that the Presbyterians must be forced to do that which they accoun-

---

prohibitions, to Sunday, the Christian dominical day (κυριάκη, *dominica*, the Lord's Day), so called and held sacred as the day of the Resurrection. See Selden *Table Talk* CXXV "Sabbath", in which Selden does in effect say that there is no obligation to take literally as applying to the Christian Sunday the injunctions in Exod 20.8–11 about the seventh day. C annotated a copy of Selden's *Table Talk* (1689), but it belonged to the Westminster Library and has not been preserved, although a transcript of at least some of the notes exists. See also *CN* I 1000D.

48[3] Cf *CN* III 4021 of c 1810: "I have no objection to a man's attending the meeting six days of the seven, if only on the *Lord's Day* he makes it the *Lord's* Day & forms the πολυφλοισβον of the Body of Christ, and a member of that Body." See also BREREWOOD and BYFIELD, and *CL* II 1189.

49[1] In the 1818 *Friend*, after quot-

ing a passage from *Unum necessarium, or, The Doctrine and Practice of Repentance* (on which C wrote 38 marginalia in that most heavily annotated of all his books, Jeremy TAYLOR *Polemicall Discourses*), C remarked upon "many passages equally gross" occurring in "a refutation of the doctrine of original sin" and concluded: "I could never read Bishop Taylor's Tract on the doctrine and practice of Repentance, without being tempted to characterize high Calvinism (comparatively) a lamb in wolf's skin, and strict Arminianism as approaching to the reverse." *Friend* (*CC*) I 434. See also *AR* (1825) 251–87, 303 and n.

49[2] Jacobus Arminius (1560–1609) rejected the Calvinist doctrine of absolute predestination or election. It was in the struggle between the Calvinists and Arminians that Grotius suffered: see BAHRDT **2** n 2.

ted Publick Perjury, or to be cast out of Trust and Office, in Church and Commonwealth. And by this means a far greater Number were laid by, than otherwise would have been; and the few that yielded to Conformity they thought would be despicable and contemptible as long as they lived. A Noble Revenge, and worthy of the Actors.

What Baxter suspected is now known to be true. The new acts were imposed by Sheldon's advice for the express purpose of ejecting all the old godly ministers, and to put in their places another generation, that might (as they effectively did), "wean the people from making *a fuss* about religion:" *i.e.* from thinking or caring about it.

51   i 387 | § 285

These Sects [of Nonconformists] are numerous, some tolerable, and some intolerable, and being never incorporated with the rest, are not to be reckoned with them. Many of them (the *Behmenists*, *Fifth-Monarchy-men*, *Quakers*, and some *Anabaptists*) are proper Fana-ticks, looking too much to Revelations within, instead of the Holy Scriptures.

Baxter makes the usual mistake of writing *Fanatic* when he clearly means *Enthusiast*.[1] The Field-Methodists are fanatics, *i.e. circà fana densâ turbâ concalefacti*; those who catch heat best by crowding together round the same *Fane*.[2] Fanaticism is the *fever* of *superstition*. Enthusiasm, on the contrary, implies an undue (or when used in a good sense, an unusual) vividness of ideas, as opposed to perceptions, or of the obscure inward feelings.

52   i 411 | § 363

2. They say, That all the World confesseth that a Vow obligeth *in re necessariâ*, to that which is antecedently a Duty: but they propound it to consideration, whether all these things following, which are in the Covenant are certainly no Duties antecedently.

The first instance in which I have found Baxter *unfair*. See the covenant itself, p. 391,[1] and you will find the oath, not for the

---

51[1] C often drew a distinction between the fanatic and the enthusiast: see e.g. BIRCH **1**, *Friend* (*CC*) I 432 and n 4, *P Lects* Lect 11 (1949) 328–9.

51[2] C translates the Latin himself. "Field-Methodists" were presumably those who responded in large crowds to Whitefield's preaching in the open fields. For the derivation of "fanatic" from "fane" see BIRCH **1** and n 4.

52[1] "The Solemn League and Covenant" is printed in full in black-letter in i 391–2. C's summary is taken almost word for word from that text.

preservation of the reformed religion in general, but for the *preservation* of the reformed religion in *Scotland*, and the *reformation* of the English Church—in other words, for the substitution of the Knoxo-Calvinistic Scoto-Genevan form of Synodical Presbytery for the Episcopal government of the Anglican Church.

53   i 412 | § 370

9. That though a Subject ought to take an Oath in the sence of his Rulers who impose it, as far as he can understand it; yet a Man that taketh an Oath from a Robber to save his Life, is not alway bound to take it in the Imposers sence, if he take it not against the Proper sence of the words.

Bo-peep with conscience. Either the robber's oath obliges or not. I think not. The guilt of the perjury lies with the *necessitating* imposer. But if it does, then it must be kept like any other binding oath or promise, *i.e.* neither in the sense of the imposer nor in that of the imposed, but in that sense which the latter understood the former to have imposed it.

54   i 413 | § 371

4. If we teach Men that the *bad Ends* of the Imposers do disoblige Men from performing Vows *materially* good, take heed lest it follow that it will disoblige them much more from obeying *Commands and Laws* materially good: And then every Subject will take himself to be disobliged, who is but confident that *Persecution, Oppression,* &c. were his Rulers Ends.

I never yet saw, heard of, or read any question in casuistry, which an honest man of sound logical head could not solve in an instant: not one, that ever had the least difficulty in it theoretically, though doubtless many where it is difficult to determine the ratio of the facts, in order to propound the question or problem.

55   i 414 | § 372

... But a Vow that is taken in my Closet, without any Man's imposition or knowledge, may be obligatory; or one that a Robber forceth me to by the High-way: The nullity of the Obligation *to take it*, is all that followeth the nullity of their Authority; which will not infer the nullity of the Obligation *to keep it*: for it maketh it but equal to a Vow which is made of a private Will without any Command of Authority at all.

Here Baxter seems to me wrong. Vows by compulsion, not a trifling one, but to avoid death, or perpetual jail, can never, never be in the same class with voluntary, still less with spontaneous vows or oaths. The sum is this: if tyrants and robbers know, that oaths compelled by them are void in conscience, a few lives may be lost, which might otherwise have been saved; but is this to be put in competition with the weakening of all tyranny, and the preservation of the essence of an oath, as either an act of duty (negatively at least) or not an oath at all? Would these Casuists be mad enough to say, that you were bound to keep an oath forced upon you by a raving madman? But, in truth, oaths altogether are bad, foolish, unchristian things, except as mere remembrancers of the guilt of deliberate falsehood, at the same time *occasioning* the affirmer to be calm and deliberate.

56　i 432–3 | § 424

It is worthy the mentioning how God's strange Judgments about this time, were turned by the Devil to his own advantage. Most certainly abundance of real Prodigies and marvellous Works of God were done, which surely he did not cause in vain! But the over-fervent spirits of some Fanaticks (Fifth-Monarchy-men) caused them presently to take them up boldly with the Commentary of their own Applications, and too hastily venting Matters of Common Report before they were tried, they published at several times three Volumes of the History of these Prodigies, in which were divers lesser Matters magnified, and some things which proved false! And though upon strictest Examination both I and all Men are convinced that very many of the Things were true (as the drying up of the River *Derwent* in *Darbyshire*, upon no known Cause, in Winter, the Earth opening and swallowing a Woman near *Ashburn* in the same County, upone her own Imprecation, the Appearance of an Army to many near *Montgomery*, and abundance more); yet were Falshoods thrust in through their heady Temerity and Credulity; whereby it came to pass, that these Wonders were so far from moving Men to Repentance, or the fear of God's Judgments, that they greatly hardened them, and made them say, "*These Fanaticks are the odious lying Deceivers of the World, that to cheat the poor People into a seditious Humour, care not to bely even God himself.*"

With what caution ought we to take the supernatural relations even of the very best and most veracious men! Baxter says, "I and all men were convinced." How? *Ex. gr.* that of the woman swallowed up, &c. Why not have given all the particulars of place, time, names and characters of the witnesses, &c.? The very same story has been told and retold repeatedly of different persons in different places and times within the last twenty-five years; and yet each so told as to leave no doubt, spite of all the pomp of witnesses, that they were each and all repetitions of the same old story. Besides, this whole hypothesis of preternatural judgment in this life is in direct opposition to a positive declaration of Christ concerning the wall that fell down and the blind man.[1]

57 i 438 | § 435

To these sad and heavy Accusations we answered, 1. The Covenant bound us to our best to reform: but did not bind us to sin, that is, to forsake all Christian Churches among us, and all Publick Worship, when we *cannot* reform as we desire. As I am bound to amend all the Disorders and Faults of my own Prayers, but not to give over praying till I can amend them.

It is impossible to read Baxter without hesitating which to admire most, the uncommon clearness (perspicuity and perspicacity) of his understanding, or the candour and charity of his spirit. Under such accursed persecutions he feels and reasons more like an angel than a man.

58 i 440 | § 437

To these I answered,

1. That it's true, that *meer Absence* is no Separation: but when a Party call and invite you to joyn with them, and you publickly accuse their way, and never joyn with them at all, you seem to tell the World that you take it to be *unlawful*...

2. Though you[r] Offices to your People cease not, yet you have your power to Edification and not to Destruction: And if a tolerable Minister be put into your Places, it's considerable whether it be not most to your Peoples Edification, Unity, Charity and Peace, to take them with you to the Publick Assemblies, and help them nevertheless

---

56[1] C's reference to "a positive declaration...concerning the wall that fell down and the blind man" is puzzling because there is no such single text. It may derive from various texts in which Jesus spoke of the inscrutability of God's working in the world and the blindness of those who do not believe: e.g. Matt 7.26–7, Luke 6.39, 47–9, John 9.39–41. For C's sustained reflection on Christ's attitude to his miraculous powers see *CN* III 3889, 3897.

at other times your selves as much as you can: And whether both helps be not more than one...

But what would come of this? Did God ever please to bring about reformation by these *passive* measures? Never! Did Luther act so? Did the Trinitarians restore the true faith by such measures, when the Arians were uppermost?

59   i 447 | § 444

[Baxter's answer to his own proposition: "Whether one that was bred a strict Protestant...may without offence to God, or Man, marry a profest Roman Catholick, in hopes of taking him off the Errour of his ways".] 5. Or if she be so happy as to escape Perversion, there is little hope of her escaping a sad calamitous Life: Partly by guilt, and partly by her grief for a Husband's Soul, and partly by Family-disorders and sins, and also by daily temptations, disappointments, and want of those helps and comforts in the way to Heaven, which her Weakness needeth, and her Relation should afford.

Popery *versus* Popery.

60   i 447

6. Supposing him to be one that loveth her Person truly, and not only her Estate (for else she must expect to stand by as a contemned thing) yet his Religion will not allow him otherwise to love her, than as a Child of the Devil, in a state of Damnation may be loved. For their Religion teacheth them, That none can be saved but the Subjects of the Pope.

This seems unanswerable if the husband be a thorough Papist. But how *could* such a one marry such a Protestant, except for her estate, or in the full intent as well as hope of using every means to con- or rather per-vert her. Either way, it must be *guilt* in a woman to marry such a man. And yet if she ever hesitated, had "*half a mind to it*," I would wager a trifle that she married him, though the Devil was grinning over the Priest's shoulder during the marriage ceremony.

61   ii 6 | ɪ iii § 15

Those that take the Oath, do (as those that Subscribe) resolve that they will understand it in a lawful Sense (be it true or false) and so to take it in that Sense: To which end they say that *nullum iniquum est in Lege praesumendum*, and that all publick Impositions must be taken in the best Sense that the Words will bear.

Oaths are 999 times out of 1000 abominations. Perhaps I need not have made the one exception, as oaths are administered in our law. "Recollect yourself! you are in the presence of the omnipresent, omniscient God, who has declared his wrath against deliberate false-hood. Do you believe this? Are you at this moment fully aware of it?" This would be a form of administering an oath, which the most rigid Quaker, if in his senses, could not object to, and would pre-clude all the evil superstitions, which now transfer the essence to the ceremony.[1]

62 ii 8–9 | § 18 "Queries upon the Oxford Oath"

Much as I love the Church of England, I have no hesitation in assert-ing (as my belief) that nothing in the history of the Inquisition was equally *wicked*, as the conduct of Sheldon and the Court, after the Restoration.[1]

63 ii 12

9. Note especially that of the *Eighth Quaere*, which implyeth divers Instances of Cases, in which *Grotius, Barclay, Bilson*, &c. say, That it is Lawful to take Arms against the King, he seemeth wholly to grant it, and maketh it but like a Cavil, to suppose that *those Cases* ever came into the Parliament's Thoughts. And I am much in that of the good Man's Mind. But if they will Swear me to an Universal, while they forget particular Exceptions, that will not make the Oath Lawful to me.

N.B. But here Baxter confounds the drawers up, or worders, of the oath, with the two Houses of Parliament, who, with the King, were the Imposers. Still, however, I could no more have taken the oath than Baxter: because it was meant to mean something beyond the former oaths, and whatever that might be, was for Diocesan Prelacy and Despotism. Oh it was a disgraceful era, both in Church and State! How grateful ought we to be for our present truly blessed Constitution in the latter, and for the mild and liberal spirit in the former! If not what a Christian Church should be, yet the Church of England injures only itself. It neither oppresses, annoys, nor interferes with those who dissent from it.

61[1] See also **55**, above, and COPY B **94**. On the Quakers generally see AURELIUS **47** n 1.

62[1] For Sheldon see **35** and n 1, above; for the Inquisition see COPY B **1** n 6.

64   ii 46 | § 103

Experience here convinced me that the Independent separating rigour is not the way to do the People good.... Two able Independents had been the setled Ministers at *Acton*; and when I was there, there remained but two Women in all the Town, and Parish, whom they had admitted to the Sacrament (whereof One was a Lady that by alienation from them turned Quaker, and was their great Patroness, and returned from them while I was there, and heard me with rest.) This rigour made the People think hardly of them; and I found that the uncharitable conceit, that the Parishes are worse than they, doth tend to make them as bad as they are thought.

Oh that this no less wise than amiable remark were more and more generally felt and acted upon! This is the sublime moral of Shakspeare's Shylock and Edmund.[1]

65   iii 55 | App III

For doubtless (tho' where Heathens were the Neighbours of the Church, many were baptised at Age, yet) no Man can name or prove a Society (or I think a Person) against infant Baptism for One Thousand Two Hundred Years at least, if not One Thousand Four Hundred: And for many Ages no other ordinarily baptized but Infants. If Christ has no Church, then where was his Wisdom, his Love, and his Power? What was become of the Glory of his Redemption, and his Catholick Church, that was to continue to the End? That Man can believe that Christ had no Church for so long time, or any one Age since his Ascension, must turn an Infidel and deny him to be Christ, if he be a rational Man. Did all the Gospel Precepts of Love and Holy Communion cease, as soon as Infant Baptism prevailed? doubtless...Christ never laid so great a stress on the outward Washing as Dividers do.... I would know the Dividers why they should think Baptism more necessary to be believed than the other Sacrament, the Supper of the Lord: Yet it is certain that all the ancient Church did purposely conceal the Lord's Supper from the Knowledge of the Catechumens; by which it appears they judged not the Belief of it essential to a Church Member: Yet I know the great thing meant by the Word Baptism in Scripture is essential to the Church-Membership of the Adult; that is, the giving up our selves to God the Father, Son, and Holy Ghost in

---

64[1] In a remark on Edmund in *King Lear* C said: "shame will naturally generate guilt". *Sh C* I 55; see also 50–2.

Covenant; but the Sign is only necessary as a Duty, but not as a means without which the thing cannot be had.

All this proves against any soul-danger in Infant Baptism, if administered and afterward acquiesced in, conscientiously. But it surely does not prove that it is not our duty to take the Sacraments as we appear to find them in Scripture. I cannot assent to Baxter's main argument: for an ordinance of admission to Christian membership, pre-requiring on the part of the competitor knowledge, repentance, and faith, is a definition that will not agree with Infant Baptism; and to deny any definition to be true which does not include the lawfulness of Infant Baptism, would be reasoning in a circle with a vengeance. The best argument is: let every man be convinced in his own mind, and agree to differ, keeping up both Love and Communion.

66   iii 57

As for my Twenty Arguments...They prove a Necessity of Profession of Consent in all adult Covenanters: But yet Parents may profess their Consent to their Childrens Covenanting or Engagement.... I would Mr. *L.* could tell me "*When the Priviledge and Duty of Parents entering their Children into the Holy Covenant with God, and solemnizing this did cease?*"

But what is all this in opposition to the positive, oft-repeated injunctions of Christ and Scripture, demanding previous faith and repentance in the subject to be baptised. Analogies are good substitutes, but they must not master when the principals are present.

Annex

John Mitford's summary of the marginalia in COPY A (BM Add MS 32566 ff 9–12) consists of 27 notes. The sequence they are written in bears no discernible relation to the order of the marginalia as they must have been written in the volume. Most of Mitford's notes can be readily identified with particular marginalia because he tends to reproduce C's characteristic single phrases; but since in these notes Mitford seems as little concerned for accuracy as for completeness, identification is not in all cases positive. His first note could represent either **5** or **39**; his 12th and 27th notes both seem to derive from **44**[i]; his 8th note is probably a version of **43** but so garbled as to look at first as though it represented an unpublished note of C's. Only two notes are not accounted for—the 4th and 22nd—and these may both represent a single marginal note of C's, not two; and for these, COPY B **24** or **88** textus is a possible location, and cf COPY B **18**.

   In all these notes Mitford has turned C's note into indirect speech, so that the "he" of a Mitford note represents the "I" of C's.

[*a*] Had he been one of the judges of Charles 1st he would have voted as they did; but he would not have put himself in the Situation: Impossible to consider in the same light, the death of Charles 1st and that of Louis XVI.

[*b*] Would have passd Sentence with Martin and Hutchinson on Charles —but how came he to have Such judges?

Copy B

Reliquiae Baxterianae &c. London 1696. F°.

Another copy of the same edition as COPY A.

Harvard University (Houghton Library)

George Frere's copy with his bookplate: "Mr G. Frere, Brunswick Square. 33"; and with his autograph inscription on p ⁻6 (p–d): "This Book was lent by me to Saml Taylor Coleridge at Hampstead & returned to me by his Ex^{ors} after his death with his Marginal Notes Geo. Frere."

George Frere (1774–1854) of Lincoln's Inn, President of the Law Society, brother of John Hookham Frere, was mentioned admiringly by C in Jun 1817. *CL* IV 740; cf 746. C's earliest surviving letter to him (5 Dec 1816) accompanied a corrected presentation copy of *SM*. *CL* IV 695. C also gave him a copy of the 1818 *Friend* and promised to bring ms corrections and an addition. *CL* IV 884. Neither copy is preserved or described. In Aug 1817 C annotated George Frere's copy of Duncan FORBES *The Whole Works* (2 vols Edinburgh [c 1755]).

Throughout the volume there are numerous X's in the margins, and marginal lines or braces in pencil appear at ii 47–8, 90, 175–6, 176, iii 56, 63; it is impossible to identify any of these as C's. A large mark "⟨" appears in the margin of i 5, 23, 32, 33 (twice), 41, 92, ii 47, 61, 143; two of these are associated with the textus of C's notes (**9** on i 23, **96** on ii 61) but there is no clear evidence that these are C's. A fist is drawn to mark a passage with special emphasis on i 76, 79, 82, 89, 127, 272; one of these is associated with **39** textus (i 127), but the fact that another is associated with C's note **76** (i 272), rather than with textus, tends to confirm the impression that these are not C's. C's corrections of simple typographical errors (i 1–15, 29, ii 96) are not here recorded in the text.

MS TRANSCRIPT. BM Ashley 4772: Gillman ms facsimile. This contains all the notes C wrote in the original copy, except for the conclusion of **98**. T. J. Wise did not appreciate that the marginalia in this copy were not in C's hand.

DATE. c 1817, 1819–25, and later. The earliest notes (usually distinguishable from the neat small hand of the later ink notes) perhaps belong to the time shortly after George Frere's first meeting with C; the Feb 1820 postscript to **5** suggests a substantial interval of time, and *CN* III 4459 (c late 1818) quotes the phrase "This hasty Inch of Time" from p 12—the page following the page on which **5** is written. Note **115** was written before C knew that the Board of Agriculture had been abolished (in May 1821). The date 1820 appears twice in the marginalia: **5** (Feb 1820), **115** (Jun 1820). The date in **91** ("20 Octr 1819") may be a slip of the pen for 1820. The date "1820" in **2** is intended as a generic date; the citation of *AR* with a page reference makes the note c May 1825. Note **82** is dated 1 Sept 1825.

1   pp ⁻5, ⁻3, pencil, overtraced

Mem. Among the grounds for recommending the perusal of our elder writers, Hooker, Taylor, Baxter, in short almost any of the Folios composed from Edward VI to Charles II[1]

1. The overcoming the habit of deriving your whole pleasure passively from the Book itself, which can only be effected by excitement of Curiosity or of some Passion. Force yourself to reflect on what you read §ph by §ph, and in a short time you will derive your pleasure, an ample portion at least, from the activity of your own mind. All else is Picture Sunshine.

2. The conquest of party and sectarian Prejudices, when you have on the same table the works of a Hammond and a Baxter; and reflect how many & how momentous[a] their points of agreement; how few and almost childish the differences, which estranged and irritated these good men![2]

Let us but reflect, what their blessed Spirits now feel at the retrospect of their earthly frailties: and can we ⟨do⟩ other than strive to feel as they ⟨now⟩ *feel*, not as they once felt?—So will it be with the Disputes between good men of the present Day: and if you have no other reason to doubt your Opponent's Goodness than the point in Dispute, think of Baxter and Hammond, of Milton and Jer. Taylor, and let it be no reason at all!—[3]

3. It will secure you from the narrow Idolatry of the Present Times and Fashions: and create the noblest kind of Imaginative Power in your Soul, that of living in past ages, ⟨wholly devoid of which power a man can neither anticipate the Future, nor even live a truly human life, a life of reason, in the Present.⟩[4]

---

a Written "how momentous & how many" and marked for transposition

1¹ C annotated the *Works* of Richard Hooker (c1554–1600) and at least five separate volumes of Jeremy Taylor (1613–67). For a convenient group of C s general comments on the Caroline divines, see *C 17th C* 134–40.

1² In the "Apologetic Preface to *Fire, Famine, and Slaughter*", composed in perhaps 1803, though put into final form in 1815, C made a similar remark about Hammond and Baxter: *PW* (EHC) ii 1104–5. Henry Hammond (1605–60), chaplain to Charles i, was deprived and imprisoned in 1648, but later set free to live in retirement with Sir Philip Warwick. There was a copy of his *Works* (4 vols 1684) in Green's library (*Green SC*—1880—598); and a copy of the *Paraphrase and Annotations upon the New Testament* (1659), traditionally C's but unmarked, was preserved in the Coleridge family.

1³ C's acquaintance with Milton's prose works was early; a few marginalia of later date are preserved.

1⁴ Cf LUTHER *Colloquia Mensalia* (1652) 61. See also *CN* iii 3590.

4. In this particular work we may derive a most instructive Lesson that in certain points, as of Religion in relation to Law, the "Medio tutissimus ibis"[5] is inapplicable. There is no *Medium* possible; and all the attempts, as those of Baxter, tho' no more were required than, "I believe in God thro' Christ," prove only the mildness of the Proposer's Temper, but as a rule would be either =0, at least exclude only the two or three in a century that make it a matter of religion to declare themselves Atheists; or just as fruitful a rule for a Persecutor as the most complete set of Articles that could be framed by a Spanish Inquisition.[6] For to "believe" must mean to believe aright, and "God" must mean the true God, and "Christ" the Christ in the sense and with the attributes understood by Christians who are truly Xtians. An established Church with a Liturgy is the sufficient solution of the Problem de Jure Magistratus.[7] Articles of Faith are superfluous; for is it not too absurd for a man to hesitate at subscribing his name to doctrines which yet in the more aweful duty of Prayer & Profession, he dares affirm before his maker? They are therefore *merely* superfluous—not worth re-enacting, had they never been done away with—not worth removing now that they exist.

5. The characteristic Contra-distinction between the Speculative Reasoners of the Age before the Revolution and those since then is this: The former cultivated metaphysics without, ⟨or neglecting,⟩ empirical Psychology; the latter ⟨cultivate a mechanical⟩ Psychology to the neglect and contempt of Metaphysics. Both therefore almost equi-distant from true *Philosophy*. Hence the belief in Ghosts,

[1]5 Ovid *Metamorphoses* 2.137: "You will go most safely by the middle way".

[1]6 For the early engagement of the Dominicans in inquisitorial activities see **105** n 1, below. An ecclesiastical Inquisition, in charge of the Dominicans, was first formally established in the thirteenth century; it was overshadowed in Spain by a Bull of Sixtus IV, 1 Nov 1478, which gave Catholic kings the right to appoint inquisitors. In Jan 1481 the Supreme Council of the Inquisition was organised in Seville. The widespread and remorseless activity of the Inquisitor quickly became a legend of terror. C's horror at the activities of the Inquisition in the late sixteenth century, and its extension to Holland and Belgium, is concentrated in his "Letters on the Spaniards" (esp *EOT—CC*—II 50–2), his principal source being the Latin chronicle of Michael Eytzinger (d 1598) *De Leone Belgico* (Cologne 1583)—a book adorned with horrifyingly specific illustrations. See *CL* III 225, *CN* III 3601.

In 1808 the Inquisition was suppressed by the French authorities. Although it was reinstituted in Spain, as C noted with revulsion in Oct 1809 (*Friend— CC*—II 141), it was permanently suppressed by a decree of 15 Jul 1834.

[1]7 "Concerning the Legal Authority of the Chief Magistrate (or Sovereign)".

Witches, *sensible* Replies to Prayer &c in Baxter, and a 100 others—[8]
See p. 81:[9] and look at Luther's Table Talk,[10] &c &c.

6. The earlier part of this Volume ~~was~~ is interesting as materials
for medical History. The [?~~true~~] state of medical Science in the
reign of Charles the First almost incredibly low![11]

2 title-page verso

The saddest error of the Theologians of this age is, ὡς ἐμοίγε δοκεῖ,[1]
the disposition to urge the histor~~yical~~ies of the miraculous actions &
incidents in and by which Christ attested his Messiahship to the
Jewish Eye-witnesses in fulfilment of Prophecies, which the Jewish
Church had previously understood & interpreted as marks of the
Messiah, before they have shewn what and how excellent the
Religion itself is—*including* the miracles, as for *us* an harmonious
part of the internal or self-evidence of the Religion. Alas! and even
when ~~th~~ our Divines do proceed to the Religion itself, as ⟨to⟩ a
something which no man could be expected to receive except by ⟨a⟩
compulsion of the senses, ⟨which⟩ by force of Logic ⟨is⟩ propagated
from the Eye-witnesses to the Readers of the Narratives in 1820—
(which Logic, viz. that the evidence of a Miracle is not diminished
by lapse of ages, tho' this includes loss of documents &c—which
logic, I say, whether it be legitimate or not, God forbid! that the
truth of Christianity should depend on the decision!—) even when

[1][8] C wrote marginalia on the subject of witchcraft in Cotton MATHER *Magnalia Christi Americana* (1702) and John WEBSTER *The Displaying of Supposed Witchcraft* (1677). His reading in the subject was wide and curious: see e.g. *CN* III 4390–6 (on Aubrey's *Miscellanies* and other works on witchcraft) and N 21½ f 56ᵛ for his use of Scott's *Discovery of Witchcraft*. On the credulity of witnesses see COPY A 56.

[1][9] See **32**, below.

[1][10] C wrote a number of notes in LUTHER *Colloquia Mensalia* (1652); see also BROWNE *Works* **54** and n 2. For C on witches, apparitions, and Luther's "ink-pot Adventure" see *Friend* (*CC*) II 115–20 (I 139–42).

[1][11] C was particularly interested in the history of medical science and how ignorance, prejudice, and superstition had persistently interfered with

scientific inquiry. At the age of thirteen or fourteen he had walked the wards of the London Hospital with his brother Luke and, thinking to become a physician himself, read medical books voraciously at that time. His early association with Thomas Beddoes and Humphry Davy consolidated both his interest and his knowledge, and turned his thought in speculative as well as hypochondriacal directions. In medical science, as in so much else, he looked for first principles, and developed views on psychosomatic illness and psychiatric treatment that are notably sensible and humane, and far in advance of the doctrine and practice of his time. See e.g. *CN* III 3431. After taking up residence with James Gillman, C read a wide range of medical books and periodicals; some marginalia in these are preserved.

[2][1] "As it seems to me at least".

our Divines do proceed to the Religion itself, on what do they chiefly dwell? On the doctrines peculiar to the Religion? No!— these on the contrary are either evaded, or explained away into metaphors, or resigned in despair to the next world where Faith is to be swallowed up in Certainty!—

But the worst product of this epidemic error is the fashion of either denying or undervaluing the evidence of a future state, and the survival of individual Consciousness, derived from the Conscience, and the holy instinct of the whole Human Race. Dreadful is this—for the main force of the Reasoning by which this scepticism is vindicated, consists in reducing all legitimate conviction to *objective* proof— whereas in the very essence of Religion & even of Morality the evidence & the preparation for its reception, must be *Subjective*. "Blessed are they that have *not* seen yet believe."[2] And dreadful it appears to me especially, who in the impossibility of not looking forward to consciousness after the dissolution of the body (Corpus *phænomenon*) (See p. 347 of my Aids to Reflection)[3] have thro' life found (next to divine Grace) the strongest & indeed only efficient Support against the still-recurring temptation of adopting—nay, *wishing* the truth of—Spinoza's notion, that the survival of consciousness is the highest prize & consequence of the highest Virtue—and that of all below this mark the lot after Death is self-oblivion & the cessation of individual Being[4]—Indeed, how a Separatist[5] or ⟨one of⟩

2[2] John 20.29 (var).

2[3] "The *phaenomenal* (i.e. merely physical) Body". See *AR* (1825) 346–7.

2[4] C seems to be thinking of *Ethics* pt 2 prop xxvi: "The effort for self-preservation is the first and only foundation of virtue...." In HCR's copy of SPINOZA *Opera* C wrote (II 59) a short note on the proof of this proposition; and in a long note on prop xxviii (II 59–61) the word *existentially* is used, for which see **8** n 1, below. See also *Ethics* pt 5 prop xxxviii–xl.

2[5] Separatist was a title first applied in c 1600 to the Brownists, followers of the Puritan Robert Browne (c 1550–1633), and later generally to the Congregationalists (or Independents) and to others who wished to renounce the episcopal authority of the Church of England. The Congregationalists held that since every Christian was a "priest unto God" (as Luther also maintained, though with different conclusions), each local congregation should be autonomous; this, they held, was the earliest form of Church order and represented the primitive and pure pattern of Christian democracy with Christ as the sole head of the Church. The Separatists (or Brownists) were driven underground in England, to flourish in Holland and America, but returned (renamed Independents) to provide the backbone of Cromwell's army. The position of the Independents was vigorously presented at the Westminster Assembly (1643), in which Baxter took part, and at the Savoy Conference (1662–3), and their position was publicly formulated with that of the Presbyterians in the Savoy Declaration (1658). Both Independents and Presbyterians were ruled Nonconformist by the Act of Uniformity (1662).

any other Sect of Calvinists, who confines Redemption to a the comparatively small numbers of the Elect can reject this opinion, & yet not run mad at the horrid idea of an innumerable Multitude of imperishable self-conscious Spirits everlastingly excluded from God, is to me inconceivable!—

Deeply am I persuaded of Luther's Position—that no man can worthily estimate, or feel in the depth of his being, the incarnation & crucifixion of the Son of God who is a stranger to the *Terror* of Nature, the *Terror* of Immortality, as ingenerate in Man—while it is yet unquelled by the faith in God, as the Almighty Father.[6]

2A i 1 | 1 i §1

... And at the same time another Neighbour's Son that had been a while at School turn'd Minister, ~~and~~ one who would needs go further than the rest, and ventur'd to preach (~~and one~~ and after got a Living in *Staffordshire*...)

2B i 2

...and at Two of the Clock in the afternoon on that Day...

3 i 2, pencil, overtraced

But though my Conscience would trouble me when I sinned, yet divers sins I was addicted to, and oft committed against my Conscience; which for the warning of others I will confess here to my shame.

1. I was much addicted when, I feared Correction to lie, that I might scape.

2. I was much addicted to the excessive gluttonous eating of Apples and Pears: which I think laid the foundation of that *Imbecillity* and Flatulency of my Stomach, which caused the Bodily Calamities of my Life.

3. To this end, and to concur with naughty Boys that gloried in evil, I have oft gone into other men's Orchards, and stoln their Fruit, when I had enough at home.

4. I was somewhat excessively addicted to play, and that with covetousness, for Money.

5. I was extreamly bewitched with a Love of Romances, Fables and old Tales, which corrupted my Affections and lost my Time.

2[6] The passage in Luther has not been traced.

6. I was guilty of much idle foolish Chat, and imitation of Boys in scurrilous foolish Words and Actions (though I durst not swear).

7. I was too proud of my Masters Commendations for Learning, who all of them fed my pride, making me Seven or Eight years the highest in the School, and boasting of me to others, which though it furthered my Learning, yet helped not my Humility.

8. I was too bold and unreverent towards my Parents.

These were my Sins which in my Childhood Conscience troubled me for a great while before they were overcome.

There is a child-like simplicity in this account of the Sins of his Childhood which is very pleasing.

3A   i 3 | 1 i §3

...And being ringing me under some more Conviction for my Sin...

3B   i 4 | §4

...being but a Superficial Scholar of himself...

3C   i 4

...though his Knowledge was not great, he would be always stirring me up to Zeal and Diligence, and even in the Night would rise up to Prayer and Thanksgiving to God, and wondered that I could sleep so...

4   i 5–6, pencil, overtraced | §5

...And the use God made of Books, above Ministers, to the benefit of my Soul, made me somewhat excessively in love with good Books; so that I thought I had never enow, but scrap'd up as great a Treasure ἔστησε ταὖτο.[1]] of them as I could. . . .

These Benefits of it I sensibly perceived. . . .

ἔστησε.] 4. It made the World seem to me as a Carkass that had neither Life nor Loveliness: And it destroyed those Ambitious desires after *Literate Fame*, which was the Sin of my Childhood! . . .

. . . And for the *Mathematicks*, I was an utter stranger to them, and ἔστησε.] never could find in my heart to divert any Studies that way. But in order to the Knowledge of *Divinity* my inclination was most to *Logick* and *Metaphysicks*, with that part of *Physicks* which treateth of the Soul, contenting my self at first with a slighter study

---

4[1] "S. T. C. the same". For C's initials written in the form of a Greek word as a name for himself see ANNUAL ANTHOLOGY **10** n 3.

of the rest: And these had my *Labour* and *Delight*. Which occasioned me (perhaps too soon) to plunge my self very early into the study of *Controversies*; and to read all the School men I could get; (for next to *Practical Divinity*, no Books so suited with my Disposition as *Aquinas, Scotus, Durandus, Ockam*, and their Disciples[)]; because I ἔστησε.] thought they narrowly searched after Truth, and brought Things out of the darkness of Confusion: For I could never from S. T. C.] my first Studies endure Confusion!... I never thought I understood any thing till I could *anatomize* it, and see the *parts distinctly*, and the *Conjunction* of the parts as they make up the whole. *Distinction* and *Method* seemed to me of that necessity, that without them I could not be said to know; and the Disputes which *forsook* them, or *abused* them, seemed but as incoherent Dreams.

5   i 11, pencil, overtraced | § 10

My chiefest Remedies are,

1. Temperance as to quantity and quality of Food: for every bit or spoonful too much, and all that is not exceeding easie of digestion, and all that is flatulent, do turn all to Wind, and disorder my Head.

For one mercy I owe thanks beyond utterance, that with all my gastric and bowel distempers, my Head hath ever been like the Head of a Mountain in blue air and sunshine.[1] S. T. C.

Alas! even this is no longer so. Feb 1820.

5A   i 11

... *Jacob Behmen* ...

6   i 14

And the result of all my Studies was as followeth: Kneeling I thought lawful, and all meer Circumstances determined by the Magistrate, which God in Nature or Scripture hath determined of only in the General. The Surplice I more doubted of; but more inclined to think it lawful: And though I purposed, while I doubted, to forbear it till necessity lay upon me, yet could I not have justified the forsaking of my Ministry for it; (though I never wore it to this day).

I am not enough read in Puritan Divinity to know the particular objections to the *Surplice*, over & above the general prejudice against all the Retenta of Popery.[1]

[5][1] In *CN* III 4459 C noted: " 'This hasty inch of Time'. Baxter's Life, p. 12."

[6][1] The "vestiarian controversy" that began in the reign of Edward VI and caused great bitterness under

7   i 22, pencil, overtraced | § 34

In the storm of this Temptation, I questioned a while whether I were indeed a Christian or an Infidel, and whether Faith could consist with such Doubts as I was conscious of. . . . For I had read in many Papists and Protestants, that Faith had *Certainty*, and was more than an Opinion; and that if a Man should live a godly Life, from the bare apprehensions of the *Probability* of the Truth of Scripture, and the *Life* to come, it would not save him, as being no true Godliness or Faith. But my Judgment closed with the Reason of Dr. *Jackson*'s Determination of this Case . . . that as in the very Assenting Act of Faith there may be such weakness . . . so when *Faith* and *Unbelief* are in their Conflict, it is the *Effects* which must shew us which of them is victorious.

§ 34. One of 1000 instances of the evils arising from the equivoque between Faith and intellectual satisfaction or insight. The *root* of Faith is in the Will. F. is an Oak that may be a Pollard and yet live.[1]

8   i 22, pencil, overtraced

1. That the Being and Attributes of God were so clear to me, that he was to my Intellect what the Sun is to my Eye, by which I see it self and all Things: And he seemed mad to me that questioned whether there were a God: that any Man should dream that the World was made by a Conflux of Irrational Atoms, and Reason came from that which had no Reason, or that Man, or any Inferiour Being was independent; or that all the being, Power, Wisdom and Goodness which we conversed with, had not a Cause which in Being, Power, Wisdom and Goodness, did excel all that which it had caused in the World, and had not all that *formaliter vel eminenter* in it self which it communicated to all the Creatures.

Elizabeth centred almost entirely upon the use of the surplice by the clergy of the Church of England. BCP of 1552 included a rubric that made the surplice the only prescribed vestment for the clergy in their ritual offices; Archbishop Parker in 1603 tried to make the wearing of the surplice obligatory for ministers in divine service, but the issue aroused such resistance that the rubric, proving unenforceable, was withdrawn from later editions of BCP.

The dispute about clerical dress provided one of the rallying points of the Puritan party by focusing attention upon the alleged Popery of its use—a matter (as C implies here) more of emotional prejudice than of historical or ecclesiastical substance. See also **73** and n 1, below, and cf *CL* i 180; *BL* ch 10 (1907) i 114.

7[1] A key statement for C's mature theological position. See *SM (CC)* 59–93 (esp 67n) and **42**, below.

Even so with ἔστησε; but whether God was existentially as well as essentially intelligent[1]—this was for a long time a sore combat between the speculative and the moral man.

9 i 23, pencil, overtraced

And *meer Deism*, which is the most plausible Competitor [to Heathenism, Mohametanism, and Judaism], is so turned out of almost all the whole World, as if Nature·made its own Confession, that without a Mediator it cannot come to God.

excellent.

10 i 23 | § 35

* All these Assistances were at hand before I came to the immediate Evidences of Credibility in the Sacred Oracles themselves. And when I set my self to search for those, I found more in the Doctrine, the Predictions, the Miracles, antecedent, concomitant, subsequent, than ever I before took notice of...

* This is as it should be. That is: first, the evidence a priori, securing the rational probability: and then the historical proofs of its reality. Pity that Baxter's Chapters in The Saint's Rest should have been one and the earliest occasion of the inversion of this process[1]—the truth of which is the Grotian Paleyian Religion, or Miniʃmum of ~~Father~~ Faith—its maxim being, Quanto minus, tanto melius.[2]

8[1] For C's account of the scholastic distinction between "essence/essential" and "existence/existential", and its place in the debate between nominalists and realists on the attributes of God, see *P Lects* Lects 9, 10, (1949) 276–7, 290–1, 434–5 (marginal note on JOANNES Scotus Erigena *De divisione naturae*). In *P Lects* 276–7 he also noticed a distinction between logical and existential in the question "whether because a thing was logically consistent it must be necessarily existent" —apparently the first use of "existential" in a sense that had become commonplace in logical discourse before the end of the century. This second sense of the word provides a bridge with the sense in this marginal note— a sense very much like that in the statement of 1817 that the separation of light and darkness was "the very first

post-creative or *existential* Act". *CL* IV 771. On C's "sore combat" see e.g. the letter of Sept 1817 to Tulk (*CL* IV 767–76) and many of the marginalia on BÖHME. The presence of God in human life is what C thinks of as existential: the coincidence of essence and existence occurs in the bond between God and man. Herbert Read held that C was the first exponent of modern existentialism before Kierkegaard: see *Coleridge as Critic* (1949) 29–30. For other uses of "existential" see e.g. BÖHME **47, 139**, *Friend* (*CC*) I 427n, *CL* V 88n.

10[1] C could have read *The Saint's Everlasting Rest* (1650) in Vol III of Baxter *Practical Works* (4 vols 1707), a copy of which was in Green's library. *Green SC* (1880) 291.

10[2] "The less, the better".

11 i 24, pencil, overtraced | § 37

And once all the ignorant Rout were raging mad against me for preaching the Doctrine of Original Sin to them, and telling them that Infants before Regeneration, had so much Guilt and Corruption, as made them loathsome in the Eyes of God: whereupon they vented it abroad in the Country, that I preached that God hated, or loathed Infants; so that they railed at me as I passed through the Streets.

no wonder. Because the Babe would perish without the mother's milk, is it therefore *loathsome* to the mother? Surely the little ones, that Christ embraced, had not been baptized—and yet of such is the K. of H.[1]

12 i 25–6, pencil, overtraced to *a*, then continued in ink | § 38

Some thought that the King should not at all be displeased and provoked, and that they were not bound to do any other Justice, or attempt any other Reformation but what they could procure the King to be willing to. And these said, When you have displeased and provoked him to the utmost, he will be your King still!... you have no power over his Person, though you have power over Delinquent Subjects: And if he protect them by Arms, you must either be ruined your selves by his displeasure, or be engaged in a War: Displeasing him is but exasperating him; and would you be ruled by a King that hateth you? Princes have great Minds, which cannot easily suffer Contradiction and Rebukes: The more you offend him, the less you can trust him; and when mutual Confidence is gone, a War is beginning: And if it come to a War, either you will conquer or be conquered, or come to Agreement. If you are conquered, you and the Commonwealth are ruined, and he will be absolute, and subdue Parliaments, and Govern as he pleaseth. If you come to an Agreement, it will be either such as you *force* him to, or he is *willing* of: If the latter, it may be easilier and cheaper done before a War than after: If the *former*, it will much weaken it: And if you Conquer him, what the better are you? He will still be King. ... These were the Reasons of many that were for pleasing the King.

Never was a stronger case made out in justification of the Regicides! Never a more complete exposure of the inconsistency of Baxter's own party! Either the Execution of this incurable Despot was constitutional or passive obedience is an absolute Duty.*a* I do not

---

a The pencil ms has been overtraced in ink to this point, evidently by C himself; the note continues in ink

11[1] Matt 19.14. Cf Mark 10.14, Luke 18.16.

recollect a clearer case in History; not one in which a plain Principle grounded on universal Reason & the constituent maxims of the Constitution was ever more distinctly confirmed by the after Events & Occurrences. For observe, that in case of an Agreement with Charles all those classes, which afterwards formed the main strength of the Parliament & ultimately decided the contest in its favor, would have been politically inert, with little influence & no actual power— I mean, the Yeomanry, & the Citizens of London—while a vast majority of the Nobles and landed Gentry, who sooner or later must have become the majority in Parliament, went over to the King at once. So with these the whole systematized force of the High Church Clergy, & all the rude ignorant Vulgar, in high & low life, who detested every attempt at moral reform—& it is obvious that the King could not want opportunities to retract & undo all that he had conceded under compulsion. But that neither the Will was wanting nor his Conscience at all in the way, his own Advocates, Clarendon & others, have supplied damning proofs.[1]

13 i 27 | § 41

... And though Parliaments may draw up Bills for repealing Laws, yet hath the King his Negative Voice, and without his Consent they cannot do it; which though they acknowledged, yet did they too easily admit of Petitions against the Episcopacy and Liturgy, and connived at all the Clamours and Papers which were against them.

How so! If they admitted the King's Right to deny, they must admit the Subject's Right to intreat.

14 i 27

Had they only endeavoured the Ejection of Lay Chancellors, and the reducing of the Diocesses to a narrower Compass, or the setting up

---

12[1] For C's close reading of Clarendon see *CN* III 3740–3742. See e.g. Clarendon *The History of the Rebellion and Civil Wars in England* (1807) III i 344–6 (Bk XI). On 18 Sept 1648 fresh negotiations were opened with Charles by parliamentary commissioners, leading to the treaty of Newport. The matters under discussion were the revocation of all the King's declarations, the abolition of the episcopacy and the Anglican liturgy, maintenance of the army by Parliament, voiding the peace with Ireland, and confirmation of parliamentary agreements with Scotland. Charles's final answer was " 'that after such condescensions, and weighed resolutions in the business of the Church, he had expected not to be farther pressed therein; it being his judgment, and his conscience.' ... And the commissioners, having received this his final answer, took their leaves, and the next morning began their journey towards London."

of a Subordinate Discipline, and only the Correcting and Reforming of the Liturgy, perhaps it might have been borne more patiently; but some particular Members concurred with the Desires of the imprudent Reformers, who were for no less than the utter Extirpation of Bishops and Liturgy ...

Did B. find it so himself? And when too he had Ch. II[nd's] formal & recorded Promise?

15 i 27, pencil, overtraced

The Bishops themselves who were accounted most moderate (*Usher, Williams, Morton*) and many other Episcopal Divines with them, had before this in a Committee at *Westminster*, agreed on certain Points of Reformation, which I will give you afterward. ... But when the same Men saw that greater Things were aimed at, and Episcopacy it self in danger, or their Grandeur and Riches at the least, most of them turned against the Parliament, and were almost as much displeased as others.

This and in this place is unworthy of Baxter. Even he, good man! could not wholly escape the Jaundice of Party.

16 i 33, pencil, overtraced | § 49

And abundance of the ignorant sort of the Country, who were Civil, did flock in to the Parliament, and filled up their Armies afterward, meerly because they heard Men *swear* for the Common Prayer and Bishops, and heard others *pray* that were against them; and because they heard the King's Soldiers with horrid Oaths abuse the name of God and saw them live in Debauchery, and the Parliaments Soldiers flock to Sermons, and talking of Religion, and praying and singing Psalms together on their Guards.

God's mercy to an age that owns[a] Jacobins were Infidels and a Scandal to all sober Christians![1]

[a] The original pencilled word is "owns" (as read by *C 17th C*), but it has been incorrectly overtraced as "our" (as read by MS TRANS)

[1] Jacobin—originally a member of a club called the Society of Friends of the Constitution, founded by monks of the Dominican Order in 1789 and holding its meetings in an old convent in the Rue Saint-Jacques. The Jacobins believed in equality among citizens, in the freedom of the individual, and in the universal brotherhood of man. But the club was suppressed by a decree of 12 Nov 1794, and "Jacobin" came to be a derogatory term for any person prepared to advance the cause of "liberty" to the point of fanaticism, and in England the umbrella-name for anybody who held convictions that were at variance with the principles England was defending

17 i 34–5, pencil, overtraced | § 51

They said to this ... 3. That as all the Courts of Justice do execute their Sentences in the *King's Name*, and this by his *own Law*, and therefore by his *Authority*, so much more might his Parliament do.

a very sound argument is here disguised in a false analogy, an inapplicable Precedent, and a sophistical form. Courts of Justice administer the total of the supreme power retrospectively involved in the name of the most dignified part. But here a Part, as a Part, acts as the Whole, where the Whole is absolutely requisite—i.e. in passing Laws; and again as B. and C. usurp a power belonging to A by the determination of A. B. and C. The true argument is, that Charles had by acts of his own ceased to be a lawful King &c.

17A i 38 | § 54

~~Tho~~. *Ric*. *Hooker*

18 i 40, pencil, overtraced | § 55

2. And that the Authority and Person of the King were inviolable, out of the reach of just Accusation, Judgment, or Execution by Law; as having no Superiour, and so no Judge.

But according to Grotius, a King waging war against the lawful Co-partners of the Summa Potestas ceases to be their King, and if conquered, forfeits to them his former share.[1] And surely if the King had been victor, he would have taken the Parliament's share to himself.—If it had been the Parliament, and not a mere Faction with the Army that tried & beheaded Charles, I could not doubt the lawfulness of the act.[2]

18A i 41 | § 57

... as also doth Mr. ~~Thomas~~ Richard *Hooker* ...

---

against Napoleonic despotism. Many, including C and RS, who welcomed and espoused the primitive theme of the Revolution, were proud to call themselves Jacobins, until the Terror and the rise of Napoleon forced them to reconsider their loyalties. For C's claim to have given "the first fair and philosophical statement and definition of Jacobinism and of Jacobin" see *Friend* (*CC*) II 144n; cf I 221n. For some strong remarks about Jacobinism made in 1804 see *CN* II 2110, 2113, 2150.

[1] Hugo Grotius, in *De jure belli et pacis* Bk I ch 4 § 13, argues that "If a King should have but one Part of the sovereign Power and the Senate or People the other, if such a King shall invade that Part which is not his own, he may justly be resisted, because he is not Sovereign in that Respect." Tr anon *The Rights of War and Peace* (1738) 121.

[2] Cf COPY A ANNEX and **24**, below.

19   i 41, pencil, overtraced

For if the Parliament have any Legislative Power, it cannot be as they are the Body or People, as Mr. *Tho. Hooker* ill supposeth ... For if once Legislation (the chief Act of Government) be denied to be any part of Government at all, and affirmed to belong to the People as such, who are no Governors, all Government will hereby be overthrown.

Here Baxter falls short of the Subject, and does not see the full consequences—of his own prior (most judicious) positions. Legislation in its high and most proper sense belongs to God only.[1] A people *declare* that such and such they hold to be law/ i.e. God's will.

20   i 47, pencil, overtraced | § 68

In *Cornwall*, Sir *Rich. Greenvile* having taken many Souldiers of the Earl of *Essex's* Army, sentenced about a dozen to be hanged: when they had hanged two or three, the Rope broke which should have hanged the next: And they sent for new Ropes so oft to hang him, and all of them still broke, that they durst go no farther, but saved all the rest ...

The Soldiers doubtless contrived this from the aversion natural to Englishmen of killing an enemy in cold blood—& because they foresaw that there would be Tit for Tat.

21   i 59, pencil, overtraced | § 85

For the very time that I was bleeding the Council of War sate at *Nottingham*, where (as I have credibly heard) they first began to open their Purposes and act their Part: and presently after they entered into their Engagement at *Triploe-Heath*. And as I perceived it was the Will of God to permit them to go on, so I afterward found that this great Affliction was a Mercy to my self; for they were so strong and active, that I had been likely to have had small Success in the Attempt, but to have lost my Life among them in their Fury. And thus I was finally separated from the Army.

It is easy to see from B's own account that his party ruined their own cause and that of the Kingdom by their tenets concerning the right and duty of the Civil Magistrate to use the Sword against such as were not of the same Religion with themselves.

19[1] See **24** and n 1, below.

22 i 62, pencil, overtraced | § 93

1. That they seem not to me to have answered satisfactorily to the main Argument fetcht from the Apostles own Government, with which *Saravia* had inclined me to some Episcopacy before; though Miracles and Infallibility were Apostolical temporary Priviledges; yet Church Government is an ordinary thing to be continued: And therefore as the Apostles had Successors as they were Preachers, I see not but that they must have Successors as Church Governors. ... Could I be sure that was the Government in the Days of the Apostles themselves, I should be satisfied what should be the Government now.

Was not Peter's Sentence against Ananias an act of *Church Government?*[1] Therefore tho' C. G. is an ordinary thing in *some* form or other, it does not follow that one particular form is an ord. thing. For the *time Being*, the Apostles as Heads of the Church did what they thought best, but whatever was binding on the Church universal and in all times they delivered as Commands from Christ. Now no other command was delivered but that all things should conduce to order and edification.[2]

23 i 66–7 | § 102

And therefore how they could refuse to receive the King, till he consented to take the Covenant, I know not: unless the taking of the Covenant had been a Condition on which he was to receive his Crown by the Laws or Fundamental Constitution of the Kingdom (which none pretendeth). Nor know I by what power they can add any thing to the Coronation Oath or Covenant, which by his Ancestors was to be taken, without his own Consent.

And pray how and by whom were the Coronation Oaths first imposed? The Scottish Nation, in 1650, had the same right to make a bargain with the Claimant of their Throne, as their Ancestors had. It is strange, that Baxter should not have seen, that his objections would apply to our Magna Charta. So he talks of a Constitution, & "unless it be part of the fundamental Law," &c—just as if these had been aboriginal or rather sans origin, and not as indeed they were, extorted & bargained for by the people. But throughout it is plain, that Baxter repeated but never appropriated the distinction between the King = the Executive Power, and the Individual Functionary. What obligation lay on the Scottish Parliament & Church to consult

[1] Acts 5.1–11.

[2] See 1 Cor 14.3, 2 Cor 10.8, 13.10.

the man, Charles Stuart's, personal Likes & Dislikes? The Oath was to be taken by him, as their King. Doubtless, he equally disliked the whole Protestant Interest—& if the Tories & C. of Eng. Jacobites had recalled James II. would Baxter think them culpable for imposing on him an oath to preserved the Protestant Church of England, & the severe penalties on his own Church-fellows?

24 i 71 | § 114

And some Men thought it a very hard Question, Whether they should rather wish the continuance of an Usurper that will do good, or the restitution of a Rightful Governour whose Followers will do hurt. But for my part I thought my Duty was clear, to disown the Usurper's Sin, what Good soever he would do; and to perform all my Engagements to a Rightful Governour, leaving the Issue of all to God ...

And who shall dare unconditionally condemn those who judged the former to be the better Alternative? especially those who did not adopt Baxter's notion of a jus divinum personal and hereditary in an Individual whose Father had broke the Compact on which the claim rested.[1]

25 i 75, pencil, overtraced | § 120[a]

One Mrs. *Dyer*, a chief Person of the Sect, did first bring forth a Monster, which had the Parts of almost all sorts of living Creatures, some Parts like Man, but most ugly and misplaced, and some like Beasts, Birds and Fishes, having Horns, Fins and Claws; and at the Birth of it the Bed shook, and the Women present fell a Vomiting, and were fain to go forth of the Room ...

This Babe of Mrs Dyer's is as no bad emblem of R. Baxter's own

---

[a] The paragraph that lies between §§ 119 and 121 is not numbered in the text

[1] *Jus divinum* is to be translated "divine right" here and in similar contexts; elsewhere, however, the phrase is better translated "divine law" because C considered the *jus divinum* to be the source from which the whole tissue of political and social morality grew. Unlike the secular metaphor of "the law of nature" that serves as premiss for much of our common law, and unlike "the divine right of kings" in the conflict between Charles I and Parliament, or "executive privilege" in a more recent issue—both principles claiming dispensation from the law in the arbitrary exercise of high authority—the *jus divinum* was in C's view all-pervasive and life-giving, flowing from the order of human life itself, an expression of human destiny as divinely conceived. See e.g. *SM (CC)* 33. For Hazlitt's attack on C's doctrine of the *jus divinum* in *SM* see *H Works* VII 121–3.

Credulity. It is almost an argument on his side/ that nothing he believed is more strange and inexplicable than his own Belief of them.

26   i 76, pencil, overtraced | § 122

The third Sect were the *Ranters*: These also made it their Business as the former, to set up the Light of Nature, under the name of *Christ in Men*, and to dishonour and cry down the Church, the Scripture, the present Ministry, and our Worship and Ordinances; and call'd men to hearken to Christ within them ...

But why does B. every where assert the identity of the new Light with the Light of Nature? or what does he mean exclusively by the latter? The source must be ⟨the⟩ same in all light, as far as it ⟨is⟩ light.—

27   i 77, pencil, overtraced | § 123

And that was the fourth Sect, the *Quakers*; who were but the *Ranters* turned from horrid Profaneness and Blasphemy, to a Life of extream Austerity on the other side.

observe the *but.*

28   i 77, pencil, overtraced | § 124

The fifth Sect are the *Behmenists.* .... Their Doctrine is to be seen in *Jacob Behmen*'s Books, by him that hath nothing else to do, than to bestow a great deal of time to understand him that was not willing to be easily understood, and to know that his bombasted words do signifie nothing more than before was easily known by common familiar terms.

This is not in all its parts true—it is true that the first principles of Behmen are to be found in the Writings of the Neo-platonists[1] after Plotinus & (but mixed with gross impieties) in Paracelsus; but it is not true that they are *easily* known, & still less so that they are communicable in common familiar Terms. But least of all is true, that there is nothing original in Behmen![a][2]

---

a 28 is written below 29 on the page, but the textus to 28 is earlier in the text than 29 textus

28[1] The earliest use of "neoplatonism" recorded in *OED* is 1845, of "neoplatonic" 1836–7, of "neoplatonist" 1837.

28[2] See BÖHME. C owned, and annotated slightly, a copy of the *Opera omnia* (Basel 1580) of Plotinus (205–70). A copy of Paracelsus *Opera* (3 vols Geneva 1658), described in *Green SC* (1880) 903 as "With 2 MS. Notes by S. T. Coleridge", is now in the Royal College of Surgeons; the notes are not in C's hand, nor is there clear evidence that the volumes were his. For extracts from Paracelsus, revolutionary medical theorist and alchemist, see *CN* III 3606, 3660. See also BÖHME **96** and n 2, BROWNE *Religio* **18**.

29   i 77, pencil, overtraced

The chiefest of these [Behmenists] in *England* are Dr. *Pordage* and his Family, who live together in Community, and pretend to hold visible and sensible Communion with Angels ...

It is curious that Lessing in the Review which he & Nicolai & Mendelsohn conducted under the form of letters to a wounded officer, joins the names of Pordage with that of Behmen. Q^y Was Pordage's work translated into German.[1]

30   i 79, pencil, overtraced | § 127

Also the *Socinians* made some increase by the Ministry of one Mr. *Biddle*, sometimes School-master in *Glocester*; who wrote against the Godhead of the Holy Ghost, and afterwards of Christ; whose Followers inclined much to meer Deism and Infidelity.

For the Socinians till Biddle retained much of the Xtn Religion, ex. gr. Redemption by the Cross—and the omnipresence of Christ as to this Planet—even as the Romanists with their Saints.[1] Luther's obstinate adherence to the ubiquity of the Body of Christ and his or rather its real presence in & with the Bread was a sad furtherance to the Advocates of Popish Idolatry & Hierolatry.[2]

29[1] Christoph Friedrich Nicolai suggested the scheme for *Briefe, die neueste Litteratur betreffend* (1759–65) and also published the work. Lessing had written 54 letters for the series by the time he withdrew in 1760: these are included in the *Sämmtliche Schriften* (30 vols Berlin 1784–98), in which C wrote four marginalia on them. Abbt took Lessing's place in the scheme, and Herder's *Fragmente über die neuere deutsche Litteratur* (1766–7) was published anonymously as a supplement. See also **105** n 2, below.

John Pordage (1607–81), astrologer and mystic, rector of Bradfield, Berkshire, is correctly associated with Böhme: his association with Jane Lead (or Leade) (1623–1704) led to the formation after Pordage's death of a Behmenist sect called the Philadelphians. German translations of at least four of Pordage's works were available between 1698 and 1715. There was a copy of Pordage's *Theologia mystica* (1683) in Green's library; the preface is signed J. L., i.e. Jane Lead.

30[1] C was well enough acquainted with the work of John Biddle (1615–62), controversial Unitarian writer, to include him in Jul 1803 in his scheme for the "Bibliotheca Britannica", with Hooker, Baxter, and Fox, as representing "the spirit of the theology of all the other parts of Christianity" —that is, other than Roman Catholicism. *CL* II 956.

30[2] For Luther's doctrine of consubstantiation see C. BUTLER *Vindication* 1 n 2. In a long note of Jun 1810 dealing with the question "Whether one of the great Ends of Christianity be not one of its Mysteries" C argued "not indeed that Transubstantiation is a Doctrine of Scripture, but that it is a mistaken conception of a true doctrine...". *CN* III 3847.

OED recognises "hierolatry"—worship of saints—as C's coinage. For

31 i 80, pencil, overtraced | § 130

Many a time have I been brought very low, and received the Sentence of Death in my self, when my poor, honest, praying Neighbours have met, and upon their Fasting and earnest Prayers I have been recovered. Once when I had continued weak three Weeks, and was unable to go abroad, the very day that they prayed for me, being *Good-Friday*, I recovered, and was able to Preach and Administer the Sacrament the next Lord's Day, and was better after it . . .

Strange that the common Manuals of School Logic should not have secured Baxter from the repeated Blunder of Cum hoc: ergo propter hoc![1] But still more strange, that his Piety should not have revolted against degrading PRAYER into medical Quackery/[2]

32 i 81, pencil, overtraced

Another time I had a Tumour rose on one of the Tonsils in my Throat, white and hard like a Bone; above the hardness of any Schyrrhous Tumour: I feared a Cancer; being it was round and like a Pease, as it beginneth . . . at the end of about a quarter of a Year, I was check'd by Conscience that I had never publickly praised God particularly for any of the Deliverances which he had vouchsafed me: And being speaking of God's Confirming our Belief of his Word by his fulfilling of Promises, and hearing Prayers . . . I annexed some thankful mention of my own Experiences; and suddenly the Tumour vanished, and no sign wherever it had been remained . . .

Before the Revolution, Metaphysics without experimental Psychology: & we here see the results. Since the Revolution, Experimental Psychology without Metaphysics: & we now *feel* the Result.[1]

In like manner, from Plotinus to Proclus, (i.e. from Commodus to Justinian) Philosophy as a substitute for Religion:[2] during the dark

---

similar compounds see COPY A **38** n 1 and CHILLINGWORTH COPY B **2** n 1.

31[1] A variant of the logical fallacy *post hoc, ergo propter hoc*—that since A comes after B, A is caused by B. C's variant: because A is found *with* B, therefore A is caused by B—or, as he puts it in *TL* (1848) 24: "the assumption of causation from mere co-existence".

31[2] See **34**, below.

32[1] See **1** § 5, above.

32[2] For Plotinus see **28** n 1, above. Proclus (412–85), was another favourite of C's, particularly for his triadic scheme; C read and annotated his work in Greek and in Thomas Taylor's translation. See PROCLUS. The period from Commodus the corrupt (161–92) to Justinian the lawgiver (482–563) corresponds roughly with the period of Neoplatonic philosophy and the emergence with it

Ages Religion as superseding Philosophy: & the Effects are equally instructive. The great maxim of Legislation, intellectual or political is—*Subordinate, not exclude*. Nature in her ascent leaves nothing behind: but at each step subordinates & glorifies. Mass, Chrystal, Organ, sensation, sentience, reflection.[3]

33   i 82, pencil, overtraced | § 133

Another time, as I sat in my Study, the Weight of my greatest Folio Books brake down three or four of the highest Shelves, when I sat close under them, and they fell down on every side me, and not one of them hit me, save one upon the Arm; whereas the Place, the Weight, and greatness of the Books was such, and my Head just under them, that it was a Wonder they had not beaten out my Brains . . .

μέγα βιβλίον μέγα κακόν.[1]

34   i 84, pencil, overtraced | § 135

But all these my Labours . . . even preaching and preparing for it, were but my Recreations, and as it were the work of my spare hours: For my Writings were my chiefest daily Labour; which yet went the more slowly on, that I never one hour had an *Amanuensis* to dictate to, and specially because my Weakness took up so much of my time. For all the Pains that my Infirmities ever brought upon me, were never half so grievous an Affliction to me, as the unavoidable loss of my time, which they occasioned.

Alas! in how many respects does my Lot resemble Baxter's! But how much less have my bodily Evils been, & yet how very much greater an impediment have I suffered them to be! But verily Baxter's Labors seem miracles of supporting Grace! Ought I not therefore to retract the note at p 80?[1] *I waver.*

---

of the Johannine Christianity. The subject of the 7th Philosophical Lecture (8 Feb 1819) was "Corrupt Philosophy...as...Opponent of Christianity...from the Antonines to the final suppression of the Philosophic Schools under Justinian". *P Lects* (1949) 227; cf 228.

32[3] A brilliant statement of the guiding thought of the *Theory of Life*. See *TL* (1848) 42–3 and cf 69–86.

33[1] "A big book is a big nuisance" or, as Burton has it in *Anatomy of Melancholy* "Democritus to the Reader" (Everyman 1932, I 24), "A great book is a great mischief". C is using the proverbial form of the saying of Callimachus (fr 465 in Pfeiffer) quoted in Athenaeus *Deipnosophists* 72A.

34[1] That is, **31**, above. A passage in i 82, underlined in pencil (which is overtraced in ink) and marked with a fist, but not certainly by C, reads: "Flatulency pumping up the Matter".

35   p ⁻5, pencil, overtraced; i 87, pencil, roughly overtraced | § 137

For my part, I bless God, who gave me even under an Usurper whom
I opposed, such Liberty and Advantage to preach his Gospel with
Success, which I cannot have under a King to whom I have sworn
and performed true Subjection and Obedience; yea, which no Age
since the Gospel came into this Land, did before possess, as far as I
can learn from History. Sure I am, that when it became a matter of
Reputation and Honour to be Godly, it abundantly furthered the
Successes of the Ministry. Yea, and I shall add this much more for
the sake of Posterity, that as much as I have said and written against
Licentiousness in Religion, and for the Magistrates Power in it,
and though I think that Land most happy, whose Rulers use their
Authority for Christ, as well as for the Civil Peace; yet in Compari-
son of the rest of the World, I shall think that Land happy that hath
but bare Liberty to be as good as they are willing to be; and if
Countenance and *Maintenance* be but added to *Liberty*, and tollerated
Errors and Sects be but forced to *keep the Peace*, and not to oppose
the Substantials of Christianity, I shall not hereafter much fear such
Toleration, nor despair that Truth will bear down Adversaries.

P. 87. §4.—especially valuable.

   Most valuable & citable §.*a* Likewise it is a happy instance of the
Force of a cherished Prejudice in an honest mind—*practically*
yielding to the truth, but yet with a *speculative,* " *though I still think,*
&c "

36   i 99 | § 144

He [Cromwell] thought that if the War was lawful, the Victory was
lawful; and if it were lawful to fight against the King and conquer
him, it was lawful to use him as a conquered Enemy, and a foolish
thing to trust him when they had so provoked him, (whereas indeed
the Parliament professed neither to fight against him, nor to conquer
him).

nonsense!

37   i 99

He [Cromwell] thought that the Heart of the King was deep, and
that he resolved upon Revenge, and that if he were King, he would
easily at one time or other accomplish it; and that it was a dishonest
thing of the Parliament to set men to fight for them against the King,

---

a The whole paragraph is marked with a pencil line in the margin

and then to lay their Necks upon the block, and be at his Mercy; and
that if that must be the Case, it was better to flatter or please him,
than to fight against him.

and was not this the truth? See Laing's History of Scotland, Vol. I.[1]

38 i 114 | § 171

But though my *fears* are never so great, that a man dissembleth and
is not sincere, yet if I be not able to bring in that Evidence to invalidate his Profession, which *in foro Ecclesiae* shall prove it to be
incredible, I ought to receive him as a credible Professor, though but
by a *Humane*, and perhaps most *debile Belief*.

And of course, therefore, with a most debile Love.

39 i 127–8, marked with a line in the margin | § 213

3. ... The *better* Causes are these: 1. I value all things according to
their *Use* and *Ends*; and I find in the daily Practice and Experience
of my Soul, that the Knowledge of God and Christ, and the Holy
Spirit, and one Truth of Scripture, and the Life to come, and of a
Holy Life, is of *more use* to me, than all the most curious Speculations. ... So the Knowledge of God and of Jesus Christ, of Heaven
and Holyness, doth build up the Soul to endless Blessedness, and
affordeth it solid Peace and Comfort; when a multitude of School
Niceties serve but for vain Janglings and hurtful Diversions and Con-
tentions: And yet I would not dissuade my Reader from the perusal of
Aquinas, Scotus, Ockam, Arminiensis, Durandus, or any such Writers,
for much Good may be gotten from them: But I would persuade him
to study and live upon the essential Doctrines of Christianity and
Godliness, incomparably above them all. ... And I think if he lived
among Infidels and Enemies of Christ, he would find that to make
good the *Doctrine of Faith* and of *Life Eternal*, were not only his
noblest and most useful Study; but also that which would require the

---

37[1] The exploits and fate of Mon-
trose, and the duplicity of some of his
followers in support of Charles I in
Scotland 1644–50, would illustrate this
principle clearly enough, as given
in Malcolm L A I N G *The History of
Scotland* (4 vols 1804) III, on a flyleaf
of which C's only surviving marginal
note on Laing is written. Relevant
passages occur in the 2-vol 1800 ed I
248–309, 323, 400–9, which are also
found in Vol III of the 4-vol 1804 ed
(pagination not identical), Vols III and
IV being a reprint of 1800 Vols I and II.
(Vols I and II of 1804 ed are a self-
contained prefatory study of the part
played by Mary, Queen of Scots in the
murder of her husband Darnley.)

height of all his Parts, and the utmost Diligence, to manage it skilfully to the Satisfaction of himself and others.

Who would deny the truth & importance of the remarks in this §.ph? But then what are the essential Doctrines, if not Sin & Original Sin as the necessitating Occasion, and the Redemption of Sinners by the incarnate Word as the Substance of the Christian Dispensation?[1] And can these be intelligently believed without knowlege & stedfast meditation? By the unlearned they may be worthily received; but not by the unthinking or the self-ignorant Christians!

40 p ⁻6 (p–d), referring to i 127–8

4. . . . had I been void of internal Experience, and the Adhesion of Love, and the special help of God . . . I had certainly Apostatized to Infidelity (though for *Atheism* or *Ungodliness*, my Reason seeth no stronger Arguments, than may be brought to prove that there is no Earth or Air, or Sun). I am now therefore much more Apprehensive than heretofore, of the Necessity of well grounding Men in their Religion, and especially of the Witness of the indwelling Spirit: For I more sensibly perceive that the *Spirit* is the great Witness of Christ and Christianity to the World: And though the Folly of Fanaticks tempted me long to over-look the Strength of this Testimony of the Spirit, while they placed it in a certain *internal Assertion*, or enthusiastick Inspiration; yet now I see that the Holy Ghost in another manner is the Witness of Christ and his Agent in the World: The Spirit in the Prophets was his first Witness; and the Spirit by Miracles was the second; and the Spirit by Renovation, Sanctification, Illumination and Consolation, assimilating the Soul to Christ and Heaven is the continued Witness to all true Believers: And if any Man have not the Spirit of Christ, the same is none of his, *Rom.* 8. 9. 127–128. Spiritual Proof of Chr^y.

41 i 128

5. Among Truths certain in themselves, all are not equally certain unto me; and even of the Mysteries of the Gospel, I must needs say

---

39[1] The question of original sin, which had vexed C's thinking as early as the *annus mirabilis*, is discussed in detail and at large in *AR* (1825) 251–87. There C's examination concentrates upon Jeremy Taylor's doctrine of sin and redemption in *Deus Justificatus* and the inadequacies of it, but it offers an analysis equally pertinent to Baxter's position if only because both Taylor and Baxter offered to C a means of defining precisely the Calvinist and Arminian deflections from orthodoxy: see e.g. *Friend* (*CC*) I 434.

with Mr. *Richard Hooker Eccl. Polit.* that whatever men may pretend, the subjective Certainty cannot go beyond the objective Evidence: for it is caused thereby as the print on the Wax is caused by that on the Seal: Therefore I do more of late than ever discern a necessity of a methodical procedure in maintaining the Doctrine of Christianity, and of beginning at Natural Verities, as presupposed fundamentally to supernatural. . . . My certainty that I am a Man, is before my certainty that there is a God. . . . My certainty that there is a God, is greater than my certainty that he requireth love and holiness of his Creature: My certainty of *this* is greater than my certainty of the Life of Reward and Punishment hereafter . . .

There is a confusion in this §. 5. which asks more than a marginal note to disentangle.

Briefly—the process of acquirement is confounded with the order of the truths, when acquired.[1] A tinder-spark gives light to an Argand's Lamp—is it therefore more luminous?[2]

42 i 129–30

11. Accordingly I had then a far higher opinion of Learned Persons and Books, than I have now. . . . But now Experience hath constrained me against my will to know, that Reverend Learned Men are imperfect, and know but little as well as I . . . And the better I am acquainted with them, the more I perceive that we are all yet in the dark: And the more I am acquainted with holy Men, that are all for Heaven, and pretend not much to Subtilities, the more I value and honour them. And when I have studied hard to understand some abstruse admired Books . . . I have but attained the Knowledge of Humane Imperfection, and to see that the Author is but a Man as well as I.

On these points, I have come to a Resting-place. Let such Articles, as are either to be recognized as *facts* (ex. gr. Sin=Evil having its origination in a Will; & the reality of a responsible & (in whatever Sense freedom is presupposed in responsibility) of a free Will in Man/ or acknowleged as Laws (ex. gr. the unconditional bindingness of the Practical Reason) or to be freely affirmed as necessary thro' their moral interest, their indispensableness to our spiritual Humanity

[1] Cf *CN* ii 3023.
[2] Aimé Argand (1755–1803), born in Geneva, lived for some time in England; invented a lamp c 1782 that gave brighter illumination by introducing a current of air into the middle of the flame through a tubular wick.

(ex. gr. the personëity,[1] holiness, & moral government & providence of God)—let these be vindicated from absurdity, from ~~all~~ self-contradiction, and contradiction to the pure Reason—& restored to simple Incomprehensibility. He who seeks for more, knows not what he is talking of: he, who will not seek even this, is either indifferent to the truth of what he professes to believe, or he mistakes a general determination not to disbelieve for a positive and especial Faith—which is only *our* faith as far as we can assign a *reason* for it.—O how impossible it is to move an inch to the right or left in any point of spiritual & moral Concernment, without seeing the damage caused by the confusion of the Reason with Understanding![2] S. T. C.

43   i 131

23. My Soul is much more afflicted with the thoughts of the miserable World, and more drawn out in desire of their Conversion than heretofore: I was wont to look but little further than *England* in my Prayers, as not considering the state of the rest of the World: Or if I prayed for the Conversion of the Jews, that was almost all. But now as I better understand the Case of the World, and the method of the Lord's Prayer, so there is nothing in the World that lyeth so heavy upon my heart, as the thought of the miserable Nations of the Earth: It is the most astonishing part of all God's Providence to me, that he so far forsaketh almost all the World, and confineth his special Favour to so few: That so small a part of the World hath the Profession of Christianity, in comparison of Heathens, Mahometans and other Infidels!

I dare not *not* condemn myself for the languid or dormant state of my feelings respecting the Mahometans & Heathen, yet know not, in what degree to condemn! The less culpable grounds of this my languor are, first, my utter ignorance of God's Purposes with respect of the Heathens—& second, the strong conviction, I have that the

42[1] "Personëity" ("person-ness"), like "multëity" ("many-ness"), is a peculiarly Coleridgian word formed on the analogy of certain scholastic terms that he found philosophically useful: see ATHENAEUM **31** n 3. Two examples, both cited by *OED*, illustrate the special function of the word: LUTHER *Colloquia Mensalia* (1652) flyleaf and Daniel WATERLAND *Vindication of Christ's Divinity* (Cambridge 1719) 254–5; HNC in *LR* IV 232, repeated by *OED*, has introduced a gloss from an unidentified source—"that is, his I-ship (*Ichheit*)". Cf EICHHORN *Neue Testament* COPY A **31** and LEIGHTON *Genuine Works* (4 vols 1819) [COPY B] I 170.

42[2] C regularly noted how the failure to distinguish between reason and understanding had prevented the earlier English divines from developing the full potential of their theological thought: see e.g. DONNE *Sermons* COPY B **29**.

Conversion of a single Pro⟨v⟩ince of Christendom to true practical Christianity would do more toward the Conversion of Heathendom than an army of Missionaries.[1]

44 i 131

25. My Censures of the Papists do much differ from what they were at first: I then thought that their Errours in the *Doctrines of Faith* were their most dangerous Mistakes as in the Points of Merit, Justification by Works, Assurance of Salvation, the Nature of Faith, &c.[1] But now I am assured that their mis-expressions, and mis-understanding us, with our mistakings of them, and inconvenient expressing our own Opinions, hath made the difference in these Points to appear much greater than they are; and that in some of them it is next to none at all. But the great and unreconcilable Differences lye, in their Church Tyranny and Usurpations, and in their great Corruptions and Abasement of God's Worship, together with their be-friending of *Ignorance* and *Vice*.

Romanism and Despotic Government in the larger part of Xtendom, and the prevalence of Epicurean Principles in the remainder—these do indeed lie heavy on my heart!

44A i 135

But when great Men write History, or Flatterieers by their Appointment, which no man dare contradict, believe it but as you are constrained.

45 i 135, pencil, overtraced

... I hartily lament that the Historical Writings of the Ancient Schismaticks and Heriticks (as they were called) perished, and that partiality suffered them not to survive, that we might have had more Light in the Church-Affairs of those times, and been better able to judge between the Fathers and them.

It is greatly to the credit of Baxter that he has here anticipated those merits which so long after gave deserved celebrity to the name and writings of Beausobre and Lardner—and still more recently of Eichhorn, Paulus, & other Neologists.[1]

43[1] For C's scepticism about the efficacy of missionary work, see e.g. *CN* III 3505, 3838, and nn. See also BLOMFIELD 3 and n 3.

44[1] In *AR* (1825) 206–7n C quoted

two paragraphs from i 131—a "golden passage"—beginning with this sentence.

45[1] Isaac de Beausobre (1659–1738), Huguenot writer, prepared a French

46 i 136, pencil, overtraced

... My own Eyes have read such *Words* and *Actions* asserted with most vehement iterated unblushing Confidence, which abundance of Ear-Witnesses, even of their own Parties must needs know to have been altogether false: and therefore having my self now written this History of my self, notwithstanding my Protestation that I have not in any thing wilfully gone against the Truth, I expect no more Credit from the Reader, than the self-evidencing Light of the matter, with concurrent rational Advantages, from Persons, and Things, and other Witnesses, shall constrain him to; if he be a Person that is unacquainted with the Author himself, and the other Evidences of his Veracity and Credibility.

I may not unfrequently doubt Baxter's memory or even his competence, in consequence of his particular modes of thinking; but I could almost as soon doubt the Gospel Verity as his *veracity*.[1]

47 i 138 | at the end of I i

The Book following (Lib. I. Part II.) is interesting and most instructive as an instance of Syncretism,[1] even when it has been under-

---

translation of the NT (Amsterdam 1718) at the command of the King of Prussia. His *Remarques historiques, critiques et philologiques sur le nouveau Testament* and the incomplete *Historie de la Réformation* were published posthumously. There was a copy of his *Historie critique de Manichée et de Manichéisme* (2 vols Amsterdam 1724–9) in Green's library, not shown as C's. Nathaniel Lardner (1684–1768) is recognised as one of the founders of the modern school of critical research into early Christian literature with his *Credibility of the Gospel History* (14 vols 1727–55). C was aware of his work as early as 1796: *CL* I 197; see also 371, 554, II 821–3, and *CN* I 851. For C's continuing admiration of Lardner, see *IS* 50, *Friend* (*CC*) I 30n. N 54 ff 5ᵛ–8 of Nov 1833 shows that C relied upon Lardner—to some extent at least—for "Quotations from the Fathers".

C annotated several works of Johann

Gottfried Eichhorn (1752–1827) as well as *Das Leben Jesu* by Heinrich E. G. Paulus (1761–1851). For "Neologist" as "one who adopts neologism in theology or religious matters, a rationalist", *OED* cites Newman in the *Eclectic Review* in 1827 for the first use; but C's use, referring generally to Eichhorn and his school, is earlier. For the "Neologic Divines" see *CN* III 4401 (c 10 Mar 1818) and n, and cf *AR* (1825) 354n.

46[1] HNC printed this note in *TT* 12 Jul 1827, adding **34** in a footnote. The distinction between "verity" (from *verus*, true absolutely) and "veracity" (from *verax*, truth-telling) is normally secured by those who use language carefully, but C saw some need to draw attention to the difference in e.g. *Friend* I 43 (II 42), *BL* ch 9 (1907) I 100, *SM* (*CC*) 46, 48. Cf **115** at n 7, below.

47[1] "Syncretism"—generally, an attempted reconciliation of opposite

taken from the purest and most laudable motives & from impulses the most Christian—its epicurean *clinamen*,[2] & yet utter failure in its object, that of tending to a common center. The experience of 18 Centuries seems to prove that there is no practicable medium between a Church Comprehensive (which is the only meaning of a Catholic Church *visible*) in which A in the North or East is allowed to advance *officially* no doctrine different from what is allowed to B in the South or West; and a Co-existence of independent Churches, in none of which any further Unity is required but that between the Minister and his Congregation, while this again is secured by the election and continuance of the former depending wholly on the will of the latter.

Perhaps, the best ~~POSSIBLE~~ state possible, tho' not the best possible state, is where both are found, the one established by maintenance, the other by permission: in short, that which we now enjoy. In such a state no Minister of the former can have a right to complain for it was at his own option to have taken the latter—et volenti nulla fit injuria.[3] For an individual to demand the freedom of the Independent Single-church when he receives 500£ a year for submitting to the necessary restrictions of the Church General, is *impudence* and Mammonolatry to boot.[4] S. T. C.*[a]

* Since the Mss Note below was written, I have seen or believed myself to see cause for qualifying the opinion there expressed. More especially since I have had the honor and happiness of a familiar acquaintance with the Revd Edward Irving,[5] I have acknowleged a

[a] Below his initials C wrote "*See above" and then wrote his afterthought at the head of the page

---

tenets or practices. The term "Syncretist" was especially applied to the theological system devised by Baxter's older contemporary Georg Calixtus in his attempt to reconcile Lutherans, Calvinists, and Catholics. C also applied it to a much earlier period "about the time of Heliogabalus" and to "those who could fain reconcile a neo-platonized Polytheism with Judaism & Christianity". N 29 f 132^v. See also *CN* iii 3605, 4251, *LS* (*CC*) 200 and n.

47[2] In order to account for the collisions between atoms that would otherwise move only directly downwards, and also to account for free

will, Epicurus postulated the principle of *clinamen* to impart a slight swerve to his atoms—though not, as in C's image, towards the centre.

47[3] "And what a man consents to cannot be considered an injury [to him]"—a law maxim cited in *LS* (*CC*) 212.

47[4] For compounds on "-latry" and "-duly" see COPY A 38 n 1.

47[5] C seems to have heard Edward Irving (1792–1834) preach first in Jul 1823 and was greatly impressed by the "super-Ciceronian, ultra-Demosthenic Pulpiteer of the Scotch Chapel in Cross Street, Hatton Garden". *CL* v 280. By Jun 1824 he and Irving were meeting

true medium between the Church of E. and the Independent Scheme—
viz. the Division or Separation of *Election* and *Selection*, the former
belonging to the congregation, the latter to the Assembled Ministers—/

48   i 141, pencil, overtraced | i ii § 11

3. That they [the *Erastians*] misunderstood and injured their
Brethren, supposing and affirming them to claim as from God a
coercive Power over the Bodies or Purses of Men, and so setting up
Imperium in Imperio; whereas all temperate Christians (at least except
Papists) confess that the Church hath no Power of *Force*, but only to
manage God's Word unto Mens Consciences.

But are not the Receivers as bad as the Thief? Is it not a poor evasion
to say—It is true, I send you to a dungeon there to rot; because you
do not think as I do, concerning some point of Faith:—but this
only as a *civil* Officer. As a Divine, I only tenderly entreat and *persuade* you! Can there be fouler Hypocrisy in the Spanish Inquisition
than this?

49   i 142–3, pencil, overtraced | § 12

In the Diocesane Party I utterly disliked 1. Their Extirpation of the
true Discipline of Christ . . . as their Principles and Church State
had made it unpracticable and impossible, while one Bishop with
his Consistory, had the sole Government of a thousand or many
hundred Churches. . . . 4. That they extinguished the ancient Species
of Bishops, which was in the times of *Ignatius*, when every church had
one Altar and one Bishop; and there were none but *Itinerants* or
Archbishops that had many Churches.

I could never rightly understand this objection of R. Baxter's. What
power not possessed by the *Rector* of a Parish would he have wished
a parochial Bishop to have exerted? What could have been given by
the Legislature to the latter, which might not be given to the former?
In short, Baxter's plan seems to do away *Arch*-bishops (ἐπισκοποι
κοινοι)[1] but for the rest to *name* our present Rectors & Vicars

---

regularly, Irving assuming the rôle of
C's pupil and admirer. C annotated
three of Irving's books: see IRVING
and LACUNZA. But c 1826 C began to
doubt Irving's integrity of purpose, and
then to question his sanity.

C's footnote to **47** seems to have

been written c 1824–5, but the annotation itself is evidently rather earlier.

49[1] "Common   (or   general)
bishops"—i.e. bishops common to
several dioceses. Baxter's proposed
change, as C notes, would be merely
in name.

Bishops.—I cannot see what is *gained* by his plan. The true difficulty is that if Church Discipline is attached to the Establishment by this World's Law, not to the form established: and his objections from § 5 to § 10 relate to particular abuses, not to Episcopacy.[2]

50   i 143, pencil, overtraced | § 14

5. But above all I disliked, that most of them [the Independents] made the People by majority of Votes to be Church-Governors, in Excommunications, Absolutions, &c. which Christ hath made an Act of Office, and so they governed their Governors and themselves.

Is not this the case with the two Houses of Legislature? The Members taken individually are subjects; collectively Governors

51   i 177, pencil, overtraced | § 37

Answ. 7. The extraordinary Gifts of the Apostles, and the Priviledge of being Eye and Ear Witnesses to Christ, were Abilities which they had for the infallible Discharge of their Function, but they were not the Ground of their Power and Authority to govern the Church. . . . But when Christ authorised his Apostles with the Power of Government, *Potestas Clavium* was committed to them only, not to the Seventy . . .

I wish for a proof that all the Apostles had any extraordinary gifts which none of the 70 had. Nay, as an Episcopalian of the Ch. of Eng. I hold it an unsafe and imprudent concession, tending to weaken the Governing Right of the Bishops.

But I fear that as the Law and Right of Patronage in England now are, the Q.[y] had better not be stirred; lest it should be found that the true Power of the Keys is not as with the Papists in hands to wch it is doubtful whether Christ committed them exclusively, but in hands to which it is certain that Christ did not commit them at all.[1]

52   i 179, pencil, overtraced

. . . It followeth not that a meer Bishop may have a Multitude of Churches, because an Archbishop may, who hath many Bishops under him.

49[2] The abuses cited in §§ 5–10 are *inter alia* that the Prelates "set up Courts more *Secular* than *Spiritual*"; they made use of force "wherein their carnal interest did . . . manage a War against the Interest of Christ and Godliness and the Souls of Men".

51[1] For the commission to Peter, from whom the apostolic succession flows, see Matt 16.19; for "the 70" see Luke 10.1.

What then does B. quarrell about? That our Bishops take a humbler title than they have a right to claim? That being in fact Arch-bishops —they are for the most part content to be styled as one of the Brethren?

53   i 185, pencil, overtraced | § 45

[In his reply to objections by the Anabaptists:] I say again, No Church, no Christ; for No Body, no Head: and if no Christ then, there is no Christ now. Take heed therefore how you un-Church, or disown the whole Church of Christ in the very frame, for so many Ages.

Baxter here forgets his own mystical regenerated Church. If he mean this, it is nothing to the argument in question: if not, then he must assert the monstrous absurdity of, No unregenerate Church, no Christ.[1]

54   i 188, pencil, overtraced | § 46

3. Or if they would not yield to this at all, we might have Communion with them as *Christians*, without acknowledging them for Pastors.

Observe the inconsistency of Baxter. No Pastor, no Church; no Church, no Christ.[1] And yet he will receive them as *Christians*— much to his honor as a Christian, but not much to his Credit as a Logician.

55   i 189, pencil, overtraced

3. We are agreed that as *some discovery of Consent* on both Parts (the *Pastors* and *People*) is necessary to the being of the Members of a political particular Church: So that the *most express* Declaration of that Consent, is the most plain and satisfactory Dealing, and most obliging, and likest to attain the Ends ...

In our Churches, especially in good Livings, there is such an overflowing Fullness of Consent on the part of the Pastor as to supply that of the People—altogether—nay, to nullify their declared Dissent.

53[1] "No Church, no Christ"—one of a family of catch-phrases current in the seventeenth century on the analogy of James I's reply to the Scottish "Millenary Petition" of 1604— "No Bishop, no King". See e.g. "*No Spirit, no God*" in *CN* I 1000G and "No Christ, no God" in *CN* II 2448. See also **54**, below, and *CN* III 4489.
     54[1] See **53** and n 1.

56   i 194 | § 49

By the Establishment of what is contained in these Twelve Propositions or Articles following, the Churches in these Nations may have a Holy Communion, Peace and Concord, without any Wrong to the Consciences or Liberties of Presbyterians, Congregational, Episcopal, or any other Christians.

Painfully instructive are these Proposals from so wise, and peaceable a Divine as Baxter. How mighty must be the force of an old Prejudice when so acute a Logiciaein was blinded by it to such palpable inconsistencies. On what ground of Right could a Magistrate inflict a penalty thereby to compel a man to *hear* what he might believe dangerous to his soul, on which the Right of burning the refractory individual might not be defended?

57   i 198–9, pencil, overtraced | § 51

To which ends .\.. I think that this is all that should be required of any Church or Member (ordinarily) to be professed, "*In General I do believe all that is contained in the Sacred Canonical Scriptures, and particularly I believe all explicitly contained in the Ancient Creed, and I desire all that is contained in the Lord's Prayer, and I resolve upon Obedience to the Ten Commandments, and whatever else I can learn of the Will of God.*"

To a man of sense but unstudied in the *context* of human Nature and from having confined his reading to the writers of the present and the last generation unused to *live* in former ages, it must seem strange that Baxter should not have seen that this Test is either *all* or *nothing*. And the Creed! a Papist would desire no better concession from a Protestant, than that he should place a Tradition of the Romish or Western Church in the same rank with the Scriptures. Could B. be ignorant that the absurdly so called Apostles' Creed was the mere *catechism* of the Catechumens in the Roman Diocese, and not the Baptismal Creed of the Eastern Church?[1] The only Test necessary is an established Liturgy.[a2]

58   i 201, pencil, overtraced | § 55

As Reverend Bishop *Usher* hath manifested that the Western Creed, now called the Apostles (wanting two or three Clauses that now are

---

a This note, like several of the pencil notes from here onward, has been overtraced in ink by HNC

57[1] On the Apostles' Creed cf *Catholick Theologie* **9** n 1, and **58** n 1, below.   **57[2]** *LR* iv 102 softens this note by elision and rewording.

in it) was not only before the Nicene Creed; but of such *farther* Antiquity, that no beginning of it below the Apostles Days can be found: So it is past doubt that in other Words the Churches had still a Symbol or Sum of their Belief, which was the Test of the Orthodox, and that which the Catechumeni were to be instructed in.

Remove these 2 or 3 clauses and doubtless the substance of the remainder must have been little short of the Apostolic age. But so is one at least of the writings of Clement.[1] The great Question is: was this the Baptismal Symbol, the regula fidei which it was forbidden to put in writing?[2] Or was it the Christian A. B. C. of the Catechumeni *previously* to their Baptismal initiation into the higher Mysteries— to the strong meat which was not for Babes?[3]

58[1] The earliest version of the Apostles' Creed known in C's day was in Marcellus *Apologia* (c 340). Rufinus (345–440), in *Commentarius in Symbolum Apostolorum*, said that the text had been preserved by the Roman Church unchanged since the Apostles and that other churches had added to it. The only work correctly ascribed to Clement of Rome (fl 96) is the first of the two Epistles of Clement to the Corinthians.

58[2] "Rule of faith"—the usual Latin equivalent of κάνων τῆς πίστεως. Cf C's use of "Canon Fidei" in **100**, below. Irenaeus used the term "Canon Fidei", and Tertullian used both "Regula Fidei" and "Symbolum Fidei", but "Symbolum Fidei" did not undisputably refer to a formulated creed until the middle of the fourth century, and it is not certain that all these terms are synonymous. See BIBLE *Apocryphal NT* **4** and n 4.

58[3] For the closing phrase see Heb 5.12–14. C had already answered "the great Question" to his general satisfaction in Jun 1810 in *CN* III 3880, drawing from the facts presented by Stillingfleet conclusions different from those of Stillingfleet himself, Baxter, Field, and Waterland. (See also **100**, below, *Catholick Theologie* **9**, and *CN* III 3964.) (*a*) The Apostles' Creed was not the *regula fidei*, but was a document used in the preliminary instruction of catechumens, in its earliest use primarily for pagan adults and later, as Christianity spread, mostly for young Christians and eventually for children. (*b*) The Apostles' Creed is a condensed account of the history of Christ almost devoid of doctrinal content; but it probably included materials that had been current in the days of the Apostles. It was a formula preserved by the Church of Rome; it appeared in different forms in other churches, showing the greatest modification where the pressure of heresy was strongest. (*c*) The *regula fidei* (or "Symbolum Fidei", as C calls it in *CN* III 3880) was "always repeated at Baptism", but since "it was forbidden to put [it] in writing" its precise nature was unknown. It was "elder than the Gospels—& probably contained only the three doctrines of the Trinity, the Redemption, and the Unity of the Church". The Apostles' Creed was "the Christian A.B.C." leading to baptism, the *symbolum* (or token of admission to baptism): the *regula fidei* was the affirmation of doctrinal belief made at the time of initiation into the central rites. (*d*) The Nicene Creed was not a relic of the *regula fidei* but "a paraphrase" of the Apostles' Creed.

59 i 203

Not so much for my own sake, as others: lest it should offend the Parliament, and open the Mouths of our Adversaries, that we cannot our selves agree in Fundamentals: and lest it prove an occasion for others to sue for an Universal* Toleration.

* That this apprehension so constantly haunted, so powerfully actuated, even the mild and really tolerant Baxter, is a strong proof of my old opinion—that the Dogma of the right and duty of the civil magistrate to restrain and punish religious avowals by him deemed heretical, universal among the Presbyterians and Parliamentary Church-men, joined with the persecuting spirit of the Presbyterians, was the main cause of Cromwell's despair & consequent unfaithfulness concerning a Parliamentary Common-wealth.[1]

60 i 222–3 | § 86 Letter to the Lady Anne Lindsey

I tried, when I was last with you, to revive your Reason, by proposing to you the Infallibility of the Common Senses of all the World; and I could not prevail though you had nothing to answer that was not against Common Sense. And it is impossible any thing controverted can be brought nearer you, or made plainer than to be brought to your Eyes and Taste and Feeling: and not yours only, but all Mens else. Sense goes before Faith. Faith is no Faith but upon Supposition of Sense and Understanding; if therefore Common Sense be fallible, Faith must needs be so.

This is one of those two-edged Arguments, which (not indeed *began* but) began to be *fashionable*, ⟨just⟩ before & after the Restoration—I was half converted to Transsubst. by Tillotson's *Common Senses* against it, seeing clearly that the same grounds totidem verbis et syllabis would serve the Socinian against all the mysteries of Christianity.[1] If the Rom. Cath. had pretended that the *phænomena* Bread & Wine were changed into the *Phænomena*, Flesh and Blood, this Objection would have been legitimate & irresistible; but as it is, it is mere sensual Babble.—The whole of Popery lies in the assumption of *a Church*, as a real Agent, a numerical Unit—infallible in the

---

59[1] On toleration see **92**, below.

60[1] The work C refers to is John Tillotson (1630–94) *Discourse Against Transubstantiation* (1684); see *CN* III 3868n. On transubstantiation see also **30** n 2, above. In Jul 1802 C referred to this notable preacher and archbishop of Canterbury as one of "the best & greatest men of the Church" (*CL* II 807), but he seldom mentioned his work. Cf a note on a back flyleaf of Jeremy T A Y L O R *Polemicall Discourses*. The Latin phrase means "in the same number of words and syllables".

highest degree, inasmuch as both what *is* Scripture and what Scripture teaches is infallible by derivation only from ~~the~~ an infallible decision of the Church. Fairly undermine or blow up this; & all the remaining ~~peculierar~~ Tenets of Romanism fall with it—or stand by their own insight, as opinions of individual Doctors.—*a*

An Antagonist of a complex bad System, a *System* however notwithstanding—& such is Popery—should take heed above all ~~other~~ things not to *disperse* himself. Keep to the *sticking* place. But the majority of our Protestant Polemists seem to have taken for granted, that they could not attack Romanism in too many places or on too many points: forgetting, that in some ~~one~~ they will be less strong than in others; and that if in any one or two they are repelled from the assault, the feeling of this will extend itself over the whole— Besides, what use of 13 reasons of a Witness's not appearing in Court, when the first is that the Man had died since his subpœna? It is as if a party employed to root up a tree were to set one or two at that work, while others were hacking the Branches, & others sawing the Trunk at different heights from the ground.

N.B. The point of attack suggested below*b* in disputes with the Romanists is of especial expediency in the present day: because a number of pious & reasonable Catholics are not aware of the dependency of their other tenets on this of the Church—but are themselves shaken & inclined to explain it away. This once fixed, the Scriptures rise uppermost: & the Man is already a Protestant, tho' his opinions should remain near to the Roman than the Reformed Church.

61　i 224

But methinks yet I should have hope of reviving your Charity: You cannot be a Papist indeed, but you must believe, that out of their Church (that is out of the Pope's Dominions) there is no Salvation; and consequently no Justification and Charity, or saving Grace: And is it possible you can so easily believe your religious Father to be in Hell; your prudent, pious Mother to be void of the Love of God, and in a state of Damnation . . . ?

The argument ad affectum Caritatis, p. 222. is beautifully and forcibly stated;[1] but yet defective by omission of the point—"*not* for unbelief

---

a Having reached the foot of the page, C has written "*Continued above, at the top of this page ‡*" and marked the beginning of the continuation with ‡

b In logical terms "above"; but physically the beginning of 60 lies "below" the closing "N.B.", which is written at the head of the page

61[1] The Latin phrase—"[addressed] to the emotion of Charity"—referring back to the opening clause of **61** textus, identifies an argument emo-

or misbelief of any article of Faith; but simply for not being a member of this particular Part of the Church of Christ.*a* For it is possible that a Christian might agree in all the articles of Faith with the Roman Doctors against those of the Reformation, and yet if he did not acknowlege the Pope as Christ's Vicar, & held salvation possible in any other church, he is himself excluded from Salvation."— Without this great distinction, Lady Anne Lindsay might have replied to Baxter—So might a Pagan Orator have said to a Convert from Paganism in the first ages of Christianity. So indeed the Advocates of the old Religion *did* argue—What? can you bear to believe, that Numa, Camillus, Fabricius, the Scipios, the Catos, that Tully, Seneca, that Titus and the Antonini are in Flames of Hell, the accursed Objects of the divine Hatred?[2] Now whatever *you* dare hope of *these*, as Heathens, we dare hope of *you* as Heretics.

62   i 224

And if it be damnable to be a *Sect*, all Papists must be damned; they being as certainly a Sect as there is any in the World: A corrupt part of the Universal Church, condemning the rest, and pretending to be it self the whole, is a Sect or Party of Schismaticks; but such are the Papists: Therefore they are a Sect, *&c.* But this is not the worst; You consequently Anathematize all Papists by your Sentence: for Heresies by your own Sentence cut off Men from Heaven: But Popery is a bundle of Heresies: Therefore it cuts off Men from Heaven. The *minor* I prove according to your Churches Principles, that Doctrine is Heresie which is contrary to a *point* of Faith: But many of the Papists Doctrines are contrary to Points of Faith: *Ergo, &c.*

This introduction of syllogistic form in a letter to a young Lady is whimsically characteristic.

63   i 225–6, pencil, overtraced

You say, "*The Scripture admits of no private Interpretation.*" But 1. You abuse the Text and your self with a false Interpretation of it, in these Words. An Interpretation is called private, either as to the

---

a C here wrote ", intending to close his statement of the "point", then extended the argument to "...Salvation" without cancelling the first "

---

tionally directed, as in *argumentum ad hominem* and the like.

61[2] Figures in the legend and his-

tory of Rome, distinguished for the part they played in the cause of order and civilisation, piety and virtue.

Subject Person, or as to the *Interpreter*: You take the Text to speak of the latter, when the Context plainly sheweth you that it speaks of the former: The Apostle directing them to understand the Prophesies of the Old Testament, gives them this Caution; That none of these Scriptures that are spoken of Christ the publick Person, must be interpreted as spoken of *David* or other private Persons only, of whom they were mentioned but as Types of Christ.

It is strange that this sound & irrefragable argument has not been enforced by the Church Divines in their controversies with the modern Unitarians as Capp, Belsham & others, who refer *all* the prophetic texts of the Old Test. to historical personages of the then time, exclusive of all double sense.[1]

I unthinkingly have called this *strange*, but I now recollect, that the Romanists' sense of the Text is adopted in our 39 articles—being one of the very few pitch-stains of Papistry, which our Reformers had not at that time discovered in their robe of Faith.[2]

64   i 226–7, pencil, overtraced

6. As to what you say of *"Apostles still placed in the Church"*: When any shew us an immediate Mission by their Commission; and by Miracles, Tongues, and a Spirit of Revelation and infallibility prove themselves *Apostles*, we shall believe them. Till then we remember that Church that was commended for *trying them that said they were Apostles, and were not, and finding them Lyers, Rev. 23.*

[1] Newcome Cappe (1735–1800), Unitarian minister, a passage from whose *Critical Remarks on Many Important Passages of Scripture* (2 vols York 1802) C copied out in Sept 1807, dismissing him as a Socinian. *CN* II 3135; see also *CN* III 3968. Thomas Belsham (1750–1829), leading spokesman for the Unitarians in their controversy with the Church of England 1815–17 and writer of Whig tracts (see *LS—CC*—181–4n), is linked by C with Priestley contemptuously in a marginal note on Jeremy TAYLOR *Polemicall Discourses* i 1074 as representing "modern Unitarianism"; also in N 37 ff 39–39ᵛ C spoke of Priestley and Belsham as the leaders of opinion among those "who regard the Christ, the Son of God, as a mere individual Man...".

[2] The text under discussion is 2 Pet 1.20: "...no prophecy of the scripture is of any private interpretation". The only Article dealing directly with interpretation of Scripture is Article VI: "Holy Scripture containeth all things necessary to salvation: so that whatsoever is not read therein, nor may be proved thereby, is not to be required of any man, that it should be believed as an article of the Faith, or be thought requisite or necessary to salvation." The Romanist's "sense of the Text" (i.e. 2 Pet 1.20) is that the Church alone, not the private person, has authority to interpret Holy Writ. C then may have in mind Article XX: "*Of the Church.* The Church hath power to decree Rites or Ceremonies, and Authority in Controversies of Faith."

This is one of those two-edged arguments,[1] which Baxter & Jer. Taylor imported from Grotius, & which have since become the universal *Fashion* among Protestants.[2] I fear, however, that it will do us more hurt by exposing a weak part to the *learned* Infidels, than service in our combat with the Romanists. I venture to assert most unequivocally that the N. T. contains not the least proof of the *Linguipotence* of the Apostles,[3] but the clearest proofs of the contrary: and I doubt, whether we have even as decisive a victory over the Romanists in our Middletonian, Farmerian and Douglasian Disputes concerning the Miracles of the two first Centuries & their assumed contrast *in genere* with those of the Apostles and the Apostolic Age, as we have in most other of our Protestant Controversies. MEM. These opinions of Middleton & his more cautious Followers are no part of *our* Church Doctrine.[4] This passion for Law Court Evidence began with Grotius.

65   i 246 | § 101 "Of Ceremonies" § 27

§ 27. The Separation that hath been made from the Church, was from the taking a Scandal where none was given: The Church having fully declared her sence touching the Ceremonies imposed, as Things not in their Nature necessary, but indifferent. But was chiefly occasioned by the Practice, and defended from the Principles of those that refused Conformity to the Law, the just Rule and Measure of the Churches Unity.!*

* To a self-convinced and disinterested Lover of the Church of England it ~~gav~~ives an indescribable horror to observe the frequency

64[1] Cf **60**, above, the opening clause of which is identical to these words.

64[2] See COPY A 5 n 1.

64[3] Against Baxter's contention that "Tongues" is one of the marks of the true Apostle, C notices that the Apostles did not in fact show outstanding "linguipotence"—tongue-power—i.e. not the "gift of tongues" but skill in strong and unambiguous use of language. Elsewhere C noticed that St Paul was especially deficient in this respect: see *CN* III 3903. *OED* ascribes the only use of "linguipotence" to C in this note.

64[4] C referred to Conyers Middleton (1683–1750) in 1796 in *The Watch-*man (*CC* 52), and to his *Letter from Rome, Shewing an Exact Conformity Between Popery and Paganism* (1729) in Sept–Dec 1805 (*CN* II 2264, 2729, 2737); here, however, he is probably thinking of Middleton's latitudinarian treatise *A Free Inquiry into the Miraculous Powers, Which Are Supposed to Have Subsisted in the Christian Church from the Earliest Ages* (1749). Hugh Farmer (1714–87) wrote *A Dissertation on Miracles* (3rd ed 1810), a copy of which, with Farmer's *Essay on the Demoniacs of the New Testament* (1805), was in Gillman's library. John Douglas (1721–1807), in the *Criterion* of 1752, attacked Hume's arguments against miracles.

with which the Prelatic Party after the Restoration appeal to *the Laws* as of equal authority with the express words of Scripture—as if the Laws, by them appealed to, were other than the vindictive Determinations of their own furious Partisans; as if the same Appeals might not have been made by Bonner and Gardner under Philip & Mary.[1]—Why should I speak of the inhuman Sophism that because it is silly in my neighbor to break his egg at the broad end[2] when the Squire & the Vicar have declared their predilection for the narrow end, therefore it is right for the Squire and the Vicar to hang and quarter him for his silliness.

66   i 248–9, pencil, overtraced | "A Defence of Our Proposals to His Majesty for Agreement in Matters of Religion" § 1

And we conceive that "*The Ancient Form of Church-Government, and the Soundness of the Liturgy, and freedom from corrupting unlawful Ceremonies,*" are Matters that are worthy a conscionable regard: and no such little inconsiderable things as to be received without sufficient trial, or used against the Disswasions of our Consciences. No Sin should seem so small as to be wilfully committed; especially to Divines. . . . And whether the *Imposor* or the *Forbearers* do hazard and disturb the Church, the nature of the thing declareth. To you it is *indifferent* before your *Imposition*; and therefore you may without any regret of your own Consciences forbear the *Imposition*, or perswade the Law-makers to forbear it. But to many of those that dissent from you, they are *sinful*; and therefore cannot be yielded to by them without the wilful violation of their Duty, to the absolute Soveraign of the World.

But what is all this good worthy Baxter! but saying and unsaying? If they are not indifferent, why did you concede them such? In short, nothing can be more pitiably weak than the conduct of the Presbyterian Party from the first capture of Charles I. Common Sense required either a bold denial that the Church had power in ceremonies more than in doctrines, or that Parliament was the Church (since it is our Parliament that *enacts* all these things)—or if they

65[1] Edmund Bonner (c 1500–69), successively chaplain to Cardinal Wolsey, bp of Hereford, and bp of London, supported Henry VIII in his attempt to divorce Catherine of Aragon by pleading the case in Rome. He was imprisoned by Edward VI for neglecting to enforce the new prayer-book and was twice deprived of his bishopric. He joined in the Marian persecution with great severity, and died in the Marshalsea. For Gardiner see COPY A 35 n 1, above.

65[2] Jonathan Swift *Gulliver's Travels* bk I ch 4.

admitted the authority lawful, and the ceremonies only (in their mind) *inexpedient*—good God! can Self-will more plainly put on the cracked mask of tender Conscience, than by refusal of obedience? What intolerable presumption, to disqualify as ungodly and reduce to null the majority of the Country, who preferred the liturgy in order to force the long-winded vanities of bustling God-orators on those who would fain hear prayers, not spouting!

67   i 249, pencil, overtraced | § 2

The great Controversies between the Hypocrite and the true Christian, whether we should be serious in the Practice of the Religion which we commonly profess? hath troubled *England* more than any other: None being more hated and derided as Puritans, than those that will make Religion their Business.

Had not the Governors had bitter proofs that there are other and more cruel vices than swearing and careless living? that these were predominant chiefly among such as made *their* religion their *business*?

68   i 249, pencil, overtraced | § 3

And whereas you speak of opening a Gap to Sectaries for private Conventicles, and the evil Consequents to the State, we only desire you to avoid also the cherishing of Ignorance and Prophaneness, and suppress all Sectaries, * and spare not, in a way that will not suppress the means of Knowledge and Godliness.

* the present company i.e. our own dear selves, always excepted!

69   i 250, pencil, overtraced | §4

Do you really desire that every Congregation may have an able, godly Minister? Then cast not out those many Hundreds or Thousands that are approved such, for want of Re-ordination, or for doubting whether Diocesans with their Chancellors &c. may be subscribed to, and set not up ignorant ungodly ones in their Places. Otherwise the poor undone Churches of Christ will no more believe you in such Professions, than we believed that those Men intended the King's *just Power* and *Greatness*, who took away his Life. *

* or like Baxter joined the armies that were showering Cannon Balls and bullets around his inviolable person! When ever by reading the Prelatical writings and Histories, I have had an over-dose of anti-prelatism in my feelings, I then correct it by dipping into the works

of the Presbyterians, &c. and so bring myself to more charitable thoughts respecting the Prelatists, & fully subscribe to Milton's assertion, that PRESBYTER was but OLD PRIEST writ large!—1

70   i 254, pencil, overtraced | "Concerning the Liturgy" § 18

1. The *Doctrine* [of Infants' Salvation] is sound. But the Apocryphal Matter of your Lessons, in *Tobith, Judith, Bell* and the *Dragon, &c.* is scarce agreeable to the Word of God.

Does not Jude refer to an apocryphal Book?[1]

71   i 254, pencil, overtraced

Our experience unresistably convinceth us, that a continued Prayer doth more to help most of the People, and carry on their Desires, than turning almost every Petition into a distinct Prayer; and making Prefaces and Conclusions to be near half the Prayers.

This is now the very point, I most admire in our excellent Liturgy.

To any particular petition offered to the Omniscient there may be a sinking of Faith, a sense of its superfluity; but to the lifting up of the Soul to the Invisible and there fixing it on his Attributes, there can be no scruple.

72   i 257, pencil, overtraced | § 29

The *Not-abating* of the *Impositions* is the casting off of many hundreds of your Brethren out of the Ministry, and of many thousand Christians out of your Communion: But the *abating* of the Impositions, will so offend you, as to silence or excommunicate none of you at all: For *e.g.* we think it a Sin to Subscribe, or swear canonical Obedience, or use the transient Image of the Cross in Baptism, and therefore these must cast us out: But you think it no Sin to *forbear* them, if the Magistrate abate them, and therefore none of you will be cast out by the Abatement.

as long as independent Single-Churches, or voluntarily synodical, were forbidden and punishable by penal Law, this argument remained irrefragable. The imposition of such trifles under such fearful threats was the very bitterness of spiritual Pride, and vindictiveness. —After the law passed by which things ⟨became as they⟩ now are, it

69[1] "New Presbyter is but Old Priest writ large"—*On the New Forces of Conscience under the Long Parliament* in MILTON *Complete Collection of Historical, Political and Miscellaneous Works* (2 vols 1738) i 171.

70[1] Jude 14–15 quotes from the pseudepigraphical *Book of Enoch*. See also BIBLE COPY B **135**.

⟨was⟩ a mere question of expediency for the national Church to determine in relation to its own comparative Interests.[1] If the Church chuse unluckily, the injury has been to itself alone.

73   i 258–9, pencil, overtraced | § 34

In Conclusion, we perceive your Counsels against Peace are not likely to be frustrated: Your Desires concerning us are like to be accomplished: You are like to be gratified with our Silence and Ejection, and the Excommunication and Consequent sufferings of Dissenters. And yet we will believe that blessed are the Peace-makers, and though *Deceit be in the Heart of them that imagin Evil, yet there is Joy to the Counsellors of Peace, Prov.* 12. 20.

Is it not strange that such men as Baxter should not see that the Ring, Surplice &c. are *indifferent* according to *his own* confession, yea, mere trifles in comparison with the peace of the Church;[1] but that it ⟨is⟩ no trifle, that men should refuse obedience to lawful authority in matters indifferent, and prefer Schism to offending their *Taste*, and *Fancy*? The Church did *not* contend for a trifle, nor for an indifferent matter, but for a principle on which all order in society must depend.

Second Thoughts. True, provided the Church enacts no ordinances

72[1] The Independents, or Congregationalists, rejected the hierarchical structure of the episcopal church and even the more democratic structure of the Presbyterians, claiming that according to the Gospels each believer was in the position of a priest, and that each congregation was autonomous, guided by private conscience and the literal understanding of Holy Scriptures. See **2** n 5, above. Under Elizabeth and the Stuarts a series of repressive acts of Parliament sought to enforce conformity, culminating in the Act of Uniformity in 1662. The Congregationalists managed to establish their identity in the "Savoy Declaration" of 1658, and the Toleration Act of 1688 gave limited relief, but the "law...by which things became as they now are" is presumably the Nonconformist Relief Act of 1779. Under this, all persons "dissenting from the Church of England, in holy orders or pretended holy orders, being a preach-er or teacher of any congregation of dissenting Protestants" were entitled to all the "exemptions, benefits, privileges, and advantages" granted to ministers of the Established Church by the Toleration Act. The only requirement was to sign a declaration of belief that "the Scriptures...do contain the revealed will of God; and that I do receive the same as the rule of my doctrine and practice".

73[1] See also **6** n 1, above. The surplice—originally a white linen surcoat worn over a fur garment, as the name implies—was mediaeval and like other vestments of the Western Church (which evolved in the fourth to the ninth century from secular Roman dress of the first century) had no Aaronical origin. From the tenth to the thirteenth century the surplice superseded the alb as the regular vestment for minister and choir in ritual offices.

that ⟨are⟩ not necessary or at least plainly conducive to order or (generally) to the ends for which it is a Church. But surely this cannot be said of the Cross in Baptizing, or the Judaical conceit implied in the Surplice, or the arranging of the Communion Table as a sacrificial *altar*. Besides the point which the King had required them to consider was not what ordinances it was right to obey, but what it was *expedient* to enact or not to enact.

74 i 269, pencil, overtraced | ɪ ii § 106 "Concerning . . . your Majesty's Concessions"

. . . we humbly prosecute our Petition to your Majesty, that the Primitive Presidency . . . may be the Form of Church-Government established among us: At least in these Three needful Points.

1. That the Pastors of the respective Parishes may be allowed, not only publickly to Preach, but personally to Catechize or otherwise Instruct the several Families, admitting none to the Lord's Table that have not personally owned their Baptismal Covenant by a credible Profession of Faith and Obedience; and to admonish and exhort the Scandalous, in order to their Repentance; to hear the Witnesses and the accused Party, and to appoint fit *Times* and *Places* for these things; and to deny such Persons the Communion of the Church in the Holy Eucharist, that remain impenitent; or that wilfully refuse to come to their Pastors to be instructed, or to answer such probable Accusations; and to continue such Exclusion of them till they have made a credible Profession of Repentance . . .

Suppose only such men Pastors as are now (most improperly whether as boast or as sneer) called Evangelicals;[1] what an insufferable Tyranny would this introduce? Who would not rather live in Algiers? This alone would make this minute History of the ecclesiastic factions invaluable, that it must convince all sober lovers of Independence and moral Self-government, how dearly we ought to prize our present Church Establishment with all its faults![2]

74[1] As a general term since the Reformation "Evangelical" refers to those groups who claimed that their doctrines were drawn purely from the teaching of the Gospels. To C "the Evangelicals" were Wilberforce and his group, the Clapham Sect, all within the Church of England. See *LS* (*CC*) 194 and n 4.

74[2] The basis of C's conservative position regarding the Established Church, as stated in *C&S* and embodied in his view of the responsibilities of the "clerisy". See **115**, below, *C&S* esp chs 5 and 6, and *AR* (1825) 290n.

75 i 270

It is necessary to the Honour of the Christian Profession . . . [to] the Purity, Order, Strength and Beauty of our Churches, the Vanity of Believers, and the Pleasing of Christ who hath required it by his Laws.

S? or Unity? or Amity?

76 i 272, pencil, overtraced

Therefore we humbly crave that your Majesty will here declare, "That it is your Majesty's pleasure that none be punished or troubled for not using the Book of Common Prayer, till it be effectually re-formed by Divines of both Perswasions equally deputed thereunto."

The dispensing power of the Crown not only acknowleged, but earnestly invoked! Cruel as the conduct of Laud and that of Sheldon to the Dissentients was, yet God's justice stands clear towards them, for they demanded that from others, which they themselves would not grant.[1] They were to be *allowed* at their own fancies to denounce the ring in marriage, and yet empowered to endungeon thro' the Magistrate the honest and peaceable Quakers for rejecting the out-ward ceremony of Water in Baptism as manifestly seducing men to take it as a substitute for the spiritual reality, tho' the Quakers no less than themselves appeal to Scripture authority the Baptist's contrast of Christ's, with the water Baptism.[2]

77 i 273, pencil, overtraced

2. We are sure that *kneeling* in *any Adoration at all*, in *any Worship*, on *any Lord's Day* in the Year, or any *Week-day between Easter and Pentecost*, was not only *disused*, but forbidden by *General Councils* . . . And therefore that kneeling in the Act of receiving is a *Novelty* contrary to the *Decrees and Practice* of the Church for many hundred Years after the Apostles.

76[1] William Laud (1573–1645) as abp of Canterbury (from 1633) pursued a stern enforcement of Charles I's policy of political and ecclesiastical absolutism. See HEYLYN's life of Laud, *Cyprianus Anglicus* (1671). In a note-book entry of c Dec 1828, C referred to Laud as "the St Dominic of the semi-protestant High Church, the vindictive, hot-headed, narrow-minded superstitious Bigot—who having sacri-ficed the peace and prosperity of the Realm to his Monkish Follies, and kindled the flames of Civil War in three Kingdoms, died remorseless with a self-approving Conscience". N 38 f 7ᵛ. For Gilbert Sheldon see COPY A **18** n 1.

76[2] See also COPY A **15** n 1.

Was not this because kneeling was the agreed sign of Sorrow and personal contrition, which was not to be introduced into the public worship on the great Day and the solemn seasons of the Church's Joy, and Thanksgiving? If so, Baxter's appeal to this usage is a gross sophism—a mere *Pun*.

78 i 308–19 | § 174 "The Exceptions against the Common-Prayer which I offered the Brethren when they were drawing up theirs"

Notes on Baxter's proposed emendations

78[a] i 308

1. Order requireth that we begin with Reverent Prayer to God, for his Assistance and Acceptance, which is not done.

1. Enunciation of God's invitations and promises in God's own words (as in the C. Pr. Book) far better.

78[b] i 308

2. That the Creed and Decalogue, containing the Faith, in which we profess to assemble for God's Worship, and the Law which we have broken by our Sins, should go before the Confession and Absolution; or at least before the Praises of the Church; which they do not.

2. Might have deserved consideration, if the People or the larger number, consisted of uninstructed Catechumeni or mere Candidates for Church membership. But the object being not the first teaching of the Cr: and Dec: but the lively re-impressing of the same, it is much better as it is:

78[c] i 308

3. The Confession omitteth not only Original Sin, but all actual Sin as specified by the particular Commandments violated; and almost all the Aggravations of those Sins. ... Whereas *Confession* being the *Expression of Repentance*, should be more *particular*, as Repentance it self should be.

3. Grounded on one of the grand Errors of the whole Dissenting Party—viz. the confusion of public *Common* Prayer, Praise, and Instruction with *dome⟨s⟩tic* and even with *private* Devotion. Our Confession is a perfect Model for christian Communities.

78[d] i 308

4. When we have craved help for *God's Prayers*, before we come to them, we abruptly put in the Petition for speedy Deliverance "*O*

God, make speed to save us: O Lord make haste to help us." without any Intimation of the Danger that we desire deliverance from, and without any other Petition conjoined.

5. It is disorderly in the *Manner*, to sing the Scripture in a plain Tune after the manner of reading.

6. "*The Lord be with you. And with thy Spirit*" being Petitions for Divine Assistance, come in abruptly, in the midst or near the end of Morning Prayer: And "*Let us Pray*" is adjoined when we were before in Prayer.

4. 5. 6. Querulous mouse-like Squeak and Nibble.

78[e] i 308

7. "*Lord have mercy upon us: Christ have mercy upon us: Lord have mercy upon us*" seemeth an affected Tautologie, without any special Cause, or Order here: And the *Lord's Prayer* is annexed that was before recited: And yet the next Words are again but a Repetition of the foresaid oft repeated General "*O Lord shew thy Mercy upon us.*"

7. Still worse—the Spirit, in which this & similar Complaints originated, has turned the Prayers of Dissent. Ministers into irreverend Preachments—forgotten that Tautology in words and thoughts implies no tautology in the *Music* of the Heart, to which the words are, as it were, *set*—and that [it]*ᵃ* is the *Heart*, that lifts itself up to God. Our words & thoughts are but parts of the Enginery which remains with ourselves. And ~~dry~~ Logic, the rustling ~~dried~~y leaves of the lifeless reflex-faculty does not merit even the name of a Pully or Leaver of Devotion.

78[f] i 308

8. The prayer for the King "*O Lord save the King*" is without any Order put between the foresaid Petition, and another General Request only for Audience "*And mercifully hear us when we call upon thee.*"

8. a trifle; but just.

78[g] i 308

9. The second Collect is intitled "*for Peace*" and hath not a Word in it of Petition for *Peace*, but only for "*Defence in Assaults of Enemies, and that we may not fear their Power.*" And the Prefaces "*In knowledge of whom standeth our eternal Life, and whose Service is perfect*

ᵃ Word supplied by the editor

Freedom" have no more evident respect to a Petition for "*Peace*" than to any other. And the Prayer it self comes in disorderly, while many Prayers or Petitions are omitted, which according both to the method of the *Lord's Prayer*, and the Nature of the *things*, should go before.

10. The third Collect intituled "*for Grace*" is disorderly, in that it followeth that "*for Peace*"; And thus the main parts of Prayer, according to the Rule of the *Lord's Prayer*, and our common Necessities are omitted ...

9. 10. Not wholly unfounded; but proceeds on an arbitrary and (I think) false assumption/ that the Lord's Prayer was universally prescriptive in form and arrangement.

78[h]

11. Most of our Necessities are passed over in the like defective Generals also in the *Evening Prayer*.

11. = 3.

78[i]　i 309

12. The *Litany* ... omitteth very many particulars. ... And it is exceeding disorderly, following no just Rules of method: Having begged pardon of our sins, and deprecated vengeance, it proceedeth to *Evil in general*, and some *few* Sins in *particular*, and thence to a more particular enumeration of *Judgments*; and thence to the recitation of the parts of that Work of our *Redemption*, and thence to the deprecation of *Judgments* again, and thence to Prayers for the *King* and *Magistrates*, and then for all *Nations* and then for *Love and Obedience* ...

12. The very points here objected to as faults I should have selected as excellences. For do not the Duties and Temptations occur in real life even so intermingled? The imperfection of Thought, much more of Language, so singly successive, allows no better representation of the close neighbourhood, ~~the Chiliagon,~~ nay, the co-inherence of duty in duty, desire in desire. Every want of the Heart pointing Godward is a Chiliagon that touches at a thousand points.—From these remarks I except the last § of 12[1]—which are defects so

78[i][1] The last paragraph of § 12 reads: "Next this, the *Bishops and Curates* are prayed for without the *Parish Incumbent, Presbyters*, or else it's intimated that *they* are but the *Bishops Curates*, or else they are called Bishops themselves; and no Man can tell certainly which of these is the sence: And the *Preface* would intimate to the People, that it is some special

palpable & so easily removed that nothing but Antipathy to the Objectors could have retained them.

78[j]   i 310–19

13. The like *defectiveness* and *disorder* is in the Communion Collects for the Day. [The Collects for 36 days are then examined.]

13. I do not see how these supposed improprieties could be avoided without risk of the far greater evil of *too great* appropriation to particular Saints and days, as in Popery. I am so far a Puritan that I think nothing would have been lost, if Christmas Day and Good Friday had been the only week days made holy days, and Easter the only Lord's Day especially distinguished. I should have added Whitsunday; but that it has become unmeaning since our Clergy have become Arminian, and interpreting the descent of the Spirit as the gifts of Miracles and ⟨of⟩ miraculous infallibility by inspiration, have rendered it of course of little or no application to Christians at present. Yet how can Arminians *pray* our Church Prayers *collectively* on *any* day? Answer. Boa Constrictor and Ox or Deer. What they *do* swallow proves so astounding a dilatability of gullet, that it would be unconscionable strictness to complain of the Horns, Antlers, or other indigestible Non-essentials, being suffered ~~off~~ to rot off at the confines—ερκος οδοντων.[1] But to write seriously on so serious a subject—it is mournful to reflect, that the influence of the Systematic Theology then in fashion with the Anti-prelatic Divines, whether Episcopalians or Presbyterians, had quenched all *fineness* of mind, all *flow* of Heart, all Grandeur of Imagination/ ⟨in *them*:⟩ while the victorious Party, the prelatic Arminians, enriched as they were with all Learning and highly gifted with Taste and Judgement, had emptied Revelation of all ⟨the *doctrines*,⟩ that can properly be ~~called~~ said to have been *revealed*—and thus equally caused the extinction of the Imagination and ⟨quenched⟩ the *Life* in the Light

great marvel for Bishops and Curates to have Grace: And after all this, there are *no particular petitions* for them, according to the nature and necessity of their Work, or of their Congregation, but only this one General Request, that they may have God's Grace and Blessing to please him. Lastly (before the Blessing) is *Chrystsostom*'s Prayer, meerly for the granting of our Requests, with two Petitions, one for *Knowledge*, the other for *Life Eternal*.

The following Prayers and Thanksgivings on particular extraordinary Occasions, are...the best composed of all the daily Common Prayers: But that these Prayers and Thanksgivings are all placed after the Benediction, is disorderly...."

78[j][1] In Homer (e.g. *Iliad* 4.350) "the barrier of teeth" provides a heroic restraint upon speech. Here the teeth seem to provide a barrier against incoming indigestibles.

by withholding the appropriate Fuel and the Supporters of the sacred Flame.[2]—So that ⟨between both parties⟩ our transcendent Liturgy remains like an ancient Greek Temple—a monumental Proof of architectural Genius, of an age long departed, when there were Giants in the Land!—[3]

79   i 337 | § 195

[The Commission, to resolve their differences, formed a group of six—three of each party—Baxter being one. Although the six were to debate in private, several of the bishops attended their meetings and boldly engaged in the arguments between the two parties.] ... and as I was proceeding, here Bishop *Morley* interrupted me, according to his manner, with vehemency crying out, *what can any Man be for any time without Sin!* ... and the Bishop (whether in Passion or Design I know not) interrupted me again, and mouthed out the odiousness of my Doctrine again and again, I attempted to speak, and still he interrupted me in the same manner.

The Bishops appear to have behaved insolently enough. Safe in their knowlege of Charles's Inclinations they laughed in their sleeves at his *Commission.* Their best answer would have been to have pressed the Anti-impositionists with their utter forgetfulness of the possible nay, very probable differences of opinion between the Ministers and their Congregations—A vain Minister might scandalize a sober Congregation with his extempore prayers or his open contempt of their kneeling at the Sacraments, &c.—By what right if he acts only as an Individual? And then what an endless source of disputes and preferences of this Minister or of that!—

80   i 341–3 | § 207 "The Paper offered by Bishop Cosins"

A way humbly proposed to end that unhappy Controversie which is now managed in the Church ... 1. *That the Question may be put to the Managers of the Division, Whether there be any thing in the Doctrine, or Discipline, or the Common Prayer, or Ceremonies, contrary to the Word of God; and if they can make any such appear, let them be satisfied.*

2. *If not, let them then propose what they desire in point of Expediency, and acknowledge it to be no more.*

This was proposed, doubtless, by one of your *sensible* men—it is

78[j][2] See AURELIUS **39** textus and n 1.   **78[j]**[3] Gen 6.4.

so plain, so plausible, shallow, nihili-n[a]uci-pili-flocci-cal![1] Why, the very phrase "contrary to the word of God" would take a month to define—and neither party agree at last. One party says—The Church has power ⟨from God's word⟩ to order all matters of order so as shall appear to them to conduce to decency and edification. But Ceremonies respect the orderly performance of divine Service— Ergo, the Church has power to ordain Ceremonies—The Church has power to ordain Ceremonies—But the Cross in Baptizing is a Ceremony—Ergo, the Church has power to prescribe the crossing in Baptism.—What is rightfully ordered, cannot be rightfully withstood—But the Crossing &c is rightfully ordered—Ergo, the Crossing cannot be rightfully omitted.—To this how easyily for would the other party deny first that a small number of Bishops could be called the Church—2ⁿᵈ that any one Church had power or pretence from God's word to prescribe concerning mere matters of outward decency & convenience to other Churches or Assemblies of Christian People. 3.—That the blending an unnecessary and suspicious act is no doth in no wise respect order or propriety. Lastly, that to forbid a man to obey a direct command of God because he will not join with it an admitted mere tradition of Man is contrary to Common Sense—no less than to God's word expressly and by breach of Charity which is the great end and purpose of God's Word.—Besides, might not the Pope and his Shavelings have made the same proposition to the Reformers in Edw. VIᵗʰ'ˢ reign, for the greater part of the idle superfluities which were rejected by the Reformers only as idle and superfluous,—& for that reason contrary to the *spirit* of the Gospel, tho' few if any were in the direct teeth of a positive Prohibition.[2]—Above all, an honest Policy dictates that the end in view being fully determined (as here, for instance, the pre-

80[1] C's coinage with Christ's Hospital undertones. Cf e.g. *CL* I 171 (to RS, 13 Nov 1795): "flocci-nauci-nihili-pilificating"; *LL* I 7, 95 (to C, 1796): " flocci-nauci-what-d'ye-call-em-ists "; *CL* v 295 (to Mrs C, Aug 1823): "flocci-nauci-nihili-pilification". *OED* cites Shenstone's use of some such compound in a letter of 1741, but C's source—and Lamb's too—is probably *An Introduction to Latin Grammar for the Use of Christ's Hospital* (1785) 167, in which a list is given of exceptions to the rule that price is expressed in the ablative: "flocci *of a lock of wool*,

nauci *of a nut-shell*, nihili *of nothing*, pili *of a hair*...". That C should use such a word to Mrs C in 1823 implies either that the rule in this form had some common currency together with the rhymed mnemonics that grammarians have devised to embrace the intransigencies of the Latin tongue (Mrs C was an effective teacher) or that it had become part of the Coleridge family dialect.

80[2] Edward VI, indifferent in matters of religion, allowed the Reformation to take its course under Cranmer.

clusion of disturbance and indecorum in Christian Assemblies) every addition to means already adequate to the securing of that end, tends to frustrate the end—and are therefore evidently excluded from the prerogatives of the Church (however that word may be interpreted) inasmuch as its Power is confined to such ceremonies and regulations as conduce to order and general edification. In short, it grieves me to think that the Heads of the most apostolical Church in Christendom should have insisted on 3 or 4 silly trifles, the abolition of which could have given offence to none but such as from the baleful superstition that alone could attach importance to them effectually it was charity to offend—when all the rest of Baxter's Objections might have been answered so triumphantly.

81 i 343, referring to i 342, pencil, overtraced | § 207 "Answer to the foresaid Paper"

7. That they are *forced* to give thanks for *all* whom they Bury, as *Brethren whom God in mercy hath delivered and taken to himself.*

8. That none may be a Preacher that dare not Subscribe that there is nothing in the Common Prayer Book, the Book of Ordination, and the Nine and thirty Articles, that is contrary to the Word of God ...

I think that the 8th might have been likewise left out:[1] for as by the words "contrary to the word of God" it was not meant to declare the C. P. Book free from *all* error, the sense must have been that there is not any thing in *such* a way or degree contrary to God's word as to oblige us to assign sin to those who have overlooked it, or who think the same compatible with God's word, or[a] who tho' individually disapproving ⟨the particular thing⟩ yet regard that acquiescence as an allowed sacrifice of individual opinion to Modesty, Charity, and Zeal for the peace of the Church. For observe that this 8th instance is additional to & therefore not inclusive of, the preceding 7. Otherwise it must have ⟨been⟩ placed as the first, or rather as the whole, the seven following being motives & instances in support and explanation of the first.

82 i 365–7

M[r] Kenyon yesterday,[1] 1 Sept[r] 1825, observed, that R. S. could not *mediate* and that I could not *militate*—that even when it ~~was~~ was

---

[a] Here C has written "(see above at II)", and at the head of the page "II continued from the Margin"

81[1] That is, Baxter's eighth point— not the vⅠⅠⅠth Article of Religion (which is "Of the Three Creeds").

82[1] John Kenyon (1783–1856), wealthy dilettante, philanthropist, and occasional poet, made the acquaintance

Southey's own purpose to sit as an Arbiter, he was sure, before he was aware, to ~~be~~ stand up as a Partisan, and drop the Scales in order to wield the Sword—while I was so engaged in tracing the diverging Branches to a common Trunk both for Right and Wrong that both Parties took ~~me for an enemy~~ to the Sword against *me*. S. saw all Difference as Diversity;[2] ~~and~~ while I was striving to reduce supposed Contraries into compatible Opposites, whose worst error consisted in their reciprocal Exclusion of each other. S. found positive falsehoods where I saw half-truths, and found the falsehood in the partial Eclipse.—S. = a Grey-hound: S. T. C. a Pointer.—I have amplified our common Friend's Observation in my own metaphorical way; but I give the conclusion in his own words—In short, Southey should write Books and you write notes on them.[3]—It may serve to confirm this Judgement, if I mediate here between Baxter & the Bishops. Baxter had taken for granted, that the King had a right to promise a revision of the Liturgy, Canons & Regiment of the Church; and that the Bishops ought to have met him and his Friends as Diplomatists on even ground. The Bishops could not with discretion openly avow all, they meant; and it would be High Church Bigotry to deny that the Spirit of Compromise ~~was~~ had no Indwelling in their Feelings or Intents. But nevertheless it is true, that they thought more in the Spirit of the English Constitution than Baxter & his Friends—This, thought they, is THE LAW of the Land, quem nolumus mutari[4]—and it must ⟨be⟩ the King with and

---

of Poole in 1808 and through him became a friend of C, Lamb, and RS. C annotated a copy of his *Rhymed Plea for Tolerance* (1833).

   82² C often distinguished between (as here) "difference" and "diversity" or (as elsewhere) between "distinction" or "distinctness" and "division". See e.g. *Friend* (*CC*) II 104n (I 177n). More searching in relation to this marginal note is the question asked in *CN* II 3154. See also AURELIUS 46 and n 2.

   82³ On C as a pointer, see his "self-excriminating" statement to RS in Nov 1795: "The Truth is—You sate down and wrote—I used to saunter about and think what I should write." *CL* I 172; cf *S Life* (*CS*) II 188–9 and *WL* (*L*) III 1231. Cf "Southey once said to me: You are nosing every nettle

along the Hedge, while the Greyhound (meaning himself, I presume) wants only to get sight of the Hare, and Flash—strait as a line! he has it in his mouth!...But the fact is—I do not care two pence for the *Hare*; but I value most highly the excellencies of scent, patience, discrimination, free Activity; and find a Hare in every Nettle I make myself acquainted with. I follow the Chamois-Hunters...but avail myself of the Chace in order to a nobler purpose—that of making a road across the Mountain...". *IS* 143–4. For RS's greyhound see *S Life* (*CS*) III 261; and for an earlier instance of the chamois-hunter see *Friend* (*CC*) II 48–9.

   82⁴ "Which we refuse to change".

by the advice of his Parliament, that can authorize any part of his Subjects to take the question of its Repeal into Consideration. Under other Circumstances a King might bring ~~the~~ Bishops and the Heads of the Romish Party together—to plot against the Law of the Land. No! We would have no other Secret Committees, but of Parliamentary Appointment. We are but so many Individuals. It is in the Legislature that the Congregations, the party most interested in this Cause, meet collectively in their Representatives.—

Lastly, let it not be overlooked, that the root of the Bitterness was common to both Parties—viz. the conviction of the vital importance of Uniformity—and this admitted, surely an undoubted majority in favor of what is already Law must decide *whose* Uniformity it is to be.

83   i 368–9 | § 239

We must needs believe, that when your Majesty took our Consent to a Liturgy, to be a Foundation that would infer our Concord, you meant not that we should have no Concord, but by consenting to this Liturgy without any considerable Alteration.

This is forcible Reasoning; but which the Bishops could fairly leave ~~it~~ for the King to answer: the contract, tacit or exprest, ~~was~~ being between him and the Anti-prelatic ⟨Presbytero-⟩Episcopalian Party, to which ~~th~~ neither the Bishops nor the Legislature had acceded or assented. If Baxter & Calamy[1] were so little imbued with the spirit of the Constitution, as to consider Charles the Second as *the Breath of their Nostrils*,[2] and this dread Sovereign Breath in its passage gave a Snort ~~where they~~ for a Snuffle, (or having led them to expect a Snuffle surprized them with a Snort), let the reproach be shared between the Breath's ⟨fetid⟩ Conscience and the Nostril's Naso-ductility. Breath's Father died a martyr to the vice of Lying: Breath inherited the Vice but ~~contri~~ chose to shift the martyrdom on the Fools that believed him—The Traitors to the Liberty of their Country who were swarming and intriguing for favor at Breda when they should have been at their post in Parliament or in the Lobby,

83[1] Presumably Edmund Calamy the elder (1600–66), puritan divine, who was one of the authors of *Smectymnuus*, written against Bishop Hall's claim of divine right for episcopacy. Like Baxter, he was a member of the Savoy Conference. For his grandson Edmund, editor of Baxter, see **115** n 5, below.

83[2] Probably an echo of Gen 2.7: "And the Lord God formed man of the dust of the ground, and breathed into his nostrils the breath of life; and man became a living soul." But cf Job 27.3–4, Isa 2.22.

§ 240. And in the Conclusion of this Busineſs, ſeeing we could prevail with theſe Prelates and Prelatical Men, (after ſo many Calamities by Diviſions, and when they pretended Deſires of Unity) to make no conſiderable Alterations at all ; the Reaſon of it ſeeming unſearchable to ſome, was by others confidently conjectured to be theſe :

1. They extreamly prejudic'd the Perſons that ſought this Peace, and therefore were glad of means to caſt them out and ruin them.

2. The Effects of the Parliament's Conqueſt had exaſperated them to the height.

3. They would not have any Reformation or Change to occaſion Men to think that ever they were in an Errour, or that their Adverſaries had reaſonably deſired, or had procured a Reformation.

4. Some confidently thought that a ſecret Reſolution to unite with the Papiſts (at leaſt as high as the old Deſign which *Heylin* owneth in *Laud's* Life) was the greateſt cauſe of all : And that they would never have loſt ſo great a Party, as they did but to gain a greater (at home and abroad together.)

§ 241. And here, becauſe they would abate us nothing at all conſiderable, but made things far harder and heavier than before , I will annex the Conceſſions of Archbiſhop *Uſher*, Archbiſhop *Williams*, Biſhop *Morton*, Biſhop *Holdſworth*, and many others in a Committee at *Weſtminſter* (before mentioned) 1641.

A Copy of the Proceedings of ſome Worthy and Learned Divines touching Innovations in the Doctrine and Diſcipline of the Church of England : *Together with Conſiderations upon the Common Prayer Book.*

Innovations in Doctrine.

1 *Quære.* WHether in the Twentieth Article theſe Words are not inſerted, *Habet Eccleſia authoritatem in Controverſiis fidei.*

2. It appears by *Stetfords*, and the approbation of the Licenſers, that ſome do teach and preach, *That Good Works are concauſes with faith in the act of Juſtification*; Dr. *Dove* alſo hath given Scandal in that point.

3. Some have preached the Works of Penance are ſatisfactory before God.

4. Some have preached that private Confeſſion by particular Enumeration of Sins, is neceſſary to Salvation, *neceſſitate medii*; both thoſe Errours have been queſtioned at the Conſiſtory at *Cambridge*.

5. Some have maintained that the Abſolution which the Prieſt pronounceth, is more than Declaratory.

6. Some have publiſhed, That there is a proper Sacrifice in the Lord's Supper, to exhibit Chriſt's Death in the *Poſtfact*, as there was a Sacrifice to prefigure in the Old Law in the *Antefact*, and therefore that we have a true Altar, and therefore not only metaphorically ſo called, ſo Dr. *Heylin* and others in the laſt Summers Convocation, where alſo ſome defended, that the Oblation of the Elements might hold the Nature of the true Sacrifice, others *the Conſumption of the Elements*.

7. Some have introduced *Prayer for the Dead*, as Mr. *Brown* in his printed Sermon, and ſome have coloured the uſe of it with Queſtions in *Cambridge*, and diſputed, that *Preces pro Defunctis non ſupponunt Purgatorium*.

8. Divers have oppugned the certitude of Salvation.

9. Some have maintained the lawfulneſs of *Monaſtical Vows*.

10. Some have maintained that the Lord's Day is kept meerly by Eccleſiaſtical Conſtitution, and that the Day is changeable.

11. Some have taught as new and dangerous Doctrine, that the Subjects are to pay any Sums of Money impoſed upon them, though without Law , nay contrary to the Laws of the Realm, as Dr. *Sybthorp*, and Dr. *Manwaring* Biſhop of St. *Davids*, in their printed Sermons, whom many have followed of late years.

Bbb 12. Some

---

6. An annotated page of Richard Baxter *Reliquiae Baxterianae* (London 1696). See BAXTER *Reliquiae* COPY B **83–86**

Houghton Library, Harvard University; reproduced by kind permission

preparing *Terms & Conditions*—![3] Had all the Ministers that were afterwards ejected, and the Presbyterian Party generally, exerted themselves, ~~with~~ heart & soul, with Monk's Soldiers, & in collecting those whom Monk had displaced,[4] and instead of carrying on treasons against the Government *de facto* by ⟨mendicant⟩ negotiations with Charles had taken open measures to *confer* the Scepter on him, as the Scotch did—whose stern and truly loyal Conduct has been most unjustly condemned—the Schism in the Church might have been prevented, and the Revolution superseded./

P.S. In the above, I speak of the Bishops, as *Men* interested in a litigated Estate. God forbid! I should seek to justify them, as Christians!

84 i 369 | § 241 "Innovations in Doctrine"

1. *Quaere*. Whether in the Twentieth Article these Words are not inserted, *Habet Ecclesia Authoritatem in Controversiis fidei*.

Strange! that the evident antithesis between *power* in respect of Ceremonies and *authority* in points of faith, should have been overlooked./[1]

85 i 369

6. Some have published, That there is a proper Sacrifice in the Lord's Supper, to exhibit Christ's Death in the *Postfact*, as there was a Sacrifice to prefigure in the Old Law in the *Antefact*, and therefore that we have a true Altar, and therefore not only metaphorically so called . . .

Doubtless, a gross Error/ yet pardonable, for to Errors nearly as gross it was opposed.

83[3] Breda, the official residence of Charles II in exile. The Declaration of Breda, issued on 4 Apr 1660—the conciliatory move that secured Charles's return to England—promised a general amnesty (which did not in fact save the regicides), liberty of conscience, and the return to Parliament of a number of important issues formerly the prerogative of the Crown. The Convention Parliament accepted the declaration, and Charles was proclaimed king on 8 May 1660; he landed at Dover on 25 May, to be met by General Monck, and arrived at Whitehall on the 29th.

83[4] George Monck (1608-70), who as Cromwell's commander-in-chief in Scotland completed the subjection of the Scots in 1652 in less than a year, was largely responsible for organising the return of Charles II to England in 1660.

84[1] Cf **63** and n 2, above.

86 i 369–70

10. Some have maintained that the Lord's Day is kept meerly by Ecclesiastical Constitution, and that the Day is changeable.

Where shall we find the Proof of the Contrary? at least, if the position had been worded thus: the ~~Expedience and even~~ moral ~~m~~ and spiritual Obligation of keeping the Lord's Day is grounded on its manifest necessity, and the evidence of its benignant effects, in ~~the~~ connection with those conditions of the world, of which even in Christianized Countries there is no reason to expect a Change: and is therefore commanded by implication in the New Testament,[1] so clearly and by so immediate a consequence as to be no less binding on the Conscience than an explicit command. A having lawful authority expressly commands me to go to London from Bristol. There is at present but one safe Road. This therefore is commanded by A: and would be so, even tho' A had spoken of another Road, which at that time was open.

87 i 370

18. Some have broacht out of *Socinus* a most uncomfortable and desperate Doctrine, *That late Repentance*, that is upon the last Bed of Sickness, *is unfruitful*, at least to reconcile the Penitent to God.

This, no doubt, refers to Jeremy Taylor's Work on Repentance—& is but too faithful a description of its character.[1]

88 i 373 | § 244

[Baxter recounts how "One Mr. *Atkins* of *Glocestershire*, being beyond Sea" with other servants of Charles I, "fell into acquaintance with a Priest, that had been (or then was) Governour of one of their [the Papists'] Colledges in *Flanders*".] A little after the King was beheaded, Mr. *Atkins* met this Priest in *London*, and going into a Tavern with him, said to him in his familiar way "*What business have you here? I warrant you come about some Roguery or other.*" Whereupon the Priest told it him as a great secret, "*That there were*

86[1] The obligation to keep the sabbath is, as C admits, implied rather than required by the NT. Luke 23.56 (citing Exod 20.10–11) is a rare instance specifying that the sabbath was for rest; but the Hebrew word *sabbath* simply means "rest". See also COPY A

48 n 2 and BREREWOOD and BY-FIELD.

87[1] *Unum necessarium, or, The Doctrine and Practice of Repentance*, for which see COPY A **49** n 1. For all his admiration of Jeremy Taylor, C often noticed his tendency towards Socinianism.

Thirty of them here in London, *who by Instructions from Cardinal* Mazarine, *did take care of such Affairs, and had sate in Council, and debated the Question, Whether the King should be put to death or not? and that it was carried in the Affirmative, and there were but two Voices for the Negative, which was his own and anothers: And that for his part he could not concur with them, as foreseeing what misery this would bring upon his Country.*" That Mr. *Atkins* stood to the Truth of this, but thought it a Violation of the Laws of Friendship, to name the Man.

Richard Baxter was too thoroughly *good* to enable for any experience to make him worldly *wise*. Else how could he have been simple enough to suppose that Mazarine left such a question to be voted pro & con & decided, by 30 Emissaries in London![1] And how could he have reconciled Mazarine's having any share in Charles's Death with his own masterly account p. 88, 89, 100?[a][2]—Even Cromwell, tho' he might have prevented, could not have effected, the sentence. —The Regicidal Judges were not his *Creatures*. Consult the Life of Colonel Hutchinson.[3]

89   i 374–5

Since this, Dr. *Peter Moulin* hath in his Answer to *Philanax Anglicus*, declared that he is ready to prove, when Authority will call him to it,

---

[a] C has written "88, 89, 100"; but "98, 99, 100" (as printed in *C 17th C*) is clearly intended

---

[1] Jules Mazarin (1602–61), Italian by birth and with Jesuit training, became a naturalised Frenchman in 1634 and entered the service of Louis XIV. Although he had never been in high orders, he was created cardinal in 1641 at Louis' instigation, and in 1642 was appointed prime minister. It does not appear that he had any direct hand in the condemnation of Charles, but the English were inclined to place a sinister interpretation upon any of Mazarin's activities.

[2] There is no note on i 98–100 in COPY A. COPY B 36 and 37 are both written on i 99, but neither provides a general comment on the whole passage referred to here.

[3] I.e. HUTCHINSON *Memoirs of the Life of Colonel Hutchinson* (1806) by his widow, Lucy Hutchinson (b

1620). Col John Hutchinson (1615–64), a regicide, was imprisoned for a time at the Restoration, but was saved from execution and from the confiscation of his property by the intervention of his kinsmen. C's supposition is confirmed by p 303: "Some of them [the gentlemen that were appointed his judges] after, to excuse, belied themselves,and sayd they were under the awe of the armie, and overperswaded by Cromwell, and the like; but it is certeine that all men herein were left to their free liberty of acting, neither perswaded nor compelled; and as there were some nominated in the commission who never sate, and others who sate at first, but durst not hold on, so all the rest might have declin'd it if they would, when it is apparent they should have suffer'd nothing by so doing."

that the King's Death and the Change of the Government, was first proposed both to the *Sorbonne*, and to the Pope with his Conclave, and consented to and concluded for by both.

The Pope in his Conclave had about the same influence on Charles's Fate as the Pope's Eye in a Leg of Mutton.[1] The Letter intercepted by Cromwell was Charles's Death-warrant. Charles knew his power; & Cromwell and Ireton knew it likewise[2]—and knew, that it was the Power of a Man who was within a yard's Length of a Talisman, only not within an Arm's length, but which in that state of the public mind would, could he but have once grasped it, would have enabled him to blow up Presbyterian & Independent. If ever a lawless Act was defensible on the principle of Self-preservation, the Murther of Charles might be defended. I suspect, that the fatal delay in the publication of the Eikon Basilike, is susceptible of no other satisfactory Explanation.[3] In short, it is absurd to burthen this Act on Cromwell or his Party. The guilt, if guilt it was, was consummated at the Gates of Hull—i.e. the first moment, that Charles was treated as an Individual, Man against Man. Whatever right Hampden had to defend his Life against the King in Battle, Cromwell & Ireton had in yet more imminent danger against the King's Plotting. Milton's

---

89[1] The "Pope's Eye"—the lymphatic gland surrounded with fat in the middle of a leg of mutton, esteemed a tidbit. The phrase was in use in the seventeenth century.

89[2] The intercepted letter—and there is some doubt whether the king wrote such a letter to the queen or that it was actually intercepted—was alleged to have been written by Charles at the time of his flight from Hampton Court to the Isle of Wight in Nov 1647, saying that he would hang Cromwell as soon as he had made what use of him he wished. Henry Ireton (1611–51), an Oxford BA with training in the law, was (according to Hutchinson) "the chief promoter of the parliament's interest in the county" of Nottinghamshire. After raising a troop of horse in Nottingham in Jun 1642, he joined Cromwell in 1643 to become one of his most distinguished leaders of horse, and in 1646 married Cromwell's daughter. Strong-minded and intelligent, he became Cromwell's most valued political adviser, and as a conservative who wished to preserve as much of the existing constitution as possible he exerted—for a time at least—a restraining influence on Cromwell's fanaticism. The alleged letter from Charles to the queen, however, finally convinced Ireton that compromise with the king could no longer be possible. He was one of the signatories of Charles's death-warrant.

89[3] Εἰκὼν Βασιλική, written perhaps by John Gauden from Charles's papers and conversation but thought by many at the time to have been written by Charles himself, was not published until the day of Charles's execution or shortly afterwards, and was largely responsible for Charles's reputation as a martyr. C annotated a copy of a 1649 ed; see also Christopher WORDSWORTH "*Who Wrote Εἰκὼν Βασιλική?*" *Considered and Answered* (1824–5).

reasoning on this point is unanswerable[4]—& what a wretched hand does Baxter make of it!

90 i 375–6 | § 250

"... *but if the Laws of the Land appoint the Nobles, as next the King, to assist him in doing right, and withhold him from doing wrong, then be they licensed by Man's Law, and so not prohibited by God's, to interpose themselves for the safety of Equity and Innocency, and by all lawful and needful means, to procure the Prince to be reformed, but in no case deprived,* where the Scepter is inherited."* So far Bishop *Bilson* ...

* Excellent!—O by all means preserve for him the benefit of his rightful Heir-loom, the regal Sceptre; only lay it about his shoulders, till he promises to handle it, as he ought!—But what if he breaks his promise & your Head? or what if he won't promise?—How much honester would it be to say—that Extreme Cases are ipso nomine not generalizable, therefore not the Subjects of a Law, which is the conclusion ⟨per genus⟩ singuli in genere inclusi?[1] Every extreme Case must be judged, by and for itself, under all the ⟨peculiar⟩ circumstances—Now as these are not foreknowable, the case itself cannot be pre-determinable. Harmodius & Aristogeiton did not justify Brutus & Cassius; but neither do Brutus & Cassius criminate Harmodius & Aristogeiton.[2] The Rule applies till an Extreme Case occurs; & how can this be *proved*? And I answer: the only Proof is Success & Good Event—for these afford the best presumption 1. of the Extremity & 2. of its remediable Nature—the two elements of its Justification. To every Individual it is forbidden/ He who attempts it

89[4] Milton *An Answer to Eikon Basilike* § 8 "Upon His Repulse at Hull": *Works* ed Birch (2 vols 1738) i 387. "...he begins an open War by laying siege to *Hull*: which Town was not his own, but the Kingdom's; and the Arms there, public Arms, bought with the Public Money, or not his own. Yet had they bin his own by as good right as the private House and Arms of any man are his own; to use either of them in a way not private, but suspicious to the Commonwealth, no Law permits."

90[1] *Ipso nomine*—literally "by the very name"; that is "by the meaning of the word ['extreme'] itself".

C expands the Latin formula in **116**, below: see **116** n 1.

90[2] Two Athenian friends, Harmodius and Aristogeiton, in 514 B.C. murdered Hipparchus, younger brother of the tyrant Hippias, and intended to kill Hippias as well. They were later considered patriotic martyrs and were accorded divine honours. The contemporaries of Brutus and Cassius, however, were not prepared to approve the assassination of Julius Caesar in 44 B.C. in the same way. See *Friend* (*CC*) ii 318, in which C noticed that an *allegation* of tyranny was not enough to justify assassination.

therefore, must do so on the presumption, that the Will of the Nation is in his Will. Whether he is mad or in his senses, the Event can alone determine.[3]

91 i 399–401 | §§ 314–17[a]

§ 314. Now concerning this Diocesan Frame of Government, the *Non-Subscribers* (called *Puritans* by many) do judge that it is sinful and contrary to the Word of God, both in the *Constitution* and in the *Administration* of it. And they lay upon it these heavy Charges, the least of which if proved, is of intolerable weight.

§ 315. 1. They say, That *quantum in se* it destroyeth the *Pastoral Office*, which is of Divine Institution, and was known in the Primitive Church: for it doth deprive the Presbyters of the third essential part of their Office: for it is clear in Scripture, that Christ appointed no Presbyters, that were not subservient to him in all the three parts of his Office, as Prophet, Priest and King, to stand between the people and him in Teaching, Worshipping and Governing . . .

§ 316. 2. . . . That it introduceth a *New Humane Species* of *Presbyters* or Spiritual Officers, instead of Christ's, which it destroyeth . . . He [Hammond] saith not that this sort had no Government of the Flock, but that they were under the Bishop in Government . . .

§ 317. 3. . . . That it destroyeth the *Species* or Form of particular Churches instituted by Christ . . . "The Churches of Christ's institution were constituted of Governing Pastors, and a Flock governed by them in Person as Holy Communion, every Church having its proper Pastor, or Pastors." But such Churches . . . are destroyed by our Frame of Prelacy. . . .

[Four additional arguments are given: (4) "That it setteth up a *New Church-Form* which is unlawful, instead of that of Christ's institution"; (5) "That it extirpateth the *ancient Episcopacy*"; (6) "That instead of the *ancient Bishops*, a later sort of Bishops is introduced, of a distinct *Species* from all the ancient Bishops"; (7) "That it maketh the *Church Government* or *Discipline* which Christ hath commanded, and all the ancient Churches practised, to be a *thing impossible* to be done, and so *excludeth* it; and therefore is unlawful".]

There is, ως ἐμοίγε δοκεῖ, one flaw in Baxter's Plea—that he useth a metaphor, which, inasmuch as it is but a metaphor, agrees with the

[a] C has made an "X" against § 317

90[3] For continuation of this thought see **116**, below.

thing meant in some points only, as if it were commensurate in toto and virtually identical. Thus the Presbyter is a *Pastor* as far as the watchfulness, tenderness, &c are to be the same in both; but it does not follow, that the Presbyter has the same *sole* power, and exclusive right of guidance—and for this reason, that his *Flock* are not *Sheep* but *men*; not of a natural, generic or even constant inferiority of Judgement, but Christians, Co-heirs of the Promises, and therein of the Gifts of the Holy Spirit, and of the interpretation of the Holy Scriptures. How then can they be excluded from a share in Church-Government? The Words of Christ, if they may be transferred from their immediate application to the Jewish Synagogue, suppose the contrary—and that highest act of Government, the election of the Officers and Ministers of the Church, was confessedly exercised by the Congregations, *including* the Presbyters and Arch-presbyter or Bishop, in the primitive Church. The ? therefore is: is a National Church established by Law, compatible with Christianity?[1] If so (as Baxter held) the representatives (King, Lords, and Commons) are or may be representatives of the whole People, as Christians, as well as Civil Subjects—and their Voice the Voice of the Church, which every individual *as* an individual, themselves as individuals, and a fortiori the Officers and Administrators appointed by them, are bound to obey ~~against whose~~ at the risk of excommunication, against which there is no appeal but to the heavenly Cæsar, the Lord and Head of the universal Church. But whether as ~~temporal~~ the accredited Representatives and Plenipotentiaries of the National *Church*, they can avail themselves of their conjoint but distinct character as temporal Legislators, to superadd corporal or civil Penalties to the spiritual sentence in points peculiar to Christianity, as heretical Opinions, church Ceremonies, and the like, thus *destroying Discipline*, even as Wood is destroyed by combination with Fire,—this is a new and difficult Question, which yet Baxter and the Presbyterian Divines, and the Puritans of that age in general, not only answered affirmatively, but most zealously not to say furiously affirmed, with anathemas to the Assertors of the Negative and spiritual Threats to the Magistrates neglecting to interpose the temporal Sword.

In this respect the present Dissenters have the advantage over their earlier Predecessors; but on the other hand they utterly evacuate the Scriptural Commands against Schism; ~~and~~ take away ⟨all⟩ sense and significance from the article ~~of~~ respecting the *Catholic* Church;

91[1] C dealt with this question in *C&S*, esp ch 6 (*CC* 50ff).

and in consequence degrade the Discipline itself into mere *Club*-regulation, or the By-laws of different *Lodges*: ~~as among Free Masons~~[2]—that very Discipline, the capability of exercising which in its own specific nature, without superinduction of a destructive and transmutual Opposite, is the fairest and firmest support of their cause. S. T. C.—

20 Oct[r] 1819.[a] This day 49 or as my Mother said and my *Wife believes, 48 years of age.[4]

* who is a year or more older in *time*, and 20 years younger in all other respects.[3]

92 i 401–3 | § 324

... we are agreed [in admitting fit persons to Communion and rejecting those unfit] 2. That sententially it must be done by the Pastor or Governour of that particular Church, which the Person is to be admitted into, or cast out of: And by the judgment of the Pastors of other neighbour Churches, when they also, as Neighbours, are to refuse Communion with him.

This ⟨most arbitrary⟩ appropriation of the Words of Christ and of the Apostles, John and Paul, by the Clergy to themselves exclusively, is the πρῶτον ψεῦδος,[1] the fatal error which has practically excluded

[a] A slip for "1820"?

91[2] For C and Freemasonry see *Lects 1795* (*CC*) 292 n 1.

91[3] Mrs C was born in 1770, but the precise date of her birth seems not to be recorded.

91[4] Mrs C and C's mother were both correct about the year of C's birth, and C is mistaken about the day of the month: he was born on 21 Oct 1772. From 1797 onwards C regularly gave his birthday as 20 Oct; in the later years he sometimes thought of himself as one year older than he was. See *CL* i 160, 303, ii 766; *CN* i 997, 1252, 1577, ii 2237, 2703; and see also BÖHME 137 (1818), N F° f 55. Since "1819" would make him actually 47, and in his own estimation 48, "1820" seems to be intended. Perhaps he wrote "9" by anticipating the 9 in "49".

92[1] C frequently used the term πρῶτον ψεῦδος to mean the first (that is, logically first or fundamental) error in a line of thinking or argument. He

translates the term in various ways, all of which point to his understanding of it as an oversight difficult to discern and of widespread infectious implication: e.g. "the fundamental error" (*CL* iv 920), "*fundamental* Errors" (CHILLINGWORTH COPY A 1), "his original error" (BÖHME **158**), the "root of my mistake" (BÖHME **137**). Cf DE WETTE **23**. The term, widely used by earlier writers (e.g. Leibniz and Kant) and by contemporary writers (e.g. De Q), comes from Aristotle *Prior Analytics* 66[a]17, at the beginning of 2.18; cf 66[a]1–15. C rightly considers the πρῶτον ψεῦδος the virus or infection of falsity, and like the source of any infection difficult to locate and identify; and in this he seems to be strictly Aristotelian in taking πρῶτος not only to mean first in temporal and logical sequence (the starting-poing of the falsity) but also virtually as the adjective of ἀρχή—the beginning as the

Church Discipline from among Protestants in all free Countries. That it is retained and an efficient power among the *Quakers* & only in that Sect, who act collectively as a Church, who not only have no proper Clergy but will not allow even ~~of~~ a Division of Majority and Minority, nor a temporary President, seems to supply an un-answerable confirmation of this, my assertion, and a strong presumption for the validity of my argument.

P.S. The Wesleian Methodists have, I know, a Discipline and the power is in their Consistory, a genuine Conclave of Priests Cardinal, since the Death of Pope Wesley[2]—but what divisions ~~of~~ and secessions this *has* given rise to, what discontents and heart-burnings it *still* occasions in their laboring inferior Minister, & in the *Classes*, is no less notorious—and ~~not~~ may authorize a belief that as the Sect increases it will be less and less effective, nay that it has decreased—and after all, what is it compared with the Discipline of the Quakers? —Baxter's inconsistency on this subject would be inexplicable, did we not know his zealotry against Harrington, the Deists and the Mystics—so that like an electrified Pith-ball, he is for ever attracted towards their Tenets concerning the ~~per~~retended *perfecting* of ~~the~~ spiritual sentences by the Civil Magistrates; but ⟨he⟩ touches only to fly off again. "Toleration! dainty word for Soul-murder! God grant that my eye may ~~be averted~~ never see a Toleration!" ~~as~~ he exclaims in his Book against Harrington's Oceana.[3]

93   405 | § 339

As for the Democratical conceit of them that say that the Parliament hath their Governing power *as they are* the Peoples Representatives, and so have the Members of the Convocation, though

origin or initiative source. There is a close link between this notion and C's recurrent image of "the queen bee in the hive of error": see BAINES **1** n 2.

92[2] John Wesley (1703–91) assumed leadership of the Methodists from his brother Charles (1707–88) in 1761. Charles strongly disapproved of John's decision in 1784 to ordain presbyters with authority to confer orders and to administer the sacraments—hence C's gibe about "Pope Wesley". The Quakers admitted no orders. C wrote more than 100 marginalia in SOUTHEY *Life of Wesley* (2 vols 1820).

92[3] Baxter attacked Harrington's *Commonwealth of Oceana* (1656) in his

A Holy Commonwealth, or Political Aphorisms (1659): see *Reliquiae* i 118 § 195 and iii 71 § 152. The quotation "Toleration! dainty word for Soul-murder!..." has not been located in either Baxter or Harrington. Whether or not "Soul-murder" is a term used by either, C used it himself in a *Courier* essay of 31 Aug 1811, "Superstition, Religion, Atheism (An Allegoric Vision)" (*EOT—CC*—ii 263), in a letter referring to the abuses he sought to help redress with his pamphlets on the factory children in Apr 1818 (*CL* iv 855), and in a note on HACKET *Scrinia Reserata* (1693) i 93.

those represented have no Governing power themselves, it is so palpably Self-contradicting, that I need not confute it.

Self-contradictory according to *Baxter's* Sense of the words, represent and govern. But every rational Adult *has* a governing power: viz. that of governing himself.

94   i 412–14 | § 370

9. That though a Subject ought to take an Oath in the sence of his Rulers who impose it, as far as he can understand it; yet a Man that taketh an Oath from a Robber to save his Life, is not alway bound to take it in the Imposers sence, if he take it not against the proper sence of the words.

9. This is a point, on which I have never been able to satisfy myself— the only safe conclusion, I have been able to draw, being the folly, mischief, and immorality of all Oaths but judicial ones—and those no farther excepted than a as they are means of securing a deliberate consciousness of the presence of the Omniscient Judge—Oaths not Vows. The inclination of my mind is, at this moment, to the principle, than[a] an Oath may deepen the guilt of an act sinful in itself; but cannot be detached from the Act—it being understood that a perfectly voluntary and self-imposed Oath is itself a Sin. The man who compels me to take an Oath by putting a pistol to my ear has in my mind clearly forfeited all his Right to be treated as a moral Agent. Nay, it seems to be a Sin to act so as to induce him to suppose himself such. ⟨*Contingent*⟩ Consequences must be excluded; but would, I am persuaded, weigh in favor of abannulling an Oath sinfully extorted; *on* PRINCIPLE.[1]

But I hate Casuistry so utterly, that I could not without great violence to my feelings put the case in all its bearings—Ex. gr. It is sinful to enlarge the power of Wicked Agents; but to allow them to have the power of binding the conscience of those, whom they have injured, is to enlarge the POWER &c/ 2. No Oath can bind on to the perpetration of *a Sin*; but to transfer a sum of money to from its rightful owner to a Villain is a Sin—& 20 other such.—But the Robber may kill the next man!—Possibly; but still more probably, many who would be Robbers if they could obtain their ends without Murder would resist the Temptation if no extenuations of Guilt were contemplated—and one Murder is more effective in rousing the

---

a A slip for "that'"

94[1] See also COPY A **55** and **61**.

public mind to preventive Measures, and by the horror, it strikes, is directly preventive of the tendency, than 50 civil Robberies by *contract.*—

95   i 413 | § 371

Answ. 1. . . . The Ends of Parliaments may be manifold and unknown, which the People cannot know, nor are bound to search after. . . . If a discontented Person should say, that the Parliaments End in the Act of Uniformity, and that against Conventicles, was Persecution and the Suppression of Religion, and therefore they are not to be obeyed, how would this hold, while *Uniformity* and *Peace* are the *published* Ends, and the rest are either uncertain or impertinent to us.

Still Baxter supposes the men collected in Parliament House a *Parliament*; but this they were not.

96   i 413

2. Whether indeed the Imposers Ends were ill, is a Controversie fit to be touched by it self. They thought such a Change of Church-Government was a good End: And for *doing it against Law* they put not that into the Swearers part, in this Clause; and professed the contrary themselves. But if they did themselves purpose to do that *against Law*, which others swear to do *"in their Places and Calling"* that is, *according to Law*, are those others therefore not obliged to do what they vowed to do *according to Law*, because the Imposers intended to do their part against Law?

But this is sheer nonsense. How could a man act according to Law against a Law?

97   i 435, pencil, overtraced | § 427

3. That the Minister be not bound to use the Cross and Surplice, and read the Liturgy himself, if another (by whomsoever) be procured to it: So be it he preach not against them.

Wonderful that so good and wise a man as B̄x̄t̄r̄ should not have seen that in this the Church would have given up the best, perhaps the only efficient Preservative of her Faith. But for our blessed and truly apostolic & scriptural Liturgy, our Churches ⟨Pews⟩ would long ago have been filled by Arians and Socinians, as too many of their Desks and Pulpits already are/.

98   ii 59 | ɪ iii § 125

. . . As also to make us take such a poor Suffering as this, for a Sign of true Grace, instead of Faith, Hope, Love, Mortification, and a

Heavenly Mind; and that the loss of one Grain of Love, was worse than a Long Imprisonment...

Here Baxter confounds his own particular case, which very many would have coveted, with the sufferings of other Prisoners on the same score, sufferings *nominally* the same, but with few, if any, of Baxter's supports, almost *flattering* supports.

99　p +1, written above—and after—**113**, referring to ii 60 | § 133

It would trouble the *Reader* for me to reckon up the many Diseases, and Dangers for these ten Years past, in, or from which, God hath delivered me; though it be my Duty not to forget to be thankful. Seven Months together I was lame, with a strange Pain in one Foot; Twice delivered from a Bloody Flux; a spurious Cataract in my Eye (with incessant Webs and Net-works before it) hath continued these eight Years, without disabling me one Hour from Reading or Writing: I have had constant Pains and Languours ... so that I have rarely one Hour's, or quarter of an Hour's ease. Yet, through God's Mercy, I was never one Hour Melancholy, and not many Hours in a Week disabled utterly from my Work ...

P. III. p. 60. The Power of the Soul by its own act of Will is, I admit, great for any one occasion or for a definite time—yea, it is marvellous.—But of such exertions and such an even frame of Spirit as Baxter's were, under such unremitting & almost unheard of bodily derangements and pains, as Baxter's, & during so long a life, I do not believe a human soul capable, unless substantiated and successively potenziated by an especial divine Grace.[1]—S. T. C.

100　ii 65–6 | § 143

2. The Reasons, why I make *no larger a Profession* necessary than the *Creed and Scriptures*, are, because if we depart from *this old sufficient Catholick Rule*, we narrow the Church, and depart from the old *Catholicism* ...

Why then *any* Creed?—This is the difficulty. If you put *the* Creed as in fact & not by courtesy Apostolic, on a parity with Scripture,

99[1] Cf **5**, above. The word "potenziated" occurs in *CN* III 4426, 4486 f 47 in Aug–Sept 1818 and 25 Feb 1819. C had already "hazarded the new verb potenziate, with its derivatives, in order to express the combination or transfer of powers". *BL* ch 12 (1907) I 189; see also *CN* III 4418 f 13ᵛ and n.

OED records "potentiate", ascribing the coinage of it to C, and assigns "potentiation" to J. H. Green *Vital Dynamics* (1840). Although *OED* notes that the root of C's word is German *Potenz*, that connexion is lost by normalising the word to "poten*t*iate".

having namely its authority in itself, & the direct inspiration of the Framers, inspired ad id tempus a et ad eam rem[1]—on what ground is this to be done? without admitting the binding power of *Tradition* in the very sense of the term in which the Church of Rome uses it & the Protestant Churches reject it? That it is the Sum total, made by apostolic Contributions, each Apostle casting, as into a helmet, a several article, as his Συμβολον, is the *Tradition*;[2] & this is held as a mere Legendary Tale by the great majority of Learned Divines. That it is simply the Creed of the Western Church, is affirmed by many Protestant Divines, & some of these Divines of our Church.[3]

Its comparative simplicity these Divines explain by the freedom from Heresies enjoyed by the Western Church, when the Eastern Church had been long troubled therewith.—Others, again, & not unplausibly, contend that it was the Creed of the Catechumens preparatory to the Baptismal Profession of Faith—which rather was a fuller comment on the union of the Father, the Son, & the Holy Ghost into whose Name (or power) they were baptized.— That the Apostles' Creed received additions after the Apostolic Age, seems almost certain; not to mention the perplexing circumstance, that so many of the Latin Fathers, who give almost the *words* of the apostles' Creed, declare it forbidden absolutely to write or by any material form to transmit the Canon Fidei, Symbolum, Regula Fidei, the Creed κατ' εξοχην,[4] by analogy of which the question— whether such a Book is Scripture or no—was to be tried. With such doubts how can the Apostles' Creed be preferred to the Nicene by a consistent Protestant.[5]

101   ii 67

2. They think, while you [the Independents] seem to be for a *stricter Discipline* than others, that your way (or usual Practice) tendeth to extirpate Godliness out of the Land; by taking a very few that can

100[1] "For that time and that case".

100[2] *Symbolon*—a token, originally the two pieces of a coin broken by contracting parties; a covenant. *Symbolon* was not used of the Creed until the middle of the third century; see **58** n 2, above. In two long notebook entries of c Sept 1821 C considers the history and uses of the word "Symbol", distinguishing it from emblem, eikon, metaphor, simile, etc: N 29 ff 57–62.

100[3] Cf N 29 f 59: "...the absurd Legend of the Creed=Symbolum or Symbola Fidei, as the Pic Nic contributions of the 12 Apostles".

100[4] The Greek phrase means "eminently". For *canon fidei, symbolon, regula fidei* see n 2, above, and BIBLE *Apocryphal NT* **4** n 4.

100[5] See also **58** n 3, above, and *Catholick Theologie* **9** n 1. In c Jul 1810 C gave another view of the nature and history of the Apostles' and Nicene creeds: see *CN* III 3964. For the Athanasian Creed see BÖHME **33** n 1.

talk more than the rest, and making them the Church, and shutting out more that are as worthy ...

Had Baxter had as judicious Advisers among his theological, as he had among his legal, friends; & had allowed them equal influence with him; he would not, I suspect, have written this irritating & too *egomet*ical §.[1]—But B. w̄ld have disbelieved a prophet who had foretold that the whole Orthodoxy of the Nonconformists would be retained & preserved by the *Independent* Churches in England— after the Presbyterian had almost without exception become first Arian, then Socinian, & finally Unitarian—i.e. the demi-semi-quaver of Xtnty, taking lax Arminianism for the Semi-breve.—[2]

102   ii 69 | §§ 144–5

After this I waited on him [Dr John Owen] at *London* again, and he came once to me to my Lodgings, when I was in Town (near him;) And he told me, that he received my chiding Letter, and perceived that I suspected his Reality [? Fealty] in the Business; but he was so hearty in it, that I should see that he really meant as he spake, concluding in these Words " *You shall see it, and my Practice shall reproach your Diffidence.*" ...

About a Month after I went to him again, and he had done nothing, but was still hearty for the Work. And to be short, I thus waited on him time after time, till my Papers had been near a Year and quarter in his Hand, and then I desired him to return them to me, which he did, with these Words, " *I am still a well-wisher to those Mathematicks;*" without any other Words about them, or ever giving me any more Exception against them. And this was the issue of my third Attempt for Union with the Independents.

D[r] J. Owen was a man of no ordinary Intellect.[1] It would be interesting to have his conduct in this point, seemingly so strange, in some

101[1] Egometical—C's coinage, from the emphatic form of "I", *egomet*. Not in *OED*.

101[2] English names for musical note-values provide wider scope for word-play than the fractional American notation, in which a semi-demi-quaver is a thirty-second note and a semi-breve a whole-note. C indicates an extreme attenuation of what in Grotius was already an attenuated Arminianism. Arminianism (for which see COPY A **49** n 2), which opposed Calvin esp on the doctrine of predestination, persisted in England among Laudians, latitudinarians, Wesleyans, and other anti-Calvinist groups. See **108** and **115** (C's footnote *), below; also *CN* I 1565, *Friend (CC)* II 280, *P Lects* (1949) 446–7. *AR* (1825) 157n, 301.

102[1] John Owen (1616–83), puritan assailant of Arminianism, was an incessant writer and one of the Triers set to purge the Church of scandalous ministers. A copy of his *Works* (28 vols 1826) was in Green's library.

measure explained. The words, "those Mathematics" look like an inuendo, that Baxter's scheme of union, by which all the Parties opposed to the Prelatic Church were to form a rival Church, was, like the Mathematics, true indeed; but true only in the *Idea*—i.e. abstracted from the Subject Matter—Still, there appears a very chilling want of open-heartedness on the part of Owen, produced perhaps by the somewhat *overly* and certainly most ungracious, *resentments* of Baxter. It was odd at least to propose Concord in the tone & on the alledged ground of an old Grudge.

103   p +5 (p–d), referring to ii 69 | § 146

I had been Twenty Six Years convinced that Dichotomizing will not do it; but that the Divine Trinity in Unity, hath exprest it self in the whole Frame of Nature and Morality. . . . At last *Mr. Geo. Lawson's Theopolitica* came out, which reduced Theology to a Method more Political and righter in the main, than any other I had seen before him: But he had not hit on the true Method of the *Vestigia Trinitatis* . . .

Part III. p. 69.

Among Baxter's philosophical merits we ought not to overlook, that the substitution of Trichotomy for the old & still general plan of Dichotomy in the Method and Disposition of Logic, which forms so prominent & substantial an excellence in Kant's Critique of the Pure Reason, of the Judgement, &c belongs originally to Richard Baxter, a century before Kant—& this not as a Hint but as a fully evolved & systematically applied Principle. Nay, more than this! Baxter **grounded* it on an absolute Idea *pre*supposed in all intelli-

* On recollection I am disposed to consider *this* ⟨alone⟩ as Baxter's *peculiar* claim. I have not indeed any distinct memory of Giordano Bruno's Logica Venatrix Veritatis; but doubtless the principle of Trichotomy is necessarily involved in the Polar Logic:[1] ~~this~~ which

---

103[1] Giordano Bruno (1548–1600), restless and unorthodox speculative thinker, was burned at the stake at Rome for heresy. Ever since C had first encountered Bruno's work in Apr 1801, he had admired it for its daring originality and fearless independence of spirit, and found in Bruno—as in Heraclitus and Böhme—a precursor of his own way of mind. He here refers to *De progressu et lampade venatoria logicorum* (Wittenberg 1587); see *CN* III 3825. For a list of Bruno's titles, see *CN* II 2264, and for C's account of his reading of Bruno see *Friend* (*CC*) II 82n and BÖHME **4** n 1. Bruno was always a prime figure in C's scheme for his intended "Vindiciae Heterodoxae". For C's view of Bruno as the founder of trichotomy and the polar logic see also *CL* IV 775 and *P Lects* Lect 11 (1949) 323–7.

gential acts: whereas Kant takes it only as a *Fact* of Reflection—as a singular & curious Fact, in which he seems to anticipate or suspect some yet deeper Truth latent & hereafter to be discovered.—[4]

again is ~~in~~ the same with the Pythagorean *Tetractys*[2]—i.e. the eternal Fountain or Source of Nature; & this being sacred to contemplation of Identity & prior in order of Thought to *all* division, ~~it~~ is so far from interfering with Trichotomy, as the universal form of Division (more correctly, of distinctive Distribution in Logic) that it implies it.—Prothesis being by the very term anterior to Thesis can be no part of it—Thus in

Prothesis

Thesis   Antithesis

Synthesis

we have the Tetrad indeed in the intellectual & intuitive Contemplation; but a Triad in discursive Arrangement, and a Tri-unity in Result.——[3]

104   ii 144 | Mr John Humphrey's *Papers given to the Parliament-Men.* "Comprehension with Indulgence"

. . . there is a *Bill* at present in the House, *a Bill for the ease of the Protestant Dissenter in the Business of Religion* . . .

There are two sorts . . . of the *Protestant Dissenters,* one that own the Established Ministry, and our Parish Congregations, and are in Capacity of Union upon that account, desiring it heartily upon condescension to them in some small matters . . .

103[2] For the Pythagorean tetractys see **103** n 1, above, and BÖHME **6** n 10. In *AR* (1825) 173n C spoke of "the Supreme Being alone, the Pythagorean TETRACTYS; the INEFFABLE NAME, to which no Image dare be attached . . .".

103[3] See e.g. *TT* 24 Apr 1832.

103[4] The principle of trichotomy is, as C says, a prominent feature of both works. Kant himself comments upon it in *Critik der Urtheilskraft* Einleitung IX (p lviin in C's copy of the Berlin 1799 ed, the passage not marked or annotated). The note is to Kant's table of faculties, which are arranged in threes. "It has been thought somewhat suspicious that my divisions in pure philosophy should almost always come out threefold. But it is due to the nature of the case. If a division is to be *a priori* it must be either analytic, according to the law of contradiction— and then it is always twofold . . . or else it is *synthetic*. If it is to be derived in the latter case from *a priori* concepts (not, as in mathematics, from the *a priori* intuition corresponding to the concept,) then, to meet the requirements of synthetic unity in general, namely (1) a condition, (2) a conditioned, (3) the concept arising from the union of the conditioned with its condition, the division must of necessity be trichotomous." Tr J. C. Meredith (Oxford 1952) 39n. There is a long note on trichotomy in N 29 ff 128^v–127^v (Sept 1820).

For the *One*, that which we propose is a farther Latitude in the present Constituted Order, that such may be received. . . . Let us suppose that nothing else were required of a Man, to be a Minister of a Parish than there is to the Parishioners to be a Member of a Parish Church, as part of the National . . .

[Farther on, Humphrey argues (p 145) that "Bishop *Laud* be confined to his Cathedrals" so that "the Ceremonies in the ordinary Parish Churches be left to the Liberty of the Minister, to use, or use them not, according to his Conscience, and Prudence toward his own Congregation".]

Seeing the great difficulties that lie in the way of increasing Churches so as to *meet* the increase of population, or even so as to *follow* it, & the manifold desirableness of *Parish* Churches, with the maternal dignity that in a right state of Christian Order would attach to them as compared with Meeting-houses, Chapels, & the like, all more or less privati Juris[1]—I have often felt disposed to wish, that the large majestic Church central to each given Parish ~~were~~ might have been appropriated to public Prayer, ~~be~~ to ~~all~~ the mysteries of Baptism & Lord's Supper, and to the quasi *Sacramenta*, Marriage, Penance, Confirmation, Ordination &c,[2] and to the continued Reading aloud or occasional Chaunting of the Scriptures during the intervals of the different Services, which ought to be so often performed as to suffice successively for the whole Population—and that on the other hand the Chapels & the like should be entirely devoted to Preaching & Expounding.

105   ii 153 | § 274

And I proved to him [a person unknown professing Infidelity], that *Christianity* was proved true many years before any of the New Testament was Written, and that so it may be still proved by one that doubted of some words of the Scripture; and therefore the true order is, to try the *truth* of the *Christian* Religion first, and the perfect Verity of all the Scriptures afterwards.

With more than Dominican Virulence[1] did Goeze, Head Pastor of

104[1] "Under their own Jurisdiction".

104[2] See BIBLE COPY B **140** n 3.

105[1] See **1** n 6, above. In the early attempts of the Roman Church to deal with heresy and before an Inquisition had been formally established, members of the Dominican Order, because of their learning and disinterestedness, were chosen to inquire into divergencies from orthodox beliefs. Their zeal and ferocity in carrying out their commission, in the thirteenth century, against the Albigensian heresy, established their reputation as merciless professional inquisitors, the fear and

the Lutheran Church at Hamburgh, assail the celebrated Lessing for* making and supporting the same position as the pious Baxter here advances—

    * His controversy with Goeze was in 1778.—~~just~~ nearly 100 years after Baxter/[2]

106   ii 155 | § 282

And within a few days Mr. *Barwell* riding the Circuit, was cast by his Horse, and died in the very Fall. And Sir *John Medlicot*, and his Brother, a few weeks after, lay both dead in his House together.

This interpreting of Accidents and Coincidence into *Judgements* is a breach of Charity and Humility only not universal among all sects & parties of this period and common to the best & gentlest men in all. We should not therefore bring it in charge against any one in particular. But what excuse shall be made for the revival of this presumptuous Incroachment on the divine Prerogative in our days?—

107   ii 180 | Additions § 9

Near this time, my Book, called, *A Key for Catholicks*, was to be Reprinted: In the Preface to the first Impression, I had mentioned with Praise the Earl of *Lauderdale*. . . . I thought best to . . . prefix . . . an Epistle to the Duke, in which I said not a word of him but Truth. . . . But the Indignation that Men had against the Duke, made some blame me, as keeping up the Reputation of one whom Multitudes thought very ill of: Whereas I owned none of his Faults, and did nothing that I could well avoid, for the aforesaid Reasons. Long after this he professed his Kindness to me, and told me I should never want while he was able, and (humbly) intreated me to accept Twenty Guinea's from him, which I did.

This would be a curious proof of the slow & imperfect Intercourse of communication between Scotland and London, if Baxter had not

---

hatred of them being concentrated in the punning name *Domini canes*— hounds of the Lord.

   105[2] In 1774–7 Lessing published from Wolfenbüttel a rationalist attack on orthodox Christianity entitled *Fragmente eines Ungenannten*, written by H. S. Reimarus. Johann Melchior Goeze (1717–86) attacked the *Fragmente* vigorously on the assumption that Lessing had written the work. Lessing replied with *Anti-Goeze* (1778) and in the same vein composed *Nathan der Weise* (1779) in praise of toleration. C became aware of this controversy when he was in Germany in 1799: see *CN* I 377 ff 22–3. The *Anti-Goeze* is included in L E S S I N G *Sämmtliche Schriften* (30 vols Berlin 1784–98). See also *Friend* (*CC*) I 34 n 1.

been particularly informed of Lauderdale's HORRIBLE Cruelties to the Scotch Covenanters:[1] & if Baxter did know them, he surely ran into a greater inconsistency to avoid the appearance of a loss.[a] And the *20 gneas*—they must have smelt, I should think, of more than the *earthly* Brimstone that might naturally enough have been expected in gold or silver from Caledonian Palm. I would as soon have picked an ingot from the Cleft of the Devil's Hoof.

Ταυτα λέγω περίθυμος: εγω γαρ μισεῖ ἐν ἴσῳ
Λαυδερδαῖλον ἔχω καὶ κερκοκερώνυχα Σᾶταν.[b2]

108   ii 181 | § 13

About that time I had finished a book called, *Catholick Theologie*; in which I undertake to prove that besides things unrevealed, known to none, and ambiguous words, there is no considerable difference between the *Arminians* and *Calvinists*, except some very tolerable difference in the point of perseverance . . .

What Arminians? *what* Calvinists? It is possible that the guarded Language & Position of Arminius himself may be interpreted into a "very tolerable" compatibility with the principles of the milder Calvinists, such as Archbishop Leighton—that true Father of the Church of Christ![1] But I more than doubt the possibility of even approximating the principles of Bishop Jeremy Taylor to the fundamental doctrines even of Leighton—much more those of Cartwright, Twiss, Owen.[2]

---

[a] A slip for "less"?
[b] C has rewritten **the** Greek epigram at the head of the page with two changes in wording: in line 1, ταῦτ᾽ ἔλεγον ("I said"); and in line 2, Λαυδερδᾶλον

107[1] John Maitland, 1st Duke and 2nd Earl of Lauderdale (1616–82), was secretary for Scottish affairs 1660–80; he pursued with spectacular rigour the policy of making the Crown absolute in Scotland.

107[2] "I say this in great anger: for I hold for Lauderdale the same hatred as for tail-horn-hoofed Satan." In *Omniana* I 197 C said that he had come across the phrase κερκοκερώνυχα Σαταν in "some Greek Hexameters (MSS)", but the attribution looks suspicious. The compound emerged in 1807–8 (*CN* II 3205) and found a place in a letter of 30 Jan 1818 (*CL*

IV 823), in a note on a front flyleaf of John SMITH *Select Discourses* (1660), and in a letter of Jun 1832 (*CL* VI 915). The English form "cercocerony-chous" is not recorded in *OED*.

108[1] Robert Leighton (1611–84), abp of Glasgow. C's annotated copies of three editions of Leighton's *Works* provided the framework for *Aids to Reflection*.

108[2] Thomas Cartwright (1535–1603) and William Twisse (c 1578–1646), both puritan divines and controversialists. For John Owen see 102 n 1, above.

109   ii 186–7 | § 44

... the Bishop of *Lincoln* Dr. *Barlow* ... told my friend that got my Papers for him, that he could hear of nothing that we judged *to be sin*, but *meer inconveniences*: When as above 17 years ago, we publickly endeavoured to prove the sinfulness even of many of the old Impositions ...

Clearly an undeterminable Controversy/ inasmuch as there is no Contra-definition possible of Sin & Inconveniences in Religion: while the exact *grade* at which an inconvenience, becoming intolerable, passes into Sin, must depend on the state, degree of Light, &c of the individual Consciences, to which it appears or becomes intolerable. Besides: a thing may be not only indifferent in itself but may be declared such by Scripture, and on this indifference the Scripture may have rested a prohibition to Christians to judge each other on the point—. If yet a Pope or Archbishop should force this on the consciences of others, ex. gr. to eat or not to eat animal food, would he not sin in so doing? And does Scripture permit me to subscribe to an ordinance made in direct contempt of a command of Scripture? ~~Must~~ If it were said—in all matters indifferent & so not sinful you must comply with lawful authority: must I not reply—But you have yourself removed the Indifferency by your Injunction. Look in Popish Countries for the hideous consequences of the unnatural doctrine—that the Priest may go to Hell for sinfully commanding & his Parishioner go with him for not obeying that command.

110   ii 191 | § 76

But after this when I had ceased Preaching, I was (being newly risen from Extremity of pain) suddenly surprized in my house by a poor violent Informer, and many Constables and Officers, who rusht in and apprehended me, and served on me one Warrant to seize on my person for coming within five miles of a Corporation, and five more Warrants, to distrain for an Hundred and ninety pounds, for five Sermons.

I cannot express how much it grieves me, that our Church Clergy should still think it fit and expedient to defend the measures of the High Church Men from Laud to Sheldon, & to speak of the ejected Ministers, as Calamy, Baxter, Gouge, Howe &c &c &c,[1] as Schis-

110[1] Edmund Calamy the elder (see **83** n 1, above), Baxter, Thomas   Gouge (1609–81), and John Howe (1630–1705) were all ejected from their

matics, Factionists, and Fanatics or Pharisees—thus to flatter some half dozen dead Bishops wantonly depriving our present Church of the Authority of perhaps the largest collective number of learned and zealous, discreet & holy Ministers that ~~ever~~ one Age & one Church was ever blest with, and whose Authority in *every* considerable point is in favor of our Church and against the present Dissenters from it.—And this seems the more impolitic, when it must be clear to every student of the History of these times, that the unmanly Cruelties inflicted on Baxter & others were, as Bishops Ward, Stillingfleet & others saw at the time,[2] part of the popish Scheme of the Cabal, to trick the Bishops & dignified Clergy into rendering themselves & the established Church odious to the Public by Laws, the execution of which the King, the Duke, Arlington, & the popish Priests directed towards the very last man that the Bishops themselves (~~for~~ the great majority at least) would have molested.[3]

111 iii 36 | Appendix II

... I confess you may say as much for the proving of the Universal Churches Practice, in this Point [i.e. the imposition of hands], as in most, it being of constant and solemn use, and none that I know of, that ever opposed it.

How likewise can it be proved that the Imp. of Hands in Ord[n] did not stand on the same ground as the Imp. of Hands in Sickness—i.e. the miraculous Gifts of the first Preachers of the Gospel? All Protestants admit that the Church retained several forms so originated, after the cessation of the originating Powers, that were the substance of these Forms.

ministries under the Act of Uniformity in 1662. But it is not clear which Calamy and which Gouge C had in mind. Edmund Calamy the younger (c 1635–85; see **115** n 5, below) was also ejected from his ministry, and so was Robert Gouge (1630–1705), son of Thomas Gouge, and Henry More's pupil; Howe represents a generation younger than Baxter and was a friend of Henry More (for whom see **115** n 9, below).

110[2] Seth Ward (1617–89), bp of Salisbury. Edward Stillingfleet (1635–99), bp of Worcester, whose *Origines Sacrae* (1675) C annotated in a copy

bound with STILLINGFLEET *Discourse Concerning the Power of Excommunition* (1662) and *Irenicum* (1662).

110[3] The Cabal, an unofficial cabinet 1667–73 (the name made up from the initials of its members: Clifford, Ashley, Buckingham, Arlington, and Lauderdale), was notorious for the part it played in the shameful secret Treaty of Dover (1670). "The Duke" is the second son of Charles I, Duke of York from 1660 until his accession as James II in 1685. Henry Bennet, 1st Earl of Arlington (1618–85), was perhaps the least scrupulous member of the Cabal.

112   iii 37–8

If you think not only Imposition to be essential, but also that nothing else is essential, or that all are true Ministers that are ordained by a lawful Bishop *per manu[u]m impositionem* [by the imposition of hands], then do you egregiously *tibi ipsi imponere* [impose upon yourself].*

* Baxter, like most Scholastic Logicians, had a sneaking affection for Puns. The cause is: the necessity of attending to the primary sense of words, i.e. the visual image or general relation exprest, & which remains common to all the after senses, however widely or even incongruously differing from each other in other respects.—For the same reason, School-masters are commonly Punsters.[1]—"I have indorsed your Bill, Sir!" said a Pedagogue to a Merchant—meaning, that he had flogged his Son William. "Nihil in intellectu quod non prius in sensu",[2] my old Master, R[d] J. Boyer, the Hercules Furens of the phlogistic Sect, but else an incomparable Teacher, used to translate—first reciting the Latin words & observing that they were the fundamental article of the Peripatetic School—"You must flog a Boy before you can make him understand"—or "You must lay it in at the Tail before you can get it into the Head.["]—[3]

112[1] On punning see Böhme **60** and n 1.

112[2] "There is nothing in the Understanding not derived from the Senses, or—There is nothing *conceived* that was not previously *perceived*"—C's tr in *AR* (1825) 218n. In the first philosophical letter to the Wedgwoods, 18 Feb 1801, C had remarked that "The nihil in intellectu quod non prius in sensu of the Peripatetics is notorious" (*CL* II 680); the germ of this widely dispersed dictum can be found in Aristotle *De anima* 427[b]16, 432[a]7–8. But C said in *BL* ch 9 (1907) I 93–4, and in *AR*, that he found it in its Latin form in Leibniz, and in both cases he gave Leibniz's qualifying phrase "praeter ipsum intellectum"—"except the understanding itself". See "Epistolae mutuae G. G. Leibnitii et F. G. Bierlingii" Letter II, Leibniz's reply: *Opera omnia* ed L. Dutens (6 vols Geneva 1768) v 359; also in *Nouveaux Essais* II 1. See also *SM* (*CC*) 67n.

112[3] James Boyer (1736–1814) was under grammar master at Christ's Hospital from 1767 until in 1776 he was elected to the upper mastership vacated by the Rev Peter Whalley (editor of Ben Jonson); he retired in 1799. See [P. J. Boyer] "An Eighteenth Century Pedagogue—James Boyer" *Oxford and Cambridge Review* No 5 (1908); there is also a corrected typescript of the article in the Bristol Central Library. Boyer's "Liber Aureus" (BM Ashley 3506) contains early ms essays and poems by C. In 1803 C's dreams were troubled by his recollection of Boyer and other Christ's Hospital figures: see e.g. *CN* I 1649, 1726. See also H. Coleridge **48A** and n 1. For Boyer's worth and severity as a teacher, see *BL* ch 1 (1907) I 4–6, *TT* 27 May 1830; and for his kindness, *CL* I 65 and 64n, *TT* 16 Aug 1832. But the savagery of Boyer's beatings was proverbial. In a note on *QR* XIX (Oct 1813) 96 C gave a more temperate version of Boyer's peripatetic adage: "You must make a lad *feel* before he will *understand*."

113   iii 45

Then "3. That the Will [must] follow the practical Intellect whether right or wrong" that is no Precept, but the Nature of the Soul in its acting, because that Will is *potentia ceca, non nata, ad intelligendum, sed ad volendum vel nolendum intellectum* [a blind potentiality, not born to understand, but to will or refuse understanding]: So that it is a most intollerable thing to grant that Man's Error can make Duty no Duty, or Sin no Sin.

This is the main fault in Baxter's Metaphysics: that he so often substantiates Distinctions into dividuous self-subsistents. So, here. A will not intelligent is no *Will*.

114   iii 55, pencil, overtraced | Appendix III

... And for many Ages no other ordinarily baptized but Infants. If Christ had no Church, then where was his Wisdom, his Love, and his Power? What was become of the Glory of his Redemption, and his Catholick Church, that was to continue to the End?

But the Antipædobaptists would deny any such consequences, as applicable to them who are to act according to the circumstances, in which God, who ordains his successive manifestations in due correspondence with other Lights & states of things, has placed them. He does not exclude from the Church of Christ (say they) those whom we do not accept into the Communion of our particular Society— any more than the House of Lords excludes Commoners from being Members of Parliament. And we do this because we think that such promiscuous admission would prolong an error which would be deadly to us tho' not to you who interpret the Scriptures otherwise.

115   pp +1–+3; footnote p +3

There are two Senses in which the words, Church of England, may be used—first, with reference to the *Idea* of the Church as an Estate of this Christian and Protestant Realm, comprizing the interests, ⟨1.⟩ of a permanent learned Class, i.e. the Clergy;[1] ⟨2.⟩ those of the proper, i.e. *infirm*, Poor, from age or sickness; and ⟨3.⟩ the adequate proportional instruction of all in all classes, by public Prayer, recitation of the Scriptures, by expounding, preaching, Catechizing,

[1] The fact that C did not use here the word "clerisy" that he used in *C&S* for precisely this concept may suggest that this note was written before he had coined the word; C used "clerisy" as early as Feb 1821: *CL* v 138. See also Blomfield 3 and n 1, *C&S* (*CC*) 46 n 1.

and *schooling*: and last not least, by the example and influence of a
Pastor and a School Master placed, as a germ of civilization and
cultivation, in every Parish throughout the Realm.—To this Ideal,
the ⟨reformed⟩ Church of England, with its marriable & married
Clergy, would have approximated, if the Revenues of the Church,
as they existed at the Death of Henry VII[th,] had been ⟨rightly⟩
transferred ⟨by his Successor.—Transferred, I mean,⟩ from Reser-
voirs, which had, by degeneracy on one hand and progressive improvement ~~and~~ on the other, fallen into ruin, & in which the said
Revenues had stagnated into ~~Public Evils~~ contagion or uselessness—
~~if (I say) they the Revenues of the Ch. had been~~ transferred from
what had *become* PUBLIC Evils to their original & inherent Purpose
of *Public* Benefits—instead of their sacrilegious alienation by transfer
to *private* Proprietors.—That this was *impracticable*, is *historically*
true; but no less true is it *philosophically*, that this impracticability,
arising wholly from *moral* causes (viz. the loose Manners and
corrupt Principles of a great majority in all classes during the Dynasty
of the Tudors) does not prevent this wholesale Sacrilege from deserving the character of the first and deadliest Wound inflicted on the
CONSTITUTION of the Kingdom: which term, in the body politic
as in bodies natural, expresses not only what is & has been evolved
but likewise whatever is *potentially* contained in the seminal principle of the particular Body, & would in its due time have appeared
but for the emasculation in its infancy.—This, however, is the first
sense of the words, Church of England.[2] The second is, the Church
of England as now by Law established, & by *Practice* of the Law
actually existing.—That in the first sense it is the Object of my
Admiration and the earthly Ne Plus Ultra of my religious Aspirations, it were superfluous to say; but I may be allowed to express my
conviction, that on our recurrence to the same Ends & Objects (the
restoration of a National and Circulating Property in counterpoise ~~to~~
of individual Possession disposable & heritable)[3] tho' in other
forms & by other means perhaps (M[r] Brougham's Motion, June
28, 1820, promises a *beginning*)[4] the Decline or Progress of this

115[2] See *C&S* (*CC*) 124–5.
115[3] See ibid 35.
115[4] A Bill for the Education of the
Poor: reported in extenso in *The
Times* of 29 Jun 1820, and declared in
A Reg for 1820 to be "one of the most
elaborate and instructive ever delivered
in parliament". Henry Peter Brougham
(1778–1868), MP from 1810, was also
a vigorous advocate of the abolition
of the slave-trade. C wrote notes on
Brougham's *Inquiry into the Colonial
Policy of the European Powers* (1803)
and marginalia in a copy of *A Speech
on the Present State of the Law of the
Country* (1828). But see *C&S* (*CC*) 61.

Country depends.—In the second sense of the Words, I can sincerely profess, that I love & honor the Church of England *comparatively* beyond any other Church, established or unestablished, now existing in Christendom: And it is wholly in consequence of this deliberate and most affectionate filial Preference that I read this Work, and Calamy's Historical Writings with so deep and so melancholy an Interest:[5] and I dare avow, that I cannot but regard as an ignorant Bigot every Man who (especially since the publicity & authentication of the Contents of the Stuart Papers, Memoirs & Life of James IInd &c)[6] can place the far later furious High Church Compilations & Stories of Walker & others in competition with the v~~e~~eracity & general Verity of Baxter & Calamy[7]—or forget that the great Body of Non-conformists to whom these great & good Men belong~~ing~~ed, were not Dissenters *from* the established Church, ~~willingly~~, but an orthodox ~~P~~ & numerous Portion *of* the Church.—Omitting then the wound received by Religion generally, under Henry 8th & the shameless secularizations clandestinely effected during Elizabeth's & the first James's Reign, I am disposed to consider the three following as

115[5] Edmund Calamy (1671–1723), nonconformist biographical historian, grandson of Edmund Calamy the elder (for whom see **83** n 1 and **110** n 1, above). Having assisted Sylvester in preparing Baxter's ms for publication, he published an abridgment of the *Reliquiae Baxterianae*, devoting ch 9— nearly half the book—to "A Particular Account of the Ministers, Lecturers, Fellows of Colledges, &c., who were silenced and ejected by the Act for Uniformity", consisting of a list of 2465 biographical sketches. For the Church of England response by Walker to Calamy's "Account" see **115** n 7, below. In 1713 Calamy issued a revised ed, and a further revision in 1727. On 18 May 1830 C began to read Calamy's *An Historical Account of My Own Life* (2 vols 1829): N 43 ff 76–75ᵛ.

115[6] *The Life of James the Second, King of England, &c.* "Collected out of memoirs writ of his own hand [by William Dicconson]. Together with the King's advice to his Son, and His Majesty's Will. Published from the original Stuart manuscripts...by the Rev. J. S. Clarke" (2 vols 1816).

115[7] In response to Edmund Calamy's "Account" (see **115** n 5, above), John Walker (1674–1747), Anglican ecclesiastical historian, collected information by query sheets for a corresponding list of deprived and sequestered clergymen. His book—*An Attempt Towards Recovering an Account of the Number and Sufferings of the Clergy of the Church of England ... Occasion'd by the Ninth Chapter of Dr. Calamy's Abridgment of the Life of Mr. Baxter*—published in folio in 1714, opened with a history of ecclesiastical affairs 1640–60 and then offered a list of 3334 names (without biographical sketches). In his preface he attacked Calamy and promised a detailed attack on Calamy's ch 9, but that was deferred and in the end was never published. Calamy treated with contempt Walker's abusive tone and his numerous errors, and in successive versions of his own "Account" quietly and diligently corrected his work from material supplied by both friends and enemies.

On "veracity" and "Verity" see **46** n 1, above.

the grand evil Epochs of ~~the~~ our present Church—1. The introduction (& after-predominance) of Latitudinarianism ⟨under the name
of⟩ Arminianism, & the *Spirit* of a conjoint *Romanism and

* i.e. Romanism or, if you please, Laudism or Lambethism in
Temporalities & Ceremonials, and of Socinianism in Doctrine, retaining the words but rejecting or interpreting-away the sense and substance of the Scriptural Mysteries.—This Spirit has ~~in~~ not indeed
manifested itself in the article of the Trinity, since Waterland gave
the death-blow to Arianism, & so left no alternative to the Clergy
but the actual Divinity or mere Humanity of our Lord[8]—& the
latter ~~it~~ would be too impudent an avowal for a Public Reader of our
Church Liturgy; but in the articles of Original Sin; the necessity of
Regeneration; ~~and~~ the necessity of Redemption in order to the
possibility of Regeneration; of Justification by Faith, and of prevenient and auxiliary Grace; all I can say with sincerity is, that our
Orthodoxy ~~is~~ seems so far in an *improving* & state, that I ⟨can⟩
hope for the time, when ⟨Churchmen will use the term,⟩ *Arminianism*,
~~will be regarded~~ as to express a habit of Belief opposed not to
Calvinism or the Works of Calvin, but to the Articles of our own
Church, and to the Doctrine in which *all* the first Reformers agreed.
—N.B. By Latitudinarianism I do not mean the particular tenets of
the Divines so called, such as D[r] H. More, Cudworth,[9] & their
Compeers, relative to Toleration, Comprehension, and the general
Belief that in the greater number of points then most controverted
the pious of all parties were far more nearly of the same mind than
their own imperfections and the imperfection of Language allowed
them to see. I mean the disposition to explain away the articles of
the Church on the pretext of their inconsistence with right Reason—
when in fact it was only an incongruity with a *Wrong Understanding*,
the faculty which S[t] Paul calls φρονημα σαρκος,[10] the rules of which

---

115[8] C refers to Daniel WATER-
LAND *A Vindication of Christ's
Divinity* (Cambridge 1719), one of two
Waterland books he annotated. See
also *CN* III 4321.

115[9] Henry More (1614–87) and
Ralph Cudworth (1617–88), both
"Cambridge Platonists". C annotated
MORE *The Theological Works* (1708),
Philosophical Poems (Cambridge 1647),
and the two pseudonymous works
*Observations upon "Anthroposophia
Theomagica"* (1650) and *The Second

Lash of Alazonomastix (Cambridge
1651). Cudworth's *True Intellectual
System of the Universe* (1678) was important to C from the early Bristol
days: see ARISTOPHANES tr Cary 1
n 1.

115[10] Rom 8.6–7. AV renders the
phrase "the carnal mind" and gives in
the margin as alternative "the minding of the flesh". In its frequent
Coleridgian use the phrase is perhaps
best translated, as he himself rendered
it in BLANCO WHITE *Letters* 1 and

Socinianism, ~~from~~ at the latter Half ⟨or towards the close⟩ of the reign of James the First. ⟨Montague, Laud & their confederates.⟩[12] 2. The ejection of the 2000 Ministers after the Restoration, with the other violences into which the Churchmen ~~were~~ made themselves the Dupes of Charles, James, ~~and~~ the Jesuits & the French Court. (Vide *Stuart Papers*).[13]—It was this that gave consistence and enduring strength to *Schism* in this Country, prevented the *pacation* of Ireland, and prepared for the separation of America at a far too early period for the true interests of either Country.—3. The surrender of the Right of taxing themselves,[14] & the Jacobitical Follies that combined with the former to put it in the power of the Whig Party to deprive the Church of her CONVOCATION—a bitter disgrace & wrong, to which most unhappily the People were rendered indifferent by the increasing Contrast of the Sermons of the Clergy from the Articles & Homilies of the Church;[15] but a wrong which already has avenged, & will sooner or later be seen to avenge, itself on the State & the governing Classes that continue this Boast of a short-sighted Policy—the same ⟨Policy,⟩ that in our own memory would have funded the Property of the Church, & by converting the Clergy into salaried Dependents on the Government pro tempore, have deprived the Establishment of its fairest Honor, that of being neither enslaved to the Court, nor to the Congregations—the same,

---

having been all abstracted from Objects of Sense (Finite in Time & Space) are logically applicable to Objects of the Sense alone. This I have elsewhere called the *Spirit* of Socinianism, which may work in many whose tenets are anti-socinian.[11]

---

in *AR* (1825) 231, "the mind of the flesh". But, depending on context, he used other versions—"the sensual understanding" in BÖHME **175** and *AR* (1825) 14, "the sensuous nature" in "*Prometheus*" (*LR* II 357), "the wisdom of the Flesh" in BÖHME **165**. In LEIGHTON *Genuine Works* (4 vols 1819) COPY B III 121, C noted that "φρόνημα σαρκός is 'the flesh'...in the act or habitude of minding". A long note in N 29 f 17, part of a detailed attack on Socinianism, is devoted to defining the Greek phrase (for which he suggests the Latin equivalent *intelligentia carnis*).

115[11] See *SM* (*CC*) 100: "It is not the *sect* of Unitarian Dissenters, but the *spirit* of Unitarianism in the members of the Established Church that alarms *me*." The relation between the Socinians as predecessors of the modern Unitarians is discussed in *SM* (*CC*) 111–12 n 5. For Socinianism see BAHRDT **1** n 1 and C's long footnote in *LS* (*CC*) 181–4.

115[12] Richard Montague (1577–1641), controversialist and bp of Chichester, was, like Laud, diligent in securing obedience to church discipline.

115[13] See **115** n 6, above.

115[14] See *C&S* (*CC*) 84.

115[15] On "the practical suppression of the CONVOCATION" by the Septennial Act, see *C&S* (*CC*) 99–100.

alas! which even now pays and patronizes a Board of Agriculture to undermine all ⟨landed⟩ property by a succession of false, shallow, and inflammatory Libels against the Tythes.—[16]

These are my weighed Sentiments: and fervently desiring (as I do) the perpetuity and prosperity of the Establishment, zealous for its rights and dignity, preferring its Forms, believing its Articles of Faith, and holding its Book of Common Prayer, ⟨and its translation of the Scriptures⟩ among my highest privileges as a Christian & an Englishman, I trust that I may both entertain and avow those sentiments without forfeiting any part of my claim to the name of a faithful member of the Church of England.　　　　　　S. T. Coleridge

Highgate—June 1820.

P.S.[a] As to Warburton's *Alliance of the Church and State* I object to the *Title* (Alliance) and to the matter and mode of the reasoning.[17] But the Interdependence of the Church and the State appears to me a Truth of the highest practical importance. Let but the Temporal Powers protect the subjects in their just rights as subjects merely: and I do not know of any one point, in which the Church has the right or the necessity to call in the Temporal Power as its ally, for any purpose *exclusively* ecclesiastic. The right of a Firm to dissolve its Partnership with any one Partner, breach of contract having been proved, and publicly to announce the same, is common to all men as social Beings.

116　p +4, possibly an addendum to **90**

Law is—Conclusio per regulam Generis singulorum in Genere isto inclusorum.[1] Now the Extremesa ~~are not included and the~~ and

---

[a] The "P.S." follows on the same line as the date but, being squeezed in between the signature and the opening of C's footnote, it was evidently written after the footnote

115[16] While he was writing *LS*, C read the Report of the Board of Agriculture for 1816 (*Agricultural State of the Kingdom in February, March and April, 1816*) and protested against the biased reports given by its members in attacking the system of tithes. See *LS* (*CC*) 213 n 1. See also *C&S* (*CC*) 161 and n 2.

115[17] William Warburton (1698–1779) *The Alliance Between Church and State* (1736). C seems to have known the book by Jun 1802 (*CL* II 802; there was a copy of the 1741 ed in WW's

library). As he was to show in *C&S*, C was opposed to Warburton's views on the relation between Church and State; in 1825 he examined in detail "The error, which 20 years ago I noted in Warburton's Alliance of Church & State" (N F° f 8); *CN* II 2440 of 9 Feb 1805 confirms the statement. See also *CN* II 2440n.

116[1] "A conclusion drawn by the rule of a Class of individuals included in that Class"—i.e. a conclusion drawn in accordance with the rule that what is true of a class of individual things is

Inclusa, are contradictory terms. There⟨fore⟩ Extreme Cases are not capable Subjects of Law a priori—but must proceed on knowlege of the Past, and anticipation of the Future, and the fulfilment of the anticipation is the proof, because the only possible determination, of the accuracy of the Knowlege. In other words, the Agents may be condemned or honored according to their intentions, and the apparent source of their motives; (so we honor Brutus) but the extreme case itself is tried by the Event.—

true of each one of the individuals in that class. See above, **90** at n 1. The truncated version in **90** is even more difficult to translate: "through the class of the individual included in the class". No such phrase turns up in the standard logic books, perhaps because the principle is so obvious as to be almost tautological.

FRANCIS BEAUMONT

c 1585–1616

JOHN FLETCHER

1579–1625

The plays of Beaumont and Fletcher may first have come to C's attention through a letter from Lamb in Jun 1796: "I can't help thinking there is a greater richness of poetical fancy [in Beaumont and Fletcher] than in any one, Shakespeare excepted." *LL* I 28–9; cf 31, 73. C said in Feb 1804 that he intended to read through "Ben Johnson, Beaumont & Fletcher, & Massinger" in order to "prove what of Shakespere belonged to his Age, & was common to all the *first-rate* men of that true Saeculum aureum of English Poetry, and what is his own, & his only". *CL* II 1054. The marginalia on Beaumont and Fletcher are closely related to C's various series of literary lectures, the notes in Lamb's copy (COPY A) being written in 1811 or earlier, and on his own set (COPY B) in 1815 and later. When C lectured on Shakespeare he often discussed Beaumont and Fletcher and Jonson— and sometimes Massinger—as a basis for critical comparison in establishing the quality, stature, and independence of Shakespeare's genius and artistic judgement. See e.g. *CL* V 25–6. Although he hoped that "I shall not ... shew myself blind to the various merits of Jonson, Fletcher, and Massinger, or insensible of the greatness of the merits which they possess in common" (*Misc C* 42), his general critical assessment in 1818 may well have been formed ten years earlier: "The plays of Beaumont and Fletcher are mere aggregations without unity; in the Shakespearian drama there is a vitality which grows and evolves itself from within—a key note which guides and controls the harmonies throughout." *LR* I 104 (*Misc C* 44).

For the distribution of marginal notes in the two copies, see "Index to the Marginalia" following. In the later years C said that he most admired and enjoyed *Monsieur Thomas, The Little French Lawyer, Rollo,* and *The Beggar's Bush. TT* 24 Jun 1827, 17 Feb 1833. In c Oct–Nov 1806 he intended some project based on *Thierry and Theodoret* (*CN* II 2931); in Mar 1810 he quoted from *Love's Pilgrimage,* a play not marked in either of the annotated copies (*CN* III 3736); in 1815 he proposed to rewrite *The Pilgrim* and *The Beggar's Bush* for the London stage (*CL* IV 599; cf 590–1).

C was well aware of the corrupt state of the Beaumont and Fletcher text and of the formidable task of setting it to rights: "The confusion is now so great, the errors so enormous, that the editor must use a boldness quite unallowable in any other case." *TT* 15 Mar 1834; cf 17 Feb 1833. For C and Lamb on the problem of assigning authorship to the 53 Beaumont and Fletcher plays see COPY A headnote.

SPECIAL ABBREVIATIONS. In the editor's notes the following abbreviations refer to later collective editions:

"Bowers"—*The Dramatic Works in the Beaumont and Fletcher Canon* gen ed Fredson Bowers, Vols I, II (Cambridge 1966, 1970). In progress.

"G & W"—*Beaumont and Fletcher* ed Arnold Glover (Vol I), Arnold Glover and A. R. Waller (Vol II), A. R. Waller (Vols III–X) (10 vols Cambridge 1905–12).

"Variorum"—*The Works of Francis Beaumont and John Fletcher: Variorum Edition* (4 vols 1904–12). The series was not completed. The plays correspond with G & W volume-for-volume except that *The False One* and *The Little French Lawyer* in G & W III appear in Variorum IV. (This ed quotes some of the marginalia in COPY B.)

INDEX TO THE MARGINALIA

	COPY A	COPY B
The Beggar's Bush		36A
The Bloody Brother (Rollo)	5–7	58–59
Bonduca		
The Captain		
The Chances		
The Coronation		66A–68
The Coxcomb		
Cupid's Revenge		
The Custom of the Country		27–28
The Double Marriage		
The Elder Brother		29–32
The Fair Maid of the Inn		71–72
The Faithful Shepherdess		
The False One		
Four Plays ... in One		
The Honest Man's Fortune		77A
The Humorous Lieutenant		37–39
The Island Princess		
A King and No King		20A–21
The Knight of the Burning Pestle		
The Knight of Malta		
The Laws of Candy	1	46–47
The Little French Lawyer		51–52
Love's Cure		
Love's Pilgrimage		
The Lover's Progress		
The Loyal Subject		41–42
The Mad Lover		40
The Maid in the Mill		
The Maid's Tragedy		12–20
A Masque at Grays-Inn		
Monsieur Thomas		
The Nice Valour		

Copy A

Fifty Comedies and Tragedies. Written by Francis Beaumont and John Fletcher, Gentlemen. All in one volume. Published by the authors original copies, the songs to each play being added, &c. 2 pts (in 1 vol). London 1679. F°.

British Museum C 45 i 7

Charles Lamb's copy. Inscribed on the title-page: "perlegi hunc Librum 29 die Decembrii 1700"; and at the head of i 1 in an early hand, scribbled over: "C. H. Kirke". Heraldic bookplate of "John Washer of Lincoln's Inn Esqre" on p ‾2.

At the head of i 63 is the signature "Martin Charles Burney". Martin Charles Burney (c 1788–1852), son of Capt (later Admiral) James Burney, was known to Lamb as early as Jul 1803 (*LL* i 357), and in Jan 1829 Lamb described him to Barry Cornwall as "on the top scale of my friendship ladder" (*LL* iii 202). In 1818 Lamb dedicated the first volume (poetry) of his *Works* to C, the second (prose) to Martin Burney with a sonnet. This copy of Beaumont and Fletcher may have been given to Burney before or after Lamb's death. Lieut-Col Francis Cunningham (1820–75), son of Allan Cunningham and editor of Massinger and Jonson, bought it at Sotheby's in Nov 1870, with five other folios, for 8s 6d. A long note, unsigned, written by Cunningham on p ‾1, states that this is the copy of Beaumont and Fletcher described in "Old China" and used by Lamb in preparing his *Specimens of English Dramatic Poetry* (1808). The Sotheby catalogue entry is pasted to the same page, together with the relevant extract from "Old China" (cut from the *London Magazine* of Mar 1823). When Cunningham bought the volume it was "in a desperately tattered state"; he had it rebacked with the original boards. In 1930 the volume was comprehensively repaired by the BM.

Lamb's textual emendations and pencil marks for transcribing appear throughout the volume; a list in Cunningham's hand of Lamb's major textual emendations is pasted to p $^{+}$5 (p–d). On Pt i sig A1^{v} Lamb has copied out in ink, at the end of "The Bookseller's to the Reader", Beaumont's *An Epitaph upon My Dear Brother, Francis Beaumont*. He has also written short notes on i 386 and ii 31; and on *Bonduca* remarked that "the red beard" is "Judas's colour in the tapestries"—a note *Misc C* ascribes to C.

Lamb was interested to some extent in the problem of assigning authorship to the 53 plays in the 1679 folio. On p [x] of his own copy he noted: "Those marked — the only ones certainly written jointly, the rest by Fletcher", and marked six titles in this way; he also noted beside the title of *The Coronation* "Shirley claims this", and beside the title of *A Masque* "by Beaumont". C, however, was not interested in this question beyond trying (not very hard) to detect Shakespeare's hand in *Two Noble Kinsmen*: "Beaumont and Fletcher … here and henceforward I take as one Poet, with two names ... ". BM Add MS 34225 ff 57ᵛ–62: *Misc C* 42.

DATE. Oct 1811: see **13**.

THE LAWS OF CANDY

1 i 314

This Play has (to my feelings) a defect which is uncommon in B. and F. It is not even *entertaining*. The Story is as dull, as the ~~incidents~~ characters are unnatural and the incidents improbable & revolting./ The diction indeed is perhaps purer & more simple than in several other of the Dramas; but there are fewer poetic lines and passages, & such as there are or were intended to be such seem to me an old coat new turned, ~~the~~ mere parodies of the same thoughts & passions better exprest in their other plays—as Cassilane's Harangues, for instance—compared with Memnon in the Mad Lover, Archas in the Loyal Subject with Theodore, & with Caratach in Bonduca.—It is remarkable, that Fletcher so exquisite in his Comedies, should so universally fail in all the Comic Scenes of his Tragedies. They not only do not re-act upon & finally *fuse* with, the tragic Interest, an excellence peculiar to Shakespere & Hogarth (See Lamb's Essay on Hogarth, in the Reflector)[1] but they are dull & filthy in themselves—

VALENTINIAN

2 i 380 | V ii 30–1

EMPEROR. *Danubius*
　I'le have brought through my body.

It is strange, that a man of Genius should have thought it worth while to steal, in this parody line, the rants of Shakespere's poisoned King John.[1]

1[1] Lamb's essay "On the Genius and Character of Hogarth" was first published in Leigh Hunt's *The Reflector* II No 3 (article viii) in 1811. See also *CN* III 4096n. C and Lamb must have discussed the comparison of Hogarth with Shakespeare; when C was reading Beaumont and Fletcher he thought of Lamb's essay, and Lamb in his essay repeats what C had to say about Hogarth in *Friend* No 16 (*CC*) II 213. In Thomas FULLER *History* **2** C grouped Hogarth with Shakespeare,

Milton, Fuller, and Defoe, saying "these are Genera, containing each only one Individual".

2[1] "Parody" in the sense of a weak imitation; C uses the word in the same sense in **1** and **8**. Shakespeare's King John, dying of poison, cried:

Poison'd—ill fare;—dead, forsook, cast off;
And none of you will bid the winter come
To thrust his icy fingers in my maw;
Nor let my kingdom's rivers take
　their course

3 i 384, written at the end of the play

A noble subject for the few noble minds capable of treating it would be this: What are the probable, what the possible defects, of *Genius* —& of each given *Sort* of Genius? And of course, what defects are psychologically impossible? This would comprize—what Semblance of *Genius* can *Talent* supply? And what *Talent*, united with strong feeling for poetry & aided by Taste & Judgement? and how are the effects to be distinguished from those of Genius?—Lastly, what degree of Talent may be produced by an intense desire of the End (ex. gr. to be and to be thought, a Poet) without any natural, more than general, aptitude for the means?—[1]

4 i 384–5, beginning below **3** in the space at the end of the play

Be it not presumptuous or taken as a proof of Self-conceit, I will affirm that no man can have formed a just idea of ⟨possible⟩ *tragic* Drama, as opposed to ~~to~~ possible *comic* Drama, & not find in this Trag. of Valent. a convincing proof, that the Writer was utterly in-capable of Tragedy—and that such instances ad contra, as may be brought, must be attributed to lucky Imitation of Shakespere, tho' blind to the *essential* excellence (which easily may be notwithstand-ing the mind is struck with *accidental* beauties) of what he has imita-ted.—In short, I scarcely recollect any scene or passage in B. & F. that is ~~very~~ exclusively tragic, that is not in a higher degree poetic— i.e. capable of being narrated by the Poet in his own person in the same words, with strict adherence to the character of the Poet.— There is a kind of Comedy which whoever produces, must be capable of Tragedy (Cervantes, Shakespere)[1]—but there is another kind, & that too highly amusing, which is quite heterogeneous. Of this Latter Fletcher was a great master.—The surface & all its flowers & open pleasures, serious or light, ~~was~~ere his Property—all his eye can see, ear hear—nothing more.

Through my burn'd bosom; nor entreat the north
To make his bleak winds kiss my parched lips
And comfort me with cold....

King John v vii 35–41. See also COPY B **5** textus.

3[1] For C's frequent distinction between genius and talent in poetry, see e.g. *CN* III 3415 (1809), *BL* ch 11

(1907) I 153, *CL* IV 667 (1816), *TT* 21 May 1830, 20 Aug 1833; and BEAU-MONT & FLETCHER COPY B **65**.

4[1] On Miguel de Cervantes Saaved-ra (1547–1616), whose *Don Quixote* C had read as a youth and came to admire as a work of genius comparable to Shakespeare, see 1818 Literary Lecture VIII in *LR* I 113–31. Cf *CN* III 4503 and n.

THE BLOODY BROTHER
[THE TRAGEDY OF ROLLO]

5　i 432 | II i 91–5

[Latorch, "Rollo's earwig", though patently a villain, gives Rollo, Duke of Normandy, comprehensive counsel, which closes with such encouragements as "Now you go right, Sir, now your eyes are open" and "Now y'are a man, Sir."]

Tho' Single Facts in History would poorly justify a Poet's introduction of anomalous Varieties, accidental monsters, Lusus Naturæ[1]— were it only that they cannot represent an *Idea*, and whatever is not ideal (i.e. partaking of the τό καθολὸν)[2] cannot be poetry.[3] Yet even in *genuine* History, such as Froissard, Comines &c[4] I remember no instance of Villains talking to their Sovereigns, in the character of Counsellors, as professed Villains.

6　i 433 | II i 64–74

LATORCH. . . . can this toucht Lyon . . .
　　But when ambition whets him, and time fits him,
　　Leap to his prey, and seiz'd once, suck your heart out?
　　Do you make it conscience?
*] ROLLO. Conscience, *Latorch*, what's that?
LATORCH. A fear they tye up fools in, natures coward,
　　Palling the blood, and chilling the full spirit
　　With apprehension of meer clouds and shadows.
ROLLO. I know no conscience, nor I fear no shadows.

[*] That men have reasoned thus to themselves after a guilty deed in order to blunt the sting of Remorse, I doubt not; but that it is

5[1] "Sports, freaks of nature".

5[2] "The universal"—C's usual error, for the adverbial καθόλου. C may here be recalling Aristotle's *Poetics* 1451[b]5–10, the well-known comparison between poetry and history.

5[3] C made this statement again in 1815 more deliberately, connecting it with the authority of Aristotle. *BL* ch 17 (1907) II 33–4. The record of C's lectures from 1808 to 1818 suggests that his definition of poetry developed around his inquiry into the relation between parts and whole, pleasure and

truth, and in general the reconciliation of opposites: see e.g. *Sh C* I 147–50, II 68. Clear Aristotelian premisses, of which this annotation is an early instance, seem to have come to the forefront of C's mind when he was working out his critique of WW in detail in *BL* ch 22.

5[4] For C's early use of Froissart in the translation of John Bourchier, Baron Berners, see *CN* I 1075 and cf *BL* ch 3 (1907) I 42n. He annotated Lamb's copy of *The History of Philip de Commines* (1674).

natural to reason thus as an inducement to perpetrate a crime, I find no evidence in History of my own experience of Men, no dim presentiment, no *germ* of its possibility in my own Heart.

7 i 433 | II ii 53–64, the Drinking Song

> *Drink to day and drown all sorrow,*
> *You shall perhaps not do it to morrow.*
> *Best while you have it use your breath,*
> *There is no drinking after death.*
>
> *Wine works the heart up, wakes the wit,*
> *There is no cure 'gainst age but it.*
> *It helps the head-ach, cough and tissick,*
> *And is for all diseases Physick.*
>
> *Then let us swill boyes for our health,*
> *Who drinks well, loves the common-wealth.*
> *And he that will to bed go sober,*
> *Falls with the leaf still in October.*

This is the original of the excellent Song, "Punch cures the Gout, the Colic, and the Phthysic"/ the Imitation is an Improvement.[1]

THE PROPHETESS

8 i 578, written at the end of the play

Were I to choose a play, that most realized the Ideal of Anti-Shakesperianism, I should fix, I think, on this: tho' perhaps half a dozen others of the same writer might be perilous Competitors. A witch, possessed of all powers & comprizing in herself all the Gods; yet ~~an aunt~~ an every-day old Aunt, only a Witch, ~~that~~ but by whose powers no one knows—working neither for good or for evil, but to secure her *Niece* a reluctant Husband—& all the rest, pasteboard puppets, ducking head, lifting arms, & sprawling legs, as she pulls the thread—nothing from within, all from without—sincere conversions to Virtue produced in an instant by unmanly terrors—no characters, no men, no women—but only mouthing Vices, or inter-

---

[1] *Come, Landlord, Fill a Flowing Bowl.* The third verse, as given in *The Frisky Songster* (which C used as early as 1798), runs:

Brandy cures the gout,
The colic, and the phthisic,
So it is to all men
The very best of physic.

locutory Entia Narrationis[1]—Explanations personified by Hat, Coat, Waistcoat, & Breeches—of course, no *Interest* (for a vulgar curiosity about—not what is to *happen* next—but about what the Witch will *do* next, whether Thunder or a Brimstone She Devil, or an Earthquake[a] ⟨cannot be called *Interest*—⟩)—Miserable parodies & thefts of fine Lines in Shakespere—and the compound, a senseless Day-dream, with all the wildness without any of the terror of a Night-mair—in short, Stupidity from malice (of self-conceit) prepense aping Madness. The proper compliment is to open one's mouth in *wonder* and lo! it ɪt was only a Yawn!

THE QUEEN OF CORINTH

9 ii 6, heavily cancelled in ink | ɪɪ i 1–7

!!! *Enter* Merione (as newly ravished).[b]

MERIONE. To whom now shall I cry? What pow'r thus kneel to?
And beg my ravisht honor back upon me
Deaf, dead, you gods of goodness, deaf to me,
Deaf Heaven to all my cries; deaf hope, deaf justice,
I am abus'd, and you, that see all, saw it;
Saw it, and smil'd upon the villain did it:
Saw it, and gave him strength . . .

OH! OH! by reading Shakespere our fancies are duped into love and admiration of his age! Yet read B. & F.—and feel how gross how [. . .]!—and (Enter Merione newly ravished [. . .][c]

10 ii 6 | ɪɪ i 22–41

Enter Theanor, Crates, *with vizards.*

MERIONE. My shame still follows me, and still proclaims me;
He turns away in scorn, I am contemned too,
A more unmanly violence than the other;
Bitten, and flung away? What e'r you are
Sir, you that have abus'd me, and now most basely
And sacrilegiously robb'd this fair Temple,

---

a CA reads "earwigmaker", perhaps with "Rollo's earwig" in mind; but "Earthquake" is clear in the ms
b Below the printed direction "*Enter* Merione (*as newly ravished*)" C has written out the same words
c About 30 words obliterated and illegible

8[1] "Creatures of the Story". Cf C's use of "ventriloquist" in COPY B 66. In his account of "sentimental" drama he said: "one author distri-butes his own insipidity among the characters, if characters they can be called, which have no marked and distinguishing features". *Sh C* ɪɪ 124.

I fling all these behind me, but look upon me,
But one kind loving look, be what ye will,
So from this hour you will be mine, my Husband;
And you his hand in mischief, I speak to you too,
Counsel him nobly now; you know the mischief,
The most unrighteous act he has done, perswade him,
Perswade him like a friend, knock at his Conscience
Till fair Repentance follow: yet be worthy of me,
And show your self, if ever good thought guided ye;
You have had your foul will; make it yet fair with marriage;
Open your self and take me, wed me now: [*Draws his Dagger.*
More fruits of villany? your Dagger? come
Ye are merciful, I thank you for your medicine:
Is that too worthy too?

Exquisite specimen of the Μισητεον σubstituted for the φοβερον![1]

11   ii 8 | ɪɪ iii 196–9

QUEEN. If all the Art I have, or power can do it,
He shall be found, and such a way of justice
Inflicted on him: A Lady wrong'd in my Court,
And this way rob'd, and ruin'd?

O flat! flat! flat! Sole! Flounder! Pla[i]ce! all stinking! stinking flat![1]

12   ii 8 | ɪɪɪ 207–16

[MERIONE expresses her gratitude to Agenor.]
     I kneel and thank ye, Sir,
And I must say ye are truly honourable:
And dare confess my Will, yet still a Virgin;
But so unfit and weak a Cabinet
To keep your love and virtue in am I now,
That have been forc'd and broken, lost my lustre,
I mean this body, so corrupt a Volume

10[1] "The Hateful substituted for the fearful!" The contrast φόβερον/μισητέον was probably suggested by the contrast δεινὸν (terrible)/μισητόν in Longinus § 9, as noted by HNC in *LR* ɪ 166 (in which HNC has probably altered C's Greek to match Longinus' text). C regularly used the form μισητεόν= "to be hated"—a stronger word than Longinus's μισητόν= "hated". C used these contrasting terms in COPY B **49** (in English, at n 4) and **58** (in Greek and English), in his notes on William Blake's *Songs* (*CL* ɪv 836, corrected from ms), and in the 1818 Literary Lectures (*LR* ɪ 166).

11[1] For a similar comment see ANNUAL ANTHOLOGY **15**.

For you to study goodness in, and honor,
I shall intreat your Grace, confer that happiness
Upon a beauty sorrow never saw yet ...

this is pretty; but it is false, & made up of incompatibles./ natural feelings, & abstract notions, wch being, such feelings can not exist.*

13   ii 9, written as though a footnote to **12**

* N.B. I ~~shall will~~ not be long here, Charles!—& gone, you will not mind my having spoiled a book in order to leave a Relic.
        S. T. C.—   Octr 1811.—¹
        ⟨ *W. W.* ⟩²

13¹ On 1 May 1821 Lamb, writing a note to C to accept an invitation to Highgate, added a curious postscript: "Extract from a MS. note of S. T. C. in my Beaumont and Fletcher, dated April 17th 1807. '*Midnight*. God bless you, dear Charles Lamb, I am dying; I feel I have not many weeks left.'" *LL* II 295. No such note is now in Lamb's copy of Beaumont and Fletcher, but the circumstantiality of an exact date, and the fact that C did suffer a sudden and alarming illness on the night of 17–18 Apr 1807 (*CL* III 11), suggest that Lamb was transcribing a note from this book—whether written in some now perished part of that ruinous volume, or part of a note written on a loose paper inserted in the book, it is now impossible to guess. In Feb 1808 DW reported that C had written to RS that he thought he was dying (*WL—M2—*I 197; cf 188, 198, 200), and two notebook entries repeat C's presentiment (*CN* III 3273, 3276). The same thought hovered in his mind in late 1809 when he was assessing his library (*CN* III 3656). "I shall soon die", he wrote in a notebook in Apr 1811 (*CN* III 4071), and on 2 May 1811 he wrote in Lamb's copy of Donne's *Poems* a note very much like this one in Beaumont and Fletcher (Donne *Poems* **61**)—all three of them at a time when his morbid suspicion of the Wordsworths was inducing him to write the bitter letters that eventually brought WW to London in the spring of 1812. There may be a connexion between the word "Relic" in this note and Donne's poem *The Relique*; see Introduction, above, p cxxi and n.

13² The initials could be "W. N.", but the reading "W. W." given by *CA* and *Misc C* is visually possible. WW was in London from 20 Apr to early Jun 1812, trying through the mediation of Lamb and HCR to resolve the bitter quarrel between himself and C. It is just conceivable that Lamb showed WW the note written in Oct 1811 as evidence of C's illness and dismay during the long crisis of 1811, and that WW initialled it perhaps as a token of his genuine desire to resolve their difficulties.

Copy B

The Dramatic Works of ... Beaumont and Fletcher ... from the text, and with the notes of the late George Colman, Esq, &c. Vols II–IV (of 4) [of *The Dramatic Works of Ben Jonson, and Beaumont and Fletcher*]. London 1811. 8º.

"Printed for John Stockdale", and referred to as the "Stockdale Edition". *The Dramatic Works of Ben Jonson* are confined to Vol I. Through an error in binding, the forepages referring to Beaumont & Fletcher that belong in Vol II have been bound in Vol I of this set between "The Life of Ben Jonson" and "The Preface" to Jonson's plays. The Contents leaf in Vol II reads "VOLUME THE FIRST"—i.e. of Beaumont & Fletcher—but the Contents leaves of Vols III and IV read "VOLUME THE THIRD/FOURTH".

British Museum C 126 i 1

Inscribed by C on a front flyleaf in each vol: "S. T. Coleridge 29 March. 1815. Calne, Wilts. £4,,10". "S. T. C." label on the title-page of each vol.
  A short note on II 245 and on III 77 may be in J. J. Morgan's hand. In the Contents page three consecutive titles are marked with a pencil stroke, possibly by C: *The Elder Brother, The Spanish Curate,* and *Wit Without Money*.

CONTENTS of the forepages belonging to Vol II but bound in error in Vol I. p [i] "Players' dedication. (Folio, 1647.)"; [ii]–iii "Mr. Shirley's preface"; [iv]–v "Stationer's address. (Folio, 1647.)"; [vi] "Booksellers' address. (Folio, 1679.)"; [viii]–xix "Preface [to Beaumont and Fletcher]. Giving some account of the authors and their writings. (Octavo, 1711.)"; xx–l "Mr. Seward's preface" (notes 1–7); [li]–lxxxvii "Commendatory poems [to Beaumont and Fletcher]" (note 8); lxxxviii–xc "Upon an honest man's fortune. By Mr. John Fletcher"; [xci]–xciii "Letter [in verse] from Beaumont to Ben Jonson"; [xciv] "Names of the principal actors who performed in Beaumont and Fletcher's plays"; [xcv]–cii "Preface to Beaumont and Fletcher"; [ciii]–civ "Extract [from Capell's Notes on Shakespeare's *Antony and Cleopatra*]".

DATE. 1815, after Mar (a few notes); the others c late 1817 to spring 1819.
  The purchase of the volumes in Mar 1815 was perhaps connected with C's hope of repeating the success of *Remorse* by making an entertaining adaptation of *The Pilgrim* and *The Beggar's Bush*. The title of a similar project, "Diadestè", written on a flyleaf of Vol II (9), tends to confirm this conjecture. In early Oct 1815 C was telling Daniel Stuart about this project (*CL* IV 590) and on 15 Oct made definite overtures about it to Byron (*CL* IV 598–9, 601n, 605). He received no encouragement for the scheme, and since there are only two short notes on *The Pilgrim* and none on *The Beggar's Bush* it seems unlikely that C wrote more than a few marginalia in this copy in 1815. The first proof-sheets of *BL* arrived in

Calne early in Oct 1815 (*CL* IV 593), and C had *The Faithful Shepherdess*
"open before me" while he was proof-reading ch 2 (*BL*—1907—I 33);
but no note is written on that play in COPY B. The marginalia in COPY B
seem to belong to the preparation for his most successful series of fourteen
literary lectures Jan–Mar 1818. Lecture VII, 17 Feb 1818, was advertised
as "On Ben Jonson, Beaumont and Fletcher, and Massinger ..."; but
as in the earlier series this was "not primarily a lecture on Shakespeare's
contemporaries, but a lecture on Shakespeare himself, illustrated by comparisons with Jonson, Beaumont and Fletcher, and Massinger". *Sh C* II
242, 247. C seems to have stopped writing marginalia on COPY B after
preparing the Feb–Mar 1819 lectures.

1   I xxi, pencil | Seward's Preface, 1750

The King and No King too is extremely spirited in all its characters;
Arbaces holds up a mirror to all men of *virtuous principles*, but
!!] *violent passions*. Hence he is as it were at once *magnanimity* and
pride, *patience* and *fury*, *gentleness* and *rigor*, *chastity* and *incest*,
and is one of the finest mixtures of virtues and vices that any poet
has drawn, except the Hotspur of Shakespeare, and the *impiger*,
iracundus, *inexorabilis Acer*, of Homer.... Bessus and his two
Swordsmen in this play are infinitely the liveliest comic characters of
!!] mere bragging cowards which we have in our language; and if
!!] they do not upon the whole equal the extensive and inimitable
humours of Falstaff and his *companions*, they leave all other characters
of the same species even Shakespeare's own Parolles far behind
them.

These are among the endless instances of the abject state, ~~in~~ to which
Psychology had sunk from the Reign of Charles the I—to the middle
of the present reign—George 3ʳᵈ—& even now it is but awaking—[1]

2   I xxvi, pencil

As Shakespeare did not study *versification* so much as those poets
who were conversant in Homer and Virgil, I do not remember in
him any striking instance of this species of beauty.

mad, Mʳ Seward! you were mad, or ignorant!

3   I xxx, pencil

[Seward compared Julia's speech in *Two Gentlemen of Verona* IV iv
163—"Madam, 'twas Ariadne passioning, | For Theseus' perjury
and unjust flight"—with Aspatia's speech in *The Maid's Tragedy*

---

[1] Cf *CN* III 3372 (9–19 Sept 1808), and BAXTER *Reliquiae* COPY B 32.

II ii 68 etc—"I stand upon the sea-beach now"—and preferred the latter.]

It is strange, to take an incidental Passage of one Writer, intended only for a subordinate part, and compare it with the same Thought in another Writer, who had chosen it for a prominent and principal Figure.

4 I xxx–xxxi, pencil

ASPATIA. . . . Do it again by me the lost Aspatia,
    And you shall find all true.—Put me' on th' wild island.

[Seward's note gives the reading of four quartos, the folio, and late octavo:]

> *And you shall find all true but the wild island.*
> *I stand upon the sea-beach now, and think . . .*

[Seward's emendation is given in the text.]

The old Reading is beyond doubt the right one. The Maiden could not imagine the bedroom a wild Island; but She might easily imagine Aspasia as Ariadne.—The words "I stand &c" evidently means to support the preceding "*but*"—viz. *Suppose* me on the Sea-beach—/ or far rather, you must substitute the Sea-beach & its scenery for the room/ all else you may copy—& that very copying of me, as Ariadne, will so influence your imagination, that you will give a corresponding character to the mere figures of your Invention/[1]

5 I xxxii, pencil

[Seward prefers the death of the poisoned Emperor in *Valentinian* V ii and the poisoned Alphonso's sufferings in *A Wife for a Month* IV i to the death of King John from poison in Shakespeare's *King John* V vii 35–43.]

Mr Seward! Mr Seward! You may be & I trust you *are*, an Angel; but you *were* an Ass.[1]

6 I xxxiii, pencil

Every reader of <u>taste</u> will see how superior this [quotation from *A Wife for a Month* IV i] is to the quotation from Shakespeare.

of what Taste?

4[1] Variorum, G & W, and Bowers all accept "the old reading" of *The Maid's Tragedy* II ii 67.

5[1] For further complaints against Seward see **21**, **31**, **32**, **42**, **60**; and against the edition in general see **40**, **44**.

7 i xl, pencil

[Seward's classification of the plays according to relative excellence.]
These 4 should surely have been placed in the very first Class/[1]—
But the whole attempt ends in a woful Failure.

8 i lxxiv, pencil | John Harris's commendatory poem *On the Death and Works of Mr. John Fletcher*

> *I'd have a state of wit convok'd, which hath*
> *A power to take up on common faith . . .*

This is an instance of that modifying of quantity by Emphasis, without wch our elder Poets can not be scanned—"Power" here instead of being one – (Pow'r) must be not indeed – –, nor – ᴗ; but –ᴗ/ ᴗ /—. The first syllable is 1¼.[1]

9 ii ⁻3

Diadestè[1]

10 ii ⁻2

We can never expect an authentic Edition of our elder *dramatic writers Poets* (for in their times a Drama was a Poem) until some man devotes undertakes the work, who has studied the philosophy of metre. This has been found the main Torch of sound Restoration in the Greek Dramatists by Bentley, Porson, and their followers:[1]

7[1] C has identified them by his marks in Seward's list: in Seward's Class ii, *Monsieur Thomas, The Chances, The Beggar's Bush*; and in Class iv, *The Pilgrim*. Seward classified all these as comedies.

8[1] The scansion applies to the words "power to take". By raising the mark for the first short syllable C indicates the extension of the word "power" with a lighter emphasis than the following short syllable "to".

9[1] The title "*Diadestè the Arabia Rite*" also appears in N 16 f 36ᵛ (c Apr 1815); the history of the project and meaning of the title are fully discussed in *CN* iii 4245n. Among the five items outlined to Byron c 25 Oct 1815 as "connected with Theatre" it appears as "3. An entertainment in two acts—the Scene in Arabia—First act finished, & the Songs for the second".

CL iv 606. Of the two existing drafts of *Diadestè*, the one at VCL may belong to 1815 (see *CN* ii 2629n and cf *CN* i 1723n), the other—BM Add MS 34225 ff 36–45—is written on the back of printed notices of the 1818 literary lectures, is entitled "Diadestè, an entertainment in one Act", and is set in "Arabian Landscape (for which consult Thalaba & the notes to it)— Sand Hills in the Distance—Groves of Arabian Trees in the immediate Vicinity—& Tent . . .".

10[1] Richard Bentley (1662–1742) and Richard Porson (1759–1808) both made notable discoveries about the metrics of Greek drama, Bentley of the metrical continuity of the anapaestic system and Porson of the rules of the iambic trimeter, one of which is still called Porson's Law. On Bentley's discovery of the application of the

how much more then in our own Tongue!—It is true, that *Quantity*, an almost iron Law with the Greek, is in our language rather a subject for a peculiarly fine ear, than any law or even rule—but then we instead of it have first, Accent, ~~then~~ 2^ndly^ emphasis, and lastly, retardation & acceleration of the Times of Syllables according to the meaning of the words, the passion that accompanies them, and even the Character of the Person that uses them.—With due attention to these, above all ⟨to⟩ that, which requires the most attention & the finest taste, the last; Massinger, *ex. gr.* might be reduced to a rich and yet regular metre.[2] But then the Regulæ must be first known—tho' I will venture to say, that he who does not find a Line (not corrupted) of Massinger's flow to the *Time total* of an Iambic Pentameter Hyperacatalectic, i.e. four Iambics ($\cup$ –) and an Amphibrach ($\cup$ – $\cup$) has not read it aright.—By power of this last principle (ret. and accel. of time) we have even Proceleusmatics and Dispondœuses[a]—proceleusmatics ($\cup$ $\cup$ $\cup$ $\cup$) and Dispondœuses (– – – –) not to mention the Choriambics, the Ionics, the Pæons and the Epitrites.—Since Dryden the metre of our Poets leads to the Sense: in our elder and more genuine Poets the Sense, including the Passion, leads to the metre.—⟨Read even Donne's Satires as he meant them to be read and as the sense & passion demand, and you will find ⟨in⟩ the lines a manly harmony.⟩[3]

---

a Here the writing has reached the foot of the page. At the head of the page C has written: "~~we have e~~ *from the bottom of the page*" and then continued the note

---

extinct letter *digamma* see H. Coleridge 4 n 1. C annotated a copy of Francis Wrangham's anonymous *Life of Richard Bentley* [1816]. Outstanding among Porson's various achievements were his masterly editions of four Euripides plays (1797–1801). C. J. Blomfield, one of Porson's followers as a textual critic, published a critical edition of Aeschylus *Prometheus* in Cambridge in 1810, using as a tribute to Porson types cut from Porson's handwriting—types that for more than a century and a half have been one of the peculiar graces of English classical and biblical studies: see Aeschylus *Prometheus*. As an undergraduate C had had some personal acquaintance with Porson, who was a fellow of Trinity and examiner for the Craven Scholarship when C was a

candidate: see *CL* i 44–5, 138, iv 803. When C met Porson in Oct 1806 he was distressed that "he took no notice of me, not even by an act of common civility". *CN* ii 2894. But he was indignant when, in 1830, *The Devil's Thoughts* and *The Two Round Spaces* were ascribed to Porson—"the tersest of Writers". *CL* vi 830. See also 36 and n 1, below.

10[2] C often mentioned Philip Massinger in his lectures on the drama and admired particularly his prosodic mastery: see esp *CN* iii 4212; cf *CN* iii 3445, *Sh C* 123, *Misc C* 42. For a small group of comments on Massinger see *C 17th C* 674–8.

10[3] See Donne *Poems*—esp 1, 24, 27—for C's comments on Donne's versification, now almost a staple of twentieth-century criticism. His con-

11 ɪɪ [7], pencil | Life of John Fletcher

In general their plots are more regular than Shakespeare's . . .

This is true, if true at all, only before a Court of Criticism which judges one scheme by the Laws of another and diverse. Shakespear's Plots have their own laws or regulæ—and according to these they are *regular*.[1]

THE MAID'S TRAGEDY

12 ɪɪ 1 | ɪ i 7–11

STRATO. As well as masque can be.

LYSIPPUS. As masque can be?

STRATO. Yes; they must commend their king, and speak in praise of the assembly; bless the bride and bridegroom, in person of some god: They're ty'd to rules of flattery.

> As well as masque *can* be.—Masque can be? Yes!
> They must commend the King and speak in praise
> Of the assembly, bless the Bride and Bridegroom
> In person of some God. They're tied to rules
> Of Flattery.—

But the metrical arrangement is most slovenly throughout.

13 ɪɪ 2 | ɪ i 42–4

MELANTIUS. These soft and silken wars are not for me:
> The music must be shrill, and all confus'd,
> That stirs my blood; and then I dance with arms.

What stranger Self-trumpeters and tongue-bullies all the brave Soldiers of B. and F. are!—Yet I am inclined to think, it was the fashion of the Age, from the Soldier's speech in the Counter Scuffle—& deeper than the Fashion B. and F. did not fathom.—

14 ɪɪ 2–3 | ɪ i 89ff

LYSIPPUS. Yes. But this lady
> Walks discontented, with her watry eyes
> Bent on the earth . . .

Opulent as Shakespear was and of his opulence prodigal, he yet

---

siNderation of metre, begun in **8**, above, continues in **28, 34, 36, 41, 68, 69**; see also **41** at n 3, below. For a detailed analysis of "the Song over the poisoned Valentinian" see BM MS Egerton 2800 f 59 (printed in *C 17th C* 660–1). For a central discussion of metre see *BL* ch 18 (1907) ɪ 49–57.
11[1] Cf *BL* ch 2 (1907) ɪ 21–2n.

would not have put this exquisite piece of Poetry in the mouth of a *no-character* or as addressed to a Melantius. I wish that B. and F. had written Poems instead of *Tragedies*.

15 II 3 | I i 112–13

MELANTIUS. I might run more fiercely, not more hastily,
  Upon my foe.

∪ ∪ – ∪ – &c I might run more fiercely not &c

16 II 4 | I ii 18–19

CALIANAX. Office! I would I could put it off: I am sure I sweat quite through my office.

the syllable *off* reminds the testy old-man of his robe—and he carries on the image.

17 II 4, pencil | I ii 88–91

MELANTIUS. ... 'Would, that blood,
  That sea of blood, that I have lost in fight,
  Were running in thy veins, that it might make thee
  Apt to say less ...

All B & F's Generals are Pugilists or Cudgel fighters that boast of their *Bottom* and of the *Claret* they have shed.[1]

18 II 5, pencil | *The Masque* I ii 172–4

CINTHIA. But I will give a greater state and glory,

  And raise to time a noble memory   nobiler
  Of what these lovers are. ...

I suspect that nobler, pronounced as an amphimacer, no bi ler, was the Poet's word.[1]

19 II 5, pencil | I ii 150–9

[Colman removes from the text of Cinthia's speech, as unworthy of Beaumont and Fletcher, and probably spurious, this interpolation of 1630:[1]]

[17][1] Among pugilists, as Byron well knew, "bottom" was staying-power or guts, and "claret" blood.

[18][1] Variorum and Bowers both read "nobler" from the 2nd Quarto.

Colman, however, gives the reading of the 1st Quarto, and G&W retains it.

[19][1] G & W accepts the interpolation, observing that the lines do not appear in the 1619 ed. Variorum (P. A.

> Yet, while our reign lasts, let us stretch our pow'r
> To give our servants one contented hour,
> With such unwanted solemn grace and state,
> As may for ever after force them hate
> Our brother's glorious beams; and wish the night
> Crown'd with a thousand stars, and our cold light:
> For almost all the world their service bend
> To Phoebus, and in vain my light I lend;
> Gaz'd on unto my setting from my rise
> Almost of none, but of unquiet eyes.

The 8 first lines are not worse, and the last couplet incomparably better, than the Stanza retained.

20   II 12, pencil | II i 313–15

AMINTOR. Oh, thou hast nam'd a word, that wipes away
    All thoughts revengeful! In that sacred name,
    "The king," there lies a terror. . . .

It is worth noticing that of the three greatest Tragedians, Massinger was a Democrat, B+F. the most servile jure divino Royalist—[1] Shakespear a Philosopher—if any thing, an Aristocrat/

A KING AND NO KING

20A   II 81 | II i 216–18

GOBRIAS.   And to me.
    He writes, what tears / of joy / he shed /, to hear   ∪ −
    How you were grown in every virtuous way . . .

21   II 94–6 | IV ii 20–2

TIGRANES. She, that forgat the greatness of her grief
    And miseries,[29] that must follow such mad passions,
    Endless and wild in women! . . .

[Seward in n 29 says that he has emended "wild as women" to "in women", and adds:] I hope, I have restor'd the true particle, which gives a very different and a very good sense to the whole sentence,

---

Daniel) accepts the lines, citing C's authority; Bowers (R. K. Turner) accepts them without comment.

20[1] For C's view of Beaumont and Fletcher as uncritical exponents of the divine right of kings see **41** at n 1, **53**,

54. In SHAKESPEARE *Dramatic Works* (2 vols 1807) [COPY D] I 415 C contrasts Shakespeare's sophistication with "the hollow extravagance of Beaum. and Fletch's Ultra-royalism".

i.e. when women, so weak to defend themselves, have such strong passions as to fly their friends, and follow a prisoner into an enemy's country, then must run the hazard of *endless* and *wild* miseries. Or if the epithets *endless* and *wild* be apply'd to passions, the sense will be much the same, and the emendation as necessary.

It would be amusing to learn from some existing Friend of Mr Seward what he meant or rather dreamt in this note. It certainly is a difficult passage—of which there are two solutions—one, that the Writer was *somewhat* more injudicious than usual—the other, that he was very very far more profound & Shakespearian than usual. His emendation at all events is right and obvious. Were it a passage of Shakespear, I should not hesitate to interpret it as characteristic of Tigranes' state of mind—disliking the very virtues & therefore half-consciously representing them as mere products of the violence of the Sex in general in all their whims, and yet forced to admire and feel or express gratitude for its exertion in his own Instance. The inconsistency of the Passage would be the consistency of the author—But this is above B. & F.—

THE SCORNFUL LADY

22 II 117, pencil | II i 98–111

SIR ROGER. Do I dream, or do I wake? surely, I know not. Am I rub'd off? is this the way of all | my morning prayers? Oh, Roger, thou art but grass, | and woman as a flower! Did I for this | consume my quarters[22] in meditation, vows, | and woo'd her in heroical epistles? | Did I expound the Owl,[23] and undertook, | with labour and expence, the recollection of those thousand pieces, consum'd in cellars, and tobacco-shops, of that our honour'd Englishman, Nic. Broughton?[24] | Have I done this, and am I done this to? | I will end with the wise man, and say, "He | that holds a woman, has an eel by the tail." |

[n 22. Colman, overriding Theobald:] We have retained the old word, *quarters*, because it may refer to *time*, as well as to Sir Roger's person.

Squares of paper—Quires.[1]

22[1] Variorum lineates this passage somewhat as C does; Bowers (R. W. Bond) prints it as prose. C's conjecture is not supported by any usage recorded in *OED*.

23　ii 117, pencil | **22** textus

[n 23:] The *Owl* is evidently some piece of Nich. Broughton's, or *some such doughty writers. Mr. Seward.*

Draytons.[1]

24　ii 117, pencil | **22** textus

[n 24, Theobald's note:] *Of that our honour'd Englishman*, Ni. Br.] The Poets, I do not apprehend, had any intention of sinking, or making a secret, of this author's name. . . . He was a voluminous writer, who, among other things, compiled an elaborate tract about Fifth-Monarchy-men. . . .

Mi. Dr. i.e. Michael Drayton.[1]

25　ii 117–18, pencil | **22** and **23** textus

Strange that neither M^r Th. nor Mr S. should have seen that this mock-heroic Speech is in full-mouthed Blank Verse![1]—Had they seen this, they would have seen that quarters is a substitution of the Players for Quires or Squares, i.e. of Paper.

> Consume my quires in meditations, vows,
> And woo'd her in heroical Epistles—

they ought likewise to have seen, that Drayton is here ridiculed, for his Poem, The Owl & for his heroic Epistles.[2]

26　ii 119, pencil | ii ii 88–93

YOUNG LOVELESS. Fill him some wine. Thou dost not see me mov'd; these transitory toys ne'er trouble me; he's in a better place, my friend, I know't. Some fellows would have cry'd now, and have curs'd thee, and fall'n out with their meat, and kept a pother; but all this helps not: He was too good for us, and let God keep him!

23[1] See **25** n 2, below.

24[1] No editor supports C's conjectural emendation. The earliest texts read "Ni. Br.", which Theobald confidently expanded to "Nic. Broughton" in his main text. Variorum reads "Nich. Breton" and Bowers "Nicholas Breton": that is, Nicholas Breton (1545–1626), a prolific writer of trifles, a few of which are remembered. See also **25** n 2, below.

25[1] See **22** n 1, above.

25[2] Michael Drayton (1563–1631) published *England's Heroical Epistles* in 1597 and *The Owle* in 1604. A submerged reference to Drayton, however, need not exclude an additional reference to Nicholas Breton as a writer of trifles; for Sir Roger, who is "Curate to the Lady", is surprised at the prospect of lovemaking, and is telling over the rag-and-bone of his chaste endeavours.

The Editors ought to have learnt, that scarce an instance occurs in
B + F of a long speech not in metre. This is plain staring blank verse.[1]

> Fill him some wine! Thou dost not see me mov'd.
> These transitory Toys ne'er trouble *me*
> &c

THE CUSTOM OF THE COUNTRY

27 II 146–7

[Note by Theobald, explaining the *lex merchetae*, which is in effect
the theme of the play:] ... Eugenius III. king of Scotland (who
began his reign A.D. 535) ordained, that the lord, or master,
should have the first night's lodging with every woman married to
his tenant or bondman. This obscene ordinance is supposed to have
been abrogated by Malcolm III. who began his reign A.D. 1061 ...

I cannot but think, that in a country conquered by a nobler Race
than the Natives, and in which the latter became villans & bondsmen,
this Custom, may have ⟨been⟩ introduced for wise purposes—as of
improving the Breed, lessening the antipathy of different Races,
producing a new bond of relationship between the Lord and the
Tenant, who, as the eldest born, would at least have a chance of
being and a probability of being thought, the Lord's Child.—In the
West Indies it cannot have these effects, because the Mulatto is
marked by nature different from the Father, because there is no
bond, no law, no custom but of mere debauchery.

28 II 148–51 | I i 144–7

RUTILIO. .... Yet if you play not fair play, and above-board too,
> I have a foolish engine here.—I say no more:
> I'll tell you what, and, if your honours guts are not enchanted—

Evidently transposed.

> Yet if you play not fair, above-board too,
> I'll tell you what—
> I ~~have~~ I've a foolish engine here—I say no more—
> ∪∪ – / ∪ – / ∪ – / ∪ – / ∪ – /
> But if your Honors guts are not enchanted—

Licentious as the comic metre of B. and F. is, far more lawless and
yet a far less happy imitation of the rhythm of animated Talk in

---

26[1] Variorum and Bowers print this speech as verse.

real Life, than Massinger's—Still it is made worse than it realy is by ignorance of the halves, thirds, and two thirds of [a][a] Line which B. and F. adopted from the Italian & Spanish Dramatists.[1]—Thus in Rutilio's

> Any man would
> Desire to have her & by any means,
> At any rate too, yet this common Hangman,
> Who hath whipt off a thousand maids' heads already—
> – ∪ ∪ –
> That he &c.[2]

In all comic metres the Gulping of short syllables, and the abbreviation of syllables ~~ra~~ ordinarily long by the rapid pronunciation of eagerness & vehemence is not so much a licence, as a Law—a faithful copy of nature—& let them be read characteristically, the *Time~~s~~* will be found nearly the same/—Thus—a thousand maids' heads (– ∪ ∪ –) is a choriambus or even perhaps a Pæon primus – ∪ ∪ ∪ / a dactyl by virtue of comic rapidity being equal to an Iambic when the Iambic is distinctly pronounced. I have no doubt, that all B. and F.'s Works might be safely corrected by attention to this rule—and that the Editor is entitled to transpositions of all kinds, & to not a few omissions—For the rule of the metre lost, what was to restrain the actors from interpolation?—

THE ELDER BROTHER

29 II 189–90 | I ii 130–3

CHARLES. . . . For what concerns tillage,
Who better can deliver it than Virgil
In his Georgicks? and to cure your herds,
His Bucolicks is a master-piece. . . .

[Colman's note:] This mistake, of mentioning those subjects, as occurring in the Bucolicks, which are treated of in the Georgicks, is noticed by Mr. Sympson.

[a] Word supplied by the editor

28[1] Variorum I 490 (R. W. Bond) prints C's comment, but commends Dyce's rejection of an editor's right "to transpositions of all kinds, & to not a few omissions".

28[2] The printed text, which both Variorum and G & W use, reads:

> Any man would desire to have her, and by any means,
> At any rate too, yet that this common hangman,
> That hath whipt off the heads of a thousand maids already,
> That he should glean the harvest, sticks in my stomach!

Fletcher was too good a Scholar to fall into so gross a Blunder. I read the words as a parenthesis, thus—

For what concerns tillage Who better can deliver it than Virgil
In his Georgicks, *or* to cure your Herds. (His Bucolics are a master-piece) But when &c.—[1]

Jealous of Virgil's Honor, he is afraid lest ~~in this~~ by referring to the Georgicks alone he might be understood as undervaluing the preceding Work—Not that I do not admire his Bucolics too in their way; but when &c

---

30   ii 199, pencil | iii iii 55–6

CHARLES. . . . She has a face looks like a story;
   The story of the Heav'ns looks very like her.

[Colman's note:] Mr. Seward, out of kindness to Charles, and that he may "not talk nonsense", would alter *story* to *glory* in both places: But, says Mr. Theobald, "I have preserv'd the word *story*, because our Authors have used the same image in their Philaster;

> —*How that foolish man,*
> *That reads the* story *of a woman's* face,
> *And dies believing it, is lost for ever!*"

—Yes! but this latter is evident sense.

   I can make sense of it as little as Mr Seward—the passage from Philaster is nothing to the purpose. But instead of Glory I should propose Astræa;

> The Astræa of the Heavens looks very like her.

---

31   ii 203, pencil | iii v 207–8

ANGELINA. . . . You're old and dim, Sir,
   And th' shadow of the earth eclips'd your judgment.

Inappropriate to Angelina; but one of the finest Lines in our Language—/[1]

29[1] Variorum ii 22n (W. W. Greg) declares that "In any case there can be no excuse for tampering with the text as Coleridge proposed to do."

31[1] For C's recollection of iii v 171–6 in 1823 or 1826 see *The Improvisatore*: *PW* (EHC) i 463.

32 II 207 | IV ii 83–5

[Theobald's emendation of Charles's speech:]

CHARLES. . . . *And lets the serious part of life run by,*
   As thin neglected sand, whiteness of name,
      You must be mine, &c.

[Seward's note:] . . . The meaning of the passage being evidently this—If you should yield, I should hate you; for I am no courtier, that gives the rein to all his wanton appetites. No; *whiteness of name, i.e.* the character and consciousness of chastity and *innocence, you must be always mine* * . . .

* Nonsense! "Whiteness of name" is in apposition to "the serious part of Life"—i.e. deservedly pure reputation. And the following line—"You *must* be mine" i.e.—tho' I do not enjoy you today, I shall hereafter, & without reproach—

WIT WITHOUT MONEY

33 II 259, pencil | I i 242–4

VALENTINE. One without substance of herself, that woman
   Without the pleasure of her life, that's wanton;
   Though she be young, forgetting it; tho' fair,
   Making her glass . . .
[Seward gives an alternative version:] ". . . *that's wanton;*
   Though she be young, forgetting it, though fair,
   Making her glass, &c."

The present Text and that proposed by Mr S. equally vile. I have endeavored to make the lines *sense*, tho' the whole is, I suspect, incurable except by bold conjectural reformation.—One without substance of herself, that's wanton. (or as we often write, i.e. wanton) Without the very pleasure of life, i.e. wantonness[1]

34 II 263 | II 93–5

VALENTINE. . . . A maid makes conscience
   Of half-a-crown a-week for pins and puppets;
   A maid's content with one coach and two horses.

[Seward's note:] As there is a syllable wanting in the measure here, I have ventured to supply it. *Pins and Puppet*-shows seem to me

33[1] Variorum records C's emendation and combines it with another of   Dyce's, but leaves the main text unaltered.

rather more expressive of a lady's pocket expences than pins and puppets.

a syllable wanting!—Had this S. neither ears or fingers? The Line is more than a usually regular, ~~more~~ Iambic Pentameter hyperacat:[1]

∪ – | ∪ – | ∪ – | ∪ – | ∪ – | ∪

---

35   II 263, pencil | II ii 97–100

VALENTINE. With one man satisfied, with one rein guided,
   With one faith, one, content, one bed⸝,   one breed—
   ~~Aged~~ ⸝S̶he makes the wife, preserves the fame and issue;
   A widow is a Christmas-box that sweeps all.

is "apayd["]=contented too obsolete for B and F?—If not, the[n]

   Content with one faith, with one bed apay'd,
   She makes the wife, &c/

or *one breed*, i.e. one set of children.

   The *Widow* is &c.

---

36   II 291, pencil

[Colman's note at the end expresses dissatisfaction with Theobald's and Seward's attempt to turn the play into verse.] We have no doubt but the play of Wit without Money was written in verse; but it is at the same time certain, that either our Authors were more licentious in this Comedy than in all their other plays put together; or else that the players, by whom, as Mr. Seward supposes, "this play was divested of its measure, in order to render the dialogue more low and farcical"... were so successful in their anti-heroic endeavour, that it appears totally impossible ever to effect a thorough restoration of the metre.

The Editors (and their contemporaries in general) were ignorant of any but the regular Iambic Verse—. A study of the Aristophanic & Plautine Metres would have enabled them to reduce B. and F. throughout into metre.[1]

34[1] For "hypercatalectic".

36[1] Bentley and Porson both did important work on Aristophanes and Plautus: see **10** n 1, above. For C's special interest in Aristophanes and his metrics, and J. H. Frere's translations of Aristophanes, see ARISTO-PHANES.

THE BEGGAR'S BUSH

36A   II 295, pencil | I i 117–20

HUBERT. ... and weak Gerrard wrought,
     But by your cunning practice, to believe
     That you were dangerous; yet not to be
     Punished by any former~~al~~ course of law ...[1]

THE HUMOROUS LIEUTENANT

37   II 331, pencil | I i 127–30

SECOND AMBASSADOR. ... when your angers,
     ~~Like~~ ∫So many brother billows, rose together,
     And, curling up ~~your~~ their foaming crests, defied
     Even mighty kings, and in their falls entomb'd 'em.

This worse than superfluous "Like" is very like ~~the~~ an interpolation of some *matter-of-fact* Critic, all pus, prose, atque venenum.[1] The *your* in the next line, instead of *their* is likewise Yours, Ye Pusfacti Homos!

38   II 336, pencil | II i 55–6

TIMON. ... But let's do what we can; tho' this wench fail us,
     Another of a new way will be look'd at.

[Colman's note:] We much suspect the poets wrote, of a new *day*. So, immediately after,

         ——*Time may*,
     For all his wisdom, yet give us a day.

For this very reason we more than suspect the contrary.[1]

39   II 339, pencil | II iii 81

LEUCIPPE. I'll put her into action for a wastcoat:
[Colman's note:] The term *wastcoateër* frequently occurs in our Authors' works. It seems to imply, a *meaner kind of strumpet*. ... It

---

36A[1] G & W reads "formal".

37[1] C has inserted into the phrase "pus atque venenum" from the opening line of Horace's *Sermones* 1.7 the English word "prose", to make "all pus, prose, and poison". The phrase at the end of the note means something like "You pus-made hombres". *Misc C* 76n provides the suggestion "Puris facti homines". Cf *CL* v 185.

38[1] Variorum agrees with C without citing him.

is probable, the epithet was derived from some particular *vest* worn
by the courtezans.

What we call a Riding-Habit—some mannish Dress.[1]

THE MAD LOVER

40   ii 434 | iv i 82–5, *Masque of Beasts*

ORPHEUS. .... This goodly tree,
An usher that still grew before his lady,
Wither'd at root: This, for he could not wooe,
A grumbling lawyer ...

Here must have been a Line omitted, rhyming to Tree, & the words
of the next have been transposed—

This goodly Tree,
(Which leafless and obscur'd with moss you see)
An Usher this, that 'fore his Lady grew
Wither'd at root—This, for he could not woo &c—[1]

THE LOYAL SUBJECT

41   ii [448]–9, beginning on the blank page facing the fly-title

It is well worthy of notice, and yet has not been (I believe) noticed
hitherto, what a marked difference there exists in the dramatic
Writers of the *Elizabetho-Jacobæan* age (mercy on me! *what* a
phrase for "during the reigns of Eliz. and James I["]!) in respect to
political Opinions.—Shakespear, in this as in all other things, himself and alone, gives the permanent Politics of Human Nature/ and
the only Predilection, which appears, shews itself in his Contempt of
Mobs and the Populace.—Massinger is a decided Whig: B. and
Fletcher high-flying passive-obedience Tories.[1]—The Spanish Dramatists furnished them with this as with many other Ingredients.

By the bye, an accurate and familiar acquaintance with all the
productions of the Spanish Stage prior to 1620, is an indispensable
qualification for an Editor of Beaumont and Fletcher—and with
this qualification a most interesting and instructive Edition might
be given.—[2]

39[1] This point is not noticed in
Variorum. A waistcoat seems never to
have been a riding-jacket, but—as used
by women—a short garment often of
costly material worn under a gown or
cloak.

40[1] Variorum quotes Dyce's approv-
ing citation of C's "ingenious remarks".

41[1] See also *Sh C* i 122.

41[2] It is not clear how extensive C's
firsthand acquaintance with early

This Edition is below Criticism.

P.S. In the metre of the Drama B. and F. are inferior to Shakespear on the one hand, as expressing the poetic part of the Drama, and to Massinger on the other, in the art of reconciling ~~rhythm~~ metre with the natural rhythm of Conversation: in which Massinger is, indeed, unrivalled. *Read* him aright, and measure by Time, not syllables, and no lines can be more legitimate, none in which the substitution of equi-pollent Feet & the modifications by emphasis, are managed with such exquisite Judgement[3]—B. & F. are fond of the 12 syllable (not Alexandrine) Line, as—Too many Fears, 'tis thought too: and to nourish those[4]—This has often a good effect. It is one of the varieties most common in Shakespear—

41A II 473 | III v Song iv

Have ye any crack'd maidenheads, to new leach or mend?
Have ye any old maidenheads to sell or to ~~change~~ lend?[1]

42 II 477, pencil | IV ii 52–3

THEODOR. Why should we have a young lady? Are women now
O' th' nature of bottles, to be stopp'd with corks?

[Colman quotes:] "And maids, turn'd bottles, cry aloud for corks." Pope.

Ben Jonson has, if my memory fail me not, the line from which Pope took this worthless double Entendre.[1]

Spanish drama was. There is discussion of "the old Spanish play" *Atheista Fulminato* and of the Don Juan theme in *BL* ch 23 (1907) II 185–8 (but the information comes at second hand from Shadwell), and Green's library contained a copy of *Spanisches Theater* ed A. W. Schlegel (2 vols Berlin 1802), not shown as C's. *Green SC* (1880) 743. Calderón is the Spanish dramatist C most often referred to (see **59** and n 1, below); and if the date 1620 is to be taken strictly Calderón is excluded, his first play having been produced in 1623. Calderón's most famous predecessors were Cervantes, who wrote 20 plays early in his career, and Lope de Vega, who wrote over 400 dramas.
41[3] For similar remarks on right

reading as an indispensable element in prosody see DONNE *Poems* **1**, **24**, **27**. See also **10** n 3, above.
41[4] *The Loyal Subject* I i 21.
41A[1] Possibly not C's hand: cf II 245. Variorum and G & W both print "change" without comment.
42[1] *The Rape of the Lock* IV 54. Cf Pope's sermon "The Dignity, Use and Abuse of Glass Bottles". A source in Jonson has not been found; since this edition of Beaumont and Fletcher includes Jonson's dramatic works in Vol I C may have made an error of association. Other parallels offered by G. Tillotson in his edition of *The Poems of Alexander Pope* (1962) 188n are: Dryden's tr of Lucretius 3.218–21, and *Measure for Measure* III ii 182–4.

RULE A WIFE AND HAVE A WIFE

43   II 506, pencil | III i (III iv 61–2)

OLD WOMAN. . . . I fear he will knock my
Brains out for lying.

[Colman's note:] Mr. Seward discards the words *for lying*, because
"most of the things spoke of Estifania are true, with only a little
exaggeration;" and "because they destroy all appearance of
measure."

Mr S. had his Brains out—the Humor lies in Estifania's having
ordered the old Woman to tell these Tales of her/ for tho' an in-
triguer, she is not represented as other than chaste—and as to the
metre, it is perfectly correct, in the Comic rhythm—

knock my— (a pause)
BRAINS out for lying.

44   II 507, pencil | III v 80–3

MARGARITA. As you love me, give way!
LEON. It shall be better, I will give none, madam:
I stand upon the ground of mine own honour,
And will maintain it.

[Seward's note:] I think it much more probable that the words
["It shall be better"] are a part of *Margarita's* speech, who finding
her *menaces* vain, endeavours to *coax* her husband into obedience,
by conjuring him by love, and promising that it should be better for
him. I therefore have restored it to her.

The meaning is: it shall be a better way first—as it is, I will not give
it or any that you in your present mood would wish.[1]

45   II 511, pencil | IV ii 9–10

SANCHIO. . . . Was she
Made to be the matter of her own undoing . . .

[Seward's note suggests "maker" for "matter".]

The error is only in the printing—

Was SHÈ made
To be the matter &c—[1]

but this Edition swarms with such & far worse Misprints.

44[1] Variorum, citing C, assigns the   45[1] Variorum divides the line as C
lines to Margarita.   does.

THE LAWS OF CANDY

46   ii 523–4, pencil | i i 4–8

MELITUS. The sadly-thriving progress of the loves
      Between my lord the prince, and that great lady,
      Whose insolence, and never-yet-match'd pride,
      Can by no character be well express'd,
      But in her only name, the proud Erota.

[Colman's note:] It is difficult, by any Etymology, to reconcile this name and character to each other. From Ερως can only be derived the attributes of *love*; and from Ηρως those of *greatness*, on which *insolence* and *pride* are indeed not uncommon, though not constant, attendants.

~~It would be curious to learn, in what Lexicon the Editor discovered~~ ~~Ηρως to mean *greatness*, or indeed any thing else than Love.~~[1] The poet intended no allusion to the word, Erota; but says that her very name, "the proud Erota", became a character & adage—as we say, a Quixot[e] or a Brutus—so to say an Erota expressed female pride and insolence of Beauty.

47   ii 525 | i ii 17–22

ANTINOUS. . . . But if now
      You should (as cruel fathers do) proclaim
      Your right, and tyrant-like usurp the glory
      Of my peculiar honours, not deriv'd
      From successary, but purchas'd with my blood,
      Then I must stand first champion for myself . . .

[Colman's note:] Mr. Theobald would read, either *from successors*, or *from ancestry* . . .

Successors = nonsense. The Poet doubtless wrote Successry/ which tho' not adopted in our language, ~~is~~ would be on many occasions, as here, a far more significant phrase then ancestry.

48   iii ⁻2, written below acquisition inscription

He is seldom up, till 12 at noon.

   Too true; and add that he is as seldom in bed, till 3 in the morning; but likewise do not forget, that from 12 to 4, from 7 to 10, and from 11 to 3, he is at work, either collecting, or correcting, or composing.[1]

46[1] Ηρως means "hero", whence perhaps greatness; Ερως (or Ερος) means "love".

48[1] A glimpse of C—in accusation and self-defence—either at Calne in 1815, during the compilation of *SL* and

49 III ⁻2–⁻1

Mem.

To note how many of the Plays are founded on rapes—how many on unnatural incestuous passions—how many on mere lunacies.

Then his ⟨virtuous⟩ Women, either ᵐ crazy Superstitions of a merely bodily negation of a having been acted on, or Strumpets in their imaginations and Wishes—or as in the Maid of the Mill, both at the same time—

In the men, the Love is merely Lust in one direction—exclusive preference of one Object—[1]

His Tyrants' Speeches are mostly taken from the mouths of indignant Denouncers of his Tyrant's character, with the substitution of I for He, and the omission of "*He acts as if he thought, or said*, Know I am far above the faults, I do—and those I do I'm able to forgive too/ Nor dare the Gods be angry at my Actions—.["]— The only feelings they can possibly excite are disgust at the Aeciuses,[2] and other Loyalists outré, or compassion—as Bedlamites.—So much for their Tragedies[a]—But even their Comedies are most of them disturbed by the fantasticalness or gross caricature of the persons or incidents. There are few characters that you can like (even tho' you should have had erased for you all the *filth* that bespatters the most likeable, as Piniero for instance)[3] scarcely any, you can *love*. How different from Shakespear—who makes one have a sort of sneaking affection for even his Barnardines, whose very Iagos and Richards are aweful, and by the counteracting power of profound Intellects rendered fearful rather than hateful[4]—and even the exceptions, as Goneril and Regan, proofs of superlative Judgement & the finest moral tact, in being utter Monsters, nulla virtute redemptum,[5] are kept out of sight as much as possible—they being indeed only means for the excitement and deepening of noblest Emotions to-

[a] Here the writing has reached the foot of p⁻2; it continues on p ⁻1 below **21**, which had previously been written at the head of p ⁻1

the writing and proof-reading of *BL*; or at Highgate, during the composition of the works he published 1816–18 and the preparation (of which these marginalia are part) for the literary lectures that began in Jan 1818. The description would fit well his earlier pattern of living at Allan Bank during the *Friend* 1809–10.

49[1] C recognised and frequently explored and refined the distinction between love and lust. See e.g. *CN* III 3293 §§ 5, 7; cf BÖHME **132** and n 1 and H. COLERIDGE **44** n 1.

49[2] Aecius is "the Emperour's Loyal General" in *Valentinian*.

49[3] "A merry Captain" in *The Island Princess*.

49[4] See COPY A **10** and n 1, and cf **58**, below.

49[5] "Redeemed by no virtue".

ward the Lear, Cordelia &c—and employed with the severest economy.
—But even his grossness—~~in~~ that which is really so independent of
the increase of vicious associations with things indifferent (for
there is a state of manners conceivable so pure that the language of
Hamlet at Ophelia's feet might be a harmless rallying or playful
teazing of a Shame that would exist in Paradise—)—yet at the worst
how different from B. and F.'s!—In Shakespear the mere generalities
of Sex, mere words oftenest, seldom or never distinct images—all
head-work and fancy-drolleries, no sensation supposed in the
Speaker, no itchy wriggling—In B. and F. the minutiæ of a Letcher—[6]

50 III ⁻1, written above the continuation of **49**

I am in a strong-hold built on a high & rugged Precipice—climb it
if you can & dare—& take it if you can—I shall then [be][a] your
Booty—But do not expect that I shall prove the Betrayer of the
Gates—or throw rope & ladder to you.—
    Clever Aminta's Temptation to Mamertus.[1]

THE LITTLE FRENCH LAWYER

51 III 2, pencil |I i 37–8

DINANT. Are you become a patron too? 'Tis a new one,
    No more on't, burn it, give it to some orator,

[Seward suggests the reading:]

    Are you become a *patron* too? How long
    Have you been conning this speech? 'Tis a new one;
    No more on't, &c.

If conjectural emendation like this, be allowed, we might venture to
read
    Are you become[b] a Patron to a new tune?
    No more on't &c.

    Patron? 'Tis a new Tune.

[a] Word supplied by the editor
[b] The margin is stained and these three words are almost illegible

49[6] Cf **57**, below, and *Sh C* I 119–20.

50[1] The reference is puzzling and uncertain. This seems to be not a *précis* but a free elaboration of some detail in the Beaumont and Fletcher text. In *The Maid in the Mill* III i and iii, Aminta gets what she wanted, but inadvertently and through a web of accident and mistaken identities rather than by temptation; similar imagery occurs in III i, but it is not used by Aminta herself. If this is the passage C had in mind, "Aminta" is correct, and "Mamertus" is a slip for "Martinus". In *The Maid's Tragedy* one character is named "Amintor", and it could be argued that in Act III he cleverly tempts Melantius; but the imagery of C's note is not directly represented in that play, and the text is in Vol II, not in Vol III, in which C's note is written.

52   III 2, pencil | I i 71–3

DINANT. Thou wouldst not willingly
>   Live a protested coward, or be call'd one?

CLEREMONT. Words are but words.

DINAN. Nor wouldst thou take a blow?

[Seward suggested:]

>   Words are but words, but *coward* is a name
>   I could not brook.

O miserable!—D. sees thro' C's gravity—& the *Actor* is to explain the "Words are but words—" is the last struggle of affected morality.

VALENTINIAN

53   III 39| I iii

It is a real Trial for Charity to read this III Scene with tolerable Charity towards Fletcher. So very slavish, so reptile are the feelings and sentiments, represented as Duties.[1] And yet remember, he was a Bishop's Son—and the Duty to God was the supposed Basis.[2]

54   III 40, the footnote and last paragraph at the foot of 41–3

Personals, (including 1. body, 2. house, 3. HOME, 4. Religion*)—Property—Subordination—Intercommunity—these are the Fundamentals of Society. Now no one of these can be ⟨rightfully⟩ attacked except when its Guardian has abused it to subvert one or more of the rest. Charles I. *deserved* Death.[a]

The reason is: that the Guardian, as a Fluent, is less than than the P̶ PERMANENT which he is to guard. He is the temporary and mutable *mean*—and derives his whole value from the *End*. In short, as Robbery is not High Treason, so neither is every unjust act of a King the converse—*all* must be attacked & endangered. Why? Because the King, as a to A, is a means of A ⟨=subordination,⟩ in a far higher sense, than a proprietor, =b, is to Property=B.

* i.e. negative so that the Person be not compelled to do or utter in relation of the Soul to God what would be, in *that* Person, a Lie—such as to force a man to go to Church, to swear that he believes what

---

a The writing having filled the foot margin of III 40, it continues at the head of that page with "* *from below*"

53[1] Cf **20** and n 1, above.

53[2] The "Preface, 1711" (p viii) records that John Fletcher was the "son of Dr. Richard Fletcher, who was created by Queen Elizabeth Bishop of Bristol, and after removed to Worcester".

he does not believe &c.—The *positive* may be a great & useful Privilege; but cannot be a *Right*: were it for this only, that it can not be pre-defined.[a] The ground of this distinction between negative and *positive* is plain—No one of my fellow-citizens is encroached on by my *not* declaring to him what I believe respecting the supersensual—but should every man be entitled to preach against the preacher, who could hear *any* preacher?—Now it is different in Loyalty—there we have *positive* Rights, but not *negative* Rights. For every pretended negative would be in effect positive/ as if a Soldier had a right to keep to himself, whether he would or would not fight.

55　III 40 | I iii 79–86

AECIUS. ... Make me worthy
　　To be your ever friend in fair allegiance,
　　But not in force: For, durst mine own soul urge me
　　To turn my hand from truth, which is obedience,
.　　.　　.　　.　　.　　.　　.　　.
　　That daring soul that first taught disobedience,
　　Should feel the first example.

Sweet Logic! Ex. gr. A stone can swallow. For without swallowing a man cannot eat—or drink—cannot therefore drink poison—but Socrates, *who was a Stone*, did drink poison—ergo, A stone can swallow.

56　III 43 | II ii 16–19

CLAUDIA. ... I'd rather make a drallery 'till thirty.
　　While I were able to endure a tempest,
　　And bear my fights out bravely; 'till my tackle　　Q^y while[1]
　　Whistled i' th' wind, and held against all weathers;

[Colman's note:] No English Dictionary, or Author that we know, exhibits the word *drallery*. That it is corrupt, therefore, is scarcely to be doubted; but we do not think with Mr. Seward, that the context absolutely requires the name of some ship ... might we not venture to read ...

　　"I'd rather make a *drollery* till thirty?" ...

The whole of this Speech of Claudia's seems corrupt—and if accurately printed (i.e. if the same in all the prior Editions) irremediablye but by bold conjecture.

---

[a] The note continues at the foot of III 42 with "(continued from over leaf)"

56[1] C's conjecture is not recorded in Variorum.

57 III 49–50, referring to *Valentinian* III i

B. & F. always write as if Virtue or Goodness were a sort of Talisman or strange Something that might be lost without the least fault on the part of the Owner. In short their chaste Ladies value their chastity as aɴ material thing, not as an Act or State of being—and this mere *thing* being a merely imaginary, no wonder that all his Women are represented with the minds of Strumpets—except a few irrational Humorists, far less capable of exciting our Sympathy than a Hindoo who had had a basin of Cow-broth thrown over him—for this, tho' a debasing Superstition, is still real—and we might pity the poor wretch, tho' we cannot help despising him. But B. & F.'s Lucinas are clumsy *Fictions.* It it is too plain, that the Authors had no one idea of Chastity, as a virtue—but only such a conception as a blind man might have of the power of seeing, by handling an Ox's Eye.—In the Queen of Corinth indeed they *talk* differently—but it is all *Talk/* for nothing is real but the dread of losing ᵗʰᵉⁱʳ a reputation. Hence, the frightful contrast between their women (even those who are meant for virtuous) and Shakespear's. So, for instance, the Maid of the Mill— a female must not merely have ᵘˢᵉᵈ grown old in brothels, but have chuckled over every abomination committed in them with a rampant sympathy of imagination, to have had her fancy so sp—wing drunk with the minutiæ of Letchery as this icy-chast Virgin, the Maid of the Mill.

THE TRAGEDY OF ROLLO
[THE BLOODY BROTHER]

58 III 139–40, beginning on the fly-title

This is, perhaps, the most energetic of Fletcher's Tragedies. He evidently aimed at a new Richard the Third in Rollo; but as in all his other imitations of Shakespear, ⟨he was not philosopher enough to *bottom* his original. Thus, in Rollo⟩ he has produced a mere personification of outrageous Wickedness, with no fundamental characteristic Impulses to make either ⟨the Tyrant's⟩ Words or actions philosophically intelligible. Hence, the most pathetic situations border on the *horrible*; and what he meant for the Terrible, is either hateful (μισητεὸν)[1] or ludicrous. The scene of Baldwin's Sentence in the Act the IIIᵈ is probably the grandest working of Passion in all B. and

---

58[1] "Hateful": see COPY A **10** n 1. The word "terrible" echoes Longinus's δεινόν.

F.'s Works; but the very magnificence of filial affection given to Edith ⟨in this noble scene⟩ renders the after scene—(in imitation of one of the least Shakespearian of all Shakespear's Works, (if it BE *his*) theat ~~scene~~ between Richard & Queen Anne)*[*] in which Edith is yielding to a few words & Tears, not only unnatural, but disgusting.

[*] Queen Anne is described as a weak, vain, *very* woman throughout.

59 III 139–40 | I i 20–1

GISBERT. He is indeed the perfect character
  Of a good man, and so his actions speak him.

This Character of Aubrey and the whole spirit of this and several other plays of the same Author, are interesting as traits of the morals which it was fashionable to teach in the reigns of James I, and his Successor who died a martyr to them. Stage, Pulpit, Law, Fashion all conspired to enslave the Realm. Massinger's Plays breathe the opposite spirit; Shakespear's the spirit of Wisdom that is for all ages. By the bye, the Spanish Dramatists (Calderon in particular) had some influence in this *respect, as well as in the busy intrigues of B. & Fletcher's Plays.[1]

* i.e. romantic Loyalty to the greatest Monsters.—

THE WILD-GOOSE CHASE

60 III 183 | II i 126–9

BELLEUR. ... that wench, methinks,
  If I were but well set on, for she is a fable,
  If I were but hounded right, and one to teach me:
  She speaks to th' matter, and comes home to the point!

[Sympson suggests *affable* for "a fable". Colman suggests:] The whole passage should be in a parenthesis, thus,

---

a C has drawn a line around the whole parenthetic clause. Since the last sentence of the note is written below a line drawn after "but disgusting", it is here printed as C's footnote to the marked parenthesis

59[1] See **41** n 2, above. C read one of the plays of Calderón (1600–81), perhaps *La Devoción de la Cruz*, in Schlegel's translation in Rome and "compared [it] with the original". *CL* III 359. A list of desiderata drawn up in Feb 1808 includes Calderón's "Comed. & Autos Sac." (*CN* III 3275; cf 3924): there was a copy of *Autos sacramentales, allegoricos y historiales* (6 vols Madrid 1717) in RS's library. *Southey SC* (1844) 3242. In 1817 C intended to translate a play of Calderón (unidentified). *CL* IV 733.

"——that wench, methinks,
If I were but well set on—(for she is *a fable,*
If I were but hounded right, and one to *teach me*)—
She speaks," &c.

Pity! that the editor did not explain wherein the sense, seemingly enforced by the next Line, consists. A Sable?—i.e. the black fox hunted for its precious fur.[1] Or *at-able*? as we now say, She is come-at-able.[2]

A WIFE FOR A MONTH

61   III 235 | IV i 609–10

ALPHONSO. Be'Twixt the cold bear~~s, far from~~ and the raging lion,
   Lies my safe way.

[Seward, who recommends the text printed by Colman, adds after elaborate argument:] And that I have therefore only restored the original is further probable from hence: The allusion to Phaeton is evidently carried on in this line, and Ovid makes Phoebus advise him particularly to avoid the *serpent,* i.e. the *constellation* that lies *betwixt the two bears.* The reverse of this therefore would naturally occur on this occasion.

This Mr Seward is a blockhead of the provoking Species. In his letch of correction he forgot the words—Lies my safe way! The Bear is the extreme pole—and thither he would travel over the space contained between it "and the raging Lion."—[1]

THE PILGRIM

61A   III 300 | IV ii 8–9

    1   5   2   3   4   6   7   8

RODERIGO. And, consider'd at the best, is but[a] a short breakfast
   For a hot appetite.[1]

a   C has drawn a curved line below "is but" evidently for exclusion from the reconstructed line if it is to make a pentameter

60[1] The sable that is valued for its fur is a marten, not a fox; and although sable is the heraldic name for black, the fur of the sable marten is brown. G & W reads "fable".

60[2] *OED* records a use of "come-at-able" in 1687.

61[1] In the constellations of the two Bears the tip of Ursa Minor's tail is Polaris, the (North) Pole Star, to which the two outermost stars of Ursa Major point. Leo, lying between Cancer and Virgo, is connected with the Bears in two senses: a line drawn southerly through the Pointers passes through Leo, and it is in Leo that the northern pole of the globe lies. The Bear, guarding the North Pole, represents extreme cold; and since the sun enters Leo on 21 July, Leo astrologically stands for what is masculine, commanding, fiery, hot, dry. G & W prints: "Betwixt the cold bear, and the raging Lyon".

61A[1] G & W follows Colman's text.

62 III 300 | IV ii 21

[Roderigo is present in a pilgrim's habit disguised as Pedro, a noble gentleman, servant to Alinda. After he has uttered a monologue in which he tries to persuade himself that he is not interested in ruining Alinda:] *Enter* Alinda.

Alinda's interview with her Father is lively and happily hit off; but *this* scene with Roderigo is truly excellent. Altogether indeed this Play holds the first place in Fletcher's romantic Entertainments (Lustspiele)[1] which collectively are his happiest performances, and is inferior only to the romance of Shakespear, As You Like It, Twelfth Night, &c.

63 III 301 | II ii 79–80

ALINDA. To-day you shall wed Sorrow,
    And Repentance will come to-morrow.

Penitence?—or—Repentance—she will come tomorrow.

THE QUEEN OF CORINTH

64 III 387 | II i 17–21

Enter Merione, as newly ravish'd.
MERIONE.[a] These tears of anger thus I sprinkle toward ye,
    You that dare sleep secure whilst virgins suffer;
    These stick like comets, blaze eternally,
    'Till, with the wonder, they have wak'd your justice,
    And forc'd ye fear our curses, as we yours.

Had the scene of this Tragi-comedy been laid in Hindostan instead of Corinth, and the Gods here addressed been the Vischnu and Co of the Indian Pantheon, this Rant would not have been much amiss.[1]

65 III 412–13, written at the end of the play

In respect of Style and Versification this Play and the Bonduca may be taken as the best, and yet as *characteristic*, specimens. Particularly, the first Scene of Bonduca—. Take the Richard the Second of Shakespear, and having selected some one scene of about the same number of Lines, and consisting mostly of long Speeches, compare it with the first scene of Bonduca/ not for the idle purpose of finding

---

a Textus marked with a line in the margin

62[1] German for "comedies".

64[1] C had found valuable material for his projected "Hymns to the Elements" in Thomas Maurice's *The History of Hindostan* (2 vols 1795) in 1796 or 1797; see e.g. *CN* I 240n.

out which is the better, but in order to see and understand the difference. The latter (B. and F.) you will find a well arranged bed of Flowers, each having its separate root, and its position determined aforehand by the *Will* of the Gardener—a fresh plant a fresh Volition. In the former an Indian Fig-tree, as described by Milton—all is growth, evolution, γενεσις—each Line, each word almost, begets the following—and the Will of the Writer is an interfusion, a continuous agency, no series of separate Acts.[1]—Sh. is the height, breadth, and depth of Genius: B. and F. the excellent mechanism, in juxta-position and succession, of Talent.[2]

THE WOMAN'S PRIZE

65A IV 134 | I ii 86–8

MARIA.   I am perfect.
Like Curtius, to redeem my ~~country~~ *sex*, have I leap'd
Into this gulph of marriage . . .

THE NOBLE GENTLEMAN

66 IV 166–7

Why have the Dramatists of the times of Elizabeth, James I. and the first Charles become almost obsolete? S excepting Shakespear?—Why do they no longer belong to the English People, being once so popular?—And why is Shakespear an exception?—One thing among 50 necessary to the full solution is, that they all employed *poetry* and poetic diction on *unpoetic* Subjects, both Characters & Situations—especially, in their Comedy. Now Shakespear's all all ideal—of no time, & therefore of all times.—Read for instance, *Marine's* panegyric on the Court, p. 168, Column 2 [ndl]—What can be more

[65][1] See *Paradise Lost* IX 1001–7:

The Figtree, not that kind for Fruit renown'd,
But such as at this day to *Indians* known
In *Malabar* or *Decan* spreads her Armes
Braunching so broad and long, that in the ground
The bending Twigs take root, and Daughters grow
About the Mother Tree, a Pillard shade
High overarcht, and echoing Walks between . . .

[65][2] For the distinction between genius and talent see COPY A 3.

[66][1] Oh, the state
And greatness of that place, where men are found
Only to give the first creation glory!
Those are the models of the ancient world,
Left like the Roman statues to stir up
Our following hopes; the place itself puts on
The brow of majesty, and flings her lustre
Like the air newly lighten'd; form and order,

unnatural & inappropriate, (not only *is* but must be *felt* as such) than such poetry in the mouth of a silly Dupe.—In short, the scenes are mock dialogues, in which the Poet Solo plays the ventriloquist, but cannot suppress his own way of expressing himself.[2] Heavy complaints have ⟨been⟩ made respecting the transprosing of the old plays by Cibber[3]—but it never occurred to these Critics to ask how it came that no one k̶n̶ ever attempted to transprose a comedy of Shakespear's./[4]

THE CORONATION

66A IV 201 | I i 284–6

SOPHIA. . . . it would seem injustice
  To allow a civil war to cut you off,
  And your own selves the instruments.

67 IV 202 | I i 340–3

SELEUCUS. Altho' he be my enemy, should any
  Of the gay flies that buz about the court,
  S/et to catch trouts i' th' summer, tell me so,
  I durst in any presence but your own—

[Colman's note:] The editors of 1750 substitute *fit* for *sit*; we think improperly. Seleucus seems to mean, "Courtiers that buz about the court, AND *sit* to catch, &c."

Pshaw: Sit is either a misprint for Set, or the old p̶r̶ & still provincial word ⟨for "set" as the⟩ participle passive of seat or set.—I have heard an old Somersetshire Gardener say—"Look, Sir! I set these plants here; those yonder I *sit* yesterday."

Are only there themselves, unforc'd, and sound,
As they were first created to this place.

C 17th C 665 follows *Misc C* in quoting incorrectly from Vol IV 168 col 1; but C's reference is to col 2, i.e. I i 64ff.
  66[2] Cf COPY A **8** n 1.
- 66[3] Colley Cibber (1671–1757), actor of foppish parts and author of about thirty dramatic pieces, is said to have adapted plays as freely as he wrote them: his adaptations of Beaumont and Fletcher include *Love Makes the Man*, from *The Custom of the Country* and *The Elder Brother*, and *The Rival*

Fools, from *Wit at Several Weapons*; he made a version of Shakespeare's *Richard III*, and his *Non-Juror* is a clumsy adaptation of Molière's *Tartuffe*. Poet laureate and butt of Pope's *Dunciad* (1742), Cibber wrote an attractive autobiography—*An Apology for the Life of Mr. Colley Cibber* (1740)—of which C owned a copy and from which he repeated an anecdote in Dec 1818 (*CL* IV 892).
  66[4] Cf Marvell's *The Rehearsal Transpros'd* (1672), from which C quoted some phrases in c Feb–Mar 1800. *CN* I 702–8.

67A   IV 203 | II i 12–13

ARCADIUS. Only to get an appetite
   To ~~thee~~, Polidora.

68   IV 203 | II i 48–54

ARCADIUS. Nay, some will swear they love their mistress, so
   ∧ they Would hazard lives and fortunes to preserve
   One of her hairs brighter than Berenice's,
   Or young Apollo's; and yet, after this,
   A favour from another toy would tempt him
   To laugh, while the efficacious hangman whips
   Her head off.

∧ They would haz, an anapæst for an Iambic. The and yet which must be read as ányet $= -\cup$ is an instance of the *enclitic* force in an accented ~~mono~~syllable, and $y\bar{e}t$ is a complete Iambic; but anyet is like spirit a Dibrach $\cup \cup$ trochēized[1] by the first accent or arsis damping (not extinguishing) the second.

WIT AT SEVERAL WEAPONS

68A   IV 285, pencil | I i 16–18

OLDCRAFT. I rushed into the world, which is indeed much like
   The art of swimming, he that will attain to't
   Must fall plump in, and duck himself at first,

69   IV 286–7, pencil continuing in ink | I i 74–83

OLDCRAFT.[a] I'm arm'd at all points against treachery,
   I hold my humour firm; if I can see thee thrive by
   Thy wits while I live, I shall have the more courage
   To trust thee with my lands when I die; if not,
   The next best wit I can hear of, carries 'em:
   For since in my time and knowledge so many rich children
   Of the city conclude in beggery, I'd rather
   Make a wise stranger my executor
   Than a foolish son my heir, and have my lands call'd after
   My wit than after my name; and that's my nature.

   a Textus marked with a line in the margin

   68[1] *OED* records this as the earliest use of "trocheized", but dates it 1834 as from *NLS*.

It would be easy to restore this passage to metre,[a] by supplying a sentence of four syllables, which the Reasoning almost demands, and correcting the grammar—"next" is a mere interpolation, otherwise "*can*" might be struck out.

> Arm'd at all points gainst treachery, I hold
> My humour firm. If living I can see thee
> Thrive by thy wits, I shall have the more courage,
> Dying, to trust thee with my Lands. If not,
> The best Wit, I can hear of, carries them.
> For since so many in my time & knowlege,
> Rich Children of the City, have concluded
> *For lack of Wit* in beggary, I'd rather
> Make a wise Stranger my Executor
> Than a fool Son my Heir, and have my lands calld
> After my Wit than name—And that's my Nature.

69A IV 286 | I i 93

OLDCRAFT. Then why should I ~~take~~ care for thee?

69B IV 286 | I i 106

OLDCRAFT. Which To prevent ~~which~~, I have sought ~~out~~ a match out [b] for her.

70 IV 287 | I i 123–8

SIR GREGORY. ... Do you think
> I'll have any of the wits hang upon me after
>   I am married once?
> None of my kindred ever had before me.
> But where's this niece? Is it a fashion
> In London to marry a woman, and never see her?

>> That I'll have any of the Wits to hang
>> Upon me after I am married once?
>> Is it a ~~London~~ Fashion in London
>> To marry a woman and to never see her.—

The superfluous "to" gives it the ⟨Sir Andrew⟩ *Ague-CHEEK* character[1]

---

[a] The note, begun in pencil, is continued from here in ink
[b] The printed text reads "To prevent which" and "out a match"; C has marked both phrases for transposition

70[1] I.e. C's "to" added before "never".

THE FAIR MAID OF THE INN

71 IV 329 | II i 126–35, 140

[Albertus has decided to cut off Mentivole's right hand in punishment for slightly injuring his son Cesario.]

ALBERTUS. . . . rash young man,
  Thou tak'st me in an ill planet, and hast cause
X To curse thy father; for I do protest,
  If I had met thee in any part o' th' world,
  But under my own roof, I would have kill'd thee.
  Within there!—Look you! Here's a triumph sent for
    Enter Physician, Surgeon, and Servants.
  The death of your young master.
SERVANT. Shall we kill him?
ALBERTUS. No;
  I'll not be so unhospitable. But, sir,
  By my life, I vow to take assurance from you,
X That right-hand never more shall strike my son.

  .   .   .   .

ALBERTUS. Chop his hand off!

X In this (as indeed in all other respects; but most in this) it is that Shakespear is so incomparably superior to Fletcher & his Friend—in Judgement!—What can be conceived more unnatural & motiveless than this brutal resolve? How is it possible to feel the least interest in Albertus afterwards? or in Cesario?—

72 IV 332 | II i 413–17

[Near the end of Act II the Mentivole–Cesario affair referred to in **70** is still in mind. Cesario speaks to his sister Clarissa and notices that she is not wearing her ring—the ring that she admits she has given to Mentivole.]

CESARIO. Then shall I ever hate thee, oh, thou false one!
  Hast thou a faith to give unto a friend,
  And break it to a brother? Did I not,
  By all the ties of blood, importune thee
  Never to part with it without my knowledge?

Precious Friends with a vengeance!—What unnatural Trash!—

THE TWO NOBLE KINSMEN

73　IV 394–5, pencil | I iii 33–5

EMILIA. . . . Since his depart, his s̲p̲o̲r̲t̲s̲,　　　　　*imports*
　　　Tho' craving seriousness and skill, past slightly
　　　His careless execution,

I conjecture, Ímports, i.e. duties or offices of importance. The flow of the versification in the speech seems to demand the trochaic ending, $\angle\,\cup$, while "since his depart, his sports", blends jingle and *hisses* to the annoyance of less sensitive ears than Fletcher's, not to say Shakespear's.

74　IV 395, pencil | I iii 86–92

EMILIA. . . . it was a note
　　　Whereon her spirits would sojourn (rather dwell on),
　　　And sing it in her slumbers: this rehearsal
　* 　(Which surely innocence wots well, comes in
　* 　Like old importment's bastard; has this end,
　　　That the true love 'tween maid and maid may be
　　　More than in sex dividual.

* Of this difficult & probably corrupt sentence not a note in explanation!—[1]

75　IV 397, referring to Act II

[After the Epilogue there is rehearsal, in a note of more than three pages, of Seward's arguments for Shakespeare's hand in this play, then Colman's conclusion:] we cannot find one plausible argument for ascribing Shakespeare any part of the Two Noble Kinsmen.

On comparing the prison scene in this act (=II) with the dialogue between the same speakers in the First, I can scarcely retain a doubt, as to the First Act's having been written by Shakespeare: assuredly

[74][1] *Two Noble Kinsmen* appears only in G & W IX, in which the text of this passage reads:

　. . . it was a Note
Whereon her spirits would sojourn
　(rather dwell on)
And sing it in her slumbers; This
　rehearsal
(Which fury innocent wots well)
　comes in

Like old importments-bastard, has
　this end;
That the true love 'tween Maid, and
　Maid, may be
More than in sex individual.

G & W has no comment on the passage except to note that the parenthesis "rather dwell on" is not present in the 1634 quarto or in the 2nd folio.

not by B. or Fl. I hold Jonson more probable than either of these Two.[1]

76 IV 435–6, pencil, written at the end of the play

The main presumption for Shakespeare's share in this Play rests on a point, to which both these sturdy Critics[1] (and indeed all before them) were blind—the construction of the Blank Verse, which proves beyond all doubt an intentional imitation, if not the proper hand, of Shakespeare. Now whatever improbability there is in the former (which supposes Fletcher conscious of the inferiority, the too *poematic* minus-dramatic nature, of his versification, and of which there is neither proof nor likelihood) adds so much to the probability of the latter. On the other hand, the *Harshness* of many of these very passages and a harshness unrelieved by any lyrical interbreathings, and still more the want of profundity in the thoughts, keep me fluctuating. S. T. Coleridge—

THE WOMAN-HATER

77 IV 472 | I ii 1–27

LAZARILLO. Go, run, search, pry in every nook and angle
    O' th' kitchens, larders, and pasteries;
    Know what meat's boil'd, bak'd, roast, stew'd, fried, or sous'd,
    At this dinner, to be serv'd directly, or indirectly,
    To every several table in the court;
    Be gone!
BOY. I run; but not so fast as
    Your mouth will do upon the stroke of eleven.
LAZARILLO. What an excellent thing did God bestow
    Upon man, when he did give him a good stomach!
    What unbounded graces there are pour'd
    Upon them that have the continual command
    Of the very best of these blessings! 'Tis
    An excellent thing to be a prince; he is
    Serv'd with such admirable variety of fare,
    Such innumerable choice of delicates;
    His tables are full fraught with most nourishing food,

75[1] The 1634 quarto assigns authorship to Fletcher and Shakespeare. Cyrus Hoy's analysis ascribes the whole of Act I to Shakespeare, as well as II i, III i–ii, v i (second part), and v iii–iv.

76[1] I.e. Seward and Colman.

> And his cupboards heavy laden with rich wines;
> His court is still fill'd with most pleasing varieties:
> In the summer his palace is full of green-geese,
> And in winter it swarmeth woodcocks.

Prose printed as Blank Verse—as elsewhere in this edition blank verse is printed as prose. *S. T. C.*

Here the verse recommences/*

> Oh, thou goddess of plenty!
> Fill me this day with some rare delicates,
> And I will every year most constantly,
> As this day, celebrate a sumptuous feast
> (If thou wilt send me victuals) in thine honour!
> And to it shall be bidden, for thy sake,
> Ev'n all the valiant stomachs in the court;

* the transition from the prose to the verse enhances & indeed forms the comic effect. Laz. concludes his soliloquy with a *Hymn* to the Goddess of Plenty.

THE HONEST MAN'S FORTUNE

77A IV 550 | III i 141–2

VERAMOUR. 'Would I might live, once more,
    To wait on my poor master!

GEORGE BERKELEY
1685–1753

Siris: a chain of philosophical reflexions and inquiries concerning the virtues of Tar Water, and divers other subjects connected together and arising one from another ... A new edition, with additions and emendations. London 1744. 8⁰.

Bound with Thomas Prior (c 1682–1751) *An Authentick Narrative of the Success of Tar-Water, in curing a great number and variety of distempers, with remarks, and occasional papers relative to the subject. To which are subjoined, two letters from the author of Siris. Shewing the medicinal properties of Tar-Water, and the best manner of making it.* London 1746.

Yale University (Beinecke Library)

The signature "W. Sherlock" is written in ink on p [3], and on the title-page an illegible signature "Ch[   ]".

The earliest record of C's reading of Berkeley is his borrowing from the Bristol Library 1–28 Mar 1796 of Vol II of the *Works* (1784). *Bristol LB* 75. This volume includes all but the *Principles of Human Knowledge, Three Dialogues Between Hylas and Philonous, An Essay Towards a New Theory of Vision,* and *Alciphron*; it may be assumed that these major works were—as internal evidence suggests—already familiar to him. C included Berkeley's name in a list of projects in Sept–Oct 1796 (*CN* I 174; cf 203), and when his second son was born in May 1799 he named him Berkeley. In the philosophical letters addressed to the Wedgwoods in Feb 1801 C regarded Berkeley as the father of modern idealism and named Berkeley, Hartley, and Joseph Butler as "the three greatest, nay, only three *great* Metaphysicians which this Country *has* produced". *CL* II 699, 703. But in 1801 C could see Berkeley's position as that of Descartes—greatly clarified (*CL* II 699); and the movement away from Berkeley towards Kant had begun almost imperceptibly before the turn of the century, perhaps through his reading of Hutton's *An Investigation of the Principles of Knowledge* (1794). *CN* I 243n. Nevertheless, *Dejection: an Ode*, composed 1802, has many Berkeleyan undertones, and C's respect for Berkeley did not decline.

For the grounds of C's later objection to Berkeley's idealism see *P Lects* (1949) 60–1 (from N 25), *CN* III 3605. A letter written to Gooden in 1820 gives an important summary of C's reading of Berkeley. *CL* v 13–14.

DATE. Possibly 1808–9, if two clusters of references to Berkeley—in *CN* III 3276, 3325 (Feb–May 1808); 3542, 3592, 3605 (Jul–Sept 1809)—are of dates similar to these annotations. There is a substantial quotation from *Siris* in the 1818 *Friend* (*CC*) I 112–13, which was not in the 1809–10 ed; and there are even later arguments with Berkeley in N F⁰ c 1825.

1 p⁻¹

This great man[1] needed only an entire instead of partial emancipation from the fetters of the mechanic philosophy to have enunciated all that is true and important in modern Chemistry.[2] ~~and~~ e Combining ~~the~~ its (= hodiernity's)[3] more accurate detail and discrimination of Facts with the more profound and vital philosophy ⟨of⟩ Heraclitus, Pythagoras, and Plato ~~he~~ he might have refined and integrated both into one harmonious System, the centre of which would be Theosophy, and its circumference Physionomy.[4] S. T. C.

1A p 56, marked with a line in the margin | § 116

§ 116. ... There are nevertheless three sorts of people to whom I would peculiarly recommend it [tar-water]: Sea-faring persons, ladies, and men of studious and sedentary lives.

2 p 144 | § 300

Plato and Aristotle considered God as abstracted or distinct from the natural world. But the Aegyptians considered God* and nature as making one whole, or all things together as making one universe.

* probably, not God sensu eminenti,[1] but the NATURE of God: while as Wisdom, and Holy Will they too might have considered God as abstracted from the *natural* World.

3 p 173 | § 365

He [Plato] further adds, as for what hath been now said, it belongs all to Socrates.

1ᵐᵘˢ Omnia.[1]

1[1] In *LS* C declared Berkeley to be "a great and good man, not less illustrious for his piety and zeal as a Christian than for his acuteness and profundity as a Philosopher". *LS* (*CC*) 192.

1[2] On the history of modern chemistry see *P Lects* Lect 12 (1949) 342–3. C made a similar complaint against the *Querist* in 1800: see *CN* I 893. C referred to *BL* ch 13 as being like Berkeley's *Siris*, "announced as an Essay on Tar-water, which beginning with Tar ends with the Trinity, the omne scibile forming the interspace". *BL* (1907) I 201.

1[3] "Today-ness"—from Latin *hodie*. *OED* records "hodiernal" but not "hodiernity".

1[4] For the family of words that "physionomy" belongs to see BLUMENBACH **1** n 3. For a similar linking of the name of Heraclitus with Pythagoras and with Böhme (instead of Plato) see e.g. *CL* IV 775.

2[1] "In the *eminent* sense". For the distinction between "eminent" and "formal" see BÖHME **12** n 1.

3[1] "[He was] the first [to say] everything".

BIBLE

Copy A

The Holy Bible, containing the Old Testament and the New: translated out of the original tongues, and with the former translations diligently compared and revised, &c. Cambridge 1790. 8º.

A. H. B. Coleridge

C's family Bible, presented to him by Joseph Cottle on 7 Oct 1795 in response to a list of desiderata received by Cottle two days after C's marriage. *CL* I 160. A hole at the top of the title-page, interposing an unnatural space between the Christian name and surname of Cottle's signature, indicates that the book was bought secondhand by Cottle.

Inscribed on the title-page: "Joseph Cottle to S. T. Coleridge" and "J. C. to S. T. C." Inscribed by C on p ‐3: "given to me by Joseph Cottle after my marriage—S. T. Coleridge". Edith Coleridge has signed her name at the foot of the page.

In addition to C's notes there are entries on two front flyleaves by Mrs C, Mrs DC, and Mrs HNC. These are given in the ANNEX.

DATE. Oct 1795 (**1**), 19 Sept 1796 (**2**), 30 Nov 1796 (**3**), 14 Sept 1800 (**4**): dated in ms. **5** is of uncertain date; see **5** n 2.

---

1   p ‐3 (p–d), first of a series of entries below C's inscription

Married at St Mary Red Cliff to Sara Fricker on the fourth day of October 1795—I being 23 years old the twentieth day following of the same month.[1]

---

2   p ‐3

September 19th, 1796. 30 minutes past two in the morning my Wife was delivered of a Son, his name Hartley Coleridge. N.B. He was born before either the Nurse or Surgeon arrived—& altogether without any aid.— — — —[1]

1[1] Again the mistake about his own birthday: see BAXTER *Reliquiae* COPY B **91** and n 3. He was in fact 23 years old on 21 Oct 1795.

2[1] For the account of HC's birth, and the intention of naming him David Hartley, see *CL* I 236. For the sonnet on HC's birth, see *CL* I 245, *PW* (EHC) I 153–4. HC died in 1849 without having married.

411

3 p ⁻³

November 30ᵗʰ, 1796 H. Coleridge was burnt across the bottom of his back by the ⟨edge of the⟩ bason, in which he has*ᵃ* being washed: which bason had been placed on the *nob* of the fireplace, to take off the *chill*. This was the first time, that his Mother had washed him with Water at all warm & it is odd, that at different times both his Mother & I had*ᵇ*¹

4 p ⁻²

Derwent Coleridge, born half past 10 °clock, Sunday night, Sept. 14ᵗʰ, 1800.¹

5 p ⁺¹
Romans IX. 19: 20, 21.¹

> Doth it our Reason's mutinies appease
> 　To say, the Potter may his own clay mould
> To ev'ry use, or in what shape he please,
> 　At first not counsel'd, nor at least controul'd?
>
> Pow'r's hand can neither easy be nor strict
> 　To lifeless clay, which ease nor torment knows;
> And where it cannot favour nor afflict,
> 　It neither justice nor injustice shows.
>
> But could have life, and life eternal too;
> 　Therefore if doom'd before they can offend,

ᵃ A slip for "was"
ᵇ The note is incomplete

3¹ On 4 Dec 1796 C told Charles Lloyd, Sr: "My Wife...and our Infant are well—only the latter has met with a little accident—a burn, which is doing well." *CL* I 264.

The next entry is in Mrs C's hand—Berkeley Coleridge's birth: see ANNEX [*a*].

4¹ C reported the birth in letters of 16 and 17 Sept. *CL* I 622, 623. On 28 Sept C said: "alas! I fear, he will not live" (*CL* I 626), and the day before noted: "The child being very ill was baptized by the name of Derwent/ The Child hour after hour made a noise like the Creeking of a door which is being shut very slowly to prevent its creeking." *CL* I 626; *CN* I 813. By 1

Nov DC had recovered and gave no further cause for anxiety: see *CL* I 646, 662. His name is discussed in *CL* I 632, 646. DC died in 1883.

For the birth of SC, DC's son, and Herbert and Edith Coleridge see ANNEX [*b*]–[*e*].

5¹ "Thou wilt say then unto me, Why doth he yet find fault? for who hath resisted his will? Nay but, O man, who art thou that repliest against God? Shall the thing formed say to him that formed it, Why hast thou made me thus? Hath not the potter power over the clay, of the same lump to make one vessel unto honour and another unto dishonour?"

It seems to show what heavenly power can do,
But does not in that deed that pow'r commend.

Davenant's *Death of Astragon*: or the Philosopher's
Disquisition directed to the Dying Christian.[2]

Annex

Five other entries have been made on the front flyleaves in various hands.

[*a*] p⁻2, in Mrs C's hand, below **3**

Berk⟨e⟩ley Coleridge born, May 10, half past 2 the Morning—1798—
⟨died Feb   1799[1]⟩

[*b*] p ⁻2, in Mrs C's hand, below **4**

Sara Coleridge born December 23ᵈ 20 minutes past 6 in the Morning,
1802.[2]

[*c*] p ⁻2, in Mrs Derwent Coleridge's hand

October 17ᵗʰ (friday) 1828. Derwent Moultrie Coleridge son of Derwent
& Mary Coleridge was born 20 minutes past 8 in the evening at Helston in
Cornwall.

[*d*] p ⁻2, in SC's hand

October 11ᵗʰ ⟨1830⟩. Herbert Coleridge, son of Henry Nelson & Sara
Coleridge, was born at Hampstead, at a little past 11 in the forenoon.

[*e*] p ⁻1, in SC's hand

Edith Coleridge daughter of Henry Nelson & Sara Coleridge—born at
Hampstead June the 29th 1832, at half past nine o'clock A.M.

5[2] William Davenant (1606–68) *The Death of Astragon* sts 83–5. C could have found this in *B Poets* IV 874; the passage is unmarked in all three annotated copies. C owned ANDERSON COPY A early enough to have copied this in by 1800, but there is no clue to the date.

[1] Berkeley Coleridge was born on 14 May 1798 at "half past one" according to C in *CL* I 407, and died 10 Feb 1799. The note of his death, also in Mrs C's hand, was presumably made some time after the event. While C was in Germany the child developed smallpox after inoculation, and "at one o'clock on Sunday morning a convulsive fit put an end to his painful existence". *Poole* I 289–92; cf *CL* I 449 and n. See *CL* I 478–9, 481–2, 490. C wrote a poem on Berkeley's death: *CN* I 625 (20), *CL* I 483, *PW* (EHC) I 312. For a group of hexameters written when C was "blind from weeping about little Berkley" see BÖHME **149**.

[2] Cf *CN* I 1310 and n. SC herself later wrote that "the entry of my birth is in my dear mother's handwriting, and this seems like an omen of our lifelong separation, for I never lived with him [my father] for more than a few weeks at a time". *SC Memoir* I 1–2.

Copy B

The Holy Bible, containing the Old and New Testaments: translated out of the original tongues, &c. Oxford 1822. 8º.

Stereotype edition: Printed at the Clarendon Press by Samuel Collingwood and Co. printers to the University, for the British and Foreign Bible Society, instituted in London in the year 1804.

New York Public Library (Berg Collection)

Inscribed on the title-page "A. Gillman" and "The Rev^nd J. Gillman from his very affectionate Mother—. Aug^st 1840". C records in **135** that he wrote the marginalia "under the Roof of my dear and under God my most precious Friends, James and Ann Gillman". A few flowers are pressed between the leaves at pp 90/91.

In Feb 1828, within the time-span of these marginalia, C said that "of all the supplemental means of comfort and of growth that it has been given me to employ, the most fruitful has been the habit of making some one chapter of the Psalms or the Prophets, or St John's Gospel, or of St Paul's Epistles a regular part of my morning and my last prayers". *CL* vi 725. A year later he complained to J. H. Green that two parts of his copy of Eichhorn's *Einleitung in das Neue Testament* were missing "just at the very time, that I am beginning my notes, chapter by Chapter, on the Epistles of Paul. For to the reading of the N.T. and collating our version with the Greek, I commonly appropriate the two last hours of my waking day." *CL* vi 784.

MS TRANSCRIPTS. (*a*) NYPL (Berg Collection): a series of transcripts in an unidentified hand on 28 small leaves of paper, paginated, the first of which is headed: "Notes by S. T. Coleridge written in a Bible belonging to the Rev^nd J Gillman". Although this set of transcripts was evidently intended to be independent of the volume, the leaves have been inserted loose at the places the notes refer to. (*b*) VCL LT 65: notes **80–82**, **135** in an unidentified hand, possibly the original transcript for the version in *C at H*.

DATE. Feb 1826 to Jul 1829: four notes are dated in ms—25 Feb 1826 (**140**), c 23 Dec 1827 (**58**), 1827 (**78**), Jul 1829 (**135**). There is some interaction between these marginalia and the notebook entries for 1826–9, principally in N F⁰ and NN 34–41, and also between these marginalia and some of the marginalia on BOOK OF COMMON PRAYER COPY B (written Dec 1827–Sept 1831).

NOTE. In the editorial notes, biblical passages cited by C are normally quoted from AV; for convenience a modern edition of AV is used except when direct quotation from C's own copy is required by the context. In the textus the editor has preserved the italics of AV—the translators' conventional indication of words and phrases not actually present in the original Hebrew or Greek. C's suggestions for improving or correcting the AV translation have been compared with *NEB*, sometimes without further comment when such a parallel illuminates or supports C's position, sometimes when a recent authoritative translation of a problematical passage is likely to be of interest to the reader.

C's knowledge of Hebrew was less confident than his command of Greek; at times he needed the help and advice of Hyman Hurwitz in resolving questions that the Hebrew text raised (see e.g. BOOK OF COMMON PRAYER 25 n 2), but he regularly consulted the Septuagint not only for hints about the rendering of Hebrew words and idioms but also for the evidence offered by the differences in order, content, and wording between the Septuagint and the Massoretic text. The Massoretic text confronts a translator or interpreter with plenty of difficulties, but the stable and authoritative nature of the text itself leaves little or no scope for conjectural emendation, even if C had been a more able Hebraist than he was; at times he drew upon the large body of traditional textual glosses (the Massorah), though whether as primary materials or as details picked out in the commentaries does not appear. In many places in the marginalia that follow and in his notebooks, C suggested improvements and clarifications of the AV wording of OT. Some of these, in BIBLE COPY B at least, he translated or adapted from the German of "The Version [of OT] by Cohen"—i.e. *Die Heilige Schrift ... nebst verbesserter deutscher Uebersetzung* ed S. J. Cohen (18 pts Hamburg 1824–7) [here cited as

"Cohen"]: the Hebrew text of OT with German translation, including Mendelssohn's. See **24** n 1, below. Where C's reliance upon Cohen can be identified with some probability, the parallel is recorded in the footnotes. In the notebooks—and probably elsewhere—he relied on such commentaries as Cocceius, Jerome, Pearson's cumulative *Critica sacra*, and the D'Oyly and Mant edition of the Bible.

The only copy of the Greek NT that C is definitely known to have owned is the edition of R. Whittaker, London 1622; he referred to it in c Mar 1828 as "my obscure old Edition of the New Testament with a Vocabularium or Lexicon, Londini Apud Joannem Billium, Typographium Regium, 1622", and valued it for some appended notes by Joseph Scaliger. N 37 f 51ᵛ—a condensation of a note of Jul 1827 in which he gives the date of publication as 1612, but there can be no doubt that the edition was of 1622 and that in both notes he was referring to the same copy of it. C's first concern was for the correct theological interpretation of a biblical text. If the details of the text were open to question, being unintelligible as they stood or pointing towards an unacceptable interpretation, he would consider rational emendation and would use any assistance that came to hand in the *apparatus criticus* of the edition he was using, in versions rendered in the languages he could read, and in the commentaries available to him. But he was not interested in textual criticism as such. There are no signs that he availed himself much of the technical niceties that had been accumulating through the eighteenth century in the tracing and examination of NT mss and that were to lead to an enormous extension of critical apparatus and to important refinements in the Greek text. Not unaware of these activities (see e.g. BIBLE *Apocryphal NT* **4** n 1), C worked from the *Textus receptus* that Tyndale (1525) and the translators of AV (1611) had used—the adulterated Byzantine "ecclesiastical" text that, with little change, was commonly used as standard from the time it was first printed in 1514 until Tischendorf's texts were published 1841–69. The Griesbach edition that C cited in his prospectus for an *Encyclopaedia Biblica* (IS 392–3)—a revised text, provided with a copious *apparatus criticus* drawn from many mss— appeared in three editions 1774–1805, but C seems not to have used any of them. Nor are there signs that he used any of the deliberate reconstructions of the Greek text available in his lifetime, e.g. Daniel Mace (1729), William Bowyer (1763), Edward Harwood (1776), Karl Lachmann (1831). Nevertheless, C had access to much detailed textual information, especially in the commentaries of Eichhorn, Rhenferd, Wetstein, and others, and made good use of it.

In the editorial notes, exegetical and historical information has been drawn principally from *The International Critical Commentary* (28 vols Edinburgh 1895–1936), *The Interpreter's Dictionary of the Bible* (4 vols Nashville 1962), the *Encyclopaedia Judaica* (16 vols Jerusalem 1971–2), *Peake* (1967), and *ODCC* (1971).

OLD TESTAMENT

1 p 5, pencil, overtraced | Genesis

How many and what important Problems do not the Eleven first Chapters of this Book offer or suggest to a thinking mind! And how few have been noticed—not to say, solved—by our Divines and Commentators![1]

2 p 11, pencil, overtraced | Gen 7.8–9

Of clean beasts, and of beasts that *are* not clean, and of fowls, and of every thing that creepeth upon the earth, There went in two and two unto Noah into the ark . . .

Q[y]. What *at this time* was the meaning of "clean" & "unclean". It *seems* like an anachronism, an antedating of the Law.[1]

3 p 11 | Gen 7.17–20

And the flood was forty days upon the earth; and the waters increased, and bare up the ark, and it was lift up above the earth. And the waters prevailed, and were increased greatly upon the earth; and the ark went upon the face of the waters. And the waters pre-

[1][1] The "Problems" raised by the opening chapters of Genesis were for C of two kinds, not entirely separable: inexhaustible questions about the creation and the relation of God's creative activity to the world (as elaborated in e.g. the marginalia on Böhme); and questions about the authorship, integrity, and age of various parts of the text of the Pentateuch, particularly as concentrated in the opening chapters of Genesis. From the earliest times, inconsistencies and anachronisms were noticed in the five books traditionally ascribed to Moses. The possibility of non-Mosaic or multiple authorship appeared in tentative form in the seventeenth century, and important questions were raised by e.g. Luther, Spinoza, Richard Simon, and Jean Astruc (for whom see Böhme 67 n 1). More important to C than any of these was J. G. Eichhorn's *Einleitung ins Alte Testament* (Leipzig 1787)—which C annotated—with its tabulation of the two strands in Genesis rep-

resented by the use of Jehovah/Yahweh and Elohim for the name of God. The theory now known as the "Documentary Hypothesis", first clearly formulated in 1833 by Eduard Heuss, was not fully articulated—by Graf and Wellhausen—until after C's death.

[2][1] The anachronism that C notices arises because the law regarding clean and unclean foods (in Lev 11 and Deut 14; see also **13** and **14**, below), as well as the name "Yahweh", was not disclosed to Moses until the revelation on Mt Sinai (Exod 13). This part of Gen belongs to the strand that Wellhausen named J (for Jehovah/Yahweh); he named two other strands E (for Elohim) and P (for an assumed later priestly source). The J and P sources take divergent views of the origin of sacrifice, J regarding the worship of Yahweh and the institution of sacrifice as already existing before the flood, P regarding the Law as Mosaic. See also *CL* v 135.

vailed exceedingly upon the earth; and all the high hills, that *were* under the whole heaven, were covered. Fifteen cubits upward did the waters prevail; and the mountains were covered.

Verses 17–20 sound to my feeling like a quotation from some ancient Poem.[1] S T C

4 p 21 | Gen 19.1

And there came two angels to Sodom at even; and Lot sat in the gate of Sodom ...

XIX. v. 1.—Compare v. 22 of XVIII. Evidently it should have been rendered: And the two Angels arrived at Sodom at even[1]

5 p 45 | Gen 36.31–6

And these *are* the kings that reigned in the land of Edom, before there reigned any king over the children of Israel. [Bela the son of Beor, Jobab the son of Zerah, Husham of the land of Temani, Hadad the son of Bedad, Samlah of Masrekah.]

Evident but *very* ancient Interpolation; the same names being found in the Samaritan Text.[1]

6 p 61 | Gen 49.4–5

Unstable as water, thou shalt not excel; because thou wentest up to thy father's bed; then defiledst thou *it*: he went up to my couch. Simeon and Levi *are* brethren; instruments of cruelty *are in* their habitations.

4. But THY precipitancy ⟨inconsiderateness⟩ was swift as a flush of Water—for this thou shall not be extolled.—5. Weapons of Violence are their Symbols of Brotherhood or Relationship.[1]

[3][1] Textual scholars now assign these verses to P, with other highly poetic sections: e.g. Gen 1.1–2, 1.4, 5.1–28, 30–2, 6.9–22. Genesis was probably the last book of the Pentateuch to receive its final form.

[4][1] AV does not unambiguously identify the "two angels at even" of 19.1 with the "two men" who "went toward Sodom" of 18.22. C expands this note in N 42 f 41[v].

[5][1] Eichhorn had made this same observation in his *Alte Testament* I 269–70. The Samaritan text is a Hebrew text of the Pentateuch written in Samaritan script and diverging only

slightly from the standard text. It was first published in Paris in 1645. Eichhorn (II 147ff) ascribed it to the time before the separation of the ten tribes after the death of Solomon in 933 B.C.; modern scholars prefer a later date, in the fifth century B.C., as suggested by Neh 13.23–31.

[6][1] C is translating Cohen's German version. *NEB* reads: "Turbulent as a flood, you shall not excel; | because you climbed into your father's bed; | then you defiled his concubine's couch. | Simeon and Levi are brothers, | their spades became weapons of violence."

7   pp 70–1, pencil, overtraced | Exodus 7.15 to 8.11

[Moses with a stroke of his staff turns the river water into blood.]
And the magicians of Egypt did so with their enchantments. . . .
[Aaron calls forth a plague of frogs.] And the magicians did so with
their enchantments . . .

Hieroglyphicè   historical.[1]   Predictiones   Astrologicæ—*Baculus
Astronomicus*[2]—Enchantments = Constellated   Talismans—Metallic
Almanachs.[3]

8   p 81 | Exod 16.23

And he said unto them, This *is that* which the Lord hath said, To
morrow *is* the rest of the holy sabbath unto the Lord: bake *that*
which ye will bake *to day*, and seethe that ye will seethe; and that
which remaineth over lay up for you to be kept until the morning.

23. Is this an historical prolepsis? Or are we to infer that the Sabbath was not first instituted but only solemnly confirmed from M.
Sinai?[1]

9   p 85 | Exod 20.8

Remember the sabbath day, to keep it holy.

XX. 8. If the Hebrew word have the same force as our "remember",
the term seems to imply a previous institution of the 7th Day.[1] The
evidence to the contrary is merely negative

7[1] "Hieroglyphically historical"—
i.e. taken from early hieroglyphic
records; but C, like his predecessors and
contemporaries, often used "hieroglyphic" as = "symbolic", and here he
evidently means that as well. For his
quizzical observation that not all
Egyptian hieroglyphic inscriptions were
as old or reliable as was claimed by
"The French *savans* who went to
Egypt in the train of Buonaparte" see
the two opening paragraphs of
"*Prometheus*": *LR* II 323–4. But this
would not apply to the biblical history
originally, as he supposed, recorded in
hierog¹yphics; on which see also *LR* II
325, *CN* III 4325. See also Böhme **164,
165.**

7[2] "Astrological Predictions—Astro-
nomic *Staff*."

7[3] Webster *The Displaying of*

Supposed Witchcraft (1677) pp 84–5
helps to explain this cluster.

8[1] The "prolepsis" occurs in that
the sabbath was not formally instituted until the Decalogue was given
to Moses on Sinai (Exod 20.8 = **9**
textus, below). In Gen 2.3 "God
blessed the seventh day, and sanctified
it" but it is not recorded that he communicated this to man until he gave
the Law to Moses. Observance of the
sabbath was evidently of great antiquity and its origins were obscure.

9[1] The Hebrew word *zokar* (rendered μνήσθητι in Septuagint and
memini in Vulgate) means "to hold in
memory, to bear in mind, not to forget". For C's interest in the sabbatarian controversy see Brerewood
and Byfield; and for his mature
view of the Christian sabbath see *TT*
19 May 1834.

10   p 88 | Exod 22.18

Thou shalt not suffer a witch to live.

18. Webster has shown clearly, that Witch (mulier inflata, bladder-woman) was a fortune-telling Ventriloquist—always in the service of the false Gods—Pythoness. So the Witch of Endor.[1]

11   p 90 | Exod 24.10–11

And they saw the God of Israel: and *there was* under his feet as it were a paved work of a sapphire stone, and as it were the body of heaven in *his* clearness. And upon the nobles of the children of Israel he laid not his hand: also they saw God, and did eat and drink.

v. 10. 11. It seems to me difficult even for a Jew but scarcely possible for a Christian to deny that the God here seen was the Son of God; and that ⟨in⟩ Christ, the Word and Jehova the same Person is expressed.[1]

12   p 90 | Exod 24.12ff

And the Lord said unto Moses, Come up to me into the mount. . . . And Moses rose up, and his minister Joshua: and Moses went up into the mount of God. And he said unto the elders, Tarry ye here for us, until we come again unto you. . . . And Moses went up into the mount, and a cloud covered the mount. . . .

We must suppose a Summit surmounting the Hill, and rising from

10[1] The Pythoness—the priestess who in a trance spoke the words of the oracle at Delphi. John WEBSTER *The Displaying of Supposed Witchcraft* ch 8 pp 165–6 (text) reads: "Concerning the Woman of *Endor*, that our English and many other Translators have falsly rendered a Witch, or a Woman that had a familiar Spirit, we have spoken sufficiently [in pp 120, 127], where we treated of the signification of the word *Ob*. And there have shewed plainly, that she is only called the Mistriss of the bottle, or of the Oracle, and that what she there did, or pretended to do, was only by Ventriloquy . . . and so changing her voice did mutter and murmur, and peep and chirp like a bird coming forth of the shell, or that she spake in some hollow Cave or Vault, through some Pipe, or in a Bottle, and so amused and deceived poor timerous and despairing *Saul* . . .". For the Witch of Endor, see 1 Sam 28.7–25. See also HILLHOUSE **1** § 3. Cf *CN* III 3753 and ARGENS **11**.

11[1] Cf John 1.18, a text of great importance to C: "No man hath seen God at any time; the only begotten Son, which is in the bosom of the Father, he hath declared him." That the Jehovah of the OT was the Word, the mediator between the transcendent God and man, is a traditional interpretation; that He was also incarnated as Christ follows from this, and is asserted by many of the Christian Fathers. See **53**, **57**, **112**, and esp **119** and nn, below.

the top of Sinai as a distinct Hill from a level plot—somewhat as the Crater-Hill from the Cima of Mount Etna.[1]

13   p 123 | Leviticus 11

[What beasts may and may not be eaten][1]

This 11th Chapter is the most difficult to reconcile with the conception of Laws dictated by the Supreme Reason. But difficulties are not Objections.

14   p 124 | Lev 11.29–32

These also *shall be* unclean unto you among the creeping things that creep upon the earth; the weasel, and the mouse, and the tortoise after his kind, And the ferret, and the chameleon, and the lizard, and the snail, and the mole. . . .

Tho' to forbid Rabbit, Hare, and Turtle, yet allow men to eat Black Beetles and Grashoppers, seems strange to us; yet the general tendency of these prohibitions is wise and beneficent.

15   p 182 | Numbers 24.17

. . . there shall come a Star out of Jacob, and a Scepter shall rise out of Israel, and shall smite the corners of Moab, and destroy all children of Sheth.*

* a far more probable Version is—and shall *cluck* together (*under his wings, as a Hen*) all the children of Seth—i.e. the members of the true Church.—[1]

16   pp 219–20 | Deuteronomy 17.14–20

[The election and duty of a king]

XVII. 14–20. "A perplexing Section, beset with difficulties whatever date be assigned to it"—such was my first thought; but I now find in

12[1] C knew about Etna at first hand from climbing it in Aug 1804: see *CN* II 2170–7, esp 2171. *Cima*—Italian for "summit". C's impulse to visualise a Palestine he had never seen is clear in **68**, below.

13[1] Here, and in similar textus references to whole chapters, the summary is given from the edition of the Bible that C was annotating.

15[1] In N 33 f 6 C ascribed this "version" to Alting. C's onomatopoeic word "cluck" matches Alting's *glocitando*. The Hebrew word in Num 24.17 is *karakar*. As early as the Targums (the Aramaic translations of the OT) the interpretation "subdue [in the sense of rule over] the children of Seth" appears; later commentators took the latter phrase to mean "the children of desolation" and gave the verb *karakar* its post-biblical sense "to break down, to crush". *NEB* reads: "a star shall come forth out of Jacob, | a comet arise from Israel. | He shall smite the squadrons [*or* heads] of Moab, | and beat down all the sons of strife."

it one of the strongest evidences of the Authenticity of the whole Book. Neither before nor after Moses could it have been written: therefore by Moses.[1]

17 p 269 | Judges 1

This and the preceding Book[1] compiled after Rehoboam but before the Captivity; but of undoubtedly ancient and authentic documents, which in "The Book of Judges" were probably narrative poems—~~War~~ Heroic Songs.[2]

18 pp 272–3 | Judges 3.15–30

[The murder of Eglon by Ehud]

It is doubtless said, that the Lord made this treacherous Assassination an occasion of Israel's Deliverance, but it is not said or even implied that the Act itself was commanded by the Lord. It was: or it was not. If it *was*, then it was the execution of a sentence passed by a rightful Judge—and itself rightful. If it was not, then it is only one of the instances, in which a righteous Cause is brought by divine providence to a prosperous conclusion, notwithstanding its commencement in an unrighteous Act. Thus, the Reformation in the adulterous Divorce of Queen Catherine.[1]

19 pp 288–9 | Judges 15.15–20

And he found a new jawbone of an ass, and put forth his hand, and took it, and slew a thousand men therewith. And Samson said, With the jawbone of an ass, heaps upon heaps, with the jaw of an ass have I slain a thousand men. And it came to pass, when he had made an end of speaking, that he cast away the jawbone out of his hand, and called that place Ramath-lehi. And he was sore athirst, and called on the LORD, and said, Thou hast given this great deliver-

16[1] *Peake* 238n sees this section as a warning to the monarchy, and says that "the king" is Solomon; so it probably belongs to the early days of the divided monarchy.

17[1] I.e. Joshua.

17[2] The evidence of composite authorship in Joshua and Judges is as copious as it is difficult to unravel; certainly some of the elements are very old.

18[1] That is, the Reformation in England coming from Henry VIII's insistence upon divorcing Catherine of Aragon. He had married her on his accession in 1509 with a special papal dispensation to marry his deceased brother's widow. Cranmer declared the marriage null in May 1533, all attempts to secure a papal annulment having failed. In 1534 the Pope declared the marriage valid and excommunicated Henry; Henry then abolished Roman jurisdiction and revenues in England, and in 1535 the dissolution of the monasteries began.

ance into the hand of thy servant; and now shall I die for thirst, and fall into the hand of the uncircumcised? But God clave an hollow place that *was* in the jaw, and there came water thereout; and when he had drunk, his spirit came again, and he revived . . .

Probably, some narrow Ghyll[1] or Rent in the mountain was named the Ass's Jaw~~bone~~ and some remarkable Rock called the Jaw-bone, which Samson by his vast strength lifted up & whirled down on the Philistine Troops winding up the Rent—. This is implied in the literal meaning of Ramath-lehi, viz. the *lifting up* of the Jaw-bone[2] —Afterwards he found a spring or collection of Rain Water in the very place, which he had layed open. It is an interesting relic of the enigmatic Narration, characteristic of the heroic age.

20 pp 309–11 | 1 Samuel 8.19–20

Nevertheless the people refused to obey the voice of Samuel; and they said, Nay; but we will have a king over us; That we also may be like all the nations; and that our king may judge us, and go out before us, and fight our battles.

v. 19. In ancient records, composed in the infancy of historic Literature, Negative proofs are of small force = ex. gr. the objection to the 17th of Deuteronomy, v. 14–20,[1] that had this passage existed in the Law-book as it came from the hand of Moses, the People would not have failed to remind Samuel, that the measure had been predicted, fore-ordained and provided for by God.—Answer. Perhaps, they did: and perhaps, the passage was known only to the more learned among the Priests. During the long anarchy & successive revolutions from the death of Joshua to the appointment of Joel and Abiah, the Hebrew Tribes had fallen into a state of ⟨great⟩ Rudeness & Ignorance. David was forced to procure Artists & Artizans from

---

19[1] On *gil*, *OED* notes that "The spelling *ghyll*, often used in guide-books to the Lake district, seems to have been introduced by Wordsworth". WW used "ghyll" in *An Evening Walk* line 54 (composed 1787–9, published 1793) and noted that the word, having the same meaning as "dingle", was (he believed) "a term confined to this [Lake] country". See also *W Prose* II 274, 280, and cf 443 n to 1220–4.

19[2] C's version comes from the marginal gloss: "That is, *the lifting up of the jawbone*, or *casting away of the*

jawbone"—a folk etymology. The literal meaning of the name is *rāmath* ("hill" and suggestive of throwing), *lehi* (a place-name, as in Judges 14, and suggestive of the jaw-bone); the gloss explains the pun.

20[1] Esp Deut 17.18–19: "And it shall be, when he [the king] sitteth upon the throne of his kingdom, that he shall write him a copy of this law in a book out of that which is before the priests the Levites: And it shall be with him, and he shall read therein all the days of his life. . .".

Tyre—Contrast this with the beautiful works finished in the Wilderness, the ornaments of the Ark &c./ on the other hand, it is far more improbable that so wise and evidently far-sighted a Statesman, as Moses, should not have calculated on the probability of such an event, and taken measures for the continuance of his Code of Laws under all forms of the Executive Power, royal or republican. And yet I see no harm in supposing these verses, in Deuter^y. to have been inserted by Samuel. See v. 25.[2]

21   pp 368–9, pencil, overtraced | 2 Samuel 24.1–15

And again the anger of the LORD was kindled against Israel, and he moved David against them to say, Go, number Israel and Judah. ... So when they had gone through all the land, they came to Jerusalem at the end of nine months and twenty days. And Joab gave up the sum of the number of the people unto the king: and there were in Israel eight hundred thousand valiant men that drew the sword; and the men of Judah *were* five hundred thousand men. And David's heart smote him after that he had numbered the people. And David said unto the LORD, I have sinned greatly in that I have done: and now, I beseech thee, O LORD, take away the iniquity of thy servant; for I have done very foolishly.... So the LORD sent a pestilence upon Israel from the morning even to the time appointed: and there died of the people from Dan even to Beersheba seventy thousand men....

This (XXIV) ch. is startling for *us*, under the present dispensation, but a profound moral is contained therein. Men are not to be *counted*; but individually weighed. Persons may not be degraded into *Things*; nor a Nation treated as a *property*.[1] S. T. C. Still it may be asked— what Law David violated?

22   p 549, pencil, overtraced | Job 3.25–6

For the thing which I greatly feared is come upon me, and that which I was afraid of is come unto me. I was not in safety, neither had I rest, neither was I quiet; yet trouble came.

not the meaning of the original exactly "Yea! (even there in my highest prosperity) I was never *quite* at ease, never *wholly* free from

---

20[2] Probably 1 Sam 10.25 (since there is no v 25 to Deut 17 or to 1 Sam 8): "Then Samuel told the people the manner of the kingdom, and wrote *it* in a book, and laid *it* up before the LORD."

21[1] C's fundamental and recurrent argument against slavery: see ANALYSIS 7 n 2.

anxiety; or without some obscure foreboding: and now the Storm of Disquiet (or Trouble) has come indeed!["]—/ This is the Spirit of the original[1]

23   p 550, pencil, overtraced | Job 5.7

Yet man is born unto trouble, as the sparks fly upward.

7. One is sorry to disturb a Rendering which has passed into a Proverb; but the context requires a different translation, viz. Man is born for the trouble (*of Man*) as the Birds of Prey to a high flight. i.e. to soar in order to pounce.[1]

24   p 552 | Job 7.12

Am I a sea, or a whale, that thou settest a watch over me?

12. Obscure. The Version by Cohen has Sea-monster instead of whale.[1] Could it be rendered—the Dæmon of the Sea? Am I any fixed part in the order of things?[2]

25   p 553 | Job 7.20

I have sinned; what shall I do unto thee, O thou preserver of men? why hast thou set me as a mark against thee, so that I am a burden to myself?

VII. 20. Have I sinned, i.e. granted, that I have sinned, yet how have ⟨I⟩ injured thee?—/[1] a most beautiful thought utterly lost in our Version.

26   pp 552–3 | Job 8.17–18

His roots are wrapped about the heap, *and* seeth the place of stones. If he destroy him from his place, then *it* shall deny him, *saying*, I have not seen thee.

22[1] Apparently a free version of Cohen, modified by the force of C's identification with Job's utterance.

23[1] A literal tr of Cohen; but the phrase following "i.e." is C's. There is a longer version of this note in N 37 f 27[v]. *NEB* reads: "man is born to trouble as surely as birds fly [*or* as sparks shoot] upwards". C copied Job 5.6 and 5.23 in one of his earliest notebook entries—*CN* I 8.

24[1] *Die Heilige Schrift...nebst verbesserter deutscher Uebersetzung* ed S. J. Cohen (18 pts Hamburg 1824–7): Hebrew text of OT with German translation, including Mendelssohn's. C refers to this edition several times in notebook entries of c 1828–9, in NN 37, 42, 45, 46, 53. Green's library included a copy in 4 vols: *Green SC* (1880) 36. For the Sea-monster see **29** and n 1.

24[2] *NEB*: "Am I the monster of the deep, am I the sea-serpent, | that thou settest a watch over me?"

25[1] *NEB*: "If I have sinned, how do I injure thee, | thou watcher of the hearts of men? | Why hast thou made me thy butt, | and why have I become thy target?"

VIII. 17. Neither Sense nor Syntax. The Poet compares the hypocrite to a Tree growing close beside a the House, and carrying the simile adds, His very Roots (i.e. the Man's inmost affections) wind round the Stones—and he gloteth on this Dwelling of Stones—18.—which is incapable of returning his attachment—.[1]

27   p 560 | Job 19.25–8

For I know *that* my redeemer liveth, and *that* he shall stand at the latter *day* upon the earth: And *though* after my skin *worms* destroy this *body*, yet in my flesh shall I see God: Whom I shall see for myself, and mine eyes shall behold, and not another; *though* my reins be consumed within me. But ye should say, Why persecute we him? seeing the root of the matter is found in me.

25. I know, my Redeemer liveth: he will survive the Last on Earth.

26. And when this Skin, this Flesh, shall have rotted away—I see God.

27. That I myself ⟨may⟩ see him, with my own eyes and not by those of strangers, is my burning Desire (= my fervent Wish.) 28. And that ye may exclaim—when ye shall have found out the true grounds of my case—Why do we persecute him?[1]

28   p 562 | Job, end of ch 21

I seem, thro' great part of this most precious as most ancient Poem, to feel that the *Clew* of the argument is yet to be given.

29   p 575, pencil, overtraced | Job 40.15, 41.1

Behold now behemoth [*gloss*: Or, *the elephant*, as some think], which I made with thee: he eateth grass as an ox. . . . Canst thou draw out leviathan [*gloss*: That is, *a whale*, or, *a whirlpool*] with an hook? or his tongue with a cord which thou lettest down?

The ignorance of natural history among the Learned of that age is

---

26[1] Suggested by Cohen. *NEB* vv 16–18: "His is the lush growth of a plant in the sun, | pushing out shoots over the garden; | but its roots become entangled in a stony patch | and run against a bed of rock. | Then someone uproots it from its place, | which disowns it and says, 'I have never known you'."

27[1] A literal tr of Cohen, except that

C writes "burning Desire" where Cohen has "innigste Wunsch". In N 37 f 24 C was "delighted that Cohen's . . . literal rendering . . . decisively favours the common interpretation" and went on to give this same tr with variations. C made another comment on Job 19.25–6 in DONNE *Sermons* COPY B **88**.

strikingly instanced in the explanation of Behemoth, evidently the Hippopotamus, by the Elephant, and Leviathan, no, the Crocodile, by the Whale!!/[1]

30 p 577 | Psalms 2.12

Kiss the Son, lest he be angry, and ye perish *from* the way, when his wrath is kindled but a little. Blessed *are* all they that put their trust in him.

12. N.B. There are four different ways of rendering *nashku bar.*—1. Submit to disciplines (Septuagint: πραξασθε παιδειας) 2. Kiss the Son. 3. Worship in purity. 4. Cloathe yourselves with innocence—!!!!—[1]

31 p 582 | Ps 17

[David craveth defence of God against his enemies. He sheweth their pride, craft, and eagerness.]

Ps. XVII. must be, I apprehend, spiritually interpreted of, or supposed to be uttered by, the Messiah himself in his humiliation, or as I rather think, by the persecuted Church Militant in her first purity with Christ as her Head.[1]

32 p 585 | Ps 22

My God, my God, why hast thou forsaken me? *why art thou so* far from helping me, *and from* the words of my roaring?...

XXII. Most deeply interesting as being the Psalm, which our Lord on the Cross *gave out* with a loud voice, for the purpose of directing the attention of his Mother & his beloved ~~discipline~~ Disciple[a][1] to the

---

a "Disciple", first written in ink, is cancelled in pencil and rewritten, possibly by C

29[1] "Of that age"—i.e. the age of the glossator. That behemoth is a hippopotamus, not an elephant, and that leviathan is a crocodile and not a whale, is agreed by modern scholars. C had attacked the question of behemoth as early as 1796 in a footnote to *Religious Musings*, but inconclusively: "...Poetically, it designates any large Quadruped." *PW* (EHC) i 119 n 2.

30[1] Septuagint reads δράξασθε, not πράξασθε, but there is no significant difference in meaning. In N 37 f 24ᵛ C renders (1) as "Exercise disciplines", and attributes (2) to Jerome's com-

mentary and (3) to Jerome's text; he attributes (4) to Cohen, but could also have found it in Cocceius, who suggests "armamini puritate" (be armed with innocence). He ends his note: "Mem. To ask Professor Hurwitz for an explanation." RV offers as gloss "Worship in purity"; RSV reads "Kiss his feet"; *NEB* reads "tremble, and kiss the king".

31[1] Ps 17 is an individual lament or prayer, uttered by one beset with enemies.

32[1] The words "My God, my God, why hast thou forsaken me" occur in Matt 27.46 and Mark 15.34, addressed

fulfilment of this prophecy; at that moment before their eyes, as a sure pledge of the equal fulfilment of the triumphant prophecy that follows.[2]

33   p 586 | Ps 23.3

He restoreth my soul: he leadeth me in the paths of righteousness for his name's sake.

XXIII. v. 3.—name's sake = for Christ's sake. See John's Gospel where our Lord himself calls himself the Name which the Father had glorified above all names even with himself—i.e. the Numen, to which he had from everlasting communicated his own deity.[1] S. T. C.

34   p 587 | Ps 27.4

One *thing* have I desired of the LORD, that will I seek after; that I may dwell in the house of the LORD all the days of my life, to behold the beauty of the LORD, and to enquire in his temple.

Ps. 27.4. If this be rightly translated, Temple, how could it be a Psalm of *David*? But a Ps. of D. must often mean no more than a Davidic Psalm: as we say, a Pindaric Ode.[1]

35   p 594 | Ps 38

[David moveth God to take compassion of his pitiful case.] O Lord, rebuke me not in thy wrath: neither chasten me in thy hot displeasure. . . .

---

to Mary and John. In *CN* III 3890 C advanced "the hypothesis...that Christ in repeating Eli. Eli, lama sabachthani, really repeated the whole 22nd Psalm". Cf *TT* 30 May 1830.

32[2] I.e. vv 27–31: "All the ends of the world shall remember and turn unto the Lord...".

33[1] John 12.28. Cf also John 17.6 and 26. C finds significance in the similarity between *numen* (spirit, will, power) and *nomen* (name), for which see also **64** and n 1, below. See also *CN* III 3954, BLANCO WHITE *Practical Evidence* 12, BOOK OF COMMON PRAYER copy B 12, and BROWNE *Works* 42. Cf "A good Father speaks to us in nomine Dei; a Mother in *numine*". N F° f 97.

34[1] Solomon began building the Temple about five years after David's death. The association of the Psalms with David is a very ancient tradition, and the ascription of the whole collection to David received rabbinical and patristic support. Of the total of 150 Psalms, 73 (including 39 of the 41 psalms in Bk I) have the superscription "*le-David*", tr "*A Psalm* of David" in AV. Whether any of these are genuinely from David's hand seems to be beyond proof, but it is not impossible that a few are. C draws a parallel with the vogue in English poetry—begun by Cowley and still alive in C's time—for reproducing the rhapsodic tone and prosodic intricacy of Pindar's own odes, in most cases an excuse for high rhetoric and loosely improvised metrics.

O let a man afflicted with disease or with self-condemnation *pray* the Psalms on his knees—& he will find, in how narrow a circle all the deep joys & sorrows of human nature are contained!—[1]

36   pp 596–7 | Ps 41.10–11

But thou, O Lord, be merciful unto me, and raise me up, that I may requite them. By this I know that thou favourest me, because mine enemy doth not triumph over me.

XLI: 10. The Psalmist must here be interpreted as typical of the God-man, the Divine Humanity struggling against the fallen Humanity, the *Corrupted* Faculties & Impulses of Man. No otherwise can these passages be reconciled with the Morality of the Gospel.

37   p 599 | Ps 49

A new translation of the Psalms is a great Desideratum. The Version in the Prayer-book is admirably suited to devotional purposes/ but this ~~does~~ is not accurate enough to compensate for its inferiority in all other respects—The 49th is erroneous throughout.—[1]

38   p 599 | Ps 49.7–8

None *of them* can by any means redeem his brother, nor give to God a ransom for him: (For the redemption of their soul *is* precious, and it ceaseth for ever)...

v. 8. For the Ransom of the Soul is a vast price, and it (i.e. the Ransom-money) will be wanting forever—i.e. it will never be forthcoming.[1]

35[1] For C on prayer in a state of self-condemnation see e.g. *CL* III 478–9 (Apr 1814), and cf *CN* III 4183 and BOOK OF COMMON PRAYER COPY B **1** n 1. On prayer generally see esp BOOK OF COMMON PRAYER COPY B **29** and n 9.

37[1] Miles Coverdale's version of the Psalms, though earlier in date than AV and less accurate in points of detail, was printed with BCP as being better "suited to devotional purposes" and continued to be the version sung and said in churches until this century. "I wish the Psalms were translated afresh; or, rather, that the present version were revised", C said. *TT* 30 May 1830.

When he made a memorandum in Jan 1830 "To try to paraphrase and apply to my own Soul and spirit the 42nd and 43rd Psalms, in one Ode, or sweet musical movement" he intended "to adopt the *Bible* Version as the ground". N 44 f 6. N 29 ff 20[v], 71 shows C using George Horne's *A Commentary on the Book of Psalms* (2 vols Liverpool 1816). Of the difficult Ps 49 there are about as many differences between AV and *NEB* as between BCP and AV.

38[1] *NEB*: "Alas! no man can ever ransom himself | nor pay God the price of that release; | his ransom would cost too much, | for ever beyond his power to pay...".

39   p 599 | Ps 49.10

For <u>he seeth</u> *that* wise men die, likewise the fool and the brutish person perish, and leave their wealth to others.
we see: one sees.[1]

40   p 600 | Ps 50

[The majesty of God in the church. His order to gather saints. The pleasure of God is not in ceremonies, but in sincerity of obedience.] The mighty God, *even* the LORD, hath spoken, and called the earth from the rising of the sun unto the going down thereof. . . .

What can Greece or Rome present, worthy to be compared with the 50th Psalm, either in sublimity of the Imagery or in moral elevation?/

41   p 601 | Ps 54.2–3

Hear my prayer, O God; give ear to the words of my mouth. For strangers are risen up against me, and oppressors seek after my soul: they have not set God before them. Selah.

LIV.—*The Seed of Christ* in the Body of the Death, the divine Germ or Spirit in Man, here speaks. The Strangers are the workings of the Alien Will, the mind of the Flesh./[1]

42   p 607

[To the chief Musician, A Psalm or Song of David.][a]

See v. 29—This Psalm could not therefore have been composed earlier than the reign of Solomon—[1]

43   p 607 | Ps 68.29

Because of thy temple at Jerusalem shall kings bring presents unto thee.

68th v. 29. How can this be explained on the assumption that it was composed by David? But these inscriptions are of doubtful age & of little authority against internal evidence.[1]

---

[a] The traditional descriptive title of the Psalm as printed in C's Bible, as regularly in copies of AV

39[1] *NEB*: "But remember this: wise men must die; | stupid men, brutish men, all perish."

41[1] For φρόνημα σάρκος, which C usually renders "the mind of the flesh", and of which "the alien will" is an unusual version, see BAXTER *Reliquiae* COPY B 115 n 10.

42[1] For v 29 see **43** textus. For the implied anachronism see **34** n 1, above.

43[1] See **42** n 1, above.

44 p 611 | Ps 73, esp v 20

As in a dream when one awaketh; so, O Lord, when thou awakest, thou shalt despise their image.

I should conclude that this, 73rd, Psalm, was written during or after the Captivity, when the inward and spiritual Sense of the Threats and Promises began to struggle thro' the cloudy shrine of the Letter.— The "image" is = the Umbra of the Greeks & Romans, the Manes.[1]

45 p 612 | Ps 74.14

Thou brakest the heads of leviathan in pieces, *and* gavest him *to be* meat to the people inhabiting the wilderness.

v. 14. It is not impossible, that some tradition may have been preserved of the inundation caused by the drawing back of the Waters during the Exodus—& that the stranded Whales or Grampuses had become food for the Nomad Tribes, as now for the Greenlanders.[1]

46 p 619 | Ps 88.5

Free among the dead, like the slain that lie in the grave, whom thou remembrest no more: and they are cut off from thy hand.

88. v. 5. *Free* in the sense, I conjecture, in which we describe a denizen as *free* of the City of London. See Job. III. v. 13–19. A Denizen of S̶h̶ Hades—made free of Sheol.[1]

[44][1] That is, as C understands the verse, the Lord when awakened to his work of redemption will treat the wicked as no more substantial or menacing than the σκία, *umbra*, the shadowy souls of the dead (*Manes*). The Septuagint reading, however— εἴκων ("image" in NT Greek), not σκία—suggests a meaning different from C's, and *NEB* gives yet a different sense to the verse: "like a dream when a man rouses himself, O Lord, | like images in sleep which are dismissed on waking".

[45][1] For C's early use of David Cranz *The History of Greenland* (1767) and of Leemius *De Lapponibus Finmarchiae* (Copenhagen 1767) see *RX* 94–101; there are in Cranz accounts of whales found dead or driven ashore and eaten, e.g. II 41, 109, 248. The reference in *AR* (1825) 97 to "the Lives of...Egede, Swartz, and the Missionaries of the Frozen World" recalls Cranz's account of the Greenland missions (which, however, does not include Swartz).

[46][1] Job 3.13–19 reads: "For now should I have lain still and been quiet, I should have slept: then had I been at rest, With kings and counsellors of the earth, who built desolate places for themselves....The small and great are there; and the servant is free from his master." The parallel is not suggested by the AV gloss. The Hebrew of Ps 48.5 is indeed obscure; *NEB* reads: "Like a man who lies dead | or the slain who sleep in the grave", avoiding the word "free".

47 p 627, brackets in pencil | Ps 104.3–6

Who layeth the beams of his chambers in the waters: who maketh
the clouds his chariot: who walketh upon the wings of the wind:
Who maketh his angels spirits; his ministers a flaming fire. . . .
Thou coveredst it with the deep as with a garment. . .

V. 3. Who archeth (or vaulteth) his Floors (or Chambers) with
Waters—
  4. Maketh the Winds his Messengers, the Lightnings his Servants.
  6. Thou coveredst the Abyss as with a Garment—[1]

48 pp 654–5 | Proverbs 8

[The fame, and evidency of wisdom. The excellency, the nature, the
power, the riches, and the eternity of wisdom. Wisdom is to be
desired for the blessedness it bringeth.]

This majestic, profound and pregnant Chapter might be illustrated
from the ~~Pro~~ Eschylian Prometheus—which in like manner, according to the Law or Idea of mythical Poesy, represents in one place
the Gift & its qualities & virtues, in another the divine Giver.[1]
Beware, that you do not degrade the latter half of this Ch. from V. 12.
by understanding it as a mere allegorical Personification of an
Abstract Term[2]—The Son of God *is* Reason (Logos), the H. Ghost
is wisdom—living substantial R and W.

49 pp 668–9 | Prov 24.17–18

Rejoice not when thine enemy falleth, and let not thine heart be glad
when he stumbleth: Lest the LORD see *it*, and it displease him, and
he turn away his wrath from him.

v. 18. I should hope, that the Hebrew would bear to be rendered

47[1] C is translating Cohen literally except that he reads "Lightnings" for Cohen's *Feuer* (fire). *NEB* reads: "and on their waters laid the beams of thy pavilion...who makest the winds thy messengers | and flames of fire thy servants...the deep overspread it [i.e. the earth] like a cloak..."
48[1] C had delivered his one paper to the Royal Society of Literature, "On the *Prometheus* of Aeschylus", on 18 May 1825; the text is in *LR* II 323–59.
48[2] C gave continual warning against the unrecognised personifica-
tion of abstractions: see e.g. *Lects 1795* (*CC*) 208–9. See esp vv 12, 14, 15, 23, 30: "I wisdom dwell with prudence, and find out knowledge of witty inventions. ... Counsel *is* mine, and sound wisdom: I *am* understanding: I have strength. By me kings reign, and princes decree justice....I was set up from everlasting, from the beginning, or ever the earth was....Then I was by him, *as* one brought up *with him*: and I was daily *his* delight, rejoicing always before him...".

"transfer" instead of "turn away". For as it now stands, it proposes a shockingly immoral and vindictive motive: while "lest you should draw it on yourself" is a motive, by which the best man might be influenced. *S. T. C.* But if so, v. 22, XXV. must be rendered—"thou shalt melt him down"—i.e. turn his hate into love./[1]

50   p 669 | Prov 26.10

The great *God* that formed all *things* both rewardeth the fool, and rewardeth transgressors.

v. 10.—Q[y]?—By taking fools and transgressors into his service a great man grieveth all—[1]

51   pp 674–5 | Ecclesiastes 1.12

I the Preacher was king over Israel in Jerusalem.

Eccl. I. 12. Is it not wonderful, that with this verse before their eyes Biblical Critics should be found, who seriously attribute this philosophical Dialogue to Solomon! tho' the principal Speaker, who acts the part of the Sceptic & Epicurean, in the Drama, announces it by —I am (i.e. represent) that Solomon who *was* King at Jer! and tho' the Hebrew is evidently of the same age with that [of][a] Esther, and the VI first chapters of Daniel.[1]

52   p 694 | Isaiah 9.6

For unto us a child is born, unto us a son is given: and the government shall be upon his shoulder: and his name shall be called Wonderful, Counsellor, The mighty God, The everlasting Father, The Prince of Peace.

a Word supplied by the editor

49[1] *NEB* of Prov 24.18 reads: "or the Lord will see and be displeased with you, | and he will cease to be angry with him". Prov 25.22 (AV) reads: "For thou shalt heap coals of fire upon his head, and the Lord shall reward thee".
50[1] AV offers an alternative reading: "A great *man* grieveth all; and he hireth the fool, he hireth also transgressors." *NEB* reads: "Like an archer who shoots at any passer-by | is one who hires a stupid man or a drunkard." In any case—and this may be why C queried it—the verse breaks the pattern of a sequence of aphorisms on fools and folly.

51[1] As part of the "Wisdom literature" Ecclesiastes was traditionally associated with the name of Solomon, but it was recognised in C's day that, although there were early elements in the book, it had been compiled, modified, and probably largely composed when the authors of Esther and Esdras and the compiler of Daniel flourished: see e.g. EICHHORN *Alte Testament* III 571 (not annotated). The consensus of modern scholarship places the date as c 168–100 B.C. For C on the date of Dan 1–6 see **70** n 1, below.

V. 6. "The Father of ages".[1] Our version tends to confound the distinctive names and attributes of the first and second Person (=hypostasis) of the Trinity.[*]

[*][a] The Word translated everlasting—In Hebrew bears only the signification—of hidden times past and hidden times to come—In Greek—the signification is for ages of ages Isai. 9–6 Everlasting Father—the Father of hidden ages past & hidden ages to come.[2] S. T. C.

53 p 696 | Isa 11

[The peaceable kingdom of the Branch out of the root of Jesse. The victorious restoration of Israel, and vocation of the Gentiles.]

Q[y]?—Do we not fix our imagination too much on Christ, personally or individually, in the interpretation of these prophecies?—Is it not more often Christ in his *Church*? rather than Christ in his divinity?— As the latter, it is himself, who speaks, who *is* the Spirit.

54 p 720 | Isa 41

[God expostulateth with his people, about his mercies to the church, about his promises, and about the vanity of idols.]

The 41st Ch. is a most pertinent *Pioneer* to the 42nd.—In no Form, to which the Gentiles could refer as God manifested, could even a plausible *Pretence* to an Epiphany of the *Divine* Nature be found. Then follows the *Contrast*—the true exegesis of God in Man.

55 pp 721–3 | Isa 42.1, 5, 8

Behold my servant, whom I uphold, mine elect, *in whom* my soul delighteth: I have put my spirit upon him; he shall bring forth judgment to the Gentiles.... Thus saith God the Lord, he that created the heavens ... I *am* the Lord; that is my name ...

a Footnote on a loose scrap of paper at pp 694/5, not in C's hand

52[1] *NEB*: "Father for all time [*or* of a wide realm]."

52[2] The Hebrew word here for AV "everlasting", *ad*, implies duration or continuity in contrast to *olam*— "of old"—of AV Gen 21.33 and of Isa 40.28. This passage is perhaps best understood, however, in the light of Isa 40.28, in which "the everlasting God, the Lord, the Creator of the ends of the earth" is conceived as lord both of the universe and of time, as distinct from "the God of antiquity" implied in "the everlasting God" of Gen 21.33: see *Peake* 448f. In the Septuagint version of Isa 9.6 there is no phrase to correspond with "the everlasting God".

This is the great, the aweful Question. "Behold *my Servant*, whom *I* uphold." Who is the Servant? who the I? The latter unquestionably is God the Lord. "I am the Lord—"[1] And it is as little a question among Christians—that the Servant of the Lord is Jesus the Christ. But according to all ~~but~~ Christians, with exception of one obscure Sect, by courtesy only admitted to the Christian Name, Jesus is likewise God the Lord.[2] The current solution of this Problem is, that in Jesus two Natures were united in one Person. But the Prophet seems to speak of two different Persons, and not of two distinct tho' united Natures. On a satisfactory Clearing up of this difficulty the right faith in Christ and the true conception of the Gospel Scheme mainly depend.[3] To assert that God the Lord means the Father in distinction from the co-eternal Son will go but a little way, & give rise to heavier difficulties than it removes. *S. T. C.*

56   p 721, pencil, overtraced | Isa 42.15

I will make waste mountains and hills, and dry up all their herbs; and I will make the rivers islands, and I will dry up the pools.

ravines?[1]

57   p 729 | Isa 50–1

There is a Sublimity, only to be fitly acknowleged by Adoration, in these passages, in which the Jehovah WORD, the Supreme *Being*, and Eternal Reason, speaks of himself, as a Servant to the Supreme WILL, the absolute Good self-affirmed in the Holy I AM.[1]

55[1] The first "Servant-Song"—Isa 42.1–4—presents a servant who is at once righteous and a rebel; the three following Songs—49.1–6, 50.4–9, 52.13–53.12—present a servant with a mission from God. A traditional belief of the Jews was that the Messiah was here represented, but Christians have traditionally identified the Servant with the Christ, as the chapter summaries in AV declare. Rationalists long before C had preferred to take Isaiah to refer to the nation of Israel—a view that modern scholars usually accept unless they identify the Servant with a particular historical person. Cf **53**, above, and **57**, below.

55[2] C refers to the Unitarians, for which see BAHRDT **1** n 1.

55[3] As in **11**, above, and **57**, below, C is arguing that the Jehovah of OT is the Son, the Word, and that the words "God the Lord" (as in Isa 42.5) can be used of either Father or Son. But this interpretation involves an inconsistency that he does not solve here (though one solution is proposed in **53**, above, and another in N 36). If the "I" of Isa 42.1 is the Jehovah/Son/ Word, and identical with the Servant, and if "God the Lord" is being used throughout the Bible to refer only to the Father, then the deity (though not the divinity) of Christ is by implication denied.

56[1] *NEB*: "I will turn rivers into desert wastes", noting that the Hebrew literally means "coasts and islands".

57[1] For the implications for C of the name of God—"I AM THAT I AM" of Exod 3.14—see **119** n 1, below.

58   p 735 | Isa 59.5

They hatch cockatrice' eggs, and weave the spider's web: he that eateth of their eggs dieth, and that which is crushed breaketh out into a viper.

V. 5. In the Standard newspaper of 23ʳᵈ Decʳ 1827 there is an extract from an American scientific journal, of an egg which on being broken contained a green snake; the Hen was opened, & a number of soft eggs found, each containing a snake.[1]

59   pp 738-9 | Isa 63.1-6

Who *is* this that cometh from Edom, with dyed garments from Bozrah? this *that is* glorious in his apparel, travelling in the greatness of his strength? Wherefore *art thou* red in thine apparel, and thy garments like him that treadeth in the winefat? I have trodden the winepress alone; and of the people *there was* none with me: for I will tread them in mine anger, and trample them in my fury; and their blood shall be sprinkled upon my garments, and I will stain all my raiment. For the day of vengeance *is* in mine heart, and the year of my redeemed is come. And I looked, and *there was* none to help; and I wondered, that *there was* none to uphold: therefore mine own arm brought salvation unto me; and my fury, it upheld me. And I will tread down the people in mine anger, and make them drunk in my fury, and I will bring down their strength to the earth.

C. 63. v. 1–6. After the ascension into Glory, all power in Heaven and Earth, i.e. the government of the whole human race, was delivered to the Son of Man = the Son of God incarnate in Jesus, and anointed High-priest and King. Henceforward, we trust in Christ, as the Personal Providence: and to the Christ or Messiah so contemplated this sublime Oracle refers, and specially to the Coming of the Son of Man in the destruction of the Jewish State, in which the Armies of the Roman Empire (Edom) were the Scourge in his hand./

60   p 740, pencil | Isa 65.17–18

For behold, I create new heavens and a new earth: and the former shall not be remembered, nor come into mind. But be ye glad and re-

58[1] Not located in any *Standard* of 1–31 Dec 1827 or 1828; the newspaper edition that C seems to refer to may no longer be extant. C's *Sancti Dominici Pallium* was published in the *Standard* of 21 May 1827: see C. BUTLER *Book of the RC Church. NEB* reads: "They hatch snakes' [*lit.* vipers'] eggs."

joice for ever *in that* which I create: for, behold, I create Jerusalem a rejoicing, and her people a joy.

Both Heaven and earth shall pass away[a1]

61 p 741 | Isa 66

[The glorious God will be served in humble sincerity. He comforteth the humble with the marvellous generation, and with the gracious benefits of the church. God's severe judgments against the wicked. The Gentiles shall have an holy church.]

I conjecture, that this last Chapter was delivered after the Return and during the building of the Temple—The last verse is of difficult interpretation/—to wit, the "going forth & look upon".—[1]

62 p 742 | Jeremiah 1.1–3

The words of Jeremiah . . . To whom the word of the Lord came in the days of Josiah. . . . It came also in the days of Jehoiakim . . .

I cannot but regret the constant use of the neuter pronoun in our Version, wherever "the Word" is the Antecedent. The *Context* plainly requires "He", and the express authority of John & Paul is decisive for the propriety of the personal Pronoun.[1]

63 p 756 | Jer 13

[In the type of a linen girdle, God prefigureth the destruction of his people. Under the parable of the bottles filled with wine he foretelleth their drunkenness in misery. He exhorteth to prevent their future judgments. He sheweth their abominations as the cause thereof.]

N.B. The most judicious Commentators suppose this and similar Incidents (Hosea I and II: Ezekiel IV. &c) to have passed in Vision.[1]

---

[a] This note is badly rubbed and almost illegible

60[1] Cf Matt 5.18, Luke 16.17.

61[1] Isa 66.24 (the last verse in the book): "And they shall go forth, and look upon the carcases of the men that have transgressed against me: for their worm shall not die, neither shall their fire be quenched; and they shall be an abhorring unto all flesh." The sense is clear enough, even in AV, if "they" refers to "all flesh". Cf *NEB*: "and they [i.e. 'all mankind' of v 23] shall come out and see | the dead bodies of those who have rebelled against me [i.e. the Lord]; their worm [i.e. the worm of 'those who have rebelled against me'] shall not die...they shall be abhorred by all mankind". Isaiah chs 56-66 is now considered to have been composed after the return from exile (538 B.C.) and probably after the rebuilding of the second Temple (520–516 B.C.).

62[1] *NEB* avoids this nice difficulty by translating: "The word of the Lord came to him...also during the reign of Jehoiakim...".

63[1] This is a view now commonly held by biblical scholars.

64　pp 756–7 | Jer 13.11

For as the girdle cleaveth to the loins of a man, so have I caused to cleave unto me the whole house of Israel and the whole house of Judah, said the Lord; that they might be unto me for a people, and for a name, and for a praise, and for a glory: but they would not hear.

V. 11. As the Filial Word to God, so should the whole of Israel have been to the Word, the Messiah—Messias diffusus—Nomen Dei, idem ac *Numen*, i.e. præsentia intelligibilis.[1] *Ye are Gods*.[2] Estis Numina/ Gloria ut Solis = Splendor sempiternè generatus: Praise, Sonus seu Verbum glorificans[3]—all three titles of the Messiah, adopted by the Cabbalists, and used by St Paul.[4]

65　p 777 | Jer 32.26–44

[. . . God confirmeth the captivity, but promiseth a gracious return.]

That the *Spirit* of these Promises will be fulfilled whenever the Jews present the moral conditions, i.e. thorough change of heart & principle in the whole race, I see no reason to doubt, & S[t] Paul's authority for affirming—but how the literal fulfilment can be reconciled with Christianity, ex. gr. Sacrifice, I do not see.

66　p 779 | Jer 33

[God promiseth a gracious return, a joyful state, a settled government, Christ the Branch of righteousness, a continuance of kingdom and priesthood, and a stability of a blessed seed.]

It is important to distinguish carefully the Word of God which came to the Prophets from the inferences, which they as unaided Men

64[1] "Messiah spread abroad—the Name [*Nomen*] of God, which is the same as his *Numen*—that is, his intelligible presence". Cf *AR* (1825) 223: "The Name of a thing, in the original sense of the word, Name (*Nomen*, Νουμενον, τὸ *intelligibile, id quod intelligitur*) expresses that which is *understood* in an appearance, that which we place (or make to *stand*) *under* it, as the condition of its real existence...". See also *CL* v 325–6, vi 896, and **33** n 1, above.

64[2] See Ps 82.6, John 10.34, and cf Gen 3.5.

64[3] "Ye are Numina (? Divine Spirits)/ a Glory as of the Sun = a Splendour eternally generated: Praise, a glorifying Sound or Word". The phrase "Gloria ut Solis", if it echoes John 1.14—"the glory as of the only begotten of the Father", i.e. the Son, and here specifically "the Word"— could also be a submerged instance of the fusion of Son/Sun, for which see Aurelius 35 n 2.

64[4] For St Paul's use of these terms see e.g. Eph 1.6, 12; 2 Thess 1.12; Heb 1–3; and cf 1 Cor 15.41. For C and the Cabbala, see Brerewood 1 n 4.

drew from the divine declarations. Thus: Jeremiah probably supposed that this splendid promise was to be fulfilled at the close of 70 years; but this is neither expressed or implied in the prophetic words themselves dictated to him by the Lord.

67   pp 786–7 | Jer 38.23

So they shall bring out all thy wives and thy children to the Chaldeans: and thou shalt not escape out of their hand, but shalt be taken by the hand of the king of Babylon: and thou shalt cause this city to be burned with fire.

V. 23. The best if not the only way of accounting for the incongruous construction of this verse is the on many grounds highly probable hypothesis of Pr. Eichhorn, that our Hebrew Jeremiah is a correctedr and more complete Copy of of Jer: Oracles made or dictated by the Prophet himself for the Exiles to take with them into Babylon: while the Greek Sep^t was translated from the original ~~or~~ copy dictated to Baruch, at different times & written on many different Rolls/ & that in v. 23 the Dictator or Copyist recurred unconsciously to the old Copy ~~without~~ forgetting that the beginning of the sentence had had its construction changed. By referring to the Septuagint (i.e. the old Copy) you will find this confirmed—.[1] It is a mistake common in dictating. Thucydides abounds with such.[2]

68   pp 800–1, pencil, overtraced | Jer 50.8, 9

Remove out of the midst of Babylon, and go forth out of the land of the Chaldeans, and be as the he goats before the flocks. For, lo, I will raise, and cause to come up against Babylon, an assembly of great nations from the north country: and they shall set themselves in array against her; from thence she shall be taken: their arrows *shall be* as of a mighty expert man; none shall return in vain.

[1] Eichhorn's discussion of the composition of Jeremiah, which C did not annotate, begins at *Einleitung ins Alte Testament* III 121. C seems to be thinking, not of 38.23 (which does not show any "incongruous construction"), but of 38.28, about which Eichhorn makes a similar remark (III 156): "So Jeremiah abode in the court of the prison until the day that Jerusalem was taken: and he was there when Jerusalem was taken." The difficulty is in the Hebrew, which Eichhorn does not translate; the offending words—

AV "and he was there when Jerusalem was taken"—are not in the Septuagint.

[2] Syntactical discontinuity is not uncommon in Thucydides, but the ascription of this to composition by dictation seems not to be an explanation given by classical scholars; C may be drawing an inference from his own experience of dictating and his awareness of the corruptions of Elizabethan dramatic texts. The discontinuities in Jeremiah could be as validly ascribed to defects in Baruch's memory.

How desirable would have been a few annotations, explaining the relative Bearings, North, South &c, from the Point on which the Prophet stood & contemplated the Scene of Events,—Medea & Persia are meant—yet it perplexes a common Reader to know, in what sense they are described as from the North. There should be a Map, having Palestine as its center, to every Copy of the Bible. But, alas! the Bishops seem &c—[1]

69 p 803 | Jer 52

[The Babylonish captivity]

N.B. The 52nd Chapter was probably written by the Author of the Book of Kings, who resided in Chaldea—& was appended to the Oracles, as a *Note*, as we now should say.[1]

70 p 870 | Daniel 2.44

And in the days of these kings shall the God of heaven set up a kingdom, which shall never be destroyed: and the kingdom shall not be left to other people, *but* it shall break in pieces and consume all these kingdoms, and it shall stand for ever.

1. Assyrian 2. Mede 3. Medo-persian. 4. Greek. And to the Grecian Empire after the Death of Alexander I apply v. 41–43—/[1]

68[1] For an example of C's habit of visualising the precise details of the setting of biblical events see **12** and n 1, above. His proposed *Encyclopaedia Biblica* was to make provision for "maps and plates chiefly illustrative and explanatory of Plants, animals, costume, Architecture &c" and "An elaborate Commentary, philo-chrono-phyto-zoo-geo-etho-theological, historical and geographical". *IS* 392. The earliest English Bible ([Marburg] 1535) included a map illustrating the Pentateuch. C's complaint here is both against the absence of a map from this edition and against the inadequacy of such biblical maps as he had seen. The fact that this Bible was printed by the British and Foreign Bible Society gives special pungency to his remark. He greatly admired the work of the Society in ensuring "that every Englishman should be able to read his Bible, and have a Bible of his own to read". *LS* (*CC*) 165n; and see 166 n 1. By "the

Bishops" C means the directors of the Bible Society: the bps of London, Durham, Exeter, and St David's were early joint vice-presidents, and in 1816 twenty of the forty-eight bishops of England and Ireland were active and influential members of the Society. See *LS* (*CC*) 201 n 1.

69[1] The last chapter of Jeremiah is compiled mainly from 2 Ki 24.18–25.30.

70[1] Dan 2.40–3: "And the fourth kingdom shall be strong as iron: forasmuch as iron breaketh in pieces and subdueth all things: and as iron that breaketh all these, shall it break in pieces and bruise. And whereas thou sawest the feet and toes, part of potters' clay, and part of iron, the kingdom shall be divided; but there shall be in it of the strength of the iron, forasmuch as thou sawest the iron mixed with miry clay....And whereas thou sawest iron mixed with miry clay, they shall mingle themselves with the

71   pp 877–8 | Dan 7.13

I saw in the night visions, and, behold, *one* like the Son of man came with the clouds of heaven, and came to the Ancient of days, and they brought him near before him.

13. The verse in Ezekiel (I.26) from which this is borrowed, proves that the true meaning of the words is—and lo! the semblance of a human form—or a form resembling that of a man.—If ~~by~~ the Son of Man had at this time been a Synonime of the Messiah, the Writer could not have said—*like* the Son of Man: for it *was* the S. of Man.[1]

Yet that this Text might have OCCASIONED the use of this phrase as to designate the Messiah, is very possible—and in this view the adoption of the Name by the Jews contemporary with our Lord furnishes a strong argument against the Socinians. S. T. C.

72   p 885 | Hosea 2.14

Therefore, behold, I will allure her, and bring her into the wilderness, and speak comfortably unto her.

V. 14. Either the Hebrew word has some other sense than our "THEREFORE"; or if it be rightly translated, some verses must have slipt out; or lastly—it is strange Logic.[1]

---

seed of men: but they shall not cleave one to another, even as iron is not mixed with clay." C lists the four empires that successively held sway in the Middle East, each to some extent dissolving into its successor. In the latter part of the first century B.C. the whole Mediterranean world fell under Roman domination. Some interpreted the fourth kingdom of the prophecy as the Roman empire, e.g. John Davison *Discourses on Prophecy* (1825). But for C the issue applied to the dating of the book of Daniel, not simply to the delineation of what he recognised as a continuing "wave-like succession of empires". DAVISON pp 522–3. Cf Henry MORE *Theological Works* (1708) 120, in which C's suggestion is consistent with the theory that the book of Daniel was written in the reign of Antiochus Epiphanes.

71[1] Ezek 1.26 reads: "And above the firmament that *was* over their heads *was* the likeness of a throne, as the appearance of a sapphire stone: and upon the likeness of the throne *was* the likeness as the appearance of a man above upon it." For Ezek 1.26 *NEB* reads: ". . .a form in human likeness", and for Dan 7.13: "I saw one like a man [*lit.* like a son of man]". The point is not the contrast between the beasts and a figure "like the Son of Man", but that a human figure coming from heaven is recognisably an angel, hence "like a man". Cf BROOKE 22 and n 1.

72[1] Hosea 2.2–17 does not comprise a single oracular utterance; C is correct in noting discontinuity. The preceding verses describe the idolatry of Israel and God's judgement upon her. *NEB* begins v 14 with "But", whereas AV has "Therefore"; Cohen reads "Doch" (yet, nevertheless).

73   p 892 | Hosea 13–14

[Ephraim's glory vanisheth. God's anger for their unkindness. A promise of mercy. | An exhortation to repentance. A promise of God's blessing.]

With many bold and original images Hosea appears of all the Prophets the fullest of repetitions of the same thoughts, and the most unconnected—at least, the connecting link of his transitions is the hardest to discover. The two last Chapters are beautiful & in their smoothness & continuity strongly contrasted with the preceding.[1]

74   p 895 | Joel 3.2

I will also gather all nations, and will bring them down into the valley of Jehoshaphat, and will plead with them there for my people and *for* my heritage Israel, whom they have scattered among the nations, and parted my land.

III. 2. must be understood figuratively. All the enemies & persecutors of the Lord's People will destroy each other by fierce & bloody Wars—as the Moabites &c—2 Chron. XX.—[1]

75   pp 906/7, a sheet tipped in[a] | Micah 5.2–6[1]

[The birth of Christ, His kingdom. His conquest.] But thou, Bethlehem Ephratah, *though* thou be little among the thousands of

---

[a] The sheet of paper, with undated watermark, is inscribed: "S. T. Coleridge Esq[re] | Grove", evidently part of a letter addressed to C

73[1] Hosea, as we have it, is indeed obscure and the text not free of corruptions. Modern scholarship recognises two authors in the book: Proto-Hosea (chs 1–3) and Deutero-Hosea (chs 4–14). Within Deutero-Hosea a further threefold division is recognised, which assigns the last two chapters (13 and 14) to the third section, except for the opening verses of ch 13, which are seen as belonging to the second section.

74[1] The Moabites and Ammonites planned to make war on Jehoshaphat; but Jehoshaphat, learning of their intention, prayed to God, and receiving encouragement from him, ambushed, slew, and plundered his enemies. Thereafter peace reigned for twenty-five years in Jerusalem.

75[1] At pp 904/5 a sheet of paper is tipped in, on which are written two copies of a note by C, not in his hand, referring to Micah 1.4—"And the mountains shall be molten under him, and the valleys shall be cleft, as wax before the fire, *and* as the waters *that are* poured down a steep place." C's note begins with the reference "Vol. 9. p. 216", and continues: "Micha I.iv. —If the Hebrew word translated wax could bear the sense of Cedar or Pine Wood, incomparably more just and sublime would the image be thus: As the Cedar-wood (or the varnished Cedarwood) in the fierceness of the dry Heat, the Valleys split—and the mountains melt under them as Waters that plunge from the Precipice.—The

Judah, *yet* out of thee shall he come forth unto me *that is* to be ruler in Israel; whose goings forth *have been* from of old, from everlasting. Therefore will he give them up, until the time *that* she which travaileth hath brought forth: then the remnant of his brethren shall return unto the children of Israel. And he shall stand and feed in the strength of the LORD, in the majesty of the name of the LORD his God; and they shall abide: for now shall he be great unto the ends of the earth. And this *man* shall be the peace, when the Assyrian shall come into our land: and when he shall tread in our palaces, then shall we raise against him seven shepherds, and eight principal men. And they shall waste the land of Assyria with the sword, and the land of Nimrod in the entrances thereof . . .

V. ⟨The following seems to me the best Rendering and to give the true Sense of this in our translation most mysterious passage— S. T. C.⟩

But thou, Bethlehem of Ephrata!
Small as thou art, to be over Juda's Thousands (4 Mos. 31.5)[2]
Nevertheless out of thee will One go forth for me
To be Ruler over Israel.

His *Stem* (Stemma, Stirps) or *Race* (*Radix* genealogice) or ⟨as⟩ we should say *His House*
His House, from out of which he goeth forth, (*or is sprung*) is very ancient of the grey Times of old.
Him (i.e. His House or Family) He (God) will make endure as long as Womb bears (*literally, a bearing woman bears*)
And further once more over Israel will his ~~Brother~~sethren be set,

And likewise will He (the King, and Shepherd of the People) step forth and rule thro' the Might of Jehovah
In the great name of this his God: and they, (the ~~ane~~ estranged Israelites) will return:
For now will he even to the Land's extreme Bounds (in the whole united Land) be great.

thunder or cannon-like explosions of the splitting Deal & Cedar-wood, yea even of the stoutest Oak & Mahogany, in the heat of Summer, must have struck & astonished every traveller in Sicily, Malta, and West Asia!— S. T. C." For other observations of the sound of splitting wood in Malta see *CN* II 2628 and *CL* VI 937. The book (commentary?) to which C's page-reference applies has not been traced. Among the likelier ones, Cocceius does not fit, nor does any edition of Jerome (on which see 76 n 1, below) so far examined.

75[2] "4 Mos."—the 4th book of Moses, i.e. Numbers: "So there were delivered out of the thousands of Israel, a thousand of every tribe, twelve thousand armed for war."

And hereon rests our Peace,
When Assur (the Assyrian) shall invade our Land
And trample down our Palaces—*a*
Then oppose we to him seven or eight of our Shepherd-princes
(our National's Shepherds)
to mow down with the Sword his own Land that Nimrod-land
with glittering Blades—3

76   pp 907–8 | Mic 5.5

And this *man* shall be the peace, when the Assyrian* shall come into
our land: and when he shall tread in our palaces, then shall we raise
against him seven shepherds, and eight principal men.

[*] V. 5. Jerom interprets the Assyrian as = the Devil, the 7 Shepherds
of the Old Testament, or the Patriarchs & Prophets, & the 8 Princes
of Men (or, as the 70, Bites of Man) of the N. T. or the Ev. &
Apostles!!!1 and by the marginal reference to Luke it seems that our
Translators had a hankering after the same ingenious mode of
making any sense out of any words ad libitum!2

a Here the sheet is marked "(see over)"; the note continues on the side marked "2"

753 Cf the *NEB* version:
But you, Bethlehem in Ephrathah,
small as you are to be among Judah's clans,
out of you shall come forth a governor for Israel,
one whose roots are far back in the past, in days gone by.
Therefore only so long as a woman is in labour
shall he give up Israel;
and then those that survive of his race
shall rejoin their brethren.
He shall appear and be their shepherd
in the strength of the Lord,
in the majesty of the name of the Lord his God.
And they shall continue, for now his greatness shall reach
to the ends of the earth;
and he shall be a man of peace.

When the Assyrian comes into our land,
when he tramples our castles,
we will raise against him seven men or eight

to be shepherds and princes.
They shall shepherd Assyria with the sword
and the land of Nimrod with bare blades...

761 "70"—Septuagint. The Greek phrase is ἑπτὰ ποίμενες καὶ ὀκτὼ δήγματα ἀνθρώπων;—lit. "seven shepherds, and eight bites of men". The only lexical meaning for δῆγμα is "bite" or "sting"; *NEB*, translating from the Hebrew, reads simply "seven men or eight". On 17 Dec 1827 C noted: "I was half provoked ⟨to anger⟩ and half to laughter—perhaps in both equally mistaken—when after vain endeavors to discover the meaning of Micah V. 5, 6. I turned at length to Sᵗ Jerom, Tom. II. & found that the Assyrian meant the Devil...". N 36 ff 18–18ᵛ. For the crucial words Jerome had given the Septuagint version in Latin—*morsus hominum*. *Green SC* (1880) 602 is a copy of Jerome *Omnia opera* (12 vols Frankfurt & Leipzig 1684 F°).

762 Mic 5.6: "And they [i.e. the seven shepherds and the eight princes] shall waste the land of Assyria with the sword, and the land of Nimrod in

77   p 920 | Zechariah 4.12–14

And I answered again, and said unto him, What *be these* two olive branches which through the two golden pipes empty the golden *oil* out of themselves? And he answered me and said, Knowest thou not what these *be*? And I said, No, my lord. Then said he, These *are* the two anointed ones, that stand by the LORD of the whole earth.

IV. 12–14. These verses help to confirm my belief, that these & the two Witnesses in the Apocal. signify the two Sacraments which the 2 golden pipes (& the two Covenants) employ &c—i.e. are the conductors of the spiritual unction.[1]

78   p 930 | Malachi 3.14–18

Ye have said, It *is* vain to serve God: and what profit *is it* that we have kept his ordinance, and that we have walked mournfully before the LORD of hosts? And now we call the proud happy; yea, *they that* work wickedness are set up; yea, *they that* tempt God are even delivered. Then they that feared the LORD spake often one to another; and the LORD hearkened, and heard *it*, and a book of remembrance was written before him for them that feared the LORD, and that thought upon his name. And they shall be mine, saith the LORD of hosts, in that day when I make up my jewels; and I will spare them, as a man spareth his own son that serveth him. Then shall ye return, and discern between the righteous and the wicked; between him that serveth God and him that serveth him not.

§ 14–18 If this passage do not declare a future state, and a judgement after the dissolution of the visible Body, it is either a most unsatisfactory or a deceiving Promise. The latter, if the great and dreadful day was promised in the lifetime of those to whom the Prophet addresses the words, Ye have said &c—and "then shall ye return

---

the entrance thereof: thus shall he[y] deliver us from the Assyrians, when he cometh into our land...". The marginal gloss *y* cites Luke 1.74: "That he would grant unto us, that we being delivered out of the hand of our enemies might serve him without fear". The reference in Micah is to the Messiah.

77[1] Rev 11.3–13, esp vv 3, 4: "And I will give power unto my two witnesses, and they shall prophesy a thousand two hundred and threescore days, clothed in sackcloth. These are the two olive trees, and the two candlesticks standing before the God of the earth."

In finding the parallel to "the two olive trees" in Zechariah's vision C is in accord with present interpretation. But it is now considered that the two witnesses stand for the Law and the Prophets.

&c.["] The former, if it was understood of a distant futurity. What satisfaction to a man in 1827 to be told, that the bad men who are alive in the year 2357 will be burnt, & the good men tread them under foot?—/ Ch. IV. v. 5 with the correspond. in Matthew XVII, most difficult.[1]

NEW TESTAMENT

79 p [932], verso of fly-title to NT, written below **93**

The everlasting Truths, the ever-present redemptive presence and mediation of the WORD who became Man, yea, σαρξ εγενετο[1]—O! how do they soften, raise, fill the soul! But what should I have known of these glad Tidings, what should I have been—if indeed I should have at all been—had not a Christian Church been established? If Christianity had not been made a *fact* of History? Now what shall we judge to be the fit means to this end? Surely, the presumption is, that the Means, which did subserve to this end, and by which this end (viz. the wide-spread & still spreading Knowlege of the Gospel) has been accomplished, were the fit, the best means! With this conviction, & with the circumstances, associations, opinions &c of the Jews "in the days of Herod"[2] before our mind, & not our own in our times, must we read & appreciate the 3 first Gospels.

80 p ⁻2

To exhibit the difficulties of the first Historians, in the absence of paper, ink &c—then in the extreme ~~diffuse~~ separate—then to consider that the knowlege of *facts* for their own sake, ~~and~~ or for mere purposes of exact chronology, & to present succession without vacua, is a refinement of modern times—In the ancient the Moral purpose was ever predominant/ and History differed from Poesy in the *materials* rather than in the *forms* of putting them together.—His Jewells were all precious Stones—i.e. *real* facts—not factitious diamonds &c—but in the *Setting* he was determined by the Object, he had in view[1]—The object of the first Evangelist (as the Gospels

78[1] With Malachi 4.5—"Behold, I will send you Elijah the prophet before the coming of the great and dreadful day of the Lord"—cf Matt 17.10–12, in which Christ says that Elijah here means John the Baptist. See also **93**, below, in which C comments on the passage in Matt.

79[1] "Became flesh"—from John 1.14—a phrase C frequently quoted, often inverting the order of the two Greek words.

79[2] Matt 2.1, Luke 1.5 (var).

80[1] A key statement of C's view of the Bible as the supreme intersection of poetry and history—a view that informs e.g. *SM*, *AR*, and *C&S*. It is also an important declaration of his

now stand) was evidently to bring the facts into a striking reference to & connection with, the Sacred Books of the Hebrews—that of Luke, to inform the Italian Converts of the Facts themselves, in order of place & hour, as far as he had been able to ascertain—that of Mark, to combine the two purposes—his Gospel being written, like that attributed to Matthew, to Jews; but not, as Matthew's, to Palestine Jews, already acquainted with the facts more or less perfectly, but to Jews settled in foreign Lands—chiefly, it is probable, to to the Jews in Egypt, especially, Alexandria.— John's alone for the Church Universal of all ages.—Under this view only can the 4 Gospels be intelligently studied./

81 pp +2–+3

It is most worthy of consideration in the thoughtful perusal of the First Gospel which in its present form was, I am persuaded, the last written, that the difficulties and improbabilities are neither in the λογοι Κυριου ἡ διδαχη nor in the παραβολαι, nor in the πραξεις, nor in the παθηματα;[1] but in passages containing the popular reports concerning the events, the *on dits*[2]—Ex. gr. Pilate's Wife's Dream sent by a messenger to Pilate while on his Bench[3]—Pilate's washing his hands more judaico;[4] the Roman Guard in C. 27 and 28[5]—&c &c— John alone assumes and sustains the character of an Eye-witness; and in his Gospel not a difficulty occurs. All is dignified, consistent, and probable. And surely, it is a fact full of consolation, that if every passage in the three first Gospels to which a learned and judicious Reader would find questionable, were omitted, not a single fact or doctrine of the least importance to the faith or practice of a Christian, not nor nor even a single incident of any the least biographical interest, would be affected. Among the many clear proofs of an overruling Providence in the Affairs of Christianity, and in the character of the extant Writings of the Apostolic Age, may be noted the mani-

---

philosophical sense of the word "fact", the rationalist appeal to which term in a narrow veridical sense he constantly deplored. See *SM* (*CC*) 28–30; cf *LS* (*CC*) 123–4n. For C's reading of historical works and his attitude to "history" in the technical sense see e.g. BROWNE *Works* 54 n 1.

81[1] "Words of the Lord or teaching/ doctrine . . . parables . . . acts . . . sufferings".

81[2] I.e. the hearsay reports. See also **99**, below.

81[3] Matt 27.19.

81[4] "In the Jewish manner". Pilate's hand-washing—a Jewish custom—is (in Matt 27.24) a sign, which the Jews would understand, that he was turning the responsibility over to them.

81[5] I.e. Matt 27.64–6 and 28.12–15.

fest correctness and clear internal evidence of our Lord['s] Discourses and Parables. From the known custom of the Jews, when they sate at the feet of any celebrated Rabbi, it might have been taken for granted, that among the constant Hearers of Him, "who spake as never man spake",[6] there would not be wanting some one or more to take notes of what he said—and the Discourses themselves fully confirm the anticipations.

82   p +5

I cannot read the two first Gospels without a deep & (I trust) grateful sense of the goodness and wisdom of the Divine Providence, in that we know nothing of our Lord's History, as a Man, beyond what ~~was~~ is necessary or profitable for us in reference to his office, as our Redeemer & as the Object so the Founder of the Church—& that ~~of~~ as to these few facts our conviction of their truth rests chiefly—I should say wholly—on the *internal* evidence, on the Moral *impossibility* that they could have been invented or even ~~first~~ conceived by the Compilers of these Memorabilia! How would it[a] tarnish and unedge the beauty and pathos of many, almost of all, our Lord's Sayings (Λογοι του Κυριου),[1] were we under the necessity of supposing, that they were all delivered ~~on~~ at one preaching on the side of a Hill, as represented in the first Gospel!—But to suppose this or to hold it necessary so to believe (tho' the contrary is implied in Luke's Gospel) argues gross ignorance of the nature & laws of historical Composition in Ancient Times/. The *Substance* is *fact*; but the *form* is the Historian's work as an *Artist*—his ~~pur~~ choice being determined by the particular purpose for which, or the View, in which he presented the facts. An Ancient Historian was a Jeweller—enough that he passed no false or paste Drops for precious Stones.[2]

83   p 937 | Matthew 5.22

. . . but whosoever shall say, Thou fool, shall be in danger of hell fire.

literally shall be $\begin{cases} \text{liable} \\ \text{subject} \\ \text{amenable} \end{cases}$[1] to the Ge-henna of the Fire—a

hebraism for the fiery Vale Hinnom, likewise called Tophet/. It was

---

[a] C has left a space because wax from a seal or candle had dripped on the paper preventing the ink from marking

81[6] John 7.46: "Never man spake like this man."
82[1] "Words of the Lord".

82[2] See **80** and n 1, above.
83[1] All three words are adequate translations of ἔνοχος.

close by Jerusalem, and infamous for the passing of children thro'
fires to Moloch./ a volcanic Valley, like the Phlegreon in Naples.[2]—
Metaphor. the state of the Damned.

84 p 940 | Matt 8.17

That it might be fulfilled which was spoken by Esaias the prophet,
saying, Himself took our infirmities, and bare *our* sicknesses.

V. 17.—It is not easy to see the application of the words.—To *remove*
a burthen, to heal Diseases—how can this be = to bear it, to take the
sicknesses on himself?[1]

85 p 941 | Matt 9.13

... for I am not come to call the righteous, but sinners to repentance.

the not in the Greek.[1]

86 p 941 | Matt 9.14

Then came to him the disciples of John, saying, Why do we and the
Pharisees fast oft, but thy disciples fast not?

IX. 14. I know not whether it has been noticed by others; but
I seem to find a remarkable harmony between this[1] & our

83[2] C is literally correct; *NEB*, however, reads "will have to answer for it in the fires of hell". The Campi Flegrei (Phlegraean Fields)—a volcanic region northwest of Naples and east of Cumae, with thirteen low craters (the latest formed in 1538) and many hot springs and fumaroles. C will have heard of the place—or may even have seen it—during his visit to Naples in Nov 1805: he may even have seen the splendid illustrations in Sir William Hamilton's *Campi Phlegraei* (2 vols Naples 1776).

84[1] *NEB* reads: "He took away our illnesses and lifted our diseases from us [*or* and bore the burden of our diseases]." Matthew is here quoting Isa 53.4 from one of the Servant Songs (see **53**–**57** and nn, above), in which the meaning is clearly that the Servant takes our sickness and infirmities upon himself—the meaning that C expects to find here because it would correspond to the Passion of Christ (as does another echo of Isa

53.4–6 in 1 Pet 2.24). In the context of Matt 8.17, however, Jesus is curing Peter's wife's mother; he does not present the figure of the suffering Christ.

85[1] *NEB* reads: "I did not come to invite righteous people but sinners." The difficulty is only in AV and perhaps not even there, for in normal English idiom "the righteous" can be synonymous with "righteous people" without meaning "*all* righteous people".

86[1] Jesus's reply to the disciples of John (Matt 9.15–17) was: "Can the children of the bridechamber mourn, as long as the bridegroom is with them? but the days will come, when the bridegroom shall be taken from them, and then shall they fast. No man putteth a piece of new cloth unto an old garment; for that which is put in to fill it up taketh from the garment, and the rent is made worse. ... " Matt 9.17 is **87** textus.

Lord's other reply to the Messenger from John—both are
αἰνιγματωδῆ.[2]

87 p 941 | Matt 9.17

Neither do men put new wine into old bottles: else the bottles break,
and the wine runneth out, and the bottles perish: but they put new
wine into new bottles, and both are preserved.

Our Lord here hints to the Disciples of John the essential difference
between their Master & himself, as the founder of a new & spiritual
covenant, between which & these Royal observances there would be
an incongruity. Even in v. 15, I understand "fast" spiritually.[1]

88 p 942 | Matt 9.22

But Jesus turned him about, and when he saw her, he said, Daughter,
be of good comfort; thy faith hath made thee whole. And the woman
was made whole from that hour.

22. from this we learn, that Luke's addition was an *inference* only
either drawn by himself or by the Eye-witness from whom he had
received the account.[1]

89 p 944 | Matt 11.11–12

had ?][1] ... Among them that are born of women there have <u>hath</u> not
risen a greater than John the Baptist. ... And from the days of
*] John the Baptist until now the kingdom of heaven suffereth
violence, and the violent take it by force.

* I.e. at the time of John's Birth. "Among them ~~that are~~ begotten of
Women there was not raised a greater &c." V. 12..?[2] No longer by
authority & with the sanction of the Church established by Law, as
before John's Preaching; but by insurgency & act of individual Will.

86[2] "Riddling". The other reply is
in Matt 11.4–6: "Go and shew John
again those things which ye do hear
and see: The blind receive their sight,
and the lame walk, the lepers are
cleansed, and the deaf hear, the dead
are raised up, and the poor have the
gospel preached to them. And blessed
is he, whosoever shall not be offended
in me."

87[1] Cf Mark 3.19, which is part of
the source for Matt 9.15–17: "Can the
children of the bridechamber mourn,
as long as the bridegroom is with
them? but the days will come, when
the bridegroom shall be taken from
them, and then shall they fast."

88[1] See Luke 8.41–8.

89[1] The verb, ἐγήγερται, is in the
perfect tense, and is so translated in AV.

89[2] *NEB* reads: "never has there
appeared on earth a mother's son
greater than ...".

90   p 945, pencil, overtraced | Matt 12.25-7

... Every kingdom divided against itself is brought to desolation; and every city or house divided against itself shall not stand: And if Satan cast out Satan, he is divided against himself; how shall then his kingdom stand? And if I by Beelzebub cast out devils, by whom do your children cast *them* out? therefore they shall be your judges.

25–27. I apprehend that this Reasoning of our Lord is in the Spirit of a majestic *Irony*, in exposure of the malignant shallowness of the Pharisee pretence.

91   p 949 | Matt 14.26

And when the disciples saw him walking on the sea, they were troubled, saying, It is a spirit; and they cried out for fear.

Gr. *Phantasm.* or *Goblin*.[1]

92   p 950 | Matt 15.15, 16.7

Then answered Peter and said unto him, Declare unto us this parable.... And they reasoned among themselves, saying, *It is* because we have taken no bread.

XV. v. 15: and XVI. v. 7. are noticeable texts, as exemplifying the very rude and crass apprehensions of the Disciples and of the Jewish Commonalty—the low state of their intellectual faculties.

93   p [932], verso of fly-title to NT, written above **79** | Matt 17.25-6

... And when he was come into the house, Jesus prevented him, saying, What thinkest thou, Simon? of whom do the kings of the earth take custom or tribute? of their own children, or of strangers? Peter saith unto him, Of strangers. Jesus saith unto him, Then are the children free.

Matt. XVII. v. 25, 26.—This is one among many passages in this Gospel, the meaning of which I am unable to determine—and Cocceius, the only Commentator in my possession, as prolix where there is no difficulty and regularly fails me wherever I need help.[1]—

91[1] The word in the original is φάντασμα—C's "phantasm". *NEB* reads: " 'It is a ghost!' "

93[1] C borrowed a copy of Johannes Cocceius *Opera omnia* (10 vols Amsterdam 1701) from a Mr Tudor c Jul 1825, was using it in Jan–Feb 1826 and in Jul 1827, and was obliged to return it apparently late in 1827. See COCCEIUS (Lost Book).

On Matt 17.26 Cocceius is indeed not very helpful (IV 25 tr): "Christ shows that neither he, who is the Son of God, is obliged to pay the tribute nor any more are his disciples, who inherit their liberty from him and are not

So likewise v. 10, 11, 12 of the same Ch./[2] Elias shall come, and restore all things. But he is already come & gone again—for John the Baptist was Elias.—How could John be said to have restored all things? Or are we to understand, that John the Baptist will appear a third time, at the second Coming of Christ *in person*?—

The more I study the 3 first Gospels & compare them, especially Matthew's, with S[t] John's, the more probable does the hypothesis appear, which considers them as 3 several Colligations of the κηρυγματα ἅ εκηρυξαν οἱ αποστολοι—[3]

94 pp 954–5, pencil, overtraced | Matt 19.12

... and there be eunuchs, which have made themselves eunuchs for the kingdom of heaven's sake.

12. not in order to obtain heaven, but for the sake of—i.e. in order the more entirely to devote their thoughts & labours to the advancement of the *kingdom* of Heaven, that is, of the Church of Christ on earth—that God's will may be done on earth *as* it is in heaven—

95 p 957 | Matt 21.20–2

And when the disciples saw *it*, they marvelled, saying, How soon is the fig tree withered away! Jesus answered and said unto them, Verily I say unto you, If ye have faith, and doubt not, ye shall not only do this *which is done* to the fig tree, but also if ye shall say unto this mountain, Be thou removed, and be thou cast into the sea, and

redeemed with money (Isa 52.3) but with his precious blood (1 Pet 18.19) and are made the sons of the living God (Hos 1.10 or 2.1), held to serve the face [on the coin?]." On vv 10–12 (see n 2, below) Cocceius has nothing to say.

93[2] "And his disciples asked him, saying, Why then say the scribes that Elias must first come?...".

93[3] "Tidings that the apostles preached". The words κηρυγμα(τα) (proclamation,pronouncement,preaching) and κηρύσσειν (proclaim, preach) often occur separately in NT and are joined into one phrase by the Fathers; the phrase for "preached the gospel" common in Mark and Matthew is κηρύσσειν τὸ εὐαγγέλιον.

Lessing, in *Neue Hypothese über die Evangelisten als blos menschliche Ges-* *chichtschreiber* (Wolfenbüttel 1778, in *Sämmtliche Schriften* xix 1–46—not annotated by C), postulated an Aramaic gospel; Eichhorn, in his *Einleitung in das Neue Testament* (3 vols Leipzig 1804–14) Vol i, postulated an Aramaic *Urevangelium* (C preferred the term *Proto-evangelium* or *Protevangelium*) that had been subject to many additions and recensions and existed in more than one translation. (He later appreciated, however, that the verbal similarities through the three synoptic gospels must be accounted for by the use of one translation.) C read Eichhorn's arguments with care and wrote marginalia on them; he was not convinced by them, but did not evolve any consistent or clear-cut theory of his own.

it shall be done. And all things whatsoever ye shall ask in prayer, believing, ye shall receive.

God be praised!—I prayed to be enlightened respecting this to *me* very difficult passage: and I believe myself to have been heard. See Micah VII. v. 1.[1]—The whole is an awful type preparing the minds of the Disciples for the withering away, and removal, of the Jewish State. Every word is pregnant. It seems clear, that the Disciples very imperfectly understood our Lord's words.

96 p 961, pencil, overtraced | Matt 23.37

O Jerusalem, Jerusalem, *thou* that killest the prophets, and stonest them which are sent unto thee, how often would I have gathered thy children together, even as a hen gathereth her chickens under *her* wings, and ye would not!

See XXIV Numbers: v. 17—The last sentence of which should have been rendered—"and shall call together, as a Hen her chickens, all the children of Seth."[1]

97 pp 1032/3,[a] apparently referring to p 961 | Matt 24.9–13[1]

Then shall they deliver you up to be afflicted, and shall kill you: and ye shall be hated of all nations for my name's sake. And then shall many be offended, and shall betray one another, and shall hate one another. And many false prophets shall rise, and shall deceive many. And because iniquity shall abound, the love of many shall wax cold. But he that shall endure unto the end, the same shall be saved.

Verse 9. See Hooker's admirable Sermon on the Perseverance of the Saints, commonly annexed to the Ecclesiastical Polity./[2]

---

[a] A leaf of notes in C's hand

95[1] "Woe is me! for I am as when they have gathered the summer fruits, as the grapegleanings of the vintage: *there is* no cluster to eat: my soul desired the firstripe fruit."

96[1] See **15** and n 1, above. In Matt 23.37 the straightforward verb ἐπισυνάγειν (to gather together) is used.

97[1] Luke 21.9–19 is a possible reference for the note, but not so good as Matt 24.9–13, which falls on the same page as **98**. Mark 13.9–13 is also a possibility, but C has written only two notes on Mark—**100, 101**.

97[2] "A Learned and Comfortable Sermon of the Certainty and Perpetuity of Faith in the Elect: Especially of the prophet Habakkuk's Faith"—the seventh of a miscellaneous group (pp 527ff) appended to HOOKER *Works* (1682). C wrote three annotations on this sermon.

98 pp 961–2 | Matt 24.24

For there shall arise false Christs, and false prophets, and shall shew great signs and wonders; insomuch that, if *it were* possible, they shall deceive the very elect.

This prophesy must be referred to an æra still future. History, at least, records many false Messiahs, but none celebrated for miracles except Apoll: of Tyanæa but he can scarcely be called a false Christ much less capable of deceiving even the Elect.[1]

99 p 968 | Matt 27.62–6, 28.11–15

Now the next day, that followed the day of the preparation, the Chief Priests and Pharisees came together unto Pilate, Saying, Sir, we remember that that deceiver said, while he was yet alive, After three days I will rise again. Command therefore that the sepulchre be made sure until the third day, lest his disciples come by night, and steal him away, and say unto the people, He is risen from the dead: so the last error shall be worse than the first. Pilate said unto them, Ye have a watch: go your way, make *it* as sure as ye can. So they went, and made the sepulchre sure, sealing the stone, and setting a watch. . . . Now when they were going, behold, some of the watch came into the city, and shewed unto the Chief Priests all the things that were done. And when they were assembled with the elders, and had taken counsel, they gave large money unto the soldiers, Saying, Say ye, His disciples came by night, and stole him *away* while we slept. And if this come to the governor's ears, we will persuade him, and secure you. So they took the money, and did as they were taught: and this saying is commonly reported among the Jews until this day.

XXVII. v. 62–6/6: XXVIII. v. 11–15. An *on dit*.[1]

100 p 978 | Mark 7.29

And he said unto her, For this saying go thy way; the <u>devil</u> is gone out of thy daughter.

98[1] Apollonius of Tyana (c 4–c 97), a neo-Pythagorean saint of pious and ascetic life, collected many disciples and travelled to India. He returned with a reputation for working miracles (some of which resemble the miracles of Christ) and was treated as a divine being, his sect—like many Neoplatonic and neo-Pythagorean groups—offering rivalry to the Christians. Lucian (b c 120) regarded him as an impostor. But Philostratus (b c 170) was commissioned to write a life of him; and C —who wrote a vivid account of Apollonius in *P Lects* Lect 7 (1949) 240–1—referred to Philostratus quizzically as an "inventor of the Life of a Founder of a Religion". N 41 f 68ᵛ.

99[1] See **81** n 2, above.

v. 29. This is not *translation*; but the Translator's own notion of the meaning. It should have been, the dæmonial *power*, or the demoniac *paroxysm*[1]

101   p 992 | Mark 16.8

And they went out quickly, and fled from the sepulchre; for they trembled and were amazed: neither said they any thing to any *man*; for they were afraid.

Here in the judgement of the best biblical Critics the Gospel according to S[t] Mark ended. The twelve last verses are not to be found in some, & are marked with asterisks as spurious or doubtful in others of the eldest MSS.—Providentially so: for these 12 verses contain difficulties that have never been fairly explained.[1]

102   p 1001 | Luke 5.32

I came not to call the righteous, but sinners to repentance.

mistranslated, by the insertion of the definite article before "righteous". Read—"I came not to call righteous men, but sinners to repentance."[1]

103   p 1007 | Luke 8.46

And Jesus said, Somebody hath touched me: for I perceive that virtue is gone out of me.

v. 46. vulgarly mistranslated. Read—"for I perceived the power passing out of me.—["][1]

---

[100][1] The Greek term is τὸ δαιμόνιον, an adjective serving as a noun—"the demonic *something*"; in classical Greek normally used of supernatural beings, and in Septuagint and NT regularly of an evil spirit. *NEB* reads "the unclean spirit".

[101][1] It is now generally accepted that Mark 16.9–20 was not an original part of that gospel. *NEB* prints the passage as a second alternative ending, the first and much shorter ending not being included in the *Textus receptus*. Some mss give both endings, some give one or the other, some give neither.

[102][1] Trinitarian and anti-trinitarian interpretations of various texts depended very much on the presence or absence of the definite article. For C's early acquaintance with the controversy see *CN* III 3275n; he annotated

Christopher Wordsworth's anonymous *Six Letters to Granville Sharp Respecting...the Uses of the Definite Article in the Greek Text of the New Testament* (1802), the second document in the controversy opened by Sharp in 1798. See e.g. *CL* II 820–1 (26 Jul 1802) and *CN* III 3933 (c Jun–Jul 1810). C has this issue in mind in **85**, above, and in **131, 139**, below.

[103][1] C's version depends upon the verb ἐξέλθουσαν in his 1622 Greek NT —a reading that is now treated as a variant. His objection to the AV tr is made clear in N 35 ff 8–11: "...our Church Version...is worse than careless, for 'I perceive, that virtue is gone out of me', implies that our Lord no longer possessed it, as if it had been a charm, or an amulet charged with Mesmer's fluid".

104   p 1030, pencil, overtraced | Luke 24.2

And they found the stone rolled away from the sepulchre.

Therefore: not alone the Soul or Spirit of Jesus—to whose exit a Stone could have been no obstacle. Yet how harmonious with this, v. 36?[1]

105   pp 1031–2, pencil, overtraced | Luke 24.25–7

Then he said unto them, O fools, and slow of heart to believe all that the prophets have spoken: Ought not Christ to have suffered these things, and to enter into his glory? And beginning at Moses and all the prophets, he expounded unto them in all the Scriptures the things concerning himself.

25–27. What a rebuke on the human presumption, which (as in the instance of an infallible Head of the Church & Judge of all controversies) would conclude that that which to us would appear most desirable & of highest use must therefore actually exist. Of what deep interest would this Discourse of our Lord have been, had it *been preserved* as well as the Sermon on the Mount.—But no—not even a pretended tradition of a single sentence.

106   pp 1032/3, in a leaf of notes, pencil, overtraced | Luke 24

[Christ's resurrection is declared by two angels to the women that came to the sepulchre. These report it to others. Christ himself appeareth to the two disciples that went to Emmaus: afterwards he appeareth to the apostles, and reproacheth their unbelief: giveth them a charge: promiseth the Holy Ghost: and so ascendeth into heaven.]

Gosp. Luke XXIV. The very difficulties of this narrative are to my mind presumptions in favor of the simple truth and good faith ⟨both⟩ of the original Narrators & of the Compiler. Here is no attempt to make one incident *fit* on to the other—this certainty as to the fact in the minds of the Witnesses superseded & prevented the desire of explaining and accounting for the particulars—ex. gr. the rolling away of the Stone[1] & the positive eating of the material food[2] &c with the sudden vanishing & the non-recognition after so few days Absence,[3] & this during a long & momentous conversation/—

[104][1] Luke 24.36: "And as they thus spake, Jesus himself stood in the midst of them, and saith unto them, Peace be unto you."

[106][1] Luke 24.2.
[106][2] Luke 24.41–3.
[106][3] Luke 24.13–25.

107   p 1036 | John 4.21–3

Jesus saith unto her, Woman, believe me, the hour cometh, when ye shall neither in this mountain, nor yet at Jerusalem, worship the Father. Ye worship ye know not what: we know what we worship: for salvation is of the Jews. But the hour cometh, and now is, when the true worshippers shall worship the Father in spirit and in truth...

IV. 22. has all the characters of an early marginal gloss that had slipt into the text. Read 21st, and 23rd in sequence: and the breach of continuity in the thought and even in the syntax, produced by v. 22nd will be *felt*.[1]

108   p 1037 | John 5.4

For an angel went down at a certain season into the pool, and troubled the water: whosoever then first after the troubling of the water stepped in was made whole of whatsoever disease he had.

It seems to have been a Blood-bath/ for "an Angel" Luke says, the ["]Finger of God."—[1]

109   p 1051, pencil, overtraced | John 13.7

[Jesus' answer to Peter's question why he washed Peter's feet:] What I do thou knowest not now; but thou shalt know hereafter.

v. 7.—Genesis Chapt. III. v. 15.[1] The Heel, the Feet, the lower[a] Nature of man polluted by the Sep Serpent, must be cleansed, before the Head of the Serpent can be crushed.

110   p 1052 | John 14.10

Believest thou not that I am in the Father, and the Father in me? the words that I speak unto you I speak not of myself: but the Father that dwelleth in me, he doeth the works.

[a] The word "lower" is repeated in pencil above the overtraced word; "+" has been inserted after the original "lower" and before the repeated word above

107[1] This point is dealt with at greater length in N 36 ff 51[v]–52.

108[1] Luke 11.20: "But if I with the finger of God cast out devils..."— which echoes the phrase in Exod 8.19, the Egyptian magicians' description of Aaron's rod, the instrument of Yahweh's power to inflict plagues on Egypt: "This is the finger of God." A bath in fresh blood was long thought to have a curative effect; the now more usual meaning of a massacre evidently is independent of this belief.

109[1] "And I will put enmity between thee and the woman, and between the seed and her seed; it shall bruise thy head, and thou shalt bruise his heel." C's interpretation grows, not from thy narrative in John, but from the clue offered by Gen 3.15 (a parallel not suggested by the gloss). C is concerned to find a deeper figurative or symbolic meaning for the act (or rite) of washing the feet; since the story is told only in John's gospel the only relevant parallel was Gen 3.15. Cf N 36 ff 62[v]–63.

v. 10. Inquire you, what "the Father" is, as one with yet distinct from & in order antecedent to, the Son? Inquire of and within yourself, what the "I Am" is, & what the Mind or Reason—the WORD of the I AM.[1]

111 p 1058, pencil, overtraced | John 19.11

Jesus answered, Thou couldest have no power *at all* against me, except it were given thee from above . . .

v. 11.—from above means from the Sanhedrin, or Jewish Senate who to gratify their malice basely betrayed & gave up their one remaining privilege—that of judging offences against their Laws Laws,[a] short of death.[1]

112 p 1059, pencil, overtraced | John 19.21

Then said the Chief Priests of the Jews to Pilate, Write not, The King of the Jews; but that he said, I am King of the Jews.

v. 21.—Even from this Text it might be deduced, that Christ was the Jehovah of the Old Testament, the true covenanted King of the Jews.[1]

113 p 1063 | Acts 2.30

Therefore [David] being a prophet, and knowing that God had sworn with an oath to him, that of the fruit of his loins, according to the flesh, he would raise up Christ to sit on his throne . . .

v. 30. Unless in anticipation of Christ's re-appearance as visible King of the Jews, in what sense could Peter conceive our Lord to sit on the Throne of David?

114 p 1071 | Acts 8.4

Therefore they that were scattered abroad went every where preaching the word.

v. 4.—Οἱ μὲν οὖν διεσπαρμενοι—the οὖν in this place has evidently the

---

[a] So the original pencil (overtraced) reads; the version on the loose sheet reads "laws short of"

[110][1] Here, as often, C connects Christ's "I am" with the I AM of Exod 3.14. See **11** and **57** n 1, above, **117** and esp **119** n 1, below.

[111][1] This note, which flies in the face of Erasmus, Cocceius, Valpy, Clarke, Eichhorn, and many other authorities, is a shorthand version of a longer note written in EICHHORN *Neue Testament* COPY B (referring to II 262); the argument appears in more extended form in *TT* 20 May 1830.

[112][1] For the "Jehovah-Word" see e.g. **11**, above, and **119**, below.

force of "thus" or "in this account"—They then having been *thus* disperse[d.] The "therefore" makes whimsical Logic.[1]

115   p 1091 | Acts 22.9

And they that were with me saw indeed the light, and were afraid; but they heard not the voice of him that spake to me.

Yet Luke had before said ⟨ix. 7.⟩ that they did hear the voice.[1] We must suppose the first to mean "hearing a sound": and the second, "not distinguishing the Words".

116   pp 1100–1 | Romans 1

It would greatly facilitate the understanding of S[t] Paul's Writings and of this Epistle in particular, if only they were *printed* as the Apostle himself, ~~Pa~~ were he now on earth, would have prepared them for the Press—viz. subjoining or annexed in the margin or at the bottom of the Page as *Notes* what are now interworded, rather than inwoven as member Parentheses. I have in writing more than once found occasion to make a note on a note, a † to a * and something like this not seldom occurs in the long parenthetic passages of the Apostles. These with other marks and effects of a full and fervent Intellect distinguishes S[t] Paul's Proper Epistles from the highly-finished Circular *Charge*, apostolico the Epistle to the Ephesians και απο των παυλοειδων pastoral charges to Timothy and Titus.[1]

114[1] C has turned the English back into Greek without consulting the Greek text, and so has changed the participle from aorist passive (διασπα-ρέντες) to perfect passive (διεσπαρ-μένοι). Οὖν—usually "therefore"—often has a much weaker force; *NEB* agrees with C in reading "As for those who had been scattered".

115[1] Acts 9.7: "And the men which journeyed with him stood speechless, hearing a voice, but seeing no man."

116[1] "Apostolico"—in the apostolic manner. The Greek phrase means "and from the Paul-like" pastoral charges. Παυλοειδής seems to be C's coinage, formed like several other of his words on the suffix -ειδης; see also **133** and n 1, below. On Ephesians (which Eichhorn described in *Neue*

Testament III 249, 285 as *Circularschrei-ben*) see **130**, below.

Though many scholars have argued strongly for Pauline authorship of the Epistles to Timothy and Titus, a more readily acceptable view is that all three epistles were compiled in A.D. 100–120, that they include Pauline material, and that they are presented as if written by Paul to Timothy and Titus. See also **133**, below. In a note dated 12 Jan 1826 C discussed "Eichhorn's hypothesis regarding the Ep. to Titus & Timothy" and hesitantly conceded that "the Hypothesis has its advantages". N F° ff 25–25ᵛ. But in his notes on BIBLE COPY B and on BIBLE *Apocryphal NT* 1 at n 2, he was much more definite in rejecting Pauline authorship of the Pastoral Epistles.

117   pp 1103–5

Faith is the proper form of the redemptive process in us—in as much as it is the contrary and ⟨the⟩ antidote to the act that constituted the Fall, or original Apostacy. To the eternal Self-affirmation of the eternal WILL, the one only absolute Good, I AM in that I AM,[1] the due response of the finite Spirits is—Thou Art; & we in thee—only in thee & thro' thee are we! Instead of this, they said—Thou art: & we too are—Our Being has its ground in our own act. We are Gods.[2] Now Faith as distinguished from Works is the habitual renunciation of this usurpation, affirming God the ground and cause of all good works, which when we ~~in~~ attribute to God, God imputeth that our act of attribution is righteousness to us. Faith therefore supposes works/—⟨Of all our Divines, Luther most fully mastered the sense & spirit of St Paul. See his Table-talk, or Commensalia.⟩[3]

118   p 1216, at the end of the text | Romans 6.21

What fruit had ye then in those things whereof ye are now ashamed? for the end of those things *is* death.

Romans VI.

Adhuc extant in visceribus etiam hominis regenerati Peccata; non ampliús autem ut *viscera*, sed ut ἐντοζωα: ascaridum instar, quæ lacessunt potius quam lædunt[1] = disturb his ease rather than injure his health. *S. T. C.*

119   p 1108 | Rom 9.3–5

For I could wish that myself were accursed from Christ for my brethren, my kinsmen according to the flesh...Whose *are* the fathers, and of whom as concerning the flesh Christ *came*, who is over all, God blessed for ever. Amen.

with the ὁ ὤν v. 5. compare Gosp. of John 1. 18.—Both our texts are

117[1] Exod 3.14. See **110** and n 1, above, and **119**, below.
117[2] Cf **64** and n 2, above.
117[3] See LUTHER *Colloquia Mensalia* (1652) esp ch 13 "That Only Faith in Christ Justifieth Before God", and 14 "Of Good Works".
118[1] "Sins still exist in the inwards even of a regenerate man; but no more as intestines, but as internal parasites: like thread-worms that irritate rather than do harm." The Latin seems to be C's. He often used the word ἐντοζωα—apparently Cuvier's word—in the later notebooks, usually writing it in Greek characters. The intestinal worm was an old figure for C: see e.g. *CL* II 1001 (1 Oct 1803).

poorly and hungrily translated.[1] The *Greek* is decisive against the Unitarian not version but perversion.[2]

120 p 1123 | 1 Cor 11.13–14

Doth not even nature itself teach you, that, if a man have long hair, it is a shame unto him?

v. 14. What would the καρηκομοωντες Αχαιοι have said to this.[1]

119[1] Rom 9.5 (*Textus receptus*): . . . ὁ Χριστὸς τὸ κατὰ σάρκα, ὁ ὢν ἐπὶ πάντων Θεὸς εὐλογητὸς εἰς τοὺς αἰῶνας; AV: "(of whom) as concerning the flesh Christ (came), *who is* over all, God blessed for ever". John 1.18 (*Textus receptus*): . . . ὁ μονογενὴς υἱός, ὁ ὢν εἰς τὸν κόλπον τοῦ Πατρός. AV: "the only begotten Son, *which is* in the bosom of the Father". The Greek idiom o ὢν—the definite article with the participle of the verb "to be" (lit. "he being") agreeing with an antecedent—is equivalent to a relative clause in English and is normally so translated, as by AV in both texts; the antecedent in Rom 9.5 is Χριστός (Christ) and in John 1.18 υἱός (Son). But for C the phrase has a special import, entirely his own and not required (or even supplied) by the syntax: for in his mind the phrase resonates with the name of God in Exod 3.14, "I AM THAT I AM", to become the *name* of the Son. (Septuagint renders the name in Exod 3.14 as εἰμὶ ὁ Ὤν. Cf *TT* 17 Aug 1833.) This is implied in a number of C's notes, but he is explicit about it in a marginal note on Daniel WATERLAND *A Vindication of Christ's Divinity* (Cambridge 1719) 279–83, saying that "o ὢν [is a phrase] which Sᵗ John every where (and Sᵗ Paul no less) makes the *peculiar* name of the Son . . .". C's highly original sense of the hidden implication of the phrase allows him to interpret it in two ways, one traditional and the other peculiar to himself, and to apply them alternatively or simultaneously: (*a*) as a statement of the identity of Jehovah as the Word of God with the Son (the "Jehovah-Word" of e.g. **11, 53–7, 110**, above); and (*b*) as a statement of the "correlativity" of Jehovah, God the Father, as "I AM" and the Son as "He is" (as e.g. in *C&S—CC*—182 and esp later in the WATERLAND note, above).

119[2] The Greek text of John 1.18 (see n 1, above) has been subject of much debate in respect of wording and punctuation, the major alternatives to *Textus receptus* υἱός being to read Θεός or to omit the word altogether. The details need not be discussed here because C accepts the reading and the punctuation that produce the AV rendering: the issue is whether "the only begotten" is named the Son, or God, or neither, and C constantly uses the phrase μονογενὴς υἱός. Rom 9.5 is more problematical because *Textus receptus* and AV clearly make Christ not only supreme but also God, not only divine but by implication the second person of the Trinity. *Textus receptus* of John 1.18 and Rom 9.5 would be less "poorly and hungrily" translated, in C's view, only by affirming as strongly as the Greek will allow the divinity of Christ and his place in the Trinity. But it is impossible to see how C's special sense of ὁ ὢν could be unambiguously embodied in an English version of either text.

120[1] "Long-haired Achaeans"—a Homeric stock phrase (e.g. *Iliad* 2.11) for the Greeks.

121 p 1124 | 1 Cor 12.3

Wherefore I give you to understand, that no man speaking by the Spirit of God calleth Jesus accursed: and *that* no man can say that Jesus is the Lord, but by the Holy Ghost.

XII. 3. How little have our latter Divines, of the School of Paley & Watson, meditated on the last clause of this verse.[1] If only by the Spirit, then assuredly not by arguments of the common Understanding grounded on miracles, which may indeed attest the historic manifestation of the great Idea of Christ's Divinity, but can never *give* it.

122 p 1134 | 2 Corinthians 7.11

For behold this selfsame thing, that ye sorrowed after a godly sort, what carefulness it wrought in you, yea, *what* clearing of yourselves, yea, *what* indignation, yea, *what* fear, yea, *what* vehement desire, yea, *what* zeal, yea *what* revenge!...

VII. 11—εκδικῆσιν *strangely* translated by *Revenge!*—The ~~meaning~~ true rendering is "exculpation", or "justification of yourselves".[1]

123 p 1136 | 2 Cor 10.8

For though I should boast somewhat more of our authority, which the Lord hath given us for edification...

X. 8. Prerogative better than authority for εξουσια.[1]

121[1] For this view of Paley see AURELIUS **38** n 1 and cf BÖHME **163** n 2. Richard Watson (1737–1816), bp of Llandaff, wrote *An Apology for Christianity* (1776) in reply to Gibbon, and in 1796 an *Apology for the Bible* in reply to Tom Paine; C spoke of making an edition of the second of these in Mar 1796. *CL* I 193; cf 197. In Jul 1801, however, he referred to him as "that beastly Bishop, that blustering Fool". *CL* II 740. Paley and Watson were both influential exponents of the argument for God *a posteriori*; hence their insistence upon the miracles as the only evidence from which faith could be derived. See also *CL* IV 813–14.

122[1] Liddell and Scott and *NT Gk Lex* together give as meanings for ἐκδίκησις "vengeance, punishment, legal remedy"; *NEB* reads "your eagerness to see justice done". C's word "exculpation" suggests that he thinks of the word ἐκ-δίκη as being let off a sentence—encouraged perhaps by the last sentence of v 11: "In all things ye have approved yourselves to be clear in this matter."

123[1] *NEB* reads "authority". The word ἐξουσία, often "power", has so many shades of meaning, even in NT, that the translation of it must be determined by context. "Prerogative", in the sense of special power or privilege, seems a reasonable suggestion here. In *SM (CC)* 96 C renders the word as "privilege" in John 1.12, and in *TT* 20 May 1830 as "jurisdiction" in John 19.10.

124 p 1140 | Galatians 1.6

I marvel that ye are so soon removed from him that called you into the grace of Christ unto another Gospel...

v. 6. q.ʸ—persuade you *to*? or recommend to you?[1]

125 p 1142 | Gal 3.19–20

Wherefore then *serveth* the law? It was added because of transgressions, till the seed should come to whom the promise was made; *and it was* ordained by angels in the hand of a mediator. Now a mediator is not a *mediator* of one, but God is one.

v. 19. 20.—the most difficult passage in all Sᵗ Paul's Writings.[1] It was the doctrine of the Alexandrian Jews that the Law was delivered by Angels; but how this, in such direct contradiction to our copies of the Hebrew Pentateuch, should have prevailed in the School of Gamaliel, is ~~diff~~ hard to understand.[2]

126 p 1144 | Ephesians 1.4

According as he hath chosen us in him before the foundation of the world, that we should be holy and without blame before him in love...

Eph. 1. 4. One of the most delightful features in Sᵗ Paul's Epistles is the doctrinal harmony with the Gospel of John. Every where Christ is the living objective Idea in which from the beginning God con-

124[1] C seems to be searching for the intended sense of τοῦ καλέσαντος (referring to "him"); in AV this is rendered "that called you"—and could hardly be rendered otherwise. Perhaps he was looking forward to 1.10: "For do I now persuade men, or God?"; but there the verb is πείθω (persuade) and the translation is literal. *NEB* perhaps improves the sense with "...canvass for the support of...". In any case, C seems not to have been looking at the Greek.

125[1] *NEB* clarifies the passage considerably: "Then what of the law? It was added [to the promise] to make wrongdoing a legal offence [*or* added because of offence]. It was a temporary measure pending the arrival of the 'issue' to whom the promise was made. It was promulgated through angels, and there was an intermediary; but an intermediary is not needed for one party acting alone, and God is one."

125[2] C's difficulty is with the angels. According to Exod (19–31) Jehovah delivered the law to Moses, and in delivering the law Moses was the intermediary between God and the Israelites; the promise was made directly to Abraham, and to Moses as an intermediary (Deut 5.5). The possibility that angels were involved as intermediaries comes from the Septuagint version of Deut 33.2 but is not in the Hebrew text—as C knew (see **135**, below). Gamaliel, the distinguished Pharisee from whom St Paul received his early rabbinical training (see Acts 5.34, 22.3), was not an Alexandrian as were the Septuagint translators; it is strange then that Paul should speak of angels here.

templated the Elect, as perfected thro' their assumption into and union with the Divine Idea, or the Word that containeth every word that proceeded from the mouth of God.

127   p 1146 | Eph 2.14–16

For he is our peace, who hath made both one, and hath broken down the middle wall of partition *between us*; Having abolished in his flesh the enmity, *even* the law of commandments *contained* in ordinances; for to make in himself of twain one new man, *so* making peace; And that he might reconcile both unto God in one body by the cross, having slain the enmity thereby . . .

v. 14. 15. 16. What a plenitude of profound truths, the fundamental mysteries of the Life of Faith, is compressed in these verses— bright & lucent yet at first view opake from the *density* of meaning— but by the water of the Spirit to be made transparent!

128   p 1147 | Eph 4.9

Now that he ascended, what is it but that he also descended first into the lower parts of the earth?

IV. 9. Our translators had unfortunately that latest interpolation of the Apostles' Creed—["] He descended into Hades" in their thoughts —but the true rendering beyond doubt is "to this our lower world" —/[1] The Greek ἀνεβῆ contains the force of re-ascended, and in this sense of the ανα the Apostle argues a previous Descent, & consequent pre-existence.[2]

129   p 1150 | Philippians

Philippi, originally named Krenides, in Macedonia, not far from the River Strymon, on the borders of Thrace, and at the foot of Mount Hæmus.[1]

128[1] *NEB* reads: "he also descended to the lowest level, down to the very earth", but adds as alternative: "descended to the regions beneath the earth". Modern scholars (with the first *NEB* reading) take this to mean that in the incarnation Christ came down even into the world. The Greek is literally "into the lower parts of the earth". Cf DONNE *LXXX Sermons* COPY B **124**. See also John PEARSON *An Exposition of the Creed* (1741) 225–6.

128[2] The word ανα means "up", and in compounds can also mean "again". But ἀνέβη already means "he went up"; if it were to mean "he went up *again*" (re-ascended), an adverb for "again" would be needed.

129[1] This information is given in EICHHORN *Neue Testament* III 303.

130 p 1153 | Colossians

Colossae (Κολοσσαι) a small Town on the Lycus in Phrygia—the Church there founded by some Disciple of St Paul's, probably Epaphras,[1] and therefore considered by the Apostle as included in his Diocese. This Epistle on many accounts interesting (ex. gr.) as an echo to the elaborate & highly finished Circular Charge, mis-named Ep. to the Ephesians,[2] and especially valuable as an antidote to the Ascetic Heresy, so early & widely injurious to the Church, and the ground of so many other Errors.[3]

131 pp 1154–5 | Col 1.12–23

... Giving thanks unto the Father, which hath made us meet to be partakers of the inheritance of the saints in light: [13] Who hath delivered us from the power of darkness, and hath translated *us* into the kingdom of his dear Son: [14] In whom we have redemption through his blood, *even* the forgiveness of sins: [15] Who is the image of the invisible God, the firstborn of every creature: [16] For by him were all things created, that are in heaven, and that are in earth, visible and invisible, whether *they be* thrones, or dominions, or principalities, or powers: all things were created by him, and for him: [17] And he is before all things, and by him all things consist. [18] And he is the head of the body, the church: who is the begin-ning, the firstborn from the dead; that in all *things* he might have the preeminence. [19] For it pleased *the Father* that in him should all fulness dwell; [20] And, having made peace through the blood of his cross, by him to reconcile all things unto himself; by him, *I say*, whether *they be* things in earth, or things in heaven.... [23] If ye continue in the faith grounded and settled, and *be* not moved away from the hope of the Gospel, which ye have heard, *and* which was preached to every creature which is under heaven ...

v. 12. εν τῳ φωτι = in the Light. Compare Gosp. John I, 5.7.9.[1]—"in the light["] = the Kingdom of the Son of God, v. 13.

130[1] See Col 1.7 and 4.12.

130[2] See **116**, above.

130[3] EICHHORN *Neue Testament* III 287–96 gives an account of the ascetic movement that Paul and C found dangerous. For other informa-tion in this note see *Neue Testament* III 283–5.

131[1] C is pointing out that in v 12 AV omits the article, which is in the Greek—not "saints in light" but "saints in *the* light", i.e. in the king-dom of God. As he notices, the definite article occurs in the same phrase in John 1.5, 7, and 9. See **102** n 1, above, on the use of the definite article in the Greek NT. The word φῶς (light) has special potency for C because of John 1.4–9. C was acutely aware of the strong Johannine flavour of Col 1.15–

v. 14. αφεσιν inadequately rendered by "forgiveness"—rather, the putting off, or the divestment.[2] So too δια = through, is not, on account of, but by the means of. (The Blood is the Life.)[3]

v. 15. worse than *inadequately* rendered. Icōn is more than Image —viz. the *substantial* Likeness or Representative—and πρωτοτοκος πασης κτισεως = ~~begotten~~ brought forth before all creation—and even this does not give the full Force of the superlative πρωτο.[4]—and I doubt our version of v. 19. Q[y] Because in him the whole Pleroma behoved to dwell.[?5] Nor do I see the necessity of giving a double meaning to the αυτου, and αυτον in v. 20.[6] See Gosp. of John II. 19.[7]

23 and prized the passage for that reason: see n 4, below. In *SM* he used this passage (Col 1.13–20) to illustrate "a state of mind indispensable for all perusal of the Scriptures to edification". *SM* (*CC*) 44–5.

131[2] AV usually translates ἄφεσις "remission" but sometimes "forgiveness". C here seems to be looking—as he often does—for a word closer to the basic meaning "sending away". Liddell & Scott has no example of ἄφεσις being used of putting off clothes, but C's suggestion is feasible.

131[3] The Greek phrase in *Textus receptus* for "through his blood" is shown as intrusive by Griesbach and in later editions: *NEB Gk* records it as a variant. The phrase "through the blood of his cross", however, occurs in v 20.

131[4] *NEB* reads: "He is the image of the invisible God; his is the primacy over all created things [*or* invisible God, born before all things]". C's "Icōn" is a transliteration of εἰκών in the Greek text. "Image" seems a weak word to convey the fact that Christ is the invisible God made visible. Heb 1.3—also using "image" —makes the point in grander language: "Who being the brightness of his glory, and the express image of his person, and upholding all things by the word of his power"—a passage that, through its use of ὑπόστασις (AV "person"), is related to **136**, below, and to Heb 3.14.

The three Greek words quoted by C are literally "firstborn of all creation" —a phrase that C was steadily con-

cerned to render with "the full Force": e.g. *TT* 17 Aug 1833. In emphasising the superlative sense of πρωτο(ς) (first) C may wish to convey not only "very first" in order of time but also the first as the beginning, ἀρχή (cf Greek of v 18—ἀρχή, πρωτότοκος), the initiative or creative source. Despite C's efforts to bring out "the full Force" of πρωτότοκος, it is virtually impossible, without a gloss, to combine the senses of priority, eternal generation, co-eternity, and creative source.

131[5] *NEB*: "For in him the complete being of God, by God's own choice, came to dwell". "Pleroma"— transliteration of πλήρωμα in the text— is a word C often used in its own right, but he sometimes translates it "fulness" (as AV does here) or "Plenitude" (as e.g. in *CN* I 928 f 29).

131[6] C's objection is to AV's introduction of "*the Father*" as gloss to the first αὐτός in v 19: in the involute sentence that begins at v 9 in AV (v 13 in *NEB*) this introduces a "double meaning" in the many repetitions of αὐτός—i.e. a double and unspecified reference, sometimes to the Father, sometimes to the Son. The αὐτός of v 16 (twice), v 17 (twice), and v 18 can be read as referring back to "the firstborn" of v 15. What C seems to want vv 19–20 to say is: "Because in him [the Son] the whole pleroma behoved to dwell and...through him [αὐτοῦ, the Son] to reconcile all things to him [αὐτόν, the Son]."

131[7] "II.19" is clearly written but seems to be a slip for "V.19", i.e. John 5.19: "The Son can do nothing

Likewise, the clause τοῦ κηρυχθεντος εν πασῇ &c. v. 23.[8] is susceptible of a far deeper and more magnificent meaning than could be conjectured from the english words by which the clause is here rendered.

132   p 1160 | 2 Thessalonians 1.12

That the name of our Lord Jesus Christ may be glorified in you, and ye in him, according to the grace of our God and the Lord Jesus Christ.

I. v. 12. Whatever may be the *interpretation*, the literal version is "of our God and Lord Jesus Christ.["]"[1]

133   p 1161 | 1 Timothy, title

The First Epistle of Paul the Apostle to Timothy.

Παύλου; ο[r][a] παυλοειδης; τὸ δεύτερον, ἡγοῦν, ως και η προς τον Τεῖτον ἐπιστόλη.[1]

134   p 1171 | Hebrews

N.B. There is no well-grounded reason for attributing this Epistle to S[t] Paul—but many and unanswerable reasons against it. It was evidently written by some converted Jew of Alexandria: by a singularly happy conjectured, Luther assigned it to Apollos. Whoever was the Author (for Luther's is but a conjecture) it is the Work of an Apostolic Man & worthy of its place in the Christian Canon.[1]

   [a] At first sight "ὁ", but Greek would require "ἠ" (or); the fact that C's writing was interrupted before παυλοειδης by the printed page-number seems to support the loss of an –*r*

of himself, but what he seeth the Father do: for what things soever he doeth, these also doeth the Son likewise." John 5.19, showing that the Father and the Son act together as one, removes the separation of Father and Son implied by the "double meaning" of αὐτοῦ/αὐτόν that C has objected to.

131[8] The words that C quotes in Greek are the beginning of the clause, "which was preached to every creature". *NEB* is perhaps "deeper and more magnificent", as well as more literal: "which has been proclaimed in the whole creation under heaven".

132[1] C is translating the ambiguous Greek τοῦ Θεοῦ ἡμῶν καὶ Κυρίου Ἰησοῦ Χριστοῦ into equally ambiguous English. Granville Sharp *Remarks on the Uses of the Definitive Article in the*

Greek Text of the New Testament (1798) 26–9 argued that the omission of the article before Κυρίου implied that "our God" and "our Lord Jesus Christ" were identical. The equally enthusiastic trinitarian C. Wordsworth in *Six Letters to Granville Sharp* (1802) 39 and T. F. Middleton in *The Doctrine of the Greek Article* (1808) 549–54 expressed doubts—Middleton more strongly. For C on the Greek article in NT see **85, 102, 131**, above, and **139**, below.

133[1] "[Epistle] of Paul? or Paul-like [epistle]? the second surely—as is also the case with the Epistle to Titus." See **116** n 1, above.

134[1] Although Jerome and Augustine treated the Epistle to the Hebrews as Pauline, it is more probable that

135 pp +3–+4, written after **81** and before **82** | Heb 2.2

For if the word spoken by angels was stedfast, and every transgression and disobedience received a just recompence of reward; How shall we escape, if we neglect so great salvation . . .

Hebrews II. 2. A noticeable passage & one of several. The assumed Facts, which form the Premise, were mere fictions of the Alexandrian or Septuagint Translation of the Pentateuch, having no shadow of a ground in the Hebrew Text—viz. that the Law was given to Moses not by Jehova but by inferior tho' angelic Beings.[1] But the deductions, the Conclusions, are not affected by this—*they* are perfectly true. We draw the same practical conclusion from the real fact. If Moses spake from Christ, but Christ under the veil, and all was confirmed; how much more are we bounden to give heed, to whom God has been *manifested* in the flesh?[2]—Take this as a rule— In sundry parts of the Epistles the Premise is *ad hominem*, i.e. according to the belief & received doctrine of the Persons immediately addressed; but the *Inference*, the practical *Conclusion*, is for all, in all times. Apply this to the forged & apocryphal Book (of Enoch) quoted by Jude.[3] The *truth* inferred is for *us*: the argument or induction for the first Readers & immediate Addresseès of the Epistle. In what other way indeed could the moral interest of the then present age have been reconciled with that of Christians in all after ages? And vice versâ the latter with the former? In the progression of vital Growth the Integuments drop off; but the stem remains & springs upward. The Grain is for a while protected by the Husk which we afterwards separate, by the winnowing of the Spirit of Truth, who has promised to be with his Church even to the end.[4]—

the author was a second-generation Christian and a Hellenist. Eichhorn *Neue Testament* iii 442–53 argues that the author was a learned Alexandrian Jew, says that Luther was the first to assign it to Apollos (on the basis of Acts 28.24) (iii 477), and concludes— in the absence of clear evidence—that Apollos was qualified to write it, that the author was a pupil of the Apostles or an unknown apostolic Father educated in Alexandria. The authorship of Apollos still receives serious support.

135[1] See also **125** and n 2, above. For the notion that angels mediated in the delivery of the Law on Mt Sinai see Acts 7.53, Heb 2.1–4, Gal 3.19; other references are to be found in the Apocrypha, and in Philo and Josephus. For C's scepticism about angels see also e.g. *C&S* (*CC*) 169 n 4.

135[2] 1 Tim 3.16.

135[3] Jude 14–15 quotes from Enoch by name, and there are other echoes of Enoch in this short epistle. Eichhorn *Neue Testament* iii 653 notices that Tertullian had so high an opinion of Jude that he thought Enoch should be included in the canon simply because it was quoted by Jude.

135[4] Matt 28.20.

The Insight into this truth constitutes the main difference between a superstitious and a truly religious use and veneration of the Scriptures.   S. T. Coleridge

July 1829

Grove, Highgate

under the Roof of my dear and under God my most precious Friends, James and Ann Gillman.[5]

136   pp 1172–3, pencil, overtraced | Heb 3.14

For we are made partakers of Christ, if we hold the beginning of our confidence stedfast unto the end . . .

a questionable rendering of ὑποστασεως ἀρχην/ The Latin Vulgate gives initium substantiæ—&c/—Still why may it not refer to the mysterious doctrine delivered in the Gospel of John C. VI?[1] the beginning of that Substratum spirituale, into which we seek to become trans-substantiated and of which the Eucharist is the Symbol?—[2]

137   pp 1194–5 | 1 John 3.4–10

Whosoever committeth sin transgresseth also the law: for sin is the transgression of the law. And ye know that he was manifested to take away our sins; and in him is no sin. Whosoever abideth in him sinneth not: whosoever sinneth hath not seen him, neither known him. Little children, let no man deceive you: he that doeth righteousness is righteous, even as he is righteous. He that committeth sin is of the devil; for the devil sinneth from the beginning. For this purpose the Son of God was manifested, that he might destroy the works of the devil. Whosoever is born of God doth not commit sin; for his seed remaineth in him; and he cannot sin, because he is born of God. In this the children of God are manifest, and the children of the devil: whosoever doeth not righteousness, is not of God, neither he that loveth not his brother.

Of the doctrines explicitly declared in Scripture, and essential to

135[5] There is a similar inscription of Aug 1818 in Böhme 1.

136[1] Vulgate reads: "Si tamen initium substantiae ejus usque ad finem firmum retineamus"; *NEB* reads: "If only we keep our original confidence firm to the end". For the "mysterious doctrine" see John 6.31–58, esp 51, 54: "I am the living bread which came down from heaven . . .".

136[2] The terms ὑπόστασις, *substan-*

tia, substratum, taken literally, played a significant part in C's exposition of his philosophy. On "*Substance*" in e.g. *Friend (CC)* i 117n, i.e. *substans*—"under-standing"—see Blanco White *Practical Evidence* 13 n 8. See also the definition of "substance" in *AR* (1825) 6n: "*Quod stat subtus . . .*". For "suppositum" in a similar use see Böhme **31** n 4.

faith, there is not one, I deem, which it is of more importance that we should understand aright, of more perilous importance that we should not misunderstand, than the doctrine of imputed righteousness.[1] It is not, we must dare think it, *our* righteousness, but the righteousness of Christ imputed to us. But yet it must be the Righteousness of Christ *in* us: for without Holiness no man can see God. —But yet again and in the best of mortal men it is the Seed of Christ germinating in "the body of the Death".[2]

138 leaf tipped in at 1032/3 | 1 John 3.6

Whosoever abideth in him sinneth not: whosoever sinneth hath not seen him, neither known him.

I. John III. 6.

We must, I humbly presume, understand the word "sinneth" of knowingly persevering in any sinful Course/ interpreting the language of the Apostle who probably *thought* in Hebrew or Syrochaldaic, tho he wrote in Greek, by the Rule of Parallelism— "Sinneth" in the 6ᵗʰ last clause of the verse being the correspondent to "abideth in him" in the preceding clause.

From the too literal understanding of these and a few similar passages in the Epistles of John the error of Novatian seems to have arisen—viz. that any Sin after Baptism excludeth from God's declared Mercies, and is no longer within the absolving power of the Church.—. Cyprian, if I recollect aright, very properly objects, that then Absolution & Baptism must be one & the same.[1]

137[1] The phrase "imputed righteousness" is derived from Rom 4.11, 22–4 and James 2.23. The possibility of misunderstanding that C notices is in vv 7 and 9. The doctrine of imputed righteousness is stated later in 1 John 3.23–4 and 4.2, 9–10, 15–17.

137[2] See Rom 7.24: "O wretched man that I am! who shall deliver me from the body of this death"—the last five words of which haunt C's late notebooks. Here, in writing "the body of the Death" he has the Greek in mind: ἐκ τοῦ σώματος τοῦ θανάτου [τούτου], ignoring the word τούτου ([of] this). For the "seed germinating" used as a resurrection image, see John 12.24 and 1 Cor 15.36; cf also ASGILL **10**.

138[1] Novatian (fl A.D. 251), Roman Stoic and bp of Rome (anti-pope), denied that it was lawful to readmit to communion those who had lapsed under persecution. As for Cyprian on infant baptism, Robert Robinson *The History of Baptism*—C's principal authority in such matters—records that the Council meeting at Carthage under Cyprian ruled that newborn infants should be allowed baptism on the grounds that, whereas circumcision was a physical dedication to God, baptism was a spiritual dedication. For Cyprian on baptism see BAXTER *Reliquiae* COPY A **8**, **44** [q] and nn. The circular argument, or *reductio ad absurdam*, seems to be C's own. Cf *CN* III 4401.

139   p 1211 | Revelation 17.3

So he carried me away in the spirit into the wilderness: and I saw a woman sit upon a scarlet coloured beast, full of names of blasphemy, having seven heads and ten horns.

v. 3, εις ερημον, into a Desert; not, as in Ch. XII, v. 14, εις την ερημον, into *the* Desert or Wilderness.[1]—N.B. Were it on account of the articles only the N. Testament requires a revised Version.[2]   °

140   pp +1–+2, corrected in pencil, in part overtraced | Rev 17.5

And upon her forehead *was* a name written, MYSTERY, BABY-LON THE GREAT, THE MOTHER OF HARLOTS AND ABOMINATIONS OF THE EARTH.

Revel. XVII. 5. It will bear a question, whether the word, Mystery, μυστηριον, belongs to the frontal title, to the inscription; or be not rather put in apposition to "name", ονομα, by the common Hebraism of two substantives for a Substantive and its Adjective—ονομα, μυστηριον for ονομα μυστηριωδες, or ὄνομα ὅ ἔστι μυστηριον—i.e. the enigmatic Name, Babylon the Great—viz. Imperial Rome.—poculis et auro Vulg. for poculis aureis—the spirit and fire (Matthew) for spiritual fire.—[1]

The sense, which sundry Anti-papal Divines of more zeal than judgement, would impose on the word, μυστηριον (Mystery)—to with,[a] Articles of Belief contradictory and incredible, Transsubstantiation for instance, of black and secret schemes and maxims of Policy, is comparatively modern, and rests on no authority of the

[a] A slip for "wit"

139[1] *NEB* reads "the wilds".

139[2] See **85, 102, 131, 132**, and nn, above, on the importance of the definite article in the Greek NT. Here there is no article before either "wilderness" or "spirit"—instances that may be symptomatic but are not significant. C often expressed the need for a new translation of NT, also of OT, and esp of the Psalms. For his long-standing project for a poetic version of Revelation see BIBLE *NT Revelation* headnote.

140[1] C suggests that "name, mystery" may be a Hebrew idiom for "mysterious name" or "name that is a mystery" as in the Latin idiom "poculis et auro" for "golden bowls" (a faulty recollection of Virgil *Georgics*

2.192, "pateris libamus et auro"); and that correspondingly the baptising "with the Holy Ghost, and with fire" of Matt 3.11 and Luke 3.16 means baptising "with spiritual fire". He had already remarked upon the possible parallel between Virgilian and Hebrew idiom in *AR* (1825) 363 (citing the Virgilian phrase correctly). C could have found the suggestion that μυστήριον is in apposition to ὄνομα and means μυστηριῶδες in EICHHORN *Apocalypsis* (2 vols Göttingen 1791) II 207. *NEB* reads "a name with a secret meaning"—"secret" being a usual meaning of μυστήριον in NT Greek.

New Testament. [1.] The primary and most comprehensive sense of Mysterium is—that ⟨which⟩ requires ⟨⟨⟩or is required⟨⟩⟩ to be meditated on in silence with closed lips, from the verb μυω, μυσω— ~~with~~ to press the lips together, whence μυστης, Mystic, μυζω to mutter, mute &c²—2. then that ⟨which⟩ cannot or must not be communicated publicly and promiscuously; ⟨that,⟩ which is not to be disclosed except to prepared and initiated persons—ex. gr. the Samothracian and Eleusinian Mysteries. 3. Then—that⟨,⟩ which *would* have ~~been~~ remained hidden⟨,⟩ if it had not been specially revealed—a revealed truth. N.B. This is, however, a doubtful interpretation. 4. An Enigma, Riddle: (private Watch-word?) 5. A Sacrament, ~~or~~ Symbol, ⟨or⟩ Symbolic Figure. N.B. Sacramentum is the translation of mustērion in the Latin Vulgate. Hence the Romish Divines render Sᵗ Paul's observation on Marriage—This is a great *Mystery*—by this is a great *Sacrament*—whence they make Marriage one of the Sacraments/³ Now in no one of these 5 senses does Mystery seem to be characteristic of the Roman Empire, or sufficiently so ~~of~~ even of Roman Polytheism, as to merit so prominent a place. For the Mysteries that were not prohibited by the Senate & Laws, were intended to counteract the popular Religion, and as antidote⟨s⟩ to the Polytheism of the Priests, by historical or physiological explanations of the Greek Mythology.⁴ But as to the

---

140² The derivation, as given by Stephanus and Scapula, is μύω (be close or be shut, esp of eyes and mouth)⟩ μυέω (initiate, teach)⟩ μύστης (an initiate), μυστήριον. According to Eusebius, quoted by Stephanus and Scapula, "Muse" derives from μυέω. In a dialogue of c 1819–20 C sought "a general and philosophical sense" for "mysticism" and rested it upon this same derivation. N 25 ff 99–8. He repeated it again in the Glossary to *C&S* (*CC* 165), in which "to muse" is also associated with these words. The derivation and meaning of "mystery" is discussed in Henry MORE *Theological Works* (1708) 1–2 (not annotated).

140³ The Church of England recognises only two sacraments: baptism and Holy Communion; see also BOOK OF COMMON PRAYER COPY B **7** n 1.

Because *sacramentum* is used in the

Vulgate (e.g. in Eph 5.32) to render μυστήριον, and can mean either an esoteric symbol or a soldier's oath, the word became important in the post-Reformation debate about the sacramental status of marriage. For C's approval of the Pauline doctrine, strongly emphasised in BCP, that marriage is "the symbol of the Union of the Church with Christ" see BROWNE *Religio* 22 and n. In Apr 1826 he gave a definition of sacrament that he considered "far more to the purpose than that which is implied in the Note to p. 55 of 'Aids to Reflection'"—i.e. *AR* (1825) 55–6n. "A Sacrament is a Symbol or Mystery consisting of a sensible Sign and a *spiritual* Substantiative Act...". N F° ff 37ᵛ–38.

140⁴ For some account of religion under the Roman empire see *P Lects* Lect 7 (1949) 230-52, esp 249; see also Lect 2 pp 89-90, and cf BAHRDT **2**. C's

Church of Rome, or the Papacy, I am content to say with LUTHER, assuredly the last man in the world to reject or n decline any tenable Handle against the triple-crowned Bishop and his Shavelings, that *by parity of reason* the words and denunciations of the Apostolic Seer may be applied or accomodated to the Papacy and the popish corruptions of the Christian Faith and pPractice;[5] but whether such is the *primary sense* of the Chapter and the proper intention of the Apostle by the Image of the Harlot, haud ita liquet ut pro articulumo fidei habendum sit.[6]—I should rely with far greater confidence on the passage in S[t] Paul[7]—if indeed it needed any Revelation to convietnce us, that a Superstition and tyranny that contradicts, perverts, and evacuates all the ⟨proper and characteristic⟩ doctrines and purposes of Christianity is *Anti-Christian*—& the Power that began, and continues this scheme of Anti-christ.[8]

S. T. Coleridge 25 Feb[y] 1826.

Grove, Highgate.

Annex

A number of passages are marked, mostly in the NT and all but one in pencil, with a line in the margin |, X, /, or //. There is no way of saying whether these are C's marks, but some of them look like marks associated with his pencil notes, and many of them involve passages in which accuracy of translation could be in question or texts that raise difficult points of interpretation.

Old Testament

p 19	X	Gen 17.15. Sarai renamed Sarah
p 60	|	49.1
p 579	/	Ps 8.9 or Ps 9
p 600	//	51.16, 17
p 602		55.23. "10" in margin

"*Prometheus*" was "an essay preparatory to a series of disquisitions respecting the Egyptian in connection with the sacerdotal theology, and in contrast to the mysteries of ancient Greece", the core of the essay having been prepared in 1820–1.

140[5] See LUTHER *Colloquia Mensalia* (1652) ch 23 "Of Antichrist" (pp 298–328), a section not marked in C's copy. C was reading LUTHER, according to N F° f 29[v], on 16 or 17 Feb 1826, only a few days before writing this marginal note.

140[6] "It is not so clear, however, that it must be taken for an article of faith". The image of the harlot is presented and interpreted in Rev 17.1–18.

140[7] 2 Thess 2.1–10 (where the name Antichrist does not occur); see also 1 John 2.6.

140[8] For C's identification of the whore of Babylon with the papacy, and for the consequences of that identification, see "On the Third Possible Church, or the Church of Antichrist" in *C&S* (*CC*) 129–45, esp 131–2.

p 619	X	89
p 620	||	89.15
p 635	X	118, 119
p 640	XX	122. One X at the foot of col 1, the other at the top of col 2
p 736	XX	Isa 60, at the beginning
p 740	|	65.17–18. = **60** textus

New Testament

p 944	X	Matt 11.12
	/	11.28, 29
p 946	|	12.40. C frequently questioned this verse
p 950	|	15.5–6. "Ask" in margin, not in C's hand
p 1035	X	John 3.5
p 1039	X	6, summary of contents. "66 Many disciples depart from him" underlined in pencil
p 1040	X	6.29. And "This is the work of God, that ye believe on him whom he hath sent" underlined in pencil
	X	6.33, 35, 37, 40, 44, 47, 51, 53
p 1041	X	6.57, 63, 65
p 1054	X	15.27, at end of ch 15 or beginning of John 16
p 1063	X	Acts 2.30. = **113** textus
p 1064	X	2.38, 42
p 1091	X	22.16
p 1105	X	Rom 6.16, 17, 19, 20, 21, 22, 23
p 1118	X	1 Cor 6.3. "Angels" underlined in pencil
p 1132	X	2 Cor 5.1
p 1159	X	1 Thess 5.9, 10, 15
p 1160	X	2 Thess 2.3. "The son of perdition" underlined in pencil and marked with X
p 1165	X	1 Tim 6.10. "Pierced themselves through with many sorrows" underlined in pencil
p 1181	X	Heb 13.17.
p 1183	X	James 2.1, 14, 26
	X	2.17. "Alone" underlined in pencil
		2.18. "My faith *by* my works", word underlined in pencil
	X	2.24. "Faith *only*", word underlined in pencil
	X	2.26
p 1184	X	3.6, 8
		3.10. "Not so" underlined in pencil
		4.5. "Us" underlined in pencil
	/	4.8
	X	4.14
p 1186	X	1 Pet 1.19
	X	2.3
p 1197	—	3 John 9, 10
p 1200	X	Rev 2.17. "To him that overcometh ... receiveth it" marked with |
p 1204	|	7.16–17

Old Testament: Psalms

A New Version of the Psalms of David, fitted to the tunes used in churches. By N. Brady [1659–1726] and N. Tate [1652–1715], &c. London 1805. 8°.

The precise issue is not identified; imprint and format are recorded in SC. This copy may originally have been bound with a copy of the Book of Common Prayer: see BOOK OF COMMON PRAYER COPY B headnote.

Not located. *Sotheby Misc Sale* 11–14 Dec 1903 item 79: "Coleridge's copy, with 12 lines of original verse [of which only four are quoted] in his hand-writing on flyleaf—".

DATE. Uncertain.

1 flyleaf

> When Moses stood with arms outspread,
> Success was found on Israel's side,
> But when through weariness they failed,
> That moment Amalek prevail'd[1]

1[1] The remaining eight lines described in the sale catalogue are not recorded. It is not certain that the verses are C's. The transcriber has mistakenly written *Amalek* as *Amalet*. The lines are the beginning of a verse rendering of Exod 17.8–14: "Then came Amalek, and fought with Israel in Rephidim. ..." This incident provided C with the central image in a personal prayer for strength to sustain his belief through prayer: SERMONS AND HOMILIES 2.

New Testament: Gospels

A Harmonie upon the Three Evangelists, Matthew, Mark and Luke, with the Commentarie of M. Iohn Calvine: faithfullie translated out of Latine into English, by E. P[aget]. Whereunto is also added a commentarie upon the Evangelist S. Iohn, by the same authour. [Title to second part:] The Holy Gospel of Iesus Christ, according to Iohn, with the commentary of M. Iohn Calvine: faithfully translated out of Latine into English by Christopher Fetherstone, student in divinitie. 2 pts in 1 vol. London 1584. 4º.

British Museum C 126 e 5

Inscribed on the title-page: "Class: 1—Shelf: 4—Nº 8" and the signature of Mathew Helme[?]. Some corrections in an early hand, presumably Helme's, have been made to the Table on sig ¶¶5ᵛ. There are unidentified underlinings on i 203–4, 542–3, 686. "S.T.C." label on the title-page and John Duke Coleridge's monogram on p ⁻2.

For C's note of c 1806 of a project that seems to antedate his owning a copy of Calvin's *Harmonie*, see *CN* ii 2971.

No work of Calvin's, other than the *Commentarie* printed with this *Harmonie*, is preserved with C's marginalia. WW's library included a copy of Calvin's *Institutio Christianae religionis* (Geneva 1569) with the "Autographs of 'S. T. Coleridge' & 'W. Wordsworth'"; in the Rydal Mount catalogue it is marked as C's. *Wordsworth SC* (1859) 204; *Wordsworth LC* 297.

In the spring of 1802 C intended an essay on "Luther & Lutheranism, Calvin & Calvinism (with Zwinglius)". *CN* i 1181. He recognised Calvin as an instance of "sincere Bigotry" as distinct from the "Bigotry from Sincerity" of "a modern popular Preacher". *CN* iii 4177. C's desire to achieve a precise definition of the difference between Arminianism and Calvinism (accentuated later perhaps by the fact that J. H. Green was an ardent Calvinist) is to be seen in many places: e.g. *CN* iii 3963, *CL* iv 566–7, BAXTER *Reliquiae* COPY B **111**, *P Lects* (1949) 446–7, N 30 ff 17ᵛ–18. Cf Jeremy TAYLOR *Polemicall Discourses* i 682 (repeated variatim in *Friend*—*CC*—i 434).

DATE. Possibly 1820. There is no definite clue to the date of acquisition, and no direct reference to this book appears except for a quotation from the "Epistle Dedicatorie" in N 23 f 17, immediately preceding an entry dated 30 Jun 1820.

1 i 3, pencil

[Calvin's comment on Luke 1.3:] *Assoone as I had searched out perfectly.* The olde translation hath (*omnia assecuto*) I having followed all things. The Greeke word is metaphoricallye deduced from them, whiche treade in others steppes, least ought should escape them. For Luke would declare unto us a diligent studie and manner of learning.

and could Luke, or any man in his senses, appeal to this & to nothing else, when according to Calvin & the οἱ πολλοι of orthodoxists he must have been conscious "*that he had written nothing but what was revealed unto him by Omniscience, & put into his Head by the Holy Ghost*". See the Argument.[1]

2   ii 7–8 | "The Holy Gospel of Iesus Christe according to Iohn"   ˉ

[Calvin comments on John 1.1, "In the beginning was the Word...":] Furthermore as God did reveale himselfe in creating the worlde by this word, so he had the same laid up in himselfe before: so that there is a double relation, the former unto God, the latter unto men. *Servetus* the proudest knave which Spayne ever brought foorth, feigneth that this eternall worde did then take his beginning, when he was revealed in the creation of the worlde: As if it were not before such time as the power thereof was knowen in the externall worke. ... Nowe whereas some do wrest the word *beginning* unto the beginning of the heaven & the earth, doe they not make Christ subiect to the common order of the worlde, from which he is flatly exempted in this place? Wherein they doe most cruell iniurie not onely to the sonne of God, but also to the everlasting father, whom they spoile of his wisdome.

Calvin in thus making the Logos a mere attribute, and of course therefore not only not divisible, but by no possibility distinguishable, from the Father, has authorized a yet grosser Heresy, & far more prolific in heinous Inferenda, than that of poor Servetus, whom in the *pride* of a French man he appropriates as "the proudest Knave that Spain ever brought forth", and ⟨in⟩ the canine rabies of his self-assumed Hyperorthodoxy howls against, as a barking Dog.[1]—

[1] The "Greeke word" is παρηκολ-ουθηκότι, from παρακολουθεῖν (meaning, to follow along closely [with the mind] what has gone before, hence to trace or investigate rigorously). C's *hoi polloi* (the many) refers to the majority or mass—of orthodoxists.

In the "Argument" Calvin had said (sig B7ᵛ): "it little appertaineth unto us to know more, then that he [Mark] is a lawfull witnesse ordained of God, and that he publisheth nothing in wryting, but that which was revealed unto him, and putte into his head by the holy Ghost ... and the same doe I judge of Luke". C is objecting to Calvin's inconsistency: if Luke had considered himself divinely inspired he would have made that claim here instead of simply appealing to his diligent study of the facts.

[1] Michael Servetus (1511–53) travelled in Italy and Germany, where he met Melanchthon and Bucer. His

In truth, Calvin's notions of the Trinity, and those of his Apostles & Disciples for near a century after, seem to have been very crude. It is the glory of the English Church to have been as equal to the Church of Rome in this main article, as in all others she is superior—. This the Romanists themselves admit by the reverence, they pay, to Bull's Defence of the Nicene Creed, which is a classical Work in their Universities.[2] S. T. C.

3 ii 8–9, marked in the margin

[Continuing the commentary on John 1.1:] Ther fore *Augustine* saith very well, that this beginning which is mentioned in this place, is without all beginning. For although the father is before his wisedome in order, yet they spoyle him of his glory, whosoever doe imagine any moment of time wherein he was before his wisdome.

The elder and more philosophical Greek Fathers far more justly appropriated the term, Wisdom, Σοφια, to the Holy Ghost[1]—

biblical studies led him to renounce the doctrine of the Trinity in *De Trinitatis erroribus* (1531). He then turned to the practice of medicine, and in 1553 published anonymously *Christianismi restitutio*, in which he denied the Trinity and the true divinity of Christ, arguing (*inter alia*) that the Logos was no more than one of the three elements in Christ's humanity. Servetus had first met Calvin in France, and in 1546–7 had a severe epistolary theological controversy with him; these letters he added to the *Restitutio*, offending Calvin. His authorship was reported to the Inquisition by an intermediary of Calvin's; he was imprisoned in April 1553 but escaped (and was burned in effigy). When Servetus was passing through Geneva on his way to Italy, Calvin had him arrested and tried for heresy. Under torture, he refused to recant and was burned as a heretic at Champel on 27 Oct 1553. (Calvin disputed with him on the day of his execution.) Calvin's savagery was not directed only towards Servetus: in a period of five years in Geneva, Calvin had 58 persons put to death, 76 exiled for their religious beliefs, and many others imprisoned. For such brutal "Hyperorthodoxy" C's figure

is not extravagant: see also FIELD **24**, but cf *TT* 3 Jan 1834.

2[2] George Bull (1634–1710), bp of St David's, provided—with Waterland, in C's view—the foundation for sound trinitarian doctrine. Attacking the Jesuit doctrine of Petavius, Bull showed, in his *Defensio fidei Nicaenae* (1685), the consonance of the pre-Nicene Fathers, particularly Tertullian, with the teaching of the orthodox theologians of Nicene (325) and post-Nicene times, a key term in the Nicene formula being ὁμοούσιος—"of the same substance". Bull's *Defensio* so commended itself to Bossuet and other French Roman Catholic theologians that he received formal tribute at the Synod of St Germain in 1686 for his defence of Catholic doctrine; Bull, however, made his personal position clear in a book entitled *The Corruptions of the Church of Rome* (1705). See also BULL.

3[1] A similar statement appears in *LS* (*CC*) 206n. See also *CN* ii 2445, in which C quotes from Horsley. Many Greek fathers use Σοφία (Wisdom) as a synonym for the Logos, on the evidence of 1 Cor 1.24 and Col 2.3; but in mediaeval theology the word is chiefly applied to the Holy Ghost.

Intellectus, Intelligibile, Intellectio[;] now Σοφια = Intellectus in Intelligibili + Actio. Νοῦς νοερὸς ἐνί Νῷ νοήτῳ + Ενεργεῖα = Σοφία, ἡ Πνευμα αγιον.—τί εστι το Πνεῦμα, φυσικῶς; Αηρ εν κινησεῖ.[2]

3[2] "Intellect, Intelligible, Intellection[;] now Wisdom (Sophia) = Intellect in the Intelligible + Action. Intellectual Intellect in intelligible Intellect + Energy (initiative) = Wisdom, or holy Spirit.—What is spirit in physical terms? Air in motion." Intellect, Intelligible, Intellection (for which Νοῦς, νοητὸς, νοερός are here the Greek equivalents) evidently correspond to the three persons of the Trinity. As for ἐνεργεία and κίνησις the one is "force from within" (i.e. force self-initiated), the other is "motion". Cf the phrase "The Spirit self-movent (αὐτοκίνητον)" in Lacunza i cv. The term ἀήρ (air) serves a double rôle, implying for a spiritual context the breath of God, and for a physical context "air" simply. The Holy Spirit, the breath of God, is Intellect + Action; physically, breath is air in motion. Action is a matter of will; movement is purely mechanical.

This formula, one of C's many attempts to draw up a schema for the Trinity, embodies convictions intrinsic to C's own spiritual life. Cf "the Spirit is whatever it is by an act of its own". *CN* iii 4186 f 34; see also 4223, 4244. C held that judgement is an *act*, and (with Duns Scotus) that faith is an act of faith rather than (as Aquinas held) a speculative state. Cf Blanco White *Letters from Spain* 1.

New Testament: Revelation

Apocalypsis graece. Perpetua annotatione illustrata a Ioanne Henrico Heinrichs. Vol II (of 2). Göttingen (1818,) 1821. 8°.

This work was also issued as Vol x (in 2 pts) of *Novum Testamentum graece perpetua annotatione illustratum a Io. Beniam. Koppe* (10 vols Göttingen 1783–1821; 2nd ed 1808–28), the "Koppian edition", to which Heinrichs had also contributed Vol VII (1798, 1803), on the Epistles to Timothy, Titus, Philemon, and Colossians, and Vol VIII (1792), on Hebrews. The Greek text is accompanied by copious textual and exegetical commentary (in Latin), followed (II 195–343) by eight "Excursus" on crucial passages and topics.

Not located. Annotations reprinted from *LR* III, except **1**, which is reprinted from William Wright *Biblical Hermeneutics* (see below).

A copy belonging to Dr William Wright (c 1794–1856), of Trinity College, Dublin.

LR simply cited "Heinrich's Commentary on the Apocalypse... Göttingen, 1821". A note in N Q ff 49–50ᵛ, written in two unidentified hands after C's death, gives the ownership of the book and the source of the transcript of marginalia, being a copy of a passage in *Biblical Hermeneutics; or, the Art of Scripture Interpretation. From the German of George Frederic Seiler, D.D.... With notes from the Dutch of J. Heringa ...Translated...with additional notes and observations, by the Rev. William Wright, LL.D. of Trinity College Dublin* (1835) 564. The note in N Q begins: "This book belonged to D[r] Wright which [he lent] to Mʳ C —and from [which] I extracted the following notes, which the Dʳ has published as a note of Mʳ C's in a work transcribed by him entitled Biblical Hermeneutics—These Notes were written in the Year 1833, about the Month of November, therefore about 7 months before his death—". The transcript of **1** in *Biblical Hermeneutics* is prefaced with the statement: "The late lamented Mr. Coleridge, the eminent poet and philosopher, having borrowed from me, not long before his death, a volume of Heinrichs' Commentary on the Apocalypse, returned it with several curious notes, scarcely legible, some written with a pen and others with a pencil, on the margin and blank leaves, from which I trust I shall be pardoned for selecting the following effusion, dated November 1833 ...". William Wright also communicated to DC for *NTP* marginalia that C had written in his copy of Johann JAHN *Appendix hermeneuticae seu exercitationes exegeticae in vaticiniis Messiam promittentibus* (2 vols Vienna 1813–15).

Although the marginalia on Heinrichs's edition were written in c Nov 1833—a date reinforced by entries in N 53 and N 54—they are associated with a project C had had in mind for a long time: see e.g. *CN* I 1646, *LS* (*CC*) 147n, and for his interest in interpretative detail in Rev see e.g. *CN* III 3793. He outlined the scheme in N 39 f 34: 1. Dedication (Rev 1.9–3.22); 2. Prologue (Rev 1.1–8); 3. The Drama (Rev 4.1–22.21 [end]). When he began his careful reconsideration of Rev late in 1833 he was entering upon his terminal illness; he wrote the marginalia on Heinrichs's edition at the time when he was composing his verse epitaph and sending copies of it to his most intimate friends. See TODTENTANZ. Whenever Wright's copy of Vol II came into C's hands, he seems not to have expected to be able to keep it for long, and wrote to Green on 28 Oct 1833, asking him to buy a copy of Heinrichs's *Apocalypsis graece*. *CL* VI 963. On the next day he told John Sterling that he had little hope of completing the *Opus Maximum* or of collecting for publication his mss on theological subjects, and continued: "I am, however, very seriously disposed to employ the next two months in preparing for the Press a metrical translation (if I find it practicable) of the Apocalypse....I am encouraged to this by finding how much of *Original* remains in my Views, after I have subtracted all that I have in common with Eichhorn and Heinrichs." *CL* VI 967–8. No part of a verse translation has come to light.

C's marginalia on Henry MORE *Theological Works* (1708) deal with issues much like those in the marginalia on Heinrichs—a fact recognised by HNC in departing from his chronological scheme for *LR* III and IV in order to print the two sets of marginalia side by side.

MS TRANSCRIPT. N 54 f 1ᵛ: C's transcript of **7** only.

DATE. Oct–Nov 1833: see above, and **7** and n 2, below. Wright states that **1** was "dated November 1833": *Biblical Hermeneutics* 564n.

COEDITOR. Merton A. Christensen.

1   II flyleaf, referring to II 23–9ᵃ¹ | footnote to Rev 13.3 and 13.11ff

Quae cuncta...nil...impediunt, quo minus et ad proconsulem Ephesinum, qui nobis taxari videtur, adhiberi possint poetae verba... nec refragabitur, quod neque de nomine huius proconsulis, neque de eius fortuna vel secunda vel adversa compertus quidquam habemus....

Ex Herderiana autem hypothesi, quae cuncta ad Judaeam et Hierosolyma refert, designatur his omnibus callidus ille Simonis comes et satelles, Joannes Leui, Gischala oriundus....Ceterum hic ψευδοπροφητης infra vbique fere locorum adesse τῷ θηριῳ legitur,

ᵃ *LR* gives the page as II 294, with textus in German from Excursus VI, but this does not connect with C's note. Perhaps a slip for II 249, for which see **1** n 1, below

1¹ Wright says in a footnote (at n 2, below): "Alluding to Heinrichs' Commentary on chap. xiii. (See Part II. pp. 23–29.)"; textus **1** is drawn from the commentary on II 23 and 29. The subject is discussed in greater detail, however, in Excursus IV with an account of Herder's advocacy of Joannes Levi of Gischala at II 249—a passage that C objected to (in N 53 f 23ᵛ) because of Herder's "historical interpretations of the Apocalypse". This suggests that this marginal note may have been written on II 249, or, if on a flyleaf, including a specific reference to II 249.

vt exitialis duumuiratus, et, accedente draconis capitis 12 ipso, triumuiratus adeo (cap. 16, 13. alibi) aduersus christianos insurgat.

[These considerations...do not prevent the poet's words from being applied to a proconsul of Ephesus also [i.e. as well as to Nero], who seems to be being brought before us...and this suggestion will not be disproved because we have no knowledge of the existence of this proconsul nor of his good or bad fortune....

But according to Herder's hypothesis, which refers everything to Judea and Jerusalem, all this points to Simon's crafty companion and accomplice, Joannes Levi of Gischala....This false prophet is said below in numerous passages to have been with the Beast, so that a deadly duumvirate, and then on the arrival of the dragon of ch 12 a triumvirate (16.13 and elsewhere) rises to attack the Christians.]

O the sad historic prosaisms of the Proconsul of Ephesus, and Johannes Levi of Gischala!*ª2*

I have too clearly before me the idea of the poet's genius to deem myself other than a very humble poet; but in the very possession of the idea, I know myself so far a poet as to feel assured that I can understand and interpret a poem in the spirit of poetry, and with the poet's spirit. Like the ostrich, I cannot fly, yet I have wings that give me the feeling of flight; and as I sweep along the plain,[3] can look up toward the bird of Jove, and can follow him, and say—

"Sovereign of the air, who descendest on thy nest in the cleft of the inaccessible rock, who makest the mountain pinnacle thy perch and halting-place, and scanning with steady eye the orb of glory right above thee, imprintest thy lordly talons in the impassive*ᵇ* snows that shoot back and scatter round his glittering shafts,—I

ª LR provides a different opening paragraph: see **1** n 2, below   *ᵇ LR* reads "stainless"

---

12 *LR* omitted this sentence (perhaps because it would have been meaningless without a gloss) and gave a different introductory paragraph: "*Euge! Heinrichi.* O, the sublime bathos of thy prosaism—the muddy eddy of thy Logic! Thou art the only man to understand a poet!"—possibly made up from one or more detached notes that were not originally part of **1**.

In Excursus IV—as in less detail in the commentary II 23–9—Heinrichs states his own preference for the proconsul of Ephesus called Latinus, and as another possibility favours V[lpius] CLaVDIVS, whose name provides

roman numerals that add up to 666: II 259–62.

13 For C's identification of himself with various birds, see e.g. *CN* III 3793 and n. In his standard conceit of the ostrich, he buries his eggs carelessly in the sand and provides feathers for the caps of others: see *CN* I 1248 and frequently thereafter. He used the low-flying bustard (ostriches and bustards being a commonplace detail in Xenophon's account of the Persian campaign) as a metaphor for his own prose style: *CL* II 814. The eagle, the emblem for John the Evangelist, appears again in **7**, below.

pay thee homage. Thou art my king. I give honour due to the vulture, the falcon, and all thy noble baronage; and no less to the lowly bird, the sky-lark, whom thou permittest to visit thy court, and chaunt her matin song within its cloudy curtains; yea, the linnet, the thrush, the swallow, are my brethren:—but still I am a bird, though but a bird of the earth.

Monarch of our kind, I am a bird, even as thou; and I have shed plumes, which have added beauty to the Beautiful,—...*a* grace to Terror, waving on the helmed head of the war-chief;—and majesty to Grief, drooping o'er the car of Death!"

2   II 91 | Rev 17.11

Καὶ τὸ θηρίον, ὃ ἦν, καὶ οὐκ ἔστι, καὶ αὐτὸς ὄγδοός ἐστι, καὶ ἐκ τῶν ἑπτά ἐστι, καὶ εἰς ἀπώλειαν ὑπάγει.

["And the beast that was, and is not, even he is the eighth, and is of the seven, and goeth into perdition."]

[Heinrichs's textual notes:] VARIAE LECTIONES: v. 11. Adnotat Wetstenius, in Versione Coptica pro ογδοος legi αγγελος quod nostrae de Diabolo explicationi favet.

[VARIANT READINGS: v. 11. Wetstein notes that in the Coptic Version αγγελος (angel) is read for ογδοος (eighth); this favours our interpretaton, that it refers to the Devil.]

[Heinrichs's footnote:] v. 11. Atque septem his capitibus, quae in rei christianae perniciem conspiravere, accedit Satanas ipse, foedusque paciscitur (*Octupel-Allianz*) tanquam dux caeterorum et antesignanus.

[And to these seven heads, which conspired for the destruction of the Christian state, Satan adds himself and seals the treaty (the Octuple Alliance) as the leader of the others and their champion.]

Among other grounds for doubting this interpretation (that *the eighth* in v. 11 is Satan), I object, 1. that it almost necessitates the substitution of the Coptic ἄγγελος for ὄγδοος against all the MSS., and without any Patristic hint. For it seems a play with words unworthy the writer, to make Satan, who possessed all the seven, himself an *eighth*, and still worse if *the eighth*:—2. that it is not only a great and causeless inconcinnity in style, but a wanton adding of obscurity to the obscure to have, first, so carefully distinguished (c. xiii. 1–11.) the δράκων from the two θηρία,[1] and the one θηρίον

a Wright prints the three points

2[1] "The dragon from the two beasts". One of the beasts rose out of   the sea, was seven-headed, and "like unto a leopard" with the "feet of a

from the other, and then to make θηρίον the appellative of the δράκων: as if having in one place told of Nicholas *senior*,[2] Dick and another Dick his cousin, I should soon after talk of Dick, meaning old Nicholas by that name; that is, having discriminated Nicholas from Dick, then to say Dick, meaning Nicholas!

3 II 122–3 | Rev 19.9

Καὶ λέγει μοι· γράψον· μακάριοι οἱ εἰς τὸ δεῖπνον τοῦ γάμου τοῦ ἀρνίου κεκλημένοι. Καὶ λέγει μοι· οὗτοι οἱ λόγοι οἱ ἀληθινοὶ τοῦ Θεοῦ εἰσί.

["And he saith unto me, Write, Blessed are they which are called unto the marriage supper of the Lamb. And he saith unto me, These are the true sayings of God."]

[Heinrichs's footnote:] και ελεγε μοι. Quinam dixisse haec credendus erit? Procul dubio aliquis ex illo οχλῳ πολλῳ, cuius mentio fit v. 1, ubi vide, et v. 6.]

["And he said to me." But who are we to believe is the speaker here? Doubtless one out of the "much people" mentioned in v 1, which see, and v 6 ("the voice of a great multitude").]

These words might well bear a more recondite interpretation; that is, οὗτοι (these blessed ones) are the true λόγοι or τέκνα Θεοῦ, as the *Logos* is the υἱὸς Θεοῦ.[1]

4 II 122–3 | Rev 19.10

["And I fell at his feet to worship him. And he said unto me, See *thou do it* not: I am thy fellowservant, and of thy brethren that have the testimony of Jesus: worship God: for the testimony of Jesus is the spirit of prophecy."]

[Heinrichs's footnote:] Est ergo, qui hic cum Joanne colloquitur,

---

bear" and the "mouth of a lion"; he bore "the name of blasphemy" (Rev 13.1–2). The other beast came out of the earth, had "two horns like a lamb", "spake as a dragon", and "exerciseth all the power of the first beast"; he caused all the world to "worship the first beast" (vv 11–12) and also caused the mark of the [first] beast to be imprinted (vv 16–18) on all whose names are not written in the book of life (v 8). The dragon gave to the first beast "his power, and his seat, and great authority" (v 2).

[2] Old Nick: see e.g. ANALYSIS 1 at n 2.
[1] "These...*logoi* [pl of *logos*]... children of God...son of God". The play on *logoi* (words, sayings) and *Logos* (the Word) connects this note with John 1 esp vv 1–34, in which Jesus is identified as both the Word and the son of God. C's first Greek phrase is prominent in John 1.12 (AV: "sons of God", literally "children of God"), the second occurs esp in Matt 27.43 ("I am the Son of God").

non insignioris alicuius ordinis angelus, sed unus multorum, e turba illa, qui extremo orbe divinum solium cinxisse leguntur c. 5. 11; cf. ad v. 9; forte unus eorum, qui morte sua martyrium pro J. C. subierant...

[John's interlocutor here, therefore, is not one of some higher order of angels, but one of many, from that crowd said to have been in the outer circle round the divine throne (ch. 5. 11...), perhaps one of those who suffered martyrdom for Jesus Christ...]

According to the law of symbolic poetry this sociable angel (the Beatrice of the Hebrew Dante) ought to be, and I doubt not is, *sensu symbolico*, an angel; that is, the angel of the Church of Ephesus, John the Evangelist, according to the opinion of Eusebius.[1]

5   II 245 | Excursus IV "De antichristo..."

[Rev 13.18: "Here is wisdom. Let him that hath understanding count the number of the beast: for it is the number of a man; and his number is Six hundred threescore and six." Heinrichs gives a Latin version of Irenaeus *Advers. haeres.* 5.30. Tr John Keble (1862): "Yea, and the name ΛΑΤΕΙΝΟΣ hath the number of 666: and it is very probable that the last Kingdom hath this Word. For they who now reign are Latini.... Yes, and TEITAN also, if you write the first syllable by the two Greek vowels E and I, is most worthy of credit of all the names which we have. For it both contains in itself the aforesaid number, and is of six letters, each syllable consisting of three letters, and it is old, and withdrawn; for neither of our own Kings hath any one been called Titan, nor any one of the idols which are publicly adored among Greeks or Barbarians hath this name ...and it hath in it a certain shew of revenge, and of one inflicting a penalty; in that he of whom we speak feigns himself the avenger of the wronged.... Since therefore this name of Titan hath such a store of plausibilities, it hath however just so much likelihood, as that we may many ways infer that he who shall come may possibly be called Titan.... But this number of his name he [John] shewed, that we should be on our guard against him when he cometh, as knowing who he is."]

It seems clear that Irenæus invented the unmeaning *Teitan*, in

---

4[1] Cf *C&S* (*CC*) 140. Eusebius, in *Ecclesiastical History* 3.23, reports the tradition that John the Evangelist was head of the Church at Ephesus; in 3.39 he doubts which John was the author of Rev; in 7.24 he quotes Dionysius of Alexandria's arguments against the Evangelist as author of Rev.

order to save himself from the charge of treason, to which the *Lateinos* might have exposed him.[1] See Rabelais *passim*.[2]

6 II 246

Nec magis blandiri poterit alterum illud nomen, Τειταν, quod studiose commendavit Irenaeus.

[No more shall we be able to favour the other name, Teitan, strongly recommended by Irenaeus.]

No! *non studiose, sed ironice commendavit Irenæus.*[1] Indeed it is ridiculous to suppose that Irenæus was in earnest with *Teitan*. His meaning evidently is:—if not *Lateinos*, which has a meaning, it is some one of the many names having the same numerical power, to which a meaning is to be found by the fulfilment of the prophecy. My own conviction is, that the whole is an ill-concerted conundrum, the secret of which died with the author. The general purpose only can be ascertained, namely, some test, partaking of religious obligation, of allegiance to the sovereignty of the Roman Emperor.[2]

If I granted for a moment the truth of Heinrichs's supposition, namely, that, according to the belief of the Apocalypt, the line of Emperors would cease in Titus the seventh or complete number (Galba, Otho, and Vitellius, being omitted)[3] by the advent of the Messiah;—if I found my judgement more coerced by his arguments than it is,—then I should use this book as evidence of the great and early discrepance between the Jewish-Christian Church and the Pauline; and my present very serious doubts respecting the identity of John the Theologian and John the Evangelist would become fixed convictions of the contrary.[4]

5[1] C wrote a similar note in Henry MORE *Theological Works* 621.

5[2] Rabelais protected himself from prosecution for his satirical attacks upon e.g. the University of Paris and the monastic orders by inventing such names as Epistemon, Panurge, the Abbey of Theleme, &c.

6[1] "Not strongly, but ironically, recommended by Irenaeus".

6[2] For other comments on Irenaeus' decipher see *CN* III 3792, 3793, and nn. In J. C. WOLF *Curae philologicae* (Hamburg 1735) 547–8 C suggested that χ′ζ′ϛ′ (666) was an acronym of Χρίστος Ξύλω Σταυρώμενος (Christ crucified on the cross)—the Roman Catholic "Image of Idolatry". But this, the "papal idolatrous Crucifix", he took for one of his own "whimsical verbal solutions". N 53 f 24ᵛ.

6[3] C made a similar remark in MORE *Theological Works* 621. The sequence of Roman emperors is given by Heinrichs in his note on Rev 17.10 (II 90–1; cf II 274): Augustus (27 B.C.–A.D.14), 2. Tiberius (14–37), 3. Caligula (37–41), 4. Claudius (41–54), 5. Nero (54–68), [Galba, Otho, and Vitellius (69)], 6. Vespasian (69), 7. Titus (69–79).

6[4] See MORE *Theological Works* 119.

7   II 265, pencil*[a]*[1] | Excursus v "De loco illo vexatissimo, cap. 27, v. 8 sqq."

19 Nov[r] 1833.—[2]

This vile, this ⟨"vel⟩ Cacatu indigna Papyrus",[3] which will not receive Plumbago (i.e. black lead pencil) and makes ~~the~~ Ink ~~run~~ go mad, ~~defacing it~~ yea, run out of its *Senses*—this alone has saved Master Heinrichs, page after page, from a sound *, †, ~~and~~ or †† flagellation for his inveterate Prosaism.—Verily, it provokes me to see such a Dodo attempting to *tread* an Eagle.[4]

---

a The location of the ms note is not certain. It may have been written at the beginning of Excursus v, referring to a nearby note written—or attempted—in ink

7[1] C's transcript of this note begins: "Pencil Note on Heinrich's Excursus V. in Apocalypsin, transcribed—in remembrance of *German* printing, Anglicè, *blotting*: Paper—".

7[2] Whether this is the date of the original marginal note or of the transcript—or both—does not appear.

7[3] "Paper unworthy even of excrement"—C's common complaint against German paper, made with variants on Catullus *Carmina* 34.1, 20; see also e.g. *CL* III 365, the extract from N R in Introduction, above, p lxxii. The one marginal note on EICHHORN *Apocalypsis* COPY B (19 Feb 1826) is on this subject.

7[4] More foolery with images of birds occurs in FABER **11, 12.**

New Testament: Apocrypha

The Apocryphal New Testament, being all the Gospels, Epistles, and other pieces now extant, attributed in the first four centuries to Jesus Christ, his apostles, and their companions, and not included in the New Testament, by its compilers. Translated from the original tongues and now first collected into one volume. London 1820. 8°.

"Printed for William Hone, Ludgate Hill"—by whom the book was edited.

Johns Hopkins University Library

Bookplate of Alexander William Gillman. On the front blue board, apparently in Anne Gillman's hand, in ink: "Notes by S. T. C." A letter from Maggs tipped in states that the book came from the library of Dr James Gillman and was "sold by Mrs. L. E. Watson"; the book is not included in the *Watson List*.

On p 248 two pencil check marks have been made, one against paragraph 3, the other against paragraph 6; these are not identifiable as C's. 1 Clement 16 is marked with ink dots in the margin; these may be associated with his notes in N F° ff 39–20.

William Hone (1780–1842), author and bookseller, was prosecuted in 1817 for publishing satirical versions of the Litany, the Athanasian Creed, and the church Catechism. When he was acquitted on all three separate charges, C applauded the acquittal, though he can scarcely have condoned the offence. *CL* IV 814–15; see also *CRB* I 214, but cf *WL* (*M2*) II 410. Lamb became acquainted with Hone in early 1819 (if not earlier), and collaborated generously with him in preparing *The Every-Day Book* (1826), which was dedicated to Lamb and puffed by RS in his "Life of Bunyan" prefixed to *Pilgrim's Progress* (1830). Everything Hone undertook tended to founder; *The Every-Day Book* and *The Table Book* failed to make his fortune. See also *LL* III 269–74. In his last years be became devout and orthodox and often preached. C may have had some slight acquaintance with him. In a note on SOUTHEY *Life of Wesley* (2 vols 1820) II 166–78 he recorded that "Hone called my 'Aids to Reflection', *a proper Brain-cracker*". A volume of six tracts including Richard Towgood's *History of Charles I* is described as having "Autograph of W. Hone, and Index in MS. by Mr. Coleridge". *Gillman SC* (1843) 435.

In spite of a savage review in *QR* and fierce attacks by Samuel Butler and Thomas Rennell, Hone's edition of the Apocryphal NT—shamelessly derivative and of questionable scholarship—sold rapidly and was reprinted several times, being the only available popular collective version in English of the "Apocryphal New Testament" and the "Apostolic Fathers". (The works that Hone had drawn upon without adequate acknowledgment—Jeremiah Jones's *New and Full Method of Settling the Canonical Authority of the New Testament* and William Wake's *The Genuine Epistles of the Apostolic Fathers*—were reprinted in 1826 and 1816 respectively but were too specialised to have wide appeal.) *QR* had referred to the editor of this "nefarious publication" as "a wretch, as contemptible as he is wicked . . . a poor illiterate creature, far too ignorant to have any share in the composition" of it, and Hone quoted the passage in his refutation in the 3rd ed of 1821. In his 1820 preface he had said that "Concerning any genuineness of any portion of the work, the Editor has not offered an opinion, nor is it necessary that he should." But to the unwary reader he presents e.g. the *Gospel of the Birth of Mary* and the Arabic *Gospel of the Infancy*—works so far removed from canonical acceptance and serious historical interest that M. R. James gave only a summary of them, and Hennecke ignored the first and represented the second only with brief extracts—as though they were of authority equal to (say) the *Epistles of Clement*. For the distinctions that would have confronted Hone if he had been a scrupulous editor see **4** n 4, below. M. R. James, the next Englishman to compile a collection comparable to Hone's, gives a forthright assessment of Hone's work in his edition *The Apocryphal New Testament* (Oxford 1953: 1st ed 1924) xiv–xvii. In fact, Hone had no scholarly pretensions whatsoever; he was a miscellaneous writer who had suffered political persecution, was usually in a state that Lamb called "painful exigency", and desperately needed something profitable to publish.

CONTENTS. Introduction (**1**); *The Gospel of the Birth of Mary* (**2**); *The Protevangelion* [or, *The Book of James*]; *The First* [or Arabic] (i.e. *Thomas's*) *Gospel of the Infancy of Jesus Christ*; *The Epistles of Jesus Christ and Abgarus*; *The Gospel of Nicodemus* [or, *The Acts of Pontius Pilate*]; *The Apostles' Creed*; *The Epistle of Paul to the Laodiceans*; *The Epistles of Paul to Seneca, with Seneca's to Paul*; *The Acts of Paul and Thecla*; *The First* (and *Second*) *Epistle of Clement to the Corinthians*; *The General Epistle of Barnabas* (**3**, **4**); *The Epistle of Ignatius to the Ephesians*; —— *to the Magnesians*; —— *to the Trallians*; —— *to the Romans*; —— *to the Philadelphians*; —— *to the Smyrnaeans*; —— *to Polycarp*; *The Epistle of Polycarp to the Philippians*; *The Shepherd of Hermas*. Table I A List of all the Apocryphal Pieces not now extant; Table II A List of the Christian Authors of the 1st four Centuries whose Writings contain Catalogues of the Books of the New Testament.

DATE. c 1–15 Apr 1826: on the evidence of notes in N F⁰ ff 39–20, 40–41ᵛ, which were written on 11, 12, and 13 Apr 1826.

1   pp xi–xii, pencil, overtraced | Introduction, footnote

. . . Sir Isaac Newton observes, that "what the Latins have done to this text, (1 John, V. 7.) the Greeks have done to that of St. Paul, (Timothy, III. 16.) For by changing ὁ into Θ, the abbreviation of θεὸς, they now read, *Great is the mystery of godliness*: GOD *manifested in the flesh*: whereas all the churches for the first four or five hundred years, and the authors of all the ancient versions, Jerome, as well as the rest, read, *Great is the mystery of godliness*, WHICH *was manifested in the flesh.*" Sir Isaac gives a list of authors, who, he says, "wrote, all of them, in the fourth and fifth centuries for the Deity of the Son, and incarnation of God,* and some of them largely, and in several tracts; and yet", he says, "I cannot find that they ever allege this text to prove it. . . . "

* Strong grounds, I admit, for ὁ instead of Θεος—and if the Syntax had allowed the masculine gender, ΟΣ, it might easily have been mistaken for ΘΣ. But ὁ, scarcely. On the other hand, the context and internal evidence are at least equally strong in favor of Θεος. With ὁ (i.e. which mystery of Piety,/ ευσεβειας is badly translated "of Godliness")[1] the text is flat & hardly intelligible!—But the Epistle itself is not a work of Paul's but of a later age[2]—& were it otherwise, it would prove no more than what is asserted in 20 other places of the N. T.—viz. that God was in Christ reconciling the world to himself,[3] and not Christ's personal divinity

2   p 1 | *The Gospel of the Birth of Mary*, headnote

In the primitive ages there was a Gospel extant bearing this name, attributed to St. Matthew, and received as genuine and authentic by several of the ancient Christian sects. It is to be found in the works of Jerome . . . from whence the present translation is made. His contemporaries, Epiphanius, Bishop of Salamis, and Austin, also mention a Gospel under this title. The ancient copies differed from Jerome's . . .

Who would not from the prefatory note suppose that *this* very Gospel was found in Jerome—and that it was the same with the Gospel of the Nazarenes attributed to St Matthew—and that this was now extant in Jerome's Works?—All which, however, are so many Blunders! Pity that Mr Hone had not referred the Reader to the Vol. and Page of St Jerome's Works, in which ⟨he or⟩ his Collector found

---

[1] *Textus receptus* of 1 Tim 3.16 reads Θεὸς, but Griesbach (1800), and later Lachmann, Tischendorf, and Tregellesius all read ὅς, as *NEB Gk* does. As C points out, ὅς (masc) cannot agree with μυστήριον (neut); but the syntax does allow ὅς if one understands it to mean—as *NEB* does—"He who". *NEB* treats the phrase "He who was manifested..." as in apposition to μυστήριον (i.e. the mystery is Christ), and considers the rhythmic closing phrase to be part of a familiar hymn or creed.

AV regularly renders εὐσεβεία as "godliness" (several times in 1 Tim, and in 2 Tim and 2 Pet), but in Acts 3.12 as "holiness". *NT Gk Lex* defines the word as "the duty that man owes to God, piety, holiness, religion". *NEB* reads "the mystery *of our religion*".

[2] For C on the authorship of 1 Tim see BIBLE COPY B **116** and n, and **133**. Here he seems to be more certain about the non-Pauline authorship of 1 Tim than in BIBLE COPY B.

[3] 2 Cor 5.19.

it.[1] Why has Mr Hone omitted to mention the Books, from which he made these reprints?[2]

3   p 122 | *The General Epistle of Barnabas,* headnote

... This Epistle lays a greater claim to canonical authority than most others. It has been cited by Clemens Alexandrinus, Origen, Eusebius, and Jerome, and many ancient Fathers. Cotelerius affirms that Origen and Jerome esteemed it genuine and canonical; but Cotelerius himself did not believe it to be either one or the other; on the contrary, he supposes it was written for the benefit of the Ebionites, (the christianized Jews,) who were tenacious of rites and ceremonies.

What is the Logic of this? How does its having been written for so good and *paul*ine a purpose prove its spuriousness. The word "canonical" in this place is an ignoranza.[1] Jerome could not think that a Book was in the Canon, which his own catalogue of canonical Scriptures does not contain: tho' he might think it worthy of a place.[2] s. t. c.

2[1] Hone is indeed confusing two gospels attributed to St Matthew. The earlier one, variously known as the "Gospel according to the Nazaraeans" or the "Gospel according to the Hebrews", was translated from the Hebrew by Jerome (*De viris illustribus* 2.3) in the belief that it was the original version of the canonical Gospel of Matthew; it has survived only in quotations by the Fathers. The one mentioned here by Hone, and to which the "Gospel of the Birth of the Virgin Mary" was an adjunct, is in Latin and may be as late as the eighth century; it is usually known as the "Gospel of pseudo-Matthew". These two gospels were accompanied by pretended letters from Jerome establishing the authenticity of them. Jeremiah Jones gave the reference to Jerome's works, but did not mention that the works in the volume that includes the "Gospel of the Birth of the Virgin Mary" are treated as supposititious (as in Migne *PL* xxx 297–305).

2[2] None of the translations is Hone's. In a few of his headnotes he made unobtrusive acknowledgment to Jeremiah Jones and Wake. When C made his notes on Clement's Epistles in N F° he recognised that that translation was Wake's.

3[1] C's quarrel here is more with Hone's logic than with his terminology; for his own distinction between "extracanonical", but "genuine", and "spurious", see **4**, below. Cf *TT* 12 Jan 1834.

3[2] Jerome established the text of the Vulgate, and thereby finally settled the canon of the NT for the Western Church. According to a tradition endorsed by Clement of Alexandria, Barnabas was the thirteenth disciple, taking the place of Judas Iscariot, and Acts shows him as the companion of St Paul in his ministry to the Gentiles. The epistle ascribed to Barnabas—more a theological treatise than a letter—is now thought to have been written, not by Barnabas, but by an Alexandrian Christian towards the end of the first century. Tertullian considered that the Epistle to the Hebrews was written by Barnabas, but C found parts of the Epistle of Barnabas "somewhat too philo-judaic, alexandrine, edging on the fantastical" to have been written by the author of Hebrews.

4   pp 122–9 | end of headnote, following directly on **3** textus

Bishop Fell feared to own expressly what he seemed to be persuaded of, that it ought to be treated with the same respect as several of the books of the present canon. Vossius, Dupuis, Dr. Cave, Dr. Mill, Dr. S. Clark, Whiston, and Archbishop Wake, also esteemed it genuine: Menardus, Archbishop Laud, Spanheim, and others, deemed it apocryphal.

Apocryphal is a taking but likewise a *take-in* Title of friend Hone's Choosing. Extra-canonical Scripture of or near to the Apostolic Age, would rightly designate the first Ep. of Clement, Barnabas, ~~and~~ Hermas, and (with aid of indicative asterisks to distinguish the admitted interpolations from the doubtful passages, and both from the probably genuine) Polycarp & Ignatius.—The remainder deserve no other title but Spurious Gospels and Epistles of uncertain date, but later than the third Century.—But I am, I confess, so far of Bishop Fell's mind[1] as to wish, that the Gospel of the Infancy concorporate with our first Gospel, that prefixed to the third, the last Chapter of the 2nd, the latter Half of the last Chapter of the 4th Gospel, the first Epistle to Timothy (if not rather all three of the Pastoral Epistles[)];[2] and the Apocalypse had formed an intermediate Canon between the New Testament, and these of Clement, & Barnabas, as having less evident internal marks of Catholicity—N.B. This would not deny that they were θεόπνευσται γραφαι;[3] but simply that ⟨the inspiration⟩ was episcopal—i.e. for particular times and occasions, not apostolic—i.e. for the Universal Church of all ages, & consequently that these Scriptures of the lower Canon were sources of edification, and of direction by accomodation according to the analogy of Circumstances—and not like the Superior Canon, measures of Faith and Practice absolutely.—The same division into Canonical of the first and Canonical of the second, order I would have applied likewise to the Books of the Old Testament[4]

4[1] John Fell (1625–86), bp of Oxford, edited the *Epistle of Barnabas*. One of the founders of textual criticism of the Bible as a science, he published in 1675 a text of the Greek NT the *apparatus criticus* of which shows variants from more than a hundred mss. Fell's protégé John Mill in his text of 1707 showed more than 30,000 variants from mss.

4[2] The three epistles 1 and 2 Tim and Titus are normally (since the term

was introduced by P. Anton in 1726) known as the Pastoral Epistles. Cf ETERNAL PUNISHMENT 16. On the authenticity of John 21 see BLANCO WHITE *Practical Evidence* 5.

4[3] "God-inspired writings"—the phrase, based on 2 Tim 3.16, often used by the Fathers to describe the holy scriptures.

4[4] In these notes C consistently uses the term "canon" (and its related and derivative forms) to refer to the list of

27 books of the NT drawn up by Athanasius in 367 and embodied in Jerome's Vulgate. He is therefore able to ignore in his discussion the historical fact that in the early centuries different elements of the scattered Church used different books and held differing views about the authenticity of certain books and about their virtues as instruments of religious life and observance. In saying that for Hone the term "apocryphal" is a "*take-in* Title" (both deceptive and over-inclusive) he accuses him of ignoring the differences among those Christian documents which were used by the churches from time to time and from place to place but were not eventually included in the universally accepted canon. He proposes a two-fold division: (*a*) "extra-canonical" writings, written in or near the Apostolic Age, genuine on the whole, though their texts may be in part corrupt and in part infected by gnosticism; (*b*) "Spurious" writings—which C calls "vulgar fabrications" (N F° f 39)—of much later date (third century and later).

Unfortunately C's term "extra-canonical" can logically be applied to both groups, as can the word "apocryphal" in the sense evolved through the centuries. The discussion can be clarified by using the term "deutero-canonical" for C's "canonical of the second order" to refer to the (variable) group of writings that might constitute a NT Apocrypha corresponding to the OT Apocrypha.

The concept of a "canon" (κάνων, a measuring rod, a standard) as a criterion both of orthodoxy and of the body of Christian scripture emerged at the end of the second century as a defence against (what Hennecke calls)"all-subversive syncretism". Historically the distinction C wished to draw was confused by the practice of the churches well into the Middle Ages—and beyond. A number of documents that combined fanciful and legendary episodic material with extracts from the central Christian writings—at worst, forgeries claiming apostolic authority—circulated widely and until the end of the second century were not discouraged by the churches. Although clearly inferior to the central writings of the NT, these spurious documents were of use in the life of instruction, meditation, and prayer, though unsuitable for public or formal use, and were considered *apocrypha* in the strict sense of that word—"secret", "esoteric". As the sense of catholic orthodoxy crystallised, many of these *apocrypha* were declared heretical and over a long period of time tended to fall under official condemnation. As a class of Christian writings purporting to give witness to the mission of Christ and his Apostles, C is here prepared to dismiss them.

C's proposal in this note is in harmony with the proposals of many Catholics and Protestants at the time of the Reformation, that a secondary canon be formed to include the doubtful books of the present NT and the OT Apocrypha. But the lists varied. Luther e.g. set apart at the end of his Bible Hebrews, James, Jude, and Revelation; the Council of Trent (1546) retained the existing canon, i.e. the Vulgate (and indeed the established order of the books in NT implies a descending order of apostolic authority and "canonicity"); yet Sextus Senensis in his *Bibliotheca Sancta* (1566) gave a list of "deutero-canonical" books of the NT different from Luther's. C, however, would have included in his NT Apocrypha ("deutero-canon") the apocryphal *1 Clement* and the *Epistle of Barnabas* (adding elsewhere the *Shepherd of Hermas*), and from the canon not only certain whole books—the three Pastoral Epistles and Revelation—but also, relying upon the resources of textual criticism, certain elements "episcopal...not apostolic" that are embedded in the NT canon—part of Matt 1, Mark 16, Luke 3, and John 21.

WALTER BIRCH

c 1774–1829

A Sermon on the Prevalence of Infidelity and Enthusiasm, preached in the parish church of St. Peter, Colchester, on Tuesday, July 28, 1818, at the visitation of the Lord Bishop of London. Oxford 1818. 8º.

Not located. Annotations reprinted from *LR* II. *Lost List*.

Henry Francis Cary's copy, presumably presented to him by the author.

Walter Birch of St John's College, Oxford, BD 1805, became a Fellow of Magdalen. In 1818, when he delivered this sermon, he was rector of Stanway in Essex. Many letters from his Oxford friend H. F. Cary are printed in Henry Cary's *Memoir of the Rev. Henry Francis Cary* (2 vols 1847). Cary told Birch on 8 Sept 1818 that he had had "the pleasure of becoming intimate [with C] here last autumn, and find him on the whole, the most extraordinary man I have met with, insomuch that I expect it will be some time or other considered among the *opprobria* of this age that he is suffered to continue in poverty, and, with regard to any public acknowledgement of his merits, almost in neglect. He remembered having met you at a Mr. Methuen's . . .". *Memoir* II 25. C had first visited the Methuens at Corsham, about ten miles from Calne, Wiltshire, in Oct 1814 and continued to be befriended by them until his removal to Highgate. C first met Cary at Littlehampton in Sept 1817.

DATE. 1818, after Jul, if read shortly after publication.

COEDITOR. James D. Boulger.

1 written perhaps on pp 2 (title-page verso) and 4 (dedication verso), evidently referring to pp 15–17

Enthusiasm, properly so called, is the offspring of presumption; of a presumption, the highest and most perilous *in kind* that it is possible to conceive; for it is essential to her nature to assume the fact, upon inadequate grounds, of an extraordinary communication of notions, figures, powers, or authority, from above. Instead of submitting her opinion on this point, or indeed on any other, to the rule of Scripture, Scripture itself is submitted to the rule of her own arbitrary interpretation, by a disparagement of reason, and a claim of paramount superiority for these internal revelations. . . . But having

494

trampled reason under her feet, she knows no control, can use or set it aside, as may suit her purpose, and roam at will in the boundless range of feeling and imagination. . . . All these things she would fain believe to be "the working of the Spirit," and is soon settled in a full persuasion that they are so. . . . She delights in high and daring speculation on matters far beyond our reach, and will seize on passages of Scripture connected with them, in order to propound doctrines, which, how contrary soever to the tenor of divine truth, must thenceforth pass for matters of undoubted certainty, to be denied by none who would avoid the brand of unbelief, or at least, of a very low degree of Christian proficiency.

In the description of enthusiasm, the author has plainly had in view individual characters, and those too in a light, in which they appeared to him; not clear and discriminate ideas. Hence a mixture of truth and error, of appropriate and inappropriate terms, which it is scarcely possible to disentangle. Part applies to fanaticism; part to enthusiasm; and no small portion of this latter to enthusiasm not pure, but as it exists in particular men, modified by their imperfections—and bad because not wholly enthusiasm. I regret this, because it is evidently the discourse of a very powerful mind;—and because I am convinced that the disease of the age is want of enthusiasm, and a tending to fanaticism. You may very naturally object that the senses, in which I use the two terms, fanaticism and enthusiasm, are private interpretations equally as, if not more than, Mr. Birch's.[1] They are so; but the difference between us is, that without reference to either term, I have attempted to ascertain the existence and diversity of two states of moral being; and then having found in our language two words of very fluctuating and indeterminate use, indeed, but the one word more frequently bordering on the one state, the other on the other, I try to fix each to that state exclusively. And herein I follow the practice of all scientific men, whether naturalists or metaphysicians, and the dictate of common sense, that one word ought to have but one meaning. Thus by Hobbes and others of the materialists, compulsion and obligation were used indiscriminately;[2] but the distinction of the two senses is the condition

---

[1] This marginal note is a central statement of C's distinction between enthusiasm and fanaticism. See also BAXTER *Reliquiae* COPY A **51** and *P Lects* (1949) 216n (from N 25). Cf *SM* (*CC*) 23. C is here countering the pejorative implications of "enthusiasm" current in his time. See also *CN* III 3366, 3372; BUNYAN COPY B **4**.

[2] See *P Lects* Lect 5 (1949) 174; cf *BL* ch 4 (1907) I 64n.

of all moral responsibility. Now the effect of Mr. Birch's use of the words is to continue the confusion. Remember we could not reason at all, if our conceptions and terms were not more single and definite than the things designated. Enthusiasm is the absorption of the individual in the object contemplated from the vividness or intensity of his conceptions and convictions: fanaticism is heat, or accumulation and direction, of feeling acquired by contagion, and relying on the sympathy of sect or confederacy; intense sensation with confused or dim conceptions. Hence the fanatic can exist only in a crowd, from inward weakness anxious for outer confirmation; and therefore, an eager proselyter and intolerant. The enthusiast, on the contrary, is a solitary, who lives in a world of his own peopling, and for that cause is disinclined to outward action. Lastly, enthusiasm is susceptible of many degrees, (according to the proportionateness of the objects contemplated,) from the highest grandeur of moral and intellectual being, even to madness; but fanaticism is one and the same, and appears different only from the manners and original temperament of the individual. There is a white and a red heat; a sullen glow as well as a crackling flame; cold-blooded as well as hot-blooded fanaticism. Enthusiasts, ἐνθουσιασταὶ from ἔνθεος, οἷς ὁ θεὸς ἔνεστι, or possibly from ἐν θυσίαις, those who, in sacrifice to, or at, the altar of truth or falsehood, are possessed by a spirit or influence mightier than their own individuality.[3] *Fanatici— qui circum fana furorem[a] mutuo contrahunt et afflant*—those who in the same conventicle, or before the same shrine, relique or image, heat and ferment by co-acervation.[4]

I am fully aware that the words are used by the best writers indifferently, but such must be the case in very many words in a composite language, such as the English, before they are desynony-

---

[a] *LR* prints "*favorem*", but "*furorem*" must surely have been the word in ms

[3] "'Enthusiasts', *enthousiastoi*, from *entheos*, 'those in whom the god is' [cf "*God in* us" of Bunyan copy b 4], or possibly from *en thusiais* [in sacrifices]". The derivation from ἔνθεος has always been accepted; the derivation from ἐν θυσίαις is not usually noted as a possibility. For C on "the original meaning" of ἐνθουσίασμος see *Friend* (*CC*) i 432n and n 4.

[4] "Fanatici", the Latin equivalent given by Stephanus and Scapula for ἐνθουσιαστικοί. "Co-acervation"— the act of heaping together. Fanatics, according to C's Latin phrase, are "people who frequent fanes, being infected with frenzy [reading *furorem*] and blowing it into flame".

mized. Thus imagination and fancy; chronical and temporal, and many other.[5]

1[5] On desynonymising terms see BAXTER *Reliquiae* COPY A 40. For the distinction between imagination and fancy see e.g. *BL* ch 13; for the distinction between reason and understanding see e.g. BAXTER *Catholick Theologie* 14 n 3 and *Reliquiae* COPY B 42 n 2. C does not seem to have developed a distinction between "chronical" and "temporal" or to have used it elsewhere; it may be a projection of the distinction between eternity and time, which he explicated at length in ETERNAL PUNISHMENT (1817) 1. "Chronical" may represent time absolute, time in the mind of God; "temporal" time worldly and relative, time in the mind of man. C may have been struck by the bifurcation of the adjective χρόνιος (usually of a long time) and the adjective *temporalis* (usually of a short interval or a point in time) from the apparently synonymous nouns χρόνος and *tempus*.

WILLIAM BLAKE

d 1694

The Ladies Charity School-house Roll of Highgate: or A Subscription of many noble, well-disposed Ladies for the easie carrying
of it on. [? London] [? 1680]. 8º.

Four engravings in facing pairs before p 1. The book has no title-page; the
title cited above is the heading to the text on p 1. The book is sometimes
catalogued as *Silver Drops, or Serious Things*, but see CONTENTS, below.
On p 292 at the end of the text: "*Written by* WILLIAM BLAKE, *Housekeeper to the Ladies Charity-School.*" The first engraving—the figure of
Charity—faces a front elevation (untitled) of the (?proposed) Charity-
School; the third engraving—the figure of Father Time—faces an engraving of butterflies with curious inscriptions above and below. William
Blake's own copy, with his notes, is in the BM: 4400 n 16.

Indiana University (Lilly Library)

James Gillman's copy with his autograph signature in ink at the head of
p ⁻3.
 William Blake, a woollen draper and considerable property-owner,
founded and was in charge of a girls' charity-school in Highgate in c 1680.
He built Nos 1–6 The Grove, Highgate, between 1682 and 1685 in what
was then the garden of Dorchester House (now demolished), intending to
endow his school by renting the houses. It was apparently on the basis of
this speculation that he announced in his book—though with almost
impenetrable obliquity—his plan for an improved charity-school. His
plans did not prosper; he mortgaged his property and was imprisoned in
the Fleet for debt; released in 1687, he sank into obscurity. The row of
brick houses that he built in The Grove—"the finest terrace in Highgate",
Pevsner calls it—remains as a quiet remembrance of him, No 3 now bearing
a plaque remembering its most distinguished occupant. James Gillman
acquired the house in the autumn of 1823. It is difficult to imagine that he
did not recognise the connexion between his house and this curious little
book, yet C does not mention this in his note.

CONTENTS. (*a*) pp 1–78: "A Subscription". After the preamble, a series
of twenty-seven letters begins on p 13; in his own copy Blake has written
in the names of all but one of the benefactresses. (*b*) pp 79–292: *Silver
Drops, or Serious Things*, in four sections: (1) "The Substance of the fine
Young Lady's answer to that Objection in the Essay; *Are these Times for
Charity* ..."; (2) "Short Hints, but Sound Truths, In great Humility";
(3) "Short Sayings of the Wise, or Q. Mary's Martyrs"; (4) "The last

and general Closing Letter, that is thus presumed to be offered ". (*c*) p [293] final plea (as given in **1** n 1, below).

DATE. 24 Dec 1829.

1   pp ⁻3––2, pencil

This is a very odd and very interesting Book.[1] The whimsical *Omnium Gatherum* of the unlearned Writer's leasing[2] of whatever he had been reading, poured out on each and every occasion, with the deep feeling of Reverence for the Rank & Station of those, to whom he pleads, elevated by the evident sense of the *Duty* of so feeling, blended with the religious earnestness with which he enforces *their* duties on them—& the simplicity & single-heartedness over all—give this old Book, for me, a sort of charm. I often dip into it: & never without being amused. S. T. Coleridge 24 Decʳ 1829 Grove, Highgate/

1[1] The book is an elaborate plea to "Noble Ladies" to give charitable support to the Charity-school in which he cared for "near forty Poor, or Fatherless Children, Born all at, or near *Highgate, Hornsey,* and *Hamsted*" (p 1). In *Silver Drops* (p 224) Blake says that he had recently recovered from an illness that he feared might be mortal; during convalescence "I did secretly resolve (if God should raise me up) to perform, or finish, this poor little scribbled (and yet serious) short, brief, and harmless Pocket-Book...". The volume closes (p [293]): "It is humbly desired, that what you or any of you, most noble Ladies, Gentlewomen, or others, are pleased to bestow or give towards this good and great design, that you would be pleased to take a receipt on the back-side of Time, or Charity [i.e. two of the engravings at the front of the book], sealed with three seales, namely, the Treasurers, Houskeepers, and Registers, and it shall be fairly recorded, and hung up in the School-house to be read of all from Time to Time, to the world's end we hope."

1[2] A sixteenth-century word, later dialect—"gleaning".

JOSEPH BLANCO WHITE
1775–1841

The grandson of an Irish Roman Catholic merchant established in Spain, Blanco White was born in Seville and christened José María Blanco y Crespo. He was ordained a Roman Catholic priest in 1800, but abandoned the priesthood and fled from Cadiz to England in 1810 during the French invasion. From 1810 to 1815 he edited *Español*, circulated in Spain by the British government in defence of the national cause. He resumed a Christian faith in 1812, and in 1814 signed the Thirty-nine Articles in order to qualify for orders in the Church of England. In 1825, after studying at Oxford and being tutor to Lord Holland for two years, he engaged vigorously in a controversy with Charles Butler: see C. BUTLER general note. In recognition of these services to the Church he received the degree of MA at Oxford in 1826, was made a member of Oriel College, and settled in Oxford. But he was never *persona grata*, and felt himself an outsider at Oriel. C probably saw little of him after 1831, when he followed Abp Whately to Dublin; he died a Unitarian in Liverpool. His best known work in English is *Letters from Spain*, a copy of which C annotated. His autobiography was published posthumously: *The Life of the Rev. Joseph Blanco White, Written by Himself; with Portions of His Correspondence* ed J. H. Thom (3 vols 1845).

Although Blanco White had known RS since 1817 or earlier, his first meeting with C occurred on 14 Jul 1825, when Blanco White, though "in very infirm health", came from Chelsea to Highgate in a glass coach and "spent the whole day from 1 o'clock till ½ past 9 with me". *CL* VI 481. After this meeting Blanco White sent C four of his books, all of which C annotated.

In Nov 1828 White sought C's help in establishing a new quarterly, the *London Review*, but it foundered after the second number. "I profoundly revere Blanco White," C said in 1830, "but his Review was commenced without a single apparent principle to direct it . . .". *TT* 10 Jun 1830.

On about 2 Sept 1829 C had noted: "Had Blanco White written nothing else [than *The Poor Man's Preservative*], and done no other service to Protestantism, the cowardly-slight encouragement, he has met with & never complained of, would remain a disgrace to the Heads of our Church . . . he ought long before this to have been a Dignitary of our Church, & that he is not such, implies not only a defect of right feeling but likewise a want of sound policy, in our Bishops/—". N 41 ff 57–57ᵛ.

500

A Letter to Charles Butler, Esq. on his notice of the "Practical and Internal Evidence against Catholicism". London 1826. 8⁰.

British Museum C 126 h 12

Inscribed on p ⁻2: "To S. T. Coleridge Esqʳᵉ with the author's best regards." "S. T. C." label on title-page verso. John Duke Coleridge's monogram on p ⁻4.

Blanco White sent this copy to C with a letter dated 21 Jun 1826, which said in part: "The advantages I have derived from your *Aids to Reflection*, are so clear to me that I promise to myself a similar effect from any thing that may come from your pen. If you were to see my copy of your *Aids*, you would scarcely find ten pages together without pen or pencil marks, which prove that I ⟨have⟩ made use of those *Aids*." Ms PML. Not until 28 Nov 1827 did C write to thank Blanco White for this book, telling him that he had written verses "on the blank page of Butler's Book of the Church". *CL* vi 713; see also 759–60. *CL* vi 759–60. For the poem *Sancti Dominici Pallium* aroused by Butler's "calumnious Abuse" of Blanco White see Charles BUTLER *Book of the Roman Catholic Church* 1. For the place of this book in the controversy involving RS, Butler, Blanco White, and others see Charles BUTLER general note.

DATE. Probably late Jun 1826.

COEDITOR. James D. Boulger.

1   pp 84–5, pencil | ix "Unfair manner in which the Author's testimony and arguments are met" [from Contents; there are no Chapter-titles]

You [Butler] betrayed yourself in your next words. "But the penal codes of Elizabeth reduced many a mother, who would not inform, in certain cases, against her child, to similar woe."

Where are we [to]ᵃ find the *proof* of this ~~which~~ if there [be]ᵃ no proof forthcoming, *infamous* Assertion? Where shall we *find*? Mʳ Butler ought not to have imposed on us the necessity of *seeking*. He was bound in conscience to have cited instances, in which a mother had been placed under the alternative of losing her own, or informing agains[t]ᵇ her Son's [life]!ᵃ—

2   p 131 | Appendix "Original Authority which proves, that the Pope at one time conceived himself . . . to be, an object of divine worship"

[In a note to p 12, Blanco White quotes in Italian from Giovanni Villani *Historie Fiorentine* (Venice 1559) 206. Tr: "At that time,

---

ᵃ Word supplied by the editor
ᵇ C has written the word inattentively as either "aguns" or "agains"

considering that the people of Palermo had done wrong, and hearing of the great preparations King Charles was making to overcome them, they [the Sicilian legates] sent as their ambassadors some monks to Pope Martin, begging him to be merciful, uttering in their mission only the words 'Lamb of God that takest away the sins of the world, have mercy on us; Lamb of God that takest away the sins of the world, have mercy on us; Lamb of God that takest away the sins of the world, grant us thy peace.' In full consistory the Pope replied to them, without any other utterance, these words written in the *Passio Domini nostri Jesu Christi*, saying simply: 'Behold the King of the Jews, and they gave him a blow.' Upon which the ambassadors departed in great confusion."] My truly learned friend [Rev Richard Garnett] adds: "The above-mentioned embassy took place in 1282, and John Villani began to write his History in 1300, only eighteen years after."

Still I do not see the proof, that the Ambassadors intended the Pope to be understood by the Words. Suppose I had thrown myself prostrate before[a]1

---

[a] The note is incomplete

21 C considers the same episode fully in Blanco White *Practical Evidence* 12.

Letters from Spain. By Don Leucadio Doblado [i.e. Joseph Blanco White]. Second edition. Revised and corrected by the author. London 1825. 8⁰.

1st ed 1822 was pseudonymous. Preface to the 2nd ed signed "Joseph Blanco White" and dated "*Chelsea, June 1st,* 1825."

Keble College, Oxford

Autograph signature "A Gillman" on the title-page. Stub of half-title.

Two cross-references in pencil in an unidentified hand on pp 243, 254, and serial numbers 1, 2, 3 on pp 243, 244, 246.

In a letter of 12 Dec 1825 C thanked Blanco White for sending him this book and the *Poor Man's Preservative*. He began reading the *Letters* "an hour before dinner—resumed it after tea, i.e. 7 o'clock—and when I heard the clock strike 2, thought it was time to undress—and did so, save and except my drawers & dressing gown, but could not lay the Book down till I had finished the last page just as it struck three. I need not say, it was a delightful work; but I should be ungrateful if I did not avow that both directly and by suggestion it has been a most instructive one to me." *CL* v 522.

DATE. [28 Nov–11 Dec] 1825 and later. The ink notes were written when the book "was first sent" to C; the pencil notes are later (see **2**).

COEDITOR. James D. Boulger.

1   pp 111–15 | Letter III

I have often heard the question, how could such men as Bossuet and Fenelon adhere to the Church of Rome and reject the Protestant faith? The answer appears to me obvious. Because, according to their fixed principles on this matter, they must have been either Catholics or Infidels. Laying it down as an axiom, that Christianity was chiefly *] intended to reveal a system of doctrines necessary for salvation, they naturally and consistently inferred the existence of an authorized judge upon questions of faith, otherwise the inevitable doubts arising from private judgment would defeat the object of revelation.

* The most *striking*, certainly, and most fearful, but far from the only, instance of the practical mischiefs resulting from the confusion of Belief and Faith—In the German the same word expresses both, viz. Glaube—a grievous defect! But even where this is not the case, as in the Latin and in our own language, by how many Divines are they regarded as Synonimes. The great Object of Christianity is FAITH—fëalty to the SPIRITUAL in our Humanity, ⟨to⟩ that, which indeed*a* contra-distinguishes us as *human*—to that Power, in which

a Written "indeed which" and marked for transposition

the Will, the Reason and the Conscience are three in One, & by which alone spiritual Truths, i.e. the only living and substantial Truths, can be discerned.[1] To this power, under the name of Faith, every thought of the Understanding, of the "mind of the Flesh["], must be brought into subjection[2]—and Beliefs of particular Dogmata, i.e. the perception of the preponderance of the arguments *for* over those against their verity, is then only essential, when such Belief is implied in the state of FAITH. Hence S[t] Paul tolerates many and those not trifling errors of Belief, even while he exposes them—Be satisfied, each of you, in his own mind—and exercise charity towards such of the Brethren, as profess different persuasions; but cling all of you to the Bond of Love in the unity of *Faith*.[3] Yet how early the dangerous identification of the two words began, we learn from the Epistle of James, who arguing ex absurdo on the assumption, that Faith means Belief, ~~un~~justly remarks—The Devils *believe*, and so thoroughly too, that they believe and tremble.[4] Belief, therefore, cannot be the proper and essential Ground of Salvation in the Soul— But Faith *is*—and by Christ himself solemnly declared to be so. Therefore, Belief cannot be the same as Faith—tho' the Belief of the truths essential to the Faith in Christ is the necessary accompaniment and consequent of the Faith. Ex. gr. I cannot sincer[e]ly trust in Christ, & entirely love the Lord Jesus, without at the same time believing, first, that he *is*: & secondly, that he is most trust- and love-worthy. But I can love him, trust in him, and earnestly desire to obey his commands, without having even heard of the immaculate Conception of the Virgin Mary, or having troubled my head respecting even her aei-partheny.[5]

2   pp 157, pencil | Letter v

[Dr Carnero, visiting a prioress who was suffering from self-imposed fasting, sent for a glass of water and put it into her hand,] with a peremptory injunction to do her utmost to drink. The unresisting nun put the water to her lips, and stopped. The physician was urging

[1][1] One of C's best terse definitions of faith. The relation of will, reason, and conscience as "three in One", and the reality of religious faith, is discussed at large in *SM, AR, CIS*, and the "Essay on Faith" (*LR* IV 425–38).

[1][2] Rom 8.7—a frequently recurring phrase in C's later writing, usually in the form φρόνημα σαρκός. See BAXTER *Reliquiae* COPY B **115** n 10.

[1][3] This sentence is a free and condensed paraphrase of Eph 4.1–17, esp vv 2–3.

[1][4] James 2.19: "Thou believest that there is one God; thou doest well: the devils also believe, and tremble."

[1][5] Anglicisation of ἀειπαρθενία: perpetual virginity. Not in *OED*. The word is not uncommon in patristic Greek.

her to proceed, when to his great amazement he found the contents of the glass reduced to one lump of ice.

I wonder, that I never asked Mʳ White, what he really meant by the insertion of this Thumper. Perhaps, I had passed over this page & the opposite, the leaves sticking: for I certainly read the Volume, when first sent to me by the Author. *S. T. C.*

3 pp 157, pencil

We had the account of this wonder from the clergyman who intro-
!!] duced us to the nun. Of his veracity I can entertain no doubt: while he, on the other hand, was equally confident of Dr. Carnero's.

Pray, was ~~not~~ Dʳ Carnero put to his oath, whether he had ascertained that it was water & not ice in the Glass, when the Attendant brought it to him?—But the more probable solution is, that Dʳ C. was humming the Clergyman.

4 p 157, pencil

Our visit to the other convent made me acquainted with one of the most pitiable objects ever produced by superstition—a <u>reluctant nun</u>.

Say rather a *diseased*

5 p 157, pencil

A sense of decorum, and the utter hopelessness of relief, keep the bitter regrets of many an imprisoned female a profound secret to all but their confessor. In the present case, however, the vehemence of the sufferer's feelings had laid open to the world the state of her harassed mind. She was a good-looking woman, of little more than thirty: but the contrast between the monastic weeds, and an indescribable air of wantonness which, in spite of all caution, marked her every glance and motion, raised a mixed feeling of disgust and pity, that made us uncomfortable during the whole visit.

& I should fear, that in this climate, cases of Nymphomania in the Nunneries are not rare.[1]

6 p 167, pencil

In the intervals of the dance we were sometimes treated with dramatic scenes, of which the dialogue is composed on the spot by the actors.

5[1] The earliest use of "nymphomania" recorded in *OED* is in a translation (1800) of William Cullen *Synopsis nosologiae methodicae* (1769) by Thomas Bateman, one of whose books was lent to C in 1814 by Dr Daniel: see BATEMAN.

This amusement is not uncommon in country-towns. It is known by
*] the name of *juegos*—a word literally answering to *plays*. The actors
are in the habit of performing together, and consequently do not
find it difficult to go through their parts without much hesitation.

* Q^y The same as the Venetian Fabas? ⟨to⟩ which Gozzi's Genius
has given celebrity?[1]

7 p 412–15 | Note A. On the Devotion of the Spaniards to the Immaculate
Conception of the Virgin Mary.—p. 22.

The dispute on the Immaculate Conception of the Virgin began
between the Dominicans and Franciscans as early as the thirteenth
century. The contending parties stood at first upon equal ground;
but "the merits of faith and devotion" were so decidedly on the side
of the Franciscans, that they soon had the Christian mob to support
them, and it became dangerous for any Divine to assert that the
Mother of God (such is the established language of the Church of
Rome) had been, like the rest of mankind, involved in original sin.

It may deserve ~~the~~ attention from the zealous advocates of the
authenticity of the Evangelia Infantiæ, prefixed to the Gospel of
Luke and concorporated with the canonical Revision of Matthew's[1]
—whether the immaculate Conception of the Virgin is not a legitimate Corollary of the Miraculous Conception of our Lord/ so far at
least, that the same reason, that rendered it incompossible[2] for him
to have a maculate Father, is equally cogent for the necessity of an
immaculate Mother.

6[1] Carlo Gozzi (1722–1806). In
May 1819 C referred to "the dramatic
Pieces of Carlo Gozzi, called (absurdly enough) the Venetian Shakespeare. Tho' no Shakespeare, he is a
delightful Fellow...". *CL* IV 940–1.
As early as 13 Oct 1815 C had tried to
secure a copy of Gozzi, and failed in
three attempts. *CL* IV 597, 633, 635,
656. He wanted to write "A Drama
from Calderon [and from] Carl
Gozzi", being convinced that "Gozzi's
PLAN properly *anglicized* and *Lon-
donized* (*not* the works themselves)
would meet with some share of [his]
Success". *CL* IV 733, 941. C may
eventually have secured a copy:
Gillman's library included the *Opere*
(6 vols Venice & Florence 1772).
Gillman SC (1843) 431.

7[1] Matt 1.18–2.23 and Luke 1.5–
2.52 give two rather different accounts
of the birth and childhood of Jesus as
preface to the gospel; both state that
Mary was a virgin. C elsewhere in his
notes refers to these "prefaces" as
separate writings and (as here) under
the title of "evangelia infantiae"
would have placed them in his canon
of the second order: see BIBLE
Apocryphal NT **4** n 4. C's point here is
that those who argue for the genuineness of the "evangelia infantiae" may
find that they must accept the doctrine
of the Immaculate Conception of the
Virgin Mary as a logical consequence.
7[2] See BAXTER *Reliquiae* COPY A
32 and n 1.

But alas! in subjects of this sort, we can only stave off the difficulty. ~~We may enlarge~~ It is a point in a circle/ on whichever side we remove from it, we are sure to come round to it again. So here. Either the Virgin's Ancestors, paternal & maternal, from Adam & Eve downward were all sinless; or her immediate Father & Mother were not so, but "like the rest of mankind, involved in original Sin.["]

But if a Sin-stained Father & Mother could produce an immaculate Offspring in one instance, why not in the other? That the union of the divine Word with the seed & nature of Man should ~~effect the extinction~~ preclude the contagion of Sin in the Holy Child, is as much to be expected on the one supposition of our Lord's Birth as on the other. So far from being a greater miracle, it seems so necessarily involved in the miracle of the Incarnation common to both, as scarcely to be called an additional Miracle. The accidental circumstance, ~~of~~ that the Unitarian party, most palpably to their own* disadvantage, reject or question the Chapters in question, is the chief cause of the horror, with which our orthodox Divines recoil from every free investigation of the point.

* The Conception by the over-shadowing of the Holy Spirit being the only plausible explanation, which a Socinian can give to the often repeated Antithesis Son of God and Son of Man, of one and the same person. The Believer in the Trinity, the incarnation of the Filial God, and ~~the~~ redemption by the Blood of the divine Mediator, has an interest therefore in the removal, rather than in the uppropment,[3] of this strongest, nay, only, Buttress of ⟨the *extreme*⟩ Heresy.—

7[3] Not in *OED*.

The Poor Man's Preservative against Popery: addressed to the lower classes of Great Britain and Ireland. London 1825. 12⁰.

British Museum C 126 d 11

Inscribed on p $^-2$: "To S. T. Coleridge Esqre from his sincere friend the Author." John Duke Coleridge's monogram on p $^-6$. "S. T. C." label on title-page.

C received this book, with *Letters from Spain*, between 28 Nov and 12 Dec 1825, when he acknowledged receipt with the comment: "The Poor Man's Preservative—to repeat the words I used in a note to my Nephew—had all the charm of Novelty for me. I am not certain that it did not please me even more than the original larger Volume. But probably, the constant lively sense of the great present utility of the Preservative, and the excellent management of the Dialogue, bribed my Judgement a little." *CL* v 522. For the remark to Edward Coleridge [6] Dec see *CL* v 520. For C's view of this book in 1829 see general note, above.

DATE. c Dec 1825.

COEDITOR. James D. Boulger.

1 p $^-1$, referring to p 23 | Dialogue I

I threw myself, in fact, wholly upon his [Christ's] mercy. My trust was not in vain; for calm was soon restored to my soul; and I found myself stronger than ever in the faith and profession which I made when I became a member of the Church of England.

P. 23. last 6 lines.—

Let X represent any given Position, doctrinal or historical—: and let a, b, c, de, e represent so many several grounds for the belief of its truth, and w, y, z certain difficulties and objections. Now it ⟨is⟩ clear, that the evidence of the former may receive such an addition in distinctness, positiveness, and cogency that the weight of the latter, m considered as counterbalance, may become $= 0$, not without any insight into the grounds & nature of their falsehood or inapplicability, and consequently, without the power of returning a satisfactory solution. The difficulties remain but the Doubt is overwhelmed.

Now the^a the Man can have reflected little on the constitution of the human mind, who does not understand, and as little on the history & processes of his own mental growth who does not know by experience, how wonderfully the clearness and evidence of grounds

---

^{a} Here, at the foot of the page, C has written: "(*turn to the top of the page*.)" and at the top of the page—the note having been begun halfway down—"*from the bottom of the page*"

and reasons in all matters not scientifically demonstrable is diminished ⟨i.e. hidden or obscured⟩ by the turbulence or inquietude of the thoughts and feelings, and revealed (& *subjectively* increased) by the stillness and genial tranquillity of the Soul. (See Aids to Reflection, p. 183: l. 20–28.)[1]

This, I think, rescues this passage (which, I confess, startled me for a moment) from all charge of mysticism or superstition. *s. t. c.*

---

2 p 82, cropped | Dialogue III

You know that one of the principal articles of the Roman Catholics is *transubstantiation*. This article would be searched for in vain in the Scriptures; for though our Saviour said of the Bread, "this is my body;" and of the wine, "this is my blood," the Apostles could not understand these words in a corporeal sense, as if Christ had said to them that he was holding himself in his own hands.

I receive the Eucharist in Bucer's sense,[1] and according to the Doctrine of our Church as expressed in her Catechism.[2] But the Sacramentary *memoria technica* Doctrine too often even by Churchmen [s]ubstituted f[o]r it is to th[e] R[ea]l[i]st Tenet[3] as [. . . . .]

1[1] *AR* (1825) 183: "In preventing the rank vapours that steam up from the corrupt *Heart*, Christianity restores the *Intellect* likewise to its natural clearness. By relieving the mind from the distractions and importunities of the unruly passions, she improves the *quality* of the Understanding: while at the same time she presents for its contemplations Objects so great and so bright as cannot but enlarge the Organ, by which they are contemplated."

2[1] "In Bucer's sense"—that Christ is spiritually, not physically, present in the elements of the eucharist. Cf *CN* III 4044 and n, and G. BURNET *History* 9. The relation of Martin Bucer (1491–1551) to Luther and Zwingli in the controversy on the sacrament is discussed in the marginalia on STRYPE *Memorials of Cranmer* (1694). C made a similar statement in *AR* (1825) 332–3.

2[2] In the Catechism the section on the eucharist begins with the statement that the Sacrament of the Lord's Supper was ordained "for the continual remembrance of the sacrifice of

the death of Christ, and of the benefits which we receive thereby". C may be thinking of what follows. "*Question.* What is the outer part of the Lord's Supper? *Answer.* Bread and Wine, which the Lord hath commanded to be received. *Q.* What is the inward part, or thing signified? *A.* The Body and Blood of Christ, which are verily and indeed taken and received by the faithful in the Lord's Supper." Article XXVIII (of the Thirty-nine Articles) denies the corporal presence (i.e. transubstantiation) but affirms the *real* presence of Christ in the eucharist.

2[3] Unfortunately the comparison is incomplete and the word "Realist" uncertain. Perhaps C is pointing out that the extreme Sacramentarian position—which he describes as the "*memoria technica* Doctrine"—can merge with the other extreme position, transubstantiation, as set forth in the textus. See also BOOK OF COMMON PRAYER COPY B 29 and *CN* III 4044. The Sacramentarians ("Sacramentary" or "Sacramentarian" being a name given to those who deny the real

3 p 83

... Saint Paul did not believe that the bread and wine were converted into the material Christ, by the words of consecration; but though he calls these signs the communion of the body and blood of Christ, he also calls them bread and cup.

The original mistake and misfortune consisted in drawing the attention which should have been ~~given~~ turned exclusively ~~to~~ on *the Act*, to the Material[1]

presence of Christ in the Eucharist) considered that the eucharist was—according to C's account here—simply a reminder of the fact of Christ's death, in his derogatory term a "mnemonic device". (Sacramentarians, however, usually also held that the eucharist was a sign or symbol.) The crucial phrase "Do this in remembrance of me" occurs in 1 Cor 11, 24, 25, and in Luke 22.19 (which *NEB* treats as an interpolation). Against the superficial notion that ἀνάμνησις (remembrance) means no more than a fixed "memorial", a recalling of the fact of Christ's death, C probably had in mind a process of calling-to-mind for purposes of meditation, for which the mechanical and arbitrary implications of the elaborate mnemonic procedures of "memoria technica" would be grossly inappropriate. For "memoria technica" as an ancient and arcane tradition known to C mostly through Bruno see BROWNE *Works* **10** n 1. Over against the Sacramentarian position C would place the Johannine doctrine of the eucharist as an inner witness of the Holy Spirit: see John 6.30–58. Paul's doctrine, as implied by 1 Cor 11.26, 12.12–27, is that in the celebration of the Last Supper "ye do shew [proclaim] the Lord's death until he come"; that Christians become members of one body—the body of Christ—in partaking of the one sacrament; and that the eucharist is a memorial of the covenant between God and man.

3[1] For sacrament as act see BIBLE COPY B **140** n 3.

Practical and Internal Evidence against Catholicism, with occasional strictures on Mr. Butler's Book of the Roman Catholic Church: in six letters, addressed to the impartial among the Roman Catholics of Great Britain and Ireland. London 1825. 8°.

British Museum C 43 b 19

DATE. [18–21] Jul 1825, and (?) later. Note 2 is dated 21 Jul 1825. Blanco White called on C on 14 Jul 1825; on 18 Jul C wrote to John Murray to thank him for sending him "Mr Blanco White's interesting and most valuable Work, with his gratifying Note". *CL* v 484; see also 481.

COEDITOR. James D. Boulger.

1   pp 72–4, pencil | Letter III

The divine commission, on which she [the Church of Rome] grounds *] these claims, runs in these words of Christ to the chief of his apostles: "Thou art Peter, and upon this rock I will build my church; and the gates of hell shall not prevail against it: And I will give unto thee the keys of the kingdom of heaven; and whatsoever thou shalt bind on earth, shall be bound in heaven, and whatsoever thou shalt loose on earth shall be loosed in heaven." [Matt 16.18–19.]

* Paley wrote his Horæ Paulinæ to exhibit the Harmony & unconscious Coincidences of the Epistles of Paul with Luke's Acts of the Apostles[1]—Would he, or some man of more depth & equal

[1] William Paley (1743–1805) *Horae Paulinae, or the Truth of the Scripture History of St Paul Evinced, by a Comparison of the Epistles...with the Acts of the Apostles, and with One Another* (1790; 10th ed 1819), which C praised in his Theological Lectures as "the most decisive piece of reasoning yet produced on a subject of Theology". *Lects 1795 (CC)* 186 and n. In 1793, as an undergraduate, when Paley's *Principles of Moral and Political Philosophy* (1785) was still required reading at Cambridge, C sent Mrs Evans a copy of the *Reasons for Contentment* (1792), calling Paley "this great and good man"; and in his 1795 lectures made use of Paley's *View of the Evidences of Christianity* (1794). By 1796, however, he was planning to write "Strictures on God-

win, Paley &c &c" (*CN* I 161[e]; see also *CL* III 720, *CN* I 1711), in 1801 considered him one of the "corrupters & poisoners of all moral sense & dignity" (*CL* II 720), and in Jul 1803 proposed to "make a dashing Review" of the recently published *Natural Theology; or, Evidences of the Existence and Attributes of the Deity, Collected from the Appearances of Nature* (1802). C was convinced of Paley's Socinianism by 1802, if not before (*CL* II 807); and from 1806 onwards— although he included *Horae Paulinae* and the *Natural Theology* in a list of books recommended to Poole in Sept 1807 (*CN* II 3145)—he spoke of Paley's doctrines in terms of contempt, linking his name with Grotius as representing a shallow and dangerous rationalism. Paley's ethical doctrines,

clearness, had ~~written~~ attempted the far more needful task of reconciling the three first Gospels, τα ευαγγελια τα κατα σαρκα,[2] *doctrinally*
with the Pauline Letters. Of ⟨the authenticity of⟩ *these* we *have*
the same kind of evidence as of Cicero's or Pliny's—for *they* have a
character of individual Genius/ & supposing the Gospels bonâ fide
apostolic or of apostolic authority, I find much that perplexes me,
in the Comparison. Ex. gr. Had Paul been aware that these words
had been addressed by Christ to Peter, in whatever sense—it seems
strange, that he should speak of Peter & his followers as he has *done*.[3]

2 pp 83–6

The belief in purgatory is so inseparable from the former tenet [of
infallibility], that I need not enlarge on the peculiar advantages which
Rome has derived from it.

It ~~wi~~ may perhaps be counted among the few benefits, which the
Fathers of the five first Centuries have conferred on pure Christianity
that they enable us to prove the novelty of the Doctrine of Purgatory.
Thank God! we know that ⟨during⟩ the three first Ages the Christian
Church was wholly innocent of the fiction—& that for yet another 3
Centuries it was but a tolerated Guess/—Nevertheless, I cannot
blame a Romanist uninformed in Church History, nor wonder at
him, if he believes himself to find in the Vth of Matthew, and one or
two of the Parables a strong confirmation of this most pernicious
Article, if not a direct Authority for it[1]—Indeed, that the bolder
members of the Unitarian Sect pretend to discover a discrepance
between the three first Gospels, Matthew especially, and the writings
of John & Paul, is my least ground of complaint against the Minimi-
fidian Heresy.[2] I should draw indeed a very different inference, even

he said, were "vile, cowardly, selfish,
calculating" (*CN* II 2627); and in 1810
he said that Paley "degrades the spirit
of honor into a mere class-law among
the higher classes originating in selfish
convenience, and enforced by the
penalty of excommunication from the
society which habit had rendered indispensable to the happiness of the
individuals" who represented that
class. *Friend* (*CC*) I 435.

1[2] "The gospels according to the
flesh"—i.e. the gospels (excluding
John) that record the life of Jesus from

a human point of view—the phrase
echoing 2 Cor 5.16 and 1 Cor 1.26.
Cf *CL* VI 784, 894.

1[3] Presumably Paul's rebuke of
Peter and his followers in Gal 2.14–17.

2[1] See e.g. Matt 5.22, 26, 29, 19.35,
Luke 17.13.

2[2] The position of one who believes
as little as possible. See *AR* (1825)
202–7: "...its object is to draw
religion down to the Believer's intellect, instead of raising his intellect up
to religion". *OED* cites this passage
as the first use of the term "minimi-

if ~~no means~~ I saw no way of explaining the *appearance*: nor can I indeed deny that it is a remarkable circumstance that it is these very passages in the first Gospel which have ~~so~~ such striking parallelisms in the Talmud and oldest Rabbinical Traditions.[a][3]

And *qu*[y]? would any real injury to Christian Faith result from the hypothesis, that our Saviour addressing himself προπαιδευτικως to the mixt multitude of his Auditors,[4] many of whom were untaught even in the first principles of common Morality, occasionally reminded them of the Sayings of their own Wise Men, or quoted parts of their own liturgical Compilations—if with condescending mercy he performed the part of a compassionate Countryman, to make *better* men even of such as were not in the number of those who were to become *other* men—to *reform* where it was not given him to regenerate?—Quærentis, non docentis, formâ hæc scripsi[5]

S. T. Coleridge 21 July 1825.

3   pp 90–1

The Reformed churches are taxed with their *variations*, as if, like Rome, they had pledged their existence upon infallibility.

The fair way of stating this point is, first, to subtract all those dis-

---

[a] Here C has written "**", and has continued in the foot margin with a new paragraph, opening with "**"

---

fidianism", expounding it in contrast to "Ultra-fidianism", which is also recognised as C's coinage.

2[3] C's knowledge of the Mishnah, Gemara, and other rabbinical texts is not yet determined in bibliographical detail, but he could have drawn much from biblical commentaries and theological works familiar to him. In Jul 1816 he was trying to get the use of a version of *Mischna, Hebraice et Latine* ed G. Surenhusius (6 vols Amsterdam 1698–1703)—see *CL* iv 657—and may have succeeded in securing a copy of his own since there was a set in Green's library. *Green SC* (1880) 620. Boyer had made C a "tolerable Hebraist" at Christ's Hospital (*BL* ch 1—1907—i 6), but C's Hebrew was probably not in very good order when he took up residence in Highgate. (The "specimens of Rabbinical Wisdom selected from the Mishna" in *Friend—CC—* ii 154–6, 170–1, 308–9 were translated from a German version by Moses Mendelssohn in J. J. Engels *Schriften*.) In late 1816 or early 1817 he made the acquaintance of Hyman Hurwitz (1770–1844), Master of the Hebrew Academy in Highgate, who was in 1828 to be appointed first Professor of Hebrew in University College, London; there are many signs in the late notebooks that Hurwitz helped C improve his Hebrew and guided him into the rabbinical literature that he needed for his biblical studies: see esp N 37 and N 38. See also HURWITZ. In Jul 1833 C could tell Mrs Lockhart that "I happen to be a favorite among the Descendants of Abraham". *CL* vi 943.

2[4] "Propaideutically"—as a preliminary to instruction. See BÖHME 46 n 5.

2[5] "I have written this in the character of an inquirer, not as an instructor".

agreements that are known to exist in the Romish Communion it-self; and then to enumerate & examine the remainder. If I am ⟨not⟩ grossly deluded, I shall find that the latter will be reduced either into bewilderments, which in Protestant Countries are pitied as harmless insanities, while they are *killed off*[1] or concealed in monkish cells under the papal despotism—or Substitutes for the Deism & Atheism which are the sole Alternative of Orthodox faith in Catholic Lands. It is most honorable to Protestantism that it has presented Chris-tianity in so amiable a Light, that even the Unbeliever seeks a pretext for retaining the names & finds it in Socinianism.

4 pp 100–1 | Letter iv

Optimism is the system of the many: a revelation which could not remove every doubt, and silence every objection, must certainly fail to suit their previous notions.

In a most valuable Book these pages from 95–100 are distinguishably *excellent*: it is good sense heightend into philosophy. Our Church has awoke, of late, rubbed her eyes, remembered who and what she was, and begins to bestir herself! And lo! Providence has sent her a Recruit & an Auxiliary worthy of her & of her good Cause. It will be worse than Cowardice if the Church do not openly avow her sense of the service by conferring some one of her Dignities on the Author of this book.[1]—*S. T. C.*

5 p 103–4

[According to the Roman Catholic theory of Papal Infallibility:] The Pope might be, in his conduct, an enemy of Christ and his gospel, and nevertheless succeed in the enjoyment of whatever privileges were granted to Peter, *in consequence* of the love which, above the other apostles, he bore to his divine master.* He might be a monster of vice, yet he did not cease to be *vicar* of him *who did no sin.* [Footnote:] * Simon, son of Jonas, lovest thou me more than these? He saith unto Him, Yea, Lord, thou knowest that I love thee. He saith unto him, Feed my lambs. *John* xxi. 15. *et seq*.

It has always appeared to me evident, that in this passage our Lord intended a mild reproof of the Spirit of Self-sufficiency & Self-over-

---

3[1] C had repeated this phrase mockingly in 1795–6, taking it up from the injudicious use made of it by William Windham when secretary-at-war. See *Lects 1795* (*CC*) 306 and n 2, *Watchman* (*CC*) 61 and n 3.

4[1] The Church of England did not bestow any honour on Blanco White: see also general note, above.

rating that still lingered in Peter/ & the strongest argument, I can think of, in favor of the Romish Doctrine of Succession, is that the same words with the same purpose may be addressed to Peter's nominal Successors. Who pretend to such superiority of Zeal, as they? but who feed the Lambs so faithlessly?—I need not remind the learned Reader, that the whole last Chapter of John by some, and the verses from the 14th verse by many, Biblical Scholars, have been considered of doubtful authenticity.[1]

6   pp 109–11

The Protestants, in fine, have *varied*, because, by restoring the Scriptures to their full and unrivalled authority, they perceived the intrinsic power of settled, recorded, *invariable* revelation; and were aware that, in spite of doubts and divisions, the light of those divine records needed no help to withstand the attacks of the gates of hell.

The Pr. have varied, first because by force of circumstances and the necessity of acting according to the Measure of Light vouchsafed them, they set up the infallibility of ~~the Bible~~ a Book against & in place of, the infallibility of a Man, without definitely settling what they meant by it, or with what qualifications & under what conditions they asserted it.—Still, however, a vast, an incalculable Gain, both immediately and in the direct consequences. They pretend to no miraculous inspir~~a~~lations, and as *mere* men, they *must* pass from papal Darkness to Gospel Day thro' a Twilight. There is the rem-~~anent~~nant of Night in the Dawn of the Morning. Or compare Protestantism to a bird-limed Lark that has worked itself loose but still has patches of the viscous Fetters sticking to its feet and wings.[1] This however was the golden time of the Reform, & few and small were the Rents in the unity of Faith.—But secondly, soon came the first results & rewards of mental emancipation—increase of *popular* knowlege, arts, industry, trade, commerce, civil & political Liberty, all tending to an exclusive exercise and cultivation of the *Understanding* and the prudential habit, to the bedimming of the Reason and the Spiritual Light.[2] And then rose sadder & more momentous

[5][1] That John 21 is an appendix and that it differs from the body of the fourth gospel in style and point of view is agreed by biblical scholars. The present consensus on grounds other than stylistic appears to be, however, that the appendix was written by John. On the authenticity of John 21 see also BIBLE *Apocryphal NT* **4**.

[6][1] C could think at times of his mind and genius as bird-limed: see e.g. *CL* II 1203, III 222, *CN* III 3661 and n, 4088 f 155ᵛ and n.

[6][2] For the distinction between reason and understanding see e.g. BAXTER *Catholick Theologie* **14** n 3.

Differences! ~~which~~ And yet ~~at~~ the worst ~~were~~ Heresies that the Genius of Protestantism disclosed were tolerable Misgrowths compared with the Atheism & Moral Deformities which Pseudo-Catholicism produced and concealed.

7 pp 202–4 | Letter VI

Indeed, among the saints of the Breviary, most will be found commended for similar [devotional] practices; and not a book of devotion, by writers of that communion exists, which does not represent some bodily exercise or distortion, as an effectual method of pleasing God.* [Footnote:]* The least morose of all Roman Catholic saints, Saint Francis de Sales, though not carrying these practices to the degree usual among professed saints, strongly recommends this kind of spiritual gymnastics to his friends. The following are his directions to a gentleman "*qui vouloit se retirer du monde.*"

"Je vous conseille de pratiquer ces exercises pour ces trois mois suivans ... que vous vous leviez toujours à six heures matin ..." Lettres de Saint François de Sales.

I would willingly believe, that De Sales had seen or suspected an indolence of Will, a languor of Volition, in this Gentleman; and hoped that by ~~rem~~ imposing on him a bodily act requiring a certain degree of exertion he might by virtue of Association call up an inward activity.—The soberest Protestant Divine might discreetly counsel a friend to substitute for praying in thought, & with the head on the pillow the practice of kneeling and distinctly articulating his prayers. I say this wholly from the spiritual character of De Sales' Writings/[1]—for alas! it would be mock-Candour to attempt any such palliation of the Romish Guides generally: whose systematic plan is that of turning religion into Superstition, and suspending all the energies of the inner man by concentring the attention on sensible Images, & exhausting the Volition in mechanical movements ~~of the body~~. This indeed is the Clue to the ~~whole~~ murky laby-

7[1] Blanco White had quoted from St Francis of Sales (1567–1622) *Lettres à des gens du monde* IV vii. St Francis is testing and tempering the spiritual aspirations of the penitent by imposing "ces petites et foibles austérités". C's defence is perhaps unusual for a Protestant: but it may be noted that St Francis's mission to convert the Calvinistic people of Chablais, before he was appointed coadjutor to the bishop of Geneva in 1596, was exceptionally successful. C acquired in Jan 1806 a copy of St Francis of Sales *Il teotima o sia il trattato dell' Amor di Dio* ed and tr Carlo Barbieri (2 vols Padua 1790–1). See also St FRANCIS.

rinth of the Anti-christian Minotaur—To disensoul[2] the whole Organism of Religion by rendering it exclusively *objective*; but as the Objective exists, *as* objective, only by its correspondence to, and as the Correlate of, the Subjective, by the extinction of the latter it loses all true Objectivity, and becomes at once spectral and sensual.[3] The whole Romish Ritual presents for to a truly spiritual Eye dead Flesh galvanized by Fraud and remorseless Superstition! S. T. C.—

8 p 204

The Roman Catholics will talk of penance *in moderation*; but where is the line drawn, where, indeed, can it be drawn, to point the beginning of excess? Must I again revive the memory of the victims whom I have seen perish in their youth, from the absolute impossibility of moderating the enthusiasm which their church thus encourages? It is chiefly among the tender and delicate of the female sex, that the full effects of these examples are seen. How can a confessor prescribe limits to the zeal of an ardent mind, which is taught to please God by tormenting a frail body? Teach an enthusiastic female that self-inflicted death will endear her to her heavenly bridegroom and she will press rope or the knife to her lips.

This, again, is one of the but one application of a R Sophism that *pervades* the Romish Apologists—viz. Whatever in any conceivable particular case may possibly be advisable for this or that Individual, is imposed as a general Rule, and defended by on the very questionable maxim—ab abusu contra Usum non valet argumento conclusio.[1]—Now where the use is comparatively trifling and of rare occurringence, while the Abuse is most mischievous & of hourly frequency, ab Abusu etiam contra Usum, vel saltem contra commendationem usûs, valida datur conclusio.[2]—The Romish Hierarchy, that seek to withdraw the Sacred Scriptures from the Laity on this pretence, ought least of all men to contravert the principle.

9 p 205

Does not the young victim read of Saint Theresa, that "... her ardour in punishing the body was so vehement as to make her use hair

---

[7] [2] Not in *OED*, but cf "ensoul", "dissoul".

[7] [3] On objective/subjective see *BL* ch 12 (1907) i 174–9.

[8] [1] "From an Abuse, no valid argument conclusion can be drawn against the Use of a thing."

[8] [2] "From the Abuse, a valid conclusion can indeed be drawn against its Use—or at least against recommending its use."

shirts, chains, nettles, scourges, and even to roll herself among thorns, regardless of a diseased constitution?"[1]

I cannot say how far it would have been expedient in a work like the present to have shewn & explained the secret Partnership of Moloch & Belial in these inhuman Self-outrages. Here as in most other things Extremes meet[2]—the Εαυτην τιμωρευμένη all too easily becomes in one and the same act an ἑαύτην-πορνευομένη.[3] Αι τῆς Θερέσης εκστασεῖς,[a] επι τινι μην τοῖς ορ⟨γ⟩ασμασι διεφερον;[4] Languages affords only the same words to describe both: and that they are not used metaphorically in the former is most certain/ from the *locality* assigned to the Sensations, and the bodily exhaustion consequent thereon. Among the prime mysteries of Darkness the Libido sui vix conscia æstu per *totum* systema nervosam diffuso, may be placed.[5]— S. T. C.

10   p 215

[Blanco White quotes from the *Exercise for Monday* "as containing a fresh and striking proof of the indefatigable industry of Roman Catholic priests, in entrapping young people to take the dangerous vow of perpetual celibacy".] "Yes, my most dear Mother! I desire to be pure all my life, as well in body as soul: I do, I say, most

[a] As the third character in this word C first wrote σ, then wrote over it the ligature for στ

9[1] Blanco White is translating from the *Breviary*. C may have turned back from p 208, in which he would have read: "The picture of St Theresa [i.e. her vision, described in the *Breviary*] fainting under the wound which an angel inflicts on her heart with a fiery spear [footnote in Latin: she 'heard Christ saying, as he held out his hand to her, "Henceforth you shall be honoured as my bride".'] were it not for the nun's weeds worn by the principal figure; might easily be mistaken for a votive tablet intended for some heathen temple; and her dying rather of love than of disease is more worthy of a novel of doubtful tendency than of a collection of lives prepared by a Christian church to exemplify the moral effect of the Gospel."

9[2] In Dec 1803 C set down what was to become his favourite proverb, "Extremes meet", intending "to de-

vote the last 9 pages of my Pocket[book] to the collection" of "instances of the Proverb". *CN* I 1725. See also *Friend* (*CC*) I 110 and n 5, and e.g. *AR* (1825) 360n. In c 1820–1 he noted: "I should like to know, whether or how far the delight, I feel & have always felt, in adages or aphorisms of universal or very extensive application, is a general or common feeling with man, or a peculiarity of my own mind. I cannot describe how much pleasure I have derived from 'Extremes meet' for instance; or 'Treat everything according to its Nature', and 'Be'!" N 29 f 56[v].

9[3] "Self-punishment [becomes] self-excitation".

9[4] "In what way did THERESA's ecstasies differ from *orgasms*?"

9[5] "Sexual desire scarcely above the conscious level, with its heat spread through the *whole* nervous system".

humbly desire it, and most earnestly beseech you, dear Lady, to obtain for me that which you so much recommend to me. I do here, prostrate, reverence you, O Sacred Virgin Mary, Mother of the Word incarnate! and together with the holy thrones and all celestial spirits, ever bless and praise you infinitely, the Morning Star, *Stella Matutina*; for that you, the most beautiful of all creatures, were the first that did vow perpetual chastity, preparing the way to so many virginal souls which have already followed, and shall hereafter follow you in so high, so glorious, and so divine an enterprise.— Hail Mary!"

Methinks, the Romish Commentators who find in so many a lucid text of Scripture as many strange Senses in sanction of their Church Whimsies, Sacraments and sub-sacraments, as Katterfelto by his Solar Microscope found animals, large as his black Cat, in a drop of transparent Water,[1] are not entitled to charge me with any unpardonable super-fœtation of Scripture if I plead—for the possibility, that these blasphemous Parthenolatries and Hyper-dulies[2] were present to our Saviour's mind when with a prolēpsis of Anger and Offence he checked his Mother's officious interference with his public and divine functions in the words, τι εμοι και σοι, γυνη[3] ⟨; my in-

10[1] Gustavus Katterfelto (d 1799), Prussian conjurer and quack doctor, appeared in London in 1782, giving demonstrations in Spring Gardens and working on the credulity of Londoners during the influenza epidemic of that year. He claimed in advertisements (which normally appeared under the headline "WONDERS—WONDERS—WONDERS") that he could show under his solar microscope the insects that caused the influenza epidemic as large as birds; in his demonstrations he used a remarkable black cat that sat on his shoulder and had prophetic powers, and other cats that ran an electric machine. By 1784 he had attracted the interest of royalty with a perpetual-motion machine but was less successful in the provinces: in Shrewsbury he was imprisoned for imposture, and having later settled in Yorkshire he was imprisoned in Kendal for a rogue. He is mentioned by Cowper in *The Task* IV 86 and by Peter Pindar. C turned Katterfelto, the solar microscope, and the black cat to the same figurative purpose as here in *LR* I 321, DONNE *Sermons* COPY B 39, and in the ms of *CIS* (see *C 17th C* 177).

10[2] "Parthenolatry" (virgin-worship)—a hostile coinage of C's; *OED* ascribes the earliest use of it to C in HACKET *A Century of Sermons* (1675). "Hyperduly" is a term in RC theological use for the superior veneration due to the Virgin Mary, of an order between the "latria" (worship) due to God and the "dulia" (veneration) offered to the saints. C will have seen the word—if nowhere else—in Jeremy TAYLOR *Polemicall Discourses* (1674) i 548 in a section "Of the Worship of Images", which he annotated. For C's use of a family of words formed on *-latry* and *-douly* see BAXTER *Reliquiae* COPY A 38 n 1.

10[3] John 2.4: "Woman, what have I to do with thee?" *NEB* more literally reads: "Your concern, mother, is not mine".

terpretation is, at least, in perfect harmony with Matth. XII. 498, 49. τις εστιν η μητηρ μου; &c.)[4] S. T. C.

11 pp 217–19, at the end of the text

When you have candidly and honestly weighed all this, decide with yourselves, if it be not the part of every ingenuous and liberal Catholic of these kingdoms, to strike out the *Roman* from his religious denomination, and place in its stead the noble epithet of Christian? Preserve, with God's blessing, so much of your tenets as may appear to you consistent with his word; but disown a church which, by her miracles, libels the Gospel history with imposture; and whose mawkish piety disfigures the sublime Christian worship into drivelling imbecility.

Let the conscientious Catholic first take from the Liturgy of the English Church all those points, as to which he is ⟨in⟩ perfect accordance: and having meditated awhile on their positive and comparative Moment, let him resume his inquest with the faith in the divine origin and authority of the Scriptures.

The Romish Church has solemnly declared that all the declarations of the Sacred Writers are true and infallible in the sense, in which they were delivered. This then is beyond controversy: for in this and in making it an article of faith both the Parties are agreed. Common Sense dictates, that a truth, to which both of two Parties, each numerous & supplied abundantly with learned Men, assent, pleno ore et corde toto (a truth, which has been admitted semper, ubique, et ab omnibus)[1] must be more *evident*, than the truth of a position asserted only by one ~~and that~~ a Party, and that too a Party temporally interested in its introduction & maintenance. In *certainty*, there are no degrees; but evidence admits of many. Now surely what is *evidently Certain* must be the most legitimate test of a disputed & therefore not in the same degree evident, *pro* Certo oblatumi.[a2] An *evident* certainty is the test even of mathematical

---

[a] C first wrote "oblatum", then dotted the first minim of the "u" and scribbled over the rest of the word

10[4] "Who is my mother?" and "Behold my mother, and my brethren!"

11[1] Assent "with clear voice and a whole heart" to a truth admitted "always, everywhere, and by every one". For the source of the "Vincentian Canon" (*quod semper* etc), the traditional ground for Catholic assent, see *CN* II 2437n. Jeremy Taylor, e.g., quotes it in *Polemicall Discourses* (1674) i 168—a passage C annotated.

11[2] Of a proposition "brought forward *as* a Certainty". C's recurrent distinction between the certain and the positive associates certainty with the

certainties; how much more then of a supposed or pretended, but at the same time & by an equal number, denied & disputed, certainty./ If this be true, & its truth is palpable, it cannot but be the duty of a rational conscientious Catholic to inquire, ~~and~~ whether the Scripture returns the compliment. The Romish Church asserts and requires you to believe, ~~all~~ the infallible truth & righteousness of all the declarations and decisions of Scripture. Now does Scripture assert and require you to believe, the ⟨infallible⟩ truth, & righteousness of all the declarations of the Romish Church? Of the words, in which your Church asserts this infallibility of Scripture, there is and can be but one meaning. It is the direct, literal, ⟨necessary,⟩ and immediate Sense of her Words.—Is there no other possible interpretation of the two or three single Texts, which you pretend ~~from Scripture~~ as the declaration of Scripture for the similar infallibility of the Romish Church? You cannot affirm this: for a multitude of eminently learned Divines, age following age, have interpreted & still do interpret these texts very differently.—But is yours the immediate sense, or ~~any~~ only a deduced sense et per consequens?—Certainly, the latter only: for you must first prove the *Romish* Church to be the true Church and ~~in that~~ not only this but to be *the* Church in *the* sense, in which Christ was then speaking of the Church.—But again—what the Scriptures are, and what are Scriptures, you may easily determine. Those which Protestant & Romanist join in receiving, *must* be Scriptures: as ~~of~~ far as the present Controversy is concerned.—But how can you even pretend to be equally clear as to who or what is the Church, in the practical application of infallibility? There are at least four different & irreconcileably different, Opinions among the Roman Catholics themselves——

What is the Conclusion? That at all events you are bound to receive the doctrines & precepts of the Scriptures. But does not this bind you by necessary Consequence to reject whatever precept & doctrines ~~ar~~ shall either contradict them, or render them of no effect?—Compare then, fearlessly and honestly, the impressions which would be left on a competent & unprejudiced mind after the careful perusal of the New Testament with those, that a circuit of the

---

reason, positiveness with the senses, as in *Friend (CC)* I 97. So in *CN* II 3095 he speaks of "the sense of *certainty*" and "the sensation of positiveness"; in *Friend (CC)* II 7 he remarks "how distinct and different the sensation of positiveness is from the sense of certainty"; and in *CL* III 48 says that he is speaking with "a *sense* of *certainty* intuitively distinguished from a mere delusive *feeling* of *Positiveness*". See esp *CN* III 3592, entitled "On Certainty".

Romish Nunneries, Monasteries, Inquisition-jails, Chapels, Oratories, &c &c would leave!—Frame to yourself a diary of the Life of St Patrick, as recorded by the authority of the successive Heads of your Church—: & then ~~turn~~hen tell me whether such a life is not of necessity incompatible with or at least making of no effect, the larger number of ⟨Scripture⟩ precepts given to all men!—

12   pp 220–2 | Notes. A. [referring to] Page 31

[Blanco White, defending RS against Butler, quotes a passage from Paulus Emilius Veronensis:] Cum apud Pontificem de hac consternatione ageretur, a Panormitanis missos ad eum oratores, viros sanctos, qui ad pedes illius strati, VELUT pro arâ hostiâque, CHRISTUM AGNUM DEI SALUTANTES, illa ETIAM ex altaris mysteriis verba supplices effarentur—"Qui tollis peccata mundi, miserere nostri:—Qui tollis peccata mundi, miserere nostri:—Qui tollis peccata mundi, dona nobis pacem." Pontificem respondisse, Panormitanos agere quod fecissent, qui, cum Christum pulsarent, eundem regem Judaeorum salutabant, re hostes, fando salvere jubentes.

[Tr C. Butler in *Book of the Roman Catholic Church* pp 131–2, as quoted by Blanco White: "The city of Palermo having grievously offended the Pope sent some holy men to him as ambassadors, who prostrated themselves at his feet, AND SALUTED CHRIST THE LAMB OF GOD, as before an altar and the blessed sacrament, and suppliantly pronounced the mystic words of the altar, 'Lamb of God, who takest away the sins of the world, have mercy upon us! Who takest away the sins of the world, give us peace.' The Pope replied by telling them, that they acted like those who, after they had struck Christ, saluted him King of the Jews; that in reality they were his enemies, although in these words they wished him health."][1]

[There follow two pages of criticism of Butler's translation; Blanco White points out that "Butler makes the whole transaction quite unintelligible" by making the ambassador address Christ, yet the Pope takes the words as addressed to him.]

I need not say, that I contemplate the blundering Jesuitry of Butler's translation with the contempt and disgust, which belong to it, and other clumsy ~~tricks of this~~ juggles of this special-pleading Sophist. Yet I cannot quite assent to the perfect accuracy of Mr White's translation, tho' it may perhaps give an equivalent sense. I should ~~render~~ explain the latin words—"who prostrating themselves at his

12[1] In BLANCO WHITE *Letter* 2 C began to write a note on this same passage but stopped without completing it.

feet, as before Altar & Host, Saluting (i.e. *in his Person as the* Representative of Christ) Christ the Lamb of God, ~~used~~ uttered likewise the very ~~same~~ words ~~as were~~ used in the Service of the Mass.["]—Had ~~Butler's~~ Mr White's sense been meant, the words must have been, veluti (or ac si) Christum Agnum Dei *salutarent*.[2]— As the words are, the passage contains a flagrant instance of the gross⟨est species of⟩ *Idolatry*, the Pope having been avowedly addressed as a visible Image representing Christ & containing in itself the *numen* of Christ.[3] P.S. Possibly, I may have required pure⟨r⟩ Latin of Paulus Emilius of Verona, than I had a right to expect: and am inclined to retract my criticism. S. T. C.

The word *"salutantes"* suffices to render Butler's translation ridiculous.[4]—A more ingenious Apologist might with less disingenuousness have interpreted the wholl~~ye~~ narrative into a piece of disgusting Flattery—& hav~~inge~~ ⟨con⟩tended that the Ambassadors meant only to express their unconditional Submission—We have offended beyond the Holy Father's forgiveness. We dare not address ourselves to him, or even look up toward him; but Lord! have mercy upon us! Christ! have mercy upon us—&c. But the *"salutantes"* baffles all attempts, & identifies the Pope with Christ too glaringly.

13   pp 234–7 | Note D.—Page 78. Transubstantiation

What appears to me most deserving the attention of philosophical observers, is the *concurrence* of two perfectly unconnected errors, in giving birth to this intellectual monster.

12² "As if *they were saluting* Christ the Lamb of God". It is difficult to see any significant difference between Butler's translation and C's.

12³ C objects to the Pope being treated as though he were an idol that somehow contained the divinity (*numen*) of Christ. Cf Blanco White's text pp 78–9: "By the combined influence of *tradition* and *infallibility*, the church of Rome established the doctrine of *Transubstantiation*. From the moment that people are made to believe that a man has the power of working, at all times, the stupendous miracle of converting bread and wine into the body and blood of Christ; that man is raised to a dignity above all which kings are able to confer. What, then, must be the honour due to

a bishop, who can bestow the power of performing the miracle of transubstantiation? What the rank of the Pope, who is the head of the bishops themselves? The world beheld for centuries, the natural consequences of the surprising belief in the power of priests to convert bread and wine into the incarnate Deity. [Then follows the long note summarised in the textus above.] Kings and emperors were forced to kiss the Pope's foot, because their subjects were in the daily habit of kissing the hands of priests...".

12⁴ C seems to mean that *salutare* is a suitable word to use of addressing the Pope, but not of addressing Christ; hence the meaning would be "saluting [him] as Christ the Lamb of God".

... Even among the early Christians ... The spiritual presence of Christ, the intimate connexion between an external and simple act of eating and drinking, and the influence of his grace on the soul of those who eat and drink by faith in his death and passion, was soon lost sight of. ...

One of the doctrines introduced by the Aristotelian system of the school, is that of *substantial forms*, or *absolute accidents*. ... This was a lucky discovery for the school divines. It explained the bodily presence of Christ in the sacrament. The *substance* of the bread and wine, they said, is converted into his body and blood; but *the absolute accidents*, the *substantial forms* of both, remain as before. Hence the word *transubstantiation*. ...

The nature of the contrary errors respecting the Eucharist seem to me abundantly clear:—First, and common to both Parties the confusion of the Phænomenon with the Noumenon, or thing in itself./[1] 2. The substituting a ~~chosen~~ select Symbol, a *Pars pro Toto*, του totius quippe et presentatrix (τα γαρ νουμενα ἔστι καθ᾽ ολον ἐν ἑκάστῳ) et representatrix,[2] for, and to the exclusion of, the universal verity symbolized. (*Romish Plethora*) 3. The ~~exinanition~~ De-substantiation of the mysterious *Symbol* into a grotesque hollow *Metaphor*. (*Arminian Marasmus*, or *Sacramentarean Atrophy*.)—[3]

I feel my courage fail at the thought of questioning the accuracy of a Spanish Divine on a statement of the Scholastic Theory of Transsubstantiation; but this distinction of Substance from Substantial Forms, as a doctrine of either Scotist or Thomist, is new to me. Des Cartes indeed bordered on this; as indeed *his* Matter is itself little more than an absolute or subsisting Accident.[4] Scotus on the other hand (as I had imagined) attributed to all Entia Substantia a formative force as a sort of radiance, *specifying* the Accidents, which were the joint product or result of this force, et virium ubique circumstantium, the harmony of which he in some places seems to ground on the omnipresence of the Deity.[5]—Now this materializing

13[1] Cf *CN* III 3725: "...when Pride will work up the φαινομενα into a *system* of *Things in themselves*, then they become most pernicious errors".

13[2] "A *Part for the Whole*, indeed both presentative (for the *noumena* are wholly in each) and representative of the whole". See **13** n 7, below, and cf *CN* III 3605. For C's use of καθ᾽ ολον for καθολου see BEAUMONT & FLETCHER COPY A **5** n 2.

13[3] On the sacrament as symbol, not metaphor or allegory, see BOOK OF COMMON PRAYER COPY B **6** and n 2.

13[4] For C on Descartes on matter see e.g. *BL* ch 8 (1907) I 88–9, *P Lects* Lect 12 (1949) 349–50.

13[5] "Substantial Beings...and of forces present everywhere about". C evidently accumulated some direct knowledge of Duns Scotus' writing

effluence, or *outerance*,[6] was retracted in the spiritual Substance of the Body and Blood of Christ—while the Divinity united with it as tota in omni parte,[7] supported the specific ground of the Accidents by sustaining, as it were, the vibration that had been given by the substance (realitate sub-stanti)[8] of the Bread and Wine.—This, it will be seen, comes very near to Berkleianism, in which the Accidents have their subsistence in the Percipient, and their specific cause in the supersensual Motors, of all whose formative motions God is the Sustainer, the Sustenance, and perpetual originating Pulse and Impulse.—According to my learned Friend's conception the Substance of the Bread & Wine would at no time have stood in any *actual* connection, much less, union, with the Accidents; but in a mere *juxta-position*.

14   p +2, pencil

Love in the mask of Emulation, between two Boy-friends—like two butterflies that climb the air as on some ladder too fine for human ken, still striving to surmount each other, and yet nor less following the brief descents.[1]

---

but it is not clear which works he read. See *P Lects* Lect 9 (1949) 280 and *CL* v 326 n 2. See also BAXTER *Reliquiae* COPY A **34** and n 1.

13[6] For C's consideration of "utterance" as "outerance" see BÖHME **100** and n 2. For a connexion between "substantial Forms" and "outerance" see *CN* III 3592.

13[7] "The whole in every part". This favourite phrase of C's crystallises the guiding notion in Aristotle's theory of form and in C's theory of imaginative structure. See also e.g. *CN* III 3962.

13[8] C points to the literal meaning achieved by dividing the word into its elements: "the under-standing".

14[1] Cf *CN* I 1428 of 16 Aug 1803: "Butterfly let loose, how very high, how madly, how purposeless/ it pushes the air under it & runs up the Stairs of Air./ 2 Butterflies, an Image of the restless Fondness of two young Lovers." See also ANDERSON COPY A **1** and n 6.

CHARLES JAMES BLOMFIELD
1786–1856

A Charge delivered to the Clergy of his Diocese by Charles James Lord Bishop of London at his primary visitation in July MDCCCXXX. London 1830. 4º.

British Museum C 61 c 9

Inscribed on p ⁻1 (inside of original paper wrapper): "From the Author"; and on the title-page in HNC's hand: "H. N. Coleridge Hampstead— *1830*." The pamphlet was evidently presented by Bp Blomfield to HNC, who wrote his name in it and then lent it to C, no doubt encouraging profuse comment.

C's first indirect connexion with Blomfield was in reading H. F. Cary's copies of Blomfield's editions of *Prometheus Vinctus* (1810) and the *Persae* (1814): see AESCHYLUS. After 1824 Blomfield was in frequent touch with the Wordsworths; after his translation to the bishopric of London in 1828 he became acquainted with HNC. C referred to him in 1830 and 1832 (*CL* VI 846, 902), and hoped to use Blomfield's influence in publishing his proposed edition of ASGILL.

DATE. 11 Sept 1830 and shortly thereafter: 11 Sept 1830 (**2**), Sept 1830 (**12**). All the notes seem to have been written at the same time.

COEDITOR. James D. Boulger.

1   pp [3]–[4], a few details pencil, overtraced

I am almost afraid, my dear Henry! that this being an Author's= presentation Copy, and this Author a Bishop, and this Bishop a Bishop of LONDON,*ᵃ* ~~that~~*ᵇ* I may be thought, at least *felt*, by you to have indulged my propensity to marginal Annotations somewhat out of place. But I cannot (n.b. the usual lying Synonime for, I *will* not) resist the temptation of observing to you, ⟨with respect to the first half of his Charge,⟩*ᶜ* how manifoldly the worthy Prelate's Reasoning is weakened, how unsteady it is thro' defect of the *foundation*, in consequence of his constantly addressing his Clergy in the character of a *Christian* Bishop, and this *exclusively*. What is the legitimate Conclusion? *Either*, that the 39 Articles & Canons

---

ᵃ This word is written in swash capitals   *ᵇ* Crossed out in pencil
ᶜ The interpolation is in pencil, overtraced in ink by HNC

526

semi-personified as the Church of England, is are the One & only saving Church of Christ—which the papal Church with undeniable *Consistency* at least, whatever may be thought of its Modesty and Charity, asserts of itself—*or* that the Church of England is a *favored Sect*, by the partiality of the two houses of Parliament allowed and authorized to exact such and such Sums from the Land-owners, Farmers &c, without any consent perhaps no consent asked on their part, indepe⟨n⟩dent*a* of their attendance on its Ministry and without any recognizable proportion to their claimants'*b* Services!—Well may the good Bishop augur that *such* an Institution stands in jeopardy.—⟨I seem to see with the clearness of an intuition, that only on the distinct conception of the 3 (only possible) Forms of a Church can our Church be *vindicated* on *principle*.—And as to Expedience— alas! tis quaking Bog-ground.⟩*c*

2 p [4]

My dear Henry, it is very easy to laugh or sneer down a literary Man who has in various forms advanced and enforced any *connexus* of (what in his earnest conviction are) fundamental Principles, or seminal Ideas/,*d* and who in treating of the appertinent Subjects, which will be numerous in proportion to the importance and comprehensiveness of The Ideas, ever refers to them, and tries every point by these as by the criterion—"Hem!—*Ideas*—antecedent grounds and conditions—Reason distinguished from Understanding"—out it comes, as inevitably as the great *Bacon* from B. M. —nolens volens,[1] or like the Patentee of the Anti-friction Powder who, on the Motion of the Planets being spoken ⟨of,⟩ observed, that he felt quite proud in admitting that the Creator was the first original Anti-frictionist![2]—But after all the *legitimacy* of this easy

---

a The interpolation is in pencil, overtraced in ink by HNC
b The deletion and interpolation are in pencil
c This sentence was added after **2** had been written; C tried to squeeze it into the space left between **1** and **2**. Because the last line of ms ("*vindicated*...Bog-ground.") had to be written between the two first lines of **2**, C has ended the insertion with the sign "ʌ =", and added " = ʌ" before "My dear Henry" to show a reader where to read next
d Written as), here printed as /

2[1] The edition of Bacon coming out from "Basil Montagu—willy-nilly". In 1802 C had helped Basil Montagu (1770–1851) prepare a selection of English prose writers (pub 1805), and had later encouraged him to prepare a new edition of Bacon—at this time in progress: *The Works of Francis* *Bacon* (16 vols 1825–37). Cf *CL* v 493 and n, vi 843–4.

2[2] The first patentee of anti-friction powder has not been traced; but the powder was presumably graphite in some form. The earliest use in *OED* (1837) is assigned to Carlyle. In Aug 1832 C said he was willing to attend the

Criticism or *proleptic* Set-down, depends on the answer to a previous question—Are the Principles or Ideas true or false?—i.e. *Are* they Ideas, or mere verbiage?? Are they fundamental?—If they are ⟨both true & fundamental⟩ how could the Man avoid recurring to them, without sacrificing truth and the duty of communicating truth to a cowardly fear of being cried down, ~~for~~ as a Pedant & a Crambist?[3]— If false & trifling, expose their falsehood & nothingness—and laugh as long as such worthless laughing-stocks can supply the stimulus. S. T. Coleridge. 11 Sept[r] 1830.

3　pp 10–11, pencil, overtraced

[Footnote:] The Bishop, upon delivering the Bible into the hands of the person to be ordained Priest, says, "Take thou authority to preach the Word of God, and to minister the holy Sacraments, *in the congregation where thou shalt be lawfully appointed thereunto.*"

Now these very words in Italic are enough to prove the necessity of distinguishing (n.b. *not* of *dividing*) the National Clerisy from the Church under Christ.[1]—The command of Christ is freely to give what from free Mercy had been received—and "offer my Gospel to *all* Nations"[2]—i.e. without respect to the Individual's birth & locality, not as our fanatics interpret the words—as if our Lord had been sending his disciples off, like so many Mungo Parks,[3] this to the heart of Africa, another to the undiscovered, but by revelation made known, continent of America. (S[t] Thomas, I believe, had this honor of Ante-columbianism.)[4]—&c &c—

christening of his grand-daughter and "to stand beside Mrs Coleridge...in proof that the lack of Oil or Anti-friction Powder in our Conjugal Carriage-wheels did not extend to our parental relations...". *CL* vi 918.

2[3] A "crambist" (not in *OED*) serves warmed-up leftovers: from *crambe bis cocta* or *crambe repetita*, twice-cooked or warmed-up cabbage.

3[1] For the history of C's word "clerisy" see BAXTER *Reliquiae* COPY B **115** n 1, and cf **74** n 2. A clear definition appears in *C&S* (*CC*) 46. Cf *AR* (1825) 290n for the "three Classes" of the "Learned Order"; also see *LS* (*CC*) 170–1, and *TT* 10 Apr 1832.

3[2] The phrase "offer my Gospel" is not found in NT. See, however, Matt 28.19 "Go ye, therefore, and teach all nations", and cf Matt 24.14, Mk 13.10.

3[3] Mungo Park (1771–1806), Scottish surgeon and missionary, made a journey (under the sponsorship of the African Association and Sir Joseph Banks) to discover the sources of the Niger in 1795–7; his *Travels in the Interior Districts of Africa* (1799) was in its 5th edition in 1807. *The Journal of a Mission to the Interior of Africa, in the Year 1805*, made up from diaries that Park had sent home before his death, was not published until 1815. For C's objection to missionary work in foreign lands see e.g. BAXTER *Reliquiae* COPY B **43** and n 1.

3[4] According to the apocryphal *Acts of Thomas* (not included in Hone's *Apocryphal New Testament*), St Thomas evangelised India but after his death

4 p 11, pencil, overtraced

When all act in conformity with the rules of one harmonious system, not interfering with, but encouraging and emulating one another, *the whole body being fitly joined together, and compacted by that which every joint supplieth, according to the effectual working in the measure of every part, maketh increase of the body, unto the edifying of itself in love.* (Eph. iv. 16.)

Now just turn to Eph. IV. 16. & you will find that Paul is speaking of the whole body of *Eccalumeni*[1]—the nearest Copy of which is, perhaps, a Quaker Community,—whereas Dr B.^{a} applies the term, Church, in the abusive sense gradually imposed on the term during the fearfully rapid Corruption of Christianity—viz. as signifying the Ministers and professional Preachers, exclusively. The Gospel *has* no PRIESTS,* *can* have no Priests: they & their sacrifices are superseded by the everlasting self-sacrificed High Priest, the Word incarnate in Christ Jesus. But every point, which Dr B. is urging, arises naturally out of the aims, & objects & duties of a National Clerisy.

* i.e. in the sense of the Greek Hiereus & the Hebrew Cohen.[2]

5 p 21

With respect to the weekly prayers on Wednesdays and Fridays, I would not willingly, in any case, sanction their discontinuance, thinly as they are now attended ...

Pauperis formâ,[1] I beg to ask, why not? Can a more senseless Waste of a Clergyman's time, a more useless inroad on a Conscientious

^{a} C wrote "Dr B." in pencil; HNC overtraced it as "the B."

was buried in the West. Hence this first evangelist is referred to as "Ante-columbian"—i.e. in America before Columbus.

4[1] The word "Eccalumeni"—ἐκκαλούμενοι (those "called out of")—does not appear in this text or anywhere in NT. In NT, καλέω is the normal verb for the call to salvation, and ἐκκλησία in classical Greek is a group called *out of* houses, fields, etc to an assembly. See rather Eph 4.17: "I say...that ye henceforth walk not as other Gentiles walk". By using the present participle passive of the verb from which ἐκκλησία derives, C provides a noun to refer to those who—being members of the Christian assembly or church (ἐκκλησία)—are by the fact of that membership "called out [of this world]" (ἐκκαλούμενοι). For the importance of this idea of the Christian Church see *AR* (1825) 166n, *C&S* (*CC*) 45, 125 n 2.

4[2] The word translated as "priest" is ἱερεύς in NT and *kohen* in OT; the principal function of both was to prepare and offer sacrifices.

5[1] "In the character of a pauper"—i.e. allowed to bring legal action without payment of costs (according to acts of 1495 and 1532, repealed 1883). C implies ironically that, as he stands to lose nothing, his criticism may not be well founded.

Clergyman's pastoral Labors, ~~upon~~ a learned Clergyman's Studies, be imagined?—Is it ⟨not⟩ a relic of Popery, grounded on the hypothesis of the Minister's being a Priest, who was to offer daily the *sacrifice* of the Mass *for* the People, the attendance of the latter being desirable perhaps, but no more necessary than their understanding the prayers uttered or rather mumbled in an unknown Language?— Our Church is not rich enough, nor perhaps, were the soul-poisoning Celibacy of their Clergy done away, would even the Romanish Church be rich enough, to maintain the number of Ministers, that the *daily* Services of the consecrated Houses would require. What can be done, our Clergy, it is to be hoped, are doing—i.e. infuse into the minds of their flock juster & more spiritual conceptions of the Christian *Church*.

6   pp 22–4

In the discharge of those duties which, in a populous parish, far exceed the physical abilities of the strongest and the most devoted minister, great assistance may be derived from parochial visiting associations, acting in subordination* to the Clergy.

* Acting in nonsense! God forgive me for my impatiency!—When and where did such an association exist but as a hypocritical party-business? Why, an Association? to visit the poor parishioner *ex officio*, like the Window-light Man or Tax-gatherer?[1]—*Titus* proposes this scheme—*Titius* another—*Tatius* a third—each has its advocates, who think it *ingenious*, or that *some thing* may be done in that way—. And then arises *Totius*, and presents a fourth *idea* (for *that* is the phrase) taking parts from each of the three former—with due compliments to the *benevolent* and pious Setter up of the same.— Well! come of this what can come! I was born to a more invidious task—viz. to propound and do my~~self~~ best to prove & elucidate, certain *truths*, at least certain *positions*, which leave no other choice to the Mind, but that of ~~d~~receiving them as truths or rejecting them as falsehoods. If the former be admitted, all *choice* is out of the Question. We must act on these truths. Now such a position I assert

6[1] The Window-light Tax, levied according to the number of windows and openings in a house, was first imposed in 1697. Between 1747 and 1808 the tax was increased six times; see *Watchman (CC)* 109. When C first visited Hamburg in Sept 1798 he was "struck with the profusion of windows, so large and so many, that the houses look all glass". *Friend (CC)* II 212; cf *CN* I 340, *CL* I 432. The tax was reduced in 1823 but continued in force until 1851, when it was finally repealed in response to violent agitation.

the difference of a National Clerical Establishment & ~~of~~ the Church under Christ to be—and the consequent necessity of distinguishing them, both in the objects and the means to be employed for their attainment. This is no *Theory*—to be superseded by another, as soon as a new fact or two is discovered, which had escaped the attention of Theorist the first.—It is either a Principle, on which all must be grounded: or it is a Falsehood. No third is possible! But that a National Church may *include* a Christian Church, I more than admit: and good Archbishop Grindal, the last of the Race of Luther & Melancthon was deprived of his See by the jealous semi-romish, Elizabeth, for supporting and indicating the means of realizing this great Idea.[2] From the failure of this ⟨at⟩tempt, and the servile generation of Oxford Churchmen under James I arose the *Dissenting Interest*, and the degradation of the Church into a dominant *Sect.*— Is it it not palpable, that D^r B's plan is a Scotch Eldership in disguise? If Knox judged rightly in this attempt to blend the characters of a Christian Church and a Clerisy by ~~human~~ common law established, why then honestly & openly adopt it.[3] But if—nay, this is not a question to be discussed *marginally*, large and tempting as the Margins of this Charge happen to be!—

7   p 22

There is a special promise of blessing annexed to ministerial service; and the sense of that specialty ought not to be effaced from the minds of our flocks, by the permitted intrusion of laymen, however pious and zealous, into that which belongs to our own peculiar office.

Where? how comes it that the worthy Prelate has forgotten to annex Book, Chapter, & Verse? If he can shew me any such text, in the *undoubted* Writings of Paul or John, I will turn Rom. Catholic the next hour; for a Deist I cannot be. *S. T. C.*

8   p 26, pencil, overtraced

[Paragraphs dealing with Education, especially the education of the poor]

6[2] Edmund Grindal (c 1519–83), abp of Canterbury, was placed under sentence of suspension from 1577 to 1582 for refusing to carry out Elizabeth's mandate suppressing "prophesyings", i.e. private meetings of the clergy to study the Scriptures. See John STRYPE *Life of Grindal* (1710).

6[3] *The Book of Discipline*, drawn up in Edinburgh by Knox's ministers in 1560 on order of Parliament, made wise and liberal suggestions for religious and educational organisation, including the Presbyterian scheme of elders.

This and the following §phs are excellent:—solid and seasonable Sense in simple yet dignified language.

9 p 30, pencil, overtraced

It is my wish that in general young persons should not be brought to me for Confirmation till they are sixteen years of age.

On the first perusal of the late Bishop's Heber's Life of Jer. Taylor, I was surprized at, and still regret, his unqualified condemnation of Taylor's short treatise on Confirmation.[1] So far from agreeing with Heber in his almost dissentinglike views of this ordinance, it appears to me indispensable in a Church which practices Infant Baptism. See Aids to Reflection, on *Baptism*.[2] S. T. C.

10 p 31, pencil, overtraced

I now proceed to ... a topic of great importance ... I mean admission into the ministry of our Church. Having laid down certain rules for my own guidance in the discharge of that part of my office, for which I am most deeply and fearfully responsible to Him, who has commanded me by his Apostle *to lay hands suddenly on no man* [1 Tim 5.22] ... it is important that my sentiments should be known to those young men, who intend to be candidates for Holy Orders in this diocese.

Mem. I am persuaded that this Advice of the Apostle's has no connection with ordination, but was a rule of Caution in the application of the Gift of Healing.[1] There is a very curious and, indeed, a very interesting and important Anecdote in the Talmud, quoted by Rhenford,[a] attesting the general belief of the power of Healing

[a] The name, correctly written by C in pencil, has been incorrectly overtraced as "Rhinford"

9[1] In his "Life of Jeremy Taylor" prefacing his ed of the *Whole Works of Jeremy Taylor* (15 vols 1822), Reginald Heber (1783–1826) said that he could not consider the "Discourse of Confirmation" "as a favourable specimen of [Taylor's] genius". See I cclvi–cclx. In the "Discourse of Confirmation" (in Pt ii of Jeremy TAYLOR *Polemicall Discourses*), Taylor, according to C, wished to "assert the inferiority... in rank and efficacy, of Baptism to Confirmation" (ii 2–6); Heber wished to reassert the sacramental priority of

baptism, as is orthodox in the Church of England.

9[2] *AR* (1825) 354–76.

10[1] In C's view, the "rule of Caution" is reinforced by the continuation of 1 Tim 5.22, "neither be partaker of any man's sins"; he apparently considers that the laying on of hands is at once an act of healing and of absolution. The laying on of hands applied originally to the ordination of elders, and was not used in the restoration of penitents until the third century. *Peake* 876b.

possessed by the Christians of the Apostolic Age, even among their most bigotted enemies.[2]

11 p 35, pencil, overtraced

Although I would not go so far as to assert, with Scaliger, that "all controversy proceeds from an ignorance of grammar" . . . yet I am convinced that no person is a competent judge of religious controversy . . . who does not possess a grammatical acquaintance with them [the Christian Scriptures] in their original tongue . . .

If Scaliger had said "from ignorance of Words or of the limits of Words", I am prepared to support the assertion in toto.[1]

12 p 36, pencil, overtraced

Upon these qualifications then I intend for the future to insist. With respect to the moral fitness of young men who apply to me for ordination, I must necessarily depend upon the testimony of others; and a serious and awful responsibility is theirs, who give their solemn attestation to a fact, of such importance to the interest of religion. But of their learning I can judge for myself. . . . Those right and pious intentions, which alone can justify any man in declaring his belief, that he is called by the Holy Ghost to take upon him this office and ministration, are so inconsistent with all apathy and in-

10[2] The "general belief" in the Christian disciples' power of healing is illustrated with "a memorable example" taken from the *Cod. Aboda Zara* f 722: Jacob RHENFERD *Opera Philologica* (Utrecht 1772) 215. (C annotated p 214.) Rhenferd prints the Hebrew original with a Latin translation. "It once happened to Ben Dama the son of R. Ishmael's sister that he was bitten by a serpent and Jacob, a native of Kefar Sekaniah, came to heal him but R. Ishmael did not let him; whereupon Ben Dama said, 'My brother R. Ishmael, let him, so that I may be healed by him: I will even cite a verse from the Torah that he is to be permitted', but he did not manage to complete his saying, when his soul departed and he died." *The Babylonian Talmud: Aboda Zara* tr I. Epstein (1935) 133.

11[1] In 1801 or 1802 C had copied into a notebook (with SH's help) a long extract from Sennertus (including an aphorism by Julius Caesar Scaliger) on the virtue of accuracy of words in thought and action. *CN* I 1000C. He used the passage as motto for the third Bristol essay "On the Principles of Genial Criticism" (1814) and again in *BL* ch 16 (1907) II 22. In precept and practice, C followed the principle that the right use of words is the key to right thinking and right action. In studying the argument and exposition of others he was vigilant to detect the delusive sophisms that, through cynical, credulous, or insensitive use of language, lead to self-deception or fragmented thinking or blur the clarity of judgement and action; in his own writing he characteristically sought to desynonymise terms and patiently to clarify the distinctions that make his thinking lucid and fertile. See esp *AR* (1825) 245; also 35–6.

dolence, that no person who has really formed and acted upon them, will present himself to the Bishop, without a competent store of knowledge, except those who are by nature unfit for the functions of a teacher. While therefore I admit, and not only admit, but earnestly press it upon your remembrance, that no treasures of acquired learning, no original powers of mind, unaccompanied by a sanctified heart, and by a zealous and humble spirit, are to be regarded as qualifying any man for the ministry, I must contend that the want of them, in a competent degree, is to be regarded as an absolute disqualification.

a paragraph equally worthy of, and appropriate for, a Bishop of the Christian & a Prelate of the National Church.

13   p 38, pencil, overtraced, written at the end of the text

Differing from the Bishop's judgement in a few minor points, I should be ashamed of myself if I felt any hesitation in declaring this an admirable Charge and worthy the best ages of our Church—quæ esto perpetua![1] is my unfeigned & fervent prayer.

S. T. C. Sept. 1830—

13[1] "And may she [i.e. the Church] survive forever".

JOHANN FRIEDRICH BLUMENBACH

1752–1840

Über die natürlichen Verschiedenheiten im Menschengeschlechte . . .
übersezt, und mit einigen Zusätzen und erläuternden Anmerkungen
herausgegeben von Johann Gottfried Gruber. Leipzig 1798. 8°.

Gruber's translation into German of Blumenbach's *De generis humani
varietate nativa* (3rd ed 1795).

British Museum C 126 c 6

Bookplate of "Jos.ʰ Henry Green" on p ⁻5 (p–d). "S. T. C." label on the
title-page.

C may have heard of Blumenbach from Thomas Beddoes before going to
Germany in 1798. As soon as he arrived in Göttingen he secured an introduction from Brandes, governor of the university, as well as from Blumenbach's brother-in-law. *CL* I 472. C not only attended Blumenbach's
lectures on physiology and natural history but also had some personal
acquaintance with him and his family, and Blumenbach's son was one of
C's companions on the Harzreise in May 1799. *BL* ch 10 (1907) I 138, *CL*
I 494, 497. See also Carlyon I 161–2, *C in G* 564. From time to time in the
later years C recalled scraps from Blumenbach's lectures and conversation
and used these to illustrate and adorn his own observations: see e.g.
IS 245, *CN* II 2544, III 4047, 4273.

In the summer of 1800 C told Davy that he thought of translating
Blumenbach's *Handbuch der Naturgeschichte* (Göttingen 1799), but he
seems not to have taken the work in hand. See *CL* I 590–1. C was later
disturbed by Blumenbach's refusal to believe in the validity of animal
magnetism. See *Friend* (*CC*) I 154–5n, *CL* IV 883, 886. C's copy of
Blumenbach's *Institutiones physiologicae* (ed not identified) was in
Wordsworth LC 438, 1188.

DATE. Jan 1828 and later: dated in ms Jan 1828 (1). A note in N 26 ff
99ᵛ–100ᵛ of c May 1827 is a less highly developed version of 4; 2–4 appear
to have been written at the same time, after 1 had been written.

COEDITOR. Lore Metzger.

1   pp ⁻3–⁻1, referring to p xx [actually xix–xx] | Dedication to Sir Joseph Banks

. . . wiewohl . . . ich jene gewöhnliche von den Physikotheologen
insgemein ausgeschmückte und gepriesene Wichtigkeit und Würde
in der Lehre von der Stufenfolge der Natur, auf keinen Fall anerken-

nen kann, so gebe ich doch sehr gern das zu, dass diese metaphorischen und allegorischen Spiele einen unläugbaren Nutzen für die Erleichterung der Methode in der Naturgeschichte haben.

Denn sie legen gleichsam den Grund für jedes natürliche System, worin die Dinge nach ihrem Totalhabitu und den äussern Eigenschaften ... geordnet werden ...

[Although ... I can on no account admit that ordinary importance and dignity in the theory of the gradation of nature which is so generally embellished and praised by the natural theologians, nevertheless I gladly concede that these metaphorical and allegorical games are undeniably useful in facilitating the methodology of natural history.

For they establish, as it were, the ground for each natural system in which things are arranged ... according to their total condition and their external characteristics...]

Page XX. Dedic. to Sir J. B.[1]

The fault common to the Systems & Systematizers of Natural Hystery[2] is, ὡς ἔμοι δοκεῖ, not so much the falsehood nor even the unfitness of the guiding principle, diagnostic or teleological, adopted in each; as that each is taking[a] as the only one, to the exclusion of others, and as adequate per se to exhibit the whole of the Subject— the Systematizer forgetting that Nature may pursue a hundred Objects at the same time, and each by a different Line or Chain of Facts from the first Hint of the Purpose to be realized to the Structure or Organ in its most perfect form, & in which the final cause of the whole Series ~~will~~ has attained its full evidence, and determines the place of all the intermediate Facts. For ~~the prophecies of~~ Nature ~~are~~

---

[a] A slip for "taken"

---

[1] Although C had no personal acquaintance with Sir Joseph Banks (1743–1820), except obliquely through Samuel Purkis in Feb 1803 (see *CL* II 919–20), he was aware in 1802 of the splendour of Banks's library and hoped to use it. *CL* II 869. Banks's library went to the BM in 1826. Gifted naturalist, he had accompanied Cook on his first voyage around the world 1768–71 (and paid for the outfitting of *Endeavour*), and would have gone on Cook's second circumnavigation if Cook had not refused to provide what Banks considered an adequate complement of musicians for the voyage. He received the honorary DCL from Oxford at the age of twenty-eight on his return from the Pacific, was elected president of the Royal Society in 1778 (he held the office for forty-one years), and was created baronet in 1781. He provided many exotic trees and plants for the Royal Botanic Garden at Kew, was instrumental in founding the colony at Botany Bay, and financed the *Bounty* for her ill-fated expedition to bring breadfruit trees from Tahiti to the West Indies.

[2] Possibly an ironic conflation of "mystery-history-hysteria": not recorded in *OED*. Cf "hyistorically" in *CN* III 4414.

interpreteds her prophecies by fulfilling them, the first step ~~being the prophecy~~ of the fulfilment constituting the prophecy.—

He forgets too or has perhaps never reflection,[a] that the continuity of Production in Nature is not bound to a continuity in Space—which is a form of *perception*, a *subjective* necessity not a Law of productive Nature. One link may be found in an inhabitant of the Baltic, and the next in the intertropical Pacific Ocean; and nevertheless, the articulation of Nature not broken; and ~~what~~ a class of phænomena which for the Physiographer lie dispersed more widely than the ~~many~~ limbs of Absyrtus, scattered by the fratricidal Enchantress, may for the Physiogonist re-unite and co-organize:[3] and the Proximity, which we seek in vain in Space, be found in Time, ~~and~~ where the ~~facts~~ several Links form, as it were, so many successive Sentences in the same Chapter of the great History of Organic Life.

Even the purposes of artificial Classification would be best attained by several distinct Schemes, and a more exact knowlege of each animal afforded by reference to the place & rank ~~in~~ which it holds, in each, than can be hoped for from any one exclusive System.—But ~~for~~ to arrive at the ends of philosophic Arrangement, there seems to be but one way—namely, to discover and bring together before the mind the ~~many and various~~ principal objects which Nature effects in the process of elevating matter into organization and *manifest* vitality—and under each of these to arrange the facts illustrative of the particular idea, as far as it extends. Thus, to give only one instance. To elicit the *quality~~y~~ies* of matter, to compel the elementary stuffs to reveal their interior Being, and their finer affinities, is an evident End in the organizing process, without reference to which it would be impossible to reduce a multitude of phænomena in the lower orders of Organic Nature to any intelligible ~~n~~ connection—.

S. T. C. Jany 1828.

---

[a] A slip for "reflected"

1[3] The earliest use of "physiogony" cited in *OED* is C's in *LR* III 158—i.e. a note on a front flyleaf of Henry MORE *Theological Works* (1708)—but "physiogonist" is not recorded, and the earliest date given for "physiographer" is rather later than this. C here distinguishes between the physiographer as concerned with the description of natural phenomena (*natura naturata*) and the physiogonist who seeks to explain the production or generation of the natural world (*natura naturans*). See e.g. "On Poesy or Art" in *BL* (1907) II 257, and *P Lects* Lect 13 (1949) 370–1. Absyrtus, son of Aeetes, King of Colchis and of Hypsea, was Medea's brother. When Medea was running away with Jason she tore her brother's body to pieces and strewed his limbs in her father's way to stop his pursuit.

2 p ⁻1 and title-page verso, referring to pp 51–2n | i *Von dem Unterschied zwischen dem Menschen und den übrigen Thieren* § 18

Die Spitzfindigkeiten der alten und neuern Scholastiker über die Sprachen der Thiere sind zahllos. Es wird genug seyn, wenn ich zur Probe Alberten, mit dem Zunamen der Grosse, anführe, der ausser dem Menschen, auch einem menschenähnlichen Affen, dem kleinen Gibbon nämlich, Sprache zuschreibt, jedoch nicht ohne eine merkwürdige Einschränkung. "*Der kleine Gibbon—sagt er—spricht, ob er gleich ein vernunftloses Thier ist, allein er disputirt nicht* (hat nicht zweyerlei Meinung über ein Ding?) *spricht auch nicht von den Dingen im Allgemeinen, sondern seine Töne sind vielmehr auf das Einzelne der Dinge gerichtet, von denen er spricht.*"

[There exist countless sophistries of ancient and modern scholastics regarding animal speech. It will suffice if, as an example, I cite Albertus Magnus, who attributes the power of speech not only to man but also to an anthropoid ape, namely the small gibbon, yet not without a notable limitation. "*The small gibbon,*" he says, "*is able to speak, although it is an animal devoid of reason, but it does not dispute* (has not two different opinions about a thing?) *nor does it speak of things in general; rather its utterances concern the particularity of the things of which it speaks.*"]

P. 51, 52. Note.—Blumenbach cites (for the purpose of ridiculing him) a sentence from Albertus Magnus,[1] in which I find nothing to laugh at, unless it be the making the Gibbon Minor the *only* exception to the position that Man only has Language. Had Albertus said: "If the power of conveying information by intelligible Signs, visual or auditory, would constitute the possession of Language, Language is common ~~is common~~ to many & various Animals; but if we use the word, language, in its only proper sense as the power of conveying not things only but the process and result of our *reflection* thereon, it is predicable of the Human Species alone," he would have said nothing but the truth.—It is an error in expression. Albertus retains the term, Language, while he admits the absence of that which is its essential constituent.[2] But his meaning is right and pertinent.

2[1] Albertus Magnus (1193–1280), *doctor universalis,* Thomas Aquinas's master, was instrumental in uniting theology and the Aristotelian philosophy as the basis of scholasticism. Neither here nor in e.g. *CN* iii 4414 does C say anything about Albertus Magnus independent of the book he is working from.

2[2] See Argens 12 and 13 n 1.

3 p +1, referring to pp 73–7 | § 34

That among the modifying Causes ab extra Climate holds a principal place, no competently informed Naturalist will deny, but yet I can not but think, that Blumenbach attributes more to it,[1] than the fact of the wide extent of Latitudes occupied by the same Race will permit. All Africa for instance, with exception of a mere slip of Coast at the Northern Extreme—and again, all America.

4 pp +1–+4

Without rejecting Bl:'s Pentad of Races[1] but likewise without attributing more to it than the merit of being the most convenient Division hitherto proposed, I am ~~unwilling~~ unwilling to detach ~~it~~ the subject from its historical Staple-ring,[2] the Noachidæ: and would therefore class the Haupt-varietäten, into the Generous, the Degenerous, and the Mixed.[3] If the mythic Curse had not disfraternized the second or middle Brother, ~~the Human Species~~ Mankind would have been, as one Species, so only one *Race*.

Prothesis

Noah

Thesis	Indifference	Antithesis
Shem	Ham	Japhet

The common Character of the Race, Historic   The Semitic or Positive Pole, the Religious-historic, Traditions secured and guarded by Rites, Institutions and Sacred Codes—. The Iapetic or Negative Pole, the literary, philosophic and sciential Historic:—The Hammonic, the Indifference of the Semitic and Iapetic: sciential, philosophic, ~~but~~ and historical, but all in the form ~~of~~ and in the service of

---

3[1] In § 34 pp 73–7.

4[1] Blumenbach's fivefold division of the races, as contrasted with Kant's threefold division, is outlined in N 26 ff 99ᵛ–100ᵛ (c May 1827) and in *TT* 24 Feb 1827: Caucasian (European), Malayan, American, Ethiopian (Negro), Mongolian. See also n 3, below.

4[2] In the "Essays on Method" C spoke of the need for "a *staple*, or *starting-post*" as "the INITIATIVE" in methodical discourse. *Friend (CC)* ɪ 455; see also *BL* ch 12 (1907) ɪ 180. He challenged Eichhorn's use of the word ἀρχή, stating that "ἀρχή signifies... the antecedent *principle*, the ground, & actuating power in one; & not a first effect:—the staple, not a Link". EICHHORN *Neue Testament* COPY A **44**. See also DONNE *Sermons* COPY B **50**.

4[3] The Noachidae—the [three] sons of Noah, implying a threefold division as against Blumenbach's fivefold scheme. *Haupt-varietäten*—chief varieties, i.e. the most general classes. See BLUMENBACH pp 203ff.

Religion—. If therefore the Semitic be distinguished as the religious & the Iapetic as the Sciential, the Hammonic would be characterized as the Symbolic. And as the Degeneracy was gradual, such in fact *was* the character of the Land of Ham, or Ancient Egypt.—At present (and in all times since the commencement of Continued History) we find, First, the Generous or Semito-Iapetic Race— comprizing the Jews, Syrians, Chaldeans, Arabians; the Persians, Greeks, Italians, and all the Gothic Nations, German, Swedish, Norwegian, Danish, English, and Scotch exclusive of the High- landers—.

To this, the Generous Race, we may subjoin, tho' in strict pro- priety a mixed Race yet as the descendant derived from inter- marriages between the descendants of Shem, Japhet, and of Ham by the branch of Canaan & in the earlier and milder form of Degener- acy, ⟨we subject in to the Generous,⟩ as a sort of linked Appendix, the Celtic Tribes—comprizing the Welsh, Erse, the French, since the first Half of the reign of H Louis the 14 XIVth, generally: ⟨and per- haps the Sclavic⟩ In the logical Pentad the Celtic would stand under Synthesis

Thesis	Mesothesis	Antithesis
Semitic	Hammonic	Iapetic
	Synthesis	
	Celtic.	

Degenerous—the Negro.
Mixed or three Products of Intermarriages in different stages of Degeneracy & in different proportions of the three Bloods

Thesis	Mesothesis	Antithesis
Mongolian	Malay	American.

Thus, the Historic or Generous Race ⟨1.⟩ consists of the Race and Co-ordinate Families, and of the Mixed and Subordinate—the Celtic and Sclavonic.

And in like manner the unhistoric and Degenerous consist of
2 The pure—=the Africans; and
3. 4. 5. The Mixed=the Mongolian, the American, and the Malay.

The advantages of this modification of Blumenbach's Scheme is are: that ⟨1.⟩ it is founded on history, at all events on an ancient and justly venerated tradition: 2. that it leaves room for historic com- binations, to be judged by the canons of credibility, and the greater or lesser success of which might be applied, as a test of the Scheme itself:—and 3. it ~~does~~ escapes the error of attributing to the Climate and the accidents of Circumstance a larger share of influence than either sound Philosophy or the Facts themselves will admit.[4] s. t. c.

4[4] In N 36 ff 59ᵛ–60 C complained that Blumenbach's distinction of five races, though given "with classical neatness" in respect of "countenance, and bodily form", had given no distinction "in respect of intellectual faculties, and moral predispositions". For other discussions of the theory of the races of men, see e.g. *P Lects* Lect 8 (1949) 254–5, *Misc C* 6–7, 11–12. A note on the front flyleaves of Steffens *Grundzüge der philosophischen Naturwissenschaft* (Berlin 1806) attempts a schematic classification, with special notation, beginning from the division into Shem, Ham, and Japhet.

GIOVANNI BOCCACCIO

1313–1375

Delle Opere di M. Giovanni Boccacci . . . In questa ultima impressione diligentemente riscontrate con più esemplari, ed all sua vera lezione ridotte, &c. [Edited by Lorenzo Ciccarelli.] Vols I–IV (of 6). Florence [Naples] 1723. 8º.

Vols V and VI were published in Naples in 1724.

N. F. D. Coleridge

Bookplate of DC on I ⁻3 (p–d). A note by EHC is inserted in Vol I: "Vols 1.2.3. Sold to Iredale 1887—Vol. iv. Among Green Books.—Vols 1.2.3. repurchased by me from Iredale. April 1890 4/–."
"S. T. Coleridge" is written vertically on the title-page of Vol IV, possibly in Edith Coleridge's hand.

Two small extracts from Boccaccio show C in Nov 1802 taking his first steps in Italian, with the help of the Wordsworths, in the *Genealogia degli Dei. CN* I 1649, 1653. The lightly annotated copy of the *Opere* may have been acquired in the Mediterranean. For C's general view of Boccaccio see e.g. *CN* III 4388. In Sept 1814 he had tried to interest John Murray in a translation of "the Prose Works of Boccaccio, excluding the Decameron"; but receiving no encouragement either from Murray or from Samuel Rogers, he had abandoned the project by Oct 1815. *CL* III 529, 562; IV 570, 592.

CONTENTS. I, II. *Il Filocopo.* III. *La Fiammetta, Il Corbaccio.* IV. *L'Ameto*; *L'Urbano*; *Origine, Vita, Studij, e costumi del chiarissimo Dante Alighieri*; *Lettere*; *Testamento*.

DATE. c 1808 or later: see *CN* II 2670 and **1** n 3, below. The reference to Boccaccio's *Vita di Dante* in *BL* ch 11 (1907) I 158 coincides with the pagination of this edition. The sentence at the end of **1** may have been a direction to himself for a lecture perhaps as late as Feb 1818.

1 I ⁺3, referring to I 8, pencil | *Il Filocopo*

Quell'eccelso, ed inestimabil principe sommo Giove, il quale degno de' celestiali regni posseditore, tiene l'imperial corona, e lo scettro, per la sua ineffabile provedenzia, avendo a se fatti nolti cari fratelli, e compagni a possedere il suo regno; e conoscendo l'iniquo volere di Plutone, il quale più grazioso, e maggior degli altri, aveva creato, che già pensava di volere dominio maggior, che a lue non conveniva: perlaqualcosa Giove da se il divise, e in sua parte a lui, e a suoi seguaci diede i tenebrosi regni di Dite, circondati dalle stigie paludi, e loro eterno esilio assegnò dal suo lieto regno: e provide di nuove generazioni da riempiere l'abbandonate sedie, e con le proprie mane formò Prometeo, al quale fece dono di cara, e nobile compagnia.

[That mighty and inestimable sovereign prince Jupiter, worthy possessor of the celestial realms, holds by ineffable providence the imperial crown and sceptre, having himself created many cherished brothers and companions to share his kingdom with him. Aware that Pluto, whom he had created greater and more handsome than the others, was already nourishing an iniquitous desire for greater power than he could allow, Jupiter gave Pluto and his followers the twilight regions of Dis, set in stygian marshes, and condemned them to perpetual exile from his own pleasant and gracious kingdom. And to refill the empty seats, he fashioned a new generation and with his own hands shaped Prometheus and made him the gift of a dear and noble wife.]

P. 8. Boccaccio from a sense possibly of poetic justice, herein followed by a goodly company of poetic Sons, Ariosto, Camoens, &c reversed the Scheme of the Early Church and the Fathers of the first Centuries[1]—they, namely, transferred the functions and attributes of the Pagan Gods and Godlings, Goddesses & Nymphs to deified 〈Bishops,〉 Monks, Nuns/—Boccaccio transferred the functions & histories of 〈Hebrew〉 Prophets and Prophetesses and of Christian Saints and Apostles, nay the highest Mysteries & most aweful Objects of Christian Faith, to the names and drapery of Greek & Roman Mythology/[2] Quote p. 8—from Quell'eccelso—to nobile compagnia.[3]

2 I ‑2, referring to I 63

[The instructor Racheo to the prince and the young Biancafiore:] E loro, in breve tempo, insegnato a conoscer le lettere, fece leggere

1[1] For C's interest in Ariosto see ARIOSTO 1 n 4. He seldom mentioned Camoëns. There was a copy of "Poems by Camoens. 1804" in Gillman's library, not shown as C's. *Gillman SC* (1843) 327.

1[2] On 15 Sept 1805, in Malta, C made a note about the "confusion of Heathen & Christian Mythology in the Poets of the 15th Century", citing Ariosto as an instance. *CN* II 2670. In Feb 1818 he included a similar passage in his notes for a lecture: see *CN* III 4388 f 146ᵛ and n.

1[3] The passage specified is printed as textus to this note. The direction "Quote p. 8..." was probably for use in a lecture. Boccaccio may have been discussed in a lecture in the 1808 series: see BM MS Egerton ff 21‑2, in *Sh C* I 183.

!!] il santo libro d'Ovvidio, nel quale il sommo poeta mostra, come i santi fuochi di Venere, si debbano ne' freddi cuori, con sollecitudine accendere.

[And having in a short time taught them to read, he made them read the holy book of Ovid, in which the great poet shows how the sacred fires of Venus can speedily be kindled in the coldest hearts.]

Deeply interesting—but observe, p. 63. l. 33. 35.

The *holy Book*, Ovid's Art of Love!!—This is not the result of mere Immorality.

> Multum, Multum,
> Hic jacet sepultum.[1]

2[1] "Much, Much, Here lies buried". In a footnote to *The Garden of Boccaccio* C noted what lies buried: "I know few more striking or more interesting proofs of the overwhelming influence which the study of the Greek and Roman classics exercised on the judgments, feelings, and imaginations of the literati of Europe at the commencement of the restoration of literature, than the passage in *Il Filocopo* of Boccaccio, where the sage instructor, Racheo, as soon as the young prince and the beautiful girl Biancofiore had learned their letters, sets them to study the Holy Book, Ovid's Art of Love." *PW* (EHC) I 480n.

HERMANN BOERHAAVE
1668–1738

A New Method of Chemistry; including the theory and practice of that art: laid down on mechanical principles, and accommodated to the uses of life. The whole making a clear and rational system of chemical philosophy. To which is prefix'd a critical history of chemistry and chemists, from the origin of the art to the present time. . . . Translated . . . by P[eter] Shaw . . . and E[phraim] Chambers, &c. 2 vols in 1. London 1727. 4º.

A translation, with copious notes added, of *Institutiones et experimenta chemiae* (Paris [?Leyden] 1724)—a book made up from notes taken at Boerhaave's lectures and published without his approval and to his great annoyance.

Not located. Annotations printed from MS TRANSCRIPT. *Gillman SC* (1843) 491.

James Gillman's copy.
   Boerhaave, a celebrated physician of the eighteenth century, held successive professorships at Leyden, in medicine and botany, and in chemistry, and at the same time conducted a lucrative medical practice that drew patients from all over Europe; he won wide acclaim as one of the foremost pre-Lavoisier chemists. For C on the transitoriness of the fame of scientists (including Boerhaave) as compared with poets see *CN* III 4197. Boerhaave's principal works were *Institutiones medicae* (1708), *Aphorismi de cognoscendis et curandis morbis* (1709), and *Elementa chemiae* (1732); the last of these was published to supersede the unauthorised *Institutiones chemiae* and appeared in a translation by Peter Shaw in 1735 as *A New Method of Chemistry* 2nd ed.

MS TRANSCRIPT. VCL BT 37: SC's transcript, prepared for *NTP*.

DATE. c May 1818 or later. Cf *CN* III 4414–4420.

1   I 43 | Pt i. Prolegomena, or the History of Chemistry
[Translators' footnote:] Some time afterward he [a chemist] gave *Helvetius* [physician to the Prince of Orange] a piece of matter about the bigness of a turnip-seed, and promis'd to see him again the next morning: But *Helvetius* wanting patience to wait his coming, cast the matter into six drachms of melted lead, which became converted into gold.

What became of this Gold? Did the gold weigh six drachms? Was it assayed?[a] It is verily a lame testimony.

2 I 43

[Translators' footnote, citing Becher:] The emperor *Ferdinand* III. says he, did himself change three pounds of mercury into two pounds and a half of pure gold; and this by means of a single grain of tincture. This notable transmutation was perform'd at *Prague*; and a medal was struck of the same gold, in memory thereof.

Had Ferd.[b] III. no political design in spreading the belief of the chryso-poietic powers?[c1]

3 I 56 | Pt ii. Theory of Chemistry. First Class of Fossils: Metals

☉ Gold		*Sol,*
☽ Silver		*Luna.*
♀ Copper,		*Venus.*
♂ Iron,		*Mars.*
♃ Tin,	or	*Jupiter.*
♄ Lead,		*Saturn.*
☿ Quick-silver,		*Mercury.*
+ Vinegar		Corrosiveness.
♁ Antimony,		The king's bath.

These characters appear to have been in use among the most ancient chemists.

Platinum might be marked ☉ ♂[d] Gold + Iron or rather Gold + (+ Iron); i.e. Iron acting positively, where + (− Iron) would signify Iron acting privatively, by diminution of specific gravity.[1]

---

[a] MS TRANSCRIPT reads: "assured? (assumed—assumed ⟨assayed⟩)"
[b] MS TRANSCRIPT reads: "Fred."; the inversion of letters is corrected from textus
[c] In both MS TRANSCRIPT and *NTP* this sentence was treated as a continuation of 1 and an inapplicable textus provided   [d] In MS TRANSCRIPT this double symbol is written ♀

2[1] Ferdinand III (1608–57), Holy Roman Emperor from 1637. The coin was struck in 1638 to celebrate his reign. He was a good administrator and had assisted in the overthrow of Wallenstein. "Chryso-poietic"—gold-making; cf "Chrysopoets" in *CN* III 4414 f 8[v].

3[1] Platinum, though used commercially in Europe from 1741, was first scientifically described in 1754 and was introduced to laboratory use by William Wollaston c 1804. The specific gravity (as given by Davy) of gold is c 19.277, of iron c 7.7, of platinum 21.3; the lighter iron, "acting positively" on gold, apparently produces a higher specific gravity. In 1818 C spoke of the metals "as hitherto not decompounded and probably all *humanly* indecomponible, in the present epoch of Nature. Possibly, they are different proportions of Carbon and Azote indifferenced by the minimum of Hydrogen or Oxygen." *CN* III 4420. Cf BÖHME 17.

4 I 58

Quicksilver evidently shews gold in the middle, or body of it, silver at top, or in the face, and a corrosive at bottom: accordingly all the *adepts* say of mercury, that it is gold at heart, whence its heaviness; that its outside is silver, whence its white colour: but that there is a pernicious, corrosive sulphur adhering to it, denoted by the cross; that if its brightness, and its corrosive could be taken away, it would remain gold; that the quantity of sulphur is here so great, as to render it wholly combustible by fire; that the more 'tis burnt, the nearer it comes to gold; and that were it perfectly calcined and purified, and its colour changed, it would be gold.

Here the sulphur must be supposed to mean the excess of Light, Light not neutralized by Gravitation super-oxygenated.—From this point of view, viz. that the thing (*phænomenon fixum sive mortuum*) was taken symbolically for the Powers, and the Materia (*Phæno-menon fluxionale*),[1] as the magnetic and electrical materiæ, the Alchemists may perhaps be decypherable into intelligible notions.[2]

S. T. Coleridge.

5 I 60

[Translator's footnote:] He [M. Geoffroy] adds, that the ashes of all vegetables afford iron, which it would be hard to suppose lodg'd

[1] "Phenomenon fixed or dead" (the thing); "fluxional phenomenon" (Materia). With the second phrase, cf "fluxional body" in BROOKE ANNEX, the "material particles" of which are "in a continual flux even as a column of smoke". The distinction is between (*a*) "the thing", matter differentiated; and (*b*) "Materia", phenomena in flux, matter undifferentiated ("chaos" in cosmological terms). "The thing" corresponds to the dynamic term "the Powers", and "Materia" corresponds to the dynamic term "the magnetic and electrical materiæ". In C's terms "the Powers" are light and gravitation (*CN* III 4420), and the "materiæ" may be the four elements explicated in *TL*— carbon and azote (magnetic), oxygen and hydrogen (electric). But the cor-respondence of these terms to an alchemical scheme does not appear. If (as seems to be proposed) for the alchemists "the body" represents the "immaterial" powers of light and gravitation, the degree of differentiation would be reversed.

[2] Cf *CN* III 4414 f 10, adapted and condensed from Boerhaave I 9–37: "Sometimes it seems as if the Al-chemists wrote [like] the Pythagoreans on Music—viz—metaphysical, in-audible Music, as the basis of the Audible—It is clear that by Sulphur they meant the solar Light or Rays, and by Mercury the principle of Ponderability—so that the Theory is the same with that of the Heraclitic Physics, or the modern German Natur-philosophie, which derives all things from Light and Gravitation, each bipolar. Grav.=N. and S. or Attraction and Repulsion: Light= E and W. or Contraction and Dilation. —Gold being the Tetrad, or inter-penetration of both, as Water is the Dyad of Light, and Iron the Dyad of Gravitation—". Cf *CN* II 4419–4420, partly from Boerhaave I 70–7.

in the plant it self, and must rather be deem'd the effect of the fire in calcination. Again, clay does not shew the least sign of any metal, work it how you will, without mixing; but add linseed oil to it, and by fire you will have a metal, which is no other than real iron.

The clay of course contained the iron, the linseed oil supplying the carbon for its separation. But with regard to plants and to the Blood, it is more doubtful, it would be so very difficult to weigh with sufficient accuracy the various volatile products, with the oxygen used in the burning.[1] S. T. C.—[a]

6 i 72 | Mercury, or, Quick-Silver

The *second character* of mercury is to be the most fluid of all bodies, *i.e.* its parts separate, and recede from each other by the smallest force; consequently, of all bodies, it is that whose parts cohere the least, or are the least tenacious; and therefore, of all others the least ductile, and malleable.

Here is an instance from which we may learn the utility of a just definition. Mercury is *è contra* the least fluid of all bodies, under an equal specific portion of heat—i.e. equally fused. For the only tenable definition of a fluid is a body the parts of which are not interdistinguishable by figure. Now mercury retains its globoseness *ad infinitum*.—So I reasoned but I see the defect of the logic (tho' I nevertheless retain my objection to the proper fluidity of quick-silver). Globoseness is the μορφη αμορφος,[1] the figure that necessarily results from the indifference or equilibrium of all dimensions. Schelling's definition of fluid is incorrect because inadequate.[2] An

---

[a] All the notes from here onward are signed "S. T. C.", but that seems to be SC's way of marking off C's notes from their textus

5[1] Blumenbach reported oxide of iron in minute quantities in blood: *Institutions of Physiology* (1817) 8. Elliotson added in a note (ibid 10): "It has been generally supposed that iron existed in the red particles of the blood as a subphosphate. Berzelius informs us...that he has never discovered iron nor lime in the entire blood, though both are so abundant in its ashes."

6[1] "Shapeless shape", "figureless figure"; cf τò ἄπειρον (unlimited, undifferentiated) in BÖHME **31** n 7. For "Globoseness" see BÖHME **24**. See also "*Prometheus*" (*LR* II 338), *CN* III 3632, and **9**, below.

6[2] See e.g. SCHELLING *Ueber den Begriff der speculativen Physik* (Jena & Leipzig 1799) p 26 (not annotated); tr: "The Formless = the Fluid. What is fluid (of the second order at least, which owes its fluidity to a higher principle) is not the absolutely formless (= the μη ov of the old Greek physicists), but *that which is receptive of any form*, and for that very reason formless (αμορφον). What is fluid must in general be defined as a mass, *in which no part can be distinguished from another by figure*....The main principle is: *the similarity of actions* (and accordingly of attractions too) *in the fluid in all directions*."

equilibrium of the whole which prevents its being parts at all, but by accidental force ab extra, not favored but counteracted by the essential character of the proper fluid. In short melting is not fluidizing.[3]

7 I 73

The parts of water do not divide so readily as those of quick-silver; and the parts of oil much less; there is a certain tenacity even in the parts of spirit of wine, which resists a separation; but there is scarce any cohesion at all, in the parts of mercury.

It is in vain to reason on these facts till we have formed *distinct* conceptions of the difference between adhesion and cohesion, attraction and contraction, dilation and repulsion, and of centrality from them all.[1]

8 I 74

[Translators' footnote:] Notwithstanding mercury receives such a degree of cold, its great separability, and fluidity prevents its congealing. Mr. *Boyle* tried various ways to bring it to freeze, by making an extream cold, and exposing an exceedingly thin skin of mercury thereto; but without effect. *Hist. of Cold.*

A warning against the use of the word, "extreme" whereas we now know, that even that degree of cold which is compatible with human life will freeze quicksilver.[1]

9 I 120 | Vulgar Stones

[Translators' footnote on "Origin and Formation of Stones":] ... A fluid seed seems a contradiction. True, a seed may be contain'd in a fluid vehicle; which we actually suppose is the case in animals: but

6[3] In c Aug–Sept 1818 C noted: "An additional argument on my side against the eminent Fluidity of Quicksilver (see Boerhave's Chemistry (M[r] Gillman's Copy) and my marginal note)/— that with this exception (relatively to Boerhave who asserts its fluidissimity) the two Series, of Galvanico-Electric Non-conductors and conductors consist all of solid bodies—Hence & from many other causes I assert that 1. solid is ℀ to hollow not to fluid—and 2. that if Quicks. were a fluid, it would be a *dry* fluid." The note is then developed as a comprehensive inquiry into "the relations and complex antagonisms of the modifying to the substantial Powers". *CN* III 4420.

7[1] On clear and distinct ideas see e.g. *CN* I 902, 1016, 1714, 1715, III 3744.

8[1] Mercury freezes at $-40°$ F., as C could have known from Rees's *Cyclopaedia* and many other contemporary sources, but perhaps more memorably from any account he had read of the Arctic travellers, especially Samuel Hearne and John Franklin.

the proper seed or stamen it self, inevitably must be a solid. This is obvious from the very notion of a seed, which is nothing but a little organiz'd body, wherein all the parts of the future production are contained in small: the production it self is only the seed enlarg'd, so as to shew its several parts to the eye. . . . 'Tis no more possible for the seed, *e. gr.* of a tree, to be fluid, and yet remain a seed, than for the tree it self to be fluid, while a tree; so that the seminal origin of stones does not seem tenable.

This question has been more recently a subject of controversy between the adherents of the justly celebrated John Hunter,[1] and the no less deservedly celebrated Blumenbach, who has adopted this argument, viz. the inconsistency of fluidity with organization, in the very conceptions of the two terms.[2] But I doubt the validity of the argument. The *conception* of a Fluid is not a, or the, Fluid: but a logical *abstract*. First, it must be inquired whether there exist in nature any substance adequate to the generic definition? And if this were affirmed, yet 2[ndly] whether the Blood, Semen &c, nay, whether the whole of an organized body during Life, be not gradative[3] media between solid figure accurately (*Rigid*)[a] and Fluid? It is clear to me that nothing vital is properly either Rigid or Fluid, but mere approximations to the one or the other, either of which realized would be death. If a perfect fluid be defined as quantitative Indifference, a fixed body or solid as quantitative Difference, a vital Organism must be

a Word not included in *NTP* text; the customary way for SC to record a doubtful reading for later consideration was to place it underlined in parenthesis

9[1] John Hunter (1728–93), surgeon and comparative anatomist, whose collections are still an ornament of the Royal College of Surgeons and in whose honour the first annual Hunterian Oration was given in 1813. Two of his pupils were Joseph Adams (1756–1818), who recommended C to Gillman's care, and John Abernethy (1764–1831), who had cured De Q of drug addiction in Jan 1808 and whom C knew from 1818 onward, his work having an important influence on *TL*. In 1818 C spoke of Hunter as "the profoundest, we had almost said the only, physiological philosopher of the latter half of the preceding century". *Friend* (*CC*) I 493n; cf 473–5. C owned a copy of J. Adams *An Illustration of Mr Hunter's Doctrine* (1814).

9[2] See, however, the long note to *Friend* (*CC*) I 493–4, in which C considers Blumenbach and Hunter as in general agreement in their theory of life, as opposed to "Stahl and others". Hunter's docrtine, which C considered "a genuine philosophic IDEA", was that the principle of life is "'independent of organization,' which yet it animates, sustains, and repairs". Blumenbach, in ch 40 of his *Institutiones physiologicae* (the handbook for the lectures that C attended)—for which see also *Friend* (*CC*) I 194—gives an account of the *nisus formativus* acting upon the fluid in the uterus and shaping the hitherto shapeless matter. See also BÖHME 79 and nn 2, 6, and *L&L* 16–23.

9[3] "Step by step". *OED* ascribes the word to John Brown (1818) and to J. H. Green *Vital Dynamics* (1840).

defined participially as a continuous Differencing of the Indifference equal to a continued Indifferencing of the Difference. Without the former no *figure*, without the latter no *Life*. The whole controversy therefore is resolved into a pseudological Logomachy or a dispute about words from a misappropriation of the words in dispute.

10   I 125 | Fifth Class of Fossils: Sulphurs

It must be owned, however, that spirit of wine, which is a sulphur, is miscible with water; but it is owing to this, that the sulphur in spirit of wine is so changed, and its parts so attenuated, and divided, as to insinuate themselves among the parts of the water, where they would not otherwise be admitted.

A good instance of a subjective and perhaps arbitrary definition understood in a term with the concrete represented by the same term. *A* sulphur with Sulphur—i.e. Brimstone.*

* A chemical Theorist might even now so extend the use of the word *sulphureous* as to include oil and alcohol, as the two antithetic proportions of carbon & hydrogen; but in no state of the science could he find an excuse for defining a genus by one of its species.[1]

11   I 126

The second [common sulphur] is *arsenic*; the most fatal of the whole tribe, as destroying all animals, both man and beast; which the word itself imports, being compounded of ανερ, man, and νικαω, I overcome.

Then it must have been *Andronicon*. Even from αρσην masculus, it would be arsenīcum, not arsĕnĭcum. Probably it is simply from αρσην—the masculine, i.e. the active, penetrating.[1]

12   I 126

[Translators' footnote:] Sulphur contains some parts which render it more inflammable than either nitre or oil; and yet abounds with acid, and vitriolic particles, which strongly resist the flame in several other bodies: the fire of sulphur, beside its common effect, seen in matches, in another capacity, acts by means of its acidity upon some

10[1] See generally the opening pages of *TL*, and the "Essays on Method" in *Friend (CC)* I 448–524.

11[1] The word ἄνηρ (man) has the root ἀνδρ- when declined or compounded. The word ἄρσην is old Attic for ἄρρην (male), hence C's "masculus". But, C argues, if in "arsenic" the -*nic* were from νικάω (conquer), the *i* would be long, whereas (as he shows in his scanning of "arsĕnĭcum") this Greek adjectival suffix has a short *i*.

metals, especially iron; and also on red rose-leaves, which are turn'd white by its fumes. *Boyle Useful. of Exper. Philos.*

Instance for Logic.[1] Here fumes are taken = Sulphur, without proof. Now *we* know that the Fumes are Sulphur + Oxygen, and B. ought to have seen, that the Fumes *might* be Sulphur + x, or an unknown something.

13 ı 236 | The History of Fire

[*Subterraneous parts the hotter the deeper they are.*] Thus, they who dig mines, wells, *&c.* constantly observe, that while they are yet but a little below the surface, they find it a little cool; as they proceed lower, it grows much colder, as being then beyond the reach of the sun's heat; insomuch that water will freeze almost instantaneously, and hence the use of ice-houses, *&c.* But a little lower, *viz.* about 40 or 50 foot deep, it begins to grow warmer; so that no ice can bear it; and then the deeper they go, still the greater the heat...

Excellent examples might be selected for my Practical Logic, *de terminis haud adhuc exhaustis*,[1] or A = B.C.D. taken as A = A.

12[1] C's scheme for his "Logic" was outlined as early as Jun 1803: *CL* ıı 947, *CN* ı 1646. He was speaking of it in Oct 1809 and again in Jan 1817: *CL* ııı 238–9, ıv 701. For a convenient, but editorially early, summary of ms references to the "Logic", see *L&L* 69–70n, which includes this marginal note and **13** following.

13[1] "Concerning limits not yet exhausted".

JAKOB BÖHME

1575–1624

The Works of Jacob Behmen, the Teutonic Theosopher. ... To which is prefixed, the life of the author. With figures, illustrating his principles, left by the Reverend William Law, M.A. 10 pts in 4 vols. London 1764, 1764, 1772, 1781. 4º.

Edited by G. Ward and T. Langcake, reprinted in the main from John Sparrow's translations. The curious plates to Vol I, and certain "figures" in the text, are Law's only contribution.

British Museum C 126 k 1

Inscribed by John Duke Coleridge on I ⁻3: "C Coleridge Heaths Court 1892 This book belonged to S. T. C." "S. T. C." label originally on the title-page of each volume.

Although there is no presentation inscription, this set was evidently given to C by De Q in Feb 1808. See *CL* III 48, *CN* III 3263, 3276. De Q reported that some months after giving the volumes to C he had seen "one volume, at least, overflowing, in parts, with the commentaries and the *corollaries* of Coleridge". *De Q Works* v 183; cf II 140.

The intricately devised plates to Vol I, with cut-out overlays to provide a series of transformations within each basic figure, are a striking feature of this "Law" edition; C remarked upon them in late summer 1809 (*CN* III 3526), and Yeats was fascinated by them when he was making his edition of Blake nearly ninety years later.

A note in pencil on III ⁻2—"Self denial p 244"—may be in J. H. Green's hand. Passages are marked in pencil, evidently not by C, on II i 18–19, 48; ii 10; iii 17–18, 91, 92; iv 8, 9, 12, 22; III i 16–17, 28, 29–30, 143, 244–5; IV i 156, 157, 169. Parts of I ii, III i, IV i, the whole of III ii, and the last four works in IV were still unopened in 1969. The volumes were rebound by the BM in 1970: see **1** n *a*, below. Before the rebinding, there was a loose sheet at III i 372/3; this has now disappeared, but see ANNEX, below. On III i 84 C has corrected "Rampant" to "Rampart" in the phrase "the Devil built up his *Fort*, Rampant, and Strong Hold".

Jakob Böhme, born near Görlitz in Upper Lusatia, gave up his craft of shoemaking when a visionary experience in adult life persuaded him that he should devote his whole time to meditation on divine things. In c 1612 he began to circulate in ms his revelations on man, God, and nature under the title of *Aurora*—a book that showed a remarkably detailed knowledge of the Bible and of alchemy. Although his book was condemned by local ecclesiastical authority, Böhme continued to pursue his inquiries into the origin of things and particularly into the nature and origin of evil. He wrote thirty-one further books and essays, of which only one small volume, *The Way to Christ*, was published in his lifetime; a collective edition of his writings was published in Amsterdam in 1675. Between 1645 and 1662 English translations by John Sparrow, John Ellistone, Humphrey Blunden, and Charles and Durand Hotham were published separately in London. The edition that C annotated was the focus of interest in Böhme in England, being the only approximately collective English edition available in C's lifetime.

In Jul 1817 C told Ludwig Tieck, with whom he had discussed Böhme when they first met in 1805, that there were certain ideas about light and sound that "Before my visit to Germany in September, 1798, I had adopted (probably from Behmen's Aurora, which I had *conjured over* at School)". *CL* iv 751. An early reading is implicitly confirmed by the title "Jacob Behmen" as fourth item in a list of C's projected writings drawn up in Dec 1795–Jan 1796, and there are signs that the early reading, even if only of the *Aurora*, was more than casual. *CN* i 174, 1000E and n. In Nov 1803 C included Böhme in a list of "Revolutionary Minds" that he intended to write about: *CN* i 1647; cf 1835 f 66. See also *BL* ch 9 (1907) i 95, and SCHELLING *Philosophische Schriften* (Landshut 1809) 442. On 21 Jan 1810, having acquired his set of Böhme two years before, he wrote Lady Beaumont a comprehensive opinion of Böhme's mind and work: *CL* iii 278–9. A notebook entry of 4 Feb 1810 records a dream "with a sense of fright" and extends the thought of the letter: "J. Boehmen's mind may be well illustrated from Dreams—there is meaning, important meaning, in both; both the exponents are almost accidental . . .". *CN* iii 3692.

CONTENTS

MS TRANSCRIPTS. (*a*) VCL H 6 (76 notes) and BT 21 (120 notes): EHC transcripts, confined to **1–134** in Vol I—i.e. almost all the notes on *Aurora* and *The Three Principles*, all the notes transcribed in H 6 being repeated in BT 21. This transcript (i.e. BT 21) is mentioned by John Muirhead in *Coleridge as Philosopher* (1930) 271 and was used by Alice D. Snyder, being the only version of the Böhme marginalia available to scholars until the Ottery Collection was transferred to the BM.

(*b*) University of California at Berkeley, 78 Rare Books Dept: ms facsimile, in an unidentified hand in a copy of the same edition as C's. R. F. Brinkley "Coleridge Transcribed" *RES* XXIV (1948) 219 suggested that the hand might be Mrs Gillman's. The notes, showing many omissions, are confined to Vol I. The copying is much less accurate than MS TRANSCRIPT(*a*), and after the first few pages most of the Greek has been omitted. In Vol III there is some underlining, and in Vol IV a few notes in another hand that do not correspond to anything in the BM original.

DATE. Feb 1808 to 15 Mar 1826. C acquired the volumes in Feb 1808. The date "1800" in **23**, anticipating the date of acquisition, needs special consideration: see **23** n 3, below. Dated notes appear in Vols I and III: Vol I—1817 (**31**), 27 Jun 1817 (**23** PS), 19 Jul 1817 (**58**), Aug 1818 (**1**), 27 Aug 1818 (**52**), Sept 1818 (**92**), 19 Oct 1818 (**137**); Vol III—9 and 10 Nov 1819 (**157** PS), 20 Jul 1822 (**149**), 15 Mar 1826 (**144**).

C evidently did not annotate these volumes by working methodically through them from beginning to end, but concentrated on certain works— esp *Aurora* and *The Three Principles*—and returned to them from time to time, sometimes reading continuously, sometimes sporadically and locally, sometimes paying close attention to his own notes, adding postscripts and new notes as his reflection extended and matured. In view of C's warning in two notes of Aug 1818 (**1, 52** PS) that a reader of the Böhme marginalia must treat with caution the notes written at "earlier dates", it would be desirable to be able to identify all the earlier notes that represent "any positions or opinions contrary" to what he took to be clear and stable in Aug 1818. A number of the notes are dated in ms (see above), and a number of others include internal evidence that is some help in dating; but the dating of many individual notes is highly problematical. The concentration of dated notes in 1817–18 does not conceal the fact that many were written much earlier and some later: once C had acquired these four volumes they were always with him.

Certain clusters of references to Böhme in *CN* and *CL* offer suggestive parallels to some of the notes. For Feb 1808–Oct 1810—*CN* III 3263, 3276, 3354, 3526, 3692, 3975; for 1815–16 (associated with a work on Böhme originally intended in 1810 as a supplement to *The Friend*)—*CN* III 4189, *CL* IV 590, 592, 656, 687, *CRB* I 88, 107; for c Jun 1817–Oct 1818 (summaries of the polar scheme of creation and the relation of God to the world)—*CN* III 4359, 4449, *CL* IV 742, 750–1, 775, 804–9, 873–6.

Many of the notes in this series, and particularly the most intricate and puzzling ones (e.g. **6, 24, 28, 172, 178**), may be seen as points of temporary focus in a continuously developing heuristic process in which C was seeking either to render the relation of God to the world or to find a symbolic scheme for representing all phenomena in the organic and inorganic realms. As part of the mental landscape of these notes, *CN* III 4418–4420 and three letters to C. A. Tulk and J. H. Green Sept 1817–Sept 1818 (*CL* IV 767–75, 804–9, 873–6) are helpful. Many of the notes are informed by C's developing, variable, and waning relations with the *Naturphilosophie*, especially the work of Schelling, Fichte, Steffens, Oken, and Eschenmayer (to mention the ones he annotated most fully). But C's mind tends to assimilate and transform whatever it takes up, and the dates of many of these notes are uncertain; his relations with the *Naturphilosophie* in these marginalia are resonant and suggestive rather than derivative; they are too complex and pervasive to allow us to ascribe with much confidence particular details in the marginalia to specific locations in the large and difficult literature of *Naturphilosophie*. A few tentative elucidations have been offered, usually in the form of parallels from C's other writings, occasionally by venturing a clarifying gloss or summary.

COEDITOR. Richard Haven.

1   I, inserted leaf[a]

To the Reader

I earnestly intreat of the Reader into whose possession or under whose perusal this Copy of Jacob Behmen's Writings should happen to fall, and who should feel disposed[b] to peruse the numerous marginal annotations added by me in my own hand-writing, that he would *first of all* read over attentively the Note occupying the Margins of pages 125, 126, and 127[1]—lest perchance I should lead him into errors from which I have extricated myself.[2] And may the Spirit and ⟨the⟩ Word with the Leading of the Father of Lights[3] enable him to ~~find~~ know in himself the truth of the Truths contained in

[a] A sheet of paper that may originally have been a flyleaf and was at some time tipped in to Vol I later became detached and was folded horizontally into the front of Vol I until all 4 vols were rebound by the BM in 1970; the sheet was then tipped in to Vol I between the title-page and sig A2 (Advertisement), with slight loss to the right-hand edge of the pencil note **2**. On one side of the sheet, now recto, two notes are written: **1** and **65** (which refers to I i 219 and has therefore been placed in the sequence of the text). On the other side of the sheet, now verso, **2** is written in pencil, and is apparently the latest of the three notes to be written   [b] Final *d* added by C in pencil

1[1] See **52**, below, the postscript to which is dated 27 Aug 1818.

1[2] In **52** C is concerned to trace the errors in the theory of creation by which Böhme—and C himself—"approaches so perilously near to Pantheism". The end of the last of the "Essays on Method" (*Friend—CC*—I 519–24), in which C examines "the ground-work...of all true philosophy"—an essay that he regarded as one of his most important—is open to mis-

interpretation through the same errors that he here discerned in Böhme. In 1818 he sent letters to several of his friends with a long "paragraph... unfortunately omitted", which is written into the annotated copies, "it's object being to preclude all suspicion of any leaning towards Pantheism, in any of it's forms". (*CL* IV 894. For the omitted paragraph and its variants see *Friend* (*CC*) I 522–3n.

1[3] James 1.17.

these Volumes, clarified from the~~ir~~ Errors of the same—and to find
within what he will in vain seek from without!⁴

> S. T. Coleridge
> under the shield and shelter of ~~m~~ his
> affectionate Friends, James and Anne Gillman,
Highgate, August ad finem, 1818.⁵

2 I, inserted leaf,[a] pencil

To the contemptuous ⟨and therefore unreasonable:
for what rea[son] for continuing to rea[d] what you despis[e]?⟩[b]
Reader

Plato and Aristotle both reprehend this point in Anaxagoras, that
having, to his immortal honor in the history of Philosophy, first
established the position of a supermundane ΝΟΥΣ, ως το πρωτον,
μεσον και ύστατον¹ he yet never makes any regular or determinate Use
of this supreme Agent in the course of his System, but does as the
Poets do who introduce a God only when their invention fails them,
or their Plot has been unskillfully laid—that is, he never introduces
the NOUS (= Pure Intelligence) but as a Deus ex machinâ to cut a
knot, he is not able to untie.²

The fault of the great German Theosopher lies in the opposite

---

[a] See **1** n *a*, above
[b] These letters, now lost from the ms, were present when the note was originally transcribed by the editor

1⁴ Cf *CN* III 3946: " . . . the words of
Lady Guyon['s] first Confession. . . .
Speaking of her discomforts, doubts &c
—'It is, because you seek without what
you have within.' " See also *SM* (*CC*)
92–3 and n 8.

1⁵ For a similar affectionate formula
written in Jul 1829 see BIBLE COPY B
135.

2¹ "MIND [or "Pure Intelligence"
in C's phrase below], as the first,
middle, and last". Cf *AR* (1825) 142.
The Greek phrase seems to be C's,
although reminiscent of many other
passages pre-Socratic, Aristotelian, and
biblical. For C's use of νοῦς and its
cognate adjectives νοερός and νοητός
see **122** n 4, below, and e.g. *CN* III
3862 and n.

2² In *Phaedo* 97ʙ–98ʙ Plato says
that according to Anaxagoras "It is
mind that produces order and is the

cause of everything. . . . As I went on
with my reading I saw that the man
[Anaxagoras] made no use of intelligence, and did not assign any real
causes for the ordering of things, but
mentioned as causes air and ether and
water and many other absurdities." Tr
Fowler (LCL 1914). See also Aristotle
Metaphysics 985ª18–22: "Anaxagoras
avails himself of Mind as an artificial
device (μηχανή) for producing order,
and drags it in whenever he is at a loss
to explain some necessary result; but
otherwise he makes anything rather
than Mind the cause of what happens."
Tr Tredennick (LCL 1933). C had
copied out the Aristotle passage
from Cudworth in late 1796: *CN* I
208. Aristotle's word μηχανή is the
"machine" of C's *deus ex machina*. See
also *P Lects* Lect 4 (1949) 145–6, and cf
Friend (*CC*) I 516n.

extreme. But this ought not to excite thy scorn. For the *Attempt* is dictated by Reason, nay even by Consistency; and if he have failed by soaring too high, magnis tamen excidit ausis[3]—and in no spirit of pride did he soar—but being a poor unlearned Man he contemplated ~~the~~ Truth and the forms of Nature thro' a luminous Mist, the vaporous darkness rising from his Ignorance and accidental peculiarities of fancy and sensation, but the Light streaming into it from his inmost Soul. What wonder then, if in some places the Mist condenses into a thick smoke with a few wandering rays darting across it & sometimes overpowers the eye with a confused Dazzle?[4] The true wonder is, that in so many places it thins away almost into a transparent Medium, and Jacob Behmen, *the Philosopher*, surprizes us in proportion as Behmen, the Visionary, had astounded or perplexed us. For Behmen was indeed a Visionary in two very different senses of that word. Frequently does he mistake the dreams of his own overexcited Nerves, the phantoms and witcheries from the cauldron of his own seething Fancy, for parts or symbols of a universal Process;[5] but frequently likewise does he give incontestible proofs, that he possessed in very truth

"The Vision and Faculty divine!"[6]

And even when he wanders in the shades, ast tenet umbra Deum.[7]

Read then in meekness—lest to read him at all, which might be thy folly, should prove thy Sin.

S. T. Coleridge

3   1 i xii | The Life of Jacob Behmen

There is a small Market-Town in *Upper Lusatia*, called *Old Seidenburg*, distant from *Gorlitz* about a Mile and half, in which lived a Man whose Name was *Jacob*, and his Wife's Name was *Ursula*. People they were of the poorest Sort, yet of sober and honest Behaviour. In the Year 1575 they had a Son, whom they named *Jacob*. This was the divinely-illuminated JACOB BEHMEN, the *Teutonic*

2³ Ovid *Metamorphoses* 2.328: "Yet he failed in a daring attempt".

2⁴ Cf *CN* I 528: "The sunny mist, the luminous gloom of Plato—". Here C's imagery of the mind interfuses with Böhme's: see also *AR* (1825) 383–5. For the way "objects look gigantic thro' a mist" see *Lects 1795* (*CC*) 52 and n, *Watchman* (*CC*) 125 and n.

2⁵ See *CN* III 3692 and cf *CL* VI 715 for a link with Swedenborg. See also

P *Lects* Lect 11 (1949) 329ff and *Friend* (*CC*) I 140–6 (II 117–21).

2⁶ WW *Excursion* I 79: *WPW* V 10.

2⁷ "But the shadow contains a God". The same passage, adapted from Statius *Thebaid* 4.425, is given at greater length in "*Prometheus*": "Ivimus ambo | per densas umbras: at tenet umbra Deum." *LR* II 349. Cf "nec caret umbra Deo" in *CN* I 1179.

Theosopher ... He ... died there in 1624, being near fifty years of Age ...

Elizabeth began to reign 1558—Shakspere born 1564/ about 11 years before Behmen; ⟨who was⟩ born in 17th of Eliz.—Shakspere died in 1616, in the 14th year of James I. Behmen in the 22nd year.— Giordano Bruno died 1601—when born, I do not recollect.[1]— ⟨32 years after the first Printing of Copernicus's works, in 1543.—⟩[a2]

4 i i xii

For in the Heat of Mid-Day, retiring from his Playfellows to a little stony Crag just by ... finding an Entrance, he went in, and saw there a large Wooden Vessel full of Money, at which Sight, being in a sudden Astonishment, he in Haste retired, not moving his Hand to it, and came and related his Fortune to the rest of the Boys, who coming with him, sought often and with much Diligence an Entrance, but could not find any. But some Years after, a foreign Artist ... skilled in finding out magical Treasures, took it away, and thereby much enriched himself, yet perished by an infamous Death, that Treasure being lodged there, and covered with a Curse to him that should find and take it away.

Was this an allegory of Behmen's—expressing that a Treasure had been discovered to him which none of his Fellows could find out even the Entrance to—but that as far as mere Philosophy was concerned, Bruno, who was burnt alive at Rome, & who published several of his Works in Germany, had mastered it ?/[1]

---

[a] The last phrase "32 years ... in 1543" has been squeezed in at the end of the note after **4** (in a different colour of ink) had already been written

3[1] Giordano Bruno, born in 1548, died at the stake in Rome on 17 Feb 1600; in *Friend (CC)* II 81 C has the date right. See also **4** n 1 and **52** n 16.

3[2] The tradition is that the first printed copy of *De revolutionibus orbium celestium* was placed in Copernicus' hands on the day of his death, 24 May 1543. A date thirty-two years later would be in 1575, the year of Böhme's birth. C's reason for thinking of Copernicus is presumably that one of the charges brought against Bruno by the Inquisition was that his system was based on the Copernican heliocentric scheme.

4[1] On the possible connexion between Böhme and Bruno see **52** and n 16, below. C for some time planned to include both in a study of "Pantheists and Mystics" that was to be part of the projected Logosophia; the Böhme marginalia were perhaps a preliminary to that study. See *CL* III 279; IV 590, 592, 656, 687; and for the projected life of Bruno, *Friend (CC)* II 81–2 (I 117–18). As early as Nov 1804 he had written in N 21 an incomplete list of Bruno's works. *CN* II 2264. In Sept 1809 he referred again to eleven works of Bruno, only six of which he said he had read, and the note was repeated in 1818. *Friend (CC)* II 82n (I 118n). Eight of Bruno's books

5 I i xv, pencil

"For I had a thorough View of the Universe, as in a Chaos, wherein all Things are couched and wrapped up, but it was impossible for me to explain the same."

explicate, develope, unfold—Germanicè auseinderandersetzen.[1] When a modern Orthodoxist of the Protestant Arminian Church will explain to me what he means by Inspiration, Inspired Penmen, Inspired Writ, &c, by something more than by *synonimes*—i.e. when he *explains* ⟨the *sense*,⟩ and not merely *construes* the *words* by help of Entick's English Dictionary[2]—then I will tell him whether I think Behmen's Writings, or the Author, *inspired*—or any portion of the former grounded in *unaided* & *partial* recollections of inspired Truths: for as such, the Author himself offers them to us—& therefore as not infallible.

AURORA

6 I i 22/23, 24,[a] beginning on the blank page facing the opening of *Aurora*

As the conditions, under which alone a man may hope to interpret the writings of this heavenly-minded Seeer, the first in account is, doubtless, a heart purified of Scorn, which is the closest Compound of the two worst elements, Self-lust, and Brother-Hate/ Now he that lusteth for himself (for Self-*love* is a Lie and Flattery in all creatures, inasmuch as God alone can *love* himself as himself) he lusteth after a lie, and a false imaginary center.[1] Eccentric and elliptical he is the Slave of two Foci, Lust and Hate, the Synthesis of which is Scorn—

> [a] Between p 22 (last page of Contents) and p [23] (first page of *Aurora*) the original binder has bound in a leaf of 4 pages: [1]r blank, [1]v engraved figure, [2]r explanation of figure, [2]v blank. C's note begins on p [2]v filling that page completely, continues on the first page of *Aurora*, and ends on p 24

were published in Germany. In c May 1810 C wished to secure from Malta or elsewhere a copy of *De progressu et lampade venatoria logicorum* ([Wittenberg] 1588). *CN* III 3825. If, as seems to be the case, **4** is an "early" note of c 1810, it looks as though the reading of Böhme had brought C back again to thoughts of Bruno.

5[1] Lit. "to set forth in distinct elements". C used the same German word in N 29 f 112v, translating it (as here) "unfold"; see also **109**, below.

5[2] John Entick (c 1703–73), schoolmaster, compiled a number of elementary English and Latin diction-

aries for school use. His *New Spelling Dictionary* (1764) went through numerous editions up to at least 1850. For the importance of desynonymising see BAXTER *Reliquiae* COPY A **40** n 1.

6[1] For mysticism and fanaticism as self-centred preoccupations that ascribed authority to notions merely idiosyncratic, see e.g. BAXTER *Reliquiae* COPY A **51** and n 1, BIRCH **1**, *AR* (1825) 381–5. On self-love see e.g. *P Lects* Lect 2 (1949) 107, *LS* (*CC*) 186–7. In Swedenborg's doctrine those in whom self-love is a commanding motive go to hell.

i.e. the Self-conceit turned sour.—Therefore, the first pre-condition is a loving and a humbled state of mind.—The second is an experience of the shadowyness and death of all mere notional Learning—a feeling, a weary feeling, if not a clear sense, that notions are but words, and excellent as signs become mendacious when they would mean themselves.[2]—The last and third pre-condition, especially requisite for these Works, is that the more educated Reader should evermore bear in mind the sentences in the ~~second~~ §̶ six first line[s] of p. xvi. of The Life of Jacob Behmen—viz.—"Whatever I could apprehend with the external principle of my mind, that I wrote down. But however, afterwards the Sun shone upon me a good while but not constantly: for the Sun hid itself, and then I knew not nor well understood my own labor."—Not *all*, nor perhaps exactly *how*, Behmen *saw*; but what, with his former associations he could reproduce in his Consciousness after the Vision had past away—have we in his Writings—and moreover he had but a scanty store of Words, so that he is obliged to repeat the same word with various predicates where more learned men would have established distinct Terms. But even this arose in part out of his deep sense of the oneness and the involution—Already however, it is plain, that he hath contemplated the very *principle* of all Philosophy, in three aboriginal Forms[3]—~~The One and All (=Abyss) O./ the~~ ⟨one & the⟩ all ~~(=Ground ⟨⚷=1.⟩)⟩[4]~~ ⟨⟨1⟩ the One in all & thro' all, and over all (=the self-existing God, having the Ground within himself—2. The Ground: το θειον, the Allmight and reality of God & potentiality of all things.[5] 3. The Father, Son, & H. G./[*]⟩

[*] The first of the three ~~of~~ is the Kingdom—
The second the Power
The third the Glory—Thine is the ~~Power~~ Kingdom, and the Power,

6[2] See *BL* ch 9 (1907) I 98: the writings of mystics "contributed to keep alive the *heart* in the *head*; gave me an indistinct, yet stirring and working presentiment, that all the products of the mere *reflective* faculty partook of DEATH".

6[3] Böhme, as the titles of his books and of the chapters within his books show, was obsessed with threefold schemes. The threefold division of *Aurora* is Philosophy, Astrology, Theology. See also e.g. 65 textus, below.

6[4] The cancelled phrases show that C sometimes, perhaps in the early years, translated Ἑν καὶ πᾶν as "the One and All" or "the one and the all". Cf BAXTER *Reliquiae* COPY A 2 n 2.

6[5] The term τὸ θεῖον ("the divine" or "divinity"), as opposed to ὁ θεός (God, as a person), is common at all periods, but C adds greatly to its significance. See *CL* IV 767–8 (Sept 1817), especially the statement that "True Philosophy begins with the τὸ θεῖον in order to end in the Ὁ Θεός." See also ARISTOPHANES 1 n 3.

Now these three are each the principle of a separate human Philosophy—the first of ~~Dionysius~~ Theosophy, the second of ~~Practical~~ Philosophy, ⟨or the love of Identity—⟩ the third of Theology—~~Theosophy being the Unity of all three.~~—The first can be attained positively by its own ~~Intuition~~ συνεστιωσις εν αυγη[7] alone/.—~~but~~ ⟨The second⟩ ~~it~~ may be learnt negatively[b] by an insight into the absurdit~~y~~ies that would follow from supposing the contrary. The Zero, or the $+0$, is the highest principle of all numbers, the Infinite of all Finition. The whole Universe must be represented as a single transparent Drop—a divine Chaos, not as the confused Commixture of all Distincts, but as the identity of them all, & therefore as the absence by pre-eminent *præsence* (quod est *præ* omnibus—non ut *ante* omnia, sed ut *præ*)[8] of all distinctions. The ○ is in the ●: & therefore the center itself IS not, ⟨i.e.⟩ *as* the center, for that *supposeth* the periphery.[9]—First, ~~thereon,~~ the positive Zero or $+0$—Second the $+-$, or -2 as the condition of $X+1$.—Thirdly, the Tetractys—or ⟨Trias—i.e.⟩ quod Deum ipsum $3=1$—quoad Deum absolutum

---

and the Glory—for thine, O Father, are the Word, and the Spirit is thine! for ever & ever—[a6]

a This appended note, written in the gutter margin of p [23], evidently refers to the place marked "[*]"

b C has written "negatively ~~it~~ may be learnt" and marked the words for transposition

6[6] Cf **52**, in which C establishes to his satisfaction that Böhme's position is fundamentally pantheistic. "Thine is the Kingdom...", familiar from the closing formula of the Lord's Prayer in the Book of Common Prayer, occurs in Matt 6.13 in the *Textus receptus*. With "the Word, and the Spirit" cf 1 John 5.7: "For there are three that bear record in heaven, the Father, the Word, and the Holy Ghost: and these three are one".

6[7] A modified fragment of the Greek quotation in **33**, below: "banqueting together in splendour".

6[8] "That is, *præ* everything—not in the sense of *ante*, but in the sense of *præ*". C desynonymises *ante* and *prae* more distinctly than classical usage seems to imply, wishing to exclude particularly the usual meaning of *ante* as "before in time". (*Ante* can also mean "in front of" in space,

can be used figuratively of rank, esteem, preference; and *ante omnia* sometimes means "in the highest degree, especially".) *Prae* ("before, in front of, in advance of") is, however, more often used figuratively; and C, by associating *prae* with "pre-eminent", seems to imply something like "transcendent presence". Cf "præpotence" in **18** n 1, below, and his note on "pre-" in "predestination" in BROWNE *Works* **43**. For C's concept of chaos as the undifferentiated, see **146** n 1, below. Cf "Chaos in the throes of self-organization" in G. S. FABER *Mysteries of the Cabiri* **13** (after n 6).

6[9] See also the first sentence of **7**, below, and the scholastic definition of God as "a circle whose centre is everywhere and circumference nowhere" in e.g. *AR* (1825) 226n. See also *CN* II 2784, in which ⊙ is also read as *Theta*.

4—i.e. Prothesis, Thesis, Antithesis, and Synthesis.[10]—Now Behmen in this work begins with the second—or the Difference in the In-difference, or primary Powers. But presupposing the first, or the intense Reality, he begins with Qualities, & maketh Quantity one of the Results—Most wisely! For Quantity is image & symbol/.— Conceive therefore the ● producing —●—: This polar Unity, of which the Magnet is the earthly Symbol, Behmen calleth the two Qualities in one—namely, Expansion or the +, and the Negation or Counter-power, = − / and this latter he calleth evil—i.e. contemplated in its separate action, and because he hasteth to the moral interest which predominates in him. But let us take them first as mere *powers*—Space and Time, Substance and Form/ and which in their struggle first become Attraction (= Time, Limit, Form, Negation) and Repulsion, (= + Space, Area, Substance, Positum)

6[10] The formula offered in this part of **6** is an early attempt to express the scheme of creation in terms of the polar (or dynamic) logic through the use of numerical symbols, following the method of the Pythagoreans and of Oken (see **52** n 15, below). In the light of C's later formulations a tentative explication can be offered. The three sections of C's scheme represent three phases (or dynamic figures) in a process rather than terms or numbers. (1) +0 (positive zero)— "The whole Universe...a divine Chaos", circumference without a centre, undifferentiated potential. (2) + − (positive, or active, negation) or − 2 (the Number 2 with negative valency), the principle of differentiation, the "condition" that allows +0 to become +1 (active Monas, God in the self-affirmation of Will). (3) One phase in two aspects: as a Trias (Trinity) "because [it represents] God himself", and is therefore 3 = 1; and as a Tetractys "inasmuch as [it represents] God as absolute"—the four terms being Prothesis, Thesis, Antithesis, Synthesis. Pythagoras, according to C, "founded the grand system of the Deity as the *Monas*...". *P Lects* Lect 2 (1949) 108–9. The four terms of the tetrad produce a figure of the Trinity: "Thus the Monas, the Dyas, the Trias, and the Tetractys are one". *CN* III 4427. See also *AR* (1825) 173n. Further application of this scheme to the theory of emanations and the Trinity occur in **105, 110, 172**, below. In **107**, below, C shows how the scheme 1 > 2 > 3 = 4 = 1 occurs in the tetrad, and how the tetrad expands to a pentad and a heptad to produce 10, "on which Nature revolves". See also BAXTER *Reliquiae* COPY B **103** n 1, on the "logical Tetractys".

The tetractys (τετρακτύς) or "set of four", traditionally ascribed to Pythagoras himself, provides the figure of the universe and the source of all things in a single diagram

that has the properties of an equilateral triangle and of producing from each of its corners the same sequence of numbers 1 + 2 + 3 + 4 = 10. "...But we do not know even what Pyth. meant by *ten*—assuredly, not the mere number, 10, as in ten guineas or ten Houses." TENNEMANN *Geschichte der Philosophie* (10 vols Leipzig 1798–1817) I 112. Cf also I 120: "The arithmoi [numbers] of Pyth. were evidently the very same as the *Ideas* of Plato." C also annotated the account of the Pythagorean philosophy in STANLEY *History of Philosophy* (1701) i 350–406.

7   i i 38–9 | Ch 3 "Of the most blessed Triumphing, Holy, Holy, Holy Trinity"

[All powers in Nature proceed from God the Father. The Father may be compared to the sun, which is at the same time the synthesis and source of all astral forces. The three persons of the Trinity should not be considered as three distinct gods.] 77. The Son is in the Father, being the Father's Heart or Light, and the Father generates the Son continually from Eternity to Eternity; and the Son's *Power* and Splendor shine back again in the whole Father, as the Sun does in the *whole* World.

As the Sun is (here conceived to be) the manifested Convergence of all the Astral Powers, subsisting from them, yet re-acting as that which is the Condition of *all* being a Whole: so the Son is the omnipresent Center of that infinite Circle, whose only Circumference is in ~~his~~ its own Self-comprehension, the eternal Act of which for ever constitutes that Center.[1] The immanent Energy of the divine Consciousness is, and is the cause of, the co-eternal Filiation of the Logos, the essential Symbol of the Deity, the substantial, infinite, sole adequate, Idea, in God, of God; in and by whom the Father, thus *necessarily* self-manifested, doth *freely* in the ineffable *overflowing of Goodness create, and, in proportion to the containing power, manifest himself to, all Creatures. But the ~~contrary~~ second Energy—in *order*, (for time attributed to the Infinite Eternal is a contradiction in thought) of the Father in and through the Son, and of the Son in and from the Father, and in and from Himself, as in and from the Father, is, and is the co-eternal Procession and Procedence of, the Holy Spirit—one God, blessed over all! Unity wh~~at~~ich *cannot* be *divided*! Tri-unity, which cannot *but* be *distinguished*.

    * "Tὸ Περισσον"[2] is ⟨one⟩ of the Pythagorean names of the divine nature.

7[1] A reference to the scholastic definition of God quoted in **6** n 10, above. See also *C&S* (*CC*) 179–80; *CL* vi 598 (var), and **171**, below. Böhme's comparison of Son and Sun, which C is here expounding, resonates with his own habitual merging of Sun and Son: see AURELIUS **35** n 2.

7[2] C translates περισσός as "overflowing" in his preceding phrase, "ineffable overflowing" (cf n 4, below); it here means "superabun-

dant". In NT Greek περισσός and its derivatives have the primary meaning of "excessive" or "abundant": e.g. in John 10.10 "that they might have life…more abundantly", in 2 Cor 8.2 "the abundance of their joy". The word is also used of "odd" numbers; the Pythagoreans equated "odd" with what makes orderly, with the Good, with the divine nature manifested in the world.

The main cause of our human aversion to conceive or admit the
personality, ~~or~~ i.e. the essential Distinctness, of the Word and the
Spirit, lies in our not devoutly attending to the infinite disparateness
of an eternal and creative Mind, whose ideas are anterior to their
Objects, from Minds whose Images and Thoughts are posterior to
the Things, and produced or conditioned by their Objects! The
latter—Effects, Shadows of Shadows, pene Nihilum a non vere
Ente![3] The former super-essential Causes, ὧν ἐν τῷ Περισσῷ,[4] (let
the imperfection of language, let the strivings of human weakness be
forgiven, the growing pains of inadequate Intellect and their accompanying Distortions) ὧν ἐν τῷ Περισσῷ, in whose excess and overflow of *Actuality* all created Things have their Reality.[5]

S. T. Coleridge

8 I i 39

97. And so the Spirit in Beasts, Fowls, and Worms, exists also; and
all has its three-fold Source in *Similitude* to the Ternary in the Deity.

97.
Vide, St Augustin, likewise Baxter.[1]

9 I i 39–40, referring to ch 3 *in toto*[a]

Böem's (or as we say, Behmen's)[1] account of the Trinity is masterly
and orthodox. Waterland and Sherlock might each have condescended
to have been instructed by the humble Shoe-maker of Gorlitz,[2] with

a This note may be a continuation of 7 or a comment on it, but it begins in a different hand

7[3] "Almost Nothing, from what does
not really Exist"—*pene nihil* being
part of a phrase ascribed to Augustine
in **110**, below. For C's distinction
between *vere non ens* (really not-
being) and *non vere ens* (not really
being) see **20**, below, and *CN* III 3861;
see also **31**, below. The "Shadows of
Shadows" may recall εἴδωλον σκιᾶς of
Aeschylus *Agamemnon* 839.
7[4] "In the superabundance of
which"—or, as C translates it himself,
"in whose excess and overflow". See
n 2, above.
7[5] The ideas in this note are close to
those in C's letter of 13 Oct 1806 to
Clarkson: *CL* II 1195–6.
8[1] But cf Augustine in Migne *PL*
XXXVIII 255 (tr): "[We have] mind,
reason, counsel, which the beasts have

not, the birds have not, the fish have
not."
9[1] "Behmen" is the standard English version, as on the title-page of this
edition. C's use is variable, but since
he may at any time use the standard
English form the variations are no
reliable guide in dating undated
marginalia on BÖHME. "Böem" occurs only here (cf "Bœm" in *CN* III
3276). "Böemen" is found in **23**, below, "Boemen" in **29**, "Boëmen" in
CN III 3354. "Bœhmen" is more usual:
CN I 1646, 1835, III 3692, 3925, 3975.
For "Behmen" see **38**, **39**, **45**, below,
and all further occurrences in these
marginalia.
9[2] C annotated Daniel WATER-
LAND *Vindication of Christ's Divinity*
(1719) and *The Importance of the*

great advantage to themselves, and to the avoidal of the perilous Errors, of which they were at least in jeopardy. Let me add to this Note, that there are three analogous Acts in the human Consciousness, or rather three dim imperfect Similitudes; and if ever we have a truly scientific Psychology, it will consitst of the distinct Enunciation, and Developement of the three primary Energies of Consciousness, and be a History of their Application and Results.[3] Humphrey Davy in his Laboratory is probably doing more for the Science of Mind, than all the Metaphysicians have done from Aristotle to Hartley, inclusive.[4] Φωνῶ Συνετοισι.[5]

S. T. C.

10 1 i 40

Even while my faith was confined in the trammels of Unitarianism (so called) with respect to all the doctrines of Sin and Grace, I saw clearly, as a truth in philosoph~~l~~yy, that the Trinitarian was the only consequent Medium between the Atheist and the Anthropomorph.[1] Spinoza, the Hercules' Pillar of human Reason, dismissed Intellect from his System: his cogitatio infinita remains always τὶ ακεντρον.[2] He was too profound a Thinker not to perceive, that there can be no

---

Doctrine of the Holy Trinity (1734), and William SHERLOCK *Vindication of the Doctrine of the...Trinity* (1690). He was impressed by Böhme's obscure birth in Altseidenberg, his boyhood as a cattle-herder, and his industrious life (for a time) as a shoemaker in Görlitz. The similarity to Hans Sachs —also a shoemaker—did not escape C's notice. As a Blue-coat boy of thirteen he had had his "*one* just flogging" for trying to apprentice himself to a shoemaker. *TT* 27 May 1830.

9[3] Self-retaining, self-containing, and self-causing—see *CL* VI 599–600.

9[4] See C's letter to Davy in Jan 1809, congratulating him on his providing evidence "of the moral connection between the finite and the infinite Reason". *CL* III 171–2.

9[5] "I declare [this] to the enlightened"—tr based on *CL* IV 942. The phrase is adapted from Pindar *Olympian Odes* 3.85, φωνάεντα συνετοῖσι, which C had used in *Lects 1795* (*CC*) 310, *CN* III 4155, 4244, *LS* (*CC*) 126,

BL chs 9, 22 (1907) I 100, II 121, *CL* IV 942, and as the original for "vocal shafts" in "The Historie and Gestes of Maxilian" (*CW* IV 446). The use in 9 and in *CL* IV 942 recalls the sardonic use Gray had made of the phrase as motto to his Pindaric *Odes* (1757) and, with even sharper edge, in his *Poems* (1768). For C's reading of Pindar see 22 n 2, below.

10[1] A view that C frequently expressed. For an early statement of it see *CN* I 922 (Feb–Mar 1801). The "medium" is between the position that there is no God and the position that God is "man-shaped"—mere man.

10[2] His "infinite thought"—i.e. Spinoza's "God"—remains always "a centreless/pointless thing". Spinoza's God is absolutely infinite (*Ethics* Pt i Def 6), a thinking thing (Pt ii Prop 1), and an extended thing (Pt ii Prop 2). C's point is that Spinoza avoids a central Intellect because he saw that this would lead him to the Trinity. See also 6, above; and cf 31 n 7, below.

Intellectus without a simultaneous Intelligibile and Intellectio/ the best possible logical Exponent of the Father, the Word, & the Spirit.[3]

11   I i 41 | Ch 4 "Of the Creation of the Holy Angels"

8. And, as I said before, all the Powers or Virtues are in God the Father, and no Man with his Sense and Thoughts can *reach* to apprehend it. But in the Stars and the Elements, as also by all the Creatures in the whole Creation of this World, a Man may *clearly know* it.

8. This is expressed finely and with philosophical precision. So far from comprehending it we are not even capable of the preparatory act of *ap*prehension.[a] We cannot even take it up into the mind. But we can *know* it. Datur, non intelligitur.[1]

12   I i 41

9. All Power and Virtue is in God the Father; and proceeds also forth from him, as Light, Heat, Cold, Soft, Gentle, Sweet, Bitter, Sour, Astringent or Harsh, Sound or Noise, and much more that is not possible to be spoken or apprehended. *All these* are in God the Father, one in another as one Power, and yet all the Powers move in his *Exit* or going forth.

10. But the Powers in God do not operate or qualify in that *Manner*, as in Nature, in the Stars, and Elements, or in the Creatures. No, you must *not* conceive it so: For Lord *Lucifer* in his Elevation made the Powers of impure Nature *thus* burning, bitter, cold, astringent, sour, dark, and unclean.

9 and 10. Nota *bene—eminently*, not *formally*.[1] For the meaning of the word "qualify" see § 3 of Chapt. 1 et seq.[2]—By Quality Behmen

---

[a] The word "apprehension" having reached the extreme outer edge of the page, C inadvertently placed his full point on the projecting edge of p 45

[10][3] Cf SPINOZA *Opera* (2 vols 1802–3) I 582–4.

[11][1] "It is *given,* not to be *understood*"—as C renders this favourite dictum in *BL* ch 8 (1907) I 91. See e.g. *TL* (1848) 36: "assumed, though not comprehended".

[12][1] I.e. Böhme is using the terms "Power and Virtue" "eminently", in a higher sense than is conveyed by the strict meaning of the words. In scholastic terminology a thing is related to its cause "formally" (*formaliter*) if its defining characteristics inhere in it (as heat in fire), or "eminently" (*eminenter*) if its defining characteristics are an inferior version of those found in the cause (as man in God). C provides his own account of the distinction in HOBBES 1. For his understanding that in Aristotle's view perception was not a mirror see *CN* III 3605. Cf "*eminenter,* in a certain transcendant mode": *CN* III 4158.

[12][2] *Aurora* I §§ 3–4: "...A Quality is the Mobility, boiling, springing,

intends that act of each elementary Power, by which it energizes in its peculiar kind. But in the Deity is an absolute Synthesis of opposites. Plato in *Parmenide* and Giordano Bruno passim have spoken many things well on this aweful Mystery/ the latter more clearly.[3]

13 1 i 41

11. But in the Father all Powers are mild, soft, like Heaven, very full of Joy, for all the Powers triumph in one another, and their Voice or Sound rises up from Eternity to Eternity.

12. There is nothing in them but Love, Meekness, Mercy, Friendliness, or Courtesy; even such a triumphing, rising Source or Fountain of Joy, wherein all the Voices of Heavenly Joyfulness *sound* forth, so as no Man is able to express it, nor can it be likened to any Thing.

11. 12. B. carries on the sublime metaphor (*plusquam* metaphora)[1] of "THE WORD": the representation by which of the Son of God is the sublimest Thought, that ever entered the Soul of man, the purest Form of Intuition—"eine mehr als geometreisrischen Anschauung".[2]

14 1 i 41

15. The Quality of Water is not of *such* a running and qualifying Condition or Manner in God, as it is in *this* World, but is a Spirit, very bright, clear, and thin, wherein the Holy Ghost riseth up, a *mere Power*.

16. The bitter Quality qualifies in the sweet, astringent or harsh and sour Quality, and the *Love* rises up therein from Eternity to Eternity.

---

driving of a Thing. As, for example, *Heat*, which burns, *consumes*, and drives forth all, whatsoever comes into it, which is not of the same Property; and again, it *enlightens* and warms all cold, wet, and dark Things; it compacts and hardens soft Things." *Works* 1 i [23].

12[3] The *Parmenides* was a rich mine for the Neoplatonists. Proclus especially selects it in *In theologiam Platonis* as the dialogue that contains the whole of Plato's theology, and based on it

his scheme of emanation (for which see 110 n 2, below). Bruno argues that ideas exist in metaphysical unity in the mind of God. C, perhaps having in mind Bruno's *De umbris idearum*, emphasises Bruno's insistence upon the principle of dynamic polarity; cf 52 n 16, below, and *P Lects* Lect 11 (1949) 323.

13[1] "*More than* a metaphor"—i.e. a literal statement.

13[2] "A more than geometrical insight".

15. 16.—What is here opened theosophically, is developed philo-sophicalled*a* in the Theoria &c of Boscovich.[1]

15 I i 41–2

18. And this, in the Deep of the Father, is like a Divine SALITTER, which I must needs liken to the *Earth*, which before its Corruption was even such a *Salitter*. But not so Hard, Cold, Bitter, Sour, and Dark, but like the Deep, or like Heaven, very clear and pure, wherein all Powers were *good*, fair, and heavenly; but that Prince Lucifer thus *spoiled* them, as you shall perceive hereafter.

18. By the *Salitter* we should understand that general Element, ⟨which⟩ whether it be an etherial Metal terrific, or an earth metallific, ~~which~~ is the centripetal Principle, ~~which~~ that, by its accersive power over the repulsional or centrifugal Elements ~~is~~ furnishes the con-ditional ~~of~~ cause of all the Forms of sense, visible, tangible, etc.[1] By this Archeus of the omne tangibile the two Airs of Ammonia and volatile Alkali, on blending pass at once into a solid Form/[2] and it may be conjectured, that the same will be discovered in the inflam-mable Air, and is the principle of this Combustible becoming water

---

a A slip for "philosophically"

14[1] Ruggiero Giuseppe Boscovich (1711–87), in *Theoria philosophiae naturalis redacta ad unicam legem virium in naturae existentium* (Venice 1763), sought to explain the material universe in terms of Newton's law that every action has an equal and oppo-site reaction. C seems to be referring here to Article 450 of the *Theoria*. See also *CN* III 3962; cf 3370n, 3953n. C had some early acquaintance with Boscovich's work (*Lects 1795—CC—* 216–17n) and in 1809–10 used Bosco-vich's edition of Benedict Stay, the notes on which contain some of Bosco-vich's most important philosophical statements: *Friend* (*CC*) II 11 and n (I 10 and n).

15[1] *Salitter*—saltpetre, potassium nitrate—was regarded by the al-chemists as a powerful creative agent. Böhme uses the term symbolically to mean the substratum of the "Divine Powers", the forces that constitute the universe, both spiritual and material.

See also **19**, below. "Accersive" (not in *OED*), from *accerso* (*arcesso*), summon forth. The concept of a "centripetal Principle" suggests the classification of substances in terms of "cohesion", earths being incoherent and metals cohesive; see **15** n 6, below, and *CN* III 4223 and n.

15[2] "Archeus" is Paracelsus' term for the vital power or ruling principle, esp of animal and vegetable organisms: see also **96** n 2, below. C renders the term "Paramount Power" in **36**, below; he also associated the term with Helmont in a letter of Nov 1816: *CL* IV 688. See also *CN* III 4136 and n. "Omne tangibile"—everything accessible to touch: see also **24** n 9, below. "Vola-tile Alkali" is the old term for am-monia; C, perhaps a little confused here, may have had in mind the reac-tion between "Volatile Alkali" and "muriatic Gas" (hydrogen chloride) described in his notes taken at Davy's lectures of 1802: see *CN* I 1098 f 21.

when combined with the Combustive Air.[3] It ~~is~~ may ~~proba~~possibly ⟨be⟩ the same in essence with the diamond or carbon[4]* and should this be made appear, it will bear full Testimony to the Truth of the Teutonic Theosophy/ as we know, that all vegetables consist[b] of the combustible, combustive, carbonic, and sodarchic Elements.

* and differ from Soda, Potash, Lime, Strontian, Barytes, by combined Water-stuff, in addition to the Combustive or Oxalkalarch Air. Arch or archic, that is, that which causes a thing to begin to be that which it afterwards is, I think far preferable to the *gen* of French Nomenclature; but for the basis I would prefix Hypo = ὑπο, sub unfortunately being pre-occupied as a diminutive. Thus instead of Oxygen &c I would say oxalkalarchic, hydrarchic, nitrarchic in the Adjective, and nitrarch, hydrarch; but the metalloid base of Soda I would [name][a] Hyposode: or else the affix yl for ὑλη, the stuff or materia prima/ Sodyl, potassyl, strontianyl &c.[5] S. T. C. P.S. It is clearly a defect in the French Nomenclature, that the same affix is put to Hydrogen & Oxygen/ for Oxygen is the proper Hydrarch, & Hydryl is the proper name of the other.[6]

16 1 i 42

20. For every Quality bears its own Fruit, *as it is* in the corrupted murtherous Den or dark Valley and Dungeon of the Earth; there spring up all Manner of Earthly Trees, Plants, Flowers, and Fruits. Also *within the Earth*, *grow* curious precious Stones, Silver, and Gold, and these are a *Type* of the Heavenly Generating or Production.

[a] Word suggested by the editor

[b] Written "consits"

15[3] "Inflammable air" and "combustive air"—old terms for hydrogen and oxygen.

15[4] C is probably drawing directly on Davy, perhaps on his article in *Phil Trans RS* of 1808 (quoted in **117** n 1, below). See *CN* I 1098 f 28[v], III 4432, which later provided C with the makings of an elaborate jest: "Cottle's Psalms with morals of his own added to each.—Diamond + Oxygen = Charcoal." N 24 f 59[v].

15[5] C recorded Davy's theories on these substances in a series of notes on Davy's first Royal Institution lectures in 1802 (*CN* I 1098 ff 17–19), but he may also have in mind Davy's article of 1808 (see n 4, above). C's use of "Water-stuff", i.e. *Wasserstoff* (the

German for hydrogen), suggests that he may also have consulted STEFFENS *Beyträge zur innern Naturgeschichte der Erde* (Freyberg 1801), in ch 1 of which this group of substances is discussed as well as ammonia. In *Lehrbuch der Naturgeschichte* p 37 Oken proposed the suffix "el" as the suffix for the metalloids obtained through the decomposition of alkalis and earths.

15[6] This discussion of chemical nomenclature is similar to that in a notebook entry of Dec 1807 beginning "I will suggest to Davy". *CN* II 3192. In c Aug–Sept 1809 C spoke with admiration of the Germans as "the great Nomenclators in all the Sciences". *CN* III 3605 f 118[v].

21. Nature *labours* with its utmost Diligence upon this corrupt dead Earth, that it might generate Heavenly Forms and Species or Kinds; but it generates *only* dead, dark, and hard Fruits, which are no more than a mere Shadow or Type of the Heavenly.

22. Moreover its Fruits are *altogether* fierce, or biting, bitter, sour, astringent, or harsh and hot, also cold, hard and evil; they have *scarce* any Spark or Spice of Goodness in them. Their Sap and Spirit is *mixed* with hellish Quality, their Scent or Smell is a very *Stink*; thus has Lord *Lucifer* caused them to be. . . .

23. Now when I write of Trees, Plants and Fruits, you must *not* understand them to be *Earthly*, like those that are in this World. . . .

24. No, but my Meaning is heavenly and spiritual, yet *truly* and *properly such*. . . .

Unde Sulphur in ovis fetidis?[1] O how gladly would I resign my Life, even were I happy, even were it not sickly and like a Sheep with the *Rot*, a victim which it would be blasphemy to bring to the Altar— but O were it what ♄:[2] would have rendered ⟨it,⟩ were it even worthy of ♄:, yet resign ⟨it⟩ I would, to procure for mankind such health and longevity to H. Davy, as should enable him to discover the Element of the Metals, of Sulphur, and of Carbon. O! he will do it! yea, and perhaps reveal the *synthetic* Idea of the Antithets, Attraction and Repulsion.[3] S. T. C.

17 ɪ i 43, referring to **15** and **16**

Appendix to the Note on the margins of the preceding Leaf.

The Salitter is Gravitation or the power of Depth, therefore truly the Powers each in the other, as the synthesis of Attraction and Repulsion, yet truly a third power, in which both the former are co-inherent and one: but it is gravitation as in the Sun, ~~the~~ at once the center of gravity and the fountain of Light—. The metals are in substance Carbon + azote, some *primarily* oxydated, others hydrogenized—but beyond the powers of the Laboratorium microchemicum[1] for that ⟨very⟩ reason. Quartz &c = N + E. Sulphur,

16¹ "Where does the Sulphur come from in foul-smelling eggs?"

16² An abbreviated form (here in cipher) of C's anagram of SH's name, Asra Schōnthinu. For the formation of the anagram see *CN* ɪɪɪ 3534; and for the use of the Hebrew letter *shin* (ש) in the anagram see *C&SH* 20 and n, and cf *CN* ɪɪɪ 4103 f 163; see also e.g. *CN* ɪɪɪ 3428,

3429. For a time C hoped that SH would bring happiness and purpose into his life: see e.g. *CN* ɪɪɪ 3430, 3472, 3508, 3551.

16³ See **17**, below.

17¹ "Microchemical Laboratory". Azote ("lifeless") is a name for nitrogen, the most inert of the gases then known.

Phosphorus, Potassium, S+W.[2] Oxygen itself, more aptly named Zoöte, is Carbon + Neg. Electricity, and azoote but the zoomet(allon) or zöium + W. or pos. Electricity.—So instead of Carbon, or Diamond, or Quartz, I should prefer inventing a name for the North polar Metal—either phytomet (met for metallon) or Phytium.

Alas! Since I wrote the preceding note, H. Davy is become Sir Humphry Davy, and an *Atomist*![3]

18   1 i 43, written directly after C's footnote to **15** without paragraph break

25. In the Divine Pomp and State are especially *two* Things to be considered: *First* the *Salitter* or the Divine Powers, which are moving springing Powers.

26. In that same Power grows up and is generated Fruit according to every Quality and Species, or Kind, viz. *heavenly* Trees and Plants....

27. The *second* Form or Property of Heaven ... is *Mercurius*, or the Sound, as in the *Salitter* of the Earth there is the Sound, whence there grows Gold, Silver, Copper, Iron, and the like; of which Men make all Manner of *Musical Instruments* for sounding, or for Mirth, as Bells, Organ-Pipes, and other *Things* that make a Sound: There is likewise a Sound in all the Creatures upon Earth, else all would be in Stillness and *Silence*.

§ 27 is admirable—the Messenger or Mercury of the Salitter is indeed Sound, which is but Light under the paramouncy of Gravitation.[1] It is the Mass-Light. The Granit-blocks in the vale of Thebais still send forth sweet *Sounds* at the touch of Light—a proof that Granit is a metallic composition/—[2]

19   1 i 43

N. B. Salitter is *Salnitter* in the original German, i.e. Sal Nitrum— i.e. the chrystallized or fixed Principle of Nitre—a better symbol

---

17[2] Cf STEFFENS *Grundzüge* ch 6, where the metals are divided into a coherent and non-coherent series, the former represented by the North (carbon), which is originally oxidised, the latter by the South, which is originally hydrogenised.

17[3] Humphry Davy was knighted on 8 Apr 1812. See *CN* III 4196n, 4221 and n; cf *CL* IV 760.

18[1] This note bears out what C wrote to Tieck in 1817 about "the idea, that Sound was = Light under the prae-

potence of Gravitation, and Color= Gravitation under the praepotence of Light...". *CL* IV 751. See also **100**, below.

18[2] The statue of Memnon in the Valley of Thebes was supposed to sing (or make a sound like a snapping string) at dawn. This has been explained as due to the expansion of the stone when struck by the warm rays of the sun. C refers to this legend also in *BL* ch 22 (1907) II 103.

could scarcely have been chosen to represent the basis, ground, or principle of BEING as distinguished from the causes of *Existing*— Salnitter may be literally translated in with relation to our present chemical nomenclature Carbonazot, the Sal = Carbon, or principle of Fixity & Coherence, by attraction, and the Nitre or Nitter = Nitrogene (or azote) by Repulsion[1]

20 I i 44–7

46. For behold the total Holy Trinity has with its moving composed, *compacted*, or figured a Body, or Image out of itself, like a *little* God, but not so fully or *strongly* going forth, as the whole Trinity, yet in some Measure according to the *Extent* and Capacity of the Creatures. For in God there is *neither* Beginning nor End; but the Angels *have* a Beginning and End, but not circumscriptive, apprehensive, palpable, or *conclusive*. . . .

47. But thou must rightly understand this. They are made and compacted together, or figured out of the *Salitter* and *Mercurius*, that is, out of the *Exit* or Excrescence.

47. Εκ Περισσῳ Θεοτητος.[1] In the Logos, or adequate Idea of the divine Beings, all Ideas possible according to Wisdom, and Goodness (which is truly all that can be meant by the words "in the nature of Things": for nature is the Creature of God, and to be the One, the Good, the Wise, is God's nature) in the Son, I say, are contained all possible Ideas *eminenter*.[2] But in him all are as one/ yet even as the divine act of Self-consciousness gave substantial Essence to his greater Idea, even so all the included Ideas produced existing Images of themselves in the power and thro' the free goodness of Deity/ for it was better that they should be, than not be. But yet by *existence*, i.e. *stare extra*,[3] they of necessity became *finite*, & therefore *inadequate*, Images of their Prototypes in the divine mind; and as finite derived their distinguishing ⟨& separate⟩ ~~Beings~~ Natures from *not-Being*: as Plato has set forth almost inspiredly.[4] Hence the Chasm

---

19[1] This may have been intended as a further addition to **15**. C uses the word "carbonazot" hereafter both as the generic term for all metals and as the representative of the "magnetic axis" the poles of which are carbon and azote (nitrogen). See **15** n 1, above.

20[1] "Out of the Superabundance of Divinity". See **7** n 2, above.

20[2] See **12** n 1, above.

20[3] "To stand outside".

20[4] In *Sophist* 256D–259D and ff; also in *Timaeus* and *Philebus*. Here, as often in his discussions of Plato, C is inclined to draw upon Neoplatonic interpretations. See also *P Lects* Lect 4 (1949) 164–5, 426n.

infinitely infinite between Deity and the Creatur[e.]*a* I merely give the order of Thought, like the anarthrous[5] Words at the head of a Chapter.—1. The existence of the Universe not necessary, all and ~~the~~ all consciousness ~~of~~ being comprize[d]*a* in the Tri-une God. 2. Thro' Grace it was created, according to the divine Ideas. 3. Bu[t]*a* the Images of those Ideas being finite and contingent had their ~~Beings~~ defined by negations—infinitely less than the vere entia, they ~~were~~ Worl[d]*a* ⟨was⟩ better than vere ~~ens~~ non ens, tho' non vere ens.[6] 4. From negation arose free Will and Desire. 5. From thence the possibility of Evil.—6. From Grace a new Creation, the 5th Article having brought in the necessity of Revelation—and thence the whole Economy of Redemption, or the reduction of Soul to Spirit, of the Image to its Idea, which could only be effected by producing in them the condition of their Ideas, namely, the being all, as one, in one/ and thereby putting off the evils of separation and finiteness. 7. Hence the necessity of the Incarnation of the Logos/ 8. And the joyous and adorable mystery of being born again in Christ[7]—for in him the Image preserved itself constant to the Idea, and only numerically distinct (but number reduced to its own mereness becomes evanid)[8]—yet as an Image ⟨Christ *Jesus* was⟩ capable**b* of combining with Images, and of uniting the regenerate Creation, as by the affinity of an Intermedium, ~~with~~ to the Infinite Idea, which is of God, and with God, and God.[10] "As I am in my Father, even so ye are in me."[11]

Then will the Spirit drink-in perfection in an eternal growth by the

* Why should this appear stranger to us, as a law of *spiritual* nature, than the incombinableness of Oil with Water without an Intermedium in *the world of the Senses*?[9]

---

a The edge of the leaf is damaged, with the loss of a few letters that the editor had transcribed while the leaf was still intact

b At * C has written: "(see the note on the other margin of this page)". His footnote is written in the gutter margin of p 46

20[5] C means "lacking articulation" —a sense not recorded in *OED*, although that is the meaning of ἄναρθρος. The first use recorded by *OED* for "anarthrous" is for the meaning "without an article", as used by T. F. Middleton in *The Doctrine of the Greek Article* (1808), for which see BIBLE COPY B **132** n 1.

20[6] For C's early acquaintance with these terms in Pico della Mirandola—"real beings", "real not-being", "not-

real being"—see *CN* I 374. Cf also **7** and n 3, above.

20[7] See John 3.3, 3.7; 1 Pet 1.23.

20[8] "Tending to vanish, transient".

20[9] As e.g. mustard in making salad dressing, or egg yolk in mayonnaise.

20[10] John 1.1.

20[11] Cf John 14.20: "At that day ye shall know that I am in my Father, and ye in me, and I in you."

beatific Vision of the Unutterable, in whose Image it was created—
eternal approximation of the Glorified to the Infinite Glory, nascent
Hope for ever losing its nature in fruition, as the Coral is said to
blush in full beauty the moment it lifts itself above the Waters. 9.
Lastly, (in this Chapter of mere Cogitanda), the two natures in
Christ, a necessity consequent on the divine Decree at the first
Creation—and henceforward from his Resurrection & Re-assump-
tion into the Bosom of his Father,[12] his perpetual Humanity/ our
heavenly King, and the Morning Star of the Flock of ~~the~~ his Redeemed.[13]

21 I i 47 | Ch 5 "Of the Corporeal Substance . . . of an Angel"

20. As there are *two* Things to be observed in God; the *First* is the
Salitter, or the Divine Powers, out of which the Body or Corporeity
is; and the *Second* is the *Mercurius*, Tone, Tune or Sound: Thus also
it is in *like Manner* and Form in an Angel.

21. First there is the *Power*, and in the Power is the Tone or *Tune*,
which rises up in the Spirit, into the Head, into the *Mind*, as in Man
in the Brain; and in the Mind it *has its open Doors or Gates*; but in
the *Heart* it has its *Seat*, Residence and Original, where it exists out
of all Powers.

20. 21. Plato's *Harmony*. Indeed throughout the co-incidence in ~~the~~
the train of Thought with so entire a difference of manner, is almost
miraculous/ if we reflect who & what J. B. was.[1]

22 I i 47

26. You should not here scorn my Spirit, for it is *not* sprung forth
from the wild Beast, but is generated from my Power and Virtue,
and *enlightened* by the Holy Ghost.

Absit peccatum! væ mihi si φαντασιαις ⟨υπεροπλοις*⟩ lasciviam!²—

* ¹ αλλα βροτων/ Τον μεν κενοφρονες αυχαι
ΕΞ αγαθων εβαλον·

20¹² "Into the bosom of the Father"
—John 1.18 (var), a phrase that C
often repeated: cf **161** n 2, below, and
esp BROWNE *Works* **39** n 1. In
altering AV "in" to "into" C is
thinking of the Greek text, εἰς τὸν
κόλπον τοῦ πάτρος. Εἰς usually means
"into", but often in NT (e.g. John
1.18) εἰς encroaches on ἐν = *in*.

20¹³ Cf Rev 2.28, 22.16, and 14.1–4.
21¹ C seems to be recalling Plato
Philebus 25c–26a.
22¹ Pindar *Nemean Odes* 9.37–42
(var): "But, among mortals, *one* is cast
down from his blessings by empty-
handed conceit, whereas *another*,
underrating his strength too far, hath
been thwarted from winning the

This alone be my Object, as this alone can be my Defence, the desire to kindle young minds, & to guard them against the temptation of the Scorners, by shewing that the Scheme of Christianity tho' not discoverable by reason, is yet accordant thereto—that Link follows Link by necessary consequences; ~~and~~ that Religion ~~only moves~~ passes out of the ken of Reason only where ⟨the Eye of⟩ Reason has reached its own Horizon; and that Faith is ⟨then⟩ but its *Continuation*, even as the Day ~~steals~~ softens away into the sweet Twilight, and Twilight ⟨hushed & breathless steals⟩ into the Darkness! ~~When~~ It is Night, sacred Night! ‡ The upraised Eye views only the starry Heaven, which ~~shews~~ manifests only itself—and the outward Look ~~is but~~ gazes on the sparks, twinkling in the aweful Depth, ~~of the sombre Hollow~~ only to preserve the Soul steady and concentered in its ~~silent~~ Trance of inward Adoration. Θεῳ Μονῳ Δοξα!³

> Τον δ'αυ καταμεμφθεντ' αγαν
> Ισχυν οικειων κατεσφαλεν καλων,
> Χειρος ελκων οπισσω, θυμος ατολμος.
>
> Pind. Nem. Ode XI.

23 I i 48

[Expounding "Of the Qualification of an Angel", Böhme begins with the five senses, which he calls "Counsellors".]

37. The *first* Counsellor is the *Eyes*; they are affected with every Thing they look upon, for they are the *Light*.

38.... The Eyes work in the Thing they look upon, and the *Thing* works again in the Eyes, and the Eyes as the Counsellor,

honours within his reach, by an uncourageous spirit that draggeth him back by the hand." Tr J. Sandys (LCL 1915). On C's continuous interest in Pindar, and especially in the intricacies of Pindar's versification, see PINDAR (ed Schmied). His slip in copying κατέσφαλεν for παρέσφαλεν suggests that on this occasion he was using the Heyne edition (4 vols Göttingen 1798–9). See *CN* III 3721 and n.

22² "Let me not sin! Woe to me if I were to wanton in overweening fancies!"

The rest of the note—with slight alterations but including the quotation from Pindar—forms the concluding paragraph of *BL*. The interlinear alterations and the appended quotation from Pindar do not seem to have been written at the same time as the original note; the revisions will have been made in May–Jun 1817, when C decided to incorporate the note into *BL*. See *BL* ch 24 (1907) II 218.

22³ "Glory to God alone!"—a formal doxology taken variatim from Rom 16.27, 1 Tim 1.17, Jude 25; often placed ceremoniously at the end of a book, e.g. Thomas Fuller *Davids Hainous Sinne* (1631). C has also written it at the end of a discussion of fame in *CN* III 3291 (Apr 1808).

bring it into the *Head* before the Princely Seat or Throne; and there it is to be approved of.

39. Now if the Spirit is *pleased* with it, then it brings the same to the Heart, and the Heart gives it to the Passages or *Issuings* forth of the Powers, or Fountain-veins in the whole Body; and then the Mouth, and Hands, and Feet, fall to work.

40. The *second* Counsellor is the *Ears*, which have their Rise also from all the Powers in the whole Body through the Spirit; their Fountain is *Mercurius* or the *Sound*, which arises from all the Powers.

The paucity and tenuity of the discoverable Nerves to, in, and from the Heart is rather a proof of the imperfection of our present Physiology than an Objection to Böemen's Position. All that can be legitimately inferred from the anatomical fact is, that the functions of the Heart are not meant to be entrusted to the ordinary processes of conscious empirical Volition. But the issuing forth of the Sensibility into the Irritability, and its retroition is strictly physiological as well as metaphysical truth: however the View may be beyond the physiology and metaphysics of the Day.[1]—Equally just and profound is the derivation of the Auditual Organismus and its Archeus from the ζωομεταλλικον,[2] and which Death does partially let fall back into formal metal, whence the Iron in the Blood after the departure of the vital energies. Hence too the hardness pre-eminent of the Bones belonging to the Ear—and its apprehension of Space by means of Time and Depth only:

S. T. Coleridge 1800[a][3]

Approved on reperusal 27, June 1817

a "1800" is clearly written

23[1] An early attempt by C, in his search for a single dynamic scheme, to discern the relation between the characteristic features of organic life and the electrical-magnetic-chemical forces that seemed to command the inorganic realm. His insistence upon not being limited by the instruments of inquiry that happen to be available is typical of his method of inquiring into complex matters. Cf *TL* (1848) 48.

With "retroition" cf the cognate words "introitive", "reintroitive", and "unintroitive" in **143** n 1, below.

23[2] "Zoometallic"—animal-metallic, on the analogy of "zoophyte" in **24** n 1. For "Archeus" see **15** n 2, above.

23[3] C cannot have written a marginal note in these volumes in 1800 because he did not acquire them until Feb 1808. Two possible explanations for the clearly written "1800" suggest themselves. He could have put a correct date for the *conception* of the idea rather than the date of his recording it here (e.g. "irritability", for which see *CN* I 924n). Or he could have made a slip in writing the date of the year in which he actually wrote the note; the least implausible reconstruction being that early in 1810 he wrote (from ten years' habit) "180", then wrote the "0" of 1810, and neglected to alter the preceding 0 to 1.

24 I i 49–50

45. The *third* Princely Counsellor is the *Nose*; there the Fountain rises up from the Body in the Spirit into the Nose. . . .

46. And as the excellent, precious, and amiable *blessed* Savour or Smell goes forth from all the Powers of the Father and of the Son, and *tempers* itself with all the Powers of the Holy Ghost, whence the *Holy Spirit* and most precious Savour rises up from the Fountain of the Holy Ghost; and flows or boils in all the Powers of the Father, and *kindles* all the Powers of the Father, whereby they are impregnated *again* with the amiable blessed Savour, or *Saving Smell*, and so generate it in the Son and Holy Ghost; *so also* in Angels and Men, the Power of the Smell rises up out of all the Powers of the *Body* by and through the *Spirit*, and comes forth at the *Nostrils* of the Nose, and is affected by all Smells or Savours, and brings them through the Nostrils of the Nose, which is the third Counsellor, into the Head, before the Princely Seat, or Throne. . . .

[The power of smell is "generated out of the *Salitter*" and is also "mixed with *Mercurius*".]

49. The *fourth* Princely Counsellor is the *Taste* on the *Tongue*, which also arises from all the Powers of the Body through the Spirit into the Tongue: For all *Fountain-veins* of the whole Body go into the Tongue, and the Tongue is the Sharpness or *Taste* of all the Powers. . . .

More recondite than the Genesis of the Auditual Life, but not less just—The Smelling is to Hearing what the South = negaPositive, Pole or Repulsion is to the North, = Negative, Pole of Magnetism, or Attraction. It is equally metallöid but S.W. = azot hydrogen-occidentized, as the Hearing is under the potenziation of the N.E. i.e. Ζωόphyte oxygenorientized.[1] The Taste is akin ⟨to⟩ the Smell, being yet more hydrogenized and Western, less to the South/ or

---

24[1] Much in this note is similar to parts of the letter to Tulk of Jan 1818: *CL* v 804–9; cf also *CN* III 4436, which has Oken in the background. "Occidentized" (Westerned) is not in *OED*, but "Orientized" (Easterned) is recorded for 1881. "Potenziation", not in *OED* in this spelling, is ascribed to C from a rather later context; see also BAXTER *Reliquiae* COPY B **99** and n 1, and *CN* III 4418 f 13ᵛ and n. "Zoophyte"—animal-plant—is an Aristotelian term (ζωόφυτον), in use in its English form from 1621, to refer to organisms classed as intermediate between animals and plants (see also **46** and n 9, below); but C, in his search for a suitable nomenclature, may be using it as "life-producing" (using the suffix *-phyte* in preference to *-gen*) for the pole opposite to "azote" (lifeless—see **17** n 1, above).

more truely it [is]*a* a more ισομερης τετρακτυς[2]—an hydrate of Carbonazot.

I use *occidentized* for the tension or ammaximation[3] of the positive pole of Electricity, or the surface sphere of Becoming; and *orientized* ⟨I use⟩ for the Negative Po~werle~. The interpenetration of both is water, or rather perhaps the ὕδωρ ἐν ὕδατι:[4] for in all real water the axis or line of Essence (*Being*, Base, Substance) must exist, as well as the spherical or rather hemispherical E. W. Line of Existence (το γιγεσθαι,*b* γενεσις,[5] Becoming, Form, Mode). Water therefore is con crete Galvanism, with no other figure, neither Length nor Breadth, of itself, but Depth only, i.e. globosity. It is the Quaternion[6] of Death and thence the necessary commencement of all Life—Solidity or rather Fixity, is the opposite Pole, of Death. Nothing wholly fluid or wholly solid does or can live.[7]

This I have written to explain the words, that Taste is an Hydrate, or the differencible[8] and still self-differencing Indifference.—Lastly, with the same Truth Böemen views the Feeling as the rudiment of, and in, all other senses—organized into Touch, but not without the aid of some one or more of the other senses—Taste at least./ There-fore because the Touch is Feeling organized, it is the transitional sense

---

a Word supplied by the editor   *b* A slip for γιγνεσθαι or γινεσθαι

24[2] "Equally divided tetractys". Since carbonazote represents one axis of C's tetractys and water the other, this scheme seems to imply a structure of four elements—carbon, nitrogen, oxygen, and hydrogen—with the two polar axes at right angles to each other. See also **45**, below.

24[3] *OED* records "maximization" for Bentham 1802 and "maximation" for 1881. "Ammaximation", not in *OED*, through the use of the prefix *ad-* (up to), provides a motor image—"the [bringing up] to a maximum".

24[4] "Water in water"; the phrase seems to be C's. Cf *CL* IV 808 of Jan 1818, in which the phrase also occurs. See also *P Lects* Lect 12 (1949) 359; *CN* III 4319 (in which water is "the noblest material image"), 4418–20, 4432–6, and nn. See **45** and n 5, below. Cf STEFFENS *Grundzüge* p 48.

24[5] "Becoming (or coming into being), genesis (or origin)". The force of the infinitive used as a verbal noun (γίγνεσθαι) is here scarcely distin-

guishable from the function of the processive noun cognate with it (γένεσις). For C's use of the Greek infinitive in preference to an abstract noun, cf θεωρεῖν/θεωρία in *CN* III 4328, ποθεῖν/πόθος in **52**, below, and *CN* III 4438.

24[6] Set of four—the Latin-derived word for tetrad or tetractys, for which see **6** n 10, above.

24[7] A starting-point for these thoughts may be noted in *CN* III 3632. See also *CL* IV 771 (Sept 1817): "Water has no figure of itself...". Cf the "single transparent Drop" that represents "The whole Universe" in **6**, above. See also **45**, below. In **175**, below, C was to say that "Only by Resistance can the Life shape itself, and give the formal and formative Channels to the Sap, that feeds its Growth". See also BOERHAAVE **9**.

24[8] Not in *OED*. Formed from the verb "to difference", for which see e.g. **121**, below.

by which the Powers of the Senses are excited ab extra.[9] With the Taste it is a Twin Birth, ~~but~~ that interdetermines[10] each the other. The Will concentered first and then sent forth in a determinate direction is itself a mighty Touching—for the Will is the Kern or neucleus of Life. Hence we say a *touching* Sentiment—nay, I doubt not that all invisible Powers being fuelled and intensified by their outward and visible Symbols, that this is the primary and the main cause, tho' not the only one, of Action and gesticulation & the aidant effects of the same, in oratory.—[a]

25 1 i 49

50. But that which is *not good*, the Holy Ghost ~~speweth~~ evomiteth *that* ~~out~~[1] as a loathsome *Abomination*, as it is written in the "Apocalypse", and as he ~~spewed out~~ evomited[b] the Great Prince *Lucifer*, in his Pride and Perdition.

25A 1 i 50

53. If so, then is it brought to the Mother, the *Heart*, which gives it to all the *Veins* or Powers of the Body, and then the Mouth and Hands

---

[a] Note 24 continued in the margin to the end of § 56; 26—beginning at the opening of § 57, to which it refers—follows directly on 24 without a break in the line

[b] Note 24 is written around 25: 25 therefore was written earlier than 24

24[9] In announcing to Poole in Mar 1801 that he had "overthrown the doctrine of Association, as taught by Hartley", C said that he was confident that "I shall be able to evolve all the five senses, that is, to deduce them from *one sense*, & to state their growth, & the causes of their difference —& in this evolvement to solve the process of Life & Consciousness." *CL* II 706. As this marginal note implies, that "*one sense*" was "feeling" as the state of indifference or union of all the senses. A number of renderings of tactual experience and reflections on it accumulated in the notebooks: see e.g. *CN* I 924, 1297, 1414, 1568, 1812, 1822, 1826, 1827; II 2398, 2399, 2405, 2468, 2495, 3215. In Sept 1801 he was prepared to state that "*tangible* ideas & sensations" are "all that forms *real Self*" and with his usual verbal scrupulosity found it necessary to refine his terms in order to embrace "touch" in an integrative theory of perception. *CN* I 979; and see **147**, below. In Jul 1802 he noticed

the importance of the tactual sense in poetic and critical process: see *CL* II 810; cf "to my *tact*" in AESCHYLUS *Prometheus* **2** and "words excite feelings of Touch" in *CN* II 2152. Cf *CN* III 3401. (For a derogatory observation on the sense of touch as proper to "finger-philosophers", see **76** n 3, below.)

In Aug–Nov 1804 C found in Plotinus (as he thought) through John Smith a phrase for the "touch of the mind"—νοερὰ ἐπαφή. *CN* II 2164; cf 3188. Even this he refined into the more intimate compound (perhaps from Proclus) συναφή, describing an intuition as "an immediate knowing, νοερος συναφη or spiritual contact". *CN* III 4351; cf 4381, and BROWNE *Works* 53. Cf David Jones: "The imagination must work through what is known and known by a kind of touch." *Epoch and Artist* (1973) 244.

24[10] Not in *OED*.

25[1] C shows his distaste for the word "spew" in BEAUMONT & FLETCHER COPY B 57.

lay hold of it. But if it is *not* good, then the Tongue *spits* ~~or spews~~ it out, before it comes to the Princely Counsel.

54. But *though* it be pleasant to the Tongue, and is of a Good Taste, but yet is not *serviceable* and useful for the whole Body, then it is *rejected* nevertheless, when it comes before the Council, and the Tongue must spit ~~or spew~~ it out, and touch it no more.

26 1 i 50

56. As *all Powers* go forth from God the Father and Son, in the Holy Ghost, and so one touches the other, from whence exists the *Tune* or *Mercurius*, so that all the Powers sound and move themselves.

57. Else if one did not touch the other, nothing would stir *at all*, and so this touching makes the Holy Ghost *stir*, so that he rises up in all the Powers, and touches all the Powers of the Father, wherein then exists the heavenly Joyfulness or *triumphing*, as also Tuning, Sounding, Generating, Blossoming, and Vegetation or Springing, *all* which has its Rising from this, that one Power *touches* the other.

58. For Christ saith in the Gospel, *I work, and my Father worketh also*. And he means this very touching and working, in that every Power goes forth from him, and generates the Holy Ghost, and in the Holy Ghost all the Powers are *already* clearly *stirred*, by the going forth of the Father.

§ 57, 58, B. supplies the fundamental position of $V^{(3}$ or the ~~Du.~~[a1] cubo-cube ⟨or Dynamodynamis⟩[2] of Magnetism, i.e. Animal Magnetism.[3]

> [a] "Du." for Δυ of Δυναμις (*Dynamis*)

[26][1] "V" evidently = *vis*, power, the Latin equivalent of δύναμις in n 2, below. "$V^{(3}$"—the equivalent, by abbreviation, of "$V^{(3}M$" in **28**, below, "VM" being *vis magnetica*. The "cubo-cube" is $2^3 \times 2^3 = 16 \times 16 = 256$, the figure of animal magnetism in **28**, below. Cf "the fourfold Four" in **97**, below.

[26][2] "Force-power", by duplication of δύναμις.

[26][3] Animal magnetism, originally called "mesmerism" after its first practitioner, F. A. Mesmer (1734–1815), was sometimes called "zoomagnetism", which—on the analogy of "zoometallic" in **23** and "zoophyte" in **24**—could refer to a power intermediate between animal and magnetic. Mesmer, although treated as an impostor by his medical colleagues, aroused so much interest and controversy by his practice and writings that the king of France in 1784 called a commission of inquiry, which included Benjamin Franklin; in the copious report of the commission Mesmer's facts as reported were endorsed but his theory contested. Among early theorists the chief issue was whether "mesmerism" involved (as the name "zoomagnetism" implies) an actual flow of magnetic current from operator to patient, effecting a direct functional modification of the patient's nervous system, or whether the operator by psychic or suggestive means obliquely altered the

27 ɪ i 50, referring to sections on the senses

The Object and Import of this section from § 35 to 62 § is greatly superior to the workmanship, which is unusually coarse. B. wishes to shew that our senses are not merel things of the Body, but have their root in the spiritual powers, and their prototypes in the most exalted Spirits. His purpose is to raise up the Body, not to degrade the Soul, or to anthropomorphosize the Deity. The motto might be taken from Plotinus—῞Η γὰρ καί ὕλη ασωματος.—[1]

28 ɪ i 50–1

Numeral Signs.

$1 = 2$ or the Birth of the Dyad, then

~~1 + 2 or~~

$1 + 2$ or the manifested Triad.

But $1 = 2 = 1$ Magnetism

$2 \times 2 = 4$ Electricity, or VM.

4×4 16 Galvanism, or $V^{(2}M$.

$16 \times 16 = 256$. Animal Magnetism or $V^{(3}M$

65,536—Spiritual Grace, prevenient and auxiliary

$D^o \times D^o$

$=$

4,294,967,206

Regeneration, or the New Creation.[1]

---

nervous system and state of mind of the patient (in a way that Freud and others found efficacious in the treatment of hysteria). In *The Friend* of 7 Sept 1809 C referred contemptuously to the fanaticism and irrationality of "the Animal Magnetists" and reprinted the statement in 1818, but in later marginalia on the passage he wrote: "N.B. *recanted* since 1817. After subtracting all exaggerated or doubtful Testimonies, these *undeniable* Facts are as important as they are surprizing." *Friend* (*CC*) ɪ 59n. In Jul 1817 he was trying to persuade Gillman to "strip himself of his professional Antibelief" in this controversial matter. *CL* ɪv 751. See also MESMER, JUNG, KLUGE.

27[1] "For matter too is incorporeal" —a variant of Plotinus *Enneads* 2.4.9: ᾿Ασώματος δὲ καὶ ἡ ὕλη—which C had quoted accurately from Cudworth in a notebook entry of Nov–Dec 1796. *CN* ɪ 201. For later variants see e.g.

CN ɪɪɪ 3824 f 112, *CL* ɪv 759 (28 Jul 1817), and Jeremy TAYLOR *Polemicall Discourses* (1674) i 183.

28[1] For "the Birth of the Dyad" see **6** n 10, above: since "2" is the "condition" of realizing "1", the figure "$1 = 2 = 1$" is called magnetism, representing a dynamic condition or state rather than a force. See also **172** n 1, below. "VM"—*vis magnetica*—appears as 2^2—electricity, the first manifestation of magnetic force. Galvanism seems to mean life-giving electricity, as was supposed in some medical practice in C's time. The last five figures increase, according to the level of "spirituality", by the square of the previous number: $2, 2^2, (2^2)^2 \ldots$ The last two numbers are correctly calculated: 65,536 is 256^2, and "$D^o \times D^o$"—i.e. $65,536 \times 65,536$—produces the last number.

With this whole note cf C's letter of Sept 1817 to Tulk: *CL* ɪv 768–9; cf 809.

29 I i 52 | Ch 6 "How an Angel, and a Man, is the Similitude and Image of God"

Now observe,

5. The *whole* Divine Power of the Father speaks forth from all Qualities, the WORD; that is, the Son of God.

6. Now that Voice, or *that* WORD, which the Father speaks, goes forth from the Father's *Salitter* or Powers, and from the Father's *Mercurius*, Sound or Tune: And the Father speaks this forth in himself, and *that* WORD is the very Splendor or Glance proceeding from all his Powers.

7. But when it is spoken forth, it stays or ~~sticks~~ inheres[a] *no more* in the Powers of the Father, but sounds or tunes back again in the whole Father in *all* Powers.

8. Now that WORD, which the Father *pronounces* or speaks forth, has such a *Sharpness*, that the Tone of the WORD goes swiftly in a Moment through the whole *Deep* of the Father, and that Sharpness is the *Holy Ghost.*

9. For the WORD, which is spoken forth, or outspoken, abides as a Splendor or glorious *Edict* before the King.

10. But the Tone or Sound, which goes forth through the *Word*, *executes* the Edict of the Father, which he had outspoken through the Word, and that is the *Birth* or Geniture of *the holy Trinity.*

Strangely as this is expressed, it does really contain the philosophic Truth/ The Λογος which is generated by the mind is distinct, tho' not divisible, from the propagation and *actuation* of the Λογος into Reality.[1] By *Sharpness,* (ill-translated) Boemen means the definiteness, the passing of the mental Word into defined tho' omnipresent Words. Every sentence spoken from a Pulpit gives an illustrative Analogon of this. B's metaphor of Sharpness, i.e. definiteness, which is the *character* of Words *sent forth*, is no more harsh, than Holy *Spirit*, i.e. the moving Air, which is conceived of as ~~its~~ the instrument and body. S. T. C.

30 I i 54

35. With this *Song* I would have the Reader *cited* into the other Life, where he will have *Experience* of it: I am not able to set it down in Writing.

36. But if thou wilt have Experience of it in *this* World, *give over*

---

[a] This part of the textus, with C's alteration, is on p 51

29[1] "The Word". There is a parallel to this note in *SM* (*CC*) 95 and n 2, 97 and n 5.

thy Hypocrisy, Bribery, and Deceit, and thy Scorning; and turn thy Heart in all Seriousness to God: *Repent* thee of thy Sins, with a true Intention and Resolution to live Holily, and pray to God for his holy Spirit. . . .

39. Thou wilt also become quite *another* Man, and wilt think thereon all the Days of thy Life; thy Delight will be more in Heaven than on Earth.

40. For the *Conversation* of the Holy Soul is in *Heaven*, and though indeed it converses in the Body on Earth, yet it is continually with its Redeemer JESUS CHRIST, and eats as a Guest with him. Note this!

§ 35–40. Here comes forth the actual Cause of the affected Contempt and sincere Hatred of the Doctrine of Theosophy.

31   1 i 55 | Ch 7 "Of the Court . . . also of the Government of Angels"
Now observe,

6. When God Almighty had *decreed* in his Council, that he would make Angels or Creatures out of himself, then he made them out of his eternal Power and *Wisdom*, according to the Form and Manner of the Ternary in his Deity, and according to the *Qualities* in his Divine Being.

OBSERVE! This § 6 contains the πρωτον (whether το πρωτον ψευδος to το πρωτον τ᾽ αληθες)[1] of Theosophy, from Heraclitus (500 A.C.) to S. T. C. ⟨(1817 P.C.)⟩[2]—viz. the eternal distinction between the Power or essential Wisdom, ⟨as⟩ *the Ground*, of the *existence* of

31[1] See BAXTER *Reliquiae* COPY B 92 n 1; and cf 70, 137, 158, below. "Fundamental (whether the fundamental error or the fundamental truth)".

31[2] C regarded Heraclitus' philosophy of flux, and particularly this distinction between the ground and God, as a turning-point in the development of philosophy; in Sept 1817 he spoke of himself as "*Heraclitus redivivus*" (*CL* IV 775), and said that "Whatever is excellent in the *Naturphilosophie* of Schelling and his Disciples and offsets, is anticipated therein [i.e. in Heraclitus' philosophy], without the aberrations of the German School." TENNEMANN I, back flyleaves. See also *CN* III 4244, 4351, and esp 4449.

Our knowledge of Heraclitus is derived only from fragments quoted by later writers. Diogenes Laertius 9.8–11 and Aetius (pseudo-Plutarch) attempted collections. Apart from any direct knowledge of these older sources, C would have information from the histories of philosophy he used, especially Stanley and later Tennemann. C may have had access to a copy early in 1810 (*CN* III 3656n) of the first systematic collection of Heraclitan fragments by F. D. E. Schleiermacher, published in Vol I of *Museum der Alterthum-Wissenschaft* ed F. A. Wolf and P. Buttman (2 vols Berlin 1807–10) under the title "Herakleitos der dunkle, von Ephesus, dargestellt aus den Trümmern seines Werkes und den Zeugnissen der Alten". See *SM* (*CC*) 20 n 1 and *CN* III 4351n.

God, and ⟨God himself, as⟩ the *existing* God, or the *living* God—
GOD sensu eminenti![3] In all Living there is ever an aliquid *suppositum*,[4] which can never [be]*a* lifted up into the intelligibile—it is the
Darkness that is the Bearer of all Light.[5] But it is peculiar to God,
that he hath the Ground of *his* Existence within himself—he is
causa sui sufficiens.[6] Now out of this Ground (τo μη ον, or τò απειρον,
which (as Plato hath taught) is rejects and opposes all existence, yet
without which nothing can exist, and therefore he forbids us to call
God the Infinite, who is more truly to be named the Measure of the
Infinite)[7] God created all things—and ⟨only⟩ in this sense of God as
the *Ground*, ⟨is it to be affirmed,⟩ that All Things are God. But to
make the Ground God is Atheism.—Αμην! Αμην! T̶h̶e̶ τò θεῖον is
the foundation, Ο Θεος αειζώων the Crown and Key-stone of all
Philosophy.[8]—And even this Truth was that which was revealed to

a Word supplied by the editor

31[3] "In the eminent sense"—*eminenter*—for which see **12** n 1, above.

31[4] Lit. "something placed *under*"
—a foundation or underpinning, or in
C's more usual term, a "ground". See
CL IV 770, *CN* III 4436, *BL* ch 5 (1907)
I 72, *LR* II 343. "*Sup*positum" is also
the equivalent of "hypothesis", as
opposed to "suffictum" or "hypopoi-
ēsis": see *CN* III 3587 and *CL* IV 467–8.
For *substans* in a similar use see
BIBLE COPY B **136** n 2.

31[5] See *CN* III 4419 and *CL* IV 771.

31[6] "Sufficient cause of himself"—
i.e. both cause and ground. C also
embodied this notion in the term
"Aseity" (from-himself-ness) in e.g.
AR (1825) 328; cf *CL* IV 837 and N
21½ f 62ᵛ.

31[7] The ground is "not-being, or
the undifferentiated". The words "he
forbids us...the Infinite" are not in
fact Plato's but F. H. Jacobi's. They are
repeated variatim in the marginalia on
Isaac TAYLOR *Natural History of
Enthusiasm* (1829) appended to *C&S*,
and the matter is unravelled in *C&S*
(*CC*) 168 n 6. C could have seen the
passage in JACOBI *Werke* III (Leipzig
1816) 211–12, a passage not annotated,
but is more likely to have mistaken it
for Plato's actual words if he had seen
it quoted in SCHELLING *Denkmal der
Schrift von den göttlichen Dingen &c.*

des Herrn F. H. Jacobi (Tübingen
1812) 96–7, the passage again not
annotated. There is a possible difficulty in the word "infinite", a difficulty
that C outflanks by using the term τò
ἄπειρον. Latin *infinitum* is the precise
equivalent of ἄπειρον (without boun-
dary); yet the Latin word—and with it
the English "infinite"—has assumed
the mentally centrifugal implication of
something so vast that its outer limits
(*fines*) cannot be determined, whereas
τò ἀπείρον, in a sense that C seems to
think of as Heraclitan as well as
Platonic, means whatever—no matter
how small—has no defining outline or
envelope. The sense of ἀπείρον that
underlies C's concept of the "infinite"
in the BÖHME marginalia and elsewhere is significant and consistent, implying what is unlimited, undifferentiated, unformed; but the translation
of the term varies with context, e.g.
"the indistinguishable" in *P Lects*
Lect 2 (1949) 97, "the Infinite" in *CN*
III 4449. In **173**, below, he describes τò
μὴ ὄν—which in this note **31** he equates
with τo ἀπείρον—as "the not-being...
unqualified, without poles".

31[8] "Amen! Amen! the DIVINE
is the foundation, The everliving God
the Crown and Key-stone". For τò
θεῖον and ὁ θεός see **6** n 5, above.

the humble and simple Child of God, the unlearned Jacob Behmen!—
"I thank thee, O Father! that thou hast not revealed these things
&c—"⁹

32   1 i 56

27. For the Powers of the Father are *every where*, from and out of
ʽΕΝΑΔΕΣ] which the Son is generated, and from which the Holy
Ghost proceeds forth: *how* should he then be generated only in the
Center of these angelical Gates?

28. This therefore is the only Ground and *Meaning*, that the Holy
Father, who is A L L, would *have* in these angelical Gates his most
joyful and most richly loving Qualities, out of which the most joyful
and most *richly loving* Light, Word, Heart, or Fountain of Powers,
is generated; and therefore has created his Holy Angels in *this* Place
for his Joy, Honour, and Glory.

The Henades, or Ἴδέαι ὑψισται.¹

33   1 i 57

31. For observe this Mystery: The Light, which is generated out of
the Powers of the Father, who is the true Fountain of the Son of
God, is generated *also* in an Angel, and a Holy Man, so that in the
same Light and Knowledge he triumphs in *great* Joy.

32. How then is it that he should *not* be generated every where, in
the *whole* Father? For his Power is A L L, and every where, even
there, where our Hearts and Senses or Thoughts cannot reach.

33. And so now, *where* the Father is, *there* is also the Son and the
Holy Ghost; for the Father every where *generates* the Son, his
holy W O R D, Power, Light, and Sound, and the Holy Ghost goes
every where forth from the Father and the Son, even *within* all the
angelical Gates, and also *without*, besides, or beyond the angelical
Gates.

I would, that § 32. 33. were substituted for our Pseudo-Athanasian

31⁹ Cf Matt 11.25 or Luke 10.21.
C quoted the same verse with reference
to Böhme in *BL* ch 9 (1907) 1 96.

32¹ "Henads...The Henads, or
highest Ideas." A distinction between
the apparent synonyms "henad" and
"monad", established in Neoplatonic
writers, is secured in the words themselves, "henad" being formed from
the numeral (one), "monad" from the
adjective μόνος (sole, single, alone). C

usually honours this distinction: see
e.g. a passage in *"Prometheus"*:
"what Moses established, not merely
as a transcendent *Monas*, but as an
individual Ἑνάς likewise;—this the
Greek took as a harmony". *LR* II
342. In **107**, below, the Monad is the
One (cf e.g. *CN* III 4427), and "henad"
can be used of any number as an idea
(cf **49**, below).

Creed: which latter is substantially *imperfect*, to say the least, and too plainly written in the spirit of hostile Disbelief—of Arian Monotheism, not in the heart and holy Seeing of positive Belief ⟨of⟩ the Unitrine.[1] Τοὺς ἐπιστημονίκους, λόγους μύθους ἡγήσεται (ἡ ψυχη) συνοῦσα τῷ πάτρι καὶ συνεστιωμένη τὴν ἀλήθειαν τοῦ Ὄντος καὶ ἐν αὐγῇ καθαρᾷ· says a Greek Philosopher.[2] i.e. Those notions of God which we attain by the process of the discursive Understanding[3] the Soul will contemplate as *mythical* (= mythological Parables) when it exists (for its own conscious⟨ness⟩)[4] in union (or copresence) with the Father, and is feasting, as a Guest in his * House, on the Truth of absolute Being, and in a *pure* Splendor.[6]

* more strictly, at or before the same *Hearth*, or *Fire-Altar*.[5]

33[1] The "Confession of our Christian Faith, commonly called The Creed of Saint Athanasius", known as *Quicunque vult* from the opening words of the Latin version, is included in the BCP. It is "pseudo-" in two senses: it could not have been composed by St Athanasius (c 296–373), and it is also a pseudo-creed, being not a detailed statement of belief but a compendium of forty theses of the doctrines of the trinity and incarnation. C normally refers to this "Creed" as "pseudo-Athanasian" (e.g. G. BURNET *History* 8). See also *CL* v 87–8 of 16 Jul 1820. For a note on the history of the creeds, written in Jul 1810, see *CN* III 3964; and for an irreverent use of the title *Quicunque vult*, *CN* II 2621. "Unitrine" emphasises the oneness rather than the threeness of the trinity; see *CN* III 4427 and cf 4436.

33[2] The source of this Greek quotation, which is quoted in part in **46** and **47**, below, and in whole in BROWNE *Works* **53**, was presumably John SMITH *Select Discources* (1660) 164–5 ("A Discourse concerning the Existence and Nature of God" ch 10), in which it is attributed to "a Greek philosopher". (The passage is not marked in C's copy.) C had drawn material from the book as early as 1804: see *CN* II 2164n and cf III 4415n.

33[3] The distinction between discursive and intuitive (for which see *CN* III 3315) is central to the difference between understanding and reason. A key statement appears in *SM* (*CC*) 69; see also 60–1 n 1 (marginal note) and *CN* III 3801.

33[4] "For its own consciousness" derives from a confusion or a pun; συνιουσα means "going together with" or "understanding". C points out the root meaning of this verb in *BL* ch 12 (1907) I 166 and n.

33[5] In BROWNE *Works* **53** C translates the corresponding words as "is feasting with him in the Truth". His efforts to give the fullest possible meaning to συνεστιωμένη are typical of C as a translator. *Hestia* (ἑστία) means "hearth, home, altar, fire, &c"; the verb, then, means "to be a guest, or to feast in the house, or at the hearth" of a person. For hearth, light, and ray see **169**, below.

33[6] C's rendering of the Greek varies only slightly from his version in BROWNE *Works* **53**, but differs from Smith's less lively translation: "The Soul will reckon all this knowledge of God which we have here by way of Science but like a fable or parable, when once it is in conjunction with the Father, feasting upon Truth it self, and beholding God in the pure raies of his own Divinity."

34   1 i 57

39. The Father's Power is all ... and the same Power every where generates the Light. Now this UNIVERSAL POWER is, and is called the *Universal Power* of the Father; and the Light which is generated out of that universal Power is, and is called the Son.

40. But it is therefore called the Son, in that it is generated out of the Father, so that it is the *Heart* of the Father in his Powers.

41. And being *generated*, so it is another Person than the Father is; for, the Father is the *Power* and Kingdom, and the Son is the *Light* and Splendor in the Father, and the Holy Ghost is the *Moving* or *Exit* out of the Powers of the Father and of the Son, and forms, figures, *frames*, and images all. ...

43. All Growing or Vegetation, and Forms in the Father, arise and spring up, in the moving of the Holy Ghost; therefore there is but ONE only GOD, and *three* distinct *Persons* in one Divine Being, Essence, or Substance.

Not only the theosophical Truth, but the formal logical and theological accuracy and discriminateness of Jac. Behmen's Explication of the mysterious Tri-unity is worthy of reverential Wonder! And herein I behold the verification of the Apostle Paul's affirmation that the Spirit in man searcheth out the deep things even of God himself.[1]

35   1 i 62 | Ch 8 "Of the Whole Body of an Angelical Kingdom"

21. First there is in the Divine Power hidden in Secret the astringent Quality, which is a Quality of the *Kernel*, Pith, or hidden Being, a sharp Compaction or Penetration in the *Salitter*, very sharp and harsh or astringent, which *generates* Hardness, and also Coldness; and when that Heat is *kindled*, it generates a Sharpness like to *Salt*.

30. ... [The astringent Quality] "*is a Key which locketh into the Chamber of* Death, *and generates Death, from whence proceed Earth, Stones, and all hard Things*."

The translation here adds to the difficulties arising from Behmen's want of words equal to the holding fast of the specific Identity in such various operations under the various influences. But the intention is clear. In the first place he makes four Qualities, that may be called Physical[1]—The first is clearly the Species of Fixity, or

---

34[1] Cf 1 Cor 2.9–11.

35[1] Böhme postulates in all seven "Nature Spirits" or "Qualities", four of which are "physical". In **35–49** C reinterprets these in scientific terms drawn partly from German *Naturphilosophie*. See the "Spiritual Chemistry" of **52**, below.

Attraction, as he himself says; but as no Power ever can subsist in nature, or really, separate, and this power seems more akin to the 3rd, he takes in contraction, or anticipates it/ for so he saw it in his spirit. Now Attraction modified by Contraction is indeed Astringency, and the cause of Hardness, (or relative Cohesion) Coherence, chrystallization, and vegetative forms—likewise of Colors—as Oxyds of the elementary Carbon.—Truly, therefore it looketh likewise into Death, & generates Death. It is the Northern Power, that accumulates Land toward the N.E./2

36 1 i 63

31. The *Second* Quality, or Second Spirit of God in the Divine *Salitter* ... is the *sweet* Quality, which operates in the Astringent, and mitigates the Astringent, so that it is altogether lovely, pleasant, and mild, or meek.

This second is clearly the Repulsive or Positive Pole, as the first is the attractive or negative Pole of the Magnetic Axis—It is the Archeus or Paramount Power of Animality as the former is of Vegetality.[1] Hence itn vegetables it is sweetness, ripeness, putrefaction—It is the South seen by Bœhmen in its ordinary declination to the West, and the cause of the Water that accumulates to the S.W.—Repulsion in its Leaning toward Dilation—Azote modifying or qualifying with Hydrogen.[2]

37 1 i 64

43. The Third Quality, or the Third Spirit of God in the Father's Power, is the bitter Quality; which is a penetrating or *forcing* of the sweet and astringent or harsh Quality, which is *trembling*, penetrating, and rising up.

The third is clearly the Eastern Power, or Contraction: of which Oxygen is the Exponent in our present state of Chemical Knowlege— tho' I deem Oxygen as much to the N. of the Equatorial Line of E.W. Hemisphere, as chlorine to is to the South.—In this Power therefore we must take in all the properties of an xy; perhaps confounded in

35[2] With the polar scheme of **35–37** cf *CL* iv 807–8. Cf also Steffens *Grundzüge* ch 3.

36[1] For "Archeus" see **15** n 2, above.

36[2] "So long back as the first appearance of Dr. Darwin's *Phytologia* [actually *Zoonomia* (1794–6)], the

writer, then in earliest manhood... saw, or thought he saw, that the harmony between the vegetable and animal world, was not a harmony of resemblance, but of contrast; and that their relation to each other was that of corresponding opposites." *Friend* (CC) i 469–70.

Oxygen or mistaken for a compound; perhaps not yet discovered/— of Oxygen; of the equatorial ⟨hemi-⟩Spherical in the Eastern Pole, likewise not yet discovered or at least discriminated; of Chlorine; of Iodine; and perhaps of an xy that may connect Iodine with Azote or the South Pole of the Magnetic Axis.—In this view, ~~will~~ no modern Chemist could give a truer description.

38　ı i 65

58. The fourth Quality, or the fourth Fountain-Spirit in the Divine Power of God the Father, is the Heat, which is the true *Beginning* of Life, and also the true *Spirit* of Life.

Behmen does not mean *Heat*, in that sense in which it is the synthesis ~~of~~ and intermedium of Light and Gravity, or Light in the 2nd Degree of Elasticity, when we take but three Degrees, or rather genera of Degrees—but the physical Basis of Combustion, from whence all corporeal Heat i.e. Fuel is derived. It is plainly the Western or Positive Pole of the Hemispherical Line of Modifying Power—~~Po~~ the Power of Dilation, Positive Electricity, Hydrogen— and truly the *Beginning* of Life, which is always gelatinous—and it continues as the Spirit of Life, even as it is of all (so called) Spirits, or ardent Spirits.[1]—When it *masters* the Southern Pole which is the specific or paramount Principle of the Brain and Nerves, instead of remaining its servant and Carrier or cherub, it produces Hydro- phobia in man and beast[2]—and is the principle of various other Poisons and virific agencies.

39　ı i 66

65. Now the astringent or harsh Quality, together with the sour, always *contracts* or attracts the other Qualities together, and so apprehend and retain the Body and dry it.

　66. For it dries all the other Powers ... and the Sweet softens and moistens all the other. ...

　67. And the Bitter makes all the other *stirring* and moveable, and parts or distinguishes them into Members. ...

　68. And the Heat kindles all the Qualities, out of which the Light

---

38[1] "Ardent Spirits"—the alchemi- cal term for inflammable liquids.

38[2] Cf *CN* ı 72: "extreme Thirst is supposed to be the cause of the Hydrophobia". In Sept 1817 C re- ferred to Gillman's "Work on Hydro- phobia" (1812) as "one of the best Monograms of recent Times". *CL* ıv 776. Gillman dismisses "Deficiency of Water" as a cause of the disease.

rises up and expands itself above in *all* the Qualities, so that the one sees the other. . . .

65, 66, 67, 68 make Behmen's sense as stated in the preceding Note, evident—: only the word, Bitter, is a false version—~~wha~~ *Acerb* is Behmen's Meaning/ or more generally contractive, individualizing.[1]

40 I i 70

112. . . . I will demonstrate to thee . . . that the astringent, sour, and bitter Quality is predominant in the *elementary* Water on Earth.

113. Take Rye, Wheat, Barley, Oats . . . wherein the sweet Quality is *predominant*, soak or steep it in the elementary Water, afterwards *distil* it, then the sweet Quality will *take away* the Predominance from the other; and afterwards kindle that Water, and then you will *see* the Spirit, which is remaining in the Water of the Unctuosity or Fatness of the Corn, which overcame the Water.

In these and the following fact-confirmations I am yet in the Dark— How far ⟨in⟩ such passages, especially those on the force of words where the German seems to be assumed as the only language, Behmen's Understanding was striving to appropriate his past intuitions, and whether they are not to be considered as mere Commentaries in which the Commentator is not *grown up* to his Author, I dare only conjecture. Even in the most startling §^{s}, those on the correspondency of Letters, and syllables, to the universal sense of words, there lies an important Truth hidden in the seeming Blunder of its exemplification.[1]

41 I i 72

135. When the Father speaks or pronounces the WORD, that is, generates his *Son*, which is always done for ever and eternally, then that *Word first* takes its Original in the astringent Quality; therein it fixes, conceives, or *compacts* itself; and in the sweet Quality it takes its Fountain . . . and in the bitter Quality it *sharpens*, and moves itself, and in the Heat it rises up, and *kindles* the Middle sweet Fountain or Source.

In this again, § 135, the distinguishable Tetractys, or two⟨fold⟩

39[1] *OED* cites a definition of "Acerb" for 1658: "sowr, or sharp", but in a general definition offers a more complex notion: "Sour, with an addition of bitterness or astringency". For an example of C's concern to establish a set of precise terms for words that recur in this translation of Böhme—acerb, bitter, sharp, biting, harsh, etc—see **64**, below.

40[1] See **57**, below.

Dynamodynamis, re-appears intelligibly—and commands me to hesitate in the utter rejection of the preceding §s, p. 71, 70.[1]

42 I i 74

156. That friendly *courteous* Love-Light-Fire goes along in the sweet Quality, and rises up into the bitter and astringent Quality, and so *kindles* it, *feeding* them with its sweet *Love-sap*, refreshing, quickening, and enlightening them, and making them *living*, or lively, chearful, and friendly.

157. And when the Light-Love-power comes at them, so that they *taste* thereof, and get its Life, O there is a friendly Meeting, *Saluting*, and Triumphing, a friendly Welcoming and great Love, a most friendly and *gracious* amiable and blessed Kissing, and well-relishing Taste.

158. There the Bridgroom kisses his Bride: O gracious amiable *Blessedness* and great Love, how sweet art thou? How friendly and courteous art thou? How pleasant and *lovely* is thy Relish and Taste? How ravishing sweetly dost thou smell? O noble Light, and *bright* Glory, who can apprehend thy *exceeding* Beauty? How comely *adorned* is thy Love? How *curious* and excellent are thy Colours? And all this *eternally*! Who can express it? . . .

173. O ye *Watchmen* of Israel! why do you *Sleep*? Awake from the Sleep of Whoredom, and dress_ or trim your *Lamps*: The Bridegroom comes, *sound* your Trumpets. . . .

177. O gracious, amiable, blessed Love and clear bright Light, *tarry* with us, I pray thee, for the Evening *is* at Hand. O truth! O Justice and *righteous* Judgment! what is become of thee? Does not the Spirit *wonder*, as if he had never seen the World before now? O *why* do I write of the Wickedness of this World? I *must* do it, and the World curseth me for it. *Amen.*

The §s from § 156 to § 177 inclusive, with the requisite elevation and varying of the phrases and images might be *metrified* into a noble Pæan, or Orphic Hymn εἰς τὸν ἀληθῆ Διονυσον διθυρον.[1]

41[1] *Aurora* ch 8 §§ 112–34. For "Dynamodynamis" see **26** and n 2, above.

42[1] "To the true Dionysus"— διθυρός as etymon of "dithyramb", the ecstatic song traditionally associated with the twice-born Dionysus, who here symbolises to C the godman Christ, eternally generated and born again as man.

43   I i 75

170. O Man! alas, O Man! why dost thou *dance* with the Devil, who is thine Enemy? . . . Why dost thou go on so securely? Is it not a very narrow *Stick* on which thou dancest? Under that small narrow Bridge is *Hell*! Dost thou not see how high thou art, and how dangerously and desperately thou goest?

> to cross a torrent
> on the ~~uncertain~~steady footing of a Spear.
> SHAKESPEAR[1]

44   I i 75

171. O thou blind Man! . . . Is not Heaven and Earth thine? Nay, *God* himself too? What dost thou bring into this World, or what dost thou take along with thee at thy going out of it? Thou bringest an *Angelical* Garment into this World, and with thy wicked Life thou turnest it into a Devil's Mask or *Vizard*.

> Not in entire forgetfulness
> Nor yet in utter nakedness,
> But trailing clouds of Glory do we come
> From God who is our Home.
> HEAVEN LIES ABOUT US IN OUR INFANCY!
> WORDSWORTH.[1]

45   I i 77–8 | Ch 9 "Of the . . . Merciful Love of God"

21. *Now observe*, The gracious, amiable, blessed Love, which is the *fifth* Fountain-spirit . . . is the *hidden* Source, Fountain, or Quality, which the corporeal Being *cannot* comprehend or apprehend, *but* only when it rises up in the Body, and *then* the Body triumphs therein, and behaves itself friendly, lovely, and *courteously*; for that Quality or Spirit belongs *not* to the imaging or *framing* of a Body, but rises up in the Body, as a *Flower* springs up out of the Earth.

22. Now this Fountain-spirit takes its Original at *first* out of the sweet Quality of the Water.

It is most carefully to be born in mind, that Behmen no where gives the syngenesis of Water; but assumes it as a form of Light, as the earthy Sun on Earth, or Gravitation under the form and presidentcy

---

43[1] *1 Henry IV* I iii 192–4: "As full of peril and adventurous spirit | As to o'er-walk a current roaring loud | On the unsteadfast footing of a spear."

44[1] *Ode: Intimations of Immortality* lines 62–6 (*WPW* IV 281), but reading "Nor yet" for "Not in" in the second line.

of Light, even as Gold is Light under the presidential Power and Form of Gravitation—. Conceived *ideally*, and anterior to its qualification by the contact and consequent interpenetration of the two surface Powers of East and West, i.e. of the negative and positive Electricities, he seems to identify it with the South or Positive Pole of the magnetic Line; ~~but~~ not, ⟨however,⟩ as antithetical—but as a Prozŏōte rather than azote or antizote.[1] At least, he appears to regard it as nearer and more akin to the positive or self-fugient Principle, tho' still near enough to the negative or self-seeking Principle to be the ponderability of all luciform Substances. Probably, however, deeper meditation may enable me to reconcile this transformability of the sweet Quality (Nitrogen, or Azot) into ~~water~~ the primary Water with its being the point of bisection in which N. and S. are equal (whi~~ch~~ence its depth-figure, as its only figure in and of itself, i.e. its globosity[)].[2]—Thus it would be the centrifugal Centripetal—or ⟨the⟩ Centrality in the circumference—the principle of Transparency and Chrystallization in the North, (the Life in the Death) and of ponderability in the South—(the Death in the Life.)[3] But as the point on the surface perpendicular to the central point, it is likewise the point of Indifference of the E. and W.—and so only is it the entire Water—or earthly Tetractys ἰσομέρης.[4]—To understand Behmen therefore, we must bear in mind that the word Water sometimes means the Basis, as the null-punct of the Magnetic Line or Line of Being, the ὕδωρ ἐν (or ὑφ') ὕδατι;[5] sometimes the indifference of the East and West, or ~~horizontal~~ equatorial Point of the hemispherical Line of Existence; and sometimes both. In all the three cases Water may be more truly affirmed to be the common base or pondus[6] of Hydrogen and Oxygen, than Hydrogen and Oxygen to be the components of Water.[7]

S. T. Coleridge.

45[1] "Syngenesis"—cited in *OED* for an earlier date but in a different sense. "Prozoote"—not in *OED*, but cf "prozoic" (1858). "Antizote"—not in *OED*.

45[2] On "globosity" see **24**, above.

45[3] Cf *Epitaph* lines 5–6: "That he who many a year with toil of breath | Found death in life, may here find life in death!" *PW* (EHC) I 492; Todt-entanz **1**. Cf "The Night-mare Life-in-Death" of *AM* line 193: *PW* (EHC) I 194.

45[4] For the "equally divided" tetractys, see **24** n 2, above. The word in this sense may be C's coinage.

45[5] "Water in/ beneath water". See **24** n 4, above.

45[6] "Weight"—"ponderability" at n 3, above.

45[7] For the theory of "a common principle in Hydrogen and Nitrogen" ascribed by C to Davy see **117**, below. In C's dynamic scheme the opposites form a *tertium aliquid*, which is not a simple combination of the elements.

46   1 i 77, 78–9, referring to 1 i 77

23. *First* there is the astringent Quality, *then* the Sweet, *next*, the Bitter: The Sweet is in the *Midst* between the Astringent and Bitter. Now the Astringent causes Things to be hard, cold, and dark; and the Bitter *tears*, drives, rages, and divides or *distinguishes*. These two Qualities *rub* and drive one another so hard, and move so eagerly, *that* they generate the Heat, which now in these two Qualities is *dark*, even as Heat in a *Stone* is. . . .

25. Now the astringent and bitter Quality, *without* the sweet Water, rub and drive themselves *so hard* one against another, that they generate the dark Heat, and so are *kindled* in themselves.

§ 23. See Remark over leaf.*ᵃ*

  § 23, p. 77.

Behmen (it should be remembered) *beheld* all things—anschaulich —vernunft-mässig¹—not in the mere lines and surfaces of the Understanding, (λογοις επιστημονικοις)² nor on the contrary, in the chaotic Concretes of the Sense or *sensuous* ~~Intuition~~ Multëity and Immediatcy; but in the interpenetrable, transparent, coinherent concrescents, in ⟨the⟩ Definites undivided, and Multeity in Unity,³ of the esemplastic Nous, or the productive imaginative Reason.⁴ Hence he seldom attends to the distinctions (which are propaideutic merely)⁵ ~~of~~ between the Lines of Being ⟨or modifiability;⟩ and the Line of Existence, Modification, or manifestation. Thus he places the *sweet* between the N. and E.—i.e. between the Attractive, as the determination of its base, and the Contractive or particulative as the specification of its Mode. But the base determinated is the South, Azote, or rather Prozote, and the mode specificated is the West, ~~or~~ ~~hy~~ the Dilative, or universative. This is strictly accurate—the Gluten (Kleber) which is the animality in wheat⁶ and in a less degree in all

---

ᵃ Because 45, beginning at § 21 on p 77, had filled the whole right-hand margin and foot margin of p 77, 46, referring to p 77, had to begin on p 78

46¹ "Intuitively—according to reason".

46² "In the process of the discursive understanding". The Greek phrase occurs in the passage quoted from John Sᴍɪᴛʜ in 33, above.

46³ For "Multeity in Unity" see Aᴛʜᴇɴᴀᴇᴜᴍ 31 n 13, above: it is intimately involved in C's theory of imagination.

46⁴ "'*Esemplastic*. . . .' I constructed it myself from the Greek words, εἰς ἕν πλάττειν, to shape into one. . .".

BL ch 10 (1907) 1 107; also 195. Both "esemplastic" and its related noun "esemplasy" are C's coinages. See also *CN* 111 4176 and n.

46⁵ "Pertaining to preliminary instruction". Cf προπαιδευτικῶς (adv) in Bʟᴀɴᴄᴏ Wʜɪᴛᴇ *Practical Evidence* 2. C's use of "propaideutic" is earlier than *OED* records.

46⁶ C read in Thomas Brande's *Manual of Chemistry* (1819) about gluten, in wheat, being "a tough elastic substance. . .when submitted

other A vegetables, has azote or the calcareous principle hydrogenized (far more philosophically we might say, disoˣxydated) as its
essential form and formal essence—oxygenate this in more and
more, and you have Starch, Sugar, Honey: the increasing viscosity
marking the influence cr potenziating of the Carbonic or Astringent
Principle—. Observe too, that Behmen's name of his first Quality is
but another instance of this ~~indistinction~~ Identity of M Essence and
Existence, Matter and Form: for the Astringent is the Attraction
contractive—and not merely the Attractive ⟨or⟩ Fixive,[7] or ⟨the⟩
Power of Coherence ⟨per se.⟩—a striking illustration ⟨exists for us⟩
in ~~the~~ Sugar of Lead[8]—Lead being in the Southern ~~or~~ Series i.e. the
series of incoherent and soft metals/ those in which the Azote is
Lord over the Carbon, ~~th~~ the zωophyteium over the phytozöium,[9]
tho' this metal is among the Northermost or Tropical metals of those
South of the Line./ This which is primarily S. (as known by its
incoherence) by W. (as known by its great fusibility) is acted on by
the N. (it is chrystallized) and by the East (oxydated, particulated &c)
and the result is a Lump of pure Sugar of Lead, perilously confoun-
dible with a Lump of refined chrystallized vegetable Sugar.—[a]

§ 25, again, is another instance, that by the sweet Water B. intends
South as West, and vice-versâ—i.e. that he identifies the ~~Azote~~
Nitrogen and Hydrogen of our present Chemists as matter and form
of the same Element/[10] and our gallicizing Laboratory Atomists
must explain the Phænomena of Rain and the various results of
Freezing more satisfactorily than they have hitherto done,[11] before

[a] The comment on § 25 follows directly on without a paragraph break

---

to destructive distillation, it furnishes
ammonia, a circumstance in which it
resembles animal products" (pp
363–4). N 27 f 63ᵛ. C was particularly
interested in the chemical interaction
at the boundaries of animal, vegetable,
and mineral. On animality in vegetation
see also *TL* 71–2.

46[7] "Fixive" is ascribed to C (1832)
by *OED*, but neither "particulative"
nor "universative" is recorded.

46[8] C used the illustration of sugar
of lead in *P Lects* Lect 4 (1949) 152
as an example of the need to desynonymise. Vegetable sugar and
sugar of lead (acetate of lead) look the
same but have different properties:
the one nourishing, the other poison-

ous. The first is a zoophyte, the second
a phytozoium: see 24 n 1, above, and
n 9, below.

46[9] "Phytozöium" (not in *OED*),
more usually "phytozoon", is in C's
use nearly synonymous with "zoophyte" (see 24 n 1, above); but he
chooses one term or the other to
indicate the relative predominance of
"animality" or "vegetality". See n
6, above. *OED* records "phytozoon"
for 1842 (zool.) and 1861 (biol.):
"zoophyte", however, is a seventeenth-
century word.

46[10] See 45 n 7 and 47, below.

46[11] C was strongly opposed to
Dalton's atomic theory and to
"French" materialism wherever he

a verdict can be brought in against the superior Insight of the humble unlearned Cobler of Gorlitz.

47 I i 79–80

39. For the astringent Quality *loves* the sweet Water. And first, because in the sweet Water the Spirit of Light is generated, and *imbibes* or gives Drink to the astringent, hard and cold Qualities; also it enlightenes them, and warms them; for in Water, Light, and Heat, the *Life consists*.

§ 39. Water is the Gravitation in its greatest proximity to Light— therefore, is Water the differencible Indifference, or Depth (i.e. Body, Base) in its most passive state of modifiability. Heat is the intermedium and Synthesis of Light and Gravity. Light itself the formative ~~and motive~~, manifestative, the vis motrix, in short, the existential principle.[1] Profoundly therefore doth Behmen affirm that in Water, Heat, and Light the *Life* consists!—

Water as Water is Death indeed, and (as before I have observed)[2] the ponderable matter of all the aeriform substances; ~~and in~~ but it is Death as the prothesis of Life, it is Gravitation in its most emancipable State—and as the ⟨ever⟩ variable, differencible Bases, it is there to receive the Light, while Heat is the sign and product of the ever continuing Process—. All beyond this is but a continued ascent of Individuation: till the system of materiality—with the xy as the central Zero (i.e. +0 because all, no number because the substratum of all numbers) as the Prothesis, Light and Gravitation as Thesis and Antithesis, and Heat as the Synthesis—the Thesis again, ~~with it~~ as secondary Prothesis, or null punct with its Thesis & Antithesis— and in like manner the Antithesis with its Thesis and Antithesis, viz. Carbon and Nitrogen as the Poles of Gravitation, and ⟨the Imponderable of⟩ Oxygen & Hydrogen those of Light, each with its proper synthesis, and both (or the Quaternion) with the common synthesis, viz. first, Metal = Carbonazot, second, Galvanismc Etherie, third, Water—till, I say, this—the system of Material Nature, vegetative, animal, and Residual is compleated.—Then comes the Discontinuity, or Revelation of a Will as the Supporter and Lord of Nature—A new Process commences—in which the

---

saw it. See *CL* IV 760–1; cf **17** and n 3, above. C may also here be referring to an experiment that he attributed to Priestley in **117**, below.

47[1] "Vis motrix"—the moving force. For "existential" see BAXTER *Reliquiae* COPY B **8** n 1.
47[2] See **24** at n 7 and **45**, above.

Thesis and Antithesis are Light as objective, and Self as subjective, with the Geist, Ghost, or Spirit, as the Identity of Both.—So must we contemplate it when we take it by ascent, or speculatively—But far more august is the religious point of view, viz. that of Descent and Fall. The latter point of view, Religion alone, solves the discontinuity—and this view therefore is the ~~the~~ true Philosophy[3]—, but the former is the necessary (in all ordinary cases at least) initiation, or προπαιδεια.[4] Behmen ~~however~~ as a favored Epopt, συνεστιωμενος την αληθειαν του Οντος ἐν ἀυγῇ καθαρᾷ,[5] was placed on the religious point of view, and therefore he beheld in all material elements their homogeneity with Spirit, instead of the homogeneity of Spirit with matter.—

48 1 i 94 | Ch 11 "Of the Seventh Qualifying or Fountain Spirit"

25. The astringent Quality is the *first* Spirit, and that attracts or draws together and makes all dry: The sweet Quality is the *second* Spirit, and that softens or mitigates it: Now the *third* Spirit is the bitter Spirit, which exists from the fourth and first.

26. And so when the third Spirit in its Rage *rubs* itself in the Astringent, then it kindles the *Fire*, and then the *Fierceness* in the Fire rises up in the Astringent. In that Fierceness now the bitter Spirit becomes *self-subsisting*; and in the sweet it becomes meek or *mild*; and in the hard it becomes *corporeal*; and so now it subsists, and is also the *fourth* Spirit.

Could it be doubted from the preceding Chapters, yet this (§ 25, 26) would make it evident, that Behmen's 4 Powers answer to those of which Carbon, Azote, Oxygen and Hydrogen are the elementary representatives. The production of the latter is explained variously by him in different parts of his Works, but not diversely—in all, its

---

47[3] Cf C's letter to Tulk Sept 1817: "...I am endeavoring to trace the Genesis...the *Birth* of Things: and this under the disadvantage of beginning...with the lowest, per ascensum: whereas the only true point of view is that of Religion, namely, per descensum". *CL* iv 769; this letter—with another to Tulk in Jan 1818 (*CL* iv 804–9)—presents in greater detail the same argument as the present note. See also *CN* iii 3263n.

47[4] "Preliminary instruction"; cf "propaideutic" in **46** n 5, above.

47[5] An epopt—lit. "onlooker"—used especially of an initiate into the Eleusinian mysteries (see **68**, below), here means an initiate into the mysteries of nature. In **89** C uses the word to enhance his meaning in calling Böhme a "Seer", and in **158** refers to Böhme as the "Cabiric Physiotheist". The Greek phrase is part of the passage quoted from John SMITH in **33** (see also **46**); C translates it "feasting...on the Truth of absolute Being, and in a *pure* Splendor". Cf "epopsy" in **120**, below.

connection with azote is maintained, and in all it is the positive, the *real*, pole of Oxygen, as the ideal, & negative.

49 I i 101

117. Yet thou shalt know this, that always in a Place suddenly *one* Quality shows itself *more powerfully* than the other, suddenly the second prevails, suddenly the third, then suddenly the fourth, suddenly again the fifth, suddenly the sixth, then again suddenly the seventh.

The birth, distinction, yet involution of Ideas, i.e. Monads, or Sums total, under the presidency of some one of the infinite figures or numbers, all contained in each—[1]

50 I i 122, pencil | Ch 13 "Of the Terrible . . . Fall of the Kingdom of Lucifer"

40. In the Middle, or central Fountain or Well-spring, which is the Heart, where the Birth rises up, the astringent or harsh Quality rubs itself with the bitter and hot; and there the *Light* kindles, which is the *Son*, of which it is always impregnated in its Body, and that enlightens and makes it *living*.

This seems to *contain* the truth respecting the genesis of Light; but not to reveal it. The antecedents in the materiâ subjectâ[1] are, says Behmen, Astringent attraction modified by Contraction on the one hand, and ⟨by⟩ the simultaneous action of all, which must needs appear to have its focus at the Center. Now this simultaneity of Act is = Gravitation. And this having been established, Light appears. The chasms of causation in this History are evident; and the cause not less so—viz. the materia subjecta is made the Agens in se,[2] exclusive of all other Agency.

51 I i 123

48. But now the qualifying or fountain Spirits in *Lucifer* did not so; but they seeing that they sat in the highest Primacy or *Rank*, they moved themselves so hard, and strongly, that the Spirit which they generated was very fiery, and climbed up in the Fountain of the Heart, like a proud *Damsel* or Virgin.

49. If the qualifying or fountain Spirits had moved, qualified, or acted gently and lovely, as they *did* before they became creaturely, as

49[1] For "Monads" see **32** n 1, above. A schematic presentation of the "birth, distinction, yet involution of Ideas, i.e. Monads" is given in **28**, above, and cf **107**, below.

50[1] "Underlying matter". Cf **31** n 4, above. On the genesis of light see *CN* III 4418, 4456, *CL* IV 771, 806–7.

50[2] "The one acting (agent) upon itself".

they were *universally* in God before the Creation, then had they generated also a gentle, lovely, mild and meek Son in them, which would have been *like* to the Son of God; and then the Light in *Lucifer* and the Light of the Son of God had been *one* Thing, one qualifying, operating, acting, and affecting, one and the same lovely Kissing, Embracing, and Struggling.

Paradise Lost, Book IInd Jacob Behmen's is far the nobler, nay, even the more poetical, conception—the proud Virgin, and then the kindled Bride, are exquisite.[1]

52　ɪ i 125–7

66. The whole Deity has in its innermost or beginning Birth, in the Pith or Kernel, a very tart, terrible *Sharpness*, in which the astringent Quality is a very horrible, tart, hard, dark and cold Attraction or Drawing together, like *Winter*, when there is a fierce, bitter, cold Frost, when Water is frozen into Ice, and besides is very intolerable. . . .

68. After such a Manner and Kind is the astringent Quality in the innermost Kernel or Pith *in itself*, and to itself alone, without the other Qualities *in God*. . . .

69. And the bitter Quality is *a tearing*, penetrating and cutting bitter Quality or Source: for it *divides* and drives forth from the hard and astringent Quality, and makes the Mobility.

70. And betwixt these two Qualities is Heat generated from its hard and fierce bitter Rubbing, Tearing, and Raging. . . .

It has become evident to me of late, ~~that~~ for I myself have partaken of the same error, that Behmen has constructed in his spirit the working of the Spirit on the faces of the Waters, and of God the Word in the Creation out of the Indistinction (Chaos) and received this as Deity in the eternal Plenitude. Hence it is, that he approaches so perilously near to Pantheism[1]—while yet, his Heart trembling truthward, there was still an unseen presence, a desiderium, a presentation by a sense of *missing* (τῷ ποθεῖν) of the more glorious Antecedent, which revealing itself at moments dazzle-dims the other Contemplation, like cross lights.[2] Then only can his Books be ~~tr~~

51[1] Presumably the account of Satan's passage from the dark abyss into light in *Paradise Lost* ɪɪ 1034ff.

52[1] C recognised that he too had approached "so perilously near to Pantheism": see **1** and n 2, above.

52[2] Cf the "intellecturition" of **122** and n 5, below—here characterised as "yearning", πόθος, the longing for something glimpsed and desired (*desiderium*). This concept, here reinforced by his use of the verbal noun rather than the noun πόθος (cf e.g. *CN* ɪɪ 2000, ɪɪɪ 3325, 4335, 4438), has intensely personal implications for C's intellectual life in his recognition of a

read with the full profit derivable from them, when this errors (*Pars pro Toto*)[3] has been detected, so that what may be affirmed of God in his eternity be separated from the far larger and more instructive portion of the Aurora and the 3 Principles, in which the initiative Act is the divine Love and the Word that went forth, but the Operation and the Steps of the Process are in the fallen Spirits, = the agonies and throes of the Creaturely Birth in the Chaos. Every now and then he catches a rayes from the Higher, but unconscious of its Alterity,[4] he blends what he should separate—At each of these momentary eradiations he perceives a contradiction, an incompatible attribute—and then bids the Reader not think so and so, without shewing him how it is possible for him to think otherwise. He takes the depth of the Creauaturely Spirit for the Fathom-line of the Highest in the Highest,[5] and seeks to cover over the error by forewarning us to understand his words in the divine sense—which is much the same as if a man should talk of Squares, Parallelograms, and Cycloids in the Godhead, and then ~~bid~~ warn you above all things not to think of material or geometrical Figures by those Words.— Thus at the beginning of this very Page, what Behmen, *startlingly* to many who walk humbly with the Lord their God,[6] entitles "the true Birth or Geniture of God"[7] is in fact the Geniture of the World ὕπο τοῦ Θέου[8]—the parturience of Chaos made pregnant by the Divine Love, Life, and Intelligence that by the ineffable Greatness of Mercy and free Grace had passed again into the Void, that by guilty Self-inanition had become without form and void[9]—and thus re-entering the darksome Womb of the Apostacy and "made it pregnant".[10]

Thus the Errors of this extraordinary Man fall under two heads.[11] The first, easily separable, as a mere scum, by the thoughtful Reader,

sexual component in πόθος—or else that the only way of rendering the feel of intellecturition is in a sexual image. See e.g. *CN* III 3989 (Oct 1810), in which SH is clearly in mind and the overt subject is "true *Love*" as distinct from "Lust". See also *CN* III 3266. Schelling's notion that the gods of the mysteries were named "hunger" is considered in **140** and n 4, below. See also **122** n 5, below.

52[3] The fallacy of taking "the Part for the Whole". See *CN* III 3451.

52[4] "Otherness". An example of C's familiar triad Ipsëity–Alterity–

Community appears in *TT* 8 Jul 1827. See also esp *LR* III 2. The concept of God as "Alter et Idem"—Other and the Same—is developed in **178**, below.

52[5] Cf *CN* III 3768.

52[6] Cf Micah 6.8.

52[7] I.e. *Aurora* §§ 81–6: I i 126ff.

52[8] "By/through the agency of God".

52[9] See **55**, below.

52[10] Cf *Paradise Lost* I 22 (var).

52[11] C passed a similar judgement on Böhme's system in *P Lects* Lect 11 (1949) 330 and in the Conclusion to *AR*.

and which calls only for a forgiving Smile, is the occasional substitution of the Accidents of his own a peculiar acts of association
(for instance, his exemplification of the language of Nature) for
the laws and processes of the creaturely Spirit in universo. The
second, componental and dissolved thro' the whole, which it requires a spiritual Chemistry, and the addition of a new ~~substance~~
ingredient to decombine and precipitate—the confusion of the
creaturely spirit in the great moments of its renascence ανακοσμησ-
έως)[12] thro' the Breath and Word of Comforter and Restorer for ~~the~~
deific energies in Deity itself.—He preposterizes[13] the Consequent of
the Fall into the absolute First, and ignorant of the only sense, in
which it is other than an Abstraction, he makes it a mere abstraction,
and then by a second lawless abstraction, that of Subject and Object
from the idea of the Absolute, he identifies the former with God as
Omneity,[14] out of which the Living Godhead evolves, as an eternal
Birth, as the Creatures ~~are~~ bud forth ⟨&⟩ individualize, each out of
its pre-impregnated Nature. In the first instance his error is radically
the same as that of Spinoza, and in both instances the same as that of
Schelling and his followers.[15] What resemblance it may have to the
system of Giordano Bruno, I have read too few of Bruno's writings
to say, and read them at a time, when I was not competent to ask the
question, but was myself intoxicated with the vernal fragrance &
effluvia from the flowers and first-fruits of Pantheism, unaware of its
bitter root, ~~satis~~pacifying my religious feelings meantime by the dim
distinction, that tho' God was = the World, the World was not = God

52[12] Probably C's coinage, meaning "re-creation", with secondary meanings of "reordering", since κόσμος means "order, adornment, world-order, universe". With this whole sentence cf *BL* ch 13 (1907) I 202: imagination "dissolves, diffuses, dissipates, in order to recreate". In *CN* III 4418 f 15ᵛ (c Aug 1818) C uses the phrase ἐκοσμησε τὸ Χάος—"he ordered Chaos" or "he made the world out of Chaos".

52[13] "He makes an after-event come first"—C's coinage (not in *OED*). For the basis of the word see **112** n 1, below. C notices other instances of Böhme "preposterizing"—but without using the word—in **63** and **112**, below.

52[14] "Allness". For the family of words in -ëity see ATHENAEUM **31** n 3.

52[15] For Spinoza's error, see **10** n 3, above. This comment on Schelling, with similar but more extensive comments in **73** and **74**, helps to date and to explain the fading of C's enthusiasm for Schelling and his followers, and marks an important stage in the evolution of his own opinions. See also *CN* III 4263, 4397, 4449–53, his comment on Schelling written to Green in Dec 1817 (*CL* IV 792), and his extended critique—also written to Green—in Sept 1818 (*CL* IV 873–6). In *CL* IV 874 C complains that "Polarity is asserted of the Absolute, of the Monad". Nevertheless, C continued to use many of the concepts of *Naturphilosophie*.

—as if God were a Whole composed of Parts, of which the World was one![16]

P.S. I earnestly intreat of whoever may hereafter chance to peruse *this* Copy of Behmen's works, that if he should find in the marginal MSS Notes, preceding or following the present note, any positions or opinions contradictory to it and partaking of the error now & here exposed, he will attribute them to the earlier date, at which they were written.

S. T. Coleridge, Highgate—27 August, 1818[17]

53 I i 173, pencil | Ch 18 "Of the Creation of Heaven and Earth; and of the First Day"

20. Herein lies the *Pith*, or Kernel; for Gold, Silver, and precious Stones, and all bright Ores of Minerals, have their Original from the *Light*, which shone before the Times of Wrath in the outermost Birth or Geniture of Nature ... And so now ... all his qualifying or fountain Spirits love the *Kernel*, or the best Thing that is in the corrupted Nature, and that they use for the Defence, Protection, and Maintenance of themselves.

See p. 222, § 38.[1] Here then the Wheel moved too rapidly. At least, B. seems to have forgotten his own just and profound distinction of the *created* Light from the Light eternally begotten.[2] But he needed

52[16] For C's reading of Giordano Bruno see **4** n 1, above. C had already stated the philosophical basis of pantheism in a comment on Plotinus in Nov 1803: "God is not all things, for in this case he would be indigent of all; but all things are God, & eternally indigent of God." *CN* I 1680.

52[17] This PS is evidently a preliminary version of the more formal and more fully developed statement in **1**, above.

53[1] *Aurora* ch 22 § 38: "I do not say that I cannot err at all. For there are some Things, which are not *sufficiently* declared, and are described as if it was from a *Glimpse* of the great God, when the Wheel of Nature whirled about *too swiftly*, so that Man with his half dread and dull Capacity, or Apprehension, cannot sufficiently comprehend it; but what thou *findest not sufficiently* declared in one Place, thou

wilt find it done in another; if not in this, yet in the other Books."

53[2] Böhme had said earlier (pp 168–9: ch 22 §§ 1, 3–5, 17–18) that gold, silver, etc had their source in the Light that was created after the Times of Wrath, yet here he says that they had their source in the Light that shone before the Times of Wrath. The distinction that C refers to is in § 18: "But seeing the Light in the outermost Birth was extinguished, the Heat also was captivated in the Comprehensibility or Palpability, and could *no more* generate its Life. From thence *Death* came into Nature, so that Nature or the corrupt Earth could no more help it, and thereupon *another* Creation of Light must needs follow, or else the Earth would have been an *eternal* indissolvable Death; but now the Earth generates or brings forth Fruit in the Power and Kindling of the *created* Light."

another distinction—he opposes *power* to *palpability*, as if these two were the only forms.[3] Had he opposed the Real to the *Potential, and derived the Palpable by the superinduction of the former on the latter, he would have antedated the World in Chaos, or fallen into the sad and common error of conceiving Chaos as a chemical Olla Podrida—[5]

* That state, I here mean, to which the apostate Will had reduced itself by willing a reality contradictory to the only Condition, under which a reality can subsist. Behmen saw this state repeatedly in the Vision, but did not master it. It is the barren Throe, the anguish of the vain striving = Tohu Bohu—Τωϝυ Βωϝυ[4]

54 1 i 174, pencil

29. But this Spirit, or this Birth has *seven* Kinds or Species, *viz.* the astringent, the sweet, the bitter, the hot: these four generate the *Comprehensibility* in the third Birth or Geniture.

30. The fifth Spirit is the Love, which exists from the Light of the Life, which generates *Sensibility* and *Reason*.

31. The sixth Spirit is the Tone, which generates the *Sound* and the Joy, and is the Spring or Source rising up through all the Spirits. . . .

32. The seventh Spirit is Nature, in which stands the corporeal Being of all six Spirits, for the six Spirits generate the seventh. . . .

1. Attraction
2 Repulsion

3 Contraction
4. Dilation.

5. Love, as Sense.
6. Love, as communication.
7 Gravitation—Centrality.

55 1 i 175, pencil

41. But now thou must *not think*, that thereupon the whole Nature or Place of this World is become a mere bitter Wrath of Gcd[.] No;

53[3] For "palpability" see ch 22 § 18, quoted in n 2, above.

53[4] "Tōhu bōhu"—C has transliterated the Hebrew term into Greek with the help of the obsolete *digamma* (ϝ)—which AV translates "without

form and void" in Gen 1.2 and Jer 4.23. See also *CN* III 4418 f 13: "des Flüssigen, an Indistinction, Chaos, or Tohu Bohu". Cf **146**, below.

53[5] Hotch-potch, mish-mash, indistinguishable confusion.

here lies the Point; the *Wrath* does not comprehend the innermost Birth or Geniture in Nature, for the *Love* of God is yet hidden in the Center, in the whole Place of this World, and so the House which Lord *Lucifer* is to be in, is *not fully* separated, but there is still in all Things of this World, both Love and Wrath *one in another*, and they always wrestle and strive one with another.

Here is *the depth.*—It was so *potentially*, and so must have remained, but that the Spirit and the Word (Logos) returned into it—but it was not possible for the Real to have passed forth into it without realizing the Wrath, as well as the Love: so that the mere⟨ly⟩ potential Wrath became (relatively) real, and the real Life and Love became *relatively* potential—this was the ineffable Mystery of the divine Self-inanition.[1] But I say again, this is the *Depth*—in which the Light is Darkness to the Dark, and the Darkness Light to the Children of Light.   *S. T. C.*

56   I i 175, pencil

45. Yet I do not say this, as if every Man was *holy* as he comes from his Mother's Womb, but as the Tree is, so is its Fruit. Yet the Fault is not God's, if a Mother bears or brings forth a Child of the Devil, but the Parent's Wickedness. . . .

47. For every Man is *free*, and is as *a God* to himself; he may *change* and alter himself in this Life either into Wrath, or into Light. . . .

§ 45. § 47.—I warn all Inquirers into this hard point to *wait*—not only not to plunge forward before the Word is *given* to them, but not even to paw the ground with impatience. For in deep stillness only can this truth be apprehended. Suffice—it *ought* to suffice—that the Will cannot be contained in *time*—that Birth *is* a form of Time—but all guilt is in and of the *Will*—therefore, it cannot be essentially connected with the Birth.[1] *How* can this *be*? The above is the Answer —viz. *How* could it be otherwise?—How can this be *conceived*?—The reply, yea, and the first step of the *solution*, is: Crede ut intelligas.[2]

55[1] Cf **52**, above.

56[1] See *AR* (1825) 73–4: "Whatever is representable in the forms of Time and Space, is Nature. . . . And by *spiritual* I do not pretend to determine *what* the Will *is*, but what it is *not*— namely, that it is not Nature."

56[2] This phrase occurs many times in St Augustine's works. A central place is his Sermon 43 on Isa 7.9 in the Septuagint version: "Unless ye believe, ye will not understand", in which "crede ut intelligas" occurs four times in §§ 3–7. Migne *PL* xxxviii 255–8. For other uses by C see *CN* iii 3888 and n and *SM* (*CC*) 97 n 1. Augustine is quoted again in **110**, below.

57 i i 195 | Ch 19 "Concerning the Created Heaven, and the Form of the Earth . . ."

133. The Word (*Nacht*) conceives itself first at the Heart, and the Spirit makes a grunting Sound with or in the astringent Quality, yet not wholly comprehensible to the astringent Quality; afterwards it conceives itself upon the Tongue: But *all the while* it grunts at the Heart, the Tongue *shuts* the Mouth, till the Spirit comes, and conceives itself upon the Tongue, but then it opens the Mouth suddenly, and lets the Spirit *go forth*.

It is too absurd to be confuted, without absurdity.—How does it apply to skotos?[1] Or where shall we find the *grunt* of the German *ch* in the English Nite? (Night.) Now Nitor, the same sound, is Shiningness, in Latin. The only possible manner~~eans~~ of retrieving, in some small measure, Behmen's character, would be to interpret all these passages—not as *instances* of the *reality*, but as elucidations of the mode: and the possibility, of the process—in the first birth and evolution of Language—ἔπεα ζ ζωοντα.[2]

And after all, it may be fairly asserted that these passages are not more extraordinary for Jacob Behmen, than the Cratylus is for Plato. Take either in the literal sense, and it is below confutation: and whatever can be imagined to clear up Plato, will mutatis mutandis apply equally to J. Behmen.[3]   *S. T. C.*

58 i i 204–6 | Ch 20 "Of the Second Day"

89. For when *Adam* spoke at the first, he gave Names to all the Creatures, according to their Qualities and innate instant Operations, Virtues or Faculties. And it is the very language of the total universal Nature, but is not known to every One.[1] For it is a hidden

57[1] C played on the word σκότος (dark) in *CN* iii 4134 f 167ᵛ and, in a more personal context, in *CN* iii 4243.

57[2] C translates the phrase himself in *CN* iii 4237 (28 Oct 1814): "living words". The phrase, used again in *C&S* (*CC*) 184 and in the Author's Preface to *AR* (1825) pp xi–xii, is a variant of the Homeric phrase ἔπεα πτερόεντα (winged words), which C used several times, often (as here) recalling the title of J. Horne Tooke's philological book Ἔπεα πτερόεντα, *or The Diversions of Purley* (2 vols 1798, 1805), in which C says he wrote an inscription. See also *CN* iii 4237n.

57[3] For other discussion of this problem, see **40, 58, 89, 92, 96**. Swedenborg also attempted analyses of biblical language; and in SWEDENBORG *De equo albo* (1758) 16, C noted a similarity of sense and "extreme dissimilarity in the two men in point of *Learning*".

58[1] This notion of Böhme's, marked in passing by C in **52**, above, is more fully considered in SWEDENBORG *True Christian Religion* (2 vols 1819) i 470–1: "Behmen's 'LANGUAGE OF NATURE', which, appearing in his first Work as a ludicrous absurdity, in each succeeding work defecates & struggles upward to a grand *Idea*. . .".

secret Mystery, which is imparted to me by the Grace of God from the Spirit, which has a Delight and Longing towards me.

Now observe,

90. The word *Wasser* (*Water*) is thrust forth from the Heart, and *closes* the Teeth together, and passes *over* the astringent and bitter Qualities, and touches them not, but goes forth *through* the Teeth, and the Tongue contracts and rouzes up itself together with the Spirit, and *helps* to hiss, and so qualifies, mixes, or *unites* with the Spirit, and the Spirit presses very forcibly through the Teeth.

This so frequent and confident recurrence to the "very language of the total universal nature", which yet consists of Behmen's observations of the shapes and motions of his organs of speech while he pronounces aloud a Syllable in *German*, and this too under the influence of a previous knowlege of the meaning of the whole Word, is to *me* at this present time (July 19, 1817) by far the most incomprehensible—*seems* to me the one *absurd*—thing in all his works. —I cannot explain it.—How is it possible, that after the appearance of the AURORA in print,[2] and during all the time he was maintaining himself by transcribing the MSS of his following and maturer works —how, I say, is it conceivable, that neither his own mind nor any of his correspondents should have put the sameimple question to him— Can the syllable *Wass* require or be accompanied by the same motions of the tongue &c as the asperated vowel *Hoo*—or the open vowel a?—And in like manner *ser* with the same as dore, and that again as qua?[3] Is the total language of Nature for the *German* only—the *German* Catholic—Are not the Greek ὕδωρ (hoodore)[4] and the Latin Aqua as good words as *Wasser*?—Behmen often speaks of Latin and Greek and Hebrew—he could not, one would think, be so very ignorant as to take the German for the only language—he must have heard, that the Old Test. was translated from the Hebrew, the New from the Greek? If he had asserted that a spiritual and genetic intuition of the thing, Wasser, of the relation, Unser Vater, &c &c[5] uttered itself forth by such and such acts of the component Powers (the seven spirits according to him) in the Throat, Palate, Tongue, Lips, Teeth, &c/ and had affirmed, that the

---

58[2] *Aurora* did not appear in print during Böhme's lifetime, but circulated in ms.

58[3] The syllables of *Wasser*, ὕδωρ, and *aqua*: "Was/ Hoo (ὑ)/ a"; "ser/ dore (δωρ)/qua".

58[4] A phonetic version of the preceding Greek word for "water".

58[5] The two opening words of the Lord's Prayer in German. See **148** textus, below.

uncorrupted Root was essentially the same in all languages, tho'
now altogether passed away, even as jour retains no one element of
Dies, nor Dies of Ημερα—or Anfang of the Mosaic Reshith—*then*
he would have asserted little more than Whiter & others have
done.[6]—But what has this to do with the *German* Syllables exclusively,
to which alone his descriptions answer? But even suppose him
⟨ημ⟩[a7] to have been so utterly ignorant, as to have supposed the
German the universal only language, yet the same syllable in the
same language could not always mean the same or similar, ex. gr.
ser in Wasser and Unser, un in unser and unhold. Te Deum and
Dich Gott—&c &c.[8]—In short, it is to me utterly inexplicable—The
Blunder is so excessively gross, if a blunder, & I find nothing like it
in the rest of his Writings, be they deliria or be they revelations: and
if noth a this blunder, I what is it? A and B. may both intend the
same act or object, at the moment that the former utters the word
Sprach, and the latter said, or dixit, or disse, or α εφη;[9] but it is
impossible, that the configurative movements of the Mouth and
Larynx can be the same.

59 I i 207, pencil | Ch 21 "Of the Third Day"

24. *Not* that the Fruits of the Earth are thereupon *wholly* in the
Wrath of God; for the one only incorporated or compacted Word,
which is immortal and *incorruptible*, which was from Eternity in the
Salitter of the Earth, sprung up again in the Body of Death, and
brought forth Fruit out of the *dead* Body of the Earth; but the Earth
comprehended *not* the Word, but the Word comprehended the
Earth. . . .

26. Thou must not think, that thereupon the outermost dead
Birth or Geniture of the Earth has got *such* a Life through the risen
Word that sprung up, so that it is *no more* a Death: No; that can
never be, for that which is *once* dead in God, that is really dead, and

a The two Greek letters are written below "him"

58[6] *Jour*, *dies*, ἡμέρα—French,
Latin, and Greek for "day"; *Anfang*
and *reshith* are German and Hebrew for
"beginning", as in Gen 1.1. For Walter
Whiter (1758–1832) and his *Etymologicum Magnum* (1800) and *Etymologi-
con Universale* (1811, 1825) see *CN* III
3762n.

58[7] A teasing phonetic transition
that equates "him" with the first
syllable of ἡμέρα, day.

58[8] *Unser* is an adjective formed by
adding -*er* to the pronoun *uns*; *un*- in
unser (our) is part of the pronoun *uns*,
but *un*- in *unhold* (ungracious, unfriendly) is a negative prefix. "Dich
Gott"—the opening words of the *Te
Deum* in German.

58[9] "Dixit" and εφη are Latin and
Greek for "said". C presumably takes
disse for the French equivalent to complete the group of three languages
noted in **58** n 6, above.

in its *own Power* can never be living again; but the Word, which qualifies, mixes, or unites with the astral Birth in the Part of the Love, that generates the *Life* through the astral Birth or Geniture, through the Death.

This[a] with § 24 argues so full an intuition of the Plenitude as the Life in God πρό τοῦ Χαοῦς, ~~in~~ contrasted with the Death in God (= Chaos) as the ὕλη or τὸ παθήτικον[1] 1st of the Spirit, and then of the Word, in ineffable Mercy condescending to and upon the *Lost*, τοῖς ἀπολλυμένοις εν τῇ ἀποστασεῖ:[2] and thus of the secondary dependent Life, the variable, beginning, ending, ever-beginning Tune, the product of the Æolus and the ÆOLIAN Lute[3]—so clear a Beholding of these Mysteries do these §§ argue, that I have need* of § 38, p. 222 (of the Aurora)[5] to be able to conceive the possibility of Behmen's frequent eclipses, and pantheistic Transfers of the throes of the Birth * and of §s 66 to 71 inclusive, p. 211.[4]

[a] I.e. § 26

59[1] "Before the Chaos...as the matter or what is passive, receptive, acted upon".

59[2] "To those lost [*or* destroyed] in the Fall"—not a biblical phrase. For ἀπόστασις see **153** n 8, below.

59[3] The Eolian lute (or harp)—the subject of a "conversation" poem of C's in 1795—is a passive instrument that speaks only when a draught of air strikes it in an appropriate way. As C came to understand the active nature of perception in imagination, he found the Eolian harp an unsuitable image for the imagination, but continued to use it (as here) for other purposes.

59[4] *Aurora* ch 21 §§ 66–71. "66. It is *not* so to be understood, as that I am *sufficient* enough in these Things, but only so far as I am able to comprehend. 67. For the Being of God is like a Wheel, wherein many Wheels are made *one in another*, upwards, downwards, cross-ways, and yet continually turn all of them together. 68. Which indeed when a Man beholds the *Wheel*, he highly marvels at it, and cannot *at once* in its Turning learn to conceive and *apprehend* it: But the more he beholds the Wheel, the more he learns its Form or Frame; and the more he learns, the greater Longing he has to

the Wheel; for he continually sees something that is more and more wonderful, so that a Man can neither behold it, or learn it *enough*. 69. Thus I also, what I do not *enough* describe in one Place concerning this great Mystery, that you will find in another Place; and what I cannot describe in this Book in Regard of the Greatness of the Mystery, and my Incapacity, that you will find in the *other* following. 70. For *this Book* is the first Sprouting, or Vegetation of this Twig, which springs or grows green in its Mother, and is *as a Child*, which is learning to go, and is not able to run apace *at the first*. [Cf *Friend—CC—*II 150 (I 20).] 71. For though the Spirit sees the Wheel, and would fain comprehend its Form or Frame in *every* Place, yet it cannot do it exactly enough, because of the Turning of the Wheel: But when it comes about again, so that the Spirit can see the first apprehended or conceived Form again, then *continually* it learns more and more, and always delights and loves the Wheel, and longs after it *still* more and more."

59[5] For *Aurora* ch 22 § 38 see **53** n 1, above.

ἐκ τοῦ Χάους[6] to the divine Self-affirmation, so catachrestically (to say the least) called by him, the divine *Geniture*.   S. T. C.

60   I i 211, pencil

64. And just such opinions and Tenets I have read also in the Books and Writings of Doctors, (*der *Doctoren*,) and there are also very many *Opinions*, Disputations, and Controversies risen about this very Thing among the *Learned*.
[Shoulder-note:] **Doct. Thoren*. Learned in Folly of verbal Trifles.
N.B. All men who possess at once active fancy, imagination, and a philosophical Spirit, are prone to *Punning*;[1] but with a presentiment, that the Pun itself is the buffoon Brutus concealing Brutus, the Consul.[2] Nor is this the only instance in which a ridiculous likeness leads to the detection of a true analogy.—But these §s (63–71) are *most* important in more important respects—viz. the insight into *Behmen's Grade*.[3]

59[6] "Out of the Chaos". For the word "Chaos" see **146** n 1, below.

60[1] The shoulder-note provides C not only with the general topic for his comment but also with an actual pun: "Doct. Thoren" means "learned fools". For a discussion of C on puns and punning see also BAXTER *Reliquiae* COPY B **112** and DONNE *Poems* **49** and n 1. Too strict a definition of punning should not be allowed to conceal the wide implications that the word and the process had for C. "There sometimes occurs an apparent *Play* on words, which not only to the Moralizer, but even to the philosophical Etymologist, appears more than a mere Play." *AR* (1825) 53n. For his "intended Essay in defence of Punning" see *CN* III 3762 (c Apr–Jun 1810); cf 3542, 3789, 3954, 4267, 4309, 4444. Increasingly aware that words, often by accidental or illogical association of sound, spelling, or sense, through slips of the pen and tongue, and through emotionally distorted recollections and conjunctions, could generate functional and semantic relations of great power and complexity, he counselled the utmost subtlety and learnedness in our use of language.

60[2] Lucius Junius Brutus, after his father and brother had been murdered by Tarquin the Proud, escaped death by pretending to be insane and was called *Brutus* for his (feigned) stupidity. In 509 B.C. he was made one of the first consuls, was responsible for proscribing the Tarquins, and is remembered as the Father of the Roman republic.

60[3] *Aurora* ch 21 § 64 is **60** textus; §§ 66–71 are given in **59** n 4, above. "63. The Simple says, *God made all Things out of nothing*; but he knows not that God; neither does he know what he is: For when he beholds the *Earth*, together with the *Deep* above the Earth, he thinks verily all this is *not* God; or else he thinks, God is *not there*. He always imagines with himself, that God dwells only *above* the azure Heaven of the Stars, and rules, as it were, with some Spirit which *goes forth* from him into this World; and that *his Body* is not present here upon the Earth, nor in the Earth." "65. But seeing God opens *to me* the Gate of his Being in his great Love, and remembers the *Covenants* which he has with Man, therefore I will faithfully and earnestly, according to my Gifts, *unshut* and set wide open *all the Gates of God*, so far as God will

61 I i 213

[The remainder of ch 21 is concerned with the operation of the "seven spirits" in the creation of material nature.]

85. Then next the *bitter* Spirit, which exists in the Fire-flash, is also in the *Matter* or Mass, and that cannot endure to be captivated or imprisoned in the dried *exsiccated* Matter, but rubs itself against the astringent Spirit in the dried Mass or Lump, so long till it *kindles* the Fire; and so when that is done, then the bitter Spirit is terrified, and gets its Life.

The word, bitter, appears ill-chosen as the continuing characteristic of the the Second quality. Nay, it is little less than a contradiction to the descriptions definitive given by Behmen with wonderful consistency. Bitter is the language of Taste for the central, the dark depth in the midmost.—The modern "Sour", Sauerstoff, *Oxy*gen, is not *much* better./ Somewhat better, however, it is, because tho' Acidity be but an accident, & not punctual East, yet it is the most usual accidental form of the Contractive. The pungent seems to me the best word.—Behmen's Sense, nevertheless, is quite plain: as to the first 4 qualities, or material Tetractys—1. Attractive = astringent. 2̶ 4. Repulsive = volatile, or ammoniacal. 2. Contractive = pungent, splitternde. 3. Dilative = fluxive, melting.—1. Carbon. 2̶ 4. Azote. 2. Oxygen. 3. Hydrogen: the 1st & 4th, the Poles of the Magnetic axis, or ——— Line of Basis; the 2nd and 3rd the Neg. and Pos. Poles of the ∩ of the hemispherical or *Electrical* Surface Line.—./[a]

The preceding was written while I was yet in hope of reconciling Behm: to the polar Scheme of NS and E.W.—Since then I have fancied that Behmen sometimes beheld Nature in this, and at other times in a different Scheme. But I am now convinced that his Division ħwas originally and continued to be N.E. and S.W.—i.e. that he considered Carbon and Oxygen as ⟨the *Substantive* Powers—⟩ now allies, and now Antagonists—but still modifications of a common principle—and in like manner, Azote and Hydrogen, ⟨as the *Adjective* Powers.⟩[1] Hence his sweet Water/ sweetness being the name he gives to Azote as the ripening and putrifying ~~power~~ Agent. It cannot be denied, that Behmen's ~~id~~ view seems more nearly corres-

---

[a] The oblique stroke is added in the blacker ink of the added paragraph

---

give me Leave." "*Behmen's Grade*"— the level of Böhme's intuition or intellectual insight.

61[1] I.e. "Repulsion and Dilation (chemically, Azote and Hydrogen)": see **137** at n 4, below. "Adjective"— dependent, not standing by themselves.

pondent to the Mosaic account—namely, of the Fire-flash as anterior to the Combustible—and then introduces the Repulsive or Dilative accordingly as the Astringency or the Contraction is the predominant. But if the Polar Scheme be too *formal*, Behmen's is too contingent—too perspective.

62   I i 213

90. But when the sweet Water can defend itself *no* longer, then "*Anguish*" rises up in it, just as in Man, when he is *dying*, when the Spirit is departing from the Body, and so the Body yields itself captive as a Prisoner to Death; just so the *Water* also yields itself captive as a Prisoner.

The genesis of the *Dilative*, the form of Growth—tho' grotesquely worded.

63   I i 214

95. And so now when the Astringent grapples with the Bitter, then the Bitter *leaps* aside, and takes the Syron's Sap[1] along with it; and then the Astringent every where presses hard after it, and would *fain* captivate it, then the Bitter rushes out from the Body, and extends itself as far as it can.

Imagine a Poet intensely watching a Tree in a Storm of Wind, unconsciously imitating its motions with his body, and then transferring to the Tree those sensations and emotions that accompanied his own gestures: and then you may understand Behmen, and his mode of describing the acts of Nature by ante-dating the passions, of which yet those acts may be, perhaps, the nascent state and fluxional quantities.[2]

64   I i 214

98. ... If in these three Qualities, *viz.* the astringent, bitter and sweet, the Wrath-fire was not kindled, then thou wouldst *plainly* see where God is.

99. But now the Wrath-fire is in all three; for the Astringent is *too very* cold, and contracts, or draws the Body *too hard* together;

[1] C is here correcting an error in the text, as §§ 91, 92 confirm. But in any case he is alert to this particular confusion of Sun and Son: see AURELIUS 35 n 2.

[2] Infinitesimal quantities: for "fluxional" see ATHENAEUM 31 n 4. Böhme's "mode", as described, is presumably an instance of "preposterizing", for which see 52 and n 13, above.

and the Sweet is *too very thick* and dark, which the Astringent soon catches and holds it captive, and dries it *too much*; and then the Bitter is *too stinging*, murderous, and raging; and so they cannot be reconciled to agree.

100. Else if the Astringent was not so much *kindled* in the cold Fire, and the Water not so thick, also the Bitter not so *swelling*, rising, and murderous, then they *might* kindle the *Fire*, from whence the *Light* would exist, and from the Light the *Love*, and so out of the Fire-flash, the *Tone* would exist. And then thou shouldst *see* plainly whether there would not be a heavenly *Body* there, wherein the Light of God would, and does *shine*.

§ 100. I could almost doubt the translation in the words "also the Bitter not so *swelling*, rising."—For it is evident that Behmen's Bitter which is the same as pungent, (even as *we* still say, a bitter blast, a bitter sharp wind, a bitter Tongue = lingua *acerba*—possibly from bite, biting) corresponds to the $\dot{x}$ of Oxygene, Chlorine, and Iodine:[1] and I remember no class of phænomena, Oxyds or Acids likely to have suggested these epithets—~~unl~~ except indeed the Action of the mineral acid on Lime, and the ebulliency of the carbonic acid Gas.—And this is sufficient: and had I recollected these before, I might have spared this Note—save only the explanation of *Bitter* which is of value to a student of Behmen's Works.—I suspect that the common opposition of sweet and bitter originated in the sense of Bitter, as a harsh Sour. What then was our present Bitter (amarum) called?—This would demand a special investigation. I guess, that it had no distinct & separate exponent—lothelysome, ugsome, deadly, *sad*, *dull*, schwery, = weary. To *wear* me down I conjecture to be a different word from *wear* to consume—Query? Süss, with the t for s seet, sweet $\dot{x}$ schwer.[2]

65   I i 215

110. The *first Three*, viz. the astringent, sweet, and bitter, belong to the Imaging or Forming of the Body; and therein stands the Mo-

64[1] "Acerb": see **39** n 1, above. *OED* supports C's etymological relation between "bitter" and "bite". The meaning of the sign $\dot{x}$ is not certain, but the two dots indicate the position of chlorine and iodine in relation to oxygen, which C takes as the exemplar of the pole of contraction and which (in **61** and **65**) he considers to be equivalent to Böhme's "bitter". In the Sept 1817 letter to Tulk C wrote: "Oxygen is probably E by North, while Chlorine, Iodine . . . are E. by S. and form a series of Links from Oxygen to Azote." *CL* IV 773.

64[2] *Schwer* can mean "heavy, clumsy"; but "weary" is derived from *werig*. C is not correct in distinguishing the two senses of "wear" as two separate words.

bility, and the *Body* or Corporeity. And these now have the Comprehensibility, or Palpability, and are the Birth of the *outermost* Nature.

111. The *other three*, viz. the Heat, Love, and Tone, stand in the Incomprehensibility, and are generated out of the first three; and this now is the inward Birth, wherewith the Deity qualifies, mixes or unites.

Bearing in mind that Hydrogen and Nitrogen are two modifications of the same Substance, in Behmen's theory, viz. his sweet Water: and that his *Bitter* is = pungent or contractive; §phs 110, 111. are sufficiently clear. His Glycydor,[1] or common Base of Hyd. and Nitrogen, + Bitter + Astringent under the power of the Astringent do truly constitute the Corporeity—and the same + Astringent + Bitter or Contractive ~~under~~ assimilating the power of the Contractive, give the Mobility. It is, however, an inconvenient perplexity —thus to distinguish the Substances independent of the potenziating Directions—& whatever chemical facilities it may supply for the solution of particular facts, yet philosophically we have an equal Right to assume a common Base of Carbon and Oxygen. Far better therefore to assume a common Base of all four—a simple Ousia[2] or potential Reality—and to preserve the Directions distinct

$$+b \ \overset{-a}{\underset{+a}{\diamondsuit}} \ -b$$

opposites in the strait lines, disparates in the oblique.

66 1 ⁻1, loose leaf,[a] referring to 1 i 219 | Ch 22 "Of the Birth or Geniture of the Stars, and Creation of the Fourth Day"

8. Before this Looking-Glass I will now *invite* all Lovers of the holy and highly to be esteemed Arts of *Philosophy*, *Astrology*, and *Theology*, wherein I will lay open the Root and *Ground* of them.

9. And though I have not studied nor learned *their* Arts, neither do I know how to go about to measure Circles, and *use* their Mathematical Instruments and Compasses, I take no great Care about that. However, they will have *so much* to learn from hence, that many will not comprehend the Ground thereof *all* the Days of their Lives.

10. For I use not their Tables, Formulas, or Schemes, Rules and

---

a See 1 n *a*, above

65[1] C's coinage from γλυκύς (sweet) and ὕδωρ (water): not in *OED*.

65[2] Transliteration of Greek οὐσία, "being"; but C provides his own meaning.

Ways, for I have *not learned* from them, but I have another Teacher, or School-master, which is the whole or total NATURE.

11. From that *whole Nature*, together with its innate, instant Birth or Geniture, have I studied and learned my *Philosophy, Astrology,* and *Theology*, and not from Men, or by Men.

12. But seeing Men *are Gods*, and have the Knowledge of God ... therefore I *despise not* the Canons, Rules, and Formulas of *their* Philosophy, Astrology, and Theology. For I find, that for the most part they stand upon a *right Ground*, and I will diligently *endeavour* to go according to their Rules and Formulas.

13. For ... their Formula or Scheme is *my* Master, and I have my Beginning and *first* Knowledge from their Formula or Positions: Neither is it my Purpose to go about to amend or cry down theirs, for I cannot do it, neither have I *learned* them, but leave them standing in their own Place and Worth.

To H. C. and D. C.

I ~~ta~~ shall be obliged to take as my motto §s 8, 9, 10, 11, 12, 13— ⟨p. 219 of the Aurora,⟩ but o! with what bitter regret, and in the conscience of such glorious opportunities, both at School under the famous Mathematician, WALES, the companion of Cook in his circumnavigation,[1] and at Jesus College, Cambridge, under an excellent Mathematical Tutor, Newton,[2] all *neglected* with still greater *remorse*! O be assured, my dear Sons! that Pythagoras, Plato, Speusippus, had abundant reason for excluding from all philosophy and theology not merely practical those who were ignorant of Mathematics. Μηδεις αγεομετρητος εισιτω—the common ~~con~~inscription over all the Portals of all true Knowlege.[3] I cannot

66[1] William Wales (c 1734–98), a Yorkshireman of humble background, was one of the two astronomers chosen by the Royal Society to accompany James Cook on his second voyage around the world (1772–5), his principal duty being to apply the first seagoing chronometers to the accurate determination of longitude. Immediately after his return to England he was appointed Master of the Royal Mathematical School at Christ's Hospital (the navigation school) and so taught mathematics to C, Lamb, and Leigh Hunt, all of whom remembered him with respect and affection. On the second voyage, Cook three times crossed the Antarctic Circle in search of a south polar continent; hence Wales was among the first to confront the marvels, dangers, and miseries of the Antarctic Ocean. One cannot help wondering how much Wales, a lover of Thomson, Milton, and Shakespeare, inadvertently contributed to C's account of the South Ice in *AM*.

66[2] Thomas Newton (d 1843), author of *Treatise on Conic Sections* and of *Illustrations of Sir Isaac Newton's Method of Reasoning*, was one of the four Fellows of Jesus who supported William Frend in the "trial" of 1793 in which C played a brief but boisterous rôle.

66[3] "Let no one ignorant of geometry enter"—by tradition the

say—for I know the contrary, and the §s above referred to express the conviction—that it *cannot* be *acquired* without the *technical* knowlege of Geometry and Algebra—but never can it without them be adequately *communicated* to others—and o! with what toil must the essential knowlege be *anguished-out* without the assistance of the technical!—[4]
S. T. Coleridge—

67 1 i 221

[26. 27. Böhme gives evidence that "the dear Man *Moses*" was not the original author of "all of Genesis".] And it is very *likely*, that the Creation, before the Flood, was *not described in Writing*, but was kept as a dark Word in their Memories, and so delivered from one Generation to another, till *after* the Flood, and till People begun to lead epicurean Lives in all *Voluptuousness*.

Whoever has read Astruc's and Eichhorn's Inquiries into concerning the diverse Authors and documents, from which the Book of Genesis was compiled—especially the remarks of Eichhorn as to the polytheism of the Author of the first Chapter (see his Einleitung in das Alte Testament) cannot but be struck with this singular coincidence by anticipation in the unlearned Jacob Behmen, 200 years before![1]

68 1 i 221

30. After these Patriarchs came the *wise Heathens*, who went somewhat *deeper* into the Knowledge of Nature. And they in their Philosophy and Knowledge did come even before the Face or Countenance of God, and yet could *neither* see nor know him.

§ 30 likewise is as admirably expressed as it is accurately stated. The Epoptæ of the Cabiric Mysteries knew the Θεῖον, and the Trinity in *their* but not in *its* Genesis out of εκ του Θειου[1]—but still the Copula

---

motto inscribed over the entrance to Plato's Academy. (The second word properly reads ἀγεωμέτρητος.) See *Watchman* (*CC*) 34n, and *LS* (*CC*) 173. Speusippus, Plato's nephew, succeeded him as head of the Academy.

66[4] C's "regret of having neglected the Mathematical Sciences" is expressed in KANT *Vermischte Schriften* (4 vols Halle 1799 etc) [COPY C] II 109 (in 1824) and SCHUBERT *Allgemeine Naturgeschichte* (Erlangen 1826) back flyleaf (c 1827). For C on the value of studying geometry, see *LS* (*CC*) 173.

67[1] Jean Astruc (1684–1766) argued in his *Conjectures sur les mémoires originaux* (Brussels 1753) that Moses was the compiler rather than the author of Genesis. Eichhorn also considered Genesis to be a compilation. See BIBLE COPY B 1 n 1.

68[1] For *epoptae* (ἐπόπται) see 47 n 5, above, and cf 89, below. For C's interest in the mystery religions see 101 and n 5, below. The Greek words mean "the Divine" and "out of the Divine": see 6 n 5, above, and esp "*Prometheus*" *LR* II 342.

or Unity was the Irrational, and the three persons three different Gods: Zeus, Dionysus and Pallas—[2]

69 ɪ i 222, pencil

43. For thou needest *not* to ask; *Where is God?* ... For wheresoever thou lookest, there is God.

If Behmen had never put a "*that*" for "*there*", who could have condemned him?

70 ɪ i 223, pencil

44. When thou beholdest the *Deep* betwixt the Stars and the Earth, *canst* thou say, that is *not* God, or there God is *not*? O, thou miserable corrupted Man! be instructed; for in the Deep above the Earth, where thou seest and knowest *nothing*, and sayest there is *nothing*, yet even *there* is the light-holy God in his Trinity, and is generating *there*, as well as in the high Heaven aloft above this World.

In this sentence, "*that* is God" and "*there* God is" are taken as equivalent, and this is Behmen's πρωτον ψευδος.[1] Would any man who knew the use of words, contend that the parings of Plato's nails were Plato? Tho' considered as growing on his fingers, ~~they~~ it might be said of them—even as these the Life of Plato *is*!—

71 ɪ i 227

[91, 92—a theosophical description of the purification of gold.]

93. II. Then secondly, the astringent Death of the Water is to be separated, from which proceeds a poisonous venomous Water of Separation or *Aquafortis*, which stands in the Rising up of the *Fire-flash* in Death, which is the evil Malignant, even the very worst Source of all in Death, even the astringent and bitter Death itself; for this is the Place where the Life, which exists in the sweet Water, died in Death. ...

The sweet water (azote) 29.77—/ The Pungent (Behmen's Bitter)= oxygen 70.23.[1]—The azote per se is clearly only the corpus Mortuum

68[2] Zeus, the supreme father-god; Dionysus, son of Zeus, god of frenzy and ecstasy; Pallas Athene, daughter of Zeus, goddess of wisdom, war, and the arts. These are the higher triad of gods, but not as represented in SCHELLING *Ueber die Gottheiten von Samothrace* (for which see **140** nn 3, 4,

below), although all are mentioned by him in his n 112 on pp 100–7. See also *LR* ɪ 186.

70[1] "Fundamental error". See BAXTER *Reliquiae* COPY B **92** n 1.

71[1] The figures correspond approximately to the proportions by weight of nitrogen and oxygen in nitric oxide.

of ~~the~~ what it was, when the pungent actuated it only as the aura ignea.[2]

72   i i 230 | Ch 23 "Of the Deep above the Earth"

18. And *these* Births or Genitures have *no Beginning*, but have so generated themselves from Eternity; and as to this Depth, *God himself knows not what He is: For He knows no Beginning of Himself, also he knows not any Thing that is like Himself, as likewise He knows no End of Himself.*

This is one of those hard offensive sayings, the error and so far the falsity of which consists in the inconvenience and ambiguity of the words rather than in the meaning. Behmen meant only to say, that God cannot know himself in his *infinite* Being as a Subject knows itself by the act of making itself an object for itself—: for this is the necessity of ~~a~~ ~~finite~~ limitation, and imperfect Being. I AM in that I AM, is God's self-affirmation, and ⟨that⟩ God verily *is*, is all we can we affirm of him; ⟨that,⟩ to which no addition can be made, when we speak of *the total God*, Θεος αβυσσος.[1]

73   i i 241, pencil | Ch 24 "Of the Incorporation, or Compaction of the Stars"

22. And at the *Fulness* or Accomplishment of this Time, God would adorn and trim this House with its Qualities, as a royal Government, and let those very qualifying or fountain Spirits *possess* the whole House, that they might, in that House of Darkness and of Death, bring forth Creatures and Images again, as they *had done* from Eternity, till the Accomplishment or Fulfilling of the whole Host or Army of the new created Angels, which were Men. And *then* God would bolt and bar up the Devil in the House of Darkness in an eternal Hole, and then kindle the whole House in its own Light again, *all but* the very Hole, Hell, or Dungeon of the Devils.

71[2] C seems to have used *corpus mortuum* and *caput mortuum* indifferently, the second being the common alchemical term for the worthless residue at the end of a chemical process. Cf *TL* (1848) 70–1. In **61** above, C had identified Böhme's "pungent" as oxygen. When the pungent (oxygen) actuates azote (nitrogen) it becomes *aura ignea*, which is apparently the life in the sweet water. Cf ESCHENMAYER **18**.

72[1] "God unfathomable". By joining this phrase to "*the total God*" C provides a link between his special use of ἄβυσσος (abyss) and the inscrutable "*sup*positum" of **31**, above. Ἄβυσσος, the negative form of βύσσος (βύθος), depth, represents "the deep" of Gen 1.2. In a long account of his scheme of creation in *CN* III 4418 f 13 C renders βύσσος ἄβυσσος as "deepless Depth". "Abyss" does not occur in AV. See also **98**, below.

23. *Now it may be asked*, Why did not God bolt him up instantly, and then he had *not* done so much mischief?

Behmen often starts a difficulty, which he cannot solve, or solves but very imperfectly. This, however, proves his sincerity and simple-heartedness. The κατάβασις τῶν πνευμάτων ὥστε ὕλη γένεσθαι, die Gerinnung des selbstvergifteten Geistes,[1] is an Idea, the Flash of which he has often reflected in his Mirror, but never mastered or kept fast hold of. Hence (in contradiction to his own assertions in other places) the sinlessness and co-eternity of the Salitter or Matter—his consequent perilous approaches to Manicheism on one hand[2] and to Pantheism on the other. Hence too his perplexities whenever the *Successive*, the Gradual in Time, is to be accounted for. Thus he supposes himself asked: But why was not this done *at once*, *instantly*? And his answer respect[s][a] only the question. Why was it done?—which is not the question in point.

Schelling and his Followers are in the same case as Behmen—only that Behmen oscillates or rather leaps from Error to the Truth or to the neighborhood of the Truth, while Schelling *settles* on the Error—.[3]

74 I i 242, pencil

36. Behold! the Stars are plainly incorporated or *compacted* out of or from God; but thou must understand the Difference between them, for they are *not* the Heart, and the meek pure Deity, which Man *is to honour* and worship as God; but they are the innermost and sharpest Birth or Geniture, wherein all Things stand in Wrestling and *Fighting*, wherein the Heart of God always generates itself, and the Holy Ghost *continually* rises up from the Rising of the Life.

This is substantially the same as Schelling says in his DENKMAL:[1] and the best that a Pantheist, and Hylotheist can say—and bad is the

---

a Letter supplied by the editor

73[1] "Descent of the spirits to become matter, the coagulation of the self-poisoned Spirit".

73[2] Manichaeism—a dualistic heresy that emerged in the third century A.D., based on the assumption of a primordial conflict between light and darkness.

73[3] See **52** and n 15, above.

74[1] I.e. SCHELLING *Denkmal der Schrift von den göttlichen Dingen*. In a note on Kant's *Vermischte Schriften* C wondered "whether Schelling took the leading idea of his Theology... namely, the establishing an independent Ground of God's Existence, which indeed God (τὸ θεῖον) but not God himself (ὁ θεός), from Kant's 'Einzigmögliche Beweisgrund' or from Behmen?..." KANT *Vermischte Schriften* (4 vols Halle 1799) [COPY B] II ⁻4, referring to II 219–20.

best.[2] For if the Absolute Good could not be without it, it becomes adorable as the Ground of the Good, or the Good ceases to be adorable as grounded in it. Or if they be both one with God, what avails *calling* this or that only by the name? But Behmen has this great advantage over Schelling, that we have only to substitute C (=the creaturely) under the renewing influence of D (=the divine Spirit and Word) for D in D, to render his Intuitions true and fruitful in many respects—whereas Schelling begins and ends in Abstractions, his physical Laws not being truly Laws, but extensions, often (I own) ingenious and happy extensions of Analogy, or disguised Generalizations.

75 I i 242–3, pencil

39. It is just such a Birth as is in *Man*; the Body is even the *Father* of the Soul, for the Soul is generated out of the Power of the Body, and when the Body stands in the anguishing Birth or Geniture of God, as the Stars do, and not in the fierce hellish Birth, then the Soul of Man qualifies, mixes, or *unites* with the pure Deity, as a Member in or of his Body.

§ 39. a woeful error; but a consequent result of the identity of the Material (=Salitter) with God. Spinoza from the same premise deduced the same conclusion. Yet in a certain sense it would be true; but then there must previously be given such ⟨a⟩ definition of Soul, as the word "Soul" would ill expression—namely, the fantastic Self, the Imagination *I*. This indeed may be truly affirmed to be generated out of the Power of the Body.[1] But this is [a]*ᵃ* deep question, which I have not yet enucleated.[2] Ψυχὴ εκ τῆς Σαρκος by the influence of the Logos—Partaking of the Father it becomes Ψυχη λογικοϛη—till depurated[3] from its Mother it passes upward into π πνε Πνευμα λογικον.[4]

ᵃ Word supplied by the editor

74[2] Hylotheist—one who identifies God with matter (ὑλή). This use by C is earlier than that recorded in *OED* (1828). "Bad is the best" is quoted from Beaumont & Fletcher *Rollo* IV ii; cf *EOT* (*CC*) I 279.

75[1] See **155**, below.

75[2] Both "enucleate" and "enucleation" had been current long before C used them. For a similar, but not synonymous, term see e.g. *auseinandersetzen* in **5**, above.

75[3] A seventeenth-century word meaning to make/ become free from impurities.

75[4] "Soul [coming] out of the flesh...logical Soul...logical Spirit" —"logical" here meaning "partaking of the Logos" or "of the nature of the Logos". The distinction between ψυχή (soul) and πνεῦμα (spirit) is consistently maintained in AV. See e.g. AURELIUS **18** n 1 and **45** n 1.

76 i i 245, pencil

73. But the holy God is *hidden* in the *Center* of all these Things in his Heaven, and thou canst neither see nor comprehend him; but the *Soul* comprehends him, and the astral Birth but half, for the Heaven is the Partition between Love and Wrath. That Heaven is every where, even in thyself.

74. And now when thou worshippest or prayest to the *holy God* in his Heaven, then thou worshippest or prayest to *him* in *that* Heaven which is *in* thee, and that same God with his Light; and therein the Holy Ghost *breaks* through in *thy* Heart, and generates thy *Soul* to be a new Body of God, which rules and reigns with God in *his* Heaven.

75. For the earthly Body, which thou bearest, is one Body with the whole kindled Body of this World, and thy Body qualifies, mixes, or unites with the whole Body of this World; and there is no Difference between the Stars and the Deep, as also the Earth and thy Body; it is all one Body. This is the only Difference, thy Body is a *Son* of the Whole, and is in itself as the whole Being itself is.

What practically vital Christian, experienced in the communion with God, and the struggles of and with the Spirit, in prayer whether passive or fervent, can read §phs 73, 74—what Philosopher, who is indeed such, can meditate on §. 75—without a profound admiration of the Writer, increased into Wonder by the reflection on his Circumstances; his want of Learning; poverty of words; lack of skill and mastery in both the Rhematic and Logical composition and sequency of Words; exclusion from the society of the Learned and Ingenious; and lastly, ⟨his⟩ scanty Means and manual labor, as a humble Shoemaker! Verily, it is worse than hardness, it is badness of Heart, to scoff at the wreaths & columns of Smoke from theis Altar or Hearthstone of Behmen's Genius[1]—with such heavy damps dripping continually thereon, and with such wet Logs for the Fuel, the marvel is that the smoke did not utterly choke and strangle the flames!—or rather that there was any Smoke even, and that the Spark was not quenched as soon as kindled! The very Delusions of such a mind are more venerable to me than the heartless Sobrieties of a Locke, ⟨a⟩ Paley, or a Dugald Stewart![2] Let it be, if you will have it so, that

---

76[1] Cf the "*Hearth*, or *Fire-Altar*" in **33**, above.

76[2] C deplored the philosophical superficiality of Locke, Paley, and Dugald Stewart (1753–1828) and in

Oct 1810 said: "Aye, poor B[öhme]! there came more Light thro' the cranny of thy Madness than ever passed thro' all the doors & windows of the Psilosophists' sober Sense, & acute pene-

poor Jacob is sometimes *out of his Wits*, and often *out of* his Senses—
Yet it is better so, than with the Fascinati, to have *lost his Reason*.[3]

S. T. Coleridge

77   i i 248, pencil | Ch 25 "Of the Whole Body of the Stars Birth or Geniture"

20. But that there *seemeth* to be a blue or azure Sphere *above* the
Stars, whereby the Place of this World is closed and shut out from
the *holy* Heaven, as Men have thought *hitherto*; yet it is *not so*, but
it is *the superior Water of Nature*, which is much brighter than the
Water below the *Moon*. And now when the *Sun* shines through the
Deep, then it is as it were of a light-blue or azure Colour.

Here as elsewhere in Behmen (and in like manner in the genuine
Reliques of Heraclitus) by Water is signified the Ὕδωρ εν ὑδατι; Aqua
intima; Ether; Materia prima; Dilatio *con*tractabilis ✕ Dispersio
*at*tractibilis; Multeitas continua indifferentialis ✕ Multeitas discreta
differentialis.[1]—So understood, § 20 is sufficiently accurate.

78   i i 249 | "Concerning the Kindling of the Heart, or Life of this World"

32. When God had brought the Body of this World in *two Days*
into a right Form, and had made the Heaven for a *Partition* between
the Love and the Wrath, then on the *third Day the Love* pressed
through the Heaven and through the Wrath, and then instantly the
old Body in Death stirred and *moved itself* to the Birth or Geniture.. . .

37. In this Revolution the Planet *Mars* came to be, whose Power
stands in the *bitter* Fire-crack for it is a Tyrant, Rager, Raver, and
Stormer, like a *Fire-crack*; moreover it is *hot,* and a poisonous
venomous Enemy of Nature, through whose Rising up and Birth or

---

tration/". *CN* iii 3975. Cf *BL* ch 9
(1907) i 93–9, 102–5, and *P Lects* Lect
11 (1949) 327–31.

76[3] C defended Giordano Bruno—
with Plato, Aristotle, Kant, and all
the great discoverers—against a charge
of "impenetrable obscurity" levelled
by "the men of 'sound common sense'
. . .those snails in intellect, who wear
their eyes at the tips of their feelers".
Omniana (1812) i 242–3. "Fascinati"
—the bewitched.

77[1] C is saying, apparently, that
when Heraclitus spoke of "the way up
and the way down" in the universe—

fire condensing into air, air into water,
water into earth, and the reverse process ever proceeding simultaneously—
he meant "Water in water; absolute
Water; ether (αἰθήρ); primal Matter;
Dilation subject to *con*traction as
opposed to Dispersion subject to
*at*traction; continuous undifferentiated Multeity as opposed to discrete
differentiated Multeity". For the first
phrase (which is not Heraclitus') see **24**
and n 4, above. On the differentiation
of chaos see **6** n 10, above. See also *CN*
iii 4448, 4420, *CL* iv 808.

Geniture in the Earth, all Manner of poisonous, venomous, evil Works and *Vermine* are come to be.

38. But seeing the Heat in the middle Point or Center of the Body was *so mighty* great, thereupon it extended itself so very largely, and opened the Chamber of Death so wide before its Kindling of the Light, that it, the S U N, is the greatest Star.

39. But as soon as the Light kindled itself in the Heat, so instantly was that hot Place *caught* in the Light, and then the Body of the *Sun* could grow *no* bigger. For the Light mitigated the Heat, and so the Body of the *Sun* remained there *standing* in the Midst or Center as a *Heart*, for the Light is the Heart of Nature, *not* the Heat. . . .

40. As far as the middle Point or Center has kindled itself, *just* so big is the *Sun*; for the *Sun* is nothing else but a kindled *Point* in the Body of Nature.

Except the § 37, which savors strongly of the astrological Age of Behmen, I see little in this Section which is not capable of being translated into as tenable a Theory, as Buffon's:[1] and §phs 38, 39, & 40 are in a far profounder Spirit, than belonged to the French Philosopher, or to his Country or his Age.

79 I i 249–51 | § 39 in **78** textus, above

The dilative ~~Power~~ Force was balanced by the contractive—the attractive by the ~~self-projective~~ repulsive—thus the two powers, ~~of~~ the Superficial, and the Central, were each balanced in its polar forces, and then became sexual Opposites, the Central ⟨=B.⟩ perfected into Gravitation, the distinctive or superficial ⟨=A.⟩ into Light—and the Sun became the seat of both. For the Contractive or −Pole of A allying itself with the Repulsive or + pole of B. became the projectile and self-projective, i.e. Light—and the + pole of A allying itself with the − pole of B. became the Globous Mass, of which Gravitation is the Function. For that Gravitation is not merely Attraction but a synthetic Power has been shewn by me elsewhere.[1] That not Heat but Light is the Heart of Nature is one of those truly profound and pregnant Thoughts that ever and anon astonish me in Behmen's Writings. That the Heat is not generated by the Blood but by the nerves has been proved experimentally within the last ten

78[1] George Louis Leclerc, Comte de Buffon (1707–88), author of *Histoire naturelle* (1749–67) (which C knew in Smellie's translation), advanced a theory that the planets resulted from the outflowing of a "torrent" caused by the collision of a comet with the sun: see **81**, below. Buffon's theory—as C understood it—did not meet with his approval. See SWEDENBORG *De cultu et amore Dei* (1745) i 8.

79[1] See **17**, above.

years.[2] But the affinity of the Arterio-muscular System, and of the Flesh and Blood generally to Light I trust that I shall make evident in my Commentaries on the first and sixth Chapters of the Gosp. of John.[3] Hence ⟨in⟩ the Logos (distinctive Energy) is *Light*, and the Light became the *Life* of Man[4]—Now [that]*[a]* the Blood is the Life, is affirmed by Moses[5]—and has been forcibly maintained by John Hunter.[6]

N.B. Heat is not identical with the Dilative—if so, Light were only a polar force, and not a bipolar Power—and we must have a Radix or Identity higher than Light, as containing both it and Heat. Heat is the Indifference of Light and Gravitation,[7] and capable therefore of passing into either.

80   I i 250, referring to **79**

The note over-leaf*[b]* is not expressed so clearly as it ought to ~~and m~~ have been—and as it might be by distinguishing the Power of Light (Lux lucifica) which is the Identity of the Contractive and the Continuous from the Thing, Light (Lux phænomenon) which is Light with the positive Pole of Gravitation for its Basis,[1] as explained over-

---

[a] Word supplied by the editor   *[b]* I.e. **79**, which began on p 249

79[2] If C refers to John Hunter (see n 6, below) he was not quite so specific: "...am apt to suspect there is a principal source of heat, although it may not be in the blood itself, the blood being affected by having its source near the source of heat. That this principle resides in the stomach is probable...but I suspect that the stomach sympathizes with those actions of the brain which form the mind, and then produces heat...". *Treatise on the Blood* (1794) 291.

79[3] C often spoke of his plan for a commentary on the fourth Gospel: see e.g. *CL* III 533, IV 589, 592, 687, 736. See also **151**, below, and BIBLE COPY B **107–112**.

79[4] John 1.4.

79[5] See Gen 9.4 and Lev 17.11, 17.14.

79[6] For John Hunter, foremost English comparative anatomist and physiologist of his day, see BOERHAAVE **9** n 1. In 1796 C wrote: "Hunter [says] that the *Blood* is the Life—which is saying nothing at all ...". *CL* I 296. Later, however, he became much interested in Hunter's vitalist physiology and in the work of his follower John Abernethy: see *L&L* 16–23. For Abernethy's assertion that fluid and semi-fluid substances have a principle of life suffused through them, see *Friend (CC)* I 474 n 4.

79[7] Cf STEFFENS *Grundzüge* p 64.

80[1] *Lux lucifica*—light-making Light; the term is Augustine's (e.g. *Contra Faustum* 22.8.9), quoted by Erigena and many others. See also **100**, below, on light and gravity. The whole matter is more elaborately developed in *CN* III 4456 of 1 Nov 1818. The position is briefly restated in *"Prometheus"*. Chaos was "the container and withholder...out of which light, that is, the *lux lucifica*, as distinguished from *lumen seu lux phaenomenalis*, was produced;—say, rather, that which, producing itself into light as the one pole or antagonist power, remained in the other pole as darkness, that is,

leaf. Likewise, it would be better to say, that the Distinctive is the Unity of the Continuous and the Divisi~~ve~~duous, as its *forms*— when the Power preponderates under the first form, the Continuous becomes the Dilative—when in the 2nd, the Dividuous becomes the Contractive, and *forces* as well as forms.

81   i i 250, pencil | "The Highest Ground of the Sun, and of All the Planets"

It is interesting to find Buffon's Theory (of the Planets having been different explosions from the Sun) in Jacob Behmen![1]

82   i i 255, pencil

97. Now as the Original and Beginning of the Life in a Creature is, so is the *first Regeneration* of the Nature of the *new* Life in the *corrupted* Body of this World. . . .

Pity! that Behmen did not keep this point more steadily in view, and more *contra-distinctly*! He would not then have so often transferred

gravity, or the principle of mass, or wholeness without distinction of parts". *LR* ii 339. For *lux* and *lumen* see **169** and n 1, below.

81[1] See **78** n 1, above. Fragments of Böhme's theory of the birth of the sun and the planets can be seen in **77** and **78** textus, above. See also **83** and **84** textus, below. C does not seem to be clear about either Böhme's theory or Buffon's.

Böhme's scheme (as set forth in *Aurora* ch 25, devoted to the birth of the sun and planets) proposes that before the creation of the sun there existed distinct from each other the Light of God and "the Body of this World". The Body of this World was in darkness and held in Death and Anguish until it had heated itself from its own Fire-source in the midst of the Body. When the Heat became very severe "the Love in the Light of God broke through the Heaven of the *Partition*"; the Love in Light captivated the Heat and changed it into "*competent* Meekness" and there was no further Anguish: "the Body of the *Sun* remained there *standing* in the Midst or Center as a *Heart*". "But

when the *Sun* was kindled, then the horrible Fire-crack went forth upwards from the Place of the *Sun*"; the Fire-crack was held in the place it now occupies as the planet Mars. The other planets were formed by "the Light" in sequence not from the sun but out of "the Body of this World"—first Jupiter, then Venus, then Saturn, then Earth.

Buffon, in a section of the *Histoire naturelle* entitled "Théorie de la Terre", based his theory of the origin of the planets on the observation that the planets move around the sun in the same direction and in almost the same plane, and that there is a harmonic distribution of the planets in terms of both mass and distance. For these elegant relations he postulated a single cause—the collision of a comet with the sun. The comet made a furrow in the sun, drove out some of the sun's matter in the form of a "torrent", and imparted motion to the torrent. The solar matter, as it moved in the torrent away from the sun, distributed itself into globules, which assumed separate orbits. Buffon did not theorise here about the primal creation of the sun;

the Geniture of the Creature to the eternal Filiation of very God from very God!

83   1 i 256, pencil | Ch 26 [no title] "Of the Planet Saturn"

1. Saturn, that cold, sharp, austere, and astringent Regent, takes its Beginning and Original *not* from the *Sun*; for it has in its Power the *Chamber* of Death, and is a Drier up of all Powers, from whence *Corporeity* exists.

§. 1. That of the Solar Satellites some ~~are~~ owe their place and separate Being to the redundancy of the Solar Power—i.e. were exploded from the Sun—and*ᵃ*1

84   1 i 259, pencil | "Of the Planet Venus"

36. From whence the Affections or *Insinuations* exist; for the Power of *Venus* makes fierce *Mars* or the Fire-crack mild, and mitigates it, and makes *Jupiter* humble, else the Power of *Jupiter* would break through the hard Chamber *Saturn*, and in Men and Beasts, through the Skull or Brain-pan; and so the Sensibility would transmute itself into High-mindedness above the Birth-right, or right Law or Order of the Geniture of the Deity, in the Manner and Way of the *proud* Devil.

Hence the Devil is imaged with Horns—the Sensibility would extend beyond itself. It would be creative, that is, become Reproductivity in its own right; and ⟨it would be⟩ motory[1] in itself, i.e. become Irritability & yet remain Sensibility. But this was impossible—and the result was a mere relative Ascent, but a positive descent into a yet meaner & more vegetative form than the Skull itself—namely Horn! and thence, by enkindling & propagation of the Productivity, manifesting itself at the other extremity, a Tail. What a Devil is a Man-beast! What a Beast is the Devil![2]

85   1 i 260, pencil | "The Center or Circle of the Birth of Life"

43. The Spirit cites the Physicians to come before this Looking-glass, especially Anatomists and Dissectors of Men, who by their *Anatomy*

ᵃ The note is incomplete

nor did he postulate an "explosion" of the sun as the origin of the planets, nor a sequence of "explosions", one for each planet.

83[1] C apparently broke off this note because he realised that Böhme had said that Saturn "takes its Beginning . . . *not* from the *Sun*".

84[1] "Motory"—that causes motion. *OED* cites Davy's use of the word in 1799, and C's in *BL* ch 13 (1907) I 197.

84[2] Cf *CN* III 3866 of Jun 1810 and 4138 of c Apr 1812. See RICHTER (Jean Paul) *Kampaner Thal* (2 pts Erfurt 1787) i 75.

would learn the Birth and Rising or Springing up of *Man's Life*, and have murdered many *innocent* Men, against the Right and Law of God and of Nature, *hoping* thereby to find out the wonderful Proportion, Harmony, and Form of Nature, that they might thereby be *useful* in restoring the Health of others.

Honest Jacob had in mind the romantic horrific stories of the Italian Painters, which in some editions of the Lie[a] were related of Italian Surgeons—all which were confidently believed in that age and by men in whom such credulity was far less excusable than in our simple-hearted and lack-learning Shoemaker.[1]

86 I i 262, pencil

64. And such a House is the whole Deep without, within, and above all Heavens; which House is called the *Eternity*. And such a House also is the *House of Flesh* in Man, and in all Creatures.

65. And this Being together comprehends the Eternity, which is *not called* God, but the Body of Nature which is not Almighty, wherein indeed the Deity is immortal or not dead, but standing hidden in the Kernel of the seven Spirits, and yet not comprehended or understood.

I can affix no other meaning to these §s, but the divine Omnipotence considered *abstractly* from the Act, Word, and Love. But it ought not to be so considered—not only because such abstraction is the ground and occasion of a Manichean Pantheism,[1] but likewise because it establishes a Potentiality in the Godhead, subversive of the eternal Perfection. For Potentiality is a Will not perfected.[2]

----

[a] A slip for "Lives"

85[1] The "romantic horrific stories" grew out of the widespread superstitious resistance, in the fifteenth and sixteenth centuries, to the precise anatomical knowledge that could be learned only by dissecting human cadavers. Vasari's *Lives of the Painters*, which C may well have in mind as Böhme's source, includes a few references to the direct study of anatomy by famous painters. See *Lives of the Painters* ed E. H. and E. W. Blushfield and A. A. Hopkins (New York 1926) II 200, 246, III 215. Green's library contained a copy of the Paris 1803–8 ed (Vols I–III, all pubd) of *Vies des peintres, sculpteurs, et architectes. Green SC* (1880) 796. C made a note based on Vasari early in 1806: *CN* II 2792. Strong revulsion at the desecration of human bodies induced Pope Leo x to stop Leonardo (1452–1519) making autopsies—and C may have been aware of this issue from William Roscoe's *Life and Pontificate of Leo X* (1805): see BARCLAY *Argenis* COPY A 3 n 6.

86[1] See **73** n 2, above.
86[2] See **177** n 2, below.

87   I i 264 | "Of Man and the Stars"

94. Now that Seed has first a *Mother*, which is the dark *Chamber* of the House of Flesh. Secondly, it has a Mother, which is the *Wheel* of the seven Spirits, according to the Kind and Manner of the seven Planets. Thirdly, it has a Mother which is generated in the Circle of the seven Spirits in the Center, and is the *Heart* of the seven Spirits. . . .

98. But the *third* Mother they cannot constantly or *permanently* shine through, for it stands in the House of Darkness. . . .

98. The *third* counted backward—or a mistake for the *first*: see §. 94.

88   I i 265

101. *First*, the astringent Spirit catches hold, and that draws together a Mass or *Lump* out of the *sweet* Water, that is out of or from the Unctuosity or Fatness of the *Blood* of the Heart, or from the Sap or *Oil* of the Heart.

§ 101. It should be borne in mind that Behmen throughout this work contemplates the W. and S., or the dynamic Hydrogen and Nitrogen as the same power in different aspects. ◊.

THE THREE PRINCIPLES OF THE DIVINE ESSENCE

89   I ii 4–[5], pencil | "Preface to the Reader"

And therefore this Author, having the true Knowledge, could well explain the Letters of the Names of God, and cther Words and Syllables, the Signification of which he says is well understood in the Language of Nature.

However heartily disposed to believe J. Behmen to have been a Seer (Ἐπόπτης)[1] in a sense that approaches to Inspired, so far that he was illuminated, yet ~~this~~ not the *idea* of his language of nature; but his exemplification and practical application of this idea forms a stumbling block which my faith can neither remove or climb over.[2] If there had been but one possible language, and that the German, it still would be contradictory—ex. mahne, a mane, or rebuke—meinet wegen, he means ways, and meinetwegen = on my account.[3] In

89[1] See **47** n 5, and cf **68**, above.
89[2] See **57** and **58**, above.
89[3] The correct form of the German word for "mane" is *Mähne*; *mahne* means "rebuke". The second example shows C's awareness of the "endless accidental modifications that accompany all existing Languages": **96**, below.

Willeram's time (1160) stinkende meant wohlriechende—Die Küssen deines Mundes sind süsser als stinkende Salben.[4]—So his *Sul* and *phur*—what becomes of it when we call the same thing Brimstone—or his *Mer cur* ius when called Quick silver/[5] The only way of saving Behmen's credit seems to be, to suppose that he had seen the truth as to the *Ideal* of Language—and had in his ordinary state confounded the spiritual, perhaps angelic, language with the poor arbitrary & corrupted Languages of men as they actually exist.[6] S T C.

90 ɪ ii 7 | "The Author's Preface"

10. *Further, We must consider the great Reasons why it is very necessary to learn to know ourselves, because we see and know that we must die and perish for our Enemy's Sake, which is God's Enemy and ours, which dwells in us, and is the very Half of Man. And if he grows so strong in us, that he gets the upperhand, and is predominant, then he throws us into the Abyss to all Devils, to dwell there with them eternally, in an eternal, unquenchable Pain and Torment, into an eternal Darkness, into a loathsome House, and into an eternal Forgetting of all Good, yea into God's contending Will, where our God and all the Creatures are our Enemies for ever.*

Behmen might have & probably had, thought of a central Fire, which radiating to all points of the circumference was the genial warmth of the Globe, and above the warmth rising cloathed it with Light—But yet to such as sunk down, & seeking a center in themselves found instead the center of all, it must be a very horrible Fire, which no creature can endure.[a] Now the Self of every Creature should be the Light or Glory of God, even his WORD & co-eternal Son—in

[a] Here C has written "ʌʌ turn to the bottom of this page—" and has continued the note with "ʌʌ"

89[4] Williram or Willeram of Ebersberg (1048–85), one of the first to write in German vernacular. C quotes the Willeram version of Song 1.2–3: "Let him kiss me with the kisses of his mouth...Because of the savour of thy good ointments"—"Cússer míh mít cússe sínes múndes...sîe stínchente mit den bézzesten sálbon". See H. Hoffmann *Williram's Uebersetzung des Hohenliedes*...(Breslau 1827) 5–6. C could also have seen this in Johann Schilter *Thesaurus antiquitatum* Vol ɪɪɪ (Ulm 1728). In modern German *stink-*ende means "stinking", *wohlriechende* "fragrant".

89[5] Böhme tries to establish a correlation between the sounds of the syllables of *Sulphur* and *Mercurius* in order to determine the character of the forces they represent. Cf **57**, above, and see **93** and n 1, below. For the alchemists on sulphur and mercury see *LR* ɪ 208–9.

89[6] Cf "...besides the language of words, there is a language of spirits (sermo interior)...". *BL* ch 12 (1907) ɪ 190–1.

whom is LIFE & that Life the creature's Light[1]—and not in the abysmal Will[2]

91 I ii 7

Who shall dare look down on the Mind, from whom this Preface proceeded? Yea, the Light of Christ covers the dark ground, as the Light-world covers the Body of Sun. Yet it is a mercy that the Light should retreat on each side, and leave rifts & chasms & feculæ— as the Spots in the Sun.—[1]

92 I ii 10, referring to **93**

§ The following was written when I was new to Behmen. ~~My~~ The solution is still the only one, I have to offer; but it is no longer satisfactory to my mind: and to this day, Septr 1818, Behmen's "language of nature" is the great stumbling-block of his works to me.—[1]

93 I ii 10–11 | Ch 1 "Of the First Principle"

6. Behold, there are especially three Things in the Originality, out of which all Things are, both Spirit and Life, Motion and Comprehensibility, viz. *Sulphur, Mercurius,* and *Sal.* . . .

7. Now to speak in a creaturely way, *Sulphur, Mercurius,* and *Sal,* are understood to be thus. *SUL* is the Soul or the Spirit that is risen up, or in a Similitude (it is) God: *PHUR* is the *Prima Materia,* or first Matter out of which the Spirit is generated, but especially the Harshness: *Mercurius* has a fourfold Form in it, *viz.* Harshness, Bitterness, Fire, and Water: *Sal* is the Child that is generated from these four, and is harsh, eager, and a Cause of the Comprehensibility.[1]

90[1] An echo of John 1.4.

90[2] Not in *OED* in this sense—i.e. the will arising from the abyss. See **72** and n 1, above.

91[1] C intends a word for dark spots in the sun ("Spots in the Sun"), referred to by astronomers as *maculae,* the counter-term for bright spots being *faculae. Feculae*—lees, dregs, impurities—may be a slip or a confusion.

92[1] The "Language of Nature" occurs at the end of **89** textus, above.

93[1] In a letter to Lady Beaumont, 21 Jan 1810, C referred to the substance of **93** and **94** textus: "It is plain, that the words and phaenomena of certain chemical experiments with Quicksilver, and Sulphur (which he learnt from Fludd, or disciples of Fludd) were present to his fancy while he was delving into the possible state of *Being* prior to *Consciousness*—(See the Three Principles, p. 10, 11 etc.) and of the association of bodily feelings, voluntarily forced, with thought, see the ridiculous Analysis of the word, Mercurius, with the separate meanings of Mer, Cur, Ri, and Us." *CL* III 278–9.

⟨§⟩*ᵃ* Here the good man bowed in his humility to the seeming knowlege of those among the Learned who alone had condescended to
converse with him, and who after a worldly form neighboured the
most on his spirit ⟨viz. the Alchemists:⟩—and therefore his outward
apprehension strove to express its recollections of the inward Seeing
in *their* Phrases—which yet were but arbitrary signs ~~for~~ and in his
use of them—even as if he had invented words, as Ab, ~~a~~ ac—adra—
&c. Thus, he divides Sul and Phur. All these are the crude efforts of
the recollective powers, blending the darkness of the ~~s~~ Night with
the impressions left by the Day. For verily Behmen's Works are
Behmen's Dreams; but his Dreams are Light gleaming, often flashing
thro' sometimes suffocated in, always struggling with, the Darkness. But the wisdom of the Empirics & Epicureans ~~are~~ is a mock
harmony of consistent Darkness, & self-sufficing Oblivion.[2]

94   I ii 11, pencil

10. . . . Mark what *Mercurius* is, it is Harshness, Bitterness, Fire, and
Brimstone-water, the most horrible Essence; yet you must understand hereby no *Materia*, Matter, or comprehensible Thing; but all
no other than Spirit, and the Source of the original Nature. Harshness is the first Essence, which attracts itself. . . . Now the Sting
and Sharpness cannot endure attracting, but . . . resists . . . and is a
contrary Will . . . and from that Stirring comes the first Mobility,
which is the third Form. Thus the Harshness . . . attracts harder and
harder, and so it becomes hard and tart . . . so that the Virtue or
Power is as hard as the hardest Stone, which the Bitterness (that is,
the Harshness's own Sting . . .) cannot endure; and then there is
great Anguish in it, like the horrible brimstone Spirit, and the Sting
of the Bitterness, which rubs itself so hard, that in the Anguish
there comes to be a twinkling Flash, which flies up terribly, and
breaks the Harshness. . . .

But § 10, and almost every where the Confusion and difficulty of
Behmen arises from his affirming intuitively, and seldom or never
reasoning logically, by aid of abstraction. Thus abstractly there are
four Powers, Astringency, Pungency (which B. calls now bitterness,
and now sourness) Repulsion, and Dilation; but really no one of

93[2] C attacks the "wisdom of the
Empirics & Epicureans" under other
names in *CN* III 4251 (May 1815); but
CN III 3605 (c Aug–Sept 1809) also
provides parallels, including the *abeste*,
Profani! of **98**. See also *P Lects* Lect 6.

these is without the other three, and the designation is according to the predominance. Not always distinguishing this he of course often confounds the names—Thus, Repulsion, the opposite of Astringency, he sometimes calls Sweetness, sometimes Fire &c.

95 ɪ ii [2], blank page facing "Preface to the Reader", referring to **94**

N.B. To tThat part of my Note to p. 10, 11, which I have written with pencil, is too important to remain entrusted to so perishable a record. I therefore repeat it here: it being a necessary clue to thread the labyrinth of Behmen's Theosophy.[1]—In all knowlege there are two points—the mode of acquiring, and the mode of communicating it: Discere, et docere.[2] The first, is in the first instance at least, is Intuition, or immediate Beholding.[3] and Above all, is this necessary in the knowlege of spiritual and metaphysical Entities. Wh Qui veré discit, videndo intuendo discit: ast intueri, sensu spirituali, vult idem ac *esse existentialiter*. Quantum sumus, intuemur.[4]—The second is logicé, by *abstraction* and consequent distinction of terms:[5] Qui bene docet, bene distinguit.[6] Now Behmen, from his want of technical education, ⟨neglected the *art* of reasoning, by acts of abstraction,⟩ which separate from the first is are indeed a mere Shadow⟨s⟩, but, like a Shadow⟨s⟩, of incalculable service in determining the remember able outlines of the Substance. ⟨He⟩ is wholly intuitive.—For example. By abstraction I designate four Powers, or

95[1] Much of the argument of this note is repeated, without reference to Böhme, in the letter of Sept 1817 to C. A. Tulk, *CL* ɪv 769–75, and in *CN* ɪɪɪ 4114.

95[2] "To teach, and to learn".

95[3] See "On the Principles of Genial Criticism": "I have restored the words, *intuition* and *intuitive*, to their original sense—'an intuition,' says Hooker, 'that is, a direct and immediate beholding or presentation of an object to the mind through the senses or the imagination.'" *BL* (1907) ɪɪ 230. See also *BL* ch 12 (1907) ɪ 166–8.

95[4] "He who really learns, learns by intuition: but to intuit, in the spiritual sense, means the same as '*to be*' in the existential sense [or *in terms of existence*]. We intuit to the

extent that we are." Possibly a rendering of a statement by Kant or Schiller. See the distinction between discursive and intuitive, with quotations from Kant's *Logik*, in *CN* ɪɪɪ 3801, and in *BL* ch 12 (1907) ɪ 190n C's objection to Kant's too exclusive definition of "intuition". The primary meaning of *intueri* is "to gaze at" or "to see into", corresponding to some meanings of θεωρεῖν. For *existentialiter* see Bᴀxᴛᴇʀ *Reliquiae* ᴄᴏᴘʏ ʙ **8** n 1. "Existential" is used in **47**, above, and **139**, below.

95[5] The "second [point]", "logicé", corresponds to "Intuition", which was "the first [point]". *Logice* ("logic") is common in later Latin.

95[6] "A good teacher makes good distinctions". Cf *CN* ɪɪɪ 4058 f 73, 4418 f 15.

rather two Powers having each two forces, which may [be]^a *diagram'd* in a cross of two lines, each bi-polar:

$$\text{D} \overset{\text{A}}{+} \text{C}$$
$$\text{R}$$

or as an Axis with an Hemisphere, North, South: East, West. Have A and R. represent Attraction and Repulsion: C and D Contraction and Dilation. But intuitivè no one of these *is* without the other three/ and the name is given by that power which is the predominant. Thus, we may take elementary Carbon, as the representative of Attraction, not that it could *be* without R. C. D; but because these are taken up into and under the predominance of A.—They are a fourfold Four: A+CRD. C+ARD. R+DAC D + ACR.—Now Behmen se beholding them as they are, is led often to confound their names. Astringency i.e. Attraction, he often confounds with Bitterness, S or Sourness, i.e. Contraction—Repulsion he sometimes calls, sweetness, sweet Water—sometimes Fire/—and so on—. He almost always however enables the attentive Reader who has mastered his meaning in the first instance, to corrects these confusions: but the attention must be great and continuous, and more than can be often expected. Therefore as few Philosophers better deserve, so none more require a running Comment: or what would be still more profitable, a rifacciamento,[7] in which by Algebraic Symbols or Symbols invented in the manner of the Algebraic the predominances with the modifying powers might be expressed—so as to preserve the unity and yet retain the distinction.—But this is done, my notes may be of great service—tho' they are mere specimens, and the reminiscences necessary in almost every page.—More especially, with regard to Fire, and Warmth—which he often confuses with Repulsion/ and with each other.—So Astringency and Bitterness—the meaning of which may be hinted in Oxyd of Carbon.—

But the mystery and depth of Behmen are in the three superadded Powers, or Spirits, and their origination out of and reaction on the primary Four, or the union of the natural with the transcendental Philosophy.[8] In this it is most emphatically true, that Fiendo dis-

---

^a Word supplied by the editor

95[7] Properly *rifacimento*, "reworking". C often used the word in this incorrect form, usually referring to the 1818 *Friend*.

95[8] "The primary Four"—i.e. the four physical qualities that with "the three superadded Powers" make up the seven "Nature Spirits" or "Qualities" of **35**, above.

cimus.[9] See the printed marginal note (f) to p. 8. of the Author's Preface to the three Principles.—[10]

S. T. Coleridge

96 I ii 12

[12ff. Böhme analyses the separate syllables of the word "Mercurius" as themselves symbols, and tries to relate their significance to their physical sounds.][1]

That B. in his first work, the Aurora, should have bedreamt himself into this absurdity by confounding the ideal* origin of words *in genere* with the endless accidental modifications that accompany all existing Languages, does not seem strange; but that he should repeat and persevere in this confusion after he had had communion with men of Learning and with the works of Paracelsus, as it is evident from his latter works that he both had and had (in style and arrangement at least) profited by—this does perplex me.[2]

* i.e. suppose man perfect; and his organs and organic Acts must have been faithful symbols of his spiritual Life and Cognition. But when men became corrupt, in their nature, then the organs themselves began as it were to *lie*, as well as his erroneous cognitions and inward Acts to communicate false impulses to the organs.—

97 I ii 15–16 | Ch 2 "Of the First and Second Principle, What God and the Divine Nature Is"

11. Behold now, when the Bitterness, or the bitter Sting (or Prickle,) (which in the Original was so very bitter, raging and tearing, when it took its Original in the Harshness,) attains this clear Light, and

95[9] "We learn by having things happen to us". Cf *CN* I 374, from Pico della Mirandola: "Tantum scit homo, quantum operatur."

95[10] *The Three Principles* 8 n *f*: "Seal that can be opened by no academic, university, or scholastic Learning; but by earnest Repentance, fasting, watching, praying, knocking, and seeking in the Sufferings of Jesus Christ by the Holy Spirit."

96[1] Cf **57, 58**, above.

96[2] C recognised that Paracelsus was a likely channel through which doctrines from the mysteries could have reached Böhme. C also knew that Böhme could find in the works of Paracelsus examples of newly coined words whose sounds bore no relation to their meaning, and which (*archeus*

being an exception) were devoid of etymological relationships. For C on Paracelsus' coinages see *CN* III 3660 and n. C's reading of Henry MORE *Antidote to Atheism* in 1801 (*CN* I 938, 941) seems to have drawn his attention to Paracelsus and back to Böhme (see *CN* I 1000E, 1000I); but his important acquaintance with Paracelsus' works began in 1808 (see *CN* III 3660). He observed that "Paracelsus was a braggart and a quack; so was Cardan; but it was their merits, and not their follies, which drew upon them that torrent of detractions and calumny, which compelled them so frequently to think and write concerning themselves, that at length it became a habit to do so." *Omniana* I 216.

tastes now the Sweetness in the Harshness, which is its Mother, then it is so joyful, and cannot rise or swell so any more, but it trembles and rejoices in its Mother that bare it, and triumphs like a joyful Wheel in Birth. And in this Triumph the Birth attains the fifth Form, and then the fifth Source springs up, *viz.* the friendly Love; and so when the bitter Spirit tastes the Sweet Water, it rejoices in its Mother (the sour tart Harshness,) and so refreshes and strengthens itself therein, and makes its Mother stirring in great Joy; where then there springs up in the sweet Water-Spirit a very sweet pleasant Source or Fountain: For the Fire-Spirit (which is the Root of the Light, which was a strong (fierce rumbling Shriek, Crack, or) Terror in the Beginning) that now rises up very lovely, pleasantly and joyfully.

12. .... And out of these six Forms, now in the Birth, or Generating, comes a six-fold self-subsisting Essence, which is inseparable; where they one continually generate another, and the one is not without the other, nor can be, and without this Birth or Substance there could be nothing; for the six Forms have each of them now the Essences of all their sixfold Virtue in it, and it is as it were one only Thing, and no more; only each Form has its own Condition.

13. .... And each Form or Birth takes its own Form, Virtue, Working and Springing up from all the Forms; and the whole Birth now retains chiefly but these four Forms in its generating or bringing forth; *viz.* the rising up, the falling down, and then through the turning (of the Wheel in the sour, harsh,) tart Essence, the putting forth on this Side, and on that Side, on both Sides like a Cross; or, as I may so say, the going forth from the Point (or Center) towards the East, the West, the North and the South: For from the Stirring, Moving, and Ascending of the Bitterness in the Fire-Flash, there exists a cross Birth. For the Fire goes forth upward, the Water downward, and the Essences of the Harshness sideways.

Tho' these §s, 11. 12. and 13. are rendered more than usually obscure and perplexed by the attempt to represent faithfully the co-inherences and mutual evolutions of the fourfold Four, yet the last 3 or 4 lines of the last (overleaf)[a] bring us back to the *meaning*, and will be sufficiently intelligible if only we remember that the Orient and Occident are taken by Behmen as the Upward and Downward.

E Fire = Oxygen

Carbon ——┼—— azote

W Water = Hydrogen[b]

[a] C means "the last 3 or 4 lines" of § 13: "the going forth...sideways"
[b] In the bottom right-hand corner of the page C has written "*turn over*"

while the horizontal Line of the Cross represents the Substantive Line, or Line of the *Essences*—i.e. the poles of the magnetic Axis— C = elementary Carbon. A = azote. C.+A. Describe a circle by making the Cross revolve on its points, and one semi-circumvolution presents it as North = C. South = A. East = O. West = H./ i.e. Oxygen, and Hydrogen.

98 I ii 16 | Ch 3 "Of ... the Birth of the Eternal Nature"

3. And although I write now, as if there was a Beginning in the eternal Birth, yet it is not so; but the eternal Nature thus begets (or generates) itself without Beginning. My Writings must be understood in a creaturely Manner, as the Birth of Man is, who is a Similitude of God. ... And my Writing is only to this End, that Man might learn to know what he is, what he was in the Beginning, how he was a very glorious eternal holy Man, that should never have known the Gate of the strong (or austere) Birth in the Eternity, if he had not suffered himself to lust after it through the Infection of the Devil, and had not eaten of that Fruit which was forbidden him; whereby he became such a naked and vain Man in a bestial Form, and lost the heavenly Garment of the divine Power, and lives now in the Kingdom of the Devil in the infected *Salnitre*, and feeds upon the infected Food.

Chapt. III. This is in the depth.[1] Abeste, profani![2] The βυσσος αβυσσος[3] may be contemplated as two in one: ~~First~~ in both = Almacht Gottes.[4] First, the deistic deific All-might realized in God by God for God, as the *ground* of his Existence which as his divine nature God alone hath in himself—is and hath! 2. As the same All-might *potential* of all other Being ⟨not in God as God: and in this sense it⟩ ~~which~~ is the ground out of which God created man, but in his own image breathing into him a spiritual life—"a living *Soul*"[5]—& so took him up out of the ground—But when man would the ground to be himself, he sunk back into the ground, & became the ground as of itself, and

98[1] The subtitle to §§ 1–8 is "The Gates of the Great Depth".

98[2] "Begone, you who are not initiates!"—a variant of *Aeneid* 6.258– 9: " 'procul o procul este, profani,' | conclamat vates...".

98[3] "Deepless Depth". See **72** n 1, above.

98[4] "All-might of God", as C renders it in the next sentence.

98[5] Gen 2.7.

not as the ground of God—but in itself it is a severe anguish, an impotent lusting, only to lust—the birth of Phantoms and false Life.[6]

99 I ii 18

11. But mark the Depth, in a Similitude which I set down thus; the harsh Spring in the Original is the Mother out of which the other five Springs are generated, *viz.* Bitterness, Fire, Love, Sound, and Water. . . .

Tho' the sequel always makes Behmen's meaning clear, and tho' he has added the words, "or sour" in this work; yet it is to be regretted that the term (Bitter) which is central, should be retained.

100 I ii 18

12. For the Spring of the great Anguish, which was in the Beginning before the Light, in the (tart) Harshness, from which the bitter Sting or Prickle is generated, that is now in the sweet Fountain of the Love in the Light changed from the Water-Spirit, and from Bitterness or Stinging is now become the Fountain or Spring of the Joy in the Light. Thus now henceforth the Fire-flash is the Father of the Light, and the Light shines in him, and is now the only Cause of the moving Birth, and of the Birth of the Love. That which in the Beginning was the aking Source, is now *SUL*, or the Oil of the lovely pleasant Fountain, which presses through all the Fountains, so that from hence the Light is kindled.

Light issueth forth out of the Depth, and the Depth becometh Gravity: and the Gravity submitteth, openeth, *utt*(out)*ereth* itself to receive the Light, and so giveth it a resting place of fixity, and the Gravity under the dominion of the Light becometh Color: and the Light in love entereth into and yielding itself to the Gravity becometh Sound[1]—So that in Love the fugitive Outward innereth itself and abideth in Color, and the stifled fixed Inward hath Outerance and flight in Sound.[2] Yet not oblivious of their O̶r̶i̶g̶i̶n̶a̶l̶s̶ matrix the

---

98[6] See **111** n 2 and **127** n 1, below.

100[1] This notion is reminiscent of Goethe's *Farbenlehre*: see C's letter to Tieck in Jul 1817 with mention of his reading *Aurora* at school. See **18** and n 1, above. Although he may indeed have read *Aurora* at Christ's Hospital, there is no evidence that he interpreted it in these terms before the period covered by the marginalia. A similar explanation of sound and colour reappears in a letter of 12 Jan 1818 to Tulk (*CL* iv 807) and in *CN* iii 4418.

100[2] "Inner" and "outer" as verbs, and the noun "outerance"—which also appears e.g. in BLANCO WHITE *Practical Evidence* **13**—represent a

Sound passeth inward, and the Color spreads itself outward, the latter meeting the humorous buxom Eye becometh the element of Form for the Fancy and is the formative Light of the Life: the former thro' the Ear by the hard metalloid bones and tight tympanum sinketh into the Understanding, and becometh the substance of the Thought.—Color = Lux centripetalis: Sonus = Gravitas centrifuga[3]

101 I ii 24 | Ch 4 "Of the True Eternal Nature"

19. ... God the Father made Man; the Beginning of whose Body is out of the (one) Element, or Root of the four Elements, from whence they proceed, which (one Element) is the fifth Essence, (or Quintessence,) hid under the four Elements, from whence the dark Chaos ... had its Being, before the Times of the Earth; whose Original is the Spring of Water, and out of which this World with the Stars and Elements, as also the Heaven of the third Principle, were created.

20. But the Soul was breathed into Man, merely out of the original Birth of the Father by the moving Spirit ... Which original Birth is before the Light of Life, which is in the four Anguishes, out of which the Light of God is kindled, wherein is the Original of the Name of God; and therefore the Soul is God's own Essence or Substance.

Behmen appears in some places to have considered the Astringent or Attractive not only as the positive* but as the sole primary power, and Fire as the offspring by an intro-action of the Astringent on itself; in his phraseology, the Child of the Anguish.—Then by the reaction of the Fire, i.e. the *Con*tractive power, on its Parent, the attractive, to have generated two powers—first, the Dilative (Fluidizing) when the Attractive, as the Principle of Cohesion Totalism,

* The polar Philosophy considers it as the Negative or Northern.

---

central psychological perception of a quintessentially Coleridgian sort. *OED* records the first two for 1890, ascribing the use to J. H. Stirling; "outerance" is not in *OED*. The punning connexion between "utterance" and "outerance" engages another favourite term, "outness"—"a word which Berkeley preferred to 'Externality'" (*CN* III 3325). See also *CN* I 1307. The term was important to C in working out his theory of perception and had served him since Sept 1801 or earlier.

See esp *CN* III 3605, and e.g. *CN* I 985, 1297, 1307, 1387, II 2540, III 3325, 3592, 3605, 4058, and *AR* (1825) 384. "*In*-ness" (corresponding to "outness") in *CN* III 4418 f 12 is recorded in *OED* with earliest date 1866. See also "to give *utterance*, an *outer* being" in *CL* V 399; "it's *utter*-ance or exoteric Half" in *CL* VI 537; and "utterance (i.e. outwardness, *Äusserung*)" in *CL* VI 756.

100[3] "Colour is centripetal Light: Sound is centrifugal Gravity".

is the Predominant—and the Repulsive, or gaseiform, when the contractive, or principle of Particularism, is paramount.[1] Hence, ⟨perhaps,⟩ he so frequently includes the Air in Fire, or puts them in apposition.

This would come very near to the original theory of Phlogiston: and has its points of superiority over the bipolar Dyad, in *realism* and simplicity.[2] The diversity in the latter between the modified or substantive and the modifying or verbal, savors more of *Logic*, of *subjective* Production, and incroaches more on the Unity of Nature: —but then it has the advantage in application, and as a form of invention and solution, more especially in the Metallology.[3] So at least it appears *at present*. But Behmen's (if it be his: for it is not improbable that, as his Visions happened to be symbolized, he adopted the one or the other) was my own original Conception: and I do not despair of reducing under it the phænomena which I have of late accustomed myself to consider under the polar Construction.[4] The intimate connection of Earth and Fire in the Vesta of the Roman mythology, the Dogma of Heraclitus, the Ceres & Proserpine of the Eleusinian Mysteries:[5] while Jupiter, Juno (= the Air in its two forms) and Neptune (= the Water-element) are rep-

---

101[1] In *OED* "fluidizing" is recorded for 1855. "Totalism" is not in *OED*. The first use of "Particularism" is ascribed to C in FIELD 36, dated 12 Mar 1824.

101[2] Phlogiston was the principle of combustibility released from a burning body during combustion, and was generally considered to be imponderable. This was Priestley's view (see also ANDERSON COPY B 19 n 2). The phlogiston theory derived some support from the discovery of the inflammable air later called hydrogen, which seemed to exhibit some of the qualities ascribed to phlogiston. Davy briefly proposed and quickly rejected a modification of the theory, suggesting that all combustibles might contain hydrogen and that in combustion this combined with oxygen to form water, the product of combustion then being not an oxide but a hydrate. *Phil Trans RS* (1808) II 362. See also **15** n 4, above. For the "bipolar Dyad" see **107**, below.

101[3] Not in *OED*.

101[4] See **139**, below.

101[5] In Roman mythology, Vesta (Hestia in Greek) is the goddess of fire, hearth, and home, and is also identified with Earth. Cf **33** n 4, above. Heraclitus does not make an especially intimate connexion between Earth and Fire, since in the sustaining sequence Water comes between Earth and Fire (see **77** n 1, above); but a direct connexion between Earth and Fire is made by pseudo-Plutarch, quoted in Stanley *History of Philosophy* (1701) pt ix Heraclitus ch 1 sec 1 (I 444): "...all things are made by the extinction of this Fire; first the grosser part of it being contracted becometh Earth, then the Earth being loosn'd by the nature of Fire, becometh Water...". Ceres is also often identified with Earth. Schelling equates Proserpine with Hestia and Flame in *Ueber die Gottheiten* 17. The myth of Ceres and Proserpine was the basis of the Eleusinian mysteries.

resented as *Births*, γεννηματα, are at least striking Coincidences.[6]—
This is at all events clear to me, that ~~the terms~~ Positive and Negative,
are *inconvenient* TERMS.

102 I ii 24

21. And if it elevates itself back into the Anguish of the four Forms
of the Original, and will horribly breath forth out of Pride in the
Original of the Fire ... it so becomes a Devil: For the Devils also
with their Legions had this Original, and they out of Pride would
live in the [i]fierce Wrath of the Fire, and so they perished, and remained Devils.

i. That is, would feel the Will as Will; and make it generate in itself,
instead of generating in the Reason. Cast the σημεν ον θε γρουνδ.[1]

103 I ii 24

22. Yet if the Soul elevates its Imagination forward into the Light,
in Meekness and Comeliness or Humility, and does not (as Lucifer
did) use the strong Power of its Fire, in its Qualification, (or Breathing,) then it will be fed by the Word of the Lord, which is the Heart
of God; and its own original strong (fierce wrathful) Source of the
Birth of the eternal Life becomes paradisical, exceeding pleasant,
friendly, humble, and sweet, wherein the Rejoicing and the Fountain of the eternal Songs of Praise spring up: And in this Imagination it is an Angel and a Child of God, and it beholds the eternal
Generating of the [o]indissoluble Band; and thereof it has Ability to
speak, (for it is its own Essence or Substance,) but (it is) not (able
to speak) of the infinite Generating, for that has neither Beginning
nor End.

[Shoulder-note:] [o]Note, what is possible to be spoken of, and what
not.

o. the περιχορησιν, and the birth of Ideas in the Pleroma Λογου;[1]
but not the self-realization of the Absolute Will, or the filiation of
the Alterity—for these are *infinite*

101[6] Γέννημα—as distinct from
γένεσις (see e.g. *CN* III 4420 f 17)—the
product or outcome of the process of
bringing into being.

102[1] English in Greek characters:
"semen on the ground"—from Gen
38.9.

103[1] *Perichoresis*, which is rendered
"intercirculation" by C in FIELD *Of*

the Church **23**, and "circumincession"
in theological contexts, is glossed by C
in *CN* III 3575 as "circular internal
Generation, in which A *is* as soon as
becomes B—and B in the very act becomes A—". The word also occurs in
CN III 4359, 4483. "Pleroma Λογου"
—the Pleroma (fulness) of the Word.

26. And thirdly, you find in all Things a glorious Power and Virtue, which is the Life, Growing and Springing of every Thing, and you find that therein lies its Beauty and pleasant Welfare, from whence it stirs. Now look upon an Herb or Plant, and consider it, what is its Life which makes it grow? And you shall find in the Original, Harshness, Bitterness, Fire, and Water, and if you should separate these four Things one from another, and put them together again, yet you shall neither see nor find any Growing; but if it were severed from its own Mother that generated it at the Beginning, then it remains dead; much less can you bring the pleasant Smell, or Colours into it.

The reader must constantly bear in remembrance Behmen's inconsistency in naming the four powers—thus in § 26 we must understand Attraction, Contraction, Repulsion and Dilation as the elementary Powers—but not noticing the absence of the Repulsion or Azote he sees the Oxygen (or contraction) and the Hydrogen (or dilation) as three, the Fire being the product between both, or Synthesis.*
His frequent oscillations between the terms Bitterness, Sourness, & Prickle or Pungency, sometimes explaining one by the other with an "or" and sometimes accumulating them, to express the one power, sufficiently prove what he was aiming at, but which from want of abstraction he could not aptly distinguish. From this cause, likewise, he does not discriminate the centrality from the surface powers— which in more than one passage greatly obscures his use of the principle, BITTERNESS—which must be, in and of itself, taken as the Absorption† of each in the other, of all the powers, just as Black

* N.B. not the Indifference: which is Water.

† N.B. Fourcroy & Vauquelin determined the Amer or Bitter principle, to be a superoxygenized hydrocarburet of Nitrogen.[1]

104[1] "Bitter Principle. This term has been applied to certain products of the action of nitric acid upon animal and vegetable matters of an intensely bitter taste." *Brande's Dictionary of Science, Literature and Art* (1842). A "superoxygenized hydrocarburet of Nitrogen" would be a substance compounded of the four elements that represent the four polar forces and would thus stand in the same relation to the tetractys as the hypothetical "carbonazote" stands to the "magnetic axis": see **19**, above. Investigations into the bitter principle made by Antoine François, Comte de Fourcroy (1755–1809), an early convert to the theories of Lavoisier, and Louis Nicolas Vauquelin (1763–1829), his assistant from 1783 to 1791, were noticed in a summary report by Robinquet entitled "Observations on Aroma" in *The Quarterly Journal of Science, Literature, and the Arts*

is in Color—and not as an antithesis to any one power—Thus
Sweetness ✗ Sourness = Oxymel—but Sweet and Bitter are ✗ , and
irreconcileable—both are tasted, & the effect is a mawkishness.[2]
The very word suggests, that the exponents of *Quantity* are exhausted: and that a *Quality* is introduced.

105 I ii 25

I would wish the Note in this ⟨page (25ᵗʰ)⟩, and others in other parts
of the volume, to be read under the modification of the Note on the
page preceding, 24ᵗʰ.[1]—. Observe, however, that both the Polar
System or Tetractys, and the Tri-une, are necessary views of the same
truth, and by no means does either invalidate the practical Results
of the other. But they should be preserved distinct: which could not
be expected of J. Behmen. Ex. gr. in § 26, Fire evidently stands for
the principle of Air—and he has the bipolar or Tetractys, in view.

106 I ii 25

29. For the Stars themselves are senseless, and have no Knowledge
or Perception, yet their soft Operation in the Water makes a seething, flowing forth, or boiling up one of another, and in the Tincture
of the Blood, they cause a Rising, Seeing, Feeling, Hearing, and
Tasting.

Astrology/ that is, the Celeste *Chemique*, is a Science in POSSE.[1]

107 I ii 26

32. But what do you think there was before the Times of the World,
out of which the Earth and Stones proceeded, as also the Stars and

---

("Brande's Journal") x (1821) Art 10,
suggesting a possible terminus *a quo*
for this note.

104[2] In a marginal note on Lorenz
O K E N *Lehrbuch der Naturgeschichte* (6
vols Leipzig & Jena 1813, Jena 1816–
26) Vol I back flyleaf C explained these
two logical symbols, as elsewhere, with
the same examples: " ✗ opposite,
Sweet ✗ Sour ✗ contrary. Sweet ✗
Bitter." "Oxymel"—from ὀξύς (sharp,
sour) and μέλι (honey, sweet)—normally a medicinal mixture of vinegar
and honey, is here used by C almost
as a technical term for the sweet-sour
antithesis as distinct from the sweet-
bitter contrariety. Cf "The little

Birds shoot out their *gushes* round |
Mellow tho' shrill, an Oxymel of
Sound". *CN* III 3831.

105[1] I.e. **101**, above.

106[1] The "Celestial *Chemistry* is a
Science in POTENTIAL FORM"—
apparently a play on the title of the
Marquis de Laplace's celebrated work
on mathematical astronomy, *La Mécanique céleste* (1799–1825). Cf "Kant's
intellectual Mechanique" in BROWNE
Works **52**. For the development of
astrology into astronomy, and of
alchemy into chemistry, see e.g.
P Lects Lect 9 (1949) 382–3; and cf *CN*
III 4414 (abstracted from Boerhaave).

Elements? That out of which these proceeded was the Root. But what is the Root of these Things? Look, what do you find in these Things? Nothing else but Fire, Bitterness, and Harshness, (or astringent Sourness,) and these three are but one Thing, and hence all Things are generated.

§. 32. It is vexatious, that from the want of one distinction, of the second Birth from the first, Behmen should have so confusedly reflected truths of which, in their unity and co-inherence, he had so clear and intuition. ⟨Hence, the appearance of Cosmotheism in his works.[1] Thus, ex. gr.⟩ ~~Here~~ Fire is ⟨here⟩ evidently ~~used for~~ inclusive of the Centrifugal, Bitterness ~~for~~ of the Center, and Harshness ~~for~~ of an Attraction which in combination with the second and opposition to the first is the Centripetal—i.e. the three primary Powers are Attraction, Repulsion, and Gravitation: ⟨but misapplied, Poles of Lines for Lines &c.⟩

The monas ($=1$) by the law of polarity generates the Dyad ($=2$), itself remaining, or representing itself by, the Indifference-point, ($=3$) whence $1=3$, or the Triad. But each pole of the Dyad generates in like manner $+$; whence the $2=4$, but the point of bisection considered as the center is a fith, whence the pentad; and again as superficial it generates the equatorial point in each hemisphere, whence the Heptad, or 7.—

The Synthesis of each Dyad with the other (Oxygen + Hydrogen with Carbon: and Hydrogen + Oxygen with Azote) constituteing the two principles of destruction, Fire and Putrifaction, ~~constitute~~ give us the Ennead, $7+2=9$—and the recommencement of the Birth, involved in and one with the destruction gives the completing Decad $=10/$ on which Nature revolves.—or as being and appearing (3) as producing and preserving (4) as destroying to re-appear and re-produce (3). $3+4=7+3=10$.—[2]

108 ɪ ii 27

37. Now you can here produce nothing more, that God should ever use any Matter out of which to create the Devil, for then the Devil might justify himself, that he made him evil, or of evil Matter. For

---

[1] "Cosmotheism"—the view that the universe (or cosmos) is God. *OED* records the first use of the word as C's in "*Prometheus*": *LR* ɪɪ 326, 350. Cf **110**, below, in which Cosmotheism is presumably represented by "3: of the World the same as God (=Indian Pantheism)".

[2] For various transformations of the tetractys see **6** n 10, **105**, **172**, and *CN* ɪɪɪ 4427n. The "Decad"—set of ten—is another form of the tetractys.

God created him out of nothing, but merely out of his own Essence or Substance, as well as the other Angels. . . . And if it was not thus, no Sin would be imputed to the Devil, nor Men, if they were not eternal, and both in God, and out of God himself.

38. For to a Beast, (which is created out of Matter,) no Sin may be imputed, for its Spirit reaches not the first Principle; but it has its Original in the third Principle . . .

39. And if you cannot believe this, take the holy Scripture before you, which tells you, that when Man was fallen into Sin, God sent him his own Heart, Life, or Light, out of himself into the Flesh, and opened the Gate of the Birth of his Life, wherein he was united with God; and being broken off in the Light (Part) (yet continued in the Original of the first Principle) he has kindled that Light, and so united himself to Man again.

These §s are not less valuable as Theology than they are profound as Philosophy. They contain the radical confutation of Socinianism— as the general term for all Heresies that deny or metaphorize the mystery of Redemption and Incarnation.[1]

109 ɪ ii 27

40. If the Soul of a Man was not (sprung) out of God the Father out of his first Principle, but out of another Matter, he could not have bestowed that highest Earnest or Pledge of his own Heart and Light upon him . . . but he could very well have redeemed or helped him some other Way.

§ 40. a necessary truth; but needs to be *unfolded*[1]— it is certain rather than evident.[a]

110 ɪ ii 27

42. If therefore you will speak or think of God, you must consider that he is all; and you must look further into the three Principles,

---

[a] Note **110** follows directly on **109** without a paragraph break

108[1] In the middle years C was much concerned to clarify his attack on Socinianism; the detailed notes made on that subject in *CN* ɪɪɪ 3581, 3675, 3817, 3870, 3968, 4300 provided the substance for his published attacks in the *Lay Sermons* and *AR*. The fact that the point of attack in this marginal note is "Redemption and Incarnation" suggests that the note is of late date. For a general account of Socinianism see BAHRDT **1** n 1.

109[1] Cf "explicate" and "auseinandersetzen" in **5** n 1, above, and "enucleate" in **75** n 2, above.

wherein you will find what God is, you will find what the Wrath, the Devil, Hell and Sin are; also, what the Angels, Man and Beasts are, and how the Separation or Variation followed, from whence all Things have thus proceeded; you will find the Creation of the World.

§ 42. is enough of itself to place Behmen in the highest rank of original Thinkers. The momentous truth of the joint dependency of the Creation on the Fall (of the Spirits: not Adam's) and on the Love = God had been *shut out*,—*negatively*, by the ordinary acceptation of the Creation, ανευ Λογου, yet δια Λογου, κτισεως absurdæ sive irrationalis,[1]—and, *positively*, by the doctrine of emanation—the most ancient, the most widely diffused and the most fruitful, of Heresies.[2] It so explains as to deny both Creation, and Evil—a fact, which of itself forms some slight presumption of a connection, of some kind or other, between the two.

Well might Augustin say, on the emanative plan, Mundum e nihilo creavit ipsum pæne nihil.[3] The common Notion is far preferable: for it is in fact rather an Act of Adhesion in the Will than a Conception in the Intellect—not so much a conversion to the Truth, as an aversion from the four enormous errors, 1. of the World as the Ground of God (=the Hesiodic Theogony):[4] 2. of the World as

110[1] Of the Creation "without the Word, yet through the Word, of an absurd or irrational creation".

110[2] The doctrine of emanation, taught in the *Zohar* (second part of the Cabbala) and e.g. by Proclus among the Neoplatonists, is ancient and widespread as an account of the creation of the world. One form of the doctrine holds that the world came into being through the eradiation of God's power but without a direct act of will on the part of God; this is pantheistic. Cf **12** n 3, above, and n 3, below. (For "another form of the emanation-system", referred to as "an epicurean Onion", see **120**, below.) For C on the pantheistic consequences of the doctrine of emanation, see *CN* III 3862, and cf 3824.

110[3] "He created the world from nothing, it being almost nothing." The meaning of C's "Well might Augustin say, on the emanative plan" is ambiguous. He evidently has in mind Augustine *Confessions* 12.8, as misquoted in Sir Walter Ralegh *History of the World* (1677) 3 (see *CN* II 3088 and n): "But all this whole was almost nothing [*prope nihil*], because hitherto it was altogether without form; but yet there was now something apt to be formed. For thou, Lord, madest the world of a matter without form; which being next to nothing [*paene nullam rem*], thou madest out of nothing; out of which thou mightest make those great works which we sons of men do wonder at." Tr LCL. By substituting "the world" for "matter without form", Ralegh—and C—have distorted Augustine's meaning.

110[4] Hesiod in his *Theogony* tried to show the development of the universe from chaos and to trace the history of the gods. C described this as "an anti-philosophic Atheism, of which a sensual Polytheism was but the painted veil". *P Lects* Chronological Assistant (1949) 72.

without God (=Epicurean Atheism)[5] 3: of the World the same as God (=Indian Pantheism): and 4. of the World co-eternal with God.—[6]

S. T. C.

111 ɪ ii 28

47. Yet in this [the first] Principle there is nothing else but the most horrible Begetting, the greatest Anguish and hostile Quickening, like a Brimstone-spirit, and is ever the Gate of Hell, and the Abyss wherein Prince Lucifer (as the extinguishing of his Light) continued; and wherein (*viz.* in the same Abyss of Hell) the Soul continues, which is separated from the second Principle, and whose Light (which shines from the Heart of God) is extinguished, and for which Cause also, at the End of this Time, there will be a Separation or Parting asunder of the Saints of Light from the Damned, whose Source will be without the Light of God.

The Ipsëity, which in all eternity God realizes in the Alterity, is here conceived as of itself—of course, as an ever baffled Act, a self-contradictory Striving, a most horrible Begetting—the center of a circumference striving to be itself circumferential.[a] Thus this same indissoluble Band, or Copula, is to the Heavenly the Principle of or Ground of Life in the Act of Life, to the Reprobate the realizing Act of Life in the everlasting Passion of Death. For Ipseity and Alterity are co-inherently the reality of each other.[1] Εν αυτῳ ἔστι η ουσια των μη οντων;[2] it is the Father of Lies, the Den of Phantoms, the potential cause of Shadows, Subjectives without Objects, and thence

---

[a] Here C has written "†", and at the head of the page "† *continued from below*"

110[5] Epicurus taught that gods exist but that they are entirely apart from the world. The Epicurean system, being purely mechanical, dispenses with divine intervention. See also **93**, above, at n 2.

110[6] C's scheme of the Spinozistic pantheism is given in Baxter *Reliquiae* copy ᴀ 2 n 2. Spinoza's atheism is more flexible than the Indian and would include both varieties 3 and 4.

111[1] The statement down to "the reality of each other" is an affirmation of C's position that God, the ground of being, acts in the polarity of Ipseity (Himselfness) and Alterity (Otherness). See the ms note quoted in **127** n 1, below, and also **172**. In this marginal

note C is rephrasing Böhme's position in his own terms in a manner consonant with his own accounts of chaos and creation. The Greek phrase that follows is an explanatory parenthesis.

111[2] "In it ["the Copula"] *is* the existence of the things that *are not*". If "the Band, or Copula" between Ipseity and Alterity is dissolved, God is no longer the ground of being. The centre of the world then becomes self and the dynamic relation is reduced to the condition of "an ever baffled Act, a self-contradictory Striving". This is "the Father of Lies...the potential cause of Shadows". See also **98** at n 6, above, and **172** at n 3, below.

comparingly opposed to them, as Thoughts to Things—whence Contrasts &c.—The Genesis of Hell, and Satan is as no less indispensable, as a formal ground, in philosophy as than in Religion.

112 I ii 28

49. So I will now write of the second Principle, of the clear pure Deity, of the Heart of God. In the first Principle ... is Harshness, Bitterness, and Fire; and yet they are not three Things, but one only Thing, as they one generate another. Harshness is the first Father, which is strong, (fierce or tart,) very sharp and attracting to itself; and that Attracting is the (Sting) or Prickle, or Bitterness, which the Harshness cannot endure, and it will not be captivated in Death, but rises and flies up like a strong fierce Substance ... And then there is a horrible Anguish, which finds no Rest; and the Birth is like a turning Wheel, turning so very hard, and breaking and bruising as it were furiously, which the Harshness cannot endure. ... And so when the Flash of Fire comes into its Mother, the Harshness, and finds her thus soft and overcome, then it is much more terrified (than the Harshness,) and becomes in the Twinkling of an Eye white and clear. And now when the harsh Tartness attains the white clear Light in itself, it is so very much terrified, that it (falls or) sinks back as if it were dead and overcome, and expands itself, and becomes very thin and (pliable or) vanquished: For its own Source was dark and hard, and now is become light and soft; therefore now it is first rightly become as it were dead, and now is the Water-Spirit.

I conjecture, that Behmen, in this strange picture-language confused with the language of sensations, meant to convey the state of the absolute Self, considered as pure unlimited Activity, anterior (in nature) to its self-consciousness—and then by a ὕστερον πρότερον[1] of the Fancy attributes to such a State of Self-action those feelings which it would have occasioned *after* self-consciousness. The twinkling flash I suppose to mean that first dawn of Consciousness, in which the absolute Self begins to divide itself (for itself; but in truth remaining one & the same) into Subject and Object. Then the Harshness, which was before the Father, now considered as the substratum of the Objectivity, to which the Subject attributes its birth, becomes

112[1] "Hysteron proteron"—a figure of speech in which the cart comes before the horse. C laid down a double scheme in *CN* III 3421: "ὕστερον πρότερον | Hind before | *preposterous* Fore behind"—see also *SM* (*CC*) 104 and n—and in **52**, above, coined the verb "preposterize" (not in *OED*) and found an example of it in Böhme in **63**. See **52** n 13, above.

its Mother: and as the intelligent Subject establishes all things reality
& Life in the absolute "*I*", and considers itself as the I, so whatever
is opposed to itself must partake of Death = passivity—it is vanquished. By the water-spirit I suppose Behmen meant the flowing
continuous *objectivity* of the *I*, not graspable but yielding & in quietness giving back the Subject *I*.[a][2]

—The above note was written, while I was but in the dim dawn of
knowlege—& wholly in the *subjective* Thinking—of course, incapable of coming near Behmen.   S. T. C.

113   I ii 28–9

§. 49. I now find admirable. Even in Chemistry, as the echo of Spiritual
Truths, it has been suspected by men of some eminence[1] that there is
a comm one interchangeable Essence common to Hydrogen and
Azote, either ⟨of which may be conceived⟩ as $X+Z$, or $X-Z$ or
$X+Y-Z$, or $X+YZ$, or $X+Z-Y$, in *relatively*. Exempli gratiâ: if
Hyd. be $X-Z$, Az. may be $X+Z$, &c. I at least confess, that notwithstanding the splendid labors of Steffens I find insurmountable
difficulties in conceiving Repulsion as a *primary* force, as a simple
Power.[2]

114   I ii 30

57. Now you may well perceive that the Birth of the Sun takes its
Original in the Fire . . .

Son[1]

115   I ii 30

58. But the Holy Ghost is not known in the Original of the Father
before the Light (breaks forth;) but when the soft Fountain springs

---

[a] The postscript seems to have been written at the same time that C cancelled this paragraph

112[2] C cancelled this note presumably because he found that it was
not correct. Out of C's pervasive discussion of subject and object a few
passages can throw light here. See
P Lects Lect 3 (1949) 116; and cf 192n.
The "burlesque on the Fichtean
Egoismus" on the theme "I, I, I!
I itself I!" in *BL* ch 9 is also to the
point; see also *BL* ch 12 (1907) I 174ff.

113[1] The reference is primarily to
Davy. See **117** and n 1, below.

113[2] The notion of a "one interchangeable Essence" helps to elucidate
46, above, at nn 7 and 8. For Steffens
the force of repulsion is represented by
nitrogen, which marks the south pole
of the magnetic polarity. See *Grundzüge*
ch 3, esp p 46.

114[1] C is correcting a misprint;
but see **7** n 1, above.

up in the Light, then he goes forth as a strong Almighty Spirit in great Joy, from the pleasant Source of Water, and of the Light. . . . Positive Action.

116   I ii 30

[§ 58 continued:] . . . and he is the Power and Virtue of the Source of Water, and of the Light; and he makes now the Forming, (Shaping, Figuring,) and Images . . . and he is the Center in all Essences; in which (Center) the Light of Life, in the Light of the Sun, or Heart of the Father, takes its Original. And the Holy Ghost is a several Person, because he proceeds (as a living Power and Virtue) from the Father and the Son, and confirmeth the Birth of the Trinity.

§ 58. Here should have been deduced one distinctive   [a] of the Creation or Universe from God—.For in God the Prothesis is not manifested for itself, but only in the Fountain which he is from all eternity because he never can subsist but with the Light in the bosom of the Fountain, whence proceeds the Spirit. But in the Creation as conditioned by the Fall of, Apostasis,[1] the Prothesis is manifested as the Hardness, the Austerity, the stone indeed of the foundation, but likewise the Stone of offence. See Matthew, Chap. 11.[2]—Hence the □ = World, the △ emblem of the Triune.[3]

117   I ii 36–7 | Ch 5 "Of the Third Principle, or Creation of the Material World"

20. And if you open the Eyes of your Mind, you will see that Fire is in Water, as may be seen in a Storm of Lightening, and yet it is no

[a] C has left a space for a word he did not supply

116[1] For "Apostasis" as "the Fall" see **59**, above, and **153** and n 8, below.

116[2] "The Stone of offence" refers to 1 Pet 2.5–8: ". . .but unto them which be disobedient, the stone which the builders disallowed, the same is made the head of the corner, And a stone of stumbling, and a rock of offence, even to them which stumble at the word, being disobedient. . .". C's reference to Matthew is a slip: the passage (source in part for 1 Pet 2.5–8) is Matt 21.42: "The stone which the builders rejected, the same is become the head of the corner. . .".

116[3] As traditional symbols, □ represents limitation, △ represents *inter alia* "the first-born of beauty" (see *BL*—1907—II 230); and both are in some sense symbols of the tetractys, □ being the figure of the quaternion (for which see **24** n 6, above) and △ the figure of "multeity in unity". In this context, where both figures represent building-stones rather than pure symbols, □ represents the stability and mass of a foundation-stone and as the symbol of limitation is also "the Stone of offence", and △ can represent a head-stone or key-stone. Perhaps, as parallel to **31**, above, □ stands for τὸ θεῖον, "the foundation", and △ stands for ὁ θεὸς ἀειζώων, "the Crown and Key-stone". For □ as "to rest" and ○ as "to move" see *CN* II 2342.

durable Fire, though it be true Fire, which sets Houses on Fire, and burns them. So also you may see that there goes forth from it a mighty forcible Air, and that they are in one another; and besides, you see that Water is generated in the Storm.

§ Water is in the ultimate truth = the bipolar Electricity, which becomes Fire in the disunion, not a durable Fire, but still a real one. So far even the present state of Chemistry harmonizes with Behmen: and as to the "mighty forcible air" let it not be rejected without first remembering that Davy, our Prince of Chemists, has strongly suspected a common principle in Hydrogen and Nitrogen.[1] Water being the two electricities in puncto indifferentiæ,[2] is it inconceivable that after disunion a slighter bond may take place, in which the negative or $-E =$ oxygen may exert an active power on the Positive or $+E =$ Hydrogen, and this by Contraction + Dilatation generate Repulsion, i.e. form Hydrogen into Nitrogen? The experiment of Priestly in freezing water nine times successively and at the 9th time produce the same quantity of Nitrogen as at the first,[3] seems to confirm it. For Ice is evidently an oxyde of Water.

118 I ii 37

22. For there is in the Original, first Harshness, which attracts, shuts up, makes Darkness, and sharp Cold; but the Tartness cannot

---

117[1] Cf Davy's Bakerian Lecture for 1809: "One of the queries that I advance, in attempting to reason upon the singular phenomena produced by the action of potassium upon ammonia was, that nitrogen might possibly consist of oxygen and hydrogen, or that it might be composed from water." *Collected Works* v 246. In a footnote added in 1808 to his Bakerian Lecture of 1807 Davy had also said that "A phlogistic chemical theory might be defended, on the idea that the metals are compounds of certain unknown bases with the same matter as that existing in hydrogen; and the metallic oxides, alkalies and acids compounds of the same bases with water." *Collected Works* v 89–90n. For C's view that water could be the common base of both hydrogen and oxygen see **45**, above, at n 7.

The exalted epithet applied to Davy in this note would indicate a date before Apr 1812: see **17** n 3, above. C's admiration was at its highest in late 1807 and early 1808 (see AURELIUS **51** n 1). Thereafter his regard for Davy declined, but his one reference to him in the 1809–10 *Friend* shows that when it was a matter of public statement his personal disappointment with Davy interfered as little with his judgement as the estrangement from WW interfered with the triumphant declaration of WW's genius in *BL*. See *Friend* (*CC*) II 251–2.

117[2] "In the point of indifference". On water see **24**, above; see also **173**, below.

117[3] Priestley's "Experiments on the Production of Air by the Freezing of Water'" was included in *Memoirs of Dr. Joseph Priestley* (1806) 265–6. Davy had referred to it in his Bakerian Lecture of 1809: see *Collected Works* v 253–4.

endure the Attracting: For the Attracting in the Cold makes in the
Bitterness a Sting, (or Prickle,) which rages and resists against the
hard Death, but not being able to come away out of the Tartness
(being its Mother wherein it stands,) therefore it rages very horribly,
as if it would break the Harshness (in Pieces;) it flies upwards and
sideways, and yet finds no Rest, till that the Birth of the Harshness
falls into an aching horrible Essence, like a Brimstone-Spirit . . .
like a whirling Wheel. . . .

The Bitterness instead of alternate Tyrannies disparts; the centripetal
and centrifugal becomes *functional* as reconciled in a Synthesis =
Gravitation. Here as every where the Prothesis (*here* = Bitterness)
has its Image in the Synthesis: thus:*a*

$$\Theta \xleftrightarrow{} A$$

where P = prothesis, Θ = thesis, A = antithesis, and S = synthesis.*

Q^y Whether the true figures of one and two are not $(,)$? or like
our written i with dot fixed on to the top? $\dot{\iota}$

  * Divide $\bigcirc$ into $($ and $)$,*b* ~~re~~concile, i.e. remove the ~~aversion~~
opposition and unite them in an † upright line; and we have $\}$. So

$$1\frac{0^{\ddagger}}{3}2$$

  † That is, the line of progression: consequently of production. In the
horizontal they would fall back into the Prothesis, & be again = 0.

  ‡ This is the +0, or nihil positivum = omneitas indistincta.[1]

119 I ii 38 | Ch 6 "Of the Separation in the Creation, in the third Principle"

2. Nay, we have it clearly and plainly to be seen in ourselves, and in
all Things, if we would not be so mad, blind, and self-conceited,
and would not be so drawn and led by a *k*School-boy, but did stick
close to the *Schoolmaster himself, who is the Master of all Masters,
for we see indeed that all Things spring out of the eternal Mother . . .
[Shoulder-note:] *k* Outward Reason.

k. der Verstand-Gespenst[1]
* der Vernunft-Geist, dessen Mutter die ewige Vernunft ist.[2]

  a A cancelled diagram precedes the final one
  b C had reversed symbols for the second and third, which he deleted

118[1] "Positive nothing (zero) is an
undifferentiated allness"—"omneitas"
being a scholastic word current in the
anglicised form "omneity" in the
seventeenth century (e.g. BROWNE
Religio 15 textus), which C translated

"Allness" in *SM* (*CC*) 60. See also
CN II 2346, III 4369.

119[1] "The Understanding-Ghost".
119[2] "The Reason-Spirit, whose
mother is eternal Reason". See **123**
and **126**, below.

120 I ii 38

[§ 2, continued from **119** textus:] ... and as she is in her own Birth, so she has generated this World, and so is every Creature also generated. And as that (Mother) is in her springing forth in Multiplication, where every Fountain (or Source) has another Center in it from the Genetrix, and a Separation (or Distinction,) but undivided and not asunder, so also this World is generated out of the eternal Mother, which now is such another Genetrix, and yet is not separated from the eternal Mother, but is come to be in a material Manner ...

In §. 2. from one mistake or rather *oversight*, and an inconvenient expression B. approaches too near to Pantheism, per consequentia: tho' in this very § he forbids the doctrine. It is not true or consistent with Behmen's own more correct recollections of his epopsy, that the material Creation is "such another Genetrix" as the eternal Mother (the Plenitude in the Alterity) or that it is properly generated out of the latter.—This would in truth be but another form of the emanation-system—or an epicurean Onion.[1] There are three moments, Creation in the Eternity—of God ⟨in the Word:⟩ Materialization—of Sin: Creation in Time, or rather Re-creation—of God *by* the Word. B's oversight is in the second.

121 I ii 39, referring to **120** textus

Q[y]? It would be hard to affirm a *separation* perhaps; but yet it not "so also" either, but *differenced* tho' not separated, the × of the eternal Mother being only interdistinguished.[1]

122 I ii 39

3. Now because this Birth (of the Sun) has a Beginning through the Will of God, and enters again into its Ether, therefore it has not the Virtue or Power of the Wisdom; but it continually works according to its Kind, it vivifies and kills; what it does, it does (not regarding whether it be) evil, crooked, lame, or good, beautiful or potent, it causes to live and to die, it affords Power and Strength, and destroys the same again; and all this without any premeditated Wisdom ...

120[1] For the "emanation-system" see **110** n 2, above. By "Epicurean" C here means "of materialistic tendency", and the "onion" signifies a logical regress. With "epopsy" (not in *OED*) —"seeing"—cf "Epopt" in **47**, above.

121[1] In **120** C takes the "eternal Mother" to mean "the Plenitude in the Alterity", and the phrase "so also" occurs in **120** textus. The symbol " × " is here the sign of multiplication or generation; or, in more specialised terms, the two axes of the tetractys potentially present before creation.

See Kant's noblest work, Critik der Urtheilskraft, and its noblest Chapter, on Teleology: as a commentary on this and similar §s in Behmen.[1] Nature (B. would say) is wise and *so far* good *essentialiter*; ⟨but not formâ propriâ:⟩[2] for her essence is in God and one with the *Allmight* which cannot but be *negatively* wise, for it and the wisdom *be* one, and yet *only negatively* wise, for in the Dyad o̶r̶f manifestation, it is the Antipole of w̶i̶s̶d̶o̶m̶ Intelligence, i.e. τοῦ Λογου, which eternally rises and raises by pressing the Irrational (το απειρον αλογον) under it.[3] This j̶a̶m̶ haud Jam Intelligens neque Intellectus (οὐ μὲν νοερὸν πότε, ουδε νοητον)[4] is however a perpetual Intellecturition, a ποθος, Sehnsucht, Yearning, Ceres,[5] which resurges to the pressure sequacious of the undivulsed[6] Suppressor—whence, as the Symbol to its Radix, all Elasticity in nature, and its proportions and relations to Hardness, (Time) Sound, Mass.—From all this it follows, that nature cannot *appear* other*wise* than *blindly* wise—an unintelligent Wisdom.[7]

122[1] C wrote only one marginal note in Kant *Critik der Urtheilskraft* (Berlin 1799). There is evidence that he read the book as early as Jul–Sept 1809. *CN* iii 3584; cf 3713.

122[2] "Essentially; but not in her proper form [i.e. not "formally"]". For the special sense of *essentialiter/formaliter* see Baxter *Reliquiae* copy B **8** n 1.

122[3] The "Logos" is here identified with Intelligence, and the Irrational is glossed with a phrase that could be rendered "the indeterminate non-Logos", or "the unrealised (i.e. undifferentiated) unreason", or "the irrational indeterminate". See **31** n 7, above.

122[4] The Latin and Greek phrases are equivalent: "This not-yet Intelligent (Intellecting) nor Intelligible (Intellected)"; cf *CN* iii 3862n. In a note on a front flyleaf of Eichhorn *Einleitung in die apokryphischen Schriften* (Leipzig 1795) C translates νοερόν "intellectual" and νοητόν "intelligible", ascribing the first—and perhaps the second—to "the Alexandrine abstraction-mongers". Nevertheless, the two terms were important to him, and in *CN* iii 4351 τὸ ἄπειρον νοητόν means "intellectual Infinity" and

νοερὸς συναφή means "spiritual contact". See also **24** n 9, above, and Browne *Works* **53** n 4.

122[5] Πόθος (for which see **52** n 2, above), Sehnsucht, Yearning, and Ceres are approximate synonyms clarifying the sense of the syllable -ur in the coined word "Intellecturition" (not in *OED*); cf "Wolf's percepturitio" in *CN* iii 3256 and "futurition" in *AR* (1825) 156. In *Ueber die Gottheiten von Samothrace* Schelling tried to prove on etymological grounds that *Ceres* originally meant "hunger": see **140** n 4, below. In a marginal note on Joseph Ritson *A Select Collection of English Songs* (3 vols 1783) i 10–11 πόθος is used for "the *being in love*".

122[6] "Undivulsed"—not torn apart. *OED* does not record this negative form. "Divulsion" is the word Sir Thomas Browne used in his account of the vulgar error that "a Bever to escape the Hunter, bites off his testicles"—a detail that C obliterated in his copy. See Browne *Works* **13B, 24A–E**.

122[7] C's most striking image of "blind Nature"—the Nature of the atheist—appears in his "Allegoric Vision". Greatly expanded, the "Alle-

123　I ii 45 | Ch 7 "Of the Heaven and Its Eternal Birth and Essence, and How the Four Elements Are Generated ..."

22. You have a Similitude (of this) in yourself. Your Soul which is Die Vernunft] in you, gives Reason to you, whereby you think, (consider, and perceive;) that represents God the Father: The Light Der Verstand] which shines in your Soul, whereby you know the Virtue (or Power in you,) and lead (and direct and order) yourself with; that represents God the Son, or the Heart, the eternal Power Der Geist[1]] and Virtue: And the Mind, in which the Virtue of the Light is, and that which proceeds from the Light wherewith you govern your Body; that represents the Holy Ghost.

124　I ii 52 | Ch 8 "Of the Creation of the Creatures ..."

22. The Sun is the Goddess in the third Principle ...

Godd*ess*, because the Sun (die Sonne) is feminine in German.

125　I ii 55, pencil

43. ... And thus the Spirit of the Stars, or the Spirit in the Form of Fire, had now by its Longing copulated with the watery (Spirit,) and two Sexes sprung out of one Essence; the one according to the *Limbus* in the Form of Fire, and the other according to the Aquaster (or Spirit of the Water) in the watery Form; yet so (blended or) mixed, that they were alike as to the Body. And so the Male was qualified according to the *Limbus*, or Form of Fire, and the Female according to the Aquaster in the watery Form.

It is curious, that Ackerman, and other of the late philosophizing Naturalists have characterized the female by the relative predominance of Hydrogen (Behmen's ~~Mother~~ Spirit of the Water) and the Man by the rel. predom. of Oxygen, (the Spirit in the form of Fire[)].[1]

126　I ii 60 | Ch 9 "Of the Paradise ..."

25. Reason (which is gone forth with *Adam* out of Paradise) asks, Where is Paradise to be had (or found?) Is it far off or near? ...

Verstand should be rather translated Understanding than Reason:

goric Vision" was printed in the *Courier* 31 Aug 1811 and provided part of the introduction to the *Lay Sermon* (1816): see *LS* (*CC*) 131–7, esp 137. See also *Lects 1795* (*CC*) 89–94, esp 93 and n; *PW* (EHC) II 1092–6, esp lines 170–99.

123[1] "The Reason", "The Understanding", and "The Spirit"; cf **119**, above, and **126**, below.
125[1] Possibly Johann Christian Gottlieb Ackermann (1756–1801), or Jacob Fidelis Ackermann (1765–1815), both physicians.

as is evident from this § 25, and indeed throughout Behmen's Works.[1] The Understanding is that faculty of man which judges according to the categories, i.e. its is own constitutive forms, and (in Behmen) includes in them the original forms of Intuition which belong to the receptivity or impressible *Sense*, viz. Space and Time.—

127 I ii 69 | Ch 10 "Of the Creation of Man, and of His Soul"

19. . . . But he [i.e. Man in Paradise] ought not to have eaten any earthly Fruit, wherein the Corruptibility (or Transitoriness) did stick. It is true he should have eaten, but only with the Mouth, and not into the Body; for he had no (Entrails, Stomach, or) Guts, nor any such hard dark Flesh, it was all perfect; for there grew paradisical Fruit for him, which afterwards went away, when he went out of Paradise . . .

I understand in this that he used the palate as a pure *organ* of distinction and distinctive Intellect, as we may still use our eyes and ears: he did not join himself or blend with the essence of the thing eaten by sensuous enjoyment.[1]

128 I ii 73

42. Now therefore in the anguishing Mind of the Darkness, is the inexpressible (or unutterable) Source . . . from whence the Name Quality exists as from many (Sources, or Wells,) into one Source,

126[1] That C wished to consult Böhme's works in the German original is also seen in **142**, **162**, and **170**, below. Böhme in fact used *Vernunft* in the sense that C—following Kant—assigns to *Verstand*, and vice versa. The German edition in Green's library, not shown as C's, was published in 1831. For C's distinction between reason and understanding see BAXTER *Catholick Theologie* **14** n 3.

127[1] In a detached ms, BM Add MS 34225 f 150[v], C provides a comment on ch 10 § 40 (I ii 72), his first paragraph being a summary of § 40. "Behmen (3 Principles), p. 72. § 40.— 1. Anguish. 2. The quality (= Multeity? essential Relativity?) 3. Mind (Individuation?) 4. The Will to grow & generate (The re-action or alternation of the Multeity on the Individuation?) 5. The vis, virtus, power or faculty. 6.

The light (distinctive Act.) 7. the forth-driving Spirit of the Light. 8. A will in the Light to generate a sui simile ["a likeness of itself"]—(a new re-active of the Individuum in the Multeity[)].—

"For the inworking of Love is to generate itself into the Deity; but the impulsion ab diverso ["from the opposite direction"] of Love under the form or tincture of the apostate will is to generate the Deity into Self—it can produce therefore only images of Self, which would be pure copies, were it not that the Individuum cannot act but with and in and under the Multeity.—Such is the clearest view, I can at present form, of Behmen's Schematism.—" This is an answer to the tentative proposition in **98** at n 6, and a clear restatement of **111** nn 1 and 2; why not written in the volume itself is a question unanswered.

and out of these many Sources (running) into one Source, springs forth the Plurality of Skill . . .

—Many passages in this work would suggest the conjecture, that J. B. had read Plotinus and Proclus;[1] but here is a proof that he was ignorant of the learned Languages—the word. Qualität, he here supposes to be derived from the German word, Quell, a source or fountain. *Qualis*, possibly from και ολος.[2]

129   ɪ ii 74, second paragraph in pencil

48. . . . Here Lucifer was very heedless, and became so very proud, that when this Brimstone-Spirit in the Will of the Mind of God was created, then he would fain have flown out above the End of Nature, and would drive the Fire out above the Meekness; he would fain have had all burn in the Fire. . . . [These Spirits] generated a fiery Will, when they should have opened their Center to the Regeneration of their Minds, and so should have generated an angelical Will.

He would have made *power* its own end, and converted Nature into freedom. Thus all the great Heroes of the world from Nimrod to Buonaparte are philosophically as well as Scripturally Children of the Devil.[1]

    N.B. J. B. uses the term, Will, to express the Potentiality, and the *Mind* for the Actuality. The Apostate Angels employed their actual Will to realize the potential.

130   ɪ ii 75 | Ch 11 "Of . . . the Temptation"

5. . . . every Quality (or Source,) would be <u>creaturely</u> . . .

this word should be always rendered *creative*, or *creator-like*.

128[1] Neoplatonism influenced the alchemists, who influenced Böhme; hence the similarities. In Jan 1810 C said that "the most beautiful and orderly developement" of Böhme's philosophical position was to be found in Proclus *Platonic Theology*. *CL* ɪɪɪ 279.

128[2] C's derivation of *qualis* ("of what kind", from which comes "quality") from the Greek for "and whole" is fanciful. It could be on the analogy of *qui* from και ó, for which see *CN* ɪɪɪ 3843.

129[1] 1 John 3.10, Acts 3.10 (var). Cf "the Marks, that have characterized the Masters of Mischief, the Liberticides, and mighty Hunters of Mankind, from Nɪᴍʀᴏᴅ to Nᴀᴘᴏʟᴇᴏɴ". *SM* (*CC*) 65–6. Napoleon, in *Friend* (*CC*) ɪɪ 162 (9 Nov 1809), is "this genuine offspring of the old Serpent"; he represents "the heart & soul of a Devil" (*CN* ɪɪɪ 3845 f 123ᵛ), and is an example of "the despotic Atheism [that] would make the Will a Law to itself, i.e. itself God". *CN* ɪɪɪ 3866.

131 I ii 76

8. Besides, if *Adam* had eaten earthly Fruit, he must then have eaten it into his Body, and have had Guts (or Entrails:) And how could such a Stink (and Dung) (as we now carry in the Body) have been in Paradise in the Holiness of God? ...

This argument, which is far too often repeated, is among the weakest and most suspicious part of Behmen's Mind. To the pure all things are pure.[1] As great Wisdom and Glory are manifested in the Entrails and Processes of Digestion, as in the Mouth & the processes of Manducation. For wise purposes the Recrements are rendered offensive to *our* sense of smelling; (yet this is in great part an *acquired* Habit—) while to the acuter Smell of the Dog the same matter does not appear offensive in the least degree.

132 I ii 89 | Ch 12 "Of the Opening of the Holy Scripture ..."

37. Behold, I give you a true Similitude: Suppose that thou wast a young Man, or young Maid, (or Virgin,) (as *Adam* was both of them in one (only) Person,) how dost thou think thou shouldst stand? Suppose thus, set a young Man of good Complexion, beautiful, and virtuous; and also a fair chaste modest Virgin, (or young Maid,) curiously featured, and put them together; and let them not only come to speak together, and converse lovingly one with another, but so that they may also embrace one another; and command them not to fall in love together, not so much as in the least Thought, also not to have any Inclination to it, much less any Infection in the Will; and let these two be thus together forty Days and forty Nights, and converse with one another in mere Joy; and command them further, that they keep their Will and Mind stedfast, and never conceive one Thought to desire one another ... and that the young Man shall will (and purpose) never to copulate with this, or no other Maid (or Virgin;) and in like Manner, the Maid, (or Virgin) be enjoined the same. Now, thou Reason, full of Misery, Defects, and Infirmities, how do you think you should possibly stand here? Would you not promise fair with *Adam*? But you would not be able to perform it.

A most unfair and inapplicable Similitude—Give both the Youth and the Maid the same deep and perfect intuitions of Deity, the same beatific Vision, in which Adam is supposed to have possessed, the

---

131[1] Titus 1.15. For a particular instance of this purity in the field of perception see *CN* III 3401.

same various and inexhaustible Insight into all the Objects of Creation—and let the command only be, that they should *love* each other
without *lust*—and instead of perceiving any impossibility of keeping
the command, I am at a loss to conceive how the conception of
breaking it could have arisen in the mind, if it had ⟨not⟩ been
suggested by the command itself. Even in our present imperfect
nature, could a man think as deeply, energetically, and continuously,
as Sir Isaac Newton: he would find no very great difficulty in preserving himself as pure a Male-Virgin as Sir I. N. is said to have lived
& died. Add to this that Adam was not yet (according to J. B.) Flesh
and Blood. If J. B. had only had 80 ounces of his Blood drawn off,
the possibility of lusting after a woman would have appeared a
greater mystery to him, than the difficulty of not doing it.[1]

133 I ii 92 | Ch 13 "Of the Creating of the Woman out of Adam"

1. ... And thus we must be ꜰbound with the Woman till we send her
to the Grave ...
[Shoulder-note:] ꜰ*Schleppen*, begirt, surrounded.

Schleppen means, to *drag along* with any thing, clog, or inward
weakness—to *drag on wearisomely with the Woman as with* a Clog.[1]

134 I ii 112 | Ch 14 "Of the Birth and Propagation of Man"

41. Behold, thou seeking Mind, that which thou seest before thy
Eyes, that is not the ᵘElement, neither in the Fire, Air, Water, nor
Earth: neither are there four, but one only, and that is fixed and
invisible, also imperceptible: For the Fire which burns is no Element,
but (it is) the fierce (stern Wrath,) which comes to be such in the
Kindling of the Anger, when the Devils fell out of the ᵘElement:
The Element is neither hot nor cold, but it is the Inclination (to be)
in God ...
*] [Shoulder-note:] ᵘThat one pure, holy, eternal Element.

* That reality, which is the basis or element even of the merest
Potential, is the continued effect or rather efficience of the Divine
Will. See Gospel of John, Cap. I.[1] But because it is so, it is an Ens

132[1] See a close parallel between
this note and two notes on love in
Kᴀɴᴛ *Metaphysik der Sitten* (2 vols
Königsberg 1797) II 39–40 and on a
back flyleaf. For C's general doctrine
of love see Bʀᴏᴡɴᴇ *Religio* 22 n 1.

133[1] "Clog" (noun)—impediment,
encumbrance—a figurative use since
the sixteenth century. Cf *WPW* I 360.

134[1] John 1.3–4: "All things were
made by him [i.e. the Word]; and
without him was not any thing made
that was made. In him was life...".
C unfolds the action of the "Necessary
Will of God" in *CN* III 3765.

reale[2]—and in its ascending into the Potential, as the water in a syphon, it becomes a Soul, the Soul of the Potential, as a partial actualizing of the same, and this becomes a Creature.

135 I ii 169 | Ch 18 "Of the Promised Seed of the Woman"

13. It is very true, according to the first Principle (*viz.* the Abyss of Hell) he has willed it [i.e. the fall of man]; but that Kingdom is not called God; there is yet another Principle and fast Inclosure between. But in the second Principle (where God appears) he has not willed it. Indeed all is God's. But the first Principle is the Band of Eternity, which makes itself; from whence God the Father goes forth from Eternity into the second Principle; and therein he generates his Heart and Son (from Eternity to Eternity;) and there the Holy Ghost proceeds forth from the Father and the Son, and not in the first (Principle;) and Man is created for the second Principle.

§. 13. This, as it here stands, contains in the fewest and plainest words the Mysteries of Samothrace[1]—and is doubtless a Polytheism rooted in a super-sensual Atheism.[2] But doubtless likewise Behmen willed it not thus; but would have gladly received the correction—the All-might, which God's Will is, and which he knoweth within himself as the Abyss of his Being—the eternal *Act* of Self-constitution,[3] in necessity of finite contemplation supposed and antecedent (in order) to his personal Reality.—*This* Swedenborgh has confounded with the paternal principle—or rather this principle he has taken instead & to the exclusion of the Father.[4]

134[2] A "real Entity". See **7** n 3, above; and cf **20** n 6, above, and **166** n 1, below.

135[1] On the mysteries of Samothrace cf **122** at n 5, above, **140** at nn 3, 6, and **158**, below.

135[2] This view of the origin of polytheism appears in the "Chronological and Historical Assistant" to *P Lects* (1949) 72, in Literary Lecture 9 (*LR* I 184–9), and in "*Prometheus*" (*LR* II 325–30).

135[3] Cf *BL* ch 13 (1907) I 202, "the eternal act of creation in the infinite I AM", and "the abeternal act of Self-realization" in ANNEX.

135[4] See ANNEX at n 3, below. This reference, like that in **161**, is to SWEDENBORG *The True Christian Religion* (2 vols 1819), which Charles Augustus Tulk (one of the editors of the volumes) gave to C in c Jan 1820. These two notes mark the first intersection of C's long-matured thoughts on Böhme with his first consideration of Emanuel Swedenborg. The marginalia on this volume, together with an extended summary note—a stray ms printed in *CL* v 88–9n—were linked with a proposal to write "a history of the mind of Swedenborg" if the Swedenborg Society could raise £200 (see *CL* v 89n).

The crucial question for C here is how to reconcile God's omnipotent will with the fact of free-will in man, and the gift of grace with the imperative of faith. Swedenborg's incorrect definition of faith was, in C's view, "the Queen Bee in the Hive of Rom.

136 I ⁺2, referring to I ii 169 | **135** textus

See p. 169. §. 13.¹—the Cabiric Theophysy or *Natura* Deorum.²

137 II ⁻2

Observe that during my earlier studies of these Works I had entertained sundry Convictions, which I have now outgrown¹—the πρωτον ψευδος or root of my mistake² being this—that in common with Newton, Kant, Schelling, Steffens &c³ I had assumed four primary forces, Attraction and Repulsion as the poles of Length, and Ɇ – and + Electricity as the Poles of Breadth—and considered Gravitation as the *Offspring* of the synthesis (not with Kant as the Synthesis itself) of Attraction and Repulsion.—This scheme leavens too many of my Notes.—At present, I admit two *primary* forces only, Attraction and Contraction, and construction Repulsion and Dilation (chemically, Azote and Hydrogen) out of the two former by the preponderance of this or that.⁴ In both there is the synthesis of both: but in Dilation there is Contraction under the predominance

Cath. [and Swedenborgian] Error" (II ⁻4): neither authority in the Roman church nor "illumination" among the Swedenborgians could substitute for the moral initiative demanded by "Luther's Doctrine". C deals positively with this issue in his marginalia on Swedenborg's chapter on "The Divine Trinity" (I 346–9).

136¹ That is, **135**, above.

136² The Cabiri—the "great gods" worshipped in the mysteries of Samothrace. The "Elohim of the Greeks were still but a *natura deorum*, τὸ θεῖον, in which a vague plurality adhered; or if any unity was imagined, it was not personal—not a unity of excellence, but simply an expression of the negative—that which was to pass, but which had not yet passed, into distinct form". *LR* II 342 ("*Prometheus*"). The Latin phrase, "the *Nature* of the Gods"—i.e. a nature made up of gods—is another version of *theophysy* (θεοφύσις), "god-nature". The Greek word seems not to occur in any dictionary nor is "Theophysy" in *OED*. Cf C's use of "Physiotheist" in **158**, below.

137¹ For C's progressive revision of

his view of Böhme's doctrines and his developing interpretation of them see e.g. **1**, above. His statement in III i (**157**) that he had read only Vol I before Nov 1819 is contradicted by this note.

137² An unusual rendering of πρῶτον ψεῦδος: see BAXTER *Reliquiae* COPY B **92** n 1. Cf **158**, below.

137³ Cf the letter of Jan 1818 to Tulk: "This oversight of Kant (in his ...System of the Heavens...) in the assumption of *two* Powers only, as Newton had done before him, was the occasion of all the errors and imperfections of his theory." *CL* IV 808.

137⁴ Cf C's letter to Green written three weeks before this note: "No wonder then, that our discrepances from the Doctors of the Absolute are far more in number than our agreements. For all our principles previous to the genesis of polarity...is one continued Discrepance: and, as we assume different Poles, and two only original Poles instead of four (N ⚥ Ɇ instead of N⚥S, and Ɇ⚥W.) all that follows must more or less partake of the Discrepance." *CL* IV 876.

of Attraction, in Repulsion Attraction under the predominance of Contraction.—

But even thus inadequate to the solution of Nature will these co-ordinate and subordinate Factors [be]*a* proved, if there be not pre-adjoined the Spirit and the Word, i.e. Ὁ Ερως ἱέρῳ ἰο Λόγῳ ἔργον ἐνώσας.[5]

S. T. Coleridge 19 Octob[r] 1818

Tomorrow, 20 Octob[r], my Birth day. 47th year! Alas! alas!— Mercy! Forgiveness! Grace!—[6]

THE THREEFOLD LIFE OF MAN

138 ii i [1] | Ch 1 "Of the Original Matrix or Genetrix"

3. So now when we consider the life, what it is, then we find that it is a burning Fire, which consumeth, and when it hath no more (fuel) to feed upon, it goeth out; as may be seen in all Fires. For the life hath its nourishment from the body, and the body from the food; for when the body hath no more food, then it is consumed by the fire of the life, so that it fadeth and perisheth, as a fair flower, when it hath no water, withereth.

⟨3 §⟩ Wonderfully did this gifted Seer fly before his Age. Even at this moment Life retarded is merged in or confounded with the vis inertiæ (=ἀντιζώη)[1] counteracted, and Life itself, the source of all spontaneity, affirmed to be a *compelled State*. Luckily, this being the exact reverse of the Truth, the Results are not greatly affected. It is but A for B. and B. for A.

139 ii i [1]–4

6. And so now we perceive, in our very great and true knowledge, that every life desireth its (own) Mother, (out of which the life is generated) for a food; as the Wood, which is the Mother of the Fire, that the Fire desireth to have, and if it be severed from its Mother it goeth out. In like manner, the Earth is the Mother of all

a Word supplied by the editor

137[5] "Love uniting its energy with the holy Word"—the closing words of the opening epigraph to the 1818 *Friend*, ascribed there to Zoroaster *Oracula* ed F. Patrizi (Venice 1593), which C found reprinted in STANLEY *History of Philosophy*: see *CN* III 4447n, and cf 4424, 4446. C has inserted the words Ὁ Ερως into the Zoroaster text; his own translation of Nov 1818 reads: "[Love] uniting thy energy with the Holy *Word*". *CL* IV 884.

137[6] For C's birthday and his (mis)calculations of his age, see BAXTER *Reliquiae* COPY B **91** n 3.

138[1] "Force of inertia (that is, anti-life)".

Trees and herbs, and they desire it; and the water (with the other Elements) is the Mother of the Earth, or else it would be dead (or barren), and there would grow neither metals, trees, herbs, nor grass out of it.

⟨§ 6:⟩ This position is just—if only it be rightly interpreted. There is no union but of Opposites, = the Law of Polarity—and the Converse follows by the ~~same~~ Law of Identity—viz. The~~ir~~re are no Opposites without a common principle—or the essence of all opposites, ex. gr. of the N. and S. Poles of a Magnet, is the unity, or that which is neither because it is the essence of both—even as ~~this~~ all manifestation of unity is by opposition. Now that which each opposite seeks in the other ⟨as ~~the~~ its own essence &⟩ in which seeking consists the tendency to union, Behmen entitles THE MOTHER, ~~that~~ because that which appears to seek or to take the active part requiring a masculine character implies the feminine or passive in that which ⟨is⟩ sought. But as that which is *here* contemplated, as being sought, is not the correspond~~enc~~et (or the opposite *as* the opposite ⟨i.e. its wife;⟩) but the common principle from which each is derived or born, Behmen calls it the Mother. Thus Oxygen and Hydrogen are the two *Poles* of the Power of Breadth, ~~or t~~ or o~~r~~f the xyz which is the essence of both: ~~or~~ i.e. the common Mother. The wood (i.e. the Hydrogen to which the wood owes its combustibility)[1] ~~is~~ contains the *Mother* of the Fire—that which is at once its Parent (*pre*suppositum ejus) and its Food.[2]—Behmen would have expressed himself more luminously, if he had borne in mind that the Hydrogen is the *positive* Pole = Positive Electricity: and Oxygen the negative = negative Electricity. The ~~wood~~ air-fire therefore is better entitled to the name of ⟨the⟩ Mother, which the wood desires to have—in other words, the Hydrogen attracts the Oxygen.—⟨N.b. I recant the last preceding sentence, which indeed contradicts what I have before more rightly observed—if the Oxygen were the feminine, an error into which the term "*negative*" betrayed me, it would still be the Wife.⟩[a] So the Trees and Herbs, as particular Organisms are Love opposed to the Earth or Soil as part of the total Organismus— in common language, organized is opposed to Inorganic—But the

---

[a] The insertion is in a different hand and ink

139[1] C is apparently following Davy's suggested modification of the phlogiston theory of combustion: see **101** n 2, above.

139[2] The Latin phrase—"its *pre*-condition"—is to be understood in terms of the explanation of "*prae-*" in **6** n 8, above, and of "*aliquid suppositum*" in **31** and n 4, above. See also **140**, below.

⟨material⟩ principle common to both is aerated ~~Carbon~~ ⟨Metal from Carbon = Diamond as one Extreme, to the base of Nitrogene at the other.⟩ and this the Vegetable seeks in the Soil/—for here and elsewhere by the word Earth Behmen means ~~Carbon, or~~ ⟨oxydated metals: more especially those toward the⟩ the negative (= North) Pole of the magnetic Axis. ~~under one or other of the two modifications, ⟨that by⟩ Oxygen or ⟨that by⟩ Hydrogen, as Symbols & embodied representatives of Negative and Positive Electricity.~~— With equal Truth is Water called the Mother of Earth. For Water is the cube of the two poles of Gravity + the two poles of Light—or ~~of =~~ the four elements, each containing the other three as under its predominance. The indifference of the two poles of ~~the~~ Magnetism, Carbon and Azote, is its *substantial* principle: the indifference of the two poles of Electricity, or Oxygen and Hydrogen, is its *existential* principle.[3] But it is the Cube of ~~Surface~~ Nature under the dominion of Light: as Metal (Gold *eminenter*)[4] is the Cube of Nature under the Dominion of Gravity.

Water therefore is truly the Mother of Earth inasmuch as it is the representative of the Chaos, or ⟨state of⟩ Indistinction quoad Naturam *superficialem*:[5] and whether the ~~Water~~ the Bases of Earths be considered as Carbon, or ⟨as⟩ Azote, or ~~as Carbon-azote~~ as primary ~~Hydrate~~ indecomponible Hydrates or primary indecomponible Oxyds of Carbon-azote, i.e. coherent or incoherent Metals; still it is by and in Water that the Bases are born into (or become) Earths.

As soon as the Darkness separated itself into Light and Gravity, each bipolar, the four elementary products of the four polar Energies became at the same instant Water under the predominance of Light, and Metal under the predominance of Gravity.—The latter again (the Metals) separated from the former, according to the degree of the predominance of Gravity—the far larger part, probably, precipitated itself by the first act and formed the nucle~~ar~~us of the Planet—others were modified by the Light in the water, and gradually deposited prepared the Humus and Surface Land—others again were held in solution, and ~~th~~ in the fitful alternations of the Powers of Light and those of Gravity were now breathed forth as Airs, and *now* precipitated as Oxyds or Hydrates—and to these after-pains we owe the after-births, or the Metallic ores and Metalloids in the veins

139[3] For "*existential*" see Baxter *Reliquiae* COPY B 8 n 1.

139[4] See **12** n 1, above.

139[5] "As regards its *superficial* Nature".

of the Rocks &c. Yet Relapses ⟨of Nature⟩ or Sinkings back from the organic and vivific Tasksensions commanded her by the word and impelled by the spirit (as briefly told in Genesis C. I. v. 9–25)[6] or her first rudimental attempts towards individuation in the Mountains and the suites of their Formations (= the Wernerian ~~Bildungen~~ Formationssuiten) would be the more significant expression.[7]

To this long physical comment I have only to add, that for the Paragraphs from § 8 to § 19 no commentary is requisite for a recipient soul, or would be of any use to the Worldling.[8] I at least remember nothing superior—scarce aught equal—to them in speculative Theology. Wonderful man!   S. T. Coleridge.

140 II i 4–5

23. But when we speak of the source (or original) of the fire, and of its kindling (we mean concerning the Fire of Life) we know for certain, that in its Original, before the kindling of the fire, it consists only in two forms, and hath but one Mother, which is harsh, and draweth to her, and yet there is nothing in herself, but a willing of the Eternal Father in the Eternal Nature which he hath appointed in himself to reveal, and to declare his *wonders*.

24. Now that Will is Eternal, and is not stirred up by any thing but by itself; and if that were not, all were nothing, neither darkness nor light: therefore seeing there is somewhat, it must needs be the Eternal Will, and that is astringent, and desirous of the *Wonders* of the *Creation*. Therefore seeing there is a Desire, the Desire attracteth to itself, and that which is attracted in the Desire maketh

139[6] Creation of the third day to the beginning of the sixth day, i.e. from the separation of water from land to the creation of animals—the creation of man following in v 26.

139[7] Cf "the suites of the (so called) Wernerian Formations" in *CL* IV 805. Abraham Gottlob Werner (1750–1817), German geologist, developed theories to explain the distribution of minerals by the chronology of their formation. He was a Neptunist, offering the theory that the earth's crust was formed of deposits from some primeval ocean —opposing the Plutonic theories that everything came from fire. Steffens gave casual endorsement to his views. This long note presents much the same

notions as C's letters of Sept 1817 and Jan 1818 to Tulk (*CL* IV 767–75, 804–9) in trying to give a "scientific" justification of the story of creation in Genesis.

139[8] *Threefold Life* ch 1 §§ 8–19. The argument may be summarised thus: While the body is subject to the stars, i.e. to natural laws, the soul that is "breathed in" from God derives its "powers" from the "eternal nature" of God. The soul must free itself from the temporal life and incline its will to God. With the Fall, the soul entered into the spirit of the temporal world instead of the eternal life of God, and a new birth is therefore required, which is possible only through Christ.

Works

665

the Will full, so that the Desire is fulfilled; for the Will is as thin (or empty) as a Nothing, and that which is attracted into the Will maketh the Will thick (or gross and full) and that is its Darkness: and the Eternal Desire standeth in the Darkness.

§ 23. Doubtless, the first conceivable manifestation of Being, its first act as it were, must be in two forms only—viz. Attraction and ~~Repulsion~~ Contraction—:[1] and the Mother ⟨of both,⟩ or the Identity in the Difference, can only be conceived as an Astringency, a hungring after Being, a ground or presuppositum of Being rather than real Being—Hence the τό ὑπερούσιον of the Platonists[2]—the Axieros and Axiokersa of the Cabiric[3] and the Ceres (~~k~~cheresh = hunger) of the Eleusinian mysteries[4]—Yea, Repulsion itself is but a form of Self-retention, without which Attraction would *baffle* itself by instant reduction to the original point +0, or ~~p~~ nihil positivum—vel prægnans.[5]

[a]The Hierokerux of Samothrace[6] could not have uttered a profounder Oracle than that in § 24.—viz. the generation of Darkness (which in Behmen always means the *principle* of Gravitation) out of Attraction & Repulsion, as a third and synthetic Power. I say, the principle or Mother of Gravitation—which manifesting itself polarized into Light and Gravity. Yet Gravity must be ~~conceived~~

[a] The comment on § 24 follows directly on without a paragraph break

140[1] This alteration is in accordance with the position adopted in 137, above.

140[2] This term (which also occurs in *CN* III 4427), meaning "that which is above being", is found e.g. in Proclus *Elements of Theology* § 138. Thomas Taylor translates it "the superessential", Dodds "the supra-existential".

140[3] The Cabiri of Samothrace were called Axieros, Axiokersa, and Axiokersos; see SCHELLING *Ueber die Gottheiten von Samothrace* (1815) 7, 16, etc; see also *P Lects* Lect 11 (1949) 322, and 174 n 1, below.

140[4] Schelling argued (*Samothrace* pp 16–17, 60–3) that the names of all three Cabiri (see 136, above) denoted "hunger" or "yearning" and that the name of Ceres (the principal goddess of the Eleusinian mysteries), whom in different forms he identified with all three, was the same as Hebrew

cheres[h]—and this he explained (p 63) as a root whose derivatives mean cultivation, seed, etc. C repeated this derivation in "*Prometheus*": "In the language of the mysteries, it [Chaos] was the *esurience*, the πόθος or *desideratum*, the unfuelled fire, the Ceres, the ever-seeking maternal goddess, the original and interpretation of whose name is found in the Hebrew root signifying hunger, and thence capacity." *LR* II 338, a passage that derived from a heavily revised section of the "proto-*Prometheus*" ms.

140[5] "Positive—or pregnant—zero".

140[6] The hierokeryx of Eleusis, mentioned in Schelling *Samothrace* 81. Samothrace, like Eleusis, Schelling continues, had its hierophant, his title being derived from the Hebrew for "Seer"—which connects with C's use of "Seer" as an epithet for Böhme (see 47 n 5, above).

taken as the first conceived of the connate Twins—tho' born in the same instant.

141 II i 5

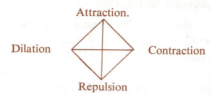

A Symbol of A—i.e. that in which A is the Ascendant = Diamond, Quartz

of C. Oxygen, Rust,

of R. Nitrogene, Phosphorus/ animal matter of the nerves,

of D. Hydrogen = vegetable Odors

142 II i 5

27. Therefore now we should speak of the forms of the sour (or astringent) dark Nature. For we understand that the Darkness hath a longing after the Light, which eternally standeth before it, but in *another Principle*.

28. For the two Forms, the sour and the bitter stinging, are the Original of *All* things, and the Eternal Will is the Mother (or Matrix) wherein they are Generated: and we are to know that the sourness always attracteth with the conception of the Will, and that *attracting* is the stinging of the stirring, which the sourness cannot well endure: for the attracting sourness desireth the sour strong *shutting up* in Death, and the stinging bitterness is the *Opener*, and yet it were a nothing in itself without the Will. . . .

30. Now these [the sour and the bitter] entering into one another so swiftly, like a sudden thought, the sting would fain *get out* from the sourness, but cannot, for the sourness generateth and maintaineth it; and not being able to get the upper hand (or get loose) it *turneth round* like a wheel, and so breaketh asunder the attracted sourness, and maketh a continual hurlyburly and mixture . . .

31. For the sour desiring attracteth and maketh penetration, and the bitterness breaketh it asunder in the turning wheel, and so there ariseth *multiplicity* of Essences . . .

§ 27–§ 31. I have not the original German; but I cannot doubt, that the Translation here is erroneous.[1] For the Sour we ought to read

142[1] If C read any of Böhme's works in the original German, it seems to have been after all these marginalia were written: see **170** and n 1, below.

the Astringent: and instead of the Bitter the Salt, Pungent or Alkaline: in modern language, the first is the power of Carbon, as the ground, and the second the power of Oxygen, as the modifying stimulant—in philosophical language Attraction modified by Contraction. The Wheel or circular motion is rightly attributed to the latter—as that (which being posterior to the projectile or length, and its punctual Antagonist) must necessarily *generate* a circle thereon:

$$\cdot = \odot^2$$

143 II i 6

33. For the vast infinite space desireth narrowness and inclosure or comprehension wherein it may manifest itself, for else in the wide stillness there would be no manifestation; therefore there must be an *attraction* and inclosing, out of which the *manifestation* appeareth; and therefore also there must be a contrary Will; for a transparent and quiet will is as nothing, and generateth nothing: but if a Will must Generate, then it must be in *somewhat*, wherein it may form, and may generate in that thing; for Nothing is nothing but a *stillness* without any stirring, where there is neither darkness nor light, neither life nor death.

§ 33 excellently setteth forth the necessity of a Negative or re-introitive Principle[1] in the infinite Nature—a self-seeking and therefore a Comprehension, whereby a Unity be arise up in the Infinity and be to it as the Act to the Substance, as the Lord to the Lordship or Signiory.

143A II i 18–19, bold pencil line in the margin | Ch 2 "Further of the Genetrix"

85. ...and here Love and Enmity ought to be considered, and how they *oppose* one another.

86. For Love is Death to Wrathfulness, and by its shining taketh

The original of the passage (§ 28) reads: "Denn die zwei Gestalten, als Herbe und Bitterstachlicht, sind der Urkind alles Wessens, und der ewige Wille ist die Mutter, in her sie sich gebaren."

142[2] See 6, above.

143[1] "Reintroitive" (not in *OED*) is one of a family of words most of which C coined for his own peculiar use. "Introitive" and "unintroitive" are both recorded in *OED*, the second ascribed to C (in another context). "Introition" (not in *OED*) appears in *CN* III 4186 and "retroition" in **23**, above. "Extroitive" (ascribed to C in *OED*) and "introition" occur in *CN* III 4272; "extroitive" and "retroitive" (not in *OED*) in *C&S* (*CC*) 180 and in N F⁰ f 77; "introitive", "exition", and "retroition" in *CN* III 4186 f 35. See also uses in *CN* III 4281, 4301.

away the Power of the Wrathfulness. And here the Power of God in Love and Anger, is rightly to be considered.

87. But that the Love may thus be Generated, is caused by the *first* Will from the still habitation; for the still and clear habitation, which is without a source, desireth no fierceness, and yet causeth fierceness: and if the fierceness were not, there would be no sharpness; and so the *second* Center (of Love) would not be generated, out of which the *supernatural* light shineth, where then the Name of God the Father and of God the Son existeth.

144 II i 142 | Ch 13 "Of Christ's Most Precious Testaments . . ."

[§§ 10–32 is a discussion of the nature and significance of the Eucharist, e.g.:]

16. And as God, in his heavenly Virgin, (out of which the heavenly Substantiality is discovered, and attaineth substance in the Tincture of the Fire) *is a substance*; which substance, God (with the Word and Heart, with the receiving in of the Tincture out of *Mary*'s blood, in which the soul dwelt) did with the word *Fiat*, as with the Eternal astringent Matrix, comprehend, and let them together become flesh and blood after a human way and manner; (understand, as the Eternal Substantiality, with the wisdom, *viz. the Eternal Virginity*, has given itself into the perished Tincture and Matrix of *Mary*, wherein was *the Promised Word*, which gave itself also in the Eternal Substantiality into the perished Tincture, (or life,) and so became *a New Man*, being strange and unknown to the Earthly Man,) so this New Body of Christ, (understand *the inward Christ*, which the outward Man which was mortal covered,) gave itself under Bread and Wine, as an Outward (thing,) into the Tincture of the Souls of the Apostles, *and became Man in the Apostles in the Tincture of the soul*; and that is the New Body which Christ hath brought us from Heaven; (of which he said, *None goeth to Heaven, but he that is come from Heaven . . .*).

15 March, 1826.[1]

Make due allowance for the Paracelsian Drapery, & *viz.* the Alchemistic Metaphors and technical terms, in which Jacob Behmen, whose Scantling of Book-knowlege allowed him little choice, had accustomed himself to think: and this section from § 10 to § 32 will be found, ὡς ἔμοιγε δοκεῖ, to convey the true Joanno-pauline doctrine

---

144[1] There are no notes on pp 7–141, and **144–148** are confined to a relatively small number of pages— five dispersed notes apparently written at much the same time.

of the Eucharist. See CONCLUSION of the Aids to Reflection by S T Coleridge.[2]

145 II i 143

17. For, to say that Christ seedeth the Soul with Spirit *without* Body, is not true; the Holy Ghost makes not a Principle, but the Eternal Substantiality in which the Holy Ghost dwells, and goes out from thence in a form of many thousand innumerable Essences, even that which is so gone forth, is the *Virgin of Chastity, viz.* the Eternal Wisdom, in which all the Wonders of this world were beheld from Eternity.

This ☞ is an important yet too generally neglected truth.[1]

146 II i 158 | Ch 14 "Of the Broad Way ... and of the Narrow Way"

40. For it is sufficiently known to us (seeing God is merely Good) that he created *nothing* Evil; for that which was not from Eternity, was not in the Creation.

§ 40. i.e. from God descended only the Eternal Actuality into ~~the~~ or upon the eternal possibility, which had *striven* aloft—even as sick men strive in a dream—not *r̸ose̸* but ~~fe~~ *strove,* and in the striving fell, and in the falling strove, and so ad infinitum—a state which the Ancient Sages expressed by Chaos, & Moses by Tohu Bohu—[1]

144[2] The "Conclusion" to *AR* opens with a justification of William Law and Jakob Böhme, and proceeds (p 379) to a discussion of the authenticity of "the fourth Gospel", esp John 6 (for which see **151**, below), and of mysticism, and an attack upon "the Mechanico-corpuscular Philosophy". *AR* (1825) 377–402.

145[1] A note referring to II i 152 was written on c 14 Mar 1826 in N F⁰ f 34ᵛ: "Αλλο μεν το ρημα, αλλο ο λογος. In which of our learned Divines shall I find more truth more nobly expressed than in the following §ph. of poor despised Jacob Behmen—Vol. II. p. 152—ad finem." C then transcribed Böhme's §§ 8, 9. The Greek phrase—presumably C's—means "The spoken word is one thing, the Word another." Elsewhere C distinguishes "the Word" from "the written ρηματα, or Scriptures": LEIGHTON *Genuine Works* (4 vols 1819) [COPY B] I 174–5. Cf a letter of Jan 1824, in which he—like

Plato in *Cratylus*—connects ῥῆμα with ῥέω (flow): "The Phaenomenon, or visual and literal Apprehension, is ῥῆμα—a fluxion." *CL* v 326.

146[1] Etymologically "chaos" means something like "gaping void". Hesiod is the first of the "Ancient Sages" in whose work the word survives (*Theogony* 116); Anaximander's concept of ἄπειρον and the theories of later cosmological philosophers evidently influenced the meaning of the word; it occurs (as "murky") in Aristophanes *Birds* (693, 698) at the place where C annotated; but not until Ovid *Metamorphoses* 1.5ff does it appear fully described as "the rough unordered mass of things...warring seeds of elements". The word "chaos" does not occur in AV; χάος occurs twice in the Septuagint. For other uses of "chaos" by C see **59**, above, and **157**, **158**, below. The term "Tohu Bohu" is discussed in **53** n 4, above.

147   II i 159

48. But the Devil awakened unto him the *Sulphur* (or Gross Matter) therein, and has set the *Bestial* spirit in the superior dominion in him; that which Man should have ruled over, rules over him, and that is his *Fall*.

What should have remained Form, Symbol, Idea became Self, i.e. Touch/[1] victoremque cupidum vicere.[2]

148   II i 175 | Ch 16 "Of Praying and Fasting"

> *Unser Vatter*   *im Himmel.*
> **Our Father** (which art) **in Heaven.**

41. When we say, *Unser Vatter im Himmel*, then the soul raises up itself in all the Three Principles, and gives itself up into that out of which it is created; which we understand, in the Language of Nature, very exactly and accurately. For *Un* is God's Eternal Will to Nature, *ser* comprehends it in the first four forms of Nature; wherein the first Principle consists.

It would have been painfully amusing to have seen poor Jacob making faces, while he was trying this cabbalistic process, sounding the syllables & watching his sensations and again expounding them in fancies of height, depth, inwardness, outwardness &c &c—Yet still it is hard to understand how he could overlook—for he could not be ignorant of the fact that the original Prayer was in Greek/— Thus the same syllable, *our*, is the english—pronoun adjective, and the beginning of the Greek word for Heaven—*Our*anos.—[1]

FORTY QUESTIONS CONCERNING THE SOUL

149   II +1, evidently referring to II ii 10–11 | "The First Question Answered"

25. . . . it beholdeth itself, and yet findeth nothing but an A, which is its [z]Eye. [Shoulder-note:] [z]In the Text, AVge, which in the German Language signifies an Eye.[1]

147[1] On touch, see **24** n 9, above.

147[2] "They defeated the lustful/ covetous victor"—source unknown. The word "covetousness" occurs in Böhme's text in § 47, and "lust" in § 49.

148[1] Cf **58**, above. C has transliterated οὐρανός—"the Greek word for Heaven".

149[1] Böhme's text II ii §§ 25–8 is devoted to the subject of *Auge*=Eye; § 30 is entitled "Eye of God, Eye of Eternity", § 31 "Eye of God's Wonders", and a plate facing II ii 24 is entitled "Philosophic Globe or Eye of the Warders of Eternity".

20 July, 1822 (28th day of Derwent's Fever. God be merciful to me!)[2]

*Eye! the Micranthrope thou in the marvellous Microcosmos![3]

Even bodily comprizing Bone, Tendon, Ligament, Membrane, ⟨Blood-⟩vessel, Gland, with the 3 forms of the Nervous Systems, Nerves of Sense, Nerves of Motion, and the gangliac Nerves—at once the Telescope, and the Mirror of the Soul, and even more *imperiously* than the Hand & Touch the Seat and Agent of ⟨the⟩ Magical Power—![4]

Already in 1799 I had written the following Lines (then blind from weeping about little Berkley, I being absent & at Ratzeburg, 35 miles N.W. of Hamburg)[5]

* I put down this harsh Hexameter in order to exemplify the effect of Accents in short'ning quantity.—Whether we read the word, Micránthrope, as a Bacchius, i.e. ∪ – –, approaching to an Amphibrach, ∪ – ∪, in consequence of the Accent on the second syllable: or *Mí*cranthrope as an *accentual* Dactyl in contempt of Quantity, (reluctante Quantitate)—still the whole Line forms an hexameter— the quasi-dactylic Micranthrope having, if it be *distinctly* pronounced, and in order to a distinct enunciation of each syllable, an accent on each—just as the tribrach, Nóbódý.

Míc rán thrópe

149[2] On 24 Jun 1822, while HC was paying an extended visit to the Gillmans, DC came unexpectedly to Highgate with a high fever that had attacked him two days before when he was in London on his vacation from Cambridge. Gillman diagnosed the illness as "a remittent, or 21 days fever". On 12 Jul, the 20th day of the fever, a critical change occurred that suggested that he had typhus; C and Mrs Gillman were forbidden to sit with him, and for a time "it trembled in the scales whether he should live or die". He was considered out of danger by 3 Aug and was beginning to recuperate. C's cry "God be merciful to me!"—eight days after the crisis— probably has less to do with DC's illness than with another crisis that the illness had precipitated in the relations between C and his sons and between the sons and the Gillmans. The whole situation was too much for HC: he liter- ally ran away and went north, never to return—one of the four "griping and grasping Sorrows" of C's life. See *CL* v 240–51. Whether in all these grievous circumstances C was annotating Böhme does not appear; this note was written on a back flyleaf.

149[3] This hexameter has not been published, but in a reflection on the implications of "detach[ing] the Eye from the Body"—a passage almost Jacobean for its tinge of horror—the substance of it appears in *AR* (1825) 389. "Micranthrope"—little man (to correspond to "microcosm", little universe)—is C's coinage: *OED* cites C's use of "Micranthropos" in *AR*.

149[4] See the passage in *AR* cited in n 3.

149[5] For the death of Berkeley Coleridge see BIBLE COPY A ANNEX [a] and n 1. The hexameters following were originally part of a verse letter written to the Wordsworths when they

O what a Life is the Eye! What a fine and inscrutable Essence!
Him that is utterly blind nor glimpses the Fire that warms him,
Him that never beheld the swelling Breast of his Mother
(Smiling awake at the bosom as a Babe that smiles in its Slumber)
Even for Him it exists! It stirs and moves in its Prison,
Lives with a Separate Life: and "Is it a Spirit?" he murmurs:
"Sure, it has Thoughts of its own, and *to see* is only a *Language*!"[6]

S. T. Coleridge

THE CLAVIS

150   II iv 17, pencil, § 131 marked in the margin | " ⊃ The Seventh Property"

1 × 7. Desire] 127. For according to the manifestation of the Trinity of God, there are but three Properties of Nature: the first is the Desire which belongs to God the Father, yet it is only a Spirit; but in the seventh Property, the Desire is substantial.

2 × 6.] 128. The second is the Divine power and virtue, and belongs to God the Son; in the second Number it is only a Spirit; but in the sixth it is the substantial Power and Virtue.

3 × 5.] 129. The third belongs to the Holy Ghost; and in the beginning of the third Property it is only a fiery Spirit; but in the fifth Property, the great Love is manifested therein. . . . [1]

131. Now these are the seven Properties in one only Ground; and all seven are equally Eternal without beginning; none of them can be accounted the first, second, third, fourth, fifth, sixth, or last; for they are equally Eternal without beginning, and have also one Eternal beginning from the unity of God.

MYSTERIUM MAGNUM

151   III i [3] | Preface to the Reader

. . . This Man of God is the inward Man, the Child of God, the hidden Man of the Heart, *Christ in us*, whose Flesh and Blood except we eat and drink, we have no Part in him. These Words of Spirit and Life he spoke when he was yet alive *upon the Earth* before his

---

were in Goslar in Dec 1798: see *CL* I 452. (The variants between this text and the received text have not been recorded: see *PW—EHC*—I 305.)

149[6] Attention is drawn in *CN* III 4073n to the close relations between C's poem *Limbo* (drafted in *CN* III 4073) and Böhme's *Forty Questions*

Concerning the Soul (Question 34) and *The Threefold Life* (ch 4 § 32)—the first two works in Vol II of this edition.

150[1] See **35** and n 1 for the four "physical" Spirits that, with these three "spiritual" Spirits, make up the seven "Nature Spirits" or "Qualities" or (as here) "Properties".

Suffering, which made his Disciples cry out, This is a hard Saying, who can bear it?

These—the whole VIth of John to wit[1]—are indeed hard sayings, alike for the disciples of the crude or dead *Letter*, and for the Doctors of abstractions & mere moral meanings. The former swallow all as it comes untasted, neithinger masticating nor ruminating: the latter expound the highest and for the outward Man the most intolerable Assertions of Christ ("Who can bear them?" exclaimed the vast majority even of his more Zealous Followers)[2] into the baldest Truisms or most familiar ethical Common-places, as if the Messiah having nothing new in substance to tell the World sought to supply the place by the strangeness of the language, and was constrained to amuse his Countrymen by making a sort of Conundrums, the merit of which consists in disguising the most palpable and familiar meanings in the most unexpected and out-of-the-way Similes! Almost miraculous, however, must be the influence of Prejudice, if their way of interpreting Scripture is not rendered ludicrous even to themselves in its application to this Chapter—the manifest object of which is to reveal to them us that Spiritual Things differ from Objects of Sense by their *greater reality*, by being more truly and more literally *living substances*—more ex. gr. that *the* Flesh & Blood of Christ, which his Redeemed must eat and drink, are far more properly Flesh and Blood, than the phænomena of the visible Body so called.[3] S. T. C.

152   III i 4

... The certain Meaning of the Words of Scripture is the *Jewel* locked up in them, not now attainable from the Apostles by *] Conversation with them. Therefore now we should apply ourselves to the *Things* they spoke of, which are to be inquired after in the *Mind*, and the Knowledge of them to be received from *God* by †] Prayer, who will open the Understanding, *For there is a Spirit in Man, and the Inspiration of the Almighty gives Understanding*, as it did to this Author, who by the Command of the Holy Spirit wrote his

151[1] John 6 includes the miracles of feeding the multitude and walking on the water; the sacramental passage is in vv 47–58. For C on the eucharist, see BLANCO WHITE *Poor Man's Preservative* 2 n 1.

151[2] C echoes John 6.60: "Many therefore of his disciples, when they had heard this, said, This is an hard saying; who can hear it?"

151[3] This argument is expanded in the long footnote to Aphorisms on Spiritual Religion XVIII: *AR* (1825) 308–9.

deep Knowledge *given* to him of God, and has therein pointed out the Way to us wherein we may understand *what in us* is Divine, and what Natural; the New Man, and the Old; which is the Aim and Scope of the whole Bible: These New Things and Old are those that the *Scribe learned* in the Kingdom of Heaven brings out of his Treasury; neither can any Knowledge be wanting to him who has Christ in him. For *in Christ are hid* all the Treasures of Wisdom and Knowledge.

* This, *this* is the cardinal point, on which all the differences between Protestants hinge: nay, I might add between Christians of all denominations. The one Set assert that Prayer and the Spirit promised to those who pray in faith, are either—1. nothing but modes of a sort of self-magnetizing, means by which the individual excites and abstracts his own intellective faculty thro' the agency of the feelings and imagination, as the Socinians and the majority of the Church Arminians: or—2. that the Spirit is indeed a præternatural influence, but yet reveals no truth *in* the mind but merely enables it to read the Scriptures intelligently—the Mind being exclusively and solely the Eye, the Spirit the Sunshine, and the Scriptures the Dial, as Luther, Calvin, and the Presbyterian Divines generally.—The other set are exemplified in their extreme, the Quakers.[a1]

I hold the Lutheran & Presbyterian Opinion as far as it is *positive*; but reject it as exclusively. In the Scriptures, but also in the mind: tho' I have full faith, that at a certain point of the spiritual progression both will unite as in the Apex of a triangle, the Base representing the ⟨Divine⟩ Spirit, one side the Spirit of man, the other the inspired Scriptures.[2] *To* the mind in and through the *mind*, the *Book* and the outward *Creation*: in all three the Spirit works and speaks to us.

153   III i 4–6 | **152** textus

† In order to command the hollowness of the Arminian Scheme we must put its different interpretations &c side by side, and see how they agree with each other. Thus, the Arminians of the present-day hold, that before their return from the Captivity the Jews had but an anthropomorphic notion of their God, as the God of Gods, πατηρ

---

a Here the note, written in the head and outer margin, is interrupted by the direction: "* see above" (i.e. **152**) and "† see below" (i.e. **153**, which is written in the foot margins of pp 4–6). The ink of this direction is black, corresponding to the body of **152**. It appears that **153** was written first in the foot-margin, then **152** in the head and outer margins, and finally **154** in the gutter margin as the only space available near its textus

152[1] For C on the Quakers generally see AURELIUS **47** n 1.

152[2] See **116**, above, for the triangle as "emblem of the Triune".

βασιλευς ανδρών τε θεών τε.[1]—Well! at another time, in confutation of another tenet of theirs, that the Old Testament contains no declarations of the immortality of Man as a living soul, I adduce the Texts—of the Soul—of the spirit—&c returning to God who gave[2]—or this of Job[3]—& then—Sessa!—Presto! the Hebrew Jehovah becomes a vague every where diffused Ether or Spirit of Animation, a Sea, out of which the bubbles rise & into which they break and are no more. In the mean time, they do not reflect, that tho' it may be consistent with the divine Wisdom to withhold for a time certain truths or the full manifestation of them, yet it is blasphemously incongruous with ~~his~~ the Veracity of the God of Truth to reveal or inspire *falsehood*.[4] Now these passages either mean the same doctrine that *Christians* believe—or a different one, preclusive of personal immortality—but if the former be true, the latter is false not by imperfection but positively false and necessarily deceptive.—To all these Remarks let this be the common accompaniment. The *toutoukosmou* Professors of Chrstnty[5] tell us, that the workings of the Spirit, the ingrafted Word, the Christ born within us, the Life that is the Light of *every* man, &c &c[6] only mean the common sense and the acquired convictions of the Understanding. We on the other hand hold and teach, that the *true* Common Sense, the only real and effective Convictions are the working of the Spirit, the Christ born in our Hearts, the Word that was with God and God, the Life that is the Light, &c.[7] They lower the divine into the ordinary human, we raise that, which is indeed and ~~un~~distinctively Human, into a participation of the divine. The Divine was originally the Base, from which the Human detached itself—(the Fall of Mean, η αποστασις)[8] then the

---

153[1] "King of men and gods"—echoing Homer's epithet for Zeus: πατὴρ ἀνδρῶν τε θεῶν τε, "father of men and gods".

153[2] Eccles 12.7.

153[3] Böhme cites Job 32.8: "But there is a spirit in man: and the inspiration of the Almighty giveth them understanding."

153[4] For C's meaning of "veracity" see BAXTER *Reliquiae* COPY B 46 n 1.

153[5] "Toutoukosmou"—transliteration of τούτου κόσμου (of this world) from John 18.36: "My kingdom is not of this world". In the dialogue between Demosius and Mystes appended to *C&S* the "Toutoscosmos" doc-

tors are the representatives of rationalism and materialism: see *C&S* (*CC*) 174–7 and cf *AR* (1825) 219n. *OED* does not record the word in either form.

153[6] With "the workings of the Spirit", cf Eph 1.19; "the engrafted Word", James 1.21; "the Christ born within us", cf Luke 17.21; and the rest is from John 1.9.

153[7] John 1.1, 1.4.

153[8] C commonly used the word "apostasis" (lit. "standing away"; cf C's "detached itself") to mean "the fall" either of man or of creation (as in **59** and **116**, above, and **158**, below). The usual Greek form is ἀποστασία, which occurs in 2 Thess 2.3 ("falling

Human became the *Base*, and the Divine the Combinant—i.e. for those who received it. "But to as many as received him, to them he delegated the power to become Sons of God." St John, C. I.—9

154   iii i 4 | **152** textus

This, however differently worded, is the whole Scope of Kant's Critique of the Pure Reason, of the *practical* Reason, of the Judicial Power, and all his other after Works: above all ~~in~~ his Relig. within the Bounds of the Pure Reason.—1

155   iii i 7 | The Author's Preface

[§§ 1–5. A likeness of the spiritual world is hidden in the visible world. Visible things proceed from the invisible, and the invisible works in and through the visible. Such is the relation of soul to body.]

   6. *Thus Man has now received Ability from the invisible Word of God to the Re-expression, that he again expresses the hidden Word of the divine Science into Formation and Separation, in Manner and Form of the temporal Creatures, and forms this Spiritual Word according to Animals, and Vegetables; whereby the invisible Wisdom of God is pourtrayed and modelized into several distinct Forms. As we plainly see, that the Understanding of Man expresses all Powers in their Property, and gives Names unto all Things, according to each Thing's Property ... so that the invisible might play with the visible, and therein introduce itself into the Sight and Sense of itself.*

This Preface, especially the first seven §s,1 is full of the profoundest truths, weightily and even scientially expressed. § 6. deserves particular attention: for it explains the dependence of Consciousness on the Body as ~~its~~ the enunciative form of the inner Man, and the condition of our intercommunion as finite Spirits: and thus obviates the strongest and most plausible Argument of the so-called Materialists; and enlists it for the opposite side. Speaking collectively and not of any one insulated person, we might with no improper boldness

---

away"), and is used by the Fathers to mean "the fall of man". Milton e.g. used "apostasy" in *Paradise Lost* vii 44 of Adam's fall.

   1539 C is glossing John 1.12: "...to them gave he power...". The Greek verb is ἔδωκεν (he gave).

   1541 Among other works of Kant, C annotated the *Critik der reinen*

Vernunft, Critik der Urtheilskraft, and *Die Religion innerhalb der Grenzen der blossen Vernunft*; his copy of the *Critik der practischen Vernunft* is only lightly marked. See KANT. For C's reading of Kant in the middle years see e.g. *CN* iii 3346, 3561–62, 3801, and nn.

   1551 For § 7 see **156** textus, below.

call the Body *the Consciousness* of the Mind. Corpus = anima jam facta sibi et sui ipsius conscia: Anima = ea, cui pote⟨s⟩tas inest faciendi se sui consciam.[2] Who has not[a]

156 III i 8

7. *As the Mind introduces itself with the Body, and by the Body into Senses and Thoughts, whereby it works, and acts sensibly to itself; so also the invisible World (works) through the visible, and with the visible World. We are not in any wise to conceit, that a Man cannot search out what the hidden divine World is, and what its Operation and essence, for on the visible Essence of the Creation we see a Figure of the internal spiritual Operation of the powerful World.*

Q.[y] *Word?*

157 III i 11 | Pt i ch 1 "What God Manifested Is"

2. ... God ... is the *One*; in reference to the *Creature* as an Eternal Nothing. He has neither Foundation, Beginning, or Abode; he possesses nothing but only himself. He is the Will of the *Abyss*; he is in himself only one; he needs neither *Space*, or *Place*. He begets himself in himself, from Eternity to Eternity ... The Eternal Wisdom or Understanding is his Delight: He is the Will of the Wisdom; the Wisdom is his Manifestation.

3. In this Eternal Generation we are to understand three Things, *viz.* 1. An *Eternal* Will. 2. An *Eternal* Mind of the Will. 3. The *Egress* from the Will and Mind, which is a *Spirit* of the Will and Mind.

4. The Will is the *Father*: The Mind is what is *conceived* of the Will, *viz.* the *Seat* or Habitation of the Will, or the *Center* to something; and it is the *Will's Heart*: And the *Egress* of the Will and Mind is the *Power* and *Spirit*.

November 9th, 1819. With great delight I find, that Behmen guided by the light of a sincere love of truth, worked himself out of the Pantheism (God = Chaos) of his earlier writings: and seems in this Tract to have emerged into the full Day./ Blest was the Hour, when first the clear Insight was given me, of the one ever open and yet ever hidden Mystery, which even here Behmen is possessed by rather than

---

[a] The note is incomplete

155[2] "Body is the soul already made conscious in itself and of itself: Soul is that which has within it power to make itself conscious of itself." For C's objection to the soul–body opposition, see DONNE *Sermons* COPY B 76. The "Materialists'" view of the body as a short-cut to a doctrine of the soul is examined in BROOKE 24.

possesses, of the $A = \Omega^1$—in the x = abcd—z, *ergo* = x. With that *ergo* Behmen *begins*, even *here*: but what a *Spring* above the verge of Chaos, but still within Chaos, at which I had left him in ~~his~~ the first Volume, the only one which I have hitherto read excepting this and the foregoing pages—[2]

158 III i 11

10 November, 1819. As I read on, I have found that this first Chapter is a deceptive Promise: that Behmen soon deviates into his original error, πρωτοψευδος,[1] and places the polarities *in* the Deity, makes them eternal, confounding, first, Correspondents with opposites, and *then* Opposites with Contraries.[2] The Kingdom of Turbulence and Darkness, the direful Hunger (= Ceres)[3] is placed *in* the Beginning, and not merely (as the truth is) *from* the Beginning. Thus the proper Deity becomes the Proserpine/ having a dark *Source*. In short, Behmen remains, I fear and as far as I have hitherto read, a Cabiric Physiotheist.[4]

Let this, however, have been fully and distinctly seen into, and heedfully borne in mind so as to be duly recollected on all due occasions, namely, at the several §s grounded on or adulterated by this Physiotheism, or anticipation of the Apostasis in the Stasis,[5] and these Books may be studied with unspeakable benefit, as a transcendental Physiology, rich in bold original Conceptions, and roots of

---

157[1] *Alpha = Omega*: the beginning is the end. Cf Rev 1.8: "I am Alpha and Omega, the beginning and the ending...". C may also have in mind the Heraclitan declaration, "The way up and the way down are one and the same." See also *"Prometheus"* (*LR* II 339): "The Phoenician confounded the indistinguishable with the absolute, the *Alpha* and *Omega*, the ineffable *causa sui*. It confounded, I say, the multeity below intellect, that is, unintelligible from defect of the subject, with the absolute identity above all intellect, that is, transcending comprehension by the plenitude of its excellence."

157[2] A mistake: see **137** n 1. But probably there was no extensive reading of Vol II before Oct 1818, and no earlier reading of Vol III or IV.

158[1] A unique form of πρῶτον

ψεῦδος, for which see **137** n 2, above, and BAXTER *Reliquiae* COPY B **92** n 1.

158[2] One of the main purposes of C's logical symbols was to keep steadily in view the difference between "opposites" and "contraries", for an instance of which see **104** and n, above. A clear definition of "the essential difference between *opposite* and *contrary*" is given in *C&S* (*CC*) 24n: "Opposite powers are always of the same kind.... The feminine character is *opposed* to the masculine; but the effeminate is its *contrary*."

158[3] See **140** and n 4.

158[4] See **136** and n 2.

158[5] For apostasis as the fall of matter in the creation cf **59, 116, 153,** above; and see especially *CN* III 4449 ff 28–29ᵛ for the place of *stasis* and *apostasis* in a Heraclitan scheme of creation. For another use cf *CIS* 5–6.

physical and vital truth not less prolific than profound. Ex. gr. p. 24. §. 17.[6]

S. T. Coleridge,
Highgate.

159 III i 23 | Ch 5 "Of the Five Senses"

10. ... And yet it is all but God manifested; who manifests himself through the *Eternal Nature* in ingredient Properties. Else, if I would say what God is in his *Depth*, then I must say that he is wholly without Nature and Properties; being an Understanding, and Original, of all *Beings*; the *Beings* are his Manifestation; and thereof we have only *Ability* to write, and not of the unmanifested God, who also were not known to himself without his Manifestation.

This is the Rock, on which Behmen still wrecks or rather bulges: and this of itself is a proof how essential to the purity and entireness of Religion a true Idea of the Trinity is—i.e. that it is the co-eternal Logos, in and by which God is manifest to himself, & without which, we may dare affirm, God would not *be*—in the same sense as we might say, that a circle would not be without a center & circumference—the LOGOS, and in it the wholly spiritual Pleroma, the unity in infinity of the Elohim, *not* the coagulation of Chaos, much less the Chaos itself. In short, there are but three possible coherent systems—*I*. That of Self-construction, according to which the Absolute organizes itself into the World. = Pantheism. II. That of ⟨Self-mechanism, or rather of⟩ selfless Formation, according ⟨to⟩ which aboriginal Chaos is everlastingly mechanized into Particulars, from which according to the degrees of harmony in the Multeity Life & Perception & finally Consciousness, result— = Atheism. (N.B. This system does not exclude Gods, or even a Supreme God, in the vulgarest sense, but makes them the *Consequent* of the World.) III. That of the Trinity: and this third is the only possible Escape from one or other of the two former.[1]

158[6] *Mysterium Magnum* ch 5 § 17: "Also there could be no Sound without a Conception; and therefore all *Forms* belong to the Sound: 1. The Desire makes Hardness. 2. The Compunction moves. 3. The Anguish does amass it into an Essence, for Distinction. 4. The Fire changes in its devouring the Grossness of the amassed Essence into a *Spirit* or Sound. 5. Which the Desire does again receive in its Softness and Meekness, and forms it to a Voice, Tone, or Expression, according to the Powers. 6. And what is conceived or formed is the vital Sound, or distinct Understanding...".

159[1] See **110**, above, for four variations of atheism and pantheism.

160   III i 24 | "The Original of Life. ♃ Jupiter"

11. The *sixth* Property of Nature, and of all Beings, arises also out of all the rest, and is manifest in the Fire through the Light in the *Love-desire*; it is Nature's Understanding, Voice, Sound, Speech, and all whatsoever soundeth, both in Things with Life and without Life . . .

12. Each Spirit desires Essence after its *Likeness*. . . . And this mutual Intercourse, Consent, and intimate intire Assimulation one with another, is the *pleasant Taste* of Love.

13. But that which is conceived in the Love-desire . . . is now the natural and creatural Understanding which was in the Word . . .

14. This Harmony of Hearing, Seeing, Feeling, Tasting, and Smelling, is the true *intellective* Life . . .

15. Therefore one only Will, if it have divine Light in it, may draw out of this Fountain, and behold the Infinity, from which Contemplation this *Pen* has wrote.

16. Now there belong to the manifest Life or Sound of the Powers, Hardness and Softness, Thickness and Thinness, and a *Motion*; for without Motion all is *still*. . . .

17. Also there could be no Sound without a Conception, and therefore all *Forms* belong to the Sound . . .

18. This is now the manifested *Word*, which in itself is only *One* Power, wherein *all* Powers are contained. . . .

19. In the Light of God, which is called *the Kingdom of Heaven*, the Sound is wholly soft, pleasant, lovely, pure, and thin; yea as a Stillness in reference to our outward gross Shrillness . . . as if the Mind did *play and melodize* in a Kingdom of Joy within itself . . . For in the Essence of the Light all is *subtile*, in Manner as the *Thoughts* play and make mutual Melody in one another. . . .

These §s from § 11 to § 19 inclusive are full of high Contemplation. +A passes into +B to lose itself, and in the next instant retracts itself in order to give an *Alterity* or to +B, and this in order to lose itself in another form by loving the self of another as another—And these are the *Fits* of extroitive and retroitive Acts,[1] in which Love *lives*.[2]—Reverse this: and −A and −B give the process, in which the selfish Principle strives.—

160[1] Outward-going and backward-going: i.e., in a different Coleridgian terminology, "ab intra" and "ad intra", centrifugal and centripetal. See 143 n 1 for the family of words to which these two belong.

160[2] See also 132 and n 1, 137 n 5, above.

161 III i 29 | Ch 7 "Of the Holy Trinity, and Divine Essence"

5. ... We Christians say, that God is threefold, but only one in *Essence*: But that we generally say and hold that *God is threefold in Person*, the same is very wrongly apprehended and understood by the Ignorant, yea by a *great Part* of the Learned: For God is no Person but only in *Christ*; but he is the eternal begetting Power, and the Kingdom with all Beings; all Things receive their Original *from* him.

This opinion, which is likewise that of *Swedenburg*,[1] has, I confess, in times past appeared just to me, and confirmed by if not directly asserted in the Gospel of S[t] John, C. 1. v. 18.[2] But deeper meditation has opened to me the error or ambiguity of the tenet, in the want of a previous definition of *Person*. If the word be confined to a manifestation ad extra, ex. gr. in the present case, to all finite Being, the tenet is still defensible—in this sense God is a *person* only in the only-begotten Son, and *this* sense of Personality S[t] John expresses by exegēsis.[3] But if it be extended to the Self-manifestation of God, as God, then it *burns*—i.e. borders too perilously on Pantheism, and gives an atheistic sense to S[t] John's *In the beginning*: whereas S[t] John clearly meant the words εν αρχη as synonymous with *Eternally* or *From all Eternity*.[4]

S. T. C.

162 III i 33 | Ch 8 "Of the Creation of Angels"

16. And we are not to understand, that the holy Angels dwell only above the *Stars* without the Place of this World, as Reason, which understands nothing of God, fancies; indeed they dwell without the

---

161[1] See **135** n 4, above. When C was offering Tulk proposals in Sept 1821 for a book on Swedenborg, he referred without apology to "Swedenborg's system of Theanthroposophy" (*CL* v 174); he discusses the critical term "begotten" in SWEDENBORG *True Christian Religion* I 2–3.

161[2] John 1.18: "No man hath seen God at any time; the only begotten Son which is in the bosom of the Father, he hath declared him." Cf **20** and n 12, above, and BIBLE COPY B **119** and n 1.

161[3] In the summary note on Swedenborg (see **135** n 4, above) C had said that he was "not partial to the word" *Person*, lamenting "the shadowy Idolism, which it does, and is liable to, occasion; but any other mode of

uttering the unutterable would, it appears to me, fall under equal objections...". *CL* v 89n; and see the different version in the letter p 88. But in TAYLOR *Polemicall Discourses* i 960–3 he said that "person" was a "most unhappy and improper term", and in DONNE *Sermons* COPY B 7 that it was an "equivocal word". He discussed the matter in detail in N F° ff 18ᵛ–19.

161[4] The two Greek words are the opening words of the fourth gospel and also of Gen in Septuagint—"In the beginning". The meaning proposed here is also discussed in notes on EICHHORN *Einleitung in das Neue Testament* (3 vols Leipzig 1804–14) II 109–10. For ἀρχή see BLUMENBACH **4** n 2.

Dominion and Source of this World, but in the *Place of this World*, although there is no Place in the Eternity; the Place of this World, and also the Place without this World, is *all one* to them.

Reason has no *fancy*; but Behmen means *the Sense*, or the Understanding under the conditions of Time and Space, a faculty which corresponding to such subjects only as ⟨have⟩ Place, and Shape for predicates, must needs make mad superstitions or engender presumptuous Disbelief when it is misapplied to Objects supersensual, the entities of the moral & spiritual World. The Reason is a Participation of *Ideas*: & strictly speaking, it is no *Faculty*, but a Presence, an Identification of Being & Having.[a]

This sentence alone (& ⟨there⟩ are a hundred such in these Volumes) would suffice to establish the sense of the word, REASON, in Behmen's use of the term, whether it be Vernunft or Verstand in the original[1]—B. uniformly means that faculty which St Paul calls φρονημα σαρκος,[2] ⟨in *oppos.* to the *Reason*:⟩ i.e. the UNDERSTANDING, or that which *stands under*, supports, and gives the form to, the *materials* supplied by the Senses[3]—just as the Skeleton of wood upon which the bricks & stones of a Bridge rest while building & receive from ⟨it⟩ that figure of the Arch, which gives the Bridge ⟨all⟩ its strength, and constitutes the Cohesion of the materials.—Now abstract from the skeleton its own corporëity,[4]—or rather try to

[a] This paragraph is squeezed in above **163**, showing that **163** was written before **162**

162[1] The German original reads *Verstand*, which is normally for Böhme the word that corresponds to C's "Reason": see **126** n 1, above.

162[2] See BAXTER *Reliquiae* COPY B **115** n 10. C sometimes uses the literal version "the mind of the flesh", and associates the term regularly with the understanding: see e.g. BLANCO WHITE *Letters* **1**, *AR* (1825) 231–2, and **176**, below. See also **175**, below: "the sensuous Understanding".

162[3] In late 1819 or early 1820 C made a notebook entry referring to this marginal note. "Without the potential moulds, ανευ μορφαις μορφογενεσι [without form-generating forms] of the Under-standing the notices supplied by the Senses would have no *substans*, no substance—could not be *formed* into Experience. Without the materials contributed by the Senses, the forms of the Understanding would have no *reality*, no content—or as the popular Language, always more philosophical than the Individuals that slight it, truly says—There is no *sense* in it.— Being thus interdependent, both are necessarily confined to such subjects as have the predicates of Time and Space—strange are the Bulls that are engendered, where the Logic of the mere Understanding is allowed to bring the entia of the supersensual World to its Procrustes Bed.—See Note MSS, in Behmen, vol. 3, p. 33." N 28 f 47.

162[4] For C's use and coinage of words ending in -eity on a scholastic analogy, see ATHENAEUM **31** n 3; but the translators of this edition of Böhme often use the word "corporeity"—i.e. body-ness: see e.g. **83** textus.

conceive the figure of the Arch as a somewhat self-subsistent; as antecedent to the material⟨ized⟩ Arch; and as the proper and effective *cause* of the material quantities being ~~any~~ that *one* thing; ~~& the true agent in all its properties~~ and then conceive it as remaining *in*, at once (as it were) lying *under*, and yet visible *through*, the materials; and you will thus obtain a just and definite notion of the interdependence of the Understanding and the Sense.[5] Without the forms (formæ formificæ, or potential moulds)[6] of the Understanding the quota supplied by the Sense & its organs (= the Senses, the Eye, the Ear, &c) would have no *substance*, no coherency: without the Sense the forms of the understanding would have ⟨no⟩ *reality*, no purport. But as our present Senses correspond to our present Understanding, so ~~are~~ do the forms of the Understanding belong to ~~the~~ our senses—& have no import except as applied to Objects of sensuous Experience. We say rightly—theyre ~~have~~ is no *sense* in them.

163   III i 47 | Ch 11 "Of the Mystery of the Creation"

5. Now the Eye of God was in *Moses*, and in the *Saints*; they have seen and spoken in the Spirit of God, and yet had not the *entire Vision* of the spiritual Birth in them, but *at times* only, when God would work Wonders ...

"Si Pergama dextrâ Defendi &c.—"[1] a profound and at the same time a *sublime* conception of Miracles. Compare with this § of the despised Sutor the cobbleries of Paley, Watson & their immediate Predecessors and Followers.—[2]

164   III i 77–8 | Ch 19 "Of the Building of the Woman"

2. For we find that the Woman was taken and formed in the *Fiat* out of *Adam's* Essence, both in Body and Soul. But the Rib betokens *Adam's* Dissolution or Breaking, *viz.* that this Body should and would be *dissolved*; for in the Place of this Rib *Longinus's* Spear must afterwards, when Christ was crucified, enter into the same,

162[5] C used the example of "the wonderful properties of the arch" as "a forcible illustration of the Aristotelian axiom...that the whole is of necessity prior to its parts". *Friend (CC)* I 496–7. Cf *C&S (CC)* 159.

162[6] "Form-generating forms"— the approximate Latin equivalent of the Greek phrase in n 3, above, which is also equated with "potential moulds".

163[1] Virgil *Aeneid* 2.291: "If Troy's

towers could be saved by strength of hand, by mine, too, had they been saved." Tr Fairclough (LCL 1919).

163[2] The "Sutor"—cobbler—is Böhme. For C's dissatisfaction with Paley's "evidences" and his conception of miracles see e.g. *CN* III 3897. For a general note on Paley see BLANCO WHITE *Practical Evidence* 1 n 1; and for Paley and Watson, BIBLE COPY B 121 n 1.

and tincture and *heal* the Breach in the Wrath of God with heavenly Blood.

Here B. seems engaged in a fruitless, probably, an impracticable undertaking—the discovering a spiritual (i.e. universal) truth in the mythus of the Rib. But such passages as these are the *Snores* of the sleeping Genius—aliquando bonus dormitat Homerus.[1]—I have sometimes conjectured that the Chapter was translated into *words* from stone Carvings, or proper Hieroglyphs[2]—and that in the latter there had been some such paronomasia as in our Children's picture-for-word Books: in which an eye stands for I, a Yew for you &c[3]—which translated back into a different dialect would make a most mysterious Mythus, like this of Eve's manufacture—tho' perhaps the picture may ⟨have⟩ meant nothing more by the rib, than a bone of the Trunk generally, and by this again nothing more than that God made the Woman in the same mould as he had made the Man, only subtracting the greater Hardness, Stiffness, and self-supporting Character of the latter.—Ŧ In the infancy of the World the Mythos was written, & for it—the simpler ⟨therefore⟩ and more childlike ~~the~~ an interpretation is, the more probable ought it to be considered.

165   III i 82–3 | Ch 20 "Of the . . . Fall, and Corruption of Man"

[§§ 3–11 deal with the temptation and such questions as: "Why did Satan choose to speak through the serpent? How was the serpent able to talk?" and so on]

It is painful to observe, how this mighty but undisciplined Spirit perplexes his own intuitions by confusion of the Letter with the Life, and of the Symbolic Life with the Letter! The II Chapter of Genesis appears to be little more than a translation of Sculptured Figures into Words—the serpent being the Egyptian Symbol of intellective Invention, idolized by the Descendants of Ham, but the same, taken separately, as the φρονημα σαρκος, the wisdom of the Flesh, in St Paul.[1] Distinctive & discursive Knowlege ~~is~~ was & by the fitness of

---

164[1] Horace *Ars Poetica* 359 (var): "sometimes good Homer nods"—C having altered Horace's *quandoque* to *aliquando* without respect for metre.

164[2] Gen 2.19–23 is indeed an earlier, more primitive, account (J) than 1.1–2.4 (P). See BIBLE COPY B 7 and n 1 and cf **165**, below, *CN* III 4325, *AR* (1825) 252n.

164[3] C uses such a pictogram for Charlotte Brent's name in *CL* III 372.

165[1] See **162** and n 2, above. In 2 Cor 1.12 AV reads "in fleshly wisdom", but the Greek is ἐν σοφίᾳ σαρκικῇ, not φρόνημα σάρκος. On the serpent symbol see *AR* (1825) 251–2n.

the symbol remains, represented in the ramifications of a Tree, full of fruit but with the Serpent (which has here a double meaning, as being significant of poison or evil secretly working) wreathing the Boughs— Thus, the Mythos speaks to the Catechumen & to the Adept.—To the Catechumen it states the simple Fact, viz. that Man fell & falls thro' the separation and insubordination of the Fancy, the Appetence, & the discursive Intellect from the Faith or practical Reason— To the Adept it conveys the great mystery, that the origin of moral Evil is in the *Timeless*, εν τῷ αχρονῳ[2]—in a spirit, not comprehended within the consciousness,—tho' revealed in the conscience of Man.

166 III i 182 | Ch 34 "How Noah Cursed His Son Ham"

12. But *Ham's* Figure according to the monstrous Spirit should not have any Dominion or *Reign* in the Life of the new Birth, but be only as a Servant, or as an Instrument without Self-Will, or any peculiar Life of Self, must serve and administer to the Use of the spiritual Kingdom; in like Manner as the *Night is hidden in the Day, and yet it is really there, but so as if it was not; and it is the *Handmaid* to the Day's Operation and Power.

* For the mere purpose of *illustration* it would be easy to justify this similè, as meaning no more than, "as the defect of self-luminous power in the sensible Objects on the surface of the Earth finds a substitute in the solar light which prevents us from feeling or noticing this defect.["]—But if, as Behmen justly teaches, this their darkness is not a mere negation, $=0$, but a positive Act of self-privation $=-1$; that is, if it be not simply αφως, but αντιφως or ens tenebri_ficum;[1] then the Similitude rises into a fair analogy.

For the purpose of elucidation, the transparent Chrystal whose

165[2] "In the *Timeless*" translates the Greek phrase. The word ἄχρονος was used in Neoplatonic and patristic Greek; the phrase ἐν τῷ ἀχρόνῳ occurs e.g. in Plotinus 6.1.16.

166[1] Not simply "*not*-light, but *anti*-light or a dark-making entity". For φῶς see also **169** and n 1, below. In BROWNE *Works* **40** Antiphōs is—as here—Gravitation. The "ens tenebrificum" (ἀντι-φῶς) evidently has its source in "Paracelsus' *Stellae tenebricosae* that shed forth sheaths of Cold and Darkness to meet and en-close whatever counter-rays of Light and Heat might come in their way". *LS* (*CC*) 243: letter of c Nov 1819 (*CL* IV 973 var). C had noted in c 1801–2, from Paracelsus by way of Henry More, that "Night is brought on by the influence of *dark* Stars that ray out darkness & obscurity upon the Earth, as the Sun does light." *CN* I 1000I and n; cf *CN* I 1674 and n, and *CN* III 4134 f 167ᵛ. With Negation ($=0$) or ἀ-φως and self-privation ($=-1$) or ἀντι-φῶς, cf the draft version of *Limbo* (c Apr–May 1811): *CN* III 4073.

proper darkness is hidden by the Light which it supports & permits itself to be permeated by, presents a more lively exponent to the imagination.

167 III i 182

14. For *Sem*'s figure passed in the Covenant upon *Abraham* and *Israel*, among whom the Word of the Covenant was manifested and spoken forth. And *Japhet*'s Figure went along in Nature, *viz.* through the *Wisdom* of Nature in the Kingdom of Nature . . . and *Sem*'s Lineage looked upon the Light in the Covenant; thus *Japhet*, that is, the poor captive Soul, which is of the Eternal Nature, *dwelt in Sem's Tent*, *viz.* under the Covenant: For the Light of Nature *dwells* in the Light of Grace, and is a Tenant or Inhabitant of the Light of Grace, *viz.* of God's Light; it is even as a Form or framed Substance of the unformed uncomprehended Light of God.

§ 14. is admirable: especially the 3 last lines.

168 III i 211 | Pt ii ch 37 "Of Abraham and His Seed"

10. For the Heathens *worshipped* the Stars and four Elements, seeing they knew that they governed the *outward* Life of all Things; their understanding of the compacted sensual Tongue . . . did also enter into the *formed* compacted . . . *Word of Nature* in them; and one Understanding moved the other, *viz.* the Human Understanding, in their Desire, moved the Understanding in the Soul of the outward World, *viz.* of the *expressed* and formed Word out of the inward dark and Fire-world, and out of the astral and elemental World; in which Soul the *Meaning* of the Sphere of Time is in the Understanding. . . .

12. From *this* Soul, *viz.* from the Horologium of the Understanding of Nature, the Heathens were *answered* by their Images and Idols, *viz.* through the Sense of the *Astrum*, which *their Faith* . . . did move and stir up.

When I consider the age and country in which these and so many other §s of equal or greater worth were written; when I recollect the notions held and doctrines enforced by the contemporary Divines, Civilians and Philosophers; and then reflect on the rank and means of *this* Man, only less contrasted with *their* circumstances, opportunities, and *bookish* acquirements than *these* principles with *their* Tenets—it seems to me, that many assertions, that have been favorably received by the Learned of the present day, have met a more decisive oppugnancy on the part of my Reason and Feelings, than the Belief avowed by the *Gichtelians, that Jacob Behmen was favored with a portion of the same spiritual Gift, the outbreathings of which in John and Paul we pronounce θεοδοτα,[2] and designate by the name of Inspiration. *S. T. C.*

* a small but most estimable and blameless Church still existing at Amsterdam, who hold Behmen & Behmen's works in the same regard as the ~~Saint~~ the Church of the New Jerusalem ~~to~~ hold Em. Swedenborg & *his* Writings.[1]

169 iii i 481–2 | Pt iii ch 75 "How Jacob . . . Blessed the two Sons of Joseph, and Preferred the Youngest"

10. *The Word became Man*; understand, the uncreaturely not natural Word of God, manifested itself in God's creaturely Word of Man's Soul, and took on him the faded Light's Image, and *quickened* or made it living in itself, and put it into God's Left Hand . . .

1 Focus ipse se ponens, το φως αει γενναων—Lucem ab eterno gignens. 2. Lux foci-genitus. 3. Lumen = Sol supercelestis. 1. κεντρον (ως του πυρειου.) 2. φως. 3. αυγη = Ηλιος—The earliest Symbol of the Tri-une God, and (all t desiderata of a Symbol considered) the best.[1] ~~What~~ More than any other ~~may~~ gains in greater exactness of

168[1] Johann Georg Gichtel (1638–1710), German mystic and follower of Böhme, founded a group called the Brethren of the Angels. Gichtel, as C implies in this note, valued Böhme's writings as highly as the Bible. The followers of Emanuel Swedenborg (1688–1772), calling themselves "The New Church signified by the New Jerusalem in the Revelation", organised themselves as a distinct denomination in 1787; C's cancelled word shows that he was aware that the leaders of the New Church were entitled "Saints". C became well acquainted with Swedenborg's work and the practices of his followers through his friendship with Charles Augustus Tulk (1786–1849), one of the founders, and the first secretary, of the Swedenborg Society formed in 1810. C first met him by chance in Littlehampton in Sept 1817. In Feb 1818 Tulk lent C a copy of his friend William Blake's *Songs of Innocence and Songs of Experience* (1794), about which C wrote a detailed letter of criticism. *CL* iv 834, 836–8. Cf C's annotated volumes of Swedenborg, at least four of which belonged to Tulk.

168[2] "God-given", agreeing with "outbreathings".

169[1] In this ch 75 Böhme is discussing the relations among Christ, God, and Man according to his interpretation of Gen 48.13; in § 10 he is glossing John 1.14. Böhme's description of man's creaturely nature as "the faded Light's image" has inspired C to construct, in terms of different aspects of light, a symbolic representation of the trinity and of the creative nexus through which "*The Word became Man*".

(A) Latin. "The Focus [Hearth] which establishes itself, (and eternally generates light)—generates light from eternity. 2. Light generated from the focus. 3. Splendour, that is, supercelestial Sun."

(B) Greek. "centre/point (as of the fiery [element?]) [i.e. figuratively *focus*,

correspondency, it loses by ~~its~~ the difficulty in being understood itself. The Will, the Mind, the Force in Actu, ~~was~~ is a repetition rather than an Exponent per aliud, or ἀλλοφανες.[2]

170　ıv sig A3ᵛ | Advertisement [to Vol ıv]

The original Text is preserved through all the reprinted Tracts, and this Volume thereby made at the least as close and faithful to the deep Sense of the Author, as delivered to us in the Old and First English Version of his Books, as the others that have preceded it.

But no where can I find any hint of a collation of the old and first English Versions with the Original German.—I *must* contrive to get some one of my Friends or *Con*quaintances, who can afford it, to go as far as 3£ for the Copy at D's, High Holborn![1]

---

hearth], ⟨ever generating the light.⟩ 2. light. 3. splendour [as tr in **33**, above, lit. "ray"], that is, the Sun".

With "*se ponens*" in (A) cf αὐτοθέτης in **172**, below. C uses *focus* (cognate with φῶς) in its ancient meanings of "hearth" and "fire" as well as in its modern senses; cf "*Hearth, or Fire-Altar*" in **33**, above, and cf **101** n 5, above. The parallel schemes establish an equivalence of *lux* and φῶς, and of *lumen* and αὐγή, and present three stages in descending order: *focus*/κέντρον, the source; *lux*/φῶς, the superior (or first) light generated from the source; *lumen*/αὐγή, the radiance or splendour of the superior light. (A later stage, after the "supercelestial sun", would be the sun in the sky, which—as though for a telescoped symbol of this whole process—C commonly identifies with the Son, as Donne and many others before him had done: see AURELIUS 35 n 1.) This scheme is associated with the sequence God—Light—Sun implied in Gen 1 as explicated by the "oldest philosophy" in the mouths of the Neoplatonists. Cf *SM* (*CC*) 95. It represents not only "the earliest symbol of the Tri-une God" but also the phases of the creative act: 1. God's creative will, 2. creative power radiating from God, 3. the splendour of power filled in the Word. See also **134** and **80** n 1, above. In C's mind there may be some connexion between αὐγή in this note and Böhme's *Auge* (eye) in **149**, above. For the "desiderata of a Symbol", see *SM* (*CC*) 30, where the dominant image is "translucence".

169[2] "The Will, the Mind, the Force in Action" repeats the schemes above, and is not an exposition of it "through something else, or *something that appears other*". Cf *SM* (*CC*) 62. In noticing that in a symbolic scheme the more exactly the symbols correspond to what they represent, the more difficult they are to understand, C seems to be saying that the scheme he has offered lies on the borderline between symbolic inscrutability and self-evident intelligibility.

170[1] Possibly J. Darcy of 42 High Holborn (1820) or R. Doyle of 7 High Holborn (1820), later Martin Doyle of 242 High Holborn (1821). C's desire to get a copy of the German original may in the end have been satisfied: Green's library contained a copy of Böhme's *Sämmtliche Werke* ed K. W. Schreiber (7 vols in 5, Leipzig 1831). *Green SC* (1880) 48. For "*Con*quaintances" see *The Three Sorts of Friends* in *PW* (EHC) ıı 1012, *CN* ı 617 and n, *CL* ııı 456 (17 Nov 1813).

SIGNATURA RERUM

171 IV i 10 | Ch 1 "How . . . Whatever Is Spoken of God Without the Knowledge of the Signature Is . . . Without Understanding . . ."

4. And then secondly we understand, that the Signature or Form is no Spirit, but the Receptacle, Container, or Cabinet of the Spirit, wherein it lies; for the Signature stands in the Essence, and is as a Lute that lies still, and is indeed a dumb Thing that is neither heard or understood; but if it be played upon, then its Form is understood, in what Form and Tune it stands, and according to what Note it is set. Thus likewise the Signature of Nature in its Form is a dumb Essence; it is as a prepared Instrument of Musick, upon which the Will's Spirit plays; what Strings he touches, they sound according to their Property.

§. 4 As a faint Glimmer of Illustration, take the figures/ $\overset{+}{0}$, 1, 2, 3, 4, 5, 6, 7, 8, 9, 1/$\overline{0}$—. These are all, and each *Unities*, Henads tho' not Monads[1]—they ~are~ may stand for what B. in this §. calls Spirits— But take 10,234,567,890—and their place gives to each its *Signature*. Observe, however, that in a yet higher relation each cypher has a place ~of~ in (Qy. a *space*?) itself in the absolute +0 or *super-numeral* 1—.[2] Thus 5, or 7, contains a *proper* signature, by which it is 5 or 7—and a common signature, as *a* number/

Both these may be entitled primary Signatures—Then comes the Signature, spoken of in §. 4—or the Signature of outward relation, the Signature *ab et ad extra.* or the former may be named the Proprium *Spatii*; the latter the Proprium *Loci*.[3]

172 IV i 12–13 | Ch 2 "Of the Opposition and Combat in the Essence of All Essences"

8. We understand, that without Nature there is an eternal *Stillness* and *Rest*, *viz.* the *Nothing*; and then we understand that an eternal Will arises in the Nothing, to introduce the Nothing into Something, that the Will might find, feel, and behold itself.

§. 8. The +0, super-essential Will, or Causa Sui, or Αυτοπατωρ.— Then the self-realized Will, the Source of Being as Being, the Effectus

---

171[1] The difference is between monad transcendant (the One) and henad as individual (i.e. any number from one to nine). See **32** n 1, above.

171[2] The number 1 is the "*super numeral*" because it is the source of all numbers. See **6** n 10 and **32** n 1, above. Cf "the supernumeral or Monad" in *CN* III 4449 f 26.

171[3] "*From and to the outside*" . . . "the Signification of *Space*" . . . "the Signification of *Place*".

Sui, πατηρ αυτοθετης—⊙./ Then the I_2,[a] the αυτογεννημα, or αυτο-υιος—in which act ⟨by its own re-action⟩ the ⊙ is itself I_1. ⟨or⟩ the Idem; as ⟨the⟩ then generated I_2 is the Alter.[1] Hence $I = 2$.—Then the Copula of the I_1 and I_2; and thus $I = 3$.—And the Pleroma of the ⊙ $= I_1$ in the ~~II~~$_2$ = ⊙, which with the ~~III~~$_3$ & by it, is itself ⟨actually⟩ $=$~~III~~$_2$; ⟨yet⟩ presents the the tetrad,—~~which~~ as the ⟨*possible*⟩ immediate Antecedent, ~~is~~ the *Possibility*, of the *Creation* or Creaturely $= V$ to IV—.—Now the Tetractys = Triad is the Divine or Eternal Nature—& should not be marked, 1.2.3.—but ~~I II III or~~ $I_1.I_2.I_3. = I$.—There is no ~~IIII or~~ I_4—the Pleroma being *in* the I_2, and no more capable of being added *to* it, or of being contemplated as co-ordinate *with* it, i.e. προς τον Λογον, than the Thoughts of my

---

[a] C has actually written "I$^{(2}$". To avoid confusion with the editor's footnote indicators, C's numerous superior numerals in this note have been printed as inferior numerals

172[1] With this difficult note, in which C tries to provide a schematic representation of the creative activity of the Trinity (Tri-une), cf **6** and n **10**, **107**, **169**, **171**, above, and the clearer exposition of part of it in **178**, below. See also *CN* III 4427, 4436. In Oken's notation (see **6**, **7** and nn, above) C explores "the *Possibility*, of the *Creation* or Creaturely" with the help of a few Neoplatonic and Christian terms and some special sigla. Super-essential will is "Cause of Self, or Self-father"; the self-realised Will is "Effect of Self, father positing self". (With αὐτοθέτης cf *se ponens* in **169**, above.) The Roman number I is the monad or first cause, or self; the remaining Roman numbers II–IX are henads, *arithmoi* (numbers), ideas, of cosmic rather than merely arithmetic import; the arabic numbers represent an order "lower", more abstract, less spiritually real than the Roman numbers, C's "substantial Numbers, or *Numeri numerantes*" (numbering Numbers). The inferior arabic numbers (they are superior in the ms, but see textual note) represent successive phases of the I (*one* or *Self*: see *LR* II 346); and ⊙ is a sign derived from **6** and **142** (**6** and **7** being closely related to this note), meaning the self-defining consciousness. In I_2 (the second phase of the One) the "self-create, or self-son" (? Logos) emerges;

in the act and self-reaction of becoming, the self-defining consciousness *is* the One in its first phase, being then both "Idem" (same: I_1) and "Alter" (other: I_2), in the terminology of e.g. **178**, below. In this way, One is two— God is Father and Son—hence the bond between One in its two phases I_1 and I_2. Again, the fulfilment of self-defining Consciousness (Pleroma of the ⊙) having come about through the identity of I_1 and I_2, the self-defining consciousness, though actually *in* I_2, becomes in its fulfilment a new number II. The Tetrad $+0, 1, 2, 3 =$ the Triad 1, 2, 3, which represents "the Divine or Eternal Nature" in as much as the numbers 1, 2, 3 arise, not from a cosmic sequence I, II, III, but through an actual-spiritual sequence of phases of self-realisation of the One—I_1, I_2, I_3. There is no fourth phase I_4 because the Pleroma that produces II (and so completes the series I, II, III) is "*in* the I_2" (προς τον Λογον echoing πρὸς τὸν Θεόν of John 1.1—"the Word was *with* God"). The Pleroma presents the tetrad, which is the possibility of the sequence 5–9, the rest of creation.

Both Αὐτοπάτωρ (Self-father) and αὐτουιος (self-son) are used by Iamblichus; πάτηρ αὐτοθέτης (father self-posited) occurs in Proclus. For another use of Αὐτοπάτωρ see *CIS* 5.

Mind can be conceived as added *to* my mind—. Only by a Prolepsis, or in *anticipative* reference to a not-god; not as aught actual, but as a possibility, is the Pleroma = *IV*. Hence in the Pythagorean Theosophy the IV is either included in the first Triad, and V.VI.VII. are the second—VIII.IX.X. the third—or it is the 10/ by the mysterious Assumption of 0 by 1—which the × (cross) only restores to the substantial Numbers, or Numeri numerantes. More plainly, ⟨the Ennead alone represents the Divine Nature:⟩ the ten is added to the perfect Ennead[2]—because out of the IV there has arisen a new reality—viz. the actualization of the *essential* eternal Potentiality, and the consequent potentialization, or disrealizing of the one essential, alone eternal, Actuality—or 1 engenerated in the ⟨ − ⟩ 0, [*] and therefore of the − 0 in the one.—This the Phantom, Matter, Self, Eccentric Center, Lie, Guilt.—[3]

[*] (− 0, or Contrary of the + 0.)

173   iv i 13

9. For in the Nothing the Will would not be manifest to itself, wherefore we know that the Will seeks itself, and finds itself in itself, and its seeking is a Desire, and its finding is the Essence of the Desire, wherein the Will finds itself.

the Not-*thing*, το μη ον, not qualified, without poles—in the rest of the Null-punct.[1]

174   iv i 62 | Ch 9 "Of the Signature, Shewing How the Internal Signs the External"

22. But I understand here the virtual Salt in the vegetable Life: *Saturn* makes the common Salt in the Water: He is an heavenly and an earthly Labourer, and labours in each Form according to the Property of the Form; as it is written, *With the holy thou art holy, and with the perverse thou art perverse.* In the holy Angels the heavenly *Mercury* is holy and divine, and in the Devils he is the Poison and

172[2] The ennead (as distinct from *henad*)—the set of nine. The word was also used by Porphyry as the title to each of his six divisions of Plotinus' writings, each division comprising nine chapters.

172[3] I.e. "the Father of Lies, the Den of Phantoms, the potential cause of Shadows" of **111**, above.

173[1] "Not qualified, without poles" is the state of "matter" referred to by Anaximander as τὸ ἄπειρον: see **31** n 7, above, and cf **111**. The "Null-punct" (nodal point or "point of indifference") is the state Böhme refers to in **172** textus as "eternal *Stillness* and *Rest*". Cf **45** and **117**, above.

Wrath of the Eternal Nature according to the dark Impression's Property, and so on through all Things . . .

Singular were it only as mere coincidence with the Cadmilus or Camillus of the Samothracian Cabiri, and the Mercury or Hermes φιλανθρωπος[1]

———superis Deorum
Gratus et imis.
Horat.[2]

175   iv i 138 | Ch 16 "Concerning the Eternal Signature and Heavenly Joy"

36. Thus there is no sufficient Ground in the Election of Grace as *] Reason holds it forth: *Adam* is chosen in Christ; but that many a Twig withers on the Tree, is not the Tree's Fault, for it withdraws its Sap from no Twig, only the Twig gives forth itself too eagerly with the Desire; it runs on in Self-Will, *viz.* it is taken by the Inflammation of the Sun and the Fire, before it can draw sap again in its Mother, and refresh itself.

*§ 36. Only by Resistance can the Life shape itself, and give the formal and formative Channels to the Sap, that feeds its Growth. But when instead of this it receives into itself the outward Life which was made present to it only that it might be resisted, then it (*not* assumes: for its evil was the defect of action; but) *suffers* the qualities of the meaner Alien, and the Twig withers on the Tree of Life, in the same manner as if it had been cut off, and layed ion the hot Hearth at the edge of a Fire.—Now the occasion of this Self-desertion is this: that the Resistance is a pleasurable energy, followed by a gladsome Self-finding (Empfindung)[1]—but the Resistee or Out-world Influence is the Condition of this resistance, as such a

174[1] "Lover of man"—an epithet for Hermes. The identification of Hermes with Cadmilus, and the Horace quotation (see n 2, below), but not the epithet for Hermes, come from SCHELLING *Samothrace* pp 20–1, 74–5; see **101** n 5 and **140** nn 3–6, above. Cadmilus was the fourth of the Cabiric deities, according to the traditional view the lowest, the servant of Axieros, Axiokersa, and Axiokersos; but according to Schelling he was the intermediary between these and the highest gods, who were all forms of Hephaestus, the Demiurge. See also "*Prometheus*" in *LR* ii 355–6, 358.

174[2] Horace   *Odes*   1.10.19–20 ("Hymn to Mercury"): "welcome alike to gods above and those below". Tr Bennett (LCL 1934). Quoted in SCHELLING *Samothrace* 75.

175[1] C's interpretation of *Empfindung* as "in-self-finding" is discussed in *CN* iii 3605n (Aug–Sept 1809), and note is taken of its use by Schelling and Fichte. C glosses the word in *CN* iii 4443: "A Sensation, a Feeling, is what I *find in* me *as* in me—Emp = intra, euphonicè for Ent;—finde." See also *C&S* (*CC*) 180.

necessary Concomitant, and then by the law of Association and the inveterate Sophism of the sensuous Understanding (φρονημα σαρκος)[2]—that, namely, of *Cum* hôc: ergo *propter* hoc,[3] it is mistaken for the proper cause, and loved and valued accordingly

OF THE ELECTION OF GRACE

176   ıv i [153] | The Author's Preface

1. When Reason hears any thing said concerning God intimating what he is according to his Being, Essence, Substance and Will, it imagines in itself as if God were some strange thing afar off, dwelling without and beyond the Place of this World, aloft above the Stars, and governed *only* by his Spirit with an omnipotent Power in the Place of this World.

Scarcely a Day in my Life passes in which I do not meet with some fresh instance of the Evils or Inconveniences arising from the misuse of the word, Reason, instead of the Understanding, or φρονημα σαρκος—[1]

177   ıv i 162 | Ch 2 "Of the Origin of God's Eternal Speaking Word"

26. Thus those Powers, which all lie in one Power, are the *Original of the Word*: For the one only Will comprises itself in the one only Power, wherein lies all hidden Secrets, and breathes itself forth through the Power into *Visibility*.

27. And that same Wisdom or Visibility is the *Beginning* of the Eternal Mind; *viz.* the every Way Discovery of itself.

§. 26.—I fear, that I have myself (thank God! the work is ⟨as⟩ yet only in MSS)[1] written incautiously on the ~~W~~ absolute Will as the same with the Ground of the Divine Existence—but this cannot be done without something of a Prolepsis. For the Will does indeed contain in itself Power (~~with might~~) and Intelligence as the Identity of both; but yet ~~all its~~ Light and Intelligence do not constitute ~~the~~ Will—they are essential to it or *of* its essence but not *its essence* which is to be causative of Reality. Now here is the Abyss, & the abysmal Mystery, that there is in the causativeness or All-might of

175[2] See **162** n 2, above.

175[3] "*With* this: therefore *because of* this", a variant of the fallacy "post hoc, ergo propter hoc".

176[1] See **175**, above.

177[1] Cf **135**, above. The mss cannot be identified with certainty: possibly the "Mysteries of Religion", or some part of the "Logosophia", or *AR*? See e.g. *Friend* (*CC*) ı 515 n 3: "...the Absolute Will, THE GOOD, the super-essential Source of BEING...". See also e.g. *C&S* (*CC*) 182.

God more than God. ~~because~~ i.e. an xy that God did not realize in
*him*self—for the Real containeth the Actual and the Potentiality—
but in God as God there is no potentia~~lity~~.—²

178   IV i 162–3

29. For the Will is the *Beginning*, and is called God the Father.

§. 29.—In ~~the latter half of~~ this period commences Behmen's Error,
and the false Leaven of his whole Theosophy. The Will *is* the beginning, ~~far rather~~ only when considered as more and higher than the
Ground of Deity ⟨or⟩ the Abyss. But ⟨when used as = the Might,⟩ it
is not to be called God, much less God the Father. It is the ~~depthless~~
Depth ⟨of⟩ the eternal Act, by which God affirmeth himself, as the
alone *Causa Sui*. The Depth begetteth not, but in & together with,
the Act of Self-realization—the Supreme Mind begetteth his substantial Idea, the primal Self (I AM) its other Self, and becometh
God the Father, self-originant and self-subsistent even as the Logos
or Supreme Idea is the co-eternal Son, self-subsistent but begotten
by the Father—while in the mutual and reciprocal act of Self-
attribution, the ~~effusorion~~ and re-fundence, the inspiration and
respiration of Love the Son is Deus alter et idem/ and these words
express the Triunity—Deus, Alter, Idem—i.e. Deus: Deus Alter:
Deus idem in Patre et in Filio, per quem Pater et Filius Unum sunt,
qui et ipse cum Patre et Filio est unus Deus.[1]

177[2] Cf **86**, above: "Potentiality is
a Will not perfected". C often quoted
the scholastic axiom that God is
"actus purissimus sine ulla potentialitate"—a perfectly pure act devoid of all potentiality—and in DE
WETTE **15** said that "God is a pure
Act". See BAXTER *Catholick Theologie*
1 n 2. There is an important discussion
of the theological implications of the
terms "Actual", "Real", and "Potential" in a letter written to the Rev
James Gillman in the margins of a
copy of *C&S*: see *C&S* (*CC*) 234.

178[1] "God, other and the same"...
"God, Other, the Same—that is,
God: God as Other: God the Same
in the Father and in the Son, through
whom Father and Son are One, who
himself also with the Father and the
Son is one God"—a statement, in
terms that in some respects correspond
to those in **169**, above, of the relation
of the persons of the Trinity in "the
mutual and reciprocal act of self-
attribution". The important new
element here is the statement at the
beginning of the note, that the Will
arises from the primal Ground. The
whole note provides a summary of
what C had said, or was to say,
elsewhere: see e.g. the "Formula
Fidei" in *LR* III 1–2, *CN* III 4427, and
ANNEX, below. C ascribed the phrase
"Deus alter et idem" to Philo: see *SM*
(*CC*) 95 and n 3, *C&S* (*CC*) 84n (in
which C calls the Logos the "alterity")
and n 3. The word "re-fundence" (not
in *OED*) means "pouring back"—
from the same root as "effusion"
(pouring out) but in a reverse direction.

179 IV i 292 | Ch 12 "A Brief Clearing of Some Questions Which Make Reason to Err"

162. Mark this well, all ye that will teach, and *suppose* ye are called to it; look well to your calling *within* you, whether ye be also called of God in Christ; whether Christ has called you with his Voice within you.

163. If not, then you are not other than *false* Prophets, who run unsent, and enter not into the Sheepfold by the Door of Christ.

164. That ye steer your Course by a *human Call*, it avails before Men, and God is pleased to *permit* what Men do, when it is done in his Order, or according to his Ordinance . . .

165. Where that is not done, and ye will stick only upon your *human* calling in your own Self-Will, then ye sit upon the Stool or Chair of Pestilence, and are Pharisees and *false* Prophets.

166. And if there were many hundred thousands of you, yet the *Office* makes you *not* to be Prophets and Shepherds of Christ, unless you enter in through Christ's living Door.

162–166. Can any thing be more congruous with good sense and sobriety of Judgement that is not less than Christianity?

180 IV i 292

169. Hearken, Reason, err not; God's Spirit suffers not itself to be *judged of Reason*: *Jonah* was born a Prophet, out of the Limit of the Covenant, and stood in the *Figure* of Christ, signifying how Christ should be cast into the Anger of God *into the Jaws of the Great Whale* of the Divine Righteousness, to fulfil it; and how he should go *into the Sea* of Death.

169. §. This, I dare assure myself, was a suggestion of Behmen's private Understanding and not an Insight in the Spirit. The Book of Jonah is an Apologue—and Jonah a symbol of the Jewish Nation, and of its characteristic bigotry, spiritual pride, uncharitableness and rebellious disposition—[1]

Annex

The following note was written by C on a sheet of paper, formerly inserted loose—and accidentally—at III i 372/3, but now no longer in the volume. It is closely related to **135, 172, 177**, but may be part of the ms fragment on Swedenborg's *True Christian Religion* printed in *CL* v 88–9n. For a direct

180[1] Cf *AR* (1825) 255n, in which C also referred to App B of *SM*. See also *SM* (*CC*) 59 and n 1, in which the details of the "Apologue" are explained and a parallel passage from N 21½ f 61 is quoted.

connexion between Swedenborg and Böhme in the subject of this note see **135** and **161**, above.

The abeternal[1] act of Self-realization[2] must, doubtless, perfect itself and be Self-knowlege. In the Language of the Finite, and relatively to the successions (or successive Apprehensions) of the Human Intellect, we may permit ourselves to say: that the Absolute Will *becomes* the Paternal Mind = the Father Almighty.[3]

Scholium. Observe, that I hereby guard and protest against the use of the term *Become*,[4] as proper to the object itself—and stand apart from Schelling and his Followers, the so called Physiosophs, or Natur-philosophen,[5] who affirm a Becoming sensu proprio[6] of God himself—.

[1] Not in *OED*. "From eternity" (as in the phrase *ab eterno gignens* in **169**, above), as distinct from "aboriginal" (*ab origine*, "from the beginning or source"), which occurs in **6** at n 3 and in **159**.

[2] Cf **135** at n 3, above.

[3] Cf, in **178**: "...the primal Self ...becometh God the Father". In **135**, above, C accuses Swedenborg of wrongly making this identity of God's will and "the paternal principle".

[4] In the ms fragment on Swedenborg (see **135** n 4, above) C said: "I acquiesce in the use of the words begotten and proceeding, each as distinguished from the other, and both as contra-distinguished from, created". But in a long note on SWEDENBORG *True Christian Religion* II 120–1 he said that Swedenborg was guilty of "either a sad misuse of Words, or mere Pantheism" in stating that

certain things, including light and heat, "are not creatable". See also **161** and n 1, above.

[5] "Physio-" provides from Greek the first component of the German word *Natur-philosophen*, and "-sophs" the second; the form of the second element may imply that in C's view the *Naturphilosophie* marked a shift from "philosophy" to "sophistry". *OED* ascribes "Physiophilosophy" to Tulk (after 1834). In the Platonic philosophy "being" is the attribute of the ideas or of God, "becoming" is the attribute of nature (*physis*). C's single word may provide a shorthand derogatory comment upon the *Naturphilosophie*; cf the term "Theanthroposophie" applied to Schelling in *CL* IV 792 (13 Dec 1817). Cf **161** n 1, above.

[6] "In the proper (i.e. unmetaphorical) sense".

GOTTFRIED CHRISTIAN BOHN

fl 1726

Gottfried Christian Bohns wohlerfahrner Kaufmann. Herausgegeben von C. D. Ebeling... und P. H. C. Brodhagen... Fünfte, gänzlich neu ausgearbeitete und sehr vermehrte Auflage. 3 vols. Hamburg 1789. 8º.

Victoria College Library (Coleridge Collection)

Signature of "Ab^m Meyer" in ink on I ⁻2. Inscribed by C in ink on I ⁻2: "S. T. Coleridge purchased these three volumes for three Sicilian Dollars, at Nº 35 under the Piazza, opposite the Treasury, La Vallette, Malta 20 Dec. 1804"; and on II ⁻2: "S. T. Coleridge La Vallette, Malta, 20 Dec. 1804".

Der wohlerfahrner Kaufmann ("The Expert Merchant") was first published in Hamburg in 3 vols, 1726–7. C's connexion with this book is curious. On 20 Sept 1798 Klopstock had taken C and WW to visit Christian Daniel Ebeling (1741–1815), one-time professor of history and Greek at the Akademisches Gymnasium, then librarian of the Stadtbibliothek, in Hamburg—"a lively intelligent man with an ear-trumpet". *CN* I 337 and n; *BL* (Satyrane's Letters) II 155. C may have seen a copy of the new ed of *Der wohlerfahrner Kaufmann* at Ebeling's house (Vols I and II run to nearly 800 pp each, Vol III is 1075 columns of tabulated detail), and recognised it when he saw a second-hand copy in Malta. In 1798, the notebook entry following the account of the meeting with Klopstock and Ebeling consists of a long list of prices of food in Germany (*CN* I 338)—domestic detail needed if Mrs C was to set up housekeeping in Germany—which could conceivably have been informed by Bohn. What use he intended for it in Malta—whether in his official work for the Governor, or conceivably to inform himself for the proposed (but unfulfilled) commission to buy corn in Russia—it is impossible to guess. He may simply have bought it for sentimental reasons.

DATE. Probably spring/summer 1808 to 30 Mar 1809: see **1** n 1, below.

1 II ⁻2, pencil, written below C's note of acquisition

Mr Estcourt	M^r ~~Phelps~~ Phips
Mr Lock	Mr Patterson[1]

1[1] These can best be accounted for as names of prospective subscribers to the 1809–10 *Friend*. The first and third names appear in the list compiled in N 62: see *CN* III 3471 ff 7, 7^v, 6, and for biographical detail see the alphabetical list in *Friend* (*CC*) II 427, 451. "Mr Patterson" may be Henry Patteson (1757–1824), rector of Drinkstone, Suffolk: see *Friend* (*CC*) II 450 (not in N 62). "Mr Lock" is a mystery: no such name appears in the list of subscribers, and a mistake for "Losh" is unlikely for a man who had been a friend for several years: see *Friend* (*CC*) II 443.

697

CLAUDE ALEXANDRE, COMTE DE BONNEVAL

1675–1747

Memoirs of the Bashaw Count Bonneval, from his birth to his death: shewing, the motives which induced him to quit the service and dominions of France . . . interspersed throughout with an entertaining diversity of secret intrigues, amorous adventures, military and political atchievements; being, in effect, the secret history of Europe for the best part of the current century. Written by himself, and collected from his papers. 2 pts in 1 vol. London 1750. 8⁰.

Pt i: tr of the spurious *Mémoires du comte de Bonneval* (London [Holland] 1750) pp 1–168. Pt ii: tr of *Anecdotes vénitiennes et turques, ou Nouveaux Mémoires du comte de Bonneval . . . par M. de Mirone* (2 vols Utrecht 1740).

Dove Cottage Library

Inscribed on the title-page: "W. Wordsworth", and below this in the hand of the poet's son "Wᵐ Wordsworth". On the front paste-down the initials "S. T. C." have been added in another hand.

Bonneval's life, marked as it was by a flamboyant opportunism and military panache surpassed only by his incorrigible insolence, was sensational enough to foster during his lifetime four sets of forged memoirs: see **1** n 2, below. He entered the army of France at the age of 13, was made colonel in 1701, and commanded a regiment with distinction in the War of Austrian Succession. But in 1704 he incurred the displeasure of the minister of war, was court-martialled, and (according to one account) sentenced to death. He managed to escape to Austria and there, in the rank of general, served Prince Eugene of Savoy with distinction, first in an action against his own countrymen, then in a number of battles against the Turks, and finally in the capture of Belgrade. Although he was rewarded with many honours by his new masters, he was soon imprisoned for insolent behaviour, and on his release left Austria for Turkey, joined the Muslim faith, and was given high military command. He became a popular figure, was showered with honours and luxurious perquisites, and was encouraged to cultivate grandiose ambitions as a statesman; but eventually he was exiled for military insubordination. After returning to Constantinople in 1739 he spent the last years of his life in fruitless efforts to negotiate his reinstatement to France. He died in Constantinople and was entombed there.

DATE. Mar–May 1810, while C was still at Allan Bank: see *CN* III 3738.

698

The second paragraph of the note was evidently written later than the first, but before his departure to Greta Hall early in May 1810.

1   p ⁻3 (p–d)

Quære. Whether to be so utter a villain, in every act and function of Life, as a man, as a Husband, as one having a country from whence he derived wealth, and rank, as a Christian &c &c—and not to know it—nay, to think himself a very amiable creature—& to write his memoirs in order to be admired—is not *proper* to a French man? —No other human Being *could* do this—Hundreds be as great Villains—but none so perfectly at ease with himself.—[1]

When I wrote the above, I did not know that these Memoirs are forgeries[2]—anecdotes picked up here & there, some doubtless from Bonneval himself, and with a much larger portion of mere Inventions, put together by one La Hode, at the Hague—La Hode was an apostate Jesuit, a most abandoned Scoundrel, Cheat, Sharper, Infidel, Debauchee &c &c.[3]

---

[1] The notebook entry that dates this reading is a sketch of an idea for *The Friend*: "Friend. Vanity, analysed in the character of Count Bonneval.— Pursue it thro' 1. The French Character...". *CN* III 3738. Such an essay was not written for *The Friend*, perhaps because—as he said in the postscript to his note—C discovered that the *Memoirs* he had been reading were a forgery. On the national characteristics of the French see *Friend* (*CC*) I 420–3.

[2] Later than the date of C's note, a few genuine writings of Bonneval were published—two short memoranda on military tactics and some letters— in the Prince de Ligne's *Mémoire sur le Cᵗᵉ de Bonneval* (Paris 1817).

[3] The Jesuit Père La Mothe (c 1680–c 1740), French historian, wrote several works during his exile in Holland, where he changed his name to La Hode. It is not certain that he was the author of any of the spurious memoirs. The Prince de Ligne dismisses the suggestion that "M. de Mirone", the "compiler" of the *Anecdotes vénitiennes* (1740), was a pseudonym of the Marquis d'Argens but does not venture any positive recommendation for authorship of "les detestables Mémoires". The source of C's information about La Hode is not known: it may have come from RS's acquaintance with Jesuit documents.

BOOK OF COMMON PRAYER

Copy A

The Book of Common Prayer. [Edition not identified.]

Not located. Annotation reprinted from *LR* i. *Lost List.*

See *LR* i 34: "These lines [of verse] were found in Mr. Coleridge's hand-writing in one of the Prayer Books in the chapel of Jesus College, Cambridge."

DATE. c 1794.

1

     ——I yet remain
To mourn the hours of youth (yet mourn in vain)
That fled neglected: wisely thou hast trod
The better path—and that high meed which God
Assign'd to virtue, tow'ring from the dust,
Shall wait thy rising, Spirit pure and just![1]

O God! how sweet it were to think, that all
Who silent mourn around this gloomy ball
Might hear the voice of joy;—but 'tis the will
Of man's great Author, that through good and ill
Calm he should hold his course, and so sustain
His varied lot of pleasure, toil, and pain![2]

[1] The opening lines are—with variations—the last five and a half lines of W. L. Bowles's elegy *On the Death of Mr. Headley*, which was first published in *Sonnets* (3rd ed 1794). For C's acquaintance with these Sonnets, see BOWLES. C has altered line 1 from "I, alas! remain"; line 5 from "Ordain'd for virtue", and line 6 from "bless thy labours, spirit".

[2] EHC rejected JDC's statement that the last six lines "practically belonged to the same poem" of Bowles, and correctly assigned them to C. There is, however, a strong echo of Bowles: see *On Mr Howard's Account of Lazarettos* lines 5–8.

Copy B

The Book of Common Prayer, and administration of the Sacraments, and other rites and ceremonies of the Church, according to the use of the Church of England: together with the Psalter or Psalms of David, pointed as they are to be sung or said in churches. Cambridge 1755. 8⁰.

[bound with] *A Companion to the Altar: shewing the nature and necessity of the sacramental preparation, in order to our worthy receiving the Holy Communion.* [Date unknown.]

Imprints: (BCP) Printed by Joseph Bentham, Printer to the University, by whom they are sold in Cambridge, and by Benj. Dod Bookseller in Ave-Mary Lane, London. (*A Companion*) London: Printed for John Beecroft, Successor to Mr. Edmund Parker, at the Bible and Crown in Pater-noster Row.

Not located. *Lost List.*

This volume was in the possession of the Gillman family as late as Nov 1893: MS Leatherhead. Some of the notes, esp **1** and **29–31**, may have been written for the instruction of Henry Gillman, James Gillman's younger son: see MS TRANSCRIPT, below.

Since both MS TRANSCRIPT and *LR* show that there were marginalia on *A Companion to the Altar*, it is reasonable to suppose that the *Companion* was bound in at the end of the Book of Common Prayer (as is the case in all copies examined in the BM), not at the beginning, as the transcribed and printed order of the marginalia suggests. Copies of the *Companion* usually have a note printed below the imprint: "Note, This Book is bound up with the *Common-Prayers* of several Sorts, and to be had at the Place abovesaid." The order of the marginalia has been altered to consort with the actual sequence of the Book of Common Prayer, with the *Companion* following the Articles of Religion (the last section of BCP).

This copy may also have had bound at the end a copy of either N. Brady and N. Tate *A New Version of the Psalms of David fitted to the tunes used in churches* Printed by A. Wilde, for the Company of Stationers, or Thomas Sternhold, John Hopkins, et al *The Whole Book of Psalms collected into English Metre . . . conferred with the Hebrew* London: printed by Charles Ackers, for the Company of Stationers.

MS TRANSCRIPT. Cornell: Healey 2619, SC's transcript of **1**, **3**, **4**, **9**, **12–15**, **17**, **21**, **25**, **29**, **30** (but in the same sequence as in *LR* III 6–18); marked at the end: "These notes were written in a Book of Common Prayer belonging to Henry Gillman—by S. T. Coleridge. The book was Published at Cambridge in the year 1755, by Joseph Bentham & by B Dod. Ave Mary Lane London." Since this transcript is evidently closer to the ms original than the version in *LR*, the *LR* text has been followed only for those notes which are not included in MS TRANSCRIPT.

DATE. 1827–31: **29** is dated 14 Dec 1827, **28** is dated Sept 1831. There may be some connexion between the notes on the Psalms (**9–25**) and the notes on the Psalms in BIBLE COPY B (**30–47**), but only Ps 68, 74, 88, and 104 are treated in both sets of notes.

1

A man may pray night and Morning: yet deceive himself. But no man can be assured of his sincerity, who does not *pray*—Prayer *is Faith* passing into act—a union of the will and the Intellect realizing in an *intellectual act*. It is the *whole* man that prays; less than this is wishing, or *lip* work, a charm, or a mummery. Pray always:—says the Apostle[1]—i.e. have the habit of prayer, turning your thoughts into acts by connecting them by an act with the idea of the Redeemer God, and even so [reconverting][a] actions *into thoughts*.

2 | Eleventh Sunday after Trinity. The Epistle: 1 Cor 15.1

Brethren, I declare unto you the Gospel which I preached unto you, which also ye have received, and wherein ye stand: by which also ye are saved . . .

Why should the obsolete, though faithful, Saxon translation of εὐαγγέλιον be retained? Why not "good tidings?" Why thus change a most appropriate and intelligible designation of the matter into a mere conventional name of a particular book?[1]

3 | 1 Cor 15.3

For I delivered unto you first of all, that which I also received, how that Christ died for our sins according to the Scriptures . . .

Christ died thro' our sins, & we *live* thro' his Righteousness.[1] He died thro' the sin, and *for* the *Sinners*. S. T. C.—

a This word, not legible to SC when she was preparing MS TRANSCRIPT, is supplied from *LR*

1[1] C repeated this injunction many times: see e.g. BROWNE *Works* 34 and *CN* III 4183. The command does not come directly from St Paul in this form; 1 Thess 5.17 reads "Pray without ceasing", but the words "pray always" in 2 Thess 1.11 are not in the form of a command. Cf Col 1.3. C may have misplaced in his mind Luke 21.36: "Watch ye therefore, and pray always"; and cf Luke 18.1: "men ought always to pray".

2[1] The word εὐαγγέλιον—translated "gospel" in AV (from OE *godspel*, "good tidings")—was carried into the descriptive titles of the four narratives of the life and ministry of Jesus. C's regret is not only that "gospel" no longer means "good tidings", but also that it has so consistently come to recall the "conventional title" of any one of four books of the NT that what St Paul evidently meant in 1 Cor 15.1 is precluded—the preaching of the Christian faith, the good tidings of the new dispensation. See also BIBLE COPY B **93** n 3.

3[1] The Greek for "died for our sins" in 1 Cor 15.3 is ὑπερ τῶν ἁμαρτιῶν ἡμῶν—that is, because of, by reason

4 | The Gospel: S. Luke 18.9

[The parable of the Pharisee and Publican:] Two men went up into the temple to pray; the one a Pharisee, and the other a publican. The Pharisee stood and prayed thus with himself: God, I thank thee, that I am not as other men are, extortioners, unjust, adulterers, or even as this Publican ... And the publican, standing afar off, would not lift up so much as his eyes unto heaven, but smote upon his breast, saying, God be merciful to me a sinner. I tell you, this man went down to his house justified*[a] rather than the other ...

* N.B. *not* justified; but justified *rather* than the other i.e. *less* remote from Salvation.[1]

5 | Twenty-fifth Sunday after Trinity. The Collect

Stir up, we beseech thee, O Lord, the wills of thy faithful people; that they plenteously bringing forth the fruit of good works, may of thee be plenteously rewarded ...

Rather—"that with that enlarged capacity, which without thee we cannot acquire, there may likewise be an increase of the gift, which from thee alone we can wholly receive."

6 | The Order for the Administration of the Lord's Supper, or, Holy Communion

Dearly beloved, on — day next I purpose, through God's assistance, to administer to all such as shall be religiously and devoutly disposed, the most comfortable Sacrament of the Body and Blood of Christ; to be by them received, in remembrance of his meritorious Cross and Passion; whereby alone we obtain remission of our sins, and are made partakers of the kingdom of heaven. Wherefore it is our duty to render most humble and hearty thanks to Almighty God our heavenly Father, for that he hath given his Son our Saviour Jesus Christ, not only to die for us, but also to be our spiritual food and sustenance in that holy Sacrament.

---

[a] This word, underlined by SC but not italicised in BCP, is presumed to have been underlined by C

---

of, our sins: this does not necessarily mean—though often so interpreted—"he died to atone for our sins". Cf e.g. 1 Thess 5.10, 2 Cor 5.15. "We *live* thro' his righteousness" is adapted from Rom 5.21, in which the preposition is διά (through), as in e.g. 1 John 4.9.

4[1] The phrase παρ' ἔκεινον means "more than, or rather than, the other". C means that neither was fully justified, but the sinner more than the pharisee—a more subtle sense than *NEB*: "It was this man ... and not the other, who went home acquitted of his sins."

Mem. In the Exhortation in our Communion Service l. 10. before "His meritorious Cross & Passion" I should propose to insert the words "his assumption of Humanity, his Incarnation and"—and in the 22nd line after "sustenance" I would insert the word "as".[1] Not in the Sacrament exclusively, but in all those acts of assimilative Faith, of which the Sacrament is a solemn, eminent and representative instance, *an* Instance and the Symbol.[2] S. T. C.

7 | The Form of Solemnization of Matrimony

[The estate of Matrimony] is not to be enterprised, nor taken in hand unadvisedly, lightly, or wantonly... but reverently, discreetly, advisedly, soberly, and in the fear of God; duly considering the causes for which Matrimony was ordained. First, it was ordained for the procreation of children, to be brought up in the fear and nurture of the Lord, and to the praise of his holy Name.

Marriage, simply as marriage, is not the means "for the procreation of children," but for the humanization of the offspring procreated. Therefore in the Declaration at the beginning, after the words, "procreation of children," I would insert, "and as the means for securing to the children procreated enduring care, and that they may be" &c.[1]

8 | The Communion of the Sick

[rubric:] *But if a Man, either by reason of extremity of sickness, or for want of warning in due time to the Curate, or lack of company to receive with him, or by any other just impediment, do not receive the Sacrament of Christ's Body and Blood; the Curate shall instruct him, That if he do truly repent him of his sins, and stedfastly believe that Jesus Christ hath suffered death upon the cross for him, and shed his Blood for his redemption; earnestly remembering the benefits he hath*

6[1] The proposed text then reads: "I purpose...to...administer...the ...Sacrament...in remembrance of his Assumption of Humanity, his Incarnation and his meritorious Cross and Passion" and "...to be our spiritual food and sustenance as in that holy Sacrament".

6[2] For the sacrament as symbol, see e.g. BLANCO WHITE *Practical Evidence* 13, DONNE *Sermons* COPY B 33, and BUTLER *Vindication* 1. C's central statement on symbol is in *SM (CC)* 30–1, summarised in 79. See also *SM (CC)* 86 and *AR (1825)* 198–9.

7[1] C noted in TAYLOR *Polemicall Discourses* i 1003: "I place the moral, social and spiritual Helps & Comforts as the proper & essential ends of Christian Marriage and regard the Begetting of children as a contingent consequence." The Church of England recognises only two sacraments—baptism and holy communion: cf BAXTER *Reliquiae* COPY B **104.**

thereby, and giving him hearty thanks therefore; he doth eat and drink the Body and Blood of our Saviour Christ profitably to his Soul's health, although he do not receive the Sacrament with his mouth.

Third rubric at the end.

I think this rubric, in what I conceive to be its true meaning, a precious document, as fully acquitting our Church of all Romish superstition, respecting the nature of the Eucharist, in relation to the whole scheme of man's redemption. But the latter part of it—"he doth eat and drink the Body and Blood of our Saviour Christ profitably to his soul's health, although he do not receive the Sacrament with his mouth"—seems to me very incautiously expressed, and scarcely to be reconciled with the Church's own definition of a sacrament in general. For in such a case, where is "the outward and visible sign of the inward and spiritual grace given?"[1]

---

9 | The Psalter, or Psalms of David. The 1. Day: Ps 8.2

Out of the mouth of very babes and sucklings hast thou ordained strength, because of thine enemies: that thou mightest still the enemy and the avenger.

To the dispensation of the twilight Dawn, to the first messenger of the redeeming Word, in the yet lisping utterers of Light and Life, a strength [and][a] a power were given "because of the Promises" greater and of more immediate influence, than to the Seers & Proclaimers of a clearer Light, even as the first re-appearing Crescent of the eclipsed Moon shines for men with a keener brilliance, than the following larger segment, previous to its whole emersion.[1] Moses, Lycurgus, Solon, Numa, compared with Isaiah, Jeremiah, &c[2] S. T. C.—

a Word supplied by the editor

8[1] The phrase "the outward and visible sign..." is from the Catechism in answer to the question: "What meanest thou by this word *Sacrament*?"

9[1] An instance of C's direct observation of the night sky. Here he is using "crescent" in its radical sense—growing, increasing—and only suggestively of the shape of the partly disclosed moon, since the moon emerging from the shadow of an eclipse is C-shaped, decrescent, the shape of the waning moon. For C's play on the words for the changes in the apparent shape of the moon, crescent (D-shaped, waxing) and decrescent (C-shaped, waning), see e.g. *CN* II 2603, 2766.

9[2] "Because of the Promises" made "to Abraham and his seed": Gal 3.16. C is contrasting the great law-givers who restored a corrupt state of society to a civilised condition with the great prophets who through their apocalyptic vision led men to personal redemption. Cf *LS* (*CC*) 223 and n.

Seventeen notes (**9–25**) are now devoted to the Psalms, a particular inter-

10 | Ps 8.5

Thou madest him lower than the angels: to crown him with glory and worship.

Power + idea = angel.
Idea − power = man, or Prometheus.[1]

11 | The 13. day: Ps 68.34

Ascribe ye the power to God over Israel: his worship, and strength is in the clouds.

The "clouds" in the symbolical language of the Scriptures mean the events and course of things, seemingly effects of human will or chance, but overruled by Providence.

12 | The 14. day: Ps 72

Give the King thy judgements, O God: and thy righteousness unto the King's son. . . .

The 72nd Psalm admits of no other interpretation except of Christ as the Jehovah incarnate. In any other sense, it would be a specimen of more than Persian or Mogul Hyperbole and Bombast, of which there is no other instance in Scripture, and which no Christian would dare to attribute to an inspired writer; we know too, that the Elder Jewish Church ranked it among the Messianic Psalms.[1]

P.S. *The Word* (in St John) and the *name* of the Most High in the Psalmist, are almost[a] equivalent terms.[2] S. T. C.

---

[a] It is not clear whether SC intended "almost" to be cancelled. *LR* omits it

---

est pursued in BIBLE COPY B **30–47** and through several of the late notebooks. Only four of the notes refer to the same Psalms as are annotated in BIBLE COPY B.

10[1] This point, central to the "*Prometheus*" essay of 1825 "with all its subtlety and all its obscurity", is nowhere so succinctly stated as here: see *LR* II 331, 343, 348, 350, 354. On the relation of angel, man, and beast, see BÖHME **84** and n 2.

12[1] Both Jewish and Christian tradition recognise Psalm 72 as messianic. In any case, C's impulse is to interpret the Psalms "by the Gospel": see **25**, below.

12[2] The reference is to v 17: "His Name shall endure for ever; his Name shall remain under the sun among the posterities...". For the identity of the Word and the name see also BIBLE COPY B **64**; and for the relation between *nomen* (name) and *numen* (power) see BIBLE COPY B **33** n 1. See also **29** at n 7, below.

13 | Ps 72.1: **12** textus

God of God, Light of Light, very God of very God, the only begotten, the Son of God and God, King of Kings & the Son of the
King of Kings[1]— S. T. C.

14 | Ps 74.2

O think upon thy congregation: whom thou hast purchased, and redeemed of old.

Mem. The Lamb sacrificed from the beginning of the world, the
God-Man the Judge and the self-promised Redeemer of Adam in
the Garden—[1]

15 | Ps 74.15

Thou smotest the heads of Leviathan in pieces: and gavest him to be
meat for the people in the wilderness.

Does this Verse attach to any tribe, to a Nation? The Psalm appears
to have been composed shortly before the Captivity of Jerusalem.[1]
S. T. C.

16 | The 16. day: Ps 82.6–7

I have said, Ye are gods: and ye are all the children of the most
Highest. But ye shall die like men: and fall like one of the princes.

13[1] The first five formulae are from
the Nicene Creed (var): they form one
group in contrast to "God, King of
Kings, & the Son of the King of
Kings", which is an expanded version
of "the King" and "the King's son"
in Ps 72.1. The contrast is between the
divine and the earthly. "King of
Kings" was originally the title of the
King of Assyria, who in fact ruled
over many vassal kings. The kingship
of the Lord, however, is declared several
times in the Psalms, in Jeremiah,
Ezekiel, Daniel, and Zechariah; and
as supreme Lord he acquires the title
of the supreme earthly king. The
formula "King of Kings" is first
applied to Christ in 1 Tim 6.15; cf
Rev 17.14, 19.16, and the use of
"King of kings, and Lord of lords, the
only ruler of princes" in the Prayer
for the King's Majesty. C sees an
unintentional prophecy in the Psalmist's prayer that the earthly sovereign(s)
will be wise and will judge well.

14[1] For "The Lamb sacrificed..."
("slain") see Rev 13.8. The "God-
Man" is called the "Redeemer of
Adam" because of the promise given
to Eve (Gen 3.15), and "self-promised"
because it was the Jehovah-Word who
gave the promise and fulfilled it as the
Christ.

15[1] In spite of the context of
national catastrophe, v 15 may well
refer not to the fact or hope of national
salvation but to God's triumph over
the primeval chaos-monster, the con-
trolling of waters, and the bringing of
order into the world. In BIBLE COPY
B **45** C considers it "not impossible"
that this verse recalls the "inundation
caused by the drawing back of the
Waters during the Exodus" and that
nomad tribes lived off the stranded
whales and grampuses.

The reference which our Lord made to these mysterious verses, gives them an especial interest. The first apostasy, the fall of the angels, is, perhaps, intimated.[1]

17 | The 17. day: Ps 87

Her foundations are upon the holy hills: the Lord loveth the gates of Sion more than all the dwellings of Jacob. Very excellent things are spoken of thee: thou city of God. I will think upon Rahab and Babylon: with them that know me. Behold ye the Philistines also: and they of Tyre, with the Morians; lo, there was he born. And of Sion it shall be reported, that he was born in her: and the most High shall stablish her. The Lord shall rehearse it when he writeth up the people: that he was born there. The fingers also and trumpets shall he rehearse: all my fresh springs shall be in thee.

I would fain understand this Psalm, but first I would collate it word by word with the Hebrew It is wholly Messianic.[1] S. T. C.

18 | Ps 88.10–12

Dost thou shew wonders among the dead: or shall the dead rise up again, and praise thee? Shall thy loving-kindness be shewed in the grave: or thy faithfulness in destruction? Shall thy wondrous works be known in the dark: and thy righteousness in the land where all things are forgotten?

Compare Ezekiel xxxvii.[1]

19 | The 20. day: Ps 104

Praise the Lord, O my Soul: O lord my God, thou art become exceeding glorious, thou art clothed with majesty and honour. . . .

I think the Bible version might with advantage be substituted for this, which in some parts is scarcely intelligible.[1]

16[1] The NT reference is John 10.34–6. See also BIBLE COPY B 64. C's notion that in this psalm "the congregation of princes" is a superhuman or angelic company is generally received.

17[1] This psalm, not generally or traditionally considered messianic, celebrates the triumph of Yahweh, as a result of which all nations may be reckoned citizens of Zion. Collation of this textually difficult psalm would presumably have been undertaken with Hurwitz: see **25**, below. There is no sign in these marginalia of C using Cohen's version; the notes were therefore presumably written before C acquired a copy of Cohen in c Mar 1828: see BIBLE COPY B 24 n 1.

18[1] Ezek 37 is the vision of the dry bones. See esp 37.12–14. For a comment on Ps 88.5 see BIBLE COPY B 46.

19[1] Ps 104 celebrates the wonder and variety of creation. Though in some ways parallel to Gen 1, it is not so much concerned with the initial acts

20 | Ps 104.6

Thou coveredst it with the deep, like as with a garment: the waters stand in the hills.

No; *stood above the mountains*.[1] The reference is to the Deluge.

21 | The 21. day: Ps 105.3

Rejoice in his holy Name: let the heart of them rejoice that seek the Lord.

If even to *seek* the Lord be joy, what will it be to *find* him! Seek me Oh Lord! that I may be found by thee.[1] S. T. C.

22 | The 23. day: Ps 110

The Lord said unto my Lord: Sit thou on my right hand, until I make thine enemies thy footstool. 2 The Lord shall send the rod of thy power out of Sion: be thou ruler, even in the midst among thine enemies. 3 In the day of thy power shall the people offer thee free-will-offerings with an holy worship: the dew of thy birth is of the womb of the morning. 4 The Lord sware, and will not repent: Thou art a Priest for ever after the order of Melchisedech. 5 The Lord upon thy right hand: shall wound even kings in the day of his wrath. 6 He shall judge among the heathen, he shall fill the places with the dead bodies: and smite in sunder the heads over divers countries. 7 He shall drink of the brook in the way: therefore shall he lift up his head.

v. 3. Understand—"Thy people shall offer themselves willingly in the day of conflict in holy clothing, in their best array, in their best arms and accoutrements. As the dew from the womb of the morning, in number and brightness like dew-drops; so shall be thy youth, or the youth of thee, the young volunteer warriors.["]1

of creation as with the created order as "given" to us. In Bible copy b 47 C offers his own translation of vv 3–4 and part of v 6.

20[1] C quotes AV against the Prayer Book version, in accordance with **19**, above. *NEB* reads: "the waters lay above the mountains".

21[1] Cf Deut 4.29, Matt 7.7, Luke 11.9. The last sentence of C's note expresses a less usual sentiment, similar to Augustine *Confessions* 11.2: "[Christ] by whom Thou didst seek us when we sought thee not, didst seek us indeed that we might seek Thee." Donne makes the point more daringly in *Holy Sonnet* xviii.

22[1] The translation and interpretation of this psalm—especially v 3—have been much disputed. *NEB* reads: "3. At birth [*or* on the day of your power] you were endowed with princely gifts and resplendent [*or* apparelled] in holiness [*or* your people offered themselves willingly (*meaning of Hebrew uncertain*), resplendent &c]. You have shone with the dew of youth since your mother bore you."

v. 5. "He shall shake," concuss, *concutiet reges die iræ suæ.*[2]

v. 6. For "smite in sunder, or wound, the heads;" some word answering to the Latin *conquassare.*[3]

v. 7. For "therefore," translate "then shall he lift up his head again;" that is, as a man languid and sinking from thirst and fatigue after refreshment.[4]

N.B. I see no poetic discrepancy between vv. 1 and 5.

23 | The 24. day: Ps 118

O give thanks unto the Lord, for he is gracious: because his mercy endureth for ever.

To be interpreted of Christ's church.[1]

24 | The 27. day: Ps 126.5

Turn our captivity, O Lord: as the rivers in the south.

Does this allude to the periodical rains?[1]

25

As a Transparency on some night of public Rejoicing seen by common day, with the lamps from within removed, even such would be the Psalms to me uninterpreted by the Gospel.[1] O honoured M[r] Hurwitz could I but make you feel what *Grandeur*, what magnificence, what an everlasting significance[a] & import Christianity gives to every part of your national History, to every page of your sacred Records[2] —S. T. C.—

<hr>

[a] MS TRANSCRIPT reads "magnificence"

22[2] "He will shake/concuss kings in the day of his anger". But Vulgate (which C seems not to have consulted) reads: "confregit in die irae suae reges." *NEB* reads: "The Lord... has broken kings in the day of his anger."

22[3] Vulgate reads: "conquassabit capita in terra multorum". The violent onomatopoeic word *conquassare* means "to smash asunder," "to squash". *NEB* reads as a variant version: "He shall punish the nations—heaps of corpses, broken heads—over a wide expanse".

22[4] *NEB* reads: "He will drink from the torrent beside the path and will hold his head high."

23[1] The imagery of vv 22 and 26 is given Christological significance in several places in NT.

24[1] A view regularly held, the periodical flooding of the Nile being an image of fertility restored.

25[1] C described a transparency that he had seen in Bristol in Jun 1814: *CL* III 512. The first use of "transparency" in this sense is noted in *OED* for 1807.

25[2] Hurwitz was a friend of C's in Highgate from late 1816: see BLANCO WHITE *Practical Evidence* 2 n 3 and HURWITZ. C relied upon him for enlargements of his scanty and long-ago Christ's Hospital Hebrew.

26 | Articles of Religion. xx "Of the Authority of the Church"

The Church hath power to decree Rites or Ceremonies, and authority in Controversies of Faith: And yet it is not lawful for the Church to ordain any thing that is contrary to God's Word written, neither may it so expound one place of Scripture, that it be repugnant to another. Wherefore, although the Church be a witness and a keeper of holy Writ, yet as it ought not to decree any thing against the same; so besides the same ought it not to enforce any thing to be believed for necessity of salvation.

xx. It is mournful to think how many recent writers have criminated our Church in consequence of their own ignorance and inadvertence in not knowing, or not noticing, the contra-distinction here meant between power and authority. Rites and ceremonies the Church may ordain *jure proprio*:[1] on matters of faith her judgment is to be received with reverence, and not gainsaid but after repeated inquiries, and on weighty grounds.

27 | xxxvii. "Of the Civil Magistrates"

...It is lawful for Christian men, at the commandment of the Magistrate, to wear weapons, and serve in the wars.

This is a very good instance of an unseemly matter neatly wrapped up. The good men recoiled from the plain words—"It is lawful for Christian men at the command of a king to slaughter as many Christians as they can!"

28

Well! I could most sincerely subscribe to all these articles.[1] September 1831.

A COMPANION TO THE ALTAR

29 ? blank verso of half-title facing title-page, perhaps referring to p 8

...I shall endeavour to shew what that *Preparation* of Heart and Mind is, which must dispose us for a worthy Participation of the blessed Sacrament: And herein I hope to remove all those Fears and Scruples which arise in our Minds about "eating and drinking

26[1] "In her own right".

28[1] Under the Test and Corporation Acts of Charles ii Dissenters and Roman Catholics were barred from national and municipal office. The acts remained on the books until 1828 but had been administered inconsistently from the end of the eighteenth century. C wrote *C&S* at a time when legislation was being formulated to remove remaining discriminatory anomalies.

unworthily, and of incurring our own Damnation thereby," as groundless and unwarrantable; and to do this I shall take occasion to explain that part of our CHURCH CATECHISM, designedly intended for our Instruction, with relation to this Duty of a sacramental Preparation, namely,

Q. "What is required of them who come to the Lord's Supper?"

A. "To examine themselves whether they repent them truly of their former Sins, stedfastly purposing to lead a new Life, have a lively Faith in God's Mercy through Christ, with a thankful Remembrance of his Death, and to be in Charity with all Men." This is that Sacramental Preparation which our Church (in as few words as is possible) hath provided for our Companion and Guide to the holy Altar....

The best preparation for taking[a] the sacrament, and better than any or all of the Books and Tracts composed for this end,[1] is, first to read over and over again, and often on your knees, at all events with a kneeling and praying heart, the Gospel according to S[t] John, till your mind is familiarized to the contemplation of Christ, the Redeemer and Mediator of Mankind, yea, and of every creature, as the living and self-subsisting WORD, the very truth of all true Being, and the very Being of all enduring Truth! the Reality, which is the substance and unity of ALL Reality! the Light that lighteth every Man,[2] so that what we call *Reason* is itself a light from that *Light, Lumen a Luce,* as the Latin more distinctly expresses this fact[3] —But it is not merely *Light,* but therein is *Life*: and it is the *Life* of Christ, the co-eternal Son of God, that is the only true life-giving Light of men;[4]—we are assured and we believe that Christ is God,

---

a SC has written "talking", which may have been the reading of the ms

29[1] Not only the *Companion to the Altar,* but also *Sermons or Homilies of the United Church of England and Ireland, as they were originally appointed to be read in churches in the time of Queen Elizabeth,* which was commonly printed in pamphlet form to be used separately or bound with the Book of Common Prayer, together with the Thirty-nine Articles and one of the metrical versions of the Psalms. C annotated a copy of *Sermons and Homilies* (1815), which is now in the BM.

29[2] John 1.9.

29[3] "Light of Light" in the Nicene Creed, used in the Communion Service. For the distinction between *lumen*/ αὐγή and *lux*/ φῶς, see BÖHME 169 and n 1: *lumen* is the derived light, *lux* the divine light, and of the two terms *Lux* is always for C the higher, or prior. Sometimes *Lux* is God, *Lumen* the Word; sometimes *lux* is reason, *lumen* understanding; in N 37 f 67 *Lux* is "the Life of the Word", *Lumen* "the Light of Truth in Man". Here reason is *lumen,* derived from *lux,* the divine light.

29[4] John 1.4: "In him was life; and the life was the light of men."

God manifested in the Flesh.[5] As God, he must be *present entire** in *every* creature; but he is said to *dwell* in the regenerate, to *come* to them who receive him by Faith in his *name*, that is, in his Light, Power and Influence: for this is the meaning of the word *Name* in Scripture, when applied to God and his Christ.[7] For where a true belief exists Christ is not only present with or among us (for so he is in every man, even the most wicked)—but *to* us and *for* us, see John's Gosp. C 1 v. 9–13—& again, my Father and I will come and *we* will dwell in you.[8] As truly and as really as your soul resides *constitutively* in your living Body, so truly, really, personally and substantially does Christ dwell in every regenerate Man—[9]

After this course of study, you may then take up and peruse, sentence by sentence, the Communion Service, the best of all comments on the Scriptures appertaining to the mystery—(This is the Preparation, which will prove, with God's Grace, the surest Preventive and Antidote to the freezing Poison, the lethargizing Hemlock, of the Doctrine of the Sacramentaries, according to whom the Eucharist is a mere *practical Metaphor*, in which Things are employed instead of articulated sounds, for the exclusive purpose of recalling to our minds the historical fact of our Lord's Crucifixion— in short (the profaneness is with *them* not with me) just the same as when Protestants drink a glass of wine to the glorious memory of William the third.)[10] True it is that the Remembrance is *one* end of

* For how can God or indeed any Spirit exist *in parts*? If that were possible we might talk of so many feet or inches of God being in this or that person.[6] S. T. C.—[a]

---

[a] SC transcribed this footnote as though it belonged to 1

29[5] Cf 1 Tim 3.16. There is a close parallel between this marginal note and *CIS* ix.

29[6] For "the whole in every part" see BLANCO WHITE *Practical Evidence* **13** n 7. Cf FLEURY 2: "A precious faith verily that is capable of fractions!"

29[7] Cf **12** and n 2, above.

29[8] "*To* us and *for* us" is implied rather than stated. See John 1.9–12. C's last phrase, "& again...", echoes John 14.23.

29[9] Note **1** and the first paragraph of **29** together represent one of C's principal reflections on prayer: see,

however, *CL* III 478–9, BÖHME **152**. Cf *CN* III 3355. Prayer was to have been carefully considered, with the eucharist and faith, in a volume supplementary to *AR* and may have become *Confessions of an Inquiring Spirit*. See *AR* (1825) 376. A short prayer was written down on 1 Jan 1828 in N 36 ff 38–38ᵛ; a much longer "Nightly Prayer" of 1831 is printed in *LR* III 3–6.

29[10] Cf *CN* II 2724, 2711 (var). See also BAHRDT **2**. The sacramentary controversy is discussed in BLANCO WHITE *Poor Man's Preservative* **2** and n 3.

the Sacrament, but it is, Do this in remembrance of *me*[11]—of all that Christ was and is, has done and is still doing, for fallen Mankind, of course of his Crucifixion inclusively, but not of his Crucifixion alone. S. T. Coleridge Dec. 14 1827—

30   ? p 9

First then, That we may come to this heavenly Feast holy, and adorned with the Wedding Garment, *Matt.* xxii. 11. we must search our Hearts, and examine our Consciences, not only till we see our Sins, but until we hate them; and instead of those filthy Rags of our Righteousness, we must adorn our Minds with pure and Pious Dispositions ...

But what if a man seeing his Sin earnestly desire to hate it, shall he not at the altar offer up at once his desire & the yet lingering sin & seek for strength?[1] Is not the Sacrament Medicine as well *as food*? Is it an *end* only or not likewise a means? Is it merely the triumphal Feast or is it not even more truly a blessed Refreshment for and during the Conflict?—S. T. C.

31   ? p 14

Which Confession of Sins must not be in general Terms only, that we are Sinners with the rest of Mankind, but it must be a special Declaration to God of all our most heinous Sins in *Thought*, *Word* and *Deed*, with all their several Aggravations, laying open our Sores to our heavenly Physician ...

Luther was of a different judgment. He would have us feel and groan under our sinfulness and utter incapability of redeeming ourselves from the bondage, rather than hazard the pollution of our imaginations by a recapitulation and renewing of sins and their images in detail. Do not, he says, stand picking the flaws[a] out one by one, but plunge into the river, and drown them![1]—I venture to be of Luther's doctrine.

[a] Probably for "fleas", a misreading or deliberate alteration by *LR*

29[11] Luke 22.19, 1 Cor 11.24; also in the Prayer of Consecration in the Communion Service.

30[1] In Apr 1814, when he had resolved to place himself in charge in order to break his addiction to opium, C said "The first outward and sensible Result of Prayer is a penitent Resolution, joined with a consciousness of weakness in effecting it (yea, even a dread too well grounded, lest by breaking & falsifying it the soul should add guilt to guilt by the very means, it has taken to escape from Guilt—so pitiable is the state of unregenerated man!)." *CL* III 479.

31[1] Not Luther, but St Francis of Sales, as quoted by Thomas Halyburton *Memoirs of the Life of... Mr. Thomas Halyburton* (10th ed Edinburgh 1797) 126–7. C copied this passage in N 29 f 71[v].

LOUIS ANTOINE FAUVELET
DE BOURRIENNE

1769–1834

Private Memoirs of Napoleon Bonaparte, during the periods of the Directory, the Consulate, and the Empire. 4 vols. London 1830. 8º.

Not located. *Parke Bernet Cat* 29 Jan 1952 lot 111: "Samuel T. Coleridge's copy with annotations and notes (some comprising several lines) in his autograph on over thirty pages. On the flyleaf is an eight-line note in his autograph, signed with initials; all in pencil." The catalogue prints one note from the flyleaf to Vol IV.

Bourrienne had been private secretary to Bonaparte, accompanying him to Egypt in 1799. He was later a diplomat and was involved in questionable financial transactions. After Waterloo he transferred his allegiance to the Bourbons. His *Memoirs* are not always reliable.

DATE. c Jul 1830. C's remarks on Bourrienne in the *TT* ms are dated 2 and 15 Jul 1830, and may include unacknowledged annotations from this copy.

1 IV flyleaf, pencil

Every so called Great Man is a measure of his age in the ratio of his accredited greatness. This is eminently true of Napoleon. The stupendous in Greatness! Merciful heaven! What must that age be for which this paltry Corsican could be great, stupendously Great?[1] S. T. C.

1[1] For C on Bourrienne as "the French Pepys" see *TT* 6 Jul 1830.

WILLIAM LISLE BOWLES
1762–1850

Sonnets, and other poems, &c. Fourth edition. Bath 1796. 8°.

Bound with one of the four known copies of C's "Sheet of Sonnets", a 16-page gathering that C put together "to bind up with Bowles's". *CL* I 252.

Victoria & Albert Museum (Dyce Collection)

This copy was presented by C to Mrs Thelwall on 18 Dec 1796, presumably with the "Sheet of Sonnets" already bound in.

Notes in an unidentified hand—presumably John Thelwall's—in ink on pp 28, 29, 30, 31, 32, 33, 36, 42, 43, 45, 46, 49, 50, 56, 57, 58, 60, 61, 62, 66; prosodic and other marks appear on pp 34, 35, 41, 44, 51, 59, 65, 67, 68, 70, 77, 80, 118, 119, 120, 121, 123, 124, 125.

In *BL* ch 1 C gave an account of how, when he had just turned seventeen, he made the overwhelming discovery of Bowles's sonnets "twenty in number, and just then published in a quarto pamphlet"; how his fellow Blue-coat T. F. Middleton, "my patron and protector", gave him a copy; and how C—too poor to buy copies—made "more than forty transcriptions" for his friends. *CL* I 29, 32; *BL* ch 1 (1907) I 8–15. (None of these transcripts has survived.) C sent Bowles a copy of his *Poems* (1797) and in Sept of that year went to Bremhill to seek his criticism. *CL* I 318, 327, 344. Even though Bowles accepted the ms of *Osorio* and persuaded Sheridan to write to C to discuss the possibility of staging the play, the visit was not a success. *CL* I 355–6, 385. For C the spell was broken in 1802: "I well remember", he told Sotheby in one of his brilliant early letters on the nature of poetry, "that . . . Southey observed to me, that you, I, & himself had all done ourselves harm by suffering our admiration of Bowles to bubble up too often on the surface of our Poems." *CL* II 855; cf 864. At Calne, until he took up residence in Highgate in 1816, C cultivated Bowles's acquaintance and received much kindness and encouragement from him and his friends in the theatre. But again, personal association was not a success, and Bowles's involvement in Tory church politics in 1817–18 became cause of serious tension between them. Yet in 1821 Bowles presented C with a copy of his *Two Letters to the Right Honorable Lord Byron*—memento of a futile literary quarrel between two men who had been influential in securing a public for C's work in the dark years 1814–15.

As further tribute to the effect of Bowles's *Sonnets* on young poets, WW told Samuel Rogers towards the end of his life that "When Bowles's sonnets first appeared, I bought them in a walk through London with my dear Brother who was afterwards drowned at sea. I read them as we went along, and to the great annoyance of my brother, I stopped in a niche of London Bridge to finish the pamphlet." Quoted in *W Life* (Moorman) I 125. WW was still reading Bowles's *Sonnets* aloud in 1836: see *CRB* II 480.

In addition to the inscribed copy of the *Sonnets* (1796), C owned a copy of the 1st ed (1789) and of *Elegiac Stanzas* (1796), and was lent or owned the *Poetical Works* Vol II (1801). Marginal notes in a copy of *The Spirit of Discovery* (Bath 1804) in Duke University Library are not in C's hand, but the book may have been his.

CONTENTS. Twenty-seven sonnets, and thirteen other pieces including *On the Death of Henry Headley* (which C "adapted" in BOOK OF COMMON PRAYER COPY A), *Monody Written at Matlock*, *Elegy Written at the Hotwells, Bristol, July 1789*, and *Abba Thule*. Of the fourteen sonnets that had comprised the 1st ed (Bath & London 1789), only the third was omitted from this collection; the others are printed in their original order, a new sonnet being placed between the original XIII and XIV.

DATE. 18 Dec 1796. On 17 Dec 1796 C had written to Thelwall: "... Item—(Shall I give it thee, Blasphemer? No. I won't—but) to thy Stella I do present the poems of my [Bowles] for a keep-sake." *CL* I 286.

1 p⁻²

Dear Mʳˢ Thelwall

I entreat your acceptance of this Volume, which has given me more pleasure, and done my heart more good, than all the other books, I ever read, excepting my Bible. Whether you approve or condenmmn my poetical taste, this Book will at least serve to remind you of your unseen, yet not the less sincere,

Friend
Sunday Morning

Samuel Taylor Coleridge
December the eighteenth
1796

HENDRIK BRENKMANN

1680–1736

LOST BOOK

Historia Pandectarum, seu fatum exemplaris Florentini. Accedit gemina dissertatio de Amalphi. 2 pts (in 1 vol). Utrecht 1722. 4⁰.

Not located; marginalia not recorded. Puttick and Simpson Sale 31 Jan 1907. *Lost List.*

Autograph notes by Coleridge in the margins.

EDWARD BREREWOOD

c 1565–1613

A Second Treatise of the Sabbath, or an explication of the fourth Commandement. Written, by Mr Edward Brerewood professor [of astronomy] in Gresham Colledge in London. Oxford 1632. 4º.

Bound as second with Richard BYFIELD *The Doctrine of the Sabbath.*

Pierpont Morgan Library

Annotations in ink in a seventeenth-century hand on pp 10, 11, 14, 16, +4.

Acquired by C c 12 Oct 1815: see BYFIELD headnote. When he returned borrowed copies of Sterne and Swift to Thomas Boosey on 25 Feb 1818, he sent this composite volume for Boosey to inspect, writing: "Brerewood's tract begins where I have put in the Slip of Paper". *CL* VI 1045.

For details of the controversy between Brerewood and Byfield see BYFIELD headnote.

DATE. Perhaps 1824–5: after the 1823 move to The Grove, Highgate. See BYFIELD DATE.

1 pp 4–6

The Lords resting on the seaventh day, is not the reason of the obligation, for that followes the decree of Gods pleasure onely; but onely of the election of the day, *viz*: the 7th; namely that for that cause it pleased him to exempt that day before any of the other, and charge it with a commandement of rest.

Q^y Is it not high time, that our Clergy should give to these words "rested the 7th day" a sense compatible with the Idea of the Supreme Being, which they themselves teach their Congregations to form?— It does not seem to me impracticable or even very difficult—and I am persuaded that ~~of~~ one of the distinguishing perfections of the Hebrew Scriptures is the double Sense of the most important passages, and yet both senses in entire harmony—.[1] How indeed otherwise could the same Scriptures have been intelligible to ~~one~~ the Childhood of the Human Race, and yet remain a Light answering

1[1] Cf BOOK OF COMMON PRAYER COPY B **25**.

Light to an Age of Science & Philosophy?[2] I am no advocate for *inventing* senses. No!—The Divine Acts are popularly expressed by the emotions & appearances, with which such Acts would have associated in human Agents—Still there is an *analogy* of the lower to the Higher, which enables the Lower to be used as *Symbols* of the Higher and this *Analogy* must be shewn, and not only the truths thus symbolized be displayed, but the Scripture Words proved to be fit and appropriate *Symbols*.[3] The three first Chapters of Genesis are instances throughout. Even the Cabbala is not *all* nonsense & mummery—in its present state it is the maggoty Corse of a defunct Science & Philosophy; but here & there a *Feature* is still discernible.[4] S. T. C.—

2 p 18, marked with a line in the margin

Christ gave no such commandement to his Apostles, for neither is any remembrance found of it in the histories of his life and doctrine, the Gospels; nor record of any such Commandement in the writings of the Apostles given or to bee given by Christ, or by his appointment to the Church, or to the Apostles.

[1][2] From the time of the Bristol lectures of 1795 C often referred to the Jewish dispensation as "the Childhood of the Human Race". See *Lects 1795* (*CC*) 113, 115, and see the similar view quoted from Estlin's *Evidences* in 116 n 1 (probably written by C): "... in the history of mankind at large, perhaps the patriarchal age may be considered as the infancy; the Jewish as the childhood; the Christian as the youth; and the final prevalence of Christianity, as the mature age of the world".

[1][3] Cf "Hard to express that sense of the analogy or likeness of a Thing which enables a Symbol to represent it, so that we think of the Thing itself—& yet knowing that the Thing is not present to us." *CN* II 2274. See also *CN* II 2319, 2320, and BOOK OF COMMON PRAYER COPY B 6 n 2, **29** at n 10.

[1][4] C's acquaintance with the Cabbala was probably from Eichhorn and other commentaries. The Cabbala, as an esoteric method of interpreting the Old Testament, could be expected to interest C sooner or later because of its suspected links with Heraclitus and Pythagoras and the Greek mystery religions, and for its discernible connexions with Christianity, Neoplatonism, and the theosophic tradition that passed through Paracelsus and Reuchlin to Böhme and Swedenborg. For C's rejection of the view that the Cabbala was a mediaeval compilation and his assertion of a view common in his day that its origin was much earlier, see *P Lects* Lect 10 (1949) 299–300 and 444 n 21. After his meeting with Hyman Hurwitz in 1816 (see BOOK OF COMMON PRAYER **25** n 2) his grasp of Hebrew doctrine and documents became much more secure, not only because of his increasing command of Hebrew but also because of his desire to find definable resonances in Greek, Hebrew, and Christian thought. Green's library included a copy of *Kabbala denudata seu doctrina Hebraeorum transcendentalis, et metaphysica atque theologica...* tr C. K. von Rosenroth (4 vols in 2 Salzburg 1677–8): *Green SC* (1880) 548.

For if it be said that Christ commanded it to the Apostles, although the Commandement be not mentioned.

1 An uncertaintie is affirmed which cannot bee proved, and Christ belied for any thing that appeareth.

§. Here begins the truly valuable portion of this Treatise. The preceding Comment, is so little capable of any practical application to Christians of these times, that it is a sufficient Objection to it, that it is at least a *disputable* Truth, if Truth—and ~~tho'~~ granting it to be true, yet for the former reason not worth the controversy, it is calculated to provoke. S. T. C.

3 p 39, pencil

There is a threefold Sabbath, 1 *Externall*, of the body from servile worke. 2 *Internall*, of the soule from sinne, from the *guilt* of sinne, freed from damnation; from the *Crime* of sinne freed from disobedience, by the merit and grace of Christ. 3 *Aeternall*, from both labour and sinne, and all the paines and passions of this life. The first was the Sabbath of the *Law*. The second of *Grace*. and the third of *Glory*.

ad fin[em]^{a1}

Annex

Five passages, marked with a pencil line in the margin in the same way as **2** textus and apparently in the same pencil as **3**, were probably marked by C.

(*a*) **1A**   p 7

Touching sanctifying of the Sabbath; The duty in generall of sanctifying it, is commanded by God: But the particular manner of sanctifying it, is not prescribed by him, but the Church; The act is Gods ordinance; The particular manner and limitation of the act touching time, place, order, is the Churches decree; The thing it self, or matter, is of divine constitution, but the manner and circumstances of that sanctification were left to the determination of the Church.

---

a Letters supplied by the editor

3[1] "Up to the end"—i.e. from p 39 to the end of this section of the argument. See p 40: "The prescription of one day in seven is but an *Imitation* of the like prescribed to the Iewes, not a divine commandement. I say, but the imitation of a divine Commandement. But yet the commandement that it imitateth, and whence it hath warrant and direction, being but ceremoniall, the imitating Commandement cannot be Morall." For a general comment on the whole tract see BYFIELD **1** PS.

(b) **1B** p 9

The word (*Thou*) importeth every Freeman, or every man as farre as he is free, and hath power to keepe it, or to dispose of himselfe. For some are free *simply*, who by their condition are so; others *Limitedly*, as servants may be by their Masters permission; namely, so farre as the disposition of themselves, or their owne actions is allowed them. In which case only Servants come under the obligation of the commandement, but yet that is not as servants, but as in some sort free, namely as they are primary authors themselves of their owne workes, and not as Ministers of their Masters worke.

(c) **2A** p 19

The Lords day seemes to bee celebrated in the Church rather by *Imitation* of the Apostles, then their *Constitution*; for we finde their example for holy assemblies on that day, but Commandement of theirs given to the Church for celebrating that day, we finde none.

(d) **2B** pp 35–6

The celebration of the Lords day had for occasion. 1. The resurrection of our Saviour that day: 2 The example of his Apostles: 3 The custome of the Church freely imitating (without Precept) that Example, who yet solemnized it not in stead of the old Sabbath, but together with it; as yet is usuall in *Aethiopia* and *Syria*; And all this while it was observed, not of necessarie obligation, or iniunction (for any thing that appeareth) but of voluntary devotion. But at last it obtained obligation by the Institution of Princes, and Synods of the Church; The first Emperour that commanded it was *Constantine the Great*... The Synode that decreed it was the Councell of *Laodicea*... *Anno Christi* 364.

The Apostles *Examples* of assembling to divine service on the Lords day, enforce no *Commandement* on the Church to doe the like (else by their example we are also to keepe the *Iewish* Sabbath) because examples have not the force of *Lawes*, which all men ought to keepe, but of *Counsells* only and perswasions, not amisse to be followed of them whose case is alike.

(e) **2C** p 38

Ob: There cannot be so many reasons for the celebrating of any other day, as the Lords day, 1. Creation of the world. 2. Nativity. 3. The Resurrection of Christ. 4. Descent of the Holy Ghost, &c. Therefore the Church could not have dedicated another day.

Sol: The argument is denied: because though these are good reasons for the *Election* of the day, why the Church should encline to make choice of that day before any other, yet not sufficient for *obligation*, to binde them to observe that, and exclude all other, for the Church notwithstanding these reasons, might have dedicated another day to that solemnity without breaking any Commandement of God.

HENRY BROOKE
c 1703–1783

The Fool of Quality; or, The History of Henry Earl of Moreland. . . .
A new edition, greatly altered and improved. 4 vols. London 1796.
12º.

Henry E. Huntington Library

Label pasted on I ⁻2: "H. E. Savage Library Highgate".

Seven footnotes or insertions into C's notes are written in pencil in an
unidentified hand; and in the same hand sixteen substantive notes on the
text, three queries, and one correction of a typographical error; these are
mostly in Vol III. Some 117 pages in all 4 vols are marked with sidelines,
underlinings, ticks, fists, and slashes; a few of these may be C's but they
are impossible to identify.

DATE. c Aug–Oct 1830, on the evidence of two detailed references in notebooks of Aug and Oct 1830 in N 44 and N 47: see **17** n 5 and **14** n 5, below.
An expanded version of **24** that may be as early as 20 Jun 1827 was
printed by HNC from an unidentified source: see ANNEX.

1 I xiii–xvi, pencil | Dedication "To the Right Respectable My ancient and well-
beloved Patron the Public"

[The Dedication opens:] "Why don't you dedicate to Mr. PITT?"
Because, Sir, I would rather set forth my own talents, than the
virtues and praises of the best man upon earth. I love to say things
that no one else ever thought of, extraordinary, quite out of the
common way. I scorn to echo the voice of every fellow that goes the
road. [Pp xiii–xvi are taken up with a fable, introduced with the
words:] . . . it was the custom of all the seers and sages, of ancient
days, to introduce truth and wisdom under the covering of fable;
and this covering was as a nut-shell; if your teeth were able to crack
it, you had the kernel for your pains. Permit me then, at least, to
imitate their manner; for, though the matter should happen to drop
by the way, the first traveller who takes it up may be bettered thereby.

An exquisite Composition is this "Dedication"—to the genius of
Swift it adds a moral geniality, a *richness* of Heart—But O! how
deceitful is the Heart in the best of us! Thro' the whole of this enchanting Day-dream Novel, the imagination, & of and the con-

722

sequent Craving for, Wealth, are fed, yea, *crammed* even to glut-
tony! The Herosoes of the Story are all rich as Crœsus/ Mr Fenton
a magnified Rothchild, all the Barings in *one*/[1] only so very good, so
very very afflicted!—But what of all this—we offer an atoning smile
of assent to our disapproving REASON, then turn to the Book &
"love it all the better."[2] *S. T. C.*

2   ɪ 43–4, pencil | Ch 1

On a summer's day as he . . . rambled into a park whose gate he
saw open . . .

—the gate of which
   Mem. "whose" is the *personal* Genitive, a valuable privilege of
our language, which it is now almost a fashion to violate, thus
giving to our prose the appearance of *flat* poetry. Miss S. *whose*
name is Susan read this Book, the Name *of which* is the *Fool of Q.*
Now too many of our modern Scribes would have written "her Book,
whose name["]—a vile affectation.[1] *S. T. C.*

3   ɪ 46, pencil | Ch 2

The language of true love is understood by all creatures, and was
*] that of which Harry had, almost, the only perception.

* ⟨read⟩—and was almost the only language of which Harry had a
full perception.

4   ɪ 100–1, concluded on ɪ +1–+2 | Ch 4

Large societies of men, nay mighty nations, may and have been
merchants. When societies incorporate for such a worthy purpose,
they are formed as a foetus within the womb of the mother, a constitution within the general state or constitution; their particular
laws and regulations ought, always, to be conformable to those of
the national system; and, in that case, such corporations greatly

1[1] Nathan Meyer Rothschild (1777–1836), financier and merchant, was born in Frankfurt-am-Main, was naturalised in 1804, and in 1805 established in London a branch of his inherited banking and mercantile business. Famous for the scope and skill of his financial transactions, he became banker for many European countries and was agent for the English government in the Peninsular War. Seven members of the Baring family, eminent statesmen and financiers, are noted in *DNB*.

1[2] Cf Fragment 48: "No matter for that! quoth S. T. C., | I love him the better therefore." *PW* (EHC) ɪɪ 1009.

2[1] See also **6A** and **7**, below, and cf *CL* vɪ 787 (c Mar 1829) to HNC.

conduce to the peace and good order of cities and large towns, and to the general power and prosperity of the nation.

In the infancy of Commerce these chartered Bodies Corporate were not only useful but perhaps necessary. So only could the power of Capital be called into action, & experience be rendered progressive. But in the adult age of Commerce these Monopolies are dead weights. The general Rule is against them—if in any case a chartered Monopoly is defensible, it must be defended as an *exception* and the Defenders have the onus probandi,[1] that it is an exception.[a]

Thus the Assailants of the E. India Company need only say—Monopolies are in the rule evils.

The E. India Company is a Monopoly—unless therefore you can shew, that it forms an exception to the Rule, the Conclusion is—Ergo, the E. India Company is an Evil.—[2]

It does not lie on us to shew the evils of the E. India Company—we may know of none ~~still~~ but we are entitled a priori to conclude it to be such.—The Defender on the other hand is bound to demonstrate the particular *good* & that it is an overbalance to the General Evil—or the particular evils that would follow from the suppression of the Monopoly & that they are greater than the good that would follow from opening the trade—or both, if he can.

My own opinion is that the strength of the East India House Cause rests mainly on the latter position—namely, the danger to the Constitution from the vast ~~increase~~ accession to the already enormous patronage of the Crown.

5   ı 172–3, pencil | Ch 5

Within a fortnight after this, Mr. James, the house-steward, furnished a large lumber-room with ~~thousands of~~ coats, out-coats, shirts, waist-coats, breeches, stockings, and shoes, of different sorts and sizes, but all of warm and clean, though homely materials.

Brook was a man of true Genius; but it would have conduced in no

---

a The note having reached the foot of ı 101, C wrote: "See *blank Leaf*", and at the head of ı⁺1: "Conclusion of MSS. note p. 101"

4[1] "Burden of proof".

4[2] Monopoly in the Indian trade was officially ended in 1813 by Lord Liverpool's Bill, which gave to the Board of Control set up by Pitt in 1784 authority over the East India Company's commercial transactions. See *C&S* (*CC*) 91–4. Earl Grey's Act of 1833 finally deprived the East India Company of its monopoly in trade with China. C could have had plenty of information about the East India Company from Charles Lamb, who served as a clerk in the India House from 1792 until he retired, and for a time from JW and the elder Capt John Wordsworth, both of whom were shipmasters in the East India trade.

trifling degree to the improvement of this work if he had borne in mind the wise adage of old Hesiod πλεον ημιου παντος, i.e. Half is not seldom more than the whole.[1]—Here, for instance, the words, "thousands of" might have advantageously [been][a] omitted.—In Vol. IV. the mondalis odi[2] *presses.*

6 I 180–1

Away flew Harry, like feathered Mercury, on his Godlike errand. Forth issued Mr. James, Frank, and Andrew; and last came Mrs. Hannah, with the house-maid and cordials.

This is Brooke's characteristic fault—a *too-muchness*—an over-heated hyperbolism in his phrases—surely, "*Humane* or compassionate Errand" was the utmost that such a service required.[1]

6A I 185 | Ch 6

On the departure of Vindex, though Ned's drollery was dismayed, his resentment was, by no means, eradicated: for the principle of Ned was wholly agreeable to the motto of a very noble escutcheon; and *Nemo me impune lacessit,* was a maxim the of whose impropriety of which not Saint Anthony, himself, could persuade him.

7 I 185–6

Full against the portal that opened upon the school-room, there *] stood an ancient and elevated chair, whose form was sufficiently expressive of its importance.

* This might, perhaps, have been justified, as a playful Personification of the Majestic Chair—but that the frequency of this vile confusion of the personal with the neuter Genetive, whose for "of which" deprives the Writer of this plea. It is a gross, tho' a spreading, Solecism that disfigures the style of some of our ablest Contemporaries—ex. gr. Scott, and Southey. The Ed. Review swarms with instances.[1]

---

[a] Word supplied by the editor

5[1] Hesiod *Works and Days* 40. C had noted this phrase in Apr 1804 (*CN* II 2003); he used it again e.g. in G. BURNET *Life of Bedell* 11 and in *CL* VI 736 (28 Apr 1828). Hesiod was not a particular favourite of C's, but WW's library included a copy of Hesiod's *Works* (Cambridge 1672) with the autograph initials "S. T. C. + W. W.".

For a general comment on Hesiod see *TT* 11 Aug 1832.

5[2] "Dislike of the commonplace". C may have in mind *mundialis odi*— "I hate what is of this world".

6[1] *OED* records "too-muchness" first in 1875. The second annotator added a comment on Brooke in pencil on p 181.

7[1] See 2 n 1, above.

8 I 208–9

[How "some parents and preceptors" use upon children "the motive of what they call emulation".] Now, though envy and emulation are often confounded, in terms; there are not two things more different, both in respect to their object, and in respect to their operation: the object of envy is the person, and not the excellence, of any one; but the object of emulation is excellence alone; as when CHRIST, exciting us to be emulous of the excellence of God himself, bids us be perfect, as our father which is in heaven is perfect: the operation of envy is to pull others down; but the act of emulation is to exalt ourselves to some eminence or height proposed: the eyes of envy are sore and sickly, and hate to look at the light; but emulation has the eye of an eagle, and soars, while it gazes in the face of the sun.

There is doubtless a wide difference between Envy and Emulation— the latter consisting in a desire to obtain equal excellence with another by exerting the same means, and without any wish to deprive the other of ~~that~~ his excellence, and without any pain in the contemplation of it. Yet notwithstanding this, I remember that the noblest minds at our school needed no such stimulus—Sympathy performed its office far better.[1]

9 II 28–9 | Ch 8

Here Mr. Longfield paused; and the judge cried out, Clerk, hand me up the examination of this prevaricator. This his lordship perused with a countenance and scrutiny, apparently inveterate. But, finding that the deponent had not touched upon the robbery, and that neither the words, *feloniously*, nor *of malice*, were inserted in that part that referred to the death of lord Stivers, he tore the examination into twenty pieces. Come, come, he cried, again, I have not yet done with this same Longfield. I perceive perfectly well, how he came by the watch and snuff-box. The transference was not difficult, from the prisoner, who stole them, to this her confederate. But, tell us, my wonderfully honest friend! how came you to keep these things

---

[1] An unusual observation about his own school experience, but central to his theory of education. A passage on p 207 has been marked in the margin in pencil, possibly by C: "Fear never was a friend to the love of God or man, to duty or conscience, truth, probity, or honour. It, therefore, can never make a good subject, a good citizen, or a good soldier; and least of all, a good Christian; except the devils, who believe and tremble, are to be accounted good christians."

from their lawful owners, for the very long space of twelve months and upwards? Why did you not, immediately, or long before now, give informations against those, whom you so suddenly take it into your head to accuse? And, why would you suffer that so exceeding chaste, and innocent lady, to labour, all this time, under the infamy with which her character, in my judgment, is still justly loaded?

To all these questions, Mr Longfield barely smiled; but bowing with his head, and making a motion with his hand to two gentlemen ... Mr. Archibald ... got up and spoke ...

The effect of such delineations as this of the Judge is dangerous in the present state of the popular mind—but it must be remembered in H. Brooke's justification that Chief Justice Page & others gave too great occasion for such portraits, & were infamous for their abusive browbeating Language on the Bench—& for their shameless partiality where the Government or the Aristocracy was concerned.[1] S. T. C.

10   II 121, pencil | Ch 11

Your story, cried Mr. Fenton ... reminds me of an observation made by Harry the IVth of France, that is equally pertinent to the subject. [Follows a long anecdote of the king sending for an old judge, much honoured for his wisdom and justice, and asking him to tell him "by what measures you have been enabled to content all parties". The Judge, after hearing all the evidence, would withdraw and settle the question by a throw of the dice. He argues learnedly for the justice of this procedure.]

It is not often, that Brook makes any story worse by his way of telling it: this however is an exception. But in this he had a mighty rival—Rabelais, the original Relator/[1]

11   II 232–3, pencil | Ch 13 "Story of the Hon. Mr. Clinton"

The world, my lovely cousin, the world is to man, as his temper or complexion. The mind constitutes its own prosperity and adversity: winter presents no cloud to a cheerful spirit, neither can summer find sunshine for the spirit that is in a state of dejection. In my youth,

---

[9][1] Sir Francis Page (c 1661–1741), not chief justice but judge of the King's Bench from 1727, was known as "the hanging judge" and was notorious for the partiality he showed to the rich. He is noticed with contempt by Pope, Fielding, Johnson, and others.

[10][1] The story appears at III 69–94 (chs 39–42) of the Gillman copy that C annotated—apparently 4 vols 1807.

every object presented me with happiness; but alas, the time came, when the universe appeared as a vault wherein joy was entombed. and the sun himself but as a lamp that served to shew the gloom and the horrors around me.

Exquisite alike in thought and expression! And yet this work, worthy of being placed on the next Shelf to our Shakespear, Spenser, Milton is only known and spoken of [as]*a* a Child's Book!—

12   iii 3 | Ch 14

A number of external successes, also, assisted to persuade us, in those days, that felicity was to be attained and ascertained upon earth. The regency of Cromwell* was administered with the strictest justice at home, while, at the same time, it became revered and formidable abroad, and extended its influence to regions the most remote.

* Alas! and to what a Wretch did the bigotry & intolerant Spirit of the Presbyterians sacrifice their own & the Nation's *Power & Freedom*![1]

13   iii 5

. . . for every kind of passion is unquestionably a kind of suffering . . .

a remark equally profound and beautiful. *S. T. C.*

14   iii 19–25

[When Matilda Golding is dying, she speaks to her husband:] I love you no longer, my Harry, she cried; I love you no longer. Your rival, at length, has conquered, I am the bride of another. And yet I love you in a measure, since in you I love all that is him, or that is his; and that I think is much, a great deal, indeed, of all that is lovely. O, my dear, my sweet, mine only enemy, as I may say! riches were nothing unto me, pleasures were nothing unto me, the world was nothing with me! . . . You, and you only, Harry, stood

a Word supplied by the editor

12[1] The injudicious excesses of the Presbyterian faction within the Church of England during the Commonwealth provide a continuous theme in BAXTER *Reliquiae* and in the marginalia on other books that deal with the political and ecclesiastical history of the period.

The second annotator added a comment in pencil: "Very little Freedom Charles had left them to sacrifice & as to national fervor, that was greater under Cromwell than under any other Jacobite Stuart family".

between me and my heaven, between me and my God. Long, and often, and vainly, have I strove and struggled against you; but my bridegroom, at length, is become jealous of you; my true owner calls me from you, and takes me all to himself!

Now this tho' a very common, indeed only not a universal, ~~Error~~ opinion among strict Religionists, appears to me a gross and even a dangerous Error—and not only without any authority in Scripture, but in the face of Scripture. If (said our divine Redeemer) ye love not your earthly Parents, when[a] ye love your heavenly Father whom Ye have not seen.[1] The true head and base, the foundation and the pinnacle of a right and truly evangelical Spirit is to love God in all things that are lovely, in order finally to love all Good things in God. I reverence the wise man, and in that wise man I revere the Father of Lights,[2] the Giver of all Wisdom—I offer my affectionate services and sympathies to a suffering fellow-christian—and my Saviour, who dwelleth in all his Elect, assures me that he himself is included in the kindness shewn to my suffering Brothers: The divine attributes shining thro' the Creatures & Works of the Invisible Creator are called in Scripture his Names[3]—And this is one & a most sublime Sense of the two first clauses of the Lords Prayer—Our Father, who art (for us in our present veil of flesh) in Heaven, who art where ever true Being is, but who especially *art*, where Spirits made perfect[4] have immediate vision of thy presence, and in this intuition have a Heaven, and beatitude past utterance!—Hallowed be thy *Name*—every name of thine, every mark and symbol in which thy Wisdom and almighty Love shine thro' for our dim eyes; but above all, hallowed be that Name which thou above all thy Names hast glorified even with thy own essential Godhead, the Name, Jesus, the *Word* Coeternal—&c[5]

15 III 113, pencil

He has given me a little money to dispose of . . . among the confined debtors . . . if you give me the sum of your debts . . . he will

[a] For "how can"?

14[1] 1 John 4.20: "...for he that loveth not his brother whom he hath seen, how can he love God whom he hath not seen?"

14[2] James 1.17.

14[3] See also BAXTER *Catholick Theologie* **10** n 3 and **14** n 2, and BOOK OF COMMON PRAYER **12** n 2.

14[4] Cf Heb 12.23.

14[5] The second annotator added in pencil: "When Jesus told us to say 'Hallowed be thy name'—did he mean his own? 'Why called thou *me* good?' was his modest & humble question—". In N 47 ff 2ᵛ–5 C wrote a reflective and expanded version of **14**, opening: "1 October 1830. Friday Night. Fool of Quality, Vol. 3. p. 19." and quoting the central part of **14** textus.

set you clear in the world. . . . Then, turning * toward me, Can you guess . . . what you undertake to do for me? I question if the charities of this Nation would be sufficient . . . to effect my deliverance.

* And ~~they~~ this, it appears, was only 700£.—One instance among scores of Brooke's hyperbolic infirmity.[1]

16   III 142–3 | Ch 17

[Ned is restored to his rightful parents, and Mrs Fielding confesses her feigned deafness.] But you look so altogether the gentleman and the kind-hearted Christian, that I think I ought to have no reserve of any kind toward you.

an inadequate excuse, I must say, for an imposture played by a newly regenerate Saint—a trick of the old trade not to mention the difficulty of Ned's presence—How could she avoid recognizing him?[1] And if she did, knowing him of course to be her Brother's child, how or why should or could she suppress her delight—but as relieving the load of guilt from her mind, and removing the main obstacles of her Brothers forgiveness? But this is cold Criticis⟨u⟩m. The F. of Q. must be read as it was composed—i.e. as a delightful Dream![2] S.T.C.

17   III 198–202

Pray Mr. Peter, were you never angry? Scarce ever, Sir, that I remember; at least on my own account; for I do not fear any man that steps upon the earth, and what is it then that should make me angry? A man may be angry, said Mr. Clement, from other motives sure, besides that of fear. God himself can be angry, and yet he cannot possibly fear.

I am feelingly assured, Sir, replied the valiant Peter, that God was never angry in his whole life . . .

This is a problem not of so easy solution, as the amiable Writer, whose religious views were those of Jacob Behmen, appears to have considered it. He takes for granted that anger *always* supposes *fear*; but this is not true.[1] There is a holy Anger, excited by the contempla-

15[1] See **5** and **6**, above.

16[1] The second annotator underlined the question and added: "five or six years had *past*".

16[2] See **1**, above—"this enchanting Day-dream Novel".

17[1] But C recognised that fear has a close nexus with *human* anger: see *CN* I 979; cf *BL* ch 2 (1907) I 19–20, *CN* II 2441. See also *CL* II 863 and *BL* ch 4 (1907) I 52.

tion of a Will freely determining itself to Evil,[2] and an ingrate & rebel Hate of the Good & the Giver of all Good;[a] ~~which~~ & this Anger so far from implying *precludeth* Fear, even in *men*—as in many of the old Christian Martyrs. Such Anger is a perfection of our Nature—& a feature in the Image of God.[3] Why then is it incredible that in a transcendent form it should be affirmable of God—in a form as transcendent to that in which it exists in the best of Men, as the divine Love transcends any Love, we can feel! And yet essentially Love must be Love, even as Truth is Truth. Were it otherwise all the attributes of God would become mere articulated sounds, not meaning what the *words* ⟨in all other instances⟩ mean, and without any other meaning, that we know of. Besides every ~~argument~~ ground, on which the Author asserts *Anger* to be incompatible with God, would apply with equal if not greater force to Pity, Mercy, Justice—I have said, that Brooke was a Behmenist—but in this respect, he has only skimmed the Cream and Sweetmeats of Behmen's System—Jacob himself entertained far other and profounder views on this point.[4] S. T. Coleridge[5]

18 III 213

Self is a poor, dark, and miserable avariciousness, incapable of enjoying what it hath, through its grappling and grasping at what it hath not ... But is it not, Sir, a very terrible thing, said Harry, for poor creatures, to be evil, by the necessity of their nature?

*] You mistake this matter, my Harry; you take the emptiness, darkness, and desire, in the creature, to be the evil of the creature. They are, indeed, the only possible cause of evil, in or to any creature; but they are exceedingly far from being an evil, in themselves;

---

a The annotator of C's notes has underlined "determining...Giver of all Good"

17[2] The second annotator placed a cross beside C's word "Evil" and added in ink: "Surely such a Will or Determination, bent upon its own misery, is an object of compassion, not of anger, even amongst men—how much more so in the eyes of God! A bad man is the most pitiable of all earthly objects—".

17[3] Cf "God by *Anger* drove out Polytheism/ This very important/". *CN* I 1417.

17[4] See e.g. BÖHME **54, 55** textus.

17[5] On 19 Aug 1830 C noted that he had seen "the necessity of asserting a double Will" and referred as example to "the exquisite passage in Brooke's 'Fool of Quality' in the discourse of Fenton & Harry after his Affair with the E. of Mansfield's Son/ a passage that deserves to [be] made a part of the Catechism for every Boy or Girl, from 12 to 15". N 44 f 68ᵛ. The reference seems to be to III 210ff.

they are, on the contrary, the only, the necessary and indispensible foundation, whereon any creaturely benefit can be built. ...

* No! Harry did *not* mistake; but the Author had not penetrated to the depth of the Mystery: tho' his Master, Jacob Behmen, had a glimmering & confused view of it.[1]

19 iii 224–5

Other states ... have been compounded, like ours, of princes, peers, and people, the one, few, and many united. But the error and failure *] of their constitution was this: The People, who are the Fountain of all Power, either retained, in their own hands, an Authority they were never qualified to wield; or deputed it to trustees without account ...

* This is either a barren Truism, or a very teeming Fallacy, according as the words are understood. The first, if physical Power be meant; the second, if the Right to demand obedience—i.e. Moral Power[1]

20 iv 3–7 | Ch 18

[Harry replies to a question put to him by Lord Portland:] To be serious then, said Harry, my father thinks, in the first place, (for I have no manner of skill in such matters) he thinks, I say, that his Majesty is one of the greatest warriors and one of the wisest statesmen *] that ever existed. He thinks, however, that he has attachments and views that look something further than the mere interests of the people by whom he has been elected; but he says that those views ought, in a measure, to be indulged, in return of the very great benefits that he has done us. He is, therefore, grieved to find, that his majesty has met with so much reluctance and coldness from a nation so much obliged.

* A common objection to W. IIIrd even among the Whigs; but in fact, it was one of that great & good man's excellencies, that he saw distinctly, that Great Britain must owe her elevation to, and preservation in, the first rank of nations, yea and as the primus inter primatos,[1] to her commercial, manufactory, and colonial superiority —and that such a nation, rather such an *empire*, could not have a

18[1] See esp Böhme 111.
19[1] In the margin of iii 225 the second annotator wrote: "In whom can the *right* to demand obedience by & for the benefit of the whole body—If

not here, where will you find it except in the divine Right of Kings—and we have not got to *that* yet—".
20[1] "First among the foremost".

separate interest from that of the great European Commonwealth of Nations—that the maintenance of Continental Protestantism, and the full independence & vigor of North Europe, in counterpoise of France always & in antagonism to despotic R. Catholic France, was a vital interest of G. Britain.[2] This the tory semi-jacobite high church Squire Westerns[3] of the Day were too stupid to see, and this even the Whigs, for the greater part, understood but partially. William's, not fault, but deficiency & misfortune, was that he was ~~en~~ not endowed with the power of communicating his superior wisdom to others persuasively, & in a way appropriate to to the genius & character of the English of that Age.—But he was a truly great & good Man.[4]

21 IV 69, pencil

... Lucifer and Adam, were ... represented by the two thieves who suffered in company with Christ ... [One accepted Christ's mercy;] the other rejected the Christ with contempt ... [yet after many ages] may be compelled to cry out, O seed of the woman! heal, heal the head thou hast crushed, and admit me also, though last, to some part, the least position of thy pardoning salvation!

Good!—

22 IV 79–81, pencil

But I shall only dwell a minute on three principal articles, first, that Messiah was to be God—secondly, that he was however to be a suffering Messiah—and thirdly, that he was to give himself to death for the salvation of sinners.

FIRST. With respect to his divinity, Daniel says: "I saw in the night visions, and behold, one like unto the SON of MAN came with the clouds of Heaven, and came to the ANCIENT OF DAYS, and they brought him near before him. And there was given him DOMINION, and GLORY, and a KINGDOM, that all people, nations, and languages should serve him; his DOMINION is an EVERLASTING DOMINION, which shall not pass away."

Sad should I be, were there no other & better proofs of the Eternity

20[2] One of the strongest statements of the political grounds for C's objection to immediate Catholic Emancipation.

20[3] Tom Jones's adoptive father in Fielding's novel.

20[4] William III (1650–1702) reigned jointly with Queen Mary from 1689 to 1694. She was the heir to the throne; he was always the admired liberal foreigner.

& Divinity of the Mediator, the Son of God incarnate in Christ Jesus, than this passage of a suspected Book![1]—& the texts from Isaiah, the truly evengelical Prophet, & of the authenticity of which there can be no rational doubt, is applied to our blessed Lord only by rhetorical accomodation.[2] But why, in the name of Common Sense, should a Christian look further than to the writings of John and Paul? In these the Divinity of Christ is the very ground and object of all their reasoning—it is asserted or implied in every chapter.[3]

23 IV 127–8, pencil

It is not, my lord, to the mourners for sin, alone, to whom comfort is promised: the state of suffering and mourning is in its nature extremely salutary, and of happy tendency to man; and it is, therfore, that the suffering JESUS hath pronounced it blessed.

The God of all love takes no delight in the sufferings of his poor and pitiable creatures; neither would he have made this state of our mortality a vale of tears and a state of misery, had it not been in order to conduct us through transitory evils to ever enduring bliss, where "he himself will wipe all tears from our eyes."

If the "nosce te ipsum,"[1] if self-knowlege be, as it is, the ground of all true & profitable knowlege, then whatever draws us inward upon our own Spirits, cannot but be salutary. Now this is the effect of Suffering & Sorrow, as long as they do not exceed the degree that permits the exercise of thought and reflection. S. T. C.

24 IV 130–1, pencil

It is no way evident to me, my lord, that body, or at least such gross bodies as we now have, are necessary to the perceptions and sensibilities of our spirit. God himself is a spirit. . . . Wherefore, as our spirits are the offsprings of his divine spirit, we may justly presume

22[1] The passage quoted by Brooke is Dan 7.13–14, a text commented on in BIBLE COPY B 71 and n 1. C doubted the authenticity of chs 1–6 but was convinced of the importance of the rest: see e.g. *TT* 6 Jan 1823, 13 Apr 1830, and *CL* VI 568–9.
22[2] Isa 53.1–9, quoted by Brooke at pp 80–1.
22[3] The second annotator added in pencil: "S. T. C. is bold—to dispute

the texts from Daniel & Isaiah will seal his condemnation as effectually in the Eyes of the thorough Saint, as probably in S. T. C.'s Eyes that of the sceptic is sealed who doubts of John & Paul".
23[1] "Nosce te ipsum"—the Latin version of the oracular precept γνῶθι σεαῦτον, "know thyself". For C's poem on this theme see *PW* (EHC) I 487. Cf *BL* ch 12 (1907) I 173–4.

them endowed with like capacities. But, if body is necessary to the preception of spirit ... we may reasonably suppose that when our spirits shall be parted from these gross and frail bodies, they shall be instantly clothed upon with more pure and permanent bodies. Or, as I rather think, that those pure and permanent bodies are already forming and pregnant within our gross and corruptible bodies; and that when the midwife death shall deliver us from the dark womb of our woeful travail and mortality, we shall immediately spring forth into incorruption and glory.

Brooke should have asked himself, what he meant by the Body? The ponderable visible particles of the Carcase?[1] Or the organic & organific movements of the invisible Life? Music will produce symmetrical Figures in Sand—and the Sand is indispensable to the visibility of the Figures. But is the Sand the Music? the Tune? Every organic Body is a *Tune*, an Air or Scheme of Life.[2]

25 IV 149–51, pencil

O, said he, as he advanced, thou true house of mourning, thou silent end of all men, how sad art thou to sense! how sad to me above all, who bearest in thy dark bosom such precious and beloved relicks!

Then, casting himself on the coffins of my lady and lord Richard, as they lay side by side; and clasping his arms about them as far as he could reach; O, he cried, my mother, my brother, my dearest brother, my dearest mother! you are gone, you are gone from me, and you never knew the love that your son and brother had for you. Ah, how did I flatter myself, what happiness did I not propose, in attending, serving, and pleasing you; in doing thousands of tender, kindly and endearing offices about you! but you are snatched from me, my mother, you are snatched from me, my brother! all my prospects are defeated and cut away for ever! You will no more return to me, but I shall go to you; and O, that I were laid with you this minute in this still and peaceful mansion, where hopes and fears cease, and all are humbled together!

I cannot but think this unnatural.

Indeed, the constant attempt to represent the Uncle himself as

---

24[1] On the distinction between Body and Carcase see ANNEX, below. Cf AURELIUS **50** and n 1, and see the playful distinction between "*me myself me*" and "Carcase Coleridge" in *CL* II 761 (22 Sept 1801). See also ESCHEN-MAYER *Psychologie* (Stuttgart & Tübingen 1817) 104.

24[2] For life as "tune" see BÖHME **171** textus, and cf **13** and **64** textus.

"a man wholly made up of Sorrows & killing griefs"[1] is the most objectionable feature of the Work. It savors too rankly of Moravian *Maudlinism*—it has a sickly musky bergamot smell/.[2] This and the extravagant overloaded Flattery to Harry, even in his own presence, are the Disease of this otherwise most exquisite Work—Nevertheless, this latter fault is so far a true portrait of Life, that of all flattery the mutual flattery of *religious* professors is the most *intense*. Never shall I forget the Amoebean Eclogue between Miss Hannah More & an Evangelical Countess, which I heard during a Breakfast at Mrs More's![3]

26 IV 272, pencil

Father, Son, and Holy Spirit, will then become co-embodied in this divine body; they will be the repletion of it, they will operate all things by it.

This is not only transscriptural, but antiscriptural, I fear.[1] Far, far too visual, too sensuously visual

Annex

As part of Lecture 12 of the Jan-Mar 1818 Literary Lectures HNC printed "Note on a Passage in the Life of Henry Earl of Morland. 20th June, 1827":*LR* I 214–16. The ms source of the note has not been identified. The note evidently refers to IV 130–1, i.e. **24** textus.

25[1] This grotesque parody of the figure of Messiah (Isa 53.3) is at IV 137.

25[2] See George LAVINGTON *The Moravians Compared and Detected*; cf *CN* II 2103, III 4169 and n. See also *LS* (*CC*) 184 n 3. "Moravians", the name commonly ascribed to that sector of the Protestant Church originally called the Bohemian Brethren and, after their "renewal" by Zinzendorf in 1722, the Moravian Brethren, were closely associated with the Lutheran Church; they have generally stood for a simple and unworldly form of Christianity.

25[3] Amoebaean—alternately answering, as e.g. in Virgil's *Eclogue* 3. See *Friend* (*CC*) I 417. Hannah More (1745–1833), author and evangelical blue-stocking, lived in and about Bristol most of her life, engaged in works of pious education and charitable improvement, and toward the end of her life was closely connected with the Clapham Sect. C told Cottle in May 1814 that he had "seen & conversed with" her and thought her "indisputably the *first* literary female, I ever met with—In part, no doubt, because she is a Christian". *CL* III 499–500. Cottle was also introduced to her but was so offended by her neglect of him in the company of persons of title that he never called on her again. C knew her *Strictures on the Modern System of Female Education* (1806) and her successful novel *Coelebs in Search of a Wife* (1809).

26[1] *OED* does not record this sense of "transcriptural". "Antiscriptural", however, is a seventeenth-century word.

The defect of this and all similar theories that I am acquainted with, or rather, let me say, the desideratum, is the neglect of a previous definition of the term "body." What do you mean by it? The immediate grounds of a man's size, visibility, tangibility, &c?—But these are in a continual flux even as a column of smoke. The material particles of carbon, nitrogen, oxygen, hydrogen, lime, phosphorus, sulphur, soda, iron, that constitute the ponderable organism in May, 1827, at the moment of Pollio's death in his 70th year, have no better claim to be called his "body," than the numerical particles of the same names that constituted the ponderable mass in May, 1787, in Pollio's prime of manhood in his 30th year;—the latter no less than the former go into the grave, that is, suffer dissolution, the one in a series, the other simultaneously. The result to the particles is precisely the same in both, and of both therefore we must say with holy Paul,—"*Thou fool! that which thou sowest, thou sowest not that body that shall be,*"[1] &c. Neither this nor that is the body that abideth. Abideth, I say; for that which riseth again must have remained, though perhaps in an inert state.—It is not dead, but sleepeth;—that is, it is not dissolved any more than the exterior or phenomenal organism appears to us dissolved when it lieth in apparent inactivity during sleep.

Sound reasoning this, to the best of my judgment, as far as it goes. But how are we to explain the reaction of this fluxional body on the animal? In each moment the particles by the informing force of the living principle constitute an organ not only of motion and sense, but of consciousness. The organ plays on the organist. How is this conceivable? The solution requires a depth, stillness, and subtlety of spirit not only for its discovery, but even for the understanding of it when discovered, and in the most appropriate words enunciated. I can merely give a hint. The particles themselves must have an interior and gravitative being, and the multeity must be a removable or at least suspensible accident.

---

[1] 1 Cor 15.36–7 (var).

HENRY PETER BROUGHAM
BARON BROUGHAM AND VAUX
1778–1868

A Speech on the Present State of the Law of the Country; delivered in the House of Commons, on Thursday, February 7, 1828 ... verbatim from "The Times" newspaper. London 1828. 8⁰.

Published Mar 1828 (*EC*).

Bound as sixth in "TRACTS 1812–30".

British Museum C 126 i 3(6)

In Malta Oct–Dec 1804 C made notes from Brougham's youthful *Inquiry into the Colonial Policy of the European Powers* (2 vols Edinburgh 1803), partly for an essay or review for the *Courier*, partly in preparing for Sir Alexander Ball "Observations on Egypt" (VCL MS F 14.3b). The notes on Brougham's *Inquiry*—C was using Ball's copy and therefore presumably could not write in the margins of it—are preserved in BM MS Egerton 2800 ff 106–8; about one third of them are printed in *IS* 292–3, 335–6.

Henry Brougham first became MP in 1810 and by 1816 was the most prominent member of the Opposition in Parliament; he was well known for his spirited defence (sometimes successful) of Leigh Hunt and his brother in 1811, and in 1820 for his vigorous defence of Queen Caroline against a politically motivated charge of adultery.

C was aware of Brougham's activities in the movement for abolishing the slave-trade (see e.g. *CL* VI 952), his efforts to provide adequate education for poor people (see BAXTER *Reliquiae* COPY B **115** n 4), and his commanding support of the campaign to establish a London University as an educational opportunity for dissenters excluded from Oxford and Cambridge. Some dissatisfaction with Brougham's educational principles induced C to point out the "One constant blunder of these New-broomers (or Broughamers)—these Penny Magazine Sages and Philanthropists, in reference to our Public Schools": see HEAD **1**. But in Feb 1827 he wrote Brougham a letter strongly recommending the appointment of Hyman Hurwitz as first professor of Hebrew in University College, London (*CL* VI 668; cf 710), and Hurwitz was appointed. Later in 1827 C's friends sought Brougham's help in petitioning for a civil-list pension; the plea failed in spite of Brougham's support. *CL* VI 681. Again in 1831, when C's friends tried to have the grants restored to the associates of the RSL, Brougham as Chancellor took C's part and, although unable to persuade

738

the King to restore the grant, offered C a grant of £200. On grounds of principle, C was not prepared to accept it.

DATE. 18 Feb 1828: dated in 2.

1   p 5

And, in his mind, that man was guilty of no error,—he was a party to no exaggeration—he was led by his fancy into no extravagance,— *] who had said, that all they saw about them, Lords and Commons, the whole machinery of the State, was designed to bring twelve men into the jury-box, to decide on questions connected with liberty and property.

* *I*[a] will say, that all ————[b] was designed to render possible the production of Othello & Co, the Paradise Lost, the Principia and the Differential Analysis; and I will undertake to maintain my point against M[r] Brougham in any logico-rhetorical ~~country~~ Tourney-Court in the realm, with Sharps or Blunts.[1]   S. T. Coleridge.

2   pp 43–6

[Brougham argues that all property should be equally available for meeting debts.] That man must be inconsistent as a reasoner, or of a very ricketty and crochetty state of mind, or else very unprincipled, who would, at this time of day, propose to uphold the dignity of the aristocracy, by converting any portion of them into fraudulent and dishonest debtors.

I not only should not form so contemptuous a judgement of the intellect of a man who should defend the existing Law in this point; but I should be disposed to retort the contempt—not indeed on the *Opiner*: in this instance that is impossible—but on the contrary Opinion, as founded on the false, mischievous, and debasing principle of a true and absolute *property* (i.e. propriety)[1] in any portion of the Land.—A landed Estate is a Trust for determinate uses—and one of the uses is the existence of *enduring* Families, and of *estates* ~~of~~ in a graduated ascent, ~~of~~ of magnitude and number in inverse ratio.[2]

---

[a] C has underlined "I" three times
[b] The long dash stands for the words in the textus "they saw about them, Lords and Commons, the whole machinery of the State"

1[1] I.e. with sharp or blunt weapons.

2[1] C proposed that the term "propriety" be used to refer to "The sum total of...heritable portions [of land], appropriated each to an individual Lineage", and that "nationalty" be used to refer to the national reserve of property, the two together comprising the "Commonwealth". See *C&S* (*CC*) 35–6, 40.

2[2] For the view that all land should be conceived as held in trust, see *C&S* (*CC*) 41, 51, and cf *TT* 31 Mar 1833.

The only valid Objection is derivable from the inconsistency of our Laws, which permit indefinite additions to landed ~~Estates~~ Property, ~~and~~ or rather (as in Thelusson's case)[3] in co-acruation of Estates.[4] Mr Brougham's ~~and~~ Doctrine, which is that of the Utilitarians generally,[5] would degrade the sacred Idea of our Country, our NATIVE LAND, into a mere general term, ~~a~~ the merely logical Unity of an Aggregate, a Sum Total, of tributary Despotisms.

S. T. Coleridge 18 Feby 1828.

2[3] Peter Thellusson (1737–97), merchant and naturalised Huguenot, was famous for his shrewd but eccentric will, according to which the main part of his large fortune was to accumulate at compound interest for two generations, with the prospect (it was calculated) of growing to £140 million. The will was disputed and declared valid in 1799 and the judgement confirmed by the House of Lords in 1805; but an act of Parliament was passed in 1800 preventing testators from devising property for accumulation for more than twenty-one years. The will was disputed again in 1859, by the end of which suit most of the estate had been consumed in litigation.

2[4] Neither "coac[c]ruation" nor "accruation" is recorded in *OED*. The normal term is "accrual".

2[5] C's hostility to the utilitarian position reminds us that John Stuart Mill, in his famous pair of essays on Bentham and Coleridge (1838, 1840), was considering in contrast the two great seminal minds of their age.

SIR THOMAS BROWNE

1605–1682

C's earliest reference, in Feb–Mar 1800 (*CN* I 690), to Sir Thomas Browne's writing is a phrase from the *Pseudodoxia Epidemica*. His discovery of Browne may have come through Lamb, for in "The Two Races of Men" Lamb derisively challenges C's claim to have been the first of his generation to admire the *Hydriotaphia*. By 1802 C had acquired his own copy of the little 1669 octavo of *Religio Medici*, but before that—and afterwards—he seems also to have relied on Lamb's copies or possibly Godwin's, or both. He wrote notes in his *Religio Medici* in 1802 and later inscribed this copy to SH; but he wrote other notes in it in about 1809.

In Mar 1804 C said that Sir Thomas Browne was "among my first Favorites" (BROWNE *Works* 1). In 1817–18, as the notebooks show (*CN* III 4367–77), he read the 1658–9 folio with care—especially the *Hydriotaphia*—and used the marginalia and notebook entries in Lecture 14 of the Literary Lectures (13 Mar 1818) on prose style (*Misc C* 218; see also 223 and *Works* headnote). One "reading" possibly accounts for the two detailed references to Browne in SHAKESPEARE *Dramatic Works* (2 vols 1807) [COPY D] II 703, 1016.

DISTRIBUTION OF MARGINALIA IN "RELIGIO MEDICI"

Text	Religio (1669)	Works (1658–9) Pt ii	Text	Religio (1669)	Works (1658–9) Pt ii
Bk I § 1		31	48	18	38
3	5–6		49		39
6	7–8		50		40–40A
7	9	32	52		41
9	10		54		42
13	10A	33	59		43
15	11		Bk II § 1		44–45
16	12–13		2	19–20	
18	13A	34	5	21–22	
19	14		6	23	44
21	14A		7	24–24A	46–47
22		35	9	25	
32	14B		10	26	
33		36	11	27	
34		37	12	28	
35	15		13	29	
36	16		14		48
39	17				

Religio Medici. The sixth edition, corrected and amended. With annotations [by Thomas Keck] never before published, upon all the obscure passages therein. Also Observations by Sir Kenelm Digby, now newly added. [Anonymous.] London 1669. 8⁰.

"Printed by Ja. Cotterel, for Andrew Crook". Fly-title to Pt ii—"Annotations upon Religio Medici"—is imprinted 1668 but the volume is paginated in a single series.

John Rylands Library

Autograph signature "S. T. Coleridge" above 3 at the head of p ⁻2. Inscribed on p ⁻7 (inner front board, from which the p–d had already been lifted), apparently in C's hand but actually in SH's: "Sara Hutchinson from S. T. C.". On the title-page below the displayed title "Religio Medici" C has written: "By Sir Thomas Brown"—the spelling he uses consistently throughout these notes. On p ⁻6, in pencil, a bookseller's or librarian's note: "Autograph copy of S. T. Coleridge. With marginal and other notes."

Before C annotated this copy, a number of cross-references had been written in, in ink in a neat hand, referring the text to the Annotations and the Annotations to the text: these appear on some thirty-five pages, and on p 31 C has written his note around one of these references. On pp ⁻2, 3, 9, 16, 18, 20, 23, 41, 49, 55, 68, 72, 127, single words are written in another hand, usually glossing hard words in the text. Although this hand is squarer and more deliberate than C's hand in this book, *C 17th C* (but not *LR*) printed as C's notes nine of these glosses, as well as two notes in the same hand—one on Byron, the other on Johnson—on pp 90 and 124. On p ⁺1 a pencil note in yet another hand comments on C's note 3: see 3 n 1, below.

It is difficult even to guess when—if ever—C gave this copy to SH. He could have given it to her in late 1801 or early 1802, with the early notes written in it, but the presentation letter of Mar 1804 in the folio *Works* implies that Browne was then new to SH and makes no reference to *Religio Medici*, although that text is in Pt ii of the folio. It is noticeable that, out of delicacy, C has crossed out in ink and rendered illegible the passage recorded in **24A** and the corresponding phrase in the Annotation—a procedure he was to use in many passages of the *Pseudodoxia Epidemica* in the *Works*. Whenever or wherever C wrote the "later" notes in this copy (**21 to 27**) it is difficult to imagine him giving the book back to SH if he remembered accurately what he had written in those notes. Perhaps the book was left at Greta Hall in 1810, and so found its way back to SH at some later date: the inscription "Sara Hutchinson from S. T. C." does not seem to have been made at the time of presentation. The notes "Communicated by Mr Wordsworth" to HNC for *LR* seem all to have been transcribed by SH; among the notes printed in *LR* from this copy six of the seven "later" personal notes are represented, though with omissions.

CONTENTS. "To the Reader"; pp 1–176 *Religio Medici*; pp [179–84]

"The Annotator to the Reader", pp 185–297 "Annotations upon Religio Medici" (anonymous, dated 24 Mar 1654); pp 301–75 Sir Kenelm Digby's Observations; pp [376–9] Postscript.

MS TRANSCRIPT. BM Add MS 46553 ff 222–222ᵛ: title on f 222ᵛ, probably in SH's hand, "Marginal Notes from Sʳ Thoˢ Brownes Religio Medici— Ed: small 8ᵛᵒ—1649". Part of an incomplete transcript of the marginalia, comprising the last part of **26** and the text of **27, 29,** and **2.** The fact that **2** was transcribed after **29** suggests that **2** was written on the back flyleaves that have been cut out (pp ⁺7/⁺8, ⁺9/⁺10 if they had survived), leaving broad double-tapered stubs corresponding to a stub between pp ⁻4 and ⁻5. HNC might have placed this note immediately after **1** to give prominence to a general comment that serves as introduction to all the notes and because of C's imaginative identification with Browne in that note. But the last paragraph of **33**, printed in *LR* I but no longer in the volume, could have been written on the missing front flyleaf, together with the date 1802 that HNC assigns to the notes. The missing note **2** is here printed from MS TRANSCRIPT since that text is evidently closer to the ms than is the text of *LR*.

DATE. 1802, c Jan–Feb in London (**1–20, 28–34**); and 1809, c Apr–Sept— at Greta Hall or at Allan Bank. HNC gives 1802 as the date of the selection of notes in *LR*, but he includes five of the "later" notes. Two passages noted in **34** as memorable appear variatim in *CN* I 1067, 1068 of c Dec 1801. The notes on love—**21, 22, 25, 26**—could hardly have been written as early as 1802: they arise out of a situation and an attitude that did not obtain, even intermittently, before "the terrible Saturday afternoon" of 27 Dec 1806 (*CN* II 2975, III 3547), or after SH's departure for Wales in Mar 1810.

1 p ⁻4

Strong Feeling & an active Intellect conjoined lead necessarily to Spinosism. T. Brown was a Spinosist without knowing it—and so indeed are almost ⟨all⟩ sincerely pious and generous minds.ᵃ1

> ᵃ The bottom of pp ⁻4/⁻3 has been torn off immediately below the last word of **1.** The missing piece may have contained **2,** and perhaps also the second paragraph of **33** (which was printed in *LR*). See MS TRANSCRIPT, above

11 C recognised that Spinoza's philosophy pointed inevitably to pantheism and so to atheism, but his admiration for the man and the purity of his thought never diminished. C's habit was to regard a philosophical system, not as an abstract and impersonal construct, but as a view of the moral world necessarily informed by the moral and intellectual commitment of the philosopher himself. He could see how the "theory" of Spinoza could become dangerous and corrupt if engaged from a moral angle markedly different from Spinoza's; he could also recognise how a man (like Sir Thomas Browne) could become an unconscious Spinozist. See *CN* III 3869 (Jun 1810). In a letter of Mar 1815, he remarked "the noble honesty, that majesty of openness, so delightful in Spinoza": *CL* IV 548. See also BAXTER *Reliquiae* COPY A 2 n 2.

2 MS TRANSCRIPT, perhaps originally p ⁻4 or ⁻3, now lost[a]

This Book paints certain parts of *my* moral & intellectual Being (the best parts no doubt) better than any other book I have ever met with —& the style is throughout delicious[1]

3 p ⁻2

If I have not all the *Faith* that the Author of the Religio Medici possessed, I have all the *inclination* to it—/ It gives me pleasure to *believe*.[1]

3A sig B1ʳˑᵛ, marked with an ink line in the margin | "To the Reader" (at the end)

It was set down many years past, and was the sense of my conception at that time, not an immutable law unto my advancing judgement at all times; and therefore there might be many things therein plausible unto my passed apprehension, which are not agreeable unto my present self.

4 p 1 | the displayed title

RELIGIO MEDICI,/,

i.e. a Physician's Religion

5 p 5 | Pt i § 3

I am, I confess, naturally inclined to that, which misguided zeal terms superstition: my common conversation I do acknowledge austere, my behaviour full of vigour, sometimes not without morosity ...

So much the worse.

6 p ⁺1, referring to p 6; marked in the margin with an ink line[b]

There are questionless both in Greek, Roman, and African Churches, Solemnities and Ceremonies, whereof the wiser Zeals do make a

---

[a] The bottom of pp ⁻4/⁻3 has been torn off immediately below the last word of **1**. The missing piece may have contained **2**, and perhaps also the second paragraph of **33** (which was printed in *LR*). See MS TRANSCRIPT, above
[b] From "that look asquint". The identification of the lines in the margins as C's is established by **17**

2[1] C used the unusual—for him— word "delicious" in a similar context in a note of 19 Dec 1801 addressed to SH in BARTRAM. See also **33**, below.
3[1] A pencil note in an unidentified hand on p ⁺1 refers to **3** and perhaps

also to **33**: "Descartes (Discours du Monde) says, It is one thing to believe, & another for man to imagine that he believes—S. T. C. in one of these MS notes adopts the idea."

Christian use, and stand condemned by us, not as evil in themselves, but as allurements and baits of superstition to those vulgar heads that look asquint on the face of truth, and those unstable judgements that cannot consist in the narrow point and centre of vertue, without a reel or stagger to the circumference.

excellent![1]

7 p 10, marked in the margin with an ink line | i § 6

Every man is not a proper Champion for Truth, nor fit to take up the Gantlet in the cause of Verity: Many from the ignorance of these Maximes, and an inconsiderate Zeal unto Truth, have too rashly charged the troops of error, and remain as Trophies unto the enemies of Truth: A man may be in as just possession of Truth as of a City, and yet be for[c]ed to surrender; 'tis therefore far better to enjoy her with peace, then to hazzard her on a battle ...

Godwin, for Instance.[1]

8 p 11, marked in the margin with an ink line (listed in **34**)

I must confess my greener studies have been polluted with two or three [heresies, schisms, or errors], not any begotten in the latter Centuries, but old and obsolete, such as could never have been revived, but by such extravagant and irregular heads as mine ...

I sympathize—'tis excellent

9 p 13 | i § 7

The second [heresie &c] was that of *Origen*, that God would not persist in his Vengeance for ever, but after a definite time of his wrath, he would release the Damned souls from torture: Which error I fell into upon a serious contemplation of the great Attribute of God, his Mercie; and did a little cherish it in my self, because I found therein no malice ...

6[1] This single word of comment is transferred from the list of notable passages written on p +1 (**34**, below). Seven other such comments have similarly been transferred from **34** to their appropriate positions in the text.

7[1] From early 1800 until a distressing quarrel in Feb 1804 (later resolved), C fostered an acquaintance with William Godwin (1756–1836), even though any early interest he may have had in *Political Justice* had rapidly waned. He never thought highly of Godwin's intellectual capacity or his philosophical acumen (see e.g. *CN* i 637, 910); yet he gave a good deal of time—not always ungrudgingly—to criticising and revising Godwin's works from 1800 to 1804, and claimed that although others patronised Godwin as a populariser, he himself had always spoken of him with respect.

To call this opinion *an error*! Merciful God! how thy Creatures blaspheme thee!

10　p 17 (listed in **34**) | i § 9

... I love to lose my self in a Mystery, to pursue my reason to an *Oh altitudo!* "O! the Depth!"*ᵃ*

So say I: so says dear W. W.¹

10A　p 27, the last four lines marked in the margin with a line in ink | i § 13

> *It is thy Makers will, for unto none*
> *But unto reason can he ere be known.*
> *The Devils do know thee, but those damn'd ~~meteros~~-meteors*
> *Build not thy glory, but confound thy creatures.*
> *Teach my indeavours so thy works to read,*
> *That learning them, in thee I may proceed.*
> *Give thou my reason that instructive flight,*
> *Whose weary wings may on thy hands still light.*
> *Teach me ~~so~~ to soar aloft; yet ever so,*
> *When near the sun, to stoop again below.*
> *Thus shall my humble feathers safely hover,*
> *And though neer earth, more then the Heavens discover.*

11　pp 30–1, marked in the margin with an ink line (listed in **34**) | i § 15

Who admires not *Regio-Montanus* his Fly beyond his Eagle, or wonders not more at the operation of two souls in those little bodies, than but one in the trunk of a Cedar? I could never content my contemplation with those general pieces of wonder, the flux and re-flux of the Sea,¹ the increase of *Nile*, the conversion of the Needle to the North; and have studied to match and parallel those in the more obvious and neglected pieces of Nature, which without further travel I can do in the Cosmography of my self; we carry with us the wonders we seek without us: There is all *Africa* and her prodigies in us; we are that bold and adventurous piece of nature, which he

---

ᵃ C has crowded these words in between the lines of type above the words "Oh altitudo!"

10¹ Cf *Tintern Abbey* lines 35–49, in which WW gives thanks for "that blessed mood | In which the burthen of the mystery...Is lightened", and "we are laid asleep | In body, and be-come a living soul", and "see into the life of things". In *AR*, however, C was to call this position of Sir Thomas

Browne's "Ultra-fidianism": *AR* (1825) 201. See also **11**, below.

11¹ Both C and WW transferred the figure "flux and reflux", a common phrase for the ebb and flow of the tide, to the activity of the mind: see e.g. *Friend* (*CC*) ɪ xl, ɪɪ 17, *BL* ch 15 (1907) ɪɪ 15, *WPW* ɪɪ 388n.

that studies, wisely learns in a *compendium*, what others labour at in a divided piece and endless volume.

This is the true characteristic of Genius—our destiny & instinct is to unriddle the World,[2] & he is the man of Genius who feels this instinct fresh and strong in his nature—who perceives the riddle & the mystery of all things even the commonest & needs no strange and out of the way Tales or Images to stimulate him into wonder & a deep Interest.[3]

12 p 32, last 3 lines marked in the margin with an ink line | i § 16

Thus there are two Books from whence I collect my Divinity; besides that written one of God, another of his servant Nature, that universal and publick Manuscript, that lies expans'd unto the eyes of all; those who never saw him in the one, have discovered him in the other: This was the Scripture and Theologie of the Heathens; the natural motion of the Sun made them more admire him, than its supernatural station did the Children of *Israel*; the ordinary effects of nature wrought more admiration in them, then in the other all his Miracles; surely the Heathens knew better how to joyn and read these mystical Letters, than we Christians, who cast a more careless eye on these common Hieroglyphicks, & disdain to suck Divinity from the flowers of Nature.

All this is very fine Philosophy, & the best & most ingenious Defence of Revelation.[1]

13 pp +1 and 33, marked in the margin with an ink line

I hold there is a general beauty in the works of God, and therefore no deformity in any kinde or species of creature whatsoever: I cannot tell by what Logick we call a Toad, a Bear, or an Elephant, ugly, they being created in those outward shapes and figures which best express those actions of their inward forms.

33—most beautiful!—

So do I hold—& believe that a Toad is a comely animal. But neve[r]theless, a Toad *is* called ugly by almost all men; & it is the Business of a Philosopher to explain the Reason of this.[1]

11[2] "Unriddle" is a sixteenth-century word, but the oblique reference is probably to Pope *Essay on Man* II 18, i.e. man as the "riddle of the world".

11[3] Cf *Friend* (*CC*) II 73–4 (I 109–10).

12[1] See also BROWNE *Works* 37. Cf *Lects 1795* (*CC*) 94, and see 94–5 n 3.

13[1] With this remark on ugliness cf AURELIUS ANNEX [*f*] pp 29–30. See also among a series of jottings from Gilbert WHITE *Natural History of Selborne* (2 vols 1802) a suggestion that toads are "*comely* animals": *CN* III 3959 f 76ᵛ (c Jul 1810).

13A　p 39, marked in the margin with an ink line (listed in **34**) | i § 18

'Tis, I confess, the common fate of men of singular gifts of minde, to be destitute of those of fortune; which doth not any way deject the Spirit of wiser judgements, who throughly understand the justice of this proceeding; and being enriched with higher donatives, cast a more careless eye on these vulgar parts of felicity. It is a most unjust ambition to desire to engross the mercies of the Almighty, not to be content with the goods of minde, without a possession of those of body or fortune: and it is an error worse than heresie, to adore these complemental and circumstantial pieces of felicity, and undervalue those perfections and essential points of happiness, wherein we resemble our Maker.

14　p 42 | i § 19

There is, as in Philosophy, so in Divinity, sturdy doubts, and boisterous objections, wherewith the unhappiness of our knowledge too neerly acquainteth us. More of these no man hath known than my self, which I confess I conquered, not in a martial posture, but on my knees. For our endeavours are not onely to combat with doubts, but always to dispute with the Devil ...

This is exceedingly striking! Had Sir T. Brown lived now-a-days, he would probably have been a very ingenious & bold Infidel/ in his *real* opinion/ tho' the kindness of his nature would have kept him aloof from vulgar prating obtrusive Infidelity.—

14A　p 45 | i § 21

I remember a Doctor in Physick in *Italy*, who could not perfectly believe the immortality of the Soul, because *Galen* seemed to make a doubt thereof.

14B　p 69, marked in the margin with an ink line (listed in **34**) | i § 32

This is that gentle heat that brooded on the waters, and in six days hatched the World; this is that irradiation that dispels the mists of Hell, the clouds of horror, fear, sorrow, despair; and preserves the region of the minde in serenity: whatsoever feels not the warm gale, and gentle ventilation of this Spirit, (though I feel his pulse) I dare not say he lives; for truely without this, to me there is no heat under the Tropick; nor any light, though I dwelt in the body of the Sun.

15 pp ⁺1, and 77 marked in the margin with an ink line | i § 35

... God being all things, is contrary unto nothing, out of which were made all things, and so nothing became something, and *Omneity* informed *Nullity* into an Essence.

77 for its exquisite absurdity!

An excellent *Burlesque* on some parts of the Schoolmen, tho', I fear, an unintentional one.

16 pp ⁺1, and 80 marked in the margin with an ink line | i § 36

Thus we are men, and we know not how; there is something in us that can be without us, and will be after us, though it is strange that it hath no history, what it was before us, nor cannot tell how it entred in us.

80–81. *Divine!*

Truly sublime and in Sir T. Brown's best manner.[1]

17 pp ⁺1, and 85 marked in the margin with an ink line | i § 39

Some Divines count *Adam* 30 years old at his creation, because they suppose him created in the perfect age and stature of man; and surely we are all out of the computation of our age, and every man is some months elder than he bethinks him; for we live, move, have a being, and are subject to the actions of the elements, and the malice of diseases, in that other world, the truest Microcosm, the womb of our mother; for besides that general and common existence we are conceived to hold in our Chaos, and whilst we sleep within the bosome of our causes, we enjoy a being and life in three distinct worlds, wherein we receive most manifest graduations: In that obscure world and womb of our mother, our time is short, computed by the Moon; yet longer then the days of many creatures that behold the Sun, our selves being not yet without life, sense, and reason; though for the manifestation of its actions, it awaits the opportunity of objects, and seems to live there but in its root and soul of vegetation: entring afterwards upon the scene of the world, we arise up and become another creature, performing the reasonable actions of man, and obscurely manifesting that part of Divinity in us, but not in complement and perfection till we have once more cast our secondine,

16[1] In a marginal note on SHAKE-SPEARE *Dramatic Works* (2 vols 1807) [COPY D] II 1016 C refers to the next section—"Relig. Medici: Sect. 37 ad finem"—in support of Hamlets' belief that "The spirit, that I have seen, | May be the devil". *Hamlet* II ii 627–32.

that is, this slough of flesh, and are delivered into the last world, that ineffable place of *Paul*, that proper *ubi* of spirits. The smattering I have of the Philosophers Stone (which is something more then the perfect exaltation of Gold) hath taught me a great deal of Divinity, and instructed my belief, how that immortal spirit, and incorruptible substance of my soul may lye obscure, and sleep a while within this house of flesh. Those strange and mystical transmigrations that I have observed in Silkworms, turned my Philosophy into Divinity. There is in these works of nature, which seem to puzzle reason, something Divine, and hath more in it then the eye of a common spectator doth discover.

85–86–87—best of all/—

This is a most admirable passage! Yes! the History of a man for the 9 months preceding his Birth would probably be far more interesting & contain events of greater moment than all the 3 score & 10 years that follow it.[1]

18   p 105 | i § 48

This is made good by experience, *which can from the Ashes of a plant revive the plant, and from its cinders recal it into its stalk and leaves again.

[*] Moll Row!!—This was, I believe, some lying Boast of Paracelsus, which the good Sir T. Brown has swallowed for a Truth.[1]

19   p 131 | Pt ii § 2

It is a happiness to be born and framed unto vertue, and to grow up from the seeds of nature, rather than the inoculation and forced graffs of education ...

a just thought well expressed.

20   p 131

... I give no alms to satisfie the hunger of my Brother, but to fulfil and accomplish the Will and Command of my *God ...

* Consider "God" as the word that expresses *the whole* of *all things*

17[1] A similar project for writing the prenatal history of a soul occurs in *CN* II 2373 (Dec 1804), but it ends with a disclaimer: "Try! it is promising!— You have not above 300 volumes to write before you come to it—& as you write perhaps a volume once in ten years, you have ample Time, my dear Fellow!"

18[1] For an amusing story about the Ottery St Mary witch Moll Row and her black cat, see Carlyon I 132–5. For Paracelsus see BAXTER *Reliquiae* COPY B **28** n 2.

& this is just. We ought not to relieve a poor man merely because our feelings impel us; but because these feelings are *just* & *proper* feelings. My *feelings* might impel me to revenge with the same force, with which they urge me to charity— / I must therefore have some rule by which I may *judge* my feelings—& this Rule is "*God*".[1]

21 p 146 | ii § 5

I never yet cast a true affection on a woman, but I have loved my friend* as I do vertue, my soul, my God. From hence me thinks I do conceive how God loves man, what happiness there is in the love of God.

* I have loved—& ⟨still do⟩*a* love—*truly* i.e. not in a fanciful attributing of certain ideal perfections to an existing Being, who possesses perhaps no one of them;[1] but as in a true & palpable sympathy of manners, sentiments, & affections. So have I loved *one* Woman; & believe that such a love of such a Woman is the highest Friendship— for we cannot love a Friend as a Woman, but we can love a Woman as a Friend.[2]

22 pp 146/7, a sheet pasted by one corner to the top of p 147, written on both sides: a postscript to **21**

* Friendship satisfies the *highest* parts of our nature; but a wife, who is capable of friendship, satisfies *all*. The great business of real unostentatious Virtue is—not to eradicate any real genuine instinct or appetite of human nature; but—to establish a concord and unity betwixt all parts of our nature, to give a Life and a Feeling & a Passion to our purer Intellect, and to intellectualize our feelings & passions. This a happy marriage, blessed with children, effectuates, in the highest degree, of which our nature is capable, & is therefore chosen by St Paul, as the symbol of the Union of the Church with Christ; that is, of the Souls of all good Men with God, the soul of the Universe[1]—"I scarcely distinguish," said once a good old man, "the

a The inserted words "still do" are written with the same pen and in the same colour of ink as **22**; they were written into the earlier note **21** when C wrote the long reflective postscript **22**

20[1] Cf part of *CN* II 2556, a long note of Apr 1805 on virtue, love, duty, and happiness: "To perform Duties absolutely from the sense of Duty is the *Ideal*, which perhaps no human Being ever can arrive at, but which every human Being ought to try to draw near unto—This is—in the only wise, & verily, in a most sublime

sense—to see God face to face". Cf C's objections in *CN* I 1705–11 to Kant's categorical imperative.

21[1] Cf *CN* III 3406; see also *C&SH* 20.

21[2] See *CN* III 3284, 3442, 4036; but cf I 1065 and III 4297.

22[1] In the summer of 1809 C paraphrased some lines from Cartwright's

wife of my old age from the wife of my youth; for when we were both young, & she was beautiful, for *once* that I caressed ⟨her⟩ with a meaner passionion I caressed her a thousand times with *Love*—& *these* caresses still remain to us!"[2]

Besides, there is another Reason why Friendship is of somewhat less Value, than Love which includes Friendship—it is this—we may love many persons, all *very* dearly; but we cannot love many persons, all *equally* dearly. There will be *differences*, there will be *gradations*—our nature imperiously asks a *summit*, a *resting-place*[3]—it is with the affections in Love, as with the Reason in Religion—we cannot go on *diffuse* & equalize—we must have a SUPREME—a *One the highest*. All languages express this sentiment. What is more common than to say of a man w in love—"he idolizes her," "he makes *a god* of her."—Now, in order that a person should *continue* to love another, better than all others, it seems necessary, that this feeling should be reciprocal. For if it be not so, Sympathy is broken off in the very highest ⟨point.⟩ A. (we will say, by way of illustration) loves B. above all others, in the best & fullest sense of the word, love: but B. loves C. above all others. Either therefore A. does not sympathize with B. in theseis most important feeling; & then his Love must necessarily be incomplete, & accompanied with a *craving* after something that *is* no *not*, & yet *might be*; or he does sympathize with B. in loving C. above all others—& then, of course, he loves C. better than A/ B. Now it is selfishness, at least it seems so to me, to desire that your *Friend* should love you better than all others—but not to wish that a *Wife* should.[4]

The Siedge: "Love is a perfect Desire of the whole Being to be united to some thing ⟨felt⟩ necessary to its perfection by the most perfect means | That Nature permits & Reason dictates—". *CN* III 3514; repeated var in *CL* IV 914 (26 Jan 1819). Cf *CN* III 3284, 4006 ff 20ᵛ–21, *CL* IV 904. Marriage as "the symbol of the Union of the Church with Christ" can be seen in Eph 5.23–32 and 2 Cor 11.2.

22[2] See a note of Feb 1810 adapted from Jean Paul: "On some delightful day in early spring or June...some of my Countrymen hallow the anniversary of their Marriage, & with Love and Fear go over the reckoning of the Past and the unknown future ...". *CN* III 3699.

22[3] The recurrence of the image of the "*summit, a resting-place*" in **26** helps to alleviate the suspicion that this note—written on a separate sheet of paper with no date in the watermark, and tipped into the book—may be separated from the other "later" notes in time and intention.

22[4] Among a large number of observations upon the inadvisability—from a husband's point of view—of female dyspathy, see *CN* III 3316, a note on rectifying "the one main Defect of Female Education"; and cf 3345. A more bitter and detached observation is found in *CN* III 4013; and cf 3618.

23   p 147 | ii § 6

Another misery *there is in affection, that whom we truely love like our own, we forget their looks, nor can our memory retain the Idea of their faces; and it is no wonder: for they are our selves, and our affection makes their looks our own.

* A Thought I have often had, and once expressed it almost in the same language;[1] ~~but~~ the *Fact* is certain, but the explanation here given is very unsatisfactory. For *why* do we never have an image of our own faces? an Image of Fancy, I mean.[2] S. T. C.

24   p 149, marked in the margin with an ink line | ii § 7

... my more setled years, and Christian constitution, have fallen upon severer resolutions. I can hold there is no such thing as injury; that if there be, there is no such injury as revenge, and no such revenge as the contempt of an injury; that to hate another, is to maligne himself; that the truest way to love another, is to despise our selves.

I thank God, that I can with a full & unfeigning Heart, utter AMEN! to this passage.

24A   p 151 | ii § 7

For there are certain tempers of body, which matcht with an humorous depravity of minde, do hatch and produce vitiosities, whose newness and monstrosity of nature admits no name; this was the temper ~~of that Lecher that carnal'd with a Statua,~~[*a*]1 and constitution of *Nero* in his Spintrian recreations.

25   pp 156–7 | ii § 9

I could be content that we might procreate like trees without conjunction, or that there were any way to perpetuate the world without this trivial and vulgar way of coition; it is the foolishest act a wise

---

a   C has cancelled these words so thoroughly in ink that they are indecipherable in this copy

23[1] Possibly *CN* I 985: "I looked intensely toward her face—& sometimes I *saw* it...except indeed that, feeling & all, I felt her as *part* of my being—twas all spectral—But when I could not absolutely *see* her, no effort of fancy could bring out even the least resemblance of her face." Or perhaps *CN* II 2079 f 36: "One remarkably affecting Dream in which I saw Sara ...how comes it I so very rarely see those I love...". See also *CN* I 986, 1250, II 2061 f 27.

23[2] Cf BROWNE *Works* **44** and n 2.

24A[1] C has also cancelled this phrase in the "Annotations": see **31A**, below. See also BROWNE *Works* **5A** n 1.

man commits in all his life, nor is there any thing that will more deject his cool'd imagination, when he shall consider what an odd and unworthy piece of folly he hath committed.

He says, he is a Batchelor, but he talks as if he had been a married man, & married to a Woman who did not love him, & whom he did not love. Taken by itself, no doubt, the act is both foolish, & debasing. But what a misery is contained in those words, "taken by itself"? Are there not thoughts, & affections, & Hopes, & a *Religion of the Heart*,—that lift & sanctify all our bodily Actions where the union of the Bodies is but a language & *conversation* of united Souls?—[1]

26 pp 163–4 | ii § 10

In brief, there can be nothing truely alone, and by its self, which is not truely one; and such is onely God: All others do transcend an unity, and so by consequence are many.

O I feel this!—& feel myself *alone*! & suffer the painful craving Void of *Solitude*! I want some being, that should be *the dearest*, the very dearest to me/ & this can not be unless by the circumstance of *my* being the *very* dearest to that Being! And this, alas! I can not be! Reciprocity is that, which alone gives a *stability* to Love!—It is not mere selfishness, that impels all kind natures to desire, that there should be some one human Being, to whom they are *most* dear/ it is because they wish some one being to exist, who shall be the resting-place & summit of their Love! & this in human nature is not *possible*, except the two affections coincide—the reason is, that the object of the highest Love will not otherwise be the same in both parties.[1]

25[1] If "Coadunation or spiritual Marriage", as in the note on KANT *Metaphysik der Sitten* (cited in AURELIUS **46** n 2), represents the state of marital union, sexual intercourse conceived as "a language & *conversation* of united Souls" transcends the loathing of bodily function uttered by Browne. See also BÖHME **132** and n 2. C's phrase "*Religion* of the Heart" may have been suggested or reinforced by his reading of Donne's *Songs and Sonets*.

26[1] See esp *CN* II 3231 f 15 (c 1807–10): "And now, that I am alone, & utterly hopeless for myself—yet still *I love*...". And *CN* III 4036 (c 1810): "But what is Love? Love as it may subsist between ⟨two⟩ persons of different sexes?...The mutual dependence of their Happiness, each on that of the other, each being at once cause & effect—You, therefore I—I, therefore you. The sense of this ⟨reciprocity of well-being⟩ that which first stamps & legitimates the name of Happiness in all the other advantages & favorable accidents of Nature, or Fortune...". Cf *CN* II 3148 and *TT* 27 Sept 1830.

27   p 165 | ii § 11

There is surely a neerer apprehension of any thing that delights us in our dreams, than in our waked senses ... for my awaked judgement discontents me, ever whispering unto me, that I am from my friend; but my friendly dreams in night requite me, and make me think I am within his arms. I thank God for my happy dreams, as I do for my good rest, for there is a satisfaction unto reasonable desires, and such as can be content with a fit of happiness ...

I am quite different: for all, or almost all, the painful & fearful Thoughts, that I know, are in my Dreams! So much so that when I am wounded by a friend, or received a painful Letter, it throws me into a state very nearly resembling that of a Dream.[1]

28   p 169 | ii § 12

> *Keep still in my Horizon; for to me*
> *The Sun makes not the day, but thee.*

thou, says the *Grammar*; THEE, says the *Rhyme/* and a Poet of course is naturally *partial* to the latter.

29   p 173 | ii § 13

[Statists that labour to contrive a Common-wealth without our poverty, take away the object of charity, not understanding onely the Common-wealth of a Christian, but forgetting the prophecie of Christ.]

O, for shame! for shame!—is there no object of Charity but abject Poverty? And what sort of a Charity must that be, which wishes misery, in order that it may have the credit of relieving a small part of it?[1] Pulling down the comfortable Cottages of independent Industry, to build alms' houses out of the Ruins!

30   p [178] (blank page facing the opening of "The Annotator to the Reader")

And Seneca *saith, Some such there are,* Qui patri obstetricem parturienti* filiae accersenti moram injicere possint.

* "Which would detain a father that was running to fetch a midwife for his Daughter in labor-pangs"—no bad Hyperbole of Master Seneca's!

27[1] See e.g. *CN* I 1597 (19–21 Oct 1803): "Nothing affects me much at the moment it happens..." and cf *CN* I 1517. C's delay in opening letters is seen in e.g. *CL* III 8n, 19.
29[1] On charity see **20**, above.

31   p +1, referring to p 204 | Annotations upon Religio Medici

So St. *Aug. Qui sententiam suam quamvis falsam atque perversam nulla pertinaci animositate defendunt, quaerunt autem cauta solicitudine veritatem, corrigi parati cum invenerint, nequaquam sunt inter Haereticos deputandi.* Aug. *cont. Manich.* 24. *qu.* 3.

[Those who defend their opinion, however wrong or misguided, without stubborn animosity, and nevertheless seek the truth with careful respect, being ready to be set right when they find it, are by no means to be reckoned among the Heretics. St Augustine *Contra Manichaeos* 24. question 3.]

204—good *quot. for my Locke Book*.[1]

31A   p 284 | Note to p 151 (24A)

This was the Temper ~~of that Leacher that carnal'd with a Statua~~.[a]

31B   p 285, marked in the margin with an ink line (listed in **34**) | Note to p 153

[Citing ii § 8: *I have seen a Grammarian toure and plume himself over a single line in* Horace, *and shew more pride,* &c.] *Movent mihi stomachum Grammatistae quidam, qui cum duas tenuerint vocabulorum origines ita se ostentant, ita venditant, ita circumferunt jactabundi, ut prae ipsis pro nihili habendos Philosophos arbitrentur.* Picus Mirand. *in Ep. ad Hermol. Barb. quae exstat lib. nono Epist. Politian.*[1]

[Some of the grammarians disgust me, for, when they have grasped a couple of roots of words, they flaunt themselves, they show off, they strut about boasting, so that they come to think that compared to them the philosophers are of no account. Pico della Mirandola in a letter to Hermolaus Barbarus which is preserved in the ninth book of the letters of Politian.]

[a] See 24A n *a*

31[1] In Apr 1801 C intended "To translate Engel's vi Stück as introduction to my Essay on Locke". *CN* I 930. The substance of this "essay" is contained in the four detailed philosophical letters addressed to Josiah Wedgwood in Feb 1801 with copies sent to Poole (*CL* II 678–703). The letters attack the admiration for Locke current in the eighteenth century and draw attention—perhaps overemphatically—to Locke's debt to Descartes. For the proposal to publish these, see *CL* II 707, 927–8. As to this now-much-expanded "*Locke Book*", and to certain other works, C bids his correspondent " 'have patience, Lord! and I

will pay thee all!' "; but no more is heard of it except as a distant echo in the proposed first treatise of the projected Logosophia in Sept 1815 (*CL* IV 589) and in Lecture 13 of the *Philosophical Lectures*. The phrase "the sandy Sophisms of Locke" in 1815 (*CL* IV 574) is typical of C's considered estimate of him.

31B[1] C copied this passage accurately, down to the word "Barb.", in N 21 in c Dec 1801, presumably when he first read the book. *CN* I 1068 (the source not noted). C quoted the passage in *Omniana* I 228. The tr here used is from *CN* I 1068n.

32   p +1, referring to p 286 | Note to p 154

[Citing ii § 8: *I cannot think that* Homer *pin'd away upon the Riddle of the Fisherman.*] The history out of *Plutarch* is thus: Sailing from *Thebes* to the Island *Ion*, being landed and set down upon the shore, there happen'd certain Fishermen to pass by him, and he asking them what they had taken, they made him this Enigmatical answer, That what they had taken, they had left behind them; and what they had not taken, they had with them: meaning, that because they could take no Fish, they went to loøse themselves; and that all which they had taken, they had killed, and left behind them; and all which they had not taken, they had with them in their clothes: and that *Homer* being struck with a deep sadness because he could not interpret this, pin'd away, and at last dyed. *Pliny* alludes to this Riddle, in his *Ep.* to his Friend *Fuscus*, where giving an account of spending his time in the Country, he tells him, *Venor aliquando, sed non sine pugillaribus, ut quamvis nihil ceperim, non nihil referam.* [Occasionally I go hunting, but not without my notebooks, so that I shall have something to bring home even if I catch nothing.] Plin. *Ep. lib.* 9. *Ep.* 36.

286—Poem on the Death of Homer[1]

33   pp −2–−1, referring (*inter alia*) to pp 376–9 | Postscript

N.B. The Post-script at the very End of the Book is well worth Reading.[1] Excepting that there is nothing particularly good after

32[1] C summarised this note on the death of Homer in N 21 in the entry immediately preceding the transcript of **31B**, with his own addition: "—his Ghost appears to the Fishermen because they each take no fish, they had gone & hanged themselves—&c—". *CN* I 1067 (source not noted).

33[1] The Postscript is at pp 376–9. "My Lord, Looking over these loose Papers to point them, I perceive I have forgotten what I promised in the eighth sheet, to touch in a word concerning *Grace*: I do not conceive it to be a Quality infused by *God Almighty* into a Soul. Such kinde of discoursing satisfieth me no more in *Divinity*, than in *Philosophy*. I take it to be the whole Complex of such real motives (as a solid account may be given of them) that incline a man to

Virtue and Piety; and are set on foot by Gods particular *Grace* and *Favour*, to bring that work to pass. As for Example: To a man plunged in *Sensuality*, some great misfortune happeneth, that mouldeth his heart to a tenderness, and inclineth him to much thoughtfulness: In this temper, he meeteth with a *Book* or *Preacher*, that representeth lively to him the danger of his own condition; and giveth him hopes of greater contentment in other Objects, after he shall have taken leave of his former beloved *Sins*. This begetteth further conversation with prudent and pious men, and experienced *Physicians*, in curing the *Souls Maladies*; whereby he is at last perfectly converted, and setled in a course of solid *Virtue* and *Piety*. Now these accidents of his mis-

p. 176—where the Religio Medici ends. Sir K. Digby's observations are those of a pedant in his own system & opinion.[2] He ought to have considered the Religio Medici ~~as~~ in a *dramatic* & not in a metaphysical View—as a sweet Exhibition of character & passion, & not as an Expression or Investigation of positive *Truth*.[3]—The Religio Medici (i.e. Religion of a Physician) is a fine Portrait of a ~~good~~ handsome man in his *best* Cloathes—it is much of what he was ~~on~~ at *all* times, a good deal of [what]*a* he was ⟨only⟩ in his *best* moments. I have never read a book, in which I felt greater similarity to my own *make* of mind[4]— active in enquiry, & yet with an appetite to believe,—in short, an affectionate & elevated *Visionary*! But then I should tell a different Tale of my ŏwn Heart; for I would not endeavor to tell the Truth (which I doubt not, Sir T. B. has done) but likewise to tell the *whole* Truth, which most assuredly he has not done[5]—However, it is a most delicious Book.—

[His own character was a fine mixture of humourist, genius and pedant. A library was a living world to him, and every book a man, absolute flesh and blood! and the gravity with which he records contradictory opinions is exquisite.]*b*[6]

a Word supplied by the editor
b This paragraph is printed from *LR*; it is not included in the incomplete MS TRANSCRIPT

fortune, the gentleness and softness of his Nature, his falling upon a good *Book*, his encountring with a pathetick *Preacher*, the impremeditated Chance that brought him to hear his *Sermon*, his meeting with other worthy men, and the whole Concatenation of all the intervening Accidents, to work this good effect in him; and that were ranged and disposed from all Eternity, by *Gods* particular goodness and providence for his *Salvation*; and without which he had inevitably been damned: This chain of causes, ordered by *God* to produce this effect, I understand to be *Grace. FINIS.*"

33[2] C borrowed from the Carlisle Cathedral Library 2 Apr 1801 to 2 Jul 1802 a copy of Kenelm Digby's *Two Treatises: the Nature of Bodies and the Nature of Man's Soule* (1645). For C's use of the book see *CN* i 1004, 1005, 1009.

33[3] For C's application of this principle to the interpretation of the Bible see e.g. BROWNE *Works* 36 and 37.

33[4] Cf "still believing mind" in *The Pang More Sharp Than All* line 5, and "most believing heart" in *To Mary Pridham* line 4: *PW* (EHC) i 457, 468. For a memorable exploration of the phrase "make of mind" see *CL* ii 1069.

33[5] For the distinction between truth and veracity see BAXTER *Reliquiae* COPY B 46 n 1. On telling "the whole Truth", see *CL* ii 762, 782.

33[6] This paragraph, added by HNC in *LR* from an unknown source, may have been written on one of the missing leaves of this volume. But since the tone of it is rather more judicial and "public" than the air of private critical innocence in the "early" notes in this volume, the paragraph may have come from some fragmentary ms associated with the literary lectures. C's self-identification with Browne gives a valuable insight into C as a reader.

34 p +1[1]

6 excellent
11
17
31
33—most beautiful!—
39
69
77 for its exquisite absurdity
80–81. *Divine!*
85–86–87—best of all/—
204—good *quot. for my Locke Book.*
285—
286—Poem on the Death of Homer

34[1] C seems to have written this list of page references before writing the annotations on the text. The brief notes attached to the list are also printed in the sequence of marginalia at the page to which each refers; when a marginal note is also written on the page referred to, the note from the list is printed as a first paragraph. For p 6 see **6**, p 33—**13**, p 77—**15**, pp 80–1—**16**, pp 85–7—**17**, p 204—**31**, p 286—**32**. It is noticeable that none of the "later" personal notes **21–27** is represented in this list.

"*Works*"

Pseudodoxia Epidemica: or, enquiries into very many received tenents, and commonly presumed truths ... The third edition, corrected and enlarged by the author. Together with some marginall observations, and a table alphabeticall at the end. London 1658. [Together with] Religio Medici: whereunto is added A Discourse of the Sepulchrall Urnes, lately found in Norfolk. Together with The Garden of Cyrus, or the quincunctiall lozenge, or net-work plantations of the ancients, artificially, naturally, mystically considered. With sundry observations. [London 1659]. 2 pts in 1 vol. F⁰.

This copy lacks the general title-page, which is imprinted: "Printed by R. W. for Nath. Ekins, at the Gun in Pauls Church-Yard, 1658." Pt ii is set in double column in a smaller type different in design from that used in Pt i. Cf Geoffrey Keynes *A Bibliography of Sir Thomas Browne* (Cambridge 1924) no 77.

"*Works*" is here used as a convenient short title for purposes of reference, although this volume does not include all Browne's works. The short title used in *CN* III is "*Pseudodoxia &c*".

New York Public Library (Berg Collection)

Inscribed by Lamb on p ⁻2: "C Lamb March 9ᵗʰ 180[4] bought for S T Coleridge". Below this in SH's hand, squeezed in between the Lamb inscription and C's remark (below): "Given by S. T. C. to S. Hutchinson March 1804". Below Lamb's note C has written: "N.B. It was on the 10ᵗʰ; on which day I dined & punched at Lamb's—& exulted in the having procured the Hydriotaphia, & all the rest lucro posito. S. T. C." Also inscribed on the title-page of Pt i: "M. Wordsworth Rydal Mount"—this signature presumably written after SH's death in 1835.

Bookplate of W. Van R. Whitall on the front paste-down, where is also written in pencil: "given to me Dec 24/19 JSH [?]".

In a ms note attached to the MS TRANSCRIPT at Dove Cottage, EHC states that "This letter to S. H. ... is the sole survivor of the correspondence" between C and SH; "Mrs Wordsworth, so her granddaughter Mrs Jane Kennedy told me, burnt all the rest of S. T. C.'s letters to Sara H." A few letters—fortunately including the verse letter of 4 Apr 1802 that became *Dejection*—and a few fragments of letters from C to SH survived, but no letter from SH to C. EHC's note continues: "The volume, which belonged to William Wordsworth the third (Bombay Bill), was sold in my presence at Sotheby's in 1896 for £30, I having bid £17." William Wordsworth (b Jan 1836), son of WW's youngest child "Willy", was at Rydal Mount when MW died in Jan 1859. *W Life* (Moorman) II 611. The book may have been given to the third William at that time, for it did not appear in the WW sale later in that year. See also *Athenaeum* I (1896) 714.

7. A flyleaf of Sir Thomas Browne "*Works*" (London 1658–9) with inscriptions by Charles Lamb, Sara Hutchinson, and Coleridge and an annotation by Coleridge. See BROWNE *Works* headnote and **3**
Berg Collection, The New York Public Library; reproduced by kind permission

The fact that C wrote notes in this copy of Browne's *Works* not only in 1808 but also on at least two widely separated occasions after he and SH had parted in the spring of 1810 raises a question whether he ever in fact gave her the book. This seems to be the copy of Browne's *Works* that was sent by mistake to the *Speedwell* in Mar 1804 (see *CN* ii 2014 f 48) and was taken to the Mediterranean. On 5 May 1809—SH and C being together at Allan Bank—she asked De Q to bring some of C's books "which were detained in London by Mr. Montagu", adding: "I know that he wants Sir T. Browne's works especially"; but she did not say it was hers. What happened to the book then we do not know; certainly it was in C's possession in 1817–18 (see *CN* iii 4366–77 and ANNEX [a]). By the time he had settled with the Gillmans in Highgate it was obviously impossible for him to send her the book without causing offence or distress. (SH met C in London in 1818, at Ramsgate in 1823, and visited him two or three times in Highgate in 1834 when she knew he was dying.) C wrote two more notes in it in Mar 1824; it was evidently in Highgate when he died.

There is no record of the book being sent to SH after C's death, but it certainly went to Rydal Mount. On 10 Jan 1835 SH sent Green "the Copies of all the notes written by Mr Coleridge in the Books at Rydal Mount" (*SHL* 439)—among them some of the notes from the 1658–9 folio "*Works*", for these were published in *LR* ii (published shortly after 11 Aug 1836) as "communicated by Mr Wordsworth", i.e. transcribed by SH. The text of the presentation letter in *LR* was taken from the original. In Jan 1848, on a visit to the Wordsworths long after SH's death, HCR "looked over Browne's *Vulgar Errors* with Coleridge's notes". *CRB* ii 673.

A copy of Browne's *Works* (1686 f°), including the *Pseudodoxia, Religio Medici, Hydriotaphia*, and *Certain Miscellany Tracts*, is described in *Gillman SC* (1843) 524 as with "Numerous MS. notes by S. T. Cole-ridge". This presumably is not the copy of the same edition in *Green SC* (1880) 302 not shown as C's and not described as annotated. The Gill-man copy was in the possession of Dr Lloyd Roberts, Manchester, in 1903 (W. E. A. Axon, *N&Q* 25 Jul 1903) but has not been reported since then and is not among the books in the Rylands Library that came from Dr Roberts's collection. Since there is no sign of a set of marginalia on Browne other than those collected by HNC for *LR*, and unlikely that HNC would not know of such a set of notes if the Gillmans had them, it is possible that this copy of the 1686 folio was a MS Facsimile containing a transcript of some or all of the notes C had written in the "*Works*" (1658–9).

MS TRANSCRIPT. DCL: Edward Quillinan's transcript of **1–3**, marked at the end: "The foregoing are written on flyleaves before the titlepage of Pseudodoxia Epidemica &c (Brown's Vulgar Errors—folio 3rd ed^n 1658 bound up with Religio Medici ⟨'printed for the Good of the Common-wealth'⟩ & a discourse on Urns—[)] in Mr Wordsworth's Library Rydal M^t." (The title-page of this edition ends, without imprint, "By Thomas Brown Doctour of Physick. Printed for the Good of the Commonwealth.") Edward Quillinan had been known to the Wordsworths since 1821, when DW befriended him and his two small children at the time of his wife's sudden death. Against WW's prolonged opposition he married Dora Wordsworth in the spring of 1841; Dora died in Jul 1847.

DATE. 1804–24. (*a*) Mar 1804: **1** dated in ms, **20**, and perhaps the deletions in *Pseudodoxia Epidemica*. (*b*) Jan–Jun 1808: **3** and **11** are dated in ms; the others seem to be **2–17, 22–27, 33, 43–52**. (*c*) 1817–18: **18, 19, 21, 29–32, 34–42**. (*d*) 16 Mar 1824: **54** (dated in ms) and **53**.

HNC dated the notes on *Religio Medici* (**31–48** omitting **44**) as "MADE DURING A SECOND PERUSAL. 1808" (*LR* II 398)—"second", that is, in relation to the other set of notes on *Religio Medici* (*LR* I 241–8), which he had indiscriminately dated "1802", although he must have noticed that some were of later date.

1 pp ⁻6–⁻4

March 10ᵗʰ, 1804. Saturday Night, 12 o'clock.—1

My dear Sara!

Sir Thomas Brown is among my first Favorites.2 Rich in various knowlege; exuberant in conceptions and conceits, contemplative, imaginative, often truly great and magnificent in his style and diction, tho' doubtless, too often big, ⟨stiff,⟩ and hyperlatinistic—: if thus I might without admixture of falshhood describe Sir T. Brown, and my description would have only this Fault, that it would be equally, or *almost* equally, applicable to half a dozen other Writers, from the beginning of the reign of Elizabeth to the end of the reign of Charles the second. He is indeed all this, & what he has ⟨more than all this⟩ peculiar to himself, I seem ~~to myself~~ to convey ⟨to my own mind⟩ in some measure by saying, that he is a quiet and sublime Enthusiast with a strong tinge of the Fantast, the Humourist constantly mingling with & flashing across the Philosopher, as the darting colours in shot silk play upon the main dye! ⟨In short,⟩ he has brains in his Head, which is all the ~~pleasanter~~ more interesting for a *little Twist* in the Brains.—He sometimes reminds the reader of

1 1 The address at the end of the letter shows that C wrote this at James Tobin's, where he made his London headquarters for more than a month while waiting for a ship to take him to Malta. See ANNUAL ANTHOLOGY 1 n 2, *CL* II 1067–8, 1077, 1098. While at Tobin's C saw much of Lamb and spent many evenings with him: *CL* II 1075, 1089. C was going to Malta in the hope of recovering his health; he also hoped that by his self-renunciatory separation SH would find her own independence:

see *C & SH* 51–3. SH, aware of both reasons, wrote him a "heart-wringing Letter", which, when C received it on 21 Feb, "put Despair into my Heart, and not merely as a Lodger, I fear, but as a Tenant for Life". *CN* II 1912. This letter of 10 Mar written to SH closes with the prayer for sleep that comes at the end of *Dejection*.

1 2 The author's name is spelled "Brown" in the title-pages of this edition.

Montaigne but from no other than the general circumstance of an ~~common~~ Egotism common to both, which in Montaigne is too often a mere amusing Gossip, a chit chat story of Whims & Peculiarities that lead to nothing,[3] but which in Sir Thomas Brown is always the result of a feeling Heart conjoined with a mind of active curiosity— ⟨their natural & becoming egotism*a* ~~in~~ of a man,⟩ who loving other men as himself, gain~~ed~~s the habit & the privilege of talking about himself as familiarly as ⟨about⟩ other men.[4] Fond of the Curious, and a Hunter of Oddities & Strangenesses, while he conceived~~s~~ himself ~~a grave~~ & with quaint & humorous Gravity a useful enquirer into physical Truth & fundamental Science, he loved to contemplate & discuss his own Thoughts & Feelings, because he found by comparison with other men's that *they* ⟨too⟩ were curi~~ou~~sosities: & so with a perfectly graceful & interesting Ease he put *them* too into his Musæum & Cabinet of Rarities—. In very truth, he was not mistaken—So compleatly does he see every thing in a light of his own, reading Nature neither by Sun, Moon, or Candle-Light, but by the Light of the faery Glory around his own Head, that you might say, that Nature had granted to him in perpetuity a Patent and Monopoly for all his Thoughts.—Read his Hydriotaphia above all—& in addition to the peculiarity, the exclusive *Sir Thomas Brown-ness* of all the Fancies & modes of Illustration wonder at and admire his *entireness* in every subject, which is before him—he is totus in illo[5]—he follows it, he never wanders from it—and he has no occasion to wander—for whatever happens to be his Subject, he metamorphoses all Nature into it.[6] ⟨In⟩ that Hydriotaphia or Treatise on some Urns dug up in Norfolk—how

---

a Written "egotism natural & becoming" and marked for transposition

1[3] At Dove Cottage 11–13 Jan 1804 C had been examining Cotton's translation of Montaigne (1743), possibly the "odd volume of Montaigne" that Lamb sent on 5 Nov 1802: *LL* I 328. Though C seldom refers to Montaigne, Lamb greatly admired his work; and the word "chit-chat" inevitably recalls the Lamb–C phrase "the divine chit-chat of Cowper". Both records of the last lecture of the 1818 series show that C mentioned Montaigne in much the same way as here: see **1** n 6, below.

1[4] Another personal parallel—cf *CN* I 1772; cf II 2830.

1[5] Cf Horace *Satires* 1.9.2 (var)— "entirely absorbed in it".

1[6] The use of **1** in Literary Lecture 14 of 13 Mar 1818 is to be seen in two records of the lecture in *Misc C* 218, 223; the first reprinted from *LR* I 235–6 (the documentary source not known), the second by "a Correspondent" in the *Tatler* of 23 May 1831. The recurrence of certain details, often verbally identical with this flyleaf note, and the presence of other details in one report but not the other, suggest that C used either the whole text of the letter from the beginning to "he metamorphoses all Nature into it" or a carefully condensed version of it.

earthy, how redolent of Graves & Sepulchres is every Line!—You have now dark mould, now a thigh-bone, now a Skull, then a bit of a mouldered Coffin/ a fragment of an old tombstone with moss in its Hic Jacet—a ghost, or a winding sheet, or the echo of a funeral Psalm wafted on a November Wind—& the gayest thing you shall meet with shall be a silver nail or gilt Anno Domini from a perished Coffin Top.—The very same ⟨remark⟩ applies in the same force to the interesting, tho far less interesting, Treatise on the Quincuncial Plantations of the Ancients—the same attention to ~~the~~ Oddities, ~~or~~ to the remotenesses, & minutiæ of vegetable forms—the same entireness of subject—Quincunxes in Heaven ⟨above,⟩ Quincunxes in Earth below, & Quincunxes in the water beneath the Earth/ Quincunxes in Deity, ⟨Quincunxes⟩ in the mind of ~~mind~~ Man/[7] Quincunxes in bones, ⟨in optic nerves,⟩ & in Roots of Trees, in leaves, & in petals, ⟨in every thing!⟩ In short just turn to the last Leaf of this volume, & read out aloud to yourself the 7 last Paragraphs of Chap. V. beginning with the words—"More Considerables"[8]— But it is time for me to be in bed/ in the words of Sir Thomas, which will serve you, my darling Sara! ~~for~~ as a fair specimen of his manner ["]But the Quincunx* of Heaven (*the Hyades or 5 Stars about the Horizon at midnight at that time) runs low, and tis time, we close the five ~~Stars~~ Ports of Knowlege: we are unwilling to spin out our waking Thoughts into the Phantasmes of Sleep, which often continueth præcogitations, making Cables of Cobwebs and wildernesses of handsome Groves. To keep our eyes open longer were to *act* our Antipodes.[a] The Huntsmen are up in America, and they are already past their first Sleep in Persia."[9]—Think you, my dear

---

[a] p ⁻5 ends with "Anti-" and the instruction "turn to the next leaf"; C resumed the note at the head of p ⁻4 by writing "Antipodes" in full

1[7] "The mind of Man", memorable from *CL* I 320, is a phrase prominent in both *Tintern Abbey* (line 99, but see 93–102) and the verse Preface to *The Excursion* (line 40, but see 35–41), in which it is declared to be "My haunt, and the main region of my song". *WPW* II 261–2, V 4. See also *Prelude* XIV 448 and the 1805–6 version of I 351–2: "The mind of man is fram'd like the breath | And harmony of music." The phrase occurs nowhere in C's poems.

1[8] See ANNEX [b], below.

1[9] Except for intentional omissions,

C quotes accurately, reading here—as the original does—"The Huntsmen are up in America"; see ANNEX [b]. C's parenthesis expands a little the shoulder-note in Browne's text: "*Hyades* near the Horizon about midnight, at that time"—a phrase with something of the savour of the gloss to *AM* (composed c 1810–15). Browne, whom C takes to task (unjustly) for objecting to the theory that the earth travels around the sun (see FIELD *Of the Church* 28 and n 1), seems to have made a reciprocal error in his calculation. Arabia and Persia are on much

Siar⟨a⟩![10] that there ever was such a reason given before for going to bed at midnight/ to wit, that if we did not, we should be acting the part of our ANTIPODES!!—and then "The Huntsmen are up in America"/—what Life, what Fancy!—Does the whimsical Knight give us thus a a dish of strong green Tea, & call it an *opiate*?—I trust, that you *are* quietly asleep,

> And all the Stars hang bright above your Dwelling,
> Silent as tho' they watch'd the sleeping Earth!—[11]
>
> S. T. Coleridge

7. Barnard's Inn, Holborn. London.—

N.B. In page 48 of the "Enquiries into common & vulgar Errors" there is a Plate of Urns & the figure of the Quincunx ✕ ~~pl~~ bound up by mistake, instead of being placed p. 48 of the last two Treatises— which is the opening of the "Cyrus Garden["], &c—[12]

2 p ⁻⁴*ᵃ*

N.B.[1] In the marginal symbols, which I have made, ⟨☉ points out a profound or at least solid and judicious Observation;⟩ = signifies that the sentence or passage in a line with it contains *majesty* of Conception or Style; ‖ signifies *Sublimity*; ⋅✕⋅ *brilliance* or ~~ign~~ *ingenuity*; Q signifies characteristic Quaintness; and F, that it contains an *error* in fact or philosophy.[2] S. T. Coleridge.

a Written below the "N.B." to 1 but in a smaller and somewhat different hand

---

the same longitude; Persia and eastern America are separated by about 140° of longitude or c 9½ hours; at midnight in England it is about 1900 hours in America and 0430 hours in Persia. The alteration (presumably C's) of "America" to "Arabia" in the *Blackwood's* version (see ANNEX [*b*]) improves matters a little: at midnight in England it would be 0430 hours in Arabia (when the diligent huntsman might well be up) but the same time in Persia. If the apparent motion of the sun is reversed, however, midnight in England would give 0500 hours in America (for the huntsmen) and 1930 hours in Persia (for those "past their first sleep")—and this may be what Browne had in mind. The detail would not matter, except that some scholars —perhaps without consulting Browne's text—have rebuked C for Browne's error.

1[10] C's slip of the pen—"my dear Sir" altered to "my dear Sara"— suggests that he had forgotten for the moment that he was writing to SH.

1[11] *Dejection* lines 130–1 (var): *PW* (EHC) I 368.

1[12] See also **20**, below.

2[1] Here the 1808 notes begin. The hand is the same as in **3**, which is written below the 1804 inscriptions by Lamb and C.

2[2] The few passages marked according to this scheme—only to i 25—are here printed in sequence through the marginalia.

3 p $^{-2a}$

It is not common to find a Book of so early date, at least among those of equal neatness of Printing, that contains so many gross typographical Errors: with the exception of our earliest dramatic Writers, some of which appear to have been never corrected; but worked off at once as the Types were first arranged by the Compositors.[1] But the grave & doctrinal Works are in general exceedingly correct; and form a striking contrast to modern publications, of which the late Edition of Bacon's Works would be paramount in the infamy of multiplied unnoticed Errata,[2] were it not for the unrivalled Slovenliness of Anderson's British Poets, in which the Blunders are at least as numerous as the pages, and many of them perverting the sense or killing the whole beauty, and yet giving or affording a meaning, however low, instead.[3] These are the most execrable of all typographical Errors.—1808.

PSEUDODOXIA EPIDEMICA

4 sig A3, pencil | "To the Reader"

We hope it will not be unconsidered, that we find no open tract, or constant manuduction in this Labyrinth; but are oft-times fain to wander in the *America* and untravelled parts of Truth. For though not many years past, Dr. *Primrose* hath made a learned and full Discourse of vulgar Errors in Physick, yet have we discussed but two or three thereof.

Is not this th[e] same person as the Physician mentioned by Mrs Hutchinson? See the Life of Colonel Hutchinson by his Widow.[1]

---

a Written below the Lamb and C inscriptions of 1804: see headnote

3[1] I.e. printed off without being corrected from proof.

3[2] Presumably *Works* of Francis Bacon (10 vols 1803), which C was using in 1807 (see *CN* II 3174); in 1808 he was using *Works* (5 vols 1765); see *CN* III 3244, 3286 f 8^v, and nn. For his own copy of the 1740 ed, which he was using in 1808, see ANDERSON COPY B **36** n 1. Bacon was very much in C's thought while he was preparing and publishing the 1809–10 *Friend* and in the 1818 revision: see *Friend* (*CC*) index. See also BLOMFIELD **2** n 1.

3[3] Anderson's *British Poets* was one of C's favourite examples of an inaccurately printed text: see ANDERSON general note.

4[1] I.e. Lucy HUTCHINSON *Memoirs of the Life of Colonel Hutchinson* (1806). The Wordsworths were reading a copy in early Feb 1807, and in a letter of 30 Jul 1807 C commended it to Josiah Wedgwood. *WL* (*M2*) I 133; MS Wedgwood. See also BAXTER *Reliquiae* COPY B **88** and n 3. The person referred to is James Primrose (d 1659), who wrote *De vulgi in medicina erroribus* (1638, tr Eng 1651, often reprinted). There is no mention of him in HUTCHINSON. C may have

4A i 4 | Bk ɪ ch 2 "A Further Illustration of the Same [Causes of Common Errors]"

For thinking by this retirement to obscure himself from God, he infringed the omnisciency and essential ubiquity of his Maker. Who ═══] as he created all things, so is he beyond and in them all, not only in power, as under his subjection, or in his presence, as being in his cognition, but in his very Essence, as being the soul of their ═══] causalities, and the essentiall cause of their existencies. Certainly, his posterity at this distance and after so perpetuated an impairment, cannot but condemn the poverty of his conception, that thought to obscure himself from his Creator in the shade of the garden, who had beheld him before in the darkness of his ·✕·] Chaos, and the great obscurity of nothing; That thought to flie from God, which could not flie himself, or imagined that one tree should conceal his nakedness from Gods eye, as another had revealed it unto his own. Those tormented spirits that wish the mountains to cover them, have fallen upon desires of minor absurdity, and chosen waies of less improbable concealment.

5 i 4

For although we now do hope the mercies of God will consider our degenerated integrities unto some minoration* of our offences, yet had not the sincerity of our first parents, so colourable expectations, unto whom the commandment was but single, and their integrities best able to resist the motions of its transgression.

* minoration, i.e. the Lessening, or extenuation.

5A i 10 | ɪ 4 "Of the Nearer and More Immediate Causes of Popular Errors"

The same words also in Greek ~~doth signifie a Testicle, and~~ hathve been thought by some an injunction only of continency, as *Aul. Gellius* hath expounded, and as *Empedocles* may also be interpreted: ~~that is, Testiculis miseri dextras subducite;~~ and might be the original intention of *Pythagoras*, ~~as having a notable hint hereof in Beans,~~ from ~~the~~ a natural signature ~~of the venereal organs of both Sexes.~~[1]

---

confused him with the Dr Plumtre, who is several times mentioned, but "he was a horrible atheist, and had such an intolerable pride, that he brook'd no superiours, and having some witt, took the boldness to exercise it, in the abuse of all the gentlemen wherever he came" (p 111). He published a book of epigrams, but enters the story only because he cured George Hutchinson of a stubborn "epileptick disease".

5A[1] The Greek phrase is usually translated "Abstain from beans"; the Latin reads: "Wretched men, take your hands from your testicles." In a

5B i 10

So he commands to deface the print of a cauldron in the ashes, after it hath boiled. Which strictly to observe were condemnable superstition. . . . In the like sense are to be received, when he adviseth his Disciples to give the right hand but to few, to put no viands in a chamber-pot, not to pass over a balance, not to rake up fire μειειν[1]] with a sword, ~~or piss against the Sun~~. nec contra solem mingere.

5C i 13, cropped | ɪ 5 "Of Credulity and Supinity"

How their faiths could decline so low, as to concede their generations in heaven, to be made by the smell of a citron, or that the felicity of their Paradise should consist in a Jubile ~~of copulation, that is, a coition of one act prolonged unto fifty years~~. seu semiseculumar[e] coitu, per L ann[os] uno et eodem act[u] continuato.

6 i 13

But if like *Zeno* he shall walk about, and yet deny there is any motion in nature; surely that man was constituted for *Anticera*, and were a fit companion for those, who having a conceit they are dead, cannot be convicted into the society of the living.

Anticera, a place famous for the growth of Hellebore, a plant supposed to cure madness.[1]

7 i 13

. . . and truth which wise men say doth lye in a well, is not recoverable but by *exantlation.

---

note on the phrase "Abstine a fabis" (Abstain from beans) C brought together, apparently from lexical sources, a number of meanings of κύαμος and words cognate with it; four of these have genital implications, but he has not included this interpretation of Browne's. N 29 f 16.

5B[1] C has constructed a Greek verb equivalent to the Latin *mingere* of his own version, by giving a Greek infinitive ending to Latin *meiere*, an alternative to *mingere*. The Greek verb is ὀμίχειν (or ὀμιχεῖν), of the same root. C has translated the cancelled

words into Latin, as also in **5C, 13B,** and **24A**; in **5A, 12A, 15A, 24B–24E** he has cancelled words in the text without providing a gloss. All these cancellations, dealing with bodily and sexual functions, may have been cancelled to spare SH's sensibilities. See also BROWNE *Religio* **24A** and **25** n 1.

6[1] The name is commonly spelled *Anticyra*. Robert Burton records the virtues of hellebore as a cure for madness, in *Anatomy of Melancholy* pt 2 sec 4 mem 4 subs 2. See also *EOT (CC)* ɪɪ 304.

* the act of drawing up, as a bucket from a well, from εξ from, and αντλον, a sewer, & thence any deep ⟨place⟩ containing water.[1]

7A i 13 | following immediately on **7** textus

It were some extenuation of the curse, if *in sudore vultus tui* [in the sweat of your brow] were confinable unto corporal exercitations, and ·※·] there still remained a Paradise or unthorny place of knowledge. But now our understandings being eclipsed, as well as our tempers infirmed, we must betake our selves to waies of reparation, ·※·] and depend upon the illumination of our endeavours. For thus we may in some measure repair our primary ruines, and build our selves men again.

8 i 14

For not obeying the dictates of reason, and neglecting the cries of truth, we fail not only in the trust of our undertakings, but in the intention of man it self. Which although more venial in ordinary constitutions, and such as are not framed beyond the capacity of beaten notions, yet will it inexcusably condemn some men, who ═══] having received excellent endowments, have yet sat down by the way, and frustrated the intention of their habilities. For certainly as some men have sinned, in the principles of humanity, and must answer, for not being men, so others offend if they be not more ... These are not excusable without an Excellency.

O me!!

8A i 18 | ɪ 6 "Of Adherence unto Antiquity"

F] They [the ancients] understood not the motion of the eighth sphear from West to East, and so conceived the longitude of the stars invariable.

8B i 18–19 | ɪ 7 "Of Authority"

Q] ... yet are their Authorities but temporary, and not to be imbraced beyond the minority of our intellectuals.

7[1] As *OED* notices, the etymology of "exantlation" is disputed between (*a*) *exanclare*—to draw (water etc) like a slave; and (*b*) ἐξαντλεῖν—to pump out (liquids) as from the bilges of a ship, for which *OED* cites this passage in *Pseudodoxia Epidemica*. The word ἄντλος means, not (as C seems to have thought when he wrote this note) a well or sewer, but the bilge-water in a ship. In Sept 1831 he made the correct connexion—recalling no doubt with revulsion his voyage to Malta in the *Speedwell*—when he alluded to "the exantlation of the mucus from the bilge of my poor crazy Lugger". *CL* vɪ 872.

9 i 20

Moreover a testimony in points Historical, and where it is of un-avoidable use, <u>is of no illation</u> in the negative; nor is it of consequence that Herodotus writing nothing of Rome, there was no such city in his time; or because Dioscorides hath made no mention of Unicorns horn there is therefore no such thing in nature.

i.e. can have no argument brought from it to prove the negative.

10 i 20

Whereas indeed the reason of man hath not such restraint; con-
F] cluding not only affirmatively but negatively; not only affirming there is no magnitude beyond the last heavens, but also denying there is any vacuity within them. Although it be confessed, the affirmative hath the prerogative illation, and <u>Barbara</u> engrosseth the powerfull demonstration.

Barbara, one of jargon-words in a Latin Verse, formed as an instrument of technical memory onf the divisions or sorts of Syllogisms in the old Systems of Logic.[1]

10[1] *Barbara*—a mnemonic used by logicians to represent a syllogism in which the major and minor premisses and the conclusion are all universal affirmatives: e.g. *A*ll animals are mortal; *A*ll men are animals; therefore *A*ll men are mortal. In mediaeval times the four vowels A, E, I, O were assigned to the four forms of categorical sentence, and the grouping of three of these letters was used to indicate the various moods of valid syllogism. *Barbara* is the first word in a doggerel Latin mnemonic that identified each of the nineteen valid forms of "strong" syllogisms by the incidence of the vowels in the key-words: "*Barbara, Celarent, Darii, Ferioque* prioris...".

In the phrase "memoria technica" in BLANCO WHITE *Poor Man's Preservative* **2**, C touches upon a complex and largely subterranean practice that passed from the Greeks to Rome and so into the European tradition, variously referred to as "technical memory", "artificial memory", or simply "ars memoriae". He was familiar with some part of this arcane tradition through his reading of Bruno (see e.g. *CL* v 332n: "Giordano Bruno —particularly...his *Mnemonic* Tracts generally"). For a detailed historical and technical account, see Frances A. Yates *The Art of Memory* (1966, 1972). Memoria technica was a method of memorising "through a technique of impressing 'places' and 'images' on memory" (Yates p xi), the "places" being committed to memory as details in a complex schematic figure, often architectural. This technique, highly cultivated by scholars to extend mental capacity, established itself at a lower level, especially among illiterate people, as a lively habit of fixing in the mind the "places" and "images" of the scriptures, whereby interrelations of narrative and doctrinal detail in the gospels, and relations between OT and NT texts, could be perceived, remembered, and elaborated, often with the help of graphic representation in emblems, sculpture, and ecclesiastical stained glass.

C recognised the value of e.g.

11 i 22 | I 8 "A Brief Enumeration of Authors" § 1

1. The first in order, as also in time shall be *Herodotus* of *Halicarnassus*, an excellent and very elegant Historian.... Now in this Author ... there are many things fabulously delivered, and not to be accepted as truths: whereby nevertheless if any man be deceived, the Author is not so culpable as the believer. For he indeed imitating the father Poet, whose life he hath also written, and, as Thucydides observeth, as well intending the delight as benefit of his Reader, hath besprinkled his work with many fabulosities, whereby if any man be led into error, he mistaketh the intention of the Author, who plainly confesseth he writeth many things by hearsay.

The Veracity and Credibility of Herodotus has increased, and increases, with the increase of our Discoveries/ Several relations deemed fabulous have been authenticated within the last 30 years from this present 1808.—[1]

12 i 22 | § 2

In the second place is Ctesias the Cnidian, Physician unto Artaxerxes King of Persia ... there are extant some fragments ... he wrote the History of Persia, and many narrations of India. In the first ... his testimony is acceptable. In his Indian relations, wherein are contained strange and incredible accounts, he is surely to be read with suspension.... Yet were his relations taken up by some succeeding writers, and many thereof revived by our Countriman, Sir *John Mandevill*, Knight, and Doctor in Physick, who left a book of his Travels, which hath been honoured with the translation of many languishesages, and now continued above three hundred years;

Quarles's elaborate conceits "on *mnemonic* grounds—as Hooks and Barbs of technical memory". N 25 f 85ᵛ; cf *Friend* (*CC*) I 21. But when he spoke disparagingly in *BL* ch 7 of "certain recent schemes which *promise* an artificial *memory*", he was thinking, not of the intricate and noble devices contrived by Renaissance virtuosi, but of some such degenerate revival as Richard Grey's widely distributed *Memoria Technica; or, A New Method of Artificial Memory* (1730 anon; thereafter several acknowledged eds in his lifetime, and kept in print with modernising revisions until c 1861). For C's awareness of the value of a figurative mnemonic to clarify and organise complex reflection, see *CL* IV 773.

11[1] C is thinking of the rapid increase in archaeological and geographical knowledge accumulated by travellers in Greece and Africa, and of the studies being made of Oriental historical records. Much of the work of Napoleon's Egyptologists tended to confirm Herodotus' description of Egypt, although C later objected to their claim to have confirmed Herodotus' report (in 2.142) of the antiquity of Egyptian records: see e.g. the opening of "*Prometheus*".

herein he often attesteth the fabulous relations of *Ctesias*, and seems, to confirm the refuted accounts of Antiquity. All which may still be received in some acceptions of morality, and to a pregnant invention, may afford commendable mythologie; but in a natural and proper exposition it containeth impossibilities and things inconsistent with truth.

Many if not most of these Ctesian Fables in Sir J. Mandevill were monkish interpolations.[1]

12A   i 23 | § 4

It were a strange effect, ~~and whores would forsake the experiment of Savine~~, if that were a truth which he delivereth of Brake or female Fearn, that only treading over it, it causeth a sudden ~~abortion~~ miscarriage. It were to be wished true, and women would Idolize him, could that be made out which he recordeth of *Phyllon, Mercury*, and other vegetables, that the juice of the Masle plant drunk, ~~or the leaves but applied unto the genitals,~~ determines their conceptions unto males.

13   i 25, cropped | § 13

[*Jeronimus Cardanus*] is of singular use unto a prudent Reader; but unto him that onely desireth <u>Hoties</u>, or to replenish his head with varieties . . . he may become no small occasion of Error.

i.e. ὅτι, *whateve*[*rs,*] that is, whatever is written, no matter what, true or false—*omniana*[—]"all sorts of Varieties["] as a dear young Lady once said ŧ to me[1]

12[1] *The Voiage of Sir John Mandevil*, putatively by Sir John Mandeville (d c 1372)—perhaps himself a fictitious figure—written in French shortly after the middle of the fourteenth century, was promptly translated into English, Latin, German, and other languages. This account of fabulous travels has for a long time been known to have been drawn from various written sources of questionable veracity. Ctesias (fl 398 B.C.), Greek physician at the Persian court, seeking to correct the "lies" of Herodotus, wrote a "history" that surpasses Herodotus in fables; it has survived only in fragments and in an abridg-ment by Photius (for whom see **31** n 1, below).

13[1] *OED* derives "hoti" (pl "hoties") from ὅτι (that), and explains it as a statement introduced by "that", hence any assertion of fact actual or alleged. But C has evidently —and legitimately—taken his word from ὅτι (whatever)—often written ὅ τι or ὅ, τι to distinguish it from ὅτι (that). The word "omniana", however, may be RS's: by the middle of Apr 1807 he had published more than a hundred odds and ends under that collective title. *S Letters* (Curry) I 448 and n; cf 449. When C used the word "Omniana" in Mar 1811 (*CL* III 306)

13A i 25 | § 14

And seeing the lapses of these worthy pens [of the learned], to cast a wary eye on those diminutive, and pamphlet Treatie~~sises~~ daily
·※·] published among us. Pieces maintaining rather Typography than
⊙] verity; Authors presumably writing by common places, wherein for many years promiscuously amassing all that makes for their subject, they break forth at last in trite and fruitless Rhapsodies; doing thereby not only open injury unto learning, but committing a secret treachery upon truth.

13B i 26 | ɪ 9 "Of the Same"

Aristotle in his Ethicks takes up the conceit of the *Bever,* ~~and the divulsion of his Testicles.~~ nempe, quod fugiens ipse testes suos divellens venatoribus reliquit.[1]

14 i 29 | ɪ 10 "Of... the Endeavours of Satan"

And if as some contend, no creature can desire his own annihilation, that Nothing is not appetible, and not to be at all, is worse then to be in the miserablest condition of something...

capable of being wished for.

15 i 31

Wherein beside that he annihilates the blessed Angels and spirits in the rank of his creation; he begets a security of himself, and a
!!] careless eye unto the last remunerations. And therefore hereto he inveigleth, not only *Sadduces* and such as retain unto the Church of God: but is also content that *Epicurus, Democritus*, or any Heathan should hold the same.

15A i 35 | ɪ 11 "A Further Illustration"

~~That the feminine sex have no generative emission, affording no seminal Principles of conception, was Aristotles opinion of old, maintained still by some, and will be countenanced by him for ever. For hereby he disparageth the fruit of the Virgin, frustrateth the fundamental Prophesie, nor can the seed of the Woman then break the head of the Serpent.~~

---

he was referring to the projected book that RS was to publish anonymously in 1812 in 2 vols under the title *Omniana, or Horae Otiosiores*, to which C contributed more than forty

of his more curious notebook entries.
13B[1] "That is, that in his flight he tore out his testicles and left them to the hunters." He was being hunted for his musk: see **24B**, below.

16   i 35

Thus ... If *Heraclitus* with his adherents will hold the Sun is no bigger then it appeareth ... he shall not want herein the applause or advocacy of Satan.

It is not improbable, that Heraclitus meant only to imply, that we ~~know only~~ *perceive* only our own sensations, and they of course are what they are; that the *Image* of the Sun is an appearance, or sensation in our eyes &c, and of course an appearance can be neither more [nor]*ᵃ* less than what it *appears* to be; that the *notion* of the *true Size* of the Sun is *not* an *Image*, or belonging either to sense, or the sensuous fancy, but is an imageless Truth of the understanding obtained by intellectual Deductions.—

⟨He could not possibly mean what Sir T. B. supposes him to have meant: for if he had believed the Sun to be no more than a mile distant from us, every Tree & House must have shewn its absurdity.⟩*ᵇ*1 S. T. C.

17   i 36, at the end of Bk I

In the following Books I have endeavoured ⟨(wherever the Author himself is in "a vulgar Error",)⟩1 as far as my knowlege extends, to give in the margin either the demonstrated Discoveries, or more probable opinions, of the present Natural Philosophy: so that independent of the entertainingness of the Thoughts and Tales and the force & splendor of Sir T. Brown's Diction and Manner, you may at once learn *from him* the history of human Fancies & Superstitions, both when he detects them, & when he himself falls into them

---

ᵃ Word supplied by the editor
ᵇ The insertion is in a smaller hand, squeezed in between the previous paragraph and the initials "S. T. C."

16¹ C's explanation is plausible, though developed in terms that are Berkeleyan or Esteesean rather than those of an Ionic philosopher of c 500 B.C. The gnomic and often ironic tone of Heraclitus' utterances (as we have them) makes it difficult to state his intention beyond question. The most likely explanations here are either that Heraclitus was demonstrating the unreliability of sense perceptions or that he was deliberately making an absurd statement in argument against some equally absurd contemporary account of the size of the sun. For Heraclitus' fragments generally, see BÖHME **31** n 2.

17¹ The running-headline throughout Pt i reads: "*Enquiries into Vulgar* | and *Common* ERRORS". The *Pseudodoxia Epidemica* was—and is—widely known as Browne's "Vulgar Errors". G. Keynes *Bibliography of Sir Thomas Browne* App II (pp 210–20) gives an account of the tradition according to which since c 1579 books had been called "Vulgar Errors" or "Popular Errors" and which Browne knew he was following.

—& from *my notes* the real Truth of Things, or at least the highest degree of Probability, at which human Research has hitherto arrived. S. T. C.

18   i 37 | II 1 "Of Chrystall"

Hereof the common opinion hath been, and still remaineth amongst us, that Chrystal is nothing else, but Ice or Snow concreted, and by duration of time, congealed beyond liquidation.

Cold = the attractive or astringent power ⟨comparatively⟩ uncounteracted by the dilative, the diminution of which is the proportional increase of the contractive. Hence the astringent or power of negative Magnetism is the proper Agent in Cold, and the Contractive, or Oxygen, an allied and consequential power—*Chrystallum/ non ex aquâ, sed ex substantiâ metallorum communi confrigatorum*.[1] As the Equator ⟨or Mid-point of the equatorial hemispherical Line ☉⟩ to the Centre, so Water to Gold. Hydrogen = electrical Azot: Azot = Magnetic Hydrogen[2]

19   i 39

... [Chrystal] will strike fire upon percussion like many other stones; and upon collision with steel actively send forth its sparks, not much inferiourly unto a flint.

it being indeed nothing else but pure Flint.

20   plate facing i 48

Misplaced—see p 48—Garden of Cyrus—towards the end of Vol:

21   i 58–9, cropped | II 3 "Concerning the Loadstone ..."

As strange must be the Lithomancy or divination from this stone [lodestone] ... and the Magick thereof not safely to be believed, which was delivered by *Orpheus*, that sprinkled with water it will upon a question emit a voice not much unlike an Infant.

i.e. To the twin counterforces of the Magnetic Power, the equilibrium of which is revealed in magnetic Iron, as the substantial, add the twin counterforces, or + and − poles, of the Electrical Power, the in-

18[1] "A Crystal [formed] not out of water, but out of the common substance of metals frozen with it".

18[2] This note, with **19, 21, 29,** and **40,** belongs to a group of "chemical" notes the background to which can be discerned esp in BÖHME **17, 46, 117, 139** (and cf **101, 107, 137**), and in BOERHAAVE passim.

difference of which is realized in Water, as the Superficial—(whence Orpheus employed the term *sprinkled* or rather affused or super-fused)[1] and you will [hear]*[a]* the voice of infant Nature—i.e. you will understand the rudimental products and elementary Powers and Constructions of the phænomenal World. An Enigma not unworthy of Orpheus—& therefore not improbably ascribed to him. ⟨*S. T. C.*⟩

P.S. − & + Magn. = Attraction and Repulsion: or Cohesion and Dispersion. − and + Elect. = Contraction and Dilation.

22   i 74 | ii 6 "Of Sundry Tenents Concerning Vegetables or Plants . . ." § 1

Many Mola's and false conceptions there are of *Mandrakes*, the first from great Antiquity, conceiveth the Root thereof resembleth the shape of Man; which is a conceit not to be made out by ordinary inspection, or any other eyes, then such as regarding the Clouds, behold them in shapes conformable to pre-apprehensions.

See Donne's *Metempsych*.[1]

[a] Word supplied by the editor

21[1] *OED* cites a seventeenth-century use of "superfused" meaning "to sprinkle or affuse; to suffuse in baptism", and also cites this marginal note, from *LR*. Browne alludes to the pseudo-Orphic *Lithica* (lines 373–4), a work of the fourth century A.D. on the magical and medicinal qualities of stones; the stone referred to here is *ophites* (serpentine), not the lodestone. C considers the idea worthy of the legendary or semi-legendary Orpheus, poet, cosmogonist, and founder of a religious movement, to whom were attributed the theogony much quoted by Neoplatonic and early Christian writers and the series of "Orphic Hymns".

22[1] The mandrake root makes a notable appearance in Donne's *Song* "Goe, and catche a falling starre", but its ambience is more mysterious in the passage C is thinking of—*The Progress of the Soule* (or *Metempsychosis. Poema Satyricon*) XIV–XVI, which ends:

So, of a lone unhaunted place possesst,
Did this souls second Inne, built by the guest,

This living buried man, this quiet mandrake, rest.

As gloss to these lines H. J. C. Grierson quotes from the *Pseudodoxia* the same passage as **22** textus, without further comment. *The Poems of John Donne* (Oxford 1912) ii 221. C quoted two passages from the *Progress of the Soule* with strong approval in *BL* ch 18 (1907) ii 65.

Mandrake (*mandragora*) is a plant with short stem, thick, fleshy, often forked, roots, and fetid lance-shaped leaves (*OED*), and bears a fruit referred to as "apples". The forked root —as Browne notes—was thought to resemble the human form, and it was said (e.g. by Shakespeare) to shriek when drawn out of the ground. Its properties are emetic and narcotic; poets variously ascribe to it properties soporific and aphrodisiac, and claim that it promotes fertility in women. Donne goes further in xv: "His apples kindle, his leaves, force of conception kill." C introduces the mandrake in the draft of *Limbo* etc: *CN* iii 4073 f 146.

23 i 82, slightly cropped | II 7 "Of Some Insects, and the Properties of Severall Plants" § 4

That *Camphire* or Eunuchates, begets in Men an impotency unto venery, observation will hardly confirm . . .

There is no doubt of the Fact, as to a *temporary* effect: and Camph: [i]s therefore a [s]trong & immediate Antidote to an [o]verdose of [C]antharides.[1] Yet [th]ere are, doubtless, [s]orts & cases of *Imp.*, which Camphire might relieve/ Opium [i]s occasionally Aphrodisial but far oftener Anti-aphrodisial—The [s]ame is true of *Bang* or powdered Hemp leaves—& I suppose of the whole tribe of narcotic Stimulants.[2]

24 i 83 | § 8

That Yew and the berries thereof are harmless, we know.

The berries are harmless; but the leaves of the yew are undoubtedly poisonous. Vide *Withering* British Plants: Taxus.[1]

24A i 91 | III 4 "Of the Bever"

That a Bever to escape the Hunter, ~~bites off his testicles or stones,~~ proprio morsu ipse suos testes divellit, is a Tenent very ancient; and hath had thereby advantage of propagation.

24B i 91

. . . the same we meet with in *Juvenall* . . .

——*imitatus Castora, qui se*
Eunuchum ipse facit, cupiens evadere damno:
~~*Testiculorum, adeo medicatum intelligit inguen*;~~

[——like the beaver, who makes himself a eunuch to avoid the loss of his testicles; so conscious is he of the drug he carries in his groin.]

23[1] The dried beetle *Cantharis vesicatoria* (Spanish fly)—used in medicine externally as a blistering substance and internally as a diuretic and aphrodisiac.

23[2] The trial that C made with Tom Wedgwood in Feb 1803 with a small quantity of *bhang* provided by Sir Joseph Banks through Samuel Purkis is recorded in *CL* II 919–20, 921, 927, 933–4. C made in the summer of 1807 some observations upon the nature and effect of the drug in Robert PERCIVAL *Account of the Island of Ceylon* (1803); his copy is now in VCL.

24[1] By Dec 1800 C owned a copy of William Withering *An Arrangement of British Plants* (4 vols 1796): see *CN* I 863. Withering's entry on *Taxus*, the "Common Yew Tree", assigns the tree to "Mountains of Westmoreland, Cumberland, and hills of Herefordshire" and cites authorities for its growing "in a truly wild state" and "in its truly natural situations" in several places well known to C. III 614. At III 615n Withering notes: "The fresh leaves are fatal to the human species. Three children were killed by a spoonful of the green leaves. . . ."

24C i 92

... we cannot maintain ~~the~~ any evulsion, ~~or biting off any parts~~ ...

24D i 92

If therefore any affirm a wise man should demean himself like the Bever, who to escape with his life, contemneth ~~the~~ a meaner loss ~~of his genitals~~; that is, in case of extremity ... we may hereby apprehend a real and useful Truth.

24E i 93

Most therefore of the Moderns before *Rondeletius*, and all the Ancients excepting *Sestius*, have misunderstood this ~~part, conceiving~~ *Castoreum* ~~the Testicles~~ of the Bever. ... The Egyptians also failed in the ground of their Hieroglyphick, whereby they expressed the punishment of adultery by the Bever ~~depriving himself of his testicles~~; which was amongst them the penalty of such incontinency. Nor is Aetius perhaps, too strictly to be observed, when he perscribeth ~~the stones of~~ from the Otter, or River-dog, as succedaneou~~sum~~ unto *Castoreum*. But most inexcusable of all is *Pliny*; who having before him in one place the experiment of *Sestius* against it, ~~sets down~~ asserts the fact in another, ~~that~~ of the Bevers of *Pontus*, ~~bite off their testicles,~~ and in the same place affirmeth the like of the Hyena.

24F i 111 | iii 13 "Of Frogs, Toads and Toad-stone"

Concerning the venemous urine of Toads, of the stone in the Toads head, and of the generation of Frogs, conceptions are entertained which require consideration. And first, that a Toad ~~pisseth, and~~ this way diffuseth its venome, is generally received, not only with us, but also in other parts. ... For to speak ~~properly~~ strictly, a Toad ~~pisseth not~~ voideth no separate, or proper urine: nor do they contain those urinary parts which are found in other Animals, to avoid that serous excretion ...

25 i 111

For the like we daily observe in the heads of Fishes, as Cods, Carps, and Pearches: the like also in Snails, a soft and <u>exosseous</u> Animal, whereof in the naked and greater sort ... Nature neer the head hath placed a flat white stone, or rather testaceous concretion.

boneless[1]

25[1] *OED* gives "exossation" only of fruit, whereas C's word clearly re-

quires the original meaning similar to Browne's "exosseous" (the only ex-

26 i 111

For although *Lapidaries* and <u>questuary</u> enquirers affirm it, yet the writers of minerals and natural speculators, are of another belief...

having Gain or money for their object.

27 i 119 | iii 17 "Of Hares"

As for the mutation of sexes, or transition into one another, we cannot deny it in Hares, it being observable in Man. For... though very few, or rather none which have emasculated or turned Women, yet very many who from an esteem or reality of being Women have infallably proved Men. Some at the first point of their menstrous eruptions, some in the day of their marriage, others many years after.... And that not only mankind, but many other Animals, may suffer this transexion, we will not deny...

a mere Disease of the κλιτορις[1] is here taken for a *Transexion*

28 i 264 | vi 8 "Of the River Nilus"

...the River *Gihon*, a branch of *Euphrates* and River of Paradise...

The Rivers from Eden were meant to symbolize, or rather meant only, the great primary Races of Mankind. Sir T. B. was the very man to have seen this, but the superstition of the *Letter* was then culminant.

29 i 272–4 | vi 10 "Of the Blackness of Negroes"

The *Chymists* have laudably reduced their causes unto Sal, Sulphur, and Mercury; and had they made it out so well in this, as in the objects of smell and taste, their endeavours had been more acceptable; For whereas they refer Sapor unto Salt, and Odor unto Sulphur, they vary much concerning colour; some reducing it unto Mercury, some to Sulphur; others unto Salt.

Even now, after all the brilliant discoveries from Scheele, Priestley and Cavendish to Berzelius, and Sir H. Davy,[1] no improvement

---

ample of that use cited by *OED*). In a remark on Blake's drawings in the *Songs of Innocence and Songs of Experience* C noticed as an occasional fault "irregular unmodified Lines of the Inanimate, sometimes as the effect of rigidity and sometimes of exossation—like a wet tendon". *CL* iv 836 (var): 12 Feb 1818.

27[1] C has transliterated the English word "clitoris" into Greek characters;

the Greek form is κλειτορίς. Fracastorius seems to have introduced the word to its present currency.

29[1] Humphry Davy was knighted on 8 Apr 1812—the earliest possible date for this note, as for Böhme **17** and other related marginalia. The principal work of Carl Wilhelm Scheele (1742–86), Swedish chemist, was on acids, and in 1777—independently of Priestley—he discovered oxygen and showed

has been ⟨made⟩ in this division, not of primary Bodies (those idols of the modern atomic Chemistry) but *of Causes*, as Sir T. B. rightly expresses them—i.e. of elementary Powers manifested in Bodies— Mercury standing for the bi-polar Metallic Principle, ~~or~~ best imaged as a line or Axis from N. to S., the North or Negative Pole being the cohesive or coherentific Force, and the South or Positive Pole being the Dispersive or incoherentic Force,[2] the first predominant in and therefore represented by Carbon, the second by Nitrogen— the Series of Metals being the primary and hence indecomponible Syntheta and proportions of both. In like manner the Sulphur represents the active and passive Principle of Fire: a i.e. the con- tractive Force, = negative Electricity, Oxygen, Flame, and the dila- tive Force = Warmth, + El. and Hydrogen/ and lastly Salt as the Equilibrium or Compound of the former. So taken, Salt, Sulphur and Mercury are equivalent to the Combustive, the Combustible, and the Combust;[3] under one or other of which all known Bodies or ponderable Substances may be classed and distinguished.[4]

30 i 314, pencil | vii 16 "Of Divers Other Relations"

And therefore what is related of devils ... that they steal the seminal emissions of man, and transmit them into there votaries in coition, is much to be suspected; and altogether to be denied, that there ensue conceptions thereupon; however husbanded by Art, and the wisest menagery of that most subtile imposter.

Sir T. Brown's doubts[a]

[a] *LR* omits the incomplete sentence

that the atmosphere is chiefly com- prised of two gases, one supporting combustion, the other preventing it. Thomas Beddoes translated Scheele's work into English in 1786. C seems not to have known his work in detail. Joseph Priestley, by isolating oxygen (1774), held the key to modern chemis- try, but his stubborn adherence to the theory of phlogiston prevented him from exploring his discovery fully. See ANDERSON COPY B **19** n 2 and BÖHME **101** n 2. Henry Cavendish (1731–1810), natural philosopher and millionaire, discovered the constitu- tion of water and of atmospheric air before 1783; he continued to experi- ment in electricity and in the density of the earth. Jöns Jacob Berzelius (1779–

1848), Swedish chemist (a corres- pondent of Davy's)—"Nature's grand inquisitor" (N 55 f 16)—formulated laws of chemical combination and the system of chemical symbols; he also discovered three new elements and was the first to isolate a number of the metallic elements.

29[2] *OED* cites the first use of "coherentific" as C's in this marginal note; "incoherentic" is not in *OED*.

29[3] *OED* assigns this use of "Com- bust" as a noun to C in this note.

29[4] For a parallel to the scheme sketched out in this note see e.g. BÖHME **94–95**. See also BÖHME **31** n 2, and *CL* iv 771–5—"a very rude sketch of the very rudiments of '*Heraclitus redivivus*' ".

RELIGIO MEDICI

31 ii [4] | Pt i § 1

For my Religion, though there be several circumstances that might perswade the world I have none, at all, as the generall scandall of my profession, the naturall course of my studies, the indifferency of my behaviour, and discourse in matters of Religion, neither violently defending one, nor with that common ardour and contention opposing another; yet in despight hereof I dare without usurpation, assume the honourable stile of a Christian ...

The ⟨*historical*⟩ origin of this scandal, which in nine cases out of ten is the honor of the medical Profession, may perhaps be found in the fact, that Ænesidemus and Sextus Empiricus, Sceptics, were both Physicians—about the close of the second Century. A fragment from the former has been preserved by Photius, and such as would leave a painful regret for the loss of the Work, had not the invaluable work of Sextus Empiricus been still extant.[1]

32 ii [6]–7,[a] cropped | i § 7

A third [error] there is which I did never positively maintaine or practice, but have often wished it had been consonant to Truth, and not offensive to my Religion, and that is the prayer for the dead; whereunto I was inclined from some charitable inducements, whereby I could scarce containe my prayers for a friend at the ringing of a Bell, or behold his corpse without an oraison for his soul ...

Our Church with ~~its~~ her characteristic Christian Prudence does not enjoin Prayer for the Dead; but neither does ~~it~~ she prohibit it. In its own nature it belongs to a private Aspiration—and being conditional, like all religious acts not expressed in Scripture, and therefore not combinable with a perfect faith, it is a something between prayer and

---

[a] ii 7 is correctly numbered, the title-page to Pt ii being p [1]. The two preceding pages were incorrectly numbered 1 and 2 instead of 5 and 6

31[1] Aenesidemus of Cnossos (c second half of first century B.C.), not apparently known as a doctor, wrote a work on the system of Pyrrho (fl 304 B.C.), the founder of Scepticism, which re-established it. Sextus Empiricus (c A.D. 200–50), whose name shows him to have been a doctor, was the chief exponent of Scepticism. Photius (c 820–91) compiled a *Bibliotheca* or *Myriobiblion*, being a summary of some 280 works that he had read before 858. Tennemann's account of Aenesidemus (v 44–100) mentions that Photius preserved a very scanty (*dürftiges*) fragment of Aenesidemus and summarised the eight books of his work.

wish—an act of natural piety sublimed by Christian Hope—that ~~dwells in~~ shares in the light and meets the diverging rays of Faith, tho' it be not contained in the Focus[1]

33   ii 8, pencil, overtraced | i § 13

... [God] holds no Counsell, but that mysticall one of the Trinity, wherein though there be three persons, there is but one mind that decrees without contradiction ...

Sir T. B. is very amusing. He confesses his past Heresies which are mere *opinions*: while his orthodoxy is full of heretical errors. *His* Trinity is a mere *trefoil* a $3\alpha = 1\beta$ which is no mystery at all, but a common object of the Senses. The mystery is, that One is Three—i.e each Being the whole God.

34   ii 10–11 | i § 18

'Tis not a ridiculous devotion to say a prayer before a game at Tables; for even in *sortilegies*, and matters of greatest uncertainty, there is a setled and preordered course of effects: it is we that are blind, not Fortune ...

But a great profanation, methinks: and a no less absurdity. Would Sir T. Brown before weighing two pigs of Lead, *a* and *b*, ⟨pray to God⟩ that *a* might weigh the heavier? Yet if the result of the Dice be at the time equally believed to be a settled & predetermined Effect, where lies the Difference? Would not this apply against all petitionary prayer? S[t] Paul's injunction involves the answer: Pray *always*.[1]

35   ii 12–13, cropped | i § 22

They who to salve this would make the Deluge particular, proceed upon a principle that I can no way grant; not onely upon the negative of holy Scriptures, but of mine own reason, whereby I can make it probable, that the world was as well peopled in the time of *Noah*, as in ours; and fifteen hundred yeares to people the world, as full a time for them as foure thousand yeares since have been to us.

But according to the Scripture the Deluge was so gentle as to leave uncrushed the green leaves on the Olive Tree. If then it was universal, and if (as admitting the Longevity of the anti-deluvians it must have been) the Earth was fully peopled, is it not strange that no Buildings remain in the since then uninhabited parts—in America for instance?

32[1] For "Focus" see BÖHME **169**   34[1] See BOOK   OF   COMMON
and n 1.   PRAYER COPY B **1** n 1.

That no human skeletons are found, may be solved from the large proportion of Phosphoric Acid in the human Bones. But Cities, Roa and Traces of Civilization?—I do not know what to think— unless we might be allowed to consider Noah as a Homo represen- tati[vus][1] [. . . . .]*a*

36 ii 15, cropped | i § 33

They that to refute the Invocation of Saints, have denied that they have any knowledge of our affaires below, have proceeded too farre, and must pardon my opinion, till I can throughly answer that piece of Scripture, *At the conversion of a sinner the Angels of Heaven rejoyce.*

Take any moral or religious book, and instead of understanding each sentence according to ⟨the⟩ main purpose and intention interpret every phrase in its literal sense as conveying, and intended to convey, a metaphysical Verity or historical Fact—what a strange Medley of Doctrines should we not educe? And yet this is[. . . . .][1]

37 ii 15 | i § 34

. . . and truely for the first chapters of *Genesis*, I must confesse a great deal of obscurity, though Divines have to the power of humane reason endeavoured to make all go in a literall meaning, yet those allegoricall interpretations are also probable, and perhaps the mysticall method of *Moses* bred up in the Hieroglyphicall Schooles of the Egyptians.

The 2nd C. Gen. from v. 4. is as evidently symbolical as the 1st Chapt. is literal. The first is by Moses himself, the 2nd of far greater antiquity, and probably translated into words from graven Stones.[1]

38 ii 19 | i § 48

How shall the dead arise, is no question of my faith; to believe only possibilities, is not faith, but mere Philosophy; many things are true

a About 12 words lost in the cropped line. An oblique stroke can be read at the end

35[1] For the cropped completion of the sentence *LR* II 400 reads: "or the last and nearest of a series taken for the whole"—which looks more like a gloss than a reading of the uncropped ms. "Noah as a Homo representati- vus" is supposed to explain the absence of traces of ante-diluvian people in those parts of the earth uninhabited since the flood.

36[1] *LR* completes the cropped sen- tence with "the way in which we are constantly in the habit of treating the books of the New Testament"—which seems to be a conjectural reconstruc- tion of the sense rather than a reading of the ms before it was cropped.

37[1] See BIBLE COPY B **1, 3, 5** and BREREWOOD **1**.

in Divinity, which are neither inducible by reason, nor confirmable by sense; and many things in Philosophy confirmable by sense, yet not inducible by reason. Thus it is impossible by any solid or demonstrative reasons to perswade a man to believe the conversion of the Needle to the North; though this be possible, and true, and easily credible, upon a single experiment unto the sense. I believe that our estranged and divided ashes shall unite again, that our separated dust after so many Pilgrimages and transformations into the parts of Minerals, Plants, Animals, Elements, shall at the voice of God return into their primitive shapes; and joyn again to make up their primary and predestinate forms. As at the Creation, there was a separation of that confused masse into its species, so at the destruction thereof there shall be a separation into its distinct individualls. As at the Creation of the world, all the distinct species that we behold, lay involved in one masse, till the fruitfull voice of God separated this united multitude into its severall species: so at the last day, when these corrupted reliques shall be scattered in the wildernesse of forms, and seem to have forgot their proper habits, God by a powerfull voice shall command them back into their proper shapes, and call them out by their single individuals: Then shall appear the fertility of *Adam*, and the magicke of that sperm that hath dilated into so many millions. I have often beheld as a miracle, that artificiall resurrection and revivification of *Mercury*, how being mortified into a thousand shapes, it assumes again its own, and returns into its numericall self. Let us speake naturally, and like Philosophers, the forms of alterable bodies in these sensible corruptions perish not; nor, as we imagine, wholly quit their mansions, but retire and contract themselves into their secret and unaccessible parts, where they may best protect themselves from the action of their Antagonist. A plant or vegetable consumed to ashes, by a contemplative and Schoole Philosopher seems utterly destroyed, and the form to have taken his leave for ever: But to a sensible Artist the forms are not perished, but withdrawn into their incombustible part, where they lye secure from the action of that devouring element. This is made good by experience, which can from the ashes of a plant revive the plant, and from its cinders recall it into its stalke and leaves again. What the Art of man can do in these inferiour pieces, what blasphemy is it to affirm the finger of God cannot do in these more perfect and sensible structures? This is that mysticall Philosophy, from whence no true Scholar becomes an Atheist, but from the visible effects of nature grows up a reall Divine, and beholds not in a dream, as *Ezekiel*, but in an ocular and visible object the types of his resurrection.

This §. a series of ingenious paralogisms

39 ii 20 | i § 49

Moses that was bred up in all the learning of the *Egyptians*, committed a grosse absurdity in Philosophy, when with these eyes of flesh he desired to see God, and petitioned his Maker, that is truth it self, to a contradiction.

Bear in mind the Jehovah *Logos*, the Ο ων εν κολπω πατρος, the Person ad extra and few passages in the O.T. are more instructive or of profounder Import/[1] Overlook this or deny it, and none so perplexing, or so irreconcileable with the known character of the inspired Writer.[2]

40 ii 20, cropped | i § 50

. . . I would gladly know how *Moses* with an actuall fire calcin'd, or burnt the Golden Calfe unto Powder: for that mysticall metall of *] Gold, whose solary & celestiall nature I admire, exposed unto the violence of fire, grows onely hot and liquifies, but consumeth not . . .

* Rather "anti-solar and terrene nature". For Gold most of all Metals repelleth Light, and resisteth that power and portion of the common Air which of all ponderable bodies is most akin to Light, and its surrogate in the realm of Antiphōs or Gravity: viz. Oxygen. Gold is *Tellurian* κατ᾽ ἐξοχήν:[1] and if solar, yet as in the solidity and dark Nucleus of the Sun.[2] Iron terrestrial or Earth[?en/y] the [. . . . .]*a*

---

a The cropped line seems to end "19" or "49"—perhaps the second, since C is here annotating § 50

39[1] In N 47 ff 4ᵛ–5 "the Jehovah-Word, the *Name*, the Son, the Glory are all Synonimes of Christ"; see also BIBLE COPY B **57**. The Greek phrase —"He who is in [the] bosom of [the] father"—is from John 1.18. C often quoted the phrase, and is here misquoting from memory rather than wishing to alter the usual meaning of it: he has omitted the articles and changed εἰς to ἐν. For his special understanding of ὁ ὤν in this text see BIBLE COPY B **119** and n 1, and *C&S* (*CC*) 182. "Person ad extra"—presumably "Deus Alter": see BÖHME

178 and n 1. The passage in the OT is Exod 33.18–20 (which C also cites in **53**, below). See also **42**, below.

39[2] See also BIBLE COPY B **11**.

40[1] "Pre-eminently".

40[2] For "Antiphōs" (ἀντιφῶς) see BÖHME **166** and n 1 and *CN* III 4418 f 15. "Tellurian"—of the earth as a planet in the solar system, Tellus being the divinity of Earth, as contrasted with the terrestrial (*terra*), specifically local, earthen or perhaps in St Paul's word "earthy" (twice repeated in John SMITH p 165: see **53**, below).

40A   ii 20

... (for things, that are in *posse* to the sense, ~~and~~ are actually existent to the understanding.)

41   ii 21 | i § 52

I thank God that with joy I mention it, I was never afraid of Hell, nor never grew pale at the description of that place; I have so fixed my contemplations on Heaven, that I have almost forgot the Idea of Hell, and am afraid rather to loose the joyes of the one than endure the misery of the other, to be deprived of them is a perfect Hell, and needs me thinks no addition to compleat our afflictions; that terrible term hath never detained me from sin, more doe I owe any good action to the name thereof: I fear God, yet am not afraid of him; his mercies make me ashamed of my sins, before his judgements afraid thereof: these are the forced and secondary method of his wisdome, which he useth but as the last remedy, and upon provocation, a course rather to deterre the wicked, than incite the vertuous to his worship. I can hardly think there was ever any scared into Heaven, they go the fairest way to Heaven, that would serve God without a Hell; other Mercenaries that crouch unto him in fear of Hell, though they term themselves the servants, are indeed but the slaves of the Almighty.

§. 52. Excellent throughout. The fear of Hell may, indeed, in some desperate cases, like the Moxa,[1] give the first *rouse* from a moral Lethargy; or like the green Venom of Copper, evacuating poison or a dead load from the inner man prepare it for nobler ministrations, and medicines from the realm of Light and Life that nourish while they stimulate.

42   ii 21, cropped | i § 54

There is no salvation to those that believe not in Christ, that is say some, since his Nativity, and as Divinity affirmeth, before also; which makes me much apprehend the ends of those honest Worthies and Philosophers which died before his incarnation. It is hard to place those souls in Hell, whose worthy lives doe teach us vertue on earth; me thinks amongst those many subdivisions of Hell, there might have been one Limbo left for these ... how strange to them will sound the History of *Adam*, when they shall suffer for him they

41[1] The downy covering of *Artemisia moxa* (mugwort) was prepared in the form of a cone or cylinder for burning the skin in the treatment of gout.

never heard of? when they derive their genealogy from the Gods, shall know they are the unhappy issue of sinfull man? It is an insolent part of reason to controvert the works of God, or question the justice of his proceedings. Could humility teach others, as it hath instructed me, to contemplate the infinite and incomprehensible distance betwixt the Creator and the Creature, or did we seriously perpend that one Simile of Saint *Paul, Shall the Vessel say to the Potter, Why hast thou made me thus?* it would prevent these arrogant disputes of reason, nor would we argue the definitive sentence of God, either to Heaven or Hell. Men that live according to the right rule and law of reason, live but in their own kind as beasts do in theirs; who justly obey the prescript of their natures, & therefore cannot reasonably demand a reward of their actions, as onely obeying the naturall dictates of their reason. It will therefore, and must at last appear, that all salvation is through Christ; which verity I fear these great examples of vertue must confirm, and make it good, how the perfectest actions of earth have no title or claim unto Heaven.

§. 54.—This is plainly confined to such as have had Christ preached unto them—but the doctrine, that Salvation is in and by Christ only, is a most essential Verity, and an article of unspeakable grandeur and consolation. Name, Nomen, i.e. νουμενον, in its spiritual interpretation is the same as power, or intrinsic Cause.[1] What? is it a few Letters of the Alphabet, the Hearing of which [.....]?[2]

43 ii 22, pencil | i § 59

That which is the cause of my election, I hold to be the cause of my salvation, which was the mercy and beneplacit of God, before I was, or the foundation of the World. *Before Abraham was, I am,* is the saying of Christ, yet is it true in some sense if I say it of my self, for I was not only before my self, but *Adam,* that is, in the Idea of God, and the decree of that Synod held from all Eternity. And in this sense, I say, the world was before the Creation, and at an end before it had a beginning; and thus was I dead before I was alive,

42[1] For the connexion between *nomen* (name) and *numen* (power) see BIBLE COPY B 33 n 1. In this note C adds another dimension to the relation by engaging *numen* with νούμενον (*noumenon*)—a participle meaning "perceived with the mind/intellect", as distinct from φαινόμενον (*phaenomenon*), which literally means "appear-ing". See also **53** and nn 3, 4, below. In the Esteesean—and Kantian—scheme the noumenal (intellectual, mental, of the mind or spirit) is distinguished from the phenomenal (of the senses).

42[2] *LR* ii 402 completes the sentence with "in a given succession, that saves?"—a possible reading.

though my grave be *England* my dying place was Paradise, and *Eve* miscarried of me before she conceiv'd of *Cain*.

Compare this with p. 8. and the judicious remark on the mere accomodation in the *pre* of predestination[1]—But the subject was too tempting for the *Rhetorician*.

44 p +1, pencil, referring to ii 23, 25[a] | ii §§ 1, 6

Religio Medici, p. 23, Column the first, on the Multitude—an admirable §.[1] p. 25 full of *fine* observations, especially Sect. 6 on

43[1] P 8: "...God hath not made a creature that can comprehend him, 'tis a priviledge of his own nature; *I am that I am*, was his own definition unto *Moses*; and 'twas a short one to confound mortality, that durst question God, or ask him what hee was; indeed hee onely is, all others have and shall bee, but in eternity there is no distinction of Tenses; and therefore that terrible term *Predestination*, which hath troubled so many weak heads to conceive and the wisest to explaine, is in respect to God no prescious determination of our estates to come, but a definitive blast of his will already fulfilled, and at the instant that he first decreed it; for to his eternity which is indivisible, and altogether, the last Trump is already sounded, the reprobates in the flame, and the blessed in *Abrahams* bosome.... What to us is to come, to his Eternity is present, his whole duration being but one permanent point without succession, parts, flux, or division." "Accommodation" in this context means "Adaptation of a word, expression, or system to something different from its original purpose" (*OED*). C means that the "*pre* of predestination" does not mean "before". For his account of *pre-/prae-* see BÖHME **6** n 8.

44[1] In *CN* III 4366 C transcribed as "Excellent" most of the following passage: "In brief, I am averse from nothing, my conscience would give me the lye if I should say I absolutely detest or hate any essence but the Divil, or so at least abhorre any thing that we might come to composition. If there be any among those common objects of hatred I do contemne and laugh at it; it is tha[t] great enemy of reason, vertue and religion, the Multitude, that numerous piece of monstrosity, which taken asunder seem men, and the reasonable creatures of God; but confused together, make but one great beast, and a monstrosity more prodigious then Hydra; it is no breach of Charity to call these Fooles, it is the stile all holy Writers have afforded them, set down by *Solomon* in Canonicall Scripture, and a point of our faith to believe so. Neither in the name of multitude do I onely include the base and minor sort of people; there is a rabble even amongst the Gentry, a sort of Plebeian heads, whose fancy moves with the same wheele as these men; in the same Level with Mechanicks, though their fortunes do somewhat guild their infirmities, and their purses compound for their follies. But as in casting account, three or four men together come short in account of one man placed by himself below them: So neither are a troope of these ignorant Doradoes, of that true esteem and value, as many a forlorn person, whose condition doth place them below their feet. Let us speake like Politicians, there is a Nobility without Heraldry, a naturall dignity, whereby one man is ranked with another, another filed before him, according to the quality of his desert, and preheminence of his

the difficulty of recollecting the images of those we most dearly love.[2]

45 ii 23, pencil | ii § 1

But as in casting account, three or four men together come short in account of one man placed by himself below them: So neither are a troope of these ignorant Doradoes, of that true esteem and value, as many a forlorn person, whose condition doth place them below their feet.

Thus 1,965. But why is the 1 said to be placed *below* the ꜧ 965?[1]

46 ii 26, pencil | ii § 7

Let me be nothing, if within the compass of my self, I do not finde the battaile of *Lepanto*, passion against reason, reason against faith, faith against the Devill, and my Conscience against all.

It may appear whimsical, but I really feel an impatient regret, that this good man had so misconceived the nature both of Faith and of Reason as to affirm their contrariety to each other.[1]

---

good parts. Though the corruption of these times, and the byas of present practise wheele another way, thus it was in the first and primitive Commonwealths, and is yet in the integrity and Cradle of well-ordered Polities, till corruption getteth ground, ruder desires labouring after that which wiser considerations contemne, every one having a liberty to amasse and heap up riches, and they a license or faculty to do or purchase any thing."

44[2] § 6 (against which C has written an X in ink) opens with a passage that recalls the notes on love and friendship in B R O W N E *Religio*: "There are wonders in true affection, it is a body of *Enigmaes*, mysteries and riddles, wherein two so become one, as they both become two; I love my friend before my selfe, and yet me thinkes I doe not love him enough; some few months hence my multiplied affection will make me be leive I have not loved him at all; when I am from him, I am dead till I be with him; when I am with him, I am not satisfied, but would still be nearer him: united soules are not satisfied with embraces, but desire to be truely each other, which

being impossible, their desires are infinite, & must proceed without a possibility of satisfaction." Then follows *Religio* 23 textus, and a little later a passage reminiscent of *Works* 32 textus: "*I* never hear the Toll of a passing Bell, though in my mirth, without my prayers and best wishes for the departing spirit: *I* cannot goe to cure the body of my patient, but *I* forget my profession, and call unto God for his soul...". On "the difficulty of recollecting the images of those we most dearly love" see also *Religio* 23 and n 1, above.

§ 5 has an X against it in pencil; it may be C's. *Religio* 21 is a note written on ii 5, and at this point 22 is pasted in on a separate sheet of paper.

45[1] Browne is evidently also using the word "men" to mean "digits". In C's number 1,965 the "troope of... Doradoes" would be represented by 965, and one "forlorn [but superior] person" by the digit 1 (in the thousands column): "as in casting account" the "one" would stand "below". $1,\genfrac{}{}{0pt}{}{965}{[000]}$ $\overline{1,965}$

46[1] See *SM* (*CC*) 59ff.

47 ii 26, pencil, cropped

For my originall sin, I hold it to bee washed away in my Baptisme; for my actual transgressions, I compute & reckon with God, but from my last repentance, Sacrament or generall absolution: and therefore am not terrified with the sinnes or madness of my youth.

This is most true as far the imputation of the same is concerned. For where the means of avoiding its consequences have been afforded, each after transgression is actual by a neglect of [. . . .]*a*

48 ii 29 | ii § 14

God being all goodnesse, can love nothing but himself, he loves us but for that part, which is as it were himselfe, and the traduction of his holy Spirit.

This recalls a sublime thought of Spinoza—Every true Virtue is a part of that Love, with which God loveth himself.[1]

HYDRIOTAPHIA

48A ii 40, col 2 | Ch 3

But *Plato* seemed too frugally politick; who allowed no larger Monu-
4] ment then would contain four Heroick Verses, and designed the most barren ground for sepulture . . .

48B ii 40, col 2, marked with a pencil line in the margin

Some finding many fragments of souls in these *Urnes*, suspected a mixture of bones; In none we searched was there cause of such conjecture, though sometimes they declined not that practise; The ashes of *Domitian* were mingled with those of *Iulia*, of *Achilles* with those of *Patroclus*: All *Urnes* contained not single ashes; Without confused burnings they affectionately compounded their bones, passionately endeavouring to continue their living Unions. And when distance of death denied such conjunctions, unsatisfied affections, conceived some satisfaction to be neighbours in the grave, to ly *Urne* by *Urne*, and touch but in their name.

---

a LR supplies "those means.", but about 8 words (illegible) have been cropped

48[1] See SPINOZA *Opera* (2 vols Jena 1802–3) II 292—*Ethics* pt V prop xxxvi: "The intellectual love of the mind towards God is that very love of God whereby God loves himself...". Tr R. H. M. Elwes (1891). Cf Prop xlii on virtue, blessedness, and intellectual love, and see *CN* III 4429. C had also thought of Spinoza when he wrote *Religio* **1**.

48C ii 41, col 2, marked with a pencil line

From animals are drawn good burning lights, and good medicines against burning . . .

48D ii 42, col 1, marked with a pencil line

In an Hydropicall body ten years buried in a Church-yard, we met with a fat concretion, where the nitre of the Earth, and the salt and lixivious liquor of the body, had coagulated large lumps of fat, into the consistence of the hardest castle-soap; whereof part remaineth with us.

48E ii 44, col 2, marked with a pencil line in the margin | Ch 4

Were the happinesse of the next world as closely apprehended as the felicities of this, it were a martyrdome to live; and unto such as consider none hereafter, it must be more then death to die, which makes us amazed at those audacities, that durst be nothing, and return into their *Chaos* again. Certainly such spirits as could contemn death, when they expected no better being after, would have scorned to live had they known any.[1]

THE GARDEN OF CYRUS

49 ii 54, cropped | Ch 3

That bodies are first spirits *Paracelsus* could affirm, which in the maturation of Seeds and fruits, seems obscurely implied by *Aristotle*, when he delivereth, that the spirituous parts are converted into water, and the water into earth, and attested by observation in the maturative progresse of Seeds, wherein at first may be discerned a flatuous distension of the husk, afterwards a thin liquor, which longer time digesteth into a pulp or kernell observable in Almonds and large Nuts.

Effects purely relative from properties merely comparative, such as edge, point, grater, &c are not proper Qualities:[1] for they are in-

---

48E[1] *CN* iii 4367–75 is a series of notes transcribing, summarising, or taking up hints from *Hydriotaphia* chs 4 and 5 (pp 44–8). *CN* iii 4367 quotes from this same chapter: "It is the heaviest stone that Melancholy can throw at a man"—which continues in Browne, "to tell him he is at the end of his nature; or that there is no further state to come, unto which this seems progressionall. . ."

49[1] Presumably C means an abrasive or scouring surface as distinct from "edge" and "point". Two passages in *The Garden of Cyrus* are noted in *CN* iii 4376, 4377 (c 1817–18).

differently producible ab extra, by grinding &c, and ab intra or from Growth.[2] In the latter instance they *suppose* Qualities as their Antecedents. Now therefore since Qualities cannot result from Quantity, but Quant. from Qual.—and as matter ♋ spirit is shape ♋ [?form ....][a] extension [...] pure Quantity[3]—Paracelsus's Dict[um] is defensible[3]

50   ii 54

The Aequivocall production of things under undiscerned principles, makes a large part of generation, though they seem to hold a wide univocacy in their set and certain Originals, while almost every plant breeds its peculiar insect ...

Written before Harvey's ab ovo omnia. Since that work and Lewenhoek's microscopium the question is settled in Physics; but whether in Metaphysics, is not quite so clear.[1]

51   ii 58, pencil | Ch 4

For that they afford large *effluviums* perceptible from odours, diffused at great distances, is observable from Onyons out of the earth; which though dry, and kept untill the spring, as they shoot forth large and many leaves, do notably abate of their weight. And mint growing in glasses of water, until it arriveth unto the weight of

---

a LR reads "matter opposed to spirit is shape by modification of extension"

49[2] "From without" and "from within".

49[3] The condition of the ms makes a reliable reading impossible and interpretation problematical: it may be "as matter ♋ spirit is shape ♋ [form, so modification of] extension [is] pure Quantity"; or perhaps "as matter ♋ spirit is shape [by a distinction in] extension [♋] pure Quantity". For the distinction between shape and form see e.g. *LS* (*CC*) 134 and n, and BÖHME Annex n 4.

50[1] William Harvey (1578–1657), in his brilliant and incisive treatise *Exercitatio anatomica de motu cordis et sanguinis* (1628), gave the first accurate account of the circulation of the blood. In his more diffuse *Exercitationes de generatione animalium* (1651) he began by formulating the previsionary principle, which could be thoroughly tested only by extensive microscopic study, that *omne vivum ex ovo*—"almost all animals, even those which bring forth their young alive, and man himself, are produced from eggs". C here accepts Harvey's first principle of biological inquiry as correct. See also EDINBURGH MEDICAL AND SURGICAL JOURNAL XXXIII 42 and *CL* IV 769. Anton van Leeuwenhoek (1632–1723), by observations with his refined microscope, established Harvey's basic inferences, and also extended inquiry into the nature and structure of blood corpuscles, spermatozoa, the lens of the eye, etc; the first representation of bacteria appears in a drawing of his in *Phil Trans RS* 1683, in which publication he issued 375 papers. His collected works were published at Leyden 1719–22, an English selection in 3 vols was published 1798–1801.

an ounce, in a shady place, will sometimes exhaust a pound of water.

How much did B. allow for evaporation?

51A   ii 58, pencil

...Though some plants are content to grow in obscure Wells; ?] wherein also old Elme pumps afford sometimes long bushy sprouts, not observable in any above-ground ...

51B   ii 61

Light unto *Pluto* is darknesse unto *Iupiter*.

52   ii 61, pencil

Things entring upon the intellect by a Pyramid from without, and thence into the memory by another from within, the common decussation being in the understanding as is delivered by *Bovillus*. [Shoulder-note:] *Car. Bovillus de intellectu.*

This nearly resembles Kant's intellectual Mechanique[1]

53   p ⁺1

The Platonists hold three Knowleges of God, 1. παρουσιη—his own incommunicable Self-comprehension—2 κατα νοησιν—of pure intel-

52[1] In Böhme **106** C had played upon the title of Laplace's monumental work *La Mécanique céleste* in suggesting that astrology—"the *Céleste Chimique*"—was "a Science *in posse*"; here the pun has stronger undertones. Laplace's *Mécanique céleste* (5 vols 1799–1825) brought the work of three generations of mathematicians on the subject of gravitation into a system that supported the invariability of planetary mean motions; in a note to his more popular *Système du monde* (1796) he had touched upon the nebular hypothesis that Kant had proposed in his *Theorie des Himmels* in 1755. In Jan 1818 C spoke of Kant's "astonishing *prophetic work*, written in his 22nd. year, entitled Himmels system (System of the Heavens) of which Le Place's Méchanique Céleste is an unprincipled Plagiarism". *CL* iv 808. In his precritical writings Kant had rejected the Leibnizian confidence that philosophy could model itself on mathematics, but in his inquiry into causality he argued that an *a priori* scheme can be inferred that brings necessity and causality into coincidence, thereby ascribing invariability to the basis of moral and philosophical judgement. Hence presumably C's phrase "the Kantean *Mechanique*" in a note on the front flyleaves of Tennemann vi. What Bovillus says here (according to Browne) reminds C of the way the *a priori* scheme arises from a combination of the *a priori* form inferred by the intellect and the *a priori* perceptive form. Cf *P Lects* Lect 7 (1949) 233.

~~ligial~~ knowlege unmixed with sense—3. κατ' επιστημην—/ or discursive intelligential knowlege[1]—Thus a Greek Philosopher:—

Τους επιστημονικοὺς λογους μύθους ἡγήσεται συνοῦσα τῷ πατρὶ, καὶ συνεστιωμένη τὴν ἀλήθειαν τοῦ ὄντος καὶ ἐν αὐγῇ καθαρᾷ[2] = Those notions of God which we attain by processes of intellect the soul will consider as mythological allegories when it exists in union with the Father, and is feasting with him in the Truth of VERY BEING, and in the pure (= the unmixed, the absolutely simple & elementary) Splendor. Thus expound, Exod. 33. 20.[3]—By the face of God Moses meant the ιδεα νοητικη which God declared incompatible with human Life—κατα νοησιν = επαφην του νοητου—the contact &c[4]					S. T. Coleridge

53[1] This marginal note is based on John SMITH *Select Discourses* (1660) 163–5; C seems to have copied this striking passage on a flyleaf of Browne's *Works* in order to have it at hand for reference or for use elsewhere. The Greek phrases are from Smith pp 163–4, introduced by "the Platonists have pointed out a threefold knowledge of God"; C gives the three terms variatim in reverse order and is glossing them as he sets them down. C's first two terms are translatable as "presence" and "by intellection"; ἐπιστήμη—usually "knowledge", "science", or "understanding" in C's sense; Smith translates the related adjective as "by way of Science".

53[2] C quoted this same passage in BÖHME 33, with slight differences in diacritical pointing and similarly ascribed (as Smith does, pp 164–5) to "a Greek philosopher". Smith's translation (p 165) reads: "The Soul will reckon all this knowledge of God which we have here by way of Science but like a fable or parable, when once it is in conjunction with the Father, feasting upon Truth it self, and beholding God in the pure raies of his own Divinity." C's translation in this note to BROWNE differs not only from Smith's but also from his other version in BÖHME 33, in which instead of "processes of intellect" he wrote "processes of discursive Understand-

ing"; instead of "consider as mythological allegories", "contemplate as *mythical* (= mythological Parables)"; instead of "exists in union with the Father", "exists (for its own consciousness) in union (or co-presence) with the Father"; and all after "feasting" reads "as a guest in his house, on the Truth of absolute Being, and in a *pure* Splendor".

53[3] "And he [the Lord] said, Thou canst not see my face; for there shall no man see me, and live." This text (which is also cited in 39, above) is quoted by Smith: see n 4, below.

53[4] Smith (p 164) reads: "The First [κατ' ἐπιστήμην] may be attain'd to in this life; but the Second [κατὰ νόησιν] in its full perfection we cannot reach here in this life, because this knowledge ariseth out of a blisfull Union with God himself, which therefore they are wont to call ἐπαφὴν τοῦ νοητοῦ a Contact of Intellectual Being, and sometimes αὐτοφάνειαν...that is, that I may phrase it in the Scripture words, *a beholding of God face to face* ...which we cannot attain to while we continue in this concrete and bodily state. And so when *Moses* desir'd *to behold the face of God*, that is, as the Jewes understand it, that a distinct *Idea* of the Divine Essence might be imprinted upon his Mind, God told him, *No man can see me, and live* [shoulder-note:] Exod. 33.20; that is, no man in this corruptible state is

54 p $^{+4}$^a

The difference between a great mind's and a little mind's Use of History—The Latter would consider, for instance, what Luther did, taught, or sanctioned: the former, what Luther, *a* Luther, would *now* do, teach, and sanction.[1]

Occurred to me Midnight, Tuesday 16 March 1824, as I was slipping into bed, my eye having glanced on Luther's Table Talk.—[2]

Item. If you would be well with a great Mind, leave him with a favorable Opinion of *You*; if with a little mind, leave him with a favorable Opinion of himself. ⌜To serve (or call even [.....] any) a ... history of [.....]⌝[b][3]

Annex

[*a*] *Blackwood's* VI (Nov 1819) 197–8 is a revised version of **1**—the letter addressed to SH on 10 Mar 1804—with a brief introduction signed "G. J.", which happens to be the reversed initials of C's host James Gillman. For the probability that the text was prepared by C to meet an oppressive commitment to *Blackwood's*, see Introduction, above, pp cxv–cxvi and nn. Since the text may have been prepared for the press by C, variants from the original (except for those remarked upon in the notes to **1**, above) are shown. A few of the variants are evidently errors of the

^a Written vertically from the gutter outward
^b This heavily obliterated sentence is almost impossible to reconstruct

capable of attaining to this αὐτοφάνεια ...". C closes his note by referring to the face of God as a "noetic idea" (not Smith's term), that is, an idea accessible [only] by νόησις; and then explains "by νόησις" by equating it with Smith's term ἐπαφὴ τοῦ νοητοῦ, the "contact of Intellectual Being". On ἐπαφὴ (contact, touch) cf Böhme **24** n 9.

54[1] C sometimes read history with pleasure (see e.g. *CL* II 829) but more often than not grumbling about the shortcomings—through shallow rationalism—of contemporary historians: see e.g. *CL* III 225–6 and indexes to *Friend* (*CC*) and *LS* (*CC*). See Macdiarmid *Lives of British Statesmen* (1807) 538–9 and *TT* 13 Jul 1832. On the philosophical reading of history, see *SM* (*CC*) 11 and n 4. A long note in N F° ff 22–23ᵛ begins: "The directing Idea of History is to weave a Chain of Necessity the par-

ticular Links in which are free Acts ...". See also *EOT* (*CC*) II 53–4. For C's view of the unique status of the Bible as history see BIBLE COPY B 80 n 1.

54[2] Two of the marginalia cn C. A. Tulk's copy of John Smith are dated 6 and 8 Mar 1824. Beginning apparently in Sept 1819, C wrote more than 100 marginalia in Charles Lamb's copy of Luther *Colloquia Mensalia* (1652); whether or not he returned the volume to Lamb from time to time, it was in C's possession when he died.

54[3] The obliterated sentence may have had some relation to C's appointment as a Royal Associate of the RSL. On 16 Mar 1824—the same date as this note—he wrote to Richard Cattermole, Secretary of RSL, acknowledging with thanks the announcement of his appointment. *CL* v 343–4.

press; but it will be noticed that the transcriber's attention seems to have started to wander by the time he was about two-thirds of the way through the ms, yet was alert enough to grapple with the astronomical figure "The huntsmen are up in America" and to delete the closing verses that might otherwise have offended SH and the Wordsworths. The printed version does not follow the ms in details of capitals, spelling, italics, or punctuation. HNC clearly did not use this version in preparing the text for *LR*.

CHARACTER OF SIR THOMAS BROWN AS A WRITER

MR EDITOR,

It is well known to those who are in habits of intercourse with Mr Coleridge, that not the smallest, and, in the opinion of many, not the least valuable part of his manuscripts exists in the blank leaves and margins of books; whether his own, or those of his friends, or even in those that have come in his way casually, seems to have been a matter altogether indifferent. The following is transcribed from the blank leaf of a copy of Sir T. Brown's Works in folio, and is a fair specimen of these *Marginalia*; and much more nearly than any of his printed works, gives the style of Coleridge's conversation.   G. J.

SIR THOMAS BROWN is among my first favourites. Rich in various knowledge; exuberant in conceptions and conceits; contemplative, imaginative; often truly great and magnificent in his style and diction, though, doubtless, too often big, stiff, and *hyperlatinistic*; thus I might, without admixture of falsehood, describe Sir T. Brown, and my description would have this fault only,[a] that it would be equally, or almost equally, applicable to half a dozen other writers, from the beginning of the reign of Elizabeth to the end of the reign of Charles the Second. He is, indeed, all this; and what he has more than all this, and[b] peculiar to himself, I seem to convey to my own mind in some measure, by saying, that he is a quiet and sublime *enthusiast*, with a strong tinge of the *fantast*; the humourist constantly mingling with, and flashing across the philosopher, as the darting colours in shot silk play upon the main dye. In short, he has brains in his head, which is all the more interesting for a little twist in the brains. He sometimes reminds the reader of Montaigne; but from no other than the general circumstance of an egotism common to both, which, in Montaigne, is too often a mere amusing gossip, a chit-chat story of whims and peculiarities that lead to nothing; but which, in Sir Thomas Brown, is always the result of a feeling heart, conjoined with a mind of active curiosity, the natural and becoming egotism of a man, who, loving other men as himself, gains the habit and the privilege of talking about himself as familiarly as about other men. Fond of the curious, and a hunter of oddities and strangenesses, while he conceives himself with quaint and humorous gravity, a useful inquirer into physical truths[c] and fundamental science, he loved to contemplate and discuss his own thoughts and feelings, because he found by comparison with other men's, that *they*, too, were curiosities; and so, with a perfectly graceful[d] interesting ease, he put *them*,

---

[a] Ms reads "only this Fault"   [b] "and" is not in ms
[c] Ms reads "Truth"   [d] "and" in ms is omitted

too, into his museum and cabinet of rarities. In very truth, he was not mistaken, so completely does he see every thing in a light of his own, reading nature neither by sun, moon, or candle light, but by the light of the fairy glory around his own head; that you might say, that nature had granted to *him* in perpetuity, a patent and monopoly for all his thoughts. Read his *Hydrostaphia*[a] above all—and, in addition to the peculiarity, the exclusive *Sir Thomas Browness*;[b] of all the fancies and modes of illustration, wonder at, and admire, his *entireness* in every subject which is before him. He is *totus in illo*, he follows it, he never wanders from it, and he has no occasion to wander; for whatever happens to be his subject, he metamorphoses all nature into it. In that Hydrostaphia,[a] or treatise on some urns dug up in Norfolk—how *earthy*, how redolent of graves and sepulchres is every line! You have now dark mould; now a thigh-bone; now a skull; then a bit of mouldered coffin; a fragment of an old tombstone, with moss in its *hic jacet*; a ghost; a[c] winding-sheet; or the echo of a funeral psalm wafted on a November wind: and the gayest thing you shall meet with, shall be a silver nail, or gilt *anno domini*, from a perished coffin top!—The very same remark applies in the same force to the interesting, though far less interesting treatise on the Quincuncial Plantations of the Ancients, the same[d] *entireness* of subject! quincunxes in heaven above; quincunxes in earth below;[e] quincunxes in deity; quincunxes in the mind of man; quincunxes in tones,[f] in optic nerves, in roots of trees, in leaves,[g] in every thing! In short, just turn to the last leaf of this volume, and read out aloud to yourself, the seven last paragraphs of chapter 5th, beginning with the words "*more considerable.*"[h] But it is time for me to be in bed. In the words of Sir T. Brown[i] (which will serve[j] as a fine specimen of his manner), "but the quincunxes[k] of Heaven (*the hyades, or five stars about the horizon, at midnight at that time*) run low, and it is time we close the five parts[l] of knowledge; we are unwilling to spin out our waking thoughts into the phantoms[m] of sleep, which often continue[n] precogitations, making cables of cobwebs, and wildernesses of handsome groves. To keep our eyes open longer, were to *act* our antipodes! The huntsmen are up in Arabia;[o] and they have[p] already passed[q] their first sleep in Persia." Think you,[r] that there ever was such a reason given before for going to bed at midnight; to wit, that if we did not, we should be *acting* the part of our antipodes! And then, "THE HUNTSMEN ARE UP IN ARABIA,"[s]— what life, what fancy! Does the whimsical knight give us thus, the *essence* of gunpowder tea,[t] and call it an *opiate*?

---

a Press error for "Hydriotaphia" *b* Ms reads "Brown-ness" *c* Ms reads "or a"

d "attention to Oddities, to the remotenesses, & minutiæ of vegetable forms—the same" omitted *e* " & Quincunxes in the water beneath the Earth" omitted

f Error for "bones" *g* "in petals," omitted

h Ms reads "Considerables" *i* Ms reads "Sir Thomas"

j Ms reads "serve you, my darling Sara!" *k* Ms reads "Quincunx . . . runs"

l Error for "ports" *m* Ms reads "Phantasmes"

n Ms reads "continueth" *o* Ms reads "America"

p Ms reads "are" *q* Ms reads "past"

r "my dear Sara!" omitted *s* Ms reads "America"

t Ms reads "a dish of strong green Tea"

[*b*] In **1** C refers to the "7 last Paragraphs of Chap. V" of *The Garden of Cyrus*. They read as follows (ii 63–4):

More considerables there are in this mysticall account, which we must not insist on. And therefore why the radicall Letters in the Pentateuch, should equall the number of the Souldiery of the Tribes; Why our Saviour in the Wildernesse fed five thousand persons with five Barley Loaves, and again, but four thousand with no lesse then seven Wheat? Why *Ioseph* designed five changes of Rayment unto *Benjamin*? and *David* took just five pibbles out of the Brook against the Pagan Champion? We leave it unto Arithmetical Divinity, and Theological explanation.

Yet if any delight in new Problemes, or think it worth the enquiry, whether the Criticall Physician hath rightly hit the nominall notation of Quinque; Why the Ancients mixed five or three but not four parts of water unto their Wine: And *Hippocrates* observed a fifth proportion in the mixture of water with milk, as in *Dysenteries* and bloudy fluxes. Under what abstruse foundation Astrologers do Figure the good or bad Fate from our Children, in good Fortune, or the fifth house of their Celestiall Schemes. Whether the Aegyptians described a Starre by a Figure of five points, with reference unto the five Capitall aspects, whereby they transmit their Influences, or abstruser Considerations? Why the Cabalisticall Doctors, who conceive the whole *Sephiroth*, or divine emanations to have guided the ten-stringed Harp of *David*, whereby he pacified the evil spirit of *Saul*, in strict numeration do begin with the Perihypate Meson, or *ff fa ut*, and so place the Tiphereth answering *C sol fa ut*, upon the fifth string: Or whether this number be oftner applied unto bad things and ends, then good in holy Scripture, and why? He may meet with abstrusities of no ready resolution.

If any shall question the rationality of that Magick, in the cure of the blind man by *Serapis*, commanded to place five fingers on his Altar, and then his hand on his Eyes? Why since the whole Comoedy is primarily and naturally comprised in four parts, and Antiquity permitted not so many persons to speak in one scene, yet would not comprehend the same in more or lesse this five acts? Why amongst Sea starres nature chiefly delighted in five points? And since there are found some of no fewer than twelve, and some of seven, and nine, there are few or none discovered of six or eight? If any shall enquire why the Flowers of *Rue* properly consist of four Leaves, The first and third Flowers have five? Why since many Flowers have one leaf or none, as *Scaliger* will have it, diverse three, and the greatest number consist of five divided from their bottomes; there are yet so few of two: or why nature generally beginning or setting out with two opposite leaves at the Root, doth so seldom conclude with that order and number at the Flower? he shall not passe his houres in vulgar speculations.

If any shall further quaery why magneticall Philosophy excludeth decussations, and needles transversly placed do naturally distract their verticities? Why Geomancers do imitate the Quintuple Figure, in their Mother Characters of Acquisition and Amission, &c. somewhat answering the Figures in the Lady or speckled Beetle? With what Equity, Chiromantical conjectures decry these decussations in the Lines and Mounts of the hand? What that decussated Figure intendeth in the medall of *Alexander* the Great? Why the Goddesses sit commonly crosse-legged in ancient draughts, since *Iuno* is described in the same as a beneficiall posture to hinder the birth of *Hercules*? If any shall doubt why at the Amphodromicall Feasts on the fifth day after the Child was born, presents were sent from friends, of *Polypusses*, and Cuttlefishes? Why five must be only left in that Symbolical mutiny among the men of *Cadmus*? Why *Proteus* in *Homer* the Symbols of the first matter, before he setled himself in the midst of his Sea-monsters, doth place them out by fives? Why the fifth years Ox was acceptable Sacrifice unto *Jupiter*? Or why the Noble *Antoninus* in some sense doth call the soul it self a Rhombus? He shall not fall on trite or triviall disquisitions. And these we invent and propose unto acuter enquirers, nauseating crambe verities and questions over queried. Flat and flexible truths are beat out by every hammer; But *Vulcan* and his whole forge sweat to work out *Achilles* his armour. A large field is yet left unto sharper discerners to enlarge upon this order, to search out the *quaternio's* and figured draughts of this nature, and moderating the study of names, and meer nomenclature of plants, to erect generalities, disclose unobserved proprieties, not only in the vegetable shop, but the whole volume of nature; affording delightfull Truths, confirmable by sense and ocular Observation, which seems to me the surest path, to trace the Labyrinth of Truth. For though discursive enquiry and rationall conjecture, may leave handsome gashes and flesh-wounds; yet without conjunction of this expect no mortall or dispatching blows unto errour.

But the Quincunx of Heaven runs low, and 'tis time [to] close the five ports of knowledge; We are unwilling to spin out our awaking thoughts into the phantasmes of sleep, which often continueth praecogitations; making Cables of Cobwebbes and Wildernesses of handsome Groves. Beside *Hippocrates* hath spoke so little and the Oneirocriticall Masters, have left such frigid Interpretations from plants, that there is little encouragement to dream of Paradise it self. Nor will the sweetest delight of Gardens afford much comfort in sleep; wherein the dulnesse of that sense shakes hands with delectable odours; and though in the Bed of *Cleopatra*, can hardly with any delight raise up the ghost of a Rose.

Night, which Pagan Theology could make the daughter of *Chaos* affords no advantage to the description of order: Although now lower then that Masse can we derive its Genealogy. All things began in order, so shall they end, and so shall they begin again; according to the ordainer of order and mysticall Mathematicks of the City of Heaven.

Though *Somnus* in *Homer* be sent to rowse up *Agamemnon*, I finde no such effects in these drowsy app[ro]aches of sleep. To keep our eyes open longer were but to act our *Antipodes*. The Huntsmen are up in *America*, and they are already past their first sleep in *Persia*, But who can be drowsie at that hour which freed us from everlasting sleep? or have slumbring thoughts at that time, when sleep it self must end, and as some conjecture all shall awake again?

GEORGE BULL
1634–1710

LOST BOOK

Defensio Fidei Nicaenae, ex scriptis, quae extant, catholicorum doctorum, qui intra tria prima ecclesiae christianae secula floruerunt, &c. (Edited by Johann Ernst Grabe.) 3 vols. Ticini 1784–6. 8⁰.

No copy of this edition examined. The title is here cited from the 1st ed, Oxford 1685 4⁰.

Not located; marginalia not recorded. *Green SC* (1880) 66: "With an autograph note by S. T. Coleridge". *Lost List*.

On 28 Dec 1884 George A. Armour of Chicago wrote to EHC: "I have a copy of Bp Bull's 'Defence'—or exactly; 'Defensio Fidei Nicaenae Georgio Bullo' Ticini 1784. (3 vols) Upon the fly-leaf of the first volume is a memorandum in the handwriting of the Poet, a copy of which I inclose you—It assists in fixing exactly a date in the journey to Sicily—and shows the state of his mind at the time." MS Leatherhead. The transcript is not now with Armour's letters. HNC had noted almost fifty years earlier that C used to read Bull "in the Latin *Defensio Fidei Nicaenae*, using the Jesuit Zola's edition of 1784, which, I think, he bought at Rome". *TT* 8 Jul 1827 n. Green's library included the folio ed of Bull's *Opera omnia* ed J. E. Grabe (1703) and a copy of *Some Important Points of Primitive Christianity* (4 vols 1713–14): *Green SC* (1880) 305, 65.

C's most extended comments on Bull's *Defensio* occur in his marginalia on WATERLAND *The Importance of the Doctrine of the Trinity*.

JOHN BUNYAN
1628–1688

Most of C's remarks about Bunyan seem to be of comparatively late date. He mentioned Bunyan in Lecture 3 of the 1818 Literary Lectures in order to clarify the use of allegory by Spenser and others (*Misc C* 33), and the ms fragment that HNC associated with that lecture serves a similar purpose: "...in that admirable Allegory, the first Part of Pilgrim's Progress, which delights every one, the interest is so great that spite of all the writer's attempts to force the allegoric purpose on the Reader's mind by his strange names...his piety was baffled by his genius, and the Bunyan of Parnassus had the better of the Bunyan of the Conventicle—and with the same illusion as we read any tale known to be fictitious, as a novel,—we go on with his characters as real persons, who had been nicknamed by their neighbours". BM MS Egerton 2800 f 49ᵛ, in *Misc C* 31; and see a small group of comments in *C 17th C* 474–6. Other remarks in 1830 are associated with the publication of RS's edition in that spring and express a strong theological interest. "Calvinism", he observed in a note on Scott's *Heart of Midlothian*, "never put on a less rigid form, never smoothed its brow & softened its voice more winningly than in the Pilgrim's Progress." Walter SCOTT *Novels and Tales* (12 vols Edinburgh 1823) x 65–6. Cf "This wonderful work is one of the few books which may be read over repeatedly at different times, and each time with a new and a different pleasure. I read it once as a theologian...once with devotional feelings—and once as a poet." *TT* 31 May 1830. The two copies of *Pilgrim's Progress*, annotated within a short period yet with markedly different emphasis, may represent this way of reading.

A copy of *Pilgrim's Progress*, ed not identified, is shown as C's in Wordsworth LC 346, marked "gone to Derwent"; this cannot be either of the annotated copies. C refers to *The History of the Town of Man-Soul* in *SM (CC)* 62, and to *Grace Abounding* in *TT* 10 Jun 1830.

Copy A

The Pilgrim's Progress. With a life of John Bunyan by Robert Southey... Illustrated with engravings. London 1830. 8⁰.

Text of Pts i and ii. Three copper-plate engravings, one after T. Sadler (1829) and two after John Martin (1830); 30 wood engravings after W. Harvey printed in the text. Published by John Murray. In this copy 17 copper-plate engravings after T. Stothard (1839, 1840) were bound in at a later date.

British Museum C 132 c 1

Inscribed by HNC on the half-title: "Henry Nelson Coleridge from John Murray. 1830"; and above this "Herbert Coleridge 1860". At the head of p ⁻2: "All the Marginalia in this book were written in pencil by S. T. C. & inked over by me. *H. N. C.*" On p ⁻6 a small label inscribed "W. H. P. Coleridge".

HNC has written short notes in ink on pp 325, 344. Typographical errors are corrected on pp 55, 341, and on p xcvii a page-reference to one of the wood engravings is written in pencil.

C said: "Southey's *Life of Bunyan* is beautiful...." *TT* 10 Jun 1830. On John Martin's engravings of the Valley of the Shadow of Death and of the Celestial City in this edition see *TT* 31 May 1830. When Lamb heard in Oct 1828 that Murray was publishing this "splendid edition of Bunyan's Pilgrim", he acknowledged that "the thought is enough to turn one's moral stomach". *LL* III 178. The letter was written shortly after Lamb had been with C.

DATE. Early Jun 1830, and perhaps later. A summary note on a front fly-leaf (1) is dated 14 Jun 1830, and a notebook entry referring to p lxvii (see **12** n 1, below) begins: "Tuesday Night, 11 ᵒclock. 8 June 1830."

1 p ⁻2, pencil, overtraced

I know of no Book—the Bible excepted as above all comparison—which I according to *my* judgment and experience could so safely recommend as teaching and enforcing the whole saving Truth according to the mind that was in Christ Jesus, as the Pilgrim's Progress. It is, in *my* conviction, incomparably the best SUMMA THEOLOGIÆ *Evangelicæ*[1] ever produced by a Writer not miraculously inspired— S. T. Coleridge. Grove, Highgate 14 June 1830.

P.S. It disappointed, nay surprized me, to find R. S. express himself so coldly respecting the Style & Diction of the Pilgrim's Pro-

---

1[1] "Compendium of *Evangelical* Theology"—an allusion to the title of Aquinas' great *Summa theologica*.

gress. I can find nothing *homely* in it but a few phrases & single words. The Conversation between Faithful and Talkative is a model of unaffected correctness, dignity and rhythmical Flow.[2]

SOUTHEY'S LIFE OF BUNYAN

2   p xv, pencil, overtraced

"We intended not," says Baxter, "to dig down the banks, or pull up the hedge and lay all waste and common, when we desired the prelates tyranny might cease." No: for the intention had been under the pretext of abating one tyranny, to establish a far severer and more galling in its stead; in doing this the banks had been thrown down, and the hedge destroyed; and while the bestial herd who broke in rejoiced in the havoc, Baxter and other such erring though good men stood marvelling at the mischief which never could have been effected, if they had not mainly assisted in it.

But would these erring good men have been either willing or able to assist in this work, if the more erring Lauds and Sheldons of very equivocal goodness had not run riot in the opposite direction?[1]— And the bestial Herd!—Merciful Heaven! Compare the whole body of Parliamentarians, all the fanatical Sects included, with the morals and manners of the Royal & Prelatical Party in the reign of Charles II.^d—*They*se were indeed "a bestial Herd"— See Baxter's unwilling, and Burnet's honest, description of the moral discipline throughout the Realm under Cromwell.[2]

1[2] On p lxxxviii RS wrote: "His is a homespun style, not a manufactured one: and what a difference is there between its homeliness, and the flippant vulgarity of the Roger L'Estrange and Tom Brown school! If it is not a well of English undefiled to which the poet as well as the philologist must repair, if they would drink of the living waters, it is a clear stream of current English,—the vernacular speech of his age, sometimes indeed in its rusticity and coarseness, but always in its plainness and its strength." Cf *TT* 31 May 1830: "The Pilgrim's Progress is composed in the lowest style of English without slang or false grammar. If you were to polish it, you would at once destroy the reality of the vision. For works of imagination should be written in very plain Language; the more purely imaginative they are the more necessary it is to be plain."

2[1] Laud, with Sheldon's support, sought vigorously to suppress the prevailing Calvinist theology and to restore the pre-Reformation liturgical practices of the Church of England. Both were Archbishops of Canterbury; Laud, for his intransigence, was impeached and executed. Cf BAXTER *Reliquiae* COPY B **76** n 1.

2[2] In BAXTER *Reliquiae Baxterianae* and BURNET *History of the Reformation*.

3 p xv, pencil, overtraced

They passed with equal facility from strict puritanism to the utmost license of practical and theoretical impiety, as antinomians or as atheists; and from extreme profligacy to extreme superstition in any of its forms.

They? Pray, how many? And of these, how many that would not have been in Bedlam or fit for it, under some other form? A mad man falls into Love or Religion, & then forsooth! it is Love or Religion that drove him mad!

4 pp xxi–xxii, pencil, overtraced

In an evil hour were the doctrines of the Gospel sophisticated with questions which should have been left in the schools for those who are unwise enough to employ themselves in excogitations of useless subtlety!

But what had Bunyan to do with the Schools? *His* perplexities clearly rose out of the operations of his own active but unarmed Mind on the words of the Apostle. If any thing is to be arraigned, it must be the Bible in *English*, the reading of which is imposed (and in *my* Judgment well and wisely imposed) as a duty on all who can read. Tho' Protestants, we are not ignorant of the occasional and partial evils of promiscuous Bible-reading; but we see them vanish, when we place them beside the good.[1]

5 p xxiv, pencil, overtraced

False notions of that corruption of our nature which it is almost as *] perilous to exaggerate as to dissemble, had laid upon him a burthen heavy as that with which his own Christian begins his pilgrimage.

* I would have said—"which it ⟨is⟩ almost as perilous to misunderstand as to deny".

6 p xlii, pencil, overtraced

But the wickedness of the Tinker has been greatly overcharged; and it is taking the language of self-accusation too literally to pronounce of John Bunyan that he was at any time depraved. The worst of what

---

4[1] C often uttered warnings against "bibliolatry": see e.g. CHILLINGWORTH COPY B **2** and **4**. His most concentrated and influential discourse on how to read the Bible was written in the form of letters and published posthumously as *Confessions of an Inquiring Spirit*.

he was in his worst days is to be expressed in a single word, for which we have no synonyme . . . he had been a *blackguard* . . .

All this narrative with the reflections on the facts is admirable—and worthy of Robert Southey—full of good sense and kind feeling—the wisdom of Love. S. T. C.

7   pp lxi–lxv, pencil, overtraced

[Bunyan argued before a court that "we can pray to God without it" —the Book of Common Prayer—adding:] "Shew me . . . the place in the Epistles where the Common Prayer book is written, or one text of Scripture that commands me to read it, and I will use it." . . . But the Sectaries had kept their countrymen from it, while they had the power; and Bunyan himself in his sphere laboured to dissuade them from it.

Surely the fault lay in the want, or in the very feeble and inconsistent manner, of determining and supporting the proper power of the Church. In fact, the Prelates and leading Divines of our Church were not only at variance with each other, but each with himself. One party, the more faithful and less modified Disciples of the first Reformers, were afraid of bringing any thing into even the semblance of a co-ordination with the Scriptures—and with the *terriculum*[1] of Popery ever before their eyes, timidly and sparingly allowed to the Church any even subordinate power beyond that of interpreting the Scriptures—i.e. of *finding* the Ordinances of the Church implicitly contained in the Ordinances of the inspired Writers. But as they did not assume infallibility in their interpretatations, it amounted to nothing for the consciences of such men as Bunyan & a thousand others. The opposite party (Laud Taylor &c) with a sufficient dislike of the Pope (i.e. *at Rome*) and of the grosser ⟨theological⟩ corruptions of the Romish Church, yet in their hearts as much averse to the sentiments and proceedings of Luther, Calvin, John Knox, Zuinglius &c,[2] & proudly conscious of their superior Learning, sought to maintain their ordinances by appeals to the Fathers, to the recorded Traditions and Doctrine of the Catholic Priesthood during the first 5 or 6 centuries—and contended for so much, that virtually the Scriptures were subordinated to the Church—which yet they did not dare distinctly *say out*. The result was, that the Anti-Prelatists

7[1] A scarecrow or bugbear—lit. a little frightener.

7[2] Luther, Calvin, Knox, and Zuinglius were all Reformers, Laud and Taylor conservative prelates who sought (as C goes on to note) to preserve ancient Catholic traditions within the Church of England.

answered them in gross, by setting at naught their foundation, that is, the worth, authority and value of the Fathers. So much for their variance with each other! But each Vindicator of our established Liturgy, Discipline &c was divided in himself—he *minced* this out of fear of being charged with Popery, and this he dared not affirm for fear of being charged with Disloyalty to the King, as the head of the Church. The distinction between the Church of which the King is the rightful Head, and the Church which hath no head but Christ, never occurred either to them or to their Antagonists;[3] and as little did they succeed in appropriating to Scripture what belonged to Scripture & to the Church what belonged to the Church. All things in which the Temporal are concerned, may ⟨be⟩ reduced to a Pentad —viz. Prothesis, Thesis, Antithesis, Mesothesis, and Synthesis. So here[a]

8   p lxiii, pencil, overtraced

He was told that he might exhort his neighbours in private discourse, if he did not call together an assembly of people; this he might do, and do much good thereby, without breaking the law. But, said Bunyan, if I may do good to one, why not to two? and if to two why not to four, and so to eight, and so on? Aye, said the Clerk, and to a hundred, I warrant you!

O dear S! how was it possible that you could read & transcribe this?, & not have your whole heart as it was when you were 4 and 20—?[1]

---

a Here C has written "=", and the diagram at the foot of the page—written in the space left between **8** (in the outer margin) and **9** (in the gutter)—is marked "="
b The words, lines, and marks in the diagram were all originally written in pencil; only the words have been overtraced in ink

7³ For C's distinction between the Church of Christ and the National Church see *C&S* (*CC*) 113–28.

7⁴ This scheme appears also in *CL* vi 816–18 (16 Sept 1829).

8¹ RS was twenty-four in 1798–9.

In 1795 C and RS had shared lectures on historical subjects in Bristol: see *Lects 1795* (*CC*) xxv, xxxiii–xxxv. C gazes across the thirty years of RS's decline from the republican sentiment of his historical lectures in Bristol into

Then you saw clearly the difference of the occasional *religious* persecutions under the Republic & the Protectorate—& the foul cruelties enacted by the Prelates for *State & Church* interests under the first & 2ᵈ Charles!

9   p lxiii, pencil, overtraced

"But there are two ways of obeying," he observed; "the one to do that which I in my conscience do believe that I am bound to do, actively; and where I cannot obey actively, there I am willing to lie down, and to suffer what they shall do unto me."

Genuine Christianity worthy of John & Paul!

10   p lxiv, pencil, overtraced

[After the Coronation, a general offer was made to suspend proceedings already in progress. Bunyan's wife presented a petition to the Judges that they consider her husband's case.] Sir Matthew Hale was one of these Judges, and expressed a wish to serve her if he could, but a fear that he could do her no good; and being assured by one of the Justices that Bunyan had been convicted, and was a hot-spirited fellow, he waived the matter.

Wretched Coward! I don't like, I never did like, that Sir M. H. It was he who fathered the jargon of the Bible being part of the Law of England.[1] Moses and Mʳ Harmer! Isaiah and "Ould Close"!![2]

11   p lxv, pencil, overtraced

Show me only a good and superior man who under whatever mistaken, but honest views he became an advocate of a bad cause, and I will look to *his* writings for the strongest, most operative,

the intolerant Toryism of the laureateship, *The Vision of Judgment*, *The Book of the Church*, and *Vindiciae Ecclesiae Anglicanae*.

10[1] Sir Matthew Hale (1609–76), friend of Richard Baxter (who wrote his life), was presiding judge over many witch trials and at the notorious conviction of two women for witchcraft in 1662; for C's revulsion at his brutal judgement in these trials see *CN* III 4390–6 and *CIS* 45–6n. On his notorious dictum about the Bible being part of the law of England, see *C&S* (*CC*) 5 and n 3.

10[2] C means that Hale would identify the Jewish law-giver with a criminal lawyer, and the poetic declamations of the prophet with the street-cry of an old-clothes man. C refers to the radical James Harmer (1777–1853)—"Alderman Harmer, the attorney, who sits on the London bench to punish petty larceny, gets £3,000 or £4,000 a year by being proprietor of the *Weekly Dispatch*, a paper which thrives on the worst of all crimes: the destruction of private and public character." Lord Broughton (in his diary 4 Dec 1833) *Recollections of a Long Life* (6 vols 1909–11) IV 327–8.

confutations and exposures of this cause. (So with R. S. in his parti-zanship for Laud, Sheldon, and the Stuarts.)[a] I am not conscious of any warping power that could have acted for so very long a period; but from 16 to near 60, I have retained the very same con-victions respecting the Stuarts & their adherents. Even to Lord Clarendon I could never quite reconcile myself.[1] *S. T. C.*

12 p lxvi, pencil, overtraced

"I followed my wonted course . . . taking all occasions to visit the people of God, exhorting them to be stedfast in the faith of Jesus Christ, and to take heed that they touched not the Common Prayer, &c."—an &c. more full of meaning than that which occasioned the dishonest outcry against the &c. oath.

Good God!! ⟨O!⟩ why does S. throw out these ipse dixi's in such en passant flashlets![1] Is it right? I love him, whatever he may think of me, & it grieves me in the Heart, because I cannot—& I try hard—yet I can not justify him. I scarcely know the quantum of bodily pain that I would not endure to have prevented R. S. from the Judgments & feelings expressed in this §ph. And it is such a *false* libel against HIMSELF. He would no more have *acted* on such principles & feelings, than ~~he~~ I or even than the most Zealous Anti-Churchman. But the *Pen* is the Tongue of a systematic Dream—a Somniloquist![2] The sunshine, Comparative power, the distinct *contra*-distinguishing judgment of REALITIES as other than Thoughts, is suspended!—During this state of continuous, not single-mindedness, but *one*-SIDE-mindedness, Writing is manual Somnam-bulism—the somnial Magic superinduced on, without suspending, the active powers of the mind.[3]

---

[a] This sentence, enclosed in pencilled brackets (not overtraced), is not included in either *LR* or *NED*

11[1] See a notebook entry of c Dec 1828: "O Heavens! What a Leash of Patron Saints have the Tory Clergy fixed on for the Anglican Church!—I. Charles the first. . . II. Archbishop Laud. . .III. Lord Clarendon—Hypo-crite, Liar in all his characters, as Man, Statesman and Historian, and the Suborner of Assassination, and unless we transfer the Guilt from the Murderer to his Stiletto, himself virtu-ally and morally an Assassin." N 38 ff 7ᵛ–8. For the grave implications of RS's altered view of the Stuarts see **12**, below.

12[1] For C's objection to the "petu-lant ipse dixi smartness & dogma-tism" that HC had "*caught* from Southey" see H. COLERIDGE **5** and n 1.

12[2] *OED* cites this passage for C's use of "Somniloquist"—a person who talks in a dream.

12[3] C wrote a long note on "Tues-day Night, 11 °clock. 8 June 1830" referring to p lxvii, which begins:

13   pp lxx–lxxi, pencil, overtraced

[Bunyan should have seen that the martyrs] had no other alternative than idolatry or the stake: but that he was neither called upon to renounce any thing that he did believe, nor to profess any thing that he did not ... that he was only required not to go about the country holding conventicles; and that the cause for that interdiction was—not that persons were admonished in such conventicles to labour for salvation, but that they were exhorted there to regard with abhorrence that Protestant Church which is essentially part of the constitution of this kingdom, from the doctrines of which Church, except in the point of infant baptism, he did not differ a hair's breadth. This I am bound to observe, because Bunyan has been, and no doubt will continue to be, most wrongfully represented as having been the victim of intolerant laws, and prelatical oppression.

Q.? More so, than when Cranmer, Latimer, and Ridley,[1] or when the Martyrs under Henry 8th, exhorted *their* Hearers to regard with abhorrence this essential part of the Constitution? Or did the Church first become a part of the Constitution when the 39 Articles were proposed for subscription?[2] Or was it not far rather those very points, which the Church of Bunyan's age had retained and inherited from the same Constitutional Church under Henry VIIIth and his predecessors, the prelatical government, to wit, and the ceremonies not sanctioned by Scripture—were not *these* the ground & objects of Bunyan's Hostility? Would that R. S. could but see as plainly as I do, that the essence of the Constitutional, i.e. of the National, Church is independent of theological dogmata!—[3]

"Southey's most interesting, and delightful but only too often (whenever the persecution of the Sectaries of the established Church...cannot be concealed, yet *will* not be condemned) one-side minded Life of John Bunyan ...". N 45 ff 21–21ᵛ.

13[1] Under the Six Articles of 1539, the first of which maintained the mediaeval doctrine of transubstantiation, Cranmer, Latimer, and Ridley were burned at the stake in Oxford as heretics. Cranmer was obliged to witness the execution of Ridley and Latimer from the window of his jail in Oct 1555, and was himself burned on 21 Mar 1556.

13[2] The Thirty-nine Articles of Religion, a series of formulae defining the doctrinal position of the Church of England, developed progressively from the Ten Articles of 1536, and reached their final form in 1571. Subscription to the Thirty-nine Articles was required of those taking holy orders and of members of Oxford and Cambridge. The Corporation Act of 1661 and the Test Act of 1673 required all public servants and officers of the Crown to be members of the Church of England; the first of these acts was repealed in 1828, the second in 1829.

13[3] See 7 n 3, above.

14 p lxxii, pencil, overtraced

He remained a prisoner twelve years. But it appears that during the last four of those years he regularly attended the Baptist Meeting, his name always being in the records ...

And yet "no victim of intolerant Laws and prelatical Oppression["]!!¹ O S! S!—would I had the couching needle—tho' verily this is a very *Niagara* of a Cataract!² No *gutta* serena, but a *mare furiosum*.³

15 p lxxix, pencil, overtraced

[A sample of one of his sermons:] "They that will have Heaven, they must run for it, because the Devil, the Law, Sin, Death and Hell, follow them. There is never a poor Soul that is going to Heaven, but the Devil, the Law, Sin, Death and Hell, make after that Soul. 'The *] Devil, your adversary, as a roaring Lion, goeth about, seeking whom he may devour.' And I will assure you, the Devil is nimble; he can run apace; he is light of foot; he hath overtaken many; he hath turned up their heels, and hath given them an everlasting fall. Also the Law! that can shoot a great way: have a care thou keep out of the reach of those great guns the Ten Commandments! Hell also hath a wide mouth; and can stretch itself farther than you are aware of! ... If this were well considered, then thou, as well as I, wouldst say, they that will have Heaven must run for it!"

It is the fashion of the day to call every man, who in his writings or discourses gives a prominence to the doctrines on which beyond all others the first Reformers separated from the Romish Communion, a Calvinist. Bunyan *may* have been one; but *I* have met with nothing in his Writings (with the exception of his Anti-pædobaptism, to which too he ~~lays~~ assigns no *saving* importance)¹ that is not much more characteristically *Lutheran*. For instance this passage is the very echo of the Chapter on the Law and Gospel in Luther's Table-talk.² S. T. C.

14¹ RS's phrase is at the end of **13** textus.

14² A couching-needle, in removing a cataract, was inserted through the coats of the eye to displace the opaque crystalline lens below the axis of vision.

14³ "No calm *tear-drop* but a raving *sea*". "Gutta serena", a disease of the optic nerve in which the lens of the eye remains clear (the cause of Milton's blindness), as distinct from "gutta opaca", cataract.

15¹ For C on infant baptism see e.g. *AR* (1825) 356–76.

15² See LUTHER *Colloquia Mensalia* ch 12, on which C wrote fifteen marginalia. See also COPY B 6.

16   p lxxix, pencil, overtraced | **15** textus

* It would be interesting and (I doubt not) instructive, to know the distinction in Bunyan's mind between the Devil and Hell.

17   p xcvii, pencil, overtraced

Bunyan concludes with something like a promise of a third part [of *Pilgrim's Progress*]. There appeared one after his death, by some unknown hand, and it has had the fortune to be included in many editions of the original work.

See p. xcix.[1] It is remarkable that R. S. should not have seen, or having seen have forgotten to notice, that this third Part is evidently written by some disguised Catholic Priest or Missionary—[2]

THE PILGRIM'S PROGRESS

18   pp 40–1, pencil, overtraced

Then I saw that one came to Passion, and brought him a bag of treasure, and poured it down at his feet; the which he took up, and rejoiced therein, and withal laughed Patience to scorn; but I beheld but awhile, and he had lavished all away, and had nothing left him but rags.

One of the not many instances of a faulty allegory in P. Pr.—i.e. that it is no allegory—The beholding *but awhile* and the change into "nothing but Rags", is not legitimately imaginable. A longer time & more Interlinks are requisite.—The allegory is a hybrid compost of usual Images and generalized Words, like the Nile-born Nondescript, with a Head or Tail of organized Flesh, and a lump of semi-mud for the Body.[1]—Yet, perhaps, these very defects are

17[1] But RS had noticed, in pp xcviii–xcix: "A stranger experiment was tried upon Pilgrim's Progress, in translating it into other words, altering the names, and publishing it under the title of the Progress of the Pilgrim... the person employed in disguising the stolen goods must have been a Roman Catholic, for he has omitted all mention of Giant Pope, and Fidelius suffers Martyrdom by being hanged, drawn, and quartered."

17[2] See *Pilgrim's Progress* ed J. B. Wharey (Oxford 1960) cxvi n 2: "A spurious Third Part appeared in 1693.

This was a brazen attempt to deceive. It described itself as 'The Third Part, to which is added The Life and Death of John Bunyan, Author of the First and Second Part; thus compleating the whole *Progress*.' Despite the strong denunciation of it printed in the form of a publisher's advertisement on the reverse of the title-page in the thirteenth edition, 1693, no fewer than fifty-nine editions of it had appeared before the end of the eighteenth century."

18[1] "Nondescript"—as a term in natural history, a species not classi-

practically excellencies in relation to the intended readers of the
Pilg. Prog.[2]

19 p 43, pencil, overtraced

Then said Christian, What means this [the dream of the fire that
blazes higher when water is poured on it]?

The Interpreter answered, This is Christ, who continually, with
the oil of his grace, maintains the work already begun in the heart;
by the means of which, notwithstanding what the Devil can do, the
souls of his people prove gracious still. And in that thou sawest
that the man stood behind the wall to maintain the fire, this is to
teach thee, that it is hard for the tempted to see how this work of
grace is maintained in the soul.

This is beautiful; yet I cannot but think, it would have been still
more appropriate, if the Water-pourer had been a Mr Legality, a
prudentialist offering his calculation of *Consequences* as the moral
Antidote to Guilt and Crime,[1] and ⟨if⟩ the Oil-instillator out of
sight, & from within, had represented the Corrupt *Nature* of Man,
i.e. the spiritual Will corrupted by taking up a Nature into itself.

20 p 45, pencil, overtraced

Then said Christian, Is there no hope, but you must be kept in the
Iron cage of Despair?

Man. No, none at all.

Chr. Why, the <u>Sun</u> of the blessed is very pitiful.

Son?[1]

21 p 52, pencil, overtraced

They told him, that custom, it being of so long standing as above a
thousand years, would doubtless now be admitted as a thing legal
by an impartial judge; and besides, say they, if we get into the way,

---

fied or not yet correctly described. Cf
CN II 2724 and I 1041 (Nile-born
frogs).

18[2] See also *Misc C* 33: "Narrative
allegory is distinguished from mythology as reality from symbol; it is,
in short, the proper intermedium between person and personification.
Where it is too strongly individualized,
it ceases to be allegory; this is often
felt in the Pilgrim's Progress, where

the characters are real persons with
nick names." Cf BM MS Egerton 2800
f 49^v, printed in *Misc C* 31 and *C 17th*
C 475.

19[1] I.e. a Paleyan. For C's distaste
for Paley's "calculation of *Consequences*" see AURELIUS 38 n 1.

20[1] Cf "God...the Sun of Righteousness" in **24**, below. For the identification of Sun and Son generally, see
AURELIUS 35 n 2.

what matters which way we get in? If we are in, we are in. Thou art but in the way, who, as we perceive, came in at the Gate; and we also are in the way, that came tumbling over the Wall. Wherein, now, is thy condition better than ours?

The allegory is clearly defective, inasmuch as "the Way" represents two diverse Meanings, viz. 1. the outward profession of Christianity, and 2. the inward and spiritual Grace. But it would be very difficult to mend it[1]

22 pp 83–5, pencil, overtraced

One thing I would not let slip: I took notice that now poor Christian was so confounded, that he did not know his own voice; and thus I perceived it: just when he was come over against the mouth of the burning pit, one of the Wicked ones got behind him, and stepped up softly to him, and, whisperingly suggested many grievous blasphemies to him, which he verily thought had proceeded from his own mind. This put Christian more to it than any thing that he met with before, even to think that he should now blaspheme him that he loved so much before . . .

There is a very beautiful Letter of Archbishop Leighton's to a Lady under a similar distemperature of the Imagination.[1] In fact, it can scarcely not happen under any weakness and consequently irritability of the nerves to persons, continually occupied with spiritual self-examination. No part of the pastoral duties requires more discretion, a greater practical psychological Science. In this, as in what not? Luther is the great Model—ever reminding the individual, that *not* he but Christ is to redeem him—and that the way to be redeemed is to think with will, mind and affections on Christ, and not on HIMSELF. "I am a sin-laden Being; & Christ has promised to loose the whole burden, if I but entirely trust in him. To torment myself with the detail of the noisome Contents of the Fardle will but make it stick the closer, first to my imagination, and then thro' that to my unwilling Will." See Aids to Reflection, p. 306.[2]

21[1] COPY B **10** refers to the same textus.

22[1] Letter IV "on a similar Occasion"—i.e. "To a Person under Trouble of Mind"—printed in the 1820 ed of Leighton's *Works* IV 437–40 (LEIGHTON COPY C only, the passage unmarked). C may be thinking of a passage on IV 439: "Believe it, Madam, these different thoughts of yours, are not yours, but his that inserts them, and throws them as fiery darts into your mind; and they shall assuredly be laid to his charge, and not to yours."

22[2] I.e. *AR* (1825) 306: "Disclaim all right of property in thy fetters! Say, that they belong to the *Old Man*,

23   p 85, pencil, overtraced

By this place Christian went without much danger, whereat I somewhat wondered: But I have learned since, that Pagan has been dead many a day; and as for the other [Pope], though he be yet alive, he is, by reason of age, and also of the many shrewd brushes that he met with in his younger days, grown so crazy and stiff in his joints, that he can now do little more than sit in his Cave's mouth, grinning *] at Pilgrims as they go by, and biting his nails because he cannot come at them.

* O that Blanco White would write, in Spanish, the Progress of a Pilgrim from the Pope's Cave to the Evangelist's Wicket Gate and the Interpreter's House!—[1]

24   pp 104–6, pencil, overtraced

Chr. . . . . Hearing is but as the sowing of the seed; talking is not sufficient to prove that fruit indeed is in the heart and life; and let us assure ourselves that, at the day of doom, men shall be judged according to their fruit. It will not be said then, *Did you believe?* *] but were you *doers* or *talkers* only? and accordingly shall they be judged.

* All the Doctors of the Sorbonne could not have ⟨better⟩ stated the Gospel Medium between Pelagianism and Antinomianism Solifidianism, (more properly named, Sterilifidianism).[1] It is indeed Faith alone that saves us; but such a Faith, as cannot be alone. Purity and Beneficence are the Epidermis, Faith = Love the Cutis vera of

and that thou dost but carry them to the Grave, to be buried with their Owner! Fix thy thought on what *Christ* did, what *Christ* suffered, what *Christ* is—as if thou wouldst fill the hollowness of thy Soul with Christ! If he emptied himself of Glory to become Sin for thy salvation, must not thou be emptied of thy sinful Self to become Righteousness in and through his agony and the effective merits of his Cross? By what other means, in what other forms, is it *possible* for thee to stand in the presence of the Holy One? . . ."

23[1] See BLANCO WHITE general note.

24[1] Pelagianism, denying the doctrine of original sin, holds that a man takes the initial step toward salvation by his own effort, without assistance of divine grace; antinomianism is the doctrine that Christians, being under the spiritual law of grace, need not observe the moral laws; solifidianism is the view that man is justified by faith alone, without consideration of "works". C's phrase "Antinomian Solifidianism" refers to a view that justification is by faith alone without reference to "works" as considered in the light of moral law. *OED* cites this note as its only instance of the use of the word "Sterilifidianism", and defines the word as "Belief in the sufficiency of a 'barren' faith". Cf *CL* v 87; see *CN* II 2434 (Feb 1805).

Christianity[2]—Morality is the outward Cloth, Faith the Lining—both together form the Wedding-garment, given to the true Believer by Christ—even his own Garment of Righteousness, which like the Loaves & Fishes he mysteriously multiplies.[3] The images of the Sun in the earthly dew-drops are unsubstantial phantoms; but God's Thoughts are Things:[4] the Images of God, of the Sun of Righteousness, in the spiritual Dew-drops are Substances, imperishable Substances.—[5]

24[2] *Cutis vera*—the true skin or *derma* underlying the epidermis.

24[3] Cf: "There is but one Wedding-garment, in which we can sit down at the marriage-feast of Heaven: and that is the Bride-groom's own Gift, when he gave himself for us that we might live in him and he in us. There is but one robe of Righteousness, even the Spiritual Body, formed by the assimilative power of faith...". *AR* (1825) 307–9, a continuation of the passage quoted in **22** n 2, above.

The parable of the loaves and fishes is told (var) in all four gospels: Matt 14.17, 15.32ff, Mark 6.35ff, Luke 9.12ff, John 6.5ff.

24[4] For thinking as "thinging" see Böhme **100** n 2.

24[5] Cf Ps 19.4–5; also Deut 32.2: "My doctrine shall drop as the rain, my speech shall distil as the dew, as the small rain upon the tender herb, and as the showers upon the grass". The phrase "the Sun of Righteousness" in its single appearance in Mal 4.2 is also a symbol of divine blessing —"with healing in his wings...". In many OT passages dew dispersed by the sun is a prime figure of evanescence, of the transitoriness of life, as e.g. in Hosea 13.3. In this marginal note C thinks of each single dew-drop as holding in itself the image of the sun; cf *SM* (*CC*) 50. After this annotation C left 300 pp unmarked.

Copy B

The Pilgrim's Progress, from this world to that which is to come . . . in three parts. Illustrated by engravings from orginal designs. With explanatory notes, by W. Mason, and others. To which is prefixed, A life of the author. London 1820. 8⁰

Published by R. Edwards, Crane Court, Fleet Street. The engraved title-page depicting "Christian assaulted by Satan, Sin, and Death" is signed "Crabb, del.ⁿ et sculpt. John Street, Blackfriars Road". Includes the supposititious Pt iii, but the editors supplied no "explanatory notes" for it.

New York Public Library (Berg Collection)

Inscribed on p ⁻5 (p–d): "Sophia Gillman from Rev⁴ J. Gillman 1854"; and in another hand "N.B. This book was given to me at the Vicarage, Sᵗ Leonard's, near Tring, on the 17ᵗʰ of July, 1883, by Mʳˢ Watson, grand-daughter of to Mʳ Gillman. It contains the autograph notes of Samuel Taylor Coleridge,—since printed in the collection of his 'Notes on English Divines'. Cuddesdon Palace July, 1883. *J. F. Oxon*:". On the same page, the bookplate of John Drinkwater; and at the top of p ⁻4 the signature "John Drinkwater 1921". Below the signature, Drinkwater has written in pencil: "Coleridge's copy of Bunyan, with many marginal notes in the poet's ms. The book was given by the Rev⁴. James Gillman, the son of C's biographer, to Sophia Gillman, who became (?) the Mʳˢ Watson referred to in the other inscription on the page opposite, in the hand of John Fielder Mackarness, Bishop of Oxford 1870–1888. . . . ." Drinkwater then gives a list of the marginalia with a comment on the exactness of the version in *NED*. A note in another hand corrects Drinkwater on the identity of Sophia Gillman: "No—Sophia became Mʳˢ Howard. Mʳˢ Watson was Lucy Gillman."

   Possibly it was through Bp Mackarness that the book returned to the Coleridge family; his daughter married Bernard, Lord Coleridge (1851–1921).

DATE. 1831, at least one note (see **10** n 2) c 21 Sept 1831. In **2** C refers to RS's life of Bunyan "prefixed to his Edition of the Pilgrim's Progress", which places the notes—if all written at one time—after 1830 and later than the marginalia on COPY A. The notes seem not to have been written at one time.

1 p ⁻2

One of the most influencive arguments, one of those the force of which I *feel* even more than *see*, for the divinity of the New Testament, and with especial weight in the Writings of John and Paul, is the unspeakable Difference between them, and ~~the extant~~ all other earliest extant Writings of the Christian Church/ ~~even those of by the of~~ even those of the same age (ex. gr. the Epistle of Barnabas) or of the next following—a difference that transcends all *degree*, & is truly a difference *in kind*.—Nay, the ⟨Catalogue of the⟩ Works written by the Reformers, and ~~by~~ in the two Centuries after the Reformation contain many many Volumes, far superior in Christian Light and Unction ⟨to⟩ the best of the Fathers—Ex. gr. How poor, and unevangelic is not Hermas, the Shepherd, in comparison with our Pilgrim's Progress.[1]

2   pp iii–v | Life

The early part of his life was an open course of wickedness.

R. Southey in the Life prefixed to his Edition of the Pilgrim's Progress has in a manner worthy of his Head & Heart reduced this oft repeated charge to its proper value.[1] Bunyan was never, in our received sense of the word, *wicked*. He was chaste, sober, honest—but he was a bitter *Blackguard*—that is, damned his own & his Neighbor's Eyes, on slight or no occasion, and was fond of a *row*.—In this our excellent Laureate has performed an important service to Morality, for the transmutation of ~~actually~~ Reprobates into Saints is doubtless possible—but like ~~other~~ the many *recorded* facts of corporeal Alchemy, ~~they are~~ it is not supported by modern experiments.

3   pp 9–11 | Pt i

As I walked through the wilderness of this world . . .

That in the Apocalypse the Wilderness is the symbol of the World or rather of the Worldly Life,[1] Bunyan discovered by the instinct of a similar Genius.[2] & The whole Jewish History, indeed, in all its detail, is so admirably adapted to, and suggestive of, symbolical use,

[1][1] For C's acquaintance with the *Epistle of Barnabas* and *Hermas the Shepherd*, see BIBLE *Apocryphal NT*. See also *CL* VI 683.

[2][1] See COPY A 6.

[3][1] "The wilderness" appears in Rev 12.6, 12.14, and 17.3, the first two referring to the "place prepared of God" where the woman in travail (? the Virgin Mary, or the Old or the New Israel) takes refuge, the third being the place where the seer is carried away to see "the judgment of the great whore" (? Jerusalem). In BIBLE COPY B 139 C comments on Rev 17.3 only by questioning the use of the definite article; the other two passages are unmarked in BIBLE COPY B and in BIBLE NT Revelation.

[3][2] Bunyan, having quoted on his title-page part of Hosea 12.10: "I have used Similitudes", also included in his prefatory couplets: "By metaphors I speak? Were not God's laws, | His gospel-laws, in older times held forth | By types, shadows and metaphors?"

as to justify the belief, that the spiritual application, the interior and permament Sense, was in the original intention of the inspiring Spirit: tho' it might not have been present, as an object of distinct Consciousness, to the inspired Writers. S. T. C.

4 pp 8–9

... where was a den. [Editor's note:] The jail. MR. BUNYAN wrote this precious book in Bedford jail, where he was confined on account of his religion. The following anecdote is related of him: a Quaker came to the jail, and thus addressed him: "Friend BUNYAN, the Lord sent me to seek for thee, and I have been through several counties in
*] search of thee, and now I am glad I have found thee." To which Mr. BUNYAN replied, "Friend, thou dost not speak truth, in saying, The Lord sent thee to seek me; for the Lord well knows, that I have been in this jail for some years; and if he had sent thee, he would have sent thee here directly."

* This is a valuable Anecdote—for it proves what might have been concluded a priori, that Bunyan was a man of too much Genius to be a Fanatic. No two qualities more contrary than Genius and Fanaticism/Enthusiasm indeed—θεος εν ἡμιν—is almost a Synonime of Genius—the moral *Life* in the intellectual *Light*, the Will in the Reason:[1] and without it, says Seneca, nothing truly great was ever atchieved by Man.[2] S. T. C.

5 pp 10–11

... and not being able longer to contain, he brake out with a lamentable cry, saying, "What shall I do?" [Editor's note:] Reader, was this ever your case? Did you ever see your sins, and feel the burden of them, so as to cry out, in the anguish of your soul, What must I do
*] to be saved? If not, you will look on this precious book as a romance or history which no way concerns you: you can no more understand the meaning of it, than if it were wrote in an unknown tongue: for you are yet carnal, dead in your sins, lying in the arms of the wicked one in false security. But this book is spiritual: it can only be understood by spiritually quickened souls, who have experienced that salvation in the heart which begins with a sight of sin, a sense of sin, a fear of destruction, and dread of damnation. Such, and such only,

4[1] "*God in* us". For a distinction between enthusiasm and fanaticism, see BIRCH **1** nn 2 and 3.

4[2] Cf *SM* (*CC*) 23 and n.

commence pilgrims from the city of destruction to the heavenly kingdom.

* Most true! It is one thing to perceive and acknowlege this and that particular deed to be sinful, i.e. contrary to the Law of Reason or the commandment of God in Scripture—and another thing to feel *Sin* within us, independent of particular Actions except as the common ground of them. And it is this latter, without which no man can become a Christian. *S. T. C.*

6 pp 36–7

Now whereas thou sawest, that as soon as the first began to sweep, the dust did so fly about, that the room by him could not be cleansed, *] but that thou wast almost choked therewith: this is to shew thee that the law, instead of cleansing the heart, by its working, from sin, doth revive, put strength into, and increase in the soul, even as it doth discover and forbid it, for it doth not give power to subdue it.

* See Luther's Table Talk—the Chapters, named, Law and Gospel, contain the very marrow of Divinity.[1] Still, however, there remains much to be done on this subject—viz. to shew, *how* the discovery of Sin by the Law tends to strengthen the Sin—and why it must necessarily have this effect—the *mode* of its action on the appetites and impetites[2] thro' the imagination & Understanding—& to exemplify all this in our actual experience.

7 pp 40–1

[Editor's note:] What, then, has the sinner, who is the subject of grace, no hand in keeping up the work of grace in his heart? No: it is plain, Mr. Bunyan was not an Arminian . . .

If by "metaphysics" we mean those truths of the pure Reason, which always transcend and not seldom appear to contradict, the *Understanding*—or (in the words of the great Apostle) spiritual verities which can only be spiritually discerned[1]—/ and this is the true and legitimate meaning of "Metaphysics", i.e. μετα τα φυσικα/[2] then, I affirm, that this very controversy of t between the Arminians

---

6[1] LUTHER *Colloquia Mensalia* (1652) ch 12 "Of the Law and the Gospel", to which C also refers in COPY A 15.

6[2] Not in *OED*. As "appetite" is a desire or seeking directed *towards*

(*ad*) something, "impetite" would be a desire or seeking directed inward.

7[1] See 1 Cor 2.13–14.

7[2] Cf "*metaphysical* science" in *Friend* (*CC*) I 440: to which n 2—a marginal note on *Friend* Copy A—provides a more detailed excursus.

and the Calvinists, in which both are partially right ~~on~~ in what they *affirm*, and both wholly wrong in what they *deny*, is a proof that without *Meta*physics there can be no *Light* of Faith.[3] S. T. C.

8 pp 42–3

I left off to watch, and be sober; I laid not the reins upon the neck of my lusts;* I sinned against the light of the word, and the goodness of God; I have grieved the Spirit, and he is gone; I tempted the devil, and he is come to me; I have provoked God to anger, and he has left me; I have so hardened my heart, that I cannot repent.

* This single paragraph proves, in opposition to the assertion in Note (k) p. 40,[1] that in Bunyan's judgement there must be at least a *negative* co-operation of the Will of Man with the Divine Grace— an energy of Non-resistance to the workings of the Holy Spirit.[2] But the error of the Calvinists is, that they ~~place~~ divide the regenerate Will in Man from the Will of God—instead of *including* it.

9 pp 46–8

So I saw in my dream, that just as Christian came up with the Cross, his burden loosed from off his shoulders, and fell from off his back, and began to tumble, and so continued to do, till it came to the mouth of the sepulchre, where it fell in, and I saw it no more.

"We know that the Son of God is come, and hath given us a dis- cerning mind (or *discernment* of *Reason*) that we may know the TRUE (*one*) and we are in the TRUE (*one*), in his Son Jesus Christ. This is the true God and Eternal Life—Little Children, BEWARE OF IDOLS.["] John I. Ep. V. 20, 21.[1] Alas! how many Protestants make ~~an~~ mental idol of the Cross ~~imagined~~, scarcely less ~~dangerous~~ injurious to the true faith in the Son of God, than the wooden

---

[7][3] Cf COPY A **24** n 1. The Arminian doctrines set forth in the Remonstrance of 1610 were a theological reaction against the deterministic logic of Calvinism, the Arminians insisting that the sovereignty of God was com- patible with real free-will in man, that Christ died for all men and not only for the elect, and rejecting the varieties of Calvinist doctrine of predestination. See **16** and **21**, below. In the Methodist movement John Wesley represented an Arminian position, George White- field a Calvinist position. See also

BAXTER *Reliquiae* COPY B **101** and n 2.

[8][1] I.e. **7** textus, above.

[8][2] See COPY A **19** textus.

[9][1] C is elaborating and glossing 1 John 5.20–1: "And we know that the Son of God is come, and hath given us an understanding, that we may know him that is true, and we are in him that is true, even in his Son Jesus Christ. This is the true God, and eternal life. Little children, keep yourselves from idols."

Crosses & Crucifixes of the Romanists, and this because they have not been taught, that Jesus was both the Christ and the great Symbol of Christ. Strange! we can explain spiritually, what to take up the Cross of Christ, to be crucified with Christ, &c means—yet never ask, what the Crucifixion itself signified—but rest satisfied in the historic image. That one declaration of the Apostle, that by wilful Sin we crucify the Son of God afresh, might have roused us to nobler thought.[2]

10 pp 49–54

. . . and besides, said they, if we get into the way, what matters which *] way we get in? If we are in, we are in: thou art but in the way, who, as we perceive, came in at the gate; and we are also in the way, that came tumbling over the wall: wherein now is thy condition better than ours?

* In this instance (and it is, I believe, the only one in the work) the allegory degenerates into a sort of *pun/* viz. the two senses of the word "way"[1]—and thus supplies Form. and Hyp.[2] with an argument, which Christian cannot fairly answer—or rather, one to which Bunyan could not make his Christian return the proper answer, without contradicting the allegoric image. For the obvious and only proper answer is—No! you are not in the *same way* with me tho' you are walking on the same Road.[a]

P.S. But it has a worse defect—viz. that it leaves the Reader uncertain as to what the Writer precisely meant or wished to be understood by the Allegory. Did Bunyan refer to the Quakers, as rejecting the outward sacraments of Baptism & the Lord's Supper? If so, it is the only unspiritual passage in the whole beautiful Allegory—the only trait of sectarian narrow-mindedness, & in Bunyan's own language, of *Legality*. But I do not think that this was B's intention. I rather suppose, that Bunyan refers to the Arminian & other Pelagians, who rely on their coincidence of their *actions* with the Gospel Precepts for their salvation, whatever the ground or root of their Conduct may be—who place, in short, the saving virtue in the *stream*, with little or no reference to the *Source*—But it is the Faith acting

---

[a] Up to this point all the notes are written in the same hand and ink. The writing changes with the PS

9[2] Cf e.g. Matt 10.38, 16.24 (and gospel parallels), Rom 6.6, Gal 2.20. But with the final phrase "by wilful Sin . . ." cf Heb 6.4–6.

10[1] See COPY A 21.

10[2] Formalist and Hypocrisy, a pair of figures "born in the land of Vain-Glory", who overtook Christian in the way after they had tumbled over the wall.

in our poor imperfect deeds that alone saves us—and even this Faith (see Galat. 1.2 c) is not ours but the Faith of the Son of God in us.[3] Illustrate this by a simile. Laboring under chronic Bronchitis I am told to inhale *Chlorine*, as a specific remedy. But I can do this only by dissolving a saturated solution of the Gas in warm water, and then breathing the Vapor.[4] Now what the aqueous vapor or steam is to the Chlorine, that our Deeds, our outward Life (βιος) is to Faith/

10A p 52

> Better, though difficult, the right way to go,
> Than wrong, though easy, where the end is woe.

11 p 52

... and the other took directly up the way to Destruction, which led him into a wide field, full of dark mountains, where he stumbled and fell, and rose no more.

This requires a comment.[a]

a wide field, full of mountains—and of *dark* mountains, where For. or Hyp. stumbled & fell/[1] the Images here are unusually obscure. *S. T. C.*

12 pp 68–70

They shewed him Moses rod; the hammer and nail with which Jae[l] slew Sisera ...

I question whether it would be possible to instance ⟨more strikingly⟩ the modifying power of a predominant Idea (that true mental kaleidoscope with richly colored Glass) on ~~the~~ every object brought before the eye of the Mind thro' its medium, than this conjunction of Moses' Rod with the Hammer of the treacherous Assassin, Jael— and similar encomiastic References to the same detestable Murder, by Bunyan and Men like Bunyan good, pious, purely affectioned Disciples of the meek and holy Jesus, yet the erroneous precon- ception that whatever is uttered ~~by a~~ by a scripture Personage is in

---

[a] This sentence is written within the text, the rest of the note in the outer margin

10[3] See Gal 2.20; cf 2.16.

10[4] On 21 Sept 1831 C, writing to Green in an interval of relief from severe bronchitis, said: "...do not forget to ask Dr Elliotson about the inhalation of chlorine in my case". *CL* vi 872–3.

11[1] See **10** n 2, above. When they left Christian, one took the way called Danger, the other the way to Destruc- tion.

fact uttered by the infallible Spirit of God makes *Deboras* of them all.[1] S. T. C. But what besides ought we to infer from this and similar facts?—Surely, that the Faith in the Heart overpowers and renders innocuous the Errors of the Understanding and the delusions of the Imagination—and that sincerely pious men purchase exemption from the practical consequences of particular Errors by inconsistency.

13 p 74

[Editor's note:] This is the best way to own Satan's charges, if they *] be true; yea, to exaggerate them also, to exalt the riches of the grace of Christ, above all, in pardoning all of them freely.

* i.e. to say what we do not believe to be true! Will ye *lie* for God? said righteous Job.[1]

14 pp 80–1

[Editor's note:] But it may be asked, Why doth the Lord suffer his children to walk in such darkness? It is for his glory: it tries their faith in him, and excites prayer to him: but his love abates not in the least towards them, since he lovingly inquires after them: "Who is there among you that feareth the Lord, and walketh in darkness, and hath no light?" Then he gives most precious advice to them: "Let him trust in the Lord, and stay himself upon his God." Isa. 1. 10.

Yes! even in the sincerest Believers, being men of reflecting and inquiring Minds, there will sometimes come a wintry season, when the vital Sap of Faith retires to the Root, i.e. to Adhesion of the Will. Tho he slay me, yet will I cling to him.[1]

15 pp 152–5, pencil, overtraced

[Editor's note, referring to the Delectable Mountains:] Fine-spun speculations and curious reasonings lead men from simple truth and

12[1] The prophetess Deborah, to whom the children of Israel appealed "for judgment", beguiled Sisera to lead his army to annihilation at the hands of Barak. When Sisera escaped from the battle and took refuge with Jael, Jael pretended to harbour him but murdered him while he slept by driving a nail through his head (Judges 4). Deborah and Barak then sang a song of triumph, "Praise ye the Lord for the avenging of Israel..." (Judges 5). Because of the magnificence of the Song of Deborah, C warns against uncritically accepting this unedifying story as justification for brutality.

13[1] Job 13.7: "Will ye speak wickedly for God? and talk deceitfully for him?"

14[1] Job 13.15: "Though he slay me, yet will I trust in him".

*] implicit faith into many dangerous and destructive errors. The word records many instances of such for our caution. Be warned to study simplicity and godly sincerity.

* and, pray, what does ~~an~~ *implicit* faith lead men into? Transsubstantiation, and all the abominations of Priest-worship. And where is the scriptural authority for this implicit faith? Assuredly, not in St John, who tells us that Christ's *Life* is & manifests itself in us as the *Light* of Man—that he came to bring *Light* as well ⟨as⟩*a* Immortality![1] Assuredly, not in St Paul, who declares all faith imperfect & perilous without insight & understanding—who prays for us that we may comprehend the deep things even of God himself.[2] For the Spirit discerned & the Spirit by which we discern, are both *God*—the Spirit of Truth for*b* & in Christ from the Father!—

16 pp [+3]–[+4] (p–d), referring to p 153

[Editor's note:] Do we see others fall into perdition by the very same sins and follies, from which God has reclaimed us? What must we resolve this into, but his superabounding, discriminating graces? One shall be taken, and another left. And, surely, it is enough to make one's eyes gush out with tears, and to melt our hard hearts into fervent love, to look back upon the many singular instances of God's distinguishing favour to us. O call them to mind, and be thankful.

P. 153. Mournful are the Errors into which the Zealous but unlearned Preachers among the dissenting Calvinists have fallen—respecting Absolute Election & discriminating yet reasonless Grace! Fearful this divorcement of the Holy Will, the one only Absolute Good, that eternally affirming itself as the I AM, eternally generatedth the *Word*, the Absolute BEING, the Supreme REASON, the Being of all Truth, the Truth of all Being, ⟨fearful its Divorcement⟩ from the Reason!—fearful the Doctrine which maketh God a Power of Darkness, instead of the God of Light, the Father of the Light, which lightneth every man that cometh into the World.[1] This we know and this we are taught by the holy Apostle, Paul: that without will there is no *ground* or *base* of Sin: that without the Law this ground or base cannot become Sin[2]—(hence we ~~are~~ do not impute Sin to the

---

a This word is inserted in ink, presumably by HNC
b C wrote "for" in pencil; it was overtraced as "thro'"

15[1] John 1.4, 5, 9.
15[2] 1 Cor 2.4–16, esp 10.
16[1] John 1.9.

16[2] See esp Rom 5.13: "For until the law sin was in the world: but sin is not imputed when there is no law."

Wolf or the Tyger, as being without or below the Law.) But with the Law cometh Light into the Will; & by this Light the Will becometh a free & therefore a responsible Will.— ~~But~~ Yea, the Law is itself *Light*, & ⟨the Divine Light⟩ becomes *Law* by its relation & opposition to the Darkness—the Will of God revealed in its opposition to the dark & alien Will of the fallen Spirit.—This freedom then is the free gift of God; but does it therefore cease to be freedom?—

All the sophistry of the predestinarians rests on the false notion of Eternity as a sort of Time antecedent to Time. It is timeless, present with & in all times.[a3]

17   pp 166–7

[Editor's note:] But how contrary to this is the walk and conduct of some who profess to be pilgrims, and yet can wilfully and deliberately go upon the devil's ground, and indulge themselves in carnal pleasures and sinful diversions?

But what pleasures are carnal? what are sinful diversions? So I mean as that I may be able to determine what are not. Shew us the Criterion, the General Principle: at least explain whether each individual case is to be decided for the Individual by his own experience of the effects of the Pleasure, or the Diversion, in dulling or distracting his religious feelings. Or can a ~~list of~~ compleat List of all such Pleasures be made beforehand?

18   pp 284–5, pencil, overtraced | Pt ii

Prud. Good boy still. But how doth God the Father save thee?
James. By his grace.
Prud. How doth God the Son save thee?
James. By his righteousness, and blood, and death, and life.
Prud. And how doth the Holy Ghost save thee?
James. By his illumination, by his renovation, and by his preservation. [Editor's note:] I cannot prevail on myself to let this part pass by, without making observation. Mr. Bunyan expresses himself very clear and sound in the faith; but here it is not so; for

---

[a] *LR* adds 21 here, without a paragraph break

The Epistle to the Romans deals extensively with the relation between the law and grace.

16[3] The confusion of time and eternity is a recurrent theme for C. Cf

e.g. ETERNAL PUNISHMENT 1 (PS), and in N 21½ f 51[v]: "The defect of Archb. Leighton's Reasoning is the taking Eternity as a *sort* of Time…".

what is here ascribed to the Son, is rather the work of the Spirit; and, indeed, the work of salvation, effected by the Son of God, is entirely left out. I am therefore inclined to think, that here is a chasm, though not perhaps in the author's original work, but by its passing through later editions. It really seems defective here, in the explanation of salvation by the distinct offices of the Holy Trinity.

N.b. I cannot see the justice or the necessity of this note. The term "Grace" appropriated to God the Father means, the ground and antecedent of our Redemption, viz: God so loved us as to send his Son &c.[1]

19 p 392 | Pt iii

I strongly suspect that this third part, which ought not to have been thus conjoined with Bunyan's Work was written by a Roman Catholic Priest, for the very purpose of counteracting the doctrine of Faith so strictly enforced in the genuine Progress.[1]

20 p 442

[A list of evils is given, against all which fasting is the proper remedy.] ... it [fasting] refines the understanding, subdues the passions, regulates the will, and sublimates the whole man to a more spiritual state of life ...

It would have been well if the Writer had explained exactly what he meant by the Fasting, here so strongly recommended. During what period of time abstinence from food is to continue, &c. The effects, I imagine, must in good measure depend on the Health of the Individual. In some Constitutions Fasting so disorders the stomach as to produce the very contrary—confusion of mind, loose imaginations against the Man's own will, &c &c.

21 pp +2–+3

There is an excellent Discourse of the great Hooker's affixed ~~to~~ with two or three others to his Ecclesiastical Polity on the final perseverance of Saints.[1] But yet I am very desirous to meet with some judicious experimental Treatise, in which the doctrine with the

18[1] John 3.16, the second of the "Comfortable Words" in the Communion Service.

19[1] *Pilgrim's Progress* Pt iii, first published 1693, is spurious: see COPY A 17 and n 2.

21[1] Cf HOOKER *Works*: "A Learned and Comfortable Sermon of the Certainty and Perpetuity of Faith in the Elect", on which C wrote four marginal notes in 1825–6.

Scriptures on which it is grounded is set forth more at large; as likewise the rules by which it may be applied to the purposes of Support and comfort without danger of causing Presumption and without diminishing the dread of Sin. Above all, I am anxious to see the subject treated with as little reference as possible to the Divine Predestination and Foresight: the arguments from the latter being a mere identical proposition, followed by an assertion of God's Prescience. Those, who will persevere, will perservere—and God foresees.—And as to the proof from Predestination, viz. that he who predestines the *end*, necessaryily predestines the adequate *Means*, I can more readily imagine logical consequences ~~that~~ adverse to the sense of responsibility than *Christian* Consequence/ such as an Individual may apply for his own edification. And I am persuaded that the Doctrine does not need these supports—i.e. according to the ordinary notion of Predestination I mean. The predestinative force of a Free-agent's own will in certain absolute Acts, Determinations or Elections, and in respect of which Acts it is one either with the Divine or the Devilish Will—and supposing the former, the conclusions to be drawn from God's Goodness, faithfulness, and spiritual presence—these supply grounds of ~~state~~argument of a very different character—especially where the Mind has been prepared by an insight into the error and hollowness of the Antithesis ~~of~~ between Liberty and Necessity.[2]

21[2] See e.g. *SM* (*CC*) 31–2.

GOTTFRIED AUGUST BÜRGER
1747–1794

Gottfried August Bürger's Gedichte. Herausgegeben von Karl Reinhard. 2 vols. Göttingen 1796. 8⁰.

A separate issue of Vols I and II of Bürger's *Sämmtliche Schriften* ed Karl Reinhard (Göttingen 1796).

Victoria College Library (Coleridge Collection)

Autograph signature "S. T. Coleridge" on the title-page of each volume.
In Jul 1796 Lamb wrote to C: "Have you read the Ballad called 'Leonora,' in the second Number of the 'Monthly Magazine'? If you have !!!!!!!!!!!!!! There is another fine song, from the same author (Berger), in the 3d No., of scarce inferior merit". *LL* I 37. William Taylor of Norwich had made in 1790 the translation that was printed in the *M Mag* of Mar 1796; the other poem referred to by Lamb was *The Lass of Fair Wone*, printed a month later. By 1798 the poem, widely known in England, had aroused Walter Scott to make his own translation, and had been parodied. For the possible influence of the translation of *Lenore* on *AM* see *RX* 336, 485–6, 567. C reported WW's discussion of Bürger's poems with Klopstock in Germany and said in Nov 1798 that "Bürger of all the German Poets pleases me the most, as yet—the Lenore is greatly superior to any of the Translations". *Friend (CC)* II 244; *CL* I 438. In the winter of 1798–9 he transcribed a substantial part of a letter from WW expressing a view of Bürger that he could not endorse. *CL* I 565–6. For C on Bürger's "most forcible combinations" in the use of language see *CN* II 3155.
This copy was bought on the evening of 22 Sept 1798 together with copies of Matthisson, Müller, Stolberg, and Lessing for a total of £1.3.6, at "The Shop near the Jungfern Stieg"—that is, at the shop of William Remnant, the English bookseller in Hamburg to whom Johnson gave C the order for £30 from which he made his first major purchase of German books. See *CN* I 340, *CL* I 417, 432.

DATE. Probably 1798–9: after 22 Sept 1798, perhaps annotated in Germany shortly after purchase.

A I 70, pencil mark | *Lenore* st 6

"Hilf Gott, hilf! Siech uns gnädig an!
Kind, bet' ein Vaterunser!——
——Was Gott thut, das ist wohlgethan.

["Help, God, help! Look on us mercifully! Child, offer a paternoster! Whatever God does is done for the best."]

B I 71, pencil mark | st 8

> Er hat es nimmermehr Gewinn!——

[He never again profited from it!]

1 I 72, pencil | st 10 lines 1–2

> "Hilf Gott, hilf! Geh nicht ins Gericht
> Mit deinem armen Kinde!..."

["Help, God, help! Do not blame Thy poor child!"]

Ps. 143. V. I[1]

2 I 72, pencil | lines 3–4

> "Sie weiss nicht, was die Zunge spricht.
> Behalt' ihr nicht die Sünde!..."*

["She does not know what her tongue speaks. Do not hold her sin against her!"]

* Acts C. 7. 59.[1]

2A I 78, pencil mark | st 21

> ——"Lasst uns den Leib begraben!"

["Let us bury the body!"]

3 I 133, pencil | *Der Raubgraf* st 9

> Ein alter Graf, fuhr Schwager Matz
> Nach seiner Weise fort,
> Vergrub zu Olims Zeit den Schatz
> In seinem Keller dort.
> Der Graf, mein Herr, hiess Graf von Rips,
> Ein Kraut, wie Käsebier* und Lips.

["An old count," continued Matz the postillion in his own way, "buried the treasure in his cellar there in Olim's time. The count, Sir, was called Count von Rips, a simple fellow like Käsebier and Lips."]

* & Lips Tullian/ Robbers[1]

1[1] "Hear my prayer, O Lord, give ear to my supplications: in thy faithfulness answer me, and in thy righteousness." Ps 143.1.

2[1] C presumably intended Acts 7.60: "And he kneeled down, and cried with a loud voice, Lord, lay not this sin to their charge."

3[1] "Rips"—a Göttingen dialect word for a strange withered creature, usually considered human. Käsebier and Lips—the nicknames of two notorious robbers. Tullian was even more notorious, being one of the nine rogues whose lives are recorded in *Des bekannten Diebes, Mörders und Räubers L. Tullian's und seiner Complicen Leben und Ubelthaten, dabey Gottes sonderbahre Schickung erhellet* (Dresden 1716). Grimm records for 1828 a use of "Tullian" as "a rogue".

GILBERT BURNET
1643–1715

Bishop Burnet's History of His Own Time. 2 vols. Dublin 1724, 1734. F°

Not located; marginalia not recorded. *Gillman SC* (1843) 512: "With MS. Notes by S. T. Coleridge". *Lost List*.

C's earliest recorded acquaintance with Burnet's writing was his borrowing of the *History of His Own Time* (1724, 1734) from the Bristol Library Society 20–7 Apr 1795; it may have been needed to help with RS's lectures. *Bristol LB* 50–1. He twice quoted from this work in *Courier* articles of Sept 1811: *EOT* (*CC*) II 291–2, 300. Later he said: "Burnet's 'History of his Own Times' is a truly valuable book. His credulity is great, but his simplicity is equally great; and he never deceives you for a moment." *TT* 15 Jun 1830.

The History of the Reformation of the Church of England. The first part. Of the progress made in it during the reign of King Henry the VIII. (The second part. Of the progress made in it till the settlement of it in the beginning of Q. Elizabeths reign.) 2 vols. Dublin 1730, London 1683. F°.

Vol I of this mixed set is a Dublin ed following the 4th London ed, Vol II is 2nd ed.

Not located. Annotations printed from MS TRANSCRIPT. *Gillman SC* (1843) 511 ("1683–1730"). *Lost List.*

In proposing the first version of *AR* to John Murray in Jan 1822 C spoke of using this work (*CL* v 198, 199); in making a somewhat different proposal to Hessey in Sept 1823 he spoke of making a "laborious Collation" of Burnet and others in preparing his "Life of Leighton". *CL* v 300. A passage "*Extracted with slight alterations from Burnet's Preface to* Vol. ii. *of the Hist. of the Reformation*" was chosen as Aphorism III of the "Aphorisms on Spiritual Religion". *AR* (1825) 180.

MS TRANSCRIPT. VCL LT 57: SC transcript used for *NTP*. The edition is there described as "2. vols. folio. Dublin. 1730"; but the page references for Vol II fit only the 1683 ed—which shows that SC was using the same mixed set as noted in *Gillman SC*.

DATE. c Sept–Dec 1823: **8** is dated 28 Dec 1823. The letter in which C spoke of collating Burnet's *History* with other church historians is dated 9 Sept 1823.

1 I i sig c2ʳ | Preface to Part I

And if a leud and wicked Pope may yet have the holy Ghost dwelling in him, and directing him infallibly; why may not an ill King do so good a Work as set a Reformation forward? And if it were proper to enter into a dissection of Four of those Popes, that sate at Rome *during this reign, Pope* Julius *will be found beyond him in a vast Ambition, whose bloody Reign did not only embroil* Italy, *but a great part of Christendom. Pope* Leo *the Tenth was as extravagant and prodigal in his expence, which put him on baser Shifts, than ever this King used, to raise Money. . . .* Clement *the Seventh was false to the highest degree; a vice which cannot be charged on this King. And* Paul *the IIId was a vile and lewd Priest, who not only kept his Whore, but gloried in it, and raised one of his Bastards to an high Dignity, making him Prince of* Parma *and* Piacenza . . .

Perhaps a Romish Wit might retort It must fare badly with your cause when four wicked Popes go to the making of one Protestant

King—or when you must extract and unite the vices of the four worst
Popes to make up the wickedness of one reforming King!—*a*

2   1 i sig c2ᵛ

*As for other things, such as the giving the Cup to the Laity, the Wor-
shipping God in a known Tongue, and several Reformations about the
Mass, though they judged them necessary to be done as soon as was
possible; they had so full a perswasion of the necessity of these, as to
think it a sin not to do them. The Prophet's words to* Naaman *the*
Syrian, *might give them some colour for that mistake, and the practise
of the Apostles, who continued not only to worship at the Temple, but
to circumcise and to offer Sacrifices . . . even after the* Law was dead,*b*
by the appearing of the Gospel, seemed to excuse their Compliance.

Here lurks a mistake. Dead it was in spiritual effiacy and as a way to
Truth. The Law therefore dared not be imposed on, or even permitted to, the Gentile Converts.[1] But on Paul and the Apostles and the
Jewish Converts generally it remained in force till the destruction of
the Temple, the abolition of the ruling Priesthood, & the dispersion
of the People, in short, the absolute extinction of the Jewish *State* in
all its constituent parts, by Vespasian and Titus.—Then when the
Heaven (the Government & Hierarchy) and the Earth (the People)
had passed away, and the Object no longer existing, the Law ceased
of necessity.[2] The Horrors of the Jewish War & the Siege of Jerusa-

---

a In MS TRANSCRIPT this note is marked "S. T. C." in pencil; but that may simply be a way of
distinguishing the textus from ms
b In *NTP* these words are printed in italics, although the body of the textus is printed in roman;
it is assumed that C underlined them

2[1] The exchange between Elisha
and Naaman, who was "captain of
the host of the king of Syria", is re-
counted in 2 Ki 5.1–19. Naaman came
to Elisha to be healed of his leprosy,
incredulously followed Elisha's instructions, and—being cured—spon-
taneously cried: "Behold, now I know
that there is no God in all the earth,
but in Israel." He undertook "henceforth [to] offer neither burnt offering
nor sacrifice unto other gods, but unto
the Lord"; but he asked to be allowed,
as a matter of duty, to accompany his
master the King of Syria to worship
in the temple of Rimmon (the Assyrian
storm-god); to this, Elisha's answer
was "Go in peace." See also Rom
6.15–23, in which Paul argues that

obedience is the link between the law
and the Gospel, yet in 7.1–6 declares
that Christians are not in servitude to
the law.

2[2] C is alluding to Matt 5.17 and 18.
In A.D. 66 Nero sent Vespasian to
reduce the Jews to subjection. Proclaimed emperor in 69, he returned
to Rome, leaving his eldest son Titus
(39–81) in command in the Middle
East. In A.D. 70 the capture and destruction of Jerusalem by Titus brought
apocalyptic Judaism to an end; thereafter Judaism became a perpetuation
of rabbinic teaching, the "religion of
the Book", a cultural rather than a
political tradition. See also *CN* III
4402.

lem with all its portentous and unparalleled incidents were the Lightnings & Thunders of Mount Sinai for its abrogation. But till this time the Law was binding, I say, on the Apostles and Jewish Christians both as a civil obligation, a duty incumbent on them as Citizens of a particular State, and by the express Command of Christ, forbidding them to make their new character as Christians a pretext for not performing their duties as Subjects.[3]

3 I i 265 | Bk III "Of the other Transactions about Religion and Reformation, during the rest of the reign of King Henry the Eighth"

Thus did Sir *Thomas More* end his days, in the 53d year of his age. He was a man of rare vertues, and excellent parts: In his youth he had freer thoughts of things, as appears by his *Utopia*, and his letters to *Erasmus*; but afterward he became superstitiously devoted to the Interests and passions of the *Popish* Clergy: and as he served them when he was in Authority, even to assist them in all their cruelties; so he employed his Pen in the same cause, both in writing against all the new opinions in general, and in particular against *Tindal, Frith,* and *Barnes* ... but reproved the corruptions of the Clergy, and condemned their cruel proceedings.

I cannot satisfy my judgment on this point, one way or the other. For the negative—there is the great improbability of the statement, from the whole cast of More's mind and character[1]—for the affirmative his latter writings and some apparently well authenticated facts, together with the admitted superstition of [Rastell].[2] But still I am inclined to believe, that the Statesman and the patriot were uppermost, and that not foreseeing the rise and power of the Third Estate, he saw in the Power of the Clergy and even in the Papal Influence the sole remaining counter-weights to the Royal Prerogative, which the Ravage of the Civil Wars, and the consequent prostration of the Nobility had left. It is possible likewise, that Henry's own overbearing and capricious character might have indisposed him to any unsettling of ancient, though not *the* ancient, landmarks.

4 III i sig b | Preface to Pt II

The second Prejudice *is, That the Reformation was begun and carried on, not by the major part of the Bishops and Clergy; but by a few selec-*

2[3] Cf Matt 5.19.

3[1] Burnet published his anonymous translation of More's *Utopia* in 1684, in a copy of which ed C wrote at least one marginal note; see Thomas MORE.

3[2] MS TRANSCRIPT reads "Pascal", evidently a mistranscription for "Rastel"—i.e. William Rastell (c 1508–65), who edited Thomas More's *Works* (2 vols 1557).

ted Bishops and Divines, who being supported by the Name of the King's Authority, did frame things as they pleased; and by their Interest at Court got them to be Enacted in Parliament: and after they had removed such Bishops as opposed them, then they procured the Convocation to consent to what was done: So that upon the matter, the Reformation was the Work of Cranmer, *with a few more of his Party, and not of this Church, which never agreed wholly to it, till the Bishops were so modelled as to be compliant to the designs of the Court. . . . The Case is not hard, if well understood: for in the whole Scripture there is no promise made to the major part of the Pastors of the Church; and there being no Divine Promise made about it, it is certain that the nature of Man is such, that Truth separated from Interest hath few Votaries: but when it is opposite to it, it must have a very small Party.*

I find it difficult to account for so very thin and languid a defence of our Reformation on this objection from the minor number of the Reformers from so sensible and powerful a reasoner as Burnet generally appears.[1] S. T. Coleridge.

P.S. The objection is not only weakly answered, but most dangerously: for first, the Parliament is almost sneakingly *insinuated*, rather than asserted, as a joint authority: and secondly, what even Parliaments were during the period from Henry VIIth to James the I, who does not know, to whom English history is not unknown? The proper answer would have been, that if the rites and doctrines abolished are false & superstitious, and those retained were, together with the interpretations of them, true, edifying and scriptural, the excellence of the Result cannot be affected by accidental coincidences of the actions of individuals, the Church representing Truth as its own evidence: But if the contrary be the case, if the Reformation were an heretical Depravation, then it should be acknowledged that the enforcement of the same on the majority of the Clergy and the Kingdom by the minority is an aggravation of the crime. Therefore, till this point be decided, the objection is premature, and, when it is decided, superfluous. For the crime needs no aggravation, and the merit no addition.[2]

4[1] Yet C chose from this same Preface the aphorism that he considered would provide "a safe criterion" for certain "*extra-scriptural* Articles of Faith": see *AR* (1825) 180.

4[2] C wrote a long note in N 30 ff 39[v]–40, referring to "Burnet's *Reform.* Vol. II. Preface, p. 10", discussing the difference between the Reformation in Scotland and in England.

5 ɪɪ i 80 | Pt ɪɪ bk ɪ "Of the Life and Religion of King Edward the Sixth"

The belief of Christ's Corporal Presence was yet under consideration. And they observing wisely how the *Germans* had broken, by their running too soon into Contests about that, resolved to keep up still the old general Expressions, of the Sacraments being the whole and true Body of Christ, without coming to a more particular Explanation of it.

Wisely? Keep up? This may have been very *prudent*, but it looks very like ʿYMBYΓ,[1] alias, No, Sir! Yes, Sir! Y,y,y-yes, Sir, N-n-n-no, Sir;—*pretty*, when prettily minced, and stammered by a young lady with downcast eye askance; but not quite so becoming in the mouth of a grave theological Reformer. Eh, Master[a] Burnet?—

6 ɪɪ i 113

The *Germans* soon saw the ill effects of this Doctrine [of Predestination]. *Luther* changed his mind about it, and *Melancthon* openly writ against it: and since that time the whole stream of the *Lutheran* Churches has run the other way. But both *Calvin* and *Bucer* were still for maintaining the Doctrine of these Decrees; only they warned the People not to think much of them, since they were Secrets which Men could not penetrate into; but they did not so clearly shew how these consequences did not flow from such Opinions.

Pity that Burnet did not inform us, how the Doctrine is to be put down! or on what principles it is to be convicted of falsehood! And if not, how Cranmer[b] & Bucer could do better, than to declare it a Truth above the human faculties, and unfit for frequent meditation, it being so likely that we should err, and the errors being so perilous![1]

7 ɪɪ i 327 | Bk ɪɪ "The Life and Reign of Queen Mary"

But above all, that Design of his, to have Seminaries in every Cathedral for the planting of the Diocess, shews what a wise prospect he had of the right methods of recovering a Church, which was overrun, as he judged, with Heresie. It was the same that *Cranmer* had formerly designed; but never took effect.

Certainly, persons formed from their Childhood, with other Notions, and another method of living, must be much better fitted

---

  a MS TRANSCRIPT reads what looks like "Méaster"—possibly to follow a correction of "Mister" to "Master" in C's ms. Perhaps C was hinting at a dialect pronunciation
  b A slip for "Calvin" (see textus), as corrected in *NTP*

  5[1] "HUMBUG" written in Greek   6[1] See 9, below.
characters.

for a holy Character, than those that have lived in the pleasures and follies of the world; who, unless a very extraordinary change is wrought in them, still keep some of their old Customs about them, and so fall short of that gravity and decency that becomes so Spiritual a Function.

Strange ignorance of human nature! And this from a Whig Bishop! To sever a body of men from all living sympathy with mankind at large, was an excellent trick for the keeping up of superstition.

8 II ii (365–8)*ᵃ* | A Collection of Records and Original Papers ... No 11 "A Declaration of certain principal Articles of Religion"

I. First; That there is but one living and true God, of infinite Power, Wisdom, and Goodness; the maker and preserver of all Things. And that in Unity of this God-head, there be three Persons of one Substance, of equal Power and Eternity; the Father, the Son, and the Holy Ghost.

Amen

II. I believe also whatsoever is contained in the Holy Canonical Scriptures.

Επεχω. *Lege*, I believe that in the holy Canonical Scriptures are contained &c. Then I answer, Amen.[1]

In the which Scriptures are contained all things necessary to Salvation; by the which also, all Errors and Heresies may sufficiently be reproved and convicted; and all Doctrine and Articles, necessary to Salvation, established.

Amen.

I do also most firmly believe and confess all the Articles contained in the Three Creeds; the *Nicene* Creed, *Athanasius* Creed, and our common Creed, called, the *Apostles Creed*; for these do briefly contain the principal Articles of our Faith, which are at large set forth in the Holy Scriptures.

Amen, not taking the damnatory Preface as part of the Pseudo-Athanasian Creed,[2] or understanding the faith required to be implicit only and not explicit.

ᵃ Between ii 368 and 369 a 4-page gathering has been inserted and is foliated "(365)" to "(368)"

8[1] The Greek word, as in BATEMAN **1**, means "I hesitate". The Latin word following it is the imperative "Read!"

8[2] For the "Pseudo-Athanasian Creed" see BÖHME **33** and n 1. In May 1827 C told Cary that "I hold the Pseudo-athanasian Creed to be pretty equally divided into four parts, under the corresponding Heads

I hold the (so called) Athanasian Creed to be not false but imperfect, but yet unfit to be a public Creed because the whole Truth in a Doctrine setting forth a one Idea is necessary to the perfection of each and every of the Truths therein contained, or of the distinct Verities contemplated in the untroubled Unity of the Idea. Now this Creed truly expresses the equality of Attributes and the Identity of the Godhead; but does not confess the subordination of the Persons.

III. I do acknowledg also that Church to be the Spouse of Christ, wherein the Word of God is truly taught, the Sacraments orderly ministred, according to Christ's Institution, and the Authority of the Keys duly used. And that every such particular Church, hath Authority to institute, to change, clean to put away Ceremonies, and other Ecclesiastical Rites, as they be superfluous, or be abused; and to constitute other, making more to seemliness, to Order, or Edification.

III. does not admit of an answer, it not being here defined, *who* the Church is, as an Executive Power. The term, Church, is here equivocal, or rather multivocal. In like manner, the term, *particular*. If the Church of England and that of Ireland be two Churches, why not York and Canterbury?

IV. Moreover, I confess, That it is not lawful for any Man to take upon him any Office or Ministry, either Ecclesiastical or Secular, but such only as are lawfully thereunto called by their High Authorities, according to the Ordinances of this Realm.

Amen—with the same faith & no other, as I confess that nothing is white that is not white.

V. Furthermore, I do acknowledg the Queen's Majesty's Prerogative and Superiority of Government of all Estates, and in all Causes, as well Ecclesiastical as Temporal, within this Realm, and other her Dominions and Countries, to be agreeable to God's Word, and of right to appertain to her Highness, in such sort as is in the late Act of Parliament expressed ...

---

of—1. Presumption, and that brimstone-colored—2. Tautology or Verbiage. 3. Nonsense. 4. Heresy". *CL* vi 684; see also v 87. The "damnatory Preface" is the two opening sentences: "Whosoever will be saved: before all things it is necessary that he hold the Catholick Faith. Which Faith except every one do keep whole and undefiled: without doubt he shall perish everlastingly."

Negatively understood, i.e. that the things of Cæsar do*ᵃ* not cease to be Cæsar's by being in and for a Church.³—Amen.

VI. Moreover, touching the Bishop of *Rome*, I do acknowledg and confess, that by the Scriptures, and Word of God, he hath no more Authority than other Bishops have in their Provinces and Dioceses: and therefore the Power which he now challengeth, that is, to be the Supream Head of the Universal Church of Christ . . . is an usurped Power, contrary to the Scriptures and the Word of God . . .

Amen.

VII. Furthermore, I do grant and confess, That the Book of Common Prayer, and Administration of the Holy Sacraments, set forth by the Authority of Parliament, is agreeable to the Scriptures, and that it is Catholick, Apostolick, and most for the advancing of God's Glory, and the edifying of God's People . . .

Amen—as far as the knowledge of its fallible origin is not contradicted by this Assent.

IX. Moreover, I do not only acknowledg, that Private Masses were never used amongst the Fathers of the Primitive Church . . . But also that the Doctrine that maintaineth the Mass to be a propitiatory Sacrifice for the Quick and the Dead, and a mean to deliver Souls out of Purgatory, is neither agreeable to Christ's Ordinance, nor grounded upon Doctrine Apostolick . . .

Amen.

X. I am of that mind also, That the Holy Communion, or Sacrament, of the Body and Blood of Christ . . . ought to be ministred unto the People under both kinds . . .

Amen.

Last of all. As I do utterly disallow the extolling of Images, Reliques, and feigned Miracles; and also all kind of expressing God Invisible, in the form of an Old Man, or the Holy Ghost in the form of a Dove; and all other vain worshipping of God, devised by Man's fantasy . . . As wandring on Pilgrimages, setting up of Candles, praying upon Beads, and such-like Superstition . . .

Amen. S. T. Coleridge, 28 Decʳ 1823.⁴

ᵃ MS TRANSCRIPT reads "to be"

8³ Mark 12.17 (Matt 22.21 var): "Render to Caesar the things that are Caesar's, and to God the things that are God's."

8⁴ C caught a severe chill in the move from Moreton House to No 3 The Grove. By 10 Dec he was troubled "with the noise as of a distant Forge-

9 II ii 386–7 | An Appendix Concerning Some of the Errors and Falsehoods in Sander's *Book of the English Schism*

But there was no occasion for *Bucer*'s saying this, ["That the Corporal Presence was so clear in the Scriptures, that no Man could deny it, who believed the Gospel"], since he never declared against the Corporeal Presence; but was for taking up that Controversy in some general Expressions.

In the Appendix to Strype's Life of Cranmer is to be found an excellent paper of Bucer's on the Eucharist, in a spirit very superior to the metaphysics of his age.[1] The result is that the Body & Blood are the Corpus νοουμενον, or actual, substantial Body, and therefore spiritual; not the Corpus φαινομενον.[2] And that in the former or noumenal sense the doctrine of the *real* (as opposed to phænomenal) presence is agreeable *with* Reason and *to* Scripture—οὗτος ἄρτος νοεῖ σῶμα ἐμον.[3]

---

hammer incessantly sounding"—an affliction that lasted for two months. *CL* v 311, 314, 327, 332. The sound could have reminded him of Greta Hall. When SC in 1852 knew she was dying and wrote for her daughter her recollections of the house where she had lived until her marriage, the two sounds she remembered hearing from her bedroom were "the river flowing, and sometimes the forge hammer, in the distance, at the end of the field".

9[1] C wrote four marginalia on this appendix, entitled "The Sententious Sayinges of Master Bucer upon the Lordes Supper", in STRYPE *Memorials of Cranmer* (1694). See also BLANCO WHITE *Poor Man's Preservative* 2 n 1.

9[2] "Noumenal Body...phaenomenal Body".

9[3] "This bread means my body". Cf Mark 14.22 and Matt 26.26, taken into the liturgy of the Communion: τοῦτό ἐστι τὸ σῶμά μου, "This is my body." See also *AR* (1825) 308–9n. C evidently means "This bread is the noumenal form of my body", νοεῖν being the active voice of the verb from which νούμενον is formed.

The Life of William Bedell, D.D. Bishop of Kilmore in Ireland. [Fly-title:] The Copies of Certain Letters which have passed between Spain & England in matter of religion, concerning the general motives to the Roman obedience, between Mr. James Waddesworth, a late pensioner of the Holy Inquisition in Sevil, and W. Bedell, a Minister of the Gospel of Jesus Christ in Suffolk. [Anonymous.] London 1685. 8⁰.

The two parts are paginated in a single series, the *Life* ending at p [260], the text of *Copies of Certain Letters* beginning at p 265. In this copy, pp 209–24 were bound in error at pp 336/7 (a note in pencil, not in C's hand, on 208 reads "turn to Pag 336").

Stanford University Library

Inscribed at the head of the title-page: "Robert Southey. Bristol. 1808", and with RS's Bewick bookplate on the verso of the fly-title to *Copies of Certain Letters*. (C refers to RS in **5**, below.) The name "Roback[?]" is written in pencil on p ⁻6. Bookplate of Stanford University: "Gift of Mrs. Timothy Hopkins." Three passages on pp 91–3 are marked in ink.

In c Jun 1810 C noted: "Read Bedell's Life & his letters to Wadsworth—delightful & excellent throughout—the very model of Judicious & truly Christian Controversy. I remember nothing comparable with it. . . ." *CN* III 3856; see also 3657, 3658, 3853, 3854, 3856, 3857, 3858, 4021. He quoted from the *Life* in the *Courier* of 6 Dec 1814, and from *Copies of Certain Letters* in the 1818 *Friend*: see *EOT* (*CC*) II 406–7, *Friend* (*CC*) I 287–8.

MS TRANSCRIPT. VCL BT 33: **6–11** only.

DATE. c Jun 1810, on the evidence of *CN* III 3856 and surrounding entries (see above). This is one of the books C annotated at Greta Hall between early May and mid-Oct 1810 in the languid but bookish interval at Greta Hall between the discontinuation of *The Friend* and his ill-fated departure for London.

1   p ⁻2, referring to pp xxvii–xxx*ᵃ* | Preface

One thing more I will add, which may afford a more general Instruction. Several years ago he observ'd a great heat in some young Minds, that, as he believed, had very good intentions, but were too forward, and complained much of abuses, calling loudly, and not very decently, for a Reformation of them: upon which he told them, the noise made about reforming abuses was the likeliest way to keep them up; for that would raise Heats and Disputes, and would be ascribed to envy and faction in them; and ill-minded Men, that loved

---

ᵃ LR and *C 17th C* incorrectly print this note as a continuation of **12**. In the ms it is written below **12** and is evidently separate

the abuses for the advantages they made by them, would blast and misrepresent those that went about to correct them, by which they would fall under the jealousie of being ill affected to the Church; and they being once loaded with this prejudice, would be disabled from doing the good, of which they might otherwise be the Instruments: Therefore he thought a Reformation of Abuses ought to be carried on by every one in his station, with no other noise than what the things themselves must necessarily produce, and then the silent way of conviction that is raised by great Patterns would speak louder, and would recommend such Practices more strongly, as well as more modestly. Discourses work but upon speculative people; and it has been so long the method of factious and ill designing Men, to accuse publick Errors, that he wished those, to whom he addressed his advice, would give over all thoughts of mending the world, which was grown too old in wickedness to be easily corrected; and would only set themselves to do what good they could, with less noise; and so to give less occasion to angry people to quarrel with them; and to justifie those abuses which are by such indiscreet opposition kept in some credit, and preserved; whereas without that they must have fallen under so general an *Odium*, that few could have the face to excuse them.

The preface—one thing more I will add—down to—face to excuse them.

THE LIFE OF WILLIAM BEDELL

2   p 8, pencil

P. Paulo went further, for he assisted him in acquiring the *Italian Tongue*, in which *Bedell* became such a Master, that he spoke it as one born in *Italy*, and penned all the Sermons he then preached, either in *Italian* or *Latine*. . . . In requital of the Instruction he received from *P. Paulo* in the *Italian* Tongue, he drew a Grammar of the *English* Tongue for his use, and for some others that desired to learn it, that so they might be able to understand our Books of Divinity, and he also translated the *English* Common-prayer Book into *Italian* . . .

Q if t[ranslation?][a] is now extant[1]

---

a Word illegible

2[1] Bedell's Italian version of BCP was not published; neither was his Italian grammar.

3 p ⁻5, referring to pp 13–14

Here I must add a passage, concerning which I am in doubt whether it reflected more on the sincerity, or on the understanding of the *English* Ambassadour. The breach between the Pope and the Republick was brought very near a Crisis; so that it was expected a total separation, not only from the Court, but the Church of *Rome*, was like to follow upon it. It was set on by *P. Paulo* and the Seven Divines with much zeal, and was very prudently conducted by them. In order to the advancing of it, King *James* ordered his Ambassadour to offer all possible assistance to them, and to accuse the Pope and the Papacy as the chief Authors of all the mischiefs of Christendome. ... *P. Paulo* and the Seven Divines pressed Mr. *Bedell* to move the Ambassadour to present King *James*'s Premonition to all Christian Princes and States, then put in *Latine*, to the Senate, and they were confident it would produce a great effect. But the Ambassadour could not be prevailed on to do it at that time, and pretended that since S. *James*'s day was not far off, it would be more proper to do it on that day. ... All that *Bedell* could say or do to perswade him not to put off a thing of such importance was in vain; and indeed I can hardly think that *Wotton* was so weak a Man as to have acted sincerely in this matter. Before S. *James*'s day came ... the difference was made up, and that happy opportunity was lost; so that when he had his audience on that Day, in which he presented the Book, all the answer he got, was, That they thanked the King of *England* for his good will, but they were now reconciled to the Pope, and that therefore they were resolved not to admit of any change in their Religion, according to their agreement with the Court of *Rome*.

P 13, 14. contain a weak & unhandsome attack on Wooton, who doubtless had discovered that the presentation of "the Premonition" previously to the reconciliation, as publicly completed, but after it had been privately agreed on between the Court of Rome & the Senate of Venice, would embarrass the Latter: whereas, delivered, as it was, it shewed the King's & his Minister's Zeal for Protestantism, and yet supplied the Venetians with an answer not disrespectful to the King.

Besides, what is there in Wooton's whole Life (a man so disinterested and who retired from all his Embassies so poor) to justify the remotest suspicion of his *Insincerity*? What can this word mean less or other than that Sir H. W. was either a crypto-papist, or had re-

ceived a Bribe from the Romish Party?[1] Horrid accusations!—
Burnet was notoriously rash & credulous; but I remember no other
instance in which his zeal for Reformation joined with his credulity
has misled him into so gross a calumny. It is not to be believed, that
Bedell gave any authority to such an aspersion of his old & faithful
Friend & Patron, further than that he had related the fact & that he
& the Minister differed in opinion as to the prudence of the measure recommended. How laxly too the story is narrated! The exact date of the
recommendation by P. Paul & the Divines should have been given[2]—
then the date of the public annunciation of the reconciliation between
the Pope & the V. Rep.—and lastly, the day on which Wooton did
present the book;—for even this Burnet leaves uncertain.—

4   p 17

And when one prest him hard in this matter, and objected that he
still held communion with an Idolatrous Church ... All the answer
he made to this was, That God had not given him the Spirit of
Luther.

See p. 161, 162.[1]

3[1] Sir Henry Wotton (1568–1639), diplomatist and poet, knighted in 1603 on King James's succession, was appointed ambassador to Venice and served there almost continuously for twenty years (1604–24). Bedell was his chaplain for three and a half years from 1607, and the incident referred to occurred in Jul 1609. C is correct in defending Wotton's integrity; the delay was owing to the Doge's illness. Logan Pearsall Smith in *The Life and Letters of Sir Henry Wotton* (1907) notices that "the falsity of 'this fine old story'" had already been proved by Dean Hickes in the seventeenth century.

3[2] Paolo Sarpi, called Fra Paolo (1552–1623), Venetian polymath, linguist, and historian of the Council of Trent, led the defence of Venice against the interdict placed upon the republic in 1605 by Pope Paul v for refusal to emend a law according to papal instruction. He led the defence with such brilliance and tenacity, with the support of "seven Divines", that after two years the Pope accepted the Venetian claim to autonomy.

4[1] Pp 161–2: "Neither let that hard term of *hypocrisie* be used of the infirmity, and sometime, of humble and peaceable carriage of some that oppose not common errors, nor wrestle with the greater part of Men, but do follow the multitude, reserving a right knowledge to themselves: and sometimes, (by the favour which God gives them to find where they live,) obtain better conditions than others can. We call not *John* the beloved Disciple an hypocrite, because he was *known to the High Priest*, and could procure *Peter* to be let to see the arraignment of our Saviour: nor call we *Peter* himself one that for *fear* denied him; much less *Daniel* and his companions, that by Suit, obtain'd of *Melzar* their keeper that they might *feed upon Pulse, and not be defiled with the King of* Babel's *meat*, and these *knew* themselves to be *captives* and in *Babel*. But in the new *Babel* how many thousands do we think there are that think otherwise; that they are in the *true Catholick Church of God*, the name whereof this *harlot* hath usurped: And although

5 p ⁻4, referring to p 26

In all that time no notice was even taken of him [i.e. Bedell], though he gave a very singular evidence of his great capacity. For being provoked by his old acquaintance *Wadsworth*'s Letters, he writ upon the points in controversie with the Church of *Rome*, with so much learning and judgment, and in so mild a strain, that no wonder if his Book had a good effect on him, for whom it was intended: It is true he never returned and changed his Religion himself, but his Son came from *Spain* into *Ireland*, when *Bedell* was promoted to the Bishoprick of *Kilmore* there, and told him, That his Father commanded to him to thank him for the pains he was at in writing it: he said, It was almost always lying open before him, and that he had heard him say, He was resolved *to save one*. And it seems he instructed his Son in the true Religion, for he declared himself a Protestant on his coming over.

p. 26. R. Southey has given me a bad character of this Son of the unhappy Convert to the Romish Church—he became, it seems, a spy on the Catholics, availing himself of his Father's Character among them—a crime which would indeed render his Testimony null and more than null—it would be a presumption of the contrary.[1] It is clear from his Letter to Bedell that the Convert was a very weak man. I owe to him, however, a compleat confirmation of my old persuasion concerning Bishop Hall, whom from my first perusal of his works I have always considered as one of the *Blots* (alas! there are too many) of the Biography of the Church of England—a self-conceited, coarse-minded, persecuting, vulgar Priest/

they acknowledge that where they live there are many abuses, and that the Church hath need of *reformation*, yet there they were born, and they may not *abandon their Mother in her sickness*. Those that converse more inwardly with Men of Conscience, on that side, do know that these are speeches in *secret*; which how they will be justified against the commands of Christ, (*come out of her, my people*) belongs to another place to consider. For the purpose we have now in hand, I dare not but account these the people of God, though they live very dangerously under the Captivity of *Babylon*, as did *Daniel, Mordechai, Hester, Nehemiah*, and *Ezra*, and many

Jews more, notwithstanding both Cyrus's Commission, and the Prophets command to depart." This passage follows immediately after **8** textus.

5[1] James Wadsworth (1604–56), son of the James Wadsworth (c 1572–1623) who was Bedell's correspondent in the Appendix that C admired (see **13**, below), was brought up and educated in Spain, where his father (the "unhappy Convert") was chaplain to the embassy and later an official to the Inquisition in Seville. The son was a government spy in England in 1625, and in Brussels and Paris in 1626 (until his imprisonment), and from 1630 onwards a common informer against Romanists.

and (by way of anti-climax) one of the first corrupters & *epigram-matizers* of our English Prose Style.[2] It is not true, that Sir Thomas Brown was the prototype of D[r] Johnson, who imitated him only as far as Sir T. B. resemble[d][a] the majority of his Predecessors—i.e. in the pedantic preference of Latin Derivatives to Saxon Words of the very same force—/ In the Balance & construction of his periods D[r] Johnson has followed Hall: as any intelligent read[er][a] will discover by an attentive comparison.[3] *S. T. C.*

6 p 89

For the selling of Indulgences is really but a commutation of Penance.

Most true! but "of Penance" in Purgatory.

7 p 158

Yea, will some Man say, But that which marreth all is the Opinion of *merit and satisfaction*. Indeed that is the <u>School Doctrine</u> ...

Alas! So far from this being the case with 99 out of an 100 in Spain, Italy, Sicily, & Catholic Germany, it is the Gospel Tenets that are the true *School Doctrine*—i.e. confined to the books & closets of the Learned among them.

8 p 161

It will be said that there are on that side many gross *errors*, many open *Idolatries*, and Superstitions, so as those which live there must needs be either partakers of them, and like minded, or else very *Hypocrites*. But many errours and much ignorance, so it be not *affected*, may stand with true Faith in Christ; and when there is true *Contrition* for one sin, (that is, *because it displeaseth God*) there is a general and implicit repentance for all *unknown sins*. God's Providence in the general revolt of the *ten* Tribes, when *Elias* thought himself left alone, had reserved *seven* thousand, that *had not bowed to the Image of Baal*: and the like may be conceived here, since especially, the Idolatry practised under the obedience of Mystical *Babylon*, is rather in false and will-worship of the true God, and rather commended, as profitable, than enjoyed as absolutely neces-

a Edge of the leaf damaged

5[2] Joseph Hall (1574–1656), bp of Exeter and Norwich, was to have been a central figure—with Jeremy Taylor and Milton—in a volume of selections "on the subject of Style both in prose & verse" proposed by C in Oct 1802. *CL* II 877.

5[3] Dr Samuel Johnson and Gibbon were also to have been included in the 1802 project, as objects of opprobrium.

sary, and the corruptions there maintained are rather in a *superfluous* addition than *retraction* in any thing necessary to salvation.

This good man's Charity joined with his Love and tender r⟨e⟩collections of Father Paul, Fulgentio,[1] and the Venetian Divines, has led him to a far, far too palliative a statement of Roman Idolatry. Not what his Pope here yet ventured to thunder forth from his Anti-Sinai; but what he & his Satellites, the Regulars, enforce to this preclusion of all true worship, in the actual practice, life-long, of an *immense* majority in Spain, Italy, Bavaria, Austria, &c &c—this must determine the point. What they *are*, not what they would persuade Protestants, is their essentials of Faith—this is the main Thing.

9   p 163

This point may give some light in a *Question* that is on foot among learned and good Men at this day, Whether the *Church of* Rome *be a true Church or no*? where I think surely if the matter be rightly declared, for the terms, there will remàin no question. As thus, whether *Babylon pretending to be* the Church of *Rome*, yea the *Catholick Church*, be so or not? or this, *Whether the people of Christ that are under that Captivity be a true Church or no*? either of both wayes if declared in these terms, the matter will be soon resolved.

Except some Man will perhaps still *object*, Though there be a people of God, yet they can be no true Church, for they have no Priesthood which is necessary to the Constitution of a Church, as S. *Cyprian* describes it, *Plebs Sacerdoti adunata*, people joyned to their Priest: They have no Priesthood, being by the very form of their Ordination, *Sacrificers for the quick and the dead*.

Strange it seems, that so good & learned a man should swallow unchew'd Cyprian's Definition of a true Church!—In what part of the N.T. did he find the Sacerdos = Priest, ~~an~~ the[a] *essential* of a church, except as far as every true Christian is a Priest? I ask, what a Priest can do, ~~which~~ but what every Christian either ought to do, or may do?—To Baptize is allowed by all Churches; to administer the Sacrament—is this denied?—Yes, or no? If yes, how can the Eucharistic *Form* be *necessary*—ex. gr. in a large Ship at Sea, the

---

[a] C neglected to cancel "an" after inserting "the"

8[1] Probably Father Fulgentio Micanzio, Sarpi's disciple and biographer. Burnet records (p 119) that Bedell took pleasure in repeating the substance of "a Sermon that he heard *Fulgentio* preach at Venice" on Christ's words "Have ye not read".

Chaplain having died? Are we saved by *Faith|* & yet not saved by Faith, unless a ceremony be performed?

10 pp 164–5

I answer, under correction of better judgments, they have the Ministry of Reconciliation by the Commission which is given at their Ordination; being the same which our Saviour left in his Church, *Whose sins ye remit, they are remitted, whose sins ye retain they are retained.*

And *could* B. Bedell believe, that this was committed to every Priest, & to Priests exclusively? Believe, that the mere *will* of a Priest could have any effect on the everlasting Weal or Woe of a Christian! Even to the immediate Disciples & Apostles could the text mean more than this—Wherever you discover by the spirit of knowlege, which I will send into you, Repentance & Faith, you shall declare Remission of Sins—& the sins shall be remitted—& where the contrary exists, your declaration of exclusion from Bliss shall be fulfilled? Did Christ say, that true Repentance & actual Faith would not save a Soul, unless the Priests verbal Remission was superadded?[1]

THE COPIES OF CERTAIN LETTERS

11 p 315 | Ch 1 "Of the Preamble. The Titles Catholick, Papist, Traytor, Idolater"

The Creed whereinto you were baptized, is it not the Catholick Faith? . . . Or is not he a Catholick that holds the Catholick Faith? That which was once answered, touching the present Church of *England*, to one in a Stationers Shop in *Venice*, that would needs know what was the difference betwixt us and the Catholicks. It was told him none: for we accounted our selves good Catholicks. . . . That we believed the Catholick Faith, contained in the Creed, but did not believe the Thirteenth Article which the Pope had put to it. When he knew not of any such Article; the Extravagance of *Pope Boniface* was brought, where he *defines it to be altogether of necessity to salvation, to every humane creature to be under the Bishop of* Rome. This thirteenth Article, of the thirteenth Apostle, good Mr. *Waddesworth*, it seems you have learned; and so are become, as some now speak and write *Catholick Roman*. That is in true interpretation *Universal-particular*; which because they cannot be

10[1] See John 20.23 (in textus), which both Burnet and C are glossing.

equalled, the one restraining and cutting off from the other, take heed that by straitning your Faith to *Rome*, you have not altered it, and by becoming *Roman*, left off to be *Catholick*.

O that the *Romanists* would weigh and apply to themselves that aphorism from Hesiod so productive in wise, so prolific in witty, applications—Νηπιοι, ουδ' ισουσιν, οσω πλεον ημισυ παντος—i.e. *their* factitious παν!!![1]

12 p ⁻2, referring to pp 381–2 | Ch 5 "Of the Safeness to Joyn to the Roman, Being Confessed a True Church by Her Opposites"

Christ our Lord hath given us amongst others, two infallible Notes to know his Church. *My Sheep*, saith he, *hear my Voice*: And again, *By this shall all Men know that you are my Disciples, if you love one another*. What shall we stand upon conjectural Arguments from that which men say? We are partial to our selves, malignant to our opposites. Let Christ be heard who be his, who not. ... That other is that which now I stand upon: *the Badge of Christs Sheep*. Not a likelihood, but a certain *token*, whereby *every Man* may know them. ... Thanks be to God: This mark of our Saviour is in us, which you with our Schismaticks, and other enemies want.

p. 381, 382.[1]

13 p ⁺2

If it were in my power, I would have this book printed in a convenient form, and distributed thro' every House, at least, thro' every Village & Parish throughout the Kingdom. A *volume* of thoughts, and of moral Feelings, the offsprings of Thought, crowd upon me, as I review the different parts of this admirable man's Life, and Creed.—Only compare *his* conduct to James Waddesworth (probably, some ancestral Relative of my honoured Friend, W. Wordsworth: fo[r] the same name in Yorkshire, from whence his Father came, is pronounced Wadsworth) with that of the priest-proud, far

11[1] Hesiod *Works and Days* 40: "Fools! They know not how much more the half is than the whole". The phrase became proverbial; and C quotes it often; see e.g. *CN* II 2003 and BROOKE 5. C continues, punning: "*their* factitious '*whole*'/'*all*'"—παν here alluding to the meaning of "Catholic" (from καθολικός "whole, universal"). He may also imply that the Catholics believe twice as much as they ought; or, that if the Roman Catholic faith were pruned of wrong beliefs, as Protestantism is, only half of that faith would remain.

12[1] The extract from *The Life of Bedell* printed in *Friend* (*CC*) I 287–8 is from pp 381–3; see also *CN* III 3856 and n (cited in headnote).

far too highly rated, Bishop *Hall*—his Letter to Hall tenderly blaming his (Hall's) bitterness to an old friend mistaken, & then his Letter to that Friend defending Hall—What a picture of goodness! I confess, in all Ecclesiastical History I have read of no man so spotless: tho' ⟨of⟩ hundreds in which the Biographers have painted them as monsters of perfection: but the *moral tact* soon feels the truth. S. T. C.

The Memoires of the Lives and Actions of James and William Dukes of Hamilton and Castleherald, etc....Together with many letters, instructions, and other papers written by Charles the I. never before published. [Together with:] An Appendix to the History of the Church of Scotland...[Half-title:] The History of the Church and State of Scotland. The II. Part. In Seven Books. 2 pts in 1 vol. London 1677. F°.

Part I of *The History of the Church and State of Scotland* is by John Spottiswoode (4th ed London 1677).

Sion College Library

On p ⁻4, a slip cut from an original endpaper and pasted onto a new end-paper in the rebound volume: "Given by Mʳ Tho. James 1711."

DATE. Autumn 1823. In N 30 f 67ᵛ there is a list of books with their shelf-marks (not in C's hand) in Sion College Library, including this one. In Sept 1823 C told J. A. Hessey that for his projected "Life of Leighton", which was to be part of *Aids to Reflection,* he had collated Spottiswoode, Heylyn, Prynne, Wharton, Burnet, and Hacket. *CL* v 300–1.

1   i 16, pencil | Bk ɪ

The Marquis [James, Marquis—later Duke—of Hamilton] discovered in that noble Conquerour [Gustavus Adolphus] an air of Majesty and Courage which could not be equalled, neither was his Prudence in Affairs inferiour to his Conduct of Armies: but those rare excellences were much soiled with insupportable Pride and Ambition, which grew with his success to an intolerable degree.

The Proofs? These rash Assertions arising out [of]*ᵃ* blind Sympathy with the Hero of his immediate Story are the greatest Blot on Burnet's character as an Historian. Had he considered that Gustavus was not a Monarch but a General & Commander in Chief of a miscellaneous Army—he would have judged at once more favorably & more justly of the best & greatest of Warriors./¹

ᵃ Word supplied by the editor

1¹ In an essay in the *Courier* of 1811 C had quoted an anecdote of Gustavus Adolphus, King of Sweden and Protestant hero of the Thirty Years' War (1594–1632), to point up a parallel between Wellington and that "commanding genius". *EOT* (*CC*) ɪɪ 157 and n. Two years earlier he had been recommending to his friends the book from which he had taken the anecdote, Walter Harte *Life of Gustavus* *Adolphus* (2 vols 1807). *CL* ɪɪɪ 200, 225–6, 241. Others who for C merited "the character of a commanding genius" included Moses, Washington, and the Bonaparte of 1800. The Napoleon of 1810, however, he might compare to Alexander the Great, but not to Gustavus. The distinction was between a "commander in chief" and a "commanding genius". See *CN* ɪɪɪ 3845 and n and cf *EOT* (*CC*) ɪ 36.

THOMAS BURNET

c 1635–1715

De statu mortuorum et resurgentium liber. Accesserunt epistolae duae circa libellum de archaeologiis philosophicis. ... Editio secunda. London 1727. 8°.

Victoria College Library (Coleridge Collection)

Inscribed by C in ink on p ⁻3 (p–d): "S. T. Coleridge".

C's ms corrections to the text of this copy seem to belong to late 1795 or early 1796, at a time when he intended to translate Burnet's *Telluris theoria sacra* (see *CN* I 61, 174 [7]) and was reading Burnet carefully to the eventual benefit of *AM* (see *RX* 461 n 61 and 502–3 n 28). C also owned a copy of *Telluris theoria sacra: orbis nostri originem et mutationes generales, quas aut jam subiit, aut olim subiturus est, complectens* (2nd ed, 2 vols in 1 London 1689), presented to him by Charles Danvers in c 1795–6 and now in VCL. He also acquired at some time a copy of Burnet's *Archaeologiae philosophicae* (1692), now in VCL, in which the passage used for the long opening epigraph to *AM*, first printed in *SL*, is marked with a sprig of *Artemisia absinthium*: see *CN* I 1000Hn.

Because of the early date of the annotations on *De statu mortuorum*, and because they represent an attempt to purify the text with a view to translation, all notes other than simple marginal corrections are treated as substantive marginalia.

DATE. Probably late 1795.

A   p 20, pencil | Ch 3

Materiam enim dicis esse Deum, et si quidem est divina, certè non erit insensibilis.[1]

[For you say that matter is God, and if indeed it is divine, surely it will not be without feeling.]

1   p 29, pencil

Quid denique perfectus ille idearum aut judex, qui tam ideas, quam earum respectus, examinat, confert, expendit, dijudicat et componit...

A[1] *Insensilis* is good Latin and occurs several times in Lucretius.

851

[What, in fact, is that commander, or judge, of ideas who examines, compares, considers, discriminates, and connects both ideas and their relationships with one another ...]

Qu prae[1]

2 p 37, pencil

... tollant solem et sydera, et quaecunque sensus nostros officiunt...

[... let them take away the sun and the stars, and whatever things get in the way of our senses...]

Qu *a*[1]

3 p 47, pencil | Ch 4

Praeterea ex tot corporibus, quae terminus in hujus vitae cursu ...

[Moreover, from so many bodies, which the end in the course of this life ...]

Qu. tenuimus[1]

3A p 58, pencil

[Quoting Clement of Rome:] "...οἱ φανερῴωθήσονται ἐν τῇ ἐπισκοπῇ τῆς βασιλείας τοῦ Χριστοῦ..."

["... they will be made manifest in the judgement of the kingdom of Christ ..."]

3B p 60, pencil

Haec autem, inquies, de Judicio generali intelligenda sunt: verum est; praeterea Judicium est secretum et particulare, quod statim à morte cujusque institutum est ...

[But these [sayings of Christ quoted from Matt 25 etc], you will say, are to be understood as referring to the general judgement: it is true; ⟨there is,⟩ besides, a private and individual judgement, which is made immediately upon the death of each person ...][1]

1[1] A noun is needed to anticipate *aut judex* (or judge): *praefectus* (overseer, commander) makes good sense, and is the reading in other editions.

2[1] *Afficiunt* (affect); *officio* usually means "impede" and takes the dative in classical Latin.

3[1] *Terminus* does not make sense. *Tenuimus* (we have had) is plausible, but other editions read *terimus* (we wear out).

3B[1] The semicolon is a misprint. C's emendation obscures the connexion between the clauses.

4 p 65, pencil | Appendix

[quoting Chrysostom on Heb 11.40:] "Nondum receperunt mercedem, sed adhuc expectant. Qui istoc modo obiêre, in tantá tribulatione, nondum receperunt illi? tantùm habent temporis ex quo vicerunt, necdum receperunt mercedem . . ."

["They have not yet received their reward, but they still wait for it. Those who died in that way in such great tribulation—have they not yet received their reward? They have had so much time since they conquered, but they have not yet received their reward . . ."]

Qu. vix-[1]

4[1] Reading *vixerunt*, "they lived"—an unnecessary emendation. Death by martyrdom was a victory in the language of the early Christians.

ROBERT BURTON
1577–1640
LOST BOOK

The Anatomy of Melancholy, what it is. With all the kindes, causes, symptomes, prognostickes, and severall cures of it. In three maine partitions with their severall sections, members and subsections. Philosophically, medicinally, historically, opened and cut up. By Democritus Iunior [i.e. Robert Burton]. With a satyricall preface, conducing to the following discourse, &c. Oxford 1621. 4⁰.

First edition. Second to eighth eds were in folio, ninth and following eds in 8⁰ and 12⁰.

Not located; marginalia not recorded. *Lost List.*

Charles Lamb's copy, noticed in "The Two Races of Men" (1820) as annotated by C but nowhere else described. The other two books mentioned in that essay as annotated by C have been preserved and have notes in them.

James Gillman gave Ludwig Tieck a copy of Burton, to which he responded by writing to C in 1818: "Mr. Gillman's valued present 'The Anatomy of Melancholy', gives me the greatest pleasure." *C 17th C* 432 n 2. It is highly unlikely that Gillman would give Tieck a copy annotated by C, or, if he did, that Tieck would not say something about it.

Wordsworth LC 970 is a copy of *The Anatomy of Melancholy* marked as C's, "Qto", i.e. Oxford 1621. It was one of the books left at Allan Bank in 1810 and never returned to C. Presumably this is the copy that left traces in the notebooks in 1800, 1802, and 1809: see e.g. *CN* I 674, 699, 1259; III 3502, 3523. As a mark of the currency of Burton's book in C's circle, it is noticeable that the sale catalogues show that there were copies in the libraries of Green, Gillman, WW, and RS.

CHARLES BUTLER
1750–1832

RS's *Book of the Church*, published in Feb 1824 as a broadside in the mounting discussion of Catholic Emancipation, set off a vigorous controversy. Charles Butler, a Roman Catholic lawyer, replied with *The Book of the Roman Catholic Church* (Dec 1824; title-page 1825), and Bp John Milner independently issued in 1825, under the pseudonym of John Merlin, a pamphlet entitled *Strictures on the Poet Laureate's "Book of the Church"*. Joseph Blanco White joined in on RS's side with *Practical and Internal Evidence Against Catholicism, with Occasional Strictures on Mr. Butler's Book of the Roman Catholic Church* in May 1825 and *The Poor Man's Preservative Against Popery* later in 1825. RS's *Vindiciae Ecclesiae Anglicanae*, in which Butler's urbanity is contrasted with Milner's scurrility, appeared in Feb 1826, closely followed in Apr by Butler's *Vindication of "The Book of the Roman Catholic Church"*; and in Apr 1826 F. C. Husenbeth (1796–1872) published an attack on Blanco White entitled *A Defence of the Creed and Discipline of the Catholic Church*. Blanco White in Jun 1826 published *A Letter to Charles Butler, Esq. on His Notice of the "Practical and Internal Evidence Against Catholicism"*. It is a curious reflection upon the conduct of nineteenth-century controversy and upon a publisher's commercial shrewdness that all these books, except Husenbeth's *Defence* and Milner's *Strictures*, were published by John Murray.

C became interested in this controversy apparently less through his relationship with RS than through the relationship formed with Blanco White in Jul 1825. He annotated all three of Blanco White's books and Butler's *Vindication*; a copy of RS's *Vindiciae Ecclesiae Anglicanae* with DC's bookplate, now in VCL, may also have been his.

The identity of the book in which C said he wrote his poem *Sancti Dominici Pallium* is discussed in *Book of the RC Church* headnote, below.

The Book of the Roman-Catholic Church: in a series of letters addressed to Rob! Southey, Esq. LL.D. on his "Book of the Church". London 1825. 8º.

A second ed was published in the same year.

Not located. Possibly a "ghost" book. Annotation printed from MS TRANSCRIPT (*b*) and (the last 16 lines) from the *Evening Standard.*

On 28 Nov 1827 C told Blanco White that he had "now before me two fragments of Letters" written to him, one in c Dec 1825, the other in Jun 1826—the second of these "with the verses written on the blank page of Butler's Book of the Church, with the motto, *Indignatio fecit*, as composed in the first Heat of my Feelings on reading the latter part of your Letter [*to Charles Butler, Esq. on His Notice of the 'Practical and Internal Evidence Against Catholicism'*], from page 80." *CL* VI 713. In all versions of the title to the poem *Sancti Dominici Pallium*, both ms and printed, C says that the book in which the poem was written was "Butler's Book of the Church". Griggs states that C "erroneously" referred to the *Book of the Roman-Catholic Church* as the book that he wrote the poem in, and that C "certainly had in mind Butler's second work, the *Vindication of 'The Book of the Roman Catholic Church'* ". *CL* VI 713–14 n 5. The poem indeed refers to material that was in the *Vindication* and not in the *Book of the Roman-Catholic Church*, but there is no reason why C should not have written his poem in the *Book* as he said he did. Since C's copy of neither the *Book* nor the *Vindication* has survived, a definitive answer to this question is not possible; at least the MS TRANSCRIPT of marginalia in the *Vindication* does not include the poem or any note of its presence in that book. The poem, written "on occasion of Butler's assent to the Calumnious Abuse of Blanco White" (*CL* VI 980), is here printed as though written "on the blank leaf at the beginning of Butler's Book of the Church", on the authority of C's repeated statement that it was so. Quite possibly, in view of the length of the poem, it was not actually written in either the *Book* or the *Vindication.*

MS TRANSCRIPTS. (*a*) Holograph transcript, possibly as sent to Blanco White: described (without note of location) in *CL* VI 713 n 4, 980–1n. (*b*) VCL MS F 1.2: a holograph transcript, entitled "Sancti Dominici Pallium", lacking the last 16 lines from the excision of all but 3/4 inch of the last leaf of ms.

DATE. c 21 Jun 1826. The occasion of C's writing the poem was his reading of Blanco White's *Letter to Charles Butler*, which was sent to him with a letter dated 21 Jun 1826. *CL* VI 713n.

1 front flyleaf

Sancti Dominici Pallium:[1] a Dialogue between Poet & Friend[a,2]

POET

I ~~mark~~ note the moods and feelings, Men betray
And heed them more than aught they do or say:
The lingering Ghosts of many a secret Deed
Still-born or haply strangled in its birth
These best reveal the smooth Man's inward Creed!
These mark the Spot where lies the treasure, Worth!

MILNER*,[3] made up of impudence and trick,
With cloven tongue prepared to hiss and lick,

* The notorious Vicar-general—*since* deceased.[4]

a MS TRANSCRIPT (*b*) continues: "found written on the blank leaf at the beginning of Butler's Book of the Church/"

1[1] "Saint Dominic's Pallium"—the pallium being a vestment granted to archbishops by the Pope. The subject of the poem is the papist persecution of heretics; the title expresses C's abhorrence through the figure of the vestment peculiar to the Roman Catholic Church and the name of the saint who was instrumental in the fratricidal crusade against the Albigenses and whose order (formed after his death) was especially associated with the Inquisition. Cf two passages in the *Courier* version (31 Aug 1811) of the "Allegoric Vision": *EOT* (*CC*) II 263, 269–70. Butler in the *Vindication* says that he does not defend religious persecution by either Catholics or Protestants, but he answers accusations against the Roman Catholic Church by citing examples of Protestant atrocities.

1[2] MS TRANSCRIPT (*a*) gives the poem a more circumstantial title: "Poet and Friend: a Dialogue occasioned by the Report of Mr Eneas M'Donnell's Speech at the British Catholic Association, Charles Butler Esq[re] being present.—See the Rev[d] Blanco White's Letter to C. B. Esq[re], *p. 80 usque ad finem*. Facit INDIGNA-

TIO Versus." Blanco White's detailed account of the meeting comprises Letter X in his *Letter to Butler* pp 99–114 and nn. The Latin motto—"Indignation inspires my verses"—is a variant of Juvenal *Satires* 1.79.

1[3] In *PW* (1834) and *PW* (1852) the names of Milner and Butler were omitted from the text; in *PW* (JDC) the name "Butler" was supplied where "Milner" was intended. *PW* (EHC) printed Milner's name on ms authority.

1[4] John Milner (1752–1826), bp of Castabala and vicar-apostolic of the western district of England, died on 19 Apr 1826. In the periodical publications of the poem in May 1827 C added a note to remove the appearance of making a personal attack on a man recently dead. In MS TRANSCRIPT (*a*) the note reads: "Tho' unnecessary, I trust, for those who know the Author, it may be hereafter proved expedient, to state that these Lines were written before Dr Milner's Death. Dr M. survives in his Publications: and it was these, as personified under the Name of their Author, that the Poet had alone in his contemplation." See *CL* VI 981.

ROME's Brazen Serpent! boldly dares discuss
The Roasting of thy Heart, O brave JOHN HUSS![5]
And with grim triumph and a truculent glee†
Absolves anew the pope-wrought Perfidy
That made an Empire's plighted faith a Lie,
And fix'd a broad Stare on the Devil's Eye—
(Pleas'd with the guilt, yet envy-stung at heart
To stand outmaster'd in his own black art!)

Yet Miln—

F RIEND.
Enough of MILNER! We're agreed,
Who now defends, would then have done, the deed.
But who not feels Persuasion's gentle Sway?
Who but must meet the proffer'd hand half-way,
When courteous BUTLER—

POET (aside)
Rome's smooth Go-between!

† truculent, a tribrach as ⟨the⟩ isochronous Substitute for the
Trochee – ◡.

N.B. *If* our Accent, a *quality* of sound, were actually equivalent
to the *Quantity* in the Greek and Latin Prosody, *then* "truculent"
would doubtless answer to an Amphimacer – ◡ –, or dactyl – ◡ ◡
at least. But it is not so. Accent shortens syllables: thus Spirit =
Sprite, Honey, Money, nobody &c.

[5] John Huss (c 1369–1415), Bohemian reformer and follower of Wycliffe. While rector of the university of Prague 1402–13, he continued to preach after Wycliffe's writings were publicly burned in 1409 and all preaching forbidden except in collegiate, parish, and monastery churches. Excommunicated in Feb 1411, he was encouraged by strong popular support to continue as rector until in 1413 his bold preaching made his position untenable. He was arrested in Nov 1414, refused to recant, and was burned at the stake on 6 Jul 1415. The Hussites, strengthened by the indignation of his followers in Bohemia, continued to exert formidable influence until the middle of the century. For "the repulsive effect" of Butler's and Milner's "Apologies for the St Dunstan, Treachery to Huss & Jerome of Prague, Massacres of Paris...&c" see N 26 f 158 (5 May 1826).

FRIEND

Laments the Advice that sour'd a *milky* Queen—
(For "*Bloody*" all enlighten'd men ~~admit~~ confess
An antiquated Error of the Press)
Who ~~with a~~ rapt by zeal beyond her Sex's Bounds
With actual Cautery staunch'd the Church's Wounds!
And tho' he deems, that with *too* broad a Blur
We damn the French and Irish Massacre,
Yet *blames* them both—and thinks, the Pope *might* err!
What think you *now*? Boots it with Spear and Shield
Against such gentle foes to take the field,
Whose beck'ning Hands the mild Caduceous*a* wield?

POET

What think I *now*? Ev'n what I thought before.
What MILNER boasts, tho' BUTLER may deplore,
Still I repeat, *Words* lead me not astray
When the shewn *Feeling* points a different way.

Smooth Butler* can say Grace at Slander's feast
And bless each Haut-gaut*b* cook'd by Monk or Priest;
Leaves the full lie on Milner's Gong to swell,
Content with half-truths, that do just as well;
But duly decks his mitred Comrade's Flanks,[7]
And with him shares th' O'GORMAN Nation's Thanks!*c*[8]

So much for you, my friend! who own a church,
And would not leave your mother in the lurch.
But if a Liberal asks me what I think;

* See the Revd Blanco White's "Letter to C. Butler, Esqre."[6]

a A slip for "Cadeuceus"   *b* A slip for "Haut-gout"
c The rest of the text is taken from the *Evening Standard*

1[6] See BLANCO WHITE *Letter to Charles Butler* (1826).

1[7] EHC adds a quotation from RS's *Vindiciae Ecclesiae Anglicanae* 228n: "'Your coadjutor the Titular Bishop Milner'—Bishop of Castabala I had called him, till I learnt from the present pamphlet that he had been translated to the see of Billingsgate." *PW* (EHC) I 450n.

1[8] I.e. Ireland, "O'Gorman" being Charles James Patrick Mahon (1800–1891), known as "The O'Gorman Mahon" or "The O'Gorman"—a colourful Irish politician and vigorous member of the Catholic Association. Since he was a prominent supporter of O'Connell in his election as MP for Clare in 1828, this reference suggests that the VCL ms is of later date than 1826.

Scared by the soot and blood of Cobbett's ink,
And Jeffrey's glairy phlegm and Connor's foam,[9]
In search of some safe parable I roam:
An emblem sometimes may comprize a tome.

Disclaimant of his uncaught grandsire's mood,
I see a Tyger lapping kitten's food.
And who shall blame him that he purrs applause,
When brother Brindle pleads the good old cause,
And frisks his pretty tail and half unsheathes his claws.
Yet not the less, for modern sights unapt,
I trust the bolts and cross-bars of the laws
More than the Protestant milk, all newly lapt,
Impearling a tame wild-cat's whisker'd jaws!

ΕΣΤΗΣΕ.

1[9] William Cobbett (1762–1835), pugnacious and virulent political journalist in favour of parliamentary reform. Francis Jeffrey (1773–1850), lawyer and editor of the *Edinburgh Review* 1802–29, was a strong supporter of the Whig party. "Connor" may be Roger O'Connor (1762–1834), Irish nationalist, but possibly a slip for O'Connell—i.e. Daniel O'Connell (1775–1847): see *CL* vi 885, 918, 925.

Vindication of "The Book of the Roman Catholic Church," against the Reverend George Townsend's "Accusations of History against the Church of Rome:" with notice of some charges brought against "The Book of the Roman Catholic Church," in the publications of Doctor Phillpotts, the Rev, John Todd, M.A. F.S.A. the Rev. Stephen Isaacson, B.A. the Rev. Joseph Blanco White, M.A. B.D. and in some anonymous publications. . . . With copies of Doctor Phillpott's fourth letter to Mr. Butler, containing a charge against Dr. Lingard; and of a letter of Doctor Lingard to Mr. Butler, in reply to the charge. London 1826. 8°

Published Apr 1826.

Not located. Annotations printed from MS TRANSCRIPT. *Lost List.*

MS TRANSCRIPT. VCL LT 66: 13 small pages, transcribed by Miss E. Trevenen.

DATE. 1826, after Apr: 4 is dated 1826. If C wrote these notes after reading Blanco White's *Letter to Charles Butler*, the date would be after 21 Jun 1826 (see BLANCO WHITE *Letter* headnote).

1 pp 191 ff [?] | Letter XVIII

8.—"With respect to transubstantiation,—We have no other words to express our opinion of him, who kneels down to a thin bread-cake, after the priest has blessed it, believing that the palpable substance is the very and material blood and bones of him who is in heaven. If we had more expressive terms than these, we would use them to describe our opinion of him, 'who taketh flour, and with part thereof he maketh bread, he eateth, and is satisfied; with part thereof he maketh a God; he falleth down, yea, he worshippeth it.' What shall we say? We may not assert that this is idolatrous and superstitious. O! no! we must repel the thought, as blasphemy! Kneel on then, and cry aloud, for it is a God; for the flour was good —and the water was good—and the priest was rightly ordained— and the worshipper believeth not his senses—nor his understanding— nor his reason—nor the Scripture." Southey

The language in which You express yourself in this passage,—I leave to the taste, the feeling and reflection of every gentleman in the world.

I wished to say nothing further upon it: but I feel it calls on me to declare, that it is a great misrepresentation of the Roman Catholic doctrine of transubstantiation. The Roman Catholic Church does not believe that "the priest maketh a God:" she believes it to be heresy, to be folly, to be impiety to say this. She believeth, that, when the priest pronounces the words of consecration, God, by his omnipotence, works the mysterious change.

Quite as rationally might I assert that the Potter is not believed by the Staffordshire folks to be a maker of Jugs and Teapots! For why? he only turns the wheel, and accompanies its revolution with certain movements of his hands—it is the power of Gravity; and of Cohesion, or the power of universal, resulting from the Sum total of specific Attraction, that properly and immediately produce the effect. Now according to the doctrine of the ablest and wisest Newtonians, this is, in truth, the present Act of the Omnipresent God—ergo, the orthodox Staffordshire People believe, that the Potter only repeats many manœuvres and pedœuvres,[1] but that it is God who by His omnipotence works the formal change. Nevertheless, I am bound in candour to say, that the difference between the Lutheran Cons: and the Trentine Trans:[2] [is]*a* only a difference between the same absurdity, with and without an attempt to transubstantiate it into sense; and yet I would prefer either to the fashionable doctrine of the Sacramentaries. The simple truth is this. The Eucharistic Act as instituted by Christ is a Symbol, i.e.—a part, or particular instance selected as representative of the whole, of which whole however it is itself an actual, or real part. Now the Sacramentaries degrade the Symbol into a Metaphor, and that too, a Catachresis, while the Romish Superstition makes the Symbol representant, the whole thing represented, and in consequence, equally with the former, destroys the *Symbol*.[3] The difference is in the substitute which with the

a Word supplied by the editor

[1] *OED* cites this as C's coinage, from *AR* (1825) 212.

[2] Luther's doctrine of consubstantiation (that after the consecration the substances both of the Body and Blood of Christ and of the bread and wine coexist in union with each other) was formulated in opposition to the mediaeval doctrine of transubstantiation (that after consecration the substances of the bread and wine were no longer present except as "accidents" —quantity, colour, taste, etc—which allowed them to remain perceptible). The doctrine of transubstantiation, re-

fined through the twelfth and thirteenth centuries, reached classical formulation in the teaching of Thomas Aquinas. At Session XIII of the Council of Trent (Oct 1551) the doctrine of transubstantiation was affirmed, and the Lutheran, Calvinist, and Zwinglian doctrines of the eucharist were repudiated. See also BAXTER *Reliquiae* COPY B **30** n 2 and *C&S* (*CC*) 106.

[3] See also BOOK OF COMMON PRAYER COPY B **6** n 2, **29** at n 10, and *AR* (1825) 198–9, *SM* (*CC*) 30. For definitions of symbol see e.g. *BL* ch 9 (1907) I 100, *AR* (1825) 254n, 308n.

Infra-protestant, is an arbitrary μνημοσυνον[4] deriving a precarious significance from a conventional understanding, or previous Agreement—with the Pseudo-catholic a *Fetisch*, an idolatrous Mummery/ Luther's mistake—(O that it had been Luther's alone!) arising from confounding the living Body (corpus intelligibile σωμα ὑποστατικον)[5] with the fluxionary conditions & media of its visibility. Southey would, I suspect, be at a loss for the text of Scripture asserting that the Body of the Son of God, the Flesh and the Blood communicated in the Eucharist, is in Heaven i.e. in a place, at an unknown distance from *the place* where we are. The Scripture tells, indeed, that the Lord incarnate had not finished his functions, as Son of Man, in the form of the suffering Messiah—that his kingdom (Dies Messiæ)[6] was yet to come when he should reappear in Power and Majesty, He, the same whom they had crucified, the triumphant Conqueror, Messiah, *King*, and that during the interval (Dies expectationis)[7] He retains his divine Humanity, and exercises all power, *as* the Son of Man, in the abode of the Perfect in Heaven. But what has this to do with the Eucharist, or the Flesh and Blood spoken of in John's Gospel C. VI?[8] I do not go as far as Bishop Horsley; but yet it would not be amiss if Southey would see what the Bishop has said of the Corpus Phænomenon of Christ after the Resurrection.[9]

---

[1][4] "Remembrance, memorial".

[1][5] "Intelligible body—substantial (hypostatic) body".

[1][6] "The Day of Messiah"—i.e. the day of the coming of Messiah, the Second Coming. The phrase is not in NT.

[1][7] "The Day of expectation"—not in NT. C here regards the Day of Expectation as the "interval" between the resurrection and the Second Coming, the "thousand years" of Rev 20.

[1][8] John 6.47–58.

[1][9] See Samuel Horsley *Nine Sermons* (1815), Sermon IV on the Resurrection (on Acts 10.40–1), in which pp 209–11 provide the substance for C's comment: "...His body was indeed risen, but it was become that body which St Paul describes in the fifteenth chapter of his first epistle to the Corinthians, which having no sympathy with the gross bodies of this earthly sphere, nor any place among them, must be indiscernible to the human organs, till they shall have undergone a similar refinement....The divinity united to him having raised him on the third day from the grave, in a body incorruptible and invisible, gave him to become visible occasionally, not to all the people, but to his chosen witnesses; to those who were chosen to the privilege of beholding God face to face in the person of his Son, of attesting the fact of Christ's resurrection, and of publishing through the world the glad tidings of the general redemption. Thus, you see, every appearance of our Lord to the apostles after his resurrection, was in truth an appearance of the great God, the Maker of heaven and earth, to mortal man."

2 p 192 [?]

Roman Catholics "do not fall down before the bread; do not worship it." They fall down before Jesus Christ, whom they believe to be present under the form and the appearance of the bread: Him, alone, they worship.

So the Canaanite fell down before Astarte whom they believed to be present under the form of the Image! Therefore they were Astartolators, but not Idolators![1] S. T. C.

3 p 238 [?] | Appendix IV. Letter on the Coronation Oath

Does it follow, that if the two Houses of Parliament should present a bill to the Monarch, for the repeal of the Laws remaining in force against the Roman Catholics, and the Sovereign should be of opinion that not to repeal those laws would bring mischief and damage to the realm, he would be constitutionally bound, in the words of the act, to make the remedy, by assenting to the bill of repeal? Would not any oath taken by the Monarch not to assent to such a bill be a nullity? Must not every such oath be necessarily understood to be accompanied by an implied condition, that nothing contained in it should oblige him to act against the principles of the constitution, or the rights or welfare of his subjects, or to forbear from assenting to any bill which enacted any measure for their good.

Then, in the name of common sense, what was the purpose, what is the use, of the Oath? I will keep it as long as I think proper! Pretty Oath! If I think proper, I will break it—that is, if it should be in my power. For unless it should have passed both Houses, it would not be in the King's power. But were the framers of the oath so ignorant of human nature, and the nature of their own constitution, as not to know that the King has and cannot but have, a great influence on the votes of both Houses: and that the Oath binds him in conscience not to use this influence to the endangerment of the Protestant Church? Or is Mr Butler so little studied in our Constitution, as not to be aware, that the Parliament, omnipotent as it may be in a Law Court, is not the Depositary of the whole power and right of the *Nation*—that the Nation *wills therefore* not to be a Republic,

---

2[1] Astarte, the goddess of fertility and one of the "gods of the people that were round about" the children of Israel (Judges 2.12, 10.6), was also one of the "strange gods" (1 Sam 7.3–4) to whom the Israelites returned whenever their devotion to Yahweh flagged, and for the worship of whom they were reproved.

governed by delegated plenipotent Proxies of the Universal Population, because it will not alienate from itself or entrust away its entire power—That the return to Popery, and change of the Evangelical
Faith is one of the Points, on which it would not entrust, even to
its Parliament, as the Representative of its principal Interests and
Estates, to decide—and that as the only practicable, safe, and peaceable mode of effecting this determination, they obliged their Sovereign
to take an oath a priori, from which he cannot release himself and
which consequently makes the Law in this respect, super parliamentary.

In my opinion, the King might without breath of his Oath remove
the existing qualifications from all Lay Catholics as Individuals,
provided that the Act declared it to be a measure of confidence, not
of Right, and declared that the discipline and Hierarchy of the
Romish Church were radically and essentially incompatible with the
spirit of the British Constitution, and provided therefore that the
Romish Clergy should never be recognised as a Body, and were incapable of becoming the Established Church of England, Scotland,
or Ireland, i.e. of forming a constituent *State* of the Realm—in the
words of Queen Elizabeth, the third, venerable Estate of the Realm![1]
But without some such declaration and provision, I do not hesitate
to affirm, that the King could not pass the Catholic Bill without
guilt of Perjury.[2]   S T Coleridge 1826

4   p 242 [?]

"The Coronation oath is made to the people, as represented by
Parliament."

Here is the mistake—The *People* are not represented in this sense *by*
Parliament, but (if at all) *in* Parliament, the King under this Oath,
being one *especial* representative. In fact, he is the only entire
representative of the *Nation*. Hence, he is the Majesty, majoritas
ἐνωμένη.[1]   S T C.

3[1] Cf *C&S* (*CC*) 42.

3[2] The Catholic Emancipation Act
—"an Act for the Relief of His
Majesty's Roman Catholic Subjects"
—passed on 13 Apr 1829 and finally
removed practically all disabilities
from Roman Catholics and admitted
them to most public offices. For C
on "Aids to a right appreciation of the
Bill admitting Catholics to sit in both
Houses of Parliament" see *C&S* (*CC*)
147–61.

4[1] "The majority made into one
figure (unified)". On the king as the
majesty or unity of the nation see
BAXTER *Reliquiae* COPY A 3 n 1 and
C&S (*CC*) 41. On the etymology and
meaning of "majesty" see *Lects 1795*
(*CC*) 295, *EOT* (*CC*) I 136 and n 2,
and *C&S* (*CC*) 20 and n 1.

5   p 242 [?]

Each of the three founders of the Protestant Church of England, Henry VIII. Edward VI. and Elizabeth swore, at their coronations, to support the Catholic religion as it was then established. Each proscribed that religion, and established another. Can any thing be alleged in defence of those alterations of the national religion by the monarchs who had thus sworn to preserve it, except that their Parliament consented to the change, and that their consent freed the monarchs from the obligations of their Coronation oaths? If this defence was available in those cases, why is it not equally available in the present?

There is but one answer to this—not quite satisfactory *in the letter*, I own, but yet true in *the spirit*. It is, that the Oaths before the Reformation were in fact framed and imposed by the Romish Hierarchy for their own temporal Interests; and that in comparison with these the Coronation Oath of William III[d] was actually the sense and positive Will of the Nation![1]   S. T. Coleridge

5[1] The Coronation Oath was often cited in the debate about Catholic Emancipation: see *C&S* (*CC*) xxxvi n 1, and cf 105 n 1. William and Mary, however, had not taken this oath. In the peculiar circumstances of James's abdication, a true Parliament could not be legally constituted and a Convention was formed to act for the time being as "the representative of the nation". In the presence of the Lords and Commons a Declaration of Rights was read to William and Mary and the crowns of England, Ireland, and France were tendered to them by the Convention. William accepted with a laconic reply that ignored the Declaration of Rights but included a statement of intent "to preserve your religion, laws, and liberties". Two months later the Scots vested their crown by Act of Settlement and proclaimed William and Mary their sovereigns, but insisted upon their taking a coronation oath and sent a deputation to Whitehall to administer it. At the clause "We shall be careful to root out all heretics and enemies of the true worship of God, that shall be convicted by the true kirk of God of the aforesaid crimes, out of our lands and empires of Scotland" William paused, said that he would not promise to be a "persecutor", and took that part of the oath only after he had been assured that the oath was not so intended. The episode was a collusive evasion, agreed beforehand, whereby William was allowed to construe the term "persecute" in a broad sense while the Scottish commissioners took it to refer specifically to capital punishment. This ambiguity was removed by the Coronation Oath prescribed by William and Mary: 1 William and Mary c 6.

JOSEPH BUTLER
1692–1752

The Analogy of Religion, natural and revealed, to the constitution and course of nature. [Edition not identified.] To which are added, two brief dissertations: I. On personal identity. II. On the nature of virtue. Together with a charge delivered to the clergy of the diocese of Durham.... A new edition, corrected. With a preface... by Samuel [Halifax], Lord Bishop of Gloucester. London 1791. 8⁰.

Of numerous editions examined, only the 1788 and 1791 editions match the pagination given in MS TRANSCRIPT.

Not located. Annotations printed from MS TRANSCRIPT. *Lost List.*

C's earliest reference to Butler's *Analogy of Religion*, in 1795, is taken at second-hand from Priestley (*Lects 1795*—*CC*—204 and n 3); but—considering that he proposed joining John Prior Estlin in an edition of the *Analogy* in Feb 1798 (*CL* I 385–6) and that in Feb 1801 he regarded Butler as one of "the three greatest, nay, only three *great* Metaphysicians which this Country *has* produced" (*CL* II 703)—it is surprising how few references C makes to Joseph Butler. In a list of desiderata drawn up in Sept 1807 the penultimate entry is "Butler's An. & Serm". *CN* II 3145. C seems to have provided himself with both—the lost annotated copy of the *Analogy* and a copy of the *Sermons* left at Grasmere in 1810 and marked in Wordsworth LC 228 as "Sent to Derwent 1827".

MS TRANSCRIPT. VCL BT 33: in SC's hand.

DATE. Perhaps between 1808 and 1815.

---

1 p 25 | Pt i "Of Natural Religion". Ch 1 "Of a Future Life" § 1

All presumption of death's being the destruction of living beings, must go upon supposition that they are compounded; and so, discerptible. But since consciousness is a single and indivisible power, it should seem that the subject in which it resides, must be so too. For were the motion of any particle of matter absolutely one and indivisible, so as that it should imply a contradiction to suppose part of this motion to exist, and part not to exist ... then its power of motion would be indivisible; and so also would the subject in which the power inheres, namely the particle of matter: for if this could be divided into two, one part might be moved and the other

867

at rest, which is contrary to the supposition. In like manner it has been argued, and ... justly, that since the perception or consciousness, which we have of our own existence, is indivisible ... the perceptive power, or the power of consciousness, is indivisible too: and consequently the subject in which it resides; *i.e.* the conscious Being.

Is the motion of a bullet from a gun divisible? If not, here is an indivisible action of a discerptible substance. I note this to shew the folly and danger of drawing arguments respecting the mind from the observed[a] properties of matter—but (or/ and) in strict logic the whole must end in a paralogism, or *idem pro alio*,[1] for what do we know of motion but as an act of our own consciousness—but as our consciousness so modified. S T C[b]

2   p 37 | i 1 § 3

Further there are instances of mortal diseases, which do not at all affect our present intellectual powers; and this affords a presumption, that those diseases will not destroy these present powers. Indeed ... it appears, that there is no presumption ... that the dissolution of the body is the destruction of the living agent. And by the same reasoning, it must appear too, that there is no presumption, from their mutually affecting each other, that the dissolution of the body is the destruction of our present reflecting powers: but instances of their not affecting each other, afford a presumption of the contrary.

This is surely a sophism. We do not imagine that the lungs are instruments of thought or of love—but of breathing—but we know that breathing is a necessary condition of the motion & proper warmth of the blood—& these of the proper functions of the brain. What wonder then if a man's brain should remain a fit instrument for thinking, while the lungs continue to permit breathing, tho' in pain. But let the disorder or a bullet destroy the lungs, the thought-organ is soon rendered useless. Butler ought to have shewn instances of diseases attacking the probable organs of thought, such as inflammations or palsies of the brain, that left the reflective powers in full vigor. This he could not do, & less than this is Legerdemain. The commonest accidents in machinery shew the folly of such reasoning—Let a furnace depend upon the air from a bellows,

---

[a] SC reads: "(obscure?)"
[b] The initials are probably an editorial identification rather than a signature; they have been omitted from 2 and 3, though present in MS TRANSCRIPT

2[1] "The same [term] for something else".

the motion of a bellows from a rope, connected by a machine—that rope may wear and wear away to the very last thread, and yet the bellows blow & furnace blaze as merrily as ever—but that last thread snapt down falls the bellows & the Fire soon goes out!—

3   p 82 | i 3 "Of the Moral Government of God" § 5

... possibly the sum of the whole strength of brutes, may be greater than that of mankind: but reason gives us the advantage and superiority over them; and thus man is the acknowledged governing animal upon the earth. ... And yet perhaps difficulties may be raised about the meaning, as well as the truth, of the assertion, that virtue has the like tendency [to obtain superiority].

... Put the imaginary case, that rational and irrational creatures were of like external shape and manner: it is certain, before there were opportunities for the first ... to form an union among themselves, they might be upon a level, or in several respects upon great disadvantage; though united they might be vastly superior: since union is of such efficacy, that ten men united, might be able to accomplish, what ten thousand of the same natural strength and understanding wholly ununited, could not. In this case then, brute force might more than maintain its ground against reason, for want of union among the rational creatures.

The excellent sense of this passage is rendered less perspicuous by the common error in our language of using Reason and Understanding (Vernunft & Verstand) as perfect synonymes. Reason & Virtue naturally involve and imply, each the other—which is not the case with understanding, an extraordinary power of which is sometimes instanced in the malignity of madmen.[1]

3[1] A central statement of the distinction between reason and understanding is in *SM* (*CC*) 59–62 and another in *AR* (1825) 208–28. See also BAXTER *Catholick Theologie* **14** n 3.

RICHARD BYFIELD

c 1592–1664

The Doctrine of the Sabbath Vindicated, in a confutation of a treatise of the Sabbath, written by M. Edward Breerwood against M. Nic. Byfield, wherein these five things are maintained: First, that the fourth commandement is given to the servant and not to the master onely. Secondly, that the fourth commandement is morall. Thirdly, that our owne light workes as well as gainefull and toilesome are forbidden on the Sabbath. Fourthly, that the Lords Day is of divine institution. Fifthly, that the Sabbath was instituted from the beginning. By the industrie of an unworthy labourer in Gods Vineyard, Richard Byfield, Pastor in Long Ditton in Surrey. London 1631. 4º.

Bound as first with Edward BRERE WOOD *A Second Treatise of the Sabbath* (Oxford 1632). The composite volume was contained in a wrapper of a single leaf of vellum written on both sides (see below), now bound in at the beginning of the volume.

Pierpont Morgan Library

Ms notes in ink in a seventeenth-century hand on pp ‾3, 89, 129, 130, 131, 201; and distinctive pen marks, apparently by the same writer, on pp 218, 219, 222, 223, 224, 225, 226.

On 12 Oct 1815 C described this book to John Matthew Gutch. "On the parchment Cover of an old Book of James Ist reign, I have found a curious fragment of the History (as I conjecture) of the miracles wrought at the Tomb of Thomas à Becket, written seemingly by one of the Monks not long after. It is in a very cramped character of monkish Latin, but the names of the persons miraculously cured are very interesting. If I can make it all out, I think of sending it to the Gentleman's Magazine." *CL* IV 593–4; 594 n 1 includes a transcript of the Latin text of one of the cures. John Aubrey has left a sad account from his own experience of the way such a ms would be found wrapping such a book. To quote abstemiously: "In my grandFather's dayes, the Manuscripts flew about like Butter-flies. All Musick bookes, Account-bookes, Copies books, etc, were covered with old Manuscripts, as wee cover them now with blew Paper, or Marbled Paper. And the Glovers at Malmesbury made great Havock of them, and Gloves were wrapt up no doubt in many good pieces of Antiquity." *Aubrey's Brief Lives* ed O. L. Dick (1972) 41–2. So much for "winding-sheets for pilchards": for which see Introduction, above, p cv.

On 25 Feb 1818, when C was returning to Thomas Boosey books that he had been using for his literary lectures and asking for others, he sent the Byfield–Brerewood volume to Boosey to examine. *CL* VI 1045.

The controversy between the brothers Byfield and Brerewood (or Breerwood, as Byfield and C spell the name, or Bryerwood) makes a tangled story. Nicholas Byfield (1579–1622) was a priest at Chester. In 1611 John Brerewood, trained by Byfield to observe the sabbath, was forced by his London employer to work on Sundays. John Brerewood's uncle Edward, hearing of the boy's plight, told him that the fourth commandment was intended to be observed only by masters, not by servants. Edward Brerewood and Nicholas Byfield then entered into acrimonious correspondence. Brerewood's opening letter, dated 15 Jul 1611 (BM Add MS 21207), was first published in Oxford in 1630 as *A Learned Treatise of the Sabaoth, Written . . . to Mr Nicholas Byfield*. Richard Byfield, younger brother of Nicholas, replied with *The Doctrine of the Sabbath Vindicated*, taking particular exception to Brerewood's spelling "Sabaoth". To this Brerewood replied by publishing in 1631 the first two letters with his own reply, expanding the original title *A Learned Treatise . . .* to include the formula *With Mr Byfield's Answer and Mr Brerewoods Reply*. He followed up that publication by issuing *A Second Treatise* (Oxford 1632).

On C's sabbatarianism see *CN* II 1968.

DATE. Perhaps 1824–5: probably after the move to The Grove, Highgate, Nov–Dec 1823.

Except for the reference to The Grove in **1**, below, no direct or internal evidence for dating the marginalia appears in the composite volume. In his letter to Boosey in Feb 1818 (cited above) C, however, did not say that the book was annotated, and it seems from his account of it that it was not already annotated. The marginalia seem to be later than the middle years, and there is no mention of Brerewood, Byfield, or Dr West in *CN* III.

It is conceivable that when C found the "monkish hand" on the parchment wrapper too difficult to transcribe, and abandoned his projected piece for *G Mag*, he continued to think of the volume as a curiosity, perhaps of some intrinsic value—which could account for his sending it in 1818 to Boosey either for a professional opinion or with a view to offering it for sale. Boosey may have reported—which is no less than the truth— that the book was not valuable enough to offer for sale and returned it; C perhaps then put it aside and thought no more about it in his preoccupation with his lectures and writing. After the move to The Grove from Moreton Hall his books were still "in confusion" as late as Feb 1824. *CL* V 328. In sorting and arranging his books in his new attic study he could have come across the volume again and have written BYFIELD **1** in the first tract and most—if not all—of the notes in both pamphlets.

1 pp $^-$4–$^-$3, first paragraph redrafted and concluded on p $^-$1

Grove, Highgate. Given me by Mr West, Surgeon; at Calne, Wiltshire—^{1} S. T. C.

1^1 No more is known about Mr West, the surgeon of Calne.

N.B. A book of of great rarity and no less value—~~It is~~ this parchment Cover which I conjecture to be part of a Record, that had belonged to Canterbury Cathedral, of the Pilgrims, Offerings, miraculous Cures &c at the Shrine of Thomas of Becket, is curious in itself,[2] & additionally so by the accident of its bringing into such close neighborhood a prime papistic with a proper puritanic Ignivomist[3]—For verily a right vehement, vituperative, & (*in his own judgement*) infallible Bigot is Master Byfield. To magnify his own Judaical Whims into essential truths of the Spirit, and then to identify himself with the very Spirit of Truth, ~~is~~ are the modest Overture and Symphony to this ~~Qoax Co~~ κοαξ κοαξ Bravura of Frogs in a Fever.[4] I ~~say Frogs~~ speak *plurally*—for tho' Master Byfield be ⟨merely⟩ singular, ~~hise name is~~ is of the Race of Legion, ~~and a~~ and his name Frog-swamp! The ~~Bigotry~~ ambition of of the ~~Tu~~Triple Crown is ~~not less~~ more arrogant than the ~~Ambition of the Triple Crown~~—Bigotry of the Conventicle Tub. If the Pope *will be* ~~Christ's the only Vicar, of the 2ⁿᵈ Person of the Trinity Master Byfield is the Vicar of the Holy Ghost~~ Christ's Vicar on Earth & ~~Thus the~~ represent the Second Person of the Trinity, our cropt Conventicler will stand in the same relation to the Third, & of course Professor[a] Breerwood's offence in first provoking his Wrath, and then in withstanding his Logic, at no safe distance from the Sin against the H. G.   S. T. C.

[b]The latter half of the MSS Note over leaf being scarcely legible, is here re-written.

κοαξ κοαξ Bravura of Frogs in a fever. I speak *plurally*: for tho' Master Byfield in his visibilities be merely singular, he is of the Race of L E G I O N and his ⟨spiritual⟩ Name Frog-swamp! The Ambition of the Triple Crown is scarcely more arrogant than the Bigotry of the

[a] This word looks more like "Profession" than "Professor"; but Brerewood describes himself on his title-page as "Professor in Gresham Colledge", and the sentence is clear enough as it stands
[b] The fair version is written on p ⁻1. In the ms the PS follows directly on the first draft on p ⁻3

1[2] For a transcript of part of the vellum ms used for the binding see *CL* IV 594n. Thomas à Becket (c 1118–70), abp of Canterbury, was murdered in his cathedral. His shrine, celebrated for its healing power, was broken up in 1538.
1[3] "Fire-vomiter". *OED* gives "ig-nivomous" and "ignivomousness", but not "ignivomist".
1[4] In the celebrated chorus of Aristophanes' *Frogs* the voice of the frogs is represented by *brech-ech-ech-ex koax-koax*. C knew the play well: see e.g. *CN* I 53, 105.

Tub. If the Pope *is* Christ's Vicar on Earth and represents the second person of the Trinity, our cropt Conventicler will stand in the same relation to the third, and the ~~learned~~ offence of a ₿ blaspheming Prelatist, ~~such as~~ a Breerwood or a Bramble-bush on the Hedge of ~~pr carnal~~ profane Learning, in arraigning the conduct and doctrine of his sanctimonious Vice-Ghostship can stand at no safe distance from the unique Sin—as indeed Master Dick Byfield, a younger Brother of ~~the~~ old Nic.[5] Byfield in more than one place of the following Work doth not obscurely intimate.

P.S. Whether Breerwood is right throughout (in the main point he certainly is) depends on what the Law of the Land was at that time—. Practically, the e only class of servants in this Country that are interested in the Question, is that of Apprentices. A Cook that should refuse to roast the Sirloin and boil the Plum pudding a Sundays, must hire herself to a Puritan or remain out of Place. But in regard to ⟨an⟩ Apprentices, I apprehend—the Law which requires him to attend divine service once at least on every Lord's Day would justify him in refusing any employment that interfered with this, and *Work* of all kinds during any part of the Day—whatever in short would preclude Rest and Refreshment, of body, mind or spirit—ex. gr. forcing a poor apprentice to attend Sermons ~~of~~ two hours long.—The ⟨Jews'⟩ Sabbath was a day of ᵽ Inaction, *Giorno di far niente*:[6] for God *rested* from the Creation—the Christian's Lord's Day is a Day of Re~~c~~restoration: for the Lord rose up and completed the new Creation.[7]

At all events it is to be regretted, that Breerwood should have placed ~~this~~ most invidious and t (I think) ~~to me~~ weakest proposition in the front of his argument. *S. T. C.*

2   pp 11–14 | Ch 2

[Byfield quotes Brerewood *A Learned Treatise* pp 5–6:] " . . . it is clearly the Lords meaning, that the Israelites should not admit of any Gentile to the participation of the Passeover, nor receive the Ammonites and Moabites into the Congregation of the Lord." [Byfield replies:] First, I reply, these Commandements are not paralell, and so your ground faileth . . . I say, this, *Thy servant shall doe no manner of worke*; and this, *No stranger shall eate of the Passeover*.

[5] A play on the name of Nicholas Byfield, the older of the two brothers, and "Old Nick", the Devil.

[6] A "Day for doing nothing".

[7] See also BAXTER *Reliquiae* COPY A 48 and BIBLE COPY B 9.

An argument lightly advanced and heavily answered; *but* answered. Let loose from the *swathe* of positive Institutes, Byfield's Reply amounts to this: Either the Moabite is supposed not to know the Obligation under which the Israelite lies—and then it is a case of Ignorance and *nihil ad rem*[1]—or he does know it & ~~its~~ regard it as sacred—and in this case he is bound not to comply with the Invitation by the moral Law which forbids him to ~~be~~ make himself accessory to a crime. Nay, tho' he should not admit the rightfulness of the Obligation himself, yet if he knows that the Israelite does, he is still bound in conscience not to join in an act by which his Neighbor is violated. For it is a decided principle in Morals, that a man becomes guilty of the crime which he might have innocently prevented. And in this ⟨instance⟩ the Moabite *perfects* the crime which but for his compliance would have rested in the intention, and which wrong intention his refusal might very probably have removed by shaming the Apostate into repentance. Previous Judgement was misled by his vivid perception of the Evils which the injunction of the sabbath would have produced, in 3 first Centuries; and he overlooked the wide difference between a Roman Slave and an English Servant, and forgot that his proposition, as far as it is true, is so little applicable to the present times, as not to be worth contending for. S. T. C.

3   pp 19-20 | Ch 4

[Brerewood's argument (p 7) quoted by Byfield:] " . . . It is therefore as cleare as the Sunne, even to meane understandings, (if they will give but meane attendance, to the tenour of Gods commandement, rather than the fond interpretations and depravations of man) that that clause of the commandement touching servants cessation from working on the Sabaoth, is not given to servants themselves, but to their masters concerning them."

In strictness of Law, Breerwood has perhaps the better of the argument in this instance; but it was a most invidious and impolitic way of carrying his point. Or rather it was unworthy of him and below his character as a Scholar and a Gentleman, to have *a point to carry*.

He should have *confined* himself to the exposure of the Sabbatical Superstition, as a Judaic incroachment on the privileges & liberty of the Christian Festival—and if he had alluded at all to his Nephew's

[1] "Nothing to the point".

Case, it should have been by contrasting the light & insignificant commission, which his Nephew was by the Puritan Minister forbidden to execute at his Master's request, with the dreary gloomy drudgery of Sermons, two hours long, Repetitions of the same after Church, long-winded Prayer-exercises, ⟨(see p. 25.)⟩[1] &c &c which the & his Party enjoin. In short, it is much to be wished, that Breerwood's "Second Treatise" had been the first and only one.

4   p 25 | Ch 5

That the servant (if not religious, which God lookes not to find, but by his word to make us such) had rather oft times worke for his master, than bee imployed in the duties of sanctification for a part, much more for all the day: for they are more irkesome to flesh and blood, than handy worke. True, that question might take more place, if it were rest alone that were aymed at, and not rest for an higher end.

an honest confession—& one to which I fully subscribe, only that for the words, "if not religious" I would read "if not a judaizing Fanatic".

5   p 47 | Ch 11

... that is no Law which is not just and right; it is perversenesse, no Law: it is not Law, but lees, but strife, but a destroyer, but error, but tiranny, any thing rather than Law, as all the learned conclude.

id est, what is wrong, cannot be right. But who is to be judge? The Conscience of the Law-giver ~~of~~ or of the Subject? Obedience may be due to a Law by force of a prior Law: as ex. gr. if each one of a 100 have agreed that the will and opinion of the minority should yield to that of the majority: if 80 vote to be Law that which 20 think unjust, it becomes a Law to the ~~20~~ whole 100 by virtue of the prior Law.

6   p 53 | Ch 12

And now observe it well, if it were absurd for God to command that good duty which wicked ones will persecute one for, then it were absurd for God to command men any good, and to this absurditie are you inevitably brought.

Strange Logic! because God will not waive a great good for a small and contingent Evil, therefore he will not avoid ~~an~~ sore evil where no adequate Good exists to overpoise it.

3[1] I.e. **4** textus. Cf **1** PS, **4**, and **7**.

7 p 57 | Ch 13

Fourthly, hee threatned the Tyrian Merchants that lodged without the gate, [Neh 13] Vers. 21. And here note, that the testification against the servants in Vers. 15. was at severall times, and upon a severall occasion from that contention with the Nobles . . .

What? if I saw a Farmer's Servants carrying home Hay on a Sunday, should I not say to the Farmer—How Why do you carry home your Hay on the Lord's Day?—Surely, and if I acted aright, to the Master and *not* to the Servants: lest I should degrade him in their eyes, when perchance on my admonition he might repent and avoid it for the future.—

8 p 61 | Ch 14

Now to reason thus, *thy pleasure* [Isa 58.13] in the worke is forbidden, but the worke may be done, if *thy pleasure* be not in it, is a most licentious doctrine; for so any wickednesse might bee done to which superiours will command us, and the doer be faultlesse . . .

This is, in truth, the only weak part of Brerewood's Argument, to which he was seduced by his private vexation. Had he limited his proposition 1. to a Christian Pagan Country—and 2.—in a Christian Country to such acts, in the non-performance of which the Law will not often protect the Servant, and which can be done without breach of the moral and spiritual purposes of the Lord's Day, his reasoning would have been unobjectionable/ and would deserve to be republished, for the consideration of the present over-righteous Sabbatarians.

9 p 178 | Ch 33

You may readily discover the Chapters, in which the Writer is pinched in the argument, by the number & virulence of the abusive terms. It would be amusing to make a collection of all the epithets and damnatory Sentences, epiphonemas[1] &c in this one treatise—and only by way of P.S. annex the harmless Proposition, which had provoked them! S. T. C.

10 pp 200–5 | "The Second Part Containing a Briefe Surveigh of Master Breerwoods Reply"

[Christians are not urged to use the Sabbath as] *a preparation* without *actuall application to holinesse*, but a present sanctifying

---

9[1] Gnomic or striking sayings. In rhetoric an *epiphonema* is a phrase added for ornament or polish; in grammar, an interjection.

themselves that day that they might be the fitter for attendance on the Lord . . .

It has often struck me that if the 4th Commandment apply to Christians, it must bind them to the very day. For the reason assigned therein is not drawn from moral purposes—namely, the duty of giving a set portion of our time to the especial service of God and our souls—& the necessity for the harmony of society that some one day and that the same should be appointed to all—which would doubtless admit the transfer of the Command from Saturday to Sunday—but that God having rested on that day from the work of C̶h̶ Creation had therefore sanctified and blessed it. Now surely this Reason so solemnly announced applies equally to all God's Creatures, capable of acting, or of being used, according to it. Thus the Oxen and Cattle and the Aliens were included. Now ⟨if⟩ iof the old Law all remains, that did not belong to the ceremonial or typical Religion and to the Jews, as a *State*, exclusively, this which equally appertains to all creatures susceptible of a Law in Heaven and in Earth, must needs remain likewise. But if not this, neither any part of that Command on account of that Command—tho' the purport of it as well as of the Decalogue throughout, remains established on the clear dictates of Reason and Humanity. Even so, the Laws of E̶n̶g̶l̶a̶n̶d̶ Solon forbid Murder, Theft, Adultery &c;[1]—but we do not therefore obey the Laws of Solon but either our own or rather the Law of God & Nature. Add too, that had S[t] Paul understood the Judaic Modifications to have been transferred from the Sabbath to the Lord's Day, would he not have given a special Command, or would not rather the Gospel have recorded such a command as given by the Lord himself after His Resurrection? Were the whole Command with all its specifications binding on all mankind, what less than a direct abrogation by God could annul a direct Command of God.—Therefore this as well as the rest of the Jewish Law w̶a̶s̶ ceased in Christ, as its *fulfilment*. The moral Law alone remained, rendered specific for spiritual purposes, according to the needs and circumstances of Christians—and this accounts for the absence of all specific precepts, except that one which was dictated by the circumstances of the Christians then few & scattered—not to neglect assembling themselves at stated times./ Hence too the celebration of the Sacrament is not confined to any day/. The perpetual Law is: A

10[1] Solon (c 640–c 558 B.C.), a civilising and liberal law-giver of Athens, the benign influence of whose laws spread over the next four centuries.

settled and adequate portion of Time at equal intervals shall be withdrawn from the Labor which is for the Animal part of Men to be devoted to their distinctive human character: namely, Love, Knowlege, Religion, Meditation and cheerful unanxious Employment. The mode, in which this may be best done, so it be done, is left to the discretion of the Church and its Rulers. One day in seven all Christians have agreed on: & this very universality moralizes it, because it cannot be deviated from without lessening the social or moral uses of the general Command. In some Countries, the Blessings of the Soil and Climate, ~~the~~ with the smaller quantity of food and cloathing needful for the Inhabitants, allow a greater number of additional Days to be consecrated than in cold and sterile Climates. In all things the Holy Day is made for Man, not Man for the Holy Day. A single Baker may enable fifty Servants ⟨or poor Wives⟩ to attend divine service & rest, & yet enjoy a comfortable meal—& the Baker himself may attend afternoon prayers. Is it not a work of Charity?

11 p 206

[Quoting Marius:]*"... for since it is of the Law of Nature that some time be peculiarly insinuated for the worship of God, it was meete, that that should be determined in the very beginning by a positive law, whence even among the Gentiles, the Religion on the Seventh Day was famous."*

In the words of Bede,[1] Christianity taking away the ceremonial Envelopes from the Law of Right Reason, and glorifying that Law by ~~additionals~~ additional spiritual, did inclusively restore the Natural Sabbath, ~~and~~ but spiritualized

12 p 211

Concerning the *authoritie that translated the Sabbath*, you say it is certaine, that the translation thereof was actually and immediately prescribed by the Church. Deale ingenuously, and shew me where; if in Scripture, then I answer that it was not immediately prescribed

---

11[1] No clear connexion with the Venerable Bede (c 673–735) appears. Presumably C has made a slip for "Beza", whom Byfield quotes in the next paragraph: "Beza affirmeth of *Iob, That as oft as his children had made an end of feasting one another in their severall houses, he sanctified* them, *and offered burnt offerings according to their number, but notwithstanding there is no doubt but that the dayly worship of God was diligently observed, besides in this most holy family, at least every seventh day was carefully sanctified, as God from the beginning of the world had appointed.*"

by the Church; for the *Apostles* were not *Authors of the institution,* but *Ministers of Christ, and pen-men of the holy Ghost.*

Curious to see this Puritan in his sabbatical Zeal running head-long into the Popish Slough of apostolical *Traditions*—so that the B̶i̶ Scriptures do not contain all needful Doctrines/

12A   p 214

That our *Saviour* intended not our Sabbath in that place of *Matthew,* because the *Apostles* call it the *Lord's day*?

12B   p 222

Could you not see that *finally* ends the *reasons* against your demand and challenge of an answer ...